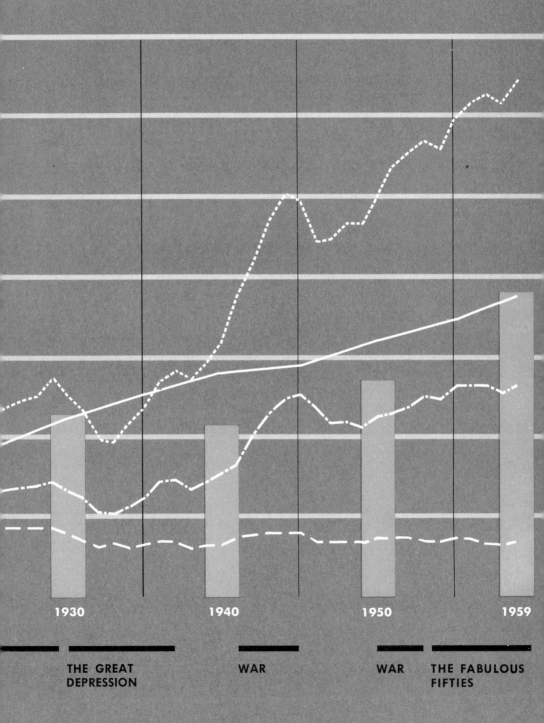

1930

1940

1950

1959

THE GREAT
DEPRESSION

WAR

WAR

THE FABULOUS
FIFTIES

ECONOMICS

An Introduction to Analysis and Policy

THIRD EDITION

E C O N

Englewood Cliffs, New Jersey

PRENTICE-HALL, INC.

1960

GEORGE LELAND BACH

Professor and Head, Department of Economics
Carnegie Institute of Technology

OMICS

An Introduction
to Analysis and Policy

ECONOMICS

An Introduction to Analysis and Policy

THIRD EDITION

George Leland Bach

Designed by Harry Rinehart

Illustrations by Felix Cooper

Preface

This edition, like its predecessors, has four major objectives, and an educational philosophy about how they can be achieved. It is aimed primarily at helping students acquire (1) a lasting interest in real-world economic problems, (2) a fundamental and rigorous tool kit for economic analysis, (3) an orderly, objective way of thinking about economic problems, and (4) the ability to use economic analysis as one major tool in reaching independent, well-considered judgments on important public policy issues. The focus throughout is on what the *student* does, on getting him interested and involved, and on getting him to learn a few things well. This is in the firm belief that only this type of learning will stay with him in the really important period long after the final examination, when he reads the newspaper and goes to the polls to vote.

If we do not manage to kindle a real interest in economics, we have lost the battle at the outset, for surely what matters is what the student does with his economics after he leaves the campus and escapes the threat of the final exam. Thus, throughout, I have tried to get the student to participate actively in the analysis of current public policy problems. In intellectual growth as in technical skills, we learn by doing, and thinking through important current policy problems is a lively way of giving students such active experience. Above all, the book tries to get every student to use the fundamental analytical tools of economics in thinking through economic problems *for himself*. Educational experience, in both economics and other fields, increasingly suggests that emphasis on the *method* of orderly thinking, on a few fundamental analytical tools, and on repeated experience in using the tools and good method in analyzing problems, provides the most promising basis for future independent thought and intellectual growth. This is my conviction.

This edition provides much that is new and completely rewritten. Over-all, about one-third of the book is completely new, another third has been substantially rewritten, and perhaps one-third is much like the second edition. The big changes are the following:

(1) I have stepped up the rigor and thoroughness of the theory presented throughout. But the previous emphasis on theory as a tool for independent *student* use in thinking through real-world problems has been maintained—in contrast to emphasis on a bare-bones theory-for-theory's-sake approach. I think there will be few elementary students who can reasonably be expected to retain and use for themselves after the course more advanced theory than is now presented. In three cases where the new theory goes farther than some instructors may want to assign to all their students, the material has been segregated in special appendixes which can be used or omitted at will.

(2) The world-wide problem of how to obtain rapid economic growth without inflation provides a central theme for this edition. This is perhaps the greatest economic problem of our day; the newspapers and the news reports demonstrate its timeliness.

More space is devoted to this problem than in earlier editions, and it is used both in examining the American economy and in comparing and contrasting alternative economic systems.

(3) In order to stimulate student interest in the exciting research developments in economics that are too new or too advanced for inclusion in an elementary text, I have added to each major section of the book a new appendix on "Current Research." These brief appendixes try to convey some of the vitality and force that make economics fascinating to economists, by telling something about samples of important recent and current economic research; they include references for those students who may be intrigued to look further. The elementary course is generally the ground on which we gain or lose the professional economists of tomorrow. I hope students can see economics as far more than the dry-as-dust exercise it has been in so many elementary courses, and that this small exposure to current research may lead some of the best minds to look further.

(4) A second innovation in the elementary textbook field (so far as I know) is inclusion of a chapter on "Managerial Economics." This burgeoning new branch of economics will be of special interest to instructors of students who are headed for business careers. But I suspect that the applications of fundamental economic analysis to managerial problems (which have already fascinated many leaders in the profession) will soon be so widespread that no thoroughly trained economist can afford to disregard them. In any case, the chapter is there for those who want it; it is so written that it can be disregarded by those who have no interest.

(5) At the end of most chapters devoted primarily to theory development, I have added a brief section, "Review—Concepts to Remember." These sections list the main analytical concepts introduced in the chapter, as a guide to the fundamental analytical tools deserving concentration. I have continued to avoid chapter summaries, because I am convinced that for many students they too readily become a substitute for studying the chapter itself. The new sections tell the student what concepts he should concentrate on understanding, rather than giving him a capsule summary to memorize.

(6) Again, the micro-economics section is written so it can be taught either with or entirely without the traditional short-run marginal-cost marginal-revenue theory of the firm. Experience with previous editions, however, suggests that most instructors prefer to cover the traditional neo-classical theory of the firm. Thus, I have changed the flavor of the second edition, which presumed that many students would have skipped this material, to a general presumption that it will be used. The result, I hope, is an arrangement that preserves the unique possibility of teaching the course without this inevitably difficult and time-consuming material for those who want to emphasize only the broad long-run allocative effects of the price system; but which removes any teaching disadvantage which the previous system of special footnotes and textual references may have had for those who cover the full theoretical treatment.

If the simpler approach to micro-economics is adopted, instructors should simply omit the following: Appendix to Chapter 20; Chapter 21; last half of Chapter 24; Appendix to Chapter 28; and the footnotes on pages 469 and 486. By concentrating the material resting on the short-run marginal-cost marginal-revenue mechanism in these pages, I hope the text will be simply adaptable for those who want to emphasize the long-run allocative effects but to do so in a rigorous fashion and with full application on major public policy issues.

(7) For both groups, a substantial amount of new material on modern business pricing practices has been added—on standard costing, cost-plus pricing, break-even

charts, rate-of-return-on-investment pricing, and so on. In addition, a new appendix to Chapter 17 describes the internal organization and decision-making processes of two typical business firms—one small and one a corporate giant—for those instructors who want to provide more institutional content for the bare-bones profit-maximizing graphs used in traditional price theory. Again, this appendix can be used or omitted to suit individual instructor preferences.

(8) Throughout, the book has again been completely updated. Not only have all figures been brought up to the minute, but fresh examples and policy problems have been chosen, which will have immediacy and meaning during the 1960's. And throughout there are a myriad of revisions—major and minor—reflecting the suggestions of literally hundreds of users, whose experiences in their widely diverse institutions have suggested the need for improvement. Not only have these suggestions been numerous and friendly; they have been a major help in making this new edition, I hope, an eminently teachable and useful book for students.

This edition is again about equally balanced between macro- and micro-analysis, and between theoretical and institutional-policy oriented material. The entire book is designed for a full-year course, with a moderate amount of time left for supplementary readings to suit the tastes of individual instructors. But it is also written with an eye to one-semester course use. Suggested outlines for three alternative one-semester courses are included immediately following the Table of Contents.

The Preface to the first edition acknowledged a large indebtedness to Dr. Mary Jean Bowman, arising out of work we had done together on an earlier book, *Economic Analysis and Public Policy.* Although the traces of earlier ideas fade with time, I am sure that much of what was said there is still appropriate. In preparing this edition I have again had the invaluable assistance and advice of many members of the economics faculty of Carnegie Institute of Technology. Very special thanks are due to Professors Myron Joseph and Norton Seeber, who have provided valuable suggestions on the entire book, and have prepared a most useful *Workbook* to supplement the text. Professors Richard Cyert, Allan Meltzer, and Merton Miller have helped to steer me straight on individual chapters. Outside Carnegie, I am especially indebted to Professors James Crutchfield of Washington, Frank Kidner of California (Berkeley), David Martin of Indiana, William McKinstrey of Miami (Ohio), and John Wilcox of Miami (Florida). And the good advice of Professors Jerome Cohen of C.C.N.Y., R. A. Gordon of California (Berkeley), Wendell Gordon of Texas, Alan Gruchy of Maryland, and Richard Ruggles of Yale on earlier editions continues to show in this one. The usual warning that only I am responsible for the final outcome needs to be added, however, for I have accepted only some of the suggestions advanced. Lastly, I want to add my appreciation to Messrs. Clarence Huizenga and Richard Young for their help on the index, and to Mr. Everett Sims of Prentice-Hall for his major role in making the book more attractive throughout.

G. L. B.

Contents

viii

PART FOUR THE DISTRIBUTION OF INCOME

Suggested Outlines
for One-Semester Course

OUTLINE A — EMPHASIZING MACRO-ECONOMICS

(Suggested readings in Parts 1 and 2 total about 300 pages, or only about 10 pages per class meeting for a typical 15-week semester. Thus, adequate time is available for supplementary outside readings or for other chapters in this text.)

Part 1   *The Foundations of Economic Analysis (complete)*

Chapter 1. What Is Economics About? *2.* The American Economy—A Summary View. *3.* The Foundations of Economic Progress: Resources and Technology. *4.* Private Enterprise, Profits, and the Price System. *5.* Straight Thinking in Economics.

Part 2   *National Income, Employment, and Economic Growth (complete)*

Chapter 6. National Income, Production, and Employment. *7.* Changing Price Levels: Inflation and Deflation. *8.* Money and the Banking System. *9.* The Federal Reserve System and the Money Supply. *10.* The Theory of Money, Income, and Prices. *11.* The Modern Theory of Income, Employment, and Prices. *12.* Economic Growth in America. *13.* Economic Fluctuations. *14.* Monetary Policy. *15.* Fiscal Policy. *16.* The Practical Problems of Stabilization Policy.

Omit Parts 3, 4, 5, 6, and 7, or select additional chapters to fit special interests. Some suggestions are:

Chapter 34. Wage-Price Policy and the Role of Government. *35.* The Public Economy. *36.* Taxes. *43.* Economic Development: The Underdeveloped Countries. *44.* Comparative Economic Systems: U.S.S.R. and U.S.A.

OUTLINE B — EMPHASIZING MICRO-ECONOMICS

(Suggested readings in Parts 1, 3, and 4 total about 325 pages, or only about 11 pages per class meeting for a typical 15-week course. Thus, adequate time is available for supplementary outside readings or for some additional chapters in the text.)

Part 1   *The Foundations of Economic Analysis (complete)*

Chapter 1. What Is Economics About? *2.* The American Economy—A Summary View. *3.* The Foundations of Economic Progress: Resources and Technology. *4.* Private Enterprise, Profits, and the Price System. *5.* Straight Thinking in Economics.

Omit Part 2.

Part 3   *Markets, the Price System, and the Allocation of Resources (complete)*

Chapter 17. Business Enterprise in the Modern Economy. *18.* Demand—The Role of the Consumer. *19.* Demand, Supply, and Market Prices. *20.* The Business Firm and Its Costs. *21.* The Business Firm—Competitive Output and Prices in the Short

Run (optional). *22.* Long-run Competitive Equilibrium. *23.* Agriculture—A Case Study in Competition. *24.* Monopoly (second half optional). *25.* Monopolistic Competition. *26.* Oligopoly. *27.* Government and Business. (Optional readings in Chapters 21 and 24 include the short-run theory of the firm, using marginal-cost marginal-revenue analysis.)

Part 4 *The Distribution of Income*

Chapter 28. How Is Income Distributed? *29.* Wages and Salaries.

Omit Parts 5, 6, and 7, or select additional chapters to fit special interests. Some suggestions are:

Chapter 35. The Public Economy. *36.* Taxes. *42.* Social Security—A Case Study. *43.* Economic Development: The Underdeveloped Countries. *44.* Comparative Economic Systems: U.S.S.R. and U.S.A.

OUTLINE C — INCLUDING BOTH MACRO- AND MICRO-ECONOMICS

(Suggested readings in Parts 1, 2, and 3 total about 475 pages, about 16 pages [one-half chapter] per class meeting for a typical 15-week semester.)

Part 1 *The Foundations of Economic Analysis (complete)*

Chapter 1. What Is Economics About? *2.* The American Economy—A Summary View. *3.* The Foundations of Economic Progress: Resources and Technology. *4.* Private Enterprise, Profits, and the Price System. *5.* Straight Thinking in Economics.

Part 2 *National Income, Employment, and Economic Growth*

Chapter 6. National Income, Production, and Employment. *7.* Changing Price Levels: Inflation and Deflation. *8.* Money and the Banking System. *9.* The Federal Reserve System and the Money Supply. *10.* The Theory of Money, Income, and Prices (optional). *11.* The Modern Theory of Income, Employment, and Prices. *12.* Economic Growth in America. *13.* Economic Fluctuations. *14.* Monetary Policy. *15.* Fiscal Policy.

Part 3 *Markets, the Price System, and the Allocation of Resources*

Chapter 17. Business Enterprise in the Modern Economy. *18.* Demand—The Role of the Consumer. *19.* Demand, Supply, and Market Prices. *20.* The Business Firm and Its Costs. *22.* Long-run Competitive Equilibrium. *23.* Agriculture—A Case Study in Competition. *24.* Monopoly (first half only). *25.* Monopolistic Competition. *26.* Oligopoly. *27.* Government and Business. (This omits all short-run marginal-cost marginal-revenue analysis.)

Omit Parts 4, 5, 6, and 7.

PART 1

The Foundations
of Economic Analysis

What Is
Economics About?

1

Economics is the study of how the goods and services we want get produced, and how they are distributed among us. This we call economic analysis. Equally, economics is the study of how we can make the system of production and distribution work better. This we call economic policy. Economic analysis is the necessary foundation for sound economic policy. This is a book about both economic analysis and policy. It is a book about the big economic problems of our time.

Concretely, economics is the study of why we are rich while two-thirds of the world's masses are bitterly poor. It is the study of inflation—of prices spiraling upward, robbing the thrifty of their savings while speculators sport diamond rings and the masses press for higher wages, speeding further inflation. It is the study of recurring mass unemployment and depressions—of millions of people out of work and hungry while factories stand idle and while farmers let crops rot because they can't pay the harvesting costs.

Economics is the study of big business—of giant concerns that sometimes benefit the consumer through mass production and research, and some-

3

times act as monopolies out to bleed the customer; that sometimes drive the little producer to the wall, but that sometimes provide the active, vigorous competition which is vital to the American private-enterprise system. Economics is the study of labor unions—of working men banded together to protect their interests against powerful employers, becoming powerful themselves in the process. It is the study of unions sometimes violent, sometimes peaceful, sometimes democratic, sometimes misled by their leaders.

Economics is the study of government spending and taxes—of the 20 to 25 cents of every dollar of your income that will go to the government if something like present conditions continue throughout your life.

What will be the big economic problems of the 1960's? No one knows. But the biggest economic problem is likely to be this: Can we win in the vast economic competition with the communist world? Will the American economic system, predominantly based on individual freedom and private enterprise, be able to demonstrate its superiority over Russia's communist system? Can we produce enough to maintain our high standard of living *and* pay the vast costs of modern defense without incurring disruptive inflation or economic collapse? Will we be able to step up our growth rate to match the spectacular achievements of the Russians over the past decade, or may the Russians slow down as they reach industrial levels closer to ours? Which system will win out among the billion people still uncommitted in the cold war between East and West?

Some economists pose still another central economic problem for America: Have we become so affluent that our demands in the marketplace will be insufficient to call forth full production and rapid economc growth? Have we become satiated with automobiles and deep freezers? Can we switch our vast productive powers to other non-market needs like education, culture, highways, and defense without undue government intervention? In short, have we become too fat and comfortable to keep our economic system virile and adaptive to change?

ECONOMICS
IN A DEMOCRACY   Throughout your life, economics will play a major role in determining what you do and how happy you are doing it. If there are depressions or inflations, you will not be able to escape them. Your income will depend largely on how effectively you participate in the economic process. Even the political stability of our democratic system may depend heavily on maintaining a reasonably stable rate of economic growth.

Thus, from a purely selfish point of view, it will pay you to understand how your economic system works. But the main reason citizens in a democracy need to understand the economic system is that they are voters. Once upon a time governments didn't interfere very much in economic life. But that time is clearly gone. Today, just about everybody agrees that the government should provide national defense, highways, education, and a score of other services not forthcoming through the private-enterprise economy; should regulate the supply of money;

should protect consumers against the excesses of monopolies; should prohibit exploitation of child labor. Fill out the list for yourself. Many people believe the government should do many more things—provide old-age and sickness protection for the poor, support the prices of farm products, legislate minimum wages, even guarantee full employment.

Even if we agree on what the government should do, there's still the big problem of how to do it. Consider the problem of speeding economic growth and preventing wasteful depressions. Should we cut taxes on businesses to stimulate investment and jobs? Should the government itself spend on investment projects? Should it go in for deficit financing if unemployment mounts? Or should it pare its expenditures and be sure to balance the budget? How about the problem of regulating monopolies? Is General Motors a monopoly that is exploiting consumers and holding back progress? How about U.S. Steel? Certainly they're both huge concerns, far the biggest in their industries. But would breaking them up into smaller units help or injure consumers and workers?

If you expect to find answers in this book on what the government should and should not do, you're in for a disappointment. *The job of a course in economic analysis is to give you the tools and the background for making up your own mind on the important economic issues of the day, not to tell you what to think.* Better understanding of how the system works will go a long way toward making you a more intelligent voter. But you should recognize from the outset that even with a thorough understanding of economics, not everybody will come out with the same answers on these problems of public policy. This is because we have different ideas on where the nation ought to be headed. Some people, for example, think avoiding inflation is the most important thing. Others believe that assuring everyone a substantial minimum income should have first priority. Any respectable economist will advise the government to do different things depending on which of these objectives is placed first. Such conflicts among the objectives of different individuals and groups are an inescapable element in the modern American democracy.

ECONOMICS AND BUSINESS ADMINISTRATION The public is understandably confused on the distinction between economics and business administration. Obviously, both deal with business and the way business operates in the economic scene. Yet economists and businessmen often come out with quite different conclusions, and sometimes with unkind words about each other.

Economics is the study of the whole economic system and how it operates in satisfying the wants of society. To the economist, the businessman and his enterprise are data to be observed—one central part of the free-enterprise economic scene, but by no means the only part. Labor organizations, consumers, investors, farmers, and government administrators are parts of the economic scene too—often very important parts. The economist tries to view the whole system from above, and to assess its performance in the light of the objectives agreed on by the democratic processes of our society. In setting these objectives, the business-man's interests are important, but they need to be balanced out against many other interests.

Business administration, on the other hand, is the study of how to operate a business concern most effectively. The business administrator sees the business firm from inside—from the president's chair. He is primarily concerned with how to maximize profits, how to keep the business alert and growing, how to weld his employees into an efficient, hard-hitting organization. Business administration studies what type of administrative organization is best for the firm, what kinds of personnel policy pay off, when it pays to borrow from the bank and when to issue new stock or bonds, how to turn out more product per dollar of expense, how to make the customer want your product. How the whole economy behaves is important to the businessman, because the rest of the economy has a big impact on any business. In prosperity, it's easy to sell your goods, and running a business has lots of bright moments. In depression, hardly anyone makes much money.

It's easy to see that economics and business administration overlap everywhere. To be any good, the economist has to have a reasonably good understanding of how businessmen operate. To be a good businessman takes a lot of understanding of what goes on outside your business. But it's easy, too, to see why business administrators and economists often don't see eye to eye. They look at the world from different viewpoints and with quite different emphases.

This is a book about economics, not about business administration. The slant of the book is essentially the citizen's slant, viewing sympathetically the problems of the businessman, the worker, the farmer, the investor, and all the others. But we need to be interested in how businessmen think and operate, because they play a central organizing role in a private-enterprise economy. We will study a little of how business concerns operate—how they keep their financial records, how they calculate costs, how they figure prices. But we will have to be content with a pretty general picture of such business practices, except for one special chapter on "Managerial Economics" later on. This is not because business admin-istration is unimportant, but because you can't learn about everything at once. So if you thought this book was going to teach you how to run your own business some day, you're in for a disappointment—though it may turn out to be more useful than you'd guess, in an indirect way.

ECONOMICS AND THE OTHER SOCIAL SCIENCES Economics and government, psychology, and sociology are also intertwined in the real world, however separate they may be in the college classroom. Consider their interactions.

The psychologist tries to explain why people behave the way they do, indi-vidually and in groups. Clearly, this explanation is important to the economist.

Why do consumers buy one breakfast food instead of another? Why do unions strike over an extra two cents an hour when they may lose more in pay during the strike than they'll gain back over the years ahead? What motivates businessmen to keep their prices stable at times when they obviously could get more (e.g., the auto manufacturers after World War II), and to boost prices at other times?

By and large, the economist tries to take people's motives and desires as given, and to explain how the system will work out on the basis of these motives and desires. Of course, he never quite does this, because often the motives are intertwined with the way the system works—for example, when there are only two or three big producers in a market and each has to worry about what the other will do (Alcoa, Reynolds, and Kaiser in aluminum production). Unfortunately, moreover, psychologists are still a long way from understanding why people behave as they do, especially when they act in groups such as unions or business firms. Hence, understanding human motivation isn't simply a matter of reading a book on psychology.

The sociologist borders closely on the social psychologist in his interest in human behavior in the entire social setting. Both he and the psychologist are likely to put more stress on noneconomic motives than economists do, and a complete understanding of the modern economic system undoubtedly calls for a better understanding of the social forces motivating human behavior than you can hope to get from this book. If you've had a course in sociology or social psychology, it should be interesting to try to fit together the explanation of behavior there with the economic slant on society here.

Lastly, as soon as we talk about public policy, some understanding of politics and the American governmental process becomes essential. Increasingly, economic pressure groups are seeking to achieve their aims through Congress and governmental administrative agencies, rather than letting the market place settle their differences. Moreover, we may as well recognize that administering an economic policy, such as antitrust legislation, may be as important as deciding on the policy in the first place. How big is too big in business is a far from simple problem for the economist, but it's still more complex for the public policy-maker. He knows that the actual administration of the policy will have to get reasonable support from widely diverse groups in society. Otherwise, antitrust simply won't have any teeth, no matter how "correct" economists are in deciding what business practices government ought to forbid in order to protect the consumer. Economic policy in a democracy can't avoid concern with the political process.

For a thorough understanding of how the economic system works, we ought to know what the psychologist, the sociologist, and the political scientist, as well as the business administrator, have to say. Unfortunately, we usually don't. So always remember that you're seeing only part of the picture when you study economics, and that intelligent citizenship and full understanding demand that you see the whole picture. This book tries to remind you of this problem whenever what the other disciplines have to say is important—for example, whether businessmen really do try to maximize their profits or not. (Many psychologists and sociologists suggest that they probably don't, a fair share of the time.) The book does the best it can for you, but when you take your economics with you to read the daily paper or to vote for your senator, it's up to you to fill in the rest of the picture.

OBJECTIVES OF THE BOOK If you're going to spend several months or a year studying a book, you deserve to know what the author thinks he is trying to accomplish. A good deal of the flavor of this book has been given in the preceding pages. But specifically, the book is aimed at these objectives:

1. *To focus attention on the major problems faced by any economic system, and to arouse an interest in these problems that will continue after you leave college.* If your use of the descriptive and analytical materials in this book ends with cramming for the final exam, the book will have failed. Its real goal is to help you read the newspaper, argue understandingly with your neighbor, and vote intelligently on economic issues over the years ahead.

2. *To provide enough descriptive material on the present economic system to give you a foundation for understanding what the problems really are.* Without understanding a problem in its whole setting, there's little chance of solving it effectively. And knowing the facts about a problem is the first step. But the book makes no pretense of supplying an encyclopedic description of the modern economy. It takes the position that your main job is to learn how to think straight for yourself, not to cram your head full of facts. A mind cluttered with transient details seldom sees the major issues. And few things will be deader 20 years from now than many of today's facts. Lastly, the evidence is that we don't remember most of the facts we memorize anyway. So learn the few main outlines of the economic system and the facts you need to understand each problem that you study. But don't make a fetish of facts.

3. *To help you develop an orderly, systematic way of sizing up and thinking through economic problems.* There's nothing unique about straight thinking in economics. But heated emotions, prejudices, and gossip are especially likely to get in the way of objectivity on labor relations, the national debt, and other such subjects. In economics as elsewhere, you have to know what the problem is before you can solve it. You need to marshal your analytical tools and use them carefully and systematically, instead of rushing blindly ahead on the first tack that comes to mind. You need to check your conclusions against other evidence and against other conclusions on the same question. And, if you want to understand more in the future than you do now, you need to stop frequently and ask yourself: What have I learned by thinking through and living through each problem?

The habit of orderly, careful thinking is something you can't learn in any one course. But a major purpose of this book is to repeat the process over and over in economics, in the hope that it will stick both here and in other fields. Chapter 5 has a good deal more to say on this important subject.

4. *To provide a few fundamental, simple, analytical economic models, principles, and concepts that will stick with you and be of real help to you in thinking about economic problems for yourself.* Unless you're going to be a professional economist, you won't remember the details of this book five years from now. The main things you can take away are those covered by the preceding three points, plus a few simple tools that you can remember and use in your day-to-day thinking. Ideally, of course, you'll learn all the finer points of economic analysis, understanding the details of modern economic theory and using them in thinking through the problems of today and tomorrow. But we know that's too much to expect from an elementary course. Throughout, therefore, there is an attempt to emphasize and re-emphasize those simple analytical models and economic principles that you can learn thoroughly and keep with you for use long after you take the final exam. Perhaps the biggest part of your job in using this book effectively is to be sure that you do get these few things firmly in mind rather than trying to memorize the details of the various problems the book considers.

PLAN OF THE BOOK   In trying to implement these objectives, the book is divided into seven parts. The Table of Contents provides a detailed outline of the book. To give a simpler picture, however, the following brief outline shows the major area covered by each Part, on the theory that if you know where you're going before you start it's usually easier to get there.

Part 1. The Foundations of Economic Analysis
Part 2. National Income, Employment, and Economic Growth
Part 3. Markets, the Price System, and the Allocation of Resources
Part 4. The Distribution of Income
Part 5. The Public Economy (government spending, taxes, and borrowing)
Part 6. The International Economy
Part 7. Some Current Economic Problems (managerial economics, social security, underdeveloped countries, comparative economic systems)

Throughout the book, whenever public policy issues are posed, you will find a recurring theme: *Decide for yourself what you think should be done!* This is not because economists have no ideas on what should be done, or because economic analysis does not suggest strongly what ought to be done. We do have ideas, often strong ones, on public policy issues, and on many of these issues economic analysis points out a clear path. But the main goal of the book is to give you the tools you will need—*and experience in using those tools to reach your own conclusions.*

On all the public policy issues, you will find that the suggested procedure is basically the same. First, carefully identify the problem that needs solution: what are the facts and what are the goals you want to see achieved? Second, marshal your analytical tools and consider thoroughly the main alternative lines of action that are open. Third, evaluate these alternatives, and then decide which policy looks best.

SOME SUGGESTIONS ON HOW TO USE THE BOOK

The most important suggestions on how to use this book are contained in the preceding sections: (1) Get a firm sight on the important goals at the outset, and (2) keep them uppermost in your mind through all the words and diversions of a long book and a busy course. But there are some tricks in using a book like this that may help you do a better job than just plowing through the assignment each day.

1. Know where you're going before you start reading. Before you start a chapter, go back and look at its place in the Table of Contents. This will give you some perspective on how it fits in with what you know already and with where you're headed. The second part of looking ahead is to thumb through the chapter itself. Get an idea of the main subjects covered and the order in which they appear. Every chapter is organized so that the major headings mark off the main parts, with sub-headings for the subsidiary parts in each main section. These headings are designed to give a summary picture of what is covered, and provide a little outline of the chapter to help you keep the main points in focus.

2. As you read, keep asking yourself, "What is the main point of this paragraph and of this section?" Some sections are largely descriptive; these are easy. Some full of tightly reasoned analysis, usually supplemented by an example of how the analysis might apply. Here, be sure you understand the main framework of the analysis. Don't let the example become the main point, since the big job is to be able to use the analytical tools yourself when new and different problems arise.

3. When you've finished reading, check to see what you've really learned. (a) A tough but very useful test is to shut the book and put aside any notes you have taken, and to write down in not more than five to ten sentences the fundamental points of the chapter. If you can do this, you've read the right way—concentrating on the fundamentals and using the rest of the chapter as a setting for understanding them. If it takes you more than a page, you may have read the chapter well, but you had better check to be sure you know what is worth remembering fully. (b) Then, using your core sentences, see whether you can honestly say to yourself that you understand their significance for the kind of problem considered in the chapter. An acid test is to see whether you can use the analytical tool for yourself on a similar but different problem from the example used in the chapter.

1. Would you expect union members and businessmen to agree or disagree on what the government ought to do about the following issues:
   a. Institute direct controls over prices to check inflation.
   b. Institute direct controls over wages to check inflation.
   c. Increase income taxes on the high-income groups.
   d. Decrease present price-support subsidies to farmers.
   e. Take more aggressive action against racketeers in unions.

   Where they disagree, which would you expect to be right? How should you go about making up your mind?

2. Suppose the federal government must raise $5 billion more in taxes because of increased spending on national defense. One group argues we should increase personal income taxes to cover the cost; another favors higher taxes on business corporations. Which alternative would you prefer? What steps are required for you to make an intelligent, orderly decision on this question?

3. If another major depression like that of the 1930's occurs, how seriously do you think it will affect you and your family? What if a rapid inflation occurs, in which prices double over the next few years? From your own point of view, which is the more serious problem for the economy to avoid?

4. List four major issues at stake in the last presidential or senatorial campaign.
   a. Which of these were predominantly or party economic issues?
   b. Choose one of the issues—for example, whether taxes should be reduced—and list as clearly and concisely as possible the reasons why you favor or oppose the measure.
   c. Find a classmate who disagrees with you, and try to determine exactly why you disagree. Is it because you differ on the facts? Because you are defining your terms differently and hence aren't arguing about the same thing? Because you have different economic "theories" about the effects of lowering taxes? Because you have different opinions on what taxes should accomplish in our society? Because of some other reason?

5. Suppose a depression occurs, producing millions of unemployed workers. A well-known economist emphasizes that the cheapest way to keep the unemployed from starvation is to give carefully planned, minimal amounts of highly nutritious (but unfortunately not very tasty) foodstuffs. An equally well-known sociologist admits that this would be the cheapest method in terms of current dollar costs, but argues that work relief that gives men jobs would be much better since it would avoid the stigma of charity and keep the men busy. Which would you agree with, and why? What other information would you want to have before making up your mind, in case you think the arguments stated are inconclusive?

FOR
ANALYSIS
AND
DISCUSSION

The American Economy— A Summary View

The United States is by far the richest nation in the world, by almost any economic measure. International comparisons of incomes and standards of living are very difficult. Incomes are measured in different kinds of money (dollars in the United States, francs in France, and so on); goods and services available for purchase vary widely over the world; and people's wants are diverse. But Table 2-1 provides a rough picture of the comparative national incomes of some of the world's nations in 1955. The figure for each nation is its total production of all goods and services (including arms and factories as well as consumer goods), valued roughly in U.S. dollars of 1955 purchasing power.[1] Because of the problems involved in such international comparisons, these data show only rough orders of magnitude. Yet they are based largely on recent United Nations estimates, and are probably in the right ball park. For the major western countries we know they are reasonably accurate.

---

[1] Data shown are actually "gross national product" estimates for the various countries. A more precise statement of just what is included and excluded in various "national income" figures will be provided in Chapter 6.

Table 2-1 emphasizes the vast productive lead of the United States economy. It is approached only by the U.S.S.R., and the communists' total production is still less than 40 per cent of ours. But such global comparisons show only part of the picture. For one thing, the proportion of total production devoted to national defense varies enormously. It is highest in the U.S.S.R., where apparently about a sixth of total output goes for military purposes. The proportion of output devoted to investment in factories and other productive equipment also varies greatly. Again, this is apparently highest in the U.S.S.R., though Germany and some of the other western European nations have also reported very high figures. Production devoted to these purposes doesn't help raise the current standard of living in consumer goods, though heavy investment means more consumer goods for the future.

Table 2-1

NATIONAL INCOMES IN 1955 *

Country	Billions	Country	Billions
United States	$387	Canada	$27
U.S.S.R	130	India	25
Great Britain	48	Japan	20
France	42	Italy	17
West Germany	34	Greece	2
Communist China	32	Peru	1

* Converted to U.S. dollars at 1955 prices. Rough estimates by author in some cases, based on United Nations and Organization for European Economic Cooperation estimates for earlier years. See footnote 1, above.

What happens when we convert these national figures to a per capita basis? This has been done in Table 2-2 on page 14. The United States retains its long lead, well ahead of Canada and more than double the highest western European countries. Russia drops far down, because her huge national product is divided up among 200 million people. But the truly shocking figures here are those for the "underdeveloped" countries of Asia, Africa, South America, and even southeastern Europe. China and India, with over a billion people between them, had per capita annual incomes (output) of only around $55 to $60. Two-thirds of the world's population—over one and three-quarters billion people—had per capita incomes of less than $200 per year, hardly enough to eke out the barest living, even when we take into account their simple life and their reliance on home-produced foods and clothing. Remember that these estimates are extremely crude, especially for the economically "backward" countries. Yet even if the estimates should be off by a wide margin, the broad picture of world-wide poverty would not be changed.[2]

[2] For a more complete table and discussion of the economically underdeveloped countries, see Chapter 43.

In looking at the figures in Table 2-2, remember that they are extremely crude estimates. To some extent, they try to compare incomparables. The Indian peasant or Chinese coolie, living in a mud hut in a tiny village, with no clothes except what he wears, with a monotonous diet of rice and fish, and who lives out his years never going more than 25 miles from his birthplace, has so little in common with the American or West European that the figures may have little real meaning. What they do say is that Americans are extremely rich by comparison with the abject poverty of the billions who live in the underdeveloped countries.

Table 2-2

WORLD PER CAPITA INCOMES IN 1955 *

Country	Dollars	Country	Dollars
United States	$2310	Italy	$460
Canada	1800	Brazil	270
United Kingdom	980	Greece	230
Australia	970	Japan	220
France	930	Peru	130
Netherlands	710	Thailand	90
West Germany	700	India	60
U.S.S.R.	630	Communist China	55

* Converted to U.S. dollars in 1955 prices. Rough estimates based on sources indicated for Table 2-1.

Another warning about per capita figures. Each figure represents only the income received by some mythical average person. Actually there is a great dispersion of incomes in most nations—a few very rich, and many poor. Thus in the United States in 1955, when average or per capita production was about $2,300, 10 per cent of all families (averaging about 3+ persons) received incomes over $8,400, while another 10 per cent received less than $900. Moreover, the average per capita figure was pulled up by the presence of a few very wealthy individuals —think what one Rockefeller, for example, does to the average. And the rough per capita figures hide a similar wide dispersion of incomes in every other country. In general, the masses received much smaller incomes than the per capita figures shown.

One last international comparison. The United States is far the richest nation. But who is growing fastest? During the past decade two very different nations have held the lead: the U.S.S.R., and West Germany, the first a communist nation and the second probably the most thoroughly private-enterprise major country outside the Americas. Each of these countries increased its total output by perhaps 7 to 9 per cent per annum over the decade. By contrast, our own total output has grown only around 3 to 4 per cent per annum, one of the slowest rates of any of the major industrialized nations. Over the past two hundred years, the achievements of the American economy have been spectacular indeed—from untrodden wilderness to the world's richest and most powerful nation. But in recent years America's power to outperform the communist world has been questioned. And the world is watching for the answer, especially the leaders of the great masses in the underdeveloped nations, whose living standards are pitifully low and who want above all else a pathway up from poverty.

INCOME AND CONSUMPTION IN THE UNITED STATES In 1958, the United States produced $438 billion worth of goods and services. About $90 billion of this went for national defense and other government services like highways and education. Another $55 billion consisted of "producers' goods"—factories, machinery, new buildings, and other equipment to produce more and better consumer goods in the future. The biggest chunk, about $290 billion, or two-thirds of the total, was made up of consumer goods and services—autos, beefsteaks, movies, clothing, medical services, and so on.

Figure 2-1 shows the incomes received by American families during 1958. The total income received by all families in that year was about $355 billion, about $85 billion less than total production. (The difference, as we shall see in Chapter 6, represented goods to replace goods that were wearing out, and other production that wasn't reflected directly in incomes received by individuals.) Figure 2-1 shows the division of this total among about 55 million family units.

At the top, 5 per cent of all families received incomes over $15,000, and the roughly 2.5 million families in this group received 19 per cent of the nation's income. Another 8 per cent of the families received between $10,000 and $15,-000, and they accounted for another 15 per cent of total income. At the bottom, even with America's prosperity, 14 per cent of all families received incomes under $2,000, and these 14 per cent got only 3 per cent of the total income.[3] Many of this lowest group were farmers who raised some of their own food and hence weren't quite so poor as they look, and many others were retired people and other "non-workers" who may have received help from families and friends. But any way you look at it, they were close to the poverty class.

Perhaps the two most striking things about Figure 2-1 are the big share of income received by the rich, and the even bigger share received by what we might call the "middle class." If we rearrange the data in Figure 2-1 a little bit, and separate out the families getting between $5,000 and $15,000 and those getting over $15,000, two facts stand out strongly: The 5 per cent of families getting over $15,000, whom we might call "rich," received nearly 20 per cent of the total income. More striking, over 45 per cent of all families fell in the $5,000–$15,000 "middle-income" group and received well over half of the total national

---

[3] If you want to convert these figures to a per person basis, divide each family into about 3 persons; single persons count as families when they live alone and operate as independent family units.

income. The rise of this "great middle class" has had profound implications for the American way of life and for the American businessman, who now finds the bulk of his market in reasonably well-off but not rich families.

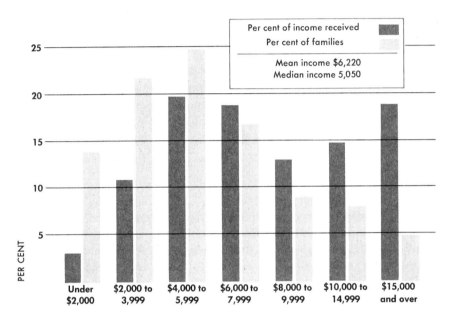

Family Incomes in 1958

Per cent of income received
Per cent of families

Mean income $6,220
Median income 5,050

PER CENT

Under $2,000 | $2,000 to 3,999 | $4,000 to 5,999 | $6,000 to 7,999 | $8,000 to 9,999 | $10,000 to 14,999 | $15,000 and over

FIG. 2-1   The United States has a wide range of family incomes. The few who are rich get far more than a proportionate share of the total national income. Half of all families got more than $5,050, and half less, in 1958. (Source: U.S. Department of Commerce.)

To appreciate how the American economy has changed, try the following little problem: The parents of a family in your home town live with their two high-school boys in a comfortable six-room suburban house, outfitted with a full line of appliances, a television set, and a car that the father drives to work. They also use the car for camping trips in the summer. The mother shops at a local super-market and at several big department stores; the boys attend the good local public schools; on weekends the family often goes swimming at a nearby beach or plays golf.

Question: What does the father do for a living? What is the social status of the family? Ten years ago you could safely have said that this was a solid middle-class family. The father was probably a professional man, a middle- or lower-echelon manager, the owner of a small business, or perhaps a successful salesman. But today you could deduce almost nothing about the family's social rank or the father's occupation. He may be a truck driver earning $5,500, a college professor earning $7,000, a plumber or skilled machinist earning $8,000, an airline pilot earning $15,000, or an executive earning $20,000. The family might be any one of perhaps half the entire American population.

The "median" American family income in 1958 was about $5,050. That is, half of all families received more, and half less, than that. The "mean" (or average) family income was about $6,200; ordinary averages are pulled up by the few huge incomes at the top. If you're interested in more facts now, look at the introductory section of Chapter 28, which considers the distribution of income in more detail.

It might seem that wealth, rather than income, would be a more fundamental measure of how well off we are economically. Actually, income seems to be more significant, since we usually don't use wealth itself, but only the income from it. Our data on wealth are sketchy. The best estimates are that our total national wealth (the value of all farms, factories, highways, houses, and so on) was somewhere around $1.5 trillion in 1958, measured in 1958 prices. This would average out to around $30,000 per family. But the questions of what you include in national wealth and how you value what you do include are so difficult that these figures shouldn't be taken very seriously. Should we include, for example, the estimated value of all undrilled oil fields in the country—and if so, at whose estimate of their value?

We do know a lot about what Americans consume with their incomes. In 1958, for example, we spent $291 billion on consumption of goods and services of all sorts. This included about $78 billion for food, $6 billion for cigarettes and cigars, $25 billion for clothing and shoes, $17 billion for medical care, $27 billion for automobiles and gasoline. Some of the smaller items may be even more interesting: $4 billion for beauty treatments, toilet articles, and haircuts, $1 billion for movie admissions, $3 billion for television and radio receivers, $3 billion for all private education, $4 billion for all welfare and religious activities, $3 billion for cleaning and pressing.

Table 2-3 summarizes the consumption part of the American standard of living. The per family figures are obtained simply by dividing the totals by the number of families. But remember that average figures obtained in this way are biased upward. A "typical" family would show substantially lower figures, and there were, of course, huge variations among families. Two additional items are shown at the bottom of the table: personal taxes and personal savings. These two, added to personal consumption expenditures, account for all the income that individuals received in 1958.

PRODUCTION AND EMPLOYMENT IN THE UNITED STATES

What does the economy produce, and who produces it?

In 1958, the economy turned out an almost infinite variety of goods and services—autos, movies, machine tools, houses, factories, bread, potatoes, haircuts, maid services, chemicals, legal services, and hundreds of thousands more. Missiles, ammunition, military aircraft, and upkeep of our armed forces made up a substantial part of this total.

We earn our livings by producing the many goods and services that we, as consumers, demand in the market. Only the government sphere of the economy provides a major exception to the private-market focus, and in our democratic system the government presumably responds to what we, as citizens, want it to do.

Table 2-4 gives a summary picture of production and employment in the whole economy. This table goes beyond the picture of personal consumption provided by Table 2-3, because total production includes a wide variety of goods and services not for direct personal consumption—machinery, factories, government output, and so on.

Table 2-3

PERSONAL CONSUMPTION EXPENDITURES, 1958 *

	All Families (Billions of Dollars)		Per Family (Dollars)	
Food and beverages	$78		$1,440	
Clothing and shoes	25		460	
Gasoline and oil	10		190	
Other nondurable goods	29		540	
Total nondurable goods		$142		$2,630
Automobiles and parts	17		310	
Furniture and household equipment	17		310	
Other durable goods	6		110	
Total durable goods		40		720
Housing	37		690	
Household operation	17		310	
Transportation	9		170	
Other services	47		870	
Total services		112		2,070
Total consumption		291		5,420
Personal taxes	43		800	
Personal saving	21		390	
		$354		$6,610

* Data from U.S. Department of Commerce. Columns may not add to totals because figures are rounded. The total per family income figure is a little larger than that in Fig. 2-1. See Chapter 6 for details.

Take a look at the industry that interests you most. If it's petroleum, only about 240,000 men are producing about $4 billion worth of petroleum and products, an annual output of around $17,000 per employee. The petroleum industry has a huge amount of capital equipment per worker—estimated at over $80,000 per production worker in 1958. This figure, compared with only about $18,000 for the economy as a whole, accounts for much of the high productivity in the oil industry. A modern gasoline refinery is about the nearest thing to an automatic factory you can imagine. There seems to be almost nobody around, except for some maintenance workers and a few leisurely people watching dial boards.

Table 2-4

PRODUCTION AND EMPLOYMENT, 1958 *

	Value of Output *	Employ- ment *		Value of Output *	Employ- ment *
TOTAL	$361	65.2	Trade	$60	12.7
Agriculture	16	5.2	Wholesale	21	3.1
			Retail	39	9.6
Mining	6	.8	Finance & Real Estate	34	2.7
Construction	19	4.1	Transportation	17	2.7
Manufacturing	109	16.7	Railroads	7	1.1
Food	9	1.5	Highways	5	1.0
Textiles & apparel	8	2.2	Other	5	.6
Lumber & furniture	4	1.0	Communications &		
Printing	5	.9	Public Utilities	13	1.5
Chemicals	8	.9	Services	40	9.0
Petroleum	4	.2	Personal	12	2.8
Basic metals	10	1.2	Medical	8	1.7
Fabricated metals	10	1.2	Legal	2	.3
Electrical machinery	8	1.2	Other	18	5.2
Other machinery	11	1.6	Government	44	9.9
Automobiles	7	.7	Federal	23	5.1
Other	24	4.0	State & local	21	4.8

* Preliminary data. Value of output in billions of dollars; employment in millions of persons. Value of output is, technically, income originating in the various industries. Figures may not add exactly because of rounding, and because some international activities are omitted. Data from U.S. Department of Commerce.

If you look at the textile industry, or at agriculture, you see a different picture. In textiles and apparel, it took about 2,200,000 workers to produce only twice the same amount of product—an output of about $4,000 per worker. Capital investment per worker in textiles was only about $6,000, far below the average for all manufacturing. In farming, 5,200,000 workers produced $16 billion of products —about $3,000 per worker.

These figures may suggest many things to you. Perhaps wages and salaries are very high in the oil industry, low in textiles and farming. Or maybe wages and salaries are about the same everywhere, but the investors take a huge cut in the oil industry on their capital investment. You may see other hypotheses in the figures. These are some of the questions about production and employment in the modern American economy that need answering later on.

The Changing Pattern of Employment.   How they make their living is as important for many people as how big their incomes are. And the ways people earn their living in America have changed drastically over the past century.

Figure 2-2 shows some of the big things that have been happening. Most spectacular is agriculture. In 1870, 54 per cent of the labor force were farmers; in 1959, only about 7 per cent. In 1870, only 22 per cent were employed in the

Percentage of Workers
in Major Occupational Groups

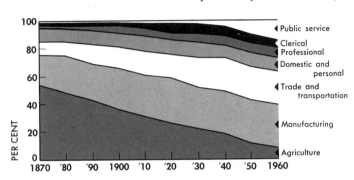

FIG. 2-2   Over the past century there has been a drastic change in the way Americans earn their livings. Agriculture is no longer the dominant way of life. Services of all sorts and manufacturing have shown the largest growth. (Source: National Resources Committee and U.S. Department of Commerce; 1960 estimated by author.)

"service" industries—trade, transportation, the professions, clerical work, domestic and personal services; in 1959, the figure was over 50 per cent. Over the whole period, manufacturing grew slowly as a percentage of total employment, although its output grew much faster in the national total, reflecting a rapid rise in productivity per worker.

Figure 2-3 shows the changing pattern of employment over the past three decades in a somewhat different way. Here you can readily see the rapid change in relative importance of the different occupations. Indirectly, this chart also suggests the high degree of mobility that has characterized the American economy.

Guns and Butter—The Heavy Hand of War.   No summary of the modern American economy is complete that does not suggest how war has dragged down our standard of living. In 1959, we spent about $46 billion—about 12 per cent of our national income—on war and preparation for war, and another $4 billion on building up foreign allies against aggression and on tidying up after past wars. If the government had merely parceled out this money equally to all taxpayers, every American family might have had about $1,000 more to spend on clothes, autos, furniture, and food. During the actual combat of World War II, federal military expenditures were higher yet, exceeding $85 billion in 1944 (at prices about half as high as in 1959, so the 1944 total would be around $170 billion in present prices). This was nearly half the total output of the economy.

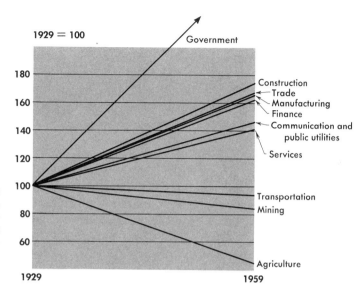

1929 = 100

Government

180

Construction
Trade
160
Manufacturing
Finance
Communication and
140
public utilities

120
Services

100

Transportation
80
Mining

60

Agriculture
1929
1959

FIG. 2-3 The pattern of employment has continued to change rapidly during recent decades. American economic growth has been characterized by a high degree of mobility. (Source: U.S. Department of Commerce.)

In a full-employment economy, we must choose between guns and butter. If we use steel and highly skilled labor to build intercontinental missiles, we can't use them to build autos or hi-fi sets. This is the dilemma in a full-employment wartime economy: Resources are scarce, but civilian wants are many. What war takes comes out of our standard of living in real goods, out of our pocketbooks in taxes and inflation.

Modern war is fantastically expensive, in money and, more fundamentally, in men and materials. The engineering design work on the huge B-58 jet bomber is said to have consumed 3 million man-hours before a single step could be taken in manufacturing the first plane. There is enough electronic equipment in the plane to provide a telephone system for a small city. The hand of war—past, present, and future—on the American standard of living is heavy indeed. Rich as we are, we would be much richer if all our resources could be devoted to peaceful pursuits—to autos and refrigerators rather than to rockets and missiles.

But we are not alone. While we devote about 10 per cent of our national production to war, the U.S.S.R., with a per capita output about one-third of ours, apparently uses around one-sixth of her national product for military purposes. In Russia the problem is even more painful than here. She has chosen heavy military outlays. We debate whether we can afford the defense we need.

FOUNDATIONS OF ECONOMIC PRODUCTION AND GROWTH

Resources and Technology. Man's ability to produce the goods and services he wants depends on the resources at his disposal and his knowledge of how to use them. The United

21

States is rich in natural resources; it is rich in produced resources, such as capital equipment, buildings, and machinery; and it is rich in human resources, the most important of all. The American worker on the production line is the best educated, best fed, and most productive in the world. American engineering and mass-production know-how have produced Detroit's fabulous auto plants, Pittsburgh's steel, Oak Ridge's atomic energy. Vast research expenditures generate a steady stream of new products and new methods. And the American businessman manages somehow to keep production going and sales booming in a way that is the mixed envy, dismay, and sometimes disdain of his less aggressive counterparts in the rest of the world. These resources and this technology are the real foundations of the American standard of living—of our sweeping growth over the centuries. We will look at them in detail in Chapter 3.

Specialization and Exchange.   To take advantage of these resources and this modern technology, the American private-enterprise system, like other highly developed economies, has developed a high degree of specialization. Charlie Chaplin immortalized the forlorn worker on the assembly line, day after day screwing his single bolt onto the cars as they went by. But specialization goes far deeper than this. The engineer who designs the plant is a specialist. So is the lawyer who sees that the title to the land is clear. So is the banker who lends part of the money for the construction. So are the accountant who keeps the records and the secretary who does the typing. So is just about everybody else. Even the boss himself is a specialist. Management has become an independent profession, and increasingly the nation's huge corporations are run by paid managers who own little or none of the businesses they administer. Only by dividing up tasks and developing highly specialized human skills and mechanical equipment can an economy obtain the benefits of "mass production" and fully utilize the basic production resources it has available.

Part and parcel of specialization is an elaborate exchange system. The lawyer, the banker, the truck driver, the engineer, the manager himself—all would starve if the intricate system of exchange that we take for granted didn't make it possible for them to buy the food they need with the incomes they earn. Even the farmer, who might eat his own carrots and potatoes, would be in desperate straits if he were really cast on his own—without electricity, new clothing, gas and repairs for his car, mail delivery, and the thousand things he gets from other specialists. Every minute of our daily lives we depend on the specialization and exchange all of us take for granted. None of us would dare specialize if we couldn't count on being able to exchange our services and products for the wide range of things we want.

Productive resources, technology, specialization, and exchange. These are the four foundation stones of the productive power of the American economy—and of every other highly developed modern economy, communist or capitalist. With-

out them, no modern economy can prosper. Only by obtaining more and better resources and by improving our technology, our specialization, and our exchange procedures can we continue to push upward our national standard of living.

All four factors are obvious. But never forget that it is the combination of these four simple factors that makes the difference between poverty and plenty. Many of the commonest economic fallacies are rooted in a neglect of these simple truths. We shall look at them in detail in the following chapters and shall return to them repeatedly.

SCARCITY: THE PROBLEM OF ECONOMIZING   The United States is rich in resources. But human wants are infinite, and diversion of part of our production potential to national defense sharpens this problem of insufficient resources to meet all wants. If nature somehow provided bountifully all the things we want, there would be no need for work, no problem of arranging for economic production. But very few things are so plentiful that everyone can have all he wants of them free. *Scarcity —i.e., not enough to satisfy everyone's complete wants free—is* the *basic economic fact.*

Since resources (including human labor) are scarce, mankind constantly faces a problem of "economizing"—of allocating scarce productive resources, consumption goods, money, time, energy, among the many alternative uses to which they might be put. We must decide which uses are most desirable and then economize, or allocate effectively, our scarce resources among them. If we spend our time or money in one way, we forego spending it in another. If we use land to produce wheat, we cannot raise corn on it. If we use manpower and machinery to make guns, we cannot use them to produce tractors. So far in history, no economy has been rich enough to escape this problem of economizing—of choosing between alternative uses of resources that are too scarce to satisfy all human wants. Probably no society ever will be. *The problem of economizing scarce resources so as to maximize wanted production for consumption is the core of the study of economics.*

The Problem of Economic Growth.   What explains America's extraordinary growth? Why are other nations growing faster now? These are complex questions. They have complex answers.

Here we need to recognize one basic fact—a fact that is intimately related to the problem of economizing. *To grow, an economy must use part of its productive resources in building up productive capacity for the future, rather than use all its capacity on goods and services for current consumption.* A higher standard of living for our children demands a willingness to live less well now than we otherwise might. If we use steel and manpower to make autos and refrigerators for today, we cannot use them to build factories and intricate machines to increase production for the future. If we devote our engineers to building TV sets, they cannot spend their time on basic research.

Here again is the central problem of economizing—of choosing among the different uses to which we can devote our scarce resources. We can't have everything. To have automatic factories for a higher future standard of living we must forego automobiles for today. To grow fast involves a real cost.

THE PROBLEM OF INSTABILITY AND DEPRESSIONS No one would deny the basic fact of economic scarcity in the world today. Yet during the depression days of the 1930's one often heard the remark, "The problem of production is solved; what we need now is to solve the problem of distribution." Though we had a vast idle productive capacity, we seemed unable to find the markets for our goods that would keep men at work. Involuntary unemployment of men and machines wasted billions of dollars' worth of potential output.

Economic growth has not come smoothly. The need to avoid instability, depression, and unemployment may be a separate social problem almost as important as that of economizing itself. But in a fundamental sense, the two problems are one. Depression unemployment and wasted production merely represent one allocation of scarce productive resources—allocation to idleness and waste.

This allocation is involuntary and unintentional. It arises out of the faulty functioning of the entire economic organization, particularly in highly industrialized, western economies. Fortunately, it is these economies that can best afford periodic waste, since their per capita real incomes are generally far above those of the unindustrialized nations. But even in the United States, the deep depression of the 1930's set back per capita real incomes to near the level of 1900; it pulled U.S. incomes down near the average level of countries far poorer in basic resources and productive ability which did not have such widespread unemployment. The problem of depression and mass unemployment is of critical importance—socially, politically, and economically. Another massive depression like that of the 1930's might threaten the very foundations of our free society.

FOR ANALYSIS AND DISCUSSION

1. What would you say are the major factors accounting for the fact that the American standard of living is so much higher than that in China? In England?

2. Suppose you are visiting abroad and are alarmed to find a large amount of anti-American sentiment, on the ground that America is extremely wealthy and could well afford to give more aid to less wealthy peoples, rather than selfishly clinging to most of the goods we produce. How would you go about explaining to the local residents why the present distribution of real income among the nations is a fair and proper one?

3. How fast do you think the American economy should grow? How would you, as dictator, go about deciding what proportion of the economy's productive resources should be devoted to current consumption and what proportion to laying a basis for higher living standards in the future?

4. A recent congressional investigation found that over half the consumer price of many food products went to middlemen at different levels—retailers, wholesalers, and so on. In some cases, as little as 20 per cent of the final price represented payments to the farmer who originally produced the food. Farm and consumer groups testifying before the committee urged action to rectify this situation.

    a. Do you agree that Congress should take some action? Why or why not?

    b. If Congress should act, what should it do?

5. What would you say are the major factors that explain the steady decline in the percentage of the American labor force employed in agriculture?

6. Compare the distribution of your family's consumption spending with the national pattern shown in Table 2-3, converting both to show the percentage spent on different items. What factors can you suggest to account for the differences between your family and the national figures?

7. Some socialists argue that the ills of the American economy could be healed by equalizing the distribution of income. This, they claim, would give everyone a generous standard of living. Calculate roughly what the income per person (or per family) would be if such a redistribution were to occur. Would you gain or lose from such a policy? Would you favor governmental action toward this type of income distribution? Why, or why not?

The Foundations of Economic Progress: Resources and Technology

3

Resources, technology, specialization, and exchange—these are the foundations of economic production and growth in every country, be it the United States, Samoa, Russia, or Bolivia. This chapter summarizes briefly where the United States stands on the first two of these basic factors—resources and technology. Chapter 4 deals with the latter two—specialization and exchange.

Production and Economic Growth Defined. *To the economist, production is the creation of any good or service that people are willing to pay for.*[1] Raising wheat is production, and so is making the wheat into flour and the flour into bread. It is also production for the local grocer to have the bread on his shelf when you want it, or to deliver the bread to your back door. The agricultural, manufacturing, and marketing services all satisfy human wants, and people are willing to pay for them.

In fact, about half the people employed in the

---

[1] In more technical language, production is the addition of want-satisfying power to goods, or the rendering of services that satisfy human wants that people are willing to pay to satisfy.

26

modern American economy are engaged in rendering services rather than in manufacturing or raising anything. Half of what you pay for many products goes for middlemen's services—the retailer, the wholesaler, the banker, the trucker, and many others. Lots of people object violently to this situation. "There are too many middlemen!" they say. Maybe there are. But if you stop and think about it you'll run head-on into this question: Are there too many manufacturers, or too many farmers? The real test for all producers is whether they satisfy a consumer demand—not how many pounds of physical stuff they produce.

There is nothing moral or ethical about production as the economist defines it. Making and selling cigarettes is production, just like raising and selling food. The test of the private-enterprise economy is the test of the market. If an act helps satisfy a human want that someone is willing to pay for, the act is production.

Economic growth means growth in the amount of goods and services produced. It may mean growth in *total* output of goods and services in the economy. Or it may mean growth in output *per capita* (or per family)—i.e., growth in the ratio: $\frac{\text{total output}}{\text{total population}}$. Although both concepts of growth are important, the second clearly gives us a more direct measure of the economic standard of living of individuals in the economy. If total output grows but population grows even faster, the standard of living of the typical individual is sliding down, not rising. You will find "economic growth" in both senses in everyday usage. *Here, economic growth will mean growth in output (or income) per capita, unless growth in total output or income is specified.*

The two definitions may give rise to quite different pictures. In this country, total output has risen about 3 per cent a year on the average over the last century, or some 35 per cent per decade. Output per capita has risen about 2 per cent per annum, or only a little over 20 per cent per decade. In India, total output has grown steadily, at a rate not far under ours in recent decades. But, since population has grown as fast as output, there has been little increase in output per capita.

MALTHUS AND RICARDO: OVERPOPULATION AND DIMINISHING RETURNS   Two Englishmen, writing a century and a half ago at an early stage of England's industrial growth, provide an interesting background for a modern look at the relation of resources and technology to production and to the outlook for economic growth.

Malthus and the Specter of Famine.   More people mean more productive power. But more people also mean more mouths to feed, more backs to clothe. In 1798, T. R. Malthus, a young British minister who was later to become a noted economist, wrote his now-famous *Essay on the Principle of Population.* He gloomily predicted that population was likely to rise far faster than the productive power associated with more people. Looking at rising birth rates, Malthus pointed out that the population could double every generation (about 30 years) if each woman had only four surviving children, half of them girls who would produce more children in the next generation. Malthus felt that this might well give a geometrical population increase, doubling each generation—2, 4, 8, 16, 32, and so on.

But the world's land could not possibly increase its food output at this rate over the long run, Malthus argued. Thus, unless population growth was checked by moral restraint, or by such disasters as war or disease, it would ultimately be checked by recurrent famine as the population out-ran the food supply. The British standard of living was hardly above the subsistence level for much of the population; unless steps were taken to control the growth of population, the outlook for improvement was bleak.

Ricardo and the "Law of Diminishing Returns." David Ricardo, another British economist writing in the same period, provided a further intellectual justification for Malthus' fears. Ricardo first stated the now-famous "law of diminishing returns." Loosely, the law says that if the number of workers applied to any fixed supply of land is increased, the crops obtained from the land will rise, but sooner or later output will increase at a slower rate than the rate at which workers were added. The implications of this "law" for the standard of living of a growing population seemed clear. Given the world's supply of tillable land, sooner or later the food output per capita would fall when the point of diminishing returns was passed in the application of more and more workers to the limited supply of land. And as population grew thereafter, food output per capita would decline steadily. (This statement of the law of diminishing returns is very rough—a more precise statement appears later in the chapter—but it shows the gloomy predictions that influenced British thinking in the early nineteenth century.)

Were Malthus and Ricardo right? If history has proved them wrong, where did they go astray? Have the rising standards of living of most countries in the western world been temporary, and will Malthus' specter reappear as population soars? Why has the United States apparently managed to avoid the results predicted, while in some other areas, like China and Indonesia, the ghost of Malthus still rides high as the precarious balance between food and population swings uneasily? Looking at the foundations of economic production will help give the answer.

POPULATION AND THE LABOR FORCE Human beings are the most important productive resource of all. In the western world, and especially in America, population has grown rapidly over the past two centuries. Although birth rates have fallen somewhat in many western countries, the average lifespan has lengthened greatly—in

America, from only about 35 years in 1800 to about 70 years now. Table 3-1, which compares the rates of population growth in different areas of the world, points up this fact. Population in Asia and Africa has grown much more slowly; birth rates are high, but lifespans are short. For the whole world, population has grown by over a billion people in the last fifty years, and the annual growth is rising rapidly.

Table 3-1

WORLD POPULATION, 1650-1959 *

Region	1650	1750	1850	1900	1959
North and South America	13	12	59	144	390
Europe	100	140	266	401	620
Asia and Oceania	332	481	751	943	1,570
Africa	100	95	95	120	230
Total	545	728	1,171	1,608	2,810

* In millions.

Figure 3-1 shows the growth rates of some individual nations, and takes a very precarious peek ahead to 1980. Population growth has so speeded in the last decades, especially in America and the huge underdeveloped countries, that the experts speak of "the population explosion." In the United States alone, the population may well grow by 100 million people in the next 25 years—to between 250 and 275 million.

For the whole world, an increase of a *billion* people over the next 15 to 20 years has been forecast by a United Nations team of experts. This would raise

Actual and Estimated Populations

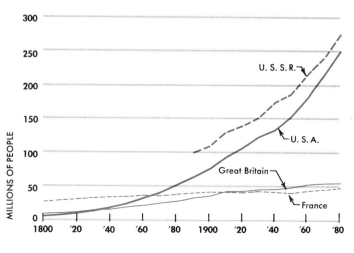

FIG. 3-1   The modern population explosion is most evident in the United States and the U.S.S.R.; inclusion of China and India would dwarf these increases, however. (Source: United Nations, National Industrial Conference Board, and U.S. Bureau of the Census; future data are about middle of alternative figures estimated by different groups.)

the world's population to nearly 4 billion by 1975. The same team suggests that world population may grow by 2½ billion more in the last quarter of the century, exceeding 6 billion by the year 2000. Most of this growth is forecast for the presently "underdeveloped" areas. China alone would have over 1½ billion people by the year 2000, compared with perhaps 350 million for the United States and 500 million for the U.S.S.R. The population forecasters haven't had a very high batting average on long-range predictions. But even if birth rates fall, modern medicine, sanitation, and generally higher living standards will surely continue to extend lifespans greatly in the world's poorer nations. Even when we make allowance for a large possible error, the term "population explosion" still sounds appropriate.[2]

In spite of this growth, population density in the United States is still low (a significant fact for Malthus' and Ricardo's analyses). It now averages about 55 persons per square mile, in comparison with about 400 in the United Kingdom, 350 in Germany, 250 in India, 550 in Japan, and over 800 in Java. Moreover, in spite of the recent population explosion, the annual percentage of population increase in the United States is still below the rate of a century ago.

Figure 3-2 shows the facts. During the first half of the 1800's our population grew at around 35 per cent per decade—about 3 per cent annually. By the decade of the 1930's the rate was down to less than 8 per cent for the entire ten years. For the 1950's it was only back up to around 20 per cent, but that meant some 30 million more people over the single decade.

To return, then, to the dilemma posed at the beginning of the chapter. More population means more mouths to feed, more consumers to satisfy. This is the denominator of the ratio: $\frac{\text{output}}{\text{population}}$, which determines the nation's standard of living. But population growth also contributes workers, who help to raise the numerator. These working members of the population are the labor force.

The Labor Force.   The "labor force" includes all persons in, or seeking, paid employment or who are self-employed. The concept provides a rough measure of the currently available work force.[3] Roughly, these are most of the men between 14 and 70 except those in school, and about a third of the women. Over the last century, the proportion of the population in the U.S. labor force has averaged around 40 per cent. In 1959, the labor force averaged about 73 million people (including 3 million in the armed services), in a population of about 178 million.

But beyond these people in paid jobs of all sorts, there were nearly 35 million housewives plus perhaps 10 million retired persons and young people in high

---

[2] Way off in the realm of pure speculation, some experts forecast a U.S. population of a billion people by 2050, less than a century away. Given the present average lifespan, this would require about 96 per cent of all women to marry and to have an average of 3⅓ children each.

[3] See Chapter 12 for a more complete definition.

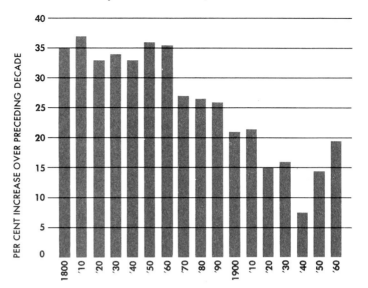

FIG. 3-2 The modern population explosion marks a big increase over recent decades. But growth rates were higher still a century ago. Each bar shows percentage increase over preceding decade. (Source: U.S. Bureau of the Census.)

school and college who were quite capable of performing productive work. Indeed, the economic contribution of the housewives who keep house and raise children, though unpaid in the market place, may be as great as that of women who hold paid jobs. The "labor force" is an obviously arbitrary, though useful, concept.

What determines the proportion of the population looking for jobs? Obviously, age distribution has a lot to do with it. Youngsters under 14 aren't counted in the labor force. Actually, few boys and girls enter the labor force, except for vacation jobs, until they are at least 17. Many of those who study for the professions continue full-time schooling until their mid-20's. At the other end, very old people seldom hold regular jobs, and retirement at age 65 or 68 is becoming standard practice in many industries. Thus, a combination of age distribution, educational standards, and retirement practices loosely sets the proportion of the male population in the labor force.

Closely related is how well-to-do the country is. When people are comfortably fixed, they send their children to college and to summer camp during vacation. When the wealthy man retires, he may try to find another job even though he doesn't have to. But when the poor man retires, with no comfortable pension waiting for him, he has to seek part-time or full-time work.

Lastly, society's attitudes toward whether women should work, when young ladies should marry, and whether wives should work after marriage are obviously important in determining the make-up of the labor force. A century ago, few women worked at paid jobs. Once married, a girl retired sedately to her new home to keep the furniture dusted, get the meals ready on time, and raise a family. Since then, there has been a slow downdrift in the average marriage age for girls, but at the same time a spectacular increase in the number of working wives. Some of the reasons for this increase are the advent of the automatic

31

washer and dryer, the vacuum cleaner, the dishwasher, and the trend toward small houses. Today, over a quarter of all married women have paid jobs; and the 22 million women at work comprise a third of the labor force.

The Labor Force in the Future.   What is the outlook for the United States labor force in the decades ahead? Nobody has a crystal ball, but some things are reasonably sure.

The labor force for 1975 has been born. Thus, the size of the labor force for at least a decade and a half will depend not on population growth but on the proportion of the total population looking for paid jobs. It is therefore significant that we are moving into a drastic shift in the age composition of the American population. For nearly two decades—through the long depression of the 1930's and World War II—marriage and birth rates fell far below normal. Today, there is a huge gap in the 20-30 age group in the labor force. But after World War II came a baby boom, a boom that has continued since. Result: a huge crop of youngsters who are now flooding the elementary and high schools and who will move on into the colleges and the labor force in the 1960's.

So the labor force will begin to rise rapidly in the 1960's. But the babies and school-age groups will probably grow even faster, so the proportion of the population in the labor force may slide even further. This likelihood is strengthened by the increased number of students going on to college, and on to even more extended graduate and professional training. What will happen to the proportion of wives who take paid jobs, only time can tell.

At the same time, old folks are living longer, and we can anticipate a steadily increasing number in the over-65 group. Some of these older people will stay in the labor force. But most will work only part time, if at all. The over-65 group now includes about 15 million (of whom only about 3 million hold full-time jobs). But although compulsory retirement at 65 to 68 has spread, many observers have begun to question whether early retirement is either economically desirable or socially and emotionally beneficial for the individuals concerned. Medical experts emphasize that at 65 some people are still alert and highly productive, others are more than ready for retirement. Perhaps more selective policies will be evolved to keep more older workers in the labor force. Even so, the growing retired group will surely push down on the proportion of the population actually working.

Shorter Working Hours?   How many hours people work a week, and how long their vacations are, influence how productive the labor force is. A century ago, the average factory worker put in 75 to 80 hours a week—generally 10 hours or more a day, including Sundays. Today he works only around 40 hours, and a standard 35-hour, 5-day work-week may not be far away.

What is the impact of shorter working hours on output per worker? Early cuts in working hours *increased* output per worker by reducing the great fatigue and inefficiency associated with long hours. But with the work-week down around 40 hours, and with at least two-week paid vacations common for regular industrial workers, it is ever less likely that shorter hours will increase the output per worker any further. (Remember, though, that other factors, such as better machinery and improved methods, may raise output per worker even with shorter hours.) The whole relationship between working hours and output is a subject of heated dispute between workers and management, and a dispute that only time will settle.

Just what is the best balance between work and leisure for the economy is a thorny problem. Short hours and long vacations may produce fewer cars and airplanes, but leisure itself, though not sold in the market place, has a real value for the persons enjoying it. Perhaps an extra hour of leisure each week is worth more than the goods that could be produced by working that hour. How fully we utilize our human productive resources—how we balance work against leisure—will affect substantially how many goods and services the American economy produces over the years ahead. The current trend seems to be clearly, though only gradually, toward an ever-increasing amount of leisure throughout the work-year.

The Quality of the Labor Force.   The productivity of any labor force depends on its quality as well as on its size. The American worker is probably the most productive in the world. One reason is the large quantity and excellent quality of the capital equipment with which he works. But the efficiency of the American worker and manager also reflects their own high quality—their high levels of health, education, and technological "know-how." America's investment in education may have been its biggest contribution to its own productivity.

The improvement in education has been phenomenal. In colonial days, few people received any formal education beyond elementary reading and writing. By 1880, only one in 15 persons of high-school age was attending school. Today this figure has risen to nearly 90 per cent, with some 10 million students in over 25,000 high schools, and with the proportion of illiterates in the population below 3 per cent. A third of all high-school graduates go on to college.

In the modern age, the scarcest of all resources has become not land or coal or even skilled workers—but brainpower. The achievements of modern science—atomic power, electronics, the "wonder drugs"—are worth the muscle-power of millions of human backs, the output of untold acres of land. Will we run out of low-cost coal and oil? If nuclear energy, and perhaps even solar energy, take their place, the world may little care. Will human needs for food outrun the world's land supply? Not if the scientists' amazing accomplishments in producing new fertilizers, hybrid high-yield crops, and new types of cultivating machines continue at their recent rates. In the ultimate improvement of human welfare one

Einstein or Steinmetz or Edison is worth thousands of ordinary mortals like most of us. Outstanding brainpower is the one resource on which we count for our major advances in technology.

The American Entrepreneur. One of the greatest human "quality" superiorities of the United States has been the ingenuity and energy of its entrepreneurs—its business innovators, managers, and risk-takers.[4] The spirit of inquiry and innovation, and the organizing and operating energy of the American entrepreneur, working in an economic, social, and political climate conducive to innovation, risk-taking, and expansion, deserve a big share of the credit for America's economic progress.

What is the outlook for a continuation of this spirit and this skill? Some observers profess to see a slackening of the proverbial American spirit of enterprise and risk-taking, as we grow richer and more comfortable. But there is little real evidence of such a decline, even though the forms of enterprise and risk-taking have shifted. The scarcity of a comparable spirit of entrepreneurship goes far to explain the slower growth of many European countries and the relative "backwardness" of many of the underdeveloped countries of the East Indies, Asia, and Africa.

NATURAL RESOURCES Our natural resources are substantially fixed in amount. We may use part or all of them, but we cannot increase their quantity. To be sure, by using fertilizers and irrigation we can improve the crop-bearing ability of land, but this must, strictly, be considered capital investment. Similarly, we may discover new natural resources previously unknown. Through improved technology we may use natural resources that have previously been useless; solar power may run the factories of tomorrow. But natural resources are limited. It was that fact, with special emphasis on the fixed supply of productive land, that underlay Malthus' worries. Since the supply of natural resources seemed fixed, how could mankind escape the inexorable law of diminishing returns as population grew?

What about the supply of natural resources in the United States and the possible impact of the law of diminishing returns here? When the first settlers arrived in the New World, they found a wealth of natural resources—fertile land, plentiful vegetation and timber, and temperate climate. From then until nearly 1900 the steady westward movement of the frontier revealed ever more supplies of fertile land, timber, mineral, and power resources. Since 1900, the discovery and settlement of new territory in the continental United States have been negligible. Yet we have an abundance of natural resources.

---

[4] *Entrepreneur* is a widely used economic term. An entrepreneur is an enterpriser, loosely a businessman who is prepared to undertake the production of goods or services when there appears to be a potential profit in doing so. For a more complete analysis, see Part 3.

Land.   We have nearly 2 billion acres of land for productive use. More than one-fifth of this vast total is valuable crop land; our agricultural resources are adequate for a vastly larger population than we now have. Another fifth is pasture land, much of which could be converted to crop production merely by plowing. Nearly a third (over 600 million acres) is covered with valuable forests, making the United States one of the world's richest timber nations. The remaining one-fourth, largely mountains or arid western plateau of little direct use in crop production, is richly endowed with mineral and power (coal, petroleum, and water) resources. Over all this territory, the climate, though varying widely, is on the whole moderate and favorable to crop production and other productive activity. And the population density of 55 per acre is low among the world's developed nations.

Minerals.   Our mineral wealth is probably greater than that of any other nation, except possibly the U.S.S.R. Our supplies of coal, iron ore, limestone, gypsum, bauxite, and molybdenum are large and seem likely to last for a long time. Copper, lead, zinc, tungsten, and most of the nonmetallic minerals are still available in large amounts, but the war drain was heavy and several of them must be viewed as conservation problems in the near future. Nickel, tin, chrome, and antimony are the only four major metals in which United States supplies are negligible relative to foreseeable needs.

As population and consumption grow, the scarcity of mineral deposits vital to industrial production may become a key problem. Compared with other nations, we are rich in mineral resources. But, as a recent major study conducted by a special presidential commission emphasized,[5] our future utilization must be more economical and efficient if we are to avoid heavy dependence on external supplies within a few decades.

Power Resources.   United States coal production is about one-third of the world total; our soft-coal resources are estimated as sufficient to last 4,000 years at the current consumption rate. United States wells produce over half the world's petroleum. But here, and in the associated production of natural gas, reserves are limited; they may not last more than five to ten decades at current consumption rates. The United States appears to have moderate deposits of high-grade uranium ores and other fissionable elements that are essential to large-scale production of atomic energy. Water-power resources are vast. United States potential hydroelectric energy is estimated at around 66 million horsepower, two-thirds of which is still undeveloped.

Adequate power sources are vital to modern economic activity. Total use of power in the American economy has grown spectacularly during the past century,

---

[5] The report provides estimates of resource uses and needs for 1975 as well as data on the present. See President's Materials Policy Commission, *Resources for Freedom* (U.S. Government Printing Office, 1952).

and the composition of power sources has changed drastically. The steadily increasing use of inanimate power to replace human workers has dominated the modern industrial revolution. This changing pattern of energy is shown in Figure 3-3.

Changing Sources of Energy in the United States: 1915-1958

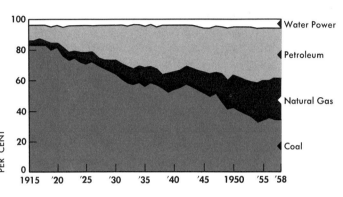

FIG. 3-3   Petroleum and natural gas have increased steadily as major sources of power for the modern economy. Will nuclear and solar power soon take over? (Source: National Industrial Conference Board; 1958 estimated by author.)

Natural Resources and the Future.   America's natural resources are bountiful. Our population density is still low. Today and for the foreseeable future, few countries rival us in natural resources.

But there is little doubt that Ricardo's law of diminishing returns will begin to take its toll, *if* other factors in the picture—more capital goods, improved technology, and improved quality of the labor force—do not offset it. Remember that substantially the same natural resources were here before the Pilgrims landed in 1620, but the American Indian's standard of living was low. Accumulation of capital goods, technological progress, and education have swamped the law of diminishing returns over three centuries. They are our big hope for the future.

CAPITAL GOODS AND CAPITAL FORMATION   The United States has the world's greatest accumulation of "capital" or "producers'" goods—buildings, machinery, equipment, and all the other "man-made" resources that produce other goods and services. Capital goods are owned mainly by businesses, since they are mostly used in producing other goods and services ultimately destined for sale to consumers. But governments—federal, state, and local—are also large owners of capital goods, such as office buildings, mail trucks, military bases, and highways. Still more important dollarwise, all the houses in the country, most of them privately and individually owned, represent a huge investment in capital goods, and turn out continuing "services" for the people who live in them.

Total United States capital goods are estimated at nearly $1.5 trillion (excluding stocks of goods held by consumers, such as furniture and clothing); this amounts to around $30,000 per family. A century ago, the figure was only around $7 billion. Looking at manufacturing plant and equipment alone, the type of capital goods that comes most readily to mind, net capital investment per wage-earner in manufacturing averaged about $18,000 in 1959, far above the figure for any other nation.

But no figures are necessary to dramatize the vast American productive capacity in the auto plants of Detroit, the steel and aluminum mills of Pittsburgh, the nation-wide railway, air, highway, and communication networks, the flour mills of Minneapolis, the huge mechanical harvesters of the wheat fields of the Northwest. American plants and equipment are renowned the world over. And America's plant is not only huge; it is among the newest and most up-to-date to be found anywhere. World War II provided a mighty stimulus to the construction of new plants and equipment, and it has been followed by the greatest accumulation of capital goods the world has ever seen. Year after year, American businesses have invested more in accumulating new capital goods than the entire national output of any except a handful of the world's major nations. Parallel to this business expansion, private individuals and builders have built new homes and apartment buildings on an unprecedented scale. Private investment in capital goods and houses in the United States in 1959 alone amounted to a staggering total of over $60 billion, and government investment accounted for perhaps $10 billion more. This was more than the entire national income of any other country in the world, excepting the U.S.S.R. and Great Britain.

Capital Accumulation—The Choice Between Present and Future. How has the United States been able to manage such a prodigious accumulation of productive capital goods? The achievement is an indivisible result of the use of labor, natural resources, invested savings, and technological advance. As the accumulation grows, old capital goods are continually replaced with different and better goods; productive capacity depends on both capital accumulation and on invention and technological improvement.

Underlying this interrelated process is a basic fact—we are rich and can set aside a substantial part of our current production each year for capital accumulation, without seriously limiting our current consumption. A very poor nation must consume all it produces in order to avoid starvation and to provide the barest minimum of clothing and shelter for its people. Such a nation cannot afford to save; it cannot afford to devote a significant part of its resources to producing capital goods that will raise the productive power and living standard of future generations. But saving is comparatively easy for us.

In "real" terms, this process amounts to diverting part of our productive resources to producing factories, houses, and machinery, rather than food, washing machines, and clothes. In "money" terms, behind the transfer of real productive resources, businesses and families save part of their incomes rather than spending all they receive on consumption goods and services. These savings are then (perhaps indirectly, through banks or insurance companies) channeled into investment in businesses which use them mainly to accumulate capital goods. Families may also, of course, invest their savings directly in new houses. The government plays a direct role, too, when it imposes taxes and uses the funds to build capital goods such as highways and post offices.

Here as almost nowhere else the old biblical adage seems to apply: "To him that hath shall be given." Thus the spread tends to widen between the haves and the have-nots among the nations. And it will widen further unless positive steps are taken to help the poorer countries stimulate the capital formation that is vital to their economic growth and development.

America's stock of capital goods has grown at an average of about 3 per cent annually over the past century. This is a rapid rate. If you stop and think about compound interest, it amounts to a doubling of the total every 25 years. But since World War II the U.S.S.R. and West Germany report rates of 8 to 10 per cent per annum, far higher than ours. How have they managed this, in spite of widespread poverty by our standards? In Russia, at least, by means that we would find intolerable. The masters in the Kremlin have simply decreed that productive resources will be used to build factories and dams, rather than to produce consumer goods. Current consumption by the masses has been held down to permit the diversion of Russia's best resources to industrialization and militarization.

The Russian experience re-emphasizes the basic choice between present and future that every economy must make, be it capitalist or communist. We make the choice one way, leaving it pretty much up to each businessman and individual to decide for himself how much to save and to invest. The Russians do it by government decision, with painful consequences for the consumer but with spectacular increases in productive capacity.

TECHNOLOGY Technological advance has come arm-in-arm with capital accumulation to help offset the steadily increasing ratio of population to natural resources. As the economist uses the term, technology is the art of combining productive resources to achieve given ends. It is the art of getting the most out of the resources available to you, through better engineering, better management, or in any other way.

There is no clear way of measuring quantitatively what the technology of the United States is today, or how rapidly it has improved over the years. The results of improving technology are inseparable from the results of the new capital goods that embody the technology and of the more productive workers who use the better techniques and the improved capital goods. But there is impressive evidence that technological advance has played a major role in offsetting the predicted impact of diminishing returns as population has soared.

By the early 1950's, capital investment per capita had increased to about 300 per cent of 1869-79. But over the same period *output* per capita rose to 400 per cent of the 1869-79 base. Looked at another way, output per unit of capital rose to only 134 per cent of 1869-79 over the period, compared with a 450 per cent increase for output per man-hour. The difference must be explained largely in terms of the improved technology that increased the average worker's output beyond the increase directly attributable to more capital goods.[6] Another series shows output per man-hour during about the same period rising roughly fourfold, while output per unit of capital only about doubled.[7]

But beyond these figures, American technology speaks for itself. Visit a modern oil refinery—millions of dollars' worth of elaborate equipment converting millions of barrels of crude petroleum to gasoline, heating oil, and other products each year, with only a few engineers sitting around watching a big panel of gauges and dials, plus maintenance workers to provide servicing and repairs when needed. Then remember that this refinery is probably only one of several in its company, linked together by a huge human organization encompassing perhaps a hundred thousand workers extending from the crude oil fields in Texas or Venezuela, along the pipe lines or tanker routes to the refinery; then through an elaborate system of distribution to storage centers and bulk stations; and finally to the local gas station where you roll up to the pumps, confident that gas will be there ready for you.

Or walk through a modern automobile assembly plant. Stop by a modern midwestern farm, complete with automatic farm machinery. Look in at the synchrocyclotron if you are a student at a large university, or visit the research laboratories of a huge corporation, such as the famous "Bell Labs" of the American Telephone and Telegraph Company. This is modern technology, the trademark of America, a source of never-ending amazement to visitors from abroad, though we ourselves tend to take it for granted.

The Role of Research and Education.   What of the future? Will technological advance continue to play such a major role? Much will depend on our research. Current annual expenditures on research and development have reached about $12 billion, a little over 2 per cent of the gross national product. The rate of research spending has skyrocketed in the last decade. More was spent during the 1950's than in all previous history combined.

The implications of these facts are enormous. The National Science Foundation suggests that in the past there has been a discernible relationship between

---

[6] Data from M. Abramovitz, *Resource and Output Trends in the United States Since 1870* (National Bureau of Economic Research Occasional Paper No. 52) (New York, 1956).

[7] S. Fabricant, *Basic Facts on Productivity Change* (National Bureau of Economic Research Occasional Paper No. 63) (New York, 1959).

research spending and, after a lag of several years, growth in output per worker in the economy. It suggests that this research may well provide a snowballing impetus to American productivity over the years ahead, and that research is clearly one of the most important single factors in the economic growth of the United States.

If the law of diminishing returns looms ominously, it is because of the fixity of natural resources as population expands. Here modern research has produced spectacular results indeed. Chemistry and modern fertilizers have vastly increased food production per acre. In America, food shortage is inconceivable, even with a population explosion. Energy sources and materials pose the major scarcity problem, if we face one. But here modern science has brought massive new sources into practical usefulness as old ones have become more and more scarce. Economic use of low-grade iron ore deposits is one example, plastics to replace wood and metals is another. Thus, although in the aggregate material resources are fixed, research promises to obtain energy and materials from plentiful resources that long seemed unusable. Food from seawater, power from the sun, may be tomorrow's answer to the law of diminishing returns.

Research is the spectacular base for advancing technology. But behind the research laboratories is the widespread American educational system—grade schools, high schools, colleges, and graduate schools. Without these, there would be few scientists for the laboratories, few engineers for the factories, few educated men to manage our factories and work in them. America has invested in mass education, with a small fringe of "class" education for the advanced pure and applied scientists, managers, and professional men at the graduate level. No one can measure precisely the productive return on investment in education. The best estimates we have suggest this may be the biggest single factor that differentiates those economies which have grown rapidly from those which have lagged. Certainly, there has been no case of rapid growth and industrialization without parallel or preceding growth in education. If this speculation is right, more investment in education could pay the highest returns of any use we might make of our resources.

RESOURCES, TECHNOLOGY, AND GROWTH: PERSPECTIVE The main objective of the preceding sections has been to fill in the important background of what our resources are and how they, with technology, support the nation's production.

The relationship between total output and population $\left(\text{the ratio: } \dfrac{\text{output}}{\text{population}}\right)$ is what determines output per capita, a rough measure of the nation's average standard of living. It is only by increasing the ratio of output to population that we can raise the average standard of living of citizens in any country. As population growth speeds up, capital accumulation, plus technological advance, plus improvement in the quality of the labor force, must proceed at an even faster pace if the average standard of living in America is to continue to rise.

SOME FUNDAMENTAL ECONOMIC RELATIONSHIPS

Scarcity: The Necessity for Economizing. The first basic fact is a repeat from Chapter 2: There are never enough resources to fill all the needs. Thus an individual, a businessman, a nation must always choose which ends it values most highly in allocating its resources among alternative uses. In all economics there is no more fundamental fact.

From this fact follows a basic relationship. *In a full-employment economy, a society can get more of one product only by giving up some other product.* Resources can be obtained to produce guns only by taking them away from producing butter. Capital goods can be accumulated only by giving up current consumption. Of course, if resources are unemployed, an economy can get more of both guns and butter, more capital and more consumption goods, by putting the unemployed resources back to work. But once full employment is restored, the basic dilemma returns.

The Law of Diminishing Returns. Ricardo's law of diminishing returns emphasized that, if an economy has a limited amount of land, the food output per worker would eventually fall as more workers were added. Although Ricardo did not state the principle very clearly, the relationship involved is a basic one in any society. It applies not merely to labor added to a fixed supply of land, but to any case where successive units of a productive resource are applied to a fixed amount of other productive resources. The law says, more precisely: *The additional output obtained from applying additional units of a variable resource to a fixed resource will generally first rise, but will always, sooner or later, fall, as more units of the variable resource are crowded onto the fixed resource.*

Modern economists sometimes state the principle more usefully in terms of *varying proportions* of different resources used together. The crucial relationship, they point out, is a change in proportions between the resources being used together. It is not necessary that one resource or group of resources be fixed while more of some other resource is added. To get the effect of diminishing returns, all that is needed is a continued increase in the *proportion* of one resource to other resources. For example, if the labor force is tripling each decade while the stock of other resources is only doubling, the principle of diminishing returns will be applicable, just as in Ricardo's case. Sometimes, therefore, the term "law of variable proportions" is now used, instead of "law of diminishing returns."

The principle (whichever way it is stated) may apply to the changing proportions of major resources for the economy as a whole—e.g., more labor applied to land and capital goods. Or it may apply within an individual firm. For example, suppose we are trying to improve service by adding more clerks in a retail store.

At first, each additional clerk improves the service considerably. But as more and more clerks line the counters, the improved service from adding one more steadily drops. We *may* even reach a point of negative extra service (returns), if, for example, the additional clerk just gets in the other clerks' way—just as we might conceivably decrease farm output by adding so many workers that they would get in each other's way.

How soon will diminishing returns set in in any real-world situation? This obviously depends on the facts of each individual case. In most real situations many productive resources are being combined, and the working of the law of diminishing returns may be hard to observe. Everyone knows that the American standard of living has not fallen as population has increased; we have seen that more capital goods and improving technology go far to explain what might superficially seem to be a contradiction of the law. Similarly, everyone knows that mass-production methods have brought lower unit costs in American industry as more labor and materials are used in a given plant, and this too may seem to contradict the principle.

But this is only to say that diminishing returns may not set in immediately. Economists have long pointed out that in many instances there may be *increasing* returns (i.e., total output may increase more than in proportion to the variable resource) for a while if the balance between the different resources is poor to begin with. An extreme example would be a plant but no workers; the addition of the first few workers would surely show increasing returns, and the improvement might continue over a large increase in workers and output in a plant designed primarily for large-scale production. But sooner or later, with a fixed plant, or with a steadily increasing proportion of some productive resource to the others, diminishing returns will set in.

Bottlenecks: The Limitation of the Scarcest Resource. The illustration just above suggests, at the level of the individual plant, another significant economic relationship—the limitation often imposed by the scarcest resource. With only five workers, even the most elaborate steel mill could turn out very little steel. Just so, for the economy as a whole the scarcest resource often plays a critical role in limiting total national production.

The United States has always had plentiful natural resources, but our output has been checked at various times by shortages of capital goods and manpower. Countries like England and Belgium have highly developed productive plants and highly skilled laborers, but they are poor in natural resources. China has abundant labor and natural resources, but little capital equipment.

Thus, what a nation lacks most may set the limit on its productive capacity and on its ability to utilize its more plentiful productive resources. Early in World War II, for example, although labor was plentiful, our war production was checked by the lack of plants and equipment to produce aircraft, arms, and ships. By 1943, these shortages had been largely overcome, full employment had been reached, and manpower had become the bottleneck—the number-one problem in expanding output. For China, for example, capital today appears to be a major bottleneck. Without more capital goods, China's vast manpower and generous natural resources will achieve little toward raising the national standard of living.

Seen from the viewpoint of the scarcest resource, this situation becomes only a special case (the increasing-returns phase) of the principle of diminishing returns. As the scarcest factor is increased in such instances, total output will increase more than proportionally until the bottleneck is eliminated—that is, until something approaching a "reasonable" balance among the productive resources is achieved. Then the diminishing-returns phase of the law begins to come into play.

ECONOMIC GROWTH: WHITHER AMERICA?

How fast will the American economy grow over the years ahead? Will the growth be stable or erratic? In short, whither America? This is a central theme of the entire book. These are questions we shall be trying to answer in chapter after chapter.

The present chapter has laid out some of the central factors underlying the present American standard of living and its outlook for the future—the supply and quality of the productive resources we will have; the technology of using these resources; the balance among them and the limitations imposed by the law of diminishing returns; and the extent to which we are willing to hold down current consumption in order to achieve greater productive capacity for the future. These are the big "real" factors determining the economy's productive *capacity* today and its growth in the future.

But further analysis is required to explain how these broad factors interact in the complex American economy, and especially to explain why we have often failed to achieve the full output potential of our productive capacity. The next several chapters will help provide this analysis for the American private-enterprise, profit-motivated economy. Then in Chapter 11 we shall come back to look in detail at the central question of economic growth: Whither America?

No less important and perhaps even more intriguing is the question: What will happen to the so-called "underdeveloped" countries of Asia, Indonesia, Africa, and South America, which will surely play a vastly more important role in the world history of the next century? How fast will they grow? What are their resources and their problems? Must they have our help as a foundation for economic development, or will they grow into powerful economic units in spite of our indifference or opposition if we choose not to help? At the end of the book, in Chapter 43, we shall come back again to this central problem of economic growth, but this time for the underdeveloped countries—one of the most vital, and most explosive, problems in the world economy today.

REVIEW—CONCEPTS TO REMEMBER

This chapter has presented a series of new analytical concepts that will be used repeatedly. Check your understanding of the following:

production   labor force
economic growth   entrepreneur
per capita output   population density
resources   capital goods
technology   producers' goods
law of diminishing returns   capital accumulation
law of variable proportions   bottleneck

FOR ANALYSIS AND DISCUSSION

1. Suppose you are interested in comparing the rates of economic growth in the U.S.S.R. and the United States. Which concept is more useful: total output or output per capita?

2. If the nation's standard of living is too low, why can't the government rectify matters by printing new money and giving everybody more to spend?

3. Make a list of the major factors likely to increase the labor force over the next twenty years and those likely to decrease it. On balance, which factors would you expect to be the most important?

4. How long should the work-week for factory workers be? What seem to you the major considerations in answering this question?

5. "Only those who work contribute to the nation's output of goods and services. Those who don't just ride on our shoulders. They shouldn't get any share of increases in the national output." Is this a fair statement? Should steps be taken to decrease the number of nonworkers? If so, how?

6. Critics of the law of diminishing returns argue that the law must be invalid since in the United States population has grown enormously over the past century while the supply of natural resources has been constant, yet output of food per capita has risen greatly. How would you answer these critics?

7. Should we cut back our consumption and expand our investment and government spending enough to widen our military and production leads over Russia? If so, how?

8. Should the federal government collect taxes to finance conservation of our natural resources—for example, by building dams to prevent soil erosion? Should you help pay the taxes if you live in New York and the proposed dam is in Nevada?

9. Only about 2 per cent of the nation's total production is devoted to research. Would it be sound policy to double this amount? If so, who should pay for it?

Private Enterprise, Profits, and the Price System

The last chapter was concerned primarily with resources and technology, two of the cornerstones of economic productivity. The present chapter provides a brief summary of the other two cornerstones—specialization and the system of exchange —on which the modern American economy rests; and roughs in a general outline of the way in which a private-enterprise, free-price system operates. In a sense, this chapter is a very brief introductory summary of all the book that follows—a map of where you are going.

How many people do you depend on to get your everyday economic wants satisfied? Your first inclination may be to say, not many. But think a minute. Who built the house you live in, and who provided all the materials to build it? How about the car you drove to school, or the shoes if you came afoot? Where did your breakfast come from —the eggs, bread, butter, milk, and so on? How many people contributed to the production of your clothes, and of the textbooks you read? Suppose you take in a movie tonight, or watch TV. How many people had a hand in making this possible?

COOPERATION
AND COMPETITION
IN A PRIVATE-ENTERPRISE
ECONOMY

Man lives by cooperating with his fellow men. In all economics there is no truth more basic than this. And in the modern economy this cooperation is indescribably broad and complex. To satisfy our simplest wants, we rely upon the efforts of innumerable people in all parts of the world, and on the labors of generations past.

Yet this vast cooperative system, as a system, has not been consciously designed by man. No human director tells the 70 million workers in the United States where to work, what to do, or how to do it. Somehow the system seems to organize itself into this intricate pattern of interdependent economic cooperation, with a minimum of central planning or directing.

Man can organize, and indeed he has organized much. Tens of thousands of workers are employed in some large industrial plants. Often many of these huge plants are joined together in a single organization. The American Telephone and Telegraph Company, for example, spreads over the entire United States, with over half a million employees and assets of over $20 billion. But in spite of the immense power of such huge aggregations, each business concern plays a comparatively small part in the total picture of organizing economic resources to satisfy human wants. And in spite of the great expansion of government controls, the private-enterprise economy still does the bulk of the job in its long-established, unplanned way.

The Incredible American Economy.   It's easy to find things the matter with a basically private-enterprise, "unplanned" economy, like the one in the United States. But thoughtful observers have long been impressed by its remarkable efficiency in producing the infinite variety of goods and services consumers want.

Consider New York City, teeming with 15 million people crowded into a few square miles. As Bastiat, a famous economist, remarked about the Paris of a hundred years ago, here are millions of human beings who would all starve in a short time without a constant flow of provisions into the metropolis. Hardly one could support himself for more than a few days without help from the far corners of the nation. "Imagination is baffled," Bastiat wrote, "when it tries to appreciate the vast multiplicity of commodities which must enter tomorrow in order to preserve the inhabitants from falling prey to the convulsions of famine, rebellion, and pillage. Yet all sleep, and their slumbers are not disturbed for a single minute by the prospect of such a frightful catastrophe."

Every day, New York City gets hundreds of tons of meat, huge amounts of fresh vegetables, coal, oil, furniture. Every year, it gets millions of shirts, automobiles, rugs, hairnets, movie films, and more products than you can think of. Yet no individual, business, or government agency plans it that way. The same is true, on a smaller scale, of every city and village throughout the country.

Who sees to it that all these millions of products are where they're needed when they're needed? What organizes this indescribably complex economy? Somehow it must be decided what to produce and when and where; then the goods and services have to be produced; then they must be distributed to consumers.

It's almost impossible to comprehend the magnitude of the problem involved. Suppose for a moment that you have just been made complete economic dictator, and that for some unfortunate reason you have not the slightest idea how much of everything is now being produced. You have to tell every one of 70 million workers just what job to do; determine how every other productive resource in the economy shall be used; decide just how much of each commodity and service shall be produced; and determine who shall get how much of what is made—all this so that the amount of everything produced will be equal to the amount demanded and no productive resources will be involuntarily unemployed!

How, for example, would you decide whether Joe Smith ought to spend his time grinding fine edges on a machine tool later to be used in manufacturing tractors later to be used in producing corn later to be fed to hogs later to be eaten as pork; or whether he ought to spend his time making fine cabinets, or running a locomotive, or operating a corner grocery store? What would you do about the minor problem of how many sheep to raise, when each sheep yields both wool and mutton, the demands for which are almost completely independent? Wool is used for clothing, blankets, rugs; mutton is used for dinner. How are you going to make them come out even, even if you have somehow decided on the total number of sheep to be raised? How would you decide who is to have tractors and corn and cabinets and mutton and wool once they are produced? This is the merest suggestion of the problems faced—and it matters not whether the economic system is capitalist, communist, fascist, or what not. Somehow these decisions have to be made.

The Organizers: Self-Interest and Competition.   In a private-enterprise economy like ours in the United States, we rely chiefly on private initiative, in search of profits or other income, to get the job done. If we as a group want something badly enough, we will be willing to pay for it. If it is shoes we want, there will be a special profit to be made in producing shoes. Businessmen, recognizing this potential profit, can be counted on to begin producing more shoes. As output increases, a point is reached when just as many shoes are being produced as consumers are willing to pay for at a price just high enough to cover the full costs of producing shoes. If businessmen compete actively for consumers' dollars, prices will be held down in relation to costs; if one or a few producers can corner the market, they may agree to put prices up instead of competing actively through producing more.

The same general pattern of production in search of profits goes on for hundreds of thousands of other products simultaneously. The relative prices and costs of producing these many commodities guide entrepreneurs to where the potential profits are largest. Entrepreneurs go where profit prospects look brightest, offering jobs and bidding raw materials and capital into those industries. Millions of workers work where they will, generally taking the jobs that offer the most pay, but tempering their decisions with all the other factors they consider important.

This is the mechanism by which the "private-enterprise, free-price system" does this indescribably complex job. It decides what's to be produced, how to get it produced, and how to distribute it to 180 million consumers. As Adam Smith pointed out in his famous *Wealth of Nations* way back in 1776, the desire for personal profit within the framework of a *competitive* economic system works almost like an "invisible hand" guiding the system toward the greatest welfare of all.

Perhaps Adam Smith was over-enthusiastic in relying so heavily on individual self-interest and competition as a beneficent invisible hand. Many people think so today. But the first big lesson to learn about a private-enterprise economy is that it gets its vast job done for the most part automatically and impersonally, through the profit and price system. Nobody decides any more than his own minute affairs. Yet everyone deciding in his own self-interest seems to do the trick. In a private-enterprise economy the absence of planning and control does not mean chaos. Rather, it means order in a system so complex that no mind could comprehend it to bring order without the price system or something like it to do the job.

But this is a lesson that must not be overlearned. We can understand and admire the way the private-enterprise, free-price system ticks on year after year, impersonally solving its millions of intertwined problems, and still not shut our eyes to its failings. And failings there are—drastic ones, some people think. Here is one of the big places for you to make up your own mind as you go through the course.

To provide a framework for the more detailed analysis to come, the next few paragraphs outline briefly the four big jobs that every economic system must somehow do. They indicate also, very sketchily, how a private-enterprise economy gets these jobs done. All the jobs lead back to the one big problem—how to use scarce resources to satisfy mankind's most urgent wants.

HOW A PRIVATE ENTERPRISE SYSTEM SOLVES THE BASIC ECONOMIC PROBLEMS

How the Price System Decides What To Produce. Under a private-enterprise, free-price system, consumers control what and how much shall be produced. The pricing process provides a way of registering consumer preferences through the amount of money consumers spend on various goods and services. The more you want something, the more money you will spend on it and the higher price you will be willing to pay for it. The relative strength of consumer demand for beefsteak, autos, and movie queens is measured in the prices and purchases of the products; and it is on this pattern that the price system decides which are the most important goods and services to be produced.

But in order to count, consumers' demands have to be backed up with dollars. No matter how badly a poor family may want a Buick and a fine house, its desires become effective in the market only when, and to the extent that, they are backed up by the ability to pay for such things. The price mechanism is hardboiled, impersonal. It produces Cadillacs for millionaires when poor youngsters have no toys. Prices reflect not how much consumers "need" goods and services, but how much they are willing and able to pay for them.

How the Price System Gets the Goods Produced. Businessmen are out to make profits. Profits are found where selling prices are higher than costs. Thus entrepreneurs will move to those industries where consumers bid prices up, and where their own ingenuity and other facts can bring costs down. Workers and owners of other productive resources will move toward higher pay away from lower-pay opportunities, insofar as it's pay they're after; if it's not pay, the system adjusts to their preference for work in lower-pay but otherwise more attractive industries. This combination of consumer demand, workers' job preferences, and the businessman's desire for profits gets the goods produced that consumers want most, at the lowest possible cost.

Thus the businessman—the entrepreneur—is essentially a link between consumers and productive resources. His social function is to organize productive activity in the most efficient (lowest-cost) way possible, and to channel productive resources toward the industries where consumer demand is strongest. Profits are the mainspring of the system—the carrot in front of the entrepreneur. In seeking profits, the entrepreneur (perhaps quite involuntarily) performs a vital social function.

How the Price System Distributes Products. Who gets the goods that are produced? The price system gives them to those who have the desire and the income to buy them. There are two steps in this process of distribution.

The first is the distribution of money income. We earn our incomes primarily by working for businessmen, helping to produce the goods and services consumers want. The price we get for our services depends on how much we are worth to the business we work for. Very roughly, competition forces the businessman to pay each of us about what we contribute to the sale value of what he is producing. The incomes we receive in this way largely determine what we can afford to buy.

The second step is the distribution of goods and services among those with money income to pay for them. The price of each commodity is bid up until the buyers least able or willing to pay for it are eliminated. This does not necessarily mean that low-income buyers are eliminated completely. Often it means that they can afford only a few units at the price established, while the higher-income groups can afford more. Poor people buy steaks, but not many. In other cases, such as mink coats and fine houses, the poor are eliminated.

How the Price System Decides Between Present and Future: Economic Growth.

Productive resources may be used to produce either for current consumption or for capital accumulation (i.e., machinery, building, etc., which will help increase future production). Here again the private-enterprise system depends largely on the free choices of consumers and the decisions of enterpreneurs, integrated through the investment and money markets, to make this choice.

Each person decides how much of his income he wants to save. Each business does the same. If the sum of all such savings is large, entrepreneurs will find it easier to borrow funds, and they will be led to invest in building new machinery and other long-term productive equipment for future production. At the same time, the switch of consumers' incomes from current consumption to saving makes the profit opportunities in producing goods for current consumption relatively less attractive. Entrepreneurs will gain by producing machinery, buildings, and factory equipment, rather than shoes, food, and tennis rackets. The pattern of production will be shifted toward capital accumulation until production of consumers' and producers' goods corresponds to the division of current incomes between consumption and saving. Economic growth speeds up. Here is a mechanism by which the price system regulates the rate of economic growth.

But here is one place where the private-enterprise system often has trouble. Sometimes when people save, enterpreneurs don't see enough potential gain in making new investments in capital goods to match, or use up, the savings. Then the savings "lie idle" instead of being respent to stimulate production of capital goods. This means unemployment and depression. Other times, businessmen grow unduly enthusiastic over a future with rosy prospects. They invest far beyond the rates at which people plan to save. This speeds up capital accumulation and economic growth. But it also often brings inflation, since the added investment spending increases the demand for resources beyond the available supply. Worse, it may lead to widespread losses, economic collapse, and unemployment when the expected profits from the new capital goods don't materialize.

Solving All the Problems Simultaneously.

These four major decisions are not made separately. Rather, they are all completely interdependent. The economic system is a huge, interconnected set of markets, each with buyers and sellers. Since most buyers buy in many different markets, what they buy of one good affects what they will buy of another. Most sellers must compete with many other sellers for the labor they hire, the raw materials they use, the dollars they borrow to build their plants. The process of production both produces goods to meet consumer demands and generates incomes for workers who are in turn consumers. Each consumer constantly chooses between buying something now with his income, or saving. All these things go on simultaneously.

The private-enterprise, free-price system, then, makes all four of its major decisions simultaneously, each composed in turn of millions of continuous, simultaneous sub-decisions by consumers, workers, businessmen, bankers, and other participants in the economic process. It is the manner in which all these complex decisions are simultaneously and continuously made in our economic system that is the core of the study of economics.[1]

THE CIRCULAR FLOW OF ECONOMIC ACTIVITY

As we suggested above, income in a private-enterprise economy flows around a circle. Businesses pay wages, interest, and other income to the public. The public, in its consuming capacity, turns around and spends this income back to businesses in payment for finished goods and serv-

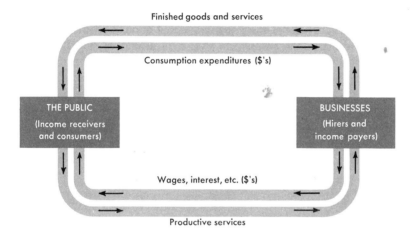

FIG. 4-1   The circular flow of economic activity.

ices. This demand, in turn, creates a further business demand for workers and for other productive resources to produce more goods and services for consumers.

Figure 4-1 is a simple picture of this circular income flow. The inside line shows money income flowing from businesses to the public as wages, interest, and so on, and then flowing back from the public to businesses as spending on consumer goods and services. The outer line shows the corresponding reverse flow of productive services (labor, capital goods, etc.) and finished consumer goods and services. On the top half, finished goods are moving from businesses

---

[1] For students versed in mathematics, it may be helpful to think of all these interdependent markets and decisions as a large system of simultaneous equations. In fact, the first clear perception of the entire process was by Leon Walras, about a century ago, who saw it just that way.

to consumers. On the bottom half, labor and other productive services are moving from the public to businesses. The circular flow of money income is the oil that greases the flow of real goods and services through the economy as the private-enterprise system fulfills the tasks outlined above.

Which comes first, business spending or consumer spending? This is a chicken-and-egg question. The main point is that neither can go on for long without the other. Consumers without jobs and incomes make for very poor business. And a business with products that no one buys is a good bet for bankruptcy. Economic activity in a private-enterprise system is a continuous flow of productive services and finished goods and services, facilitated by a matching counter-flow of money, and guided by the price system into thousands of different product channels within the main outer stream shown in the diagram.

You can readily see that this picture is oversimplified. The government has been left out. And there's no place for savings and production of capital goods that aren't sold to consumers. But the simple picture points up the central role of the circular flow process. Unless there is a continuous flow of money-spending by businesses to the public and by the public to businesses, we're in trouble.

The problem of the *over-all level* of income, employment, and consumer spending—i.e., the total level of money income flow—is the subject of Part 2. The *composition* of national output—what goods and services get produced—is the subject of Part 3. And Part 4 analyzes the question of how the national income is distributed—who gets the goods and services produced. These problems are all closely related. Never forget that they are all solved simultaneously in the day-to-day working of the economy, even though we look at them one at a time.

INDIVIDUAL FREEDOM AND THE ROLE OF GOVERNMENT   The French and American revolutions that gave us political democracy provided the ideological framework for economic individualism. Political democracy and modern private-enterprise economics arose in the same historical setting, part of the same broad sweep of history.

Individual freedom and enlightened self-interest were at the core of this broad revolution of the eighteenth and nineteenth centuries. In politics, every man should be free to vote as he pleased—to look out for his own interests at the ballot box. In economic life, again every man should be free to seek his own self-interest—to work where he wished at whatever he pleased. Enlightened self-interest and individual initiative were the driving forces for the common good in both the political and economic sense. The ballot box in politics and the market in economics were the ultimate, impartial arbiters of differences of opinion.

This philosophy assigned to government only a small role. The less that government interfered with individual freedom, the better. This was the "laissez-faire" philosophy of the nineteenth century. To be sure, individualism never went so far as to exclude government intervention altogether. True freedom necessarily involves certain restrictions on freedom. A society that gave you freedom to murder your neighbor whenever you felt like it would end up either in anarchy or in an agreement to restrict individual freedom.

So it was in the economic sphere. Clearly the government needed to establish and enforce a few "rules of the game" for the free-enterprise system. One basic rule was the guarantee that no one should be deprived of life, liberty, or property without due process of law. Another was the longstanding rule against fraud and against default on contracts. But the rules should be simple, and government should have no business in economic life outside these rules.

As time passed, the public's outlook changed. More and more questions were raised about the ability of an automatic, uncontrolled price system to make vital economic decisions acceptably. Mass production and the modern corporation swept away the possibility of an economy of tiny, highly competitive firms. Huge and powerful unions replaced the individual worker in bargaining with big business. Throughout the economy, concentration of economic power and reliance on group activity spread steadily.

At the same time, common concern grew for the individual who couldn't take care of himself. Willingness to abide by the impersonal income allocations of the market steadily diminished. Desire to "do something" about booms and depressions became widespread. A subtle shift in the meaning attached to the words "individual freedom" marked the changing tenor of the times. The rules of the game have grown into an intricate mass of law and administrative controls. The government has become an active participant in the economic game, as well as the umpire.

THE MIXED ECONOMY Today, ours is a mixed economy—still basically private enterprise but with important areas of government control and direct participation. It's up to you as an individual to decide whether you like what's been going on—whether you want to move back toward the traditional private-enterprise system, or on toward a more administered, planned economy, or in some other direction.

This is no ivory-tower, academic issue, dreamed up for college classrooms. It is the basic issue of public economic policy today. Should we try to shore up the free-price system and its individualistic implications? Or should we accept the new power groupings and set up government procedures to work with them toward a more administered economy? Clearly the government must step in to build battleships and roads, but how about slum-clearance and low-cost public housing? Almost everyone agrees the government should provide free schooling for all children, but how far should it go toward assuring equal opportunity for the poor on other fronts? How about assuring minimum health standards and old-age security? Everyone agrees that we need to level off booms and depressions. Can the government take on this job and still perform in a manner consistent with the basic philosophy of private-enterprise nonintervention? Should the government step in to push our growth rate up toward the Russians', even if it means more government control over our personal spending decisions?

In the complex world of today, "individual freedom" and freedom from regulation are no longer simple concepts. Every step toward a more intricate economy brings new problems and economic interrelationships—more calls for the government to regulate this and to stabilize that. Few Americans want a socialist system, where productive resources are state-owned and the government dominates economic life. But how to implement a workable private-enterprise economy, consistent with democratic ideals and with the realities of modern mass production and modern economic power groupings, is a hard question. It is a question that can be answered only by looking in detail at the many kinds of problems that arise in the real world around us.

At the end of this book, we shall step back and compare the private-enterprise system with the socialist approach, which is a powerful economic, social, and political force in the world of today. Some people, of course, feel that the American economy is already far down the primrose path to socialism. But compared with most of the rest of the world, private enterprise is still rampant in America. As a college student and as a citizen, you need to do a lot of careful, unemotional thinking about where the American economy really is, and which way you want it to go.

CAPITALISM TODAY "Capitalism" is a term often used but seldom defined. Words so used often generate more heat than light, and "capitalism" has over the years become a fighting word for many who advocate and oppose it. Recourse to the dictionaries and to the learned treatises of economists and historians unfortunately does not resolve the dilemma of just what we should mean when we say capitalism, for these authorities are far from agreement.

So, instead of talking about capitalism, this book uses such less colorful but perhaps more descriptive terms as the "private-enterprise, free-price system" and "profit-motivated behavior" to refer to central aspects of the modern American economy. But, though we shall generally eschew the emotionally colored term, a brief note on "capitalism" may help you to understand all the controversy about it.

Many writers agree that a "capitalist" economy is marked by at least three major characteristics:

(1) Private ownership of property prevails.

(2) Large blocks of property have been accumulated by individuals and businesses, and this accumulated "capital" provides incomes to its owners.

(3) Individuals and businesses are free to seek their own economic gain; the profit motive plays a central role in economic life.

(4) Some writers add to this list, a highly developed banking and credit system.

But once we look at these points in detail, the trouble begins. How free must individuals be to own and use property if a system is to be termed "capitalism"? Is an income tax that takes away part of your property each year, depending on how much you earn, inconsistent with capitalism? How about a requirement that you spend part of your income each year on federal old-age insurance, whether you want to or not? How free must individuals be to seek their own economic gain? Does a federal law that limits the degree of monopoly power that a "capitalist" can acquire violate the tenets of capitalism?

Should employers be free to use all their economic power to keep unions from organizing their workers? If, as in the American economy, the law restrains employers from exercising this power, has an essential element of capitalism been lost? If businesses seeking to borrow money from individual savers are required to disclose their affairs in detail through a government agency—the Securities and Exchange Commission—has an economic freedom vital to capitalism been violated? Is government operation of the postal system or of the T.V.A. going too far in invading the realm of private profit-seeking? And so on.

We shall be concerned with all these issues. The major goal of this book is to help you reach reasoned judgments on the major public-policy problems of the day. But there seems little to be gained by debating just which measures are and which are not consistent with "capitalism" when there is so little agreement on just what the term does mean. Instead, we will concentrate on trying to decide what, if anything, should be done to solve the economy's major problems. Are proposed policy measures good or bad on their merits, taking into full account the different social goals held by different groups in America today? In talking about a "private-enterprise, free-price system" throughout most of the book, we will be talking about the system many writers call "modern capitalism." If you like the term, use it. But don't let your emotional attachment or antagonism toward it get in the way of your thinking objectively about the issues.[2]

[2] Note to instructors: Instructors who prefer to cover major institutions in the opening section or who prefer to cover the elements of business accounting before reaching national income analysis may prefer to use Chapter 17, "Business Enterprise in the Modern Economy," next.

1. Suppose American college students were to develop a craze for pork chop sandwiches, instead of hamburgers. Trace through as carefully as you can the impact of this craze on the allocation of the economy's productive resources. How would you go about assessing the quantitative importance of the shifts you outline?

2. Leading movie stars receive annual salaries up in the hundreds of thousands of dollars. Some baseball players receive $50,000 to $100,000 for the eight-month season. Yet an intelligent, skilled, hard-working

FOR
ANALYSIS
AND
DISCUSSION

nurse or carpenter will ordinarily earn not more than $5,000 or so per year.

   a. How can such differences come about in a private-enterprise, free-market economy? Are they results of the free-market system, or do they reflect breakdowns in the functioning of the system?

   b. Whatever your answers to (a), do you approve of such inequalities in the distribution of income? Why or why not?

3. The price system allocates resources where consumers spend their dollars. Thus the rich man has far more influence than the poor man. Is this compatible with the democratic presumption that every man is equal?

4. The federal government and most state governments levy heavy taxes on liquor, partly to obtain revenue and partly to discourage drinking. Should Congress try to influence how you spend your money this way? How about your state legislature?

5. "Man lives by cooperating with his fellow men. In all economics there is no more fundamental truth than this."

"The core of the competitive, free-market system is the driving urge of most men to get ahead in the world, to rise above their fellow men."

Are these two statements about the American economic system consistent or contradictory? If they are consistent, how do you reconcile their apparent contradiction?

6. Is the American economy characterized by substantial equality of economic opportunity? If your answer is no, what are the main areas where opportunities are not equal, and what do you believe ought to be done about them?

Straight Thinking
in Economics

Straight thinking is hard work. Few of us have acquired the careful, orderly mental habits and discipline demanded by habitual straight thinking on all issues.

For many people, straight thinking in economics is especially hard. Not that economics is inherently more difficult or more complex than many other fields. It isn't. Economics doesn't require anything like the rigor and discipline needed for advanced mathematics, for example. But economics is so mixed up with our everyday lives that without realizing it we've accumulated a mass of opinions, ideas, hearsay, and half-truths that subtly dominate our minds when economic questions come up.

When we want to build a bridge, it never occurs to us to start without calling in expert engineers to design it. If we want expert advice on physics, we ask the physicists. Few people would consider themselves experts on bridge-building just because they drive across a bridge twice a day going to and from work—or on physics just because they live in the midst of the physical world. Yet many people, especially if they've "met a payroll," somehow feel that they know most of the important things about economic affairs simply because of their experience in earning a living in the economic world.

This tendency for every man to be his own economist is strengthened by the fact that economics is so close to the pocketbook. It's hard to be objective about things that affect you intimately. We're disinclined to recognize anybody else's expertness when he tells us things we don't like to hear, unless we are convinced that we have to. If you're the corner grocer struggling to keep afloat against competition from the big chain stores, economists who talk about the beneficial economies of large-scale enterprise aren't going to rate very high with you. If you're the manager of a chain store, you won't feel much better toward economists who want a strong antitrust division in the government to keep a close tab on big businesses.

All this, of course, frustrates economists no end. They point out, quite rightly, that running the corner grocery doesn't make the grocer a reliable expert on how desirable antitrust laws are against big business, and certainly not on how the banking system affects the economy's behavior in booms and depressions— any more than having teeth makes us experts on dental health and how to fill cavities. Economics is concerned with the way the whole economy works, not with how to run a better grocery or bank. And these are quite different things.

The purpose of this chapter is to help give you a framework for thinking straight about economics. It has two parts:

1. The first sets out some positive guides to straight thinking in economics. These positive guides consist mainly of (a) an introduction to the role of analytical "models," or theory, and (b) some suggestions about an orderly way of sizing up and reaching conclusions on public-policy ("action" or "decision") questions.

2. The second part warns against some common fallacies that often slip in to sabotage our thinking, in economics and in many other areas of our everyday lives.

Most of this chapter applies equally well to fields outside economics. Straight thinking is pretty much the same wherever you go.

SOME GUIDES TO STRAIGHT THINKING The most apparent fact about economic reality is its complexity. There are millions of businesses, 180 million consumers, hundreds of thousands of different products, many stages in the production of nearly every product. Faced with this overwhelming complexity, we obviously have to find some way of simplifying things down to manageable proportions, or turn the job over to geniuses with huge electronic calculating machines.

Use of Simplified Models: Theory.   The economist, like other scientists, begins by developing an analytical framework or model, which singles out the main elements and main relationships in the complex real economic world. These abstract models of the economy, and of the sub-parts which make it up, are generally called "theory." Such models make no pretense of being accurate descriptions of any part of the economy. If they were completely accurate, they'd defeat their own purpose by getting back to all the detail. Instead, they are intended as highly simplified abstractions of the main elements of the reality they are related to.

The notion of a model may be illustrated by a physical example. Suppose you want to understand how a bicycle works. You could study every detail of a single bicycle, or a large number of them, examining the tires, the handlebars, the sprocket, the paint, and so on. But if you could instead get a simple diagram, or a stripped-down working model, of a bicycle, you'd get to the essentials quicker. This diagram wouldn't be concerned with all the details of paint, style, quality of steel, and so on. Instead, it would show the essential parts of a bicycle —wheels, frame, sprocket, driving chain, brake—and the basic relationships among these parts. The diagram would show how pressure applied to the pedals turns the sprocket wheel; how the chain connects the large sprocket to a smaller sprocket wheel at the center of the back wheel of the bicycle; and how pressure on the foot pedal exerts a multiplied pressure in turning the back wheel through the difference in the size of the sprocket wheels. (If you knew a little elementary physics, it would help to have explanatory notes on the diagram indicating that the principles of mechanical advantage are used, with the pedal being a second-class lever and the relative sizes of the gear wheels being crucial in determining the speed and power resulting from any given foot pressure on the pedals.)

So it is in economics. A model is a simplified diagram indicating the main elements in any situation and the main causal relationships among these elements. We can state them very simply, just by identifying the main elements and talking in a common-sense way about their relationships. Or we can specify precisely the relationships connecting the elements, as when the specific physical principles are used in explaining the operation of the bicycle. In this book there is some of both, but for the major economic problems we will try to specify at least the major causal relationships connecting the elements.

An economic model may be stated as a diagram, and many graphs are used in the pages ahead. It may be stated in words, as in the bicycle case, either generally or precisely; and this approach is used repeatedly. It may also be stated in mathematical terms. Except for the simple geometry used in the diagrams, this approach is not used here, since only a few economics students have had much algebra or calculus. Most models may be stated in any one of these three ways.

The economist doesn't apologize for the fact that his theory doesn't describe the real world precisely and in detail. On the contrary, like any other scientist, he says that it's a skeleton stripped of much of the real-world detail we see around us. Without such abstract, skeleton-type models, we would get nowhere in trying to understand the intricate complexity of the modern world. With such theory, we have at least a framework for organizing our study of the economy and the public-policy problems it poses.

"Other Things Equal" and "Equilibrium."   In common with many other scientists, economists use two major concepts in working with models. One is the concept of holding "other things equal." The other is "equilibrium."

In the chemistry laboratory, we hold "other things equal" all the time. We put two elements (say hydrogen and oxygen) together in a test tube *under controlled conditions,* and get water if the proportions are 2 to 1. In the bicycle example above, we hold friction, gravity, air pressure, and various other factors constant (or assume them away altogether) in analyzing the way the bicycle works. So it is in economics. To understand, say, the impact of an increase in demand for potatoes on the price of potatoes, we may want to hold constant many other things—for example, the weather, the supply of money, and so on. In the real world they may not stay constant; but by assuming temporarily that they do, we can isolate the impact of the demand change we are studying.

This is closely related to the concept of "equilibrium." In chemistry, after we've combined hydrogen and oxygen into water, the water is an equilibrium state of the two elements until something else disturbs it. So economists generally think of the economic system tending to move toward equilibrium when some disturbing change occurs; and in analyzing the movement toward equilibrium, they commonly hold many "other things equal" to isolate the factors under analysis.

Take a simple example. A potato farmer is producing 1,000 bushels a year and the price is $2 a bushel. Now the demand for potatoes increases and the price goes up to $2.50. If we know his costs of production at different levels of output, and if we hold constant a variety of other factors such as the weather and the behavior of the government, we can use a model to see how he will raise his output to a new level of, say, 1,500 bushels annually in striving to maximize his profits. This would be a new "equilibrium" situation, which would then continue until demand, costs, or some other related factor changed again. *We mean by equilibrium a situation in which everybody is satisfied to keep on doing what he is doing. In economic equilibrium, there's nothing at work to change the output and prices under consideration.*

In the real world, of course, a thousand things would happen between now and the time all these equilibrating adjustments were completed. Consumer demand would shift again, farm costs would go up or down, the government might put in a potato price support program, and so on. *To keep matters simple enough to work with, the economist therefore makes the analytical assumption "other things equal."* This means that we trace through what *would* happen *if* all other things in the economic system remained unchanged until this change in demand had worked itself out fully to a new equilibrium. No one thinks the world really behaves this way, with only one thing going at a time. But it's the only way we can keep things simple enough to be able to trace through completely the consequences of one particular change, such as the increased consumer demand for potatoes. This is one approach to the scientists' old problem of isolating the effects of particular causes.

Economics and the Laboratory Sciences.   If you've studied chemistry or physics or biology, you know one way the physical and natural sciences get around this difficulty. They run controlled experiments. You can put two chemicals together in a test tube at a controlled temperature and see what happens, even though this simple situation might never occur outside the laboratory. The social scientist, unfortunately, seldom has this possibility open to him. We can't get everything else in the economy to stand still while we raise income taxes 10 per cent to see just what would happen. Nor can we get at the results by putting a few people off in a closed room and raising their income tax 10 per cent.

So the social scientist is never as sure and precise as the physical and natural scientist can be on lots of matters. But it's easy to overstate the differences too. Much of modern atomic physics, for example, was developed by means of abstract theory, in principle quite like the simple models (or theory) described above in the potato example. Using certain assumptions based on observed reality, scientists theorize (think through) the results that can be expected from certain causes, or (conversely) the causes that may have led to observed results. Theorizing, in cooperation with careful observation of available real-world and laboratory data, has been the foundation of nearly all the world's major scientific advances.

The Uses of Models (Theory).   What can we really achieve with models (theory)?

Their main use is to provide an *analytical framework* for analyzing any particular real-world situation. Here the theoretical model can serve a very useful purpose. Without some such model, we would be lost in the mass of detail in most real-world situations. Every real-world case is different. The model suggests some of the important questions to ask, some of the important places to look, some tentative conclusions to be investigated. This is the major use made of models in this book. But useful as the model is, it has its dangers. It's easy to let the theory tell you what you "ought" to find, and thereby miss seeing what is really going on in the real world.

Second, some people try to use models to *describe* the real world in summary fashion. This is dangerous business, since at best the theory is an abstraction, a highly oversimplified picture of reality.

A third use of models is as a *predicting,* or *forecasting,* device. In economics we're mainly interested in what will happen tomorrow, not in what happened yesterday. If you have a theoretical model, you can use it to extrapolate from where you are to what may happen in the future. For example, we have a simple model of the business cycle in Part 2. We could use this model to predict where we will be in the cycle a year from now. In one sense, this is nothing but one application of the model as a framework for analyzing the real world. But predicting is treacherous business, and you have to be very careful that you don't end up with the model taking on a lot more reliability and reality than was put into it when it was created.

But in a related sense, we use models all the time in predicting, and quite properly. We use them to predict "what would happen if. . . ." Suppose, going back to the potato farmer, we now change the "other things equal" assumption to eliminate his costs of production. We now ask, *if* his costs increase 10 cents a bushel, what will happen. The model then will help us predict, say, that his output will be only 1,200 bushels with the new higher demand. We use the theory to predict what will happen *if* . . . , still holding all other things equal. This is very different from predicting that the farmer will actually raise 1,200 bushels next year. To be safe in predicting that, we would have to be sure that the weather will stay unchanged, there will be no government crop-restriction program, and so on. These are the things we comfortably assumed unchanged in the model. Unless we're really sure they'll be unchanged, the model isn't a reliable basis for making actual predictions. But it does help us make *conditional* predictions.

Tests of a Good Theory. There are two ways of testing how good a model, or theory, is. One is to examine the assumptions on which it rests and the internal logic that it builds on those assumptions. The other is to make a pragmatic test of how well it actually does predict in the real world.

Look first at the first test. It asks two questions: (1) Do the assumptions on which the theory is built correspond to the reality to which it is being applied? (2) Is the internal reasoning of the theory logically correct? If both these conditions are met, the theory should be a useful one, both as an analytical framework and as a predicting device. But there are problems.

As a practical matter, economists are inclined to rely more on the second test—how well does the theory actually predict? This is primarily because we are seldom sure what the *crucial* assumptions are in looking at complex economic phenomena. In the real world, there are multiple causes and intricate interactions in most cases. Thus, even though the assumptions used in building a model may be demonstrably accurate, they may not be the really important assumptions in the real-world situation. For this reason, economists usually try a model out to see what it predicts, and then check the prediction against the real world they are trying to explain. If the prediction is poor, they distrust the model, no matter how beautiful its logic. If a model based on what appear to be dubious assumptions gives good predictions, they are inclined to use it, at least tentatively. But then they are uncomfortable about whether it predicts well because it is sound or merely by chance in that particular situation. In such cases, more research is needed to establish how much the model can be trusted under what conditions.

This statement may sound alarming, and lead you to wonder why economic models are worth studying at all. It shouldn't. Most of the simple models in this book are intended primarily as frameworks for analysis, and are not intended to provide direct real-world predictions without a careful look at the individual case concerned. Moreover, they are generally models that have been widely used and accepted in the economics profession for a good many years, and have thus stood the test of time. A lot of them have been checked out as conditional predicting devices. Where a special warning is needed about the newness or limited usefulness of a model, the text provides it.

One last introductory comment concerning theory. You often hear the comment, "That's good theory, but it doesn't work in practice." What the speaker must mean, if he is talking sense, is either that it is not good theory because it doesn't help explain the real world, or that it is good theory but it is being inexpertly used. Theory (use of abstract models) is only good when it *does* work in practice—that is, when it is useful in helping to understand the problem on which it is being used.

The Dangers of Models (Theory).   As you go on, you'll be using several economic models. They are simple ones, since they are intended primarily as general analytical tools, not as accurate descriptions of any particular real-world situations. The biggest danger in model-using is not that the model will be too simple, but that it will be improperly used.

1.   The first warning, therefore, is against slipping into the assumption that such simple analytical models really describe the real world. Since they make no pretense of accurate description except in the most general sense, any conclusion drawn from them can be no more directly usable than are the models themselves.

Suppose, for example, that we have a simple model of how a monopolist might behave in pricing his product so as to maximize his profits. This model may suggest that he would respond to increased consumer demand mainly by pushing up prices and by increasing output very little. This a bad situation, you say. Call out the antitrust authorities! But maybe the monopolist knows about the antitrust authorities too, and in fact increases prices very little and output a great deal to avoid investigation. Or perhaps he fears potential competition if his prices and profits get any higher. Or maybe he has his heart set on having a giant company, so that volume is the apple of his eye. None of these factors is in the model. Maybe in general they're not very important. But in this particular instance they would obviously throw your conclusions off if you blindly reasoned from the simple profit-maximizing monopoly model.

2.   The second danger is that the model may subtly become a kind of "norm" or "ideal" to which a good society "ought" to correspond. For example, later on

we will look closely at a model of the way a highly competitive economy would work. Many people think a highly competitive economy would be wonderful. But if you agree with them, it should be because you've thought through all the consequences and not because you've let a neutral analytical model become your master instead of your servant. We all have a tendency to believe in what we are most familiar with. This is understandable, but often it is not conducive to straight thinking.

3. The most subtle danger of all is that the analytical model may close your eyes to other ways of looking at the world. Most of the economic models in this book focus around prices and production of goods and services. Labor unions, for example, are viewed largely as organizations trying to push up wages, sometimes with resulting reductions in both output and employment. But maybe this way of looking at them is beside the point. Maybe the main significance of unions is that they give the worker a chance to stand up to his boss without fear of reprisal, to be a member of a group of men with common interests and ambitions, to feel that he's an important individual rather than just another cog in a big, impersonal, industrial wheel. If you become too adjusted to typical price-output analytical models, you may never stop to think of these quite different considerations. The book tries to avoid this subtle danger of looking at the world through "blinders" by reminding you frequently of other factors. But the danger is one that you will meet everywhere you go, far from economics. It is hard for most of us to see familiar problems in new and different lights.

ECONOMIC ANALYSIS AND PUBLIC POLICY

One major objective of this book is to help you understand how the modern economy operates. Economic theory is useful for this purpose. Another objective is to help you learn to make up your mind intelligently on economic policy issues—what should we do to make this work better, or to achieve some desired result? Here too theory is useful, but there's lots more to this type of "action" or policy problem.

There is no one best way of thinking straight to solve problems—e.g., the problem of what should be done to check an inflation. But most people who have thought carefully about straight thinking agree that an orderly, systematic job of thinking through a "decision" or "action" problem of this sort (be it in economics or any other field) must include the following broad interacting steps:

1. *First, you have to define the problem.* In reaching decisions about economic policy, defining the problem usually consists of two parts: (a) understanding thoroughly the situation in which the problem exists, and (b) clarifying the objectives you want to achieve through policy actions. Put in other terms, you need to clarify where you are and where you want to go. Unless you're straight on these two questions, you're likely to behave like a headless horseman, rushing

this way and that, trying one tack after another, but getting more exercise than results. Unless we know where we are and where we want to go, our chances of getting there are poor.

Consider the problem of fighting inflation. The first step in defining the problem is to look thoroughly at the inflation in progress, using the analytical models (to be studied in Part 2) in isolating the important elements of the inflationary process. Second, we need to clarify what our goals are in trying to check the inflation. Do we want primarily to insure that the inflation won't lead to a depression? Is our main goal to protect the creditors, bondholders, and widows on pensions, who get paid dollars with lower purchasing power in an inflation? Or do we want mainly to protect the poor against losing their share of the national income to those who are already better off? These are all perfectly proper objectives. But once you've studied inflations, you'll see that they may be at least partially incompatible, and that they may call for quite different anti-inflationary steps.

2. *The second step is to map out what appear to be the main alternative ways of achieving the stated objectives—the alternative paths from where we are to where we want to be.* In the inflation case, for example, analysis of the problem might suggest three major approaches: cut down on the public's spending power through raising taxes, reduce the money supply by forcing banks to call in their loans, or put ceilings on prices and wages by legislation. No one can see in advance what all the fruitful alternatives may be, but a plan that covers systematically the major alternatives suggested by preliminary analysis of the problem will usually save time and help avoid losing sight of the forest for the trees.

3. *The third step is to analyze carefully the alternative policies outlined broadly in step two.* To analyze means to trace through carefully the effects of the different policies. Here the analytical models you've learned will come in handy again. For example, you'll learn that the banks may in effect create money when they make loans and wipe the money out when the loans are repaid. You'll understand the circular flow of money income through the economy, and the implications of more or less money, more or less taxes, and so on, for the level of total expenditures. Economic theory should help you assess the alternative paths available for checking inflation, and help you make a tentative choice on the best steps to take. Perhaps in the analysis of your three main alternatives you'll hit on a fourth one you hadn't even thought of at first. Although it's important to systematize your thinking, it's equally important to keep it flexible and to remain alert for new alternative solutions to any problem you're handling.

4. When you've finally got a tentative solution to the problem (for example, pass a law that puts ceilings on all prices and wages), don't stop! *The fourth step is: Check your solution*—both against flaws in your own analysis resulting from fallacies or blind spots, and against past experience. The world has had inflations before, and governments have tried to check them by passing laws against price increases. Usually, this solution hasn't worked very well. Whatever your solution is, go back and look to see how it has worked out in the past, and what

light past experience may throw on the present problem. It's no fun to have to throw out a solution after you've gone through a lot of analysis to get it. But if your checking suggests that something is wrong, take another long look at whether you've really picked the right path to get where you want to go. It's better to find out for yourself if you're wrong than to learn it more painfully from your boss (if you're in a job) or from some other unsympathetic part of the world (such as the impersonal market place) if you've made a bad decision on prices or general economic conditions.

5. *Lastly, although it's not a part of the job of solving this problem, it's usually a good idea to stop after you're done and ask: "What have I learned from this that will help me solve the next problem better and faster?"* We learn mainly from what we do, intellectually as well as physically, and it's a good idea to try to organize and recognize what it is you're learning from experience. Some things are worth labeling in red because they look important for future use. Maybe you'll remember them anyway, but this fifth step may help in systematizing your learning from experience.

THE PROBLEM OF SOCIAL GOALS

Over and over, this chapter has emphasized the necessity for having clearly defined objectives as a basis for making an intelligent choice among alternative courses of action, and as a basis for evaluating the kind of economic system we have. In a free society, every person has the right, and the duty, to make up his own mind about what he likes and what he doesn't. Maybe the rest of the country won't agree with you if you believe that the government ought to expropriate the fortune of everyone getting more than $10,000 a year and pass it out to the poor people. But you have a right to your own views.

Does the present "mixed" economic system do a good job? Nobody can honestly answer this question until he has thought through just what it is that he wants the system to accomplish. In the same way, you can't judge whether a piece of furniture is doing a good job until you specify what you want—color, design, comfort, durability, strength, and so on. If you put major weight on how the chair looks and your roommate on how it feels, you may end up arguing about whether or not it's a good buy. And someone else who says durability is all-important may come out with a still different answer.

So it is with the economic system. If you're a good conservative Republican who looks back longingly to the 1920's when the government kept its nose out of economic affairs, and if your neighbor is a strong New Deal Democrat, you're in for some lively disagreements over economic policy. Some of these disagreements may be caused by differences in analysis. These you should be able to get straightened out. But many of them may go back to fundamental differences in what you think the system ought to do. You're a great believer in rugged free enterprise and the rewards to the man who can earn them; your neighbor is worried about the poor fellow who never seems to make enough money to keep the roof patched and the bills paid. You think that unions are a bunch of monopolists out to bleed the employer and the consumer; he sees unions as a chance for the working man to win security and real economic equality.

Since economics is the study of allocating scarce means (resources) to satisfy competing ends (demands), we have to decide what the most important ends are before we can judge whether the economic system is allocating its resources wisely and well. And we can be sure of two things: First, with 180 million people there will be many different ideas on what we want the system to achieve. Second, most of us as individuals will want many different results without being able to specify very precisely just how heavily we weight each and how we would resolve a conflict between them. No economic system is going to be able to please everybody about everything.

Some Tentative Social Goals.   Consider the following list of objectives for the American economic system:

1. A rising standard of living.
2. Economic freedom.
3. Economic security.
4. Production in accordance with consumer demands.
5. An equitable distribution of income.

Would a system that accomplished these five things look good to you? If you're a typical American of today, it might, since this list is an attempt to mirror some criteria that seem to be most generally used in evaluating our system. But make up your own list. The main purpose in presenting the list above is to give us something to work with, not to suggest that you ought to have the same list.

But if you think about the list a minute, you'll see that it's going to get us into trouble. For one thing, the words are vague: What does "economic freedom" mean? You and your neighbor may have quite different ideas. For another, it doesn't take a Bernard Baruch to see that the objectives may conflict with each other. Take the freedom and security objectives, for example. Or what do we do if the incentive of high profits and big incomes is the only way to get maximum production when our equitable-income-distribution criterion calls for more equal incomes?

There are no easy answers to these questions. The facts are that we do have different "value judgments" about what is most important in the world, and that most of us have conflicting value judgments even within our own minds. It's your job as an individual to straighten out your own thinking by clarifying what ends you think are most important, and by weighting them when you have to give up some of one to get more of another. It's the job of a democratic system to compromise the different judgments of different individuals in order to reflect the wishes of the majority while respecting minority views.

To provide a common basis for analysis, throughout this book we will use these five *tentative* criteria for judging how well our system works. But first, consider briefly some of the things the different objectives may mean to different people.

A Rising Standard of Living.   Suppose, for the moment, that we define the standard of living as the goods and services we as individuals have. Then getting a higher standard of living is mainly a question of raising the economy's output per capita. By and large, there is little disagreement on this objective. But some tough questions arise as to how added leisure should be balanced against more output, and as to how fast the economy should grow when rapid growth means giving up consumption goods now.

This objective clearly involves not only continued long-run growth in output, but greater economic stability as well. Mass unemployment is the greatest peacetime blow our national standard of living can suffer; and wasted resources in depression—poverty when we have excessive productive capacity—are the greatest paradox of modern industrial society. On the other side, inflationary booms may help increase total national output, but following depressions may more than offset the excesses of the booms.

Economic Freedom.   Individual freedom to think what you like, to work where you like, and to spend your money as you like, is the core of the American economic and political tradition. Americans want to do what they please, not what somebody tells them. Nobody is likely to get very far in our society who runs against this tradition any more than seems clearly required by the circumstances. In war, we tolerate direct controls over production, where we work, and what we buy. But we don't like them, and they go as fast as we feel it's safe to get rid of them when peace returns.

Still, the concept of individual freedom has been undergoing a subtle change in American thinking over the past few decades. Security from the hazards of depression, of sickness, of old age has increasingly been accepted as part of the "good society." Franklin Roosevelt's famous "Four Freedoms" included freedom from want and freedom from fear, along with the traditional freedoms of speech and worship. We give up individual freedom to spend our money as we please when we, by law, pay social security taxes to guarantee us against poverty in old age. Is freedom from control or from insecurity more basic? Defining individual economic freedom to get widespread agreement poses a very tough problem, and potential clashes with the next objective of "economic security" arise everywhere.

Economic Security.   The depression of the 1930's threw nearly one-third of the entire labor force out of jobs, destroyed years of planning for old age and sickness, brought abject poverty to millions. It is little wonder that economic security came to parallel the goal of freedom itself after that cataclysmic decade.

With the return of prosperity and full employment through the 1940's and 1950's, some of this concern over economic security has receded into the background. But it is plain today that economic freedom and economic security hold positions of comparable importance in the minds of many millions of Americans.

What does economic security mean? Reasonable protection against unemployment? Security against discharge for arbitrary or personal reasons? Security against poverty in old age? Protection against disaster from injury or ill health? Many Americans jest about Britain's "cradle to the grave" social security program. But we have moved steadily in the same direction, though much more slowly.

Production in Accordance with Consumer Demands.   During the nineteenth century, private-enterprise economics put great emphasis on allocating resources in accordance with consumers' wishes. This "consumer sovereignty" was viewed as an integral part of the dominance of the individual, parallel to his control over political processes through the ballot box. Individuals were assumed to be better judges of their own interests than anyone else could be. It was widely agreed that the free-price system, powered by self-interest and the never-ending search for profits, provided production in accordance with consumer demands as they were expressed in the market place.

But here again conflicts arose, and modern thinking has been less ready to accept this position. For one thing, the position takes the distribution of income as given; the rich man has millions of dollar votes on what is produced, the poor man only a few. Moreover, we increasingly dictate through the government what citizens should spend their money for. We say that everyone must go to school until he is at least sixteen, that most workers must buy old-age and unemployment insurance, that everyone must help pay for defense and modern highways, and so on down a long list. Government taxation and spending to rechannel the use of resources is in effect a control over the way we allocate our resources. And today this procedure controls the allocation of about one-fifth of all our productive resources. How far shall we go to replace the rule of the market place by the rule of the ballot box through the tax collector?

An Equitable Distribution of Income.   This is possibly the toughest problem of all. Everyone is for an equitable distribution of income. But what does it mean in practice? More wages and less profits? More for the poor and less for the rich? About the incomes people have now? The incomes people get before the government redistributes them through its taxation and spending? Incomes in accordance with how hard people work?

At least three alternative definitions of "equity" have been widely used:

1. Implicit in the free-price thinking of the nineteenth century was the idea that most people would earn just about what they were worth. The price system

would reward each in accordance with the value of his economic contribution. Most people's main economic contribution is their own personal services. Some who are more fortunate get rewards from land, investments, or other productive resources they own. The price system takes both into account.

By and large, this looks like an argument for the status quo. Let people keep what they earn. It is certainly an argument for a highly unequal income distribution. Some people have more ability than others. Opportunity is far from equal to all; the rich have a long running start on the poor. And huge incomes from property tend to make the rich even richer, absolutely and relative to the poor.

2. "Equity" means to many people merely some distribution less unequal than the present one. If you asked them how much less unequal, they probably couldn't give you any precise answer. Certainly the fact that we have relied heavily on progressive income taxes (taking a larger percentage from rich than from poor) since the 1920's is evidence that our elected representatives believe in taxing the upper-income groups hard before they take funds away from the poor. But the tax system already goes a long way toward leveling out the extremes of the income distribution before taxes. How much, if any, further most people want to go is a moot question.

3. Most people favor guaranteeing at least a bare minimum income to everyone who isn't just a lazy ne'er-do-well. We don't let people starve. This feeling of responsibility for the very poor and for those unable to take care of themselves underlies our extensive governmental program of old-age insurance, widows' and orphans' pensions, special aid for the blind, county poor farms, and so on. Only a couple of decades ago, the present provisions for these groups would have seemed generous indeed. Today, however, it is clear that much greater government intervention toward lessening income inequality is welcomed by millions of voters.

How the total economic pie is cut up into income shares each year is perhaps the hottest and most difficult issue in the entire field. What do you think is the most equitable distribution of income?

Try to straighten out your own feelings about which, if any, of these objectives you want to accept for our economic system. And whatever your objectives are, keep using them as standards to evaluate how well you like the way the economic system works.

SOME COMMON FALLACIES The preceding sections have outlined the positive job of straight thinking. But the path is full of turns and byways. This section is intended to point up some of the more common fallacies lying in wait for the unwary. As with the previous material, they show up everywhere you go, not merely in economics. Two or three are especially dangerous in economics.

The Dog and the Bone.   Consider the following syllogism, as this particular form of reasoning is called:

Major premise: All dogs like bones.
Minor premise: Roger likes bones.
Therefore: Roger is a dog.

How about it? Is Roger a dog? You should see in a minute that the conclusion doesn't follow from the premises at all. Roger may be a man, or a woodchuck, or anything else that likes bones. Maybe he's a dog, but this reasoning doesn't give you any basis for believing it.

Now try this syllogism:

Major premise: All dogs like bones.
Minor premise: Roger is a dog.
Therefore: Roger likes bones.

Here our logic is airtight. If the first and second statements (the premises) are true, it necessarily follows that the conclusion is true: Roger likes bones. Why? Because the major premise states that *all* dogs like bones; and the minor premise states that Roger is a dog and hence included in the group covered by the major premise. If Roger is included in the group described by the major premise, anything that is true of all the major-premise group must be true of Roger.

The fallacy in the first syllogism is called the fallacy of the "undistributed middle." The minor premise doesn't get Roger included under the major premise. Hence, we don't know whether statements about the major-premise group are also true of Roger.

This may seem to have very little to do with economics, but in fact syllogistic reasoning crops up constantly in our daily conversations. Consider this example: "Necessities shouldn't be taxed, so potatoes should be exempted from sales taxes." If you look at it, this is nothing but a syllogism with a missing minor premise:

Major premise: Necessities shouldn't be taxed.
Minor premise:
Therefore: Potatoes should not be taxed.

Set up this way, it is obvious that the minor premise has to be, "Potatoes are a necessity," to make the reasoning sound. If in fact potatoes aren't a necessity, the conclusion won't necessarily follow. To be sure, it may be desirable to avoid taxing potatoes, but the conclusion cannot be demonstrated from the major premise stated.

This example is a very simple one. Most syllogisms are not quite so easy to detect and clear up; often the conclusion is stated first, with the premises following "because" or some other similar word. And there are many other types of syllogism—"if this is true, then this must be true" types of reasoning. Keeping your eye out for fallacious syllogistic reasoning is an effective way to ferret out crooked thinking.

Facts That Aren't Facts.   The second syllogism above looks airtight, but can we really be sure that Roger likes bones? The answer is, yes,—if . . . if the statements in the major and minor premises are in fact true. Do all dogs like bones? Many people wouldn't think to question the "fact" in the last section, and a lot of other "facts" get by us in the same way.[1]

When is a fact a fact? One of the most frustrating things about economics is that so often different people make flatly contradictory statements about the "facts." This is a word to be on guard against. When people want you to believe something, they tell you, "It's a fact." This is an old trick of argument. Always be on guard to look behind and check up on the "facts" presented to you.

In the economic world, there are very few facts like the major premise above: "All things are this way," or "This is *always* thus and so." An accurate statement is much more likely to be: "Most dogs like bones," or "The best evidence is that about 80 per cent of all dogs like bones." In any case, we seldom have any sure way of telling that *all* things are any particular way, since our information about the real world is always partial, never 100 per cent complete.

This immediately plays havoc with airtight syllogistic logic, but unfortunately that's the way the world is. Don't throw your knowledge about syllogisms out the window, however. You can still use it just as before, except that your statements generally need to be *probabilistic* rather than absolute. If 80 per cent of all dogs like bones (assumed to be an established proposition) and if Roger is a dog, we have *a priori* a four out of five chance that Roger will like bones. This is a pretty high likelihood, but you still have to be cautious about the fifth chance.

In the real world, most statements must be probabilistic, in other fields as well as in economics. There isn't time here to go into statistics and the rules of statistical inference that tell just what it's safe to conclude from combinations of probabilistic statements. But you should get used to the fact that facts are seldom absolute facts—that they are usually "almost always" true, or maybe only 60 per cent true. Often they're true under some circumstances and false under others. This kind of world makes flatly "right" or "wrong" conclusions less common than many people like to think.

Generalizing from Small Samples.   "Red-headed people are hot-tempered. I know! I have two red-haired friends and they're both hot-tempered." Or go

---

[1] Note that these are the same two warnings issued a few pages back in evaluating theoretical models: Be sure the basic assumptions are sound, and that the reasoning is logically correct.

back to the dog-and-bone case: "I know that dogs like bones, because I have a dog and he likes bones!" How often have you heard this kind of argument?

To generalize about all red-headed people or about all dogs on a sample of one or two is extremely dangerous, unless you have some definite reason to suppose that this tiny sample is representative of the whole universe of red-haired people or dogs. There is probably no commoner fallacy than that of generalizing unthinkingly from very small samples. We are continually learning from what we see and do; this is the commonest way of extending our knowledge. Thus we inevitably build up tentative generalizations about the world from our everyday experience. But don't let yourself be too sure about the generalizations you build up from your own limited experience. It may or may not be typical. The safest generalizations have been established by careful, systematic observation of a large number of cases. The same question again: When is a fact a fact?

Black, or White, or Gray?   There is a closely related fallacy to be avoided. If one is not wary, he can go astray by (explicitly or covertly) assuming that there is no middle ground between two extremes. For example, someone may say, "Is the statement true?" Suppose you say, "Well . . . no." "Then," he will assert, "it must be false."

But in the real world, a statement is often partly true and partly false. On a foggy day, someone asks, "Is it raining?" You reply, "No." "Then," he retorts, "it must be a fair day." But of course it may just be foggy. There often is a perfectly logical middle ground between what appear at first glance to be two mutually exclusive alternatives; the alternatives stated may not exhaust the possible situations.

So for straight thinking keep up your guard against being trapped by assertions of "facts" that are really only partial facts. The wise observer of the economic scene is the one who sees the grays in their proper shadings—not the one who sees everything as black or white, true or false.

Reasoning by Analogy.   One of the most effective ways to explain something is to use an analogy. For example, in trying to explain the effect of continued repression on human behavior you may say, "Not letting someone express his feelings is like building up steam in a boiler." This certainly conveys a vivid impression; if those feelings aren't let out, our subject is going to burst like an overheated boiler.

Is the analogy a fallacy, or a very useful means of communication? It may be either, depending on how closely a human being with repressions actually corresponds to a steam boiler. It would be difficult to communicate without using analogies, but don't let the analogies lead you farther than can be justified by careful analysis. Analogies are everywhere. For example, is a monopolist in economics a robber baron?

Wishing It Were So. One of the commonest of human frailties is to believe the things we want to believe. The boss believes his employee-education program is opening the workers' eyes to the necessity of large profits for continued prosperity—and he may be a surprised man next time the wage contract comes up for renewal if he's just been wishing it were so.

This is one of the most insidious fallacies. We tend to talk to people who agree with us, to read the newspaper that reports things the way we like, and to run away from information and conclusions that are painful to us. Confronted with two interpretations of an event, one favorable and the other unfavorable, most of us will choose the favorable one. The union members believe the company could pay lots higher wages if only it would. Top management believes that all right-thinking people see that management is right and labor wrong in most wage disputes. Just wishing it were so?

Post Hoc, Propter Hoc. Suppose there's a bad depression. The government pays out large sums on public works projects. Six months later we're on the way up. Was the government spending the cause of the recovery?

Many people would say yes. The government spent, and recovery came. What could be clearer? But maybe the recovery was on its way anyhow, and the government spending did no good at all. The observed evidence tells us that government spending *may* have caused the recovery. But the mere fact that one event precedes another doesn't necessarily mean the first caused the second. To assume that causation can be determined as simply as this is the fallacy of *post hoc, propter hoc*—"after this, therefore because of this." Keep your ears open and notice how often people rely on this sort of reasoning. It's an especially widespread fallacy on economic problems.

The Fallacy of Composition. Suppose one rancher increases his cattle production. He can reasonably expect that the increase will bring him in more money when marketing time comes round. But suppose all ranchers decide to raise more beef cattle this year. Will they get more money for the cattle in total? Quite possibly not. More cattle coming to market will, other things equal, push down the price of cattle. If prices fall a long way because of the increased production, the total revenue to all cattle farmers may be less for the larger output of cattle. Clearly what is true for one rancher alone is not necessarily true for all ranchers taken together.

Consider another example. Saving is obviously a sensible procedure for most families. It stores up funds for the rainy day, for old age, for a new house, and for other important purposes. But suppose in a depression everyone decides to increase his savings. What this will mean, other things equal, is that everyone will cut down on his consumption expenditures. Unless these saved funds are somehow returned to the income stream (as in Figure 4-1), merchants' sales will fall off further. More people will lose their jobs—all as a result of individually wise decisions to save. How can a decision that is so obviously sound as an individual matter have such perverse results in the aggregate?

To assume that what is true of one part will necessarily be true of the whole is the fallacy of composition. Somehow it doesn't seem reasonable that when we aggregate everybody together, everything goes topsy-turvy from the way it looked when we took someone alone. But it does in economics, in a surprising number of cases. We have to look at consumers and businesses as individual units, and also at the total production of the economy as a whole. It's easy but fallacious to assume that what you learn about the individual will necessarily tell you what is true for the whole economy.

REVIEW—CONCEPTS TO REMEMBER

Be especially sure you understand the following concepts introduced in this chapter:

model	fallacy of *post hoc, propter hoc*
theory	fallacy of composition
"other things equal"	syllogism
"equilibrium"	

FOR ANALYSIS AND DISCUSSION

1. "Theory is all right for college professors, but not for me. I'm a practical man. Give me the facts and they'll speak for themselves." Do you agree or disagree with this sentiment? Why? How do facts speak for themselves?

2. In recent years there has been a great deal of argument over whether the federal government should build a huge system of high-speed highways. Suppose you were a senator called on to vote on this issue. How would you go about deciding which way to vote?

3. Analyze the validity of the following statements. In each case, explain carefully why you accept or reject the statement.
   a. What goes up must come down. (Used in speaking of prices.)
   b. Sales taxes burden the poor, so they are inequitable taxes.
   c. In the past, booms have always been followed by depressions, so we can look forward to a real depression in the next few years.
   d. Liberia is a republic, so it must have a president.
   e. Millions are hungry in Asia, but government-owned wheat rots in storage bins. The administration's farm policy couldn't be more nonsensical.
   f. American industry is owned by the man in the street. A recent study by the New York Stock Exchange shows that over 11 million Americans own stock in corporations.

4. How do you decide who is a reliable authority:
   a. On what medicine you should take when you are sick?
   b. On whether redheads have hot tempers?
   c. On whether the sun will rise tomorrow morning?

5. Do you believe everyone should be required to attend school until he is 16? That everyone should be required to have a smallpox vaccination? That everyone should be required to work eight hours a day, five days a week, after he reaches age 21? If your answers are different to the three questions, explain carefully the basis on which you distinguish among them in deciding how far the government should control our behavior.

6. Should wealthy citizens of New York be taxed to provide schooling and food for poor sharecroppers in Alabama? To provide better housing for slum-dwellers in New York?

7. Suppose it becomes feasible to reduce federal taxes by 20 per cent next year. What taxes would you advocate reducing? Why?

PART 2

National Income, Employment, and Economic Growth

National Income,
Production,
and Employment[1]

6

The economic history of the United States is a great success story. In less than two hundred years, our country has grown from a few struggling colonies into the world's richest nation. In the first six decades of the present century alone, our total national output (adjusted to eliminate the effect of price inflation) has risen about sixfold.

But it has been a bumpy ride up. There was a major financial crisis in 1907; a big inflation after World War I; a severe depression from 1929 to 1939; and another big inflation during and after World War II. We can be proud of our success, but we must face the fact too that our rapid economic growth has been marked by inflationary booms and depressions.

Economists once took it for granted that our private-enterprise system would automatically restore itself to full-employment prosperity whenever it got far off the track, provided that the government simply assured a reasonably stable

---

[1] Some instructors may prefer to use Parts 3 and 4 on micro-economics and the distribution of income before Part 2 on macro-economics. These Parts may be used in either order.

79

supply of money. But no more! Economists today have grave doubts that the system is self-stabilizing, and since the 1930's *the* biggest economic issue has been to devise government policies that will eliminate booms and depressions. Since 1940, we have had two decades of substantially continuous prosperity, the longest stretch in our history. Maybe we have solved the problem of obtaining stable economic growth. But maybe not. Even since 1940, we've had three minor recessions and a large amount of inflation.

Part 2 analyzes the determinants of the over-all level of production, income, and employment in our economy. In nontechnical terms, the problem is why we grow rapidly or slowly, and why we have booms and depressions—and then, what we can do about them. The purpose of this chapter is to provide some of the major analytical concepts you need to understand these problems—basically, the concepts of the "national income" or "social accounts."

MEASURES OF NATIONAL PRODUCTION AND INCOME   To understand the behavior of an enormously complex economy, we need some measure of its performance. Perhaps most important of all, we need a measure of its total output of goods and services, and a measure of the total income received by all its people. But in addition, we need more detailed measures—of how much people have left to spend after paying their taxes, of corporate profits, of family and business saving, and so on.

The "national income accounts" provide these measures. We'll start with the "gross national product," the measure of the economy's total production of goods and services, and work down to some of the more detailed measures, like personal income and savings.

Gross National Product.   *Gross national product is the nation's total production of goods and services* (*usually for a year*), *valued in terms of the market prices of the goods and services produced.* This concept goes directly back to the definition of production in Chapter 3: production is whatever people will pay for, and what they pay is an economic valuation of the worth of the production. Gross national product (abbreviated "g.n.p.") includes all the economic production in the economy in any given time period.

Gross national product is stated in money terms, since this is the only meaningful way of adding together the output of such diverse goods and services as carrots, machine tools, maid service, movies, and Buicks. Strictly, then, g.n.p. is the money value of total national production for any given period.

Gross national product may be viewed from the other side—that is, as the nation's total expenditures on goods and services produced during the year. Each unit of goods and services produced is matched by an expenditure on the unit. Most goods and services produced are bought outright. But how about the ones produced but not sold? If we regard these as having been bought by the producers who hold them, as inventories, then it is clear that the production and expenditure totals are identical.

We can look at this same total in still a third way: as the total incomes received by all sellers of goods and services. What someone spends on current output, someone else receives as income.

Thus, it doesn't matter whether we look at gross national product as (1) the value of all goods and services produced, (2) total expenditures on those goods and services, or (3) the (gross) incomes received for producing the goods and services. Since they are the same thing, we get the same total either way.

The central notion of gross national product is simple, and it is the central notion that's most important to remember. But if you're to use the concept properly, there are certain problems that you must be aware of. One is the importance of avoiding double-counting.

One way the g.n.p. is estimated each year is by summing up all expenditures on *final* products sold to consumers or to businesses for final use as producers' goods—on potatoes, factories, autos, missiles, legal services, and so on. Note the word "final." In one year, miners dig a certain quantity of iron ore out of the ground and sell it to Bethlehem Steel. Bethlehem makes the iron ore into steel and sells the steel to Westinghouse. Westinghouse makes the steel into refrigerators and sells them to you and me. We don't count the value of the iron ore, then the value of the steel, and then the value of the refrigerator. That would involve, in effect, counting the iron ore three times. Everything that is used in another product during the year shows up and is counted only in the *final* product (in this case, refrigerators), since the value of the final product will reflect the value of all the raw materials, labor, and other productive services included in it. Producers' goods, like machinery, bought by businesses, pose an obvious problem here, since they are not directly incorporated into the final consumers' goods the way raw materials are. We count such machinery and other producers' goods once, when they reach their final buyer—for example, when Ford buys a new punch press. (Some further notes on this below, under "net national product.") This process of summing up all final purchases is called the "final-product approach" to estimating g.n.p.

To get a cross-check, gross national product is also estimated each year by using another (equivalent) approach: the "value added method." Here the estimators establish the value added to each product by each firm or separate individual, and then sum up all these values. Each worker's contribution is valued at the wage or salary he is paid. Each business' contribution is measured by its net income. For example, in converting the iron ore to steel above, Bethlehem adds something to the value of the product it passes along. This added value is the difference between Bethlehem's costs (what it pays for the ore, coal, labor, and other resources that it uses) and the price at which it sells the steel to Westinghouse. Similarly, we can compute the value added by Westinghouse. And so on for each productive unit in the economy. By adding together all the values added, we come out with the gross national product, again avoiding double-counting. Each individual and business producer shows up in gross national product in terms of the value it adds to the final product. Either way, goods still in process at the end of the time period are counted as inventories (purchased by the owner as an investment) in the latest stage they have reached.

Table 6-1, using the final-products approach, breaks down gross national product according to who buys the goods and services, a useful procedure in a private-enterprise economy where production is mainly in response to monetary demand. Purchasers are divided into three big groups: consumers, businesses (buying "investment," or "producers'," goods), and governments.

Table 6-1

U. S. GROSS NATIONAL PRODUCT, 1958 *

Purchases Group	In Billions
Consumer purchases	$291
Business investment expenditures	56
Government purchases	91
Total	$438

* Data from U.S. Department of Commerce.

To provide historical perspective, Figure 6-1 presents the data on who bought the goods and services in the gross national product from 1929 to 1959. Take a look at the three major segments of the chart:

1. The biggest part of total production has consistently been goods and services for direct purchase by consumers—electric fans, stoves, dresses, movies, medical services, hats, and all the other things that we buy as consumers. This is segment A.

2. The next group is investment in "producers'" or "capital" goods—segment B. These are goods used in the production of further goods or services—buildings, machinery, equipment, and other producers' or capital goods. Such investment goods are purchased primarily by businesses. But houses are also included in the investment-goods category, on the grounds that they are so durable that in effect they represent investment goods rendering consumer services, even though they are owned directly by consumers in many cases.[2]

Three warnings about the private investment category.

First, note that it includes *gross* purchases of investment goods. It includes production that merely replaces depreciating buildings, machinery, and equipment,

---

[2] Although it is reasonable to treat new private housing as investment, you should recognize that houses differ only in degree from such durable consumer goods as autos, refrigerators, and vacuum cleaners, which are treated as consumption goods.

as well as production that represents a net increase in society's stock of capital goods. We come to the *net* increase in the nation's capital goods in the "net national product" below.

Second, "investment" means the purchase of real investment goods (buildings, machinery, and so on) *produced during the year.* For example, if you buy a ten-year-old house or machine tool, this is not investment; the building or tool was included in the gross national product ten years ago, when it was built.

Third, investment does not include mere financial transfers,

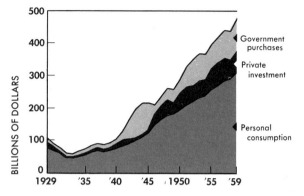

FIG. 6-1   Consumers buy most of the gross national product. The other third is government purchases and private investment, with government somewhat the larger of the two. (Source: U.S. Department of Commerce.)

such as the purchase of stocks and bonds. For example, if you buy a share of General Motors stock from me, this is not investment for purposes of the national income accounts, since it does not reflect any new production.

3. Government purchases of goods and services, segment C, cut across consumption and investment goods. Federal, state, and local governments buy food, police services, and other current consumption items, as well as investment goods like roads, buildings, and parks. But notice that government purchases of goods and services do not include all government expenditures. Governments spend large sums on "transfer payments" (e.g., unemployment insurance and social security payments) that are not payments for currently produced goods and services and are hence not included in gross national product.

To summarize, then, the three components of gross national product are: (1) consumer goods and services produced for private purchase, (2) investment goods produced for private purchase, and (3) a combination of both consumer goods and investment goods produced for purchase by the nation's governments. In all three categories, remember that it is only goods and services *produced during the year* that count; transfers of existing assets are not included.

Net National Product.   Gross national product is a measure of the total production of final goods and services in the economy. But it includes some producers' goods that just go to replace already existing producers' goods that are "depreciating" or wearing out. If a tank truck lasts ten years, we might say that one-tenth of it is used up every year, and the oil company that owns it would consider this tenth as an annual cost to be included in its selling price for oil that year.[3] So it is with all other producers' goods; they wear out. Thus, before the firm or the economy as a whole adds anything *net* to its stock of producers' goods, part of the new trucks, buildings, and machines each year must go to replacing the ones wearing out.

Net national product is the net production of goods and services during any time period. Net national product is identical with gross national product except that it omits those goods that merely replace depreciating buildings and machines. In 1958, for example, gross national product was $438 billion. Depreciation (sometimes called "capital consumption allowances") was estimated at $40 billion. Thus, *net* national product was $398 billion, about 9 per cent less than gross national product. In other words, about 9 per cent of our total output went to replace depreciating producers' goods and houses. Net national product measures the total production of goods and services for current consumption and for adding to our stock of producers' equipment, including housing.

National Income.   *National income is the total of all income payments received by the "factors of production"—land, labor, capital, and management.* The national income is basically the gross national product viewed from the income side. National income is always somewhat less than the gross national product, however. The factors of production (laborers, managers, machinery, and so forth) do not actually receive as income the full value of their output, for two reasons: (1) Income is almost invariably quoted "net" in American accounting practice. Thus, as we indicated above, part of the national output must be set aside to replace depreciating productive resources before the nation has a net national product to count as income. (2) The businesses that hire factors of production must pay indirect taxes (sales taxes, excises, and property taxes) to the government, which cut down on the income left to pay to the factors of production. If we subtract from g.n.p. these two major deductions—depreciation and indirect business taxes—we have left the total national income that goes to all factors of production. In 1958, the indirect tax deduction was $39 billion. Deducting this from net national product of $398 billion, we get a national income of $361 billion.[4]

Table 6-2 shows the share of the national income earned by each major factor of production. Note the large share that came through salaries and wages—70 per cent in 1958. This percentage has been quite stable through prosperity and depression; it hasn't varied far from two-thirds of the total national income,

---

[3] Accountants have more complicated depreciation plans, which recognize the fact that buildings and machines do not necessarily wear out at constant rates.

[4] The apparent discrepancy of $3 billion is accounted for by some minor items that need not concern us, and by a small statistical discrepancy. Remember that all these figures are only statistical estimates, albeit very painstaking and elaborate ones, and that the "value added" and "final product" approaches are different ways of building up to the same totals that must be reconciled when the estimates don't agree.

though there seems to have been a gradual upward trend in recent decades. The other three sources of income fluctuate more widely through business cycles. 1958 was a recession year, and profits were relatively smaller than in most other recent years. If you want to see how the different income shares have varied over the last quarter-century, look ahead at Figure 28-2, in Chapter 28, which shows the income shares over the entire period. A still more detailed breakdown, by industrial source of income, is given for 1958 in Table 2-4, Chapter 2.

Table 6-2

UNITED STATES NATIONAL INCOME IN 1958 [a]

Source of Income	In Billions	Percentage of Total
Total	$361	100
Wages, salaries, and other compensation	254	70
Net income of unincorporated business [b]	57	16
Corporation profits [c]	36	10
Interest	13	9

[a] Data from U.S. Department of Commerce.

[b] Including farmers and professional men in business for themselves. This includes rental income as well as business earnings.

[c] Of which $19 billion was paid out in income taxes and $5 billion was plowed back as reinvested earnings. Dividends paid out to stockholders were $12 billions. The 1958 drop in profits showed up especially in the low earnings plow-back figure.

Personal Income and Disposable Personal Income. *"Personal income" is the total income received by all individuals in the economy—what individuals actually have to spend, save, or pay taxes with.* For many purposes it is important to know how individuals and households use their incomes. Do they pay taxes with them, spend them, or save them? To study such problems, personal income is the crucial total.

Personal income is less than the national income, mainly because national income includes total corporation profits whereas individuals receive only part of these profits in dividends. As the last footnote to Table 6-2 indicates, a big chunk of corporation profits goes to Uncle Sam as corporation income taxes, and part of what's left is plowed back into businesses rather than paid out to individual stockholders. We must subtract these amounts from national income to get income actually paid out to individuals. On the other hand, individuals receive large transfer payments (social security, interest on the national debt, and so forth), which are income to them although they are not part of the national income (since they don't reflect any current production). These transfer payments must be added in to get total personal income.

In 1958, total personal income was $354 billion. Table 6-3 shows what people did with this money. First, they paid their personal taxes. What they had left we call "disposable personal income". Most of this they spent on consumption and the rest they saved. The concept of "disposable personal income" (what people have left after they pay their taxes) will be important later on in our analysis of consumer spending and saving behavior.

Table 6-3

UNITED STATES PERSONAL INCOME IN 1958 *

Distribution of Income	In Billions
Total personal income	$354
Less: Personal income taxes $43	
Equals: Disposable personal income	312
Of which:	
Personal consumption expenditure	291
Personal saving	21

* Data from U.S. Department of Commerce. Totals do not subtract exactly because they are rounded.

Data on gross national product, national income, and personal income all have their uses. In general, personal income provides the best measure of the total income people have available for spending, saving, or tax-paying. Gross national product provides a better measure of over-all production. During World War II, for example, one of the most pressing problems was to find how far total production could be increased and how large a portion of the total could be diverted to war uses. In studying this problem, gross national product and its component parts were the key concepts. But in estimating whether the supply of consumer goods produced would be sufficient to satisfy rising consumer demands without inflation, it was necessary to turn to the concept of total personal income and to how much consumers paid in taxes, how much they saved, and how much they spent on scarce consumption goods.

The Integrated Social Accounts.[5]   If you have the concepts of gross national product and personal income (with disposable personal income) well in hand, you're prepared to cope with a good many common problems. For example, most newspaper stories and business magazines focus on these measures. But for clear thinking in some of the following analysis, you need to have a good grasp of the relationships between the various parts of the social accounts. Table 6-4 summarizes the complete set of interconnections for 1958, beginning with the gross

[5] Within the last few years, a new set of social accounts has been released in preliminary form by the Federal Reserve System. These accounts, generally called the "flow of funds accounts," include all transactions in the economy, including payments in the stock market, for other financial transfers, for existing assets, and for a variety of other purposes not included in the national income accounts. When the new money flows accounts are integrated with the present established national income accounts in a few more years, we should have a much more complete picture of money payments throughout the economy.

national product total; the following paragraphs explain the transition from one concept to another. For those who like pictures better than tables, Figure 6-2 shows the same set of interconnections as a flow diagram, tracing the entire income-and-payments flow.

Table 6-4

THE NATIONAL INCOME ACCOUNTS FOR 1958 *

			In Billions
1.	*Gross National Product*		$438
2.	Deduct: Capital consumption allowances (mainly business depreciation allowances)	$ 40	
3.	*Net National Product*		398
4.	Deduct: Indirect business taxes	39	
5.	Miscellaneous and statistical discrepancies	−2	
6.	*National Income*		361
7.	Deduct: Corporation profits	36	
8.	Social security taxes	14	
9.	Add: Govt. transfer and interest payments	31	
10.	Dividends	12	
11.	*Personal Income*		354
12.	Deduct: Personal taxes	43	
13.	*Disposable Personal Income*		312
14.	Of which: *Consumption Expenditures*		291
15.	*Personal Saving*		21

* Figures may not subtract exactly, because they are rounded. A few minor items are omitted.

The reasoning behind these computations is as follows:

1. *Gross national product,* by definition, is the total value of goods and services produced in 1958 (measured at current market prices), eliminating double-counting but including production that replaces depreciating capital goods.

2, 3. To obtain *net national product,* we deduct the portion of total production that merely replaces depreciating capital goods (depreciation on business plant and equipment and on housing). According to our accounting conventions for private firms and for national income purposes, no *net* product arises until existing capital stock has been maintained intact.

4, 5, 6. *National income* is the net income paid to the factors of production—the net cost of producing the national product. Although this is a figure commonly quoted in popular discussion, it is in many respects the most arbitrary of the group. The custom is to take as national income the figure *after* payment of indirect business taxes but *before* payment of personal and corporate income taxes. Thus to derive national income from net national product we subtract indirect taxes (for example, sales and excise taxes) paid by business.

7, 8, 9, 10, 11. To obtain *personal income,* we must convert the national income *produced* into income *received* by persons in the economy (excluding corporations from the category of persons). To do this, we subtract from national income those parts of it (7 and 8) which do not represent income paid out to individuals; and add items (9 and 10) which represent transfer payments to individuals that are not payments for services rendered in the national income accounts.

First, the deduction items. Total corporation profits are included in national income, since they represent income to businesses on the money side and they represent part of the value of goods produced on the goods side.[6] But they are not income payments to individuals except for dividends transferred to individuals; hence corporation profits are subtracted but dividends are added back in (item 10). Similarly, funds paid to the government for future social-security benefits (usually withheld from wages) do not become current income to individuals and must be subtracted.

Partially offsetting these deductions, corporations pay out part of their earnings to individuals as dividends: these (10) are added back in. Similarly, the government makes a variety of "transfer payments" to individuals (social security, unemployment benefits, interest on the national debt, and so on) that represent income to the individuals but do not reflect goods and services currently produced.

12, 13. To obtain *disposable personal income,* we subtract personal income taxes from personal income. Disposable personal income is what people have left to spend or save after they have paid their taxes.

14, 15. Disposable personal income goes for *consumption expenditures* or into *personal savings.*[7]

Figure 6-2 shows the same set of interconnections visually. Begin with gross national product of $438, as in Table 6-4. $40 billion of capital consumption (depreciation) allowances drains off as a form of corporate saving, leaving $398 billion of net national product. From this, another $39 billion drains off to the government through indirect business taxes, leaving national income of $361 billion. From this, a variety of other payments are drained off (to the government in taxes and into corporate saving through reinvested earnings), while interest on the government debt and other transfer payments are added back into the income stream to make up $354 billion of personal income. This is reduced to personal disposable income through the payment of personal income taxes, and then part of disposable income goes into personal savings while the bulk goes on into consumption expenditures. These consumption expenditures in turn become part of gross national product. So do the private savings that flow into investment

---

[6] An adjustment (called an "inventory valuation adjustment") is made on reported corporation profits to eliminate paper profits or losses on inventories arising merely from price-level changes.

[7] For a more detailed discussion of the national income accounts, see *U. S. Income and Output* (U. S. Department of Commerce, 1959).

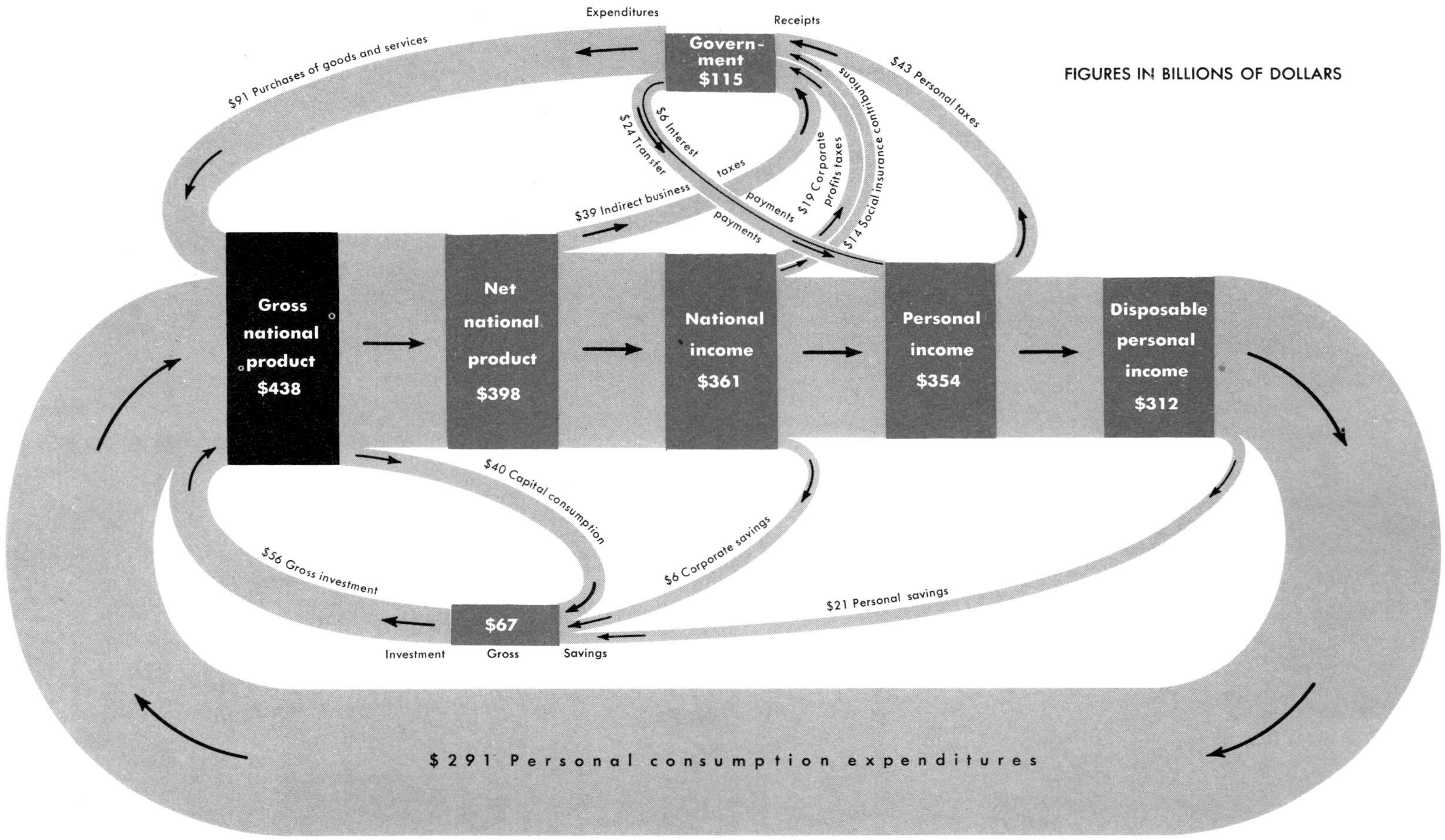

FIGURES IN BILLIONS OF DOLLARS

Disposable personal income $312

Personal income $354

National income $361

Net national product $398

Government $115

Gross national product $438

$67

$43 Personal taxes

$14 Social insurance contributions

$19 Corporate profits taxes

$6 Interest payments

$24 Transfer payments

$39 Indirect business taxes

$91 Purchases of goods and services

Receipts

Expenditures

$40 Capital consumption

$6 Corporate savings

$21 Personal savings

$291 Personal consumption expenditures

$56 Gross investment

Gross Investment

Savings

FIG. 6-2 National income and expenditure make essentially a circular flow, with many side loops. This is a more complete version of the simple circular money flow introduced in Fig. 4-1. Figures shown are for 1958.

expenditures and the government receipts that flow into government spending on goods and services. Together these three make up gross national product. A look back at Figure 4-1, in the introductory section, will show that this is merely a more elaborate picture of the simple circular flow of income shown there.

GROWTH AND FLUCTUATIONS IN OUTPUT America's economic success story can be told in two simple statements:

1. Total production has grown rapidly and vigorously, far more so than in any other country.

2. Total production has grown far more rapidly than the number of people at work—that is, output per worker has risen steadily and rapidly.

But a black mark has to be chalked up too:

3. Economic growth has been spasmodic and uneven, interrupted by depressions and recessions with wasteful unemployment of men and machines.

Growth in Total Output. Figure 6-3 shows the growth in gross national product since 1869, the first year for which these data are available. The sharply rising line represents gross national product in terms of the prices that actually prevailed each year. But prices today are much higher than in 1869, so a substantial part of the increase shown is merely higher prices. The other curve—gross national product in constant (1958) dollars—shows the growth in *real* gross national product over the period. The second curve values all output in 1958 prices, and thus shows only the actual growth in real goods and services produced. (The procedures for making such a constant price adjustment will be explained in the next chapter.)

Figure 6-3 tells its own story. Gross national product in actual prices rose from $7 billion to over $470 billion in only 90 years. If you take out the price inflation, the growth is less. But it's still phenomenal—from about $25 billion to $465 billion in constant (1958) dollars. This is a nearly twenty-fold increase in less than a century. On an annual basis, gross national product grew between 3 and 3½ per cent. This doesn't seem much in a year, but it compounds fast as the decades go by, in a geometric progression. Take $1 to start and do the arithmetic to see what it amounts to in 90 years. An annual growth rate of 3½ per cent gives roughly a 50 per cent increase each decade.

Figure 6-4, which takes an even longer look at American economic history, emphasizes the importance of thinking about annual growth rates. The left-hand portion shows real national income—in constant (1956) prices—from 1800 to 1959, as far back as these data go. This chart makes it look as if the growth rate had speeded up enormously in the last half-century. The line goes almost straight up, with an increase of over $300 billion in the last 50 years.

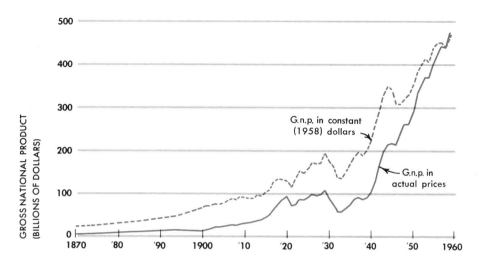

FIG. 6-3 Gross national product has grown rapidly, but spasmodically, over the past century. Part of the rise has been merely higher prices, but most has been increase in real output. (Source: U.S. Department of Commerce, National Industrial Conference Board, and U.S. Department of Labor.)

But take a look at the right-hand portion. This shows exactly the same data (real national income since 1800, in constant prices). But it does so on a "ratio" or "logarithmic" scale. This scale, shown along the vertical axis, gives equal distance to equal *percentage* increases. This is in contrast to regular charts, which

Real National Income Since 1800

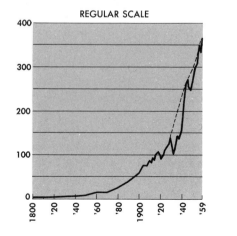
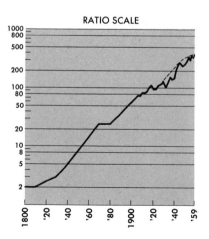

FIG. 6-4 Both halves of the chart show the same data—national income in constant dollars since 1800. But the ratio scale shows that the annual growth rate has been quite stable over the past century, not rising sharply as the regular scale suggests. (Source: U.S. Department of Commerce, National Industrial Conference Board, and U.S. Department of Labor.)

give equal distance to equal *absolute* increases. Thus, on the ratio scale an increase from 5 to 10 takes about a third of an inch vertically, and an increase from 100 to 200, or from 500 to 1000, takes the same third of an inch.

The most useful thing about this ratio scale is that it permits easy comparison of annual growth rates over the long period. A constant percentage increase—say 3 per cent per year—will show an equal vertical increase each year—a steadily rising straight line. If the growth rate rises to 4 per cent, the line will rise more rapidly. If it drops to 2 per cent, the line will rise more slowly.

When we look at the right-hand part of Figure 6-4, we see the past in different perspective. What looks like a big increase in the recent growth rate on the regular scale turns out to be just about the same growth rate as over most of our history when seen on the ratio scale. To make the comparison easier, a dotted line is plotted through the actual figures in recent peak years. Since this line connects the high points, it shows roughly the growth in full-employment capacity of the system, and the actual gross-national-product data below the dotted line show how far actual output fell short of full-employment potential.

Growth in Output per Worker and per Capita. This growth in national output has come in part from the steady increase in the number of people working. But increased output per worker is still more important. Over the past century, of the 3+ per cent annual growth in real output, about 2+ per cent has come from increased output per worker and only about 1 per cent from the increased number of workers.

Look at the chart just inside the front cover of this book. The top line shows real gross national product soaring upward. But right under it is output per man hour, climbing steadily too. A worker today turns out about 2½ times as much per hour as he did in 1900, and nearly 6 times as much as a century ago. But don't make the mistake of attributing all this just to more skilled and intelligent workers. That's part of it, all right. But improving technology, more and better machinery and equipment, better management, and a variety of other factors all share in the achievement. Later on, when we analyze the causes of economic growth, there'll be more to say about who gets how much of the credit.

Closely related to output per worker is output per capita. These are not the same thing, since only about 40 per cent of the population is in the labor force. But output (or real income, which is substantially the same thing) per capita is in many ways the best single measure we have of what is happening to the economic well-being of a nation.

Figure 6-5 shows the growth in real income per capita since 1800. As in the other charts, data before the present century are rough, and are plotted only once each decade to give a picture of major trends but not of detailed fluctuations. The slight drop in the early 1800's is of dubious significance because the data are so rough. Note the big increase in recent decades—but remember that this is a regular chart, not a ratio scale.

Economic Fluctuations.   Figures 6-3, 6-4, and 6-5 also illustrate how spasmodic our economic growth has been. The area under the dotted lines in Figure 6-4 may not look like much, but it has been estimated that we lost at least $200 billion worth of output (in today's prices) in the 1930's alone through unemployment. This was equal to three full years of actual output during the depression years. Even the recession of 1958 probably cost us $50 billion in lost income, compared with the substantially full-employment economy of 1955 or late 1959.

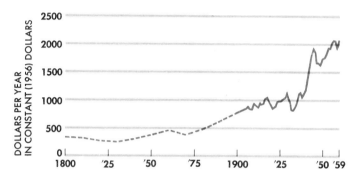

U.S. Per Capita Real Income Since 1800

FIG. 6-5   Per capita real income has grown rapidly but erratically over the past century, but less rapidly during the nation's early history when capital was scarce and population was expanding rapidly. Note the big World War II spurt. (Data from Fig. 6-4, divided by population for each year.)

In Figure 6-5, notice the drop in per capita real income from 1929 to 1933, and then the huge increase from the depression to high-pressure full employment during World War II. Maybe the war peak involved overemployment, with too much overtime and too many youngsters, wives, and old folks pressed into the labor force. It took us almost a decade to get back to that per capita real income level under more normal peacetime work habits. But the enormous waste of underemployment and depression is vividly portrayed by the very curves that show our persistent and rapid growth. (The booms and depressions don't show before the last half-century, since the earlier data are plotted only once each ten years.)

GROSS NATIONAL PRODUCT AS A MEASURE OF ECONOMIC WELL-BEING   Continuing growth in real gross national product provides one good measure of the rise in the nation's economic well-being. Certainly this is the figure you see most often in the newspapers and the news magazines, and we will use it repeatedly as a measure of economic growth. But some warnings are in order:

1.   As we have seen, wide price-level fluctuations have been common. To get a meaningful measure of actual growth in output, we must use data valued in constant prices. More about this in the next chapter.

2. G.n.p. data cover for the most part only goods and services that pass through money transactions. They take no account of such important items as non-paid housewives' services. If Mrs. A. and Mrs. B. both do their own housework, neither's services show up in gross national product. If they simply exchanged housework and paid each other $3,000 a year, neither would be better off; yet gross national product would be $6,000 higher. For the economy as a whole this would amount to billions of dollars. Only in a few cases, such as the estimated value of services from owner-occupied homes, has it proved practicable to include real production that is not sold for money.

3. Durable consumer goods (for example, cars and refrigerators) are included in gross national product when they are produced. Yet many of them are used over several years. The statistics imply that all consumers' durables are used up and represent income only in the year in which they are produced. Thus the real income actually received by using durables is greater than is shown by gross national product in depression years, when few new durables are produced but many old ones are in use; and it is lower than reported by g.n.p. in booms when consumers' durables are produced faster than they are used.

4. Gross national product places no value on leisure. Over the past century, the average work-week has been cut nearly in half—from 75 hours to about 40. No accurate monetary value can be placed on this gain, but to disregard it would be a gross error indeed. The unprecedented national output of the war years was attained only through widespread overtime work. This longer work-week surely cut down on the satisfaction received from the rapidly rising g.n.p.

5. Still more difficult to value, and lacking from money income figures, are those undefinable satisfactions sometimes termed "psychic" income. For example, a research scientist receives a regular salary (money income), with which he obtains goods and services (real income). But many researchers also derive special satisfaction from the type of work they do. They like the continued search for knowledge, the contact with other scientists, and the comparative freedom to allocate their time the way they want. Such non-monetary satisfactions constitute part of the psychic income of research. How important such income is depends largely on the individual. Some researchers sincerely enjoy their work, others work only for the pay.

6. Gross national product says nothing about what goods and services get produced. Most economists presume that goods produced through the private economy reflect roughly the desires of the buying public, weighted by the size of their pocketbooks. But there are some questions about this. Is a dollar spent on producing tailfins for a new auto as important to our economic well-being as a dollar spent on food or clothing? Do we really want the tailfins more? The vast amount of goods and services produced for the government (particularly in wartime) raises related problems. In 1944, real g.n.p. was about twice the 1929 peak level. About half the total 1944 output was munitions, services of troops, and other activities directly associated with winning the war. Was the economy twice as well off economically? How much did the production of tanks and battleships

contribute to our economic well-being? Should they be included dollar for dollar with beefsteak and Buicks? How about schools and highways?

A comparable problem arises as our economy increases in complexity. Now we build complex subway, elevated, and street transport systems in our cities. They provide incomes to thousands and serve millions daily, contributing possibly $1 billion to the annual gross national product. Does this $1 billion reflect increased well-being for our city-dwellers, or instead does it reflect a huge amount of resources devoted to the painful necessity of getting around in crowded cities? How does our economy compare with that of a rural nation that has a lower g.n.p. partly because it has (and needs) no elaborate city transport systems? Is the rural nation as much worse off economically as the g.n.p. figures suggest?

7. For many purposes, gross national product is more useful on a per capita or per family basis. Ultimately g.n.p. has economic usefulness to the individuals in a nation. A big nation like China may be poor with a large g.n.p.; a small one like Switzerland may be rich with a small g.n.p. Moreover, as population grows, the national output must be divided among more people. With modern rates of population growth, rising g.n.p. figures alone can be seriously misleading.

It is important to remember all these problems in using g.n.p. as a measure of national well-being. But with all their failings, g.n.p. data are a very useful first approximation for this difficult job of measurement.

REVIEW—CONCEPTS TO REMEMBER

This chapter introduces many of the most important concepts in economics. The following checklist is to help you make sure that you have them firmly in mind:

gross national product	depreciation allowance
"real" gross national product	national income
"value added"	personal income
"final-products approach"	disposable personal income
gross private investment	personal savings
personal consumption	social accounts
net national product	ratio scale
capital consumption allowance	logarithmic scale

1. Using Figure 6-2, explain each diversion from the main circular flow of income, and trace through the way in which it returns to the main stream. Are there side-streams which involved net additions or subtractions from the main flow in the year shown? Explain.

2. Is gross national product, net national product, or personal income a better measure of the over-all performance of the economy? Why?

3. What happens to national income over the years ahead will be a

**FOR
ANALYSIS
AND
DISCUSSION**

good predictor of most individuals' incomes. (True or false?) Do you think your own personal income will change about in proportion to changes in national income over the next decade? Why or why not?

4. Some observers have recently argued that it is dangerous for the government to try to tax away more than 25 per cent of the national income. Using the statistical data in this chapter, indicate what seems to you the most meaningful measure of "the share of nation's income taxed away by the government." Is this concept identical with "the share of the nation's output of goods and services consumed by the government"? If not, compare the two shares.

5. The steady growth in service workers is a sign of weakness in our economy, because they produce no *real* goods output comparable to farm output of food and raw materials. (True or false? Why?)

6. "When the economy is at 'full employment,' the only way to increase total output is to increase efficiency." Do you agree? Why or why not?

7. In measuring the increase in the average individual's economic well-being over the years, is per capita personal income or per capita disposable income a better measure? Defend your answer.

Appendix
National Income Accounts Data

This Appendix presents some background data on the g.n.p. accounts, and the actual data over most of the past century.

Table 6-5 presents some of the major national income accounts since 1869, the first year for which reasonably reliable g.n.p. estimates are available. Data for the related series not shown in the table may be found in the references indicated for historical material, and in the monthly *Survey of Current Business* (U. S. Department of Commerce), *Federal Reserve Bulletin* (Board of Governors of the Federal Reserve System), and *Economic Indicators* (Joint Economic Committee of Congress) for current data. *Economic Indicators* provides a simple, up-to-date summary of most important national economic series. The *Survey of Current Business* and the *Federal Reserve Bulletin* are far more complete, but, because they include so many different series, are also more difficult for the non-expert to use.

How accurate are all these data that make up the national income accounts? Nobody knows exactly. The Department of Commerce and private research workers have spent years improving techniques for estimating the magnitudes involved. Most of the components are estimated directly from sample information. For example, the business inventory estimates rest on current samples of businesses maintained by the Department of Commerce and the Securities and Exchange Commission. Wages and salaries are estimated from samples of different sectors of the economy. Tax payments are estimated directly from current government

Table 6-5

UNITED STATES NATIONAL PRODUCT, INCOME, AND EMPLOYMENT

Year or Yearly Average	Gross National Product [a] (In Billions of 1956 Dollars)	Gross National Product [b]	National Income [b]	Dis- posable Personal Income [b]	Consumer Expendi- tures [b]	Total Employ- ment [c] (In Millions)
		(In Billions of Current Dollars)				
1869-78		7	7			19
1879-88		11	10			23
1889-98		15	13			27
1899-1908	82	22	20			32
1909-18	110	40	36			39
1919	130	78	68			42
1920	121	87	70			43
1921	112	71	52			39
1922	127	73	60			41
1923	144	85	70			44
1924	141	84	69			43
1925	153	90	74			44
1926	161	96	77			46
1927	159	94	76			46
1928	165	96	79			46
1929	187	104	87	83	79	48
1930	170	91	75	74	71	45
1931	157	76	59	63	61	42
1932	133	58	42	48	49	39
1933	130	56	40	45	46	39
1934	144	65	49	52	52	41
1935	158	72	57	58	56	42
1936	179	85	67	66	63	44
1937	191	90	74	71	67	46
1938	182	85	67	66	65	44
1939	196	90	73	70	67	46
1940	214	101	81	76	72	48
1941	247	125	104	92	82	51
1942	279	160	137	117	91	55
1943	310	193	168	132	102	55
1944	330	211	182	147	112	54
1945	324	213	183	151	123	53
1946	288	204	178	159	147	56
1947	288	232	202	169	166	58
1948	302	260	223	188	177	59
1949	301	256	217	186	180	59
1950	329	283	239	204	194	60
1951	353	328	276	223	206	61
1952	368	346	290	235	218	61
1953	385	365	304	250	231	62
1954	379	361	300	255	237	61
1955	407	387	323	269	252	63
1956	419	419	349	291	269	65
1957	424	440	364	305	284	65
1958	412	438	361	312	291	64
1959 [d]	440	470	385	325	305	66

[a] Data before 1929 from John Kendrick, in *Studies in Income and Wealth,* Vol. 16 (National Bureau of Economic Research); thereafter from U.S. Department of Commerce. Data before 1929 are slightly understated.

[b] Data before 1919 from National Bureau of Economic Research, and National Industrial Conference Board; thereafter from U.S. Department of Commerce. Data before 1929 are slightly understated.

[c] Total civilian employment. Data prior to 1914 from NICB; thereafter from Bureau of Labor Statistics.

[d] All 1959 data are preliminary estimates by the author.

tax receipts. Personal savings are estimated by the Department of Commerce and the Securities and Exchange Commission, with checks from Federal Reserve Board estimates. All these estimates are cross-checked as thoroughly as possible, both by dual methods of estimating and by using different sources. And after a year or so, more complete data for checking become available from individual and business federal income-tax returns.

But the series are only estimates, and often estimates that are based on rather skimpy samples. Perhaps large chunks of income are omitted entirely (though this seems unlikely). The absolute level of the aggregates is hard to check, because only during national censuses do we get anything that approaches complete coverage of the population, and the information collected on censuses only partially meets the needs of the national income calculators. Income-tax returns fill in a mass of data, but they miss a substantial part of the population—and there is always a question about how much income goes unreported. Probably the year-to-year changes in the national income data are more reliable than the absolute levels, since any classes of income missed probably stay missed. Certainly, the farther back the figures go beyond the last quarter-century, the less reliable they become. But whatever their failings, these national income accounts are the best we have, and they are probably superior to those available anywhere else in the world.

7

Changing Price Levels: Inflation and Deflation

Everybody knows that a dollar will buy a lot more some times than others. In 1933, a man could buy a respectable shirt for a dollar; today he is lucky to get one for three times as much. Pork chops, radio repairs, movie tickets, and just about everything else cost far more than they did a quarter-century ago. Indeed, after two decades of almost continuous inflationary pressure, price inflation is said by many to be our number-one economic problem.

The only way we can add together in a meaningful way the apples, oranges, locomotives, and legal services that make up g.n.p. is to put them all in money terms. But when prices change, g.n.p. expressed in terms of dollars is no longer an adequate measure of the real goods and services produced. A 100 per cent increase in real national output would mean a great rise in the national standard of living (barring its use for such purposes as war). But a doubling of g.n.p. through a doubling of prices is no real economic gain at all. In fact, the sharp change in prices might cause severe economic disruption. In order to separate "real" from merely "dollar" changes in individual and national incomes, we have to make an adjustment for price-level changes. Figure 7-1 indicates the violent fluctuations in prices in the United States over the last two centuries. The problem of price level changes is no minor one.

**PRICE INDEXES
AND PRICE-LEVEL CHANGES**

What Is a Price Index? In 1929, a family income of $1,300 would have bought a group of goods and services called a "subsistence standard of living." In 1933, you could have bought the same collection of goods and services for about $900. By 1959, you would have needed well over $2,000.

If all prices changed in the same proportion in the same direction at the same time, measuring price-level changes would be simple. But the world of real prices is not simple and orderly. Even in a big price rise like that of the past decade, some prices declined and others rose at very different rates. Yet, even though not all prices rose, we say that the "price level" rose because there was a rise in the average of all prices. The price of the same market basket of goods was higher than before.

Table 7-1 shows a hypothetical "price index" for a "market basket" of four commodities, to show whether their price level went up or down between 1955 and 1960, and by how much. A price index is a measure of price level changes.

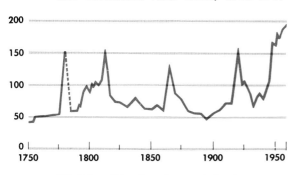

U.S. Wholesale Price Level, 1750-1959

FIG. 7-1   Prices have fluctuated sharply throughout our history. The big peaks have come during or after major wars. So far, there has been no slump following World War II. (Source: U.S. Department of Labor.)

Using 1955 as the "base year," the price of each item in that year is 100 per cent of itself. This is what people mean when they say, "Take 1955 as 100." Then we compute what percentage each 1960 price is of the 1955 price. For example, eggs at 6 cents each are 120 per cent of the 1955 price. This 120 per cent is the 1960 "price relative" for eggs, since it shows the 1960 price relative to that in 1955. To find the change in the price level (the average of all four prices), we simply take the average of the four 1960 price relatives, which gives us 108 per cent for the 1956 price level. (The percentage sign is usually omitted for convenience.) Of course, most price indexes include more commodities, but they are made in a generally similar way.[1]

---

[1] The final index numbers merely indicate the relation of average prices in the two years. We could just as well have taken 1960 as 100, in which case the 1955 index would have been 93. Although the actual index numbers would have been different, either set shows equally well the relative price levels in the two years: $93/100 = 100/108$. Thus the year chosen as 100 has little significance.

This very simple method of calculating price-level changes is likely to give misleading results, however. It tacitly assumes that eggs, hamburger, turnips, and apples are of equal importance. A 10 per cent change in the price of hamburger influences the index exactly as much as a 10 per cent change in the price of turnips or apples. Actually, hamburger is more important in most budgets than turnips, and it seems logical that a change in the price of hamburger should affect the index more.

Table 7-1

PRICE INDEX FOR 1960 WITH 1955 AS BASE YEAR

Product	1955	1960	
Eggs, each	5¢ = 100%	6¢ = 120%	⎰ of the 1955 price
Hamburger, per lb	40¢ = 100%	50¢ = 125%	"
Turnips, per lb	9¢ = 100%	6¢ = 67%	"
Apples, per lb	10¢ = 100%	12¢ = 120%	"
	4) 400%	4) 432%	
	100% = price level in 1955	108% = price level in 1960	

Thus, in most price indexes, each price is "weighted" according to its importance in the group of commodities involved. For example, the U.S. Bureau of Labor Statistics weights the prices in its well-known consumers' price ("cost-of-living") index as follows. They take a "market basket" of the goods and services bought by typical families around the $4,000 income level during the late 1940's. Choosing some 300 of the most important prices, they weight each roughly in accordance with the proportion of the family's total expenditure made on that commodity. If the family bought lots of potatoes, potatoes make up a sizable part of the weekly market basket; rent is a big item in the basket.

Having decided on the contents of the hypothetical market basket, the B.L.S. gets its price index by comparing the cost of the basket from one week to the next. The index now uses 1947-49 as a base period (100). So a weekly index reading of 120 means that the cost of the market basket is up 20 per cent from the 1947-49 price level for those goods and services.

In effect, the market-basket approach weights the price of each commodity by the amount spent on that commodity weekly. The process can easily be illustrated with our little 1955-60 price index, to show how much difference weighting may make. Suppose our family bought the four commodities shown, and that in 1955, 40 per cent of its expenditures were on hamburger, 30 per cent on eggs, 29 per cent on apples, and 1 per cent on turnips. We might then weight the price of each commodity according to its importance, and recalculate the 1960 price index as in Table 7-2, on page 102.

The calculations are simple. First compute how much each individual price has changed from the base year; this gives the same "price relatives" as in Table

7-1. Then multiply each price relative by the weight assigned to it, as shown under $R \times W$. Then add this column, and divide the total by the total of the weights assigned all the prices (100 in this case). This gives the 1960 hypothetical weighted price index of 121.

Table 7-2

WEIGHTED PRICE INDEX FOR 1960 WITH 1955 AS BASE YEAR

Product	1955 Price	1960 Price	1960 Relative	1960 Weight	1960 $R \times W$
Eggs, each	5¢	6¢	120	30	3,600
Hamburger, per lb	40¢	50¢	125	40	5,000
Turnips, per lb	9¢	6¢	67	1	67
Apples, per lb	10¢	12¢	120	29	3,480
				100	) 12,147

Weighted price index for 1960 121

The weighted index shows a substantially bigger price rise than does the un-weighted index, because it gives more emphasis to the three major products (whose prices rose) and very little emphasis to turnips (whose price fell). For most purposes, the picture given by the weighted index is more useful, but other sets of weights might be preferable for other purposes—say a different group of consumers. Certainly if our typical family's consumption pattern changes drastically, a new set of weights will be needed. The Bureau of Labor Statistics frequently re-examines the weights it uses to keep them up-to-date, since the weights obviously may influence the level of the index.

Price Indexes for Different Price Levels. Since a price level is merely an average of a group of prices, we can speak of many different price levels. One price level may reflect the prices paid by a particular group of consumers (their cost of living); another, the prices paid by wholesalers; another, the level of wages in manufacturing; and so on.

Figure 7-2 shows the movements of four important price indexes from 1929 to 1959. What price level is most significant depends on what you are talking about. If you want to measure changes in the cost of living for a particular group, the logical choice is an index of the prices of the goods and services the group consumes. If you want to study business fluctuations, an index of wholesale prices may be more useful, because it fluctuates more quickly and widely in response to changing business conditions. Other purposes call for different indexes.

In any case, it is essential to remember that an index measures accurately only changes that occur in the prices included. It is a common error, for example, to assume that the B.L.S. consumer price index measures the cost of living for the whole economy. It does a good job for lower-middle-class families in big cities, but it may be a long way off for bank presidents or farmers, who buy quite different things.

Given the wide diversity of price movements, it is hard to devise any single price index that will give a significant measure for the whole economy. The closest approach is a new index developed by the Department of Commerce to eliminate the effects of price-level movements from the gross national product. This adjust-

Different Price Levels, 1929-1959

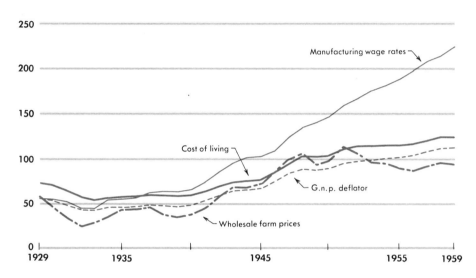

FIG. 7-2   Different prices move diversely in the modern American economy. The g.n.p. deflator series comes closest to showing the movement of prices of all currently produced goods and services. Note the movement in wage rates. (Source: U.S. Departments of Labor and Commerce.)

ment is spoken of as "deflating" the g.n.p. Special indexes are computed for the different major sectors of g.n.p., and then are combined to obtain the "g.n.p. deflator," as the index is often called.

To see how big a difference price adjustments make, look back at the actual-dollar and constant-dollar g.n.p. curves in Figure 6-3. For many purposes price-adjusted series are better than unadjusted data. But since price indexes diverge substantially, it is important to use the right price index. Be on guard to check whether a sensible index has been used in making the adjustment.

**PRICE LEVELS
AND THE VALUE OF MONEY**
The value of money varies inversely with the general price level. Suppose that all prices (retail, wholesale, wages, rents, securities, and

so forth) exactly doubled. There would be no question about the purchasing power, or value, of a dollar. It would be cut exactly in half. And if all prices were to fall by 50 per cent, the purchasing power of a dollar would double. The value of money, like the value of other things, is measured by what we can get in exchange for it. A rise in the average level of all prices is a fall in the value of money. The two are simply different ways of saying the same thing.

But to measure changes in the value of money in the real world is much harder than this example suggests. Money represents generalized purchasing power over all goods and services. To measure changes in the value of money itself, therefore, we ideally need an index that summarizes the movement in all prices.

Such an index is just about impossible to work out as a practical matter. Remember that prices of all existing assets, as well as g.n.p. items, would have to be covered. But we can construct indexes accurate enough to show that the value of money has fluctuated sharply. The rough data on wholesale prices back to 1750 shown in Figure 7-1 demonstrate vividly that the dollar has not been a stable standard of value. On the contrary! It is as if our yardstick had intermittently stretched to six feet and then contracted to eighteen inches.

THE IMPACT OF INFLATION When price levels move up and down, who gains and who loses? Does inflation ruin everybody except a few sly profiteers? Is deflation a fine thing for creditors, who can then collect dollars that have stepped-up buying power?

Inflation is often discussed with more heat than light. One reason is the wide range of definitions that people have in mind when they talk about it. When you use the word inflation to mean a rise in the price level of consumer goods, and your neighbor uses it to mean an increase in the amount of money printed by those irresponsible fellows in Washington, it's no wonder you don't succeed in talking much sense about it—especially if neither of you bothers to make clear (to yourself or to the other) just how you are defining inflation? Socrates said, "If you want to argue with me, first define your terms." And he was right. There are several respectable definitions of inflation, so we have to be very clear about what definition we are using.

"Inflation," in this book, means a rise in the price level of all currently produced goods and services—that is, a rise in the average price of all goods and services in the gross national product. This definition is used because it is simple and direct, because we have a readily available index to measure it (the Department of Commerce g.n.p. deflator series), and because it is perhaps the closest to what the man-in-the-street means when he talks about inflation.

But it is important to recognize what is *not* included in this definition. Higher prices in the stock market aren't included. Neither are higher wages. Neither is more money and credit. All these things are usually found when inflation, as we define it, occurs; but when we say inflation we shall mean the rise in g.n.p. commodity and service prices *per se*. Some people prefer a more complex definition—for example, one that says inflation is an over-extension of credit. These definitions often raise serious problems of measurement and clear analytical use; what is "over-extension"? But the main point is to decide just what definition one is using, and then stick to it.

Inflation and the Level of Real Output.   Inflation is a complex phenomenon, with complex results. Nevertheless, the next few pages take a preliminary look at the impact of inflation—both because inflation is important in its own right, and because this is a good chance to begin using some newly learned economic concepts in analyzing the problem.

Broadly speaking, the economic impact of inflation can be analyzed by asking two questions—(1) Does it increase or decrease the real output of the economy? (2) How does it affect the distribution of that output? As you learn more about economics, you will find that these same two big questions are useful in thinking through a wide range of economic problems. Remember them!

Does inflation increase or decrease the real g.n.p. of an economy? Look separately at the short-run (say within a year or so) and the long-run (economic growth) effects.

Short-run Effects. First, back to some fundamentals from Part 1. We can get more output only by (a) using the productive resources we have more effectively, or (b) increasing the quantity or quality of those productive resources.

If we are already fully employing all our men and machines at the peak output permitted by our technological and managerial know-how, obviously there is nothing inflation can do in the short run to increase total output.

But if we have unemployed resources, it is possible to increase output merely by putting them back to work. Will inflation do this? It may help, but history doesn't show clearly that it helps very much. As we shall see later, increased total spending in an underemployed economy can indeed put resources back to work. But it is usually the increased spending, rather than the higher prices themselves, that has the major output-increasing effect.

But how about the other side—may not inflation *reduce* real output, especially by leading to a boom and bust? Here again, complete analysis has to wait for more tools later on. But, outside the big runaway inflations, history provides little evidence that inflation reduces output and efficiency significantly while the inflation is in progress. Inflations do seem to feed on themselves, however, and speculative buying that looks to a profit on rising prices rather than on economic production does tend to spiral upward, setting the stage for a collapse. The more rampant the speculation on price increases, the more likely the price rise is to overshoot reasonable levels. Such speculative spirals may occur in commodity prices (which we have defined as inflation), or in other prices—for example, the stock market or the real estate market.

Conclusion: In the short run, inflation may help to stimulate more output in times of unemployment, but this effect is uncertain. In full-employment periods, it can do little good and may do much harm by helping to precipitate a recession. Either way, remember it's the impact on the employment of real resources that counts.

Long-run Effects—Economic Growth. There is one big difference in the long run. Then the quantity and quality of productive resources can be increased significantly. The main ways are through growth in the labor force and technological progress (where inflation is unlikely to be a major factor), and through capital accumulation (where inflation may have a real effect). If inflation slows the rate of saving and capital accumulation, it reduces real output over the long run. If it increases the rate of saving and capital accumulation, it speeds economic growth.

What is the evidence? Mixed, and subject to lots of argument. But there is increasing agreement on three points: First, really rapid inflation cuts down on saving and productive investment. Second, only moderate, or "creeping," inflation apparently has little effect one way or the other on the level of saving and investment. Third, the critical relationship in determining the effect of moderate inflation on growth is between selling prices and wages. If prices rise faster than wages and salaries, profits expand and more investment is induced. But if wages and other costs rise as fast as selling prices, inflation provides no inducement to more saving and investment. Over the past several centuries, wages have frequently lagged behind prices, and inflation seems often to have stimulated economic growth. But in the recent creeping inflation, wages have risen faster than selling prices, reversing the traditional stimulus to growth.

We must leave more detailed analysis to later chapters. *But again, note that the critical question in analyzing inflation's impact on economic growth is its impact on real productive resources, their accumulation, and their use.* Don't forget this in a maze of argument and counterargument about the monetary aspects of rising prices.

Inflation and the Distribution of Income.   In a full-employment economy, inflation cannot increase total output. But it can change who gets the output. Think of real g.n.p. as a big pie. Under full employment, inflation can't increase the size of the pie (except possibly over a long period), but it can affect the size of the pieces that different people get. Inflation's effect on the distribution of the national output is our second big question.

Notice a very fundamental fact. Given the size of the real g.n.p. pie, inflation cannot make people either better or worse off economically in the aggregate. If someone gets a smaller piece, someone else is bound to get a bigger one. Moving up from a $500 billion to a $600 million g.n.p. merely because of inflation does not make the economy either better *or* worse off in terms of real income, if full employment prevails both before and after.

The central principle about how inflation affects the distribution of income is this: Those whose incomes rise faster than the average get bigger pieces of the real g.n.p., and those whose incomes rise slower or not at all get smaller pieces. In a full-employment economy, inflation usually means that prices rise at about the same rate as money g.n.p. The man whose income just keeps pace with rising prices will keep about the same-sized piece of pie. The man whose income lags behind rising prices will get a decreased share of the total output. And the man whose income rises faster than prices will get an increased share. This is the same basic proposition stated somewhat differently at the beginning of the paragraph.

But the principle is too simple, because different people buy different things whose prices may rise faster or slower than the average. So how well off an *individual* is depends on the increase in *his* income *relative to the increase in the prices of the goods he buys,* not relative to some general price index. And the principle is too simple for another reason. Some people have accumulated savings and others don't. Those with accumulated savings may draw on them to maintain their consumption even though their incomes lag.

But in general these propositions about how inflation affects different shares in the national product provide a good first approximation of a full-employment economy.

In an underemployed economy, real g.n.p. may expand with inflation. But the principle controlling the distribution of real income is the same: Those whose incomes rise fastest relative to the prices they pay increase their percentage shares of the national output; and those whose incomes rise slower relative to the prices they pay get smaller percentage shares. Here everybody's real income may be rising; nobody has to lose just because someone else gains. Since the pie may be growing, everyone can have a bigger piece, even though he may lose relatively. And this is what generally happens when inflation comes in periods of rising total output, except for those people on completely or substantially fixed incomes.

These general principles are cold and abstract. Let's see what they mean for five big income groups.

Fixed Incomes. At one end of the spectrum is the fixed-income receiver—the widow living on a fixed pension, or the charitable institution with a fixed income from interest on government bonds. If the price level goes up, their purchasing power goes down whether total output increases or not. Old people and employees of nonprofit institutions (governments, churches, schools, etc.) are the two major groups whose incomes lag the most in inflation. Their incomes generally aren't fixed—government old-age pensions are gradually adjusted upward, and non-profit-based salaries are raised gradually—but they lag badly.

Salaries. In inflation, most salaries get adjusted upward, but often with a lag of a year or two, or more. Temporarily, the stenographer or the schoolteacher is in the same position as the fixed-income widow, but not permanently. This is true of most salary-earners. Their incomes lag, to varying degrees.

Wages. For years, people have been saying that wage-earners lose purchasing power when prices go up and gain it when prices go down, because wages move up and down more slowly than prices. But this statement is now of dubious accuracy. There are two things wrong with it: First, even when wage rates lag behind rising prices, the real income of labor as a group often rises in inflation, because higher prices come with better business conditions which make more jobs available. Second, in recent years organized labor has grown much stronger, and wage rates have generally not lagged behind rising prices. In fact, they have substantially outpaced prices in some inflation years. This may be a real change in the inflation picture for the future.

Shares of National Income in Inflation

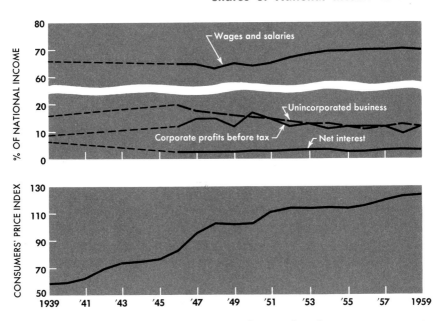

FIG. 7-3   The shares of major groups in the national income have been reasonably stable through two decades of inflation, but since World War II wages and salaries have grown faster than the others. (Source: U.S. Department of Commerce.)

Businessmen and Stockholders. Traditionally businesses have gained from inflation (at least as long as the inflation is relatively mild), and suffered in deflation. Many profits rise in inflation because businessmen add a standard percentage mark-up on their rising costs in setting prices. Or if businessmen's payments for productive services (i.e., their costs) lag behind rising selling prices, business profits rise more rapidly than prices. Moreover, rising prices during periods of unemployment have often been associated with increasing output and employment. Often, therefore, businesses make increased profits with rising price levels.

Stockholders are the owners of business corporations, and corporation profits are incomes to them. These profits fluctuate directly with changing price levels and business conditions. The stockholder reaps large dividends in good times; in depression he may go empty-handed.

But the picture may be changing. If wages rise more rapidly than prices in inflation, business profits may be squeezed in inflation (at least relatively and possibly absolutely), rather than swelling comfortably as in the past.

Farmers. Lastly, the farmer, another type of businessman. Prices of farm products have usually risen faster in inflation than the prices farmers have to pay. Thus, the farmer's real income has generally soared in inflationary periods. Moreover, if he has a mortgage his payments are easier, since they involve giving up less real purchasing power. And if the farmer owns his farm, he is able to sell or rent it at a higher figure because of the improved prospects for making a profit. Few groups gain more from rising prices than do farmers. But the long-run decline in the relative importance of agriculture has exerted a steady downpull on farm incomes that has more than offset any special advantages from inflation in recent years.

Figure 7-3 shows the shifting shares of the national income for different groups over the past twenty years. The gradual rise in the wage and salary share during the postwar inflationary years is striking. The offsetting decrease is largely in incomes of unincorporated businesses (farmers, small businessmen, and professional men), and to a lesser extent in corporation profits. But two warnings in looking at the chart: First, it doesn't necessarily follow that inflation *caused* these income shifts, just because they occurred during an inflationary period. Still, at least the inflation wasn't a strong enough counterforce to offset them, if indeed it did not encourage them. Second, remember that all these income shares rose substantially in real terms. Real g.n.p. more than doubled over the two decades, so even the unincorporated business sector had a larger real income in 1959 than in 1939—though not very much larger.

Inflation may seriously disrupt the traditional patterns of income distribution. But over the past two decades of persistent creeping inflation, most major income groups have managed to protect their positions surprisingly well. (See Figs. 7-3 and 28-2.) Wages, salaries, profits, and most other incomes have moved up roughly apace. Most participants in the market, as workers or businessmen, have managed to put up their prices fast enough not to fall far behind, if at all. In perspective, the economy may have shifted substantially to an inflation-adjusting basis. Older folks and employees of nonprofit institutions appear to be the two big groups suffering the greatest lag. They don't have any prices to put up in the market as inflation progresses. But even they are beginning to get on the bandwagon. Older folks have brought pressure to increase federal old-age benefits. They are converting their investments from fixed-income bonds into stocks. Universities are raising tuition and getting higher legislative appropriations to raise salaries. Governments are raising taxes to pay their workers more.

Are these inflation developments good or bad? If we reach the stage where no one's income is severely hurt by inflation, will resistance to it vanish? These are questions to keep in mind.

Inflation and the Distribution of Wealth—Savers, Debtors, and Creditors.   In addition to its impact on the distribution of current income, inflation transfers wealth from creditors to debtors and from savers to spenders.

Table 7-3

MONEY DEBTS IN THE UNITED STATES—MAJOR CATEGORIES [a]

	In Billions
Government securities (federal, state, and local)	$ 425
Bank deposits and currency	241
Short-term personal and business debts	196
Real-estate mortgages	171
Corporation bonded debt	112
Life insurance [b]	90
Saving and loan shares	47
Government social security [b]	37
	$1,319

[a] January 1, 1959. Data from Survey of Current Business, Federal Reserve Bulletin, National Industrial Conference Board, and estimated by the author.

[b] Accumulated reserves. The face value of life insurance in force at the beginning of 1959 was approximately $510 billion, excluding U.S. Government G.I. Insurance.

Inflation can play havoc with accumulated savings. Between 1939 and 1959, the B.L.S. consumer price index roughly doubled. The thrifty retired couple who had saved up enough to purchase a comfortable lifetime annuity of $2,000 per annum in 1939 found themselves destitute in 1959. A life insurance policy that looked big 20 years ago provides only half as much protection today. A hundred dollars invested in 3 per cent government bonds in 1939 had a purchasing power of only about $80 ten years later, even when about $40 of interest was added on to the $100 originally invested. The total loss in purchasing power attributable to the inflation between 1939 and 1959 has been estimated at well over half a trillion dollars for all holders of assets with fixed dollar value—money, bonds, insurance policies, and so on. Although their huge loss of purchasing power did not represent loss of real wealth to society as a whole (since real income and wealth were not reduced correspondingly), it did reflect a massive shift of buying power over society's current output and accumulated assets from savers to others whose buying power rose with the inflation. (Remember even here, though, that most people are both spenders and savers, so the redistributional effect was far less drastic than if savers and spenders had been two separate groups.)

Inflation also means a transfer of wealth from creditors to debtors. Rising prices mean that the purchasing power of each dollar is falling. Debtors can pay off their debts in dollars of reduced purchasing power. If I lend you $1,000 today and the price level doubles before you repay, I get back only half the real purchasing power I gave you.

In the modern economy there is a great mass of money debts. So long as these debts lie quiescent, they are not affected by changes in the value of money. When debts become due, however, they involve current cash payments and the value of money becomes a prime consideration to debtors and creditors.

Table 7-3 indicates the major items that comprised the $1⅓ trillion of money debts in the United States at the end of 1958. At one extreme, bank deposits are money that can be spent any time, and their real value is immediately affected by inflation. At the other extreme, life insurance "debts" to policyholders will generally not be paid for many years, and current changes in price levels are of much less consequence to their holders (except when they are paying current premiums). In between, the other debts are more or less immediately susceptible to erosion by inflation. But in the end, inflation gets them all.

HOW BAD IS INFLATION? How bad is inflation? This is a complicated question, and one you should be able to answer for yourself at the end of the course. Clearly, inflation may lead to economic collapse if it reaches virulent, runaway proportions. More moderate inflation, especially when it is based on speculation and large credit extension, may lead to recession. Inflation may speed or slow the rate of economic growth—which it will do, is not always clear. Inflation shifts the distribution of income and wealth. Whether you like the new distribution better than the old will have much to do with how bad you think inflation is. Some people think inflation is good, since they want to see debts eroded and non-workers (such as retired folks and bond coupon-clippers) pressured to work and invest their funds more productively.

Try the following exercise to test how well you understand the central principles of the preceding analysis. Evaluate this statement by a well-known senator: "Inflation reduces the buying power of every dollar, and impoverishes the American people. It is a national disaster!"

There is no doubt about the first half of the first sentence. It is true by definition—by our definition, at least. We defined inflation as rising prices, and higher prices do reduce the purchasing power of any given dollar. Thus, aside from the possibility of spending a dollar on particular items whose prices have not yet risen, the first clause is clearly valid. But the second half of the sentence calls for closer scrutiny, in spite of its apparent plausibility. Does it follow from the acceptable first portion that inflation impoverishes the American people? A reasonable first step is to look at history.

Consider 1940 to 1950 as an example. Over the decade there was a major inflation. In 1940, national income was $81 billion; in 1950, it was $239 billion. Consumers' prices (B.L.S. "cost-of-living index") rose from 100 to 171. If we adjust the 1950 national-income figure downward to eliminate the price increase, we get a 1950 real income of $140 billion in 1940 prices. This was an increase of $59 billion (almost 75 per cent) over the 1940 income. Even allowing for possible error in the B.L.S. price index, it is hard to see how this inflation impoverished the American people as a whole. Although one dollar would buy less in 1950 than in 1940, the increase in incomes received far outdistanced the loss caused by rising prices. History clearly shows that inflation does not necessarily impoverish the American people.

To return to a first principle, it is the goods and services produced in an economy that basically determine the national standard of living. Higher prices mean that the purchasing power of any *given* national money income is less than when prices are low. But the basic test is the real output produced and consumed, in total or per capita.

Should we conclude, then, that inflation is beneficial? Not necessarily, of course. In the first place, these statistics don't show that the inflation *caused* the increase in output, so we certainly are not justified in giving inflation credit for the extra goods and services produced. In the second place, even though the public as a whole (and per capita) clearly had more real income in 1950 than in 1940, many people were harmed by the inflation—people whose money incomes were relatively fixed. Inflation, as always, altered the distribution of the national output, so that even with a larger pie to divide, some pieces were smaller in 1950 than in 1940.

Putting the whole picture together, was the senator right—is inflation a national disaster? In summary, first you need to look at the impact on real national output as the best single guide to what happened to national economic well-being. Second, you need to ask what happened to the distribution of real income; the critical consideration here is the rate at which the individual's income changed, not whether he is a worker or coupon-clipper, a merchant or farmer, a rich man or poor. Then, you must decide whether the redistribution was good or bad. Third, ask what happened to the distribution of wealth—the differential impact on debtors and creditors, and the position of savers as against spenders. Last, you need to look to the future, to see whether the inflationary developments have set the stage for an economic downturn or have slowed the rate of economic growth. In retrospect, the inflation of the 1940's escapes condemnation on this fourth point too; the long prosperity of the 1950's can hardly be classified as disastrous.

How about the senator's statement? Make your own preliminary judgment. But emphasize the analytical concepts and questions, not the experience of the 1940's in itself. Many different factors were at work in that decade, as in any other. What happened was the result partly of inflation and partly of these other factors. The different environment of another decade may make the end results of inflation look quite different. But you can still do your own thinking about any decade with the help of such analytical tools.

Hyper-inflation. To illustrate how different inflation can look at different times, it is useful to review briefly one of the great runaway hyper-inflations.

In the great hyper-inflation in Germany following World War I, the government had to make large expenditures (including heavy reparations payments to the victorious allies). It chose to finance these payments by printing paper money rather than by making drastic tax increases. This new money increased total spending and sped the upward price spiral, for the war-torn German economy could not rapidly increase its output of goods. As prices spiraled, so did government costs, requiring further recourse to the printing presses. Prices, government spending, and new money soared to fantastic levels.

At the end of the inflation in 1923, a trillion German marks had about the same purchasing power as one pre-war mark. Postage for a local letter cost 100 million marks. A loaf of bread cost a wheelbarrow full of money, unless one had the new huge billion-mark notes to which the government increasingly turned to save the cost of paper and printing-press time. By 1923, the total quantity of German marks in circulation had risen to about 500 quintillion from the pre-inflation level of about 2 billion. Useful economic activity was completely disrupted. All prices, including wages, had to be adjusted every day, and many were adjusted several times a day. A large portion of the population turned to the major activity of spending all money received before it became worthless. Speculation and hoarding of goods became the best way of making a living. Savings were completely wiped out. The middle class especially lost everything it had accumulated. The inflation was a crushing disaster to the German economy.

Similar great inflations have occurred in other countries—for example, in central and eastern Europe following both world wars and in China during the 1940's. Even the United States has had major inflations, though none of such virulence. After the Revolutionary War the paper "continental" was drastically overissued, and became almost worthless; overissue of currency reached similar extremes in the South during the Civil War.

Two common elements link all these runaway inflations: They are associated with war or its aftermath, especially in defeated countries. And they are financed by great issues of paper money to cover huge government expenditures. Although such hyper-inflations may seem a far cry from the problems of America today— and they are—history does provide a vivid warning that inflation can get out of hand.

Does hyper-inflation require a new set of analytical concepts and tools? No, but of course the results of our analysis may vary with varying degrees of inflation. Few people would deny that the great German inflation was a national disaster. Answering the four questions at the end of the preceding section will give a clear answer why.

THE IMPACT
OF DEFLATION

What about the impact of deflation—falling prices? Try working out the analysis for yourself. Use the same general pattern that we used for inflation: What effect are falling prices likely to have on total production and employment? What effect are they likely to have on the distribution of the nation's output and wealth? You will find that the impact of deflation turns out to be generally the reverse of the impact of inflation. But there are two important exceptions: First, prices that are flexible upward don't always show the same downward flexibility—e.g., union wage rates. This means that the impact of deflation on the distribution of output and wealth may be considerably different from the impact of inflation. Second, and more important, although inflation may or may not stimulate increased employment and output, serious deflation has always been accompanied by falling employment and output.

With Chapters 6 and 7 as background, we are now ready to analyze the forces that determine the level of production, employment, income, and prices in the modern American economy.

REVIEW—CONCEPTS TO REMEMBER

This chapter adds some important new analytical concepts to those developed in earlier chapters. Be sure that you understand especially the following:

price level   inflation
price index   deflation
value of money   hyper-inflation

FOR
ANALYSIS
AND
DISCUSSION

1. "The American public as a whole is economically worse off today than in 1950 in spite of the apparent huge rise in national income, because inflation has eaten away more than the nominal increase in total income." (True or false? Check the facts for yourself, using the *Federal Reserve Bulletin* or *Economic Indicators*.)

2. Suppose three classes of individuals comprise the total population of an economy: (1) Wealthy, high-income individuals who live entirely on income from their bond coupons; (2) low-income wage and salary earners; and (3) businessmen who employ the workers and live on the profits they make. Analyze the likely effects of an inflation on the three income groups in this economy. Who, if anybody, is hurt by the inflation? Who, if anybody, is helped by it? State clearly any assumptions you make in your analysis.

3. "Inflation is a disaster. It impoverishes the average man and reduces the national standard of living." Do you agree or disagree with this quotation from a newspaper editorial? Make a careful list of the facts and/or assumptions on which your answer rests.

4. From the following data on disposable personal income and the consumer price index, compute disposable personal income for the years shown in constant (1947-49) dollars. Did "real" disposable income fluctuate more or less than money disposable income?

	Current disposable personal income	*Consumer price index (1947-49 = 100)*	*Disposable personal income in 1947-49 dollars*
1929	$ 83 billion	73	_____
1933	46 "	55	_____
1939	70 "	60	_____
1949	188 "	102	_____
1958	312 "	124	_____

5. Suppose that prices for the following products in 1949 and 1959 were as follows:

	1949	1959
Round steak (per pound)	$ .80	$ 1.00
Butter (per pound)	.80	.75
Men's suits (each)	50.00	60.00
Ford sedans (each)	1400.00	2100.00
Student notebooks (each)	1.00	1.00

a. Construct a price index showing the change in the price level of these commodities from 1949 to 1959. If you feel you need further data, explain why, make a reasonable assumption on the data, and then construct the index.

b. Does this index give a reasonably good picture of the change in the cost of living between 1949 and 1959? Why or why not?

c. Does the index reflect reasonably the change in your own (individual) cost of living? If not, what changes would need to be made to have the index reflect with absolute accuracy changes in your own cost of living?

Money
and the
Banking System[1]

Without money, our complex exchange economy would grind to a halt. Without financial institutions like banks, insurance companies, investment brokers, and savings and loan associations to link together savers and investors, the circular flow of income would stagnate.

Think for a minute about what life would be like under a barter economy. Suppose you have a pig. But what you really want is a spool of thread, two new shirts, a movie, and a newspaper. You hear that B down the road has made some shirts. But unless B happens to want some pork chops, you're still out of luck. Your neighbor, C, wants a pig, but he has only lumber to trade. If you're lucky, you may be able to get lumber from C and to swap that to B for shirts. But it's going to take some fancy haggling to work out a fair trade with such indivisible products, even if you all have a basic desire to swap. With money as a medium of exchange and as a standard unit for quoting

---

[1] Chapters 8 and 9 may equally well be postponed until after Chapters 10 and 11 by those instructors who prefer to cover the determinants of the level of income and employment first.

exchange prices, it's easy to avoid this kind of difficulty. Money is a universally accepted unit of purchasing power, freely spendable and easy to store if you want to postpone spending your income. If it weren't, we'd be in trouble.

Money is also used as a store of value, by which people can accumulate and hold generalized future purchasing power. If people decide to increase their money holdings for this purpose, they keep some of their current income instead of going out each pay-day and spending all of it. In so doing, they derail the circular flow of income-payments through the economy, and reduce the amount of money spending on the next round unless there's some offset to replace the income withdrawn. Similarly, if people decide to decrease their money holdings as a store of value, they add to the circular flow of income by spending more than they currently receive.

Money is of central importance in any market-type economy like ours. So are the financial institutions that affect the supply of money and the efficiency with which we use it. The next two chapters deal with money and financial institutions, and with government controls over them.

MONEY AND NEAR-MONIES

What do you think of when you hear the word money? Coins and paper bills, most likely. But for hundreds of years cattle served as money in the ancient world. In the Late Roman Empire small, square pieces of leather were used. Two hundred years ago, hides and skins, wampum beads, cowrie shells, and numerous other objects served as money in the North American colonies. Only recently has the world widely adopted the coins and paper notes that we now use; and today we are moving away from using metal coins for any except very minor purposes. There is nothing inherent in the things that we call money today that necessarily makes them money. By the same token, money cannot be defined merely in terms of the substances that we happen to use for it.

Any useful definition of money must be based on what money *does,* not on what it *looks like.* According to one common definition, money is anything that passes freely from hand to hand in an economic area as a means of payment irrespective of the credit of the person presenting it. But this definition is too narrow to be useful, for it would include as money only coins and paper bills issued as money by the government (commonly termed "currency"). Actually, around 80 per cent of all payments in the United States today are made by bank checks, only about 20 per cent by currency. We Americans have become so accustomed to using bank checks as money that for practical purposes payment by check is the equivalent of payment by currency, even though the check is a "credit" instrument that is good only if the bank is prepared to pay the sum indicated.

A better definition of money, then, is the total of currency and bank checking deposits, since these two comprise the nation's generally acceptable media of payment. The top part of Table 8-1 shows the amount of these two major types of money in existence in 1959.

Table 8-1

MONEY AND NEAR-MONIES IN THE UNITED STATES *

		In Billions
Money		$145
Currency	$ 29	
Checking deposits	116	
Important Near-Monies		384
Savings deposits	98	
Savings and loan shares	48	
Liquid U.S. government securities	148	
Insurance policies (cash value)	90	

* As of Jan. 1, 1959. Only government securities redeemable on demand or due within one year are included. Data from *Federal Reserve Bulletin* and *Life Insurance Fact Book.*

Only a thin line separates actual money from a variety of "near-monies" that are readily convertible into currency or checking deposits. Bank savings deposits, savings and loan shares, short-term U.S. government securities, U.S. savings bonds redeemable on the owner's demand, and the cash surrender value of insurance policies are probably the most important of these near-monies. But there are many more only a little less easily convertible, including the great mass of longer-term government bonds.

Any of these near-monies serves one function of money reasonably well—that of a store of value. In one way, they are better than money, for the holder receives interest on most near-monies and none on money itself. Balanced against this, the near-money must be converted into actual money before it can be spent. This always involves some inconvenience or delay, and sometimes a risk that the near-money can be converted only at a loss—for example, when government securities must be sold before maturity. The factors that induce people and businesses to shift back and forth between money and near-monies will be of considerable importance later on in our investigation of how well the economic system works.

PRIVATE FINANCIAL INSTITUTIONS Many kinds of private financial institutions have developed over the years to make it easier for money payments to flow through the economy. Some of these, such as the mutual savings banks and insurance companies, receive long-term savings and channel them on into real investment in buildings, equipment, and the like. Others, such as the ordinary ("commercial") banks, serve as depositories both for currently used funds and for longer-term savings.

If you are interested, you can find a detailed listing of these financial institutions and their individual specialized functions in any money-and-banking textbook. All we need here is a brief summary of how these institutions help channel current money savings into real investment (or, sometimes, how they block the channel), and then more detailed analysis of how commercial banks operate. Their function differs significantly from that of other private financial institutions.

Banks. There are now about 14,000 banks in the United States. Most of them are ordinary "commercial" banks, which accept both "savings" (or time) accounts and "checking" (or demand) accounts. About 500 are "mutual savings banks" which have no checking deposits. The theory is that savings accounts represent funds put in the bank for relatively long periods of time, while checking accounts are for funds that you expect to use promptly. Thus banks sometimes feel freer to make long-term loans when their savings deposits go up than when they have an increase in checking accounts. Technically, banks can require depositors to give 30 or 60 days' notice before withdrawing savings deposits, but they almost never do. Actually, the dividing line between savings and checking deposits is not very sharp once the funds have been deposited in the bank. But there *is* one fundamental difference: Checking deposits are spendable money, since depositors can write checks on them. Depositors cannot write checks on savings deposits. A savings deposit can be spent only by withdrawing it in the form of hand-to-hand currency or by transferring it to a checking account.

Harking back to the simple circular income flow diagram in Chapter 4 (Figure 4-1), it's obvious that saved funds have to be passed along to someone who will spend them currently if money income is to continue to flow smoothly through the economy. Do the banks actually succeed in passing current money savings on to borrowers who will spend them back into the income stream? This is a crucial question. The answer is: Sometimes they do, and sometimes they don't. Often the commercial banks actually increase or decrease the nation's money supply by their own actions, as we shall see below.

Other Financial Institutions. Financial middlemen have grown up to accommodate about every imaginable type of saver and borrower. Savings and loan associations are much like the savings departments of commercial banks; they draw mainly the savings of lower- and middle-income individuals and make mainly real-estate loans. Life-insurance companies are huge financial intermediaries. Total premiums paid on life-insurance policies and annuities in 1959 were about $13 billion, of which almost half represented savings—that is, accumulation of reserves by the insurance companies against future policyholder claims. Insurance companies invest these funds in many ways—government bonds, real-estate and business loans, and direct real-estate and business investments.

"Consumer finance," or "sales finance," companies get most of their funds second-hand from the banks and insurance companies, and then lend these funds directly to consumers at higher rates.

Another purely financial middleman is the "investment banker." Investment bankers are essentially marketers of corporate securities, rather than bankers in the ordinary sense of the word. When corporations want to sell securities, they usually engage investment bankers to do the job. Typically, the investment banker or syndicate of several investment bankers buys the securities outright from the corporation and sells them to the public at a slightly higher price, keeping the difference as payment for marketing services. The investment banker, like the sales finance company, receives no deposits from the public—he is purely a middleman who helps borrowers to obtain saved funds.

The federal government itself, though it's out of place in this section on private institutions, has become one of the primary financial middlemen between savers and investment. During the 1930's and 1940's, in order to finance government expenditures not covered by taxes, the government borrowed almost $90 billion net from individuals and non-financial businesses. Some of these savings were invested in roads, schools, postoffices, and so on. But the funds were not segregated from other government receipts. By and large, they were "invested" in fighting the depression of the 1930's and the war of the 1940's. Much the same kind of government channeling of savings into investment occurs whenever the government runs a deficit and uses the funds in ways that can be termed "investment." In fact, some observers have called taxes collected by the government "forced saving."

Direct Conversion of Savings.   Many times, no financial middleman is involved in the investment of savings. Every year, businesses re-invest billions of dollars of their own earnings in buildings, equipment, and other investment goods. Individuals buy new houses, which are considered a form of investment in the national income accounts. Individual savers also make direct loans on a small scale, or they may invest directly in stocks and bonds.

Financial Investment and Real Investment.   It is important to recognize that the term "investment" may be used in different ways. In Chapter 6, dealing with the national accounts, "investment" was clearly defined to include only spending on currently produced producers' goods, including housing. This is the sense in which the term will be used throughout the rest of the book, unless another meaning is specified.

In the sections just above, the term has been used in a different, and somewhat slippery, way. Part of the time, it has been used to mean real investment—actual investment in currently produced capital goods, as in the national income accounts. But other times it has been used to mean merely "financial" investment—

for example, when an individual or insurance company buys a government bond. This transaction is an investment for the insurance company, but from the overall viewpoint it is merely a financial transfer—not actual investment in new capital goods. Financial intermediaries sometimes make direct real investments—for example, when an insurance company erects an office building. More commonly, however, they merely make loans or financial investments, transferring the funds on to borrowers who may or may not then use them to finance real investment in new capital goods.

The same distinction exists where individuals do their own "investing." If I use my savings to build a new house, that's real investment. But if I buy General Motors stock, that's only financial investment, which passes my savings on to the man who sells me the stock, or to General Motors if it's a new stock issue. The question then is: What does that man, or General Motors, do with the funds? Obviously a lot of different things can happen to a dollar saved. Its path on to investment in new capital goods is by no means a sure one.[2]

THE SUPPLY OF CURRENCY (GOVERNMENT-ISSUED MONEY) In this elaborate system of financial institutions, what actually determines the supply of money (currency and deposits) that people have to spend? This question has two quite different answers: one for currency and one for deposits. First, consider currency (government-issued money).

Currency comprises about one-fifth of the United States money supply. The proportion between currency and checking deposits has been generally stable, except for short-period aberrations like the one that occurred in the financial panic of 1932-33. Since people are free to decide whether they want to hold their money in currency or deposits, this appears to be about the ratio they prefer.

The types of currency in circulation on January 1, 1959, are shown in Table 8-2. About $3 billion of this currency was held by commercial banks as "vault cash" for day-to-day needs. All the rest was in the hands of the public, either in active circulation or held more or less idle for one reason or another.

Federal Reserve notes, which comprise about 85 per cent of all currency outstanding, are paper money issued by the Federal Reserve Banks. They range in denomination from $5 to $10,000. The law requires the Federal Reserve to hold at least 25 cents in gold for each dollar of notes issued, plus the remainder of the note's value in government securities, commercial paper, other banking assets, or gold (see Chapter 9). Silver certificates are $1 and $5 bills issued by the Treasury Department against identical amounts of silver stored in government vaults. All currency is now issued either by the Federal Reserve Banks or by the Treasury,

---

[2] Remember, too, that purchase of *existing* capital goods (e.g., houses) does not count as investment in the national income accounts. It is only a transfer of funds against already existing capital goods.

although during the nineteenth century private "bank notes" comprised a large portion of the currency in circulation, and such notes could be issued by privately owned banks until 1935.[3]

Table 8-2

UNITED STATES CURRENCY IN CIRCULATION [a]

Types of Currency	In Billions
Federal Reserve notes	$27.3
Silver certificates	2.2
Coins	2.2
Other [b]	.5
Total	$32.2

[a] January 1, 1959. Data from *Federal Reserve Bulletin*. Includes about $3 billion of currency held by banks as "vault cash." Subtraction of vault cash from the total gives the $29 billion currency holdings of the public shown in Table 8-1.
[b] Includes older forms of currency, mainly being retired from circulation.

What Determines the Amount of Currency in Circulation?   During the past century, the "gold standard" prevailed in many countries. The presumption was that the quantity of money would vary directly with the amount of monetary gold in the country. If more gold came in, say from abroad or from the mines, it would either be used as currency itself or would serve as the basis for issuing new currency or credit. If gold flowed out, the money supply would be contracted. To an important extent this was the case in the United States through the nineteenth century and to a lesser extent into the 1920's. Then gold had a direct impact on the quantity of currency outstanding.

Today, however, neither the United States nor any other major country is on a gold standard. Even gold coins were retired from circulation in the United States in 1933.[4]

Gold is used today as a monetary base in the United States only indirectly, and the amount of gold held by the government has little direct influence on the amount of currency in circulation. The Federal Reserve must have gold on hand equal to at least 25 per cent of the Federal Reserve notes in circulation, but the

---

[3] During the years when many different types of currency were circulating, the government declared some but not all to be "legal tender." Under the law, legal-tender money must be accepted at face value in payment of obligations. This requirement does not mean that the debtor is freed from his obligations if the creditor refuses to accept the legal-tender money; it merely means that the debtor cannot be forced to offer any other kind of money and that he is not liable for interest or collection fees on the debt after legal tender has been refused. Since 1933, all kinds of currency have been legal tender, even for obligations contracted before that date.

[4] The gold standard is discussed in more detail in Chapter 14. As that chapter indicates, the actual gold is now held by the federal government, while the Federal Reserve holds only "gold certificates."

relation between the government's gold supply and the amount of currency issued has varied widely. In 1914, the gold stock was about half the amount of currency in circulation. Through the 1920's, the amount of gold rose until it almost equaled the $4 billion of currency. The vast gold inflows of the late 1930's led to gold holdings nearly 250 per cent of the $8-$9 billion of currency then outstanding. But during World War II the unprecedented currency expansion surpassed even the nation's $20-billion gold stock. Currency outstanding now substantially exceeds our monetary gold stock.

The vast amount of gold owned by the federal government still serves in a general way as security for the currency outstanding. But you can no longer obtain gold in exchange for other money unless you want to use it in international transactions or in industry and the arts. Domestically, the main monetary function of gold is to maintain confidence in the money outstanding, and even here it is less important than people used to believe.

What, then, does determine the amount of currency outstanding? *In fact, the amount of currency outstanding is determined more or less automatically by the demands of the public for currency for current use and for hoarding. When people want to convert their bank deposits into currency, they simply go to the bank and get it. If more currency is issued than the public wants, it simply flows back to the banks in deposits.* The Federal Reserve mechanism makes it possible for the public to convert bank deposits into currency, and vice versa, at will. Although the Federal Reserve and the Treasury have discretionary authority to issue and withdraw currency, they almost never use this authority except to satisfy the currency-using habits of the public.

Remember, though, that we're talking only about the amount of currency outstanding, and that currency is only a small part of the total money supply. The total amount of money (deposits plus currency) depends largely on the actions of the banking system in making or contracting loans and investments.

THE SUPPLY OF BANK MONEY: CHECKING DEPOSITS

Commercial Banks and the Creation of Credit. Currency is government money issued directly by the Treasury and the Federal Reserve. But the great bulk of our money is not issued by the government at all. Rather, it is provided by the commercial banks in their day-to-day business of making loans and investments. *The distinguishing feature of modern commercial banking is its ability to create and maintain demand deposits (checking accounts) through making loans and investments, which deposits serve as money.*

Savings banks, insurance companies, and other financial middlemen obviously "create" no checking deposits—their activities neither increase nor decrease the amount of money in existence. But the commercial banks (that is, the banks we all know and deal with) operate differently. In good times, they may lend more money than we have deposited in them. In bad times, they may call the same loans for payment, contracting the deposits created when the loans were made. Far from being a passive link in the savings-investment process, commercial banks may drastically affect the flow of funds from savers into investment.

To understand this rather startling statement that commercial banks "create" checking deposits, you need to know something about how a commercial bank works. The easiest way to get this picture is to look at a simplified balance sheet of a bank, and then to trace through a few transactions. This will give you a better idea of the nature of deposits and how they get created.

The Bank's Balance Sheet. Banks, like other business institutions, keep a running financial record of what they own and what they owe to other people. What they own and what is owed to them are their "assets." What they owe to other people are their "liabilities." The difference between the two is the "net worth" of the business to its owners, the stockholders. When these three main categories are put together in one statement, they are called a "balance sheet."

A typical bank balance sheet looks something like this, except that we have omitted a lot of minor items to make the essential categories stand out.

REPORT OF CONDITION

VICTORY BANK AND TRUST COMPANY
Victory, U.S.A.
December 31, 1959

Assets		*Liabilities and Net Worth*	
Cash	$400,000	Demand Deposits	$900,000
Bonds	800,000	Time Deposits	600,000
Loans Outstanding	400,000	Capital Stock	100,000
Building and Fixtures	50,000	Surplus and Undivided Profits	50,000
	$1,650,000		$1,650,000

What this balance sheet says is that on December 31, 1959, the bank owned cash of $400,000, bonds valued at $800,000, and a building and fixtures valued at $50,000. In addition, it had loaned out $400,000 to customers, who owed the money back to the bank. These were its *assets*.

Offsetting these assets, the bank had deposits of $1,500,000, partly demand and partly time deposits. These deposits represent *liabilities,* because they are sums the bank promises to pay out to the depositors on demand or on due notice.

The difference between the assets and liabilities was $150,000, which was the estimated *net worth* of the bank. Part of this net worth was originally paid in by the stockholders when they bought stock to start the bank. The rest is surplus and undivided profits, which are mainly the profits made by the bank and not paid out to the owners.

POTENTIAL CREATION OF CREDIT BY AN INDIVIDUAL BANK If we make some highly simplified assumptions, the basic operations of the Victory Bank are laid bare. Assume for the moment that: (1) the bank is on an isolated island where there are no other banks and no communication with other countries; (2) all payments on the island are made by bank check, and no currency is used by the public (the "Cash" item on the balance sheet may be gold or any other type of reserve); and (3) there are no laws to control the volume of loans the bank can make.

Suppose now that you, a substantial businessman on the island, go to the banker and ask to borrow $1,000. Your credit is good, and he agrees to make the loan. What happens to the bank's balance sheet?

On the assets side "Loans Outstanding" go up $1,000, and on the liabilities side "Demand Deposits" go up the same amount. Remember that all payments are made by check, so you will simply take your loan as an addition to your checking deposit at the bank. The balance sheet still balances, as it always must. *But now there is $1,000 more spendable money (checking deposits) in existence merely as a result of the bank's making a loan to you. There is no change at all in the amount of "cash" (reserve money) in existence. The bank has taken your promise to pay (which could not serve as money) and has given you its promise to pay on the order of your check (which is widely acceptable money).*[5]

This is shown readily by a simplified bank balance sheet (sometimes called a T-account), listing only the *changes* that take place in this transaction. It shows that loans have increased $1,000 on the assets side and that deposits have increased $1,000 on the liabilities side.

Assets		Liabilities	
Loans	+ $1,000	Deposits	+ $1,000

Chances are you are borrowing the money because you want to spend it. What happens when you do spend it? Say you buy some machinery from John Jones, and write him a check for $1,000. When Jones presents the check at the bank for payment, $1,000 is taken out of your account and put in his. Since all payments are made by check, he will not want any currency to take home; he merely wants the $1,000 in his checking account so he can spend it when he likes. The new $1,000 of checking deposits has been spent once and is still going strong.

A few days later, Jones buys a new roof for his house, and pays for the materials with the $1,000. Then the $1,000 is transferred again, from Jones' account

---

[5] Banks ordinarily deduct interest on loans in advance. Thus the bank would give you perhaps $970 and keep the other $30 for interest; you would repay the full $1,000. This process of deducting interest in advance is called "discount" rather than charging "interest." Suppose for simplicity, however, that the bank gives you the full $1,000.

to the roofing company's account. Now the $1,000 loan has financed $2,000 of transactions, and the money is as ready for spending again as if the bank had printed up a thousand one-dollar bills and lent them to you. Obviously the new deposit can be spent over and over as long as it is in existence.

In the meantime, what has been happening on the bank's balance sheet? Nothing. The $1,000 checking deposit has been moving from one account to another, but the over-all totals on the balance sheet have remained unchanged since your loan was first entered on the books. The additional deposit was created by the loan. It remains outstanding until the loan is paid off, and may be spent (transferred) any number of times in the meantime.

Some day your loan will come due. If you're a sound businessman, you will have built up your own checking account in preparation for the day by holding onto receipts you get from your customers. On the due date, you go in to see the banker and write him a check for $1,000 on your own account. He returns your promissory note to you, and the loan is paid off. But now what has happened to the bank's balance sheet?

Loans are down by $1,000, since the loan to you is no longer outstanding. And deposits are down by $1,000, since you have written a $1,000 check against your account and this check is not transferred to any other depositor. Repayment of the loan just reverses the original entries that were made when you borrowed the money. The loan was made by giving you a deposit account to write checks on. Repayment of the loan wipes out that checking account. The whole transaction has been perfectly businesslike. It has thousands of counterparts every day in the United States. Yet, in effect, the bank has acted like a little mint, creating the checking deposit it lends you and wiping it out when you repay the loan.

Look at the T-account now. It still shows the +$1,000 in loans and deposits from the initial loan. But now we add a −$1,000 for both deposits and loans. The balance sheet is back to its original position, but the economy had an extra $1,000 of money while the loan was outstanding.

Assets		Liabilities	
Loans	+ $1,000	Deposits	+ $1,000
	− 1,000		− 1,000

How many other loans can the banker make simultaneously? Obviously, there is no reason why he has to stop with you. Since the public does all its business by check, and since there is no other bank on the island, he has no need to worry about cash withdrawals. It is hard to see just what will put a ceiling on the volume of loans the bank can extend. And he could just as well extend credit by buying bonds. Suppose that instead of lending $1,000 to you he buys a new $1,000 bond issue by the island government. The bank enters a $1,000 checking account for the government, which the government can spend when it pleases. The checking deposit is created in exactly the same way, and it stays in existence (however often it is spent) until the bank is repaid for the bond. Since the bank collects interest on every loan or investment made, this looks like a very good thing indeed for the banker and his stockholders.

But it all sounds a little like never-never land. You probably suspect there's a catch in it some place. If people could draw out currency, you say, the banker couldn't go around creating money like that just by writing down entries on his books. And you'd be right—partly right. We need to go on and explore what happens when people can withdraw currency for hand-to-hand use. But before you throw out our whole simplified example, remember one fact from a few pages back: About 75 to 80 per cent of all transactions in the United States today are made by bank check. The simple example may not be so far off on that score after all.

LIMITS TO CREDIT CREATION BY AN INDIVIDUAL BANK

Why don't banks keep on expanding their loans and earning more interest indefinitely, if all they have to do is create new checking accounts by making entries on their books? Now remove the simplifying assumptions of our island economy, one by one, to get a real-world situation like the one that exists in the United States today.

Currency Withdrawals. Suppose we keep our other assumptions unchanged but assume that the island's money-using habits are like those in the United States today. The people want to hold about a fifth of their total money supply in the form of currency.

Now the banker is going to have to be more careful. His balance sheet shows he has $400,000 of cash, which we will assume to be either currency or something readily convertible into currency. If he is reasonably sure that the 4-to-1 ratio between deposits and currency wanted by the public will continue, he can calculate roughly how far it is safe for him to go in extending new credit. Every time he adds $5 to his deposits he can count on the public to withdraw $1 of it in currency. Thus he might be safe in expanding his deposits nearly $2,000,000, of which he would expect to lose about $400,000 in currency, in case he didn't mind seeing his cash account go down to almost zero.

Actually, the banker wouldn't want to run anywhere near that close on his currency lest the bank be unable to meet unexpected depositors' demands for their funds and "go broke." Bankers are traditionally conservative people who try to be very sure that they have plenty of cash to meet their obligations. Nevertheless, the basic relationship of the cash to potential credit expansion is clear. Whenever there is a chance of a currency drain, the bank must be sure it has enough currency to meet the requests of depositors who want currency instead of checking deposits. This public demand is typically small relative to the total volume of deposits, but the *potential* currency demand imposes a real restriction on the banks. After a banker has been in the business a while, he develops a pretty good feel for how heavy currency drains will be at different times of the year and under different circumstances, and governs himself accordingly as a normal part of his business operations. But he also usually keeps a good wide margin of safety.

There is one other question about our island economy that we should answer before going on to remove the next assumption. What if people lose confidence in the bank and make a "run" on it for currency? The answer is painfully clear. The depositors who demand the first $400,000 can be paid off, but the rest are out of luck. In a fractional-reserve banking system—i.e., one where the total cash reserves are only a fraction of the system's deposits—the banks cannot pay off all their depositors in currency, for the simple reason that they don't have that much currency. This fact has been faced with painful regularity during past financial crises and depressions in the United States. The worst was in 1932-33, when a spreading panic of bank "runs" forced the government to close all the banks in the country temporarily to protect them all from bankruptcy. At the end of the "bank holiday," public confidence had been restored enough to permit banks to reopen on a gradual basis.

This situation re-emphasizes the basic fact: Bank deposits represent largely credit extended through banks' making loans and investments, not the deposit of currency in banks. This is obviously true in the Victory Bank, since it has only $400,000 in cash but deposits of $1,500,000. It is equally true in the United States today, where the total cash reserves of all banks are about $40 billion and total deposits are about $200 billion.

Legal Reserve Requirements.   Suppose now that the islanders get to worrying about whether their bank is sound (or maybe they hear about the way things are done in the United States), and pass a law requiring the bank to hold cash reserves equal to at least 20 per cent of its deposits. (Before reading further, ask yourself whether you would favor this law. Make a list of the reasons why you would or would not.)

This legal requirement puts a real crimp in the bank's expansion possibilities. With $400,000 of cash, the bank can have only $2,000,000 of deposits. It already has $1,500,000, so the limit of its new deposits (credit extension) is $500,000. The actual working limit is less, because the banker needs to worry about likely currency drains as well as about the legal reserve requirement. Thus, imposition of a legal cash-reserve requirement against deposits puts an upper ceiling on the amount of credit the bank can extend, since new loans and investments mean new deposits.

How many deposits can be supported on any given cash reserve depends on the level of the reserve requirement. With a 20 per cent reserve requirement, the bank legally can have five times as many deposits as it has cash reserves. If the reserve requirement is 50 per cent of deposits, then the bank can only have twice as many deposits as it has cash reserves. If the reserve requirement is 10 per cent, deposits can be ten times cash reserves. In fact, the 20 per cent legal cash-reserve requirement is about what we now have in the United States banking system.

The real function of bank reserve requirements is to limit the total volume of bank credit that can be extended, even though many people think of reserve requirements as a device to assure that depositors can withdraw their funds whenever they want to. Although bank reserves do serve this depositor-safety purpose to some extent, it should be clear by now that nothing short of 100 per cent reserves would guarantee the continuous availability of cash for all depositors. With much smaller cash reserves, the thing that really keeps the banking system solvent is the confidence of the public in each other's checks. So long as nobody wants much more currency than usual, the banks get along fine. But if everyone tried to get currency for his deposits at the same time, the 20 per cent legal reserve requirement would be of only minor help in paying off the depositors.

A few institutional details about legal reserve requirements are worth attention, although they don't change the basic principles stated above.

(1) Only "cash" is counted in computing banks' legal reserves. Government securities and other assets may be nearly as liquid as cash, but they are *not* part of a bank's legal reserve. They become reserves in the eyes of the law only when they are converted into cash.[6]

(2) When a bank has more cash reserves than the law requires it to have, the excess is termed *"excess reserves."* Whenever a bank has excess reserves, it feels some pressure to expand its loans and investments. Idle reserves earn no interest. Thus the banker generally tries to keep excess reserves at the lowest level consistent with the availability of safe loans and investments.

(3) There are different reserve requirements for different banks and for different types of deposits. Banks that are members of the Federal Reserve System have their reserve requirements set by that federal authority. "Non-member" banks have their requirements set by state laws or state authorities. In either case, reserve requirements are generally higher on demand deposits than on time deposits, and on large city banks than on small country banks.

Adverse Clearing Balances. Now drop the last special assumption—that there is only one bank doing business—and return the Victory Bank to the U.S.A. Here there are lots of other banks in operation, and the Victory Bank needs to take this fact into account. If the Victory Bank makes loans to its customers, there is a good chance that they will write checks to people who do busi-

---

[6] In the United States, a bank's legal reserves are usually less than the cash shown in its balance sheet. Cash on the balance sheet includes currency in the bank's vault and deposits at other private banks and in the Federal Reserve Banks. For Federal Reserve member banks, only cash on deposit with the Federal Reserve Bank is considered legal reserve (though a bill to include vault cash is in Congress as this is written). Since this detail is unimportant for many purposes, we will consider all cash shown to be reserves. But this assumption won't work if you try to use actual published banking statistics.

ness elsewhere. And whenever this happens, the Victory Bank has to give up cash to the other bank. This is a most important change in the bank's position.

In a many-bank system, the most important limitation on the power of an individual bank to expand credit to the legal limit permitted by its excess reserves is the fear it will lose reserves to other banks. If Bank A has to pay cash to Bank B when they settle up the checks written back and forth between their customers, we say that Bank A has an "adverse clearing balance." And to Bank A an adverse clearing balance is just like a currency drain—it takes away cash reserves.

Ordinarily, the checks written against any bank and the checks it has to collect against other banks roughly balance off. You send $500 to Philadelphia to pay a bill, but your neighbor ships livestock to Philadelphia and gets a check back in payment. But if the Victory Bank expands its credit more rapidly than other banks do, it's almost certain to lose reserves on balance. Recognizing this likelihood, few bankers would make new loans and investments amounting to anything like $5,000 on $1,000 of excess reserves unless they had some special reason to suppose that they would not lose reserves through adverse clearing balances. Indeed, bankers ordinarily hesitate to extend new credit beyond their excess reserves —in this case, beyond $1,000.

To summarize what we have said so far about banks and the supply of money: (1) One function of banks is to convert savings into investment. This activity has no direct effect on the volume of money. (2) Commercial banks are distinguished from savings banks and other such institutions in that, as a group, they do not simply lend out the money that people have deposited, but actually "create" credit by giving borrowers current spending power in exchange for future promises to pay the bank. (3) The power of an individual commercial bank to expand credit on its reserves is limited by (a) legal cash-reserve requirements, and by the dangers of (b) cash withdrawals by customers and (c) adverse clearing balances.

CREDIT CREATION BY THE BANKING SYSTEM Any one bank that expands loans and investments when other banks are not expanding is sharply checked by adverse clearing balances. *But when we view the banking system as a whole, the limitation imposed by adverse clearing balances disappears. This is because an adverse clearing balance (loss of reserves) for one bank is a favorable clearing balance (gain of reserves) to some other bank.* (Still another example of the fallacy of composition from Chapter 5.)

The Individual Bank and the Banking System. If no bank lends more than its excess reserves, how can the banking *system* expand credit four-fold on its excess reserves? Assume again that the Victory Bank has $1,000 excess reserves, and that all other banks have made loans up to their legal limits. As the Victory

Bank begins to make new loans and investments, its reserves are gradually drawn away to other banks, and its credit expansion possibilities are limited. But the reserves the Victory Bank loses, some other bank gains. Suppose Victory makes a new loan of $1,000, just the amount of its excess reserves. Its excess reserves are now reduced to $800, since $200 of the total becomes required reserve against the $1,000 of new deposits created by the loan. The T-account looks like this, including the original $1,000 of excess reserves. Consider first only the entries above the dotted line.

VICTORY BANK—STAGE I

Excess Cash Reserve	$1,000		
Loans	+ 1,000	Deposits	+ $1,000
. . . .	. . . .	. . . .	. . . .
Cash	− 1,000	Deposits	− 1,000

Soon the borrower writes a check for the entire amount, and the check is deposited in Bank B. This action transfers both the $1,000 deposit and the cash reserve to Bank B; the Victory Bank retains merely the $1,000 of increased loans, offset by a decline of $1,000 in cash reserve (so its balance sheet still balances; remember that we began by showing only the $1,000 excess reserve item). Looking back to the Stage 1 T-account, deduct $1,000 from cash and from deposits, as shown below the dotted line, to see the Victory Bank's position.

Bank B now has $800 of excess reserves, as well as $1,000 of additional deposits; only $200 of the $1,000 cash it has received is needed as required reserve against its new $1,000 deposit. Obviously, it is safe in extending $800 of new loans, since it has that much excess reserves. We can set up a T-account for Bank B, showing +$1,000 for both the new cash and deposits, above the first dotted line.

BANK B—STAGE 2

Cash	+ $1,000	Deposits	+ $1,000
. . . .	. . . .	. . . .	. . . .
Loans	+ 800	"	+ 800
. . . .	. . . .	. . . .	. . . .
Cash	− 800	"	− 800

So it makes a new $800 loan, creating $800 of additional deposits. This is shown on the Bank B T-account, below the first dotted line.

Now suppose the borrower spends the money, and the $800 in deposits and in reserves is shifted to Bank C. Bank B now retains the $1,000 original deposit created by Victory plus $200 of new reserves from Victory; it also has $800 of its own new loans. The deposit transfer is shown below the second dotted line on Bank B's accounts.

But Bank C now has $800 of new deposits and the $800 of new reserves from Bank B. This is shown in a new T-account, set up for Bank C.

BANK C—STAGE 3

Cash	+ $800	Deposits	+ $800
Loans	+ 640	"	+ 640

The total of new deposits has now risen to $1,800, matched by $1,800 of new loans, even though no bank has lent a penny beyond its available excess reserves. Bank C, moreover, now has $640 of excess reserves ($800 new reserves, of which only $160 is required to back its $800 of new deposits). On these excess reserves it can safely make at least $640 of new loans, shown below the dotted line on its T-account. This will raise the total of new deposits to $2,440 against the original $1,000 of excess reserves. (The $2,440 total includes $1,000 in Bank B and $1,440 in Bank C at this stage.) And the expansion process can obviously continue.

This process of cumulative deposit expansion is diagrammed in Figure 8-1. Assume that Bank A receives $1,000 of new reserves, say because $1,000 of newly mined gold is deposited. This $1,000 deposit requires only $200 of new reserves, so Bank A is entirely safe in expanding its loans and investments by $800, as shown in the diagonal-hatched bar for Bank A.

Now Bank A's new borrower writes a check to a customer of Bank B, and the $800 is transferred to Bank B. Bank B now has $800 of new deposits and $800 of new reserves, which means that it has excess reserves of $640 since required reserves increase by only $160. It is perfectly safe in lending out an additional $640, and does so, as shown in the diagram. This $640 may now be transferred to a customer of some other bank (C), which then has new deposits and excess reserves on which to expand its loans. At each stage, the deposits created by previous transactions are piled on top, in the dotted sections, to show the cumulative increase.

As the diagram shows, this process can continue, piling up new deposits that arise from new loans, until a total of $5,000 of new deposits is reached (the tall unshaded bar at the right), including the original $1,000 deposit produced by the gold deposit. This is just what we would expect: $1,000 of new reserves has been able to support $5,000 of new deposits, given a 20 per cent legal reserve requirement against deposits. The tall shaded bar at the right shows the $4,000 of new loans and the $1,000 of new reserves, just using up the original $1,000 of new gold reserves. Moreover, this expansion has taken place even though no individual bank has ever lent out more than the excess reserves it actually has on hand. So when your banker tells you that he would never lend out more money than he has in excess reserves, he may be quite correct. Yet the banking system as a whole creates deposits equal to many times its cash reserves.

The Banking System Not Limited by Adverse Clearing Balances. Thus, multiple credit expansion can occur on new reserves, even though no individual banker ever "lends more than people put in"—that is, never lends beyond his excess reserves. Whatever reserves one bank loses, another gains. Thus, for the banking system as a whole there are no adverse clearing balances; the only overall drain on reserves would come from currency withdrawals.[7] *The $1,000 of*

Process of Deposit Expansion

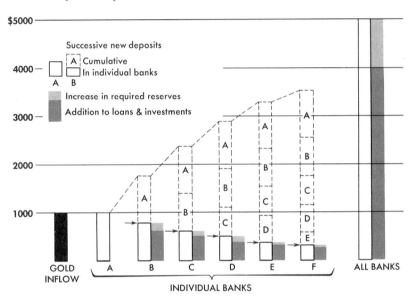

FIG. 8-1   One thousand dollars of new reserves ultimately serves as the foundation for $5,000 of new deposits, as banks make new loans and investments—even though no bank ever loans out more than its own excess reserves.

excess reserves would not permit one bank acting alone to expand credit much beyond $1,000, but the banking system as a whole may expand to the full $5,000 on a 20 per cent reserve requirement because it is not limited by adverse clearing balances. Only a loss of reserves (say, through currency withdrawals or gold shipments abroad) reduces the power of the system as a whole to expand deposits.

Bank purchases of government securities, rather than bank loans to businesses, have accounted for much of the vast expansion of deposits since 1933, especially during the war years. From 1940 to 1946, the banking system created $94 billion net of new deposits by purchasing government securities (extending loans to the

---

[7] Additional drains may come from international gold flows or from Federal Reserve or Treasury policies. These possibilities will be considered later.

government), as compared with a pre-war deposit figure of less than half this amount. During each "War Loan Drive" the commercial banks bought billions of dollars of new government securities. As the banks bought, say, $4 billion of Governments, $4 billion of new deposits might be created in a single day, simply through the banks' entry of $4 billion of deposits to the government's account on their books. Never before had this country seen such mass creation of deposits, and never before had the process of bank-credit creation been demonstrated with such straightforward simplicity.

CONTRACTION OF CREDIT BY THE BANKING SYSTEM If one dollar of reserves is the basis for five dollars of outstanding bank loans and investments, the loss of each dollar of reserves may force contraction of five dollars of loans and investments. If banks are fully "loaned up" to their legal reserve limit, loss of reserves must cause a contraction of loans and investments (deposits). As on the expansion side, mass credit contraction occurs when many banks simultaneously call in loans and liquidate investments.

The disastrous results that attend mass contraction of bank credit were clearly indicated by the financial panic between 1929 and 1933. Bankers, alarmed that customers would be unable to repay loans as rapidly as desired, called for payment of outstanding loans and refused to make new loans. To pay off their loans, customers were forced to dump many securities for sale on the open market. Simultaneously, people were withdrawing cash (reserves) from the banks to hoard in safe-deposit boxes, mattresses, and elsewhere. This forced the banks to call still more loans for payment and to liquidate investments to get enough cash to meet the withdrawals. By calling for payment of loans, the banks compelled borrowers to dispose of their inventories at forced sale, just when deepening depression and pessimism made buyers scarce. Funds could be obtained only by taking large losses on securities and goods sold. And the greater the losses sustained, the more worried the bankers became about the security of outstanding loans, and the harder they pressed for repayment, thus reinforcing the downward spiral of deflation and liquidation. Worst of all, each dollar of currency withdrawn removed the reserve base for several dollars of loans and deposits.

Some critics have emphasized that the private banks act like little individual "mints," coining and destroying deposits just as the federal mints coin and destroy currency. This criticism should be aimed not at the bankers themselves, but rather at the banking system. Bankers, in search of profits, expand loans and investments during boom times; in crises they are forced to contract loans and investments to maintain the solvency of their banks—even though this expansion and contraction intensifies the severity of booms and depressions. The creation and destruction of deposits are possible only because banks do not have to hold 100 per cent reserves to cover their deposits. The lower the percentage of reserves required, the greater becomes the possibility for expansion in good times and for drastic contraction in bad times.[8]

MONEY AND THE CREATION OF NEAR-MONIES
Only commercial banks can "create" money, because by law only they can hold demand (checking) deposits. But savings deposits, savings and loan shares, and other near-monies are close substitutes for money as a store of purchasing power. And other financial institutions can "create" near-monies.

Suppose Joe Doaks, seeing an ad promising 4 per cent at a savings and loan association, saves part of his paycheck and buys a $100 savings and loan share, which is much the same thing as putting a $100 savings deposit in the association. Or he may just withdraw $100 from his own checking account and transfer it. Either way, he transfers $100 from a commercial bank to the savings and loan association. But that association just redeposits the $100 in its own checking account at a commercial bank, so it can spend or lend the money itself.

Results: First, commercial bank reserves and demand deposits are unchanged in total. But second, Joe has a fine $100 money substitute in his savings and loan share; this will presumably decrease the amount of actual money (currency and checking deposits) he needs to hold at any given time to carry on his transactions and have a reasonable margin of liquidity. It thus increases the amount of money available for active use. Third, the savings and loan association has $100, most of which it will now feel free to lend out to new borrowers. Joe's decision to substitute a near-money for actual money in his own financial position has *both* increased the nation's total supply of money plus near-monies, *and* increased the total lending power of all financial institutions, since the commercial banks have lost no reserves and the savings and loan association has gained $100 in additional lending power (less whatever part of the total it feels it must hold as a ready cash reserve).

Thus, we must add to the money-creating powers of the commercial banking system a similar power of numerous other financial intermediaries (for example, mutual savings banks and insurance companies) to "create" near-monies, as

---

[8] In view of the important part bank-credit expansion and contraction play in business cycles, some economists advocate requiring 100 per cent reserves behind all bank deposits. They argue that this step would do much toward lessening the severity of business fluctuations. They point out that businessmen and others who wish to borrow could continue to do so, through "savings and loan organizations" that would receive savings from the public. These organizations could lend only as much as savers deposited, rather than being able to create credit as the banks do at present. The present banks might be split into two parts. One part would act as a storehouse for funds that savers simply wanted to keep idle for checking or other purposes (on which depositors would probably have to pay storage charges). The other part would act as a savings and loan organization to receive savings (paying interest on them) and to lend these savings to borrowers at a somewhat higher rate of interest.

individuals and businesses transfer money-holdings into near-monies. In total, therefore, the power of the financial system to generate money plus near-monies far exceeds the limits on its money creation.

Some economists argue that only money proper is very important, since only it can be spent. But many others emphasize that near-monies play an important role, since in effect they free part of the money stock for more active use in current spending. The near-monies may satisfy much of the public's need for a store of purchasing power, leaving checking deposits largely available for current spending.[9]

THE GOVERNMENT AND THE MONEY SUPPLY

The money supply plays an important role in determining the level of national income, employment, and prices. At the least, as we shall see, an expanding money supply is typically necessary for a growing gross national product, even though money may be only a passive factor. At the most, the amount of money in existence may be one of the central, active factors determining g.n.p. And the role of financial institutions in linking together savers and investors is central to the continuous circular flow of income.

Yet the government controls directly only one minor component of the money supply (currency), and even here it passively responds to the demands of the public. It has little or no direct control over the generation of near-monies. With money as important as it is, you probably suspect that the government somehow has more to say about how much money we have—and you are right. The federal government, acting primarily through the Federal Reserve System, can provide new reserves for the banking system when it wants to stimulate banks to make new loans and investments. It can wipe out bank reserves when it wants to restrict credit expansion. These are powerful devices. To understand them, we need to go on to the next chapter.

---

[9] As we shall see in Chapter 10, given any stock of money, the effect of this function is to speed up the turnover rate, or velocity of use, of the money.

REVIEW—CONCEPTS AND INSTITUTIONS TO REMEMBER

Among the important concepts and institutions introduced in this chapter, be especially sure you understand the following:

money	credit
currency	commercial banks
demand deposits	financial middleman
checking deposits	investment banker
savings and time deposits	financial investment
near monies	Federal Reserve notes

silver certificates

credit creation

bank reserves

excess reserves

reserve requirements

adverse clearing balance

credit contraction

1. Why is currency worth more than its value as paper and ink?

2. If banks hold cash reserves equal to only a small fraction of their deposits, are you safe in depositing your money in a bank? Explain why or why not.

3. Get a copy of a recent balance sheet from one of your local banks. What main types of credit does this bank extend? Which of these types of credit would you expect to be most liquid (most readily convertible into cash) in case of a serious recession in over-all business activity?

4. If you were a banker, would you favor reserve requirements higher or lower than the present requirements? How do you, as a citizen, feel about this same question? If there are differences in your attitudes, why do they arise?

5. In a small, isolated economy (i.e., no foreign trade) with money-using habits comparable to those of the United States, there are five identical banks. Each bank's balance sheet is as follows:

FOR
ANALYSIS
AND
DISCUSSION

Cash	$ 5,000,000	Deposits	$13,000,000
Loans	4,000,000	Capital and	
Government		Surplus	2,000,000
Securities	6,000,000		
	$15,000,000		$15,000,000

The law prescribes that banks must hold a 20 per cent cash reserve against deposits. There is no central bank.

    a. A customer of Bank A mines $100,000 of gold (considered as cash for reserve purposes) and deposits it in his bank. Trace through any *likely* expansion of the money supply by Bank A and by the entire banking system. What would be the *maximum* expansion possible? Specify clearly any assumptions that you make, and state your reasoning carefully and precisely.

    b. Is the banking system in a more or less *sound* position as a result of the gold deposit and the consequences you have predicted above? Explain why or why not.

6. Most bankers deny that they lend out more than depositors put in their banks. Can this statement be correct if, in fact, the banking system creates deposits? Explain.

7. Explain how the transfer of your $100 deposit from a commercial bank to a savings and loan association can increase society's stock of liquid assets (money plus near-monies).

The Federal Reserve System and the Money Supply

9

In 1789 the new federal constitution gave Congress the power to "coin money and regulate the value thereof." Since then Congress has established numerous institutions to deal with the monetary and financial affairs of the country. Of these, the most important is the Federal Reserve System, established in 1914 after years of painful experience with repeated financial crises and after major study by a "National Monetary Commission." This chapter deals primarily with the ways in which the Federal Reserve does its job in regulating the banking system and the supply of money so as to help promote stable economic growth.

THE FEDERAL RESERVE SYSTEM The Federal Reserve is the major agency established by Congress to provide currency for the nation's economy; to furnish a wide variety of financial services to the government and to the economy; and, most important, to regulate the total amount of money (currency plus deposits) in the economy and to maintain "monetary and credit conditions favorable to sound business activity in all fields—agricultural, industrial, commercial." [1]

Organization. The Federal Reserve System is made up of the following:

1. The Board of Governors.
2. The 12 Federal Reserve Banks.
3. The Federal Open Market Committee.
4. The Federal Advisory Council.
5. The member banks.

1. The Board of Governors is composed of seven members, appointed by the President and confirmed by the Senate. Members receive a salary of $20,000 and are appointed for 14 years. One term expires every two years, an effort to safeguard the Board as far as possible from political pressure groups. In most matters, the Board of Governors is ultimately responsible for the major policies of the 12 Federal Reserve Banks; and, since the Federal Reserve Banks in turn supervise and regulate the member banks, ultimate responsibility for the entire system is largely centralized in the Board of Governors.

2. Each of the 12 Federal Reserve Banks serves a certain district in the United States. The banks are located in Boston, New York, Philadelphia, Cleveland, Richmond, Atlanta, Chicago, St. Louis, Minneapolis, Kansas City, Dallas, and San Francisco. Each Federal Reserve Bank was founded by the sale of stock to member banks, which are required to buy stock. As stockholders, member banks receive 6 per cent dividends and elect six of the nine directors of each Federal Reserve Bank. Of these six, three may be bankers, and three must represent business, industry, and agriculture within the district. The other three directors are appointed by the Board of Governors to represent the public. Though technically they are thus privately owned, the Federal Reserve Banks are operated in the public interest, not for profit.

3. The Federal Open Market Committee consists of the seven members of the Board of Governors, plus five of the presidents of the Federal Reserve Banks. This 12-member committee determines the system's policy on open-market operations—that is, the purchase and sale of government securities in the open market. These open-market operations, explained below, are one primary means by which the Federal Reserve authorities attempt to control the volume of bank credit. Although the Board of Governors does not determine open-market policy independently, its seven members constitute a majority of the Open Market Committee.

4. The Federal Advisory Council consists of 12 private commercial bankers selected annually by the 12 Federal Reserve Banks. The Council meets with the

---

[1] *The Federal Reserve System: Its Purposes and Functions* (Board of Governors of the Federal Reserve System), p. 23. This little booklet provides a simple, authoritative statement of the aims and operations of the Federal Reserve System.

Board of Governors periodically, but its powers are purely advisory. The major purpose of the Council at present is to make sure that the views of the bankers of the 12 districts are brought to the attention of the Board of Governors at regular intervals.

5. The member banks include all national banks (chartered by the federal government) in the United States and those state banks that want membership and conform to the requirements set up for member banks. In 1959, about 6,300 of the roughly 13,500 commercial banks in the United States were member banks, but the non-member banks were almost all small ones, representing only about 15 per cent of the total deposits of the banking system.

The officers and employees of the Federal Reserve Banks spend most of their time performing regular service functions. The major policy decisions on what monetary conditions will be most conducive to economic prosperity are made primarily by the Board of Governors and Open Market Committee in consultation with the Federal Treasury and other government agencies. These policy decisions are our major interest, but the service functions deserve a brief survey.

SERVICE FUNCTIONS OF THE FEDERAL RESERVE

Holding Member Bank Reserves. Each member bank must by law keep its legally "required" cash reserves on deposit at the Federal Reserve Bank in its district. It may also keep "excess" reserves there if it wishes—i.e., reserves above the legally required amount. These reserve balances at the Reserve Banks are essentially checking accounts that the member banks maintain with the Federal Reserve, just as an individual has a checking account with a commercial bank. A member bank must always keep the reserve required by law, but beyond this requirement it is free to draw on, or add to, its reserve account as it wishes. If it needs currency to pay out to its customers, it simply draws the needed amount from its excess reserve balance at the Federal Reserve Bank. Member banks receive no interest on their reserve balances.[2]

Furnishing Currency for Circulation. All currency in the United States is now created either by the Federal Treasury or by the Federal Reserve Banks. Treasury currency—silver certificates, metal coins, and United States notes— make up 15 per cent of the total. It is issued by the Treasury but is placed in circulation largely through the Reserve Banks and the commercial banks. The Reserve Banks themselves issue Federal Reserve notes, which make up 85 per cent of the total stock of currency. These Federal Reserve notes are liabilities of the issuing Federal Reserve Bank, and also of the federal government. Each Federal Reserve note must be backed fully by collateral held by the issuing Bank.

---

[2] This use of the word "reserve" is quite different from that in ordinary business accounting, as we shall see in the Appendix to Chapter 17.

At least 25 per cent must be gold; the other 75 per cent may be gold, government bonds, or other designated acceptable security.[3]

Furnishing currency for circulation is a continuing operation. New currency is constantly being put into circulation to replace old, worn currency. Increases in the amount of currency in circulation can be predicted at certain periods of the year, such as Christmas, harvest time, and the Fourth of July, when people and businesses want more hand-to-hand cash. This currency is put into circulation very simply. The banks draw on their reserve accounts at the Reserve Banks and then pay out the money to customers who make withdrawals. The Reserve Banks always keep large supplies of all sorts of paper money and coin on hand to meet the needs of member banks. Following periods of exceptional demand, the currency flows back to the member banks and is returned by them to their reserve accounts in the Reserve Banks. The Federal Reserve thus stands ready to furnish currency for circulation whenever the member banks need it.

Clearing and Collecting Checks. Most money payments in the United States are made by means of bank checks. And most bank checks drawn on out-of-town banks are "cleared" through the Federal Reserve System to avoid shipping currency. Suppose Jones in Chicago sells a $100 bill of goods to Smith in Detroit, and is paid by a check on Smith's Detroit bank. Jones deposits the check at his bank in Chicago. The Chicago bank sends the check to the Chicago Federal Reserve Bank, which increases the reserves of the Chicago bank by $100 and decreases the reserves of the Detroit bank by $100. The check is then sent to the Detroit bank, which decreases Smith's account by $100. Jones in Chicago has his $100; Smith in Detroit has $100 less. And since both banks keep their reserves with the Chicago Federal Reserve Bank, the check is cleared simply by increasing the reserve account of the Chicago member bank and decreasing the reserve account of the Detroit member bank. No currency has to be shipped around the country.

When Jones and Smith are in different Federal Reserve districts (say Chicago and New York), the process is identical except that the New York and Chicago Federal Reserve Banks must settle their accounts. They offset the checks due to each other through an "Interdistrict Settlement Fund."

To give some idea of the magnitude of this clearing function, in 1958 the Federal Reserve System handled nearly 4 billion checks, with a total value of about $1.2 trillion. This total included many checks on non-member banks, which are permitted to use the Federal Reserves check-clearing facilities.

Supervising Member Banks. Banks in this country are supervised by several authorities. The Federal Reserve supervises all member banks. The Comptroller of the Currency (in the Treasury Department) supervises all national banks.

---

[3] Actually, the gold is stored mainly in Treasury vaults; the Federal Reserve holds instead paper "gold certificates."

Each state supervises all state banks chartered by it. The Federal Deposit Insurance Corporation supervises all banks that have their deposits insured. Thus the same bank may be subject to supervision by as many as three authorities. Generally, these various authorities cooperate, but on occasion they adopt contradictory policies.

Each Federal Reserve Bank examines the member banks in its own district. The examiners make detailed reports to the Federal Reserve Bank on the management, the loans and investments, and the general condition of each member bank. If any member bank refuses to conform to the standards of sound banking practice specified by the Federal Reserve, the Board of Governors may remove its officers and directors or take away its right to make use of Federal Reserve credit facilities. These punitive powers seldom need to be exercised.

Fiscal Agent for the Federal Government.   The Federal Reserve Banks are bankers for the federal government. They carry most of the government's checking accounts; they handle the issue and redemption of government securities; and they act as fiscal agent for the government in numerous other ways.

The government is continuously receiving tax funds, borrowing, paying out funds for salaries, planes, and so on. It issues and redeems huge volumes of securities. These activities keep a good many of the Federal Reserve personnel busy.

THE FEDERAL RESERVE AND THE SUPPLY OF MONEY   In the United States, the Federal Reserve is the central bank. It is the agency charged by Congress with the responsibility for maintaining sound monetary conditions which will help maintain a stable, growing, prosperous economy.

Federal Reserve control over the supply of money is exercised largely through control over the volume and utilization of member-bank reserves. Without excess reserves, commercial banks cannot extend more credit. Plenty of excess reserves make possible, but do not assure, expansion of bank earning assets and deposits. Thus Federal Reserve powers are designed largely to control the volume of excess reserves.

The Fundamental Nature of Central Banking.   A Federal Reserve Bank is a central bank—a banker's bank. Member-bank reserves *are* member-bank deposits at the Reserve Banks. Thus Federal Reserve control over the volume of member-bank reserves is in fact control over the volume of its own deposits.

Prior to establishment of the Federal Reserve as a central bank in 1914, the nation's commercial banks faced periodic crises. Mass withdrawals by depositors in times of stress exhausted cash reserves and forced widespread bank failures, because there was no way to convert good but illiquid loans and investments into cash on short notice. The Federal Reserve was established largely to remedy this situation. Member-bank reserves were to be held by the Reserve Banks, and the Reserve authorities were given power to create new reserves (extend credit) for member banks in times of need.

The ability to create new banking reserves and to provide liquidity to commercial-bank assets is the distinguishing feature of a true central bank. The Federal Reserve Banks can extend credit to member banks, just as member banks extend credit to businesses and individuals. Each Federal Reserve Bank must hold a reserve of gold certificates equal to at least 25 per cent of the deposits (member-bank reserves) it holds. One dollar of gold in the Federal Reserve can thus serve as backing for $4 of member-bank reserves. Assuming a 20 per cent average member-bank reserve requirement, the $4 of member-bank reserves could in turn support $20 of member-bank deposits. This credit expansion on a small gold base (roughly $1 of gold underlying $20 of bank credit in this case) is often called the inverted pyramid of credit. (See Figure 9-1 on page 144.)

Main Federal Reserve Powers.   Within the limits imposed by the law and the availability of its own gold reserves, the Federal Reserve attempts to control the volume and direction of commercial bank lending and investing, and hence the volume of bank deposits, through the following seven major channels. The first three are aimed largely at controlling the total supply or "quantity" of money, through regulating the commercial banks' excess reserves. The others are aimed more at controlling the flow of credit to particular uses, such as speculation. These latter are thus called "selective," or "qualitative," credit controls.

In regulating the supply of money, Federal Reserve actions also influence interest rates—the "cost" of money. While little is said of this effect here, later on we shall see that it too may play a vital role.

Open-Market Operations.   Purchase and sale of United States government securities in the open market has been the major device used by the Federal Reserve since the 1920's to control the volume of member-bank reserves. By buying Governments, the Reserve authorities increase member-bank reserves; by selling Governments, they reduce member-bank reserves.

1. *The Federal Reserve can create new reserves for the commercial banks* (*thus stimulating the banks to extend new loans and investments*) *much as commercial banks create deposits for individual and business borrowers.* Assume that the Federal Reserve wants to encourage more bank loans. It goes into the open market and buys $1,000 worth of government bonds, say from a commercial bank. To pay for these bonds it simply gives the bank a $1,000 deposit credit (new reserve balance) at the Federal Reserve. The commercial bank has $1,000

of new reserves, and of new excess reserves, since its deposits have not been changed by the transaction. The Federal Reserve has created $1,000 of new commercial bank reserves in exchange for a $1,000 government bond. The bond now shows on the asset side of the F.R. balance sheet, offsetting the new $1,000 of deposits (member-bank reserves) on the liability side.[4]

Consider the T-accounts for the commercial bank and for the Federal Reserve Banks:

COMMERCIAL BANK		FEDERAL RESERVE BANKS	
Cash + $1,000		Bonds + $1,000	Member Bank Deposits + $1,000
Bonds − 1,000			

Does this all seem a little like black magic—commercial bank deposits created out of nowhere on the basis of reserves which in turn are created out of nowhere by the Federal Reserve Banks? In a sense, it is. But each dollar of new reserves (at the Federal Reserve) and new deposits (at the commercial banks) is matched by an asset (a government bond at the Federal Reserve or a borrower's promise to pay at the commercial bank).

Is there a limitation on how many new reserves the Federal Reserve can create in this way? Yes. The Reserve Banks must, by law, have 25 cents in gold for each dollar of member-bank deposits (reserves) they hold. Thus, ultimately the nation's gold stock limits the volume of bank reserves, which in turn limit the volume of commercial bank loans, investments, and deposits. This is the pyramid of credit shown in Figure 9-1. One dollar of gold will support $4 of member-bank reserves, which in turn (at a 20 per cent average reserve requirement) will support $20 of commercial bank deposits. This all assumes that none of the gold has to be diverted to back up new Federal Reserve notes because the public decides to convert some of its deposits into currency. Actually, the Federal Reserve Banks' balance sheet looks something like this, omitting a number of minor items (which would make the balance sheet

The Inverted Pyramid of Credit

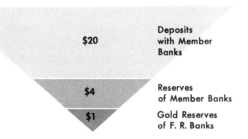

FIG. 9-1   One dollar of gold serves as the basis for $4 of member bank reserves, which in turn back $20 of deposits at the member banks. This assumes no currency drain.

---

[4] There is substantially, but not quite, the same effect if the Reserve buys the bond from a business or individual. Trace through the effect for yourself. Section (2) below will suggest the analysis if you need help.

balance exactly). Obviously about one-third of the gold is held to back Federal Reserve notes.[5]

FEDERAL RESERVE BANKS
Jan. 1, 1959
(In billion dollars)

Gold	$20	Deposits	$19
U.S. Securities	26	Federal Reserve Notes	28

How effective is the Federal Reserve in stimulating new commercial bank loans and investments when it provides new reserves through open-market purchases? More reserves push a banker to extend new credit, for no banker likes to lose the interest he might earn on idle reserves. But if excess reserves are already large because bankers don't see any "sound" borrowers looking for loans, still more excess reserves may not do much to increase bank lending. The analogy has been suggested that you can hold a balloon down by tying a string to it, but you can't push a non-buoyant balloon up by pushing on the string. This may be about right for business loans when there isn't a good loan demand.

But don't forget that banks can also buy government bonds. If their excess reserves are increased when no desirable loans are available, they may well increase the volume of deposits by buying up government bonds. Either way, the money supply increases. And history suggests that with rare exceptions commercial bankers have managed to increase their loans and investments about as far as their excess reserves permit. The big exception was the depression of the 1930's, when the commercial banks held billions of dollars of excess reserves for nearly a decade.

2. How about the Federal Reserve's power to restrict credit expansion? *When the Open Market Committee wants to decrease member-bank reserves, it sells government securities in the open market to whoever bids for them—individuals, businesses, or banks. This reduces commercial bank excess reserves when the Federal Reserve is paid for the bonds.*

If a member bank buys the bond, it pays by transferring $1,000 cash (reserves) to the Federal Reserve; on the bank's balance sheet, "cash" goes down and "bonds" go up. Thus the bank loses a full $1,000 of excess reserves, since its deposits remain unchanged. If a business or individual buys the bond from the Reserve, the effect is almost the same. If he pays in currency, he directly reduces the amount of currency in circulation. More likely, he pays by a check on his bank. If so, his bank's reserves are reduced by $1,000 when the Federal Reserve presents the check for collection. The member bank's deposits also drop by the $1,000 transferred from the bond buyer's account to the Federal Reserve. Since

---

[5] On rare occasions the Federal Reserve has faced the danger of running out of gold. For what happens in such cases, see Chapter 14.

the bank loses $1,000 in both deposits and reserves, its required reserves are $200 lower but its excess reserves drop by $800. The contraction of excess reserves is a little less than in the bank-purchase case just above, but the general effect is similar. If the bank buys the bond, the T-account entries are as shown above the dotted line. If a customer buys it, the entries are as shown below the dotted line.

Cash	− $1,000		
Bonds	+ 1,000		
. . . .	. . . .	
Cash	− 1,000	Deposits	− $1,000

Federal Reserve open-market sales can limit bank credit expansion when they reduce excess reserves to low levels. The Federal Reserve may face a serious problem if banks have large excess reserves on hand, for the banks can then lose reserves and still have an adequate base for new loans and investments. But in recent decades the Federal Reserve has had plenty of Governments to absorb all the excess reserves of the banking system. Even if the Federal Reserve could not sop up all excess reserves, by selling bonds it could force bond prices down and interest rates up, thereby somewhat restricting the flow of funds to bank borrowers.

Rediscount Rate Changes.   When a member bank runs short of reserves, it may borrow from its Federal Reserve Bank, just as you and I borrow at a commercial bank. In such a case the member bank would "rediscount" notes. The member bank has made loans to customers on customers' promises to repay, called "notes," or "commercial paper." It can "rediscount" these notes with its Federal Reserve Bank—i.e., it can use the note as collateral to borrow additional reserves. The rate of interest, or discount, charged by the Federal Reserve to member banks is called the "rediscount rate." Or member banks may borrow, using government securities as collateral. In rediscounting, the initiative is in the hands of the commercial banker to increase his reserves.

The Reserve authorities raise the rediscount rate to discourage member-bank borrowing and lower the rate to encourage it. But few bankers like to borrow, and most will borrow only when they need to in order to get additional reserves. During the 1920's, commercial banks frequently borrowed from the Reserve Banks. Nowadays, they are more likely to sell part of their short-term, low-rate government security holdings to get reserves when they run short. Thus the rediscount rate is now of relatively minor importance, although banks do borrow from the Federal Reserve from time to time; and changes in the rediscount rate still have an important psychological effect on the banking and business communities.

Changes in Member-Bank Reserve Requirements.   In 1933, a drastic new power was given to the Board of Governors—the power to change legal reserve requirements for member banks from the then-existing levels of 7 per cent, 10 per cent, and 13 per cent for country, city, and large city banks, respectively. At present, the Board of Governors has the power to vary legal reserve requirements between the old levels and levels approximately twice that high.

By raising reserve requirements, the Board wipes out member banks' excess reserves and directly restricts credit expansion. Suppose a member bank has $1,000,000 deposits and $200,000 reserves, the required legal reserve ratio being 16 per cent. A comfortable $40,000 of excess reserves is left. If the Board raises the legal requirement to 20 per cent, the reserve required against the same deposits is increased to $200,000 and the bank's excess reserve is completely eliminated. Conversely, lowering legal reserve requirements increases excess reserves.

The effectiveness of changes in reserve requirements depends on much the same conditions as for open-market operations. Increasing excess reserves when the supply of reserves is already excessive may help induce bankers to put idle funds to work, but the stimulation to new loans is likely to be limited. If increased reserve requirements reduce excess reserves to levels the bankers consider dangerously low, credit expansion will be checked or contraction will be induced. Changing reserve requirements is a heavy, blunt tool of credit control, compared with the gradual, flexible way in which open-market operations can be used. Thus, the Reserve authorities change reserve requirements only infrequently, depending instead primarily on open-market operations.

"Selective" Credit Controls.   The above controls aim to regulate the over-all volume of bank credit, rather than the particular use made of it. But the Federal Reserve Act specifically directs the Federal Reserve authorities to guard against the undue use of bank credit for speculative purposes. For the most part, reliance is placed on the judgment of the individual banker to see that the loans made are "sound." But, in addition, the Board of Governors has been given special powers to control the use of bank credit for particular purposes.

These controls aim at regulating the use made of bank credit, rather than the total volume extended. Such "selective," or "qualitative," controls may have an important direct impact on particular sectors of the economy. But their effectiveness is limited. A special control may restrain direct bank loans to finance stock-market speculation, but it cannot prevent the use of other bank credit for this purpose. If you borrow $10,000 at your bank for a regular business purpose, there is no restriction on how the funds are used once you spend them. The next recipient may speculate to his heart's content. This inability to restrain the flow of funds between sectors of the economy severely restricts the power of any qualitative credit-control device.

Selective controls have another big weakness, if you believe in free individual choice. They directly restrict individual choice among alternatives. Special controls on housing credit, for example, mean that the government diverts consumers away from buying houses to other ways of spending money. General controls, by contrast, limit the total amount of money, but they don't try to influence what kind of spending the borrower does.

Control of Stock-market Credit: Margin Requirements. Many times, customers buy stocks and bonds "on margin." This means that they pay the broker a cash "margin" (down payment) and borrow the rest of the purchase price from the broker, leaving the newly purchased securities as collateral for the loan. The broker, in turn, typically borrows from commercial banks what the security buyer does not put up as margin (cash). The smaller the margin required, the more the "speculators" can borrow of the purchase price. If margin requirements are raised, therefore, the use of bank credit for purchasing securities is restricted. If margin requirements are lowered, it becomes easier to use credit in buying securities.

Since the Securities and Exchange Act of 1934, the Board of Governors has had power to set minimum margin requirements for dealings on the major securities exchanges, ranging up to 100 per cent cash payment. In spite of their limited area of impact on the economy, since 1934 margin requirements have undoubtedly exercised an important restrictive influence on security speculation, as contrasted with the uncontrolled period of the late 1920's. In the big stock-market boom of the 1950's, security prices rose higher than in the 1920's. But with margin requirements at from 50 to 100 per cent, nearly all buying was on full cash payment, and there was little of the wild speculative fervor that characterized the late 1920's when most stock was bought on margins of 10 per cent or less. Nearly everyone agrees that Federal Reserve margin requirements exercise a healthy restraint on speculative stock purchases in a boom.

On the other side, however, if the stock market is in the doldrums and needs stimulation, reducing margin requirements does little to induce new borrowing to purchase securities. Here again, the Federal Reserve's power to check credit extension is far greater than its power to stimulate expansion.

Control of Consumer Credit. More credit extended to consumers by sellers has the same effect on consumer buying power as would direct bank loans to consumers. In fact, merchants and other sellers often finance their credit extensions by themselves borrowing from the banks.

Consumer credit, like stock-market credit, has proved highly volatile in booms and depressions, expanding rapidly in good times and contracting sharply in bad. Total consumer credit, for example, fell from about $6 billion in 1929 to $3 billion in 1933, and then rose spectacularly to $45 billion by 1959. Consumer borrowing to buy automobiles, refrigerators, television sets, deep freezers, and just about every other major "hard good," thus increased demand for durables by billions of dollars during the postwar booms. Buying "on time" has invaded almost every area of the consumer market, from false teeth to vacations in Bermuda with 18 months to pay.

In World War II, the Federal Reserve was given power to impose minimum down payments and maximum payment periods for all consumer goods purchased on installment terms. Raising down payments makes the purchase harder to make without cash in hand. Shortening the payment period raises the monthly payment required. For many buyers who seldom pay cash, these steps appear to restrain buying more than would a rise in the product's price.

The World War II goal was partly to restrain inflationary consumer demand for scarce goods, partly to divert consumer demand away from durables that competed directly with war production. But many people objected, especially the lower-income groups who couldn't afford to pay cash for everything. Why, they asked, should the few cars and refrigerators go exclusively to the rich? In wartime, shouldn't rationing or some other more equitable system of distributing scarce goods be adopted, rather than merely shutting out the poor by imposing drastic consumer-credit controls?

Consumer-credit controls lasted through the war and as long afterward as inflationary pressures continued strong. But after protracted argument, in 1952 Congress eliminated them, and has repeatedly refused to restore this power to the Federal Reserve in spite of requests from both the Board and the President for reinstatement of regulatory authority at least on a "stand-by" basis.

Control of Real-estate Credit. During the Korean War, Congress temporarily gave the Federal Reserve power to establish minimum down payments and maximum pay-off periods for mortgage loans on residential properties. The purpose was both to limit new credit extensions and to discourage the use of scarce materials in the construction or repair of houses. Experience with the regulation was too brief to permit generalizations. But there was evidence that the regulations had a good deal of bite against low- and middle-income home buyers. For them, it's the down payment and monthly payment that often matter more than the quoted price. As with other qualitative controls, real-estate credit control made little pretense of influencing the level of over-all spending, but was aimed instead at one particular sector of the economy.

New mortgage credit added over $100 billion net to the public's spending on construction over the past decade, on a base of only $73 billion of mortgage credit outstanding in 1950. Some economists advocated re-establishment of real-estate credit controls to check this expansion. But there was little support for the proposal. Indeed, other government agencies, especially the Veterans Administration and those established by Congress to encourage better housing, pushed strongly in the direction of easier housing credit.

"Direct Pressure" or "Moral Suasion." There is one last channel of Federal Reserve influence. When the Federal Reserve authorities want to restrict bank lending, they may use "direct pressure" or "moral suasion" on the bankers. Bank examiners may be instructed to tighten up their requirements for "good" loans and investments. Reserve officials may send letters to member banks, pointing

out the dangers of "speculative" loans and investments; and particular offending bankers may be singled out for special letters or interviews. Reserve officials may make public statements warning against loans for speculative purposes. In extreme cases, the Reserve Banks may simply refuse to lend to offending member banks that need additional reserves for expansion. There is not much evidence that such moral suasion is very effective.

Similarly, Federal Reserve officials can try to persuade bankers to make more loans in hard times. They may make public statements pointing out the need for business expansion; they may relax examiners' standards of "good" loans and investments; and so on. But such moral suasion to increase bank lending has had very little success indeed in expanding the volume of bank credit.

CONCLUSION   In perspective, as the Federal Reserve System nears the half-century mark in its history, how powerful have its credit controls proved? More important, how effectively have the Federal Reserve officials used these powers toward achieving stable economic growth?

It is clear that the Federal Reserve has enormous powers to check any credit expansion—indeed, to force mass contraction—if it chooses to use them. By dumping all its more than $20 billion of government securities on the market and by raising reserve requirements to their legal limits, the Federal Reserve could bring on a massive deflation sure to send the entire economic system into chaos. Of course, the Federal Reserve officials would never consider such a foolish action. But this extreme points up the great power inherent in the Federal Reserve's restrictive measures. Here the main problem is to use the controls effectively, not to seek more powerful weapons. One big question: Does the freedom of non-commercial bank financial institutions to generate near-monies seriously undermine the Federal Reserve's restrictive power? We shall look at this question presently, in Chapter 14.

In stimulating expansion, the story is different. Here the Reserve authorities' job is much harder. Their ability to create reserves is great—and can readily be made even greater by Congress. But will the banks make new loans in depression merely because they receive new excess reserves? The evidence raises grave doubts. Nor are the qualitative controls of much use in encouraging credit expansion. By flooding the banking system with excess reserves the Reserve authorities can almost surely expand the nation's money supply, since the banks will buy government securities even if they won't lend to business concerns and consumers. But if direct loans to business and consumers are needed to stimulate investment and consumption, the problem may be more recalcitrant.

How well have the Federal Reserve authorities used the tools that Congress has put at their disposal? For the answer to this—the $64,000 question—we need to wait until Chapter 14, after we have had a look in the next four chapters at the complex forces that determine the level of income, employment, and prices in the American economy.

REVIEW—CONCEPTS AND INSTITUTIONS TO REMEMBER

This chapter has introduced several important concepts and institutions, of which the following are particularly worth remembering:

Board of Governors	open-market operations
Open Market Committee	rediscount rate
Federal Reserve Banks	general (quantitative) credit controls
member banks	selective (qualitative) credit controls
gold reserves	margin requirements
"creation" of bank reserves	consumer credit

1. In what ways are the objectives of a central bank (like the Federal Reserve) different from those of a commercial bank?

2. We don't have government agencies to regulate in detail the operations of most business concerns. Why, if at all, are the banks different enough to require the Federal Reserve in our private-enterprise economy?

3. The unsung service functions of the Federal Reserve comprise its greatest contribution to the national welfare. (True or false? Explain.)

4. The powers of the Federal Reserve to restrict credit expansion in booms are greater than those to stimulate credit expansion in a depressed period. (True or false? Why?)

5. Suppose the Federal Reserve takes the following actions. In each case, explain what will be the likely effect on the total money supply:
   a. It sells $1 billion of government securities to the banks.
   b. It lowers reserve requirements to 10 per cent for all member banks.
   c. It buys $1 billion of government securities from individuals and business concerns.
   d. It buys direct from the United States Treasury $1 billion of newly issued government securities.
   e. It lowers rediscount rates by 1 per cent.

6. Suppose we should become involved in war again and Treasury borrowing from the banks plus increased demand for currency "used up" nearly all the gold available for backing Federal Reserve notes and member-bank deposits (reserves) in the Federal Reserve Banks. Would you then advocate lowering the present 25 per cent gold reserve requirement against Federal Reserve notes and deposits, as was done under similar circumstances in 1944? Why or why not? If not, what policy would you advocate?

7. Suppose the Federal Reserve wants to tighten credit and raise interest rates. Evaluate the following possible measures:

FOR
ANALYSIS
AND
DISCUSSION

    a. Federal Reserve sales of government securities to commercial banks.

    b. Federal Reserve sales of government securities to the public.

    c. Raising member-bank reserve requirements.

    d. Raising rediscount rates on commercial paper.

    e. Raising margin requirements covering stock-market purchases.

8. Suppose the economy is in a serious depression. The commercial banks have substantial excess reserves. What steps would you advocate that the Federal Reserve take to help stimulate lending and recovery? Why?

10

The Theory of Money, Income, and Prices[1]

W hat determines how fast an economy grows? Why do we have booms and depressions? For over a century economists have examined these problems from every side. Today, though we have a reasonably good understanding of both, so many unanswered questions remain that they probably get more attention in current economic research than does any other area.

This and the following chapter present the theory of income, employment, and prices—the analytical models that have proved most useful in understanding economic growth and fluctuations in the American economy. No section of the book is more important for you to understand thoroughly.

Economists all agree that, fundamentally, the "real" productive capacity of any economic system sets the upper limit to its performance at any time. These real factors are productive resources, technology, and economic organization. But his-

---

[1] This chapter may be omitted by those instructors who prefer to emphasize only the income-expenditures approach presented in Chapter 11. Or it may be equally well used after Chapter 11.

tory shows clearly that some systems are able to increase their productive capacity rapidly, by exploiting the productive possibilities of these real factors, while others seem to get nowhere. Equally, history shows that nations often fall far short of obtaining the maximum production possible from their economies. Sometimes massive depressions throw up to a third of the labor force out of work.

One large group of economists has focused on money as the key to the explanation of how well we use our productive capacities. Money demand is the driving force in a private-enterprise economy. Thus, in this monetary approach the spotlight is on the supply of money and how it is used. More recently, many economists have become dissatisfied with this strong focus on money *per se,* and have devised more complex models which pull in many other factors that influence the rate of spending in our economy.

To simplify matters, the older "monetary" approach is presented separately, briefly, in this chapter. Some economists now consider this approach mainly of historical interest. But many others believe that it still offers the simplest and best approach to understanding booms, depressions, and inflations, plus at least some aspects of economic growth.

Chapter 11 presents a more complex model of the determinants of income, employment, and prices—called the "income-expenditures" approach—along lines primarily developed during the past quarter-century. This approach incorporates some aspects of the "monetary" approach, and adds a number of additional important variables and relationships.

There is nothing contradictory about the two approaches. You don't have to be for one and against the other. Most economists find them complementary, and useful for different purposes. Both are included here, partly because they give some historical perspective on how economic thinking has developed, and partly because you may find them helpful in thinking through real-world problems.

THE FACTS First, a look at the facts about money in relation to gross national product and the price level. Figure 10-1 summarizes these relationships since 1900.

The bottom line shows the growth in the money supply, averaging 5¾ per cent per annum since 1900. The next two lines show that "real" gross national product (i.e., g.n.p. in constant prices) rose at about 3¼ per cent per annum over the same period, while actual (money) g.n.p. rose at about 5½ per cent annually. The top line shows that the price level rose by an average of about 2¼ per cent annually, the difference between money g.n.p. and real g.n.p.

It is clear that the increase in the money supply on the average paralleled closely the growth in *money* g.n.p.; and that about two-thirds of the growth in money g.n.p. was growth in real output while about one-third was inflation.

Deviations from these average (trend) growth lines are perhaps as interesting as the trends themselves. The big inflation of World War I is clearly visible. The money supply shot up from 1915 to 1920, as new money was created to finance the war, and prices soared roughly apace. The money supply began to fall below the economy's 3¼ per cent real long-term growth rate about 1927, and the long depression of the 1930's began two years later. The worst collapse of that depression (in both output and prices) came from 1929 to 1933, when the money supply was contracting severely.

Money, Gross National Product, and the Price Level, 1900-1958

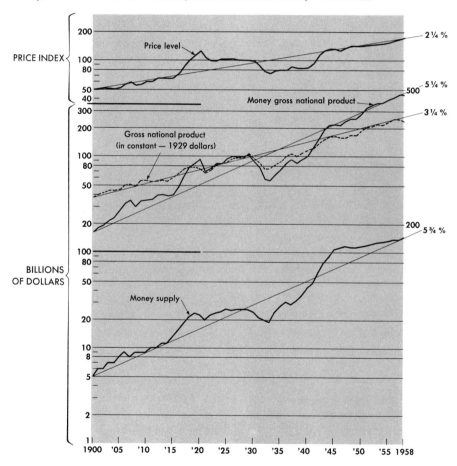

FIG. 10-1   The money supply has risen about 5¾ per cent annually, and money gross national product just a little slower. G.n.p. in constant dollars has grown only about 3¼ per cent annually, however, and a price rise of 2¼ per cent annually accounts for the difference. Has the excess of money supply over the growth in real g.n.p. caused the inflation? (Sources: Federal Reserve Board, U.S. Department of Commerce, and Raymond Goldsmith, *A Study of Saving in the United States,* National Bureau of Economic Research, 1956.)

The World War II experience differed from that of World War I. Again the money supply was expanded rapidly through selling bonds to the banks to obtain war finance. But widespread price and wage controls held inflation to a creep during the war, and it was not until their removal after 1946 that prices rose rapidly. Thus, if the new money generated inflation, it was far more spread out than during World War I. Strikingly, the growth in the money supply leveled off around the mid-1950's, and from 1955 to 1957 the money supply was substantially constant. This preceded the recession of 1957.

Many economists infer from these facts that the money supply exercises a powerful effect on the level of real output and prices. They argue that when the money supply rises much faster than the growth in the economy's real output potential, inflation results. When the money supply fails to rise as fast as real output potential, depression results. Growth in the money supply parallel to growth in potential real g.n.p. (about 3¼ per cent per annum over the past half-century) will go far to ensure stable economic growth. But others say this is too simple an analysis of a highly complex problem.

THE
MONETARY APPROACH

The monetary approach says that money is the center of the income and employment problem. It takes money to buy things. However much you may want something, unless you either have money or can get it your desires won't influence producers very much.

The classical economists—the long tradition from Adam Smith, through David Ricardo, John Stuart Mill, and Alfred Marshall, up to the decade of the 1920's—had a relatively simple view of the matter. In a nutshell, they thought that a free-market economic system would ordinarily tend to be self-equilibrating at something like full employment. They reasoned that whenever resources are unemployed or unsold, their market price moves down until it falls low enough so that everything offered is hired or sold. There may be temporary deviations from full employment, and indeed these deviations may involve violent crises or inflations. But they will be aberrations, explained largely by special external factors such as wars or famines, by cumulative, herd-like sweeps of expectations that lead to gluts of overproduction or to depressions, and especially by the erratic behavior of the monetary system.[2]

Suppose that an economic system always tends toward full-employment equilibrium. Then if there is a lot of money available for spending, the average price per unit of goods sold will be high. If there is little money, the price level will be low. Thus, with real output and employment roughly set by full-employ-

---

[2] These remarks do less than justice to the classical economists, but the purpose here is merely to give some background on economists' emphasis on money as a central factor in the cycle, not to paint a complete picture of what different economists thought.

ment capacity, the classical economists felt that fluctuations in the money supply would lead primarily to fluctuations in the general price level. More money (for example, government-issued money to finance war) would mean price inflation. Less money (for example, when the "run" on banks forced many of them to close during the early 1930's) would mean price deflation.

To be sure, the classical economists didn't think that money affected only the price level. They knew that price inflation and deflation are interrelated with the over-all level of economic activity, that financial crisis means unemployment and bad business as well, and that inflation means price speculation, high employment, and a disruption of productive relationships. Thus, by the 1920's, economists were beginning to see that changes in price levels, production, and employment were all interrelated parts of the same process. Their interest shifted gradually from money as a determinant of the price level, to money and other factors as determinants of the price level, employment, and production.

In looking at money as the center of the problem, economists have concentrated on two related analytical models—the income-velocity model, and the cash-balances model. We will consider these two monetary models separately, though they are closely related. In using them both, people are often vague on whether they are talking about money as a cause of changes in the price level or as a cause of changes in total income and employment. We shall try to avoid this confusion by focusing first on money as a determinant of the total level of expenditures (say of money gross national product). Then we can ask later when expenditures mean more output and when they merely mean higher prices.

THE INCOME-VELOCITY MODEL The income-velocity model emphasizes two factors in explaining the level of total expenditures—(1) how much money people have, and (2) how fast they spend it. A simple "equation of exchange" (proposed by Professor Irving Fisher a half-century ago) points up the relationships involved in this approach. The equation is:

$$MV = PT$$

M stands for the amount of money in the hands of the public; V for the average velocity of circulation, or the number of times each dollar is spent per time period; P for the price level, or average price per unit sold; and T for the number of units sold during each time period—the "real" volume of transactions carried out at average price P.

For example, in a very simple hypothetical economy, suppose M is $1,000. Suppose further that during some year 2,000 units of physical goods, a mixture of many sorts of goods, are produced and sold, and that their average price is $2. The T in our equation would then be 2,000, and the P would be $2; PT

equals $4,000, the total amount paid for the goods sold. We have left the V, the average number of times per year each dollar is spent on the average. Here the V is obviously 4, since total expenditures on the goods sold were $4,000 ($P$ times T), so each of the one thousand dollars must have been spent four times during the year on the average to account for the $4,000 of expenditures. The whole equation is then:

$$M(\$1,000) \cdot V(4) = P(\$2) \cdot T(2,000)$$

If you think a minute about this equation, you will see that the two sides are defined so that they will always be equal. MV is simply the total amount *spent* on goods and services during the time period—the total number of dollars multiplied by the average number of times each dollar is spent in the period. PT is the total amount *received* for goods and services during the period—the number of units sold multiplied by the average price per unit. The two are identical; what is spent, someone receives. If we now add another $1,000 in our example, and keep V and T unchanged, clearly P will have to be $4 to make the equation balance at $8,000. In economic terms, prices would be twice as high on the average because expenditures doubled but only the same physical volume of goods was sold.

This relationship underlies what is often called the "quantity theory of money." In its crudest form, this theory states that any change in the quantity of money will be followed by a proportional change in the price level. This necessarily follows, the equation shows, only if V and T remain constant, or just offset each other. In the real world, they certainly may not remain constant; indeed more money may stimulate both to rise. Thus, more sophisticated economists have developed more careful analyses in the tradition of the quantity theory, as indicated below.

The equation of exchange is obviously a truism. It just says that every dollar spent by someone is received by someone else. Why, then, is it a significant analytical tool, or model? The answer is, because it sets out four important variables on which attention may usefully be centered in analyzing booms and depressions, inflations and deflations. And it sets forth these variables in a way that points up some of their broad relationships—e.g., it is the amount of money people have, multiplied by the average number of times each dollar is spent, that gives the total annual amount of spending. The equation certainly doesn't provide any answers, but it is a simple framework for looking at the complex real world.

Gross National Product and the Equation of Exchange.   What we want to get at is total expenditures on goods and services currently produced—at gross national product. We can do this by defining T to include just those units of goods and services that enter g.n.p. *Then MV and PT become measures of gross national product. In this case, on the MV side we can count only expenditures on goods and services that enter into current g.n.p.; obviously V must apply to the* *same transactions as* P *and* T *if the equation is to hold. So defined,* V *is often called "income velocity," since it measures only those spendings that enter into the national income accounts. Similarly,* PT *becomes goods and services currently produced and valued at their current prices.*[3]

M and V in the Equation. The equation of exchange focuses attention on *M* and *V* as determinants of the level of total expenditures. Suppose we think of the receipts (*PT*) side as by and large passive, as the classical economists did. Then the equation suggests that an increase in the amount of money will lead to a higher volume of expenditures, unless it is offset by a decrease in the velocity at which the money is spent. Thus it points a finger at the government as one of the major forces controlling the supply of money; another finger at private borrowing from the banks as another source of increase in the money supply; and another finger at any other force that influences the money supply.

During World War II, for example, the money supply (currency plus checking deposits) increased from about $36 billion to $110 billion, largely because we financed the war in considerable part by creating new money. The equation of exchange warns you to look up such figures as these if you want to understand what happened to g.n.p. during the war. It suggests that you investigate the behavior of the commercial banks in making loans and investments during the war, and the behavior of the governmental agencies influencing the amount of new money created. In short, it says that if you want to understand what happened to income, employment, and prices, you need to understand what caused this great increase in the nation's money supply.

Second, the equation tells you that with such a big increase in the money supply, g.n.p. rose in the same proportion unless income velocity rose or fell during the war.

What did happen to income velocity (*V*), the other spending factor emphasized by the equation of exchange? It declined gradually throughout the war period. People spent their dollars more slowly; on the average, they held each one longer before spending it. This was partly because many goods were unavailable, partly because there was a lot of patriotic pressure against spending, and partly because incomes rose very rapidly relative to prices, which made saving easier. As a result, total expenditures on g.n.p. (*MV*) rose only from $91 billion

---

[3] If we wanted to, we could include in T *all* transactions during the period, adding in purchases of stocks and bonds, of existing houses, of second-hand automobiles, and so on. This would greatly increase the dollar figures on each side of the equation, since there is a huge volume of transactions each year that do not represent expenditures on current output. In 1959, g.n.p. was about $475 billion, whereas total expenditures on all transactions were estimated roughly at $3 to $5 trillion—perhaps ten times g.n.p. If we were to use this broader approach, *V* would reflect spending on all transactions, and might be called "transactions velocity." We would have to use this approach, for example, if we were interested in the general price level, including prices of existing assets as well as of currently produced goods and services.

to $211 billion, a good deal less, proportionately, than the increase in the money supply. The equations of exchange for 1939 and 1946 are shown below:

$$1939: M \text{ (\$ 36 billion)} \cdot V \text{ (2.5)} = PT \text{ (\$ 91 billion)}$$
$$1946: M \text{ (\$110 billion)} \cdot V \text{ (1.9)} = PT \text{ (\$211 billion)}$$
$$1958: M \text{ (\$140 billion)} \cdot V \text{ (3.1)} = PT \text{ (\$440 billion)}$$

The equation for 1958 shows what happened as the long postwar boom continued and as money became "tighter." The Federal Reserve's "easy money" policy was gradually discontinued in the early 1950's, and both business and consumers found it harder to borrow at banks. Interest rates rose, providing an inducement to put idle cash balances to work. Businesses were forced to "economize" cash balances, running with smaller cash balances relative to their sales. V rose, back above the level of the booming 1920's.

We looked in detail, in Chapters 8 and 9, at the banking mechanism that increases or decreases M in the equation. Getting at the determinants of V is a tougher job. Other monetary theorists, using a "cash-balances" approach, focused on that problem, as we shall see in the next section.

MV = PT and Forecasting g.n.p.   The equation of exchange also helps in forecasting the level of total expenditures for the future. It suggests that if you want to predict, you had better concentrate on examining the forces that determine the money supply and those that determine the rate at which people spend their money. Professor Fisher argued that by and large his V (which was a little different from ours) was relatively stable over long periods, so that changes in M could be expected to have roughly proportionate effects on PT.[4] This expectation simplified the job down mainly to predicting M, and M is something the government can control reasonably well. He emphasized, however, that over short periods V might fluctuate sharply, largely because people's expectations about future prices and business conditions might shift in response to temporary conditions. Still, these shifts would be temporary, and the stabler long-term V was the basic force.

Has the evidence borne Fisher out? Yes and no. Over the long pull, V, when adjusted to a per capita basis, has been surprisingly stable, although there has been a gradual downward drift. Seldom have wide shifts away from this long-term trend of V lasted for more than a few years. On the other hand, the temporary fluctuations in V have been whoppers, and attempts to predict them have not been very successful. In general, both M and V have dropped sharply in depressions and have increased in booms. The World War II experience cited above provides an instructive example of how far astray any such simple generalization can lead you if you use it as an automatic predictor.

---

[4] In fact, Fisher went further and argued that changes in M would generally lead to corresponding changes in P, since T as well as V would be roughly stable—a simple version of the "quantity theory of money."

Figure 10-2 summarizes the facts about income velocity since 1900. It has indeed been relatively stable as a long-run matter. But the short-run fluctuations seem to many economists to throw grave doubts on its usefulness as any except the most general long-run predictor of the relationship between the money supply and total spending on g.n.p. The chart shows clearly the tendency of velocity to rise and fall with booms and depres-

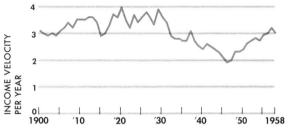

FIG. 10-2   Income velocity is relatively stable over the long run, but it rises and falls with booms and depressions, and sometimes falls drastically for special reasons— look at the World War II period. (Calculated from data for Fig. 10-1 by dividing the money supply into money g.n.p.)

sions, except when interrupted by special factors like the war conditions of 1940-46.

$MV = PT$ is a simple and clearly a rough model. It needs to be used with care. Certainly the crude quantity theory of money (that prices always change in proportion to the stock of money) to which the equation is sometimes tied is not acceptable; nor does the quantity theory necessarily follow from the equation. But simple as it is, $MV = PT$ provides a useful framework for thinking about money in relation to prices and output, especially over the long run and when big changes in the money supply occur.

THE CASH-BALANCES MODEL   Most economists who believe that money is a central factor in determining the level of total spending feel that the income-velocity model doesn't go far enough in analyzing V. We typically don't decide how fast we are going to spend our money. Rather, we decide how much we can afford to spend in relation to how much money we have and expect to receive. In a nutshell, these economists say, the crucial question is this: How big are the cash balances that people feel they need to hold? Nobody wants to hold cash for its own sake —you can't eat it, drink it, or use it directly for anything. If people decide they don't need to hold as much cash as they have on hand, they will spend it. But if they feel that they need larger cash balances, they will hold down their expenditures to build up their cash balances.

Obviously, this approach is closely related to the income-velocity approach. If the public becomes wary of the future and decides it needs a bigger nest egg in cash balances, the level of expenditures will indeed be reduced. The income-velocity man would say, "Of course, because V decreases." The cash-balances man says it's because the public decides to build up its cash balances. The latter is probably a more realistic description of what motivates people's behavior. But in principle, you can get the same result either way.

Studying the motives that lead people to hold more or less money can provide insight into what determines the level of total expenditures. The cash-balances model emphasizes the "transactions" motive (having enough money for day-to-day individual and business purposes), the "precautionary" motive (having money on hand to be prepared for unforeseen contingencies), and the "speculative" motive (holding money because you think the prices of things you want to buy are coming down). When these motives are growing stronger, you can be pretty sure that total expenditures by individuals and businesses are going to drop. Conversely, when the motives for holding money are weakening, you can look for increased spending. These motives give a framework for analyzing the cash balances that people will try to hold. Combine them with an analysis of what determines *M,* and you have the core of the cash-balances approach.[5]

Suppose, for example, that you have a current cash balance at midmonth of $1,000, and that you receive a monthly salary of $500 at the end of each month. Obviously the level of your cash balance will fluctuate monthly, jumping up when you are paid and gradually drifting down through the month. But what will lead you to change the *average* level of your balance, assuming your income stays the same?

A simple example: Suppose you are planning an expensive vacation trip in a couple of months. This will probably lead you to build up your cash balance (by cutting back current expenditures). Here is the transactions motive at work; you need more cash to take along and pay the bills on your trip. But it may have a precautionary element as well. You will want to take more than enough cash along to pay exactly the expenses you estimate for the trip. Your car may break down, or you may get sick; in such a case you don't want to be caught a thousand miles from home almost broke. And you may even be influenced by a small speculative motive; maybe you feel that prices are likely to drop on some espe-

---

[5] The cash-balance enthusiasts also use an equation, first developed at Cambridge University in England and hence often called the "Cambridge equation." If you think in terms of algebra, it may be helpful to you. The equation is

$$P = \frac{M}{kR}$$

Here P and M may be roughly the same as in the Fisher equation above. But k and R are different. R stands for "resources"—the total of resources (goods) held by the society. Loosely, it might be thought of as society's total stock of real wealth. k is the proportion of that total stock over which people want to hold control in the form of money (current purchasing power).

Thus, the equation says that, given any amount of money and total supply of resources, an increase in people's desire to hold purchasing power over resources by increasing their cash balances will lower prices. Conversely, a decreased desire to hold money (purchasing power over resources) will raise prices as people spend their money to decrease their cash balances.

The k in this equation focuses attention on people's demand for money to hold, and the way it is defined suggests that the main reason people hold money is to hold control over R (real wealth). The emphasis on the three motives for holding money indicated in the text above came after the equation was first developed. Note also that the P here must be the price level of all R (resources), just as in the Fisher equation the P must refer to the goods and services included in the rest of the equation.

cially attractive items along the way, and you want to be ready to buy if that happens. This very simple example is intended merely to illustrate how these motives may show up in individual decisions on building up or spending down cash balances.

Some broader examples now may help show how this analysis of the motives for holding cash can contribute to thinking through real-world problems. Suppose businessmen expect business to pick up and decide they need to increase their cash balances to handle increased needs for working capital (*the transactions motive*). The model suggests that, unless some other factors change too, this behavior will decrease total spending and prices, as businesses hold back income to try to build up their cash balances. Or suppose individuals and businesses increasingly expect a rise in the prices of the goods they buy. Here the *speculative motive* for holding cash is weakened; holding cash becomes less attractive than holding goods when the price of goods is expected to rise. Result: Other things equal, spending will increase and prices will rise (as expected). Increased uncertainty and wariness about the future (a rise in the *precautionary motive*) tend to reduce spending and prices, as people withhold income to build up cash balances against the uncertainty.

Suppose now that everyone decides to build up his cash balance by decreasing his rate of expenditures relative to his income. Will the result be higher cash balances all around? If your inclination is to say yes, stop and think again. With any given supply of money, there can be no change in the *total* amount of cash balances held, because there isn't any more or less money for the public to hold. Thus the result of a general attempt to build up cash balances is merely a decrease in total expenditures, *not* an increase in total cash balances, as long as nothing happens to change the total amount of money available. In velocity terms, the result is a lower V. (Remember the fallacy of composition.)

Will this concerted attempt to accumulate cash be completely thwarted? The answer is no. By pulling down total expenditures, the public's desire to build up cash balances will ultimately decrease prices (as well as production and employment). As prices fall, the existing amount of money will give command over more and more real goods and services. Thus the public will in fact increase the *real* purchasing power of its cash balances to the desired higher level, even though it cannot increase the total *dollar* amount. Perhaps people haven't planned it that way, but they have increased the real value of their cash balances by bringing on deflation and lower incomes, and perhaps lower output and employment.

MONEY, GOODS, AND BONDS   One of the great attractions of the monetary approach to the analysis of income, employment, and prices is that it promises a ready guide to monetary policy. Suppose we want to raise spending on goods and services. If the desire to hold cash balances is constant (alternatively stated, if V is constant), putting more money into the hands of the public will increase spending proportionately. But now we need to introduce a serious complication, to be explored fully later on—the V may indeed *not* stay constant.

Suppose the government simply prints new money and passes it out as unemployment relief. The recipients may spend it on goods as predicted. But they may instead spend it on bonds or other securities, instead of on goods and services. If so, they will bid up the prices of bonds, thereby (what is the same thing, as we shall see later) bidding down interest rates, without having any effect on spending for goods and services. This result doesn't seem very likely, because the new money increases the spendable income of the recipients.

But suppose instead that the government puts the new money into circulation by buying up bonds which the public holds. In that case, the public's spendable income is not increased. It merely exchanges near-money (bonds) for money. Will this increase in cash balances lead to increased spending on goods and services? Or merely to an increase in the price of bonds—a decrease in V, so far as income velocity is concerned? The decrease in V seems likely in this case.

This questions the whole cash-balances approach, which implies that people decide between two alternatives—spending money on goods and services, or holding it. It introduces a third possibility—spending money on bonds. Perhaps people determine their basic spending on goods according to their incomes, and merely shift their liquid balances between money and near-monies as the government (banking system) increases or decreases the supply of money. Many modern economists think so. And this is one of the main possibilities leading to the adoption of the income-expenditures approach in the next chapter.

HOW IMPORTANT IS MONEY AFTER ALL? People who use the monetary approach usually assume two things—implicitly or explicitly. The first is that the MV side of the monetary equation is the active side, while the PT side is by and large passive. The second is that by looking primarily at money we are getting at the central determinant of the spending decisions that individuals and businesses make.

Recently, many economists have become convinced that they need to go beyond this focus on money to understand spending decisions. They argue that individuals' *incomes* are the dominant factor that determines how much they spend. Similarly, they suggest that past and prospective business orders and profits or other such factors, not the money supply, are the basic determinants of business spending.

Does this mean that money isn't really very important after all, and that the monetary approach outlined in this chapter won't help much in understanding real-world problems?

Some of the older economists probably over-emphasized the supply of money as the central force determining the level of spending. But the relatively stable long-run relationship between the money supply and the total level of spending is hard to brush off. And in the big inflations, money has always played a central role. Runaway increases in the money supply have invariably been associated with soaring prices, usually in a dog-chasing-his-own-tail upward spiral where more money leads to higher prices, which lead the government to print more money to pay its bills, which leads to still higher prices, and so on. In such spirals, the cash-balances analysis, too, is highly relevant. The speculative motive takes over; people want to get rid of their cash as fast as they can convert it into goods because they expect prices to rise further.

Lastly, one fact about the importance of money stands out: Expanding total output has come only when the money supply was growing at least *roughly* at the same rate as the productive capacity of the economy. Perhaps the growing money supply has been merely an unessential concomitant of economic expansion, though few economists would rate it so unimportant. Perhaps monetary expansion is merely a necessary condition for a growing real g.n.p., albeit not a major causal force. Perhaps monetary expansion is a vital, active, causal factor. Nobody is sure which, but either way, money is important.

Thus the simple monetary approach outlined above is worth the effort to understand. (1) It is still the simplest framework for thinking about many real-world problems that you read about in the newspaper every day. (2) The equation of exchange is a valuable guide to straight thinking about money, prices, and real production, even though you may want to use other more elaborate models as well. And (3) the supply of money may turn out to be a dominant factor after all in some of the world's most important problems, especially inflation.

REVIEW—CONCEPTS TO REMEMBER

The following new concepts are worth careful review:

equation of exchange

velocity of circulation

income velocity

transactions velocity

cash balances

transactions motive

speculative motive

precautionary motive

quantity theory of money

1. In a period of uncertainty, everyone is likely to decide to build up his own cash (money) balance. In the absence of government action, how will this affect:
a. The total amount of money?
b. The total volume of money payments?
c. The price level?
Explain your answers, using the equation of exchange $(MV = PT)$.

FOR ANALYSIS AND DISCUSSION

2. Suppose the Federal Reserve holds the quantity of money constant over the next decade. Would you expect a constant, rising, or falling price level? Explain.

3. Many economists estimate that by 1970 gross national product may be $750 billion. How big a money supply would you estimate will be required for a g.n.p. of that size? Would you expect the required increase to be produced by the commercial banks in response to business and consumer demands for loans? What role, if any, should the Federal Reserve play?

4. By and large, would you expect prices to rise in proportion to any major increase in the quantity of money? Why or why not?

5. What are the major factors that lead you to increase or decrease the size of your cash balance? Would these same factors apply also for other individuals? For business firms?

6. "In depression, an increase in the money supply leads to more jobs; in full-employment periods, to inflation." Is this quotation correct? Does the equation of exchange help in analyzing it?

11

The Modern Theory of Income, Employment, and Prices

Most modern economists emphasize the circular flow of expenditures and incomes—from consumers to businesses back to consumers, as pictured in Figure 4-1. Joe Smith gets the money to spend on a car by working in the local steel mill. The steel company gets the money to pay Joe's wages by selling steel to General Motors. And General Motors gets the money to pay for the steel by selling cars to Joe and other consumers. Look back at Figure 6-2 for a more complete picture of this circular flow.

The modern theory of income, employment, and prices—often called the "income-expenditures approach"—stresses that what people spend on consumption and investment depends primarily on the incomes they receive, and only secondarily on such other factors as what their cash balances are. This approach, which grew out of the cash-balances analysis of motives for spending and saving, was first popularized by a noted economist, John Maynard Keynes, during the depression of the 1930's. Some of Keynes' new analytical tools have survived the test of time; others have vanished. But the approach has been developed and modified by hundreds of different economists who have worked with it, and it is now the most widely used model for analyzing the level of income and employment.[1]

The income-expenditures approach divides total spending into three big parts —private consumption, private investment, and government, as in the gross national product accounts. It focuses on each separately, and on their interrelationships. Leaving out government spending for the moment, this chapter looks first in detail at private consumption and private investment expenditures. What forces control them in an economy like ours? Second, it presents a simple analytical model interrelating the two sets of decisions as they combine to compose the private gross national product. Third, it asks: When will increases in spending mean more real output and employment, and when only inflation? Lastly, it brings the government back into the picture.

CONSUMPTION EXPENDITURES   What determines the total volume of consumer spending? The income-expenditures approach says that the most important single determinant is the income that consumers receive, and this seems reasonable. We would all like to have lots more things. But the painful fact is that most of us don't have big enough incomes to buy everything we want, and it is our incomes that generally put the ceiling on how much we can spend.

The Relation of Consumption to Income.   Careful studies have been made of what happens to consumption expenditures when incomes rise and fall. As far back as our data go, they show consumption rising with rising incomes and falling when incomes fall. This relationship is shown in Figure 11-1, which plots the relationship between total personal disposable income and total consumption expenditures in each year from 1922 through 1958. Disposable personal income (i.e., income left after paying personal income taxes) is used rather than total income, since most families presumably feel that income taxes must be paid, and choices between spending and saving are made only after allowance has been made for income taxes. This is especially appropriate for the great mass of wage and salary earners whose federal income taxes are withheld from their paychecks and sent directly to the government by employers.

In Figure 11-1, the dot for each year shows consumers' disposable personal income and what they spend on consumption. For example, in 1956 disposable personal income (read off the bottom scale) was about $291 billion and personal consumption expenditures (read off the vertical scale) were about $270 billion.

---

[1] Keynes achieved wide fame because he was one of the earliest outspoken advocates of fighting depression with deficit spending. Whatever you think about this issue—it's a subject for major investigation in Chapter 15—you should understand that the present chapter deals only with neutral analytical tools that can help you understand economic growth and instability, but that say nothing at all about what should be done about them.

Consumer Expenditures
and Disposable Personal Income

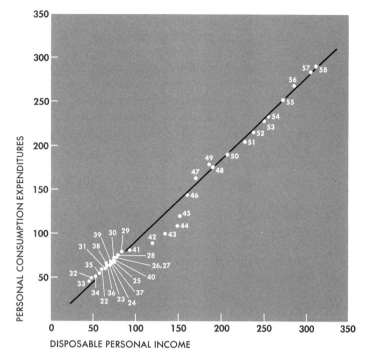

FIG. 11-1   In the depression, people spent nearly all their disposable income on consumption. During World War II they saved a large proportion. In peacetime prosperity, the relationship between disposable income and consumption looks stable. (Source: U.S. Department of Commerce.)

For 1933, the lowest year, disposable income was only $45 billion while personal consumption expenditures were about $46 billion, slightly higher than disposable personal income. People used accumulated savings and went into debt to keep themselves fed, clothed, and housed when incomes plummeted in the depression. The line running from southwest to northeast on the chart is drawn to "fit" the dots plotted. The fact that most years fall about on the straight line shows that the relationship between disposable income and consumption spending was a rather stable one. But the fact that some years are substantially off the line shows equally that in those years the stable relationship did not hold. During World War II, for example, consumption spending fell far below what would normally have been expected for the high incomes received during those years.

The Consumption Function.   The relationship between personal disposable income and consumption expenditures is generally called the "consumption function." It is also sometimes called the "propensity to consume," although this term is not an entirely happy one, since it implies plans or inclinations to consume, though we often want to look backward at what actually did happen.

As Figure 11-1 indicates, the consumption function is not always a simple, stable relationship. In analyzing consumer behavior, economists have learned to distinguish between two related but different things. Suppose disposable income in some year is $200 billion and consumer spending is $160 billion. Then we

169

might say that the_*average propensity to consume* is $160/200 = .80$, or 80 per cent. This is the relationship shown by Figure 11-1.

Now suppose that disposable income rises to $210 billion, an increase of $10 billion. Out of this increase, consumers spend $9 billion and save the other $1 billion. The way they divide their extra, or "marginal," income between spending and saving may not be the same as the way they have divided their previous income. Since we are often interested in analyzing *changes* in economics, we define separately consumers' *marginal propensity to consume*—the proportion of extra or marginal income spent on consumption. In the example, this would be $\frac{\text{change in consumption}}{\text{change in income}} = 9/10 = .90$, or 90 per cent. Of course, the marginal and average propensities to consume may be identical, but often they are not.

The Saving Function.   Consumers may spend or save their disposable income. Disposable income less consumption expenditures equals saving. Thus, from the consumption function we can automatically get a saving function. It is the proportion of disposable income saved, and it too may be viewed as either an *average* "propensity to save" or a *marginal* "propensity to save." In the example above, the average propensity to save would be .20 and the marginal propensity would be .10.

Figure 11-1 suggests that the relationship of consumer spending to disposable income is fairly stable. Figure 11-2, using a larger scale, shows directly the average propensity to save from 1929 through 1959.

Figure 11-2 again shows the special position of the war years, when saving rose to around 25 per cent of disposable income. But disregard the war years. What does the rest of the chart show?

It shows that during the postwar period the average propensity to save has been quite stable, at around 5 to 7 per cent. But when incomes were very low, in the depression of the '30's, savings almost vanished. In 1932 and 1933 the points are actually below the zero line, indicating that savings were negative; consumers spent more than their disposable incomes. In the other years of the '30's, the propensity to save was still very low, never getting above about 5 per cent, as consumers devoted almost all their incomes to consumption spending.

What Determines Consumption Expenditures?   The preceding section suggests that income is a major determinant of the level of consumer spending. But it also warns that income isn't enough to explain all the changes in consumer spending. A list of major factors that would command considerable agreement among economists now would include the following.

Income—Present, Past, and Future. Most economists agree that present income is the biggest single factor determining current consumer spending. The major evidence has been summarized above, and these data are strongly supported by common sense and by reflection. But careful statistical work over the past decade has suggested that more sophisticated relationships give a better explanation of consumption spending than present income alone.

The influence of past income is persistent. Once families have become used to any consumption level, they are reluctant to slide back down to a lower level, even if their income drops. Rather than cut back on consumption, they will (at least temporarily) reduce their saving levels substantially as income falls, well below the amount they would have saved at that income on the way up.

Consumer Saving as Percentage of Disposable Income

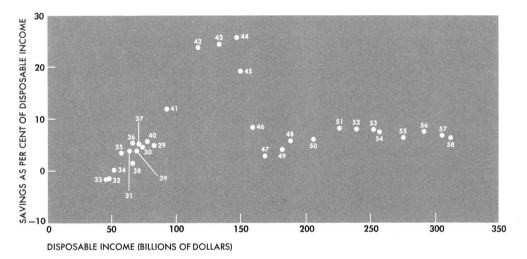

FIG. 11-2   Saving has been a stable percentage of disposable personal income in peacetime prosperity, but has fluctuated sharply in periods of severe depression and war. (Source: U.S. Department of Commerce.)

Expectation of future income is also apparently important, though this effect has not yet been so clearly established. Elaborate consumer surveys have been conducted regularly since 1946 to ascertain consumer income expectations and other expectation factors, and to determine their effect on consumer spending and saving. The surveys suggest that expectations of higher income tend to raise current tendencies to spend, but the results are far from conclusive.

Recently, sophisticated research workers have suggested that consumption spending is a substantially constant and similar proportion of disposable income for average families at all income levels, *if* we abstract from major disruptions like war and mass depression, *if* we include consumer durables with saving, *and if* we consider their "permanent" or "life-span" incomes rather than the particular income of any given year that may be distorted by special factors.

In one version, this approach says that families, consciously or subconsciously, estimate their long-range income over the years ahead (perhaps over their entire life cycle), and adjust their consumption spending and saving to their rough expectations. As a college professor, I have a pretty good idea how my salary will rise over the years ahead to retirement, barring major calamities and other such special factors. The same is true for many other families, though by no means all. Thus, during the early marriage years most families spend most of their income and even go in debt to start families and set up households. A little later, as income rises and these special expenses have been passed, they begin to save more, for retirement, to send their children to college, and so on. After their households are well furnished and their children are educated, they commonly save at a much higher rate. Late in life, as they retire partly or fully, saving drops again and often becomes negative. Looking over this life span, the average ratio of consumption to income is, if the investigations of this group stand up under further scrutiny, surprisingly similar and stable for typical families at all income levels. By the same token, it is a quite stable function of income for the population as a whole.

The "permanent income" hypothesis is closely related. It says that families base their consumption on what they expect their "permanent" income to be. Temporary deviations in income up or down from this permanent expectation will generally not affect consumption spending greatly. Rather, if income falls temporarily, the family will cut back its savings, use up its liquid assets, or go into debt to maintain consumption. If income bulges temporarily, the bulge is likely to go mainly into saving (including consumer durables). Just how families decide what their "permanent" income outlook is, is not very clear. Neither is the basis on which they estimate their life-span incomes above. But both these approaches are supported by empirical research findings that are highly promising in the search for deeper understanding of consumption behavior.

Liquid Assets. If a family has a large accumulation of liquid assets (currency, bank deposits, government bonds, and so on), it will feel freer to spend out of current income than it would otherwise. If its liquid assets are low, the reverse will be true. This seems like a reasonable hypothesis.

And there is some empirical support for it. During World War II, government borrowing placed nearly $250 billion of new liquid assets (money and government securities) in the hands of the public. After the war, this huge accumulation began to burn a hole in the public's pocket. Between 1945 and 1946, the propensity to consume rose from 81 to 92 per cent, and in 1947 to 98 per cent. Then, as incomes and prices caught up to a more normal relationship to liquid assets, the propensity to consume eased back down to previous full-employment peacetime levels.

But just how much weight should be given to liquid assets is problematical. Skeptics point out that other factors (especially the pent-up demand for consumer durables unavailable during the war) may explain the postwar spending burst, and detailed studies of family behavior have failed to establish that current spending is heavily influenced by *moderate* changes in liquid asset holdings. On the other hand, hark back to the cash-balances approach of the last chapter. The argument there was that when cash balances got *far* out of line with what the public felt was reasonable, they led to higher spending. People don't like to just hold big cash balances when there are so many other things they'd like to own. Best evidence to date is that when cash balances and other liquid assets get far larger relative to current income than the public is used to, they exert a strong pressure toward higher spending. But small variations in liquid assets don't play a very important role.

Consumer Credit. One way of getting around the limitation of income is to borrow money or buy on credit. A net increase in consumer credit correspondingly increases consumer spending power, beyond that provided by consumer incomes. Until the last couple of decades, consumers did little credit buying except in purchasing homes. But since World War II a huge volume of consumer durables—especially automobiles—has been bought on credit. By late 1959, families were nearly $45 billion in debt on consumer goods, compared to $6 billion in 1929 and about the same level in 1946. This growth represented a net addition to total consumer spending power over the period. Rising mortgage debt on houses added another $120 billion by 1959, up about $100 billion since 1946. In total, such new credit thus increased family buying power some $140 billion over the 1946-59 period.

But the deeper consumers are in debt, the less they can count on increasing this padding for their current income in future periods, and the greater is the potential inroad on current consumption spending if the debt should be "called." If you are in debt, part of your income must be used to pay it off rather than for consumption expenditures. By 1959, the proportion of current disposable income committed in this way had crept up to 12 per cent.

Availability of Goods. During World War II, you just couldn't buy lots of "hard goods" like refrigerators and automobiles, because their production was cut back or eliminated by the war. Reflecting this and other factors, the economy's propensity to consume dropped to below 75 per cent in 1943 and 1944. By 1946, consumers had accumulated an enormous backlog of demand for such consumer durables. The family car or gas stove can always be made to last a little longer, but repairs pile up and the old models get further and further out of date. Thus, the immediate postwar years saw an unprecedented boom in the demand for durables. This pent-up demand clearly played a major role in pushing up the postwar propensity to consume far above what most observers expected—to a peak of 98 per cent in the boom year of 1947 when normally such high income would have brought a much lower consumption-income ratio. Such long, severe shortages of consumer durables are rare. But their impact on consumer spending can be drastic.

Consumer Stocks of Durable Goods. Consumer spending on nondurables (food, clothing, etc.) and on services (personal care, housing, and utilities, etc.) is relatively stable, but spending on durables (automobiles, refrigerators, TV sets, etc.) fluctuates sharply with fluctuations in income. The fact that such durables last—that they can readily be used an extra year or two in most cases—means that their purchase can be postponed far more readily than the purchase of food or services. Thus, after consumers have engaged in a big buying spree on durables (for example, the 8-million-unit auto year in 1955), they are likely to slack off their buying until the new durables are at least a few years old, even though consumer income holds up. This is clearly true of any individual family; after you have a new refrigerator in the kitchen and one in the basement, it's pretty hard to sell you another new one next year. For the whole economy this effect evens out a good deal. But the bunched purchase of consumer durables nevertheless sometimes produces significant following changes in the propensity to consume.

Price Expectations. If you expect prices to rise, now is the time to buy before things go up. If you expect deflation, better hold off postponable purchases until prices go down. Changing expectations of future prices can bring violent shifts in the consumption-income relationship. Immediately after the outbreak of the Korean War in 1950, for example, current consumer saving dropped almost to zero as consumers rushed to stock up before prices skyrocketed and hard goods vanished from the market. Such drastic expectation shifts are rare, but they do occur. And when they do, they can dominate the more stable consumption-income relationships that generally prevail.

Long-run Stability and Short-run Instability. Where do all these considerations leave us on the determinants of consumer spending? At the risk of oversimplification, we can say that over the long pull the consumption-income relationship has been stable. At full-employment levels it has generally varied from the 92-95 per cent range for long only in response to strong, identifiable forces (such as war and postwar shortages). In spite of wide short-run fluctuations, consumers appear to adjust their consumption habits to rising incomes over the long run so as to maintain about the same average propensity to consume as in past prosperity periods. Will this tendency persist over the years ahead? Nobody knows. But like the long-run general stability of income velocity (the V in Chapter 10), the historical relationship has prevailed long enough to make it a reasonably good bet.

But in the short run, the American propensity to consume has been unstable and uncertain. Until the last few years, it was generally alleged that rising incomes in the upswing of booms have brought an increased propensity to save, and conversely with downswings into depression. This prediction rested primarily on the experience of the 1920's and 1930's. But the postwar boom ran just opposite to these predictions, and the mild recessions of 1948, 1954, and 1958 didn't set the propensity to consume back much. The consumption function is a useful analytical concept, but not one that gives quick and easy answers, especially for short-run predictions. Used with caution, it provides a useful tool for focusing thinking on the determinants of total consumption spending.

One other word of warning. Don't forget that businesses save too. In explaining consumer saving we are explaining only one part of total saving, just as consumer spending is only one part of total spending. In the real world, it's total saving in relation to total investment that will matter most.

PRIVATE INVESTMENT EXPENDITURES Investment spending is largely business spending—on plant, machinery, equipment, and inventories. Only one component of investment spending is made by individuals—that on new family-size housing—and this has seldom run over a quarter of total investment. So investment spending represents primarily the decisions made by businessmen—presidents, finance committees, boards of directors, and others, all the way down to the corner grocer.[2]

Investment spending has been the most dynamic, unstable major component of the gross national product. Most economists think it plays a central role in explaining both economic growth and fluctuations. Figure 11-3 shows the fluctuations of investment spending since 1929. The top line is gross, or total, investment spending. The lower line is net investment spending, which subtracts from the gross figure for each year the allowance to replace capital goods worn out (depreciated) during that year. The latter, of course, represents the net addition to our capital stock each year.

U.S. Investment Spending, 1929-1959

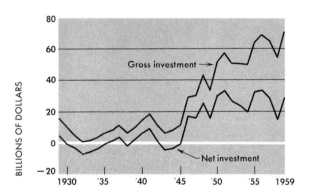

FIG. 11-3   Private investment spending fluctuates sharply. It now is far higher than ever before, but is about the same percentage of private g.n.p. as in other prosperity periods. (Source: U.S. Department of Commerce.)

What Determines Investment Spending?   What determines business investment spending? Lots of things—and probably different things at different times. Most simply, we might say that expected profits determine how much a business will spend on investment. When a businessman thinks he can invest funds in a new machine

---

[2] If consumer durables are included in investment, the proportion determined directly by consumers is higher, but still only about one-half.

and get back over the life of the machine what it cost, plus running costs, plus interest on his money, plus some extra return (profit), he will probably make the investment. In more technical economic terms, the businessman will invest when the expected rate of return on his invested capital exceeds the going interest rate—i.e., exceeds the return he could get by lending out or investing the money elsewhere.

The Marginal Efficiency of Investment.   Economists call the expected net rate of return on any investment the "marginal efficiency of investment." Suppose, for example, a businessman is thinking of buying a new milling machine for his plant. He knows the machine costs $10,000, and his engineers estimate that the machine will increase the annual output of the plant by about $2,000, with unchanged costs for labor and materials. To maintain the machine, however, will cost about $500 a year. (To make the example easy, assume the machine lasts indefinitely.) Thus the expected annual net return on the $10,000 investment in the machine will be $1,500, excluding the interest involved in using money to buy the machine. The marginal efficiency of investment here would thus be 15 per cent (i.e., $15 return annually on every $100 invested). Following the preceding paragraph, if he could borrow money at, say, 5 per cent to buy the machine, it looks like a good investment.[3]

What factors determine the marginal efficiency of investment in typical cases? Some of the major ones are:

Expected Product Demand. Note that it is *expected* net return on investment that matters. Thus, whenever a businessman *expects* the demand for his product to rise, this expectation increases the *expected* rate of return he can get by investing in new plant and equipment that will increase his output or improve the quality of his product. The fact that expectations govern the marginal efficiency of investment makes the marginal efficiency subject to wide fluctuations, depending on how the world looks to the businessman from day to day. If the world looks black, down goes the marginal efficiency of investment. Unfortunately, one of the things we don't know much about is just how volatile the effective expectations of responsible businessmen are. Much observation suggests that, though subject to wide swings, they are less volatile in response to day-to-day events than you might think, especially when major, long-range investment projects are under consideration.

Technology and Innovation. Research and development provide a big upward push for the marginal efficiency of investment. Obviously, the technical quality of the capital equipment under consideration is of central importance. If a new machine promises to lower costs or improve product quality dramatically, this

---

[3] For a more complete and precise analysis of how to compute the net rate of return on investments and on how businessmen sometimes look at the investment problem, see Chapters 32 and 41.

promise will be reflected in an anticipated large net return on the investment. Some investment is justified just to replace old machinery with duplicate equipment, but technological advance is the foundation of most present-day investment in plant and equipment.

Taxes. With modern corporation income tax rates, nearly all businessmen are primarily concerned with the expected rate of return on investment *after taxes.* In 1959, all corporations except the smallest paid income taxes of 52 per cent on their profits. (If we take this factor into account in the milling-machine example above, the investment loses a lot of its glamour.) An increase in corporation tax rates, other things equal, will lower the marginal efficiency of investment; a decrease in taxes will raise it.

General Outlook. It is never possible to estimate precisely all the factors involved over the life of a major investment. Will demand for the final product really be what we expect? Will tax rates stay the same? Will the government step in and regulate our business? Will a new machine come along next year that will make this one obsolete? With all this uncertainty, the general outlook of the businessman undoubtedly plays a big role in his final decision on whether or not to invest. History suggests that businessmen are optimistic souls. We usually think of General Motors, Procter and Gamble, and other such successes when we think of "business." But the statistics show thousands upon thousands of business ventures that fail each year, and very few that turn out to be General Motors, or anything like it. It's fortunate for the private-enterprise economy that so many businessmen are willing to bet they'll end up in the winner's circle.

Interest Rates—"The Cost of Money."   So much for the marginal efficiency of investment. The other side of the picture is the interest rate—the cost of the money needed to make the investment under consideration. If the businessman has to go to the bank or into the open market to borrow the funds needed, we can get a direct figure for the cost of money—maybe it's 5 per cent. But even if he has the money already, possibly in retained earnings from previous profits, he must still figure "implicit" interest on the funds used, since when he ties them up here he will be foregoing interest he could earn by investing them elsewhere. Here the proper interest rate to charge is a good deal harder to estimate, and, as we shall see below, some special considerations come in. But our hypothetical businessman must settle on some figure for his calculation.

The Investment Schedule and Investment Decisions.   At any time, many alternative investment opportunities are open to any business, some promising high rates of return, some low. We can graph these investment opportunities as in Figure 11-4 on page 178. Curve *II* is the investment schedule, showing that a few dollars could be invested at a high expected net rate of return, and that at lower expected rates more and more dollars can find promising outlets.

Figure 11-4 shows how the final investment decision will be made by our hypothetical businessman. Suppose the interest rate he must pay or charge himself is 4 per cent. Then any investment opportunity on his investment schedule above its intersection with the 4 per cent interest line is a profitable one, and he should take it, borrowing money if necessary. If the relevant interest cost is 5 per cent, the number of profitable investment opportunities is smaller—only those on *II* above the intersection with the 5 per cent line. At 4 per cent he should invest about $300,000 this year; at 5 per cent, only about $140,000.

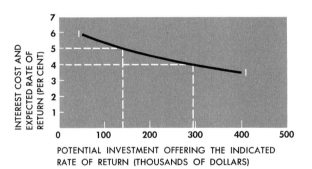

Interaction of Investment Schedule and Interest Costs

POTENTIAL INVESTMENT OFFERING THE INDICATED RATE OF RETURN (THOUSANDS OF DOLLARS)

FIG. 11-4   The curve, *II*, shows the amount of investment it will pay to undertake for each level of the interest rate.

This analysis is straightforward enough, and the logic is impeccable. In the business world, however, most businessmen seem to insist on introducing a big "safety factor" that is not included in our analysis, or they may call it something else. Company after company insists on an expected return of 15 or 20 per cent on new investment before it will take action, even though it can go to the banks or to the open market and borrow money at 5 per cent or less. What is the answer to this paradox?

Taxes are part of the story. They take half of most business profits. Another answer is the safety factor suggested above. Businessmen say they never know whether things will turn out as well as expected. Another answer is the reluctance of many businessmen to go into debt, even when it is directly profitable to do so. A fourth possibility is that businessmen calculate the effective cost of money to themselves as much higher than current market rates, especially if they must issue new stock to get funds. But these questions get further into business finance than we can go at this point. All we can do is note the real-world fact that most businesses want an expected rate of return well above the market rate of interest before they will invest. This fact does not change the general principle indicated above, but it does greatly reduce the number of investment opportunities that businessmen will consider attractive at any given time.

To summarize: The amount of investment in any given time period is determined by the marginal efficiency of investment in relation to the interest rate. Many business firms consciously go through the type of analysis outlined above for each major investment considered. Others make their calculations much more roughly. Some operate by hunch and intuition. For present purposes, assume that our model gives a rough approximation for the economy as a whole.

Business Saving and Investment Plans.   Many businessmen are reluctant to borrow money, even when they might use the funds profitably in their businesses. Throughout American business, firms have increasingly financed their expansion programs out of their own savings—that is, by reinvesting the depreciation funds they accumulate and by "plowing back" earnings into the business rather than paying them out to stockholders as dividends. These two sources—depreciation funds and undistributed profits—make up business saving.

Business saving during the past two decades has comprised well over half the economy's total savings. In 1958, business saving totaled about $45 billion, compared with personal savings of about $20 billion.

When businesses are reluctant to borrow money, their ability to finance investment out of their own savings may significantly limit their investments. Business saving depends heavily on profits in preceding years, and on the proportion of profits paid out as current dividends to stockholders. Businesses may increase their savings markedly by holding down dividends, in order to finance their investments. Eastman Kodak and B. F. Goodrich are two companies that have grown rapidly largely through reinvestment of retained earnings.

Since we usually think of business saving as flowing directly into real investment, attention here is focused primarily on business investment decisions. But business savings *may* pile up uninvested, and we dare not forget that they comprise a major part of the economy's total saving.

A MODEL OF NATIONAL
INCOME DETERMINATION   Leaving government spending and taxes aside for the moment, we now have the elements for constructing a simple model of the way consumption and investment spending decisions interact to determine the level of total spending and income. Begin with two simple, but central, propositions.

1. National income (in our simple case) by definition equals consumption spending plus investment spending. (Government will be introduced later.)

2. *In our economy, consumption and investment decisions are made, by and large, by different people.* Consumption and personal savings decisions are made by all of us, largely but by no means entirely, on the basis of the incomes we receive. Investment decisions are made primarily by businessmen, on the basis of many considerations, some related and others unrelated to current consumer spending. There is no reason to suppose that business decisions to invest will exactly match consumers' and businesses' decisions to save at any given time. *This is a crucial point.*

Simple Static Income-Determination Model.   Figure 11-5 shows a consumption function and a saving function. Consumption and saving here are functions solely of income. Line *CC* on the left-hand chart plots consumption spending against income at different income levels. The chart is drawn so that at any point on the 45° line, total consumption will just equal total income; there will be no saving. (This is true because every point on the 45° line is equidistant from the two axes.) Whenever consumption is below the 45° line, part of income is being saved. For example, at an income of 200, the economy would spend about 160 on consumption and save about 40. But if income were as low as 50, people would spend more than their full incomes on consumption; they would dissave. (For the moment, assume that all saving is done by individuals.)

The Consumption and Investment Schedules

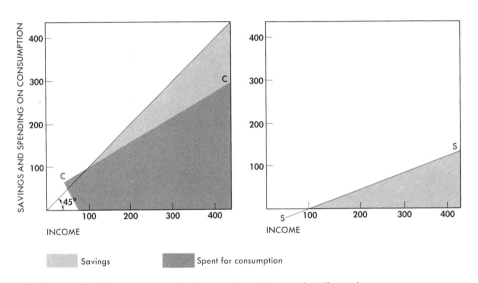

Savings   Spent for consumption

FIG. 11-5   The left-hand part of this diagram shows that people will spend a smaller proportion of their income on consumption as income rises, and save a larger proportion. The right-hand portion shows the same saving behavior by itself.

The right-hand part of Figure 11-5 shows the corresponding saving schedule. This is drawn simply by taking the amount saved at each level of income and consumption from the left-hand portion. Saving will be negative at low income levels and will become positive as income rises. The *SS* curve will, of course, cross the zero line at the same income level as the *CC* curve cuts the 45° line—about 100 in this case.

Figure 11-5 gives us the consumption and saving picture, then. Now we need to add investment spending. For simplicity, assume first that investment spending is determined "autonomously"—that is, by forces entirely independent of the level of consumer spending. Thus, assume that in this year investment spending will be 100 whatever the level of national income.

Now combine the different forces. On Figure 11-6 we plot investment spending in line *II*. This line is horizontal at a level of 100 because by assumption investment is the same amount regardless of the level of income. It intersects the *SS* curve at an income of about 350, and it is this income that is the equilibrium level. That is, 350 is the level toward which income will move if it is at any other level. No other income level will be a stable one, under the assumptions we are making.

Why is 350 the only equilibrium level? Because at this level the amount people want to save is exactly offset by the amount businessmen want to invest. Thus, the circular flow of income will be complete and stable. Consumers will receive 350 each time period, and (reading from the left-hand portion of Figure 11-5) will spend 250 on consumption and save 100. Each time period, business will invest 100, just equal to the amount consumers save; and so on for the succeeding time period. If income were any higher, people would be withholding more from the income stream than was being put back by investment spending, and the level of income would fall back toward 350. If income were lower, investment spending would be adding more to the income stream each period than was being withheld as consumer saving, and income would rise toward 350. Equilibrium will be achieved only when the amount consumers want to save is exactly equal to the amount businesses want to invest.

Figure 11-7 shows another and more complete, way of demonstrating the same result by looking at the whole income-consumption-investment picture. Here we have added to consumption spending (the *CC* curve of Figure

How Saving and Investment Determine Income

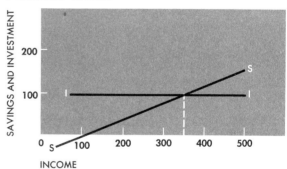

FIG. 11-6   Equilibrium income is established where the public wishes to save just enough to match the amount being invested.

11-5) the 100 of investment spending at each income level. Thus *C* + *I* equals consumption plus investment for each level of income. At an income of 350, *C* + *I* cuts the 45° line. That is, the sum of consumer spending plus business spending just equals national income. Try an income lower than 350, and you will see that something is wrong. The sum of consumption plus investment decisions is above the 45° line, and actual income will rise as consumption plus investment spending pushes it up. The opposite is true for an income higher than 350. Put in common-sense language, Figure 11-7 says that only at an income of 350 will consumer spending plus business investment spending put back into the income stream each period just the amount being received by consumers and businesses. Each period,

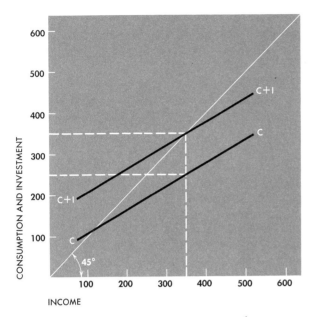

CONSUMPTION AND INVESTMENT

600
500
400
300
200
100

C+I
C
C+I
C
45°

100 200 300 400 500 600

INCOME

FIG. 11-7   Equilibrium income is established where the sum of consumption and
investment spending (on the vertical axis)
just equals national income (on the horizontal axis). This gives the same equilibrium
level as Fig. 11-6.

250 of consumer goods are produced and bought by consumers;
and 100 of new investment goods
are produced and bought by businesses, in effect using consumer
savings. Figures 11-6 and 11-7
show the same thing. They are
just different ways of looking at
the adjustment process.

*One reminder: All the above
analysis assumes that consumption and saving are passive functions of income received. If consumption spending changes for
any other reason, the equilibrium
level of income will be changed.*
In the model, such a consumption
change could be included as a
change in the propensity to consume.

**Equilibrium Not Necessarily Full
Employment.**   It is important
to recognize that this equilibrium
does not necessarily imply that the system is at full employment. Perhaps it would
take total spending of 400 per period to give a job to everybody in the labor
force. If so, an equilibrium income of 350 is an "underemployment equilibrium,"
and a higher real income could be obtained by increased spending that put the
unemployed back to work. On the other hand, if 350 at present prices is the full-
employment level, clearly a higher real income can be achieved only by increasing productive capacity, perhaps by drawing more people into the labor force,
working longer hours, accumulating more capital goods, or technological advance. More spending (say 450) without such real capacity expansion merely
means inflation.

Equilibrium is thus a neutral analytical concept. It does not imply anything,
either good or bad, about how well the economic system is performing.

Changing Investment—The Multiplier.   Suppose now that businessmen decide
to increase their spending on investment, perhaps because of a new invention.
This decision will raise the *II* curve in Figure 11-6 and the *C + I* curve in Figure
11-7. The result, common sense will tell you, is a higher equilibrium level for
income after the increase in investment. Conversely, a decrease in investment
spending will lead to a lower equilibrium level of income.

These results are obvious enough, but one additional fact may not be: *Each dollar of increase in investment will increase income by a larger, or multiplied, number of dollars.* This is because as each new dollar of investment is spent, it becomes income to a consumer who saves part but respends the rest on consumption. His respending then becomes income to someone else, who in turn saves part but respends the rest. And so on. The number of times the final increase in income exceeds the new investment is called the "multiplier." For example, if one dollar of extra investment spending generates an extra four dollars of income, the multiplier is four.

This process bears further study. Begin with our equilibrium income level of 350 and assume that the marginal propensity to consume is .75. Businessmen decide to increase their investment spending by 10. When the 10 is spent on new investment (say plant construction), it becomes income to workers. They spend 7.5 on consumption and save 2.5. The 2.5 is withdrawn from the income stream, but the 7.5 becomes income to someone else who in turn respends 75 per cent (5.6) and saves 25 per cent (1.9). The 5.6 becomes income to someone else, and so the process goes. We finally get a table like this: [4]

	New Income	New Consumption	New Saving
Initiating New Investment	10	7.5	2.5
On Round 2	7.5	5.6	1.9
On Round 3	5.6	4.2	1.4
On Round 4	4.2	3.2	1.0
	.	.	.
	.	.	.
	.	.	.
	.	.	.
	40 *	30 *	10 *

* The formula for an infinite geometrical series, to be used in finding the sum of each of the columns in the table, is:

$$1 + r + r^2 + r^3 + \ldots\ldots\ldots\ldots\ldots r^n + \ldots = \frac{1}{1-r}$$

The table shows only the first four rounds, but it gives the general picture. The 10 of new investment generates a respending chain—called the "multiplier" effect—that leads to new income of much more than 10. Actually, if you carry the arithmetic to its conclusion (or use the series shown in the footnote), you will find that the total new income is 40 (including the 10 of new investment). Of this total, 30 is spent on consumption and 10 is saved, in accordance with our consumption function. This means that the new equilibrium income will be 40

[4] This example implicitly assumes that the investors get the funds for the extra 10 of investment either by drawing on past accumulated savings or by borrowing newly created funds from the banks.

higher, total consumption 30 higher, and total savings and investment each 10 higher than before. Adding these on to the original equilibrium, we get a new total income equilibrium level of 390.

This result is shown in Figure 11-8. The consumption, investment, and *C* + *I* curves before the increase in investment are shown as solid lines, reproduced directly from Figure 11-7. Now we add 10 more of investment at each level of income. In other words, *C'* + *I'* (the dashed line) is now consumption plus 110, instead of plus 100. The *C* line is unchanged because it was originally drawn to show what level of consumption corresponds to every level of income, whatever the level of income. But the new equilibrium level of income is 390, up 40. This is where the new *C* + *I* curve cuts the 45° line, even though investment has increased only 10.

Equilibrium after Multiplier Effect

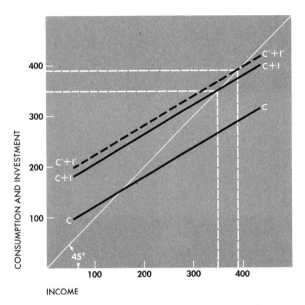

FIG. 11-8 An additional 10 of investment raises the C + I curve to C' + I', and brings a new equilibrium income of 390, up 40 from the previous equilibrium. The investment multiplier is 4.

The precise nature of this multiplier effect of new investment on consumption and income needs to be examined. Merely to say that respending of any new investment income will raise total income by a multiple of the new investment doesn't tell us much. Under what conditions is the effect powerful, and when is it weak? Can we state the multiplier principle more precisely? There are four important points:

1. The multiplier effect hinges on the fact that people respend part of each increment of income they receive. If at any point they save all their income, the respending spiral stops short.

2. The larger the proportion of its new income that the public respends on consumption, the larger will be the multiplier effect. Conversely, the more income that is withdrawn each round through saving, the smaller will be the multiplier effect.

3. The size of the multiplier effect is given precisely by the formula:

$$\text{Multiplier} = \frac{1}{1 - \text{Percentage of Extra Income Consumed}}$$

Thus, if the marginal propensity to consume is .75, the multiplier will be

$$\frac{1}{1 - .75} = \frac{1}{.25} = 4$$

Thus an increase of $1 in investment would mean an increase of $4 in income. If the marginal propensity to consume were .90, the multiplier would be 10. (Work out the .90 case in the equation, and check yourself by working out a table like the one in the preceding section. You will find that the formula merely summarizes the arithmetic.) An easy way to look at it is this: The multiplier is the reciprocal of the propensity to save, still assuming our simple case with the government absent. Thus if consumers save ¼ of their income, the multiplier is 4. If they save 1/10, the multiplier is 10. And so on.

4. What is the economic reasoning behind our statement that total income will always move toward the equilibrium level given by the multiplier on investment? For example, with a marginal propensity to consume of .75, why is the new *equilibrium* level of income just four times the level of new investment? Because at any lower level, income will continue to rise; at any higher level, income will fall. This is because at any income level below equilibrium, people will not yet have drawn enough out in savings from the income stream to offset the spending on investment, and the respending effect of investment will force the level of income up. At any income level above equilibrium, people will be saving more than enough to offset the investment spending, and this withdrawal of funds from the income stream will force the level of income down. *Equilibrium is achieved only when the public's income is such that it wants to save just enough to offset the amount being invested. Only if these two just match will the circular flow of income be continuous and stable.*[5]

The multiplier gives major stress to investment spending as the active force in changing income levels, and properly so. There is a great deal of evidence that investment decisions are a fluctuating and often independent (or "autonomous") element in the total spending picture, and that they often stimulate even wider swings in total income. But investment is by no means the only force that can change equilibrium income levels. Any of the many factors influencing consumption spending can also set up expansionary or deflationary spending changes. Only if consumption is solely a function of the level of consumer income does

---

[5] Remember that equality between decisions to save and decisions to invest guarantees equilibrium only when the propensity to consume is fixed. Even with decisions to save and to invest equal, equilibrium will be disturbed if there is a change in the consumption function—for example, a change financed by buying on credit, which would not involve a corresponding decrease in decisions to save.

investment play the unique role in setting total income implied by the examples above.

The Multiplier Further Examined. We now need a small digression on the application of multiplier analysis in the real world. It does not alter the basic reasoning above but complicates it statistically.

Since the marginal propensity to consume under high-employment conditions is usually in the 90-95 per cent range, it would appear that a multiplier of over 10 would generally prevail. This would provide an enormously powerful upward thrust of any increment to investment. But in fact, no such huge effects are observed. Instead, crude observation suggests multipliers in the range of 2 or 3. That is, when we see investment rising $1 billion, total income (g.n.p.) generally seems to rise in the range of $2 to $3 billion.

The answer lies in the fact that the .9 propensity to consume is out of *disposable personal income,* while the multiplier effect we observe is on *gross national product,* a different and much larger figure. Thus, consumption spending is usually around two-thirds of g.n.p. The difference between consumption and g.n.p. (see Table 6-3) is a combination of consumer saving, business depreciation allowances and undistributed profits, personal and business taxes, and a variety of smaller items. Loosely, this other one-third may be thought of as withdrawals from the g.n.p. income stream, comparable to the consumer saving withdrawal in the simple model above. Thus, the propensity to consume out of g.n.p. is about two-thirds, which gives a multiplier of three, roughly what we observe.[6] Actual statistical work with national income data, of course, must trace through the various segments of g.n.p. in detail to analyze fully the multiplier effects of investment. But the simple model above provides the essential reasoning.

Induced Investment and Dynamic Processes. Thus far, we have assumed that investment decisions are autonomous—that is, determined independently of the level of income and consumption. Actually, recent consumer spending and the resulting business profits are surely an important determinant of business investment plans. If we make investment dependent on consumer spending in the preceding period, we get what economists call dynamic analysis. In that case, the new equilibrium level in Figure 11-8 would not be a true equilibrium at all, since the higher consumer spending would in turn induce more investment, which would lead to a further multiplier effect on income and consumption. Intuitively,

---

[6] Many economists dislike to speak of the propensity to consume out of g.n.p., because consumers don't base their consumption spending directly on what happens to g.n.p., but rather on their own personal incomes. Thus, any observed relationship between consumption spending and g.n.p. is a purely statistical one, not based directly on individual consumer decisions, and subject to wide variations because of many factors independent of consumer spending decisions (such as business depreciation allowances, tax rates, and so on). Still, the notion of relating consumption to g.n.p. is a useful one for some rough multiplier purposes, once you recognize the dangers involved.

it looks as if such a process might spiral upward indefinitely, and under some conditions it would. But under others, we can explain why the spiral would die out, or even reverse itself and start a downward spiral.

This study of dynamic processes is the essence of the study of business fluctuations—of booms and depressions, or business cycles, as they are sometimes called. It is better to postpone such dynamic analysis temporarily until we have equilibrium analysis clearly in hand, and then return to dynamic processes a little later.

MONEY AND THE LEVEL OF EXPENDITURES

The preceding income-expenditures analysis has been carried on with no mention of the stock of money. Implicitly, we have assumed either (a) that just the right amount of money has been available in the economy to finance the transactions discussed, or (b) that it really doesn't matter what the stock of money is. But both common sense and the reasoning of Chapter 10 suggest that money *does* matter, and that the stock of money may at least sometimes rise or fall independently of the forces just discussed as determining the level of total spending. Thus, even though money may play a secondary role in the income-expenditures flow, we need to fit it in.

Many economists believe that a proper stock of money is a necessary condition for any level of national income, but that this is no great problem because the banking system will generally provide about the right money stock by responding to business and consumer demands for loans. If firms want to invest more and need more cash, they will go to the banks for loans, and these loans will create the additional money needed to finance the larger volume of spending. For example, in order to increase investment spending by 10 in Figure 11-8, business firms somehow had to get money above their receipts, either by borrowing new money or by drawing on previously idle cash balances. In the final new equilibrium position with total spending up by 40 each period, either new money or a faster spending rate for previously existing money is necessarily implied. Maybe 10 of new money created by bank loans would be just right to support the new spending level; this would imply a turnover rate of 4 per period for the new funds, assuming that turnover of old funds remains constant. But maybe 10 of new money would be more or less than is required. If that occurs, what will be the effect?

Suppose that the amount of bank lending creates more money than is "needed" to finance the new equilibrium level of 390 in Figure 11-8. That is, people and businesses find their cash balances higher than they had anticipated and higher than they want to hold at their new incomes. What do they do? One possibility is that consumers increase their spending (their propensity to consume rises) and businesses further increase their investment spending. Either result will give total spending a further stimulus, moving the system on up above 390 to a still higher equilibrium level. The exact level will, of course, depend on the precise increase in investment and the precise change in the propensity to consume.

The other possibility is that people and businesses will spend their excess cash balances on securities (financial investments), rather than changing their consumption and investment plans. The income-expenditures analysts suggest that this is the more common case. Since, they argue, consumption and investment depend largely on previous income and on real profit possibilities for investment, if people get too much cash they will simply buy stocks or bonds, or put it in the savings bank where it will draw interest. The result would then be to bid up the price of securities and (what is the same thing) to bid down the interest rate, or yield on securities.[7] As the interest rate falls, the incentive to convert cash into interest-bearing securities weakens. (Remember the strong positive motives for holding some money—for transactions, precautionary and speculative purposes —listed in Chapter 10.) The spending of cash on securities continues until the interest rate falls just far enough to induce the public to hold its larger stock of cash. The equilibrating effect of the excess money would be on the bond market and interest rate, without increasing the 390 total spending on goods and services shown in Figure 11-8.

Which way consumers and businesses react to changing money balances obviously determines how important money is in determining the level of total spending on goods and services. In the first case, the new money raises the new equilibrium level of income above 390, but does not affect the interest rate and prices of securities. In the second case, the new money has no effect on the equilibrium income level but lowers the interest rate and raises the price of securities. Either type of equilibrating approach is logically defensible. The real-world evidence on the point is not clear, although it leans toward the second alternative in most cases where cash balances don't get far out of line with what the public considers normal. This, of course, is precisely the same issue as was faced in the final section of Chapter 10.[8]

To be logically complete we must trace matters one step further in case 2. Even though the new money there doesn't directly raise the 390 level of income, it may have an indirect effect. By lowering the interest rate, it will make investment more attractive, other things equal. In our model, investment is profitable whenever the marginal efficiency of investment exceeds the interest rate. Thus, a lower interest rate expands the range of profitable investment opportunities. This

---

[7] Suppose the security is an outstanding $100 government bond paying 3 per cent (i.e., $3) per year and due in 10 years. If the price is bid up to 110, the annual real yield falls to about 2 per cent. This is because offset against the annual interest payment of $3, the bond buyer must place the $10 he will lose when he gets back in 10 years only $100 for the $110 he paid. Spreading this "capital loss" evenly over the 10 years takes away $1 of return per year, lowering the effective annual yield to $2, which is an effective interest rate of 2 per cent. (Actually, it is a little less than 2 per cent, since you only get $2 per year on an investment of $110.) The same type effect holds for other securities. For a more complete analysis, see Chapter 32.

[8] For more details, see the discussion of monetary policy in Chapter 14.

should raise investment above the originally assumed 10, which in turn will induce a further multiplier effect and a new equilibrium income above 390. But this indirect effect via the interest rate may be uncertain, depending on how strongly businessmen react to the lower interest rate. If their investment plans depend largely on other considerations, the stimulus to investment may be negligible.

RISING EXPENDITURES, TOTAL OUTPUT, AND INFLATION

When does more spending mean more output and employment, and when merely inflation?

When unemployment is widespread, increased spending generally means more jobs and more output. In depression, producers are happy to find buyers at existing prices; they're more interested in volume than in higher prices. Even labor unions, always anxious for higher wages, are unlikely to push hard and effectively for wage increases with many of their members out of work. Getting jobs for the men takes first priority.

As the economy approaches full employment, higher spending increasingly means higher prices and wages as well as more output. With most workers employed, wage rates are bid up. Materials cost more. With mills and factories approaching capacity, costs rise and prices are put up. Sometimes wages push upward on costs, leading to higher prices. Other times, businessmen, especially "administered price setters" in oligopolistic industries, push up prices faster than costs to increase profits. It's hard to say just when wage-push or administered prices are the villain, because they interact as spending rises. But as long as unemployed men and capacity remain, output generally increases as well as prices.

But what happens when total spending exceeds the output possible even with full employment of men and machines? Then pure inflation is the result. This situation is shown in Figure 11-9 (on page 190). Assume that 400 is the full-employment output. But here, obviously, the equilibrium income is nearly 500, where the $C + I$ curve cuts the 45° line. At the 400 output level, total spending is above the 45° line by 40. This difference is sometimes called the "inflationary gap." Since output cannot be increased beyond 400, the excess spending produces merely higher prices and higher money incomes.

Will the 500 national income be an equilibrium level, with prices staying at their new inflated level? Probably not, unless the government or some other factor intervenes to reduce total spending. At the 500 level, consumer and business incomes are higher, which induces continued higher spending on consumption and investment. Higher investment pushes money income still higher, and with rising prices the propensity to consume is also likely to rise. Since 400 per period is the maximum real output, the inflationary gap remains or widens, and prices and wages will be bid up even further as consumers and businesses compete for the 400 of goods and services in the next period. This is the inflationary spiral, which

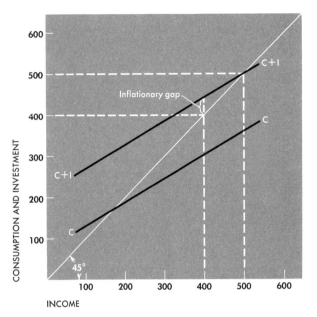

FIG. 11-9   When consumption plus investment spending exceeds full employment output of 400, the result is inflation. At full employment level, spending exceeds possible output by 40, driving prices up.

has appeared in its most extreme form in the war and postwar inflations of Germany, China, and other countries.

But three amendments must be added to this inflation model. The first is that inflation is unlikely to go far without a roughly corresponding increase in the money supply. Clearly, consumers and businessmen can economize on cash balances and speed up the use of the existing money supply to some extent if no more money is forthcoming. But these possibilities are limited, and history shows no cases of runaway inflationary spirals without vast increases in the stock of money. Thus government (Federal Reserve) action to permit increased bank lending is essential for a major inflationary spiral. Increasingly tight money, with rising interest rates, otherwise drags on investment and consumer credit, pulling the spiral to a halt.

Second, full employment is never the precise limit implied by this question. As wages and prices rise, housewives, college students, and older people enter the labor force, full or part-time. Present workers put in longer hours. Industrial engineers find ways of increasing output per man-hour. Normal repairs and maintenance may be postponed to avoid shutdowns. Production managers push plants beyond their quoted capacities for months, even years. With enough pressure, there are many ways of getting a little more output. The full-employment ceiling on output is a mushy one.

Lastly, a factor we are temporarily omitting: Capital accumulation is necessarily implied in net investment. Over a period of time, this fact, coupled with improving technology, steadily increases the output capacity of the economy for any given labor force. This is the process of economic growth, which we are neglecting in the present introductory analysis of income determination under essentially static conditions. Neglect of growth in capacity doesn't do much violence to common sense in any given year, but over a longer period it changes full-employment output substantially. In the American economy, full-employment output increases some 2 or 3 per cent annually from capital accumulation and improving technology. The growth process is examined in detail in the next chapter.

The Impact of Falling Expenditures. In the American economy, prices move upward more easily than they come down. This is partly because many industries are partially monopolized, and prefer to sacrifice volume to price in trying to maintain profits. Perhaps more important, labor unions fight wage-cuts with all their might—and wages make up around two-thirds of total costs for the whole economy. In highly competitive areas, prices come down faster with declining demand, but even there union resistance against wage-cuts means that many costs stay up. As a result, it is hard to cut prices even in competitive areas without incurring losses. And behind all these market forces there is an increasing tradition for the government to step in to prevent drastic price declines, both in the aggregate and in particular industries. Support prices for agricultural products, minimum-wage legislation, and state fair-trade legislation to prohibit price-cutting on "price-fixed" items are examples of this apparently pervasive philosophy. All in all, it takes a real slump in demand to force prices down far in the modern economy. When prices stay up, falling demand means fewer units sold.

Usually, therefore, a decline in total spending forces down production and employment more than prices. But mixed effects are the order of the day throughout the economy, and each industry needs to be investigated as an individual case to obtain a safe prediction.

THE ROLE OF GOVERNMENT So far, we have left out the government. Now, we can readily introduce it into the model by adding government spending to private consumption and investment spending, and by adding government taxes to private savings as a drain on the income stream. Thus, for the earlier equation $C + I = C + S$, we now have $C + I + GS = C + S + GR$, where GS is government spending and GR is government tax receipts.

You can readily visualize the role of government by going back to Figure 11-7. Merely reduce the present $C + I$ by the amount taxes cut private spending and add government spending on top of the new $C + I$ curve, to get the new $C + I + GS$ total spending curve. $C + I + GS$ may fall directly on the previous $C + I$ curve, or above or below it, depending on whether government spending is more or less than the amount by which taxes reduce private consumption and investment.[9] Where the new total spending curve cuts the 45° line will be the equilibrium level, for exactly the same reasons as explained the $C + I$ equilibrium

---

[9] Actually the problem is a little more complicated. Since consumption is probably a function of disposable income (after payment of income taxes) rather than total income, a change in taxes may affect the ratio of consumption to total income. But this complication may be postponed to Chapter 15.

level. Put in language, the equilibrium condition is: *Gross national product (total spending) must be such that intended private saving plus government tax collections are just offset by private investment plus government spending, where consumption spending is solely a function of income.*

A separate diagram may help to clarify this role of government taxes and spending. Look ahead to Figure 15-1, on page 273. There we have added 10 of government spending from new money, *which therefore does not correspondingly reduce private spending through tax collections.* With a marginal propensity to consume of .75, the multiplier is 4, and total income is increased by 40, to a new equilibrium level of 390. To repeat, the equilibrium condition with the government in the picture is $C + I + GS = C + S + GT$. Government taxes have the same effect as private saving, and government spending the same effect as private investment.

There is, of course, no reason why government taxes and spending must exactly balance in each time period. The government budget may be unbalanced, just as private saving and investment may be. When taxes exceed government spending, the result is a negative multiplier on the level of income. When government spending exceeds taxes, as in Figure 15-1, the result is an upward multiplier effect. This is the foundation for government fiscal policy to raise or lower the economy's equilibrium level of income and employment, which is discussed at length in Chapter 15.

The government's other major channel for influencing the level of total spending is its control over the supply of money. This channel, as was indicated above, is more indirect and perhaps more uncertain than the tax and expenditures channels, which have a direct impact on the income stream. But it has some counteradvantages too. The effects of both monetary and fiscal policy can be analyzed by using the theoretical models developed in this and the preceding chapters; this analysis will be made in Chapters 14 and 15, on monetary and fiscal policy.

REVIEW—CONCEPTS TO REMEMBER

This is a major chapter. Its analytical concepts and models are used through all the rest of the book. Be sure you understand the basic reasoning in the chapter, and the following new concepts:

income-expenditures approach
consumption function
average propensity to consume
marginal propensity to consume
saving function
average and marginal propensities
    to save
marginal efficiency of investment
interest rate

implicit interest
investment schedule
business saving
equilibrium income
underemployment equilibrium
the multiplier
autonomous investment
induced investment
inflationary gap

1. Is your own spending rate primarily a function of your recent income, of the size of your cash balance, or of other factors? Would you say the income-expenditures approach or the cash-balances approach is more helpful in explaining your own spending behavior?

FOR
ANALYSIS
AND
DISCUSSION

2. How would you expect the marginal propensity to consume to compare for families at the same income level (say $6,000 per year) at the following ages for the head of the family: 25, 40, 60, 75? Explain your answer.

3. Assume that gross national product is $500 billion. Total investment is $100 billion. Total consumption expenditures are $400 billion. Assume no government participation in the income stream:
   a. If investment rises to $120 billion, with the marginal propensity to consume .8, what will be the new equilibrium level of gross national product?
   b. Explain why this will be an equilibrium level—i.e., the level that will be established unless other unspecified factors intervene.

4. Would you expect that decisions to save for the year ahead in the economy would ordinarily be about the same as decisions to invest? Why or why not?

5. Changes in investment cause changes in saving for the economy as a whole, rather than vice versa. (True or false? Why?)

6. Assume the following summarized conditions to be in effect:

(Current annual rates, in billions)

Gross national		Gross national	
product	$500	product	$500
Consumption	300	Consumption	300
Saving	200	Investment	200

Suppose now that the level of investment rises to $220 billion and remains there:
   a. What will be the new equilibrium level of gross national product? Why? Do you need any further information to answer? If so, assume it.
   b. What is the "multiplier" in this case?
   c. How long will it take for that level to be reached?
   d. Suppose that before the new equilibrium is reached there is another increase or a decrease in the level of investment. How would you handle this in analyzing the likely effect on gross national product?
   e. Suppose that after a new higher equilibrium gross national product is reached, investment returns to the original level of $200 billion, but the economy's propensity to save rises slightly but permanently. Will the new equilibrium gross national product be higher or lower than the original one? Explain.

7. Until full employment is reached, we are safe in stimulating more investment without danger of inflation. (True or false? Why?)

8. If the money supply is increased 10 per cent through Federal Reserve open-market purchases of bonds from the public, what change, if any, would you expect in g.n.p.? Explain.

9. Suppose that in an hypothetical economy income is running at an annual rate of $500 billion g.n.p. Other major items in the national income accounts are as follows:

Consumption	$320 billion
Investment	60 "
Savings	80 "
Gov't. Expenditures	120 "
Taxes	100 "

The marginal propensity to consume is three-fourths. (For purposes of this problem, take the three-fourths marginal propensity to consume against income before taxes.)

Suppose that the government now balances its budget through a reduction in government expenditures while maintaining taxes at the level of $100 billion. What will be the effect on the levels of income, consumption, and savings? Explain.

Economic Growth in America

We Americans think of ourselves as the richest and most progressive nation in the world. We have a right to. Starting from nowhere only two centuries ago, the United States economy has produced spectacular results by any standards. Our total production (g.n.p.) in 1959 was nearly one-third of the world's total, with only 6 per cent of the world's population. It was well over double our nearest competitor's, the U.S.S.R.; and on a per capita basis it led by a wide margin.

Since World War II, the American economy has continued to grow, indeed at a somewhat faster rate than during the preceding century. The annual growth in real g.n.p. has been about 4 per cent, compared to less than 3 over the longer period. But on growth, nevertheless, we now find ourselves in the unaccustomed, and uncomfortable, position of being not merely second-best, but well back with the also-rans.

Table 12-1 provides rough estimates of the annual growth rates in real gross national product for some of the world's leading nations during the decade of the 1950's. The precise figures, and hence the exact rankings, shouldn't be given too much weight. But the estimates are almost certainly of the right order of magnitude.

Why are we so low on the list? Are the other countries merely spurting temporarily because they are still recovering from the devastation of World War II? Does the U.S.S.R.'s rate of growth, in particular, augur real danger that Khrushchev's boast will be realized—that the U.S.S.R. will bury us, not with arms, but with international economic defeat? On the gloomy side, the U.S.S.R.'s recent performance is doubly impressive because she has been able, year after year, to devote a far higher proportion of her total output to capital investment (in dams, machinery, and heavy industry generally) than we, in spite of a far lower per capita income. If we look only at industrial production (omitting lagging Soviet agriculture), the annual growth rate apparently was an amazing 9-12 per cent. And while many of these industrial facilities are aimed at military production, the bulk can be used for civilian purposes as well. Soviet steel production in 1958 (an American recession year) was nearly three-fourths ours; they hope to catch us in a decade. A 4 per cent annual growth rate implies a doubling every 20 years; a 7 per cent rate, nearly a doubling every decade. Moreover, the Russians claim more than a 7 per cent rate.

Table 12-1

ESTIMATED ANNUAL GROWTH IN REAL GROSS NATIONAL PRODUCT
DURING THE 1950's *

Country	Percentage	Country	Percentage
West Germany	8	Netherlands	5
U.S.S.R.	7	Canada	5
Japan	7	France	4
Austria	6	United States	4
Italy	6	United Kingdom	3

* Includes period 1950-1959. Estimates based largely on United Nations, Committee for Economic Development, and U.S. Joint Economic Committee data.

The postwar years have awakened many Americans from comfortable complacency to alarm. Whether we need be alarmed depends largely on what is viewed as critical—military potential, or the race for a high standard of living. On the former, the space age gives us little basis for complacency. On the latter, we still have a huge lead. How well we preserve it, and how clearly western superiority is demonstrated to the world's vast "uncommitted" millions, will depend substantially on how well the American economy performs over the years ahead.[1]

---

[1] Chapters 43 and 44 provide a detailed look at growth prospects in the U.S.S.R. and in some of the world's "underdeveloped" countries.

AMERICAN
ECONOMIC GROWTH:
HISTORY AND OUTLOOK

How fast has the American economy grown? How fast will it grow? How fast should it grow?

Over the last century, our growth rate in real gross national product has been about 3 per cent per annum; in per capita output, about 2 per cent. Since World War II, the rate has been faster—nearly 4 per cent for total output and 3 per cent per capita. Since history is the main basis for predicting the future, most economists look for growth rates of 3 or 4 per cent over the decades ahead. Some argue that we should strive for 5.

Past and Projected U.S. Real Gross National Product, 1900-1975

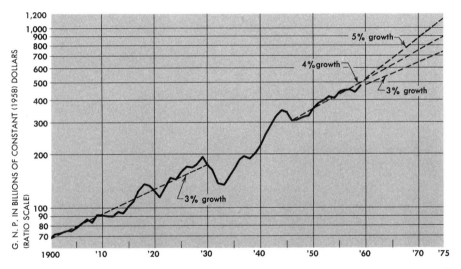

FIG. 12-1   Real g.n.p. has grown at about 3 per cent per annum since 1900, but nearer 4 since World War II. The annual growth rate makes a big difference as to where we'll be by 1975.

A difference of one or two per cent per annum piles up amazingly fast over a quarter-century, even over shorter periods. Figure 12-1 graphs American real gross national product since 1900, and extends alternative trend lines to 1975, showing separate paths for 3, 4, and 5 per cent growth annually in the future. The dotted line fitted to the years 1900-1930 shows a 3 per cent growth rate then. Skipping the depression and war years, the dotted line from 1945 to 1959 shows a 4 per cent rate for the postwar years. If we extend the recent 4 per cent trend out to 1975, we get a g.n.p. of about $900 billion in 1958 prices, about twice the 1959 level. Three per cent will give only about $740 billion. Five per cent runs up to $1,150 billion—over a trillion dollars—only about fifteen years hence. All these figures assume stable prices. If you expect inflation, raise the dollar figures accordingly.

By 1975, U. S. population will be somewhere between 220 and 245 million, if the recent growth rate continues. By 1985, the total may well be 280 million, an increase of 100 million people in only 25 years. But these spectacular population growth estimates don't imply equal growth in real output, since vast millions of the new population will be babies and youngsters, still below working age. They will be consumers, but not workers. Indeed, the labor force for 1975 has now been born, so what happens to the birth rate from now on will only affect the number of consumers among whom the nation's 1975 product must be divided up.

Both population growth and the real g.n.p. growth rate will thus play powerful roles in determining 1975 *per capita* production. If the 3 per cent g.n.p. growth rate and the maximum population figures materialize, 1975 per capita g.n.p. will be about $3,000, compared to about $2,500 in 1959. But if the 5 per cent g.n.p. growth rate and the minimum population figure turn out to be right, per capita g.n.p. will be $4,800, nearly double the 1959 figure. A percentage point or two either way in the annual growth rates can go a long way toward determining how well you will live fifteen years hence.

THE PROBLEM OF ECONOMIC GROWTH

What determines how fast an economy grows? Many things. Fundamentally, it is the "real" things that matter—the accumulation of productive capital goods, research and technological advance, education, growth in the size and efficiency of the labor force, better management. Increases in these real variables increase the basic capacity of the economic system to produce goods and services.

But in a private-enterprise economy, money demand matters too. In such an economy, money demand directs the allocation of productive resources. It induces research and development, aimed at producing more, better, and different goods and services more cheaply. It leads people to work harder and longer. It stimulates families and businesses to invest their savings where desirable returns can be obtained. In a private-enterprise, profit-motivated economy, unless money demand is adequate to take goods off the market, they will not long be produced. And unless prospective money demand promises reasonable returns on investment in capital goods, research, and development, the new capital goods necessary for economic growth are unlikely to be forthcoming.

Thus, *in real terms* the problem of economic growth is to increase the productive capacity of the economy: through diverting resources from current consumption to investment in capital goods, research, education, and other activities that increase future capacity; through increasing the size and improving the performance of the labor force; and through improving the economic organization. *In terms of money expenditures,* the first problem is to be sure that adequate total money demand exists each period to bring high-level utilization of the productive capacity that exists. Otherwise, the available output is not obtained, and new investment looking toward the future is reduced (as it usually is in recession and depression). The second problem at the monetary level is to channel money-spending away from consumption into saving and investment, so that society's stock of capital goods will be built up to increase output for the future. Thus, on the money-spending side, both the total level of spending $(C + I + GS)$ and the proportion going into private investment and the investment component of government spending are crucial in the analysis of economic growth.

REAL FACTORS   **Accumulation of Capital Goods.**   In order to grow, an economy must save. It must use part of its current output to build up productive capacity, rather than currently consuming its entire output. History suggests that the economic growth rates of the major countries correspond roughly to the proportion of their total outputs they allocate to net investment (leaving aside the special cases of war and recovery from depression).

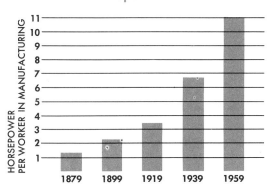

Added Investment per Worker Speeds Economic Growth

HORSEPOWER PER WORKER IN MANUFACTURING

1879   1899   1919   1939   1959

FIG. 12-2   Horsepower per worker in manufacturing, which has nearly doubled every 20 years and has risen nearly tenfold in the last 80 years, provides one indication of the vast increase in capital invested per worker.

For a wealthy nation, as for a wealthy individual, saving and investment are easy. For the poor, they are hard. Back in colonial days, America was poor and capital was scarce. Only with the help of borrowed capital from Europe could we build the early factories, railroads, and other capital goods that were the forerunners of today's industrial economy. Thrift was a painful necessity if individuals, and the nation, were to accumulate enough savings to afford even a modest house, much less a small shop or factory.

Today America is rich! By 1959, total national tangible wealth was estimated at over $1½ trillion. Capital investment per production worker averaged $18,000. In 1959 we saved over $75 billion gross and about $35 billion net. Over

$20 billion of it was saved by individuals and families, the remainder by corporations that plowed back savings into bigger and better buildings, plant, and equipment. At the same time, consumers purchased over $300 billion worth of goods and services, and federal, state, and local governments spent nearly $100 billion providing goods and services for the public, of which less than half represented military spending. Compared to other nations, our aggregate saving was enormous. But as a percentage of total income, it ranked well below several more rapidly growing nations.

Should we devote more of our resources to capital accumulation, and thereby increase productivity and the standard of living of the future? Or should we save less, shifting resources to provide an even fuller life economically for today? Rich as America is, miles upon miles if slums remain in our cities. Millions of families wear shabby clothes and have little beyond the barest necessities of life. How should we value the present against the future?

Basically, this question will be answered by millions of rich and middle-class families, and by the managers of the nation's business firms. For it is they who make most of the nation's saving and investment decisions. The poor, who might have the strongest preference for more present consumption, will have little to say on the issue, for anything beyond small savings is out of the question for them. Total saving (individual and business) has grown enormously during the present century, but not as a percentage of total income. Business saving has increased somewhat relative to business income, as businesses have increasingly financed their own capital expansion programs by retained earnings. Individuals, as we have seen, as a group have had surprisingly stable saving habits over the long run. Savings have seldom varied far from 5-10 per cent of disposable income for all consumers in full-employment periods.

But the rate of capital accumulation is not entirely left up to individuals and businesses even in the private-enterprise American economy. Every year, our governments tax away billions of dollars from individuals and businesses to be used in constructing and maintaining capital resources—schools, highways, public buildings, airports, parks, land conservation, and other such investments. In addition, new military equipment might be viewed as a temporary accumulation of national capital. In 1959, probably over $10 billion was channelled into nonmilitary capital accumulation in this way through the government. In an economy like the U.S.S.R.'s, of course, virtually all saving and capital accumulation are determined directly by the state.

What will happen to America's saving habits in the future, and hence to the rate of real capital accumulation? This is one of the biggest questions in predicting the rate of economic growth.

Research and Technology. Increasingly, research workers agree that the rate of technological advance is probably the most important single factor in explaining the rate of economic growth in America. Since 1900, production has risen twice as fast as the input of labor and tangible capital goods combined. While improved worker skill and education surely account for some of this difference, technological advance on every front—science and engineering, managerial methods, equipment—seems to emerge as the dominant explanation, more important even than the vast accumulation of capital goods.[2]

How much will we spend over the years ahead on research and development to speed technological improvement, and what will be the impact of this spending? Figure 12-3 shows the spectacular growth of spending on research and development in the United States since World War II. Although only rough estimates are available, it seems clear that research and development spending by the government and private industry has grown by more than 10 per cent annually. Well over half of all the research spending in the history of the United States has been done since 1950.

The National Science Foundation suggests that such research has a lagged effect on real output that may produce spectacular results in the near future. Indeed, automation is here. The impact of computers and electronic devices of all sorts is thought by many to be the beginning of another industrial revolution.

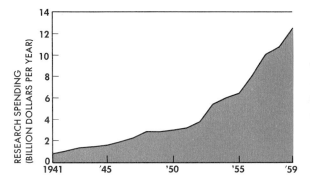

Spending on Research and Development in the U.S., 1941-1959

FIG. 12-3   Research is the newest major industry in the United States. It has grown by leaps and bounds since World War II, though most of the total shown is applied research and development, very little basic research. (Source: The National Science Foundation.)

Atomic power runs sea-going vessels and is already generating electric power for commercial use. Solar energy has been captured and is running small mechanisms like watches and telephones. Space satellites are circling the earth, and have reached the moon. Surprisingly, on the farm modern chemistry and machinery have increased output per man-year even more rapidly than in industry. New products are everywhere—drugs, plastics, synthetic fibers, panel lighting. It is hard to separate the science-fiction magazines of a few years ago from the reality of today.

Among the biggest economic problems facing the United States over the next half-century may be the depletion of energy resources (coal, oil, wood, and gas) and materials (iron ore, copper, bauxite). This is the law of diminishing returns

---

[2] For further evidence, see also p. 39.

again. How do we surmount the basic fixity of natural resources as population grows? World population may reach 6 billion before the end of the century. By the year 2000, world demands for materials and power will be enormous. Over the last century, horsepower per production worker has increased more than tenfold (see Figure 12-2), and the rate of substituting mechanical-electrical power for human labor has been steadily increasing.

But here again research and science may supply the answers. Basic research, especially in chemistry, is rapidly making previously unusable raw materials useful—fertilizers for poor soil, techniques for refining low-grade metallic ores, and dozens of other steps forward. Even more important, science has persistently opened up new power sources for economical use—oil, then nuclear energy, perhaps solar power next. Sea water can produce useful chemicals and probably eventually food. In effect, the supply of natural resources is being expanded. The science of the year 2000 would be as unbelievable to us now as atomic energy and space flight would have been back in 1900.

Thus far, a major portion of the *basic* research in America has been financed by the government (often through military funds) and performed in universities or government installations. Industry, which spends huge sums annually, does little basic research. It has concentrated largely on developing the basic research of others into commercially profitable applications—with a few notable exceptions. In total, most fundamental research and over half of all national research and development spending appears to be financed directly or indirectly by federal funds. Many major innovations from industry were originally stimulated and financed by government contracts—large digital computers, many drugs, atomic energy, missiles, and virtually all aviation developments are examples. Even the famous "Bell Labs" are not quite purely private enterprise at work, since telephone rates are regulated by the public utilities commissions to provide a "reasonable" profit above all costs, including Bell Labs research.

Who *should* finance the fundamental and applied research that underlies the growth in the nation's standard of living? Government, the universities, or private industry? Private industry can be relied on for most developmental and applied research behind saleable products. But to rely on private industry for basic research would run a serious danger, since truly basic research is often unpredictable and expensive, and seldom has direct commercial profitability. Even if a company does make a major basic breakthrough, it is seldom able to protect this discovery from development by its competitors.

Yet the mores are strong against government's undertaking ventures beyond areas directly and necessarily within the government domain. The public fears government domination of the universities, who now receive much of their research support from government agencies. Yet without extensive outside support, the universities can support only limited research. A surprising portion of modern American technological developments can be traced back to basic research done in pre-war European universities, or done here by European-trained scientists.

The proper environment, organization, and financing for research are essential in accelerating technological advance. The best answer is not yet clear.

The Labor Force and Productivity.   The rate of economic growth depends on the size and efficiency of the labor force—on the number of workers and on productivity, or output per worker. As was suggested in Chapter 3, the first of these we can predict reasonably well. The second is much harder.

The Labor Force. The "labor force" includes all persons over 14 years of age who hold or are actively seeking paid employment, or who are self-employed. Thus, the labor force includes only those who have jobs or are looking for them. It does not include the millions of young people, housewives, and retired folks who are not seeking work, even though they are perfectly capable of working.

Figure 12-4 shows what has happened to the labor force since 1900. It has grown persistently and, except for big bulges during the two major wars, steadily. The average annual increase has been about two-thirds of a million people. But this figure was much lower in the early years, and recently has run up toward a million persons a year. The big increase has been in non-agricultural jobs.

U.S. Labor Force, 1900-1959

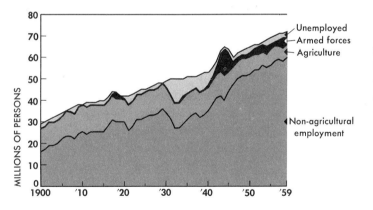

FIG. 12-4   The U.S. labor force has grown steadily, with temporary bulges during major wars. Most workers have non-agricultural jobs. Note the big unemployment pocket during the 1930's. (Source: U.S. Department of Labor.)

About forty per cent of the population has been in the labor force during recent decades. More women working have steadily pushed the percentage up, but longer education and earlier retirement have roughly offset the rise. Unless this ratio changes drastically, over the decade or two ahead rapid growth in the labor force seems sure. This is because the big marriage and baby boom of the late 1940's will begin to hit the labor market by the mid-1960's.

Up to a few years ago, many observers predicted a real excess of labor supply when that happens. But the birth rate of the last few years has continued to produce an unparalleled new baby boom. Now prevailing opinion holds that the higher birth rate will continue, and total population will rise so fast that the percentage of total population in the labor force will fall gradually, rather than rising for the foreseeable future. Thus, in spite of the big increase in total output possible with the rising labor force, the baby boom may prove a real drag on increasing per capita incomes, at least until the babies reach working age.

Growth in U.S. Output per Man-Hour, 1850-1959

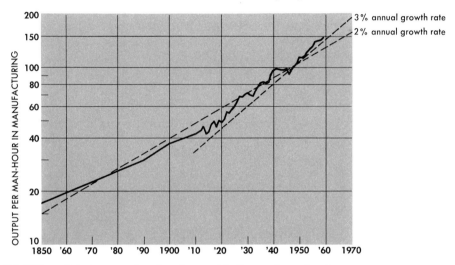

FIG. 12-5   Output per man-hour has risen persistently over the past century —at about 2 per cent annually up to World War II and nearly 3 per cent annually since. Which rate is more likely for the future?

A reminder from Chapter 3 may be useful on some of the uncertainties about just how fast the labor force will grow. Longer education and earlier retirement are continuing trends, at least for the years just ahead. But how far will they go? Even harder are the questions about women. Will they continue to marry younger? How many will turn to careers instead of marriage? Will the proportion of married women working continue to rise? The experts disagree. But one thing seems certain: The flood of new workers after the mid-1960's will roll over any changes arising from these factors, and the annual growth in the labor force will rise from around 1 per cent to at least 1½ per cent annually. This will mean over a million new workers, or at least job-seekers, annually.

Productivity. How about the annual increase in output per worker (productivity)? Here forecasting is precarious. This rate has fluctuated erratically in the past, and no wonder! Output per worker is the net resultant of all the other factors—research, education, amount of capital investment per worker, hours worked per week, efficiency of both management and labor, effectiveness of the economic organization in promoting specialization and exchange, everything that affects total output except the number of workers in the labor force. Sometimes productivity is used to mean output per man-hour of work. Then the average number of hours worked per year must be considered with the labor force. (Don't let the common practice of using "productivity" to mean output per *man* mislead you into attributing all the increased output to workers. We could equally well do a productivity calculation showing output per unit of capital, by dividing total output by the number of units of capital employed.)

The record of the past century is summarized in Figure 12-5. The dotted line roughly fitted to the output per man-hour shows 2 per cent per annum growth from 1850 to 1930; actually the rate was lower in the early years, if the data are right. The dotted line since 1930 shows 3 per cent annual growth.

Additional information is shown by Table 12-2, which points up the wide fluctuations from decade to decade. Rough data going back to 1850 suggest similar fluctuations in the nineteenth century. Annual increases vary from as high as 12 per cent to negative figures.

Table 12-2

AVERAGE ANNUAL GAIN IN PRODUCTIVITY IN THE
UNITED STATES, 1909-1959 *

Decade	Average Annual Gain in Productivity
1909-18	0.5%
1919-28	2.7
1929-38	2.4
1939-48	2.1
1949-59	3.0

* Data from National Industrial Conference Board, except for 1958-59, estimated by the author. "Productivity" is output per man-hour.

Don't put too much faith in the precision of the data. Various research workers come up with substantially different figures for the same or overlapping periods. The basic trouble is that detailed information on productivity per worker in the economy as a whole and in particular industries, especially reaching back beyond the last couple of decades, is extremely scarce. Thus, irregular fluctuations may be explained in part by poor data, rather than by unknown forces that inexplicably raise or lower productivity. But the data provide a roughly reliable picture.

Predicting future changes in productivity is made still more difficult by the fact that the economy-wide figure for any year covers up wide differences among different industries. For example, during the postwar period, average output per man-hour has increased about 3 per cent a year. But Figure 12-6 shows the increase in different major sectors of the economy, using 1947 as a base. Inclusion of data on individual industries and firms within industries would show an even more dramatic spread.

In the labor force, these changes mirror a drastic shift from man to machine power, and from low-grade to skilled and managerial jobs. The number of telephone operators has declined since 1950 in spite of a 54 per cent increase in annual telephone conversations. Ford's highly automated engine plants at Cleveland and Dearborn are said to use 1,800 fewer direct laborers but nearly 1,000 more skilled maintenance men and technicians than conventional plants with similar productive capacity. Since 1940, the ratio of "production" to "non-production" workers (salesmen, clerks, managers, professional workers, etc.) has fallen substantially in every sector of the economy.

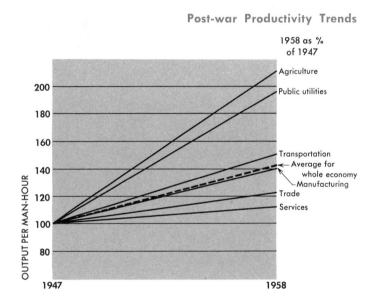

Post-war Productivity Trends

FIG. 12-6   In recent years, productivity has increased at widely differing rates in different sectors of the economy. (Source: U.S. Joint Economic Committee.)

A look at Figure 12-6 will show that occupational shifts themselves may significantly affect the average annual growth in productivity. The persistent shift of manpower out of agriculture, for example, has meant a move of workers from faster- to slower-growing productivity industries. The recent relative increase in spending on services has similarly held down the average productivity growth rate.

Nobody has a crystal ball to tell what will happen to productivity over the years ahead. The major factors are those already outlined in Part 1—resources, technology, specialization, and exchange—all woven together in the complex process exemplified by the history of economic growth. Calm economic analysis suggests that the future increase in output per man-hour will depend more on technological advance and capital investment per worker than on the specific skills of the workers in the plant. The unions often dispute this, especially at wage-bargaining time when the issue is how the fruits of advancing productivity shall be divided between wages and profits. And it is surely true that improving education and skill for the working man can contribute significantly to increasing productivity. But the case for focus on education and skills becomes far stronger if we emphasize the role of the engineer, the scientist, the planner, and the manager, than if we think of the worker in the factory as the prototype of the labor force.

Investment in Education. Education is in some ways our biggest industry and biggest investment. Today over 40 million students, teachers, and others are involved in substantially full-time educational activity—about 25 per cent of the population. This does not include a large amount of on-the-job training and other such educational activities.

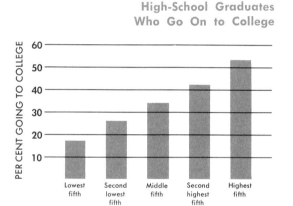

High-School Graduates
Who Go On to College

RANK IN HIGH-SCHOOL GRADUATING CLASS

FIG. 12-7   Although over a third of all high-school graduates go to college, nearly half the students of highest ability drop out after high school. (Source: Commission on Human Resources and Advanced Training.)

The impact of investment in education over the years is hard to measure. Its direct effects on improved worker skills on the assembly line are only a small part of the total value, though this direct effect should not be minimized. It is clear that the American worker is one of the most skilled and ingenious in the world. But the major significance of investment in education is in its broader aspects. Education is the foundation for advanced work by our scientists, engineers, managers, doctors, government officials, and other highly skilled people on whom much of our progress basically rests. Undoubtedly educational training pays off—at the high-school, college, and more advanced levels—for those with the ability to profit from it. Measured by life earning power, education is a high-yield personal investment, according to survey after survey. From the nation's point of view, investment in education is equally important—the highest long-term yield to be had on investment dollars anywhere, some competent observers believe.

Figure 12-7 pictures the challenge in education that still faces America today. Only 53 per cent of the top fifth of their high-school graduating classes go on to college; only 42 per cent of the second fifth; only 34 per cent of the third fifth. Although most boys and girls now finish high school, thousands of potentially more useful youngsters are lost through pre-graduation drop-outs every year. To repeat the theme from above, brainpower is our scarcest resource. One Einstein or Fermi may be worth a million more ordinary mortals in improving the welfare of mankind over the next century, measured in cold dollars-and-cents terms. To lose nearly half of all our most able youths from further education at the end of high school is a waste of resources that America can ill afford! High-grade education that pushes our ablest youths to their utmost is one of the cheapest and surest investments in progress.

What will happen to education in America? Low pay for school teachers and the shortage of qualified teachers throughout the educational system must be corrected if the nation is to have the level of education it can readily afford. The teacher shortage will be a major crisis by the 1970's, if it is not already. Better education for the masses, and, perhaps even more important for the future economic growth of the nation, more effective discovery and training of the most able youths—these hold a key to more rapid economic growth, as well as to a more effectively functioning democracy in the future.

Economic Organization and Social Environment.   Looking backward, it is clear that the economic, political, and religious atmosphere of the American scene since colonial days has been peculiarly favorable to individual initiative, hard work, and the pursuit of material reward generally. Success in business has been a mark of distinction. The "Protestant ethic," which looks upon work as a good in itself, has played an important role in establishing our mores. And the basic tradition of each man for himself has provided an inviting setting for individual attempts to rise to higher economic levels. Experts trying to help the so-called "underdeveloped" countries raise their living standards are increasingly impressed with the importance of the economic and cultural climate as a prerequisite to rapid economic growth. (Some fascinating contrasts are pointed out in Chapter 43.)

American economic institutions have shown unusual flexibility in adjusting to the needs of the growing economy. Banking and financial institutions developed rapidly in response to the need to encourage saving, to accumulate savings in forms that would be available to business units, and to provide the money to finance the economy's growth. Development of the modern corporation facilitated the accumulation of capital for business ventures without undue risk for a large group of non-managerial investors. Risk-taking was encouraged by the rapid development of insurance arrangements and by financial intermediaries which shared and spread the risk in order to make investments more attractive to private savers.

Individual freedom for a man to work where he wished, to set up in business when he liked, to invest his savings as he preferred, provided a setting unique in the modern world. It was a setting ideally designed to stimulate initiative, risk-taking, and personal effort. And it was coupled with unparalleled political freedom and social flexibility for the man who could win out in the open competition of the new economy.

Reflecting the entire economic, social, and political scene, government has been generally friendly and encouraging to vigorous, open competition and to business activity conducive to rapid economic growth. Emphasis on the preservation of peace and order, protection of property rights, general maintenance of laissez-faire conditions, and provision of necessary government services such as education, highways, and communications, were all strong governmental policies that encouraged vigorous economic activity. On the regulatory side, the government has largely limited itself to checking undue restrictions on competition. Only with the long depression of the 1930's did far-reaching governmental concern with economic security begin to encroach substantially on the strong tradition of support for individual initiative in the market place.

Will the attitude of the public as a whole, and of the government that reflects public opinion, continue to be basically friendly toward individual initiative, business, remunerative investment, and a vigorous profit-oriented economy? Will American economic institutions continue to adapt flexibly as changing times call for new ideas, new institutions, new ways of doing things? Or has the American economy become comfortable, rigid, and tradition-bound—less inclined to compete vigorously and less open to the newcomer and the new idea? Has the desire for security replaced the traditional American aggressive individualism as the banner of American economic policy?

On these questions you can find many viewers-with-alarm. Maybe they'll turn out to be right. Most observers, however, see in the American economic organization a still impressively vigorous, flexible, adaptive machine—an environment generally favorable to rapid economic growth. Whoever turns out to be right, there is agreement on one point: The general economic environment, and the governmental attitudes and policies which it produces, can give a big boost or lay a dead hand on economic growth in the future. Sir Henry Clay, a noted economist, has put the problem provocatively: "The so-called capitalist system, so far from failing, has been almost too successful in the interests of its own survival; it has encouraged the great mass of our population to believe that the increase of wealth is easy and inevitable, and depends no longer on incentives and appropriate organization but on scientific research, adequate education, and public direction." [3]

MONEY-FLOW FACTORS   It is the "real" factors—resources, technology, and economic organization—that set the economic capacity of a nation. But ours is a market economy, in which goods are mainly produced in response to money demand and the desire for profit. And we know from experience that money demand has not always kept the economy expanding at a steady rate. Sometimes demand has fallen far short of total pro-

---

[3] Address at Wharton School of Finance and Commerce, University of Pennsylvania, January 10, 1947.

ductive capacity, as in the 1870's and the 1930's; then the pall of depression hangs over the land, investment and growth slow or halt completely. Other times, money demand has far exceeded the economy's productive capacity, producing inflation. The rate of saving and the diversion of funds from consumption to investment have fluctuated widely.

Can we count on total money demand to be roughly sufficient to implement the future expansion that individuals and businesses show they want through their saving behavior? Can we count on an adequately high rate of money investment to give the growth we want? It is by no means clear that we can.

How Fast Do We Want to Grow?   Rapid growth sounds fine. More goods for everybody. But the problem is not so simple. There may be ways of growing without cost, but it's not obvious what they are. We can grow more rapidly if we work harder and longer, and especially if we divert more of our current output to investment—to building up future productive power. This means, unfortunately, having less leisure and less to consume and enjoy now. Thus, the problem of economic growth is in large part the problem of choosing between present and future.

Perhaps the payoff on investment in research and development will prove quick and spectacular. If so, rapid growth may be obtainable with only minor diversion of resources from current consumption. But even with great research successes, the resulting new plants and new methods often require heavy capital investment per worker. On the whole, increased productivity has required steadily increasing investment per laborer, not merely major technological advances. Investment in education, in better highways for transportation, in modern computers, will speed productivity upward. But as yet there appears to be no easy road to success. Better living for tomorrow means giving up consumption today.

Economics has no magic answer to the question: How fast should we grow? The answer depends largely on how we weigh the present against the future—our own comforts against those of our children. It depends on how we value work and more goods versus more leisure. It may depend too on how we assess the international picture. If the U.S.S.R. grows at 6 or 8 per cent per annum, can we afford to grow at only 3 or 4? Partly the answer may hinge on military considerations. Partly it may rest on our assessment of the impact of this picture on the world's other nations—our allies, our critics, and the uncommitted neutrals.

What Money Demand Is Needed for Stable Economic Growth?   Assume that we want continuous high-level employment, a roughly stable price level, and growth of 4 per cent a year in aggregate output. Are these compatible goals? If so, how do we achieve them?

So far as total money demand is concerned, the answer is clear. Total spending should rise at the same rate as the expansion of total high-employment capacity, and the division between consumption and investment spending should match the division between consumption and saving decisions (omitting government taxes and spending and assuming satisfactory levels of employment and prices at the outset). More total spending will mean inflation. Less will mean underemployment and waste. A malallocation of spending between consumption and investment is likely to generate short-run fluctuations in the economy that may lead to serious booms or depressions. These statements would not change if the desired growth rate were 3, 5, or any other per cent, although the division of output, income, and spending between consumption, saving, and investment would, of course, be different.

To grow more slowly than is desired because we waste resources through unemployment is foolish! For that is a case where more rapid growth would be not only costless, but actually better for everyone than slower growth. Thus, we must avoid a shortage of total spending that means unemployment both because of the current waste it generates and because it will reduce total saving and investment as income falls.

In summary (leaving the goverment aside), we must induce the public to save voluntarily just the amount needed for the desired growth rate, and count on just adequate private profit-motivated investment to convert these savings into economic growth. Conversely, we must avoid the undersaving (overinvestment) that means inflation.

Begin with the following simplified full-employment economy for 1960.

	In Billions
Total g.n.p.	$500
Consumption	325
Investment and saving	75
Government taxes and spending	100

We want to grow at 4 per cent yearly. What must 1961 look like? To simplify, assume arbitrarily that government taxes and spending increase just 4 per cent. Then clearly, private spending must also rise 4 per cent if 4 per cent additional output is to be taken off the market at a stable price level. If the proportion between consumption and investment remains stable, 1961 would look about like this, with total spending up 4 per cent.

	In Billions
Total g.n.p.	$520
Consumption	338
Investment and saving	78
Government taxes and spending	104

It does not necessarily follow, of course, that a 4 per cent increase in investment this year will produce a 4 per cent increase in total output next year. The exact relationship between current investment and increases in future output is uncertain and variable. Perhaps 1962 total full-employment capacity will be up only 3 per cent, perhaps 5 or 6. But whatever amount it is, the full-employment-without-inflation condition then again is total spending in balance with capacity output. If by 1962, the growth rate seems to be lagging below 4 per cent, this is evidence that we must step up our saving-investment rate. If the growth rate is running ahead of 4 per cent, we can afford to consume a larger proportion of current output and still achieve the 4 per cent goal.

In principle, there is no reason why we need to have a stable price level with our full-employment and 4 per cent growth rate. If, for example, total spending rises only 2 per cent while capacity grows by 4 per cent, full-employment output can still be maintained if the price level falls 2 per cent. Conversely, if total spending rises 6 per cent, full-employment output can be maintained with a 2 per cent increase in average prices.

As a practical matter, as we saw in Chapters 7 and 11, widespread price reductions without serious disruption seem unlikely in the modern American economy. With downward cost and price rigidity, inadequate total spending means unemployment of men and productive capacity. Thus, few economists now believe that total spending can safely grow less than in proportion to total capacity. Constant total money-spending with a 4 per cent annual growth in capacity could mean something like 20 per cent unemployment of men and capacity in only 5 years. This is, indeed, roughly what happened between 1929 and 1939, when the latter year saw 8 million unemployed with the same g.n.p. as in peak-prosperity 1929. Whether we can have gradual inflation with full employment and a stable growth rate is a more widely disputed issue; more on this later.

A look ahead to 1970 will illustrate some of the magnitudes involved in such growth. Assume stable prices at 1959 levels. Then a 4 per cent growth rate, coupled with the assumption of roughly constant proportions between consumption, saving-investment, and government taxes-spending, gives 1970 totals that look roughly like this:

	In Billions
Total g.n.p.	$750
Consumption	490
Investment and saving	110
Government taxes and spending	150

Can we count on consumers to buy the enormous volume of food, clothing, washing machines, automobiles, and other goods and services implied in a $500 billion consumption total? Perhaps more important, since investment is the driving force of economic growth, can we count on private investors to spend over $100 million in 1970 on profit—seeking new plant, equipment, and construction, remembering that this 1970 figure implies they spent nearly as much in 1969, only a little less in 1968, and so on back down to the then-peak level of around $60 billion in the late 1950's. And after $110 billion in 1970, will they invest the $115 billion in 1971 and $120 billion in 1972 that will probably be needed, on our assumptions, to maintain economic growth and offset the growing savings made at g.n.p. levels above $750 billion? Lastly, will we want government to take away $150 billion in taxes and spend it for us? If not, private spending will have to grow even further to take up the slack.

Since private investment plays the key role in growth so long as we stick largely to private enterprise, Table 12-3 is useful in providing perspective. Table 12-3 shows the level of private investment for selected years since 1919, in constant (1954) dollars. It's clear that the $110 billion total hypothesized for 1970 is a whopper, even when it's scaled down to about $100 billion in 1954 dollars. But we should remember too the levels of the 1950's were never dreamed of a decade before.

Table 12-3

PRIVATE GROSS INVESTMENT, 1919-1959 *
(In billions of 1954 dollars)

Year	Total	*Residential Construction*	*Other Construction*	*Producer's Durable Equipment*	*Net Inventory Change*	*Net Foreign Investment*
1919	34	5	3	13	7	6
1924	29	10	6	10	2	1
1929	35	9	12	11	3	0
1934	7	2	3	5	−3	−1
1939	22	7	5	9	1	0
1944	12	1	3	9	−2	−7
1949	39	11	11	20	−4	−1
1954	49	15	14	21	−2	0
1957	58	16	17	24	1	3
1959	68	20	17	23	5	2

* Data from U.S. Department of Commerce, except purchasing power adjustment before 1929 and all data for 1959 estimated by author. Rows may not add to totals because of rounding.

CAN WE HAVE STABLE ECONOMIC GROWTH? Many people nowadays want continuously high-level employment, a roughly stable price level, and a stable annual growth in total production of not less than 4 per cent or so. What are the chances of achieving these results simultaneously?

Private Enterprise Will Do the Job: The Optimists. To many, the past points to a bright future. The free-enterprise, profit-motivated American economy has been the world's greatest success. With this kind of system, we have had recessions and inflationary bulges. But there is no reason why they need be serious disruptions, the optimists say. And private investment plus individual private enterprise provides the brightest hope for a rapidly and solidly growing economy. Provide conditions favorable to private saving and investment, reasonably competitive conditions to assure spreading the fruits of progress, and a money supply gradually rising as total capacity expands. Then reasonably full employment, reasonably stable prices, and the most rapid growth compatible with these and private freedom will come more or less automatically from the American economy. Vast opportunities lie ahead for expanded consumption and profitable private investment, say the private-enterprise optimists.

This point of view stresses two centuries of success with major reliance on private investment and private enterprise. It stresses the importance of providing conditions conducive to continued vigorous private investment. It denies that we need be concerned about the availability of adequate investment outlets for the huge savings generated by rising national incomes. The baby boom is a powerful expansionary force. Low-cost housing, atomic energy, plastics, electronics, jet propulsion are samples of the vast range of new profitable investment possibilities, if reasonable price-cost relationships prevail. We do indeed need to be concerned that costs are not forced up too high to make new investment profitable. But this is the issue—not the possibility of running out of "investment outlets." [4]

Writers who take this general position are not necessarily complacent. Many have stressed the following factors especially:

1. *Favorable "Climate" for Private Investment.* If private investment is to be forthcoming on an ever-larger annual scale, institutional and political conditions must be conducive to profitable investment. Businessmen cannot be expected to venture capital on large-scale projects if they feel the political and economic cards are stacked against them. "Anti-business" government regulation, confiscatory tax policy, politically inviolate labor restrictive practices, and uncertainty about the future value of money will discourage any businessman. If you want an explanation of the stagnation of the 1930's, here is a big part of it, argue the optimists. But, they say, we need not let it occur again.

2. *Open Markets and Active Competition.* Open markets and active competition are conducive to dynamic growth, say most private-enterprise optimists.

---

[4] In response to worries that we may be running out of investment opportunities, the optimists are fond of quoting the following statement by the United States Commissioner of Labor during the depression of 1886: "Industry has been enormously developed, cities have been transformed, distances covered, and a new set of economic tools has been given in profusion. . . . It is true that the discovery of new processes of manufacture will undoubtedly continue, but it will not leave room for marked extension, such as has been witnessed over the past fifty years, or afford remunerative employment of the vast amounts of capital which has been created during that period. . . . The day of large profits is probably past. There may be room for further intensive, but not extensive, development of industry in the present area of civilization."

Monopolies may slow the rate of innovation and new investment. Under effective competition, any firm obtaining a new invention or process will introduce it as soon as prospective profits with the new method surpass those with existing methods. Such innovation means new investment. Other firms throughout the industry must meet the new lower-cost competition by replacing outdated equipment. But the monopolist can go on producing inefficiently with the old methods without fear of being undercut. Before introducing new methods and machines, he will take fully into account the resulting obsolescence on his existing machinery and equipment, a consideration that need not deter the competitive innovator, since it is primarily his competitors' equipment he makes obsolescent through his innovation.

3. *Facilitation of Savings-investment Process.* Savers and investors are often different persons in the modern American economy. Most corporate savings tend to move directly into real investment, usually through internal re-investment. But only a small portion of individual savings flows directly into real investment, except in residential construction. Individual savings are typically placed in bank accounts or used to buy insurance or securities. Increased savings in bank accounts have in themselves no direct effect on either the volume of deposits or the volume of excess reserves—they merely slow down the velocity of circulation of deposits, other things equal. There is nothing in the situation that will necessarily induce bankers to make new loans or investments. Savings paid into life insurance or annuity premiums augment the cash holdings of the insurance companies. But insurance companies are restricted by law and custom to real-estate and conservative security investments. Opening further the institutional channels for the flow of individual money savings into new real investment would remove one possible impediment to the effective operation of the private-enterprise, private-investment process.

The Danger of Lagging Growth and Underemployment: The Pessimists.   But not everyone is so confident. The long, massive depression of the 1930's was foreboding. Unemployment reached 13 million, over one-fourth of the labor force, and never fell below 7 million during the decade. Only World War II with its massive government spending restored prosperity and economic growth. Even with the modest recovery of the late 1930's, total output in 1939 was no higher than in 1929.

For a while, the pessimists agree, the post-World War II boom went great guns, and the economy grew rapidly. But by the mid-1950's the growth rate began to slacken, and underemployment began to spread. The recession of 1954 was a forerunner. Even in the great boom of 1955-57, unemployment seldom fell much below 3 million. The recession of 1958 quickly ran unemployment up over 5 million, and even the rapid recovery of 1958-59 barely managed to get the figure below 4 million. Actually, they say, unemployment was higher than the official figures show, because of many workers on part-time jobs and others marooned at starvation wages on farms but not technically unemployed. While money-spending rose during the 1950's, it was insufficient to offset rapid technological improvement and the growing labor force.

This bodes ill for dynamic growth, say the pessimists. Indeed, the waste of underemployment during the 1950's alone, often claimed to be a boom decade, was at least $200 billion, enough to raise the income of every family by $4,000 over the period. This was because actual production, called forth by insufficient money demand, fell far below true full-employment capacity. In 1958 alone, for example, this group estimated full-prosperity output at around $475 billion while actual g.n.p. was only about $440 billion, a waste of $35 billion of potential output.[5] A full-prosperity growth rate would have been nearly 5 per cent a year. The actual figure even for this "boom" decade was only 4.

Why has the growth rate fallen short of its real potential? Why does unemployment creep up, even in good times? The answer lies, one group argues, in shortage of money-spending, and particularly of consumer incomes and consumption spending. These "underconsumptionists" see low wages and low farm incomes as the weak link, providing inadequate consumer power to take full-employment output off the market. Investment will be forthcoming, they argue, if consumer spending goes up. Put up wages and farm incomes, is their answer.

Others, agreeing that more rapid growth is needed, believe that the big necessity is to stimulate investment directly. Investment spending is the big source of growth and new jobs, they argue. To raise wages and consumer incomes at the expense of profits and other inducements to invest is short-sighted indeed, because investment will dry up and with it jobs and consumer incomes. If we follow that policy, only government spending can then provide the incomes required for total spending needed to maintain full employment with technological advance and a growing labor force. Getting full employment and satisfactory economic growth is a foreboding problem.[6]

The Danger of Excess Spending: The Inflationists.

As prices continued to creep upward during the postwar period, the danger of inflation loomed ever larger in many minds. They worry not about too little money demand, but

---

[5] This general argument is advanced by different groups. One very active advocate is the "Conference on Economic Progress," a group composed largely of government officials, labor leaders, and economists once associated with the Democratic leaders of the Roosevelt and Truman administrations. See, for example, *Consumption—Key to Full Prosperity*, Washington, D. C. (1958). A more moderate, and more widely representative, group emphasizing the need for rapid growth was a special study commission of the Rockefeller Brothers Fund, which reported in *The Challenge to America: Its Economic and Social Aspects* (New York: Doubleday, 1958).

[6] The 10-year depression of the 1930's produced these arguments in even more vigorous form. For a leading statement of the then-stylish argument that our economy faced long-range "stagnation," see Alvin H. Hansen, *Fiscal Policy and Business Cycles* (New York: W. W. Norton, 1941).

about too much. Private and government spending together seem always to go up, and faster than total output. Right after World War II, inflation was probably inevitable, given the vast accumulation of new money created to finance the war and the great backlog of unsatisfied consumer and business demands. But long after these effects had worn off, the price indexes crept up, a few percentage points year after year.

The inflationists point to three major factors which make creeping inflation increasingly probable:

First, the government has accepted responsibility for maintaining full employment (in the Employment Act of 1946). This, say the inflationists, in effect means that the government will step in with new money and deficit spending whenever unemployment goes above moderate levels. If unions push up wages and businesses raise prices, instead of permitting both to price themselves out of the market into unemployment the government will see that new purchasing power is added—even though it supports the inflation.

Second, labor unions, businessmen, and farmers are increasingly effective in pushing up their prices and in resisting cuts. Wage-push by the unions and administered price-setting by businesses boost costs and prices when demand is strong, and block declines when demand weakens. All groups rely increasingly on government action to support and push up their wages and prices faster than they themselves could in the market. Minimum-wage laws and farm-support prices have become an accepted part of government's role. Even more fundamental, unions and businessmen increasingly realize that government spending and government support are in the background to bail them out if too-high wages or prices bring on unemployment and recession. Thus, the main restraint to inflationary behavior—the fear of pricing yourself out of the market—is greatly weakened. "Declining" areas and industries like agriculture and coal run to Washington for expansionary government spending to help solve their particular problems.

Third, government spending goes up and up! War—past, present and future—is the biggest cause. It now accounts for two-thirds of total federal expenditures, and nearly half for all governments. But actually, since 1953 the amount spent on national defense has not risen. The big increase in recent years has been on civilian government services—roads, schools, farm aid, welfare payments, and the like. The American people want lots of things from their governments, even though they criticize government spending. Any group in trouble looks for government aid. Increasing taxes can help reduce the inflationary impact of rising government expenditures. But governments find tax increases unpopular. And even when they come, workers and businessmen increasingly consider them costs to be passed on in the form of higher wage rates and prices.

Couple these factors and you have an economy that operates on a price ratchet. The cost of living goes up when demand is strong and when unions and other organized groups jack up prices, but prices catch there and stick even when demand weakens. Then when demand and other pressures pick up, prices move on up again from the higher level.

Full employment has won out over the honest dollar, say the inflationists. But worse, we may well end up having *both* inflation and unemployment. Unions, businessmen, and farmers all know they can count on large government spending to bail the economy out of any widespread tendency toward unemployment. In olden times, even the most powerful seller had to think a long time before he would risk losing his market by putting his price too high. But nowadays this fear is largely gone, with the government on hand to guarantee plenty of purchasing power and little or no inclination to curb the power of the big private pressure groups. Thus each group grabs for more income, and the result is merely higher prices and money incomes all the way round—inflation without any more real goods and services to divide up. And this attempt to grab bigger pieces of the national pie may come long before full employment is reached, as more and more of the economy is organized into monopolistic power groups.

This is the picture painted by the inflationists.

"Cost-push" and "demand-pull." If inflation has become a pressing economic problem, is it because unions have become so powerful they push up wages and hence prices, or merely because the old inflation cause, excess monetary demand, is at work? In short, is the cause of inflation cost-push or demand-pull?

The answer is, some of both, and it's hard to tell just how important each is. At the extreme, it's clear that no matter how strong the unions may be, rapidly rising wages would merely price workers out of jobs and their employers out of markets sooner or later if total purchasing power were not expanded to take goods off the market at the higher prices. This means, basically, that government (the Federal Reserve) must acquiesce in the inflation, since only through Federal Reserve action can the banks obtain reserves to create new money. At the other extreme, it's clear that even without any unions, strong excess demand (e.g., created by large government deficit spending) would soon lead to higher prices and higher wages as employers competed for workers to meet the enlarged demand. Demand-pull inflation can exist without wage-push, but wage-push alone cannot produce continuing inflation without at least support from the money supply side.

Over the postwar period, evidence exists for both hypotheses. In the late 1940's, demand-pull was strongly at work as the excess liquidity of the war period poured onto the market. Demand-pull was clearly evident again during the Korean War period, partly from private spending and partly from large government deficits. In the late 1950's, wage-push was at least partly responsible. Wage rates rose more rapidly than productivity, and rose while substantial unemployment existed. The timing of wage and price increases in major industries suggested the push of wages on prices, rather than the reverse.

The term "wage-push" may convey a burden of guilt on unions that should be shared by the business firms who push up their prices in the absence of strong demand-pull. Unions claim that business firms often jack up prices more than in response to rising wage costs, and that wage increases are therefore results rather than causes of rising living costs. During the 1950's there was much criticism of major industries for their "administered" prices, which (it was alleged) they raised faster than was justified by rising costs. In recognition of the combined union-business responsibilities for higher wages and higher prices, some economists call the recent price rises "sellers' inflation," instead of "wage-push." But, at least during the latter 1950's, union wage demands pretty clearly did much of the pushing. Even when business pricing practices are included with wages on the push side, it is still hard to separate the push from the demand-pull forces in allocating responsibility. In the last analysis, strong demand may not be the sole culprit, but it is necessary for cost-price push to account for substantial inflation.

The Prospect Ahead.   Who will be right about the future—the optimists, the pessimists, or the inflationists? Can we have all three: full employment *and* a stable price level *and* rapid growth?

It is clear that we can grow faster by devoting a larger portion of our resources to investment. But how we accomplish this in a free, basically private-enterprise economy (especially without inflation) is less clear.

One way is to lower the interest rate and make funds for investment easily available. Another way is to lower taxes on business profits and to take other steps to make business investment more attractive. Still another is to provide government subsidies, say for research and development spending. Some argue that one way is to stimulate consumption spending, but in a full-employment economy it is hard to see how this can shift resources toward investment.

A different approach is to have the government do part of the investing itself —through "fiscal policy." By increasing taxes and using the funds for investment, the government can reduce consumption and stimulate growth. Or the government may spend without raising taxes; in an underemployed economy this may stimulate growth without reducing consumption by putting unemployed resources to work, but in a fully employed economy it means inflation as the price of diverting resources to investment. This whole approach is difficult, because Americans typically dislike government entrance into the fields of business where growth investment seems most promising; research and development and education are partial exceptions.

These approaches are considered in detail in Chapters 14, 15, and 16. In a fully employed economy, they all must be based on the realization that more investment and faster growth can come only with temporary sacrifices of current consumption.

What about the problem of inflation? Would a continuing small excess of total demand, with creeping inflation, help to produce a higher growth rate? Should we consciously plan such a policy, rather than fighting against it? This, again, is a problem for Chapters 14, 15, and 16. In advance, it should be clear that persistent excess demand, assuming full employment, will help only if it does divert resources from consumption to investment. Inflation with lagging wages might well have that effect, through swelling business profits. This result has apparently obtained in numerous past inflations. But if there is no wage lag (for example, if wage-push is a major cause of the inflation), profits may not expand relatively, or may even contract. In such cases, there is little reason to expect inflation to speed economic growth. The creeping inflation of the late 1950's may be such a case. In perspective, more inflation may be likely, but that we will get much impetus to growth from the inflation is less likely.

One other big question needs to be faced: Is rapid growth, with high-level investment, compatible with *stable* growth? Historically, growth has come in spurts—in investment booms, followed by slowing-down periods of recession or depression. Many economists feel that this is the way a profit-motivated private economy must grow if it is to grow rapidly. They see instability as the price of progress. To damp the investment boom might prevent the following recession, but it would also damp down the rate of growth. This is the problem of business fluctuations—what they are and what causes them—to which the next chapter is devoted.

A CONCLUDING NOTE The forces determining the rate of economic growth are many. Their interactions are complex and often obscure. Yet few problems are more central to the welfare of the American economy over the years ahead. Against this broad view of the process of American economic growth, we need to ask a concluding question:

Does the whole chapter, focusing as it does on *economic* growth alone, miss the main point involved in any fundamental look at human progress? Man does not live by bread alone. Many observers abroad, and not a few here, argue that other economies, far poorer in economic wealth, are richer than we are culturally, spiritually, and in terms of human happiness. Is a ride in a Cadillac worth more than a leisurely walk down the road? Does a national income that includes vast advertising expenditures designed to make people want more than they have really reflect human progress? Are we happier than our forefathers, struggling to wrench a living from the wilderness two centuries ago? Not to ask these questions is to risk wearing blinders in studying man's striving for progress, even though few of us show much willingness to give up the American standard of living for the "simple" but poor life.[7]

---

[7] Some instructors may wish to go directly on to the problem of growth in the "underdeveloped" economies, Chapter 43. The chapter may be used in that order.

1. How fast do you think the American economy should grow over the decade ahead? If you think our growth rate should be speeded up or slowed down, what steps would you propose?

FOR
ANALYSIS
AND
DISCUSSION

2. Is it important for us to grow as fast economically as the U.S.S.R. does? What is the most significant measure of growth for such a discussion? G.n.p.? Private g.n.p.? Total personal consumption? Per capita consumption? Investment? Some other measure?

3. How much of your personal income are you willing to use to build up the productive capacity of the nation for the future? Do you feel that the government has a right to dictate to you a rate different from the one you prefer?

4. In looking at the growth of the United States economy since 1900, would you say that "real" factors or "monetary-flow" factors have been more important determinants of the level of total real output? Explain why you answer as you do.

5. "More rapid growth in population in the United States would mean a more rapid rise in our national standard of living." Do you agree? Explain.

6. By 1975, total United States population may be 200 million. Assume that the same proportion (about 40 per cent) of the population is in the labor force as in 1959; that the average propensity to consume out of gross national product remains at about 2/3; that output per worker rises at about 2 per cent per year; and that the price level remains constant:

   a. What level of gross national expenditure will be required in 1975 to assure full employment? Why?
   b. What level of private investment would be required, assuming government spending to remain at its 1959 level of about $90 billion?
   c. Suppose that with the gradual aging of the population only 35 per cent of the population is in the 1975 labor force. How would your answers to a. and b. change?
   d. Suppose both this and a reduction of the work-week to 30 hours should occur. How would your answers to a. and b. change? How would per capita real income in 1975 compare with that in 1959, when population was 177 million?

7. Life-insurance premiums paid in 1959 totaled over $14 billion. At the beginning of 1959, the entire physical assets of the United States Steel Corporation (such as blast furnaces, equipment, and buildings), for example, were valued at less than $4 billion. If annual reports of major business concerns are available in your library, compute roughly how many leading business concerns' total physical assets could be completely replaced by insurance premiums alone over a five-year period if all insurance savings were invested in this way.

8. "The growing strength of labor unions constitutes the greatest single threat to maintenance of full employment and a stable value of the dollar." Do you agree or disagree with this statement? Defend your position.

Economic
Fluctuations

The long pull of American economic growth is impressive. But that growth has been unstable. It has come spasmodically, in spurts separated by breathing spells or even by major depressions. Prosperity, with heavy investment spending, means rapid economic growth. Unemployment and recession means lagging economic growth.

ECONOMIC GROWTH AND FLUCTUATIONS In perspective, the booms and depressions of American history are thus fluctuations around a long-term growth trend. And this is the right way to look at them. For seldom has the trough of a recession been lower than the peak of the boom before last. Growth has been more dominant in our history than fluctuations. But this doesn't mean that booms and depressions have been unimportant. Far from it!

Are There Business Cycles? Are there business cycles—regularly recurring economy-wide booms and depressions? The answer is no, if you stress the "regularly." It is yes, if you mean only that there are intermittent periods of prosperity and recession from previous peaks. Since there is wide variation in the timing of successive bursts of total output and setbacks, many economists have dropped the words "business cycles" in favor of the term "fluctuations," which doesn't connote such regularity.

"The business cycle" also connotes a *common* cycle or movement in all business. In big booms and big depressions, this is substantially true. From 1929 to 1933, just about everything went down—employment, wages, rents, construction, investment, consumption, prices, you name it. Conversely, in the big Korean War boom of 1950-53, just about everything went up. But even in these cases, some activities went down or up a lot faster and farther than others. And in smaller "boomlets" or recessions, some series commonly go up while others are stable or go down. For example, during the recessions of 1954 and 1958, corporate profits and private investment dropped sharply, employment and spending on consumer durables dropped moderately, personal income and total consumption spending temporarily leveled off their growth, while consumer spending on services kept right on going up. An even more dramatic mixture appears if we look at individual products—for example, rockets, electronic computers, automobiles, TV sets, and bread.

Moreover, not all series turn from up to down at the same time. The National Bureau of Economic Research, a leading compiler of facts about business fluctuations, emphasizes that there is a continuous spectrum of individual economic activities at any given time, ranging from those rising rapidly to those fading badly. The Bureau says that the turn from boom to recession is best put where the majority of a big list of important series has shifted from upward to downward direction. Others are willing to focus more simply on one or two of the aggregate measures, like gross national product or total unemployment.

Growth and Fluctuations in America. Look back at Figures 6-4 and 12-1 and the graph inside the front cover to get a feel for the long sweep of strong, irregular growth in America. Against this background, it is possible to analyze business fluctuations more thoroughly by separating them out from the long-term upward trend. This is done in Figure 13-1, which shows the fluctuations in industrial production since 1900.

Industrial production is a major sector of the modern American economy. It is also one that fluctuates widely in booms and depressions. To construct Figure 13-1, first a "trend" line was drawn through the actual monthly data for industrial production over the period—a rapidly and irregularly rising series. A trend line is a line drawn roughly through the middle of the fluctuating series— roughly so the readings on the industrial production curve above the trend line about equal those below it.[1] If, then, we lay the trend line out flat, so to speak,

---

[1] Any elementary statistics book will provide information on the precise statistical techniques used in "fitting" trend lines to data. There are several techniques, which may be considered substantially equivalent for our purposes.

it becomes the zero, or normal, line in Figure 13-1. Thus, all periods when in-dustrial production was above the trend line are shown above normal, and con-versely for those below.

All the data are shown as percentage deviations from "normal." Thus the prosperity of 1955-57 runs about 10-15 per cent above normal, as does that of 1905-07. In absolute terms, of course, industrial production for 1955-57, and its expansion from the preceding low, were many times what they were for 1905-07. The vast areas below normal in the 1930's and above normal in the 1940's and 1950's on the chart are thus far smaller in comparison with earlier cycles than they would be plotted in absolute, rather than percentage deviation, terms.

U.S. Industrial Output Since 1900—Percentage Deviations from Trend

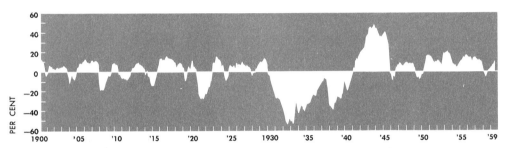

FIG. 13-1   The curve shows percentage deviations from the long-term upward trend of U.S. industrial production. Areas above the zero line are above trend, and similarly for readings below. (Source: The Cleveland Trust Company.)

The Anatomy of Business Fluctuations. The big booms and depressions in America have all involved major swings in *production, employment,* and *income.* Until the last quarter-century, *prices* would have been added to this trio. But recently prices have become very "sticky" against downward adjustments, and have not fallen appreciably even with substantial drops in the other major series. And some important booms have occurred without major increases in the price level.

Figure 13-2 shows employment and the three major components of production in the United States over the past thirty years. Their roughly synchronous be-havior is obvious. Equally obvious is the fact that production of durable goods fluctuates far more violently than nondurables, services, or employment. In fact, fluctuations in total production and employment come largely in the capital goods and durable consumer goods industries—in such "capital goods" as steel, elec-trical machinery, and locomotives, and in such "durable consumer goods" as automobiles and refrigerators. They are much milder in shoes, clothing, foods, and other relatively nondurable consumer goods. And the stability of spending on services is remarkable; the growth curve hardly wobbles since 1945, in spite of three recessions. This does not mean that nondurable consumer goods industries are unaffected by cyclical fluctuations, but the heart of the problem lies in the capital and durable consumer goods industries.

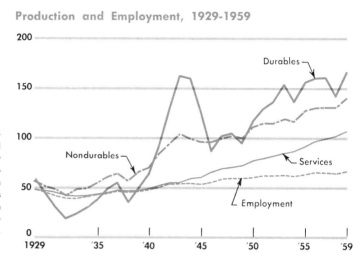

Production and Employment, 1929-1959

FIG. 13-2   The major components of production and employment fluctuate roughly together, but with very different amplitudes. Figures on production are index numbers (1947-1949 = 100); those on services and employment are actual data. (Source: U.S. Department of Commerce.)

Some economic series—for example, hog production, construction, and shipbuilding—apparently have cycles of their own, partially or largely independent of general business activity. The most important of these is construction, which showed a surprisingly regular 15-20 year pattern of deviation from its "normal" growth rate over the century preceding World War II. The war upset the cyclical pattern, and it is too soon to tell whether it has been reestablished. Peaks of the construction cycle have contributed strongly to alternate 6-12 year swells in general business activity; and major downturns in construction have often shortly preceded major business downturns. A high level of construction activity reaches back into almost every sector of the economy—directly into steel, lumber, plumbing, roofing, concrete, glass, furniture and furnishings, and many others; indirectly into associated areas, such as highway construction, utilities, and sewage systems. Widespread prosperity with a sick construction industry has been rare.

Figure 13-3 shows both the commonness and the cyclical diversity of a number of smaller components of economy activity during the 1952-59 period of two recessions and recoveries. Note that both the amplitude of fluctuation and the timing differ. All are plotted on a logarithmic scale to give equal weight to equal percentage changes.

The Perpetual Postwar Boom?   After a big boom has gone on for a few years, the economy usually undergoes a substantial setback—sometimes a major

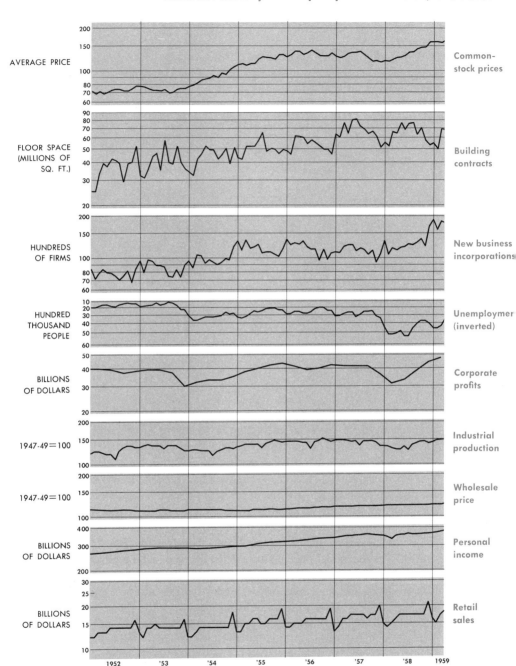

FIG. 13-3 Different components of economic activity move up and down roughly together in business fluctuations. But their timing and amplitude vary greatly. Series at the top are often thought to be "leading" series in signalling changes in business activity; those at the bottom slower movers. All data are on ratio scales.

depression, sometimes only a moderate recession. And there are good reasons for expecting this to happen, as we shall see later on in this chapter.

But the 1940's and '50's amazed just about everybody. Ever since 1940, the American economy has been sailing along in a full-fledged boom, far longer and bigger than ever before in history. Only for a brief period at the end of World War II did employment and output fall sharply, reflecting an enormous cut-back of nearly $100 billion in the annual rate of federal government spending. Even then, g.n.p. fell by only about $40 billion as private spending spurted. After that it was onward and upward. Brief "recessions" in 1949, 1954, and 1958 only temporarily halted the steady upsweep of total output, although they did produce temporary swells in unemployment when new workers coming into the labor force were not absorbed by growing total demand.

In its early years, this was unmistakably a war boom. And the Korean War in 1950-52 provided a substantial further impetus. But private spending on consumption and investment, plus a steady, solid growth in government spending on public services like roads and schools, have been the biggest factors in the amazing American prosperity of our generation.

Both the experts and the man in the street repeatedly predicted that the crash was just around the corner. At the end of World War II cataclysmic depression with unemployment of at least 10 million was widely predicted. It never happened. The economy took reconversion in its stride. By 1949, the immediate postwar burst of spending on durables seemed to have run its course and inventories piled up in factories and on dealers' shelves. But a continued rise in consumer buying offset the temporary drop in business investment. Again in 1951 it was clear that businesses were heavily overstocked with inventories, and indeed there was in 1951 and 1952 one of the biggest drops in inventory investment in American history. But it scarcely fazed the surging economy; business spending on plant and equipment and new construction sailed along at record high levels, and the irrepressible consumers kept right on each year buying more than the year before.

In 1954, things looked more serious. 1953 had again brought clear overstocking of inventories; record business investment in plant and equipment had gone on for nearly a decade without serious halt; any pent-up war demand for consumer durables had long since been filled; and it scarcely seemed possible that the economy would keep on buying new houses at those rates. What happened? Inventories slumped as predicted, and federal government spending was sliced $10 billion. But private investment hardly faltered, and consumer spending climbed steadily upward.

The 1957-58 recession looked dangerous again. The drop was sharp in inventory and other private investment spending. Even consumer spending slumped a little, but not much before it resumed its climb. This time government spending held up and provided support against the downswing. By 1959 the boom was on its way again.

Figure 13-4 shows the major elements in the long Amercan prosperity since 1940, plotted in "real" terms to eliminate the additional large rise in dollar terms arising from the postwar price inflation. As the figure shows, the biggest single burst came with the huge increase in government spending in World War II, and again in the 1950's government spending was important. But the persistent increase in consumer expenditures, year after year, no matter what happened to investment and government spending, is perhaps the most amazing development in the amazing period—followed closely by the continued high level of investment expenditures that have refused to slump seriously in spite of every indication from historical experience that they would long before this.

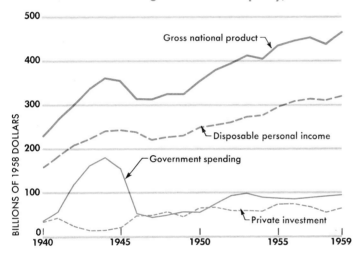

The Amazing American Prosperity, 1940-1959

FIG. 13-4 Through two decades of prosperous growth, the amazing American economy has hardly faltered except briefly after World War II. Personal income has shown the most stable growth. (Source: U.S. Department of Commerce.)

Is the business cycle obsolete? Have we at last found the secret of permanent prosperity, or had it thrust upon us through government policy or private action? Maybe. There are many who believe another massive depression like the 1930's will never again darken the land. But others have their doubts. The pessimists of Chapter 12 point to the stubborn persistence of some unemployment, even in the booms. And many old-timers remember the 1920's, when most people also thought permanent prosperity had been achieved. You should be in a better position to evaluate these arguments by the time you have finished this chapter.

BUSINESS-CYCLE THEORIES

Ever since booms and depressions began, people have been trying to figure out why they happen. Professional economists have worked out a variety of theories. Businessmen, financiers, labor leaders, and the man in the street have their business-cycle theories too—although they'd be horrified if you told them so. The man who says, "The bigger the boom the bigger the bust!" has an implicit theory about how booms and busts are related. The man who says, "What goes up must come down!" also has at least a partial theory about the relation of booms and depressions. Try asking yourself why people say, "The bigger the boom, the bigger the bust."

Different writers have emphasized everything from sun spots to Wall Street as the primary cause of economic fluctuations. But a quick survey of five major theories will give some perspective on the problem. These summaries are extremely rough. Their purpose is merely to suggest lines of reasoning—not to give a careful picture of the reasoning in each approach.

Psychological Theories.   One group says that the main thing is people's psychology and expectations, especially businessmen's. If businessmen expect times to pick up, they will expand output, increase investment, and times will in fact improve. Similarly, if consumers expect better times and rising prices, this will itself induce more spending, which will help bring about the expected better times.

Expectations are cumulative and self-reinforcing upward or downward, once they get well under way. Improved expectations lead to increased spending, which further improves expectations; and conversely on the downswing. But the further expectations go in either direction, the more extreme and more susceptible to reversal they become. Finally, any small shock or any failure of extreme expectations to materialize will be enough to reverse the whole process. Thus, a whole theory of cumulative sweeps up and down and of turning points at both extremes can be built around psychological changes and expectations. But there's a problem. The theory isn't very clear on just what are the basic determinants of the psychological attitudes it emphasizes.

Monetary Theories.   Another group says the supply of money is the key to the whole problem. When people have plenty of money, they will spend it—on both consumption and investment. Easy bank reserves and low interest rates encourage expansion in borrowing and spending. But when reserves run out and money tightens, business and individual spending are squeezed, and the boom tops off. Reduction in the money supply at a minimum impedes further business expansion and generally brings about a reduction in the over-all level of spending, the reverse of the upswing process.

This is the general approach suggested by the monetary models in Chapter 10. The basic reasoning is simple—too simple, say its critics. If this theory is right, it makes control over the level of economic activity relatively easy, since the supply of money is one of the economic variables most susceptible to government control, both directly and through the commercial banking system.

Underconsumption Theories.   Next to the monetary theories, the commonest man-in-the-street explanation of depressions has been that people save too much money and hence don't spend enough to keep workers employed. This under-consumption argument in its most naive form assumes that all individual and business profits and savings are withdrawn from the income stream and held uninvested, an obviously fallacious oversimplification. In more sophisticated versions it introduces the propensity to save with results something like this: As times get better, the proportion of income saved rises with rising income. Al-though investment may also rise, the large dollar volume of saving will become increasingly hard to offset by investment, until the point is reached where in fact the savings are a net withdrawal from the income stream. Then consumption spending is too small and saving too large to maintain the existing level of output and employment. Conversely, on the downswing, falling incomes mean a steady increase in the proportion of income spent on consumption. Thus the downswing will be slowed, and it becomes increasingly easy for savings to be more than offset by new investment.

Investment Theories.   Most professional economists emphasize investment as a crucial driving force in the cycle. It's the instability of private investment that is the core of the problem. Consumption spending is by and large a passive function of income received, but not investment. This emphasis is based on both empirical observation and theoretical analysis.

Some economists argue that investment booms when a big new *innovation* is brought into the economy—the canals, the railroads, the automobile—and that the boom peters out when this big upsurge ends. Others agree, but doubt that big innovations of this sort are essential. Instead, they point to the natural *bunching of real investment;* a few successful investments raise income payments and im-prove expectations, leading on to exploitation of other large and small investment opportunities. After such a boom has gone on for a while, producers' and con-sumers' stocks are well filled and the boom becomes increasingly susceptible to a downturn. This group often argues that *overinvestment* late in the boom turns out more goods than will be consumed as the new productive capacity comes into operation. The result is a drop in investment, followed by a negative multiplier spiral downward until something stimulates investment again.

Investment thus plays a central role in both growth and fluctuations. High in-vestment brings prosperity and rapid growth, but also the danger of recession if investment overshoots.

External Shocks.   Some economists say that economic fluctuations can be explained mainly by the external "shocks" that come along from time to time—wars, political events, gold discoveries, and so on. These shocks give an upward or downward impetus to the economic system, which may be strengthened by cumulative internal factors. These external shocks, coming more or less at random, are alleged to give a reasonably good explanation of the booms and depressions we have had. Indeed, some mathematical economists point out that theoretically a series of random shocks can set up oscillatory responses in economic or other systems. The analogy of a freely swinging pendulum is often used, where a blow from any direction or at any interval will set the pendulum swinging.

Which Theory Is Best?   Some economists are convinced that one or the other of the above approaches is the major key to explaining business fluctuations. But increasingly economists agree that all these factors may be important from time to time. Every fluctuation is different, and there is no reason to suppose that exactly the same factors are uppermost in every one. On the other hand, there is enough sameness to succeeding booms and depressions to suggest that a common analytical framework may be useful, at least as a device for raising some of the important questions we should ask in trying to explain modern business fluctuations.

The main purpose of the following sections is to suggest a tentative framework for your own thinking when you have to make up your own mind about whether good times or bad lie ahead. And you'll have to make up your own mind frequently—in deciding what job to take, in buying a house, in predicting the sales of your business, in deciding how to invest your savings, in deciding whether the government should raise or lower taxes, in judging when is a good time to hit the boss for a raise.

THE CUMULATIVE   The essence of a cyclical upswing is a cumula-
UPSWING   tive interaction between expanding investment and consumption expenditures, reinforced by new bank credit. New investment generates larger incomes through the multiplier process. These incomes induce more spending on consumption, which makes business better and induces a further increase in investment. This in turn further increases incomes and consumption through the multiplier process. And so the upward spiral goes. But it normally could not go far without additional bank credit to finance the new investment and the higher volume of total expenditures. Thus, the banks too play a central role in the cumulative upswing.

Rising Consumption.   *Rising Consumption Through the Multiplier.* To begin, assume a period of recession and an externally caused increase in investment (perhaps because a new product or machine has been invented). This new investment spending will generate a multiplied amount of income and consumer spending, through the multiplier explained in the last chapter. Just how much consumption rises for each dollar of new investment depends, of course, on the economy's marginal propensity to consume. This ratio is generally high in bad times, such as we are assuming at the outset. At the bottom of a bad depression, consumption may be nearly 100 per cent of disposable income, pointing toward a large multiplier effect, other things equal. As incomes rise into prosperity, though, the marginal propensity to save rises, reducing the multiplied effect of each additional investment dollar.

Other Inducements to Rising Consumption. As people come out of a hard depression, more jobs and more take-home pay are the only things likely to give a major boost to consumption spending. But if the revival takes hold, there are three special factors that may push the consumption-income ratio up, and keep it there.

First, consumers may have a big backlog demand for all types of consumer durables—refrigerators, stoves, autos, radios, and so on—piled up from the depression. You can use the same refrigerator a long time if you're good at minor repairs and don't mind foregoing the latest improvements, but you're not likely to be very happy about it. And try as you will to avoid it, the day will come when you have to buy another refrigerator or have the food spoil in hot weather. The postponement of purchases of durable goods is one reason depressions last. Catching up on these postponed purchases is one of the big lifts in revival.

Second, as revival moves along and prices begin to rise, consumers may begin to wonder whether still higher prices lie ahead. In 1947, you could buy a new Ford or Chevvy for $1,200 or so. Today it takes twice that much. Expectations of rising prices generally speed consumer buying, especially *if* incomes are high enough to provide some savings margin; but this is a boost we can't count on with any confidence until the upswing is well under way.

Third, as consumers and businesses borrow to finance revival spending, the public's money holdings will rise. With rising liquidity, consumers' ideas of what they can afford slide up, especially if liquidity rises faster than incomes and prices. Readily available consumer credit is a closely related support for higher consumer spending.

These three special boosts may come into play simultaneously, separately, or not at all in the upswing. The first is likely to be strongest early in revival and then gradually weaken as revival sweeps upward. The second is unpredictable, but it may exercise its strongest effect after the boom is in full swing and rising prices are widespread. The third depends on the behavior of the monetary system. Easy money for consumers and business, which gives a boost to the boom, is most likely to come with improving expectations and rosy hopes. But this factor, too, may be a transient one, since the day may come when the monetary system runs out of reserves for further expansion. Then tightening money squeezes consumer borrowing and spending.

Rising Investment. *The "Accelerator."* Rising sales generally stimulate more investment. This effect of more consumption spending in inducing more investment we call the "accelerator," or the "acceleration effect." It provides the link to complete the interaction underlying the cumulative upswing—more investment

⟶ more income ⟶ more consumption ⟶ more investment, and so on. In summary, the upswing is a cumulative multiplier-accelerator process.

Unless the original burst of investment with its multiplier effect induces more investment, there will be no cumulative upswing—only a hump on the floor of the depression. Common sense tells us that rising income and consumption should stimulate more investment. But it doesn't always work out that way. Remember that in a depression no one is quite sure what's going to happen next. There's lots of idle capacity. Accumulating inventories doesn't look like very good business.

If the rise in spending does produce a substantial accelerator effect, then the revival is on. The further induced investment in turn produces a multiplier effect, which in its turn may induce further investment. How big the acceleration effect is and how repetitive it is, are crucial questions in determining whether the revival will grow or wither. If both the multiplier and the accelerator are large, any revival that gets started will be an explosive one, with consumption and investment interacting vigorously. If either is zero, that's the end of the upswing.[2]

How strong will the acceleration effect be? The answer is, different at different times. In general, we can say that rising sales will induce new investment whenever they make the *desired* amount of plant and equipment to produce output larger than the *actual* stock on hand. Thus, if sales rise and the producer has no excess capacity, his desired stock of plant and equipment will clearly rise above his present stock, since without more capacity he can't meet the expanded demand. But if he begins with excess capacity, he probably has more plant and equipment than he currently wants, so even increased sales won't necessarily raise his desired stock above what he has.

Pragmatically, when the economy is just emerging from a serious recession, the outlook for a large accelerator effect from rising sales is bad, for two reasons:

1. Idle capacity is widespread during depression, and moderate increases in demand can often be met by using existing idle equipment.
2. Businessmen, whatever the capacity and inventory situation is, may cautiously sit and wait to see whether the increased demand is permanent. If they do, no acceleration effect will occur. Their desired stock of capital depends on the permanence they attach to the increased demand.

But as revival progresses and as idle capacity vanishes, further increases in consumer spending are more and more likely to stimulate new investment. History and theory both suggest that the acceleration effect can be powerful.

In some cases, an increase in consumer demand may stimulate a much more than proportional increase in investment spending on plant and equipment. Sup-

---

[2] The Appendix to this chapter presents a formal model of the cumulative multiplier-accelerator process which shows that under different (not unrealistic) assumed conditions, the combination of accelerator and multiplier effects can induce cyclical fluctuations in national income even when the original stimulus of investment does not fluctuate.

pose, for example, that the shoe industry produces 100 million pairs of shoes per year; that it has 1,000 shoe machines, each producing 100,000 pairs per year; and that the average life of shoe machines is 10 years. This means that 100 machines wear out and have to be replaced each year.

Now suppose that consumer demand rises by 10 per cent next year, to 110 million pairs. To meet this demand, if they have no excess capacity or extra inventories, shoe manufacturers will have not only to replace the regular 100 machines wearing out but also to buy 100 new machines to produce the additional 10 million pairs demanded. In this hypothetical case, a 10 per cent increase in final product leads to a 100 per cent increase in the demand for plant and equipment.

But the acceleration principle is not a reliable booster for the upswing. Suppose consumer demand stays at 110 million in the third year. Now manufacturers will have the productive capacity needed to meet this demand if they replace only the regular 100 worn-out machines. (None of the extra new machines needs replacement yet, of course.) Thus the demand for new machines drops back to the original level of 100 per year, a drop of 50 per cent, even though consumer demand stays unchanged at the new higher level.

Worse, assume that in the fourth year consumer demand for shoes drops below the original level, to 90 million pairs annually. Then manufacturers don't have to buy any new shoe machines at all. They don't even have to replace the ones that wear out that year. The demand for machines drops to zero as a result of a relatively small drop in the demand for shoes.

This shoe illustration is purely hypothetical of course. It does indicate, however, how modest shifts in consumer demand can, through the acceleration effect, give rise to big lumps of induced investment or to correspondingly steep slumps, even though neither is likely to be permanent.

Rising demand for such durable goods as houses is also likely to have a marked acceleration effect. For example, if houses ordinarily last 50 years, each year about 1/50 of all houses may be replaced (say, 1 million houses annually). Assume that as the result of a revival, 1 million young couples who had been living with relatives decide they want new homes. This increase of 1/50, or 2 per cent, in the total stock of homes demanded will result in a 100 per cent increase in the demand for new homes. Here again, note that the induced new investment in houses is a temporary lump that will vanish the next year unless there is a further increase in the number of young folks setting up their own houses.[3]

The acceleration effect can account for a big part of the observed changes in investment. But it won't account for all of them. Some other determinants of the cyclical behavior of investment need to be included.

Shifting Cost-Price Relationships. Back in Chapter 11, we said that decisions to invest depend fundamentally on the relationship between the marginal effi-

---

[3] Examples like these two are tricky and are to be viewed only as illustrations of possible results. Slight changes in the assumptions can give drastically different results.

ciency of investment and the interest rate (or cost of money). Rising consumer demand will clearly increase the marginal efficiency of investment and the desired stock of capital, other things equal. But common sense says that the marginal efficiency of capital depends on something else too—on the cost-price relationships involved in making the product concerned. If costs rise faster than demand, rising consumer demand won't stimulate much new investment.

Suppose, for example, the economy is just beginning a revival. Then new investment can be financed without incurring higher construction or operating costs, or bidding up interest rates—because there is still much unemployed slack in the economy. But now suppose a boom is in full swing, with little excess capacity and limited unemployment. Then further increases in consumer demand may still lead to higher marginal efficiency of investment and a higher desired stock of capital. But making new investments means *both* forcing up the cost of money (interest rates) as demands for funds increase *and* probable increases in other associated costs (such as materials in building the new plant and labor in operating it). Thus the likely return on the investment may be squeezed by rising costs as the recovery turns into boom. Cost-price relationships are an important factor in investment decisions.

Innovation and the Development of New Industries. Historically, most big booms have centered around the development of one or a few important new industries. For example, during the 1800's railroad-building, with the resultant demand for iron and steel products, was especially important. The boom of the 1920's centered around the auto and electrical industries. Actually, the inventions underlying these industries had been made years before. It was the utilization of these inventions on a large scale through developmental investment that produced the booms they dominated.

Was the development of new industries at those particular times induced by the revivals then beginning, or were the revivals created by the new industries? This is not an easy question to answer. The effect probably runs both ways.

Whether such innovations actually set off the revival or not, they play a major role in most big booms. Once a few entrepreneurs have braved the uncertain paths of introducing new products and new methods and have successfully undertaken new investments, others are eager to follow. Investment has generally come in spurts in our economy. And the spurts have been followed by slack periods. With big new industries, booms are long and lusty. Without them, the chances for lusty prosperities are weaker and growth may well slow down.

Inventory Investment and the "Inventory Cycle." Investment in business inventories plays a very special role in business fluctuations. Fluctuations in inventory investment comprise one of the most regular and predictable sub-cycles in economic activity. The "short cycles" of two to four years' duration mentioned in the historical survey are predominantly inventory cycles. When inventories become scarce, businessmen's desired inventory levels shoot up. Businesses tend to overbuy in building them up, and thus overshoot what they consider desirable inventories. Trying to unload these excess inventories, they generally overshoot again, plummeting themselves into a position where inventories are short—and they're all ready to start up again. This is too simple a picture, but it is a reasonably accurate central framework.

Figure 13-5 shows the persistence and violence of these inventory fluctuations. Note that the chart shows changes in *net* inventory investment; this is in accordance with the national income accounts, which count as inventory investment the net increase or decrease in the total stock of inventories held by business. Thus any figure above the zero line shows inventories building up; any figure below zero shows inventories being depleted. If you compare Figure 13-5 with the earlier data on total investment and g.n.p., you'll see that plummeting net inventory investment accounted for much of the recession drops of 1949, 1954, and 1958, of the upswings in 1950, 1955, and 1958-59. If, as some argue, we are beginning to get major cyclical fluctuations under control, the inventory cycle may be our biggest remaining cyclical problem.

Fluctuations in Inventory Investment

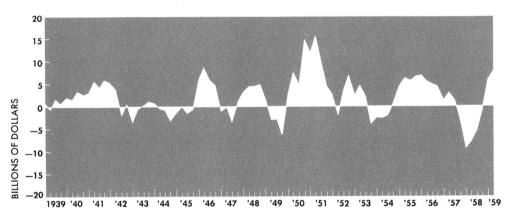

FIG. 13-5   The inventory cycle shows sharp, large fluctuations in inventory investment, which are a major factor in explaining many minor swings in aggregate economic activity.

In essence, the inventory cycle amounts to this: When businesses are accumulating inventories, production is running ahead of consumption. Obviously this can go on only for so long; the day of reckoning must come. Conversely, when business inventories are declining, consumption is running ahead of production. Obviously this too can go on for only so long. In 1959, business inventories in the whole economy (at all levels—manufacturers, wholesalers, and retailers) totaled about $90 billion. Over the long pull this total can be expected to rise with the growth in total economic activity—at perhaps 3 or 4 per cent a year.

But you can be sure that any inventory accumulation much faster than that won't last for long. And you can be equally sure that if total inventories begin to fall far short of that level, there's going to be an upswing in inventory investment.

Construction as a Special Factor. Investment in business and residential construction has bulked large in many boom periods. Construction activity reaches back into almost every corner of the economy. As was indicated above, semi-independent construction cycles averaging around 15-20 years have been evident for the past century. Thus, construction booms have strengthened some general upswings and weak construction has retarded others. This semi-independent construction cycle is particularly evident in residential housing; business plant construction shows a closer affinity to general business activity.

The reasons for this construction pattern are far from clear. They are apparently linked with the average durability of buildings and are probably related closely to the cycle in general business activity. After a vast construction boom, like that of the 1920's, construction needs are satiated. Not only were millions of houses erected, but a tremendous volume of office and industrial construction was completed in the space of a few years. Under the impetus of inflated expectations, speculative building activity spread like wildfire. Enough skyscrapers were erected in three years to serve the country's needs for five times that long. With this supply of residential and business housing, little need for new construction had developed by 1933-37, when the next revival in business activity occurred. The market was still satiated, and construction contributed little to the revival.

But by the end of World War II, expanding population and the long period of low-level construction activity had created a strong demand for new housing. Rising incomes in the boom led to housing demands which contributed strongly to the postwar boom. The construction cycle is far from independent of more general business fluctuations, whatever the exact causal relationships between the two.

The Banking System in the Upswing.

The cumulative upswing in production, employment, and income may be financed by the existing money supply for a while, as businesses and consumers draw on idle balances and speed up the use of funds. But before long, new money is needed to finance the growing volume of business. Businesses need more working capital to expand operations and longer-term funds to finance new investment in plant and equipment. With higher incomes consumers want to hold larger cash balances.

The commercial banks, and behind them the Federal Reserve, are the only source of new money for the system as a whole. And every major upswing has been marked by a substantial increase in the volume of bank credit. Bankers dislike to hold excess reserves, which earn no return. Thus, as their customers' demand for loans increases and as better times lessen the apparent risks in lending, bankers are glad to expand loans as far as they have excess reserves.

As revival progresses, the demand for bank credit rises apace. Loans expand

and more currency moves into hand-to-hand circulation as incomes rise. Excess bank reserves are drawn down to levels that induce bankers to look more carefully at new loans and investment possibilities. One sign of this situation is rising interest rates, as well as a tendency on the part of bankers to "ration" their remaining credit to preferred borrowers. By the prosperity stage, prices are generally rising, inventories large, and working-capital needs high, so additional bank credit is likely to be a *sine qua non* for continued business expansion. Unless the Federal Reserve provides new reserves, credit stringency will gradually impose a ceiling on the upswing.

UPPER TURNING POINT OR STABLE PROSPERITY? Prosperity is wonderful. Why can't it go on forever? Maybe it can, and there are good reasons for believing our chances are a lot better than ever before. But history warns us to expect a downswing sooner or later. Some reasons have been suggested on the preceding pages.

The cumulative upswing is many-sided and interacting. Early in the rise, everything seems to work together toward prosperity. But as the boom continues, the economic system becomes more and more "vulnerable" to shocks that may precipitate a downturn. Inflationary booms typically produce distorted patterns of activity that are difficult to maintain indefinitely.

What actually turns economic activity downward? Sometimes there is a spectacular financial crisis, as in 1907 and 1929. But economic change is complex, and often many phases of economic activity have turned down while others are still moving lustily upward. Sometimes it is hard to say whether the economy is still moving up or has turned down; it depends on where you look.

So the experts have become increasingly wary of predicting just what particular factor is likely to spark the downturn. Rather, they stress that a series of developments gradually set the stage for a downswing, and in such a setting it is increasingly likely that something will give the push that sets the economy unmistakably downward, even though we may not recognize it until months later.

The "environmental" factors they stress are:

1. Piling up of inventories.
2. Accumulation of large stocks of new durables in consumers' hands.
3. Consumer resistance to rising prices.
4. End of upward "acceleration" effect.
5. Rising costs.
6. Accumulation of vast amounts of new productive capacity.
7. Utilization of available new technological developments, and growing scarcity of promising large-scale investment outlets.
8. Exhaustion of excess bank reserves.
9. Weakening of confidence and expectations.

Sometimes a boom keeps going until it faces all these hurdles simultaneously. Sometimes the downturn comes when only two or three seem to present serious problems. Basically, the boom ends when the entire conjuncture gradually shifts over from favorable to unfavorable—when the driving forces of the upswing (especially investment and spending on consumer durables) give way to disappointed expectations and uncertainty in the face of increasingly saturated markets.

All this has left the government out of the picture. Yet, increasingly, government action seems to be becoming the most critical consideration in turning points. Big changes in government spending and tax policies or in Federal Reserve monetary policy may help induce turning points. More important, fiscal and monetary policy may be used to avoid the downturn and recession. Such government action will get extended attention in the next three chapters. If we are to achieve stable economic growth at full employment without inflation, it's clear we need positive government assistance to turn the trick.

THE DOWNSWING   A recession looks pretty much like a boom in reverse. Both the multiplier and the acceleration effects work downward instead of upward. Decreasing investment pulls out the support for a multiplied amount of income. Falling incomes mean falling consumption expenditures, which in turn reduce the incentive to invest. The cumulative upward spiral that made hearts glad seems diabolically designed as it races downward into depression.

Once a downswing gets under way, the path toward depression may be direct and cumulative. Businessmen, somewhat disappointed in sales and profits as prosperity levels off, are uneasy. Under such conditions, it takes only a downturn in expectations to undermine investment and production plans. Attempts to unload inventories and to obtain cash lead to the very price declines that sellers are trying to "beat" and to still worse expectations for the future. The breakdown of expectations may be especially severe when costs have risen relative to prices during the boom.

On the other hand, not all downturns turn into major depressions, just as not all recoveries soar into full-fledged booms. Since World War II, sustained consumer spending on nondurables and services has proved a massive block against a downward spiral. Business investment in plant and equipment has been more resistant to panic cutbacks than in earlier decades. Perhaps most important, changes in the government tax and expenditure system have built in quick tax liability reductions when incomes fall and automatic transfer payments to maintain personal incomes against collapse; and private unemployment insurance plans have supplemented this support.

The behavior of the banking system is especially important in the downswing. Traditionally, recessions led to "runs" on the banks, as people lost confidence in their safety and withdrew their deposits in currency. This loss of reserves came at the same time as bankers saw the business prospects of their customers deteriorating. Thus, they called for payments on loans, both because reserve pressures forced them to do so and because they feared for the safety of their funds. But this very pressure, of course, intensified the downward spiral. Borrowers were in no position to pay. Bank pressure forced them to liquidate inventories and securities to obtain funds, just when the demand for both was sagging. This induced further declines in prices, employment, and incomes, thereby further worsening expectations and speeding the downward spiral.

Since the monetary reforms of the 1930's, there is strong reason to hope that recession-period banking pressure that forces mass liquidation has been eliminated. Federal deposit insurance has substantially eliminated the likelihood of widespread runs on banks. And the Federal Reserve authorities now have both the power and the stated intention of providing the reserves to member banks needed to avoid economy-wide credit contraction at such times. If the terrific downward monetary pressures of past depressions have been eliminated, our chances of avoiding major depressions have been greatly increased.

Upturn or Stagnation?   If a major depression occurs, will business activity turn up again, or will the system bump along the bottom indefinitely?

Take the list of hurdles facing a boom as it reaches its peak and reverse them, and you have a picture of the potentially favorable forces that make an upturn increasingly likely. The gradual buildup of potential demand for consumers' and producers' durables as old stocks wear out is one of the surest and most powerful forces. But many economists doubt the certainty that the economic system will turn itself up without a prolonged massive depression if it is again permitted to reach the depths of the early 1930's. The effectiveness of positive government action to check the downswing and turn the system back up has become the dominant question in any consideration of lower turning-points.

ARE DEPRESSIONS OBSOLETE?   Are depressions obsolete? Does the long prosperity of the 1940's and '50's represent the beginning of a new era of permanent prosperity? Do we have to have another depression?

The preceding pages suggest a variety of reasons for expecting boom conditions sooner or later to give way to recession. Yet, as the prosperity of the postwar decade has weathered one predicted downturn after another, many businessmen and economists have come to believe that at least massive depressions like those of the 1870's and 1930's are a thing of the past. In spite of reminders by the "doubting Thomases" of the permanent-prosperity slogans of the late 1920's, just before the crash, they point to the following impressive list of factors in support of their belief:

1. Businessmen now manage their firms more efficiently and make their investment plans on a longer-range basis. Thus, investment plans are less susceptible to short-term swings in expectations which might earlier have set off contraction and investment cancellations. Long-run growth is widely recognized as a dominant factor in business planning, and this factor will keep business investment plans from serious short-run collapse. (So much wishful thinking! say the doubters.)

2. Consumers in America have become adjusted to a high and rising standard of living, and they will not be panicked into cutting back their spending even though business conditions weaken. If incomes slide off and jobs become more scarce, consumers will draw on liquid assets and borrow to protect their living standards, looking forward to a resumption of better times in the near future. This fact has been demonstrated repeatedly during the postwar years when consumer expenditures have continued to increase through thick and thin. Here is a massive support against recession. Moreover, the public now holds a huge stock of liquid assets (currency, deposits, and government securities) that did not exist in 1929, or in any other previous period. These assets help to cushion temporary drops in income. But the doubters ask: How long can consumers keep on spending if they lose their jobs and don't get them back after a few weeks—and isn't there going to be a day of reckoning when they go into debt deeper and deeper to buy things they can't afford? The liquid-asset stock is large, but only about normal in relation to the huge modern levels of g.n.p. if we compare the present with earlier prosperities.

3. Around $100 billion of spending annually by federal, state, and local governments provides a massive, stable component of spending that can be counted on to oppose any recession tendencies. Never before has there been such a huge, stable block of investment spending. (Maybe, say the doubters. But we'd like to see government spending and taxes cut back, and we're not at all sure how state and local government spending on schools, highways, and other such capital items will hold up if a slump comes and tax receipts fall off.)

4. Federal government tax collection and spending arrangements now have a large element of automatic built-in counter-cyclical flexibility against depression. Even if economists can't predict the cycle very well, with our present tax system personal and business tax liabilities fall rapidly if incomes drop. In recession, federal tax liabilities, especially under the income tax, fall more than in proportion to income. Hence, disposable personal income drops far less than do wages, salaries, and other income before taxes. Similarly with business profits after tax. Moreover, federal government spending on unemployment insurance and price-support payments to farmers is geared to increase automatically if employment and prices fall. All things considered, built-in federal fiscal flexibility will automatically absorb maybe a third of the shock of any drop in national income. (Maybe, say the doubters. The one-third estimate looks high; but even if it's right, how about the other two-thirds?)

5. The banking and financial system has been greatly strengthened since the crash of 1929, and we need never again have the enormous credit contraction that was the core of the 1929-33 collapse. Federal insurance of bank deposits has substantially removed the danger of runs on banks. Government supervision of banking practices is far closer than before. The debt situation in the economy today is far from the extended position of the 1920's, when both the stock-market and real-estate booms were largely financed on bank credit. (Some truth in this, say the doubters, but bank loans can still go sour and bankers still have to look out for the safety of their deposits even if it means embarrassing their borrowers. Moreover, aggregate debt levels in the economy are at alarming levels, especially for consumer credit and mortgages on homes, even though they're not so spectacularly excessive as just before 1929.)

6. Most important, we have learned how to fight depression effectively through government monetary and fiscal policy. We now are able to understand and forecast business slumps far better than in 1929, and we have powerful tools to check any slump in private spending. These tools include a greatly strengthened Federal Reserve System to prevent financial panic and to see that plenty of money is available. More important, there is now general recognition that government deficit spending can provide buying power when private spending slumps. This was the lesson of World War II, when mass government spending rapidly bailed us out of unemployment into peak production and employment. The lesson is supported by the better understanding we now have of the components of total spending and the interrelationships among them. (That's what you said back in the 1920's when the Federal Reserve was a sure guarantee of permanent prosperity, say the doubters. And how can you be so sure that deficit spending will guarantee prosperity? It didn't when the New Deal tried it in the 1930's. Maybe the war was just a special case that wouldn't work in peacetime.)

How shall we balance off these arguments? No one knows for sure. But nearly every competent observer believes we're in much better shape than before to prevent really big depressions. They hasten to add, though, that there's every reason to suspect we're still highly susceptible to little recessions, and possibly to middle-sized ones too. The inventory cycle alone, for example, is big enough to give us some nasty bumps, and no one has much hope yet of eliminating inventory fluctuations. The weight given to the arguments listed above generally increases as you go down the list.

That brings us right up against the biggest question of all: Do we really know enough now about business fluctuations, and do we have enough tools in our government stabilization kit, to avoid major depressions and to assure stable economic growth? Fortunately, there is much ground for hoping that we can do a good deal to cure the evils of instability without a complete understanding of its causes—just as Dr. Salk was able to devise an effective polio vaccine without a clear understanding of what causes polio. Government powers to help achieve stable economic growth are the main subject of the next three chapters.

1. Are depressions obsolete?

2. Why can't a boom go on forever? Or can it? If your answer is yes, what change promises to make the future different from the past?

3. Describe briefly the inventory cycle.

4. One group of business-cycle analysts argues that booms and depressions are caused by expansions and contractions in the quantity of money. Can you see any important weaknesses in this argument? If so, what are they?

5. "The bigger the boom the bigger the bust." Is this often-heard statement true or false? Support your answer by a careful analysis of reasons why or why not.

6. The following factors are generally agreed to play important roles in cyclical upswings. Analyze how the force of each changes as national income rises from depression levels to prosperity, and how, if at all, each gradually helps set the stage for the upper turning-point:

   a. The banking system.
   b. The public's propensity to consume.
   c. Consumer and business price expectations.
   d. Induced investment (the acceleration effect).
   e. Cost-price relationships as they affect investment.
   f. Inventory levels.
   g. Consumer and business "psychology."

7. How many factors can you list that might reasonably be expected to provide a strong impetus to an upswing from a long, deep depression? Evaluate the likely force of each.

8. Using the last *Economic Report of the President* or the *Federal Reserve Chart Book,* compare the increase in consumer credit and mortgage debt since 1946 with the increase in personal income. Does the result lead you to suppose that consumers are dangerously in debt? How would you decide when the level of debt becomes dangerous?

Appendix

A Formal Multiplier-Accelerator Model

This Appendix presents a simple formal model to illustrate the types of dynamic interaction that may occur between the multiplier and the accelerator.

Suppose, in Table 13-1, that we begin with national income at 1,000. Now, for some reason (say because there is a temporary war scare), businesses increase their investment rate by 100 in periods 1 and 2. The war scare then vanishes, and businessmen are prepared to drop their investment spending back to the original level. What will be the impact of this one-time bloc of new investment?

Table 13-1

DYNAMIC INCOME—EXPENDITURE MODEL

		Change from Original Level in:		
	Total Income (1)	Investment (2)	Consumption (3)	Income (4)
Original level	1,000			
Period 1	1,100	+100		+100
Period 2	1,180	+100	+80	+180
Period 3	1,224	+80	+144	+224
Period 4	1,243	+64	+179	+243
Period 5	1,229	+35	+194	+229
Period 6	1,198	+15	+183	+198
Period 7	1,147	−11	+158	+147

Assume: Original autonomous investment of 100 in periods 1 and 2 (in Col. 2).

Thereafter: Consumption equals .8 of income during preceding period.
Investment equals the increase (+ or −) in consumption (i.e., business sales) in preceding period over the next preceding period. For example, investment in period 3 is +80, because consumption was 80 higher in period 2 than in period 1.

Thus: Col. 1 equals 1,000 (original income) plus Col. 4 (change in income).
Col. 2 equals 100 in periods 1 and 2 (new assumed investment), and change in Col. 3 in preceding period for all succeeding periods (since induced investment equals the preceding change in consumption).
Col. 3 equals .8 of Col. 4 during preceding period (since consumption is always .8 of the national income of the preceding period).
Col. 4 equals Col. 2 plus Col. 3 (since national income equals investment plus consumption).

Assume, for this example, that the marginal propensity to consume is .8 out of the income of the *preceding* period (perhaps a more reasonable assumption than that consumption is related to current income). Assume also that businessmen are led to make new investments (say in inventories, plant, and equipment) when business improves, and that such new induced, accelerator-type investment is just equal to the rise in consumption (i.e., business sales to consumers) during the immediately preceding period.

On the basis of these *illustrative* assumptions, we can now trace through the dynamic results of this original "shot" of assumed autonomous business investment.

In Table 13-1, the 100 of new autonomous investment in period 1 becomes income to its recipients in that period, raising the period 1 total-income level to 1,100. This rise in income increases consumption in period 2 by 80, which is .8 of the new income in period 1. The burst of autonomous business investment continues in period 2, by assumption. Adding together the new investment and new consumption in period 2, we get 180 of new income over the original level; this gives a total income of 1,180 for period 2. The higher income in period 2 in turn raises consumption in period 3; in addition, the preceding rise in consumption induces 80 of new business investment, raising total income to 1,224. And so the process goes.

This cumulative upward expansion arises out of the interacting multiplier and accelerator effects. Common sense tells us that if we increase the strength of either the multiplier or accelerator we will get a more rapid income expansion. If we weaken either, the rise in income will be slower. And these results can readily be checked by substituting a different propensity to consume or a different accelerator in the table.

This dynamic model provides a simple framework that may help you understand the cumulative upswing of the boom and the downswing of depression. But, once it's started, why does national income ever stop going up or down? Notice that income rises ever more slowly from period 1 through period 4. Since induced investment depends on the *change* in consumption, induced investment gradually falls and the acceleration effect gradually weakens, in spite of the continued upward multiplier effect of whatever new investment there is. By period 5, new investment has dropped off substantially, and the drop in investment is enough to more than offset the continued rise in consumption. Thus, total income falls slightly in period 5, and the expansion has reached its upper turning point. Moreover, once consumption begins to fall, investment becomes a negative figure (by our accelerator assumption). This sets off a negative multiplier effect, and the downswing is under way. The bloc of autonomous investment has set off an upswing, which has eventually checked itself and has become a downswing.

The dynamic model in Table 13-1 gives some idea of the possible results of interacting multiplier and acceleration effects. But don't be too impressed with it. Changing the values of the accelerator and multiplier can drastically change the pattern you get for national income over a series of time periods. If you increase both—the multiplier to a very high marginal propensity to consume, and the accelerator to 3 or 4—you will find that national income "explodes" upward once anything starts it up. If you trace out the exact model given in Table 13-1 for about 15 periods, you will find that income "damps" back down toward the original income level of 1,000. If you use lower values for the multiplier and accelerator, national income will return to the 1,000 level faster. Moreover, if you make induced investment a function of the *level* of national income in the preceding period, rather than of the *change* in national income, you will get a still different pattern of interaction.[4]

Thus, the purpose of this simple dynamic model is not to show how business fluctuations really work. Rather, it is to focus attention on the importance of the propensity to consume and on induced investment, on the factors that influence these key variables, and on some possible interactions among the critical factors.

---

[4] For *constant* values of the multiplier and accelerator, a rise of investment to a new higher level will induce (a) an explosive, continued rise in income when both the multiplier and accelerator are large, (b) no cumulative upward process when either the multiplier or accelerator is zero, and (c) cyclical fluctuations around the new income level if one is weak and the other strong. In some cases under (c), the fluctuations will be "damped"—i.e., they will gradually die out. In others, they may be constant or expanding in amplitude. For a precise statement of these cases, given different constant values for the multiplier and accelerator, see P. A. Samuelson, "Interactions Between the Multiplier Analysis and the Principle of Acceleration," in *Readings in Business Cycle Theory* (Philadelphia: Blakiston Press, 1944).

Monetary Policy

14

No economic questions have occasioned more bitter dispute during the present century than how to cure major depressions and how to maintain full employment without inflation. Depression and mass unemployment bring waste and human misery. Inflation erodes the value of savings and leads to disruptive speculation. Almost everyone agrees that we want high-level employment and a reasonably stable price level. But how to achieve this combination is less clear.

On such complex problems we must be content with less than final answers. The experts themselves are far from complete agreement. But fortunately, there is substantial agreement (far more than the general public often realizes) on some broad lines of monetary and fiscal policy for stable economic growth. We may not know just what leads people to venture over their depth in swimming, but we can agree that it's good policy to have a competent lifeguard on duty.[1]

---

[1] The report of a special Subcommittee on Public Issues of the American Economic Association, "The Problem of Economic Instability" (published in the *American Economic Review*, September, 1950) spells out this wide area of consensus on major governmental policies to combat economic instability.

247

Since the massive depression of the 1930's, we have come to take for granted government action aimed at avoiding depression and reducing instability. Yet for well over a century the United States has experienced booms and depressions, some of them very severe. Never before the 1920's was there any serious governmental attempt to check booms, and never before the 1930's was there a major governmental attempt to "cure" depressions. Rather, events were largely left to run their course and "cure" themselves. In spite of this fact, we revived from each depression to go on to a succeeding prosperity. Much the same was true in the other Western industrial nations.

If revival came more or less automatically from past depressions, why need we enact government policies now to achieve this end? Because few human tragedies are as great as the mass unemployment, poverty, and collapse of self-respect in a major depression. Figure 14-1 shows the repeated heavy burden of unemployment on the economy. If wise governmental policy can speed recovery, surely government action is desirable.

Inflation, since it seldom involves the waste of unemployment, is a less sweeping social tragedy, unless it reaches runaway proportions. Yet it too may bring widespread misery and arbitrary redistribution of income and wealth. The persistent erosion in the purchasing power of the dollar is pointed up by Figure 14-2. Here again, the case for government action seems clear. Most individuals, acting alone, cannot protect themselves effectively against either depression or inflation.

Unemployment as Percentage of Civilian Labor Force

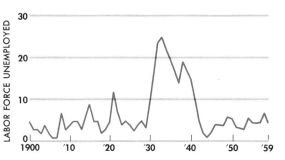

FIG. 14-1   Unemployment has soared in every recession and depression. In the great depression it reached massive proportions. What is a reasonable minimum unemployment percentage for us to shoot at? (Source: U.S. Department of Labor and U.S. Joint Economic Committee.)

But what to do is a harder question. The experience of the 1930's was not encouraging. The hodge-podge of New Deal measures may have done as much harm as good. Wartime developments demonstrated beyond doubt that government spending financed by the creation of new money can induce and maintain prosperity, if we spend enough. But they demonstrated too that it is easy to create too much money and to spend too much—easy for the government itself to stimulate full-blown inflation.

Since the New Deal days of the 1930's, government fiscal policy (taxation, borrowing, and spending) has been the stabilization device most popular among economists. But everyone has a plan to achieve full employment and avoid depressions. In the 1920's and early 1930's, stabilization through control of the money supply was the mode, and emphasis on money has revived in recent years. To some, direct controls over wages and prices look like the answer.

It is unfortunate but true that we still don't know enough about business fluctuations and their basic causes to be *sure* what are the best ways to achieve stable economic growth. With the long prosperity of the 1950's, confidence grew that we had at last found a combination of policies to avoid major depressions and inflations. Most economists share this optimism to at least some extent. Only time will tell how well-founded it is. If it is well-founded, it will be largely because the monetary and fiscal measures considered in this and the next two chapters turn out to be generally effective. For there is little evidence that the private economy itself has suddenly developed new practices and attitudes that free it from its past tendencies toward recurring booms and recessions.

Decline in Purchasing Power of the Dollar, 1900-1959

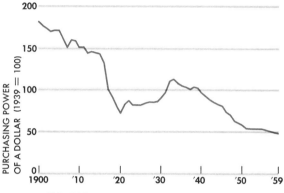

FIG. 14-2   Inflation has persistently eroded the purchasing power of the dollar, with the biggest declines coming after wars. If we had started at an inflation peak (say 1865) the apparent decline in the value of the dollar would be much less; 1900 was a low-price year. (Source: U.S. Department of Labor.)

THE GOALS OF STABILIZATION POLICY   High-level employment and a reasonably stable price level are widely accepted goals. But there is far from complete agreement on them, especially when they seem to conflict. Shall we sacrifice a stable dollar to eliminate unemployment? Or is this really the choice? Add on widespread differences over how important it is to achieve a higher rate of growth, especially at the cost of inflation, and the problem of the goals of stabilization policy looks a good deal less simple than is implied by the first sentence of this paragraph.

Possible conflict between these goals will be a major subject in Chapter 16, after we have had a look at the potentialities of monetary and fiscal policy for regulating the level of employment, prices, and growth. Chapters 14 and 15 presume a consensus on the desirability of high-level employment without inflation, and temporarily skim over the underlying possibilities of goal conflicts. After you have seen something of the way monetary and fiscal policy work, you'll be in a better position to understand some of the dilemmas policy-makers must face.

CENTRAL-BANK (MONETARY) POLICY

Central-bank Policy, Interest Rates, and the Money Supply. Even in the heyday of the gold standard, there were many who argued against leaving the supply of money to this impersonal mechanism, which increased the supply of money when gold flowed in and decreased it when gold flowed out. Instead, they argued, a "central bank" should be responsible for controlling the supply of money so as to minimize inflations and depressions. The Bank of England is generally considered the forerunner of other central banks, and the "Old Lady of Threadneedle Street" (as the Bank is often called) has played a significant part in influencing British monetary conditions for nearly three centuries. The United States was one of the last major nations to establish a central bank. The Federal Reserve was not set up until 1914.[2]

Thus for many years people have relied on central-bank policy, in addition to a metallic standard, to avoid the excesses of inflation and to maintain sound financial conditions. By raising interest rates and tightening credit through the banking system, central banks were expected to pinch off speculative, inflationary borrowing. If times turned bad, lower interest rates and easy money could stimulate borrowing and business activity. Government outlays were normally expected to be covered by current receipts, and central banks were often considered as watchdogs against too easy spending by the government, since they could make credit hard even for governments to obtain. Widespread importance was attached to central-bank credit policy. A higher central-bank discount (interest) rate was interpreted as a sign of impending general monetary tightening. Thus public psychological reactions helped to implement credit policy, sometimes more than the actual effect of the higher or lower interest rates *per se*.

Modern economic theory has clarified these channels of central-bank influence on the level of income, employment, and prices. Suppose first that the Federal Reserve wishes to check an inflation, which is developing because total private investment and consumption spending exceeds the goods and services available at present prices. Chapter 9 pointed out that the Reserve authorities have two broad channels—general controls to limit the total supply of credit, and selective controls to limit particular kinds of credit expansion. Consider them in that order.

---

[2] Two earlier government-sponsored banks (the First and Second Banks of the United States) had only brief lives and did not act as full-fledged central banks.

Policies to Check Inflation. *General ("Quantitative") Restraint.* In an inflationary boom, more money is essential if the upsurge is to continue. Businesses need more money for "working capital"—to finance larger inventories, to meet higher payrolls, to buy more materials. They need more money to finance fixed investment for expansion—new machinery, equipment, buildings. Some of this money comes from rising sales and profits. But to expand the level of operations and to finance large new investments, funds in addition to regular receipts are clearly needed. Thus, business must draw on savers outside the firm or on new credit from banks to finance expansion.

Consumers may also draw on outside financing to step up their collective marginal propensity to consume. New consumer credit from businesses or from the banks permits consumers to raise consumption spending more than in proportion to income without drawing on past savings. But businesses in such periods are generally short of working capital, so in the aggregate they can extend more consumer credit only by increasing their own borrowing from banks or other financial institutions. Thus, both businesses and consumers ultimately rely on the banks for the additional funds required to continue the upswing.

In this setting, the Federal Reserve can limit commercial bank credit by raising reserve requirements and by selling securities in the open market (open-market operations). The former directly reduces the banks' excess reserves. The latter has the same effect, because either bank or nonbank public payment for the securities sold by the "Fed" transfers cash reserves away from the commercial banks to the Federal Reserve. There is no doubt of the Fed's power to limit the total amount of credit the banks can extend.[3]

What do the commercial banks do when their excess reserves are squeezed by central-bank action? One possibility is to put up their interest rates—to raise their prices on money. This action raises the cost of money to borrowers. Since investment depends on the relation between the interest rate and the marginal efficiency of investment (Chapter 11), higher interest rates should reduce business investment. And restriction on investment will slow or reverse the boom. (Trace through the effect yourself, using Figures 11-6, 11-7, and 11-8 from Chapter 11.)

As a practical matter, banks often "ration" credit to their customers before they raise interest rates as reserves become tight. Instead of putting up rates so the customer willing to pay the highest interest will get the available credit, the banks allocate scarce credit to their oldest and best customers. They consider this sound long-run policy, just as many businesses don't try to squeeze the last penny out of good customers in periods of temporary shortages.

---

[3] Raising the rediscount rate, a third general restraint, often has more symbolic, psychological impact than direct effect in restricting bank lending. Small increases in the rediscount rate merely raise the cost of member-bank borrowing at the Federal Reserve to that extent, but they are widely viewed as indicative of the Fed's general attitude on credit conditions.

Such "credit rationing" has the same effect in limiting business expansion as do higher interest rates. In fact, credit rationing has a surer and quicker effect. In a boom businesses may be willing to pay higher interest rates for money without appreciably reducing their investment spending; their profit expectations are so high that the soaring marginal efficiency of investment overrides the rising-interest-cost side of the comparison between interest cost and marginal efficiency of investment. However rosy profit prospects may seem, credit rationing shuts off the supply of new money.

Both banks and businesses try to avoid such credit rationing. Bankers often sell off part of their government securities and use the new reserves to permit loan expansion, because interest rates on loans are higher and because they don't want to alienate long-standing business customers. But banks can switch from bonds to loans only if they can find someone to buy the bonds at reasonable prices. If bond prices fall drastically when banks begin to sell, their capital losses in selling bonds are so great as to eat up all the prospective profits on loans. And an inflationary boom is not an easy time to convince the public to convert its other assets into bonds. (Remember that the Federal Reserve by assumption will not buy bonds; this would merely negate the measures it is taking to check the inflation by tightening up on bank reserves.) Thus, banks may partially escape Federal Reserve pressure by selling their government securities, but the possibilities are limited as long as the Federal Reserve keeps the pressure on.

As credit becomes tighter, businesses and consumers try to avoid the pinch by economizing on cash balances—that is, by reducing their cash balances to the barest minimum needed to carry on their transactions and meet precautionary needs. In the aggregate, this makes the same amount of money do more work, speeding up velocity and avoiding the restraint of tighter money. The higher interest rates are forced by the credit squeeze, the greater is the inducement to convert idle savings from money into interest-yielding forms like securities and savings deposits. These shifts make previously idle money available for active use, directly or through financial institutions receiving the previously idle money.

Figure 14-3 shows this effect clearly. The dot for each year shows the average interest rate on "prime" short-term loans and the average turnover (or velocity) of demand deposits at some 400 city banks outside New York City (which is eliminated to avoid the huge volume of stock-market transactions there).[4] As interest rates rise, so does velocity. With low interest rates, velocity is low—for example, during the depression years. You should note that these figures include many transactions not included in the g.n.p. accounts, and thus are only a very imperfect approximation to changes in income velocity. But in some respects they are more interesting, since they show what happens to the total use of demand deposits when interest rates are raised or lowered.

---

[4] Actually, the data are only approximations to velocity figures for demand deposits, since they include some transactions, like transferring funds from one account to another in the same bank, which we would usually not consider an expenditure.

But, as we pointed out in the closing sections of Chapter 10, there are limits on how small working-cash balances can reasonably be. The public and the banks can avoid the pressure of Federal Reserve restraint temporarily, but only temporarily if the authorities make money tighter and tighter. It should be clear that the central-bank authorities can ultimately have as strong an impact as they wish, by raising reserve requirements sharply and by selling a large enough volume of government securities.

Interest Rates and Velocity of Money, 1919-1958

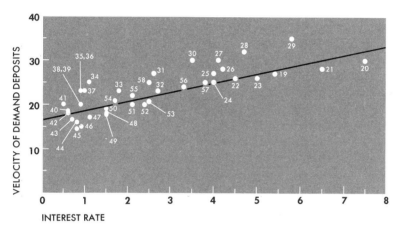

FIG. 14-3   As interest rates rise, the turnover of demand deposits goes up. It pays people to economize on the use of money and to reduce their idle balances. (Source: Federal Reserve Board.)

Don't jump from this to the conclusion that the job of the Federal Reserve is easy. Its power to check economic expansion is enormous, but overly drastic action may throw the baby out with the bathwater. The Federal Reserve's job is to check the inflation and level off the boom, not to plunge the economy into depression. Tightening up credit just enough to level off consumption and investment, or to keep their growth at just the right rate, calls for both extraordinary skill and luck.

Consider the Federal Reserve's central decision problem in fighting inflation. The problem breaks down into two big questions: First, where is economic activity now, and where is it going in the absence of further monetary policy action? Second, what shall we do to affect this expected pattern so as to provide stable economic growth without inflation? Look at Figure 14-4 on page 254, which provides a very rough picture of a business fluctuation, and put yourself in the position of a member of the Federal Reserve Board.

First, you have to decide where business activity is now. Is it at *A, B, C,* or *D?*

You don't know for sure, and neither does anybody else. Suppose you think it's probably well along in a strong business upswing—say at about *B*. Then the problem is, how near the top? And how long will the inflation and prosperity continue if you do nothing? This is even harder than deciding where we are now. Maybe the boom is about over, and prices are leveling off. Maybe the upswing has months or years of healthy prosperity left in it, and it would be a shame to damp it. Maybe it's going up so fast that speeding inflation will bring an early downturn unless prices are leveled off. If only you knew!

Second, given your best decision as to where we are and where we're headed, you have to decide what the Federal Reserve should do now. Suppose you suspect we're around *B*, and that inflation poses a serious problem. Should you raise reserve requirements? Sell bonds in the open market to tighten reserves? Or is the safe thing just to wait till we're clearly at *D* and then fight the recession, on the ground that it's better not to risk killing off prosperity?

Note that here you face two

The Problem of Timing Stabilization Policy

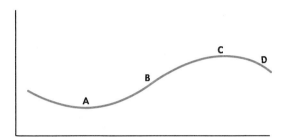

FIG. 14-4   The Federal Reserve authorities seldom know where we are in the cycle, or just how long it will take their actions to exercise their full effect. What is the right monetary policy if you think we're probably at B, but there's a good chance it may be C instead?

sub-problems. One is, what effect will any Federal Reserve action have on the course of business activity? If you sell $1 billion of government bonds, will this drastically check bank lending, or only slow it slightly? How about raising reserve requirements 10 per cent? The second is, even if you know what the effect will be, how long will it take for the full impact of tighter money to be exercised? If you sell bonds tomorrow, they may only gradually shut off lending and their full effect may not be felt for six months. By that time the boom may have turned down. Then the (lagged) effect of tight money would be to speed the downturn into recession. And unfortunately, a six-month lag seems not at all implausible. Worst, how can you know how long the lag is?

There are many lags and uncertainties between Federal Reserve decisions and their final impact on total spending. How long will it take the banks to react to tightened reserves? Will they try to sell off government securities and thus temporarily evade the desired restriction on business borrowing? How fast will businesses react to tighter credit? Will they manage to economize cash balances further? Will higher interest rates draw many or few idle dollars into the market? Will Federal Reserve action quickly hit the public's optimism in the head and drastically worsen business and consumer expectations? The Federal Reserve never knows the answers to these questions and others like them. But it has to act, or let things go their way without control. What would you do? Timing is a tough problem.

We will look further at these practical operating problems of stabilization policy in Chapters 15 and 16.

Selective ("Qualitative") Restraint.   Fear of a shotgun approach leads many observers to prefer selective, or qualitative, restraints to check inflationary booms. They argue that the problem is usually centered in some particular sector of the economy, and that to use general restraint is to risk killing off the whole boom in order to get at the offending sector. For example, perhaps consumers are borrowing and spending excessively on autos and other consumer durables. Or perhaps there is a credit-fed housing boom. Or stock-market speculation may be rampant.

Suppose the problem is a residential housing boom that seems to be running so fast as to endanger the whole prosperity. But soft spots remain in òther parts of the economy. Advocates of selective controls argue that the thing to do is adopt real-estate credit controls, by which the Federal Reserve can prescribe minimum down payments on houses and maximum lengths for mortgages, rather than making credit generally scarce enough to check the use of mortgage credit. With the speculative mood in real estate, it might take very high interest rates to damp real-estate demand and these would risk killing off the entire boom.

But direct control over real-estate credit, the argument runs, could nip the overexpansion there with little danger to the rest of the economy. Nearly all houses are bought on credit. The down payment and monthly installment are the crucial financial considerations for most borrowers. By putting up the minimum down payment to 20 or 30 per cent, many marginal buyers will be squeezed out of the market. By shortening the maximum payoff time for housing mortgages, the monthly payment is raised, with the same effect. Neither of these steps requires forcing up interest rates generally.

Is this a sound argument? The answer depends on several things.

First, how clear is it that the housing industry is really the sole trouble-maker?

Second, is the public willing to accept this direct regulation over how it spends its money in peacetime? Is it clear that the central bank knows better how we should spend our money than we know ourselves? Federal Reserve officials say that if I buy a house now, I will unstabilize the economy. But I've been planning for the house a long time, and I want it. Isn't this a free country? Unless the measure has general support, enforcement is very difficult to impose on hundreds of thousands of individual small borrowers and lenders. Remember that commercial banks make only a part of the loans, and to regulate them while leaving other lenders free would be inequitable.

Third, are we willing to have the housing lenders take the brunt of checking the housing boom? What would keep people from borrowing money on other security, and then using the funds to pay for houses, even though direct mortgage loans are controlled? New credit extended in other areas—say to businessmen or for stock-market buying—can easily be used for buying housing after it has first been spent for its original purpose. The economy has no money-tight compartments, and no selective control alone can hope to go far toward checking total spending in the economy.

Where does this leave the question of selective controls? There is no clear answer, but most Americans apparently view direct government regulation of spending patterns with distrust.[5] Direct regulation of down payments and repayment terms on consumer credit stirred widespread resentment, although it worked reasonably well during the war periods. Unions criticised the regulation bitterly, as discrimination in favor of the rich (who can buy on cash) against the working man (who must use credit). A great deal of credit extended in other areas slopped over into consumer buying. Equitable, equal enforcement posed enormous problems.

The issues about selective controls are partly ethical, where the economist has no more right to decide them than anyone else; partly economic, where most economists agree that selective controls can play a useful though modest role in restraining particular kinds of credit extension; and partly political, where the issue is whether such measures can be enacted and enforced effectively. Uneven enforcement is one of the major dangers of such special controls. No one who understands the problem thinks that selective controls are a real substitute for general credit restraint when an economy-wide inflationary boom is the problem.

Policies to Stimulate Recovery.   *General Credit Ease.* The power of monetary policy to stimulate recovery is generally less than its power to check overexpansion. The Federal Reserve can flood the banks with reserves in recession, but it has only limited power to make bankers want to lend and businesses want to borrow. You can hold a gas-filled balloon down by pulling on its cord, but pushing up on the string doesn't help much if the balloon collapses.

Suppose the Federal Reserve wants to reverse a major recession. Its first act is to be sure the banks have plenty of reserves. It lowers reserve requirements and buys government securities in the open market, providing new bank reserves in paying for its purchases. Moreover, it offers to rediscount any reasonable commercial paper the commercial banks may bring, thus guaranteeing adequate liquidity to the banking system.

This behavior has one major result. It eliminates the possibility of another 1929-33 debacle, when mass liquidation of bank credit forced the downward spiral ever deeper. But whether it will start a recovery is another matter.

Again, a critical question is, what will the bankers do? With growing excess

---

[5] Selective control over margin requirements in the stock market is a clear exception. This control is widely accepted.

reserves they will want to lend, since idle reserves earn no return. But they will lend only if there are desirous borrowers who are good risks. With the economic horizon darkening, such borrowers are scarce. Business needs to borrow when it is expanding, not when it is contracting. Banks can lower their interest rates and let their customers know that credit is available. But that may or may not produce more loans.

What bankers *can* do is buy government securities. These are always substantially safe, and they pay interest. So flooding the banks with reserves will almost certainly lead to increasing the money supply, bidding up the price of bonds, and (what is the same thing) bidding down the effective interest yield on the bonds.

More money is fine, but the new deposits may just go into idle balances. If the previous bondholders were content to hold bonds as quasi-liquid investments, offering higher prices for the bonds may lead them to sell out—but will they then take the money and buy shoes or new machinery? In recession the likelihood seems low.

Similarly, reduction of interest rates is a step in the right direction. But it doesn't guarantee more investment, if the marginal efficiency of investment is even lower. Remember that it's business expectations that count in determining the marginal efficiency of investment, and these may be for even worse times ahead. Under such conditions, no positive interest rate may be low enough to make new investment appear worth while.

Whether monetary policy is effective against recession thus depends largely on how responsive borrowers are to lower interest rates and readily available credit. Here economists differ widely; the evidence is simply not clear. Almost everyone agrees that easy money is a good thing, but estimates vary widely as to whether it will do much more than remove the pressure toward forced liquidation.

Lower interest rates are more likely to stimulate long than short term borrowing. On a long loan, like a 30-year mortgage, a small reduction in the interest rate makes a big difference in the monthly or yearly payment. Thus, lower interest rates may help appreciably to stimulate borrowing to finance construction. Similarly, they may help stimulate investment by state and local governments, which usually must borrow to finance highways, schools, sewage systems, and other such long-term projects. Some types of business investment cover long periods—for example, construction of major public utility facilities. The list where lower interest rates may help is not trivial.

On the other hand, lower short-term interest rates are less likely to stimulate business spending. Cheaper money lowers the cost of borrowing for working-capital purposes—to meet payrolls, carry inventories, and so on. But here interest is a tiny part of the relevant costs. Similarly, plans to acquire new plant and equipment depend heavily on customer demand and on expectations. Though lower interest rates help to establish an attractive ratio between interest and marginal efficiency of investment, the ratio is apt to be dominated by marginal-efficiency considerations. If new machinery doesn't promise high-level use and a reasonably prompt payout, few businesses will be led to buy it by a drop of 1 or 2 per cent in the interest rate. And it's hard for the businessman to see the need for new plant and equipment when recession has his present plant running at half capacity.

Selective Controls. Selective controls face the same problems in trying to stimulate recovery. Merely to make credit easier doesn't help much if there's no demand for the credit.

But proper monetary policy may help some, especially if selective controls have been used to restrain the preceding boom. Then removing restrictions on housing and consumer credit will help make spending more attractive in both areas. If no selective restraints are in effect, the only way to help selectively is through some form of subsidy, which goes beyond the sphere usually thought of as monetary policy.

In fighting recession, credit ease across the board makes sense. But here, as in fighting inflation, there may be the danger of too much as well as too little. The above paragraphs imply the need for an all-out attack on recession. But often there is just a little recession, and it is unclear whether the problem a year hence will be unemployment or renewed inflation. Then all-out credit ease may indeed turn the recession around, but also pile up inflationary pressures in the process. Here the Federal Reserve authorities face all the problems of prediction, lags, and uncertainties outlined above for the anti-inflation case, but in reverse.

The Supply of Money and Economic Stabilization.   Some economists emphasize the *stock of money* as the crucial variable for economic stabilization. History shows that changes in the money supply per capita have closely paralleled short-run fluctuations in the level of income and employment over at least the last century. Seldom have there been sharp reversals of upswings or downswings without a simultaneous or preceding reversal in money supply per capita.[6] The evidence is far from conclusive. But it does suggest that the volume of money per capita exercises a strong effect on total business and consumer spending, whether or not the channel is through the interest rate.

The reasoning behind this relationship is simple; it harks back to the simple monetary approach of Chapter 10. The more liquid the economy becomes, the more likely it is to raise its spending on consumption and investment. When people and businesses get more money one way or another, they feel a strong urge to spend at least part of it, unless some strong reason to the contrary holds them back. This view suggests that if you can somehow get the money supply up, whether or not by stimulating business and consumer borrowing, higher spending is likely to follow.

---

[6] See Albert G. Hart, *Money, Debt, and Economic Activity* (Englewood Cliffs, N. J.: Prentice Hall, Inc., 1953), Part III.

Most economists feel uncomfortable with this theory, however, unless they can trace through the specific ways in which more or less money influences the level of spending. And for this purpose, the preceding sections raise the relevant questions.

Monetary Policy and Economic Growth. Economic growth depends on many things, but especially on the rate of investment. If monetary policy discourages investment, it slows the rate of economic growth. If monetary policy encourages investment, it speeds economic growth. Booms are generally periods of rapid growth, recessions of slow growth. Thus, in deciding on its stabilization policies, the Federal Reserve is consciously or unconsciously adopting a policy on the best rate of economic growth.

Low interest rates encourage economic growth both because they push toward full employment and because they stimulate investment more than consumption. If the economy's basic tendency is toward underemployment stagnation, low interest rates are clearly good for both prosperity and growth. But if the economy is already fully employed, low interest rates push toward inflation, which then becomes the price of more rapid growth. Conversely, high interest rates to check inflation may have the side effect of slowing economic growth. Here again is the problem of balancing off competing social goals.

The Federal Reserve authorities have said little about their policy on economic growth. They content themselves with working to eliminate major booms and recessions, by implication at least leaving the growth rate up to the saving-investing decisions of the public. But this separation between stabilization and growth is often not feasible. Even though you believe that the free decisions of businesses and individuals should determine how fast the economy grows, you may not be able to keep the government out of the picture if you want an active economic stabilization policy. More about this dilemma in Chapter 16.

THE LESSONS OF MONETARY EXPERIENCE What has history taught about the effectiveness of monetary policy in the United States, and about the problems of using it? It may be useful for us to take a brief look at the past.

The 1920's—Boom and Bust. World War I was followed by a sharp inflationary boom and then by a short sharp inventory liquidation that briefly drove prices spiraling down. By 1922, the economy had begun a long upward pull— almost a decade of good times and substantially full employment. In 1924 and again in 1927, prosperity was broken by slight hesitations. And increasingly as the boom continued, observers questioned whether times were not a little too good. Real-estate prices climbed as construction activity reached peaks never before dreamed of. After 1926, construction turned downhill. But the stock market more and more reflected the prevalent spirit of permanent prosperity. By 1928, security prices began to soar far above levels previously considered reasonable in relation to the earnings of the companies involved. The man in the street, the businessman, and the financier, became speculators "in the market". As stock prices spiraled upward, easy profits were available for the taking, especially since stocks could be bought on margin for only a tiny fraction of their sale price.

In the midst of this speculative fever, calmer voices questioned whether such a speculative boom could last. Industrial production leveled off in 1928 and construction activity slumped substantially. Federal Reserve authorities were divided among themselves on what was the best policy. Finally, in 1929 they took mild deflationary action, in spite of widespread criticism, raising rediscount rates and speaking out against the excessive use of bank credit for speculative purposes. In late 1929 came the stock-market crash, triggering the worst deflation and depression of America's history.

Lesson: When times are good it's hard to know what's the right policy vis-à-vis speculation and minor fluctuations—what would you have done? And when the boom gets roaring, steps to check it are generally unpopular. The life of a central banker is not easy.

The 1930's—Crash and Stagnation.

As the economy spiraled downward, it was far from clear whether this was a major depression, a temporary stock-market setback, or merely a regular cyclical readjustment after a long period of rapid economic growth. The Reserve authorities reduced discount rates to ease credit in the deflation. By early 1931, there was considerable evidence that the worst was over and that a new footing had been reached for recovery of basic industrial activity.

But a further financial crisis in mid-1931 set the spiral off again. Gold began to flow out of the country, following major financial collapses in Europe. The Reserve authorities adopted a tight-money, high-interest policy to protect the nation's gold stock, which made money hard to get at home. In spite of a reversal of this policy only a few months later, the spiral of financial liquidation which developed could not be checked again. Unemployment soared. Runs on banks developed everywhere. On his inauguration day, Franklin Roosevelt's first major act was to declare a nation-wide "bank holiday," closing all banks until the panic could be calmed and arrangements could be made to keep the financial system from complete collapse.

Following 1933, with Franklin Roosevelt's new appointees running the system, the Federal Reserve adopted easy money and low interest rates to fight the depression. Excess reserves were pushed up to $3 billion by late 1935, and then, as recovery seemed on the way, pulled back down to $1 billion in 1937. As the boomlet of 1936-37 crashed precipitously back to mass unemployment in early 1938, again there was widespread criticism of the preceding Federal Reserve increases in reserve requirements to restrain rising prices in spite of continued heavy unemployment.

Although it was by no means clear that Federal Reserve policy played a major part in ending the recovery of 1937, from then on the banks were flooded with reserves. Excess reserves exceeeded $5 billion by the outbreak of war in 1939, in comparison to an average level of under $500 million through the 1920's. But bank loans rose only slightly from their 1933 lows, and bank purchases of government securities fell far short of the levels permitted by their growing excess reserves. In 1939, gross national product was at about the same level as in 1929; 8 or 9 million people were unemployed; net private investment for the entire decade was a negative figure.

Lessons: (1) When mass deflation sets in, don't hesitate to flood the economy with liquidity. Hindsight makes it clear that the Reserve authorities made a fatal error in moving so slowly to eliminate the pressure of financial liquidation that swept the whole economy downward. (2) When times are bad, it's still hard to know what is the best policy vis-à-vis minor fluctuations. (3) In a major depression, flooding the economy with liquidity at least checks further financial liquidation and helps to stimulate total spending; but bankers may simply pile up excess reserves rather than expanding loans, investments, and deposits. The life of a central banker is not easy.

World War II—War Finance, Gold, and the Congress. During the ten years before World War II, our gold reserves increased from $4 billion to $23 billion, as gold flowed in from abroad for investment and safekeeping during the troubled 1930's. The gold entering the United States was sold to the government through the Federal Reserve Banks. Each dollar of gold increased the reserves of the commercial banks by $1, as the seller of the gold deposited the check paid to him by the government. It also increased the Federal Reserve's supply of gold to back a further credit or currency expansion by $1 as the member bank turned the gold over to the government. (See Figure 9-1.) By 1941 the commercial banks had huge excess reserves, and the Federal Reserve also had gold reserves far beyond the legal requirements against currency outstanding and member-bank reserves.

With soaring war expenditures, the government raised taxes, but only enough to cover about a third of the war's costs. The Treasury began to borrow to cover the difference. About half the government bonds were sold to the public, drawing away already-existing money. The other half were sold to the commercial banks, creating new deposits to be spent by the government. This deposit expansion rapidly ate into the excess reserves of the commercial banks; withdrawal of currency into hand-to-hand circulation drained away reserves even faster (currency alone increased $20 billion during the war period).

By 1942, the commercial banks' excess reserves were nearly gone. The war blazed on and Treasury borrowing needs skyrocketed. What would you have done? You'd have found some way to permit the Treasury to sell more bonds to the banks in order to get money to finance the war, and that's just what the Federal Reserve authorities did. They could have lowered the reserve requirement ratio to provide more excess reserves. But the currency drain was so rapid that it alone would have drained out all existing bank reserves in about two years. So the Reserve Banks began to buy government securities in the open market, to create *new* bank reserves on which the commercial banks could then buy five times as many newly issued government bonds from the Treasury. Remember the pyramid of credit in Figure 9-1.

This was money-creation with a vengeance. Preceding a typical "war loan drive," for example, the Federal Reserve went into the open market and bought enough securities to build up commercial banks' excess reserves. The banks could then buy all the bonds the Treasury could not sell to the non-banking public. On a set day during the "drive," bank subscriptions for new bonds from the Treasury would be opened and the bonds allocated. Suppose the Treasury allocated $5 billion to the banks. Then the next day, the banks' balance sheets throughout the country would show $5 *billion* of new deposits for the Treasury, offset by $5 billion of new government bonds held by the banks. If you didn't quite believe that banks created deposits back in Chapters 8 and 9, World War II provided a vivid and irrefutable demonstration on a grand scale.

Between 1941 and 1945, the Federal Reserve created $23 billion of new member-bank reserves through open-market purchases. With these additional reserves, the commercial banks bought $70 billion of government securities and paid out $20 billion of new currency. As was to be expected, each dollar of new reserves served to support about four dollars of new money.

But each new Federal Reserve note took 40 per cent gold reserves, and new member-bank reserves took 35 per cent gold reserves. By 1944, therefore, the Federal Reserve itself began to run short of gold. It still had about the same amount of gold, but this gold was "used up" by legal requirements. Without more gold, its power to provide more currency and more bank reserves to help finance the war was threatened.

What would you have done? The Reserve and Treasury authorities went to Congress with the problem, and a suggested solution. There was little dissent. Congress lowered the gold-reserve requirement for Federal Reserve Banks to 25 per cent against both Federal Reserve notes and deposits, so that Federal Reserve support of the Treasury's war borrowing could be continued. The Federal Reserve again had excess gold reserves. The needs of war finance had triumphed over the tradition of gold and financial orthodoxy.

Lessons: (1) tne Federal Reserve plus modern fractional reserve banking provides an easy way to manufacture money in almost any desired amount. (2) In wartime, it's hard to keep the dangers of excess money-issue and inflation from being lost sight of in the press of winning the war. (3) Gold provides an ultimate limitation on the money-creating powers of the Federal Reserve, under present law. But Congress makes the law and Congress can change it, even on gold.

The Federal Reserve and the National Debt—1946-1951. At the end of World War II, over $275 billion of government securities were outstanding, nearly $100 billion of them held by the banking system. Between $50 and $75 billion of the national debt came due for refunding each year. The Federal Reserve faced a dilemma. (1) If it used its traditional powers to check the post-war inflation, the squeeze would induce banks to dump their low-yield government securities on the market to get new reserves to make higher-yield business loans. This would force down the price of government securities, with cries of anguish from the Treasury and the public. (2) On the other hand, if the Federal Reserve did not act to check bank-credit expansion to private borrowers, it could ease the Treasury's job in refinancing the national debt, but it would be lying down on its job as the government's monetary spearhead against inflation.

Until 1951, the Federal Reserve chose the latter path. It stood ready to buy government bonds from the commercial banks at par, maintaining their price against declines. This action kept the interest cost of the national debt low, and made it easy for the Treasury to refund the maturing debt. It also meant that the banks' huge holdings of government securities were as good as excess reserves, since they could be converted into cash at no risk at any time. Bank loans to private borrowers soared.

The Treasury, anxious to maintain confidence in the government's credit, liked this policy. A huge volume of short-term securities was outstanding, and the holders might demand cash at maturity if Governments didn't remain attractive. Losing confidence, banks and non-bank holders might also try to sell their longer-term securities. Refunding would have to be done at sharply increased interest rates, and the future market for government securities might be seriously weakened. Political repercussions from government bondholders could be very unpleasant for the administration in power if bond prices slumped.

Many economists argued, however, that higher interest costs and sagging bond prices were a proper price to pay for the restoration of effective monetary controls. The Federal Reserve increasingly took this view. If monetary policy was to check inflation, it was reasoned, the Reserve must tighten the over-all credit supply, including a rise of interest rates to the federal government itself, unless some way could be found of insulating Treasury borrowing from the rest of the money market.[7]

---

[7] Various proposals were made to "freeze" existing government security holdings in the commercial banks. This action would have removed them from the category of substantially excess reserves by eliminating their free convertibility into cash, and the Federal Reserve would then be free to tighten up on other bank credit without fear of forcing down the price of Governments. See, for example, the *Annual Report of the Board of Governors of the Federal Reserve System for 1946,* which urged a policy of this sort.

The Federal Reserve authorities tried gradually to tighten up the money market. Finally, in 1951, in an open break with the Treasury, Federal Reserve support of the price of government bonds was substantially withdrawn. Governments fell below par, but bank credit was tightened and interest rates rose. Federal Reserve control over the money supply was partially restored.

But even then, the Reserve officials made it clear that they would continue to work closely with the Treasury. Why? In spite of their "nonpolitical" status, the Federal Reserve Board members are appointed by the president and are responsible to Congress. They recognize fully their primary role as part of the government. Were they actively to combat the government's (Treasury's) financial policy, or even fail to cooperate satisfactorily, there would always be the chance that Congress might simply abolish the semi-independent status of the Reserve authorities. With the major portion of the nation's money supply outstanding against Treasury borrowing, it is clear that Federal Reserve monetary policy and Treasury debt policy must be made cooperatively.

Lesson: There are many considerations that must be weighed in forming wise monetary policy. One of the most difficult problems is the weight to be given to Treasury (government) financing needs when they conflict with other stabilization objectives. The life of a central banker is not easy.

The Dilemma of Inflation or Unemployment—The 1950's. Basically, the decade of the 1950's was a long period of prosperity. But in 1954 and again in 1958 came short recessions reminiscent of 1924 and 1927. After 1954, unemployment hovered around 3 million, until the recession of 1958 shot the figure up to 5 million, the highest since the immediate post-World War II conversion peak. Recovery in late 1958 and 1959 failed to restore high-level employment completely. Technological progress and greater managerial efficiency substantially reduced the number of workers needed to turn out any given output. In the meantime, the U.S.S.R. grew at 7-10 per cent compared to our 3-4 per cent for the decade, and consistently outpaced us in the space race. Yet, over the decade in America prices crept up nearly every year.

Was monetary pressure to avoid inflation holding down the rate of economic growth and causing unemployment? The Federal Reserve generally saw inflation as the major danger, though reiterating its goal of fighting both recession and inflation. From 1955 on, it permitted the money supply to grow only slowly, although it quickly eased credit in the recession of 1958. Increasingly, unions and Democratic politicians attacked the Reserve authorities as barriers to a healthy, growing economy. To many, the choice was: stable prices or full employment. They believed that tight money was short-sighted, for it put the fetish of a stable price level over the productivity and human happiness of full employment. Others, including the Reserve authorities, saw the problem differently. Only stable money could provide the foundation for continuing saving and prosperity.

Lesson: Even prosperity has its problems. The hardest choices of all are between widely accepted goals which appear to be conflicting. The central banker who places price stability above booming prosperity and rapid economic growth reaps many harsh words. The old refrain: The life. . . .

The next in this little series of historical vignettes might be entitled "The 1960's —Peace and Permanent Prosperity?" Will we really achieve rapid economic growth, high-level employment, and stable prices concurrently? Or must we sacrifice one for the others? Only time will tell.

THE GOLD STANDARD [8]   Our look at monetary experience would not be complete without at least a passing glance at the gold standard—the cornerstone of United States monetary policy and of worldwide financial arrangements for most of the 19th century and much of the 20th. Although the gold standard in its pure form no longer exists, a brief look at how it operated and why it was cast aside for more discretionary policies can provide valuable historical perspective. Moreover, gold has not vanished from the monetary scene.

In 1785, Congress established the dollar as the country's standard monetary unit, and soon provided for its coinage in both gold and silver. Since 1834, gold has comprised the main metallic support for the nation's money supply. Except for the period 1862-79, the country was continuously "on the gold standard" until 1933.

While the gold standard prevailed in the United States and most major European nations, it provided, in theory, an automatic, "single-rule" mechanism for controlling the volume of money. Actually, the gold standard was never as automatic in operation as in theory. But it did provide a constraining framework for almost all monetary-policy thinking and action over a long period of years. Its influence on modern thinking is still substantial.

What Was "The Gold Standard"?   The gold standard accepted by most of the Western world had two major characteristics. First, changes in the total amount of money (currency plus deposits) were roughly proportional to changes in the quantity of gold. Gold itself was not the only kind of money. As new gold was received by a country, it would serve as the basis for additional currency or deposits. On one dollar's worth of new gold, two, four, ten, or some other number of dollars of new money might be issued by the government or the banks. Similarly, an outflow of gold would reduce the nation's money supply, in the same ratio.

The second major characteristic was that each unit of money was "worth" (convertible into) a certain number of grains of gold. Until 1934, for example,

---

[8] This section is written so that it may be omitted by those instructors who prefer to do so.

each United States dollar "contained" 23.22 grains of fine gold; that is, 23.22 grains of gold could always be obtained at the Treasury for one dollar, and vice versa.[9]

The Gold Standard as a Safeguard Against Inflation. The main argument for the gold standard in most people's minds is that it will safeguard the economy against inflation.

But United States history illustrates clearly that the gold standard is no guarantee against sharp price-level changes. The graphs in Chapter 7 show the great inflation that took place during and following World War I, the precipitous drop following that inflation, and the sharp drop from 1929 to 1933, all while we were firmly on the gold standard. The quantity of money (M) fluctuated widely. This was partly because of big swings in our gold stock. But also, as was noted above, as a practical matter the banking system could expand and contract the money supply over a wide range for any given amount of gold reserves.

On the other hand, it *is* true that adherence to the gold standard would insure against any such runaway inflation as occurred in Germany after World War I, *if* sticking to the gold standard were politically and economically possible under such circumstances. However, under such drastic circumstances it is hard to imagine that any country could remain on a gold standard. The drastic monetary disturbances of that period were as much a symptom as a cause of the difficulties of the German economy.

The gold standard has one major advantage in the eyes of those who fear excessive reliance on governmental discretionary authorities. It takes the monetary management out of the hands of individuals (in whom we may have limited faith) and puts it on a more or less automatic basis (according to gold flows). But whether gold flows provide the best guide to how much money the economy needs is another question. If we want to remove power from the hands of government authorities lest they unwisely bring on inflation, there may be better automatic guides—for example, full employment, or outright stabilization of the price level. Modern economists are unenthusiastic about the gold standard. It may have some virtues in avoiding discretionary control of monetary policy, but it does not insure against sharp changes in the price level, nor does it permit authorities to use independent monetary action freely against cyclical business fluctuations.

The Abandonment of the Gold Standard. It was the desire to "do something" to mitigate business fluctuations that largely explains the abandonment of the gold standard in the 1930's. During the 1920's, countries were increasingly loath to accept deflation as they lost gold. Avoidance of hard times and unem-

---

[9] For an examination of the gold standard and international economic adjustments, see the section, "International Adjustments Under the Gold Standard," in Chapter 38.

ployment became a major policy goal. In the financial crisis following 1929, European countries faced huge gold drains into hoards and to the United States. These drains forced a tremendous contraction of the money supply, making the deepening depression still worse. In 1931, England, long the financial center of the world, went off the gold standard. Remaining on gold meant having to contract the money supply as gold was withdrawn. Off the gold standard, England could expand her money supply to check the depression and falling price level, regardless of gold flows.[10]

England's abandonment of the gold standard was a terrific blow to the confidence of the financial world, especially in those troubled times. The next major country to be hit by gold hoarding was the United States. Hundreds of banks failed as the result of this drain on their reserves. Within a few months, our monetary authorities were forced to choose between staying on the gold standard (contracting the volume of money as gold was lost) or giving up the gold standard to be able to expand the money supply in the face of a falling gold stock.

They chose to stay on gold, as we saw in the preceding section, and national income plummeted again. But finally, in 1933, as part of Roosevelt's emergency program to check the wave of bank failures, all gold was called out of monetary circulation into the Treasury. The United States officially went off the gold standard. Most of the countries of Europe had already taken this step. Some, like France, clung to gold longer, but today no major country retains the prewar gold standard.

Today, nations seem unlikely to tie their monetary systems rigidly to gold again. The advantages of mitigating domestic booms and depressions bulk larger than those of the international gold standard. This does not mean, however, that gold is unimportant. Even though monetary systems are no longer tied directly to gold flows, gold still performs two major functions: (1) It helps maintain confidence in the nation's money, even though you can't get gold except for export or use in the arts. (2) It serves as the basic means of settling international balances. Every country in the world is glad to get gold in exchange for goods and services, for gold is still everywhere acceptable as payment in international trade.

The Problem of Too Little Gold.   A country can have too little gold, if a shortage of gold keeps the money supply undesirably low, as in 1931-33. The New Deal recognized the need to raise the price level as an integral part of a recovery program. In 1934, the President declared that henceforth a dollar should contain only 13.71 grains of fine gold instead of the previous 23.22 grains, a power that had been given him in emergency legislation. This "devaluation" of the dollar to 59 per cent of its previous gold value was equivalent to raising the price of gold to $35 per ounce from its previous price of $20.67. Since the

---

[10] By abandoning the gold standard, she also hoped to gain a special advantage in international trade, to be discussed in Part 6.

amount of gold in each dollar was diminished, it now takes more dollars to equal an ounce of gold. This bookkeeping transaction increased the dollar value of the government's gold stock from about $4 billion to about $6.8 billion. It raised the government's power to follow a policy of monetary expansion.

Again in 1944 we ran short of gold, with the results indicated above.

Are we likely to run short of gold again? Although this is an ever-present problem for most nations, it seems unlikely to face the United States for the foreseeable future. During the late 1950's, we lost gold at a rate above $1 billion a year. But this was a temporary drain. With about $20 billion in gold, there is no reason why gold shortage should dictate our monetary policy. Under the law the president can restrict gold exports if the national interest requires; we have a large excess of gold now; and Congress could always change the legal reserve requirements against Federal Reserve notes and deposits if necessary.

The Problem of "Too Much" Gold.   May a country have too much gold? Did we take too much gold during the great inflow of the 1930's? Are we "stuck" with it now, or are we likely to be in the future? For the answer to these questions we must wait for a fuller analysis of the international functions of gold flows in Part 6. But two results of the massive gold inflow may readily be understood:

1. We gave foreigners goods, services, and investments for the gold they sent us, and then carefully buried the gold in Fort Knox and paid soldiers to guard it. The fable of King Midas, who finally found he could not eat his gold, may be uncomfortably relevant.

2. The effects of the gold inflow on the domestic monetary situation have been mixed. During the early war period, the excess reserves piled up by entering gold added to inflationary pressures. Later, the excess gold allayed public alarm over the monetary expansion needed to finance the war. With less gold, Federal Reserve gold requirements would have had to be reduced sooner and farther.

Whether new gold inflows will prove convenient or embarrassing to future domestic monetary policy remains to be seen. Generally, the Federal Reserve now offsets gold flows in or out by open-market operations if the flows threaten undesirable effects on the domestic economy. The Reserve authorities can easily adjust to most gold flows if this is desirable. Ultimately, if we are willing to change our legal rules that relate gold to the monetary structure, gold flows need never cause unwanted domestic monetary effects.

GOLD, SILVER, AND THE MIXED STANDARD   No single monetary "rule" now prevails in the United States to replace the old gold standard. A law passed in 1934 prescribed that the metal backing held by the Treasury for the money it issues shall consist of 75 per cent gold and 25 per cent silver. But the law does not prescribe what the *total* metal backing for money shall be. And the law does not apply to Federal Reserve notes and to bank deposits.

Silver has little remaining monetary function. Since, in 1934, the Treasury held less than the prescribed 25 per cent of silver, it set about buying large amounts of silver, and it has been buying ever since—to the tune of over $5 billion, most of it at prices well above prevailing world-market prices. The main result has been a continuing subsidy to the small group of silver-producing states. Silver long ago passed from importance as a major monetary metal.

In summary, the impact of gold and silver reserves on national monetary policy is now indirect and subject to wide discretionary authority. Changes in gold and silver stocks have a direct impact on commercial bank reserves, unless they are offset by governmental counteraction. Gold and silver may influence the decisions of the Federal Reserve and Treasury concerning reserve policy. But monetary management is the order of the day.

1. Does the federal government have a responsibility to do everything it can to assure full employment in the American economy?

2. Would you say that the Federal Reserve's chances of preventing a severe depression are any better now than they were in 1929? Why or why not?

FOR ANALYSIS AND DISCUSSION

3. Suppose creeping inflation of about 3 per cent a year continues. You are a member of the Federal Reserve Board. What should the Board do? Defend your policy and evaluate its likely success.

4. Suppose you were a banker with a balance sheet roughly like that of the Victory Bank in Chapter 8. Now the Federal Reserve raises reserve requirements to tighten credit just when the demand from loans from your long-standing business customers is rising. What would you do?

5. Do you think the Federal Reserve officials were right in supporting the price of U.S. government bonds at par through World War II even though this action helped create a huge volume of new money? How about their continued support of the bonds during the five years after the war? Should the Federal Reserve now support government bond prices to ease the Treasury's debt financing problem and to hold down the interest cost on the national debt?

6. When inflation and unemployment coincide, sensible Federal Reserve action would be to raise reserve requirements while buying bonds in the open market. True or false? Explain.

7. Restrictions on consumer credit to help check inflation during World War II were vigorously protested by many labor-union leaders on the ground that such restrictions discriminated in favor of the rich against the working man by reducing his ability to get his fair share of the scarce hard goods (autos, refrigerators, and so on) available. In your judgment, was this argument a sound one? Why or why not?

8. Since the Federal Reserve Board is in effect part of the federal government, why should there be any formal gold requirements against its notes and deposits, especially since Congress can change the gold requirements at any time? Is this a superfluous requirement?

9. There is a direct correspondence between our domestic money supply and gold flows into or out of the United States. (True or False? Explain your answer.)

10. (a) On the basis of your analysis of the functioning of the United States monetary system, how would you describe and evaluate the role of gold in the system?

(b) Does the United States have too much, too little, or just the right amount of gold now? What are the criteria you use in deciding, and why do you use these criteria?

(c) Would you advocate any change in the present federal law governing the relation of gold to the money supply? Explain and support your answer.

15

Fiscal Policy

Back in the pre-1930 days, only 10 per cent or so of the national income flowed through the public economy. But in World War II this figure soared to over 50 per cent, and during the 1950's it fell back to only 20-25 per cent. Federal, state, and local government receipts and spending of more than $100 billion a year today provide an enormous leverage to influence the level and direction of the nation's economic activity. And there is little reason to expect a return to the 1920's.

Before the 1930's, almost no one questioned the wisdom of balancing the federal budget every year. Sometimes the government didn't manage to do it, but everyone was apologetic about the failure. But as the depression deepened in the 1930's, the federal government just couldn't balance the budget, try as both Mr. Hoover and Mr. Roosevelt would. We had deficit financing because we couldn't help it. But an increasing number of people, led by the now-famous economist John Maynard Keynes, began to argue that the government's excess spending was actually a good thing in depression. The earliest argument went something like this.

271

Pump-priming.   The government should prime the pump of private spending in depression. Everyone can agree that it would be foolish to try to have government receipts just equal expenditures every day or every week. Would it be foolish to take a month as the period for balancing the budget? Surely so. Why, then, should the budget be balanced every year, instead of every two, or five, or ten years? Wouldn't the sensible thing be to balance the budget roughly over the length of the business cycle? Government deficit spending in depression would help increase total spending and prime the private pump. Later, excess government taxes to pay off the debt in prosperity would help hold down the boom. The deficit would be a temporary expedient.

Compensatory Government Spending.   As the long black years of the 1930's dragged on, faith in both monetary policy and government pump-priming waned. Talk of the stagnant economy and a chronic deficiency in private investment spread. Emphasis shifted to continuing "compensatory" government spending, aimed to fill in the deficiency of private investment. According to the compensatory spenders, the private economy couldn't carry itself forward to prosperity even when primed by doses of government investment. Government deficit spending should be continued as long and as heavily as necessary to attain and maintain full employment.

The Basic Case for Fiscal Policy.   Fundamentally, the potential stabilization role of governmental fiscal policy is a simple one. When private spending on consumption and investment falls short of high production and employment levels, the government can increase total expenditures by spending more than it currently collects in taxes. At the extreme, it can finance this net addition by creating new money so as to assure a net addition to private spending. Or it can borrow existing funds from the public, hoping to draw on funds that would not otherwise be spent. Or it may even increase total spending by increased government spending financed by new taxes, though the success of this method is doubtful. How big the stimulation is will depend largely on the size of the resulting multiplier effect. Conversely, when total private spending is too high, the government can withdraw funds from the income stream by taxing away more than it spends, generating a negative multiplier effect. At the extreme, it may simply hold or destroy this net surplus. Or it may use the surplus to pay off government debt, hoping that the bondholders will not rush out and spend the funds they receive.

Total spending on gross national product is made up of private spending on consumption and investment *plus* government spending (g.n.p. $= C + I + GS$). To summarize the preceding paragraphs, if the government increases its spending on goods and services without reducing either private consumption or investment spending, clearly this increases g.n.p. If increased government spending generates increased private spending through the multiplier, the effect is correspondingly larger.

This relationship is shown in Figure 15-1. Let the *CC* and *C* + *I* lines be identical with the lines in Figure 11-7, back on page 182. Equilibrium income would then be 350. Now suppose the government enters the picture and, without collecting any taxes, begins to spend 10 (perhaps raising the funds by borrowing at the banks). We can thus draw a new government layer on top of the *C* + *I* curve. This new *C* + *I* + *G* curve is 10 higher at every point. But this new government spending becomes income to the private economy and has a multiplier effect just like private investment. Thus the new equilibrium level is 390, because the multiplier effect raises total income four times the original investment on the assumed marginal propensity to consume of .75 in Figure 15-1, carried forward from Chapter 11. Note that this gives a new equilibrium income identical with that in Figure 11-8, where the new investment of 10 was private rather than government.

**Multiplier Effect
of Increased Net Government Spending**

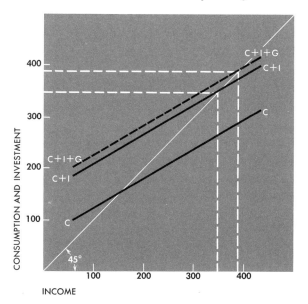

FIG. 15-1   Net new government spending of 10 adds 10 of "investment" and, with a multiplier of 4, raises total income by 40—up to a new equilibrium of 390. This is identical with the multiplier effect of 10 new private investment in Fig. 11-8.

Of course we need not have started from a purely private economy. A comparable effect would occur if we added government net spending in a situation already including government taxes and spending. But note the crucial assumption that the government spending is a net addition to private investment. If private investment falls, the multiplier effect is partly offset. Thus increased government spending financed by higher taxes is a more complex case, with a much less certain multiplier effect, to be considered presently.

This basic framework for stabilizing fiscal policy through government surpluses and deficits is simple and appealing. Surely it is the government's responsibility to help provide economic stability for the nation. No private business or agency has the vast powers necessary to tackle this job.

But there's many a slip 'twixt cup and lip. Counter-cyclical fiscal policy in the 1930's was no great success. The huge government expenditures of World War II demonstrated beyond doubt that government spending can generate high national income and high-level employment. But it demonstrated also that expansionary fiscal policy can generate inflation problems for the future (1946-50). And the 1950's saw continuing problems of how best to use fiscal policy in attaining rapid growth and high-level employment without inflation. Fiscal policy is far from simple to operate successfully. But it is a powerful tool against economic instability.

FISCAL POWERS AGAINST UNEMPLOYMENT

In depression, the job is to raise the level of total spending. (1) The government can add directly to the income stream by spending more than it collects in taxes (i.e., run a deficit), hoping for a big multiplier effect. (2) Even with a balanced budget, it can try to tax otherwise idle funds and thus finance new government spending without reducing private investment or the propensity to consume. (3) It can try to increase total private spending by redistributing income from the rich to the poor, through taxes and transfer payments.

For (1) to work effectively, government spending must represent a net addition to private investment and not reduce the economy's propensity to consume. If the government finances expenditures by creating new money, the spending is pretty clearly a net addition to investment and there is no reason to expect it to lower the propensity to consume. If the government borrows existing funds from the public, private investment *may* be slowed and the propensity to consume *may* be reduced. If the government wants to be sure of expansionary results, it had better rely on creating new money. But, as World War II showed, it had better recognize too that it may be storing up inflationary headaches for the future.

Making (2) work is a much tougher job. In principle, the government can raise the level of income by raising both taxes and spending to a higher level, without creating a deficit. Suppose income is 100, the budget is balanced, and unemployment exists. The government increases taxes by 10, and spends the 10 putting the unemployed to work. This payment to the unemployed creates 10 of additional income. The taxes cut down the spending of taxpayers, but the previously unemployed now spend their new income. If we assume that private investment is not reduced by the new taxes and that the propensity to consume of the newly employed is identical with that of the taxpayers, then the new consumption spending of the newly employed will just offset the drop in consumption by the taxpayers and total income will be increased to 110 by the 10 of increased government spending.

No one denies that this "balanced-budget multiplier" of one may occur. But it depends on a number of assumptions (for example, that private investment is unaffected, that the propensities to consume of taxpayers and newly employed are identical, and that government spending is on goods and services rather than on transfer payments). Most economists believe that deficit-financed government spending is a far surer road to increased total expenditures.

Making (3) work is hardest of all. Taxing the rich in order to subsidize the poor may stimulate consumption—but a counteracting decline in saving and investment spending by the rich is uncomfortably likely. Moreover, *marginal* propensities to consume of poor and well-to-do families are far less different than are the *average* propensities of the same families, and the net effect of income redistribution on consumption depends on the comparative *marginal* propensities involved. Taxing businesses in order to subsidize consumers runs the same risk of reducing investment as much as it increases consumption. You may think the distribution of income ought to be more equal on ethical grounds. But the effect of such redistribution on total spending and employment doesn't look very impressive, on the evidence we now have.

Underemployment Revenue Sources.   Where should the government get the money to increase its spending against underemployment? The preceding analysis points clearly toward new money creation—borrowing from the banks. Then nothing cuts into private spending. But a little more detailed look at alternative money sources is worth while.

Taxes. Collection of any tax is deflationary, because it withdraws funds from the income stream. Expansion, not deflation, is needed when underemployment is the problem. And taxes that draw directly on the income stream are worst of all. Sales taxes, excises, and payroll taxes are direct levies against spending. Income taxes, especially on high incomes or business profits, *may* be paid out of current or accumulated savings, and thus not reduce current private spending. But this result is far from sure. And many observers believe that high personal and business income tax rates impose a serious drag on private investment.

Summary: Financing government expenditures through taxes primarily involves taking funds from one group (taxpayers) to provide benefits for other groups. The primary effect is to redistribute, not to increase, the gross national product.

Borrowing from the Public. If the government needs money and can't get it from taxes, it borrows. Government borrowing from the non-bank public differs from taxation as a depression revenue source in two major respects. First, borrowing is more likely to tap idle funds, and thus less likely to reduce private spending, than are taxes. Individuals and businesses ordinarily won't stop spending on things they want just to lend to the government. If they voluntarily buy government bonds, the funds usually come out of savings. Second, when the government borrows, the lender gets a bond instead of a tax receipt. Holding the bond as a semi-liquid asset, he is likely to spend more of his current income than if he has only a fading tax receipt; his marginal propensity to consume is higher. Government borrowing from the non-bank public doesn't alter the money supply, since the borrowed funds are promptly spent back to the public. But it does increase the public's supply of liquid assets by the bonds issued.[1]

Summary: Borrowing from the public represents a drain on potentially spendable funds of the lenders, just as taxes do. But it is more likely to draw on savings than are taxes. And borrowing gives the public bonds to hold rather than tax receipts.

Bank Borrowing—New Money. The most direct way for the government to augment total spending is to create and spend new money. One way would be to print new currency and spend it. But in the modern economy, flooding the public with currency would merely lead to piling up excess bank reserves as unneeded currency was returned to the banks. Creating new bank deposits is simpler. Moreover, government printing of "greenbacks" arouses widespread public fear of unsound financial practices, whereas similar creation of deposits through borrowing from banks seems to cause little alarm.

Borrowing from the commercial banks is thus a convenient, effective way of assuring that deficit spending will have a positive multiplier effect. And once the money is created and spent by the government, it stays in the hands of the public as part of an enlarged money supply. The larger the public's cash balance, the higher will be its propensity to consume and invest out of current income, other things equal. (To work, of course, government borrowing must avoid replacing loans to private borrowers.)

An even more direct way to create new money is for the Treasury to borrow directly from the Federal Reserve, obtaining newly created deposits at the Federal Reserve in exchange for bonds. Direct government borrowing from the central bank is widely distrusted. It is called unsound and inflationary. It certainly is inflationary, since new funds are created for the government without any reduction in the public's spending power. Would this be bad in depression?

Historically, experience with direct borrowing from central banks has been concentrated in violently inflationary periods. For example, the central European hyper-inflations of the early 1920's were fed by central-bank printing-press money when taxes fell far short of financing government needs. Thus, antagonism toward this practice is understandable. Yet, for any given volume of borrowing, reliance

---

[1] This liquidity, of course, carries over into succeeding boom periods, when it may be a source of acute embarrassment to those who are attempting to curb inflationary developments. The inflationary experience after World War II was a vivid example.

on credit creation by the Federal Reserve is no more inflationary than credit creation by the commercial banks.[2] The central bank gives the Treasury a deposit credit in payment for securities, just as do commercial banks.

Summary: Insofar as spending financed by new money simply increases employment and production rather than raising prices, it is a "burdenless" form of financing. Under those circumstances, no one bears any burden of financing the expenditures (for there is no depreciation in the value of money and no taxation); and the purchasing power of some groups is increased by the added income resulting from the government spending.

Underemployment Expenditure Policies. Where should the government spend its money to get the greatest expansionary multiplier-accelerator effect against unemployment?

Public Investment. "Regular" government expenditures in normal times include extensive investment in highways, parks, education, and so on. These public projects are presumably undertaken because they fill a greater social need than do alternative uses of the resources. Citizens' dollars are diverted through taxation from private to government spending, on the vote of democratically elected representatives.

Public-investment projects in depression should be considered in the light of these "regular" needs. Such "net-social-gain" public-investment projects should be the ones undertaken first in depression periods unless there are strong counter-arguments. Next, public projects that were marginal in periods of full employment may be worth while when the need for expansionary spending arises. For example, a new highway that could not quite be justified on its own merits might become clearly desirable when it could double in brass as a recovery stimulant. If the depression is long and severe, the government may get down to investments of seriously decreasing intrinsic merit.

As recovery from the recessions of 1954 and 1958 failed to produce full employment, and as our growth rate lagged behind the U.S.S.R.'s, many economists advanced a new argument. First, they said, many public services are badly needed in our society—for example, better education—while we waste billions creating obsolescence each year through bigger tailfins on cars and new styles for refrigerators. Worse, in the affluent modern American society, even our vast attempts to create new demands can't induce enough consumer spending to keep the economy operating satisfactorily near full employment. The conclusion? The government should tax away a higher proportion of the national income and use the funds to provide badly needed public services. This would reduce private spending little, since the basic limitation for much of the economy is a substantially satiated de-

---

[2] Assuming that steps are taken to prevent further credit expansion on the new member-bank reserves provided by Reserve Bank purchases.

mand for many products. The result would be fuller employment and a better balance of public services with private output produced for the market.[3]

Enthusiasts for public investment point to many urgently needed public services —education, highways, flood control, parks, slum clearance, low-cost housing, and many others in addition to defense. Part 5 looks at these areas of public spending in some detail. Here we focus mainly on their usefulness against unemployment.

1. Public-works outlays directly stimulate the durable-goods and construction industries, where unemployment is usually centered. Public expenditures "bunched" on public works provide a big stimulus to demand in the durable-goods industries (construction, steel, lumber, and so on), in contrast to direct relief payments spread thinly over millions of unemployed. Perhaps the military strategy of massed forces against selected objectives is appropriate for depression-period fiscal policy.

2. Another important advantage of public investment is that, unlike relief payments, it gives us "something to show for our money." Modern schools, parks, and highways are valuable in their own right, beyond the help they provide in putting people back to work.

3. By providing jobs for otherwise unemployed workers, public-works projects help maintain the morale, self-respect, and skills of workers. Even with a dole or unemployment compensation to avoid starvation, worker morale suffers severely from unemployment; self-respect is lost; idleness becomes habitual; skills become rusty or vanish. Such social losses are a major cost of depression.

On the other hand, public-investment projects have serious limitations:

1. Flexibility in timing is hard to maintain. Public-works projects are often slow to get started and hard to stop once the need for them is past, both because of the physical nature of the projects and because of their political setting. How many projects shall there be, and where? Every locality and political group demands its share. Moreover, it is not practical to cut off many projects short of completion, once they are begun. A bridge halfway across a river, or a partly built schoolhouse, must be completed to avoid the appearance of flagrant waste even if depression has turned to inflation.

2. Public-works projects may perpetuate or worsen undesirable relative price-cost maladjustments in the heavy industries where public-works spending is centered. Especially in the construction industry, wages and many monopolized prices (costs) rise rapidly in boom times but stay far out of line when recession forces more flexible prices downward. Large government construction projects keep these costs up.

---

[3] See, for example, Professor J. K. Galbraith's popular *The Affluent Society* (New York: Houghton Mifflin, 1958), which led the best-seller lists in 1958.

3. Some types of public works may compete with, rather than induce more, private investment. This objection has been advanced most strongly against government construction of low-cost housing and of such combined power, reclamation, and flood-control projects as the Tennessee Valley Authority. This subject has generated more heat than light over the past two decades. Whatever the answer on many public-works projects, a wide range of available outlets, such as education, highways, parks, and resource conservation, are clearly noncompetitive.

4. Lastly, public investment is an expensive way of providing relief in periods of unemployment. Public-works outlays may need to be as much as double direct relief payments to provide any given amount of extra direct dollar income for the unemployed.

Relief Payments. Direct relief payments or unemployment benefits to unemployed workers are the cheapest and most direct way to get funds to the needy and to assure that these funds will be promptly respent. Few relief recipients will hold idle the funds they receive. On the other hand, the effect of a "dole" on morale is bad, and it fails to maintain work habits and skills for re-employment. If unemployment benefits are too high, they may leave little incentive to look for a job.

Reflecting the strong sociological and economic objections to direct relief, government-supervised "unemployment insurance" has taken over the major role in providing transfer payments to the unemployed.

Tax Reduction in Depression.   An alternative way to stimulate total spending is for the government to reduce taxes (while maintaining its own spending rate). While this does nothing directly to increase spending and leaves the government the problem of how to finance its deficit, the policy is widely favored to fight unemployment. The reasons are that it avoids direct government interference in the economy through increased spending; it permits private consumers and businesses to spend their excess funds as they please; and it is more flexible than government spending.

But here too there are counterarguments. The biggest is that merely reducing tax collections may not greatly stimulate private spending, especially private investment. At the lower income levels where saving is small, tax reductions may immediately stimulate spending by almost the amount of the reduction. But for the economy as a whole, to obtain any desired stimulative effect a deficit created by tax reduction must probably be considerably larger than one created by increased government spending.

Perspective on Fiscal Policy Against Unemployment.   If the goal is to increase total spending, government deficit-financed spending is better than a balanced budget. The deficit may be obtained by lower taxes, higher spending, or any combination of the two. The lower-taxes approach has major advantages in flexibility and minimization of government intervention; the increased-spending approach is generally more powerful, and may provide public services valuable in their own right.

As with monetary policy, one of the toughest problems for fiscal policy comes on the "in-between" cases—where it isn't clear whether unemployment or inflation is the major problem. The need for accurate forecasting is even more crucial than with monetary policy, since (as we shall see presently) fiscal policy is largely made by Congress and is hard to turn on or off fast. To adopt deficit financing too late and continue it too long may readily turn recession into booming inflation. To act too slowly against recession may permit the downswing to build momentum that is very hard to check.

This problem of slow congressional action, on top of the difficulty in forecasting what size deficit will be needed to do the job, has led many economists to push "built-in flexibility" in fiscal policy. This approach, considered in detail in the next chapter, favors a tax and expenditure system that will *automatically* run a deficit when national income falls, and will *automatically* reduce the deficit as recovery progresses. This trick is achieved through using taxes whose yield falls sharply when national income declines, and expenditures (for example, unemployment insurance) that rise automatically at the same time. The idea is to remove the necessity for economists to forecast just what actions will be needed and for Congress to act promptly on these forecasts.

In summary, most economists now believe that fiscal policy provides a very powerful weapon against major depressions like those of the 1930's. Government deficit spending is a blunt, often cumbersome tool. Except through built-in flexibility, there is little evidence yet that fiscal policy can be used flexibly to avoid minor cyclical swings. But if the depression is bad, massive deficit-financed spending can almost surely put millions back to work and push the economy back to reasonably high-level employment. Massive deficit financing is not costless. It may build up vast inflationary pressures for a later day. And it may involve far-reaching government intervention in the economy through the government spending needed. But if we are willing to use it to the hilt, it is a powerful weapon against general unemployment.

FISCAL POWERS TO CHECK INFLATION

The government's fiscal powers to check inflation are essentially the reverse of its powers to check deflation. The most direct attack on inflation is to withdraw funds from the income stream through taxes, and to hold or destroy the money. Whether the budget surplus (excess of tax collections over government spending) is obtained by raising taxes, reducing government expenditures, or both, is of secondary importance. *The crucial thing is a drain on the income stream that is not replaced through government spending.*

This is *not* the same thing as saying that the government should pay off the national debt in boom periods. On the contrary, the most anti-inflationary action the government can take with a surplus is *not* to pay off the debt, but merely to hold the budget surplus immobilized as its own cash balance.[4] If the Treasury pays off debt held by the general public, the funds are returned to private hands, where they may be spent again. If the Treasury pays off bank-held debt, the banks regain the reserves lost when the taxes were paid to the government, and they may re-expand credit on the reserves. *It is the tax withdrawal of funds from the income stream that exercises the deflationary pressure. What debt is retired thereafter merely determines how much, if any, of the deflationary impact is negated through returning funds to the public and the banks.*

The general principle is simple. A Treasury surplus is anti-inflationary because it involves either reduced government spending (with a negative multiplier effect) or increased tax withdrawals from the private sector (with reduced private spending on consumption and investment), or both. But, as with anti-depression policy, there are problems.

One, as with monetary policy, is the problem of flexibility and getting the right action at the right time. Raising taxes and cutting government spending are not popular acts for congressmen, and Congress does neither with much enthusiasm, even when inflation is a present problem. But the problem goes still deeper. Even if Congress posed no barrier to prompt action, someone would still have to say just when how much surplus was needed to avoid inflation without generating unemployment and recession. Against massive inflation a shotgun surplus approach is fine. But when there is only a little inflation, coupled with worry lest prosperity turn down, a rifle is needed. Delicate manipulation of tax and government spending rates poses major problems. Changing any tax rate involves large administrative difficulties. Starting and shutting off government investment on short notice is obviously wasteful and disruptive in many cases, especially where a valuable public service is involved and in public-works projects. Moreover, we don't know much about just how fast government surpluses work, and how powerful they are.

These difficulties, like their counterparts in combating unemployment, push many economists toward built-in flexibility as a major approach to fiscal policy. Such automatic responses don't predict and may react somewhat slowly and weakly. But they are automatic, and are certainly in the right direction most of the time.

A related major problem is what taxes to use, if taxes are to be increased against inflation. The choice hinges mainly on whose spending you want to cut down, and on the negative multiplier effect from different taxes. A tax on lower-income families is sure to cut consumption spending, because such families have

---

[4] Paying off government debt held by the Federal Reserve also avoids putting funds back into the hands of the public.

no appreciable savings on which to draw. Taxes on the rich may have less direct effect on consumption, though they will reduce savings; and remember that marginal propensities to consume differ less than average ones. Taxes on business provide a still more complex problem, depending on whether they come out of business-retained profits, dividends to stockholders, or are passed on to customers through higher prices. Even cutting down saving will retard investment, though the effect may be lagged and uncertain. The surest attack on business investment may be higher corporation income taxes. But anti-inflation effects must be weighed with the other goals of taxation, especially equity in the over-all impact on taxpayers.

Ten years ago, in spite of these difficulties, most economists would have said that government surpluses provide a generally reliable tool against major inflation, if only we have the political courage to use them. Today there are major doubts, arising mainly from the problem of "cost-push" inflation. If price rises are induced by cost-push rather than by excess demand, reducing aggregate demand through government surpluses will check inflation only at the cost of unemployment. If wages are pushed up in spite of reduced total demand, either employers must raise prices (with resulting declines in sales volume and worker layoffs) or employers may temporarily meet the higher wages out of profits. But obviously this can work only temporarily, and even then reduced profits may well reduce private investment and generate a business downturn that way.

The old assumption that substantially full employment could be taken for granted in inflationary periods no longer seems safe. And with it goes the comfortable certainty that fiscal policy provides a reliable anti-inflation weapon. But it is nevertheless probably the best and most powerful weapon we have. The practical problems of making stabilizing monetary and fiscal policy work are the focus of the following chapter.

FISCAL POLICY
AND THE BALANCED-BUDGET
TRADITION

The reasoning thus far suggests that government deficits and surpluses are powerful tools in fighting unemployment and inflation. Yet, until the 1930's scarcely anyone questioned the proposition that the government's budget should be balanced every year. And today most people probably believe a balanced budget is the best thing. Thus, a more detailed look at the fiscal consequences of this traditional policy is worth taking.

A balanced-budget policy is, in one sense, a "neutral" government policy. The government feeds back into the income stream just what it withdraws—no more and no less.[5] Thus a balanced budget seems appropriate when we are satisfied with the existing level of total expenditures—roughly, in periods of full employment without inflation.

---

[5] Though remember the possible "balanced-budget multiplier" effect noted above.

But suppose recession appears. What does the balanced-budget policy call for? With falling national income and unchanged tax rates, the government's tax receipts will fall. A deficit will automatically be created unless corrective steps are taken. To correct the deficit, the government must raise tax rates to get more money, or reduce expenditures to match its reduced tax receipts. If you believe that the government ought to be trying to *expand* total spending in order to check the recession, the balanced-budget policy is clearly wrong. *Reduced* tax rates and *increased* spending would contribute most to raising the level of total spending, but the balanced-budget policy leads to exactly the opposite action.

Similarly, inflation will generate a budget surplus, leading to tax reductions and increased spending under a balanced-budget policy. Again, this seems clearly the wrong prescription for stabilization purposes.

If a balanced-budget fiscal policy is likely to give the wrong answer so often, why did it take so long to discover its weaknesses? There are probably two answers: (1) an analogy with personal finance, where your income must cover your expenditures if you are to stay on good terms with your creditors; and (2) a pervasive feeling that by and large the economic system would itself correct any deviations from full employment without help from government fiscal policy. You should be able to form your own judgment on the latter point by now. On the former, we shall have more to say in analyzing the effects of a large public debt in the next chapter. For the moment, keep an open mind, and remember that almost any major corporation has a large amount of debt outstanding. Business borrowing is one of the standard ways to get funds for operating and long-term expansion purposes, and the volume of private debt has grown steadily over the past century.

Cyclically Balanced Budget.   This kind of reasoning led, during the 1930's, to the proposal that the budget should be balanced not annually, but over the length of the business cycle. On reflection, there seemed to many observers no great virtue in one year as an arbitrary accounting period. A cyclically balanced budget would permit government fiscal policy to play a positive stabilizing role, and at the same time maintain the basic character of a balanced budget. Only the accounting time period would be changed.

Is there anything the matter with this sensible-sounding policy? Business-cycle history suggests one problem. What if the government runs a big deficit fighting a long, severe depression, and then the following boom turns out to be a half-hearted affair that doesn't even get up to full employment? Should the government then feel obliged to try to collect a large surplus to match the preceding deficit, even though to do so would seriously depress the economy? A cyclically balanced budget policy would presumably say yes, but common sense rebels at the idea of a big government surplus when the problem is to avoid slipping back into large-scale unemployment.

If booms just offset depressions, the cyclically balanced budget policy will work out just right. Even if the two don't balance out exactly, the general notion of roughly offsetting deficits and surpluses in depressions and booms may be a useful guide to government policy. But, say the critics, what if the two needs for fiscal policy turn out not to balance out at all? Won't the cyclically balanced budget philosophy expose us to the same false prescriptions as annual budget balancing?

"Functional Finance." The "functional finance" advocates say yes. Forget about balancing the budget as a separate goal, they say. Use the government budget in whatever way is needed to help provide full employment without inflation. If the economy stagnates and the policy means more deficits than surpluses, a rising government debt is a small price to pay for the avoidance of mass unemployment. If the economy is too buoyant, continued government surpluses are fine. The major goal is economic stability, and we shouldn't become so preoccupied with our tools that we lose sight of our objectives. This approach is called "functional finance" because it views the problem of government finance purely functionally, as a means toward the goal of economic stability.

This policy is the logical conclusion of looking at government fiscal policy as a means of compensating under- or over-spending in the private sector of the economy. It gets a lot of support from modern economists. But will it really work? The answer is not so clear. Wait for Chapter 16, which looks at some of the major operating problems.

FISCAL POLICY AND ECONOMIC GROWTH Federal fiscal policy can exert a powerful influence on the rate of economic growth, both through the size of the deficit or surplus and through the particular taxes and expenditures used. The most critical question is the impact on the rate of investment.

Expansionary fiscal policy that helps generate prosperity raises the rate of growth, since investment is generally higher in prosperity than in recession. Conversely, fiscal policy that damps the boom slows the rate of growth, whether or not this is a conscious objective. But the particular taxes and government investment policies used may have as much impact as the size of the surplus or deficit. High income taxes on businesses and individuals may directly discourage private saving and investment. Increased taxes on lower-income groups, whatever their equity, check investment less than consumption.

Thus, it is not easy to use increased taxation to check inflation while simultaneously encouraging a high growth rate. In general, this double goal calls for an increased total tax burden (given any level of government expenditures), coupled with heavier taxes on consumption relative to those affecting investment. This prescription is unlikely to be politically palatable. And a surplus big enough to check the inflation may simply be incompatible with taxes on investment low enough to produce the desired growth rate.

Careful choice of government spending policies can also affect the rate of growth, given any total level of taxes and spending. Investment in basic research and education, both largely government functions now, promises high growth returns. Highways, resource development, and other such projects to improve the efficiency of the economic organization are obviously more stimulating to investment than are veterans benefits and general government expenditures.

1. Should the government guarantee substantially full employment? Justify your answer.

2. If gross national product is $50 billion short of a full-employment level, if the public's marginal propensity to consume is .95, and if private investment is constant, about how much additional government investment, financed by bank borrowing, would be necessary to raise gross national product to a full-employment level? Explain why, indicating clearly any assumptions you make.

3. Suppose the situation is as in the preceding question, but the level of private investment is not held constant. Would you then expect the amount of government investment required to be larger or smaller? Why?

4. State carefully all the advantages and disadvantages you can think of in balancing the federal budget (a) weekly; (b) annually; (c) biannually; (d) over the cycle; (e) over a 50-year period; (f) only when current business conditions are at the desired level, regardless of how often this occurred. Which alternative would you choose on the basis of your analysis?

5. You are asked to speak before a local businessman's group on whether federal taxes should be increased, lowered, or left unchanged for next year. Outline the talk you would give, indicating briefly how you would develop each of your major points.

6. Assume that international tensions require a $50 billion increase in military expenditures over the next two years. Would you recommend that the federal government raise the $50 billion by borrowing, or by approximately doubling the present tax revenue from personal and corporation income taxes? Evaluate each alternative in terms of its impact on total production, the public's standard of living, and the distribution of income and wealth. Is there a better alternative than either of these two?

7. Suppose you believe that a growth rate of at least 5 per cent per annum is essential for the American economy to meet the economic challenge of the U.S.S.R. What federal fiscal measures would you advocate to achieve that growth rate?

8. As an economist for the President's Council of Economic Advisers, you are asked to prepare a set of recommendations for action in case a recession develops in the near future. Outline the recommendations, explaining your reasons for supporting these measures.

**FOR
ANALYSIS
AND
DISCUSSION**

16

The Practical Problems of Stabilization Policy

In principle, monetary-fiscal policy to mitigate booms and depressions and to provide stable economic growth is simple. But will it really work?

The first thing to note is that there isn't much evidence yet. We have had only about twenty-five years of experience since the government first consciously tried to use government fiscal policy as a counter-cyclical device, and its use has been a constant source of controversy. Congressional and public opinion only gradually accepted the idea of counter-cyclical budget policy, and advocates of an annually balanced budget are still powerful. Thus counter-cyclical budget actions have been controversial, halting, and spotty—far from the orderly plan laid out by the functional-finance programmers.

The results thus far have been less than spectacular. Chalk up the 1930's as poor but hardly a reasonable test of combined monetary-fiscal policy, the 1940's as so-so, and the 1950's as promising. A quarter-century is a short period; and it would be surprising if a new stabilization tool like combined monetary-fiscal policy had proved fully successful on its trial run, especially with such an

286

unsystematic trial. The World War II experience did demonstrate unmistakably the enormous expansionary power of large-scale deficit spending financed by bank credit. And from 1940 to 1960 there was no major recession—the longest general prosperity in our history. But there was inflation, and much slower growth than in many other countries. Increasingly, the dilemma of how to hold down inflation while stimulating employment and growth has become the great unsolved problem of monetary-fiscal policy.

THE PROBLEM OF LONG-RUN GUIDES TO POLICY *Ad-hoc* monetary-fiscal policy, dealing with each situation as it arises rather than on the basis of any settled set of principles, has not been conspicuously successful, unless the 1950's mark the beginning of success. Operating on such a basis, we have repeatedly found ourselves trying to "cure" depressions and inflations after they have occurred, rather than preventing their occurrence. The gold standard, while it lasted, provided a broad framework for the formulation of monetary policy. With the demise of the gold standard, monetary-fiscal policy was left without a formal framework. During the 1920's, price-level stabilization was widely favored as a supplement to the gold standard as a guide to domestic monetary policy. During the 1930's, just getting people back to work was the dominant goal. By the 1950's, it was "full employment without inflation" and "stable economic growth."

"Full Employment." The Employment Act of 1946, adopted after long congressional controversy, in effect announced that it is the policy of the federal government to help achieve and maintain the "maximum" production and employment consistent with maintaining a free, private-enterprise economy. Advocates of a "full-employment" policy argue that whenever unemployment exceeds some minimum frictional level (say 2 or 3 million), expansionary fiscal and monetary policies should be adopted. When we have full employment, monetary-fiscal policy can be neutral or, with caution, deflationary. Here, they say, is a simple, easily understood long-run guide to monetary-fiscal policy for Congress and the administrative officers of the government.

Some of the questions that need to be asked about this long-run policy have already been raised. Is monetary-fiscal policy alone sufficient to maintain total demand at full-employment levels? What of the long history of great bursts of real investment? Can capital accumulation and economic progress continue at a steady rate without booms? How can monetary-fiscal policy eliminate the short cycles of inventory accumulation and de-cumulation?

And adoption of an all-out "full-employment" policy guide would raise one big additional problem: Wouldn't this policy be an open invitation to organized labor, business, and agricultural groups continually to press for higher prices and incomes? The government's full-employment policy would be a guarantee that any unemployment created by wage or price increases would be bailed out by expansionary fiscal measures—by more government spending to push up total incomes enough to assure full employment at the higher price and wage levels. There would be a constant incentive for each producer group to attempt to increase its own income absolutely and relatively by raising its own prices.

Even the present somewhat ambiguous "maximum" employment and production policy under the Employment Act runs this danger. Some observers think it has encouraged unions and businesses to push up wages and prices with little concern for pricing themselves out of the market. What if unions and business do push up costs and prices when others are still unemployed? The all-out full-employment policy says, take expansionary measures. Put the unemployed back to work. But the result is inflation. The inflation-unemployment dilemma is the great unsolved problem of modern stabilization policy.

Price-level Stabilization. Fear of the inflationary consequences of a full-employment policy leads some economists to advocate instead stabilization of the price level (generally an index of major wholesale or cost-of-living items).[1] Like the advocates of a full-employment policy, they argue that booms and depressions are easier to prevent than to cure. They say that watching the price level gives the best signals for action. If recession sets in, prices will soon begin to fall, which would be the signal for expansionary government action. If prices rise above the set prosperity level, the inflation would be a signal for deflationary policies. Advocates of price stabilization agree that the basic goal is high-level employment and output. They favor price stabilization because they feel that it could achieve the basic goal without inviting inflationary pressures.

Under price stabilization, money wages could rise as fast as worker productivity increased. If unions pushed wages up faster, unemployment would be the painful result. If businesses raised prices "too high," sales would fall off. In either case, there would be no government action to bail out self-seeking sellers from the consequences of their actions. Government monetary-fiscal policy would guarantee total spending sufficient to maintain substantially full employment at the accepted price level, and no higher.

This is a Spartan policy. It would accept temporary unemployment as the price paid for forcing sellers to forego unjustifiable wage and price increases. But its advocates argue that in our economy it is the only real alternative to creeping, then cumulative, inflation, as powerful labor unions and businesses steadily push wages and prices ever higher, abetted by a government afraid to risk unemployment resulting from restrictive fiscal measures.

---

[1] This policy involves only stabilization of the average level of prices. Individual prices would be left completely free to move relative to one another; stabilization would be achieved entirely through controlling the level of total monetary demand, not through fixing individual prices.

The critics point to another difficulty. With powerful unions and administered prices, it is no longer clear that consumer or wholesale prices will fall promptly if recession develops. Unemployment may pile up before many prices are cut. The price level goes up for many reasons, but it comes down only in response to major recession and unemployment.

Not many economists now advocate price-level stabilization as the sole guide to monetary-fiscal policy. But many would like to see it put into the Employment Act as another guide along with maximum employment and production.

High-Income Budget Balance—"Built-in Flexibility." Recently, a new policy has been suggested. It would set tax rates at the level required to finance some desired stable level of government expenditures when national income provided essentially full employment, and keep tax rates there. Assuming that the federal government should spend, say, $50 billion annually, tax rates would be set to yield about $50 billion when national income was at about a full-employment level. Heavy reliance would be placed on income taxes, whose yield would vary directly and strongly with national income fluctuations.

Under this plan, if national income fell below the full-employment level, tax income would automatically fall rapidly from $50 billion. Government expenditures would be maintained, however, so the scheme would automatically create a deficit whenever one was needed to check contracting income and employment. The deficit could be financed by commercial or Federal Reserve bank borrowing. If national income soared above the full-employment level, taxes would rise above $50 billion and an automatic surplus would result. Expenditures would be held at $50 billion in either case, except for unemployment and other such automatic anti-depression benefits, which would help stabilize the economy by automatically rising in depression and falling in booms. The plan would provide "built-in budgetary flexibility." [2]

Proponents of the plan claim that they are facing political and economic realities that other approaches gloss over. The built-in flexibility plan would require no action on the part of Congress or the administration in forecasting business developments and in changing tax and expenditure policies accordingly. There would be no need to delegate congressional power over tax and expenditure levels to get quick action. Under the built-in flexibility plan, Congress need only establish the basic expenditure level to be maintained and enact the tax rates set to cover those expenditures at high-level employment. The rest would be automatic.

The biggest question about the plan is whether it could provide enough built-in flexibility with stable tax rates and expenditures to maintain income stability if

---

[2] This plan was advanced by the Committee for Economic Development, a progressive group made up of the top executives of leading business concerns, in its policy statement, *Taxes and the Budget* (Washington, D. C., 1947), and revised in a later statement, *The Budget, The Economy, and Tax Reduction in 1956.*

strong unstabilizing forces should develop. Most economists agree that the answer is no; and most flexible budgeters agree that when drastic inflation or deflation develops in spite of built-in flexibility, functional finance becomes the order of the day. And everyone agrees that the plan does not get away from the basic unemployment-inflation dilemma.

Even if the built-in flexibility proposal alone is inadequate, it does suggest a useful approach. The more stabilizing flexibility we can build into our tax and expenditure systems, the less will we have to rely on imperfect forecasts and notoriously slow and unpredictable congressional action to produce the right fiscal measures at the right time. Nearly all economists agree that we should push toward more built-in flexibility on both the tax and expenditure sides.

The 3 Per Cent Money Supply Rule.   Another group, also despairing of our ability to forecast accurately or even recognize promptly incipient booms and recessions, urges that primary reliance be put on simply increasing the money supply about 3 per cent per annum, no matter whether times look good or bad. The 3 per cent roughly parallels the growth in full-employment-level output. With stable velocity, it would provide growth in total spending just about right to support stable growth in g.n.p. with full employment and a stable price level. The new money could be inserted into the economy either through government deficit spending or through bank loans to private borrowers. Monetary policy would be the big gun; fiscal policy would serve merely as a device for inserting money into the income stream.

This policy would not, its advocates admit, iron out small fluctuations. But they say it would provide a sound, stable growth in total spending—and, they argue, attempts to fight every little fluctuation probably do more harm than good anyway.

Everyone agrees there is a good deal of sense in having a gradually expanding money supply. But most economists feel that with wide fluctuations in velocity, to count on a stably growing money supply alone to provide stable income growth is giving too much weight to the quantity of money. Even most who doubt our ability to forecast very well believe we can do better than just increase the money supply 3 per cent a year, no matter whether times are worsening or improving. But the money-supply advocates point to the record (see Figure 10-1); the correlation between the major changes in the per capita money supply and in the level of total spending has been surprisingly good.

This policy, like the others, comes a cropper on the unemployment-inflation dilemma. If union wages and administered prices are pushed up to produce inflation when unemployment exists, shall we stick with the 3 per cent money rule, regardless of the unemployment? Or increase total demand a little more to eliminate unemployment, even at the cost of more inflation?

THE UNEMPLOYMENT-
INFLATION DILEMMA:
WAGE-PUSH
AND ADMINISTERED PRICING

Monetary-fiscal policy, properly used, can go a long way to prevent major depressions and spiraling inflation. If the problem is massive depression, the answer is easy. Fire both barrels of expansionary monetary and fiscal policy. But with the return of reasonably good times, expansionary policy to take up the remaining unemployment slack and to push up the rate of growth provides an ideal setting for wage-push and administered-price inflation. Unions press for wages beyond productivity increases. Businesses pass on the higher costs, and may add a bit more to push up profits. Higher prices rather than more employment are the major result of expansionary monetary-fiscal policy. This is sometimes called "bottleneck inflation," because cost and price increases appear at bottlenecks throughout the economy before full employment is achieved. These bottlenecks need not involve strong unions or monopolistic business price-setters. But strong unions and administered pricing increase the likelihood of inflation.

Suppose, in a full-employment economy, inflation arises because of wage-push. Then the government faces the painful choice of holding down total spending and letting the higher wages and prices generate unemployment; or putting in extra spending power to validate the new higher wage and price structure. Which would you do?

Suppose you decide that unemployment is a worse evil than inflation, and pump in some new money, through more bank reserves or government spending. But now unions increase their wage demands still further, far beyond productivity increases. Businesses, after a proper show of resistance, give in, and then put up prices to cover the higher unit costs. What now? Will you give in again, and pump in more spending power to justify the new level of inflation to avoid unemployment?

If your answer is yes, the logical conclusion of the questions is obvious. Would your monetary-fiscal policy just lead everyone on to jack up his wage and price demands even faster? Put yourself in the union's shoes. Would you hold down *your* wage demands to help the nation avoid inflation? As a businessman, would you take a costly strike to avoid inflation, even if you felt you could get the higher price for your product? Is there any level of sellers' inflation which the government should refuse to support? Where is the stopping-point? Unemployment means lost jobs and lost production that is gone forever; inflation mainly only redistributes income and wealth. Certainly widespread unemployment seems the greater evil of the two. Yet what does the stairstep wage-price inflation gain anyone? Wouldn't almost everyone be better off if it were stopped?

Many observers suggest that annual wage increases about big enough to cover increasing productivity should be approved, but that bigger ones are inflationary and should not be bailed out by the government. In a rough way, this makes good sense. But it's not as simple as it looks. Productivity increases at very different rates in different industries. If productivity increases are high in the pattern-setting industries, such as steel and autos, wages geared to rising productivity may be non-inflationary there. But as these wage increases spread to low-productivity industries (say construction and the services), they are far in excess of productivity increases there and mean rising unit costs and prices. And unfortunately for price stability, many of the strongest unions are in high-productivity industries which are wage pattern-setters.

Suppose, alternatively, we decide to stand our ground against wage-push by holding down total monetary demand. How much unemployment would it take to check wage-push and administered-price inflation? Nobody knows. Some economists estimate that wage-push would substantially vanish with around 5 per cent unemployment. Others put the figure higher. Surely, if we are willing to keep a substantial unemployed labor pool, we can take the edge off wage-push. Maybe the cost would be only 2 or 3 million out of work to do the job, but 5 million or so seems more likely. Few people think this is a satisfactory answer to the sellers' inflation problem. But no one has come up yet with a good solution, unless direct controls over prices and wages are it. For that alternative, we must wait until Chapter 28, after we've looked at the functioning of the whole price system in more detail.

THE PROBLEM OF SHORT-RUN FLEXIBILITY: PLANNING AND POLITICS

Effective monetary and fiscal policy depends on accurate timing: knowing when to do what, and then doing it at the right time. Any honest economist will admit a lot of uncertainty on just what measures should be adopted when. Economic forecasting is still a long way short of reliability. It's hard to know even where we are in the cycle, much less tell where we'll be a year hence.

Even when we know what lies ahead we're not sure of the exact impact of different combinations of taxes and government spending. Is a $5 billion surplus gentle restraint or a sledgehammer against inflation in a $500 billion economy? Lastly, there's a big uncertainty as to the lag before either monetary or fiscal policy has its full impact on income and unemployment.

The Federal Reserve can act promptly, once the need is diagnosed. But the job of getting Congress and the administration to adopt the right tax and expenditure measures at the right time is a tough one, even after we know what should be done. Never forget that in the United States the power to tax and the power to spend are firmly held by Congress. The president and his administration can influence what taxes Congress passes, but only to a limited extent. The executive agencies have a freer hand in spending, but once every year they have to go back to Congress for more money for the next year.

Once Congress and the administration see the unemployment lines lengthen, getting government spending stepped up is probably not a serious problem, whichever party is in power. Tax reductions may come rapidly too. Cutting taxes makes everyone happy—the congressman and the voters back home. Only fear of an unbalanced budget might seriously deter tax cuts, and deepening depression is not an environment calculated to make legislators or government administrators theorize about the possible calamity of a growing public debt.

Prompt congressional action to stop inflationary booms is more dubious. Four to six months is the normal time to put a major tax bill through Congress. Appropriations bills may take almost any amount of time, depending on how controversial the project is. If influential groups are against either type of bill, a few congressmen may prolong indefinitely the time required for enactment. Remember that nobody is very enthusiastic about damping a boom. Boom periods are wonderful. Legislators voting for heavier taxes to slow the upswing may not have a happy or long political life.

With a full-employment economy, it is obvious to even the uninitiated that inflation can only cut up the real-income pie into different pieces, and that everyone suffers a cut in the real value of his accumulated money savings. But the prospect of being blamed for a depression strikes horror to the heart of any elected official. Don't put the blame too readily on "those politicians." Ask yourself what you'd do if you were president, or a senator, or chairman of the Federal Reserve Board, and it looked like inflation ahead but there was a 25 per cent chance that the real problem would turn out to be depression within six months. To make your answer easier, assume that you don't even care about being re-elected at the end of your term, and that all you care about are the best interests of the people as a whole. What would you do?

Thus, except in extreme cases, the political process is unpredictable. With creeping inflation and 3 to 5 million unemployed in the late 1950's, Congress and the administration were both split on whether to fight inflation or unemployment. Unless the need is crystal-clear, it's safe to expect lots of argument and delay in getting counter-cyclical fiscal action. And the same need is seldom crystal-clear simultaneously to 600-odd legislators and the key administration officials.

Some progress toward a broad policy agreement was made in the Employment Act of 1946, in which Congress tried to spell out the basic directives that government agencies should follow in their economic stabilization activities. And we have moved toward more "built-in flexibility" in taxes and expenditures—an approach which commands almost unanimous approval among professional economists, though it is clearly only a partial answer. But the major discretionary powers, except for monetary policy, still lie firmly in the hands of Congress. And how much attention Congress pays to its own policy directives is up to the congressmen themselves. A public-opinion poll would probably still show a confused mixture of the annually balanced budget, cyclically balanced budget, and functional-finance approaches in most people's minds. Counter-cyclical fiscal policy is far from clear to the man in the street or to the typical congressman, even after two decades of heated discussion in the newspapers and in Congress.

THE PROBLEM
OF EXPANDING
GOVERNMENT CONTROL

If the economy persistently tends toward underemployment, compensatory fiscal policy would mean steadily growing government spending. Many Americans don't like this alternative, because they feel that it would mean expanding government control over private economic affairs. If the economy fluctuates between boom and depression, however, aggressive fiscal policy need not involve any long-run growth in government control over economic affairs.

Views differ violently as to whether increased government spending involves undesirable interference with the affairs of private individuals and businesses. One school points out that the government is directly responsible to the people, and we can always vote the rascals out if we don't like what they're doing to us. The other argues that increased government spending is the primrose path to socialism—step by step the government takes over direction of our economic lives. Make up your own mind.

One thing is clear on the record to date. The biggest expansions in government spending and control have come with war and preparations for war, not with attempts to avoid depression. Even the New Deal of the 1930's channeled only a small fraction of the national income through the government in this worst of all depressions, compared to the spending of World War II days. Still, there is little doubt that it is much harder for the government to stop spending than to start. The anti-recession projects of today may easily turn into the regular government expenditures of tomorrow—the farm income and price support programs of the 1930's are prominent examples.

THE PROBLEM
OF THE PUBLIC DEBT

Much of the controversy over fiscal policy arises because people fear the rising public debt that comes with deficit financing. Since the 1920's, the public debt has increased by over a quarter-trillion dollars. In 1959, interest on the national debt was about $8 billion, more than the total federal budget for 1929 and over one dollar of every ten spent by the federal government in 1959. Should we view this with alarm?

The answer is, not with as much alarm as most people have, but with some. Consider six common objections to a large national debt.

"It Just Passes the Burden on to Future Generations." Many people say that borrowing to pay our government bills just passes the cost on to future generations. But this concern is clearly a fallacy, as a little careful reasoning will show.

Suppose we are fighting a war. The *real* economic cost of the war is the resources used up. If we use steel to produce jet engines and missiles, we can't use it for autos and refrigerators. A further real economic cost is the wartime disruption and destruction. However the war is financed—by taxation, by borrowing, or by just printing new money—these real costs are substantially the same. They are borne by the war generation. They cannot be passed on to future generations except insofar as wartime disruptions and destruction may impoverish future generations, and that effect is largely unaffected by the form of war financing. The dollar cost of the war may be higher if new money or debt financing generates inflation, but the real cost of resources used up for war is unaffected.

But may not borrowing impose a special burden on future generations,[3] even if it cannot remove the burden from the present generation? The answer is that payment of interest and principal by any future generation is just a transfer or redistribution of income within that generation. If the debt is paid off, the future generation is taxing itself to pay itself. The redistributive effects may be very important and they may increase or decrease employment, production, and prices at that time. But there is no necessary reason why the redistribution will decrease the total wealth and real income of the future generation. If the debt is refunded, the result again is a redistributional one, and indirect transfer effects are minimized. The crucial factor determining the economic well-being of the future generation is its accumulated real capital and its current real output. Having a money debt from earlier generations does not reduce either, and hence imposes no aggregate real burden on the future generation.[4]

The Danger of Bankruptcy and Economic Collapse.   May too much government borrowing eventually bankrupt the government and lead to economic collapse? "Bankruptcy," as the word is generally used, means inability to pay one's debts when they are due. In this formal sense, the federal government need never go bankrupt, because it always has the power to tax or print money to service or repay the debt. It never needs to default.

But can a big public debt bankrupt "the economy"? This too appears to be an unfounded worry. Payment of interest and principal involves essentially a redistribution of income within the economy so long as the debt is domestically held. It is conceivable, of course, that the government debt might become so large as to lower drastically the credit standing of the government among investors. But United States government bonds are still considered the world's ultimate "gilt-edged" investment. Even with its huge debt, the government obtains funds at the lowest interest rates of any borrower. And whatever interest rate the government must pay to borrow, there is nothing involved that will "bankrupt the economy," whatever this vague term actually means.

---

[3] To simplify matters, a "future generation" is assumed to be one that does not overlap with the present generation. The basic reasoning is similar if the generations overlap, but the results may be more complicated because then we need to consider the relative positions of working and retired people in the two generations.

[4] If the war generation borrows funds outside the United States, and the future generation has to pay foreign bondholders, then it may be justifiable to speak of a burden of payment being placed on the future generation in the United States.

In looking at the problems raised by a large government debt, it is important to look at the debt *relative to current national income*. A $1 billion debt in a $1 billion economy would be roughly parallel to a $400 billion debt in a $400 billion economy. On this score we're much worse off than we were back during the 1920's, when we paid the federal debt down to about $16 billion in a roughly $100 billion g.n.p. economy in 1929, but much better off than at the end of World War II. In 1960 the debt eased up toward $300 billion in a $500 billion economy. Figure 16-1 shows the comparison since 1900.

Federal Debt
and Gross National Product Since 1900

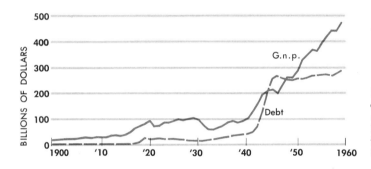

FIG. 16-1   The U.S. government debt has spurted upward in war periods, and has generally declined relative to gross national product in peacetime.

Where do we stand compared to other nations? Pretty well. Great Britain's ratio of public debt to national income is more than twice ours. We compare favorably with most other industrialized Western nations.

In perspective, our debt has soared astronomically in the last quarter-century, but so has our national income. If the g.n.p. grows at only 3 per cent a year over the period ahead, this will mean around $15 billion annually. Thus, the public debt could increase $10 billion a year, or $100 billion in only ten years, and still merely maintain the present ratio of debt to gross national product.

The Transfer Burden of Interest Charges.   A big government debt has its problems, even if the dire predictions of economic bankruptcy are overdone. One is the big annual interest on the debt. To be sure, this is only a transfer payment within the economy—from one of our pockets to the other, considering the nation as a whole. But the taxpayer and the interest receiver may be very different people. To the individual taxpayer, higher taxes to finance interest payments on the debt are just as real a cost as to finance a new guided missile or schoolhouse.

Heavy taxation tends to distort people's behavior. If the government takes a big chunk of each additional dollar earned, your incentive to work, as against leisure, probably goes down. Taxes on particular items raise their cost relative to other items, and shift demand away from the taxed goods. Nobody knows just how important such distortions are, but they look substantial. And they surely go up as the tax share of the national income goes up from where we are now.

Lastly, given our present tax system, taxing to pay interest on the debt tends to shift income from the poor to the rich. Soaking the poor to pay the rich sounds unjust to many people. It probably has a mild deflationary effect on the economy, since the poor would almost certainly have spent most of their tax dollar while the rich are more likely to save their interest receipts.

How large an interest transfer is feasible without seriously damaging the economy? This is primarily a function of two factors: (a) the relation of the interest burden to total national income, and (b) the taxes used in relation to the composition of interest recipients. A $10 billion interest transfer in a $400 billion income economy probably raises no more problems than a $1 billion transfer in a $40 billion economy. The ratio of interest cost to national income provides a first approximation to the importance of the interest burden. On this test, the United States is a little worse off than before World War II, with the ratio now about 2 per cent as compared with an average of about 1.5 per cent over the 1920-40 period. Our ratio is much lower than that for many other nations.

Psychological Deterrents to Private Investment.   Alarm over a large government debt may deter new private investment. Many writers have stressed this possible effect. Direct facts are hard to come by on the issue, but most evidence suggests that the danger is easy to overstress. Business investment depends far more on consumer demand relative to productive capacity than on the size of the public debt.

The business community and the general public adjust surprisingly quickly to changes in the general economic environment. One of the writer's first memories of economics is the bitter controversy that raged in the early 1930's over whether a public debt as huge as $50 billion could conceivably be borne without utterly destroying organized economic activity. No one seriously dreamed the debt would ever go so high—the argument concerned a hypothetical ultimate upper limit. By 1936 or so, the $50 billion had been upped to about $100 billion, as New Deal borrowing gradually increased the debt outstanding. Fifty billion no longer seemed to mean certain disaster. By 1941, the debt of $50 billion was forgotten in the mad scramble for materials, labor, sales, and profits as government and private spending soared. Soon the question, no longer an issue of burning interest, was, what about a $200 billion debt, then $300 billion?

With the postwar debt at over $275 billion and the economy operating at boom levels, general public concern over national bankruptcy has vanished, at least temporarily. The need to reduce the debt is still widely voiced in conservative financial circles, and increases are strongly resisted by many. But there is little reason to believe that if a further increase in income-generating debt were required we would not adjust "psychologically" to it as we have to previous increases. The businessman who foregoes otherwise profitable investments because of the $285 billion debt item on the Treasury daily statement is hard to find.

Debt Management and Monetary Policy.   A huge federal debt increases the difficulty of using monetary policy effectively. Billions of dollars of government bonds held by the commercial banks provide a facile base for inflationary credit expansion if the Federal Reserve supports government bond prices. Even if it does not, bank bond holdings represent a huge stock of semi-liquid assets. The governments held by the public also create a vast backlog of spending power for inflationary spending sprees, making control through monetary-fiscal policy, price ceilings, or any other device more difficult.

If stagnation lies ahead, all this liquidity may be helpful. But with inflation looming on the horizon and with continued Treasury refunding and new borrowing ahead, Federal Reserve officials can hardly help feeling hampered by the present big debt. When the Treasury needs to refund between $75 and $100 billion of federal debt annually, in addition to any new borrowing, it clearly hopes to have security prices high and interest rates low. But these are precisely the conditions that encourage inflation and increase the liquidity of the outstanding public debt. The Federal Reserve can only fight inflation by making the Treasury's job harder.

"The Lessons of Monetary Experience" in Chapter 14 tell something of what has happened. Through World War II and up to 1951, the Federal Reserve supported the market for government securities and gave up the monetary fight against inflation. But since then it has pursued a more independent policy. It has tightened money against inflation and forced the Treasury, like other borrowers, to pay higher interest rates. Result: By the late 1950's the controversy raged again as to whether the Federal Reserve should lessen its pressure against inflation and support the government bond market more aggressively in order to hold down interest costs on the federal debt. As long as a big government debt and inflationary pressures coexist, the problem can hardly vanish. The life of a central banker is not easy!

Encouragement of Government Waste.   As a matter of practical politics, too easy reliance on borrowing invites easy spending. Experience has shown that absence of the pressure of making expenditures conform to regular government receipts usually leads to growing waste and inefficiency in government administration. This is a homely but important argument against too easy reliance on continued deficit financing.

How Big Should the Public Debt Be?   How big should the public debt be? There is no single answer to this question, or to the related question—how big can the public debt be? Government debt *per se* has certain disadvantages. They are not overwhelming, and by no means the same as the disadvantages of a large individual or business debt. But they still may be serious, and they create a general presumption against increases in the public debt and for decreases. *Probably the most important principle, however, is that changes in the level of public debt —either increases or decreases—ordinarily exercise a much more direct and forceful effect on the level of current national income than does any given level of existing debt.*

Current fiscal policy (which may incidentally result in an increase or decrease in the public debt) is thus generally more crucial than is the level of existing debt. If the major aim is to achieve and maintain high-level output and employment, the level of public debt in itself becomes a residual effect of stabilizing fiscal policy. Paying off the debt, viewed in this fundamental fashion, is a secondary reason for running a budget surplus. Whether a budget deficit or surplus is desirable depends predominantly on whether a deflationary, expansionary, or neutral effect on current national income is needed. Once we have the public debt, its major effect has been felt.

For an interesting exercise to test your understanding of the basic point in the preceding paragraph, assume that the government pays off $50 billion of its debt over the next five years, half to banks and half to individuals. Analyze the effects of this transaction, beginning with the tax collections from the public which provide the government surplus used to retire the debt. Would you favor such a debt-reduction policy?

The Public Debt and the Money Supply. The preceding exercise should have pointed up a fundamental fact. Much of the nation's money supply was issued against the government debt now outstanding, and to retire bank-held debt would reduce the money supply accordingly.

Since 1800, the nation's money supply has increased from a few million dollars to $140 billion. Over this long period the government and the banks have provided about as much money (currency and deposits) as the economy "needed" to handle its current transactions and other monetary needs. Unfortunately, this provision of money primarily through the commercial banks involved sharp expansion in boom periods and sharp contraction in deflation. The net result has been economic growth, but also instability and inflation.

An increasing money supply is clearly essential to a rapidly growing economy. Over the years ahead, can we count on fortuitous circumstances or business-loan demands at banks to provide the gradual monetary expansion that is needed? Perhaps, but unless private borrowing calls forth new money at about the required rate, government debt management may have to help do the job. Nearly half of our money supply is now outstanding against bank-held government securities. Cooperative work by the Federal Reserve and the Treasury will be required to guarantee the money supply we need.[5]

---

[5] Some economists have pointed out that if the government debt held by the general public were gradually monetized, say by Federal Reserve purchases, two troublesome birds

CONCLUSION This chapter has dealt with the problems faced in using stabilizing monetary and fiscal policy. The problems are real ones, and no one should assume we have the matter of stable economic growth firmly in hand. Yet to end on a negative note would be unfortunate. Combined fiscal and monetary policy now provide a powerful tool against economic instability that should read the death sentence to massive depressions and help substantially against smaller fluctuations.[6]

could be killed with one stone. The problem of providing an appropriately expanding long-run money supply would be solved. At the same time, the publicly held interest-bearing debt could in effect be retired and replaced by non-interest-bearing securities held by the Federal Reserve.

[6] To instructors teaching one-semester courses: Chapters 34 (Wage-Price Policy and the Role of Government), 35-36 (The Public Economy), 42 (Social Security), and 43 (Economic Development: The Underdeveloped Countries) provide material that follows naturally to fill out the semester, if needed. They are written to be usable at this point, as well as where they appear in the book.

FOR
ANALYSIS
AND
DISCUSSION

1. Should the Employment Act of 1946 be amended to include stability of consumer prices as an objective of national policy equal in importance to "maximum production, employment, and purchasing power"?

2. In the last three decades labor unions have become much more powerful than before. Under these circumstances, according to some economists, a government guarantee that total spending will be kept up to full-income levels would be in effect a guarantee of continued inflation. Why, if at all, would this be so? Does it seem to you a serious danger? How would you go about assuring full employment without inflation?

3. How would you rate the availability of the following for quick action to fight a recession: monetary policy, tax reductions, and increased government spending? Recognizing the differential lags before these measures have their full effects on the level of income and employment, where would you put your main reliance in fighting a recession that is just developing?

4. If you were a congressman, would you vote to delegate the power to change tax rates to the President? To the Secretary of the Treasury? To the Federal Reserve Board? To anyone? Explain.

5. You are asked to give an hour's talk before your local Kiwanis Club on the subject, "What Should We Do About Our National Debt?" Outline your talk, indicating briefly under each point how you would develop it. Bear in mind the backgrounds and opinions of the group in planning your talk.

6. The National Association of Manufacturers has stated: "A government cannot continue indefinitely to run at a deficit without creating an inflationary trend which will in time undermine public confidence in its obligations." Do you agree or disagree with this statement? Why? To

what extent does your answer depend on your expectation of persistent stagnation or inflationary pressures?

7. Economic growth over the years ahead will mean large personal and business savings year after year. Unless savers have attractive outlets for these funds, investment will not offset the savings and depression will result. While savings may be invested directly, most personal savings go into bank deposits, insurance policies, stocks, bonds, or other such assets. Therefore, debt (public or private) must rise steadily over the years ahead to absorb the savings that will be made. Proposals to pay off the federal debt should be viewed with alarm. Instead, we should plan to increase it steadily to support stable economic growth.

Evaluate this argument, and its policy conclusion.

Current Research

The main job of an elementary economics textbook is to stir up interest in economic problems, to present the central analytical tools of economics, and to provide some guided experience in using them to reach independent judgments on current economic developments and on public-policy measures. I hope that the preceding pages, especially those on public policies aimed at providing stable economic growth without inflation, have conveyed some sense of the lively urgency of the problems with which economics deals, and some sense of the manner in which modern economics helps to solve them.

Economists spend much of their time using the kinds of tool presented here and helping to devise public policies that will make our economic system better serve the needs of mankind. But one of the further things that makes economics exciting to economists is research—the fascination of probing for new understanding, new knowledge, and new insights into how the economic system works and how it might be made to work better. Economics is far from a dead, stable body of theory and knowledge. It is the research of today that will make the better textbooks and the better world of tomorrow.

It is the purpose of these brief appendices at the end of each Part to convey a brief impression of some of the kinds of research currently under way in economics. Some of the research cited is readily understandable by a good student at the elementary level; other parts are difficult and technical. But the purpose is not to provide references that all beginning students should read. Rather it is to suggest some samples of economic research that may be intriguing to students who want to look beyond the text and who want to know more of what economics is and what economists do. Pick out two or three and look at them. If they don't hit the spot, try another. The goal is to interest you and make you want to read further.

The following paragraphs report briefly a small sample of research on some major problems covered by Part 2. It is important to recognize that these are only a sample. There is no intention at all to imply that they represent the best, or the most important, research under way on the problems covered. They are merely samples of research that one economist thinks might be interesting, and hopes may be intriguing, to curious students getting acquainted with economics. A major criterion in selection has been variety. Not one, but a half-dozen other comparable lists could readily be provided—and indeed your instructor may be happy to provide one he feels is superior.

Inflation. For an introduction to research in the area of inflation, try the symposium on "The Problem of Maintaining Price Stability" in the *American Economic Review* for May, 1960. In it, four distinguished economists survey where our knowledge stands in the area, and look forward to the unanswered questions. Professors P. A. Samuelson and Robert Solow of M.I.T. present a theoretical approach; Professor Lloyd Reynolds of Yale looks at the relation of unions and wages to inflation; and Dr. Arthur Marget of the Federal Reserve reports on what we have learned from studying foreign inflations. For a more advanced analysis at the theoretical level, try the Samuelson-Solow article on inflation in the March or June issue of the same journal.

A much more encyclopedic picture of recent research is provided by *The Relation of Prices to Economic Stability and Growth,* a compendium of 44 papers prepared by as many different economists for the Joint Economic Committee of the United States Congress, in 1958. Sample the volume by looking through the table of contents or thumbing through the pages. You will find a wide range of approaches, from abstract theoretical to careful empirical analysis, laced with a generous supply of suggestions to the Congress on how to handle the inflation problem better. The papers by Drs. Hickman (pp. 143 ff.) and Eckstein (pp. 361 ff.) provide good starting points.

If you are interested in quantitative and statistical analyses, and especially if you know some mathematics, four pieces (by Drs. Cagan, Klein, Lerner, and Selden) in *Studies in the Quantity Theory of Money* (Milton Friedman, editor; University of Chicago Press, 1956) provide careful analyses of the role of money in the inflationary process in different countries and different periods. Chang Kai-Ngau's *The Inflationary Spiral: The Experience in China, 1939-50* (John Wiley & Sons, 1958) illustrates a way of studying hyper-inflation in an underdeveloped economy.

A broader look, which tries to combine economic, social, and political factors, is illustrated by G. L. Bach's *Inflation: A Study in Economics Ethics and Politics* (Brown University Press, 1958).

Beyond these, keep an eye out for the forthcoming reports of the Commission on Money and Credit, a significant nonpartisan citizen's commission established under a large Ford Foundation grant to look into the whole problem of money, credit, and financial institutions in relation to the attainment of stable economic growth and stable prices.

Money and Monetary Institutions. Research on money is closely linked with research on inflation. The work of Professor Milton Friedman, of the University of Chicago, who tries to re-establish the validity of the quantity theory of money in a more sophisticated modern form, is summarized briefly in "The Supply of Money and Changes in Prices and Output," in the Joint Economic Committee compendium referred to above, and in "The Demand for Money—Some Theoretical and Empirical Results," in the *Journal of Political Economy* for August,

1959. A very different, and equally controversial, approach is that of Professor Edward Shaw of Stanford and Dr. John Gurley of the Brookings Institution, who emphasize the role of near-monies and financial intermediaries and minimize the importance of money as such. For an early summary, see their "Financial Aspects of Economic Development," *American Economic Review,* September 1955. Their book presenting a more complete picture should be available in 1960.

Two studies illustrating the participation of federal agencies in research are *Financing Small Business* (published by the Committees on Banking and Currency of the U.S. Congress, 1958), and *Consumer Installment Credit,* 6 volumes (Board of Governors of the Federal Reserve System, 1957 and 1958). Both include intensive work by economists within the Federal Reserve System and outside it, at both empirical and policy levels, focused on understanding better business and consumer credit and their regulation in the modern economy.

Another major Federal Reserve undertaking, which began with the work of Professor Morris Copeland of Cornell, is the provision of an entire new set of national accounts on a "money-flows" basis, to supplement the present national income accounts. The new accounts provide data on all money expenditures and receipts, including purchase and sale of assets and separate information on different business and financial groups not shown by the national income accounts. For an introduction to the continuing work, see *Flow of Funds in the United States, 1939-53* (Board of Governors of the Federal Reserve System, 1955).

A quite different type of historical research is reported in *Benjamin Strong, Central Banker* (Brookings Institution, 1958), by Professor Lester Chandler of Princeton. Strong was a dominant figure in the early years of the Federal Reserve System.

Theory of Growth and Fluctuations. Modern developments in economic theory involve partly the extension of theoretical models and concepts, and partly careful empirical testing of theoretical constructs already at hand. On the consumption function, two recent parallel analyses have challenged accepted views. Professors Franco Modigliani of Carnegie Tech (in "Utility Analysis and the Consumption Function," in *Post-Keynesian Economics* (K. Kurihari, editor; Rutgers University Press, 1955) and Milton Friedman (in *A Theory of the Consumption Function:* Princeton University Press, 1957) have presented similar theories that consumption is a stable long-term function of income. Modigliani emphasizes a life-cycle approach in relating consumption to income; Friedman a "permanent income" hypothesis that relates consumption to the expected permanent component of family income. To sample a mathematical-statistical ("econometric") analysis of the demand for particular commodities, see Daniel Suits, "The Demand for New Automobiles in the U.S.," in the *Review of Economics and Statistics* for August, 1958.

On investment decisions, *The Investment Decision* (Harvard University Press, 1957), by John Meyer of Harvard and Edwin Kuh of M.I.T., presents a path-breaking statistical-theoretical analysis of investment behavior for plant and equipment over recent years. Try also A. Kisselgoff and Franco Modigliani's "Private Investment in the Electric Power Industry and the Acceleration Principle," *Review of Economics and Statistics,* November, 1957.

A different approach to the problem of long-term growth, with primary emphasis on gathering complete empirical data, is that of the National Bureau of Research, a major source of factual information on economic growth and fluctuations. See especially Solomon Fabricant's report, as director of research, in the introductory section of the Bureau's 39th Annual Report, *The Study of Economic Growth* (1959); also his *Basic Facts on Productivity Change* (1958), and John Kendrick's *Productivity Trends in the United States* (1959), both published by the National Bureau.

Two important recent books reflect current economic theory on growth and fluctuations as it evolves: James Duesenberry's *Business Cycles and Economic Growth* (McGraw-Hill, 1958) and William Baumol's *Economic Dynamics,* 2nd ed. (Macmillan, 1959). Duesenberry uses theory against the complex pattern of history to explain growth and fluctuations. Baumol places primary emphasis on the development of theoretical models, using a good deal of mathematics.

Last, look at Geoffrey Moore's *Business Indicators* (National Bureau of Research, 1960), as a study in both the theory of business cycles and the problem of forecasting booms and depressions. Moore's approach is through a detailed statistical analysis of the lead-lag relationships of different economic series in past business fluctuations, with the presumption that these statistical patterns provide the best guide to the future.

Markets, the Price System, and the Allocation of Resources

17

Business Enterprise in the Modern Economy

In a private-enterprise economy, the businessman is at the center of the economic process. He decides what shall be produced, and how much of it. He decides how many employees to hire and how much he is willing to pay them. It is he who responds to consumer demands, sees to getting the goods and services produced, and pays out most of the incomes. Within the framework of rules established by society, his decisions and policies determine most directly how effectively the private-enterprise economy functions.

In America today, government controls over the operations of business concerns are numerous —so numerous that some businessmen protest violently that their traditional freedom is gone. Government produces some goods and services itself. And labor unions press increasingly for a share in the traditional prerogatives of management. But the businessman, harassed though he may be, remains a central organizing factor in our economy.

The purpose of this chapter is to provide a factual background on modern business enterprise, preliminary to a more extended analysis of how the private-enterprise economy gets its job done.

309

Business enterprises are called "firms." John Brown and his family run a farm; the farm is his firm. United States Steel is a firm, with steel mills in many cities, with iron and coal mines, with ore ships on the Great Lakes. The important characteristic of the firm is that it is owned and controlled essentially as a unit, however diverse its parts.

The function of making fundamental policy decisions in a firm is generally called "entrepreneurship." The entrepreneur decides when to establish a firm, how to combine productive agents, what goods to produce, how the concern will be financed, what price policies to follow, and so on. A firm is thus a business unit under one coordinated "entrepreneurship."

In the independent corner grocery store, the proprietor is the entrepreneur. He decides whether to borrow funds to remodel his store, what prices to set on his merchandise. In more complex forms of business, it is harder to pick out the entrepreneur. For example, who is the entrepreneur of American Telephone and Telegraph? The 1,600,000 stockholders? The board of directors? The finance committee of the board of directors? The president? Here it is impossible to pick out any person or group of persons as the entrepreneur; the functions of the entrepreneur are performed in a coordinated way by the various individuals and groups concerned.

A "plant" is a group of buildings and other more or less fixed physical equipment that are used together in production—perhaps a shoe-manufacturing plant or an auto-assembly plant. The Ford Motor Company is a firm with plants in Dearborn, St. Louis, Kansas City, and so forth. John Brown's farm, on the other hand, is a firm with only one plant.

An "industry" is harder to define. Usually we use the word to mean all the producers of any "commodity." Farmer Brown is part of the wheat industry if he produces wheat, part of the corn industry if he produces corn. General Motors is part of many industries. The trouble comes when we try to be precise. Shall we consider a "motor-vehicles industry," or an "auto industry," or a "low-priced auto industry"? For elementary purposes, the fineness into which we divide up commodities is not a major problem. You will seldom get in trouble here if you let common sense be your guide and if you stick to the same definition of "commodity" and the associated "industry" throughout the analysis of any problem.

The Shifting Legal Organization of Firms. The legal forms of business firms have changed with the times. When small-scale business was the rule, the individual proprietorship was dominant. This was simply an arrangement in which an individual put up the money, started his own business, ran it himself, and got the profits and losses. There are still more individual proprietorships in the United States than any other form of business organization—some 9 million in all. Of these, some 4 million are in agriculture, and most of the rest are small-scale retail concerns and service enterprises, such as cleaning establishments, filling stations, doctors, lawyers, and so on.

As the need for larger capital funds increased, partnerships became popular. These were simply cases where two or more people assumed joint proprietorship —usually joint provision of funds, joint management, and joint financial responsibility. This arrangement had substantial advantages over the single proprietorship, but it still fell short of providing enough capital for really large-scale business operations in modern times, except where the partners were very wealthy. And it shared one serious drawback with the single proprietorship: The partners were personally liable for all the debts of the business. Thus, in most cases, each partner was personally liable to an *unlimited* amount for the deeds of the other partners—a somewhat precarious position at best, and definitely not suited to drawing in funds from absentee investors. Partnerships have never been a very important form of business organization in the United States, though there are some 700,000 in existence. About half of them are in retailing; the rest are widely scattered.

THE
MODERN CORPORATION
The modern corporation, conceived largely to meet the needs of large-scale business organization and to avoid the drawbacks of its predecessors, has become the dominant form of American business enterprise. Although there are only about 600,000 business corporations, they do the bulk of the nation's business. Corporations account for about two-thirds of the nation's privately produced income. They do virtually all of the business in public utilities, manufacturing, transportation, and finance; around half in trade and construction; but less than a quarter in services and agriculture.

The biggest modern corporations are true Goliaths. In 1959, for example, the assets of the American Telephone and Telegraph Company (the world's largest business) approached $20 billion. Those of Standard Oil of New Jersey approached $10 billion, and those of General Motors $8 billion. General Motors in 1958 had sales of nearly $10 billion, an amount larger than the entire gross national product of most of the world's nations. In 1959 there were some 50 nonfinancial corporations with sales over a billion dollars.

Many financial corporations (banks and insurance companies) are as large, though most of their assets consist of investments in corporate and government securities and of direct loans to businesses and individuals. In 1959, the total assets of the Metropolitan Life Insurance Company, the largest insurance company, were over $18 billion. Those of the Bank of America, the Chase Manhattan Bank, and the First National City Bank, the three biggest banks, ranged from $8 billion to $11 billion.

Modern finance and industry are heavily concentrated in the hands of large firms, as we shall see in Chapter 26. Nevertheless, there are still many more small business concerns than large ones, and there is little evidence that big business has been appreciably increasing its share of the total market over the past two decades.

What Are Corporations? A corporation is an organization that exists as a "legal person" apart from the individuals who own and control it. A corporation may carry on business in its own name, enter into contracts, sue and be sued, own property, borrow and lend money. In general, it may as a business unit do all the things that any individual person may legally do in business.

Many of the earliest corporations were religious, fraternal, and educational institutions. For a long time, corporation charters specified rather closely what the purpose of the corporation was to be. Today, however, the corporation charters granted by most states are so broad in their grants of power and so vague in their statements of corporate purposes that they exercise little restraint over corporate activities. Indeed, since corporations pay fees for charters and special taxes to the chartering state, some states have competed in making corporation charters more and more lax in the attempt to get more fees and taxes.[1]

No matter where a corporation takes out its charter, it is permitted by the interstate commerce clause of the federal Constitution to carry on business in any other state. Thus it is hard for any state to regulate corporation practices effectively. The corporation can simply move legally to a more lax state, and carry on the same business in the same places as before.

The main advantages of the corporate form of organization center around its financial arrangements. Briefly, these advantages are:

1. Stockholders who invest money in corporations have no liability for the debts of the corporation; at worst, they can lose their original investment—unlike the unlimited liability involved in single proprietorships and partnerships. Moreover, the corporation's ability to raise large sums is enhanced by the wide range of securities it can offer, to tap different sources of investment funds, and by the substantial liquidity of corporate securities, which are continuously bought and sold on organized markets. These advantages are spelled out below.

2. In a corporation, management is delegated to a board of directors elected by the stockholders. The directors in turn supervise the salaried officials who actually run the business. Thus the individual stockholder need not concern himself with the details of managing the concern unless he wishes to—quite unlike the continuous attention required in a single proprietorship or partnership. Freedom to delegate power and responsibility to expert "managers" is essential to the operation of today's mammoth business enterprises.

3. Since corporate securities are readily transferable, no matter how many

---

[1] Delaware granted the United States Steel Corporation a charter permitting it to engage in any kind of business in any part of the world.

individual stockholders die or lose interest in the corporation the life of the business can go on unaffected.

Financing Corporate Enterprise—Stocks and Bonds.   Since college students come largely from middle- and upper-income families, many of your parents probably own corporate stocks or bonds. General Motors, IBM, duPont, Sears Roebuck, and other such companies are household words. Millions of Americans own part of them, as well as work for them and buy their products.

Corporations are financed by investments in "corporate securities." Individual investors may be part-owners of the corporation, or they may simply lend money to the business. Corporate securities fall into two corresponding broad classes: stocks, which represent ownership in the corporation; and bonds, which represent money lent to the corporation by bondholders. There are many variations within each of these two categories, and at the margin they run together. The most important differences in types of securities are in: (1) the owner's claim on the income of the enterprise relative to other security-holders; and (2) the owner's right to vote on personnel and corporate policy, and hence his power to control the corporation.

Common stockholders are the owners of a corporation. Common stock is usually "voting stock." The stockholders have the right to elect the board of directors and hence to control the policies of the corporation (except under special circumstances). They are entitled to any income remaining after prior claims of creditors and other owner-investors have been met. If the corporation is dissolved, they are entitled to all that remains (if anything) after everyone else has been paid. The common stockholders are the "residual claimants" to the corporation's income and property. They gain the most when income is high, and they are the first to lose when things don't go so well.

Net income earned and paid out to stockholders is called "dividends." Although the net income of the business "belongs" to the stockholders, often the corporation does not pay it all out, but instead re-invests part in the business. This is called "plowing back" earnings. Whether the net income is paid out or re-invested, it accrues to the benefit of stockholders, since re-invested earnings increase the value of the business.

Bondholders are creditors of the corporation. Bonds represent money lent to the corporation. Corporations often borrow money from banks. But when they want to borrow large sums for long periods, they commonly issue bonds that are sold to persons or institutions having funds to invest. Bonds are nothing but promises by the corporation to repay the funds to bondholders, at some specified future date with a set rate of interest.

If you own a bond, you are merely a creditor. You will ordinarily have no voting power to elect directors and control the corporation's policies. You will take less risk than the stockholders, since the interest on your bonds must be paid before they get any dividends. On the other hand, you will receive only your set rate of interest no matter how big profits are. Bondholders also have a prior claim on the assets of the corporation in case of liquidation. Many bonds contain provisions that if a corporation fails to pay interest when due, voting power is automatically given to bondholders so that they can protect their interests by having a voice in directing the policies of the business.

There are numerous types of bonds, and large corporations often issue several types. Some are mortgage bonds, backed by specific pieces of physical property; some are backed just by the general assets of the corporation; and so on. The important factor in determining the degree of risk or security of a particular issue of bonds in a given corporation is usually not whether or not the bond has some specific backing, but whether it has first, second, or third claim on the income and property of the corporation. In each corporation there is a definite rank of priority of claims on earnings, with first-mortgage bondholders ordinarily having "first lien"—that is, first claim to payment. All securities can be ranged in order of priority of claims on earnings and assets in a continuous series from first-lien bonds to common stocks.

Preferred stockholders have a position intermediate between that of the common stockholder and that of the bondholder. Preferred stock sometimes carries a vote; more often it does not. Typically, it has a set rate of dividends, say $6 per share, that must be paid before any dividends can be paid on the common stock. It also has priority over common stock in case of liquidation. On the other hand, preferred stock is definitely inferior to bonds in priority of claim on income and assets.

Who Controls the Corporations?   Suppose you own 100 shares of General Electric stock. How much control do you have over how General Electric is run?

The answer is, for practical purposes, none. Not because anyone is cheating or hoodwinking you—least of all the G.E. management, which makes a continuous effort to keep stockholders informed and to get them interested in company affairs. It is because of a combination of factors. In the first place, you own only a tiny fraction of 1 per cent of the company's stock. Moreover, you don't and can't know much about the operations and internal policies of G.E., a $4 billion corporation producing thousands of products, most of them involving complex scientific processes and know-how. Besides, G.E. is paying good dividends on your 100 shares, and that's what you bought them for. You haven't the slightest intention of spending a lot of money and time on an obviously fruitless trip all the way to Schenectady, New York, to try to tell the management how to run company affairs, or to throw them out for a new management.

To be sure, even if you don't go to the annual stockholders' meeting, you are entitled to send a "proxy," a person of your choice whom you designate to vote for you. Before each annual meeting, you will receive from the management a proxy form, suggesting that you designate either a management representative or someone else to vote in case you don't plan to be present. You may throw the proxy in the waste basket. If you do send it back, the chances are you'll designate the person suggested—partly because you don't know whom else to designate—thereby giving the present management the votes to re-elect themselves.

Surprisingly enough, you will be acting like the typical stockholder when you do this, even though you assume there are many other interested "big" stockholders who are keeping a sharp eye on the operating management from a stockholder viewpoint. A.T. & T. now has over 1,600,000 stockholders, no one of whom owns as much as 1 per cent of its stock. U.S. Steel has over 250,000 stockholders, Westinghouse over 150,000. On the other hand, a few well-to-do people own large blocs of stock in many well-known companies.

This wide dispersion of stock ownership, coupled with the lethargy of most stockholders, goes far to explain the substantial control over most large corporations exercised by relatively small groups of active stockholders, and often by the operating management "insiders" who may themselves own very little stock. This divorce of active control from ownership is a major development of modern business enterprise. It is probably inevitable in the large corporation. It certainly does not provide a very effective "democratic" government of corporation affairs in most cases, however good may be the intentions of the management on this score.

Of course, stockholder lethargy does not always exist. In some smaller companies, most stockholders take an active interest in the conduct of the business. Even in large corporations, conflicts and sharp struggles for proxies sometimes occur, with the control of the corporation at stake. A spectacular example was the unsuccessful effort in the 1940's, and the successful second try in 1955 of a bloc of stockholders to oust the very conservative Sewell Avery from the management of Montgomery Ward. But for the most part, minorities in control can feel sure of their ability to retain effective control without holding more than a small fraction of the voting stock. They are on the ground; most of the stockholders are far away and little interested.

Probably as little as 10 to 20 per cent of the voting stock is adequate to assure normal working control of most major corporations. In many, existing managements maintain their positions and effective control of corporate affairs with less. The most complete study on this point, made in the 1930's, covered the 200 largest nonfinancial corporations in the United States.[2] In 6 per cent of the corporations, control was exercised by nearly complete stock ownership; in 23 per cent, control was by minority stock ownership; in 21 per cent, control was by legal devices enhancing the power of minority or managerial groups; and in 44 per cent, control was by the management without material stock ownership. Moreover, the 44 per cent of the corporations that were management-controlled had 58 per cent of the collective wealth of the entire 200. More recent studies indicate little change in this situation. Cases where the "management" (directors

---

[2] A. A. Berle and Gardiner C. Means, *The Modern Corporation and Private Property* (New York: The Macmillan Company, 1934), p. 94.

and officers together) hold more than 3 to 5 per cent of the company's common stock are the exception rather than the rule.[3]

What proportion of the over-all public owns corporation stock? By 1959 there were about 12 million individual stockholders in "publicly owned" corporations, plus probably 1 to 2 million more in "privately owned" companies whose stock was held entirely by family or private control groups. The comparable total for 1952 was only about half as high.

Thus, something over 10 per cent of all adults now own stock in business corporations. This is a large number, and many big companies have more stockholders than employees. But it is still a small fraction of the population. This fact, together with minority and "insider" control of actual operations even in most widely owned corporations, makes it clear that America's corporations are still largely controlled by a few people. Most of the 12 million stockholders are small owners. A large portion of the total individually owned stock, as we shall see at the end of the next section, is held by only a few thousand wealthy individuals and families.

BUSINESS CONSOLIDATIONS AND COMBINATIONS Many of today's big corporations are the result of consolidations and mergers of separate companies. Over the past century, business combination has been a persistent, though irregular, trend. It moved through the stage of the "trusts" in the late nineteenth century, the "holding companies" in the early 1900's, outright consolidations in the decade of the 1920's, and mergers again since World War II. Today, the once-popular business "trusts" have almost vanished from the scene. But holding companies remain a prevalent form of organizing financial control over large aggregations of capital. They are less obvious than the huge corporations we all know in manufacturing, but in some ways their control is even more far-reaching. And mergers and consolidations reached record-breaking levels during the 1950's.

The Trusts. A trust involves the holding of property by a trustee who has power to administer it and to receive the income from it; both property and income are used by the trustee as directed in the trust agreement. This scheme has often been used by persons who wish to have funds held safely for the benefit of their children, and for other similar purposes. The business trust was ordinarily a corporation formed to hold stocks in a number of other corporations. Owners of stock in the controlled corporations turned their securities over to the trustee corporation and received "trust certificates" on which dividends were paid. Technically, they remained owners of the stock, but their power to vote was transferred to the trustee organization.

---

[3] R. A. Gordon, *Business Leadership in the Large Corporation* (Washington, D. C.: Brookings Institution, 1945), Chapter 2.

How might a business trust be set up? Suppose that companies A, B, and C are railroads competing with one another. A promoter sets up a trust, to which the controlling stockholders in railroads A, B, and C turn over their shares. In return, they receive "trust certificates." Control of the three competing roads could then be centralized in the hands of the trust, which might operate them so as to maximize profits and minimize competition among the three. The earnings of the roads would be returned to the original stockholders in the form of dividends on the trust certificates.

Such arrangements were often advantageous both to the promoters (who generally managed to obtain fat fees for their part in setting up the trusts and often retained part-control in them) and to the stockholders in the original operating companies (who benefited by the elimination of competition among their companies). Sometimes the trust itself did nothing but hold control of the operating companies. Sometimes a large operating company would also act as trustee for the stock to control other operating companies.

In the decade of the 1880's, the trusts grew rapidly. Most famous of the big business trusts was the Standard Oil Company, under John D. Rockefeller. Some of the others were the whisky, cordage, national lead, and sugar trusts. In most cases, the great trusts represented highly centralized control by small numbers of "insiders," who often were primarily interested in obtaining maximum returns for themselves, at the cost of other security-holders, as well as of consumers. One of the most common abuses was the issuance of "watered stock." Here the securities issued to set up the controlling trust carried a much higher face value than was justified by the assets of the trust. By selling such "watered" securities, promoters were able not only to obtain funds to buy competing companies, but also to retain large sums for themselves as commissions and salaries.

The Holding Companies.   The Sherman Antitrust Act of 1890, plus popular and judicial antagonism to the big trusts, led to a shift away from the trust form in the 1890's. Then the holding company became the dominant tool for concentrating control.

The holding company was similar to the trust, with one primary difference. The trust simply holds the shares of the controlled companies as trustee; it does not own them outright. The holding company buys up stock in the companies it wants to control. As the name indicates, the holding company typically owns and holds securities of other corporations; it frequently owns no land, machinery, or other such operating property itself.

Figure 17-1 illustrates how a holding company might be used to concentrate a high degree of control over a vast amount of capital with a minimum of investment. Suppose there are 12 railroads, A through L. Each is capitalized at $100 million, of which half is bonds, one-fourth is non-voting preferred stock, and one-fourth is common stock. Suppose we want to get control of these railroads, but we don't have enough money to buy control of each. The maximum total investment required to get control of railroad A is just over $12.5 million, which is the value of half the voting stock. We would need the same amount for each of the other railroads, if we assume that half the common is actually needed to maintain control. (A smaller amount would probably do.)

In this situation, we can form holding company X to buy up control of railroads A, B, C, and D. The total capital required is $50 million, since $12.5 million is needed to get control of each of the four roads. To raise this fund, suppose we sell $25 million of bonds, $12.5 million of preferred, and $12.5 million of common, in a new holding company X. Since only half the common stock outstanding is required to control company X, we need buy only $6.25 million of the common ourselves to hold control. We obtain the rest of the funds from the public. Then

Hypothetical Holding Company Structure

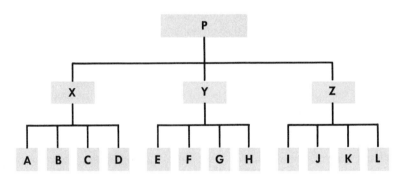

FIG. 17-1   Holding companies provide a device for holding control over a large amount of corporate assets with a relatively small investment.

suppose we do the same with holding companies Y and Z to buy up control of railroads E, F, G, and H, and I, J, K, and L, respectively. We now have gained control of all 12 railroads, with a capital of $1.2 billion, through having invested $19 million, the amount necessary to control holding companies X, Y, and Z, which in turn control the 12 operating railroads. Since X, Y, and Z hold the stock of operating companies directly, they would be called "first-degree" holding companies.

But we can go still further. To control the three holding companies, $19 million is necessary. Suppose we form a "second-degree" holding company, P, capitalized at $20 million, to raise these funds (as shown in preceding table). In forming company P, we issue $10 million of bonds, $5 million of preferred, and $5 million of common. Since only half the common is needed to control, we need put up only $2.5 million to retain control of P, with the remainder of the securities sold to the public. With this $2.5 million investment, we now have control over the entire $1.2 billion set of operating railroads. Since many stockholders fail to vote their holdings, we might be able to do the job with even less cash.

Total investment of $1.2 billion controlled by an investment of $2.5 million in the second-degree holding company, P:

Each operating company (A-L) has:

Total capitalization of	$100,000,000
Bonds	50,000,000
Preferred stock	25,000,000
Common stock (voting)	25,000,000

Each first-degree holding company (X, Y, Z) has:

Total capitalization of	$ 50,000,000
Bonds	25,000,000
Preferred stock	12,500,000
Common stock (voting)	12,500,000

The second-degree holding company (P) has:

Total capitalization of	$ 20,000,000
Bonds	10,000,000
Preferred stock	5,000,000
Common stock (voting)	5,000,000

This hypothetical example probably seems fantastic. As a matter of fact, it is not. Huge holding-company pyramids have been built up in the past few decades where the proportion of investment to total capital controlled is even smaller. For example, in the 1930's a court found that Howard Hopson, a shrewd promoter, had managed to hold control of the billion-dollar Associated Gas and Electric holding-company system with approximately $100,000 of voting stock. Especially in the public utilities and railroad fields, holding companies attained an almost unbelievable complexity. A chart of the companies included in the famous billion-dollar Insull utility holding-company empire in the late 1920's would take up three or four of these pages in normal-sized print. This was one of the most blatant cases of "insider" control and self-seeking. Small and large investors lost every cent of their investments in the Insull holding-company securities in the great crash of the early 1930's. Such abuses led to the Public Utility Holding Company Act of 1935, which ordered gradual dissolution of all such public-utility holding-company systems.

Such familiar companies as American Tobacco, U.S. Rubber, American Can, and U.S. Steel were established as holding companies around the turn of the century. Since then, however, the holding-company approach to consolidating economic control has waned outside the financial area, and direct consolidations and mergers have accounted for most inter-corporate combinations. Especially during the 1920's, and again since World War II, mergers have been widespread. But small business prospered too during those periods, and there is no clear evidence of increased dominance by big business since the 1920's.

Financial Control Groups in the Modern Economy.   By means of large investments coupled with extensive use of financial holding companies and other minority control devices, a few very powerful financial groups have attained tremendous power over the corporate structure of the nation. Grouping the 50 largest financial corporations with the 200 largest nonfinancial, the National Resources Committee found in the late 1930's that out of total assets of $115 billion for the group, the J. P. Morgan-First National Bank of New York interest group controlled over $30 billion, and that the Kuhn Loeb investment banking interests controlled over $10 billion, primarily railroads. Of the purely family groups, the Rockefeller interests controlled over $6 billion; the Mellon interests over $3 billion; and the duPont interests over $2.5 billion. By the mid-1950's it was estimated that the stock holdings alone of the duPont family exceeded $4 billion and those of the Rockefeller and Mellon families $3 billion each. Since the extent of corporate control was undoubtedly far larger, the assets controlled by such wealthy family groups were enormous indeed.

The upshot is that ownership of today's big corporations is widespread, and increasing steadily; but the holdings of most individuals are small, and a large part of the total is owned by a small portion of the population. Sketchy surveys suggest that the top 1 per cent (about 550,000) of the families hold around two thirds of all privately held stock. Most stockholders own only a few thousand dollars' worth of stock.

A big, and growing, share of all corporate stock is held by financial institutions —pension funds, trusts (usually managed by banks), insurance companies, and the like. They probably now hold around a third of the total. To date, such financial institutions have been reluctant to intervene directly in corporate control and management. But as private savings pile up in such institutions, their potential power becomes enormous, far exceeding that of even the wealthiest families. Even corporations' and unions' own pension funds, amounting to billions of dollars, are now being invested in corporation stocks, posing intriguing problems of future corporate control. Who should watch over the managers of these vast accumulations of funds?

CONCLUSION   Concentration of business administration in the hands of a small number of professional, salaried managers who have little direct contact with most of the owners of business is one of the major developments of twentieth-century industrial society.

Coupled with this development is a high degree of concentration of financial control over the modern financial and industrial worlds by a small fraction of the population, although stock ownership is widespread among small holders.

It would be a mistake to infer from these facts that the "insiders" are using their influence and operating control to the disadvantage of either other stockholders or consumers. On the contrary, there appears to be good reason to suppose that many big business concerns are managed both more efficiently and with a greater view to the social welfare under the present class of professional salaried managers than they were under the direct control of owner-operators. If you have $5,000 invested in Standard Oil of New Jersey, it is very doubtful that your interests would be better protected were Messrs. Eugene Holman and M. J. Rathbone (the top executives of Standard Oil) larger stockholders than they in fact are, or if you could personally participate in the management of the business. In Messrs. Holman and Rathbone you are hiring a much-admired team of experts in managing a huge corporation. In general, it seems safe to assume that their goals are roughly what yours would be (maximizing profits, for example), and that they are more expert at achieving the objectives than you would be.

Similarly, today's growing group of professional managers seems more concerned with serving the public well than was the typical captain of industry a half-century ago. Certainly the drive to "feather his nest" on a large scale is less dominant with the professional salaried manager, because he personally has so much less chance to gain from such behavior than did the more picturesque industrial tycoon. The earlier avowed attitude of "the public be damned" may still exist in some companies, but it has been largely replaced by a more responsible attitude among the professional managers. Nor is there much evidence that the dominant large stockholders use these positions to exploit other stockholders or the public. Indeed, many investors prefer such companies as duPont and Alcoa partly because they want the watchful guidance given these companies by the duPont and Mellon families. And, whatever the abuses of big business over the years—and we shall see that there have been many—the industrial research and vast mass production underlying the present spectacular American standard of living generally trace back to these same industrial giants, whose monopoly powers consumers may have grounds to fear.

There is little likelihood that the modern corporation, with its vast accumulations of capital and its professional management divorced from most stockholders, will soon disappear from the American scene. This raises a big problem for every thoughtful observer. How shall we obtain the obvious advantages offered by such huge industrial concerns while at the same time avoiding the excesses which the American public has typically feared from large concentrations of economic power? This is the problem we will come to a few chapters later on.

The concepts in this chapter deal largely with institutions and legal forms. Be particularly sure that you understand the following:

entrepreneur	common stock
plant	preferred stock
firm	bond
industry	trust
individual proprietorship	holding company
partnership	merger
corporation	

Appendix A

The Elements of Business Accounting

In order to understand the workings of modern business enterprise and of the modern economy, you need to know something about the elements of business accounting. Although the details of modern accounting are extremely complex, its fundamentals are simple. Only a knowledge of these fundamentals is essential for our purposes.

The Balance Sheet. A balance sheet is a cross-section picture of the financial position of a firm *at some given point of time*. It is an instantaneous snapshot, in contrast to a picture that summarizes the concern's operations over a month or year or some other time period. A second sort of picture, discussed below, is an "income" or "profit-and-loss" statement that does summarize the firm's operations over a time period.

The balance sheet of any business rests on a fundamental equation. One side of the balance sheet shows what the business owns—its assets. Exactly corresponding to the value of these assets must be their ownership, which goes on the other side of the balance sheet. Obviously the two are always equal—the balance sheet always balances.

It is not easy to say just *who* "owns" the assets of the business. At the one extreme, the common stockholders are commonly considered the "residual owners"—that is, the ones who would get all the cash left over if the business were liquidated and its debts paid off. But this consideration makes it clear that the various creditors of the business (for example, the bank that has loaned it funds or the supplier from whom it has bought on credit) also have a claim on the assets. Such "creditors," to whom the business owes money, are at the other extreme of the claimants on the business' assets—they generally get their funds first, certainly in a going concern. Bondholders, whose interest is contingent on satisfactory earnings, have a less preferred claim on the assets; preferred stockholders are still further down the list of claimants. It is easy to see that the line between "creditors" and "owners" is very indistinct. The two groups shade into one another as a continuum of claimants on the business' assets.

Commonly, business balance sheets are set up with the right-hand (claims) side divided into at least two major parts. The first group of items includes all "debts" owed by the business. The second is "capital and surplus"—the balance-sheet value of what would be left for the stockholders (common and preferred) if all debts, or "liabilities," were paid off through use of part of the assets. But, as suggested in the preceding paragraph, too much significance should not be attached to the distinction between "debts" and "capital and surplus" on the claims side of the balance sheet. Indeed, there is evidence that even this two-part breakdown of the claims side is gradually giving way to a mere listing of the claimants, with capital and surplus items last.

Table A

GADGET MANUFACTURING COMPANY
Balance Sheet, December 31, 1959

Assets		*Liabilities and Proprietorship*	
Current assets:		Current liabilities:	
Cash	$2,000,000	Accounts payable	$ 500,000
U.S. government		Accrued taxes	900,000
securities	1,000,000	Total current liabilties	$ 1,400,000
Accounts receivable	2,000,000	Bonds outstanding	3,000,000
Inventories on hand	2,000,000	Capital and surplus:	
Total current assets	$7,000,000		
Fixed assets:		Preferred stock	
		outstanding	$1,000,000
Investment in affiliated		Common stock	
company	300,000	outstanding	2,000,000
Plant and equipment	3,000,000	Surplus	3,100,000
Patents and goodwill	200,000	Total capital and	
		surplus	6,100,000
Total	$10,500,000		$10,500,000

Table A is the balance sheet of a hypothetical Gadget Manufacturing Company, as of December 31, 1959. On the left-hand side are all the assets of the company—everything of value that it owns. On the right-hand side are all claims against these assets, broken down into two groups: first, its liabilities (what it owes); and second, its capital and surplus accounts (sometimes called its "net worth" or "proprietorship") on this date.

Once you see the basic equation underlying the balance sheet, most of its items are self-explanatory. For convenience, assets are often arranged beginning with the most liquid (the most readily convertible into cash) and ending with the least liquid. Those assets that are readily convertible (say within one year) are grouped together as "current assets." The others are called "fixed assets."

Of these assets, the last calls for special explanation. Two hundred thousand dollars is the value attached, for accounting purposes, to the patents and goodwill accumulated by the company since its inception. Obviously this is an estimated figure, a more or less arbitrary valuation determined by the company's officials and accountants. The item is so obviously intangible, albeit of tremendous importance for such well-established products as Coca-Cola and Lucky Strikes, that it has become accepted conservative business practice to place a very low value on it.[4]

Actually, this item is only the most conspicuously estimated of the list; others are estimated too. The current value placed on plant and equipment, as we shall see, is particularly susceptible to the vagaries of managerial and accounting judgment, because the "current value" shown is generally nothing but the original cost of the asset less an estimated amount of depreciation.[5] Current assets can be valued somewhat more precisely; but only cash, at the extreme, is clearly and inevitably "worth" exactly the figure at which it is carried.

The liability side seems a little more tricky at first glance. "Accounts payable" is easy—these are debts owing to suppliers and others from whom the company buys. "Accrued taxes" represent tax liabilities that have been incurred but that have not yet been paid. The liabilities that will come due within a year or so are grouped together to facilitate comparison with current assets. Such a comparison gives a quick picture of the short-run financial position of the company—its "current ratio."

"Capital and surplus" consists of three items in this particular balance sheet. Part of the company's funds were obtained by sale of preferred, part by sale of common, stock. The amounts shown for each are the "par," or "face," value of the stock outstanding. This value is presumably the amount for which the stock was originally sold, though this is not always so.[6] Surplus reflects profits of the company that have not been paid out as dividends to stockholders.

Surplus is a peculiarly misleading word. It seems to connote an extra fund of

---

[4] United States Steel and American Tobacco (Lucky Strikes) for example, carry "goodwill and patents" at $1. Coca-Cola, on the other hand, carried goodwill, trade marks, formulae, etc., at their cost—$40 million in 1958.

[5] See the discussion of "depreciation" charges in the following section.

[6] In the 1800's, it was common practice to set a fictitiously high value on the capital stock. Part of this stock was issued to original founders who provided not money but goods or services that were overvalued. The term "stock-watering" in reference to this practice came from the then common practice of inducing cattle to drink as much water as possible just before being marketed in order to increase their weight temporarily. Although supervisory control now exercised by the United States government (through the Securities and Exchange Commission) has made such watering very difficult for stocks "listed" on the major exchanges, it still can be done with unlisted stocks, and not all the water has been "squeezed out" of earlier stocks.

cash lying around somewhere, but such is far from the case. Surplus is nothing but a formal accounting sub-item as part of the general capital and surplus (proprietorship) category. It could just as well be lumped in with common stock; its segregation is only a matter of accounting custom. Total "capital and surplus" is nothing but a derived figure that follows from the values placed on assets, less the company's "liabilities," which may also be partly estimated (for example, the item reserve for contingencies shown on some balance sheets). The fact that capital and surplus on December 31, 1959, was $3,100,000 more than the paid-in value of the stock reflects past earnings not paid out in dividends.

There is no reason to suppose that these past profits now repose in the cash account. More likely, as part of the firm's regular operations, they have been "re-invested" or "plowed back" into inventory, plant and equipment, securities, or some other assets. Or they may be reflected in a reduced level of the firm's liabilities. *It is absolutely essential to understand that there is no direct correspondence between individual items on the two sides of the balance sheet. Any attempt to link up individual items directly will lead to fallacious conclusions.*[7]

One other crucial warning, suggested above: The values placed on almost all the assets, and hence on the capital and surplus group as well, are *estimated* values. *If* every one of these values is accurate, then the capital and surplus figure is accurate. But it by no means follows even then that every asset could be liquidated (sold) at the value at which it is carried on the balance sheet. Many of the items have a "going value" only as part of the operating concern. If the concern were to close down, it would be very doubtful whether many of the assets could be sold separately for their stated values (for example, semi-finished gadgets in the inventory item). This situation is reflected in the fact that going concerns are seldom completely liquidated even when they "go broke." Instead, if their going-concern value is greater than their liquidation sale value, concerns are generally reorganized with the injection of some new capital, or transferred as a unit to some going concern, in order to maintain as much as possible of their going value.

The Income (Profit-and-Loss) Statement. The income, or profit-and-loss, statement is the accountant's summary view of a firm's operation over some given time period, say a year.

Table B shows a hypothetical income statement for the Gadget Manufacturing Company during the year ending December 31, 1960, the year following the balance sheet shown in Table A. This is a straightforward account of the gross income received during the year and what was done with it. The first part of the statement summarizes the income from [8] and expenses of operations; then sepa-

---

[7] The common argument that higher wages should be paid out of surpluses is an example of such an inadequate understanding of the elements of accounting.

[8] The net sales item corresponds to the revenue from sales shown by the "demand curves" in the following chapters.

Table B

GADGET MANUFACTURING COMPANY
Income Statement for Year Ended December 31, 1960

Net sales		$10,000,000
Manufacturing and selling costs:		
Materials	$2,000,000	
Labor cost	3,000,000	
Depreciation	500,000	
Maintenance and repairs	400,000	
Administrative and selling costs	1,000,000	
Taxes (other than income taxes)	600,000	7,500,000
Net profit from operations		2,500,000
Other income—interest and dividends		150,000
Interest charges—on own bonds outstanding		50,000
Net income before federal income taxes		2,600,000
Provision for federal income taxes		1,500,000
Net income (or profit)		$ 1,100,000
Allocation of net income:		
Dividends on preferred stock		$ 100,000
Dividends on common stock		400,000
Increase in surplus		600,000

rate items are included for other income and expenses; then federal income tax liability is deducted, which gives net profit after taxes for the year 1960.

The last part of the statement shows how the corporation allocates this profit. Only $500,000 is paid out as dividends. The other $600,000 is re-invested in the company. Capital and surplus (net worth) will now be $600,000 higher than if all the profits had been distributed to the stockholders. Common stockholders —the corporation's "owners"—may thus be as well off one way as the other. In one case, they get cash dividends; in the other, the value of their investment accumulates. Such plowing-back of earnings has long been commonplace in American industry, and many industrial giants such as Eastman Kodak and Ford have grown almost entirely through re-investment of earnings.

One warning about the profit-and-loss statement: The income and costs shown are not necessarily *cash* receipts and outlays; the profits are not necessarily *cash* profits. This distinction between cash transactions and accounting records is illustrated by the "materials" item. The materials used may have been purchased long before and already have been in inventory at the year's beginning. Or materials purchased during the year might have been double the $2,000,000 shown, if the firm had chosen to build up its inventories during the year. The $2,000,000 materials cost is the accounting figure for materials *used,* not for materials *bought* during the year.[9]

---

[9] The income statement shown implies that the business neither accumulated nor used up inventories on balance during the year. If there is a net increase or decrease in inventories, it can easily be taken into account in the income statement.

The same point is well illustrated by the cost item "depreciation." Every engineer and accountant knows that plant and equipment depreciate. If a truck bought in 1960 is expected to last five years, after each year it has one year less life. At the end of five years it has only scrap value if the original estimates of length of life were accurate. Actually, the concern will not have to buy another truck until 1965, but if it does not figure the using up of the truck as a current expense it is obviously understating its costs and overstating its profits in the intervening years. If no current depreciation is charged, in 1965 the entire cost of the new truck would have to be charged against that year's income. Hence accountants "charge" depreciation annually, even though no cash outlay may be involved. Thus one-fifth of the value of the truck might be charged off as a current cost each year, or some more complicated depreciation formula might be used.[10] No cash expenditure need match the depreciation shown.

Since cost and income items are accounting items rather than cash transactions, obviously there is no necessary cash accumulation at the year's end equal to net profit earned during the year. The firm's cash may be higher or lower, depending on what has seemed to the managers the best use of available funds. It is only essential that the managers be sure they have cash on hand to meet their obligations, one of which is dividends when dividends are to be paid. In fact, dividends may be paid in years when no profits have been made. American Telephone and Telegraph, for example, paid its regular dividend of $9 per year straight through the depression of the 1930's, even though annual profits fell well below $9. Capital and surplus, of course, declined by the excess of dividend payments over net profits.

Relation Between Income Statement and Balance Sheet.   These observations tell us a good deal about the relation between the income statement and the balance sheet. Suppose now we draw up a balance sheet for the Gadget Company at the end of 1960—another spot picture, linked to the earlier one by our income statement.

During the year, assets have been continually used up in the production of current output; sales or other sources of funds have continually rebuilt the firm's assets. Since a net profit of $1,100,000 after taxes was made during 1960, total capital and surplus (net worth) was up by this amount before payment of dividends. As emphasized above, the increase in assets over the year may have come in cash, inventories, accounts receivable, or any other item—or there may have been a decrease in liabilities. All we know from the income statement is that, on balance, assets less liabilities are up $1,100,000.

This $1,100,000 is reduced to $600,000 by payment of dividends—on the asset side the reduction is in the cash item when cash is paid out; in the capital

---

[10] The U.S. Treasury permits the use of any reasonable depreciation formula for computing taxable income, but the firm must stick to the same formula once it has chosen it.

and surplus accounts it is in the surplus item, which would have shown a steady increase through the year if monthly balance sheets had been made.[11] This leaves the surplus account up $600,000 over December 31, 1959. Together, the income statement and balance sheets provide an over-all accounting of the firm's financial operations and status for the period.

Table C

GADGET MANUFACTURING COMPANY
Balance Sheet, December 31, 1960

Assets		*Liabilities and Proprietorship*	
Current assets:		Current liabilities:	
Cash	$2,100,000	Accounts payable	$ 400,000
U.S. government		Accrued taxes	800,000
securities	1,200,000	Total current	
Accounts receivable	2,600,000	liabilities	$1,200,000
Inventories on hand	2,000,000	Bonds outstanding	3,000,000
Total current assets	$7,900,000	Capital and surplus:	
Fixed assets:		Preferred stock	$1,000,000
Investment in affiliated		Common stock	2,000,000
company	300,000	Surplus	3,700,000
Plant and equipment	2,500,000	Total Proprietorship	6,700,000
Patents and goodwill	200,000		
Total	$10,900,000	Total	$10,900,000

There is one other tricky spot. On the income statement, $500,000 depreciation was charged as a cost. This means that "plant and equipment" will be carried at only $2,500,000 in the December 31, 1960, balance sheet, $500,000 less than before. Actually, many firms would show the entire calculation on the balance sheet, thus:

Plant and equipment		
Original cost	$8,000,000	
Less reserve for depreciation	5,500,000	
Net plant and equipment		$2,500,000

Here the $5,500,000 is the total amount of depreciation charged against the original cost of the company's existing plant and equipment to date; $500,000 of it was charged in 1960. The "reserve for depreciation" is carried as a deduction item on the asset side of the statement. It is crucial to remember, however, that the reserve is *not* a cash fund set aside and available for expenditure. It is merely the summation of depreciation costs charged against assets used for profit-

---

[11] Concerns sometimes carry an additional item, "undivided profits," which reflects current profits, rather than having them show directly in the "surplus" account. At stated intervals (generally quarterly, semiannually, or annually), the increase in the undivided profits account is allocated to dividends, surplus, or other uses.

and-loss calculations to date. Neither is it necessarily re-invested in plant and equipment. Whether and how it is ultimately re-invested will depend largely on the profit expectations of the concern's officials.

Throughout this Appendix, we have been primarily concerned with the mechanics of business accounting. Stop now and look for a moment at what this all means economically. During 1960, the Gadget Manufacturing Company had a good year. It made $1.1 million of profits on a total invested capital (capital and surplus) of $6.1 billion at the beginning of the year. This is around a 17 per cent return on net investment, even after paying taxes. Before taxes, the return was more than twice as high. If you were to compare this rate of return with that of many leading American corporations, you would find that it looks very good.

How did this good year show up for the common stockholders? They collected $400,000 of dividends on $2 million stated (or "par") [12] value of the common stock outstanding. This would be a return of 20 per cent on money invested in the stock at that price, a phenomenally high rate. We can safely assume that the price of the stock has been bid up in the market by investors to reflect this high rate of return. Although market prices of common stock fluctuate widely, depending on many circumstances, an effective dividend yield of 4 or 5 per cent on good small companies would have been reasonable in 1960; this would imply a market price for the company's shares totaling $8 million to $10 million, on which the $400,000 dividends would amount to a 4 to 5 per cent return. The price *per share* would depend on the number of shares into which the company's capital stock had been divided. Suppose there were 200,000 shares (giving an original issue, or "par," value of $10 per share). At current market prices we might expect these shares to be selling for perhaps $40 to $50 apiece ($8 million or $10 million total value divided by the 200,000 shares).

The stockholders also gained from the $600,000 of profits plowed back into the business, which show up on the December 31, 1960, balance sheet as $600,-000 additional surplus in the "Capital and Surplus" section. It means that the company now has either that many more dollars' worth of productive assets (machinery, equipment, inventory, and so on) with which to operate, or that much less debt, or some combination of both. This condition should make it a more profitable company in the future, with larger total profit figures in the years ahead. And generally this fact would be reflected in a correspondingly high value for the company's stock on the market. Investors who are thinking about buying Gadget Manufacturing Company stock will see that less than half the profits are paid out in dividends and will recognize that total profits accrue to the benefit of common stockholders. Thus the market price of Gadget stock might be even higher than $40 or $50 a share, though plowing back half or more of total corporate profits is by no means uncommon among corporations of all sizes.

---

[12] This is a technical term often used in corporate accounting. Although this definition isn't quite accurate, you can take "par" as generally the price at which the corporation's stock was first issued.

Business Accounting Statements and Private Investment. If you feel the urge to take your newly acquired knowledge about securities and rush out to buy a few shares of common stock, don't! This Appendix deals with only the most elementary aspects of business accounting. These fundamentals are the basis for any further study of business accounts in analyzing how the economic system functions. They are also the basis for analyzing the securities of individual concerns for private-investment purposes.

But they are only the beginning. When you analyze individual corporate published statements with an eye to picking "good buys" in stocks and bonds, you need to make an intensive and detailed study. Competent investment planning must be based on a background of judgment for making inter-firm comparisons. Moreover, published corporate statements often conceal as much as they reveal, certainly to the untrained eye. Try analyzing the published statements of some actual concern in which you are interested, in the light of your study of these pages. But if you feel the urge to invest your money, the best advice is to get the help of an expert before you buy. And don't forget that what counts most is the future, not the past. What you've learned about business fluctuations and the uncertain rate of economic growth should suggest some of the problems in predicting what businesses will prosper in the future.

Appendix B

The Internal Structure and Operation of Business Firms

Economics is about business firms and how well they do their jobs. Yet economists in general spend little time on the details of how business firms operate in their day-to-day work, or on just how decisions are made within the firm; these are largely the province of business administration. For the most part, in economics we view the firm as a simple organization in which the manager rationally decides what to produce, how much of it, and how much to charge for it—generally trying to maximize profits in the process.

The purpose of this Appendix is to provide a brief glimpse into the insides of two typical business firms—one small and one large—to see how they are organized, how decisions get made in them, and how they operate. This Appendix is here because a concrete example may add reality when the later chapters talk abstractly about the cost, price, and output decisions of the firm; because you need to know something of the decision-making process to judge how much emphasis to put on different models of the firm's behavior; and because in our society, as an educated person, you should have at least some idea of what goes on inside business firms.

With all their differences, most firms carry on two basic activities. They produce a good or service, and they sell it. These activities are the focus of economic analysis. To get some impression of how they are actually performed, consider first a very simple, small manufacturing firm; and then briefly the complexity of Westinghouse Electric, one of the world's largest corporations.

The Small, Single-Product Firm: Acme Paint Co. [13]   This is a small paint company, typical of many small manufacturing-type firms. It has about a hundred employees, and annual sales of about $1.5 million. It has only one plant, and sells almost its entire output in northern Illinois and Wisconsin, where it competes with national firms and other smaller producers. Paint production involves no great economies of large-scale production once moderate size is reached, although the firm finds many difficulties in competing with the giants on the marketing side, in view of their elaborate distribution channels and national advertising programs.

The firm's common stock is not "listed" on the national exchanges, but it is spread among some forty investors in the middle-sized city where it operates. The president is the largest single stockholder, with about one-third of the shares. Thus, ownership and management are to a considerable extent merged. Although over half the stock is held by outsiders, most of them are local people who are on a first-name basis with the president.

The company's organization chart is reproduced in Figure 17-2. This shows the major divisions and indicates the number of people employed in each, with some indication of what each part of the company does. As you would expect, over half the employees are in the production department, but only about half are actually production workers. About 20 people, not counting secretaries, are in sales, and about the same number in finance and accounting. The company is small enough for the president to know every employee by name and to know just about everything that goes on in the plant, though he finds it harder to keep up with sales conditions in the various cities and towns where the company's paint is sold.

Who makes the decisions in the company? On major questions, like plant expansion, the president and the board of directors (which includes all three vice-presidents as well as the president). On operating questions, the president and the three vice-presidents. But, as in most companies, most of the day-to-day operations go along in a routine that doesn't require frequent major decisions. The salesmen sell as much paint as they can; they get paid on a mixture of salary and commission, and are prodded constantly by the sales directors and the sales VP. The salesmen report back orders to the plant; and the general foreman,

---

[13] Not the company's actual name.

working with the production-scheduling people, sees that the paint is shipped on schedule. He keeps an inventory of standard sizes and colors, and complains bitterly when salesmen phone in rush orders for odd colors and can sizes since they require special runs, jack up his unit costs sky high, and upset the normal operations of the plant.

Acme Paint Company

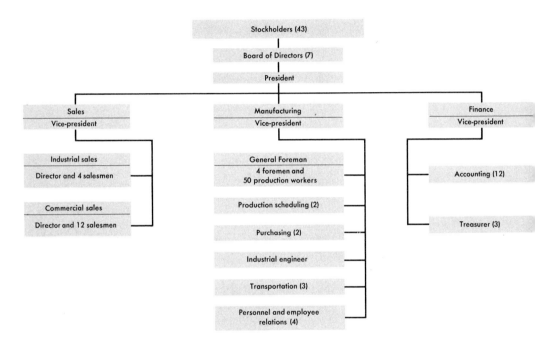

FIG. 17-2

The salesmen, in turn, protest that they often lose sales because they can't get quick enough delivery. How much inventory to hold of each paint is a major problem, because inventory takes up space and ties up scarce working capital, as the vice-president for finance is fond of pointing out. Probably no other question gets as much time in the almost constant informal meetings of the four top-management people. Company prices are agreed on in periodic conferences among the eight or ten people most involved, from all parts of the firm, but quick conferences of the top brass with the general foreman are not uncommon when a salesman phones that a big order hinges on a little price shading.

When there's a crisis, everybody gets in the act. The president doesn't sit in splendid isolation, making policy, in a company this size. If a critical machine breaks down just when a big order is on the verge of being late, he's out in the plant with the sales and manufacturing VP's and the general foreman, peering over the repairman's shoulder and maybe even giving a hand, since he came up through the paint-making business himself the hard way. The president and the sales VP spend a fair amount of time themselves in the field, calling on major customers and keeping up good will toward the company.

Where is the company economist? There isn't any. The finance VP puts together a report every quarter on the financial problems and prospects of the company, and the sales VP does the same for sales prospects. The chief accountant went to business school, and part of his job is to keep up on general business conditions as they may affect the company. But he doesn't have much time left over for the assignment, and the officers and directors go on what the salesmen report plus their general reading in *Business Week,* the *Wall Street Journal,* and the paint-industry trade journals. The industrial engineer has produced some rough cost estimates for paint runs of different sizes, working with one of the accountants, but top management relies largely on experience and "feel" developed over the years in deciding just how far to go in changing prices, introducing new manufacturing equipment and methods, and other such problems.

A Major, Multi-Product Corporation: Westinghouse.　　Now look at another company, one of the world's corporate giants. The 1958 sales of the Westinghouse Electric Corporation were nearly $2 billion. Instead of one product, the company has literally thousands, ranging from flashlight bulbs through electric meters, washing machines, and small motors, to huge turbines, generators, and atomic reactors. These products were produced and sold by some 115,000 employees; the company had an even larger number of stockholders—over 150,-000. The outcome of all this activity was a profit. Earnings were $75 million after taxes in 1958.

Figure 17-3 shows the Westinghouse organization chart as of 1959. The left-hand page shows the top-management structure of the company, indicating the major groupings of management responsibility. The bottom row of boxes shows the main operating units of the company—seven for domestic operations, plus Canadian Westinghouse and Westinghouse International. The main lines of operating authority lead up from these nine groups through two major vice-presidents, Messrs. Hodnette and Huggins, to the president of the corporation. The chart also has 18 other boxes, connected to this main "line" of operating authority by lighter black lines. These men are generally called "staff" officers, in contrast to the operating "line" responsibilities of the others. Forget them for the moment and concentrate on line operations.

The right-hand page lists the major domestic operating divisions, which fall under the groups in the bottom row of the top-management chart. For example, the "Apparatus Products" group, shown at the bottom middle of the left-hand

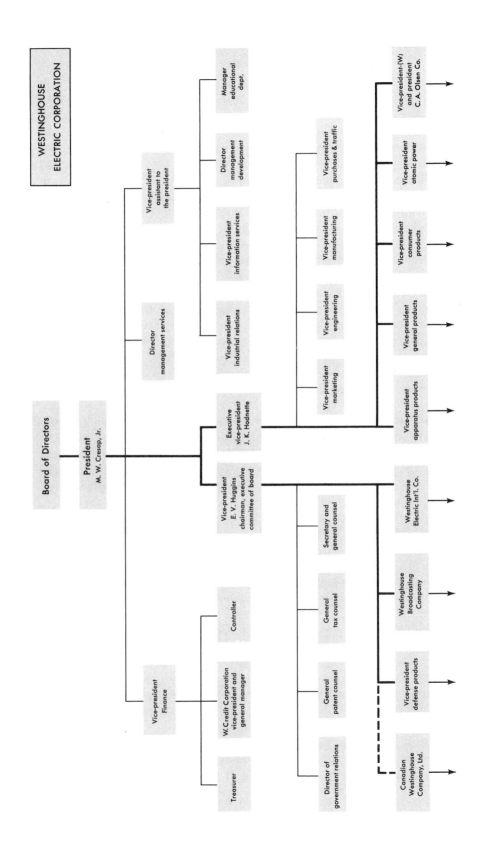

WESTINGHOUSE ELECTRIC CORPORATION

Board of Directors

President
M. W. Cresap, Jr.

Vice-president
Finance
- Treasurer
- W. Credit Corporation vice-president and general manager
- Controller

Vice-president
E. V. Huggins
chairman, executive committee of board
- Director of government relations
- General patent counsel
- General tax counsel
- General counsel
- Secretary and general counsel

Executive
vice-president
J. K. Hodnette
- Vice-president marketing
- Vice-president engineering
- Vice-president manufacturing
- Vice-president purchases & traffic

Director
management services

Vice-president
assistant to the president
- Vice-president industrial relations
- Vice-president information services
- Director management development
- Manager educational dept.

Canadian Westinghouse Company, Ltd.

Vice-president defense products

Westinghouse Broadcasting Company

Westinghouse Electric Int'l. Co.

Vice-president apparatus products

Vice-president general products

Vice-president consumer products

Vice-president atomic power

Vice-president-(W) and president C. A. Olsen Co.

Westinghouse Electric Corporation Organization

BASIC PROFIT CENTERS, EXCLUDING MARKETING ORGANIZATIONS
(Method of reporting to vice-presidents shown at bottom of opposite chart)

APPARATUS PRODUCTS GROUP (30*)

East Pittsburgh Division

Switchgear Apparatus Departments
Assembled Switchgear and Device Dept.*
Power Circuit Breaker Dept.*
Distribution Apparatus Dept.*
Carrier Microwave Dept.*
Porcelain Products Dept.*

Power Apparatus Departments
Large Rotating Apparatus Dept.*
Rectifier and Traction Equipment Dept.*
Mica Products Dept.*

Component & Printing Departments
Component Products Dept.*
Printing and Publications Dept.*

Gearing Division*

Manufacturing & Repair Divisions

Sunnyvale Manufacturing Division
Electrical Products Dept.*
Mechanical Products Dept.*

Regional Manufacturing & Repair Division
(41 plants)*

Buffalo Divisions

Motor Dept.*

Control Dept.
General Purpose Control Dept.*
Systems Control Dept.*
Director Systems*

Copper Wire Dept.*

Transformer Division
Power Transformer Dept.*
Distribution and Instrument Transformer Dept.*
Specialty Transformer Dept.*

Materials Manufacturing Dept.*

Steam Division
Heat Transfer Dept.*
Small Turbine Dept.*
Large Turbine Dept.*
Industrial Gas Turbine Dept.*

Meter Division
Meter Dept.*
Relay Dept.*
Instrument Dept.*

GENERAL PRODUCTS GROUP (11*)

Standard Control Division*
Small Motor Division
Industrial Dept.*
Aviation Dept.*
Lighting Division*
Micarta Division*
Welding Dept.*
Elevator Division*
Bryant Electric Company*
Sturtevant Division*
X-Ray and Industrial Electronics Division
Industrial Electronics Dept.*
X-Ray Dept.*

CONSUMER PRODUCTS GROUP (10*)

Electric Appliance Divisions
Major Appliance Division*
Portable Appliance Division*
Refrigeration Specialties Division*
TV-Radio Division*
Lamp Division
Large Lamp Dept.*
Photo-Miniature Lamp Dept.*
Lamp Parts Dept.*
Ken-Rad Lamp Dept.*
Electronic Tube Division*
Semiconductor Dept.*

DEFENSE PRODUCTS GROUP (4*)

Aviation Gas Turbine Division*
Baltimore Divisions
Electronics Division*
Air Arm Division*
Ordnance Dept.*

ATOMIC GROUP (6*)

Atomic Power Division (Bettis)*
Atomic Equipment Dept.*
Atomic Fuel Dept.*
Atomic Power Dept.*
Westinghouse Test Reactor*
Plant Apparatus Dept.*

OTHER (3*)

C. A. Olsen Company*
Air Conditioning Division*

Westinghouse Broadcasting Company*

* Indicates Basic Profit Center. (A Basic Profit Center exists at the first level in the organization at which the functions essential to profit on a product line come together.)

FIG. 17-3 The Westinghouse Electric Corporation organization chart as of 1959. Left page, top-management structure of the company. Right page, major operating divisions of the company.

page, includes seven major "divisions," which are expanded at the beginning of the right-hand page. These divisions in turn include 30 "profit centers," each of which is a semi-independent center of management responsibility for the production and sale of a single major product line (for example, power circuit breakers).

At first glance, this may not look much more complicated than the Acme Paint Company. But the pictures are misleading. The Westinghouse consumer products group, which occupies a small space on the right-hand page, alone apparently had sales of nearly half a *billion* dollars in 1958. For competitive reasons, Westinghouse doesn't publish figures on its sales of individual products, but it's easy to see that the whole Acme Paint Company could readily be tucked away in a corner of any one of the Westinghouse divisions within the consumer products group.

Thus, if we pictured the Westinghouse organization in the same detail as Acme's, it would cover page after page of this book. The Electric Appliances Division in the Consumer Products Group, for example, is headed by a vice-president who manages four major plants, each big enough to dwarf dozens of Acmes. In many ways, he is like the president of Acme, though with a many times larger domain to manage. He has a big sales organization concerned with getting people to buy Westinghouse appliances. In each plant, he has industrial engineers, foremen, personnel men, and production workers, all under a plant manager. And he has a staff of experts on marketing, production methods, and so on, reporting directly to him and ready to help out on problems anywhere within the division.

But the Appliances Division VP is different from the president of Acme. He's part of a larger organization. He reports not to the board of directors, but to another (group) vice-president, who is in charge of all consumer products— refrigerators, lamps, tubes, TV-radio, and so on. Much of the marketing effort for Westinghouse consumer products is planned and coordinated at this level; general policies on production methods, inventory policy, and other operations within the consumer products group, are developed. The group vice-president has experts on his own staff to advise on optimal policies for the whole group, and to pitch in on particular problems that arise in the various plants and marketing areas.

But the basic operating decisions are largely decentralized to the individual divisions. They are called "profit centers" (each shown by an asterisk on the chart), and their individual managers have a lot of leeway to make their own decisions, within the general policies developed at the group level for all consumer products. They are judged on the results. Division managerial bonuses are related to the profitability of the individual divisions, and top management takes a hard-boiled look at results when promotion and salary-revision time comes around.

If you remember that there are 64 major profit centers in the company, reporting through five group vice-presidents, plus four other major quasi-independent operations (Canadian Westinghouse, Westinghouse International, Westinghouse Broadcasting, and C. A. Olsen Co.), you begin to get some impression of the job of top management in coordinating and pulling all these widespread parts together into a profit-making organization that will compete on the one hand with G.E. (which is even bigger), and on the other with the thousands of small firms in individual areas where Westinghouse sells.

The president, Mark Cresap, manages Westinghouse and is responsible to the Board of Directors. The top-management group, we can assume from the chart, consists of Messrs. Cresap, Hodnette, and Huggins. As is common in large corporations, Gwilym Price, the Chairman of the Board of Directors, was previously president of the company—and it is safe to assume that he still participates actively in top-management policy-making, though he is no longer directly responsible for Westinghouse operations.

What do these men do? Mainly plan for the short and the long run, lay out broad lines of policy, devise procedures for seeing that the policies and plans are carried out, and watch over the profitability of the company generally. Much of their time is spent in talking with other upper-level company officials, in committees and informally—and with people outside Westinghouse, like big customers, government officials, and other top industry officials. They travel a lot, to keep in touch with their managers one, two, and three levels down, and to keep a first-hand "feel" for how operations are going. Above all, they are interested in people, in getting the right people to run the various divisions and carry out major company objectives; and in watching over the major lines of company development. What big new areas should be investigated for the future? Which lines are showing the best return on investment? Which fall short of reasonable profit objectives? In both cases, why?

The annual budget provides a major tool of planning and control. Each year, a careful review of all company operations underlies plans for the next year, and more broadly for the next five years. The funds allocated to each division for expansion, for special sales activities, and so on are budgeted. Targets are set for each major activity, and management bonuses depend largely on success in meeting or bettering those targets. There is never enough money to go around. Group and division managers always have more projects they would like to exploit than can be financed with the funds becoming available. Thus, this intra-company competition for funds provides top management with a major opportunity to evaluate the success of the many parts of the company, and to guide company activities through controlling the allocation of funds for further expansion.

Now come back to the "staff" functions on the top-management chart. These are the ones branching off to the sides, and connected to the main operating "lines" by lighter lines—marketing, engineering, finance, industrial relations, and so on. These vice-presidents report directly to top management. They have only small staffs of their own, and have no direct authority over the operating divisions of the company. Their job, instead, is to participate in top-management determination of company-wide policies in their respective areas, where they provide top expertise and continuing contact with new ideas and developments; and to help the operating divisions on a kind of consulting basis in carrying out company policies and in solving special problems. Thus, the Atomic Power Division of the Atomic Group may have a tough problem in production scheduling, or in purchasing. It can turn to the vice-presidents for manufacturing and for purchasing for advice and help. Conversely, the staff vice-presidents keep in contact with the operating managers to suggest, and sometimes push, adoption of practices in line with what top management thinks is best company-wide policy. But the division manager has a lot of authority to make his own decisions if he disagrees.

Where do some typical decisions get made? Westinghouse hasn't published its operating procedures in detail, but some general comments are probably roughly accurate. Who decides how many 100-watt light bulbs should be made next month? Probably the production scheduling people in the lamp division, in consultation with the division manager if there are any special questions at stake. Basically, the answer will depend on current orders flowing in from the sales people in the field, adjusted somewhat for inventory considerations. Who decides the price on light bulbs? Probably the division manager, in consultation with his sales and cost people, following general pricing policies laid down by top management—and in consultation with the group vice-president and the marketing vice-president of a major policy issue is involved. Who decides what to bid on a big new transformer for a public utility? Probably the senior sales people in the Power Transformer Department, in consultation with their cost analysts, and possibly with the division manager if the order is a big one and involves some unusual questions.

Who decides whether to build a new elevator plant? Here the answer gets more complex. The proposal would probably first be developed in the Elevator Division, with people from all parts cooperating, and using the services of at least the marketing and manufacturing vice-presidents. A special task force might well be set up to study the problem. Sooner or later, after informal discussions with top management, a specific detailed proposal would go to the President, who would review the proposal thoroughly, using all the special help needed from the staff organization and from the Elevator Division. If he approves, he will recommend the project to the full 20-man Board of Directors, which is comprised of a few of the top Westinghouse management plus leading businessmen, bankers, and lawyers from outside the company, all elected by the stockholders. Who decides on whether Westinghouse should go into a new space-travel project? Probably a large group of the people most concerned, using somewhat similar procedures if the project is a major, expensive one.

All this may seem complicated and roundabout as compared to Acme's procedure. Managing a huge corporation is a complex process, and the red-tape danger is very real. Top management may get isolated from the people down in the factory and out in the customers' offices. But the advantages are real too.

Westinghouse has vast research laboratories which Acme couldn't dream of. It has top experts in the special fields of planning, manufacturing, finance, purchasing, marketing, and so on. With its great sales volume, it can afford the latest large-scale machinery and automated processes. National advertising keeps "You Can Be Sure If It's Westinghouse" in millions of customers' eyes. When it needs funds, it can go to the banks or the open market with a name nationally known and respected. Westinghouse hopes to gain the advantages of size, while at the same time maintaining the advantages of small-scale managerial initiative by decentralizing much authority to the "profit-center" level throughout the country.

Acme Paint Company is reasonably typical of thousands of small companies in the way it is organized and managed. Among the giant corporations, every one is organized and managed differently, reflecting different products, different management philosophies, different histories. But Westinghouse provides a reasonably typical picture of how many big American corporations organize themselves and go about getting their work done. In the last analysis, Acme and Westinghouse face the same test, the test of the market. Each must produce what the consumer wants and must sell it at a competitive price. Otherwise, each will be just a name in the history books before many years have gone by. The fact that both have survived and grown suggests that not all the advantages are on the side of either big or little business.

REVIEW—CONCEPTS TO REMEMBER

The Appendices have introduced several important new concepts. You will meet many of the following terms not only throughout the course but in the newspaper as well:

balance sheet	profit-and-loss statement
assets	income statement
liabilities	dividends
proprietorship	"plowed-back" earnings
capital	depreciation
surplus	

1. Suppose you are planning to set up a small bakery. Will you be better off with a single proprietorship, a partnership, or a corporation as your legal form of business? What are the main considerations involved in choosing?

2. Single proprietorships and partnerships predominate in retailing and agriculture, while corporations dominate the manufacturing industries. How do you account for these differences? How can you reconcile the above statement with the great success of such retail giants as A&P and Montgomery Ward?

FOR
ANALYSIS
AND
DISCUSSION

3. Public-opinion polls repeatedly indicate that the majority of the public view common stocks as a speculative and somewhat uncertain investment. How do you account for this fact, in view of the great growth in the aggregate value and earnings of American corporations over the past century?

4. If you are a stockholder in General Motors, would you prefer to have earnings paid out to you as dividends or directly re-invested by the management? Why?

5. Should individual stockholders in business concerns take a more active part in the management of the concerns involved? Why or why not?

6. a. Arrange the following items into a balance sheet. The figure for surplus is missing, but you can calculate it once you have assembled the rest of the balance sheet.

(000's omitted)

Buildings and equipment	$700	Goodwill	$ 20
Accounts payable	160	Reserve for taxes	50
Accounts receivable	180	Cash	110
Common stock	250	Surplus	
Loan from bank	100	Stock in subsidiary	100
Inventories on hand	60	Bonds outstanding	200
U. S. Government bonds	10	Reserve for taxes	30

b. Suppose now the company pays out $10,000 in dividends. Will this change the balance sheet? If so, how?

7. The Widget Corporation reports the following information concerning its situation as of Dec. 31, 1959, and its activities during the year 1960:

(In thousands)

Sales	$10,000	Common stock	
Bonds outstanding	4,000	outstanding	$ 3,000
Inventory on hand	2,500	Labor costs	2,500
Depreciation	900	Accounts receivable	1,000
Accounts payable	1,900	Patents and goodwill	100
Cash on hand	3,000	Plant and equipment	4,500
Selling costs	1,100	Property taxes paid	400
		Maintenance	800

The net income for the year 1960 was allocated half to dividends and half to surplus, after funds were set aside to pay federal income taxes equal to 50 per cent of net income. Using this information, construct the following:

a. The firm's balance sheet as of Dec. 31, 1959 (before allocation of net income).

b. Its income (profit-and-loss) statement for the year 1960.

(Note that not all the items on the balance sheet and income statement are supplied, but the missing items can be inferred from the information given.)

Demand—
The Role
of the Consumer

18

In our economic system the businessman is in business to make money—maybe not exclusively, but surely as one of his major objectives. By and large, he can make money only by producing goods and services that people want to buy— autos, radios, dry cleaning, movies, lamp shades, and thousands of others. If there is no consumer who is willing and able to "lay cash on the barrel-head," the businessman is pretty much out of luck. Maybe the government will temporarily come to his rescue with a subsidy, or maybe he can keep going by using up his own invested capital. But over the long pull, it is the customer who is willing and able to buy who directs production in a private-enterprise economy.

He directs it by the way he spends his money— the way he allocates his income among alternative goods and services. If consumers want yellow electric refrigerators, the chances are good that yellow electric refrigerators will be produced. If consumers want Bibles engraved on the heads of pins, it will not be long before some enterprising individual is turning out Bibles on pinheads.

Consumer Behavior.
Individual Demand.
Aggregate or Market Demand.
Elasticity of Demand.

341

Consumer demand is the mainspring of economic activity. But never forget—it is the consumer with money to spend who counts! Most of us would like to have a Cadillac, and T-bone steak for dinner. But unless we have the money and are willing to spend it on these estimable objects, our desires have little significance for General Motors or the corner meat market.

This means that your "vote" on what gets produced in a private-enterprise economy is largely determined by your income, unless you have accumulated funds to supplement your income. The mill hand is going to have a lot less influence than the rich man, even though the former may be a virtuous, hardworking father of five needy children and the latter a ne'er-do-well who has inherited his money through no effort of his own. This is not to imply that virtue resides in poor rather than in rich souls, but merely to emphasize that the private-enterprise economy responds to what people have to spend, not to who they are.

Table 18-1 shows who had the buying power in 1958. It emphasizes again the huge buying power of the "middle class" in America. Define the middle-income group as you like and make your own computation. If you take the group with incomes between $4,000 and $10,000, they had $175 billion of income, a whopping 54 per cent of the total. If you raise the "middle-income" limit to $15,000, the figures go up to $227 billion and 67 per cent of the total—though this is stretching the definition of middle class by any reasonable statistical measure. Only 2.5 per cent of all families had incomes over $15,000 in 1958.

Table 18-1

FAMILY INCOMES, 1958 *

Income of Spending Unit	Number of Spending Units (In Millions)	Total Personal Income (In Billions)	Percentage of Total Income
Under $2,000	8	$ 9	3
$2,000-3,999	12	37	11
$4,000-5,999	14	67	20
$6,000-7,999	9	64	19
$8,000-9,999	5	44	13
$10,000-14,999	4	52	15
Over $15,000	2	65	19
Total	54	$338	100

* Data from U.S. Department of Commerce. A spending unit is a family or individual operating as a separate financial unit.

But Table 18-1 points up the extremes too. Twenty million spending units, over a third of the total, had incomes of less than $4,000. These families had only 14 per cent of total personal income—far less than their proportionate say over what gets produced for the market. At the other extreme, the top 6 million spending units (a little over 10 per cent of the total) received incomes over $10,000 and

34 per cent of total income, giving them a huge leverage over what the system produces.

We are a rich nation, where the great bulk of the people are above the poverty level. The very well-to-do have a good deal more to say about what gets produced than the very poor. But it is the great middle class who dominate the American market—a middle class that is rich by the standards of most other nations.

One last bit of perspective on consumer demand. Look back at Table 2-3, which summarizes all the goods and services consumers bought in 1958. Those are the demands we now need to look at more analytically.

CONSUMER BEHAVIOR You may have heard of "the economic man" —a mythical individual who carefully calculates just what he should buy before he spends each dollar, comparing the satisfactions obtainable from every conceivable expenditure before he parts with his cash. Most of us don't operate this way, and just about everyone knows it. In fact, the belief that economists generally assume such a man as typical represents mainly a failure to read and understand what economists do say about consumer behavior.

Most of us face a real problem of how to allocate our incomes among far more goods and services than we are able to pay for. Perhaps the Aga Khan buys everything he wants without concern for what it costs. But for most of us available income is limited when we match it against the vast number of things we would like to buy. In varying degrees, all of us calculate how to divide up our incomes among the things we want to buy. You may devote most of your income to nourishing foods, college tuition, and durable clothes; I may spend most of mine on books, phonograph records, and airplane trips; our neighbor may prefer a dissolute life of wine, women, and song. Probably none of us is the human calculating machine envisaged in "the economic man," though the less money we have the greater the pressure is to act in a careful, calculating way.

The economist does not pass judgment on which pattern of expenditure is the proper one. Nor does he pretend to tell you how you should spend your income to lead a happier, healthier, more learned, or other kind of life. What he does do is assume, for most purposes, that you spend your money on the things you want most. Thus, if you spent a dollar on the movies this afternoon, he is willing to take that as evidence that you preferred going to the movies over going to a prize fight at the same admission or over buying a new dollar necktie. If you stop and think about it, any other assumption leads to very strange results, as long as we assume freedom of individual action in spending incomes.

Some economists have worried about a lot of special difficulties in this connection. For example, if you buy a suit on the installment plan, is your payment of the five-dollar installment four weeks later a fair measure of your preference then for the suit over other five-dollar purchases, in case you decide in the meantime you don't like the suit? [1] You can figure out a variety of such cases. But they are not very important for our elementary purposes, since all we care about is the general proposition that what people *do* spend their money on reflects what they *want* to spend their money on.

These rather obvious observations become important later on when we try to evaluate how well the economic system works, since one of the main tests we will apply is: How well does the system respond to consumer wants? Unless we can assume that consumers' expenditures generally reflect what they want most, we will be at a loss for any measure of how well the system does in fact allocate its scarce productive resources in fulfilling consumer wants.

INDIVIDUAL DEMAND Since consumer demand is so central to the functioning of a private-enterprise system, it is important to define "demand" accurately before we begin to use the concept. *"Demand" is the whole schedule of amounts of any product that buyers will purchase at different prices during some stated time period.* This takes some explaining, since it obviously isn't quite what the word means in everyday conversation.

The individual buyer is the ultimate consumer. It is the "individual demands" of all the individual buyers that make up the "aggregate" or "market" demand to which producers respond. For most consumer goods, no one consumer is a big enough buyer to be very important in his own right; it is only the aggregated demand of many consumers in a market that greatly influences producers. Beginning with individual demands and adding them up to a total market demand is a systematic procedure.

What is your demand for sirloin steak? A little thought will tell you that this is a meaningless question until you at least ask, "At what price and over how long a time?" How much you will buy at 50 cents a pound is likely to be quite different from how much you will buy at $1.00 a pound; and obviously some time period needs to be specified. Recognizing this need, we might construct a hypothetical "schedule" of amounts you would buy at different prices during any time interval, say next week.

When we speak of your "demand" for steak, we mean this entire schedule of amounts that you would buy at various prices. It is meaningless to say that your demand is one or three pounds a week. By "demand" we mean instead your entire state of mind as to how many pounds you will buy at a whole series of possible prices, other things remaining unchanged. In principle, we might list every possible price from zero to infinity, with the amount you would buy at each price. Table 18-2 pictures your demand only over the price range shown.

---

[1] This is a case where at the time of expenditure you don't have real freedom to allocate your income. If you view the expenditure as in effect being made at the time you bought the suit, the difficulty is avoided.

Table 18-2

INDIVIDUAL DEMAND FOR SIRLOIN STEAK

Price per Pound	*Pounds Bought—per Week*
$1.20	0
1.00	1
.80	2
.60	2
.50	3
.40	4

This state of mind (your demand) toward sirloin steak next week may be shown graphically, as in Figure 18-1. If we plot price on the vertical axis and pounds bought on the horizontal axis and connect the points with a curve, we can read off the curve how many pounds you will buy at any price shown. Thus, at $1.20 you will buy no steak, at $1.00 you will buy one pound, and so on down the curve, just as the schedule above shows. If you haven't had much experience with graphs, it may be useful to practice plotting and reading off a number of such points.

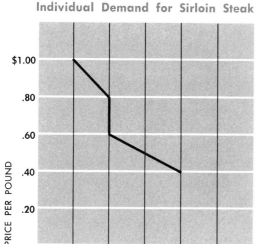

Individual Demand for Sirloin Steak

FIG. 18-1   The demand curve shows how many pounds of steak this individual will buy in a week at different prices. He will buy more at lower than at higher prices.

Whether we use the schedule or plot the points graphically is a matter of convenience. They show the same thing. In making the graph, we merely join the plotted points. Since we knew only the points shown in the schedule in plotting the graph, the readings from the curve between the points are only approximations. Only if the plotted points were very close together (say at one-cent intervals) would the curve properly be a continuous line, with the reading at every point meaningful and accurate. But most demand curves are shown as continuous lines because they are easier to work with that way and are ordinarily good enough approximations for our purposes between the points specifically plotted.

But watch out for one tricky point, whether you use schedules or graphs! Going back to your demand for steak, suppose the price is $1.00 and you are buying one pound per week. Now the local grocer lowers the price to 80 cents and you step up your weekly purchases to two pounds. *This is not a change in demand.* Your demand (your state of mind toward steak) has not changed. You have merely moved to a different point on your demand schedule or curve as a result of the lower price, just as is indicated in the original demand schedule or curve. This increased purchase at a lower price is merely a reflection of the downward slope of your demand curve.

Why Demand Curves Slope Downward. It seems obvious that you will buy more of anything at a low price than at a high one. Thus, on the kind of graph we have drawn, the demand curve will slope down, from northwest to southeast. Why? First, at a lower price for anything you can *afford* to buy more of it out of any given income. Second, at a lower price you are likely to *want* to buy more of it because it becomes relatively more attractive compared with other things you might spend your money on. You will want to substitute sirloin for hamburger as their prices converge. And at low enough prices you may find new uses for sirloin —for example, feeding sirloin instead of bones and dog biscuits to your dog. Thus, for both reasons, the quantity bought will increase as the price falls.[2]

Looked at another way, the downward-sloping demand curve says that you will be willing to pay a high price for a little steak each week, but the more steak you have the less you're willing to pay per pound to increase your weekly consumption still further. Many economists have associated this tendency with a decreasing satisfaction for each additional pound of steak you add to your weekly diet. More generally, they call it *the law of diminishing utility.* Utility here means want-satisfaction obtained from each additional unit of some commodity per unit of time. The additional utility per unit falls as you get more units.

Changes in Demand. Remember that your "demand" for steak is your set of intentions about buying steak. These depend on how much money you have and how you evaluate steak compared with other things. Now suppose that as time goes on you get tired of steak and develop a taste for seafood. You will no longer buy as much steak as previously at the various prices shown. *This change in*

---

[2] Three exceptions should be mentioned: (1) "Prestige goods" such as mink coats or exotic perfume may be bought largely because their price is high. A decline in price might lead some persons to buy less as the goods came down into a price range open to the less wealthy. (2) Some goods, called "inferior," are bought by poor people simply because they are cheap and useful. Potatoes in Ireland are the classic example. If the price of the food staple, potatoes, goes up, the Irish peasants may have to buy even more potatoes, which are still the cheapest food, because they have even less left than before to buy other more expensive foods. (3) When price drops, people may buy less because they expect the price to decline still further. This is a dynamic effect that depends not on whether price is high or low but on the way it is changing. We saw the importance of this expectations effect in the analysis of business fluctuations.

attitude is a change in demand. It is a change in the amounts of steak you will buy at the old prices.

A change in demand is illustrated most easily by using demand curves. Begin with the curve in Figure 18-1. Your switch to seafood would be reflected in a new demand curve, to the left of, or below, the old curve. You will now buy only one pound of steak per week at 60 cents and none at any higher price; only two pounds at 50 cents; and so on. This new, lower demand curve is shown in Figure 18-2 as curve *BB;* the original demand curve is *AA.* If something happens to increase your demand for steak, say a fatter paycheck to finance such delicacies, the new, higher demand might be as indicated by *CC.*

Changing Demand for Sirloin Steak

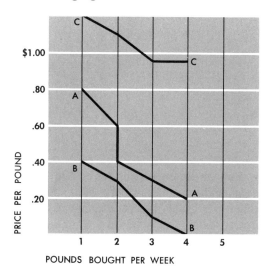

POUNDS BOUGHT PER WEEK

FIG. 18-2   Curve CC shows an increase in demand from AA. Curve BB shows a decrease. How much steak would each demander buy at $1 per pound?

Why would your demand for beefsteak, or Buicks, or neckties change? There are three major reasons. First, your tastes may change. You simply decide you don't like beefsteak, or that now you prefer Buicks to other cars. Second, your income may change. As a beginning office clerk, you may have to be satisfied with a secondhand Ford. With a doubled paycheck you may be in the Pontiac class. Third, changes in the availability and prices of other commodities may change your demand for steak. If a hog shortage takes pork off the market entirely, your demand for steak will rise because you can't get pork to fill out part of your weekly diet. Even a rise in the price of pork will probably have somewhat the same effect.

You will see later on how many economic fallacies are perpetrated through slippery use of the concept of "demand." Try checking your own grasp with a few questions such as these: (1) Production of sheep rises and consumers buy more mutton. Is there an increase in the demand for mutton? (2) Chrysler comes out with a new, more powerful engine and Buick sales decline. Is there a drop in the demand for Buicks? (3) Philco raises the price of its TV sets and sales drop off. Is there a drop in demand? (4) Congress puts a new tax on movie admissions and movie attendance drops. Is there a drop in demand?

AGGREGATE
OR MARKET DEMAND
The local department store probably isn't much concerned with your personal demand for Arrow shirts. But it is very much concerned with the aggregate demand for Arrow shirts over its entire market territory. *Aggregate, or market, demand is simply the summation of all the individual demands in the market under consideration.*

Table 18-3

CROSSROADS DEMAND FOR SUGAR

| | Purchases per Week by: | | | | | |
Price per Lb.	A	B	C	All Three	Total Expenditures	Demand
20¢	3 lb	1 lb	2 lb	6 lb	$1.20	Elastic
15¢	4 lb	2 lb	4 lb	10 lb	1.50	Unitary
10¢	6 lb	3 lb	6 lb	15 lb	1.50	Inelastic
5¢	6 lb	4 lb	7 lb	17 lb	.85	

Consider the market demand for sugar at the crossroads store of an isolated village with only three families. The demand schedules of the three families, and the total demand, might look something like Table 18-3. The aggregate demand schedule for sugar, as seen by the crossroads grocer, is the sum of the individual demands of his customers. It could be plotted on a graph just like the individual demands. The total-expenditures column shows the grocer's total weekly sales of sugar at different prices. (For the moment, disregard the right-hand column.)

ELASTICITY
OF DEMAND
Suppose ordinary table salt sells for 10 cents a pound and you use about a pound a month. If the prices goes up to 15 cents, how much less salt will you use a month? Probably no less at all. Unsalted beans and potatoes don't taste very good, and the fraction of a cent saved each day by not salting your food is trivial compared with the better taste of flavored cooking.

What does this fact do to our propositions about downward-sloping demand curves, which show that people will buy less at higher prices? Table salt at low prices for most consumers is a limiting case, where price changes probably have little or no effect on the amount purchased. Thus, plotted on a graph the demand curve for table salt at the local grocery store might be substantially vertical over the 10 to 15 cent price range. Try drawing it. We say that the demand for table salt is very "inelastic" over this price range. There is very little response, or stretch, in the quantity bought in response to a change in price.

At the other extreme, take your demand for beefsteak at the local A&P if you are substantially indifferent about whether you eat beek or pork. Suppose beef is $1.00 a pound and rises to $1.50, while other prices remain unchanged. The chances are you will cut back your steak purchases sharply—perhaps cut them out entirely—and substitute pork. Here your demand for steak would be highly "elastic." There would be a great response, or stretch, in your purchases to the increase in price.

Loosely, "elasticity" is a measure that tells how much demand will "stretch" in response to a change in price. More exactly, elasticity of demand is a measure of the responsiveness of quantity bought to changes in price. It is one characteristic *of any given demand curve or schedule.* To say a given demand is elastic or inelastic is merely to describe it, just as you might describe your next-door neighbor as tall or short.[3]

For an illustration, look back at the last column of Table 18-3. A 25 per cent price cut from 20 to 15 cents a pound for sugar led to a 67 per cent increase in sales—from 6 to 10 pounds a week. Obviously the demand over this price range is relatively *elastic,* since a relatively small price cut led to a relatively big increase in sales. But a 50 per cent price cut from 10 to 5 cents a pound induced only a relatively small (13 per cent) increase in sales. Over this 10 to 5 cent price range the crossroads demand for sugar is *inelastic.*

This example illustrates what we mean by elasticity. It also illustrates that the same demand curve or schedule may be elastic in some price ranges and inelastic in others. In most cases, it isn't safe just to speak of a demand curve as elastic or inelastic. You need to specify what price or prices you are referring to.

Total Revenue and Elasticity of Demand.   The concept of elasticity of demand helps us to predict what effect price changes will have on total expenditure on a commodity. Look again at the sixth column of Table 18-3. It's obvious that the crossroads storekeeper would be foolish to cut the price of sugar from 10 cents to 5 cents. Although he would sell more sugar, his total revenue on sugar would decrease by almost 50 per cent, because the quantity bought would rise very little in comparison with the big percentage cut in price *where demand is highly inelastic.* On the other hand, a price cut from 20 to 15 cents might make more sense, since this change *in the elastic demand range* would bring in a substantial increase in total revenue.

By now, if you're reasonably good at figures, you will have seen that one measure of elasticity is what happens to total revenue when price changes. *Specifically,*

---

[3] Strictly, we should call this concept "price elasticity of demand." There is a related concept, "income elasticity of demand," that measures the response in quantity bought to a change in income received. However, throughout this book, whenever we are talking about elasticity of demand, we shall use "elasticity" to mean "price elasticity." At a more advanced level, we can also speak of "cross-elasticity" of demand. This is the percentage change in the amount of product A that will be bought in response to a given percentage change in the price of product B.

if demand is inelastic, total expenditures on a commodity will change in the same direction as a change in price. If demand is elastic, total expenditures will change in the opposite direction from a change in price. Examine the reasoning.

1. *Inelastic Demand—Total Revenue Moves in the Same Direction as Price.* When the crossroads grocer cuts his sugar price from 10 to 5 cents, he takes 50 per cent less for each pound of sugar. Yet his sales volume increases by only 13 per cent. Obviously the volume increase, with such inelastic demand, is not great enough to offset the lower revenue per pound sold. Total revenue drops with a cut in price. Now reverse the process over the same price range. Suppose he raises the price from 5 to 10 cents. Here he will get 100 per cent more per pound of sugar and sales will drop by only 2 pounds, about 12 per cent. Clearly, total revenue will increase. It will move in the same direction as the price change, since demand is unresponsive—inelastic.[4] The change in amount bought is not enough to offset the effect of the change in price in either direction. The grocer had better keep his price up at 10 cents, or higher; certainly he'd better not lower it.

2. *Elastic Demand—Total Revenue Moves in the Opposite Direction from Price.* Now look at what happens when he cuts the price from 20 to 15 cents. Although he gets 25 per cent less per pound, he sells 50 per cent more pounds. Total revenue increases, since the increased sales volume more than offsets the decrease in price. Demand is elastic. Reverse the process over the same price range. If he raises his price from 15 to 20 cents, this 33 per cent price increase will be more than offset by the drop in volume. Total revenue will fall, moving in the opposite direction from the change in price. Demand is elastic.

3. *Unitary Elasticity—Total Revenue Is Unaffected by Price Changes.* The borderline case between elastic and inelastic demand we call "unitary" elasticity. This is where an upward or downward shift of price is just offset by a proportional change in quantity bought, so that total revenue remains unchanged. The crossroads demand for sugar between 10 and 15 cents is a case in point. Total expenditure on sugar is identical at either price, since the shift in amount bought just offsets the change in price.

The Real-world Importance of Elasticity. The elasticity of demand for his product is a prime concern of every businessman, whether or not he uses that technical term. Consider two important real-world examples.

First, the farmer. The demand for most basic farm products is apparently inelastic over the relevant price ranges. What does this mean if farmers all work

---

[4] Notice that the percentage change in price from 20 to 15 cents is different from what it is from 15 to 20 cents—25 per cent compared with 33 per cent. This is because the base with which we compare the 5-cent change varies with the direction in which we are calculating. The difference really doesn't matter for our purposes, since the effect on total revenue will always give the right answer. Obviously, the discrepancy between the two ways of figuring percentage change will gradually vanish as we take smaller and smaller price intervals–for example, a price change between 99 cents and $1.00. See the more precise formula on p. 352.

hard, the weather cooperates, and a bumper crop rolls out? It means that the *total income* of farmers from selling their crops will be *lower* as a result of this bonanza, because the bigger crop can be sold only by cutting prices substantially. This simple fact goes far to explain the continuing stream of crop-reduction plans, beginning with the New Deal AAA program, aimed at raising total farm income. With inelastic demand, even a moderate crop restriction may induce a substantially higher price, thereby increasing total revenue from crop sales.

Contrast this with the depression-period attempts of the railroads to increase their total revenues by raising passenger fares in the 1930's. Unfortunately for the railroads, the customers stayed away in droves. Either they stayed at home, or they traveled by bus or car. Demand turned out to be elastic and total revenue moved down, not up. Only when fares were cut did total revenue actually rise. Although this experience was also influenced by changing levels of national income, the impossibility of filling the coffers by raising price in an elastic demand market is plain to see.

If you were a manager, would you want the demand for your product to be elastic or inelastic? Which way would it be easier to make money? We'll look at the answers to these questions a good many times through the rest of the book. A hint: the answer may vary according to who you are, what you're selling, and when you're selling it.

What Makes Demand Elastic or Inelastic?   Why people want what they want is beyond the realm of the economist. By and large, we take people's wants as given, leaving it up to the psychologist and others to explain this particular why. But we can say some things about circumstances where demand is likely to be elastic or inelastic. Briefly, demand is likely to be *inelastic* where (1) your outlay on the object is small, (2) your want for it is urgent, (3) good substitutes are unavailable, and (4) it is wanted jointly with some complementary good. For example, matches don't cost very much, and you want them badly if you smoke a pipe or cigarettes in case you don't have a functioning lighter. Unlighted tobacco doesn't make smoke. In general, wants are most urgent for goods and services for which no close substitutes are available. Nobody's want for Esso gasoline is likely to be terribly urgent so long as a similar grade of Gulf can be had for the same price across the street.

Conversely, demand is likely to be *elastic* where (1) the outlay involved bulks large in your total expenditures, (2) your want is not urgent, (3) close substitutes are available, (4) the commodity is durable or repairable, and (5) the commodity has multiple uses. The first three statements are reasonably obvious. You think a long time before you pay a 10 per cent higher price for a radio-phonograph, but not so long for a candy bar. You stop buying if the price of something you don't care much about goes up—say a certain brand of corn flakes. Maybe you just don't care much for corn flakes, or maybe you consider another brand a substantially identical product.

The points on durability and multiple uses may take a little more thought. Autos are durable and repairable. At any given time, you can usually drive your old car a few thousand miles more; a new set of tires plus a motor tune-up costs a lot less than a new car. This alternative is likely to increase the elasticity of your demand for new cars. Lastly, any commodity that has multiple uses (like butter) is likely to have an elastic demand, because as price falls new uses and buyers may come into the market. At $1.00 a pound butter is out of sight for any use at all by lots of families. Others can afford it on bread, but not on vegetables or for cooking. At 50 cents, the first group may start using butter on the dinner table, and the second may move butter on beans from the luxury to the everyday-use class. And so on for other uses as the price fulls further.

A More Precise Measure of Elasticity.   For some purposes it is useful to be able to say just how elastic or inelastic demand is. A ready measure can be worked out from the previous reasoning. Elasticity depends on the relative changes in quantity and price. If the *percentage change* in quantity bought is more than the *percentage change* in price, total revenue moves in the opposite direction from price; demand is elastic. Thus, we can easily get a numerical value for elasticity by the formula:

$$\text{Elasticity} = \frac{\% \text{ change in } Q}{\% \text{ change in } P}$$

For example, if a cut in the price of steel ingots from $80 to $76 per ton (5 per cent) leads to an increase in sales from 100 million to 101 million tons (1 per cent), by inserting the 5 per cent and 1 per cent in the formula we get an elasticity of demand of .2.[5] Any elasticity less than 1 (unity) is called inelastic demand. Any elasticity of more than 1 is called elastic demand. Unitary elasticity of demand means exactly offsetting changes in quantity and price. Go back and try out this approach on Table 18-3 to get the precise demand elasticities at different prices. The main point to watch in this kind of calculation is the one mentioned in the footnote on page 350.

Elasticity in Graphical Presentations.   A perfectly inelastic demand curve would obviously be vertical. The same quantity would be bought at every price.

---

[5] Since price and quantity move in opposite directions, elasticity will always be a negative figure. The minus sign is customarily dropped in using elasticity measures.

Strictly, our formula needs to be applied only to very small changes in price and quantity. For changes that are infinitesimally small (as those who have studied college mathematics will recognize), the exact formula is:

$$\text{Elasticity} = \frac{\dfrac{dQ}{Q}}{\dfrac{dP}{P}} = \frac{dQ}{dP} \cdot \frac{P}{Q}$$

where dQ is an infinitesimal change in quantity and dP is an infinitesimal change in price.

An example might be your demand for insulin over a wide price range if you need the insulin to keep alive. Highly elastic demand would be a nearly horizontal demand curve. Very small changes in price would lead to very large changes in the quantity bought. But in between these extremes, trying to read elasticity by the slope of a plotted demand curve is dangerous business. Look, for example, at the following two charts. Both show the demand schedule seen by our old friend the crossroads grocer, but they use different horizontal and vertical scales. Exactly the same demand is shown on both.

Demand for Sugar, Showing Different Scales

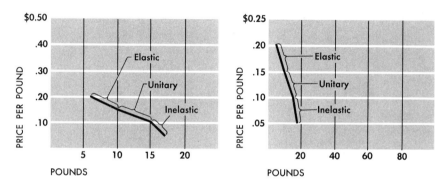

FIG. 18-3   Trying to judge elasticity of demand by looking at the slope of a demand curve is tricky. These two curves show identical demands, plotted on different scales.

Because the left-hand graph uses an extended horizontal scale, the demand curve is relatively flat throughout. Yet it is exactly the same demand as in the right-hand graph, and the elasticity at every point along it is identical with the corresponding points on the right-hand graph. Both curves are marked to show the elastic and inelastic areas. Again, the point emphasized is the danger in trying to generalize that flat demand curves are elastic whereas steep ones are inelastic. You have to remember that elasticity is a matter of *relative* (percentage) changes in price and quantity. Elasticity changes continuously even along a straight, diagonal demand curve. Check it for yourself if, as is likely, this statement seems to you intuitively wrong.

Interacting Demands.   If you buy a car, your demand for gasoline is pretty sure to increase. But, assuming your total income stays unchanged, your demand for some other things (say bus rides) will drop.

The example illustrates the two main kinds of interrelationship among demands for different things: (1) complementary or joint, and (2) substitutive or competitive. When you buy the car, you take on a "complementary" demand for gasoline to run it. But now you don't need to ride the bus. Bus rides are "competitive" with cars in your demand pattern.

In the broadest sense, since your income is fixed, the car must be a substitute for other expenditures lumped together. In this sense, all goods and services are competitive, or substitutive, since incomes are limited and any expenditure you make reduces your power to buy other things. But in many instances this effect may be quite remote; for example, your car purchase may have little effect on your demand for potatoes. By contrast, the substitution of car rides for bus rides is very direct.

REVIEW—CONCEPTS TO REMEMBER

This chapter has presented a string of important new analytical concepts that will be used repeatedly. Check to be sure you have them clearly in mind:

demand	the economic man
individual and aggregate	competitive demands
demand	complementary demands
elasticity of demand	inelastic demand
elastic demand	

FOR ANALYSIS AND DISCUSSION

1. How elastic is *your* demand for the following, near the present price for each?

Required textbooks	Lighter fluid
Gasoline	Silk shantung suits
Airplane tickets home	Lipstick
Cigarettes	Ford convertibles

In each case, see if you can isolate the factors that make the elasticity what it is.

2. Since consumers basically direct production in America, it is consumers who are responsible if our economy produces "wasteful" products like elaborate chrome trim on automobiles. Do you agree or disagree?

3. Calculate roughly how big a voice people in your own income group have in the allocation of the economy's resources. Does it seem to you to be a fair share? (Check the income data in Figure 2-1.)

4. Does consumer demand justify the high income received by TV stars? By large cotton farmers? By corporation presidents? By gangsters in control of numbers rackets? If you answer differently for different groups, why?

5. Should the American public spend a higher proportion of its income on education and nutritious food? A lower proportion on cigarettes and whiskey? How about gambling?

6. Do you act like the mythical "economic man" in allocating your income among alternative uses?

7. Suppose unsold stocks of gasoline are piling up in the storage tanks of the major refineries. If you were regional sales director of one of the major companies, would you recommend a marked reduction in the filling station price? How would you go about deciding?

8. What effect would a successful advertising campaign by the Campbell Company have on the elasticity of consumer demand for Campbell's tomato soup? Explain your answer.

Demand, Supply, and Market Prices

Chapter 4 was a bird's-eye look at how producers respond to consumer demands in a private-enterprise, free-market economy. This chapter looks in more detail at this linkage, and especially at the role of the market place and market prices in connecting consumers and producers. If you thought economics was going to be about "supply and demand," this is it.

THE ROLE OF THE MARKET AND MARKET PRICES In a loose way, it is easy to see how consumer demands get the goods and services produced that consumers want. If consumers demand more red barn paint, the immediate result is increased sales for paint dealers. These gentlemen, who ordinarily get their paint from wholesalers, will probably at least replenish their stocks; if the increased demand promises to last, they may step up their normal inventory of barn paint. The wholesalers in turn will generally order more paint from the manufacturers. And the manufacturers, with joy-

356

ous hearts, will turn out more red barn paint, since their profits depend on producing and selling paint.

Just how strong an impact will be reflected back to the paint manufacturer is hard to say, because of the several links between him and the consumer. The retailer or wholesaler may scale down or step up the increase in farmers' demands for paint. But it would be a rare case where a substantial increase in consumer demand didn't get reflected back to the paint-makers. The linkage may be jerky and imperfect, but without it the private-enterprise economic system would fall down on its job. Sometimes the linkage between consumer and producer is direct. An example is the local laundry. More often, consumer demand has to pass through several links before it hits the ultimate producer. An example is consumer demand for steel nails, which goes through at least the local hardware store and a wholesaler before it gets to (say) the American Steel and Wire Company, which makes nails. But this is only part of the picture. American Steel and Wire in turn has to reflect back the nail demand to its suppliers of iron ore, coal, and the other ingredients of steel, to say nothing of its related demands for steel-making machinery, buildings for its operations, adding machines for its cost clerks, and stationery for its typists. Yet nails are a relatively simple commodity.

Try thinking about automobiles, or new house construction, or air travel. If you chart the branching-out relationship that starts with consumer demand, you will soon find yourself rapidly running out of sheets of paper. The complex interdependence of the modern economic system surpasses the comprehension of even the most systematic human mind. Yet consumer demands must be relayed to producers through this intricate web if the system is really to turn out what consumers want to buy.

What ties all these myriad links together is a structure of markets and market prices. The grocer knows you want sugar when you walk into his store and buy 5 or 10 pounds at the prevailing price. The wholesaler knows when the retailer places his order. And so on down the chain. All consumers going into all retail stores represent roughly the direct consumer market for sugar. Consumers are the demanders, and the retail grocers are the suppliers. The market price is simply the prevailing price for sugar. For such a standard commodity, this price will be reasonably uniform at any given time, when we allow for differences explained by special services rendered by some stores and not by others (delivery, charge accounts, elegant surroundings, convenient shopping locations, and so on).

Similarly, there is a market that links retailers and wholesalers; one that links wholesalers and sugar-refiners; one that links sugar-refiners and sugar-growers. And in each market, sales take place at prices.

It is market price that acts as the adjuster between demand and supply. You will buy different amounts at different prices, and sellers will offer different amounts at different prices. It is common sense that, other things equal, people will buy more sugar at a low than at a high price. It is also common sense that, other things equal, more sugar will be offered for sale at a high than at a low price.[1] *It is this interaction between demand, supply, and price that is the core of the self-adjusting mechanism of the private-enterprise system.*

The world is far too complex to understand if we try looking at it all at once and in all its details. Thus, it is useful to concentrate first on some very simple cases, or models, of markets. The problem of understanding the real world is then one of using these models to help understand the more complex markets in the real world—and then linking together the various markets that join up consumers and producers in any particular case. In many respects, these markets differ widely. But they all boil down to pretty much the same central problem of interaction between demand, supply, and price. A good understanding of the old-fashioned, much-cited "law of supply and demand" is a powerful tool indeed for understanding how the modern economy works.

SUPPLY
Supply is analogous to demand. *Supply is a schedule of amounts that will be offered for sale at different prices during any given time period, other factors remaining unchanged.* Supply can be plotted on a curve, as can demand. But it differs from demand when it is plotted, since the supply curve ordinarily slopes uphill whereas the demand curve ordinarily slopes downhill. The slope of the supply curve reflects the fact that usually more units will be offered for sale at high than at low prices, in contrast to the reverse demand relationship.

Upward-sloping supply curves may seem obvious to you. Or they may seem anything but obvious. You may think of the economies of mass production, and suspect that the more units produced the lower the price can be. This may, of course, be true under some circumstances, and sometimes—for example, in the automobile industry—to a very significant extent. But there is much evidence that firms commonly operate at levels where supply curves are roughly horizontal or upward-sloping. And some firms will generally have higher costs than others, which may mean a rising supply curve as the higher-cost firms are drawn into the market (as is indicated by the following example).

The relation between firms' costs and the supply curves for their products is a major subject in economics. It will be examined in detail in the following chapters. For purposes of this chapter, take it on faith that most supply curves are flat or upward-sloping, with the reasons to be examined later. And even if supply curves should turn out to be downward-sloping in some cases, the type of interaction between supply, demand, and price described in the following pages would still be generally applicable and useful.

---

[1] This second statement is a much more tricky proposition. Sometimes the entire response to increased consumer demand comes merely through more production at the same price. But usually, increased demand bids up the price, and this higher price helps in calling forth added supply to satisfy the increased demand. Chapters 20 and 21 provide a more detailed look at this problem.

A simple example may help to show how supply curves work. Suppose there are three dairy farms nearby. At various milk prices each will produce and offer different amounts for sale, as in Table 19-1. For the moment, we merely assume that each farmer will produce and offer more milk as the price rises.[2]

Table 19-1

SUPPLY SCHEDULE FOR MILK

	Number of Quarts Supplied per Week by:			
Price per Quart	A	B	C	All
20 cents	50	50	20	120
15 cents	40	50	20	110
10 cents	40	40	0	80
5 cents	30	35	0	65

This supply schedule can be plotted on a graph just as the demand schedule was. Again putting price on the vertical axis and quantity on the horizontal one, we get the market supply curve shown in Figure 19-1.

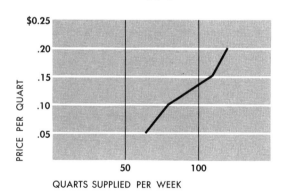

Market Supply Curve for Milk

PRICE PER QUART

QUARTS SUPPLIED PER WEEK

FIG. 19-1   The supply curve shows how many quarts will be supplied each week at different prices.

It is important to remember some of the same warnings on supply that apply to demand: (1) Supply is a schedule, not a single amount. Thus, more output at a higher price may be merely a movement to a new point on the supply schedule, not an increase in supply. A change in supply is a change in the schedule (or curve). (2) Supply has meaning only with reference to some time period. The period should always be specified. (3) A supply schedule or curve is always drawn on the assumption of "other things equal." Just what "other things" we hold constant will vary from case to case, depending partly on the time period involved. For a one-day period, the number of cows and the amount of mechanical equipment the farmer has must be taken as constants. If we're talking about supply per year,

---

[2] Probably Farmer C is what some economists call a "marginal producer." He comes into the market only if the price rises to a relatively high level.

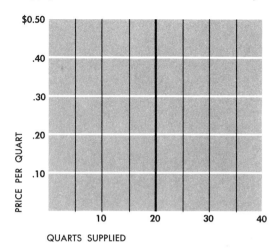

QUARTS SUPPLIED

FIG. 19-2   This chart shows completely inelastic supply. The same number of quarts is offered at any price shown.

obviously such matters become variables. This would lead you to suspect that the supply curve per year might look quite different from the supply curve per day—and it does, as we shall see presently.

Elasticity of Supply.   Supply can be elastic or inelastic, just like demand. If the amount supplied is highly responsive to price changes, the supply is elastic. If the amount offered is little affected by price variations, the supply is inelastic. Except that the amount supplied and the price ordinarily move in the same direction, whereas the amount demanded and the price move in opposite directions, the two concepts are parallel.

Elasticity of supply and the time period involved are closely related. Take an extreme case of inelastic supply first. Suppose you have a strawberry patch and a roadside stand, but no overnight refrigeration. If you picked 20 quarts this morning, your only alternatives are to sell them at whatever price you can get or to let them spoil (neglecting the possibilities that you may eat them fresh yourself or preserve them). Thus your supply curve for the day may be completely inelastic —a vertical line at 20 quarts of strawberries. You're willing to sell your 20 quarts at any price from zero up—the higher the better, of course. Figure 19-2 pictures this simple assumption, where cost of production appears to play no significant role.

Now take a case at the other extreme. Suppose some simple commodity like lead pencils can be reproduced almost without limit at some cost, say 3 cents per pencil, merely by duplicating existing manufacturing facilities, materials, and workers. Given enough time to

FIG. 19-3   This chart shows infinitely elastic supply. Given a long time to adjust, any number of pencils can be produced at a cost of 3 cents per pencil.

Supply of Lead Pencils, Given a Long Time to Adjust

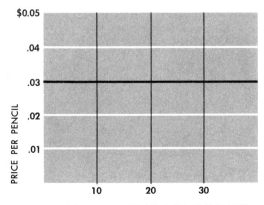

PENCILS SUPPLIED PER YEAR (IN THOUSANDS)

build new facilities, almost any given number of pencils will be produced for sale at a price of 3 cents or above. Thus the supply curve might be completely elastic— a horizontal line, at 3 cents per pencil, as in Figure 19-3.

This case, like that of the strawberries, is oversimplified; cost per pencil may not be so constant in the real world, and the resulting supply curve may not be perfectly flat. But both cases serve to indicate the kinds of situations that may prevail in the supply of different kinds of commodities, depending on the time period considered. Most cases and most time periods, of course, fall somewhere between these two extremes.

The pencil situation suggests again, too, that the shape of any producer's supply curve depends on his costs of production. This is clearly true in most cases, though the strawberry situation temporarily appears to be an exception.

DEMAND, SUPPLY, AND MARKET PRICE You may have visited the "wheat pit" at the Board of Trade in Chicago, which is one of the world's major wheat-trading markets. Here millions of bushels of wheat are bought and sold daily by a relatively small number of men, acting largely as dealers and agents for others. Suppose the supply and demand for wheat in the pit on some particular day are as shown in Table 19-2, and that these schedules are constant for the entire day.

Table 19-2

SUPPLY AND DEMAND FOR WHEAT, CHICAGO, ON A GIVEN DAY

Millions of Bushels Offered	*Price*	*Millions of Bushels Demanded*
18	$3.00	8
16	2.50	11
14	2.00	14
12	1.50	17
10	1.00	20

Suppose that the first bid on this day is $1.50 a bushel. It's pretty clear that at this price there's going to be trouble, because buyers will demand 17 million bushels whereas sellers are willing to offer only 12 million bushels. Table 19-2 shows that lots of buyers are willing to pay more than $1.50 if they have to. And they have to, because offerings are 5 million bushels short of demand at $1.50. As these buyers bid higher prices, the price will gradually move up toward $2.00. As the price rises, some buyers will drop out and new sellers will come in, until at $2.00 the amount offered for sale just matches the amount demanded. There is no reason to suppose that the price will be bid higher today, because everyone who is willing to pay $2.00 is getting his wheat and everyone who has wheat for sale at $2.00 sells it.

Try starting with a price of $3.00 to see whether that price could last long in this market. Where does the price stabilize?

This same analysis can be done graphically just as well, if you prefer pictures. Figure 19-4 graphs these same demand and supply schedules. The curves intersect at a price of $2.00 with 14 million bushels traded. This is the only price at which the amount demanded just matches the amount supplied, and it is the price that will be reached through bargaining in the market. The reasoning is exactly the same as with the schedules. At any higher price, there will be too many sellers for the buyers, and sellers will shade their prices in order to find buyers. At any lower price, buyers won't be able to get the wheat they demand and will shade up their offering prices.

Actually, of course, demand and supply seldom stay constant for long in an active market like the wheat pit, and one price may be hardly established before demand or supply changes and price slides up or down toward a new equilibrium level. Changes like this are easy to illustrate. See Figure 19-5. Keeping the same supply curve as before, suppose that war

Supply and Demand for Wheat

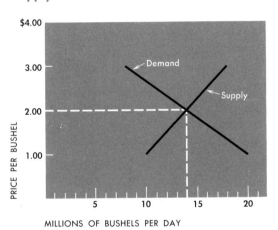

FIG. 19-4   With these demand and supply curves, the equilibrium price will be $2.00, with 14 million bushels exchanged.

news sharply increases the demand for wheat on successive days. Common sense tells you that with constant supply and increased demand, the price will be bid up—and so it is. On the second day, with demand D^1D^1, the price is bid up to about $2.50 with about 16 million bushels bought. Although the supply curve is constant, more wheat is supplied at the higher price. The result of the increased demand is *both* a higher price and more wheat traded. On the third day (demand D^2D^2) the price is still higher—up to nearly $3.00 with almost 18 million bushels bought.

Equilibrium Price.   *Whenever a price is established that just clears the market, economists call it an "equilibrium price." The amount offered just equals the amount demanded at that price. Price is in equilibrium when, with the given demand and supply curves, it stays put at that level. At any other level, price* will not be in equilibrium, since the amounts demanded and supplied will not be equal and price will move up or down toward an equilibrium that will make them equal.

A simple analogy may help clarify the notion of equilibrium and the inter-relations between demand, supply, and price. Suppose you have a round mixing bowl and three wooden balls. If you put the balls in the bowl, they will all move toward the lowest point, in the middle of the bowl. But they can't all be there, since there is only one lowest point and it's not big enough for all three. The balls will settle down into some equilib-rium position, depending on their relative sizes and weights. And there they will stay until someone disturbs them.

Now suppose you substitute a larger, heavier ball for one of the three. This will obviously disturb the old equilibrium position, not only of the changed ball but of all three. Just so, a change in supply or demand will change the equi-librium relationship involving all three. If both demand and supply change simultaneously, as they often do in the real world, the new equilibrium situation will de-pend on the new curves. Price may end up higher or lower; quan-

Supply and Demand for Wheat— Changing Demand

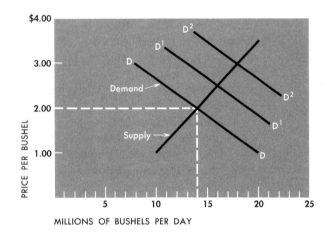

FIG. 19-5   Increases in demand to D^1D^1 and D^2D^2 cause increases in both price and quantity traded. The new equilibrium with D^2D^2 involves a price of \$3.00 and 18 mil-lion bushels exchanged daily.

tity sold may be larger or smaller. It all depends on how much and which way the two curves shift, just as in the bowl it depends on the sizes and weights of the new balls.

Supply and Demand: Some Special Cases.   *Completely Inelastic Supply.* Some extreme cases may help to clarify what is involved in these demand and supply relationships. Take first a case where the amount supplied is absolutely fixed. A favorite economists' example is that there are only four corners at State and Madison Streets in Chicago, sometimes called the busiest corner in the world. The supply curve for building space on this corner is thus completely inelastic— there's no more land available on the corner no matter how high land prices or rents may go.[3] Suppose we graph the supply of land on this corner in square

---

[3] Though you can get around this limitation partially by building higher skyscrapers.

feet and the demand (*DD*) for it, on either a purchase or rental basis. The picture might look roughly like Figure 19-6, with annual rents in equilibrium at $1,000 per square foot.

Now suppose the demand for space on the corner increases, because prosperity booms, or the population of Chicago grows. The demand curve moves up to D^1D^1. Property-owners can now charge $1,100 per square foot. The amount of land rented is identical before and after the increase in demand. This outcome in very nice from the landowner's viewpoint, not so good from the consumer's.

But if the demand falls, the full burden also falls on the landowner. The price (rent) going to the supplier (landowner) is determined solely by the demand. The supply in this extreme case, and only in this case, has no active role in determining the price.

Completely Elastic Supply. Now take the other extreme—the pencils from several pages back where the amount supplied could be increased at a constant cost merely by duplicating productive facilities. Given a long enough time period, the supply curve here would look perfectly flat, as in Figure 19-7. If *DD* is the demand, the price of pencils will be 3 cents and 10,000 per day

**Supply and Demand
for Rental Space (Inelastic Supply)**

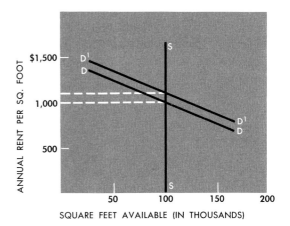

FIG. 19-6   With completely inelastic supply, increased demand means merely a higher price.

will be made and sold. Suppose now that demand increases to D^1D^1. What happens, according to the graph, is that the price remains unchanged while production and sales rise to 12,000 daily. And this is clearly sensible. Since more pencils can be produced at the same cost, the increased demand will simply call forth more pencils without bidding up the price. This is the other extreme from the land-rent case above—here the consumers can be happy. Rising demand has no effect on price but only an effect on quantity produced and sold. With the land, changing demand had no effect on the quantity sold but only an effect on the price.

Most real-world cases lie between these two extremes—though many commodities approximate the case of the pencils, given a long time period for adjustment. If increased output can be obtained only by constructing more expensive facilities, or by paying higher prices for raw materials and supplies, the supply curve will slope upward. This is the case that economists call "increasing costs." If the increased output can be produced at the same cost, the supply curve will be flat. This is the case of "constant costs."

Try working out the results of increased demand in these cases. You will see that it makes a good deal of difference to you, the consumer, which kind of product you want more of. In one case, you get more at the same price; in the other, you get more only at a higher price. (With *decreasing* costs and a *downward*-sloping supply curve, which we have temporarily ruled out, the consumer could be happier still, since then increased demand could mean more goods at a lower price.)

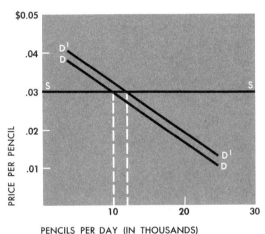

Supply and Demand for Pencils (Elastic Supply)

PRICE PER PENCIL

PENCILS PER DAY (IN THOUSANDS)

FIG. 19-7   With infinitely elastic supply, increased demand leads to more output, not to higher price.

Before going on to the next section, try one more exercise on these simple supply and demand cases. Begin with the pencils. Suppose the government imposes a tax of 1 cent on each pencil produced. What effect will this have on the price and output of pencils? Now answer the same question where pencils are an increasing-cost industry. Lastly, what would be the effect of a new tax on the land at the corner of State and Madison in Chicago, the case of perfectly inelastic supply?

"Free Goods." How is it that air, without which we should all die, is free, whereas most other things, which are much less essential, command a price? The answer is obvious once you try a demand and supply analysis. What is the supply of air? It is substantially unlimited at zero cost. The supply curve would rise above the zero cost line only at some very high-quantity figure for most real-world situations. Thus, even though we might be willing, if necessary, to pay a very high price for air, it just isn't necessary. Since the air available at zero cost is practically unlimited, any demand curve would cut the supply curve at a zero cost and price.

Aside from its use as a simple supply and demand example, the case of air as a "free good" illustrates a very fundamental economic principle: Value depends on (1) utility, (2) scarcity, and (3) cost of production. Unless an article has utility (want-satisfying ability), no one will be willing to pay for it. Unless an article is scarce, consumers will be unwilling to pay for it, however useful it may be. Unless an article requires cost to produce, its supply will be for practical purposes infinite, and no one will need to pay for it.

THE ECONOMICS OF PRICE-FIXING   The law of supply and demand states that market price and quantity sold are determined by supply and demand under competitive conditions such as the wheat-market case above. But lots of times, people—labor unions, farmers, businessmen, congressmen—don't like the prices and quantities set by market demand and supply. And they want to do something about it. What then?

Price Ceilings.   Most people don't like high prices when they're on the buying side. When inflation sweeps prices up, the pressures mount on Congress and the president to check price increases. "How can I pay $1.00 a pound for butter and $125 a month rent for a poor apartment when my income is only $3,000 a year?" asks the mill hand. And he's not going to be very happy about getting an answer from the politicians in Washington that the law of supply and demand says it has to be that way. He wants something done, or he's easy picking for the opposition party next election.

So sometimes Congress enacts a price ceiling on commodities and rents. Suppose Congress slaps a price ceiling on butter at existing levels, and demand for butter continues to grow as incomes rise. In your town, the demand for and supply of butter may look like Figure 19-8. The equilibrium price would be about $1.00 a pound. But Congress has passed a law setting a maximum price of 80 cents. What now?

At the legal price ceiling, clearly the amounts demanded and supplied don't match. People want a lot more butter than they can buy. The price system is tied down—it can't allocate the butter by equilibrating supply and demand through higher prices. Who gets the butter?

"First come, first served" may be the answer. Housewives get the children off to school early and head for the grocer's, or keep an eagle eye out for the dairy delivery truck on its way to the local A&P. They stand in lines in the grocery store. This solution is not calculated to make anyone very happy, least of all the grocer who fast loses his friends when there isn't enough to go around, and the working wives who can't do their shopping till evening.

In frustration, grocers may set up informal rationing systems of their own—say, only a half-pound to a customer. Or they may decide to protect their regular customers, so they put away a few cases of butter for them. This is hard on wives who shop around, and disastrous for families that move to new neighborhoods. Another possibility is to sell butter only to those who buy at least a certain amount of other products—though this will get the grocer in trouble if he gets caught, since such "tie-in" sales are generally illegal under the federal law.

If enough people get unhappy enough, the government may have to step in with a formal rationing plan, where the customer has to have a ration ticket as well as money to buy a pound of butter. Nobody is very happy about being rationed, and everybody complains about the red tape. Unless the government officials are both skillful and lucky, the number of ration tickets issued won't exactly match the supplies available, and a good many mixups can be counted on.

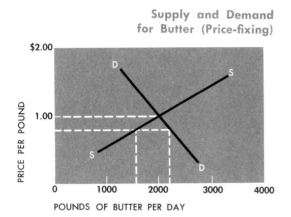

Supply and Demand
for Butter (Price-fixing)

POUNDS OF BUTTER PER DAY

FIG. 19-8   When the government sets the legal maximum price below the market equilibrium, there's trouble. More butter is demanded than is supplied at the artificially low price.

But where supplies of "necessities" become very short, government-sponsored rationing seems to appeal to more people than informal grocer rationing—a sort of "lesser of two evils" solution.

Lastly, the price system may sneak in the back door again and take over part of the equilibrating job outside the law. "Black markets" may develop. It's pretty hard for well-to-do consumers not to offer the corner grocer a little extra for an extra pound of butter. And it's pretty hard for the grocer, pinched between rising costs and fixed price ceilings, to refuse. Short of a regimented system like Hitler's Germany, it's hard to see how rigid price ceilings can be tightly enforced when inflationary pressures are strong. In World War II, such ceilings worked reasonably well in the United States, partly because of intense patriotic pressures and partly because the government gradually raised ceilings as pressures built up on various commodities. The surprising thing to most economists was not that black markets developed, but that the public's basic sense of fair play was so strong that black markets didn't blow the price-control system apart.

Whether the job is done by informal seller rationing, official government rationing, or black-market price increases, someone or something has to decide who is to get the butter when a price ceiling is imposed below the equilibrium market price. A price ceiling works no magic. It just transfers the equilibrating job to some other channel. You can't get rid of the basic supply and demand forces at work by passing a law. But you may well be able to hold the price below its free-market level *if* you are willing to see the product allocated by some other mechanism—*and if* you are willing to use vigorous enough enforcement measures to see that the price in fact doesn't exceed the legal ceiling.

Price Floors and Income Supports. Some people—usually sellers—worry because prices aren't high enough. Labor unions often try to set wages above free-market levels. Some business associations do the same thing with their prices.

The government is a large-scale participant in the game of putting floors under prices above the free-market level; parity farm-support prices and minimum-wage legislation are two examples.[4]

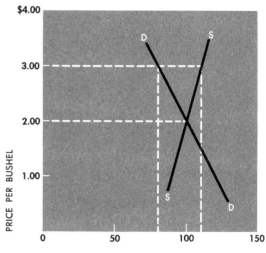

Supply and Demand for Wheat (Price Supports)

Suppose that the government, under pressure to help farmers, decrees that wheat shall not sell for less than $3.00 a bushel. But suppose the free-market price would be only $2.00, as pictured in Figure 19-9. It's clear that there is going to be a lot of unsold wheat around—about 30 million bushels. Some buyers will pay $3.00, but a lot more just won't.

Suppose the government price floor is enforced and nobody undercuts the stated $3.00 price. Are wheat farmers better or worse off as a result? First, only about 80 million bushels will be bought. Second,

FIG. 19-9 When the government puts a minimum price above the market equilibrium price, the result is trouble. More is offered than customers will buy, so the government steps in to buy the surplus or to cut back production.

our old friend elasticity of demand re-enters. If demand is inelastic, total expenditures on wheat are larger at the higher price and total farm income is up (even though consumers get less wheat to eat). But if demand is elastic, the higher price leaves everyone worse off. Farmers get less total income from their wheat, and consumers get less wheat.

But even if demand is inelastic over the price range involved, this simple form

---

[4] This is not to say that parity price supports or minimum-wage rates are always above free-market levels. They are not. But if they weren't intended to be at least part of the time, there would be little reason for their existence.

of government price edict isn't likely to prove very satisfactory. Suppose you are one of the farmers with the millions of bushels of wheat that nobody bought. The higher total income of wheat farmers is going to be small solace to you when you have no income at all. You want the government to help you, too.

So the governmental income-support program will probably take one of two basic courses. Either (1) the government will support the legal price through purchasing otherwise unsold wheat. Or (2) it will impose some kind of restriction on wheat production to reduce supply to a point where the new free-market price will approximate the legal-edict price, maybe through a "soil-bank" plan like the one that is currently stylish. Other approaches or combinations are of course possible.

In approach (1), the government ends up buying the 30 million bushels of wheat at $3.00 a bushel—at a cost of $90 million to the taxpayers. This is nice for the farmers but not so nice for the taxpayers. Remember, too, where the consumer stands in this plan—with less wheat and a higher price for what he buys. Moreover, unless something changes, the government will keep on piling up stocks of wheat indefinitely.

In approach (2), this situation is avoided by having 30 million fewer bushels of wheat produced. Farmers will get more or less income, depending on the elasticity of demand. If the government merely decreed a cut in wheat production and required everybody to cut production by the required percentage this would be the end of the matter. But actually, the government may well be expected (at least by some of the farmers) to pay those farmers who wanted to produce wheat but couldn't because of government restrictions. This was the case in the basic New Deal AAA farm programs through the 1930's, and it seems to be no less the case today. Here again the taxpayer picks up the bill for the subsidy paid to farmers for not producing the 30 million bushels of wheat. As under approach (1), consumers get fewer bushels of wheat. The government can keep the price up—if it's willing to buy up the surplus or cut back the supply appropriately.

SUMMARY: THE LAW OF SUPPLY AND DEMAND A sure-fire way to sound like an expert in economics is to observe sagely, "You can't repeal the law of supply and demand!"—whenever a difficult problem of economic policy is under discussion. This is especially good if the argument is running against you and you need a devastating blast against the political party in power or against some economic group you don't like.

The preceding pages should help to clarify both how meaningless such a statement is until it is carefully applied to the problem at hand, and how powerful an analytical tool supply and demand analysis can be. The "law" or "principle" of supply and demand can be stated in many different ways. But however it is stated, it is nothing more than an analytical tool that can be used in thinking through an economic problem. It doesn't provide ready-made answers to problems. Obviously the government and private groups can control market prices—they do it every day. But unless they recognize that they must do it ultimately through controlling either supply or demand, they're headed for some unhappy surprises.

The law of supply and demand states that the market price and the quantity sold will be determined by supply and demand in competitive markets. Many modern economists prefer to state that, given demand and supply, price and quantity sold will tend to move toward equilibrium levels that will clear the market. This latter statement is no different, but it puts more emphasis on the interrelated equilibrating process. We will see in succeeding chapters a variety of ways in which the simple analytical concepts of supply and demand can be brought to bear on widely diverse problems. A good deal of what follows boils down to analyzing:

1. Why demand and supply are what they are in particular cases.

2. The results of particular kinds of demand and supply conditions—for example, when a few monopolists get control of the market for a particular product.

3. How demand and supply conditions can be changed through public-policy measures to get results the public likes better than those produced by the free market.

REVIEW—CONCEPTS TO REMEMBER

Recheck your understanding of the major new concepts introduced in this chapter. They are:

market	equilibrium price
market price	law of supply and demand
supply	constant costs
elasticity of supply	increasing costs
supply curve	

FOR ANALYSIS AND DISCUSSION

1. Explain carefully what is meant by saying that an equilibrium price "clears the market."

2. When demand is large, we can be sure the price of the commodity will be high. True or false? Why?

3. Is it demand or supply that primarily determines price? If your answer is different in different cases, give an example in which you would expect each to be the dominant force.

4. Why are pearls so high-priced, when they serve for the most part only as decoration?

5. Are the factors determining the price of a Cézanne painting the same as those determining the price of potatoes? Explain your answer.

6. Suppose that the demand for sugar is very inelastic and a new tax is imposed on sugar. Would it be relatively hard or easy to pass the tax on to consumers through higher prices? Compare this with a product for which the demand is highly elastic.

7. Assume that the demand for wheat is inelastic. If you were a farmer, would you favor government policies to keep the price higher than its free-market level? Is there any distinction between your individual interest and the interests of all wheat farmers as a group?

8. Suppose the demand for oleomargarine increases, without any corresponding increase in the supply. What effect, if any, would this have on the demand for butter?

20

The Business Firm
and Its Costs

General Motors supplies Chevrolets. You and I buy them. Westinghouse supplies light bulbs and we buy them. In many cases, a firm manufactures a physical product, and we can think loosely of a supply-demand relationship in which the manufacturer is the supplier and consumers are the demanders. In most such cases, however, wholesalers and retailers intervene. And in lots of other instances, consumers demand services—e.g., shirt laundering and air travel. This is considerably different from the manufacturing company as an indirect supplier. In fact, in one sense, individuals, not businesses, are the most important suppliers in the economy. Most of us work for somebody else; we supply our labor services to those who demand them.

Obviously, there are many different kinds of suppliers. To simplify, the next few chapters consider manufacturing firms as suppliers and consumers as demanders, with no intermediaries. This is unrealistic, but it gives a simple first approximation to the working of the market system. There is time to come back later to the intermediaries, and to the individuals who sell their own services

372

to earn incomes. The same general type of supply and demand analysis helps in all such cases, but the specific applications are different.

WHY WORRY
ABOUT COSTS?

The question, "Why worry about costs?" may sound like a foolish one. But it's worth thinking about a minute. From a businessman's viewpoint, the answer is clear: Because, other things equal, the higher your costs are, the less of your income will be left for profits. As economists, though, we are primarily interested in profits as inducements to businessmen to produce what consumers want, rather than just in seeing how rich they make the businessmen. So we need to take a broader look at costs.

Viewed fundamentally, costs are important because they exercise a restraint on production. If nothing cost anything to produce, we could get unlimited supplies whenever we wanted them. But since it does cost to produce almost everything, we can't expect everything we want free. And how far any business will go in producing what we want will depend on how much that article costs to produce relative to what we are willing to pay for it.

Business costs are important for another reason. Looked at as wages and salaries, rent and interest payments, business costs *are* the incomes of workers and resources of owners. In explaining business costs, therefore, we are explaining why most people receive the incomes they do.

This chapter considers the kinds of costs faced by typical business concerns. In Chapter 21, the focus is on how these costs influence business production and pricing practices.

WHAT ARE COSTS?

Back in the profit-and-loss statement on page 326, costs were broken down into materials, labor cost, depreciation on plant and equipment, maintenance and repairs, selling and administrative costs, taxes (other than income taxes), and interest payments on borrowed funds. Every business has its own way of classifying costs, but these main categories show up in most such statements.

Most of these costs represent direct cash outlays—wages; payments for materials, heat, light, and repairs; property and payroll tax payments to governments; and so on. But it is important to remember that cash outlays are by no means identical with costs.

Depreciation is an example of this distinction. Depreciation is merely a bookkeeping entry estimating how much of the value of plant and equipment has been used up in producing goods during a certain time period. It is not a cash outlay at all.

Cost of materials is another illustration. This item shows the cost of materials *used* during the period. It may be more or less than the cost of materials *bought* during the period. For example, a business with big materials inventories might run a whole month without buying any materials. Yet it should obviously consider as costs the costs of the materials used up from inventory during the month. A related problem: How to estimate the cost of materials used out of inventory when the inventory has been bought at different prices (e.g., steel scrap bought at prices ranging from $40 to $60 a ton)? A lively dispute on the best way to handle such costs has been raging among accountants and businessmen for years. Only rarely will the accounting cost figure arrived at match the cash outlays for materials during the accounting period.

These examples emphasize another point. Many important business costs are necessarily *estimated* costs. What the accountant tries to do is to get the best possible approximation of the cost of producing one ton of steel, or one Ford, or one quart of milk. But this is a more complex problem than it sounds, both because it is hard to allocate many types of cost accurately to individual units of output, and because cost per unit in most companies varies with the scale of output and the passage of time. The problem is especially acute when a company uses the same facilities, officials, and labor to produce a variety of products. For example, how much of the president's salary should be allocated to plows, harrows, and harvesters, respectively, in the International Harvester Company?

Alternative Costs.   The accountant is usually interested in costs as one component of a profit-and-loss statement to compute the firm's profit over some time period. He computes profit along the lines outlined in Appendix A to Chapter 17, dealing with the difficulties indicated above as best he can. Some accountants ("cost accountants") try to isolate the "unit costs" of particular products within the company. They may do this to help management control the costs of particular operations, to determine the profitability of particular lines, or to provide a basis for pricing particular products.

The economist is interested in these calculations. But his concern with the over-all allocation of resources in the economy leads him on to some further questions.

Thinking in "real" terms, the basic fact of scarcity drives the economist to the conclusion that the "real" cost of producing anything is the alternatives that are foregone. For example, the *real* cost of producing a radio is the other commodities given up that might otherwise have been produced with the same steel, copper, wood, and labor. *The real cost is an "alternative cost"—the alternative uses of the resources that are given up when the resources are used in producing radios. Sometimes alternative cost is called "opportunity" cost.*

This fact is most obvious in a war economy, when the guns-or-butter alternative stares us in the eye. We can get more tanks, but only at the cost of giving up trucks. The real cost of the tanks is the alternative use of steel and labor foregone—trucks, refrigerators, or other civilian hard goods. The same thing is true in a peacetime economy, so long as unemployed resources are not available. If we use our resources for one thing, we can't use them for another.

This concept of alternative or opportunity cost can be put into money terms. Thus, the cost of producing one TV set is the amount of money necessary to get the factors of production needed for the radio away from alternative uses. For example, as a TV manufacturer, you will have to pay enough for cabinet makers to get them to work for you rather than for chair and table manufacturers. You have to pay enough for mechanics to get and keep them away from auto and radar plants. You have to pay enough for copper wire to bid it away from telephone companies and toy manufacturers. And so it is for every resource used in producing TV's. *In economic terms, the total cost of the TV set is the amount necessary to bid all the required resources away from the strongest competing uses.*

Accounting and Economic Costs.   Use of an alternative-cost concept leads economists to different cost figures from the ones that businessmen and their accountants work with. These differences arise primarily because the economist includes several items that the accountant ordinarily doesn't consider as costs when he draws up his profit-and-loss statements.

A simple example is the independent corner grocer, who has bought the store with his own funds and runs it himself. In addition to the regular business costs in the profit-and-loss statement, the economist would say:

"How about a return on your own investment and a salary for yourself? If you didn't have your money tied up in the store, you could be earning 5 per cent on it in another investment. If you weren't working in the store, you could earn $5,000 a year working for Krogers. You ought to account as costs a 5 per cent return on your investment and a $5,000 salary for yourself before you compute your profit for the year, because these reflect real alternatives that you're giving up when you stay in your own business."

If the grocer does not include these costs and finds he's making a $4,000 annual profit, he may think he's doing well—but actually he's kidding himself. The $4,000 doesn't even give him the salary he could earn working for someone else, much less the return he could get by investing his money somewhere else.

A similar difference, though much less obvious, is found in business corporations. Corporations pay salaries to their officers and employees, so there's no trouble there. And they pay interest to their bondholders, which is considered a cost in computing profits. But what about the interest on the owners' (stockholders') investment, just as on the corner grocer's investment?

The usual accounting calculation of corporation profits omits the alternative cost of using the stockholders' capital in this firm rather than elsewhere. Profit is calculated before any payment is made to stockholders. *The economist, how-*

ever, includes in the firm's costs a reasonable rate of return on stockholders' investment (measuring the alternative return that is foregone elsewhere). He therefore considers as "economic profit" only the excess income over and above this basic alternative cost, because a reasonable rate of return is part of the cost required to keep funds invested in any business.[1]

The accountant's way of computing profits leads to some peculiar inconsistencies. Take two identical corporations, one financed by $1,000,000 of 4 per cent bonds and $1,000,000 of stock, the other by $2,000,000 of stock. Suppose each earns $100,000 after all other costs are covered. Corporation A will now show an accounting profit of only $60,000, because the bondholders' interest takes $40,000 of the $100,000. Corporation B, identical except for financing arrangements, shows profits of $100,000. Not the least important consequence is the big difference in income tax liabilities of the two substantially identical firms, since the law permits firms to deduct bond interest as a cost in calculating profits for income tax liability, but not implicit return on stockholders' investment.

Through the rest of this book, we shall use the alternative-cost concept. Thus, costs of production will include the reasonable (or "normal") rate of return on investment necessary to keep the funds invested in any given concern rather than elsewhere. Costs will include the entrepreneur's own salary if he is self-employed. Broadly, they will include all costs required to get and keep resources in the occupation under consideration. Most costs will be the same as those used by the accountant, but the differences noted above must be kept in mind. *Especially, remember that the production-cost data and curves used here include a "normal" return on investment, if you want to avoid some dangerous pitfalls later on.*

COST OF PRODUCTION
AND THE RATE OF OUTPUT [2]

Imagine a small company that produces a single product, say fine radio-phonograph-television combinations. Suppose the only costs the company has are raw materials, labor, depreciation on plant and equipment, maintenance, and return on stockholders' investment. Suppose further that, if we look at costs over the month ahead, we find that depreciation and a normal return on stockholders' investment are "fixed" for the month—they go on whether the company operates at full capacity, part capacity, or shuts down. The other costs are "variable," depending on the company's rate of output.

Assume that the "fixed" costs amount to $1,000 per month, and that the "variable" costs vary with changes in output as in Table 20-1.

---

[1] In economics, costs that show up in the usual accounting procedures are often called "explicit" costs, while alternative costs (like a return on stockholders' investment) which are not usually recorded in modern accounting are called "implicit" costs.

[2] The Appendix, "Physical Production Relationships Underlying Cost Curves," pp. 388-392, provides the logical foundation for this cost analysis, for those instructors who prefer a detailed and rigorous treatment in this and the following chapter.

Table 20-1

FIXED, VARIABLE, AND TOTAL COSTS

Output	Total Fixed Cost	Total Variable Cost	Total Cost
1	$1,000	$ 2,000	$ 3,000
2	1,000	2,500	3,500
3	1,000	3,000	4,000
4	1,000	4,000	5,000
5	1,000	5,000	6,000
6	1,000	6,600	7,600
7	1,000	10,000	11,000
8	1,000	16,000	17,000

These costs are shown in Figure 20-1. Cost is shown on the vertical axis, output on the horizontal one. *TFC* is total fixed cost of $1,000, which is the same no matter what output is produced. On top of this, we need to put total variable cost—zero at zero output, $2,000 for one set, $2,500 for two, and so on. *TC,* the total-cost curve, thus shows total cost as the sum of total fixed and total variable cost at each level of output.

It is easy to see that *TC* does not rise at an even rate. It doesn't cost much more in total to produce two sets than one, or three than two. But as the firm gets up to six or seven sets per month, total cost begins to rise much more rapidly. It is obviously total variable cost that begins to shoot up. The reason may be that the company was set up with a "capacity" of only five or six sets a month, and to exceed this capacity may involve expensive readjustments in equipment, hiring of expensive overtime labor, subcontracting of component parts, and other such special problems. Or there may be some other explanation. But beyond this one observation, the total-cost data shown aren't very illuminating.

FIG. 20-1   Total fixed cost is $1,000 at all outputs. Total variable cost rises as output increases. Total cost for any output is the sum of fixed and variable cost; it rises rapidly once "capacity" of the plant is reached.

Total-Cost Curves

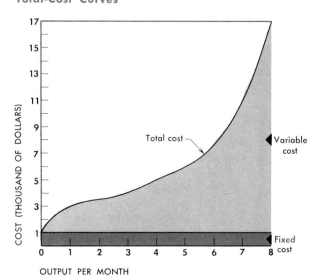

OUTPUT PER MONTH

Fixed, Variable, and Total Cost Per Unit. One reason is that the data don't show costs per set produced, and you probably think of business output in terms of cost and selling price per unit. You may already have divided through the total-cost figures by the number of sets produced to see what the cost per radio is at different levels of output. If you haven't, it's a sensible thing to do. The result is shown in Table 20-2.

Table 20-2

FIXED, VARIABLE, AND TOTAL COSTS PER UNIT

Output	Fixed Cost per Unit	Variable Cost per Unit	Total Cost per Unit
1	$1,000	$2,000	$3,000
2	500	1,250	1,750
3	333	1,000	1,333
4	250	1,000	1,250
5	200	1,000	1,200
6	167	1,100	1,267
7	143	1,430	1,573
8	125	2,000	2,125

These are, of course, just hypothetical figures. But their general character is important, because in some ways they are typical of all such cost data.

Fixed cost per unit will always be a steadily decreasing series, because the constant total-fixed-cost figure (here $1,000) is divided by a steadily rising volume of output. This is what is commonly known as "spreading the overhead." The drop in fixed cost per unit is very rapid at first, but as volume grows the cost reduction per unit steadily decreases in importance.

Variable cost per unit will generally fall at the outset, then flatten out some what, and then rise again as plant "capacity" is approached and passed. To produce one set, the company has to have labor and materials of all the types needed for the set. On the labor side, it will clearly be inefficient to try to call each type of skilled labor in just long enough to work on one set. If we try to use two of three jack-of-all-trades, we get less efficient work than we would if we divided the labor up among experts on the various parts of the job. Similarly, it may be cheaper to buy materials in larger quantities than it would be to buy just enough to produce one set per month. It's not efficient to produce only one or two sets a month.

At the other extreme, once the "capacity" has been reached for which the plant was planned, costs are likely to shoot up rapidly if we try to produce still more sets per month. "Capacity" is seldom an absolute limit in a plant. For example, steel plants often operate above 100 per cent of capacity; rated capacity allows for an average amount of shut-down time for maintenance and repairs, which can be postponed temporarily. But expansion of output beyond plant "capacity" often means drastic reorganization of operations, expensive overtime work, hiring of additional lower-skilled workers, more spoilage under pressure of speed-up, and a variety of other such factors.

Thus, without going into details at the moment, it seems reasonable that *with any given plant* (which we have assumed) variable costs per unit will rise rapidly at some point beyond "capacity" output. Just when this point is reached depends, of course, on the individual firm. In many industries, variable costs per unit are apparently flat over wide ranges of output. In others, where small-scale operations are advantageous, increase in output beyond low levels may lead quickly to rising unit costs.

Total cost per unit is simply the sum of fixed cost per unit and variable cost per unit. Or it can be obtained by dividing total cost by the number of units produced. The decreasing fixed cost per unit will always pull down on total unit cost as output rises. At first, as long as both fixed and variable costs per unit are declining, clearly the total cost per unit is declining. But at some point total unit costs will begin to rise, often after a long flat area in which the fixed cost per unit declines slightly and the variable cost per unit is substantially constant or slightly rising. The rise in total unit cost will begin when variable cost per unit turns up more than enough to offset the downward pull of declining fixed unit costs. This point is at the sixth unit in our radio plant. Total unit cost is relatively stable over the output range of three to six units, with the minimum cost per unit at an output of five sets per month.

This simple example should warn you against one common fallacy—the idea that each firm has *a* cost of production for its product. In every firm, cost of production per unit varies with output. This is certain at the extremes of very low and above-capacity output. It often occurs over the range of normal variation in operations.

A good many firms now use what they call "standard costs" in pricing their products and in keeping control over their production processes. A "standard cost" for our radio set would be an estimate by our accountants and production men of how much it should cost to produce one set at a normal, or typical, rate of output. If we think of 4 sets monthly as about normal operation, our standard cost figure would be $1,250 per set (if we include implicit return on investment). Standard cost is not necessarily minimum cost.

Such standard-cost estimates can play a useful role in modern industry; we will meet them again in the chapters ahead. But they can also lead to confusion and wrong conclusions, both in business management and in understanding the over-all operations of the economic system. Confusion will occur unless the user is careful to remember that standard-cost estimates are only *arbitrary estimates* of unit costs *at some selected level of output.*

UNIT-COST CURVES All these per unit cost data can readily be plotted on graphs as cost curves. They can be plotted either as total-cost curves for the firm, or as curves showing cost per unit of output. Both ways have their uses, but concentrate here on how the cost curves look when they are plotted on a per unit basis.

Unit-Cost Curves

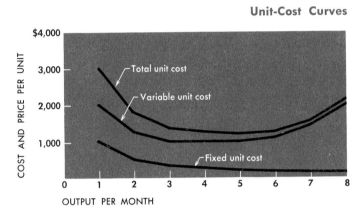

FIG. 20-2   Unit-cost curves are derived by dividing the corresponding total-cost curves by total output. Here fixed unit cost slopes downward continuously as the constant total fixed cost is spread over more units of output. Other curves are U-shaped.

Figure 20-2 shows the cost data for our radio firm. TUC is the total-unit-cost curve, VUC the variable cost per unit, and FUC the fixed cost per unit. The shape of these curves corresponds, of course, to the data. Fixed cost per unit falls steadily as the constant total cost is spread over more and more units. Variable cost per unit and total cost per unit are both U-shaped, for the reasons suggested above. In most firms, the TUC curve is probably a good deal flatter than in this hypothetical case. That is, there is a wider range of output over which total cost per unit is substantially constant, between the low-output inefficiencies at the left of the graph and the above-capacity inefficiencies at the right.

Be sure you know just what the graph means. For example, at an output of five units next month, the fixed cost per unit will be $200 and the variable cost per unit $1,000, for a total of $1,200. This happens to be the lowest point on the total-unit-cost curve. It is called the "least-cost combination." It is the lowest cost at which these hi-fi sets can be made, given the existing plant and the firm's other commitments for the month ahead.

"SHORT-RUN"
AND "LONG-RUN" VIEWS
OF COSTS

Economists are fond of talking about the "short run" and the "long run." Time is an extremely important variable in the analysis of economic problems, and this distinction is an attempt to clarify the assumptions being made about the time period involved in any case. We will mean by the "short run" any time period in which certain costs (e.g., rent and interest on borrowed funds) are fixed and do not vary with changes in the firm's output. We mean by "long run" a time period long enough so that *all* costs become variable with changes in output. *Thus the distinction is essentially an analytical one. A short run in one case may be longer than a long run in another.*

Some examples will clarify this distinction. In our hi-fi example, next month is clearly a "short run." During that month certain costs are fixed no matter how many radios we produce—depreciation on the factory building, for example. Given a longer time period, the existing plant will depreciate away or it may be sold, so the capital tied up in the plant becomes available for other uses. Similarly, managerial salary may be a fixed cost for the next month or year, but over some longer time period the manager's contract will expire and his salary will become a variable cost. If a firm has a large commitment for fixed costs extending for years ahead, the "short run" for the firm may be a long time. At the other extreme would be a firm with no plant of its own, no leases or salary contracts, and no other forward commitments. The commonest way to think of the "short run" is the time period over which a firm has a plant and equipment to which variable agents such as labor and materials are added to achieve different output levels. This is not a very precise way of drawing the distinction, but it will convey the general idea.

In the "long run," by contrast, *all* the firm's costs become variable. The entrepreneur can decide to build a new plant of different size if he likes. He can transfer his investment from one industry to another. He has complete freedom to move.

The Optimum Scale of Enterprise. The "long run" is thus a planning period, free from the short-run limitations imposed by fixed plant and other commitments. The big long-run planning problem is: What is the "optimum scale of enterprise" for the firm? This means how big a fixed plant, how big a labor force, how much equipment, what kind of management organization—it means everything related to the planning of the enterprise's scale of operations in the future.

Businesses seldom find themselves in a position to make all these decisions on future scale at one time. But they are continually re-evaluating their positions and planning specific long-run changes So they may replan their over-all scale of enterprise much more frequently than would appear from a superficial glance.

Each possible scale of enterprise for any given firm can be shown as a flattened U-shaped total-unit-cost curve associated with that scale. Clearly some scales of enterprise will be too small for reasonable efficiency. We may suspect that our radio maker of the preceding pages is such a producer, though we've made him a somewhat special case by assuming a luxury, high-quality product. As the scale of enterprise becomes larger, more of the advantages of mass production and specialization of functions can be realized, bulk buying becomes possible, skilled management can be afforded. The least-cost point on the cost curve for this larger plant will be lower than the least-cost point on the curve of a smaller enterprise. But after a certain size is reached, it seems reasonable to suppose that the firm may get too big. The least-cost point for the jumbo-sized firm may well be higher than for a somewhat smaller scale. Why, we shall consider in the next section.[3]

A set of five possible planning curves, showing expected costs for five different scales of enterprise, is given in Figure 20-3. Actually, there could be a much larger number of such curves, representing different scales of operation. Each of the *TUC* curves corresponds to a given scale of enterprise—a plant of certain

Unit-Cost Curves for Firms of Different Sizes

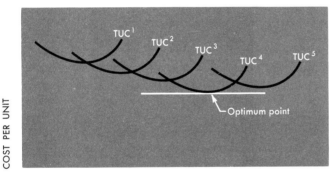

FIG. 20-3 Larger firms have lower minimum total-unit-cost points until the optimal scale of firm is reached. Then still larger firms face higher minimum *TUC*'s.

size, equipment of certain sorts, and so on. The scale of enterprise giving the cost curve at the extreme left is obviously too small to be advantageous except for a very small market. In this figure, the scale corresponding to the fourth cost curve gives the lowest possible least-cost point. A firm of this size is the "optimum scale of enterprise," in the sense that it provides the possibility of the lowest cost per unit of output of any possible scale of enterprise.

HOW BIG IS OPTIMAL? Why are manufacturing companies typically bigger than dry-cleaning establishments? Why is retailing still mainly small-scale enterprise? Why do some firms remain small and stick to a limited line of goods, while others expand into an elaborate range of products?

---

[3] Throughout, we must assume some standard product to be produced to keep the different scales of operation comparable.

These are hard questions, and the answers are complex. The primary answers may be classed under four headings: technology, management, market opportunities, and financing channels.

Technology and the Size of Enterprise.   America is the land of mass production. American industry is admired the world over for its fabulous equipment and its technical know-how. The mass-production revolution pioneered by Henry Ford with the famous Model T has never stopped spreading. Today's huge steel mills, oil refineries, and auto plants are increasingly taken for granted in the United States. Their basic advantages boil down to four factors:

1. *Specialization and Division of Labor.* Adam Smith pointed out in 1776, in his famous *Wealth of Nations,* that specialization and division of labor in making pins would reduce the cost of pins, compared with the cost of having one man do the whole job. This principle underlies mass production. Extensive specialization and division of labor are feasible only in reasonably large firms. Such specialization will pay off most where the product being turned out is complex and where many different skills and operations are involved. The auto plants of Detroit are a spectacular example of how far such specialization can profitably go.

2. *Use of Elaborate, Expensive Machinery and Equipment.* No small gasoline refinery can compete effectively with the massive, automatic, multi-million-dollar refineries now used by all the major oil companies. Only a large company can afford a multi-million-dollar "cat cracker." The machinery for a modern, efficient steel-rolling mill is very expensive; it is available only to a big firm that is able to spread the cost of the equipment over a large volume of output. No small establishment could afford to use such equipment, for without large-volume output the cost per ton produced would be prohibitively high.

3. *Balancing of Processes.* In a large firm, the various stages of a productive process can be fitted together to take advantage of the optimum scale for each stage of the operation. Suppose machine A feeds machine B, but A processes 100 units per hour while B handles 150 at optimal rates. The big company can install three A machines in line with two B machines, and thus be able to use all at maximum efficiency levels. The small company, unable to use more than one machine of each type, must either keep B idle part of the time or put A on an extra-shift basis of some sort.

4. *Utilization of By-products.* The big firm can make effective use of many by-products that may be wasted in small concerns. For example, a big meat-packing firm uses cattle hoofs to make glue and other products. In a small company the number of hoofs is too small to make this recovery worth while.

All these technological considerations point toward large concerns as being more efficient. But economies of size don't continue indefinitely. After division of labor has reached a certain point, further expansion of output merely leads to duplication of workers. The same thing is true in the use of expensive equipment, balancing of processes, and utilization of by-products. Once a company is big enough to take full benefit of all these factors, it can realize no further cost reduction on technological grounds from growing still bigger.

Management and the Size of Enterprise.   Someone has to manage every business firm, and good managers are scarce. Large firms can afford highly skilled managers—in purchasing, sales, production, finance, personnel. This kind of managerial specialization is quite similar in principle to the technological specialization and division of labor mentioned above. And it's a big advantage.

But there is one big difference. Somebody in every business has to pull the whole business together. At some point any business may get so big that managerial efficiency drops—though this point may come only after the firm is very large indeed; witness the efficiency of General Motors. The larger the firm and the greater the specialization of activities in the firm, the more essential and the more difficult coordination becomes. It becomes harder to reconcile conflicting views on major policy problems. No matter how expertly the large organization is managed and the various aspects of its activities coordinated, this process is likely at some point to become too complex. There is too much red tape; there are too many levels between the managers in the executive office and the workers in the factory or on the road; the structure becomes top-heavy and inflexible. Modern management emphasizes decentralization of authority and responsibility to avoid this central managerial problem. And this approach has accomplished much. But the potential diseconomies of management in larger enterprise are a major problem for giant firms. Look back at the problems of managing Westinghouse, in Appendix B to Chapter 17.

These possible management diseconomies may be stated in a different way. We can speak of the positive advantages of managing a small business. In the small firm, major decisions can be made more easily and more quickly. There are few specialists to consult, fewer difficulties in arriving at a mutual understanding of the problems faced. This fact gives a special advantage to small firms in fields where changes must be made frequently, as in the production of style goods like women's dresses. Channels of communication are more direct between worker and management, and supervision is easier. Blind spots where wastes are occurring are less likely to persist. Not least important may be the special interest, energy, and enthusiasm of men who manage their own businesses. But whether these match the managerial advantages in bigness is unclear. Sometimes yes, sometimes no.

Market Opportunities and the Size of Enterprise.   The size of the market may limit the size of firms. In some cases, the potential market may not be big enough to permit even one firm to expand to its optimal scale. An example might be the light and power company in a small city. Often, where numerous firms compete for shares of the total market, the share available to each places a direct limitation on the scale of enterprise. Such situations often lead to attempts by individual firms or groups to drive out competition in order to get the larger market needed to permit lower-cost production.

The big firm has obvious advantages in selling its products—large-scale advertising budgets, sales specialists, nation-wide sales organization. Similarly, big firms can often buy more cheaply through ordering large quantity lots, as well as through having more expert buyers. Often, large firms integrate vertically so that they themselves can produce many of the materials used in their own processes, whereas smaller concerns must buy their materials in the market.

All these factors may lower costs for big concerns. But it's easy to over-emphasize them. The small seller retains many advantages, especially in retailing—personal contact with the customer, special services, and so on. And expected advantages of vertical integrations have sometimes turned out to be disadvantages. Many big firms have found to their dismay that they were better off going back to the market for their raw and semi-finished materials, after they had attempted to integrate the production of the materials into their own operations. There is no magic in producing steel for yourself if you are an auto manufacturer. The question is whether you can make the steel sheets cheaper than you can buy them from a steel company; and this will depend on many factors, including your own scale of enterprise in steel-making relative to that of the regular steel producers.

Financing Channels and the Size of Enterprise. It may be hard to get the funds necessary to start a big business. But once a big business is well established, it is likely to have an advantage over little businesses in getting more funds. This is partly because of its added prestige and attractiveness to investors, partly because the organized security markets are in effect accessible only to quite large firms, partly because the costs of making large loans are less per dollar than for small loans.

How Big Is Optimal? The above considerations suggest that how big is optimal varies widely from industry to industry, and such is the case. Careful research studies and evidence presented in antitrust cases where firms have been accused of being overly large and monopolistic make it clear that very large plants and firms are required in some industries to obtain peak efficiency—for example, in autos, cigarettes, petroleum, and steel. But the evidence is also clear that in many industries medium-sized, or even small, firms manage costs as low as, or lower than, the giants. Rates of return on invested capital do not appear to be consistently larger for huge than for medium-sized or small firms, though some of the giants are among the most profitable firms. An indirect test of the optimal scale of firm is provided by what size of firm grows in relative importance in any industry. Here again the evidence is mixed. For the economy as a whole, there is no clear evidence that the share of market obtained by the largest firms is growing appreciably, though nearly all firms are getting bigger as the economy grows. In only a few industries are the giants clearly increasing their dominance—autos is one major example, where the big three have largely squeezed out other firms. But in steel, another industry where huge size is clearly needed for efficiency, the share of market held by U.S. Steel, the biggest firm, has fallen substantially over the last several decades. The empirical evidence shows clearly that there is no pat answer to the question, how big is optimal?

Do Businesses Operate at Optimum Scale? If we were to look at all the firms in any particular industry, we would probably find a wide divergence in size. Why aren't all the firms operating at the "optimum" scale?

There are many reasons, several of which we will be concerned with later. But a summary might look like this:

1. Optimum scale is only the lowest-cost scale of enterprise. It is not necessarily the most profitable scale in all market situations. In many cases, the market simply isn't big enough to permit all firms to operate at optimum scale. In such cases, a firm may in fact operate at lower costs per unit with a small plant than it would with a large plant that was used at only partial capacity.

2. Firms may become "overexpanded" as part of a drive to attain dominance in their industry. When a firm gains a dominant position in the industry, it may be able to exploit this position through influencing both its buying and selling prices to its own advantage. For example, it is commonly believed that the big tobacco companies have been able because of their dominant position to hold up the prices of cigarettes and to push down the prices paid to tobacco farmers.

3. Some firms just want to be big. Quite apart from profits, or even at the expense of profits, men with dreams of industrial empire may expand beyond optimum scale in their drive for bigness and prestige. It is hard to measure this factor, but the last century of United States history produces many cases where this motive appears to have been important.

4. Sometimes fear of government action holds back firms from expansion. This is true when a firm gains partial monopoly powers and fears that further growth may bring government action to break it up, under the Sherman Antitrust Act or other anti-monopoly legislation. It is often alleged that this fear is what keeps General Motors from taking a still larger share of the automobile market.

5. Probably most important of all, errors in judgment and the inevitable slowness in adjusting to changed conditions mean that at any time most firms will not be at optimum scale. The most careful estimates in establishing a new plant are inevitably imprecise on the multitude of factors involved: new technology to be incorporated, future wage rates and materials prices, scale of market available, managerial personnel characteristics, and so on. And even if the esti-

mates could be precise, the process of change is inescapable in economic life. Before long, new situations will arise, new markets will appear, new technological changes will be suggested. Replanning of optimum scale is a continuous process for the well-managed firm, and actual adjustments never catch up with the latest plans.

But economics and good business management are predominantly forward-looking. The businessman can't call back yesterday's decisions—they're water over the dam today. Whether they were right or wrong, the problem now is the future. Policy today cannot affect what happened yesterday—only what will happen tomorrow. Thus, for much of economic analysis it is the planning curves for tomorrow that matter—the adjustments that businessmen will make to the events of today. The same is true of business management.

REVIEW—CONCEPTS TO REMEMBER

This is another chapter of important concepts which will be used throughout the analysis of business-firm behavior. Be sure you understand the following:

cost	variable costs
alternative cost	total costs
opportunity cost	fixed cost per unit
real costs	variable cost per unit
accounting costs	total cost per unit
economic costs	short run
money costs	long run
fixed costs	optimum scale of enterprise

1. The XYZ Company has the following costs. From this information prepare a table showing the following: fixed cost per unit, variable cost per unit, and total cost per unit.

FOR
ANALYSIS
AND
DISCUSSION

Total fixed cost per month $10,000
Total variable costs:

Units Produced	Variable Cost
20	$1,000
21	2,000
22	2,800
23	3,500
24	4,000
25	4,800

Then plot your data on a graph.

2. If you were operating a drugstore, would there be any significant difference between your cash outlays per month and your costs per month? If so, list the items that would account for any differences.

3. Suppose you are considering the possibility of setting up a hot-dog stand near the local ball park. Make a careful list of all the costs you ought to have in mind in estimating whether the expected demand will produce a profit.

4. Which of the costs in question 2 would be fixed regardless of how many hot dogs you sold, and which would vary from week to week with sales volume? Using this dichotomy, draw rough approximations of your fixed and variable cost curves per hot dog, indicating the general shape you would expect the curves to have. From these curves, draw a rough approximation of your total cost (per hot dog) curve.

5. If your total-unit-cost curve is U-shaped (that is, if it first slopes down and then at some sales volume rises again), explain why you would expect your cost per hot dog sold ever to rise as sales volume increased. What would be the primary factors determining how high your sales could run before you met rising costs per unit sold?

6. Make a list of the reasons why manufacturing concerns are typically bigger than dry-cleaning establishments. Can you reconcile your list with the observed fact that some dry-cleaning establishments are bigger than some manufacturing companies?

7. "By and large, the competitive system sees to it that every firm is near the optimal size for producing its product." Do you agree with this statement? Explain carefully why or why not.

Appendix
Physical Production Relationships
Underlying Cost Curves [4]

This Appendix provides a brief statement of part of the "theory of production," which underlies the cost of production in a firm and provides a foundation for understanding the distribution of income to different factors of production. The purpose here is to examine rigorously the physical and technological relationships involved as the businessman combines the various factors of production in turning out his product.

The simplest case arises when one variable factor of production (say labor) is applied to a fixed amount of some other factor of production (say land). Consider then the results of applying an increasing number of units of labor to a fixed plot of land, abstracting from any other factors of production that may be required, such as fertilizer, tools, and so on. Table 20-3 shows what might happen in a hypothetical case.

---

[4] The Appendix is intended for those who want a rigorous physical-output foundation for the previous and following sections on business costs. It should not be assigned by instructors who plan to skip Chapter 21.

Table 20-3

VARIABLE OUTPUT WITH INCREASING INPUTS

Units of Input (Labor)	Total Output (Bushels)	Average Output per Unit of Labor (Bushels)	Marginal Output of Labor (Bushels)
1	100	100	100
2	350	175	250
3	702	234	352
4	1152	288	450
5	1700	340	548*
6	2190	365	490
7	2604	372*	414
8	2908	364	304
9	3114	346	206
10	3240	324	126
11	3300*	300	60
12	3300	275	0
13	3250	250	−50
14	3080	220	−170

* Denotes highest point for each output series.

Column 1 shows the number of laborers used. Column 2 shows the total production, say bushels of wheat, obtained as more workers are added. Total product rises until at some point (11 or 12 workers with 3,300 bushels of output in this example) so many laborers are being used on this small plot of land that they get in each other's way and thereafter there is actual *decrease* in the total output of wheat. Depending on the size of the piece of land, this point might be reached soon, or only after a very large number of laborers was used. Obviously, no intelligent farmer would ever carry production of wheat beyond this point, because by hiring more laborers he would actually decrease the total crop he obtained.

Column 3 shows the average product (bushels of wheat) per worker applied to the land. This average product rises at first, because total product rises more than in proportion to the number of workers used. But the average output per worker reaches a peak (at 7 workers and 2,604 bushels in this example), which gives the maximum output per worker of 372 bushels. Thereafter, even though total product continues to rise, the average output per worker falls.

Column 4 shows the "marginal product" as more workers are used. This column simply shows the *additional,* or "incremental," output obtained by adding each additional worker. Thus by adding the first worker the marginal product is 100 bushels. By adding the second worker the marginal product is 250 bushels, *i.e.,* the increase in total product is from 100 to 350. Marginal product reaches its peak at 5 workers. After this, adding further workers continues to increase total product, but not as rapidly as before: so the increment per additional worker falls.

These relationships can be seen readily in Figures 20-4 and 20-5. Figure 20-4 shows total product as additional workers are hired. It rises rapidly at first, as production becomes more efficient, then gradually levels off, and finally (after 11-12 workers and 3,300 bushels) turns down, for there are just too many workers to avoid getting in each other's way.

Figure 20-5 plots average product and marginal product from Table 20-3. It is clear that marginal product reaches its peak first and then turns down as the rate of growth of total product begins to slow. Average output per worker shows a similar inverted U, but the peak is reached with more workers, as Table 20-3 shows.

Note that the marginal-product curve cuts the average-product curve at the latter's highest point. This is no accident. It is necessarily true because as long as marginal product is higher than average product, each additional worker hired is adding more to total product than the average of all workers up to that point. As soon as the marginal worker adds less to total product than the average up to that point, the marginal-product curve will be below the average-product curve. Thus it will always cut the average-product curve at the highest point of the latter.

The other significant point is when marginal product becomes zero. Comparing the two figures, we see that this is at 12 workers, *which is just the point where total product turns down*. This is clearly to be expected, because marginal product is merely the amount by which total product increases as additional workers are added. Thus, when adding another worker decreases total product, marginal product becomes negative.

Total Product with Increasing Inputs

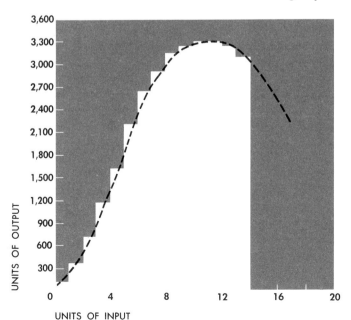

FIG. 20-4 Total output rises fast at first as variable factors are added to a fixed factor, then levels off, and eventually turns down.

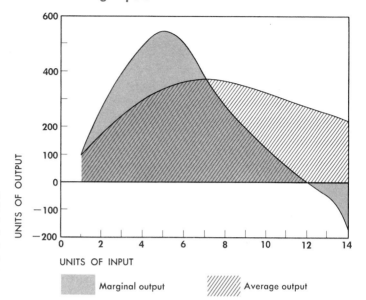

Marginal and Average Product with Increasing Inputs

FIG. 20-5 Marginal output shoots up rapidly as total output grows fast when the first variable factors are added. It turns down as the growth in total output slows, and becomes negative when total output turns down. Check it with Fig. 20-4.

UNITS OF OUTPUT

UNITS OF INPUT

Marginal output   Average output

This extremely simple example is a microcosm of what happens when factors of production are combined in more complex situations. It illustrates the "law of diminishing returns," or what is now more commonly called the "law of variable proportions." In its most general form, the law states that as the proportion of one factor of production to other factors of production increases, the average product of the relatively increasing factor will first rise and then fall persistently; and that the marginal product of the relatively increasing factor will also first rise and then fall, cutting the average-product curve at its highest point. It is important to recognize that these relationships hold whenever the *proportions* among different factors are varied in a production process; it is not essential that one or more factors be fixed in supply. Of course, if all factors used are increasing, the peak level of *total* output is also increased. If all are increased in proportion, the law of diminishing returns may be avoided altogether.

The significance of these relationships for costs of production may be indicated briefly. Assume that the market prices of all factors of production are fixed—labor, raw materials, and other items used in producing the high-fi sets described in Chapter 24. Then the total-fixed-cost curve in Figure 20-1 is obtained directly by multiplying the fixed amount of land used by its rent per acre. The total-variable-cost curve is obtained by multiplying the number of workers (variable agents) by the wage per worker.

These total costs can readily be converted to the *per unit* cost curves of Figure 20-2 by dividing through by the number of units produced. Thus, the variable-unit-cost curve will be the inverse of the average-product-per-worker curve, since wage per worker is constant. When average product per worker is rising, variable cost per unit of output falls (continuing to assume that workers are the only variable cost involved). When average product per worker begins to fall, variable cost per unit of output begins to rise. Fixed cost per unit (rent on the land in the example above) steadily falls as more bushels are produced with the same total fixed cost for land.

The combination of the persistently declining fixed-cost-per-unit curve with the U-shaped variable-unit-cost curve gives the (flatter) U-shaped total-unit-cost curve. Thus, given the prices of the factors of production, the physical production relationships determine the shape of the fixed-cost-per-unit, the variable-cost-per-unit, and the total-cost-per-unit curves in any situation. The unit-cost curves are the inverses of the physical-production curves in Figures 20-4 and 20-5.

Chapter 20 has made no use of the marginal-product curve indicated above. This curve will become the physical basis for the "marginal-cost" curve introduced in Chapter 21.

The physical productivity of varying combinations of factors of production will become of major importance again in Part 4, which considers the distribution of income—the prices received by the various factors of production for the services they render. This is because what entrepreneurs are willing and able to pay in wages, rent, and so on, depends directly on the contributions different factors make to total production, as well as on the prices at which the products can be sold. In determining unit costs of production in the present chapters, we take wages, rents, and the prices of the other factors of production as given; this means that the shapes of the various cost curves depend largely on the physical production relationships involved. In Part 4, we reverse this process and take final product prices (demand curves) as given, and then analyze entrepreneurs' demands for the various factors of production. There again, these same underlying physical production relationships will play a fundamental role in determining how many units of each factor of production it will pay entrepreneurs to hire, and how much they can afford to pay for each.

21

The Business Firm: Competitive Output and Price in the Short Run[1]

The emphasis on costs in the last chapter is justified mainly because costs influence the output and price decisions of business firms. This chapter examines how demand on the one hand and costs on the other together influence business output decisions and prices. The chapter focuses on firms in highly competitive industries, leaving until later a look at the monopolized sectors of the economy. But a good deal of the analytical core here will be equally useful when we come to the areas where lesser degrees of competition prevail.

THE THEORY OF THE FIRM

Traditionally, both economists and business advocates of the private-enterprise system have pictured the business firm as, by

---

[1] *Note to instructors:* This chapter covers the traditional neoclassical short-run "theory of the firm," using the equation of marginal cost to marginal revenue in setting output and price. For those instructors who prefer to omit it, the Preface indicates the other sections of the book which rest logically on this chapter and which should also be omitted if Chapter 21 is not assigned.

and large, trying to maximize its profits. If we accept this position, the "theory of the business firm" is a relatively simple affair.

Our "model" or "theoretical" firm wishes to maximize profits. Profits are the difference between total cost and total revenue. Hence, the firm does what it can (within the legal and moral rules of society) to maximize this difference. It tries to get customers to spend more on its own product and it tries to keep its own costs as low as possible (i.e., it tries to produce as efficiently as possible for any given level of output). Whenever the firm can increase its profits by increasing its revenues or by reducing its costs, it will try to do so. Only when it is maximizing its profits (at least to the best of its own knowledge) will the manager be satisfied. Then the firm will be in "equilibrium"—in the sense that it will not change its own policies or actions unless conditions change. Of course, external conditions (e.g., consumer demand, costs of materials, and wage rates) do change frequently, so the business firm will seldom, if ever, actually reach an equilibrium state and stay there for long. But the firm will always be aiming at this maximum-profit position in conducting its day-to-day affairs and in making its long-run planning decisions.

We know, of course, that not all firms behave this way, and at the end of this chapter we will take a more detailed look at just how much this assumption may need to be modified. But for the moment, assume that firms have a single goal of profit-maximizing, and that they go about it in an efficient way. What, then, can we say about how they would make their decisions?

THE COMPETITIVE FIRM IN THE SHORT RUN In trying to maximize its profits, the firm tries to maximize the difference between its income from sales and its costs. Since we are assuming highly competitive conditions, in which our individual firm represents only a very small part of the market and turns out a product just like its competitors', we will assume that it must take the product price as given—fixed in the market by

Table 21-1

TOTAL COST, TOTAL REVENUE, AND PROFIT

Output	Total Cost	Total Revenue	Profit
1	$ 3,000	$ 1,800	−$1,200
2	3,500	3,600	100
3	4,000	5,400	1,400
4	5,000	7,200	2,200
5	6,000	9,000	3,000
6	7,600	10,800	3,200
7	11,000	12,600	1,600
8	17,000	14,400	−2,600

total demand and supply conditions over which no one firm has any significant control. Under this assumption, our firm can ask a higher price than the one prevailing in the market. But if it does it just won't sell any goods at the higher price, since consumers can get all they want at the prevailing price from other sellers. This means that the firm sees the demand curve as a horizontal line at the prevailing market price. This assumption may seem to you rather extreme, and it is the limiting case of what economists call pure competition. But it is an instructive case with which to begin. We will drop the assumption in later chapters.

Maximum-Profit Output Shown by Total-Cost and Revenue Curves

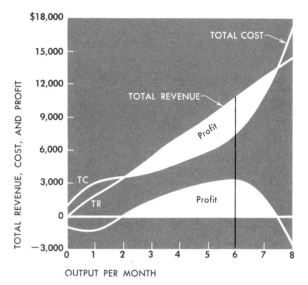

FIG. 21-1   Maximum profit is where the total-revenue curve is farthest above the total-cost curve. Potential profit range is from 2 to 7 sets per month.

Comparison of Total Costs and Total Revenue. If the hi-fi firm from Chapter 20 wants to maximize profits, it can compare its total cost with total revenue at each level of output, and thus determine the most profitable number of sets to produce. This is done in Table 21-1, where the market price is arbitrarily assumed to be $1,800. (Obviously the estimated total-revenue curve will be different at different prices for finished hi-fi sets, since total revenue is merely output multiplied by the price.) Using these data, the maximum profit output is 6 sets per month. At only 1 set per month, total revenue doesn't even cover costs. When the plant gets up to 8 sets a month, its costs shoot up so fast that they exceed even the big sales income. In between, any output is profitable, but some more so than others.

This same comparison may be made graphically, as in Figure 21-1. *TC* is total cost, plotted from the first column of Table 21-1. *TR* is total revenue, plotted from the second column. The maximum-profit output is the output where the vertical distance between the two curves is greatest—here at 6 units. The white area between the two curves shows the range over which a profit is possible. The same area is shown at the bottom of the chart, where it is easy to see where the vertical distance (height of white area) is greatest.

Marginal Analysis: Marginal Costs.   Economists and some businessmen have developed another approach to determining the maximum-profit output. It focuses on prices and costs per unit of output, which for some purposes is more convenient than the total cost–total revenue comparison above.

The businessman uses cost data for a multitude of purposes. Some of his decisions are big ones—to operate or shut down, for example. Most of his output decisions, however, are marginal ones—to take this new order at the going price or to refuse it; to cut back output 5 per cent or 10 per cent as price falls or inventory piles up. In such decisions, how much additional cost is involved in expanding output moderately, or how much is saved by cutting output a little, becomes of special interest. The concept of "marginal cost," or "incremental cost," has been developed to help in this kind of analysis.

Marginal cost is simply the *addition* or *increment* to total cost involved in expanding or contracting output by one unit. For example, going back to the radio-phonograph cost data in Table 20-1, if the total cost of producing 3 sets per month is $4,000 and that of producing 4 sets $5,000, the marginal cost of expanding production from 3 to 4 units is $1,000. That's how much *extra* it costs us to get the fourth set produced.[2]

Using this concept, we can construct a table (Table 21-2) to show marginal cost at the various levels of output in our radio plant.

Most economic adjustments are marginal adjustments of some sort. Comparison of gains and losses "at the margin"—for example, comparison of the marginal income and marginal cost associated with increasing output from 4 to 5 sets monthly—is the core of intelligent decision-making, in economics as elsewhere. The principle is the same as when you weigh the advantages of another hour's study before an exam against the disadvantages of giving up the hour's sleep. Applications abound in every field. In building a bridge, for example, the engineer must constantly weigh the advantages of getting increased strength against the related disadvantages of incurring additional weight and expense.

Maximizing Profits in the Short Run.   Table 21-3 reproduces the cost data for the radio-phonograph firm from Chapter 20, adding a column to show the marginal (incremental) cost involved in increasing output by one set at each stage. Assume now that the market price of radio consoles of the sort we make is $1,800. How many sets per month should we produce? Try to figure it out for yourself.

---

[2] Thus marginal cost is the logical counterpart of marginal product described in the Appendix to Chapter 20. Other things equal, marginal cost will be lowest when marginal product is highest, and vice versa. As more variable productive agents are added to the fixed plant, the marginal product attributable to the variable agents first rises and then falls. At given prices of the productive agents, conversely marginal cost will first fall and then rise. The full connection between these two concepts is developed in Part 4, on distribution theory.

Table 21-2

TOTAL AND MARGINAL COSTS

Output	Total Cost	Marginal Cost
1	$ 3,000	
2	3,500	$ 500
3	4,000	500
4	5,000	1,000
5	6,000	1,000
6	7,600	1,600
7	11,000	3,400
8	17,000	6,000

The answer is 6—neither more nor less. The figures for 6 sets are underscored in the table. The marginal-cost column tells how much extra is added to total costs by increasing output one more unit. On the revenue side, each unit we produce can be sold for $1,800. Since this is a purely competitive market, we can sell all we produce at the market price; we need not worry about forcing down the price by overproduction. This concept of incremental income is similar to the

Table 21-3

HYPOTHETICAL RADIO PRODUCER

Output	Fixed Cost per Unit	Variable Cost per Unit	Total Cost per Unit	Marginal Cost
1	$1,000	$2,000	$3,000	
2	500	1,250	1,750	$ 500
3	333	1,000	1,333	500
4	250	1,000	1,250	1,000
5	200	1,000	1,200	1,000
6	167	1,100	1,267	1,600
7	143	1,430	1,573	3,400
8	125	2,000	2,125	6,000

concept of marginal cost. *Economists call the $1,800 added to total revenue by each additional set sold the "marginal revenue." Marginal revenue is the extra revenue added by the production of one more unit.*

So long as producing more units adds more to total revenue than to total costs, it pays to keep on increasing output. This is the same as saying that it will pay to keep on increasing output so long as marginal revenue is larger than marginal cost. At all levels of output up to and including 6, producing another unit adds less than $1,800 to costs. But production of the seventh unit would add an extra $3,400 to costs, and only $1,800 to revenue. Clearly we would be foolish to produce the seventh unit.

What are total profits at 6 units? Total cost is about $7,600 (average unit cost of $1,267 times 6 sets). Total revenue is $10,800 (price of $1,800 per set times 6 sets). Profit is thus $3,200. This is, of course, identical to the answer obtained by comparing total costs and total revenues in Table 21-1.

The principle is: Profit will be maximized by carrying production up to the point where marginal cost equals marginal revenue (here, the price), and no further.

Ask yourself one more question, to be sure you understand why. Why wouldn't we be better off to produce 7 units instead of 6, getting the profit on the seventh, since the $1,800 price exceeds the total unit cost of $1,573 at 7 units of output? The marginal cost–marginal revenue comparison gives the answer—the seventh radio adds $3,400 to cost and only $1,800 to revenue. The fact that price is above total unit cost tells us that we can make *a* profit at the output level, but not that we will make our maximum profit at that level. An attempt to pick up the profit on a seventh set would be misguided, since it would actually involve adding more to cost than to revenue; total unit cost would be higher on all 7 units if we increase output to 7. Compute the total profit at 7 units and you'll see that it's only about $1,600 ($12,600 revenue less about $11,000 cost), much less than at 6 units.

Minimizing Losses in the Short Run.

With the market price at $1,800 we're in clover. But suppose consumer demand for high-grade hi-fi sets nose-dives, and market price falls to $1,100. It takes only a quick look at Table 21-3 to see that we're going to lose money at this price, no matter what we do. The lowest total unit cost at which we can produce is $1,200, at an output of 5 units.

What should we do to minimize our losses? One possibility would be to shut down. This way we'd lose $1,000 a month, the amount of our fixed costs, which continue next month whether we operate or not. But if we operate, producing 3, 4, or 5 units, we'll be getting $1,100 per set produced and only having to spend $1,000 per set in variable (out-of-pocket) costs. This will provide $100 per set left over to apply on our fixed costs, which we have to pay in any case. So we'd better operate, even though we lose money. By operating, we lose less than by shutting down altogether.

If the marginal cost–marginal revenue principle is a sound one, it ought to tell us now how many units to produce again this time. And it does. The answer is 5. Producing every unit up to and including the fifth adds more to revenue ($1,100) than it does to costs. Marginal revenue for the fifth unit is $1,100; marginal cost is only $1,000. But marginal cost for the sixth set is $1,600, above marginal revenue. Our total loss at a 5-set production rate figures out at $500 ($6,000 total cost less $5,500 total revenue), or only half the loss involved in shutting down completely. The principle for minimizing loss is the same as for maximizing profit: *If you operate at all, carry production up to the point where marginal cost equals marginal revenue, and no further.* Compute the loss at any other level of output, and you'll see that the rule is right.

The Decision to Shut Down in the Short Run.   Would it ever pay us to shut down in the short run? Obviously yes. If price falls below $1,000, which is the lowest variable unit cost we can manage at any output level, we'd better close up shop. Suppose price is $900. No matter how many units we produce, our income is not even going to be enough to cover our variable costs, much less provide anything to help cover the $1,000 of fixed costs. Suppose we produce 3

**Maximum Profit Output
Shown by Marginal-Cost and Revenue Curves**

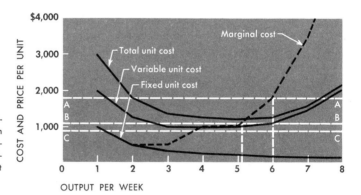

FIG. 21-2   Profit is maximized by carrying production up to intersection of marginal-revenue and marginal-cost curves—if you operate at all.

units. They will cost $4,000 but will bring in only $2,700 leaving a loss of $1,300 compared with only $1,000 if we just shut down. *At any price below the lowest variable-unit-cost point, we will minimize losses by shutting down altogether.* This doesn't contradict the marginal cost–marginal revenue principle for maximizing profits, since that principle tells us only how to do the best thing *if* we operate at all.

Graphical Analysis of Short-run Behavior.   All this discussion can readily be put in graphical form for those who like pictures better than tables. The cost curves in Figure 21-2 are plotted from Table 21-3, and are the same as in Figure 20-1 except for the addition of the marginal-cost curve. The marginal-cost curve, of course, shows the increment to total cost involved in increasing output by one unit at each stage. For example, the marginal cost involved in stepping up output from 4 to 5 units is $1,000; in going from 5 units to 6 it is $1,600.[3]

Three horizontal lines, *AA, BB,* and *CC,* have been added to show the market prices of $1,800, $1,100, and $900, respectively. These lines are the demand curves as seen by our firm when those are the prevailing market prices. The lines are also, of course, marginal-revenue curves at the respective prices, since sale of one more radio set adds just its price to our total revenue.

With this graph, we can readily determine the maximum-profit or minimum-loss output for any given market price. The principle is the same as before: It will pay to increase output so long as marginal revenue is more than marginal cost, if we operate at all. We will minimize losses by shutting down completely if price falls below our lowest variable cost per unit.

Suppose the market price is $1,800 (line *AA*). At that price the marginal-cost curve is still below marginal revenue (price) at 6 units, but above it at 7. We can tell merely by looking at the graph, therefore, that 6 units is the most profitable level of output. Since the $1,800 price line is above the total-unit-cost curve at this point, we can also tell that this is a profitable situation. The actual profit can be computed by multiplying the profit per unit ($533) by 6 units, giving the same $3,200 profit we got by using the tabular computation.

Similarly, with price at $1,100 (line *BB*), 5 units is the output that will minimize loss. Up to 5 units the marginal-cost curve is below the marginal-revenue (price) curve; at 6 units, it is above it.

And a quick glance at the $900 price situation will tell us to close down immediately. The $900 price line (*CC*) is everywhere below the variable-unit-cost curve. At $900 we can't even get enough revenue to cover variable costs, let alone accumulate anything to apply on fixed costs.

For a quick answer to the most profitable levels of output, the graphical approach has real advantages. For computing exact profit-and-loss figures, tabular data are often more satisfactory. But which you prefer really doesn't matter. The answers are the same either way.

SHORT-RUN COST CURVES AND SUPPLY CURVES

If firms try to maximize profits in the short run, we can tell from a firm's cost curves what output it will produce at any given price. The firm's marginal-cost curve will be its short-run supply curve anywhere above the minimum point on the variable-unit-cost curve. Thus, our radio firm at any price

---

[3] For mathematically inclined readers, marginal cost is the first derivative of total cost (not of total cost per unit). The marginal-cost curve will always lie below the *TUC* curve when the latter is falling, and above it when the *TUC* curve is rising, cutting *TUC* at its minimum point. In nontechnical terms, this is because the marginal cost is the increment to total cost. As long as this increment to total cost is less than the existing cost per unit, the cost per unit must be falling. As long as the increment is larger than the existing cost per unit, the cost per unit must be rising. The same reasoning holds for the relationship of the marginal-cost and variable-unit-cost curves.

below $1,000 will supply zero units. At prices from $1,000 to $1,599, it will supply 5 units. At prices from $1,600 to $3,399, it will supply 6 units. And so on up the marginal-cost curve. *The short-run marginal-cost curve is the firm's short-run supply curve.*

If this is true for all firms, it is easy to get a short-run market supply curve for any industry, by adding together the short-run supply curves (or schedules) of all the individual firms. Suppose there were 1,000 identical firms in the radio industry. Then the short-run industry supply schedule would look like Table 21-4. At each price the supply offered would be just 1,000 times the supply offered by our own little radio firm.

Table 21-4

SHORT-RUN INDUSTRY SUPPLY SCHEDULE

Price	Output of Typical Firm	Industry Output
Under $1,000	0	0
1,000-1,599	5	5,000
1,600-3,399	6	6,000
3,400-5,999	7	7,000
Over $6,000	8	8,000

Now that we have so systematically developed the short-run output behavior of a profit-maximizing firm, and have constructed the industry short-run supply schedule from the analysis, a note of warning is in order: Don't forget that our model of the precise and rational profit-maximizing firm is only a model. Do firms really try so logically and precisely to maximize their profits?

DO FIRMS TRY TO MAXIMIZE PROFITS? Anyone who has spent much time around a business concern knows that this is only a rough approximation of the way businesses behave. A variety of deviations from the simple profit-maximizing model are easy to see, even in highly competitive industries. We will look later at some further deviations likely to occur in monopolistic situations.

1. The businessman who continuously adjusted his output and prices in response to every little change in affairs outside and inside the firm would have his business in a continual state of turmoil. He might also find himself over-adjusting to small changes, and hence end up in a lower profit position as a result of his over enthusiastic adjustment endeavors. Many businessmen follow a wait-and-see attitude; their responses are often far behind what an instantaneous adjustment theory would presuppose.

2. Businessmen never know for sure what costs and demand in the future will be. They can only estimate, or sometimes merely guess—and sometimes they're wrong.

3. Cases of inefficiency in business, where better management could get production at lower costs, are easy to find—at least until competition squeezes them out.

4. The firm may find, at least temporarily, that it can't readily get the funds to undertake potentially profitable investments that require heavy cash outlays.

Use of a Profit-maximizing Model of the Firm. Where does this leave the model of a firm busily maximizing profits? Certainly any reasoning based on the assumption that every firm is striving exclusively to maximize profits at every moment should be suspect, and anyone who uses such reasoning as a description of reality deserves the scorn often heaped by the man in the street on "armchair economists." Yet through all these aberrations there is impressive evidence that the desire for profits is a dominant motive in most business concerns. Perhaps some businessmen don't carefully try to maximize profits. But it is unlikely that they consistently and knowingly adopt policies calculated to cut profits substantially below levels they could otherwise achieve.

Indeed, one of the major arguments for the competitive system is that businessmen are *forced* to act *as if* they were trying to maximize profits, whether they want to or not. Any firm that continues to operate inefficiently will be undersold in the market and will be driven either to bankruptcy or to greater efficiency. Any firm that does not respond to consumer demand will vanish from the business scene before very long. Thus, even though businessmen may not be very efficient or conscious profit-maximizers as individuals, a competitive market will force them by and large to behave the way the profit-maximizing model pictures them.

What can we conclude from these observations? Two things: First, a profit-maximizing model of the firm is likely often to be unreliable as a guide to immediate, short-run conclusions for any particular firm (for example, in answering the question: Will an increased tax on business profits be passed on immediately to consumers?). Second, the profit-maximizing model is probably a good deal more applicable in highly competitive industries than where competition is less pressing.

Bearing all these warnings in mind, we shall use an analytical model of business firms that act to maximize profits *as a first approximation* in our analysis of a competitive, private-enterprise economy. Remember, however, that here, as in every case where "theory" or a "model" is used, the model is primarily useful as a guide to the important questions to ask in analyzing any situation. No theory or model can give ready answers to real-world questions. The theory says only, *if* conditions are as they are postulated in the model, *then* the real-world results will be as described in the model. But it is up to the user to see for himself in any given case how closely the real-world problem corresponds to the model he is using. The model suggests some of the important facts to look for, some important questions to ask, some tentative conclusions to investigate.

The role of the model of the profit-maximizing firm is thus to give you a helping hand in organizing your thinking. It can be a very useful guide. But if you use it as more than that, or if you blindly accept conclusions that rest on this model, you may turn out to be very wrong indeed in any given individual case. Economic theory is an aid to independent thinking—not a substitute for it.

THE FIRM AS A BUYER OF PRODUCTIVE SERVICES

Before ending this chapter, it is important to look at the short-run output policies of the firm from a different angle. Whenever businessmen decide to produce one, ten, or a thousand units of output, they simultaneously decide to buy or hire the "inputs" of productive services needed to produce those units—labor services, raw materials, machinery, and so on.

If we liked, thus, we could do our analysis of the most profitable level of production in terms of units of productive agents used, rather than in terms of units of output. For example, to simplify, assume that our plant needs only labor and raw materials, and that these are conveniently hired in units costing $100 per unit—perhaps one worker per week plus the material he uses. For each number of units of input, there will be some corresponding output of radio sets. Thus, our cost schedules above could have been stated in terms of cost to hire varying amounts of labor plus materials input rather than in terms of producing 1, 2, 3, or more radios per week as output.

Consider the problem of how many units of input to hire each month. The marginal cost–marginal revenue principle holds here as before. So long as adding one more unit of input adds more to revenue than to cost, it pays to increase inputs and hence output. As soon as another unit of input adds more to cost than to revenue, you'd better stop expanding, because you've come to your best profit level. The marginal revenue–marginal cost principle here again tells you what is the maximum-profit or minimum-loss production level.[4]

Looking at the firm's decision-making in terms of hiring labor and other productive services is particularly useful in analyzing how wages are determined. The costs of the business firm *are* the incomes of its workers and the owners of the resources it uses. Thus, as we shall see in Part 4, these two simultaneous ways of looking at the firm's price-output decisions provide a way of integrating all of price and distribution theory. But for the time being we are interested in the firm's own adjustment to consumer demands. Hence, the analysis in terms of output, as in this chapter, is more useful.

---

[4] The marginal revenue from hiring an additional unit of variable input is based directly on its "marginal product," as described in the Appendix to Chapter 20, although of course the marginal product needs to be converted to dollar terms to become marginal revenue.

REVIEW—CONCEPTS TO REMEMBER

The essence of this chapter is the way a profit-seeking firm would try to maximize profits by carrying production up to the point where marginal cost equals marginal revenue, and no further, *if* it operates at all. Check your understanding of the following concepts:

profit maximization
marginal cost
marginal revenue

incremental cost
unit of input of
   productive services

FOR ANALYSIS AND DISCUSSION

1. From your own personal experience, would you judge that businessmen do their best to maximize profits? What kinds of evidence would you look for in making such a judgment?

2. You operate a roadside fruit stand. You have been selling raspberries at 60 cents a quart; they cost you 50 cents to produce. It is now mid-afternoon and raining. With customers scarce, you now estimate your demand scedule for the rest of the afternoon as follows:

Price	Quarts
60¢	70
55	80
50	110
45	130
40	140
35	160

You have 140 quarts on hand and no storage facilities to avoid spoilage before tomorrow. What price should you charge to maximize profits? Explain.

3. You are managing the radio plant shown in Figure 21-2, and are currently producing four sets a month. You have an order for one additional set a month, but the customer will only pay $1,050 a set, less than your minimum total cost per set. Should you accept the order? Show both graphically and through arithmetical calculations why your answer is sound.

4. Explain in common-sense language why it pays to increase production up to the point where marginal cost equals marginal revenue, and no further.

5. "A rational businessman will always disregard his fixed costs in setting his prices and current rate of output. Sunk costs are water over the dam." Do you agree with this quotation from an economics textbook? Explain fully why or why not.

6. Should businessmen be more concerned with making their companies "good citizens" in their communities or with maximizing profits?

7. A competitive firm will always maximize profits by producing at the lowest possible total unit cost. True or false? Explain.

22

Long-run Competitive Equilibrium

What economics has to say about long-run competitive behavior is more reliable than what it has to say about short-run behavior. In the short run, individual entrepreneurs may engage in all sorts of unpredictable behavior. They may mistakenly adopt inefficient production methods. They may sell below costs. They may try producing unwanted products. They may decide to accumulate cash rather than to keep their funds turning over. They may give all their workers six-month vacations with pay. In most cases, entrepreneurs probably do act roughly as if they were trying to earn the largest profits they can—but they *may* act quite differently.

In the long run in a highly competitive market, on the other hand, we can be pretty sure how businessmen will act. They will act *as if* they were trying to maximize profits—by meeting consumer demands and by producing goods at the lowest possible costs—because if they don't, competition will drive them out of business. And the long run is a period long enough for this to happen.

This is the kind of long-run competitive pressure that led Adam Smith, in his famous *Wealth of Nations,* to speak of the "invisible hand" that leads businessmen who seek only their own profits to produce the goods consumers want and to sell them at the lowest possible prices. It is the intellectual core of the support for the private-enterprise economic system today. Although a purely competitive system has never actually existed, the model of such a system has long provided a loose approximation of how a largely competitive system might work, and many observers believe that the model is a good first, albeit rough, approximation to our own system. For some, it has been a "norm" of ideal behavior against which actual economic conditions can be measured.

The main purpose of this chapter is to examine in some detail how a purely competitive system would work in terms of long-run tendencies, and to consider some of the major virtues and failings of such a system. On the basis of this examination, you can judge for yourself whether you think Adam Smith set economists and the public off on the right track with his talk about the "invisible hand" that guides a competitive system to fulfill the needs of consumers at minimum prices—or whether he gave us a bad steer.

But before looking in detail at the long-run outcome of a purely competitive system, we need to be clear on two important points that have been glossed over so far. The first is, precisely what we mean by "pure competition." The second is, just what we mean by "long-run equilibrium."

COMPETITION AND MONOPOLY

No business firm is free from competition. A.T. and T., for example, is often cited as a complete monopoly in the field of telephone communication in most communities. This is true in one sense, but if people get unhappy enough with telephoning they can write, telegraph, or radio. There are only four major firms that produce aluminum today. But quite aside from the competition among the four, for many uses steel, copper, magnesium, and other metals are potential substitutes for aluminum. Alcoa, Reynolds, Kaiser, and Olin Mathieson are acutely aware of this fact. Competition is inescapable in business.

Nevertheless, it is obvious that competition is a lot more active in some industries than it is in others. The only grocery in an isolated rural village is a good deal less exposed to competition than is the corner grocer who has Kroger and A&P supermarkets in the next block. At the competitive extreme, far from A.T. and T., we find the individual farmer producing such standardized products as wheat, corn, and hogs. He has millions of other competitors, and his product is so standardized that the buyer has no interest in who the producer is—he is interested merely in the price he has to pay. If Farmer Jones prices his No. 2 hard northern wheat at one cent a bushel more than other farmers are asking, he just won't sell any.

There is a whole spectrum of market positions between the protected monopoly position of the public utility and the extreme competition of farmers. Most of the real world lies somewhere between these two extremes, and we will look at the spectrum in detail beginning with Chapter 24. Here we want to examine how the economy would function under "pure competition"—roughly the situation of the wheat farmer above.

Pure Competition.   The essence of pure competition is that no single seller is important enough in the market to have any appreciable influence over market price. Specifically, pure competition is characterized by:

1. Many sellers, each acting independently and each so small relative to the market as to have no appreciable effect on market price.

2. An identical product, so that the consumer is indifferent as to the seller from whom he buys.[1]

3. Freedom of entry for new sellers who wish to enter the market. (This assumption is not logically necessary where (1) and (2) hold, but most economists include it in analyzing pure competition.)

The same conditions define pure competition on the buyers' side of any market.

When there are many sellers of identical products, and when no one of them *acting alone* can exert a significant influence on the market price, each producer must adjust his activities to the market. Given his costs and the market price, he will decide how much wheat to produce. But although he acts as if he has no influence on market price, in fact the *summation* of all the individual producers' actions has a great influence on market price. If prevailing costs and market price lead each individual firm to restrict output, the summation of all the thousands of individual cutbacks will drastically reduce market supply and, other things equal, will raise the price. Thus, the quantity produced and sold, and the market price, are "automatically" determined by the impersonal mechanism of the competitive market as it responds to consumer demand.

Why Study Pure Competition?   It's clear that there aren't many purely competitive industries in the modern American economy. Even agriculture, which has long been the standard example, doesn't represent quite pure competition any more, since the government has increasingly intervened to set prices and output levels. Why study pure competition, then? There are three reasons:

1. Economics is concerned especially with the over-all performance of the economic system, and with the allocation of society's resources among competing alternative uses. To get at these problems, we must have some over-all picture of the way the various parts of the economy fit together, at least as a framework for analysis and possibly as a "norm" for evaluating the actual performance of the system.

---

[1] The added assumption is also usually made that all buyers and sellers have full knowledge of prices being quoted over the entire market.

The purely competitive model, in which we assume that all markets are competitive, has a great virtue. It provides a reasonably simple and understandable picture of the way markets interrelate to channel consumer demands to producers, and of the way producers respond to those demands. Many observers, economists and others, believe that this picture also provides at least a first approximation of the "ideal" way in which a private-enterprise system ought to work. They thus use the model as a standard of comparison to ferret out those areas of the actual economy that aren't operating as well as they ought to.

Most economists agree on the usefulness of the purely competitive model in providing an understandable, over-all tool for studying the resource-allocating procedures of a market-price system. But there is a lot of disagreement on whether the purely competitive model is a proper norm against which the working of the actual economy ought to be judged. This disagreement becomes particularly sharp when public-policy measures are at stake—for example, enforcement of the Sherman Antitrust Act or enactment of labor union legislation. Remember the warning in Chapter 5 against letting models subtly slip over into becoming "norms" when you haven't really decided that they ought to be.

2. Pure competition, though almost nonexistent in its pure form, does provide a reasonably close first approximation to the behavior of important sectors of the modern economy. Most of agriculture, broad areas of retailing, wholesaling, and service establishments, and important sectors of manufacturing where moderate scale of plant is big enough for efficient production, come reasonably close to the pure-competition model. To be sure, their products are not quite identical, and any one producer usually has some control over the price at which he can sell his product. But the pressures of competition are very strong, and if he gets far out of competitive line the individual producer is likely to find himself steadily losing out in the market.

3. We have to begin somewhere, and the pure-competition case is in many respects the simplest and easiest to understand. The basic analytical tools are pretty much the same in the competitive and quasi-monopoly cases. Whether the pure-competition model is directly applicable in most cases or not, the insights gained with this case will come in handy later on, when we look at the more complex and more realistic quasi-monopolistic cases.

LONG-RUN EQUILIBRIUM AND EQUILIBRIUM TENDENCIES

Long-run equilibrium is an abstract analytical concept. Here, as with the equilibrium concept elsewhere, equilibrium means the situation that would be reached and maintained by the competitive system unless some external force came along to disturb it. For example, suppose we want to know how a purely competitive system would respond to a change in consumer demand, beginning from some equilibrium position. Assume we can hold everything else constant—the supply of productive resources, society's technological know-how, all legal and social factors—and the consumer demand for strawberries increases. The new position to which the economic system would move in response solely to the changed demand for strawberries would be its new long-run equilibrium position.

Formally, we should consider all the millions of interrelated effects throughout the economic system. But once we get far from the strawberry industry, these effects are likely to be negligible. Thus economists generally concentrate their analysis on the effects on the industry directly concerned, here the strawberry industry. This emphasis leads us to a concept of the "equilibrium of the industry," and of the firm within the industry. For some purposes we are not safe in stopping with the industry, and should instead go on to study the effects on other related industries, looking toward "general equilibrium" for the economy as a whole. For the time being, we shall concentrate on the conditions of equilibrium for the industry, and for firms within the industry.

The *immediate* (very short-run) adjustment to a higher strawberry demand might be primarily a higher price for strawberries. The *short-run* adjustment would give time for existing strawberry farmers to increase their outputs if they wished, but not to vary their fixed costs. In the *long run* there would be time for new firms to move into strawberry-producing, for existing firms to vary their whole scale of operations, and for all productive factors in the economy to adjust fully to this shift in demand. Even in the long run we assume that no other changes except the new strawberry demand interfere with the full working out of the adjustment process. We hold "other things equal" analytically—even if they don't stay that way in the real world. Long-run equilibrium is the new stable position finally reached by the industry, other things being held unchanged except as they may change in response to the increase in strawberry demand.

Of course, in the real world there is no way to hold "other things constant." And the real world never reaches a state of economic equilibrium. Before farmers can get thoroughly adjusted to this increase in demand for strawberries, consumers switch to raspberries. Or scientists invent a new, cheaper way of producing strawberries. Or war may be declared. Or any one of a million other things may happen to set new adjusting forces in motion before equilibrium is reached in response to the shift in strawberry demand. Yet this analytical device of isolating the effects of a particular event is the best way we have for getting at them in a real world so complex, interrelated, and ever-changing as ours is.

When we talk about long-run equilibrium, therefore, we are talking about the new situation *toward which* the industry is moving and which would ultimately be reached if no other forces interfered. Long-run analysis should give us clues to the *ultimate* effects of particular changes—for example, the ultimate effects of a new tax on cigarettes, of increased demand for sugar, of improved technology in quick-freezing vegetables. Will the lower costs of improved quick-freezing technology be passed on to the consumer? Will more or less frozen food be produced and sold? Will more or fewer workers be employed in the frozen-food industry? In agriculture? Analysis of the way a competitive system moves toward new equilibrium positions gives us strong clues to the answers to such questions in a competitive world.

LONG-RUN EQUILIBRIUM:
THE CONTINUOUS SEARCH
FOR PROFITS

The mainspring of the private-enterprise economy is the businessman's continuous search for profits. This does not imply that the proprietor of the local grocery spends every waking hour worrying about how to squeeze the last nickel out of his business; or that the farmer doesn't decide to go visit his friends some afternoons when he could be installing a new fence. But it does imply that, by and large, the desire to earn profits is a dominant one, and that, by and large, business concerns will orient their policies predominantly toward those production and price policies that will produce the largest profits for the company.

In the short run, some costs are fixed. The businessman's search for profits is limited by this fact. He can only make the best possible adjustment to market demand by varying output from his existing plant and other fixed productive agents. If he has hired a group of employees on an annual basis, he must make the best of the arrangement until the end of the year. With his given plant and managerial force, he can expand production only so much.

In the long run, however, all costs become variable. Existing plant and equipment wear out, and new plant and equipment can be added. Wage and salary contracts come up for renewal. Long-term contracts for supplies and materials expire. Long-term bonds and short-term bank borrowing come due for payment or refinancing. With all costs variable, the entrepreneur is completely free in making his output decisions. He can expand, contract, change the nature of his productive processes, or go out of business altogether.

Thus, in the long run, firms will move into or drop out of any purely competitive industry until expectations of profits or losses have been substantially eliminated—until it is no longer possible for anyone to better his position by moving into or out of the industry.[2] Firms will move into the industry as long as the expected market price is above the minimum point on the firm's expected total-unit-cost curve. If the entrepreneur expects market price to average around $1 on widgets and he figures he can build and operate a plant to turn out widgets at a minimum cost of 90 cents, he will enter the industry. If his calculations show a planned minimum cost of $1.10, he's unlikely to set up shop.

Thus, as long as the expected market price is above the expected minimum cost of producing a commodity, firms will move into the industry. Output will be increased, and the price will gradually be forced down to about the minimum-

---

[2] Remember that a "normal," or "going," rate of return on investment is included in the costs of each firm.

cost point. As long as expected market price is below the minimum expected cost of producing the commodity, firms will gradually drop out of the industry, output will decline, and price will gradually rise toward the minimum-cost level. *Under pure competition, with firms free to leave and enter the industry, market price cannot in the long run stay higher or lower than the minimum cost of producing the commodity. This is the long-run equilibrium price and output level toward which the industry will move.*

Three points need special emphasis here.

1. It is *expected* market prices and production costs that matter. Change is the essence of economic life. Past and present prices and costs matter only insofar as they provide evidence to the businessman of what the future will be like. If you are deciding whether to drop out of the widget business and move to the gadget business, the prices and costs that interest you are the ones that will prevail after you have made the shift. Unless you are clairvoyant, you will probably pay a good deal of attention to the past in making these future estimates. But many a business fortune has been made by seeing that the future will be different from the past and present. The man who invested in the profitable buggy industry in 1910 is in sad shape today if he stuck with his 1910 cost-price data. The man who writes off today's new products because present costs at the developmental stage far exceed obtainable market price is clearly running a big risk by so using present costs and prices as guides to the future.

2. Any alert businessman will tell you that it is the long pull that matters. The businesses that last and pay good dividends to their shareholders year after year are seldom out to "turn a fast buck." They are the ones that hold back new products until they have worked out all the bugs, even though short-run profits are foregone. They are the ones who say that the customer is right, even when they're burned up at his unreasonable demands on return privileges. To assert that most businesses try to maximize profits each day, or month, or even each year would be naïve indeed. But this is not to say that the continuous search for profits is not pervasive in the competitive areas of the business world.

3. In assuming pure competition, we assume not only that each firm is too small to influence market price significantly, but also that there are no artificial barriers to the free movement of firms and resources into and out of the industry on a par with those already there. This assumption, like the others of pure competition, is clearly an extreme one that is seldom found true in its pure form. But, like the others, it is often approximately true, and it can serve as part of the purely competitive analytical model, subject to the same warnings that apply to all other theoretical models.

Competitive Equilibrium—The Firm and the Industry.

The business firm is in long-run equilibrium when there is no incentive for it to increase or decrease its output, either by varying utilization of existing plant or by changing the scale of plant. This equilibrium will be reached when (1) the firm is producing in the most efficient way available (otherwise there would be an advantage in shifting to more efficient operations), and (2) market price is equal to the least-cost point on the cost curve for that most efficient scale of enterprise. In this equilibrium position, both actual and potential profits have been eliminated by competition (remember that costs include a "normal" return on investment), and the firm will continue using just the same amount of productive resources as it is now.

The entire industry is in long-run equilibrium when each firm is in equilibrium and there is no incentive for firms either to enter or leave the industry. We can thus define long-run equilibrium either in terms of movement of firms or of movement of productive resources. In long-run equilibrium, there is no incentive for firms or for productive resources to enter or leave the industry. There is no incentive for entrepreneurs to hire more or fewer resources in the industry. Owners of productive resources (including people who sell their own labor services) have no incentive to enter or leave the industry, since the returns they can earn there are just about what they can earn in comparable circumstances in other industries—comparable working conditions and security for labor, comparable risk for capital investment, and so on.

Survival of the Fittest and Pressures Toward Cost Minimization.

The competitive market is an impersonal arbiter of who survives and who vanishes from the business scene. With a perfectly standard product, such as oats, the buyer is indifferent to who the producer is. He will pay the market price, and no more. Any farmer who is so inefficient that his production cost per bushel is above the market price simply takes a loss, and in due course will vanish from the scene unless he improves his efficiency or receives a subsidy from someone. The fact that he may be a hard-working, God-fearing farmer with a wife and six small children is irrelevant in the eyes of the market. If his neighbor is a thoroughly unpleasant individual who throws stones at small children and refuses to contribute to the community chest but nonetheless produces oats at 10 cents less per bushel, his neighbor will still prosper in the market. In long-run equilibrium, only those who can produce at a cost as low as market price will survive, and this price will be no higher than the least-cost point on the cost curve of firms using the most efficient methods.

At any time, any industry obviously includes firms of widely varying efficiency, with different levels of profits and losses. This situation is partially explained by the dynamic nature of the economic world. Some firms are on the way up, some on the way down. Partly it is due to the fact that many industries are far from being purely competitive; the firms do not have free access to markets and technological know-how. *But if a purely competitive long-run equilibrium position were actually attained, although there might still be differences among concerns the lowest total-unit-cost points of all firms would be the same.*

It is easy to see that in the long run inefficient firms will be eliminated by competition. But it would be unreasonable to assume that all firms become identical. Some entrepreneurs are more efficient than others. Some firms are located near good markets and pay high rents, whereas others are more distant but pay lower rents. Some firms are small, and obtain efficiency through close personal supervision; others are large, and count on mass-production methods to provide low costs. Such differences may exist in long-run equilibrium. It is not necessary that all firms be identical or have identical cost curves. It is only necessary that the method of production used by each permit it to produce at a total unit cost as low as its competitors. Persistent differences between firms are consistent with uniform minimum total unit costs because there may be compensating advantages and disadvantages.

For example, suppose that one manager of a textile firm is more effective in handling men and organizing production than any other man in the industry. His firm makes substantial savings that are not available to other producers. Won't this firm continue to make a profit even in the long run, and won't its costs remain below the costs of other firms, since none of the others can duplicate its efficiency? The answer is no. When the manager is hired, his firm will have to pay him a higher salary than other managers receive in order to keep him away from other firms; his salary will be bid up until it is higher than that of a less efficient manager by roughly the differential advantage of his services. If the entrepreneur himself is the efficient manager, he must charge as a cost a salary for himself equal to what he would be able to get in alternative opportunities; this "implicit" or opportunity cost would be the compensating factor. This is true for all productive resources.

Illustration of Response to an Increase in Demand. Suppose that the purely competitive desk-blotter industry is in long-run equilibrium and that consumer demand for blotters increases. How will the industry respond?

The immediate effect will be improved profit opportunities for the firms already in the industry. The *short-run* adjustment will involve the following steps: (1) The price of blotters will rise. (2) Each firm will increase its output, since with a higher price it is now profitable to produce more blotters.[3] (This is a move up along the industry short-run supply curve.) (3) As output increases, prices will fall back somewhat, but will probably stay above the original level because in the short run output from existing firms can be increased only moderately to meet the higher demand. (4) In the new short-run equilibrium, price will be higher, output larger, and profits in the industry greater than before the increase in demand.

This short-run adjustment is pictured in Figure 22-1. The left-hand portion shows the short-run aggregate supply of desk blotters (S^1S^1), the initial demand

---

[3] The exact increase in output by each firm in the short run and hence the exact slope of the short-run supply curve depend on the marginal analysis of the following footnote. This more exact information is not necessary for the general argument.

(D^1D^1), and the new increased demand (D^2D^2). The increased demand pushes up the price from $.06 to $.08, and calls forth increased production from the firms already in the industry—from 50,000 to 62,500 blotters. This increase results from the independent actions of the many purely competitive firms producing blotters.

Increased Demand: Adjustment Before Entry of New Firms

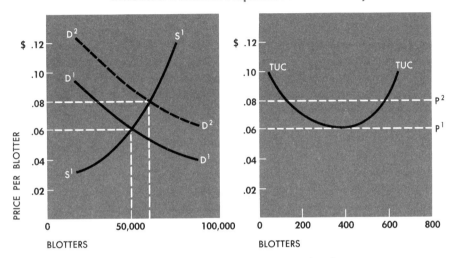

FIG. 22-1   Increased demand (D^2D^2) raises the market price and makes increased output profitable for the individual firm.

As seen by any individual firm, the increase in demand produces a higher price, which makes it profitable to produce more blotters. In Figure 22-1,[4]

---

[4] The exact pattern of short-run adjustment by the typical firm in the industry can be indicated through the marginal cost–marginal revenue adjustment mechanism of Chapter 21. When price rises to $.08, as shown in Figure 22-1, the new higher price will interest the firm's marginal-cost curve at a larger output than before. This is shown in the accompanying diagram, which is simply the right-hand portion of Figure 22-1 with the marginal-cost curve added. At the original price of $.06, the firm would produce 400 units. At $.08, the most profitable output will rise to 500 units. The firm's profit at the higher price is shown by the light blue area. As each firm increases output along its marginal-cost curve, industry output increases along the short-run industry supply curve in Figure 22-1, which is merely the summation of all the individual-firm marginal-cost curves.

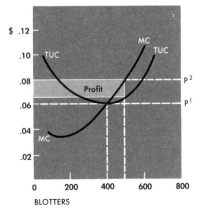

the right-hand portion of the chart shows the position of a typical firm after the price increase induced by increased demand. With price at $.08, the profit picture is bright.

But this situation is obviously unstable. Not only will existing firms want to increase output to take further advantage of the new price, but new firms will be attracted to the industry by the generous profits available. As new firms enter and productive capacity is expanded, the industry supply curve (*SS*) will gradually move to the right; more will be produced at the same price as more resources move into the blotter industry.

With this expansion of output, the price of blotters will gradually fall back toward its original level. If unlimited productive resources can be attracted without having to pay more for them (that is, if new firms can enter without bidding up costs in the blotter industry), the new long-run equilibrium will be back at the original price but with more blotters being produced. Actually, however, the entrance of new firms will probably raise costs for all firms, as higher payments are necessary to attract labor, materials, and other resources from other industries. As the price of the product falls back and costs rise, profits are gradually squeezed out. When the price is again equal to the anticipated lowest total unit cost of a new firm, there will be no further inducement for new firms to enter. The new equilibrium will probably be at somewhat higher costs and price than originally, with a substantially larger output.

These long-run adjustments are shown in Figure 22-2 on page 416. S^2S^2 is the new short-run aggregate supply curve after new firms have had time to come into the industry. Under these conditions, supply and demand are equal at a price of $.07 per blotter, with an output of 70,000 blotters in the industry as a whole. This is the new long-run industry equilibrium. The position of the typical firm is now changed, as shown in the right-hand part of the figure. Its cost curves have risen, and the price it receives is greater than before the increase in demand, but less than when the first impact of that demand was felt. That is, price rose from $.06 to $.08 and then fell back to $.07. In the new equilibrium, the typical firm is again producing the same amount as before, just at its lowest total-unit-cost point.[5] But since there are more firms than before, the aggregate output of the industry is much greater than it was initially. In response to their increased demand, consumers are getting 20,000 more blotters and are getting blotters at the lowest price that will cover costs. But they have to pay $.01 more per blotter because that much more was necessary to attract more productive resources from other uses into blotter-making.

---

[5] Figure 22-2 shows the new equilibrium output of the firm identical with the old—i.e., the new average-cost curve is merely raised by $.01 for each level of output. This will be the result if the costs of all factors of production rise in the same proportion. This need not, of course, be the case, and the particular type of cost increase shown is not important for the basic analysis of the industry's response to an increase in demand.

The adjustments following a *decrease* in demand would be the exact reverse. In the short run, price would fall and firms in the industry would suffer losses. After some firms had been eliminated, price would rise back toward its original level, to a new equilibrium at the lowest point on the new total-unit-cost curve. Consumers would be getting fewer blotters, possibly at a lower price than before the decrease in demand if the smaller number of productive resources could be hired at lower prices.

Increased Demand: Adjustment After Entry of New Firms

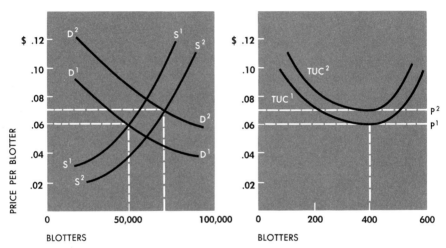

FIG. 22-2   Increased demand draws new firms into industry and produces new equilibrium for the firm and the industry at price of 7 cents.

"Constant-Cost" and "Increasing-Cost" Industries.   If an industry is very small, its chances of expanding output without bidding up productive service prices (wages, raw-material prices, and so on) may be good. Even if the industry is a large one, in the long run expanding output may not encounter substantially rising costs. If we assume that the total spendable income of society is constant, then more spending on blotters will mean less spending on something else—say books. Thus, the expanding blotter industry can get needed workers and materials previously employed by the now contracting book industry. Insofar as productive resources are relatively unspecialized (that is, are usable in one industry as well as the other—for example, common labor), this shift can be made easily and without appreciable change in the prices paid by the expanding industry. But if the blotter industry needs specialized resources (e.g., skilled machinists) who are not available from the contracting book industry, it will probably have to bid up the wages of machinists to induce more workers away from other industries.

Thus the degree of specialization of resources needed, more than the size of the industry, is the critical factor in the shape of the long-run industry supply curve, though the two are often closely related. If we make the long run long enough to permit retraining of workers and shifts in production of raw and semi-finished materials, the vast majority of industries can expand output over a wide range with only negligible increases in long-run costs. If these possibilities are not admitted, then most expanding industries will soon meet rising costs.

Industries that face rising costs as output expands are called "increasing-cost" industries; those that can expand without rising costs are called "constant-cost" industries. Actually, most industries are probably constant-cost industries over some range of output and increasing-cost industries thereafter, as they bulk larger and larger in the total economy. The safest general assumption for most problems (say in analyzing the effect of increased consumer demand for shoes, or of a tax on bread) is probably that of slightly increasing long-run costs, though the facts of each case should be considered individually. In any case, the importance of the problem to the consumer should be obvious. More output in increasing-cost industries can be obtained only by paying a higher price; increased demand for the product of a constant-cost industry can be met without any increase in the long-run equilibrium price.

Fluctuations about Long-run Equilibrium of the Industry. Adjustments toward long-run equilibrium do not actually progress with the smoothness implied in the preceding sections. Too many firms may enter a profitable industry, so that by the time they are turning out finished products the market price has dropped below cost. Too many firms may then withdraw, producing the opposite effects. Agriculture, with its annual revision of production plans and its relative flexibility as between different crops, is a leading example. Fluctuations of this kind are an important example of how faulty entrepreneurial anticipations may intervene in the processes of adjustment toward long-run equilibrium of the industry. Faulty anticipations may, on the other hand, slow up the adjustment process instead of exaggerating it. Given enough time, these faulty anticipations will usually even out toward a long-run equilibrium position.[6]

Another real-world reason the long-run equilibrium may not be reached is that "other things" do not remain constant. Consumer demand changes again before the adjustments are more than well started. Technology changes. Prices of productive factors vary. But for each significant change in these given circumstances, we can figure out what the resulting changes in the long-run equilibrium position would be.

---

[6] Under some conditions, if entrepreneurs overshoot in their production adjustments long-run equilibrium will never be reached. Instead of converging toward long-run equilibrium, the output of the industry will move into wider and wider fluctuations. For the moment, however, we need not be concerned about this case of explosive oscillatory behavior.

EQUILIBRIUM OF A COMPETITIVE ECONOMY   So far we have looked at only one industry at a time. This is commonly known as "partial-equilibrium" analysis—analyzing part of the economy while holding the rest constant. For many purposes, this procedure is satisfactory—for example, in analyzing the impact of a new excise tax on sugar. But for others we want to look at the whole economy. This broader approach is what economists call "general-equilibrium" analysis.

Suppose the entire pattern of consumer demands for the economy have frozen, and a full adjustment were worked out in a purely competitive economy. What would be the main characteristics of the resulting equilibrium situation? These were suggested above, when we considered the long-run equilibria of individual purely competitive industries.

1. Competition will have forced the price of every commodity down to the lowest total cost of production that is consistent with known technology and with the prices of productive resources used in the industry. Economic profits will have been eliminated.

2. All productive resources in the economy will be employed in those industries where their contribution to fulfilling consumer demands is greatest. If any productive resource were otherwise employed, some entrepreneur, seeking profits, would bid it away to an industry where it could contribute more to satisfying consumer demands as measured by the dollars that consumers spend.

3. All owners of productive resources (including labor) will be earning the maximum return consistent with consumer demands for final products and consistent with the owner's own preferences as to type of occupation. They will earn this maximum when productive resources are allocated as indicated in (2). The costs of business firms are the incomes of workers and resource owners.

4. Allocation of productive resources between consumer-goods and capital-goods production will match the division of incomes between consumption spending and saving. This condition follows from our earlier assumption of a stable economy with constant total income. As we saw in Part 2, this point becomes much more complex in a fluctuating economy.

"The Invisible Hand."   Such is the case for pure competition. Entrepreneurs, seeking their own profits, try to produce what will sell best on the market and produce it at the lowest cost. Consumers, expressing their preferences through market demands, determine what commodities can be sold at what prices. And resource owners, deciding in what industries and at what jobs they prefer to work, maximize their own incomes, thereby partially determining the costs at which different commodities can be produced. In the end, entrepreneurs organize the resources of society so as to produce the things that consumers want most, in the most efficient way consistent with the preferences of resource owners as to occupation. Everyone looks out for his own interests. The result is an organization of society's scarce resources that looks amazingly as if it had been guided by some invisible hand for the welfare of society as a whole.

Look at the results in a little more detail. In a free society we can reasonably assume that how each individual spends his income gives a reasonably good picture of his preferences. If he buys something for a dollar, we can infer that he prefers that article to anything else he might have bought with the dollar. Thus, if he spends a dollar for a necktie we can assume that he would rather have the necktie than anything else that might have been produced for him with a dollar's worth of productive resources.

Similarly, we can reasonably assume that if John Smith takes one job in preference to another, he prefers the one he takes. In this purely competitive world, the wages entrepreneurs are prepared to offer him will reflect both consumer demands for things he can help produce and his own skills and capabilities. He takes his pick among the available jobs. If one job is in coal-mining and he doesn't like being underground, he will probably refuse to dig coal unless the wage is considerably higher than for cabinet-making or store-clerking. If many people dislike coal-mining, their attitude will be reflected in the costs of mining coal, and in the allocation of society's resources between coal-mining and other industries.

With millions of consumers and millions of owners of productive resources, each with his own preferences, the profit-seeking entrepreneur and the free market settle these myriad differences by balancing them out at the margin in the market. Each consumer allocates his spendable income among the various commodities available, so as to maximize the total satisfaction he gets. This maximum will occur when he cannot get more satisfaction by shifting the last dollar spent on any commodity to another. Each resource owner, faced with many employment possibilities, balances out their relative attractiveness at the margin in terms of money return and other considerations, including the value he puts on leisure. No individual consumer or resource owner has any appreciable influence over what gets produced and how much of it, but in the mass they determine the allocation of society's resources among all possible alternative uses. Individual incomes, outputs, and prices are simultaneously determined. And at the center of the process, trying to buy cheap and sell dear, is the entrepreneur, continually in search of profits and thereby (perhaps unwittingly) providing the organizing service that merges and compromises all these millions of different interests.

PURELY COMPETITIVE ECONOMY—EVALUATION The case for a purely competitive economy is an impressive one. If we want consumer demands as reflected in the market to guide what shall be produced, this impersonal system looks good. If we want resource owners to be free to choose where, when, and for whom they work, the system also looks good in the way it reflects these preferences impersonally in the costs of producing different goods. Over-all, if we want to avoid authoritarian control over what gets produced, where we work, and how we invest our savings, the purely competitive private-enterprise system offers a "non-political" way of making the extremely complex and interrelated decisions and compromises required among the millions of different interests involved.

Can we do better than Adam Smith's "invisible hand," the profit motive in competitive markets? Still assuming that pure competition might actually be attained for the entire economy and still putting aside the problem of business fluctuations, what are the drawbacks, if any, to the purely competitive economic system? Several have been suggested.[7]

Income Distribution and the Allocation of Resources.   In a purely competitive economy, there would be a sort of "consumers' sovereignty" over what got produced and how productive resources were used. It would be a "one dollar, one vote" system—not a "one person, one vote" system such as we have in our political affairs. In the dollar-vote system the rich man has a lot of votes. With unequal incomes, steam yachts may be produced while millions are underfed and ill-clothed, all quite consistently with consumers' sovereignty in a purely competitive economy.

Since income distribution is a controlling factor in the allocation of society's resources under a purely competitive economy, how incomes are distributed becomes a vital question. This is the main subject of Part 4, and a complicated question it is. But a rough indication of the answer for a purely competitive system has been suggested above. Workers and other resource owners would get paid what their productive services are worth to entrepreneurs who are trying to make profits by satisfying consumer demands. The entrepreneur will hire additional workers, or other productive resources, as long as the additional cost is less than the additional revenue obtained through increasing output. Thus, entrepreneurs will bid up the wages of any grade of labor to roughly the marginal contribution a worker of that grade makes to the revenue of the business. This net addition, usually called "marginal productivity," provides a rough measure of the "economic contribution" of the worker, or other productive resource.

In a stable, purely competitive economy, every man's income would rest on the "economic contribution" made by his own services or those of his property. If the worker's primary desire is for money, he will be drawn to the job where the marginal productivity of his labor (and hence his "economic contribution") is the greatest. Non-human productive resources will move in the same way, with a similar income result. Thus, the distribution of incomes according to the "economic contributions" of productive resources in their most remunerative

---

[7] A comparison of these results with the type of "mixed" economy now existing in the United States is found in Chapters 24-26. A comparison with quite different types of economic systems is included in Chapters 43 and 44.

employments, and the allocation of resources in accordance with consumer money demands, are merely two sides of the same process.

Some people argue that such an income distribution is an eminently just and efficient arrangement. Reward according to "economic contribution," they say, is the soundest and fairest system. It provides both incentives and equity for all.

Whether or not this is so you can decide for yourself. Under a purely competitive system, incomes would still be unequally distributed. (1) Some people receive large incomes from inherited or accumulated property, whereas most of us have to get along on what we can earn. (2) Productive abilities of individuals vary greatly. (3) Individuals have unequal oportunities to develop and utilize their potential capacities even in the absence of monopolistic restriction, partly because of the inequalities that already exist. (4) Some people work harder and longer than others.

Most modern societies act to reduce income inequalities by their governmental tax and spending policies. For the moment, however, let us accept the distribution of income as given. In a stable, purely competitive economy, would there be any failings in the response of the system to the money demands of consumers?

The Problem of Minimum Size for Efficient Production. Pure competition requires that no one seller be large enough to have appreciable influence over market price. If he gets very big, there is a danger that he may react to increased consumer demand by putting up price and trying to shut out new competitors, rather than by expanding output.

This requirement means that there have to be lots of firms in every industry. How, then, can we talk about pure competition in many of the big mass-production industries that comprise only a few huge firms? Take the flat-glass industry, for example. Most of the evidence suggests that eight or ten huge furnaces and glass-making tanks, together with appropriate modern rolling equipment, can furnish all the flat glass the economy can use at peak production levels for the foreseeable future. Transportation costs are high for glass, so actually not more than half of these plants are in active competition in any one part of the country. Older methods of making flat glass are still usable, but only at substantially higher costs than the modern methods.

Representatives of the glass industry argue that more than a few major firms in the flat-glass industry would hurt the consumer far more than they would help him, because modern low-cost production methods can be used only if the market is served by a small number of large companies. The same argument is used by many other modern, highly mechanized, mass-production industries.

Even in small concerns, there is sometimes a conflict between competition and productive efficiency. For example, in a small town one large A&P supermarket may be able to sell at a lower price than would be forthcoming if the market were divided among four local grocers.

Where there are important economies of large-scale production that are unobtainable with a competitive number of firms, the public is faced with a difficult choice. Should we insist on competition even at a somewhat higher production cost than could be obtained under a monopoly arrangement—or should we tolerate the monopoly and hope that the lower price theoretically obtainable with large-scale production will in fact be passed on to consumers? This is one of the central problems of public policy in the economic area, and we will return to it in Chapter 27.

Resource Allocation When Social Costs Differ from Private Costs.

To get the proper allocation of resources among different products, the price of each product to the consumer should cover the cost of producing the product. In some cases, there are hidden costs that are not paid by the producer and hence do not enter into the commodity's price, but are borne nevertheless involuntarily by the rest of society. In such cases, price is lower than it should be and output is larger than is socially justifiabie.

One of the commonest examples is the smoke and dirt problem associated with many industrial plants. The smoke and dirt represent real costs to residents of the vicinity—through higher cleaning and painting bills, possibly through impaired health, and certainly through lessened contact with sunshine and fresh air. Yet these costs don't enter into the firm's accounting costs of producing its product. The added cost to society of the plant's dirt and smoke isn't included in the manufacturer's price to his consumers. There are "social costs" not included in the manufacturer's "private" costs.

The converse may also occur, where society gets special benefits from a producer for which it does not pay in the price of his products. Here a common example is in soil-conservation practices in agriculture. Suppose you own farm land along a stream, and you carefully plant and terrace your property to prevent erosion. This costs money. Everyone downstream from you benefits from your outlays through the decreased likelihood of floods. Yet you have no way of collecting from them in the revenues you receive from the sale of your product.

Divergences between "private" and "social" costs are widespread. They may not be very important in most industries, but in some instances they clearly are. Divergences between private and social revenues appear to be somewhat less common. But both represent instances where a purely competitive system would fail to produce an "ideal" pattern of resource allocation, from society's viewpoint.

Imperfect Information and Resource Immobility.

For the purely competitive system to work well, consumers must be well informed about the goods and services that are available at different prices, and resource owners must be well informed on the employment opportunities that are open to them. Farm workers in Montana may know nothing of the shortage of laborers in Detroit's auto assembly plants. Information may be imperfect even within the same occupation.

Stenographers in Chicago may not know about much better jobs of the same type in St. Louis.

If the Montana farm worker knows about the auto jobs in Detroit and decides to stay in Montana, even at lower pay, his decision is perfectly consistent with "ideal" resource allocation under pure competition. The competitive system aims to reflect people's preferences among types of work as well as among consumption goods. But if the farmer stays in Montana because he just doesn't know about a better job in Detroit that he would have preferred had information been available, the situation is different. Then imperfect knowledge has blocked complete competitive adjustment of resources to consumer demands. The farmer is worse off as an individual. And too many of society's resources are being allocated to producing wheat in Montana, too few to producing cars in Detroit.

The same malallocation results if resources are immobile, even though information is freely available. If our farmer has a big family and no savings, he may be quite unable to take the better Detroit job, no matter how badly he wants it. The cost of getting from Montana to Michigan, of supporting his family between jobs, and of going through a retraining period may make the change utterly impossible. Yet both the farmer and society would be better off if he could somehow get over the hump into the new industrial job.

Both imperfect information and imperfect mobility are widespread in the modern economy, especially among the lower-income groups. They both block the economy from carrying out the wishes of both consumers and resource owners.

Competitive Equilibrium in an Unstable Economy. What remains of the idea of general competitive equilibrium if we drop the assumption of a stable level of total income for the economy? Not much, may be your answer. Certainly cumulative upward and downward swings in the over-all level of economic activity imply that there is no point where the system will come to rest. Any precise notion of purely competitive equilibrium, like the model developed in this chapter, is inapplicable.

Yet the basic forces allocating resources toward the competitive result would remain in a purely competitive economy. Resources would continuously move toward the latest anticipated patterns of consumer demand, unstable as these anticipations were. Uncertainty would be much greater for entrepreneurs and resource owners—the pattern of their response to shifting consumer demands would be correspondingly less certain. But if we compare this situation with a partially monopolized system, the basic competitive forces allocating resources would still be strong.

The greatest breakdown of the resource-allocating mechanism in an unstable economy comes in the allocation between consumer goods and capital goods. The uncertainties of a fluctuating economy show up especially in fluctuating investment decisions. But this breakdown is part of the process of business booms and depressions, as we saw in Part 2. It is not peculiarly attached to either monopoly or competition. In broad outline, the basic allocative mechanism of the competitive system continues even in an unstable economy.

REVIEW—CONCEPTS TO REMEMBER

Be sure you have a firm grasp of the new analytical concepts introduced in this chapter:

pure competition	equilibrium tendencies
long-run equilibrium	constant-cost industry
equilibrium of the firm	increasing-cost industry
equilibrium of the industry	social costs
general equilibrium	private costs

FOR ANALYSIS AND DISCUSSION

1. "A purely competitive economic system would be ideal." Do you agree? Why or why not?

2. Suppose a tax of 1 cent per blotter is imposed on all blotter producers. Beginning from the situation in Figure 22-1, with price P^1P^1 and demand D^1D^1, trace through the adjustment to a new equilibrium.

3. "Under pure competition, the consumer is king. Prices can never stay for long above the minimum cost of producing any article." Is this quotation sound?

4. Under a purely competitive system, what incentive, if any, would remain for businessmen to do an efficient job, since competition would eliminate profits?

5. As a cigarette purchaser, would you prefer the industry to be one of increasing, constant, or decreasing long-run costs (assuming for the moment that the industry approaches pure competition)? Explain your answer carefully.

6. "Most people would agree that a dollar means more to a poor man than to a rich man. Since this is so, an economic system that merely reacts to the number of dollars spent is a grossly unfair system in the way it allocates resources." Do you agree or disagree? If you disagree, how might you modify the system to get around the problem indicated?

7. Suppose you are part-owner of a steel company. The city government asks you to install expensive smoke-control equipment in your mill to eliminate an alleged smoke nuisance which the mill has been creating. The cost will be $5 million, and most of your competitors in other cities have no such smoke eliminators. Would you agree to install the equipment? If you were a citizen in the community, would you favor a city ordinance requiring the mill to install the smoke eliminator?

Agriculture—
A Case Study
in Competition

Agriculture is the area of the American economy that comes closest to the model of pure competition. For most major farm products—wheat, corn, cotton, hogs, and many others—substantially the conditions of pure competition prevail, except insofar as the government has stepped in to alter them. How well has substantially pure competition worked in agriculture? What accounts for the far-reaching government intervention in agriculture to help solve "the farm problem"? In fact, is there any special "farm problem" that the forces of competition would not resolve adequately if left alone to work themselves out?

CHANGING FORTUNES
IN AGRICULTURE

Some historical background will help you understand the present situation. Back in colonial days, farming was the backbone of the American economy. As late as the Civil War, half of all Americans were in agriculture. But take a look back at Figure 2-2. This percentage has dropped steadily. It has been below 10 per cent since 1950,

425

and is still sliding. Of course total farm output has risen steadily with the growth in population. For the nation, it was more than double the 1900 level by 1960. But as a percentage of g.n.p. it has declined every decade. As America has become richer, we have spent an ever smaller percentage of our income on agricultural products.

Add on two more big facts and you have a summary of farm history in the United States over the last century. First, rapid technological advance has meant that more and more food could be produced by fewer and fewer farmers. In 1940 one farmer could feed 8 people; by 1960 he could feed more than 16. In 1940 one farmer could harvest 27 acres; by 1960 more than double that. More tractors and trucks, electrification, new fertilizers, hybrid seed, modern chemicals, better farming methods, and improved disease control add up to a rate of technological progress even faster than that in industry. Over the past quarter-century, output per man-hour has risen at the phenomenal rate of around 6 per cent in agriculture, compared to a little over 3 per cent in manufacturing and considerably less in the service industries. At this rate, fewer farmers could take care of even a rapidly expanding demand.

The other big fact about changing fortunes in agriculture is its high susceptibility to economic instability. In booms, agriculture rides high, but in depressions the bottom falls out. World Wars I and II, plus the Korean War, provided the biggest agricultural booms of modern times. Prices for wheat, corn, cotton, and hogs soared, far higher than those of industrial products. Farm land values reflected this prosperity. War demand helped, but even in peacetime booms agriculture has gained relatively more than the rest of the economy.

But the depression of the 1930's was the other side of the picture. Farm prices fell to 44 per cent of 1929 levels, but mortgage costs and taxes stayed up. Demand for many crops was insufficient to pay even for harvesting them. Mortgage foreclosures swept the country, until in desperation farmers in the Midwest began a wave of forcible resistance to foreclosures. Farm money incomes plummeted below subsistence levels, and many farm families survived only by living off their land.

With industrial depression, urban jobs were hard to find and there was little point in going to the city for work. Population "backed up" on the farms in disguised unemployment; millions of workers earned scarcely enough to avoid starvation. Farm incomes hovered below $200 per capita, and at least half the nation's farm families averaged annual money incomes of $500 or less for the decade. Desperately fighting for income, farmers continued to *expand* their output, helped by continued technological advance and by Henry Wallace's newly developed hybrid corn. By 1939, total farm output was one-third above 1929 prosperity levels. But farm incomes and prices were still at pre-World War I levels.

The depression decade of the thirties pointed up a significant difference between agriculture and industry. In industry, depression sends production and employment down, but prices fall more moderately; this response reflects the widespread industrial tendency to sacrifice volume to price. But in agriculture, just the reverse is true. Production drops very little or even goes up in depression, but prices nose-dive. Table 23-1 summarizes these diverse changes in the two areas from the boom of 1929 down to the depression depths of 1932 and back up to the moderate recovery of 1937. Agricultural production in 1931 actually rose to 106 per cent of 1929 in spite of a drop in the farm price index to 60. This farm response to declining demand reflected the high degree of competition in agriculture, and the general inelasticity of demand for major farm products. Farm prices are set in impersonal, highly competitive markets. When demand goes down, the first impact is on prices. No farmer has any control over them. He can only adjust to them.

Table 23-1

FARM AND INDUSTRIAL PRODUCTION AND PRICES *

	Agriculture		*Industry*	
Year	*Production*	*Prices*	*Production*	*Prices*
1929	100	100	100	100
1933	99	44	53	70
1937	108	83	103	85

* Figures are index numbers, 1929 = 100. Data from *Agriculture and the National Economy,* Temporary National Economic Committee, Monograph No. 23, p. 39.

What would you have done if you had been a farmer and prices dropped? You'd have been as likely to increase output as to decrease it. By planting more acreage next year you'd hope to increase your income enough to offset the lower price. But there, alas, enters the villain, inelastic demand. With inelastic demand, more total output sends prices and total farm income nose-diving further.

So relatively declining demand, rapid technological change, and high sensitivity to instability have dominated the history of American agriculture over the past century. Even when times were good, the persistent long-term downtrend ate away at the farm prosperity generated by high demand for farm products from consumers and industry.

THE FARMER'S ECONOMIC STATUS The changing economic fortune of agriculture is summed up in the statistics on farm income. The heart of the farm problem is an income problem. Many farmers have made a lot of money since the 1930's, and most are better off absolutely than they have ever been before. The "big" farmer is very big and very wealthy indeed. But the millionaire livestock ranchers in Texas, the farmers with private airplanes in the western wheat plains, and the Cadillacs in farm garages in the corn-hog belt are the exception, not the rule. When you think of the Iowa corn farmer with his 640 acres of rich rolling land, of the Texas rancher with his vast herds of cattle, and of the prairie wheat farmer with his modern wheat combine, you have a pleasing picture of American farm life. But it takes in only about 10 per cent of all farmers. Put in the Arkansas farmer trying to eke out an existence on the side of a hill, the white and Negro small farmers and sharecroppers in the South, the tenant farmers struggling along far from the fertile lands of the Midwest. Then you'll begin to get a truer picture of the total farm population. Seventy-five per cent of the total farm production comes from a quarter of the nation's farms. The well-to-do farmers are well-to-do indeed, but there aren't many of them. The least efficient 50 per cent of the nation's farms produce only 8 per cent of total farm output. About a third of all full-time farms have total *sales* (not profits) of less than $2,500 per year.

Figure 23-1 sums up the economic position of farm families over the past half-century. It compares farm and non-farm per capita incomes in the United States since 1910, including money income and estimates of home-produced consumption. Even allowing for lower farmhouse rentals and other such compensating advantages for farmers, on the average farmers were phenomenally poor in depression years and way below the non-farm population even in booms. The gap is wide and apparently getting wider as agricultural demand continues to decline relative to the rest of the economy.

Figure 23-1 also re-emphasizes agriculture's high susceptibility to booms and depressions. Farming is a boom-and-bust industry. To paraphrase the poem about the little girl with the little curl, "When times are good, they are very, very good; but when they are bad, they are horrid."

Increasingly, industry is the chief buyer of agricultural products. When industry is prosperous, manufacture absorbs a vast amount of agricultural raw materials, and its wage-earners, fully employed at good wages, buy large quantities of food products. When industry is depressed, the bottom drops out of the market for farm products. This does not mean that an exclusive causal relation runs from industrial to agricultural activity. Good and bad times in the two economic areas are interacting. But for agriculture to dominate general business activity in the United States would be a clear-cut example of the tail wagging the dog. Prosperity makes the gradual relative decline of farming easy to adjust to; in depression the adjustment is dragging and painful.

"THE FARM PROBLEM" Is there a "farm problem"? Or are the relatively low farm prices and incomes just evidence that the competitive system is working the way it's supposed to, pushing resources out of an area where consumer demand has fallen steadily relative to the rest of the economy? Is agriculture a sick industry, or merely one that must look forward to a comparatively stable size in an economy that is growing all

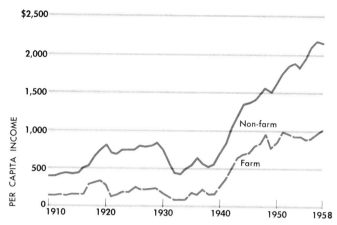

Per Capita Farm and Non-farm Incomes

FIG. 23-1   Per capita farm incomes have long been far under non-farm incomes. (Source: U.S. Department of Agriculture.)

around it at a rapid rate? Whether you call agriculture sick or not, are its difficulties to be blamed on the fact that competition doesn't really work, or that it works very well indeed?

In a competitive economy, we would expect declining relative demand to force resources into other areas where consumer demand is growing. And this has happened in agriculture. In prosperity, people have migrated heavily from rural to industrial areas and jobs. During the 1920's, nearly 2 out of every 5 farm young people reaching the age of 20 moved to towns or cities. During World War II and the 1950's, the same shift went on. And there has been considerable responsiveness to shifting consumer demand in the pattern of crops and animals produced by farmers.

But in depression, the pattern is different. The traditionally high farm birth rates pile up people on the farms; they have no place else to go. And even with heavy out-migration, the population left in agriculture has continuously been too large to earn average incomes equal to more than about half those in the rest of the economy.

Why does this situation persist, contrary to what we would expect from our description of the workings of a competitive economy? America's 4 million farm families differ widely, personally and in the crops and products they bring to market. Thus, any summary of the problems facing farmers as a whole will inevitably be wide of the mark for some families and some products. But insofar as there is a "farm problem," it appears to arise primarily from a combination of the following circumstances:

1. Demand for farm products declining relative to the rest of the economy.
2. Inelastic demand for most farm products.
3. High birth rates among farmers, and inadequate mobility out of farming (producing an inelastic supply of farm labor).
4. Unusually rapid technological advance.
5. Inelastic supply of farm land.
6. Active competition among farmers, with no one farmer big enough to do more than adjust to the market price.

7. Instability in farm prices, magnified by cyclical fluctuations in business and industry.

8. The uncertain weather.

If agriculture is sick, it boils down pretty much to this—too many resources in agriculture relative to the rest of the economy, especially too many people. With high farm birth rates, rapid technological progress, and soft demand, agriculture faces a major adjustment problem.

Not everyone would agree that farmers have a harder time adjusting to declining demand than other groups do. Some people say farmers just talk louder about their troubles and have more representatives looking out for them in Congress. Economists who believe that agriculture's problem in adjusting to declining demand is especially tough generally emphasize the following from the above list:

1. *Inelastic supply of farm labor.* The biggest current cost in farming is farm labor—primarily the farmer himself and his family. The farmer and his family are not easily transferable out of agriculture, especially in bad times. Although his cash income is used up by his variable costs and by just keeping his family going, he is likely to cling to the farm.

Partly, he may just like farming and detest the thought of city life; many farmers don't want to be factory workers any more than factory workers want to be farmers. Equally, he may simply have no idea of what else he could do, especially if he is middle-aged or older. The fact that he must move his family geographically to shift occupations further impedes mobility. As important as any of these reasons, often there simply aren't many other jobs to move to. In an industry where continuous heavy out-migration is required, these factors are serious. Surplus population piles up at an alarming rate when movement away from the farm stops.

2. *Inelastic supply of other farm resources.* The other major cost involved in farming is the farm itself. Buying a farm takes a lot of money, which farmers usually have to borrow. Since few people have the foresight or the financial backing to buy farms in bad times, purchases are concentrated in rising- and high-price periods. As a result, mortgages are often big, with correspondingly high interest and principal payments. This is all right as long as times are good, but a drop in demand and farm prices converts these fixed debt liabilities into millstones around the farmer's neck. His income drops and the payments to the bank or insurance company stay up. Farm taxes are another big fixed cost.

Suppose the farmer can't meet his payments. He goes broke, and his creditors foreclose. But farm foreclosure doesn't mean that the farm drops out of production. There's nothing much to do with a farm except to farm it. The financial institution that takes possession immediately rents it out to someone, often to the family just foreclosed. The pain of financial collapse may be severe, but it does little to reduce farm output. Supply is inelastic.

The same inelastic supply of farm resources keeps output up when demand falls, even if farmers own the land outright. There is little incentive for the farmer to withdraw his land from farm production. What else would he do with it? Quite the contrary, falling farm prices are likely to stimulate increased production, in a self-defeating attempt by farmers to hold up their incomes.

3. *Inelastic demand for farm products.* The situation is intensified by the inelastic demand that prevails for many farm products. If nature is kind and if farmers work hard, their reward is more production and less total income. If demand falls while farm production stays up, the effect is the same as if production had been increased with a stable demand. The farmer seems to be between the devil and the deep blue sea. To help himself he must produce more; this is his major hope for more income. But if everyone produces more, all are likely to get less income. What to do? The competitive model says resources should see the better rewards elsewhere and get out of farming, but somehow many of them just don't seem to go.

AGRICULTURE'S CLAIMS TO SPECIAL AID   Farmers suggest lots of bases to support their claims to special aid. Consider a few of the major ones.

1. *Low-income status.* Low farm incomes are usually the main argument supporting special aid to farmers. But if you think about it, the farmer's case for special aid here rests on his being a human being with a low income, not on his being a farmer. If you believe that everyone should have at least some minimum income, this is understandable. But, although many farmers are in the lowest income groups, many others are not, and helping all farmers on the income score may be a shotgun approach that confuses personal needs and farming as an industry. As a practical matter, under both Democrat and Republican farm programs, the rich farmers have received the big government checks, not the poor farmers. Aid programs have been based on price supports for products (where the biggest producers gain most from higher prices) and on cutting back previous production (where a proportional cut for the big fellow pays him more than it does the little fellow). Moreover, aid programs based on staying in agriculture (i.e., aid to the "industry" rather than to needy persons) perpetuate the basic cause of low farm incomes by making farmers stay in farming to get government aid.

2. *Special susceptibility to business fluctuations.* Farmers are certainly hard hit by depressions. To be honest about it, remember too that as a partial offset they come out pretty well in booms. Does agriculture have a special claim for help in smoothing out this roller-coaster ride? Surely the main approach must be through greater stability for the economy as a whole. But farmers argue that they deserve special help, especially to smooth out incomes during depressions. Make

up your own mind. This argument, you should note, is easy to confuse with the general low-income argument above. Don't count the same thing twice.

3. *The uncertain weather.* In one sense, farming is the most unpredictable business there is. The vagaries of nature upset the best-laid plans. The droughts and the floods come. There's nothing new about this problem, of course. Thousands of years ago the emperors of China sought to establish something surprisingly like the modern "ever-normal granary" storage plan, to save up surpluses in bumper years for the shortage years to come. There's no doubt that the weather can make things tough for the farmer. ("Well, he can always move out and take a job somewhere else if he doesn't like it," say the objectors.)

4. *Special aid to offset advantages of other groups.* Farmers may claim that they are injured by special privileges for other groups, and hence that they deserve offsetting special assistance. The high American tariff on industrial products has long forced the farmer to pay higher domestic prices while his own foreign markets are weakened by the same tariffs. Monopolistic conditions have been tolerated by government officials in many industries, in spite of laws purporting to outlaw monopoly. Labor unions are encouraged to raise wages. This raises the prices paid by farmers and restricts movement from the farm to urban occupations. But the farmer sells in a highly competitive market.

Many economists object to this argument for special aid to agriculture. They maintain that the answer lies in removing special privileges for other groups rather than in building up still more special privileges and restrictions. Fighting evil with evil leads to a self-feeding spiral of special privileges and restrictions, according to this counter-argument.

5. *The need for soil conservation.* Most Americans agree that it is good business to conserve our natural resources. Often the advantage of conservation to society as a whole far exceeds the dollars-and-cents return to the farmer in undertaking soil-conservation measures; this is a case where the social benefits exceed those to the individual producer. Thus, much of the farm-aid program has been justified as soil conservation (e.g., conserving soil by not planting part of the land each year). In fact, much of the conservation talk has served to disguise programs whose main goal is to raise farm income. And at the moment the problem is too much farm land rather than too little. But the conservation problem may be an important one.

In part, a genuine soil-conservation program involves educating the farmer in methods of farming that will maintain his soil to his own long-run profit as well as to the advantage of the general public. In part, collective action at public expense is needed to prevent soil erosion and wastage, as in flood control and reforestation projects. Whether farmers should be offered special subsidies to follow soil-conservation policies that are to their own ultimate profit is a debatable issue. Much depends on how society values present output against future needs.

6. *Agriculture as a way of life.* Many people look on agriculture as a stable,

sound way of life, harking back to the ways of our fathers—an anchor to windward in a hectic world of assembly lines, tenements, skyscrapers, and neuroses. The farmer is still an individual, not just a cog in a social and economic machine. This, they feel, is a way of life worth preserving.

Here is an argument obviously outside the scope of economics. Weigh it for yourself. However strong the case may be, it raises some economic dilemmas. The very traits of the farmer and his life that are admired most in this view are the ones associated with small-scale, often inefficient, family farming. Large-scale commercial farming that promises a higher farm standard of living compromises these very virtues. Experts agree that only the bigger farms can provide reasonable family incomes with today's mechanized farming methods.

A closely related argument hinges on large farm families. There is no provision in the price system, say some, for paying farmers for the outlays of money and effort they make in bearing, rearing, and educating a large number of children who later move into other economic areas. Economically, the argument runs, human beings are capital resources of the nation just as much as are buildings and machines. Here, they say, is a sound economic and sociological argument for special aid to farmers.

On closer examination, this, like the low-income argument, is logically a personal, not an industry, argument. If we want to encourage and pay for large families, all right. But if we do, the aid should be based on size of family, not on the number of bushels of wheat produced. Perhaps we think farm children are especially healthy and well brought up; if so, focus the aid to large farm families. Or perhaps the thing to do is subsidize education in rural areas. Keeping logic and emotions separate on such claims for special aid is essential if we expect public policies to do what we want them to do. (The headless horseman again.)

THE FARM-AID PROGRAM

Farmers have never been silent politically. All through the 1800's, they obtained from Congress special concessions that they wanted, often as part of a compromise with the "industrial east." In the 1920's an upsurge of farm demands for help led to special government credit institutions and low-interest loans for farmers. Also, surprisingly enough, the beginnings of the New Deal crop restriction and farm price-support programs are found not in the New Deal but in the Coolidge-Hoover administrations of the late 1920's. In 1929, the Federal Farm Board was set up with $500 million to promote "orderly marketing" by buying up farm surpluses in order to support weakening farm prices. The disastrous failure of the program, which ended up with tons of wheat and cotton and no money, pointed up the difficulties in supporting farm prices without curtailing production, and laid the basis for the New Deal farm program that followed it when the Democrats took over in 1933.

"Parity." The core of the New Deal farm-aid program was the concept of "parity"—parity between farm incomes and prices and those in the rest of the economy. Parity is still the foundation of the farm-aid program today.

As it was developed in the New Deal legislation, farm parity meant that prices paid and received by farmers should be in the same ratio as in the "normal" years 1909-14. If farm prices drop *relative to* other prices (or don't rise as fast as other prices), government action should push the farm prices back up to parity.

If you're a skeptic, you will recall that 1909-14 was the golden age of agriculture. You may ask, why not a parity program for buggies and women's high-buttoned shoes, based on 1905-06, a peak year for the buggy and high-button shoe industries? But if you're a friend of the farmer, you'll argue that since World War I we have continually been upset by excesses of one sort or another—wars, booms, depressions, and whatnot—so that 1909-14 is really the last normal period on which to base parity. Many observers have found it hard to believe that any normally perceptive adult is really kidded into taking the "parity" talk based on 1909-14 as anything more than a disguise for subsidies to farmers—but you would begin to wonder again every time another farm-aid bill goes through Congress.

In the 1950's Congress finally enacted an arrangement by which the parity base was to be shifted to the ten years preceding the year in question. But at the same time it inserted wage rates and taxes in the index of prices paid by farmers, which effectively increased the rise in that index and with it the height of the parity price for farm products. Congress also provided elaborate safeguards to spread over at least ten years the transition from the old to the new base, wherever the new base might produce lower farm parity prices than the old. At the end of the 1950's, the transition was still in progress.

To the man from Mars, the parity farm program would be a strange phenomenon. It would be hard to explain to him why we should pay people not to produce things and buy up available food to hold prices at levels where people won't consume it. But the New Deal farm program was comprehensive. According to a joking description then current in Washington circles, the AAA paid the farmers not to raise the crops, then the Commodity Credit Corporation paid them (through loans) to store any surplus that AAA didn't prevent, and the Federal Surplus Commodities Corporation bought up and gave away what surplus was left over. Though only a half-truth, the description had an uncomfortably penetrating ring. And the basic nature of the government's farm-aid program is much the same today.

Production Control and Marketing Quotas. The core of the New Deal farm program was the effort to prevent crop "surpluses" and to hold up prices by restricting production. The primary method used was limitation of acreage planted, supplemented by a system of marketing quotas in cotton, tobacco, wheat, rice, and vegetables. The arrangement thus was strikingly similar to private industrial cartels where total output is limited, the market "divided up," and price maintained by agreement.

The production-control rationale of the program was plainly stated in the original Agricultural Adjustment Act of 1933. Payments were made to all farmers who restricted acreage in accordance with the allotments made by AAA administrators; the payments were financed by a processing tax on the commodities involved. No legal compulsion was imposed on farmers to cooperate in the program, but the large benefit payments, coupled with the social opprobrium attendant on non-cooperation, brought a high percentage of participation.

The original AAA was thrown out by the Supreme Court in 1936, on grounds that taxing one group (processors) to subsidize another was unconstitutional. But succeeding acts have been similar in general design, without the forbidden special tax. Since then, the general taxpayer has picked up the tab for helping the farmer.

How effective have these production-control and marketing-control schemes proved? The answer is, not very. Not because smaller supplies would not have raised prices and farm incomes; with inelastic demand they would. But because the programs weren't very successful in restricting output. Acreage restrictions cut back the number of acres planted to wheat or corn, but at the same time farmers figured out ways to increase yields per acre. Development of hybrid seed corn alone offset the acreage-restriction program on corn; better fertilization and land-use practices worked in the same direction; and in addition farmers used the freed land to raise substitute crops (such as soybeans) which were also fed to hogs.

Thus, production has stayed up or increased, while prices are held above levels where demand would clear the market. The result has been continued government accumulation of surpluses, leading to immense storage problems and costs in addition to the basic costs of buying up the surpluses. Since the government cannot sell its stocks on the open market without depressing the supported parity price, it holds the surpluses, while consumers pay the high supported prices. Thus the public pays two ways—through taxes to buy up the surpluses at supported prices, and through the higher prices on farm products at the supermarket or as raw materials.

To get around part of this difficulty, both Truman's Secretary Brannan and Eisenhower's Secretary Benson proposed plans whereby the government would, in effect, guarantee the farmer a supported price but still sell its surplus stocks at less than parity price. Thus the surpluses would not go to waste and consumers would get farm products at lower prices. What if this action produced a market price below the support level, as it almost certainly would? Then the government would give the farmers an open subsidy for the difference. But these plans got only lukewarm support, especially from farmers. Visible subsidies are not popular, even if they're a cheaper way of getting the same results.

Crop Storage and Loan Plans. One major device for supporting farm prices has been crop storage "loans" for farmers, through the Commodity Credit Corporation. It works like this: The farmer can get a government loan on his major crop at, say, 85 per cent of the parity price. He then seals the crop in storage. Anytime he likes, he can take the crop out of storage, sell it off, and pay back the government.

The exceptional thing about these storage loans is that they give the farmer a "Heads I win, tails you lose" set-up. For example, if a farmer has a $2 a bushel loan on his wheat and the market price falls to $1.75, he can turn the wheat over to the government, let it bear the loss, and keep the $2 as, in effect, a price for his wheat. On the other hand, if the price goes up to $2.50, he can sell the wheat, pay back the $2 to the government, and pocket the difference. Thus, the crop "loan" program is in effect a guaranteed minimum price for the farmer, plus an option on any higher price that may appear—and it has recently been the major way of paying support prices to farmers.

The "Soil-Bank" Program. The Eisenhower administration entered office resolved to reduce parity support prices and to restore freer market conditions in agriculture. But it soon found that getting its program through Congress was easier said than done. Consistent pushing for moderate reductions in rigid support prices for major crops made some progress, but the basic support policies of the preceding administrations were little changed—and surpluses continued to pile up in mountainous quantities. In 1956, President Eisenhower proposed a "soil-bank" program, under which farmers would be paid for taking land completely out of cultivation, allegedly to build up a soil bank of fertility for the future but primarily to cut back the volume of crops going into government surplus. The proposal was new in name, but hardly in substance. Its emphasis on soil conservation was hardly separable from its Democratic predecessors, except for the important related Eisenhower push for lower support prices.

The effects of over a quarter-century of price-support and production-control plans are hard to assess in detail. Presumably farm prices have been higher than they otherwise would have been. Billions after billions of dollars have gone into supporting farm prices and into paying farmers not to produce, mainly through withholding land from the production of particular crops. Since nearly all these plans have been based on maintaining prices or on percentage reductions of previous acreage, they have consistently provided large benefits to the large farmers (with large crops to sell and large acreage to cut back) who need them least and small help for the little farmers who need help most. There is no clear evidence that total farm production has been held below the levels that would have prevailed without the programs. Many competent observers believe that the various government programs adopted have done more to stimulate farm production than to reduce it.

But one result is crystal-clear—the huge volume of surpluses piled up by the government. Figure 23-2 summarizes the evidence on this score for the last decade. By 1959 crop surpluses held by the Commodity Credit Corporation, the main agency accumulating such stocks, totaled over $8 billion. About 1.3 billion bushels of wheat and 1.5 billion bushels of corn were stored in converted tankers floating along the east and west coasts, in circus tents, and even in huge piles covered with canvas, as well as in every available grain storage facility. Daily government storage costs for wheat alone are over $500,000.

Commodity Credit Corporation Investment in Farm Crops

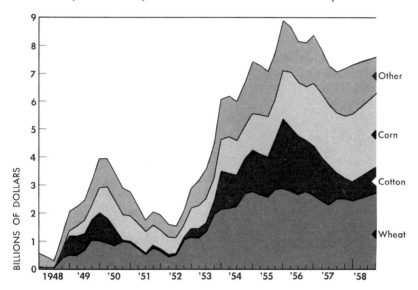

FIG. 23-2   This chart shows the total amount of government funds tied up in farm-crop loans and surplus stocks for each year.

Figure 23-3 on page 438 looks at the problem another way—what percentage of the annual crop is loaned on or bought up for government surplus each year? The federal price-support program isn't nibbling at the edge of farm production. The C.C.C. bought up (directly or through loans) nearly a third of the entire wheat crop over the past decade, and nearly half the cotton crop during the late 1950's. Wheat, cotton, and corn are the big three of the price-support program, but the legislation covers a total of 20 crops.[1] Even with a major program to dispose of the surpluses here and abroad through sale and gift, this is what piles up the surplus stocks.[2]

---

[1] The others are barley, beans, butter, cheese, dried milk, honey, peanuts, flaxseed, sorghum, oats, rice, rye, soybeans, tung oil, tobacco, wool, and mohair.

[2] Surpluses are sold mainly abroad (where the world price is under the U.S. support price) and at low prices domestically when deterioration threatens. The average loss has been about 25 per cent of the C.C.C. investment.

Special Credit Arrangements. Since the 1920's the federal government has established a wide-ranging group of special government-financed credit agencies to assure easy credit and low interest rates to the farmers. The Federal Land Banks and Federal Farm Mortgage Corporation (which was recently merged into the Federal Land Banks) have played leading roles. They are government corporations, which borrow money and lend it out to farmers, usually at rates lower than private banks charge on comparable loans.

How big a government subsidy to farmers is buried in these loans is not clear. In some cases, federal credit has filled a need of farmers that is not met by other sources of funds except at exorbitant rates, especially on loans of intermediate length. On the other hand, private lenders argue that they are unable to compete on equal terms with government agencies that meet expenses from federal funds. At its best, the program has stimulated more active competition in a lending field where price (interest) competition had long been limited.

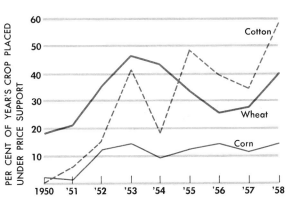

Wheat, Cotton, and Corn Placed Under Government Price Support

FIG. 23-3 A big percentage of the total annual crop of these major products has been bought up or loaned on every year. Note the peaks for cotton and wheat. (Source: U.S. Department of Agriculture.)

Export Subsidies and the Trade Agreements Program. A slumping foreign market was a big cause of the American farmer's distress in the 1930's. To meet this problem, the government moved along three lines. First, it tried to encourage a general lowering of tariffs in order to promote international trade of all sorts. This program was sure to help the farmer especially, since he depends more heavily on foreign markets than do most other producers. Second, the government gave "export subsidies" to American farmers on products for export. These were special subsidies to make up the difference between the actual price farmers could get abroad and the standard government-support price in America. Lastly, the government bought up some surpluses here and "dumped" them abroad for what they would bring on the foreign market, or gave them away to foreign governments (especially India) faced with disaster conditions.

These ways of expanding markets are considered at length in Part 6. Suffice it to say here that the Trade Agreements Program and more recent trade-expansion programs have borne lasting fruit, but the export subsidy and dumping approaches succeeded mainly in getting other nations to increase their barriers against American products.

Direct Subsidies to Farmers. Back in the depression days, Congress voted one small program of direct cash subsidies to low-income farmers, through the Farm Security Administration. If farm subsidies are to be paid, this approach is an admirable one. The subsidies are out on the table for everyone to see. They can be adjusted to the needs of the recipients. Every voter can judge for himself whether he wants his tax money spent this way.

But nobody liked the direct subsidy program much—least of all the farmers. They resent aid that looks like charity. They want to think, and to have the world think, that they are earning and entitled to the prices and incomes they get. They don't want to lay themselves open to the charge that they are raiding the public treasury. Moreover, the well-to-do farmers would have a hard time keeping their share if the subsidies were out in the open. So. . . . farm aid has generally been elaborately camouflaged, although most of the schemes have been more costly to the taxpayer than equivalent direct cash subsidies to farmers would have been. The widespread opposition to the Brannan and Benson plans among well-to-do farm groups may have reflected much of this same attitude against open subsidies.

Crop Insurance. Mother Nature is the cause of many of the farmer's worries. It rains at the wrong time, or it doesn't rain at all. The boll weevils come and eat up the cotton. Hail storms beat down the wheat.

Beginning in 1938, the Department of Agriculture offered an experimental crop-insurance program to farmers. Payments to farmers substantially exceeded premiums collected over the first few years, and Congress called the program off in 1944. But soon thereafter it was reinstituted, and it now covers most major farm crops for farmers who choose to participate.

In principle, the plan is comparable to life insurance. Only crop yield is insured, not the price. Premiums are supposed to cover losses over a period of years, although the taxpayer puts up the administrative expenses. In fact, it has proved hard to estimate likely crop losses, and premiums have had to be set roughly; by 1959, the plan was nearly $100 million in the hole, though for the last decade premiums have nearly covered losses paid. In spite of this, the program has never been extremely popular among farmers; over 20 years, a total of about 5 million individual insurance contracts were written, and total premiums and payments in recent years have run only around $15-20 million annually.

Programs to Promote Efficiency. Long before the government set out to raise farm incomes by restricting production, the Department of Agriculture was busy telling farmers how to increase production. A broad program of scientific research, on-the-ground help for farmers through nation-wide Agricultural Experiment Stations, advice on soil-conservation practices, and a variety of other measures have played a big role in raising the efficiency of American agriculture.

But by carrying out this eminently sensible program, the Department of Agriculture has been sabotaging its own crop-restriction programs. The American farmer is nobody's fool, and he has taken full advantage of modern methods to increase yields even while he is cutting back acreage under income-support programs. From an individual point of view, that's the way to have the best of both worlds. What would you do if you were a farmer?

AGRICULTURE IN THE POLITICAL ECONOMY   In its fiscal year 1959, the federal government spent almost $7 billion on agriculture. This was 8 per cent of total federal expenditures, and 20 per cent of federal expenditures excluding national security. It was more than the government spent on any other non-defense function except interest on the national debt. Yet in 1959 there were only about 4.5 million farms and farm families in the United States, out of a total of some 55´million family units.

How can such a huge government expenditure for such a small special-industry group be justified? Agriculture may have some valid claims to special aid. Most occupational groups do. But, at least by the standards of a free-market competitive economy, this is far from a blanket justification for helping the farmer every time he finds himself in trouble. If he speculates unwisely in land or raises lemons when the customers want oranges, does he have any more claim to special government help than any other businessman who guesses wrong? Even more fundamentally, if consumer demand for non-farm products grows faster than for farm products, and if, simultaneously, farmers have lots of children, does the farm population have any more economic claim to being supported comfortably in agriculture all their lives by a government subsidy than had the buggy and bloomer manufacturers when consumer demand passed them by? In a competitive economy, resources must follow consumer demand. The basic farm economic problem is adjustment to shifting consumer demands and mobility of productive resources out of agriculture, not ways to get subsidies to maintain an uneconomically large allocation of resources in farming.

In perspective, two big facts stand out about the farm legislation of the past quarter-century: One is the farmers' success in getting what they want. As one Washington correspondent put it, "As long as they act together the farmers can get anything out of the government short of good growing weather—and the government is working on that through cloud seeding and crop insurance plans." Anomalously, to give the individualistic farmers the things they wanted, the government had to make them the core of the first big central-planning movement in its peacetime history. But their own organizations had a big hand in the process. Never forget that the political process is a major part of political economy. Stuart Chase summed it up this way: "If any American believes that the New Deal agricultural legislation was the product of dreamers, long-haired professors and agents from Moscow, he is a pretty good dreamer himself. It was the product primarily of local farmers crying to be delivered from free competition." [3] Never before has the nation seen a more effective industry lobby group in getting continued subsidies from the federal treasury.

The second striking fact is the widespread failure to distinguish between the *economic* problem of resource allocation and efficiency, and the *ethical* problem of income distribution. On the economic side, there can be little doubt that agriculture has been overexpanded in the American economy over the last quarter-century, except during war periods; the direction pointed by the price system has been clear and unequivocal. Economically, our efforts should have been devoted to increasing the mobility of resources left in agriculture. On the ethical side, you have to make up your own mind on whether farmers' incomes ought to be subsidized by the rest of the population.

Most farm aid has been consciously or subconsciously aimed at the farm-income problem, though it has focused on holding up farm prices. Failure to think through the separate economic and ethical aspects of the problem has, as might have been expected, produced unsatisfactory results on both scores. On the economic side, farm-aid legislation has by and large required farmers to stay in farming as a condition of receiving aid. They have been paid for not raising crops, and have been guaranteed prices that include government subsidies. If they leave agriculture, these subsidies vanish. Moreover, the acreage-reduction programs have generally called for standard percentage reductions by all. This means laying idle part of our best land while busily keeping in production part of the marginal land.

On the income (ethical) side there have been some queer results too. Benefit payments have mainly been tied to products, not to people. By raising farm prices, the program has given the biggest benefits to the biggest farmers, since they have the most to sell. By paying farmers for cutting back production in proportion to acres farmed, the program has handed the biggest benefit checks to the highest-income farmers. This adds up to the anomalous result of passing out benefits in inverse relation to the need for help. A peak check of $278,000 to one farmer for wheat restriction in one year was reported by C.C.C., but annually dozens of farmers have received government subsidies exceeding $50,000. One farmer, one of the world's largest, collected $1.2 million in benefits in four years, and in addition received over $14 million a year for storing nearly 150 million bushels of surplus wheat and other grains. Legislation to hold subsidy payments below $50,000 has repeatedly been stalled by farm groups in Congress, although a bill to limit annual payments to $50,000 *per crop* per farmer was finally passed in 1959 (with some loopholes for larger payments). Only the unpopular Farm Security Administration program of direct aid to low-income families got directly at the low-income problem. Rural electrification, subsidies to rural schools, and

---

[3] *Democracy Under Pressure* (New York: Twentieth Century Fund, 1945), p. 99.

other such programs may roughly get the same results. But only by recognizing the low-income subsidy objective as such, if that is a major objective, can we hope to make efficient use of government funds.

There is no necessary contradiction between the economic objective of efficient resource allocation and the ethical objective of leveling up low incomes. Why, then, have not more consistent farm-aid programs been worked out on the basis of these separate objectives, rather than running everything together in a mélange that sometimes seems to spend billions of dollars without achieving either result very effectively? We could pay direct subsidies to low-income farm families, finance greater mobility out of farming, and encourage the lowest cost production possible for the production that does meet the profitability test in a free-price market. It is intriguing indeed that our farm-aid programs have helped most the better-off few among the farmers, yet they have apparently been popular vote-getters among the millions of farm voters. It is easy to see why the political parties, in power and out, court the farm votes in the key agricultural states that have swung many an election. Why the farm voters have not been more percep-tive about who is helped how much by what farm aid is harder to understand.

But the real world is not sharp and precise. Government policy is nearly al-ways a compromise of conflicting interests, usually influenced heavily by the most vocal and influential groups concerned. The spokesmen for broad groups seldom represent equally everyone in the group. The Farm Bureau and the National Grange look out for their members, by and large the higher-income farmers. But who looks out for the share-croppers and the little farmers across the nation?

In a problem as complex as that of modern agriculture, with so many different economic, political, and ethical values involved, there are seldom any absolutely "right" or "wrong" answers. Whether in some total sense America would be better off had the farm situation been left entirely to competitive market forces, no one can say with certainty. Compromise of conflicting interests is the essence of the democratic process. But economic analysis points to severe weaknesses in the expensive American farm program.

FOR ANALYSIS AND DISCUSSION

1. Is there a "farm problem" that public policy needs to be concerned about? If so, what is it?

2. In a competitive economy, resources are supposed to move where consumer demand is strongest, as individuals seek higher incomes. In the light of the comparative incomes shown by Figure 23-1, how do you explain the fact so many families stay in agriculture?

3. Would you favor government-sponsored output restriction to guar-antee minimum, or "parity," prices to paint-manufacturers in the event that paint prices and associated profits begin to fall? Do you see any important distinctions between this proposal and the comparable parity program for farm commodities?

4. If the demand for basic farm products is in fact substantially

inelastic, is there any way the government can help farmers except through output-restriction programs?

5. Does the Eisenhower "soil-bank" program appear to you a fundamental attack on the farm problem? If not, what would you suggest, and how would you go about getting it adopted by Congress?

6. Some critics of recent governmental farm programs argue that if we are going to have output-restriction measures, at least we should stop spending money to teach the farmers more efficient ways of producing more farm products. Do you agree with these critics? Why or why not?

7. There are only about 4½ million farm families in the United States. Yet Congress repeatedly votes costly benefits to farmers. Some observers argue that this is because the rural areas are heavily over-represented in the Senate, where each state has two votes no matter what its population is. Would it be a wise policy to restructure our system of congressional representation in order to reduce the political powers of minority pressure groups?

Monopoly

24

$\mathbf{M}$onopoly is something like sin. Everybody says he's against it, but a lot of people aren't very clear just what it is they're against. Like sin, monopoly has to be defined before one can talk much sense about it, or decide what, if anything, ought to be done about it.

The Spectrum from Competition to Monopoly. In one sense, every producer who isn't selling in a purely competitive market is a monopolist. This definition of monopoly as any situation other than pure competition would have some advantages— but it certainly would leave most of the world in the monopoly category. At the other extreme, a single producer of some distinct commodity for which there are no substitutes might be considered the only one with a monopoly—"one seller," as the Greek derivation of the word suggests. This definition goes to the other extreme and leaves us with very little of the world in the monopoly category. Worse, although it's the most commonly used definition, it's somewhat ambiguous, because there is no commodity or service that doesn't have some substitutes, more or less close, and we have no sharp criterion for measuring how close the substitute can be before we no longer have a monopoly. The Aluminum Company of America, up to World War II, was often called a monopoly in this sense. There was no other appreciable American producer of basic aluminum. But it is obvious that steel, wood, copper, and lots of other materials are possible substitutes for aluminum, and if the price of aluminum gets too high, people will begin to use the substitutes.

Pure Monopoly.   In spite of these problems, economists have defined a situation they call "pure," or "simple," monopoly. Consider the local power and light company in most small towns, as an example. It is the only producer of electricity in the town, and the substitution of candles, oil lamps, or gas lighting by consumers who rebel at high prices is not a very serious likelihood. (The big-city public utility is likely to be more exposed to potential competition, since industrial users of electricity do have less remote substitutes.) Alcoa's position was similar, but considerably less protected against competition. Similarly, the United Shoe Machinery Corporation for many years had, through patents and technical know-how, substantially exclusive control over several of the most vital types of shoe-making machinery. There were ways of making shoes without these machines, but they were very inefficient alternatives. Clearly, the United Shoe Machinery Corporation wasn't in as strong a position as is a public-utility company, but both fit reasonably well into the pure-monopoly classification, which is characterized by:

1. Only one seller of the good or service.
2. Rivalry from producers of substitutes so remote as to be insignificant.

Under these circumstances, the pure monopolist is in a position to set market price himself. But even he has to face up to the realities of elasticity of demand. He can put his price where he wishes. But unless demand is perfectly inelastic, the higher he puts his price the less he can sell. Partly, you will recall, the elasticity of demand for any product reflects the presence of potential substitutes, and there is no monopoly so pure, or perfect, that it can escape completely the possibility of partial substitutes. Thus, completely pure monopoly is never quite found in the real world, and "pure monopoly" shades imperceptibly into "monopolistic competition" at the monopoly extreme, just as "pure competition" shades into lesser degrees of competition at the other extreme.

The analogy to pure monopoly on the buyer's side is sometimes called "pure monopsony," which means one buyer. This case might prevail where there is only one buyer for labor services—say the mill in an isolated mill town. But like pure monopoly, pure monopsony is hard to find, since most cases involve more or less close competition from other buyers—e.g., workers are always free to move to another town if the monopsonist exploits his position too much.

Monopolistic Competition and Oligopoly.   The spectrum from pure competition to pure monopoly is a maze of special arrangements. In the simplest categorization, markets range from one seller to many sellers, all selling the same commodity. But, usually, producers have somewhat different commodities to sell. For example, breakfast-food manufacturers don't make just breakfast food. They make Post Toasties, Wheaties, Cheerios, and all the rest. Even corn flakes aren't just corn flakes; Post and Kellogg put them in different-colored boxes under different names, and to the buyer they are at least somewhat differentiated. The degree of "product differentiation" gets to be more substantial for, say, television sets. Philco, RCA, Sylvania, and Majestic may all show the same picture on the same-sized tube when tuned to Channel 4, but neither the makers nor the customers believe the sets are the same. *Where there are a good many producers selling the same (or only slightly differentiated) products, we call the situation "monopolistic competition."*

Another way of dividing up the big field that lies between the competitive and monopolistic extremes is by the extent to which sellers compete or cooperate. Obviously General Motors, Chrysler, and Ford have to pay a lot of attention to each other's policies in setting price and production plans, even though their products are all somewhat differentiated. Firms in such industries may compete actively, or they may get together formally or informally to agree on prices and on sharing the market. Economists usually group together as *"oligopoly"* such cases, where *there are only a few competing producers and where each producer must take into account what each other producer does.* Oligopoly means, literally, few sellers.

In between pure competition and pure monopoly lies almost all the American economic system. Each industry seems to be a little different. The complexity of special arrangements is enormous. Yet we need to classify this huge "in-between" area into some major groups if we are to make any headway in analyzing how it operates. In looking at the world of monopolistic competition and oligopoly, economists often emphasize the following four questions:

1. *How many producers are there of any given commodity?* The larger the number, the more likely competition is to be active.

2. *How close are the substitutes for the commodity?* The closer the substitutes are, the less real monopoly power any firm can exercise without losing customers.

3. *Do the producers involved compete on prices, or through non-price channels such as quality and advertising?* In some cases producers may not compete at all—they may sell a standardized product and agree to maintain fixed shares of a market at some agreed price. But in the vast majority of cases firms do compete in some way—either through price, or through quality of product and services, or through advertising to increase their share of the market, or in some other way.

4. *How easy is it for new firms to get into the industry, or into producing close substitutes for the industry's product?* A monopoly that can be invaded by anybody on short notice isn't much of a monopoly.

If we consider these the critical questions, we can immediately see some important sub-classes under monopolistic competition and oligopoly. For example, the monopolistic-competition group is usefully subdivided into cases where competition is primarily on prices, and where it primarily takes the form of non-price competition and competitive "demand creation" through advertising and selling activities. Oligopolies seem to fall into three groups depending on whether they "get together" on prices and output (in which case they are often called "cartels"), follow a "leader" on price-setting, or compete actively on prices and quality of product.

We come out with a division like this: [1]

I. *Pure competition*—many sellers of an identical product (wheat).

II. *Monopolistic competition*—a substantial number of sellers of identical or closely substitutable products.
   a. Price competition (vegetables in local grocery stores).
   b. Non-price competition and demand creation (beer, men's suits).

III. *Oligopoly*—a few sellers of identical or closely substitutable products.[2]
   a. Competition—on prices and through non-price competition and demand creation (television, automobiles).
   b. Collaboration.
      1. Formal collaboration on prices and output—"cartels" (nickel, internationally).
      2. Price leadership or informal price stabilization (steel, gasoline).

IV. *Pure monopoly*—one seller of a product without close substitutes (local water company).

The industries indicated are intended merely to provide some concrete impressions to go with the analytical categories. Few real-world cases fit neatly and exclusively into any one of the intermediate categories. For example, there is some demand creation, and quality competition as well as price competition, in groceries (case IIa); and there is surely price as well as non-price competition in both beer and men's suits (case IIb). The main purpose of the classification is to give us some models, or frameworks, to organize analysis of the various types of market behavior. Where actual industries are hybrids, we need to use two or more of the analytical models in thinking about them, through the next several chapters.

---

[1] In Part 4, which discusses the incomes people earn by selling their productive services, we use comparable divisions to classify the buyers of productive services—monopsony for one buyer; oligopsony for a few buyers; and monopsonistic competition for a substantial number of buyers, but still short of pure competition.

[2] Where there are only two sellers, another Greek word, "duopoly," is used. This is a special case of oligopoly.

THE BASES The basic test of an effective monopoly is its
OF MONOPOLY power to exclude competitors from the market.
If a firm can keep out potential competitors, it
can proceed with relative impunity to raise prices and to increase its profits at the
consumer's expense. The nearer the substitutes that competitors can put on the
market, the weaker the firm's monopoly position. The ideal monopoly (from the
monopolist's viewpoint) would be one over an absolutely essential product for
which there are no effective substitutes. Almost no one has such a pure monopoly,
but almost every firm has at least some small degree of monopoly.

Government Action as a Basis for Monopoly. The strongest monopolies are
the public utilities. A long-term exclusive government franchise is about as airtight a protection as any monopoly can hope for. This arrangement is found in
most localities for water, electricity, gas, and telephone companies. Even where
multiple companies are permitted by law, the market territory is usually divided
up by law or regulatory commission. Having granted this enviable monopoly position, however, governments invariably regulate the prices the monopoly can
charge. Often they maintain supervision over the company's whole operations, to
be sure that the public's interest is furthered by granting the exclusive franchise.
Otherwise, the stockholders of the local water or gas company would be in a
happy position indeed.

Government—federal, state, and local—intervenes in many other less obvious
ways to provide partial bases for monopolies. The federal farm-aid programs of
the past two decades have supported prices and induced farmers to behave like a
cartel in restricting output. On the local level, building codes, manifestly intended
to protect the public against unsafe construction and poor work, in fact provide
a widespread basis for monopolistic practices by building contractors and suppliers and by building-trades unions. Codes specify particular types of construction and particular materials, which are often outdated now by the new methods
and materials; only producers who use the prescribed methods and sellers who
offer the prescribed materials can enter the market. Practical exclusion of pre-
fabricated housing in many areas is an example. Local sanitation regulations are
another example of dual-purpose local ordinances where the practical effect is to
establish and provide monopoly positions for particular producers. The entire
federal patent system protects the monopoly position of the inventor, subject only
to some special restriction on how he uses the patent.

Patents and Research. The patent law gives to the inventor exclusive control
over any invention for 17 years. If a patent, or group of patents, gives effective
control over production of some commodity, competition is almost impossible.
The law has gradually limited the use of patents as a basis for monopoly practices,
but patents can still provide a powerful basis for monopoly powers.

The classic case of a monopoly based on patents is the United Shoe Machinery Corporation. The company was formed a half-century ago by a merger of all the leading manufacturers of shoe machinery. The new company manufactured between 95 and 100 per cent of all basic shoe machinery made in the United States. Instead of selling its machines, the company leased them to shoe manufacturers. Then it required any manufacturer who used any of its machines to agree to a "tying lease," which prevented the manufacturer from using shoe machinery made by other companies. Such use of tying leases in connection with its basic patented machinery permitted the company to extend its exclusive market control into additional parts of the shoe-manufacturing business, where previously other manufacturers had been well established. The situation was described by the Temporary National Economic Committee of Congress in the 1930's as follows: [3]

> The shoe manufacturer, who could obtain a lasting machine only by leasing it from the United Shoe Machinery Corporation, was compelled to turn to it also for his welter, stitcher, and metallic fastener, and the independent producers of those machines were robbed of their customers. The device operated also to continue far beyond the statutory 17 years the protection afforded the company by its patents. As long as any one of these patents granted it the exclusive right to produce a single machine, the tying clause in its contracts extended its monopoly to each of the others.

In 1955, after a long trial, the courts ordered the company to "cease and desist" from some of these practices, including refusal to sell the machines and the use of tying leases.

Key patents underlie the industrial position of many major American concerns, even though their position and operations are not like those of the United Shoe Machinery Corporation. Research has become part of the American industrial scene, and the "blue chips" of American industry come automatically to mind when we think of technological advance—General Electric, DuPont, General Motors, Standard Oil. These firms maintain their leading positions in oligopolistic industries in no small part by being first with the best in research. Over the past 20 years almost two-thirds of all patents have gone to corporations. General Electric alone, for example, received about 13,000; A.T. and T. about 10,000.

Research is an expensive and cumulative process. It's hard for the little firm to compete. DuPont's research laboratories alone would swallow up most of the business firms in the United States, and their stable of top-notch industrial scientists is the hopeless envy of all except a few leading rivals. As research and rapid technological advance become more important, it becomes harder and harder for new small firms to invade established industries, whether or not the industrial leaders actually take out restrictive patents on their research developments. Increasingly, the research is more important than the patents. Many in-

---

[3] *Competition and Monopoly in American Industry,* TNEC Monograph No. 21, p. 73.

dustrial patents are made obsolete by new developments long before their 17-year life expires.

Control of Raw Materials. If you can get exclusive control over the raw materials needed to make your product, you're sitting pretty—at least until someone figures out a substitute material. A few major firms have managed to get such exclusive control. Two examples described in the late 1930's by the Temporary National Economic Committee are still effective.[4]

> The International Nickel Company of Canada, Ltd., owns more than nine-tenths of the world's known reserve of nickel. The company produced more than 92 per cent of the world's output of nickel in 1929.
>
> Molybdenum is an element which finds its principal employment either in competition or in combinations with other alloying metals, in the production of steels of exceptional toughness and strength. In Bartlett Mountain in Colorado, the Climax Molybdenum Company owns 95 per cent of the world's known store of commercially workable deposits of this metal.

Financial Resources and the Capital Market. The money needed to set up an efficient firm in many industries today is tens and even hundreds of millions of dollars. Not very many people have this much money, and it's hard to borrow ten million dollars unless you're already a very well-established person or firm, no matter how engaging a picture you paint of your prospects.

In a "perfect" capital market, funds would be available for new ventures whenever the prospective borrower was willing and able to pay the going rate of interest on loans of comparable risk. In fact, however, it is hard for newcomers to raise funds in the market either by floating new securities or by borrowing from banks or insurance companies. Lenders are skeptical of unknown faces. Capital is rationed out to "desirable" borrowers rather than "sold" on the basis of the borrowers' willingness to pay the quoted interest rates. Moreover, borrowing is especially expensive for small, new borrowers, even when they can get the funds.

The fact that modern industry often requires large sums for minimal investments in new firms gives an important protection to monopolists already in the industries concerned. The imperfection of the capital market, which often makes it especially hard for the newcomer and small producer to get funds, increases this protection.

Advertising. Advertising by itself would have a hard time establishing or even maintaining an existing monopoly on any product. But the entrenched positions of names like Alcoa, Cadillac, and RCA-Victor in the mind of the American consumer are doubtless a cause of dismay to prospective competitors. Modern advertising has become increasingly "institutionalized" in many fields.

---

[4] *Ibid.*, pp. 79, 81.

Ads aim primarily at building up the company's name and prestige in the consumer's mind, rather than at selling a particular product. Large-scale prestige advertising—national or local—costs money, and only big and successful companies can afford it for long. The big company, which is often at least a partial monopolist, may find advertising a potent weapon for maintaining and extending its dominant position. Business outlays on advertising are huge. They have exceeded $10 billion every year since 1956.

Unfair Competition. Running the little fellow out of business by unfair price-cutting in order to eliminate competition is one of the charges commonly brought against big business. If A&P prices groceries very low, it is accused of a devious intent to run the independents out and then to boost its own prices when competition is gone. And you don't have to look very far back into history to find plenty of cases where big business behaved exactly this way. Such discriminatory price-cutting, aimed to eliminate competition rather than to help the consumer, often put price well below cost. Often prices were cut only in areas where competition existed; high prices in other areas were used to keep profits up while competitors were being forced to the wall. The old Standard Oil Company, around the turn of the century, provided some of the most spectacular cases of such behavior—and with great success. But the practice was widespread during at least the late nineteenth and early twentieth centuries.

Such unfair price competition is now illegal. But the line between legitimate price-cutting as a result of efficient operation, and unfair price-cutting merely to eliminate competition, is hard to draw in many cases. The more efficient producer always tends to eliminate the inefficient—unless, as is said to be the case in some modern industries, the dominant firm is already so big that it voluntarily chooses to encourage other firms to lessen the chance of antitrust prosecution by the government.

Large-scale Production and Decreasing Costs. Low-cost mass production is the trade-mark and the pride of American industry. In industry after industry (steel, electrical equipment, automobiles, chemicals, and so on), maximum efficiency can be obtained only by large firms, each producing a substantial share of the total amount that can be sold on the market. In local areas, taking advantage of the economies of large-scale production may mean one or a few monopolistic firms—for example, the one grocery store a small town can reasonably support.

In extreme cases, the total market is not big enough to permit even one firm to operate at the optimal scale of output. Until a firm reaches this optimal scale, it is operating in its range of "decreasing costs." That is, by increasing output it can cut its cost per unit produced. This is described in common terminology as the "economies of large-scale production."

If the economies of large-scale production are so great in an industry that the market is not big enough to support even one optimum-sized firm, will these decreasing costs be the basis for a pure monopoly in the industry? Probably not, unless the government intervenes to make the industry a public utility.

Figure 24-1 represents such an industry. The *TUC* curves are simply total-unit-cost curves for different scales of enterprise for a firm in the industry, say a local gas company. Scale TUC^3 is the most efficient scale in this case; its least-cost point is the lowest of any possible scale of enterprise. Each cost curve is drawn in a heavy line through the range in which it is lower than any other. The heavy scalloped line is therefore a curve that indicates the total unit cost at which each output can be produced as the size of the firm increases. The industry will be characterized by decreasing costs if demand is small relative to the scale of enterprise (TUC^3) —for example, if demand is D^1D^1 or D^2D^2. This is a "decreasing-cost" industry because the economies of scale of enterprise within the single firm have not yet been fully exploited at any output less than *OM,* the least-cost point on TUC^3.

A Decreasing-Cost Industry

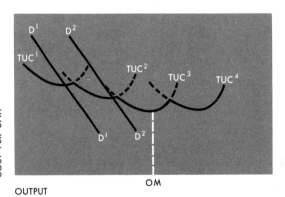

FIG. 24-1 This industry has decreasing costs up to output M. For any demand short of that, competition is unlikely to work effectively.

Under what conditions will our gas company (or any other such industry) remain a one-firm monopoly? The first firm in a decreasing-cost industry is of course happy if it has a complete monopoly. But suppose its profits are large and a new firm is attracted. In this market, with demand D^1D^1 it is obviously impossible for two or more firms to cover costs if they compete actively. Demand for gas in the area isn't big enough to support even one of them at optimum scale. If they get into a price war, the likely result is bankruptcy for the weaker, with the stronger taking over the whole market again.

In such circumstances, instead of competing aggressively, the two firms may enter into a formal agreement or unspoken understanding to maintain price and to restrict output. This arrangement is obviously wasteful of resources. Each firm is producing gas at a higher cost per cubic foot than if one firm alone were to produce the same total output. But under this market-sharing arrangement both companies may be able to make profits, and profits are likely to be the first concern of the managers. The social advantage of limiting the industry to one firm is obvious; this is the basis for most exclusive public-utility franchises.

How widespread decreasing-cost industries really are in the economy is a moot issue. There are some who claim that numerous firms outside the public-utility fields could be still more efficient if they were to expand further and take over still more of the market. It is common gossip, for example, that General Motors could undersell the entire auto industry and eliminate all the other firms if it were not held back by possible antitrust action and public resentment of such elimination of competition. But even if this rumor were true, in most industries the market appears to be quite adequate to support more than one firm of optimum size. Whether the market is big enough to support enough firms to guarantee effective competition is another question—a much more difficult one that we will consider in detail a little later.

PURE MONOPOLY [5]

Where we draw the line between pure monopoly and monopolistic competition is arbitrary, since it depends on how close available substitutes are to the product involved. In the American economy, except in the public utilities, we seldom find only one firm, no available substitutes for the commodity produced, and no possibility that other firms may invade the market. Yet looking at such an extreme case is useful, because it shows up clearly some of the attributes of monopoly. It gives some insight into what the world might be like if pure monopolies were tolerated without regulation. It suggests rules for controlling public utilities. And it may be a quite realistic description of the short-run position in which many firms temporarily find themselves because of special location advantages, development of new products ahead of competitors, or other such circumstances.

Imagine a single electric-power company in an isolated community, free to charge whatever rates it pleases. Suppose you are the owner-manager of this hypothetical concern. Waiving the fear that the local government will begin to regulate your rates, how would you go about maximizing your profits?

Costs.   First, you'd want to know your costs. Your engineers and accountants will probably have estimates at hand. If they haven't, they can produce some for you. Recognizing that these estimates are probably pretty rough, suppose the cost schedule looks like the one in Table 24-1 on page 454. To simplify matters, the table shows only the estimates for producing at rates from 1,000,000 to 1,600,000 kilowatt-hours, in intervals of 100,000 kilowatt-hours. (To simplify the language, we will use merely the word kilowatt hereafter, for kilowatt-hours.) [6]

The table is largely self-explanatory. Columns 1 and 2 are the basic total-cost

---

[5] The remainder of this chapter rests directly on the marginal cost–marginal revenue analysis of Chapter 21.

[6] Electricity producers often face demands that fluctuate widely through the day and seasonally. For simplicity, we neglect this problem here.

estimates. Column 3 is simply 2 divided by 1, to convert total cost to cost per unit. Column 4, marginal cost per 100,000 kilowatts, shows the additional cost involved in producing an extra 100,000 kilowatts. For example, it costs an extra $2,000 to up production from 1,200,000 to 1,300,000 kilowatts weekly. Column 5 converts this marginal cost per 100,000 to marginal cost per kilowatt, by dividing column 4 by the extra 100,000 kilowatts obtained in each jump.

Table 24-1

HOMETOWN ELECTRIC COMPANY—COST SCHEDULE *

			Marginal Cost	
		Average		
		Cost per	*Per 100,000*	*Per*
Kilowatts	*Total Cost*	*Kilowatt*	*Kilowatts*	*Kilowatt*
(1)	*(2)*	*(3)*	*(4)*	*(5)*
1,000,000	$50,000	5.0¢	. . .	. . .
1,100,000	52,800	4.8	$2,800	2.8¢
1,200,000	55,200	4.6	2,400	2.4
1,300,000	57,200	4.4	2,000	2.0
1,400,000	60,200	4.3	3,000	3.0
1,500,000	64,500	4.3	4,300	4.3
1,600,000	70,400	4.4	5,900	5.9

* Unit-cost data are rounded to the nearest tenth of a cent.

Sales Revenue.   All this cost information doesn't do you any good unless you know something about the demand for electricity. So you have your sales and market-research people get you the best estimates they can on the prices at which you can sell these various amounts. To simplify matters again, assume that you sell at the same price to everyone (not discriminating between residential and commercial users). Table 24-2 shows the same output range as Table 24-1.

This table is the counterpart of the cost table. Column 2 shows the prices at which different amounts of electricity can be sold. Column 3 shows the total revenue obtained by selling at those prices. Column 4 shows the extra revenue obtained by selling an additional 100,000 kilowatts—for example, $3,400 extra obtained by boosting sales from 1,100,000 to 1,200,000 kilowatts. And Column 5 converts this marginal revenue to a per kilowatt basis, by dividing the marginal revenue per 100,000 kilowatts by 100,000.

There is one special point in this table that merits attention. Under pure competition, price and marginal revenue to the seller were identical. If the farmer sold an extra bushel of wheat at $2 a bushel, he added $2 to his total revenue. *But for the monopolist, marginal revenue is always less than price, assuming he sells his product at the same price to everybody in any given time period. This is because he must lower his price to sell more units, and he must lower it not just on the marginal unit but on all units sold.*

For example, you can sell 1,500,000 kilowatts at 6.1¢ per kilowatt. To increase sales to 1,600,000 you must reduce the price to 5.7¢ on all 1,600,000 kilowatts. Thus your marginal revenue is your income from selling the extra 100,000 kilowatts (100,000 times 5.7¢ = $5,700) less the .4 of a cent loss on each of the other 1,500,000 kilowatts (1,500,000 times .4¢ = $6,000). In this case, then, marginal revenue on the 100,000 kilowatts is actually negative. Your total revenue will be $300 less if you cut price to 5.7¢ in order to increase sales

Table 24-2

HOMETOWN ELECTRIC COMPANY—CUSTOMER DEMAND SCHEDULE

| | | | *Marginal Revenue* | |
Kilowatts (1)	*Price* (2)	*Total Revenue* (3)	*Per 100,000 Kilowatts* (4)	*Per Kilowatt* (5)
1,000,000	8.0¢	$80,000	. . .	. . .
1,100,000	7.6	83,600	$3,600	3.6¢
1,200,000	7.25	87,000	3,400	3.4
1,300,000	6.9	89,700	2,700	2.7
1,400,000	6.5	91,000	1,300	1.3
1,500,000	6.1	91,500	500	.5
1,600,000	5.7	91,200	−300	−.3

to 1,600,000 units, even though you sell an extra 100,000 kilowatts at 5.7¢ each. At other points in the demand schedule, marginal revenue is also less than price, for the same reason, though only when sales get over 1,500,000 is marginal revenue actually negative.[7]

This relationship between price and marginal revenue is fundamental for every seller who is not in a perfectly competitive market. Whenever he faces a downward-sloping demand curve, he must recognize that to sell more he must cut price both on the extra units he hopes to sell and on the units he could otherwise sell at a higher price. His gain from cutting price is never as big as it appears to be at first glance.

Maximizing Monopoly Profits.   The monopolist can set his price where he pleases, and sell what the market will take at that price. Or he can decide how many units to produce, and sell them by asking the price at which consumers will

---

[7] Marginal revenue is always zero when elasticity of demand is unity, positive when demand is elastic, and negative when demand is inelastic. Why? From this proposition it obviously follows that no perceptive monopolist will ever increase his output into the range where demand is inelastic.

buy them. But, given the market demand schedule, he cannot set both the price and the number of units he will sell. The market will determine one or the other for him.

How could you maximize your profits, if you were the electric-power monopolist above?

One answer is simple. You compare estimated total cost and estimated total revenue at each different level of output. When you find the level that gives the biggest total profit (revenue minus cost), that's it. You plan to produce that many units and sell them at the price indicated.

This calculation is shown in Table 24-3, whose first four columns merely reproduce the total-cost and total-revenue figures from the two preceding tables. It's plain that your profit is largest if you produce 1,300,000 kilowatts weekly and sell them at a price of 6.9¢ per kilowatt, which gives a profit of $32,500. Expected profit would be lower at any other level shown—though there is the possibility that some level within the 100,000-kilowatt intervals on either side of 1,300,000 might be better.

Table 24-3

HOMETOWN ELECTRIC COMPANY—PROFIT CALCULATIONS

Kilowatts	Price	Total Cost	Total Revenue	Total Profit	Marginal Unit Cost	Marginal Unit Revenue
1,000,000	8.0¢	$50,000	$80,000	$30,000	. . .	. . .
1,100,000	7.6	52,800	83,600	30,800	2.8¢	3.6¢
1,200,000	7.25	55,200	87,000	31,800	2.4	3.4
1,300,000	6.9	57,200	89,700	32,500*	2.0	2.7
1,400,000	6.5	60,200	91,000	30,800	3.0	1.3
1,500,000	6.1	64,500	91,500	27,000	4.3	.5
1,600,000	5.7	70,400	91,200	20,800	5.9	−.3

* Maximum total profit.

Another way of calculating your maximum-profit position is by comparing marginal costs and marginal revenues. This comparison is made in the right-hand side of the table. As long as the marginal revenue from adding an additional unit of output is greater than the marginal cost of producing the unit, obviously profit is increased by producing the extra unit. This increase is clear when you increase output from 1,000,000 to 1,100,000 units, on up to 1,200,000 units, and then to 1,300,000 units. But if you try 1,400,000 units, the marginal cost is 3¢ per unit and the marginal revenue only 1.3¢. This is a profit-reducing move, since it adds more to cost than to revenue—even though total profit would still be substantial at 1,400,000. The marginal approach gives us the same answer as the approach that compares total cost and total revenue. The two are simply alternative ways of getting the same profit-maximizing answer. Still a third way of getting the same answer would be by comparing marginal cost and marginal revenue per 100,000 units, instead of on a per unit basis.

Which way is better? It doesn't make much difference. Economists calculate such matters on a per unit basis, and a lot of business concerns do the same. The per unit approach fits in better with the cost accountant's approach to many industrial problems, and has important advantages for many internal business control purposes. We'll use the per unit approach much of the time, but you're welcome to use the other if you like it better.

Graphical Analysis of Profit Maximization.[8]   If you think best in terms of graphs, you may ask your staff to present the cost and revenue data to you graphically. This is easy. Figure 24-2 plots the relevant per unit data for calculating your maximum-profit position. *DD* is the estimated market-demand curve for your electricity. *MR* is the associated marginal-revenue curve, per unit, which shows the increase in your total revenue associated with each additional unit sold.[9] *TUC* is the estimated total-unit-cost curve for your optimal scale of enterprise. And *MC* is the associated marginal-unit-cost curve, showing at each point the addition to your total costs associated with increasing output one unit. The solid part of each curve represents the data from Table 24-3; the dotted lines extend the curves hypothetically beyond the range of data we have.

Be sure you know how to read the various curves. Take an output of 1,200,000 units, for example. Reading from the graph, at 1,200,000 units output the total cost per unit is about 4.6¢. According to the demand curve, this output can be sold at a price of about 7.25¢ per kilowatt. Obviously this is a profitable level of output—the demand curve is above the total-unit-cost curve. Now look at the marginal curves. The marginal-cost curve shows that to increase output by one

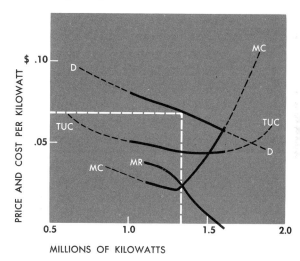

Monopoly Output and Price Decisions

FIG. 24-2   The monopolist maximizes profit by equating marginal cost and marginal revenue—here an output of about 1.32 million kilowatts to be sold at a price just under 7 cents.

---

[8] This section repeats the same analysis for those who find graphical analysis helpful.

[9] As was explained in the text above, the marginal-revenue curve is always below its demand curve, and sloping downward more steeply.

kilowatt—to 1,200,001 kilowatts—would involve an addition to total cost of about 2.4¢. This additional unit would add about 3.4¢ to total revenue, according to the marginal-revenue curve. Thus, we can readily see from the graph: (1) that an output of 1,200,000 kilowatts is profitable, and (2) that a larger output would be still more profitable, since at the 1,200,000-kilowatt level marginal cost is still below marginal revenue.

Going on, you can easily determine the maximum-profit position. It will be the output at which marginal cost just equals marginal revenue. This would be a little above 1,300,000 kilowatts, which you could sell at a price of about 6.8¢, reading off the demand curve at that output. If you wanted to compute your total profit from this graph, you could. At the most profitable output you would find your profit per unit by taking the distance between the selling price and your total unit cost, and then multiplying this profit per unit by the total number of units sold. This would give a profit of about $33,250—roughly 2.5¢ per kilowatt on 1,330,000 kilowatts.

You will note that this is a slightly higher profit than the maximum showed by Table 24-3. The graph, which gives you data for *all* levels of output rather than just one estimate each 100,000 kilowatts, tells you to produce an extra 30,000 kilowatts. The price for the larger output will only be 6.8¢, but the cost per kilowatt stays at about 4.3¢, and your total profit is about $750 larger than at 1,300,000 kilowatts.

This conclusion is suggestive: *If* in fact your cost data are smooth and continuous between the original cost estimates at 100,000-kilowatt intervals, and *if* the demand curve is also smooth and continuous between your original market-research estimates, then you'd be money out to base your calculations solely on the few intervals at which you have estimates in the original tables above. The graph, with the points connected to form accurate, continuous curves, gives you a quick guide to the maximum-profit level of output and prices. Whether you use the graph or not, you clearly need to make calculations to include possible outputs within the 100,000-kilowatt intervals used in the tables. The graph is only a short cut to these finer calculations.

PURE MONOPOLY— EVALUATION   A look at the consequences of unregulated pure monopoly, protected against entry of competitive enterprises, illustrates the extreme case of monopoly's impact on the economy.

Resource Allocation.   If one industry is monopolized and the rest of the economy is competitive, resources will be badly allocated from the consumer's point of view. Competition will not force a monopoly price down to the least-cost point on the optimal-scale cost curve. At the higher monopoly price, fewer units of the product will be sold. Thus, too few resources are hired into the monopolized industry. Consumers get fewer resources devoted to producing the monopolized product than would be optimal to meet their demand for it, relative to other products.

Conversely, too many resources will be used in other sectors of the economy. Resources shut out from the monopolized industry seek employment elsewhere. In restricting his output, the monopolist is failing to bid resources away from competitive industry, even though the marginal contribution the resources would make to satisfying consumer wants would be greater in the monopoly than in the competitive sector of the economy.[10]

Income Distribution.   Monopoly tends toward inequality of income. Monopoly profits swell the incomes of businessmen and stockholders in monopoly concerns at the expense of the rest of society. Monopoly output restriction cuts the demand for labor and reduces average wages and prices of other productive services. Remember that what the business pays out in costs is the income of its workers and suppliers. Only if monopolists were, at the outset, the low-income group in society, or if monopolies merely offset monopsonies in buying (for example, where the monopoly is a labor union dealing with a single employer in an isolated community), is inequality not increased by monopoly.

Efficiency and Progress.   In highly competitive industries, competition forces each firm to be reasonably efficient or to perish. If new production techniques or improved products are developed, the laggard who fails to keep up with the leaders soon loses out in the market and his capital erodes with his losses. Under monopoly, these pressures are weak. It does not necessarily follow that monopolies are inefficient or uninterested in progress. It only follows that they are relatively free from strong competitive pressures.

Many observers feel that the absence of strong competitive pressures does usually lead to inefficiency and lessened interest in meeting consumer needs. Rightly or wrongly, they cite the public utilities—railways, electric power, gas companies, and so forth—as slow to adopt new ideas and techniques, slow to respond to new consumer needs. Some argue that monopolists have intentionally retarded the development and introduction of new products that might weaken their monopoly position or that might increase the obsolescence rate of their existing equipment. The evidence on these points is inconclusive. But it suggests that monopolies in the absence of at least moderate competition often lag behind more competitive industries in efficiency and interest in rapid progress.

But remember one earlier qualification: If the market is so small that only a few firms can be supported at efficient scales of operation, insistence on many

---

[10] The difficulty in making a precise comparison with competitive price and output in such a case should be clear. Since the market is unlikely to be large enough to support a large number of producers, each with a least-cost point as low as the large monopolist's, we cannot demonstrate rigorously that monopoly price is higher than competitive price would be.

competitive firms would lead to less efficient operations and probably to oscillating instability through periodic price wars. Limited markets may seldom justify pure monopoly. But they may often mean that fewer firms exist than would be needed for active price competition. These intermediate cases of monopolistic competition and oligopoly need careful examination in the next two chapters. They are the common cases in the world around us.

REVIEW—CONCEPTS TO REMEMBER

Most of the major concepts used in this chapter were introduced in earlier chapters. But there are a few important new ones:

pure (simple) monopoly
monopolistic composition

oligopoly
decreasing-cost industry

FOR ANALYSIS AND DISCUSSION

1. A noted economist has argued that without government support, there would be little serious monopoly in America today. He cites public utilities, government support of unions, government-sponsored cartelization in agriculture, and "fair-trade" laws to hold up prices in retailing. How sound is this argument? Can you cite counter-examples?

2. Can you think of any pure monopolies among the firms you know? What proportion of the firms you as a consumer buy from seem to you to have a substantially monopolistic position in selling their products?

3. Select three of the firms included above, and make a list of the factors on which their respective monopolistic positions appear to rest.

4. From your observations, would you say there are significant differences between substantially monopolistic and substantially competitive firms on how hard they try to maximize their profits? On how they treat their customers? What bases do you have for your comparisons?

5. How strong a factor in building up and maintaining a monopoly position would you expect advertising could be? Can you cite examples on which your belief rests?

6. Assume for the moment the correctness of the widespread belief that General Motors' costs are so low that it could run the smaller independent auto producers out of business by cutting prices if it wished to do so. You are the president of General Motors. Would you cut prices in order to get the market away from the small independents? Why or why not?

7. If a monopoly is not making excessive (i.e., above-normal) profits, it is doing no serious harm to the public. True or false? Explain.

25

Monopolistic Competition

Almost nobody has a pure monopoly. But lots of firms have partial monopolies. The corner druggist has a partial monopoly in his neighborhood. He can charge several cents more a quart for ice cream than the big dairy stores downtown. And he can get it—because he is so conveniently located for people in the neighborhood.

Coca-Cola has a partial monopoly. No one else can make a drink exactly like Coca-Cola without infringing the law, and for years "a Coke" has been the habitual mid-morning and mid-afternoon drink of millions. But Pepsi-Cola, Royal Cola, Crown Cola, and a good many others look and taste enough like Coca-Cola to have made Coca-Cola's share of the soft-drink market decline appreciably in the last two decades. The Coca-Cola people would undoubtedly tell you they're a highly competitive field.

Bayer Aspirin has a partial monopoly. For years Bayer's held a substantial monopoly in the retail sale of aspirin, based largely on effective advertising that identified Bayer Aspirin with aspirin, even though all commercial aspirin is substantially identical. But here too other companies stand

461

ready to compete for the customer's dollar, and have in fact been doing so with increasing success by whittling away at the impression that only Bayer's is really aspirin.

A large part of the American economy is in this range between competition and monopoly—partly protected from competitors by trade names, location, tradition, quality of product, but far from perfectly protected; exposed to new competitors, but much less exposed than, say, the wheat farmer. This is the area of "monopolistic competition." In it, each firm's product is "differentiated" from its competitors', but not differentiated far enough to keep them from active competition—on prices, selling costs, quality, or all three. As was indicated above, monopolistic competition does not include those cases where there are only a few firms in an industry.[1] This few-firms case is called "oligopoly." Many products sold at retail (e.g., soap and beer) are good examples of monopolistic competition, except in small, isolated communities where there are so few retailers that the situation approaches oligopoly. The automobile and heavy electrical machinery industries are examples of oligopolies.

Before going on to examine the impact of monopolistic competition in this chapter and of oligopoly in the next, we need to pause in the following section to ask an important question that applies to both.

DO PARTIAL MONOPOLISTS MAXIMIZE PROFITS?

Do these partial monopolists, operating with various degrees of protection from market competition, try to maximize their profits? Maybe businessmen in highly competitive industries don't try to maximize profits. But if they don't make a fairly good stab at it, competition will remove them from the scene in due time. With the monopolist, we can't count so fully on competition to exert this pressure. We need to know more about the firm's motives and patterns of behavior if we are to understand how the partially monopolized sectors of the economy work.

If you asked most businessmen whether they try to maximize profits,[2] they would probably tell you, "Yes, but. . . ." The "but" might refer to lots of things, but especially to the fact that few businessmen like to say that they exploit their position by charging the last penny the traffic will bear. Playing for the long pull makes sense to many managers. It may be good business to forego higher profits today in the interest of long-run earnings.

But recognizing the fact that most businessmen see the importance of the long run as against exclusive emphasis on short-run profits, do partial monopolists

---

[1] Remember that "industry" is usually defined loosely to include all firms producing reasonably close substitutes, such as the aspirin industry, the ice-cream industry, the steel industry.

[2] In the language of Chapter 21, the question might be: Do you always try to equate marginal cost and marginal revenue? But since many businessmen never heard of these technical words, the question in the text may serve as a reasonable substitute.

generally maximize profits? Back on pages 401-402, several reasons were listed why even under pure competition many firms may not be maximizing profits at any given time. These apply equally here:

1. It takes time to adjust to change.
2. Businessmen never know what costs and demand in the future will be. They can only estimate, and often they're wrong.
3. Sometimes managers just aren't very efficient. They don't do a very good job of either minimizing costs or increasing revenues.
4. Firms sometimes can't get funds to undertake potentially profitable investments that require substantial cash outlays. The capital market is much more open to large than to small firms.

Beyond these four, there are some others that apply especially to firms holding partial monopolies, where the pressure of competition may be weaker:

5. Unusually large profits may be an invitation to new competitors, lured by the hope of winning some away. This poses a real problem to the monopolistic competitor whose position isn't very secure. Shall he reach for more profits and invite more competition?
6. Unusually large profits may bring special scrutiny from the government's antitrust officials, who may suspect illegal monopoly behavior as the basis for the profits, especially if the firm is dominant in its industry with only a few major competitors.
7. Historians point out many instances of firms that have grown big as the result of the promoters' and managers' desire for bigness as such, in spite of the dubious profitability of such behavior. Many observers of the modern scene rate growth *per se* as the most dominant single objective of large corporate management (though it is important to recognize that the growth may be generally profitable).
8. A more sophisticated argument runs that often big businesses lose potential profits because they reach the stage where top managers no longer can really make the decisions within the firm. Instead, the various departments and divisions of the firm have their own existences, each pursuing partially the broad goals set by top management but each also interested in its own problems—looking good as a department, promoting its own interests against those of other departments, and so on. Ask the president of a big corporation what he does, and you'll find that very little of his time goes to deciding how much to produce and what prices to charge. These day-to-day (short-run) decisions are typically made down in the works. Even on major, long-range issues, the decisions of top management may be pretty much determined by the actions of the various departments and by the information fed up to the top. The bigger the firm, the more serious this problem becomes.

9. Lastly, some observers emphasize the fact that the modern hired manager (as distinct from the owner-operator) may have important objectives in addition to profits—the desire for a comfortable life, undisturbed by too many new problems; the desire to get along well with others in the company; the desire to avoid ulcer-producing arguments with the union; perhaps most important, the desire to avoid looking foolish by being wrong when he takes risks. Top management has more freedom to follow these other motives if it is sheltered from vigorous competition.

A leading business executive recently described, somewhat satirically, three of these non-profit objectives as: "Empire Building," "Ivory Tower Perfectionism," and "Maginot Line Building."

The Empire Builders want to be big—leaders in their field. They want, above all, to keep chalking up one new sales record after another, or to swell their share of the market year after year, or to have the newest and biggest plant in the industry. The Perfectionists have their eyes glued on the goal of "efficiency," but sometimes on efficiency even at the expense of profits. They insist on keeping credit losses to a minimum (though more generous credit terms might increase sales enough to increase profits); they insist on keeping scrap losses down to 5 per cent (though this may actually increase over-all production costs more than it saves). Traditional rules-of-thumb about "efficiency" are all too important for the Perfectionists. The Maginot Line Builders, on the other hand, pass up profits because they are afraid to take risks. Never willing to go out on a limb with a new problem, they always keep cash and liquid assets at "conservative, safe levels." These are all sub-cases of points (2) and (4) above. Poor management isn't confined to small firms.

Some managements engage in "business statesmanship." They concentrate on improving the community where they exist, or on promoting better international understanding, or on advancing industrial relations. "Business statesmanship" and "social-minded management" have become very stylish in recent years. Service to the community and the nation is a commonly stated goal of big and little concerns. These motives are admirable. Whether they are more admirable than the traditional business objective of making profits is a subject of dispute. Some stockholders feel that management's first responsibility is profits, and that in putting this responsibility aside management actually fails to serve either stockholders or the general public as effectively as if it stuck to its traditional job of making profits for the company's owners. Management generally answers that these policies help long-run profits.

The fact is that nobody knows just how hard firms outside highly competitive areas try to maximize profits, or how well they succeed. Clearly, there are wide differences from firm to firm and industry to industry, and any simple generalization is almost sure to be wrong. In the following pages, we will assume that by and large the drive of quasi-monopolies for profits is a major factor in their behavior—as it appears to be. But, in using the profit-maximizing models that get the most attention here and in most current economics texts, you must be careful not to forget all the other motives management may have, and all the slips that occur between wish and achievement in maximizing profits.

In many ways, (2) above poses the toughest problems for the businessman who's doing his best to maximize profits. Maximum-profit estimates are no better than the consumer demand and cost estimates on which they rest. Estimating the future is never easy, and it's the future that matters. Business concerns spend thousands, even millions, of dollars keeping track of their costs in great detail and trying to get accurate forecasts of what costs and demand will be at different levels of output. Huge corporations like U.S. Steel have thousands of employees in their cost-estimating and cost-control departments. Yet many businesses lose more potential profit through inability to forecast their cost and demand situations accurately than through failure to act effectively on the basis of the cost and demand situations they estimate.

Business decisions have to be made on the basis of inadequate information and hunches more often than most people realize. The businessman seldom knows what the demand for his product is at different prices today, much less what it will be a year hence, after he builds a new plant. Often he is unsure of his present costs; he never knows what they will be very far in the future. When he has to guess at both future costs and revenues, no executive can calculate exactly what his optimum price and output positions are going to be. Yet he has to make these decisions, day in and day out. What does he do?

Different people do different things. Many of them look for some reasonable guiding rule to avoid the necessity of starting from scratch in solving each price-output problem. The practices of "standard costing" and "cost-plus pricing" have come into widespread use to meet this need.

"Standard Costing." Cost per unit of output varies at different output levels, and you're never sure just what your output is going to be very far in the future. Yet you can't be jiggling your price up and down all the time, and usually you have to quote advance prices to customers. So what a lot of businessmen do is ask their accountants and engineers to estimate as closely as possible the total cost of one unit of output at something reasonably near capacity operations. This estimate they call the "standard cost." It is the cost figure used in many of the firm's calculations, for both internal control purposes and external purposes such as price-setting, even though output may vary markedly from the near-capacity level postulated in the estimate and even though cost-component items may vary substantially from day to day or from month to month.

"Standard costing" may not be very precise, and many economists have pointed to cases where it may lead the firm to make less profit than it could, in principle, make by calculating all costs and revenue anew for each individual transaction. But standard costing is a way of getting the day's business done.

It's a rule-of-thumb short cut, albeit an imperfect one. Without such rules of thumb, the complexity of modern big business operations might lead to utter confusion and organizational breakdown rather than to a more perfect approach to profit maximization.

"Cost-Plus Pricing."   Using standard costs as a basis, many firms engage in "cost-plus," or "full-cost," or "mark-up," pricing. This means, in essence, that they price their product by taking their standard-cost estimate and adding on some allowance or mark-up—5, 10, 20, or 50 per cent—to provide a reasonable profit.[3] They are likely to use this same "full cost" to quote prices on all orders, regardless of substantial variations in the actual cost of filling the orders. This approach leads to reasonable simplicity in business operations, but it should be easy to see how it can also lead to less than maximum profits.

Actually, businessmen are often better economists than they care to let on. When standard-cost pricing gets them too far out of line with the results they would get through using an analysis based on a more direct cost calculation, they often modify, or give up entirely, their standard-cost pricing. For example, in booming markets where standard-cost pricing clearly undershoots what the market will bear, larger mark-ups or upward revision of quoted standard costs often result. In a serious depression when competition is sharp, pricing well below "full cost" becomes commonplace.

"Break-Even Charts."   Some firms use another simplifying approach, "break-even charts" or "break-even analysis." In its simplest form, this technique compares total revenue at some fixed price with total cost, at different levels of output. Total revenue will rise by a constant amount, say $5 for each unit sold if the price is $5. But total cost will rise at a different rate. The total cost (remember, *not* total cost *per unit*) is comprised of two parts. Fixed cost is the same at any level of output—say $100 per week for rent and managerial salary. Variable cost in many firms seems to be about constant per unit of output over a considerable range—say $3 per unit for wages and materials. In such a case, total cost at any output is $100 plus $3 times the number of units produced.

Figure 25-1 gives us a simple break-even chart. Line TR shows total revenue, growing at $5 per unit sold. Line TC shows total cost, beginning at $100 for zero output and rising steadily at $3 per unit thereafter. The "break-even point," is at an output of 50 units. The light blue areas show that a loss will occur at any output less than 50, and a profit at any higher output. The profit or loss is the vertical distance between the total-cost and total-revenue curves at any given output.

---

[3] Often the standard-cost estimate covers only manufacturing costs. In such cases, the mark-up percentage must cover all non-manufacturing costs, as well as an allowance for profits.

Using this chart, the businessman can see quickly about what he would make or lose at any output, given his costs. Using different prices with resulting different *TR* lines on the chart, he can compare how well off he would be at different prices he might charge. The chart is one tool to help decide the best price to set.

It is easy to see that, as described at least, it is a very crude tool. Even though it permits comparison of revenues at different prices (by using different revenue lines), its assumption about costs as a straight line is at best a rough approximation, and surely total cost would rise faster after plant capacity was reached. Still, the chart provides a guide to pricing and output decisions, short of doing a special analysis for each pricing and output decision. And the more sophisticated businessman can insert more accurate, curving estimates of his costs, if he wants to do more elaborate studies.

Break-even Chart

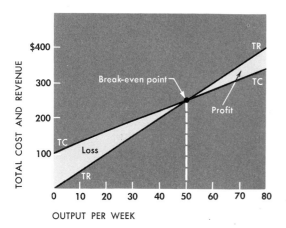

FIG. 25-1   With price at $5, *TR* is the total-revenue curve. Comparing this with the total-cost curve *(TC)*, the break-even point is 50 units per week. The firm makes a profit at any higher output.

Return on Investment.   Increasingly in recent years, big corporations appear to have used some "target" return on capital investment as a rough guide to pricing policy (and to capital investment in new ventures as well). DuPont and General Motors have for years followed this policy. G.M., for example, shoots for 20 per cent on invested capital after taxes. This, of course, doesn't give any automatic guide to setting prices, but it does throw out some guidelines to the men who do the price-setting. The company doesn't expect to get that return each year, through good times and bad. It takes the long view, and expects to do better than the target some years, worse in others. Thus, current pricing and plans for expansion are all wrapped up in the same general process, in which the test of effective performance is whether it meets this profit rate standard.

Why does G.M. choose 20 per cent as the target rate? U.S. Steel is reported to use 8 per cent after taxes, a very different figure. Alcoa is reported to use 20 per cent before taxes; General Electric 20 per cent after taxes. Maybe you'll say that, in effect, each is out to maximize profits, and their target rates are merely about the peak they think they can earn. Certainly we need to know more about how the targets are set to evaluate their impact on pricing. But for better or worse, lots of big businesses seem to use this approach as one major guide in pricing and investment planning generally.

Conclusion.   The businessman holding a partial monopoly is partially, but by no means entirely, free from the pressures of competition. Under pure competition he produces at minimum possible cost and prices accordingly, or he is driven out of business. With less active competition there is more freedom on both productive processes and pricing policies. For all the reasons indicated, we are less sure that the partial monopolist will price to maximize his profits and will minimize his costs for whatever output he chooses.[4]

PRICES AND OUTPUT
UNDER MONOPOLISTIC
COMPETITION

The Bases for Product Differentiation.   The essence of monopolistic competition is that each firm's product is a little different from those of its competitors, but not very different. Each producer tries to differentiate his product and increase the demand for it. To the extent he succeeds, he can get away with charging a little more for his product. He has set himself apart in a partially protected position.

Sometimes product differentiation involves actual physical differentiation. For example, Schlitz beer tastes different from Pabst; a Frigidaire is different from a G.E. refrigerator. But often the differentiation hinges on the things that go along with the product—convenience of the corner grocery's location, thick carpets on the floor of the best dress shops, smiling, well-groomed waitresses in some restaurants, doormen with circus-band coats at stylish hotels, easy credit terms and delivery service at some stores. Sometimes the differentiation is almost purely illusory—it exists in the mind of the customer but not in fact. The case of aspirin has been cited above. Most smokers can't tell one standard cigarette brand from another when they are blindfolded. If you can really tell the difference between the various high-test gasolines in your car on the road, you're better than most of the experts. Often when you think you're getting special easy-credit terms you're paying just what is normal in the trade.

Some bases for product differentiation are more fundamental and longer-lasting than others. But whatever the reason—physical difference in product, services, location, style, or just illusion—whenever one seller is differentiated from others in the customer's mind, that seller is able to charge a price higher than his competitors without losing all his market.

---

[4] There is a large literature on business pricing practices. Some of the main policies are summarized in these two chapters. For an interesting, easy-to-read account of some current big business pricing policies, see A. D. H. Kaplan, Joel Dirlam, and R. F. Lanzillotti, *Pricing in Big Business* (Washington: The Brookings Institution, 1958).

Short-run Output and Prices. Given his costs, the monopolistic competitor's problem is to set his price so as to maximize his profits. He has some freedom to raise price above what his competitors charge for similar products, but if he goes too far his share of the market will drop sharply. The more successful he is in differentiating his product, the less elastic his demand curve will be. With a highly inelastic demand curve, he can boost his price sharply without a corresponding drop in sales. But it's hard to convince customers that no substitute will do.

The firm's optimal price-output decision in the short run under these conditions is hard to specify. It will generally try to maximize the difference between total revenue and total costs, by producing efficiently and by stimulating demand for its own product.[5] Each firm's demand curve will depend on two major factors— consumers' total demand for the whole group of slightly differentiated products, and the firm's share of the total. Palmolive can increase and steepen the consumer demand curve for its soap only by getting customers away from Lux, Sweetheart, and the rest, unless it can somehow increase total consumer demand for toilet soap. If Palmolive succeeds in convincing people they should wash their faces oftener, this may increase the demand for other soaps as well as for Palmolive. The trick is to be sure you get the big share of the benefit if you go in for

---

[5] Given the firm's cost and demand curves, the technical conditions for maximizing profit in the short run are identical with those for the monopolist described in detail in the last half of Chapter 24. Thus, in the adjoining figure, to maximize profits the firm will set price and output where marginal cost equals marginal revenue. This gives output *O* to be sold at price *P* as the optimal position. To produce less would forego additional profits because increasing output would add more to revenue than to cost. To produce more than *O* would reduce profits because it would add more to cost than to revenue.

You may wonder whether this logical, marginal cost–marginal revenue approach to maximizing profits can really be used by businessmen, whatever their degree of monopoly, if it's so hard to estimate costs precisely for varying levels of output. If you took a sample of 100 corporate executives in the country and asked each whether his company maximized profits by equating marginal cost and marginal revenue, you probably wouldn't find ten who understood what you were talking about. But any business firm that is making a reasonably good stab at maximizing its profits is, in effect, doing what the economist means when he talks about equating marginal cost and marginal revenue. Even though the businessman may never have heard of those terms, and even though he may draw no demand and cost curves of any sort, in maximizing profits he is doing a reasonable job of making extra cost and extra revenue approximately equal. The issue is thus not whether businessmen use these terms, but whether they act *as if* they were equating marginal cost and marginal revenue. Elaborate calculations based on marginal cost and marginal revenue have little place in modern industry, but the basic "feel" of marginal analysis may be much commoner than it would appear to be on the surface. And increasing numbers of firms are making explicit use of marginal (or "incremental") cost and revenue analysis in making decisions.

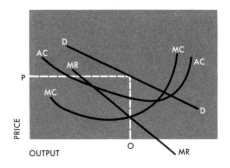

this kind of advertising. Conversely, increased advertising by Lux, or improved quality by Sweetheart, may leave Palmolive with a lower, flatter demand curve, even though Palmolive soap is just as good as before. Under monopolistic competition, it should be clear, the level and elasticity of any firm's demand curve depend on what it does and what all the other firms in the industry do as well.

Just how much any monopolistic competitor will spend on demand creation, trying to raise his demand curve and make it more inelastic to increase his profits, is hard to tell. Presumably he will increase his expenditures on advertising and other demand-creating activities as long as he estimates the results will add more to his income than to his costs. But, under monopolistic competition, partial protection from the pressures of competition, coupled with uncertainty about the complex interactions between each firm and its competitors, makes short-run output and price behavior hard to predict. As under pure competition, we are on safer ground when we look at longer-run adjustments.

Long-run Adjustments Under Monopolistic Competition. In the long run, new firms enter industries and old firms leave. The search for profits goes on, with productive resources freely transferable throughout the economy. Monopolistic competition is like pure competition in that new firms can enter the industry at will. It is different in that new firms cannot exactly duplicate the product of existing firms—they can only approximately duplicate it. For example, a new drugstore across the street from an established one might provide very close substitutes. A new women's wear store that sets up in competition with Saks Fifth Avenue will have a tougher time. For one thing, drugs, candy, and ice cream are relatively standardized as compared with women's clothes. For another, few drugstores have the prestige, glamour, and location associated with Saks.

But whether new firms can provide very close or only moderately close substitutes, high profits in any monopolistically competitive field will draw new competitors. As more firms enter, the total market is divided up more ways. The demand curve for each established firm is moved downward (to the left). Profits per firm are reduced by this sharing of the market. Gradually, if new firms continue to enter, profits tend to be eliminated, just as under pure competition. A new equilibrium with economic profits eliminated may be achieved at least temporarily.

This sounds just like pure competition. But it is different in one respect. In this temporary equilibrium, under monopolistic competition each firm is restricting output a little to take advantage of its product differentiation. Each firm is producing inefficiently; it is operating below its optimal capacity and producing at a cost above the least-cost point on its optimal-cost curve. As a result, the equilibrium market price is higher than it would be under pure competition, when price would be forced down to the least-cost point on the cost curve for the firm; and resources are wasted through the excess capacity in each firm.

This result is illustrated in Figure 25-2. Suppose that case 1 pictures a typical firm in a monopolistically competitive area. The firm is making a good profit. Since its demand curve is well above its total-unit-cost curve over a substantial range, the manager can make some profit even if he isn't very alert in choosing the best short-run price and output. The demand curve is downward-sloping, because this product is differentiated from its competitors.

What will happen? Competition will pick up. As new firms enter the market, the demand curve for each old firm moves downward as its share of the market falls. Eventually, the demand curve for typical firms will be pushed down far enough to be just tangent to the cost curve. All profit has been eliminated, and there is no further apparent incentive for new firms and new resources to enter

Individual Firm Under Monopolistic Competition

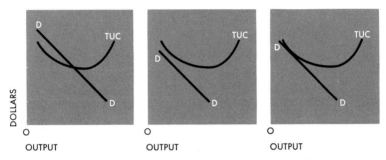

FIG. 25-2   Figure shows firm making money on left, losing money in middle, and in no-profit temporary equilibrium on right.

the industry. Neither is there any incentive for existing firms to leave, unless some especially attractive opportunity opens up elsewhere in the economy. This is case 3 in Figure 25-2.

But note that here each firm is operating to the left of the minimum point on its cost curve. Cost, and hence price, are higher than they would have been under pure competition. As long as the demand curve for each firm is downward-sloping (as it must be when each firm is big enough and different enough to have an independent influence on price), it must become tangent to the cost curve to the left of the minimum point. In economic terms, each firm will end up restricting its output below the competitive level to try to take advantage of its differentiated position—but market competition from new firms will wipe out any special profits it might have hoped for.

Suppose we started with case 2 in Figure 25-2. Here existing firms are making losses. As firms gradually drop out of the industry, the demand for the products of each remaining firm gradually rises. It continues to rise until a no-loss situation has been reached, when there is no further incentive for resources to move out of the industry. This, again, is case 3.

The similarity of these results to those under pure competition stems primarily from the relatively free entry of firms into the industry. Incentives to maximize efficiency and to develop products to meet consumer needs are strong. The only important differences evident so far are the somewhat higher price to the consumer under monopolistic competition because of product differentiation and the excess capacity built into each firm. But neither of these differences is likely to be of major importance if the competing products involved are close substitutes.

But this is not the end of the story; the equilibrium is almost surely only temporary. If you were running a grocery store and were in position 3 in Figure 25-2, what would you do? Maybe you'd just sit in stable equilibrium. But probably you'd try to figure a way to get more business. You might try improving your service to customers. Or putting in air conditioning. Or advertising more vigorously in the local papers. All these attempts would (a) cost you money. They might (b) bring you more customers—i.e., they might raise your demand curve—probably by drawing customers away from competitors. And they would (c) disturb the equilibrium situation shown in case 3. Such attempts to increase or create demand for products are apparent everywhere, keeping equilibrium (with the demand curve tangent to the cost curve) from being achieved or maintained. Competitive demand creation and quality competition are everywhere on the American scene, under monopolistic competition, under oligopoly, and even under monopoly.

QUALITY COMPETITION

Every housewife knows about quality competition. She knows which stores have the freshest vegetables, and where there are enough clerks to provide quick service. Schoolboys can tell you with surprising accuracy which drugstores in town sell the biggest ice-cream cones. When you buy a suit, you go to a store you know will stand behind it if something goes wrong. All these are examples of quality competition, just as much as the more obvious cases of using better materials and better workmanship in the physical construction of products.

Alert businessmen are very much interested in knowing what quality consumers want. They spend thousands of dollars on market research to find out whether consumers want softer seats in autos, cellophane around fresh vegetables, more carbonation in ginger ale. A shrewd businessman will improve the quality of his product whenever he believes customers want the improvement badly enough to pay for the extra cost—and a little bit more. He will put chromium trim on automobiles, foam-rubber cushions on sofas, or fancier packages around candy, if he thinks these steps will get him additional customers enough or let him charge enough higher prices to increase his profits. He will reduce product quality—for example, by putting his store on a cash-and-carry basis—whenever he believes that most customers would prefer to pay less and go without the higher quality. But he will do more. He will spend large sums to induce present and potential customers to want the particular qualities he provides in his product.

Some observers believe that quality competition is the pervasive form of competition in modern America, and that price competition is of secondary importance. There is much to support this point of view. Filling stations have long since learned that a clean rest room is more important to a touring family than a half-cent off the price of gas. Twenty years ago, having the attendant wipe off your windshield and check your tires without being asked was a striking quality innovation in the filling-station business. Today it is taken for granted. The first air-conditioned movie had an enormous quality advantage. Now the non-air-conditioned movie is the exception.

Such is often the case in quality competition. Once one firm pioneers, others feel they must follow—or risk losing their customers as a consequence of holding out. The result is higher quality all around, and, since quality usually costs money to provide, ultimately higher prices to consumers to cover the higher costs. Then every manager starts scratching his head to figure out a new improvement that will give him at least a temporary jump on the field again.

Quality competition is a perfectly valid type of competition, just as much as price competition. There are some, however, who view the movement with alarm because they feel that most such competition produces more illusory than real quality improvement. What good does more chrome on a modern auto do? they ask. And what about the buyer who would prefer a simple stripped-down model at a lower price? Why should the consumer be forced to pay for two or three fancy "crisper trays" in a new refrigerator when he could buy a less elegant storage dish himself at a third the cost? Why should you have to pay for a fancy cut-glass bottle each time you want to buy some perfume?

Behind these criticisms there lies a real danger—that higher "qualities" may become so standardized that the buyer who prefers a lower-quality product at a lower price will be unable to buy it. It's just about impossible to buy a Buick without chrome. But some retail stores quote you separate prices on merchandise, depending on whether you pay cash or buy "on time." And you can either go to a cash-and-carry supermarket, or order from the corner grocery that delivers. Ideally, for freedom of consumer choice quality differentials should be available separately and charged for only when taken. To carry this principle to the extreme might lead to chaos, but to disregard it entirely leads to a serious restriction on free consumer choice and consumer direction of resource allocation.

COMPETITIVE DEMAND CREATION Businessmen advertise to increase the demand for their products at least as often as they improve quality, in monopolistic competition, in oligopoly, and even in monopoly. Actually, advertising and quality improvement are closely related, and sometimes indistinguishable. Advertising makes no change in the physical nature of the product or in the services that go with it. But advertising may increase the desirability of the product in the consumer's mind, just as much as if the product were really better or were really wrapped up in a fancy box. The line between quality competition and advertising is a hazy one.

Selling Costs and Production Costs.   The costs discussed in previous chapters were production costs, incurred to make products that meet expected consumer demands. By contrast, selling costs are costs incurred in trying to increase the demand for a product. Production costs include costs of manufacture, transportation, financing, storage, and all other activities that are required to produce the commodity and to get it to the consumer. Selling costs include all forms of advertising and demand-creating activities—newspaper, radio, television, magazine, and direct-mail advertising, window displays, salesmen on the road and in the home office, prize contests and give-away shows, and so on.

The distinction between production and selling costs is an important one. When all costs are production costs, the demand seen by any firm is not changed by the firm's own activities. But with selling costs, the seller can always increase the demand for his product by spending more money. Whenever he tries, he is almost certain to cut the demand for his competitors' products, and you can guess what his competitors do then. They retaliate.

Competitive Advertising—An Example.   When Chesterfield advertises, the main effect is to take customers away from Lucky Strike, Camels, and Old Golds. The ads may also induce new people to take up smoking or get present smokers to smoke more, but these are probably not very important results. (Look at a few cigarette ads and see how you would assess their likely impact.) Given any level of total national spending, advertising that sells more cigarettes necessarily means less sales for someone else. This shift of demand will probably be away from other cigarette companies. But it may be away from candy makers, movies, or some industry that seems only remotely in competition with cigarettes for the consumer's dollar.

Imagine a monopolistically competitive milk industry in a good-sized city, with 15 milk companies of about equal size and no advertising. Company A begins an advertising campaign. It gets more customers by luring a few away from each of its competitors. Although A's costs are now higher, its profits are up because of increased volume, or perhaps because it can raise its price since its milk is now differentiated as superior.

It doesn't take a business genius to predict the reaction of the other companies. After spending a few well-chosen words on the manager of Company A, they will get busy on their own advertising campaigns, designed at least to get their customers back and (hopefully) to lure new customers into the fold. If every company just matched A's advertising, we might think of a new equilibrium situation, with each producer having back just his original customers, but with every company's cost higher by the amount of the advertising and with price correspondingly higher to the consumer or company profits correspondingly lower.

Equilibrium Uncertain Under Competitive Demand Creation.   But having tasted success, A is unlikely to be content to sit quietly at the restored equilibrium. So are B, C, D, and all the others. Each will be busy contriving a new and better advertising campaign—if not to expand his sales at least to protect them against the selling campaigns he strongly expects from his rivals. If another round of advertising expenditures start, the result is likely to be similar. Everybody ends up advertising more. Nobody ends up with many more customers, or with any more profits. And consumers end up with higher prices. Now they're buying advertising along with their milk—without having anything to say about whether they really want to buy advertising or not. And nobody can tell where the whole process will stop.

If we started from a long-run equilibrium situation, with no profits in the industry, substantial outlays on advertising (or other forms of demand creation) will raise problems for somebody. Maybe (a) the advertising increases total milk consumption, raising the sum of the demand curves for all producers. If so, a new, higher price equilibrium may be reached temporarily. But if (b) the advertising merely succeeds in shuffling the existing total demand around among the 15 companies, somebody is going to end up running at a loss. Costs are higher, but there is no more demand. If prices go up and total demand for the industry remains constant, total milk consumption will drop. This situation may lead to more advertising by the losing firms, in a new attempt to get more customers. Or it may lead to a price war, with some firms trying to build up sales through lower prices without advertising. Or the losing firms may gradually drop out of the industry. Any way you look at it, it's clearly not likely to be a very stable situation.

Even case (a) above, where the advertising campaign increases total spending on milk, raises the same kind of problem. Where do these additional funds for milk come from? Maybe the milk advertising stimulates total spending and raises the total level of income and employment, but this seems unlikely on the basis of our look at the determinants of national income and employment in Part II. If total spending is unchanged, obviously increased demand for milk must mean decreased demand for something else. Producers in these other industries will need to recapture customers to regain their previous positions. They are likely to fight back to regain their sales. This will cause another reshuffling of demand, with still other industries (possibly including milk) losing customers to the newest advertisers.

Over-all, it is difficult for any firm or industry to gain more than temporarily from large advertising outlays in an economy in which counter-advertising is general. The over-all effect of advertising, on which we spent over $12 billion in 1960, is to devote this part of our productive resources (men, ink, billboards, and so forth) to producing advertising rather than to producing other goods and services.

Why Not Give Up Advertising? If advertising is so largely neutralized by counter-advertising, why don't competitors simply call the whole thing off? One big reason is that each hopes to stay ahead in the race and none dares to drop out. There is usually an advantage in leading, and always a danger in curtailing— especially because it is so difficult to measure the results of advertising, particularly advertising aimed at "goodwill" and "repeat customers." Every firm tries to get customer goodwill. Once it has customers firmly tied to its product, it can afford to cut back on its advertising outlays for this purpose. But how to know when this is safe? Its repeat customers may be lured away any time. A good customer is far easier to keep than to get back once he's been lost. All this uncertainty leads to reluctance to experiment with reduced advertising outlays.

DEMAND CREATION, "WASTE," AND THE ALLOCATION OF RESOURCES   Over $12 billion spent annually on advertising is a huge amount of money. No estimates are available of the amount spent on other demand-creating activities, but the sum is undoubtedly enormous. What do we get for our money? How do we, as consumers, come out in the end?

Advertising and Consumer Information.   One obvious advantage of advertising is the information it makes available to consumers on the products advertised. When consumers are well informed about products, they are able to spend their money efficiently in satisfying their wants. The better informed consumers are, the better they are able to force producers to cater to their wants by spending on only those products that actually meet their needs. Just how many resources should be devoted to making consumers better informed is a difficult question. The price mechanism doesn't provide a measuring stick by which consumers can automatically make the decision on this use of resources, since consumers don't have a chance to buy the information separately.

Advertising that informs consumers about new products is also useful. By spreading such information rapidly, advertising may both change consumers' ideas as to what goods are most desirable and speed consumer acceptance of new products to the point where low-cost mass production is possible. In a rapidly changing economy, this service might be hard to get in any way other than through advertising.

But only part of modern advertising makes much of a contribution to consumer information. Unfortunately, many advertisers are more concerned with attracting consumers away from competitors than in providing information on which consumers can make more intelligent choices. Watch a TV set through an evening and record all the information you get that is of value in helping you decide among the products advertised. Read a copy of one of the big-selling magazines. Look at the billboards. Try the morning newspaper.

You will see ads of all sorts. Magazine and TV advertising is increasingly institutionalized—aimed at building up general goodwill and the prestige of the advertiser. You probably won't get much real information from the billboards. For specifically useful information, newspaper advertising is likely to come out best, largely because it is more local in nature and concentrates more on specific products with pictures, descriptions, and prices. Many observers of the modern scene are pretty discouraged with the level and usefulness of modern advertising; they put radio-TV "soap operas," patent medicines, and singing commercials at the bottom of the totem pole. But other people like them. You can judge for yourself.

Outright dishonest advertising has been cut down substantially by the protection given by the Federal Trade Commission and by the Pure Food and Drug Acts of 1906 and 1938. But plenty of it still exists. And many ads imply qualities which the advertised products don't have and wouldn't dare to claim directly. Spectacular cases of this sort have had to do with extreme claims made for cigarette filters, cosmetics, patent medicines, and special food products.

Lastly, advertising not only provides information (helpful or misleading), but it also does much to mold the social customs and values of modern society. The movie-star glamour that graces myriads of soap ads each month in the women's magazines has a real impact on teen-agers and housewives alike. Few people can look day after day at advertisements for new automobiles, refrigerators, and washing machines without gradually coming to believe that every American (or at least he himself) should have these products. Some observers worry lest all this create social dissatisfaction and neuroses, since, alas, not everybody has the money to buy all the shiny new things he sees advertised, or a complexion to match the movie stars'.

Advertising as a Basis for Monopoly.   Advertising, whether based on real differences or illusions, helps provide increased opportunities for profit by setting apart the seller's product. Whether the result is monopolistic competition or oligopoly, exaggerated product differentiation through advertising lets each firm boost its price somewhat through restriction of output. Sometimes the result may approach pure monopoly—the classic case of Bayer Aspirin, which kept dominant control of the market even when competitors sharply undercut its price on pharmaceutically identical aspirin, was mentioned above. Although advertising is seldom so successful, cases of very strong consumer attachment to trade names are commonplace. Aggressive advertising serves both to keep alive these consumer attachments and to discourage new firms from competition.

The Use of Resources in Demand Creation.   Is demand creation wasteful? In a full-employment economy, we must choose between alternative uses of resources.

For our advertising dollar (paid in the price of the product) we get Perry Como, billboards, singing commercials, the funny papers, the New York Philharmonic, soap operas, and a wide variety of other services, the worth of which might be disputed vigorously by different persons. Advertising expenditures make possible 5-cent daily papers, and a 15-cent *Saturday Evening Post;* $12 billion spent in a year on advertising provides many useful services and some perhaps not so useful. Moreover, the amount spent on demand creation has soared astronomically. In 1940, total expenditures on advertising were less than $2 billion; by 1950 they were $5 billion; by 1960 they were $12 billion. Is this too much? How much, if any, of it is waste?

From the standpoint of resource allocation, the real question is: Are the services provided by advertising the services we want, and are we most effectively utilizing our resources by spending $12 billion annually on these services? No firm answer is possible. $12 billion would buy a lot of other things—schools, highways, houses, medical research. We can only say firmly that by financing the services through advertising, little effective choice is left to the consumer as to what services he buys. The Camel smoker buys "The Camel Caravan" whether he has a radio or not; the Burma Shave user buys jingles or roadside signs even though he never ventures beyond the city limits. Still, almost everybody buys many advertised products and enjoys some of the fruits of advertising and demand creation. Perhaps, aside from the cases of misleading and monopoly-inducing advertising, everything pretty much evens out and consumers get just about the information and "entertainment" they would have bought anyway with their advertising dollars. But this seems unlikely, and such easy generalizations seldom face the issues. A careful analysis of the use of the consumer's advertising dollar in relation to his desires would be required for a more useful answer.

Lastly, some critics of modern quality competition and demand creation view with alarm the gradual relegation of price competition to a lesser role. Although price competition, quality competition, and demand creation may all be practiced actively in the same industry, in many areas (for example, cosmetics) open price competition has been largely abolished in favor of quality competition and active demand-creating activities of all sorts. Some manufacturers have sought special legal protection through "Fair Trade Laws" to forbid retailers to use price competition in selling their products. Here again there are conflicting interests at stake, and we will look more thoroughly at the problem of "Fair Trade" legislation in Chapter 27. Prices to the consumer are higher under modern demand creation and quality competition than they would be with more active price competition.[6] But here again it is up to you to make up your own mind. The econ-

---

[6] You often hear the argument that advertising actually lowers prices through widening the market and making possible the economies of mass production. This may be true, but note that the position is logically defensible only for decreasing-cost industries, and there only when the lower costs produced by a larger market more than offset the advertising costs involved.

omist can only point up the consequences of alternative practices; he cannot tell you which one you ought to like best.

Demand Creation and Materialism in America. At a more philosophical level, critics of the current scene point to vast expenditures on demand creation, to cars too long and low for convenience and laden with functionless fins and wings, to induced obsolescence and the elaborateness of modern consumer goods generally, as symptomatic of the materialism that dominates modern America. Foreign critics accuse us of being more interested in TV shows than in man's soul, more concerned with conspicuous consumption than with functional performance, more devoted to conformity than to individuality. Gangsters, give-away shows, and gaudiness appear as the trademarks of modern American society, to replace the dignity of man and the stress on individual freedom of the Declaration of Independence and the Emancipation Proclamation.

Perhaps these criticisms are far overdrawn. There is nothing immoral about air-conditioned cars and automatic washers; nothing spiritual about a loin cloth and poverty. Yet symbols sometimes attain deep importance in the minds of men, and the voices of the critics are persistent, especially those abroad. The questions they raise are worth thinking about.

REVIEW—CONCEPTS TO REMEMBER

Be sure you have the following new analytical concepts from Chapter 25 firmly in hand:

standard costs	quality competition
cost-plus pricing	demand creation
break-even point	selling costs
product differentiation	

1. Since most business executives never heard of marginal cost and marginal revenue, how can any reasonable person argue that marginal cost and marginal revenue explain how businesses set prices and output rates? How would you answer this question, which was asked by a well-known critic of modern economics?

2. "The widespread use of standard costing, cost-plus pricing, and break-even charts in American industry invalidates the marginal cost–marginal revenue analysis used by many economists." Do you agree or disagree? Explain.

3. It is often alleged that quality competition is increasingly replacing price competition in the American economy. From your own observation, is this a valid observation? Insofar as it is valid, is this development advantageous or disadvantageous for the consumer?

FOR
ANALYSIS
AND
DISCUSSION

4. As a consumer, would you like to see aggressive price competition among sellers of all the products you buy? Do you think that under such competition you would get the same breadth of display, return privileges, and charge-account arrangements now provided by major department stores?

5. "As long as there is relatively free entry to an industry, I can't get worried about the dangers of monopoly in that industry." Do you agree with this implication that society need only be concerned with protecting free entry into industries, so far as the monopoly problem is concerned?

6. Is the absence of unreasonable profits in an industry satisfactory evidence that monopolistic competition is not injuring consumers of the product concerned? Explain your answer to a non-economist.

7. Advertising men often argue that without the economy's present large expenditures on advertising, we could never have developed the mass markets that make modern, low-cost, mass-production methods possible.

    a. Do you agree or disagree?

    b. Insofar as you agree, does this reasoning suggest that the public would be better off if advertising expenditures were increased still further?

8. Do you get your money's worth out of the advertising expenditures for which you indirectly pay?

Oligopoly

Four companies—Alcoa, Reynolds, Kaiser, and Olin Mathieson—make nearly all the aluminum produced in the United States. General Motors, Ford, and Chrysler produce most of the automobiles. The top four companies account for over 95 per cent of all tin cans produced, of all copper smelted and refined. Over 75 per cent of the total business in the industry is done by the top four producers in cigarettes, linoleum, automobiles, rubber tires, and flat glass. In dozens of major industries, from half to three-fourths of the total business is done by fewer than ten firms. These are the oligopolies—industries where a few firms dominate the industry, though there may be many small firms that generally follow the leaders, or take what is left over. Figure 26-1 summarizes the degree of market domination by the leading four and eight firms in a number of major industries.

These examples are all on a national scale. The number of oligopolists in local markets is far larger. Building materials (such as cement and bricks), for example, are produced by hundreds of different firms scattered all over the country. But in any one local market, production is usually concentrated in one or a few firms. The two or three druggists in a small town are oligopolists so far as drugs are concerned—though possibly not on ice cream and soft drinks (where groceries and others compete). Other examples are commonplace. The more important transportation costs are and the harder it is for customers to shop around, the more likely local oligopolies are to be found.

THE FOUNDATIONS OF OLIGOPOLY

At bottom, most oligopolies rest on two factors: (1) the necessity of large-scale production (relative to the size of the market) for low-cost output, and (2) barriers against the entry of new firms into the industry.

If total market demand will support only a few firms of optimum size, aggressive price competition is unlikely. Any of the large firms will be able to undersell its smaller competitors, and there will always be an incentive for some individual firms to cut prices in order to increase their share of the market and to move to a lower point on their unit-cost curves. But there are impressive reasons why each firm will hesitate to start a price war, as we shall see. In many such industries, the most important barrier to the entry of new firms is the sheer size needed for efficient production. Newcomers trying to set up a new aluminum plant need more capital than most groups can raise. But technological know-how, patents, established marketing organization, and control over raw materials all may help to keep out newcomers. The bases for oligopoly power are similar to those for other monopolies, as indicated in Chapter 24.

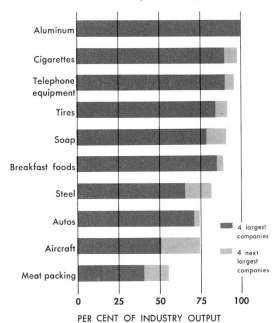

Market Domination by Leading Firms

PER CENT OF INDUSTRY OUTPUT

■ 4 largest companies

▨ 4 next largest companies

FIG. 26-1   The four largest firms dominate the industry's output in leading American industries. (Based on U.S. Department of Commerce and Federal Trade Commission data—1954.)

Still, dominant firms in an oligopoly are seldom completely safe from potential competition. For example, General Electric long held most of the basic patents in the electric light-bulb industry. It licensed these patents to small firms on condition that total production be controlled, and to Westinghouse under fewer restrictions. G.E. and Westinghouse dominated production and prices, and the market was, for all practical purposes, shared between them in rather stable proportions and without aggressive price competition. Finally, G.E.'s control was weakened by expiration of the 17-year period on some patents and by threatened antitrust action. Sylvania Electric, a small but alert firm, decided to brave the uncertainties of competition. It bought up certain free patents, stressed efficient technology and aggressive selling, and by the end of World War II had become the third major firm in the industry, though still far smaller than General Electric and Westinghouse.

The big five meat-packers maintain control of a big part of the market by controlling the major stockyards. But their control is imperfect; a large amount of meat is processed by other slaughterers and packers, especially in local markets. In the early 1900's, the meat-packing industry, like many others, used discriminatory price-cutting intermittently to provide temporary protection against newcomers. The Big Five, or as many as happened to be represented in a given territory, arranged to cut prices in rotation, a day or a week at a time, to crush independent competitors. Thus the burden distributed among the packers was relatively light, but the pressure on small competitors was overwhelming as long as the discrimination continued. Such practices aren't legal today, and oligopolies are harder to maintain.

On the other hand, two concerns have almost exclusive control of Central-American banana-producing areas, and thereby dominate the United States banana market. Their position, like others resting on exclusive control over raw materials, is relatively secure.

OLIGOPOLY PRICES, OUTPUT, AND PROFITS   Analytically, the crucial thing about an oligopoly is the small number of sellers that makes it imperative for each to weigh carefully the reactions of the others to his own price and production policies. Firms may be selling identical, or closely competing, commodities and services.

Absence of Aggressive Price Competition: Administered Prices.   Suppose you are the manager of a local brick works, and that you have two competitors in the area. You are making a reasonable profit, and so are your competitors. Each of you sets the price at which he sells—an "administered" price. Each of you knows he could make a larger profit if he could manage to increase his share of the market, because each of you is operating below capacity. Will you cut your price to get customers away from your competition?

Maybe you will. But you'd better think twice before you decide to try it. Unless they're strange fellows, your competitors will surely retaliate by meeting your price cut. Maybe they'll undercut you if you stir them up by disturbing the stability of the market. Your price advantage can't last more than a day or two before they know about it, and you can't get very rich in that length of time. Heaven only knows just what will happen if you start a local price war, but one thing looks reasonably sure: All three of you will end up with lower prices; none of you will have lured many customers away from the others; and everybody's profits will have taken a beating. In the end, you might just glower at each other in the local Rotary Club meetings, but probably you'd get together and agree to put prices back up to some reasonable level near where you started.

This is only a small-scale, hypothetical example. But the questions are the same ones that the presidents of huge corporations ask when they consider cutting prices in oligopolistic markets, in steel, automobiles, plate glass. With only a few firms in the industry, the forces toward letting well enough alone are strong. Most oligopolists hesitate to cut prices except to meet a price cut by another firm. Price reductions are likely to come only under severe pressures—seriously weakened over-all market demand in depression, for example. When firms do cut, they usually do so in the expectation that their cut will be met by rivals. Thus the cut is made with the intention of moving the whole industry price scale to a lower level, in the hope of stimulating over-all demand for the industry's product. In many cases, one major firm in an oligopolistic industry acts as a "price leader," both upward and downward, in exactly this way. How closely and consistently this leadership is followed depends on the dominance of the leader, the nature of costs in the industry, the strength of consumer demand at the time, and the personal and institutional qualities of the other managers and firms in the industry.

It is not certain that oligopolistic price will be higher than competitive price would be in the same industry. Oligopolists may price on a standard-cost markup system; they may shoot for a "satisfactory" return on capital investment; they may just follow customary price leaders. But active competition is what forces price down toward the minimum point on the unit-cost curve. In the absence of such active price competition, the likelihood seems strong that oligopoly price will be at least somewhat higher. If the industry has recently gone through a couple of violent price wars in which everyone has temporarily lost his shirt, there will be an especially strong tendency for everyone to let price alone at a level high enough to provide a "reasonable" profit. Price policy may also be affected by public opinion, and by the federal antitrust authorities lurking in the background.[1]

Such a "live and let live" policy makes sense to most producers—and to many government officials and men on the street as well. It leaves room for each firm to try quality and advertising competition to increase its share of the market. It leaves room for some price shading and juggling when times are hard or when

---

[1] For more detailed accounts, see Kaplan, Dirlam, and Lanzillotti, *Pricing in Big Business,* noted above; and Joe Bain, *Barriers to New Competition* (Cambridge: Harvard University Press, 1956).

one firm is losing out badly in the market. But aggressive price competition will probably blow the situation wide open.

Oligopoly Theory: The Kinked Demand Curve.

Economic theory helps present the price problem that faces the oligopolist, and the alternatives he must consider. Go back to the brick-works case above. The current price is 20 cents a brick, and you are selling 10,000 bricks per week. As you sit in your office, you try to imagine what your demand curve looks like, as a basis for deciding whether to change your price. Chances are you will come out with something like Figure 26-2, a "kinked" demand curve.

Kinked Demand Curve

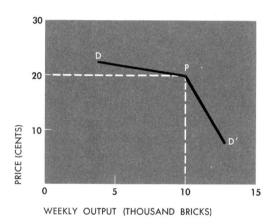

WEEKLY OUTPUT (THOUSAND BRICKS)

FIG. 26-2   Kinked demand curve suggests that you will lose total revenue if you either raise or lower price. Demand is elastic above 20 cents, inelastic below it.

It says that if you raise your price and the others don't follow, your sales will fall off sharply because your customers will desert you. On the other hand, if you cut the price, you can be almost sure your rivals will follow to avoid losing customers to you. Thus, a lower price may increase sales a little, since the market will take some more bricks at a lower price; but there's little reason to suppose you'll get a bigger share of the market away from your competitors. In other language, your demand curve is likely to be highly elastic at any price above 20 cents; much less elastic at any price below. This situation obviously puts a high premium on keeping the price where it is, just as the common sense reasoning above suggested.

Note now the critical assumptions. The first is that if you raise price, your rivals *will not* follow. It is this assumption that underlies the highly elastic curve to the left of the "corner" *P*. If, by contrast, you are a price "leader" and your rivals will follow your increase, the *DP* section of the curve will be much less elastic, and will probably just extend directly on up from *D'P*. This is because you won't lose share of market to the others. The only loss in sales volume comes for the market as a whole, because fewer bricks will be bought at the higher price.

The second crucial assumption is that if you cut price, the others *will* also cut. If they do not, then *D'P* of your demand curve will probably be highly elastic, as your rivals' customers switch to you. Then the "corner" in the demand curve will again vanish and your D'P will just be an extension of *DP*. This would be a wonderful situation for you, but it is not very likely to happen unless you can temporarily hide your price cuts from your rivals. And that's hard in an oligopoly.

In summary, then, the kinked demand curve exists because you assume a *different* reaction from your competitors when you raise than when you lower your price. If you are the recognized price leader, there will be no kink, and you are merely moving price up or down the demand curve for the whole industry (here only three firms). If you are so little that nobody reacts to your price changes, there is also no kink; but this case is really a violation of the oligopoly situation, since the essence of oligopoly is the existence of so few competitors that each must be concerned with the others' reactions. Lastly, your freedom to move price without immediately risking rivals' reactions may be larger if your product is somewhat differentiated, and consumer reaction to competing cuts may be somewhat different from an identical product case; but the general analysis is similar in both cases.[2]

Price-fixing and Market-sharing Arrangements (Cartels).

The line between not competing aggressively on price and agreeing to stabilize price is a nebulous one. In olden days, before the antitrust authorities appeared on the scene, major firms got together and agreed outright to fix prices at profitable levels. Nowadays, this practice is strictly illegal. But even though formal price-fixing and market-sharing agreements are no longer legal in the United States, analyzing a formal cartel agreement suggests some results of the common less formal oligopoly price-stabilization arrangements. And formal cartels are a dominant form of market organization in many European countries.

Cartels with Free Entry—a Simple Model. Assume a hypothetical furnace industry, in which there are only 10 firms. We want to analyze the long-run results caused by the establishment of a cartel in the industry, in which the 10 firms agree to "stabilize" prices at a higher level and to share the market equally.

---

[2] Where the demand curve is kinked, the corresponding marginal-revenue curve has a break, or discontinuity. The footnote graph shows the demand and marginal-revenue curves from Figure 26-2. Note that given this marginal-revenue curve, the marginal-cost curve (illustrated by *MC*) could move up or down considerably without logically leading the firm to change its price. This fact may further explain the observed oligopoly tendency toward price stability, even when costs change substantially. (The lower half of the *MR* curve need not be negative, though of course it will be if *D'P* shows inelastic demand.)

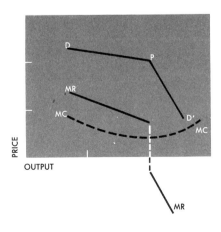

In effect, the firms will act like one pure monopoly in setting price and then divide up the business. Assume that the competitive price for furnaces of a particular type would be $400, the lowest point on the total-unit-cost curve of each producer. At $400, consumers would buy 30,000 furnaces monthly. But by restricting output, the 10 firms can make substantial profits under a cartel arrangement. So they agree to raise the price to $500 where 20,000 furnaces are sold monthly, this price being estimated as the one that will maximize total profits for the group as a whole. Then each firm sells only 2,000 furnaces monthly, but at the higher price it reaps a profit of, say, $75 per furnace (the difference between the $500 price and the $425 total unit cost at the 2,000 output level).[3]

Price is now higher than the competitive level; output is lower; employment of labor and raw materials is lower; and production is less "efficient" (i.e., plant and other fixed equipment is not optimally utilized), since each firm is operating to the left of its minimum total-unit-cost output. By agreeing to eliminate price competition, the furnace-makers gain; but consumers, workers, and resource owners lose. If the producers can keep new competitors out, they're sitting pretty.

But suppose new firms can't be kept out. Oligopoly profits lure them in. The entry of new firms will divide up the same total sales among more and more firms. With 10 firms, each producer could sell 2,000 furnaces monthly; with 12 firms, individual monthly sales can be only 1,667 (assuming each firm gets the same share of the market). Thus profits are eliminated as new firms enter, not by price reductions but by reducing output in each firm to a less and less efficient level. New firms will continue to enter, cutting down the market available to each, until finally the cost per unit has risen to equal the cartel price of $500 at an output of 1,333 for each of 15 firms.

This situation is illustrated in Figure 26-3, in which the total-unit-cost curve of a typical producer is shown. When the cartel is formed, the members agree to stabilize the price at $500. This price permits each producer to sell 2,000 furnaces monthly, and to make about $75 per furnace. But as more firms enter, building similar plants, the sales allotted to each producer fall lower and lower, until with 15 producers each can sell only 1,333 furnaces monthly. At this output the average cost per furnace has risen to $500, the cartel price, because each producer's plant is used so far below the optimum level of output. Profits have been eliminated.

Now look at the results. Consumers and resource owners (workers, investors, and so forth) are just as badly off as under the original 10-firm cartel, since price is still up at $500 and output is still restricted. And with the entry of more firms the profits of the oligopolists have been eliminated. Thus the producers are no

---

[3] Logically, the cartel as a whole would maximize its profits by estimating its costs and revenues, and then setting price and output where marginal cost equals marginal revenue. For the procedure, see Fig. 24-2 and Table 24-3 in Chapter 24 on "Monopoly."

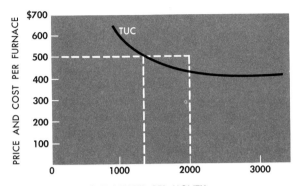

FURNACES PRODUCED PER MONTH

FIG. 26-3   At the cartel price of $500, firm first makes $75 profit per furnace. As more firms enter, each firm's market share and profit diminish.

better off than under competition, consumers and resource owners suffer all the results of monopoly, and society bears the loss of extensive "overinvestment" in the industry since far more productive facilities have been built than are required. *Such a cartel arrangement with free entry, it might thus be argued, is not a halfway point between competition and monopoly, but rather an arrangement that combines the worst characteristics of each and the benefits of neither.*

Obviously, this "equilibrium" would be highly unstable. Each producer sees a big potential gain from cutting his price, and he has little inducement to remain in the agreement since profits have been eliminated. Thus formal cartels without effective restrictions on entry seldom last long. Those with strong restrictions are more durable.

This example overstates the evils of cartels by failing to recognize the likelihood of quality competition. Cartels seldom fix market shares rigidly. Thus producers, seeing their profits vanishing, would probably try hard to attract customers through quality improvements and other non-price competition. These efforts would benefit at least some consumers, and might be a substantial offset to the cartel's price rigidity—though they would also raise costs.

OLIGOPOLY IN THE AMERICAN ECONOMY   Collaboration among firms to keep prices at profitable levels has been common since the earliest records we have of market-type economies. In the American economy, the "pools" of the nineteenth century were a formal cartel arrangement in which all the output of the industry was pooled together, then priced and sold as if the industry were essentially one monopoly. The profits were divided among the members. Economic historians have compiled a long list of pools—in steel rails, lumber, whiskey, brass, iron pipe, envelopes, window glass, petroleum products, wallpaper, and many others. Most of these pools temporarily prospered, then broke up into price wars as more and more competitors tried to invade the industry.

After the turn of the century, "price stabilization," with more informal sorts of market-sharing, gradually supplanted the formal pools and the "trusts" that followed them. The prosperous decade of the 1920's saw price stabilization entrenched as sound business policy. The New Deal policies of the 1930's encouraged cartel-type arrangements in agriculture, coal, and in industry generally through the National Industrial Recovery Act—the famous N.I.R.A. Trade associations of firms in various industries became a means of sharing information within the industry, and at the same time an effective device for facilitating price-stabilization and market-sharing arrangements.

Price Wars and Price Stabilization in High-fixed-cost Industries.   High-fixed-cost industries have played a major role in the history of American oligopoly. Consider the case of the railroads between New York and Chicago before railway rates were regulated by the federal government. There were four main routes. Each had an enormous fixed investment in right-of-way, stations, rolling stock, and so forth. Variable costs associated with adding a few more cars to any given train, or even adding whole trains, were inconsequential compared with the fixed costs. The *TUC* curve for each (for ton-miles of freight or for passengers) was downward-sloping far beyond the traffic level any one of them could realize.

Under these circumstances, the New York Central could boost its profits spectacularly if it could get New York-Chicago traffic away from the Pennsylvania. Shippers of heavy products are sensitive to freight costs. The conclusion was easy —by cutting its prices, the New York Central could attract business away from its three competitors. But exactly the same thing was true for each of the others. It was not surprising, therefore, that cut-throat competition was the rule rather than the exception.[4]

You might suppose that after about the third price war the railroads would have got together and agreed on a market-sharing price-stabilization policy. And they did periodically. But the lure of profits was great, and those were the days of the swaggering industrial tycoon. It was not until the government stepped in with the Interstate Commerce Commission to regulate rates that the price wars were ended and price discrimination against short-haul shippers was eliminated.

The steel industry today is an example of a comparably high-fixed-cost industry. The cost of a modern steel mill has to be spread over an enormous tonnage to keep cost per ton down to a reasonable figure. Steel demand is highly sensitive to business fluctuations, and only in good times do the steel companies run near capacity. Thus, much of the time each company can increase its profits markedly by increasing volume, since its *TUC* curve is downward-sloping until reasonably high-level operation is reached.

Long ago, the leaders of the major steel firms recognized the problems involved. Price stabilization, with U.S. Steel acting as a "leader" in setting prices on basic products, has been the rule since the early part of the century. Over half a century, basic steel has avoided aggressive price competition most of the time—first

---

[4] Throughout, the railroads kept up their short-haul rates to shippers who were served by only one of the four roads and who therefore had no alternatives. In many cases, it cost more to ship freight a few hundred miles between intermediate points than to ship the same freight all the way from Chicago to New York.

by formal agreements, then by the famous "Gary dinners" (at which steel leaders apparently came to price agreements at sumptuous stag dinners given by Judge Gary, president of the leading steel company), and most recently by more informal, tacit, "go-along" attitudes, facilitated by the American Iron and Steel Institute as the industry's trade association.

But the difficulties of avoiding aggressive price competition in a high-fixed-cost industry like steel have repeatedly led to undercover price-cutting and periodically to open price wars. In the depression of the 1930's, for example, the quoted base prices on steel became scarcely more than a beginning point for bargaining between the steel companies and major consumers, to determine how much the price would be shaded or what other special concessions would be made. The published prices confronting the little fellow might be firm and unyielding, but in effect steel had two price systems—the published prices and the actual bargains arrived at with big buyers. Even the NRA, which wrote into law a ban on price-cutting, was very hard to enforce, especially against the smaller companies who saw their very survival threatened by huge losses while productive capacity lay idle.

Administered Prices in Depression and Inflation.   Price stabilization was evolved largely to avoid the excesses of price competition when there was not enough demand to go around. During the great collapse of 1929-33, of the 784 prices in the Bureau of Labor Statistics wholesale price index, 35 changed only one or two times; and about half changed less than 10 times during the whole boom-and-bust cycle from 1926 to 1933.

It would be a serious mistake to infer that all sales actually were made at the quoted prices. When times get tough, businesses find ways to get around the system. Discounts are offered to old customers and on large orders to new customers. Trade-in allowances are stepped up. Concessions are made in credit terms. Delivery costs are absorbed. Secret rebates or other concessions are given. Price-shading by these means generally precedes cutting of list prices. Even in good times, list prices are actual prices only for small, irregular buyers in many industries. Price stabilization as a business policy by no means eliminates all price competition, though it keeps it within restricted bounds as long as the "orderly market" holds.

The long inflation of the 1940's and 1950's turned the problem around. Then widespread complaints were heard that the "administered prices" of the big oligopolies, especially steel and autos, led the inflationary spiral by raising prices faster than costs went up. Congressional investigations probed into oligopoly pricing practices, and pointed fingers at both big business and big unions in forcing up prices.

The evidence on these accusations has been mixed, and we will look at it further in Chapter 34. During the late 1940's, for example, it is clear that the auto companies kept their prices far below what the market would have stood during the big postwar restocking rush. At other times, product prices seem to have been pushed up faster than rising costs would have required. Over-all, perhaps the best evidence is that profits in major oligopolistic industries appear to have risen about apace with other profits during the last two decades. And they appear to have been squeezed by rising wages to about the same extent as other profits when the wage share has outdistanced profits during the postwar decade. All prices outside purely competitive areas are to some extent administered—that is, set by sellers rather than established impersonally in the market. While many oligopoly prices, especially in manufactured industrial products, did rise faster than the major price indices during the inflation, it is not clear that they rose faster than was justified by the rapidly rising costs in those industries. Pending further evidence on the behavior of oligopoly prices in inflation, the main significance of oligopoly price-stabilization and price-leadership practices seems to be in avoiding competitive downward price reductions.

Price stabilization has been widespread in retailing, as well as in manufactured products. In the depression of the 1930's, aggressive price competition drove so many retail stores to bankruptcy that traditions of live and let live became not only important for business survival but a mark of social respectability as well. The cut-rate druggist was looked down upon by the business community as not quite respectable. The "best" stores and manufacturers don't engage in aggressive price-cutting in many other lines.

Price stabilization in retailing was bolstered during the depression by the passage of "fair-trade" legislation, which forbade retail price-cutting below levels established by manufacturers for their products. Discount houses seriously undermined these agreements. Moreover, the constitutionality of the acts was challenged, and their status now varies from state to state. But traditions of price stabilization are not dropped readily, even though the law changes. The desire to avoid price wars is strong throughout the business world.

PRICE STABILIZATION AND MARKET-SHARING— EVALUATION Evaluation of oligopoly price-stabilization and market-sharing policies is particularly hard because of the absence of any simple standard to compare them against. In many oligopoly industries, anything approaching pure competition is out of the question, because the optimal size of enterprise is so large relative to the market. Thus, we would be misled to suppose that because the oligopoly price-output outcome doesn't match that of an imaginary pure competition, the industry is somehow out to beat the consumer or the worker. Yet not to match oligopoly price-output policies at least loosely against some such standard may lead us to a whitewash verdict. "Stabilization" and "sharing" are such good-sounding words.

Some of the major consequences of price-stabilization and market-sharing arrangements have been suggested above. They may be summarized as follows:

1. Adjustments to changing consumer demand are made in production and employment, more than in prices. Thus stable-price industries show wide fluctuations in output and employment over business cycles, in comparison with flexible-price industries.

2. Oligopoly prices are usually above the minimum points on the total-unit-cost curves of the firms involved. How much above depends on the industry in question —how tight the ban on new competitors is, how essential the product is, the traditions of the industry, public and governmental attitudes, and so on. If price is higher than the minimum TUC point, output must be correspondingly lower to maintain the higher price. Too few "variable" resources are used in the oligopoly industry to accord with consumer wishes; too many are excluded and forced into other sectors of the economy. On the other hand, there is too much investment in "fixed" plant in the industry, since each firm operates below its optimal scale.

3. By the same token, restricted oligopoly output reduces the demand for labor and other productive services, and lowers wages and other productive service incomes, both in the oligopoly and throughout the economy.

4. Competition is diverted toward non-price channels. Quality competition and advertising are emphasized, often with a substantial allocation of resources to demand-creating activities.

5. Whether oligopoly price-stabilization policies mitigate or intensify over-all economic instability is a moot question. On the surface, price-stabilization policies would appear to be helpful in preventing or at least slowing down cumulative price deflations. But this very stabilizing effect on prices may intensify the effects of fluctuating demand on production and employment. Unless oligopoly pricing can help stabilize ultimate consumer demand, it probably intensifies business recessions by focusing the impact of contracting demand on reducing employment and production. On the upswing, oligopoly administered pricing may speed, or retard, the cost-price inflation spiral. Over-all, the extent of oligopoly in the economy is probably not a major determinant of the severity of business fluctuations.

CONCLUSION— THE MIXED ECONOMY

The real world has little pure competition and little pure monopoly. It is predominantly a mixture of monopolistic competition and oligopoly, reaching toward the extremes of pure competition and pure monopoly in many sectors. Over-all, how does this mixed economy look in comparison with the purely competitive model presented in Chapter 22?

Resource Allocation. No matter how many or how few firms there are in an industry, businessmen must ultimately face the test of market demand. If people don't want your product, no degree of monopoly will do you much good. Moreover, even when people want your product, demand is never as inelastic as you would like it to be—when you raise the price you always run the risk of sending customers away to substitute commodities.

Under pure competition the productive system's response to consumer demands would be good; at the same time, it would take into account the preferences of resource owners on where they want to work. In the mixed economy there is this same tendency for businessmen to bid resources to where consumers most want them, as measured by consumer spending in the market. But in the mixed economy it is doubtful that resources are optimally allocated. As has been indicated several times, precise comparisons are difficult because in many monopoly and quasi-monopoly areas no realistic, highly competitive "norm" can be imagined with which the actual situation can be compared. Recognizing this difficulty, we are probably still safe in concluding that the partially monopolized industries use too few "variable" resources (labor, raw materials, and so forth), and that too many of such resources are forced out into the more competitive sectors. On the other hand, the partially monopolized industries are generally characterized by "overinvestment" in "fixed" plant and equipment. Since firms usually operate to the left of the minimum point on their total-unit-cost curves, they waste fixed resources.

How important quantitatively are these malallocations? We have no reliable quantitative estimates. Most economists who have studied the problem believe the malallocation involved represents a serious waste of society's productive resources, and certainly individual industries can be cited where this appears to be true. All in all, the malallocation is probably modest where monopolistic competition prevails with products only slightly differentiated (for example, in much of wholesale and retail trade). It is probably more important in oligopolistic industries where a few major firms have significant powers to maintain highly profitable prices with corresponding reductions in output, and where laws forbid price competition—for example, in "fair-trade" pricing of drugs.

Lastly, in the mixed economy a substantial block of resources is devoted to advertising, and to quality competition only slightly separated from advertising. That all these resources are used in accordance with consumer wants seems highly unlikely. The allocation might well be significantly different if more direct channels were open for the implementation of consumer preferences.

Income Distribution. In a competitive economy, resource owners would tend to receive incomes measured roughly by their own and their resources' marginal contributions to income produced. Although income distribution is the main business of Part 4, three tentative generalizations about the mixed economy may be suggested here:

1. Wherever partial monopolists raise price and restrict output, they reduce their own demand for labor and other resources, and force productive resources out into competitive areas where the extra supply will force down the average

price (or wage) received by productive resources. This is a direct consequence of the "inefficient" allocation of resources that results from deviation from consumer wants.

2. Businessmen and stockholders in partial monopolies often reap special monopoly profits at the expense of consumers, and possibly at the expense of resource owners. This is true, however, only where the entry of new competitors can be restricted in some way or other. With free entry, consumers may have to pay monopoly prices and accept an inefficient allocation of resources, but businessmen generally make little or no more profit than in highly competitive areas.

3. Inflexible prices in quasi-monopolized areas, coupled with highly flexible prices in competitive areas, probably increase the disparity in fluctuations of different incomes over the course of business cycles. Farm incomes, for example, traditionally fluctuate much more sharply than manufacturing wages and salaries.

Economic Stability and Growth.   The degree of monopoly is probably not a major determinant of the level of total income, employment, and prices. Widespread business fluctuations might occur in a highly competitive economy, a highly monopolized one, or a mixed one like ours. Economists are not agreed on whether widespread quasi-monopolistic pricing, especially in oligopolies, mitigates or intensifies business fluctuations; much depends on the other characteristics of the economy.

But whatever the answer is on monopolistic competition and oligopoly as such, our *mixture* of price stabilization and price flexibility is probably cycle-intensifying. If all prices were "stabilized" by business policy, there is a good chance that sharp sweeps in business and consumer price expectations might be mitigated, thereby lessening the chance that severe depressions or inflations could get under way. Or if all prices were highly flexible, over-all economic adjustments to shifting aggregate demand might come promptly, especially if the monetary system were reasonably stable. But with a mixture of the two, there is a fair chance that we get the possible benefits of neither, and the disadvantages of both—the destabilizing effect of many flexible prices that intensify expectations of cumulative price changes, coupled with the focus of fluctuating demand on output and employment in industries where prices are inflexible.

But perhaps the biggest question of all concerns growth. Do oligopoly and monopolistic competition speed or retard investment and economic growth, compared to a highly competitive society? The unfortunate answer is that we don't know yet for sure. Pure competition is clearly preferable in terms of rapid introduction of technological improvements, once they have been discovered. Under strong competition there is no possibility of holding back, whereas under oligopoly there may be. But this is only part of the picture.

Before technological change can be introduced, it must be discovered. Most research on technological processes is done in large firms, not small. Modern research is expensive, and the results are uncertain. No firm could afford G.E.'s research labs under anything approaching pure competition. Many discoveries are made by individual inventors, far from the modern laboratories of big firms. But it would be unrealistic to suppose that many modern technological advances could have been developed by small firms.

Equally important, much of modern technology is so complex that small firms could not afford to introduce the changes, even after they are known. Certainly this would be true of firms small enough to fulfill the requirements of pure competition. The problem would be less serious, though still real, as we substitute "workable" degrees of competition for pure competition.

Does this tip the scales toward oligopoly as most conducive to investment and rapid growth? In spite of the obvious advantages of big business in research, development, and introduction of major technological changes, many economists have their doubts. These doubts center around the danger that actual progress will be slower whenever the pressures of competition are lessened. Clearly there is no black-and-white answer as to which is best. An optimal combination of the size essential to effective research and utilization of modern technology, together with maintenance of as much competitive pressure as possible, may be the outcome suggested by this comparison of a purely competitive with the modern mixed economy.

REVIEW—CONCEPTS TO REMEMBER

This chapter re-uses most of the analytical concepts introduced throughout the whole section on price theory. Beyond these, be sure you understand the following new ones:

administered prices   price leadership
cartel   price stabilization
kinked demand curve   the mixed economy

1. Competition is likely to be more vigorous among the few leading firms in an industry than among the many small concerns, who often are relatively inefficient. Do you agree or disagree? Can you cite any examples to support your position?

2. "The big oligopolies like General Motors, General Electric, Swift, and Alcoa have been primarily responsible for making better goods available to consumers. Breaking them up into smaller units to obtain more active price competition would be disastrous." Do you agree or disagree? Support your position against a critic.

3. It is sometimes argued that cartels are worse for the public than would be an outright monopoly of the industry by a single firm, since the cartel charges the high monopolistic price anyhow and also involves a large waste of resources through excess capacity. Evaluate this argument. If it seems sound, would you propose that cartels be converted into pure monopolies in the industries concerned?

FOR

ANALYSIS

AND

DISCUSSION

4. Suppose you were manager of one of the furnace firms originally forming the cartel described in Chapter 26. What policies would you follow to promote your own best interests as additional new firms entered the cartel?

5. In most of the major oligopolistic industries, entry is difficult for new firms because of both the technical know-how and the large financial investment required for effective competition. Can you suggest desirable ways to overcome these difficulties, which reduce the degree of competition?

6. Suppose that you are president of the largest firm in an industry where the great bulk of the business is done by the five largest firms. As the industry leader, your firm ordinarily initiates any price changes in the industry.

    a. How would you go about deciding what price to charge for your product?

    b. Is there a conflict or community between your interests and those of the other four firms in the industry?

    c. Would consumers be betters off, by and large, if there were active price competition rather than price leadership in the industry?

27

Government
and Business

Why should government interfere at all in business affairs? Adam Smith had one answer: Because the benefits of enlightened self-seeking can be obtained only if a competitive system channels these efforts to the common good. Seldom do merchants gather together, he wrote, that their talk does not turn to means of getting higher prices for their produce. Without competition among sellers, more consumer dollars may mean higher profits and not more products. It is the job of the government, representing all the people, to see to it that reasonable competition prevails.

Everyone agrees, moreover, that in an individualistic society there have to be some rules of fair play in business practice, just as in personal behavior. Without common consent to eliminate fraud, to respect property ownership, and to honor contractual promises, business dealings would labor under a great handicap. By general agreement, it is the job of government to establish and enforce these basic rules to enable men to deal effectively together; just as it is the government's job to establish and enforce laws against murder, theft, and arson to enable men to live securely and

497

peacefully together. Among the nineteenth-century liberals, "laissez-faire" never meant that the government should do nothing, but rather that it should leave economic affairs alone *within* a framework of basic moral and governmental rules of the game.

Perhaps we can agree on these two basic governmental functions in relation to business affairs—to insist on competitive behavior and to establish the basic rules of the game. But what do they mean in practice? Does enforcing competition mean enforcing *pure* competition as we have defined it? Obviously not, for this would leave almost the whole economy outside the pale. Does it mean breaking up General Motors, G.E., and U.S. Steel? Maybe, but if it does we'd better think such a violent step through carefully before we take it. Does it mean getting after the trade associations, where producers in the same industry may pool information on costs and markets?

The economic analysis of the preceding chapters comes out with a strong presumptive indictment against monopoly. Monopoly malallocates resources, raises prices and restricts output in the monopolized industry, and lowers wages of workers employed in the industry and elsewhere. This all seems quite clear from the theoretical models used. But a familiar warning: Don't forget that those models don't necessarily represent the real world, certainly not in any detail. Remember too that most of the real world falls into the "in-between" areas that are neither pure competition nor pure monopoly, and that the results suggested by the theoretical models in these in-between cases are much less clear than at the two extremes. And don't forget the assumptions we made, which may or may not hold in any given case. Lastly, don't forget the basic requirements for active price competition, including a market big enough to support many firms each operating near its "least-cost" point.

Economic theory gives no clear answer to just how much competition is enough —just how big is too big. It suggests a basic presumption against all types of business monopolistic arrangements, viewed from the consumer's and the worker's angles—except maybe on the score of technological advance. But models as such can tell us nothing about the magnitudes involved—how big is the cost to consumers and to workers, how much higher is the oligopolist's price? And don't forget that the real world is an unstable one, where businessmen as well as consumers are looking for a rope to windward when the going gets rough. All in all, expert economists who have spent years studying the problem of "workable competition" come up with a reasonable consensus on some broad outlines of public policy against excessive monopoly, but they admit frankly they are perplexed about what to suggest on some of the "in-between" situations.

BIGNESS, MONOPOLY, AND PUBLIC OPINION   In 1958, the General Electric Company had assets of $2.4 billion, and reported profits before taxes of over $485 million on sales of $4 billion. It had 250,000 employees. Its president received a salary plus bonus totaling about $400,000, plus a valuable option to purchase G.E. stock on favorable terms. Although no exact figures are available, G.E. apparently accounted for nearly half the total sales in the country of heavy electrical machinery, light bulbs, and other major categories of electrical equipment. It was rivaled only by Westinghouse, another giant, with assets of $1.4 billion and sales of about half of G.E.'s. Big companies like Allis Chalmers in heavy equipment and Sylvania in bulbs, electronics, and lighter equipment absorbed another sizable chunk of the market, but they were far short of the two leaders in over-all size and market power.

Is G.E. a monopoly? Should it be broken up into several smaller concerns in the public interest?

Now consider Jones' Grocery Store, situated on the crossroads corner of an isolated village in northern Minnesota—population 150. Jones' total sales in 1958 were about $12,000, on which he realized a return after paying all costs (except his own salary) of about $3,000, as near as he could figure it. Jones had one employee—himself. His service was so-so, and the selection depended partly on the growing season, partly on what Jones remembered to order when the traveling salesmen stopped by infrequently. There is no other grocery store within 35 miles.

Is Jones' Grocery Store a monopoly? Should it be broken up into several smaller concerns in the public interest?

No reasonable person would answer that Jones' backward roadside store ought to be broken up by anti-monopoly policy in order to provide more competition in the village. This would be nonsense. The village can't support one respectable grocery, let alone two or three. Yet Jones' monopoly power over the customers in that village may far exceed G.E.'s power over its customers. If Jones doesn't like the Widow Smith down the street and charges her an extra price on flour or slips in some bad potatoes with every peck, she's pretty much out of luck. She can say what she will about Jones—and it may be plenty—but he knows perfectly well that's about all she can do about it. Let G.E. treat one of its customers that way, and Westinghouse or Allis Chalmers will get a phone call the next day from the insulted purchasing agent.

How about G.E.? If you think the Antitrust Division ought to look into G.E., why? Because G.E. clearly has a dominant position in the industry, with around half the market for many of its major products, and you suspect that it's fattening its profits on the consumer? Or because G.E. just seems to you too big—because you feel that no one business ought to control so much wealth, with the far-reaching economic and political power that goes with it?

It may be that you can't get very excited about G.E. one way or the other, if you're like a lot of other Americans today. G.E. is indeed a huge business, and you may sympathize with the workers when they strike for higher pay and shorter hours. But you know that G.E. has long been a pioneer in research and development of new and better products for consumers. It may make lots of money, but

it turns out high-quality, reliable products, and you have at least a sneaking suspicion that it got that big by being better than its competitors. You know, too, that
for every G.E. product you know about, you can find competing ones from Westinghouse, Sylvania, Philco, and a bevy of other companies, depending on the item.
That talk about heavy electrical machinery sounds pretty technical, and you're
not much interested in 10,000-horsepower turbines anyway. G.E. is certainly an
oligopolist by the economist's definition, but it seems to be doing a pretty good job
of serving the American consumer—and of providing a lot of well-paid, stable
jobs to American workers in the process.

If you stop to think about these two cases, you'll see that two different issues
are involved. One is the question of how strong a monopoly does the seller hold;
this is largely an issue of the size and dominance of the seller *relative* to the
market in which he sells. The second is the question of *absolute size,* which bears
no necessary relationship to the degree of monopoly the firm possesses. Jones'
Grocery is a pretty effective monopoly according to the economist's definition
back in Chapters 22 and 24, but it's a tiny concern in absolute size. G.E. clearly
holds some monopoly powers too—it's an oligopolist according to our definitions
—but its monopoly power in its markets is probably less than that of Jones'
Grocery. The striking difference is G.E.'s absolute size and economic power. The
company affects immediately millions of consumers and hundreds of thousands
of employees and stockholders by its economic actions. Its managers exert enormous power—the power of $2 billion—over the lives of nearly 300,000 workers,
over the communities in which they live, and over the consumers who buy electrical products. Never forget that our analytical monopoly and quasi-monopoly
models refer to the firm's positions *relative to its market.* The issue of absolute
size and power in the economy is related but analytically separate.

These chapters are devoted primarily to helping you do your own straight
thinking on the *economic* aspects of monopoly and quasi-monopoly. But it's important to recognize that public opinion—that potent force in controlling government action—often isn't very precise and logical. It often doesn't separate out the
issues very sharply. If we could tap the conscious and subconscious thinking of
the mythical man on the street about "monopoly," we might get something like
this:

1. Is more competition practicable? Would breaking up the big companies
really give the consumer better products at lower prices? The cheapest products
seem to come out of the mass-production industries.

2. How many firms does it really take to insure reasonable competition? Certainly not the infinitely large number required by the economist's "pure competition." Maybe only three or four big producers with several little ones nipping at
their heels.

3. Some of those corporation presidents certainly do get big salaries.

4. Can you really trust anybody with the power that goes with a billion dollars?

Big business has taken it out on the worker and the public lots of times in the past. They'd probably do it again if they could get away with it.

5. The little fellow deserves a break. We ought to help him a little against the giants.

6. The "blue chips" of American industry are the ones that have produced most of the good products that underlie our high standard of living—automobiles, nylon, refrigerators, streamlined trains, and so on. Still . . . there are those stories about how they hold products off the market—razor blades that would last two years, storage batteries that would never wear out.

7. They say that the big corporations dictate a lot of what goes into the laws made by Congress and the state legislatures. All that money surely gives them a way to buy votes that the little man can't afford.

8. Oh well, maybe with unions as strong as they are now, big business and the unions are about in balance.

This picture may not be accurate, but it does suggest the complex mixture of objectives, reasoning, and hearsay that makes up current American public opinion on "big business" and "monopoly." For the economist, big business and monopoly are far from synonymous. But the man in the street may not distinguish between them very sharply. And as the famous Abraham Lincoln saying goes: "God must have liked the common people. He made so many of them."

Elmo Roper, the public opinion pollster, has summarized what he has found over the years to be the man-in-the-street's feelings about big business. Briefly, his conclusions are: (1) Americans on the whole believe that big business is good for the American economy, and that on balance it does a good job of turning out good-quality products. (2) The American public doesn't quite trust big business, and feels that we need a government that keeps an eagle eye on the big business-man to see that he doesn't abuse his enormous potential power over workers and the public.[1]

**THE LAW
AND COMPETITION**

The law is more than what is written down in the statute books. It is what the courts say it is, what the long rows of past court decisions suggest, altered as much as the judge thinks proper in any particular case. It is what the sheriff or the Justice Department investigator thinks it is; most law is enforced without ever coming near a court room. It is what the president and his advisers think it is, through the way they instruct the government's law-enforcement branches. Above all, it is what the people will obey and support. In our democratic system, no law that does not command widespread public support can long be enforced. Often the law itself is changed when it lacks support, but

---

[1] "The Public Looks at Business," *Harvard Business Review,* March, 1949.

equally often the strength of its enforcement varies to mirror the tenor of the times.

This description is especially accurate in the field of government-business relations. Here much of the law is nowhere on the statute books. It is in the mass of court decisions, and in the practices and policies of the government's administrative agencies. Both reflect (with lags) what the public wants and what it will stand for—often more accurately than we realize. Our antitrust laws seldom change by formal congressional action. But in fact they alter constantly—with changing congressional appropriations for enforcement, changing antitrust personnel, changing judicial attitudes—often to the frustration of businessmen and their lawyers, who protest that no man can tell when he is violating the law until he sees whether the government takes him to court and the judge finds him guilty.

The Common Law.   Until 1890, there was no federal legislation that declared monopoly illegal. Nor did the states have any anti-monopoly laws of consequence. Under the common (unwritten) law inherited from England, contracts entered into to restrain trade unreasonably or to raise prices were illegal and unenforceable. Corporations formed to control other corporations in order to obtain monopoly power were similarly illegal. But the common law did not hold such monopoly practices to be criminal, nor did it even provide for damages to those harmed by the restraint of trade. The contracts were merely unenforceable.

Some judges went further than others to make things difficult for the monopolists. But the common law provided little protection to the consumer or to the little competitor who got squeezed out by combinations in restraint of trade. Some judges held extreme and vicious forms of competition to be illegal, as an extension of the law against fraud and misrepresentation, but these decisions were of little general import.

Legislation.   The last half of the nineteenth century was the era of the trusts. Standard Oil, American Sugar, American Tobacco, and dozens of others amassed huge empires that held almost complete monopolies over the products concerned. Standard Oil at its peak controlled over 90 per cent of the country's oil-refining capacity, and the bulk of the pipelines. American Sugar controlled 98 per cent of the country's sugar-refining capacity. American Tobacco had virtually complete control of tobacco manufacturing.

Moreover, the means used to build up these monopolies aroused widespread ire and fear. Standard Oil, for example, relentlessly drove smaller competitors to the wall by cut-throat competition, then bought them up or forced them into the trust, and then raised prices above competitive levels. Competitors who resisted found themselves up against ruthless force. Standard, with its vast resources, cut local prices to one-half and one-third of cost and make up the losses in noncompetitive areas. It bought up pipelines and refused transportation to competitors, or charged exorbitant prices. Through its vast power, it forced railroads to give it rebates of 25 to 50 per cent, not only on its own shipments but *on the shipments of its competitors.* When competing pipelines tried to gain a foothold, Standard bought up the refineries they served and refused to take oil from the pipelines. Violence and destruction of property were used ruthlessly when they were needed to win the trust's battles.

The Sherman and Interstate Commerce Acts. With half a hundred trust giants on the American scene, popular resentment was reflected in two major acts—the Interstate Commerce Commission Act (1887) and the Sherman Antitrust Act (1890). The Interstate Commerce Act established federal control over railroad rates and services for the first time, eliminating the cut-throat competition and rate discrimination that had long characterized this industry. The Sherman Antitrust Act was aimed at industrial monopoly. It declared illegal every monopoly and every contract or combination in restraint of interstate trade. The Antitrust Division of the Department of Justice was charged with enforcement.

These two pioneer acts are worth considering briefly, both because they still form the cornerstones of our federal monopoly regulatory policy and because they demonstrate two major alternative approaches to the problem.

The Interstate Commerce Act takes the alternative of strict, comprehensive government regulation of an industry that will not operate satisfactorily on a competitive basis. By the late 1800's, it had become abundantly clear that competitive regulation of interstate railway rates and service was impracticable. At most, only two or three roads serviced most communities, and in large areas one railway had a complete monopoly. Even where two or more roads competed, as between Chicago and New York, competition was unsatisfactory because railroads are almost invariably decreasing-cost concerns and price competition leads to price wars that drive rates far below total average cost (see page 489). The market in such cases is simply not big enough to support two or more railway systems each operating near its minimum-cost levels for the various types of shipping. Thus either oligopoly price stabilization prevails, or price competition leads to cut-throat competition and heavy losses until either price stabilization is restored or the weaker competitor goes under.

Under such circumstances, there was little point in trying to enforce competition. Instead, the Interstate Commerce Act in effect made the railroads public utilities, with their rates, services to the public, and certain other activities under the regulation of a new government commission, the Interstate Commerce Commission. General operating responsibility is left with the management elected by the private stockholders, but prices and output (i.e., rates, and amount and quality of service) must be approved by the I.C.C. as in keeping with the public interest. Under this approach, the railroads are guaranteed approved monopoly positions, but how they use their monopoly powers is carefully regulated.[2]

---

[2] With modern truck, bus, and airline competition, some economists now suggest that the day has come to try freer competition again, on the argument that competition provides more stimulus to efficiency than does government regulation.

The Sherman Act was aimed at the other part of the economy, where competition could be expected to do a reasonably good job of regulating prices, output, and quality for the public good. Thus the Sherman Act's approach was exactly the opposite of that in the I.C.C. legislation. In order to enforce active competition, the Sherman Act outlawed restraints of trade, monopoly, and attempts to monopolize, as follows:

> Section 1. Every contract, combination in the form of a trust or otherwise, or conspiracy, in restraint of trade or commerce among the several states, or with foreign nations, is hereby declared to be illegal. . . .
> Section 2. Every person who shall monopolize, or attempt to monopolize, or combine or conspire with any other person or persons, to monopolize any part of the trade or commerce among the several states, or with foreign nations, shall be deemed guilty of a misdemeanor. . . .

This was broad and sweeping language. Inevitably, a wide range of questions arose over the years as to just what was actually outlawed. What is covered by "restraint of trade," by "monopolize, or attempt to monopolize"? Another complex set of questions arose over just what activities were included under "interstate" commerce, since the federal government's power to regulate covers only commerce between different states.

As with all other such legislation, such questions have been answered primarily through a long series of court rulings interpreting the law. We will look at some of these rulings in the following section, in observing how the Sherman Act has worked out in actual practice. But here it is important to recognize the basic problem of regulatory policy which the Sherman Act illustrates. No legislation regulating the complex modern economy can hope to specify in detail every case and situation that is to be covered. Instead, Congress must do its best to state its intentions clearly, leaving to government administrative officials, to regulatory commissions, and ultimately to the federal courts the job of applying the general intent to individual cases. The substance of regulatory law is often developed more in its interpretive application over the years than through the original congressional action.

The Clayton and Federal Trade Commission Acts. One of the biggest problems in making the Sherman Act effective was the difficulty everyone had in defining just what it was that was illegal. Thus in 1914 two new acts were passed—the Clayton Act and the Federal Trade Commission Act—to clarify this situation by specifically prohibiting certain unfair and monopolistic practices, regardless of the group or individual engaging in them, and by setting up new enforcement procedures.

The Clayton Act listed specifically as unfair and illegal (1) discriminatory price-cutting; (2) tying contracts, which require buyers to purchase all items in a line as a condition of getting one item; (3) acquisition of stock in competing companies to obtain monopoly powers; and (4) interlocking directorates in competing corporations. But each of these was prohibited only "where the effect may be to substantially lessen competition or tend to create a monopoly. . . ." Thus, the Clayton Act cleared the picture slightly by defining some illegal acts. But it still left open the basic problem of interpretation for the courts in many individual cases.

The Federal Trade Commission Act created a commission to act as a watchdog especially against unfair competitive practices aimed at creating monopoly and injuring competitors. The Commission was given power to hold hearings and to issue "cease and desist" orders that require offending firms to discontinue illegal practices. When the first major appeal from a Commission ruling against a business firm reached the Supreme Court in 1919, however, the Court held that the same rule-of-reason approach must be applied in all F.T.C. rulings as is used by the courts, and that it is for the courts, not for the F.T.C., to make the ultimate decisions in interpreting the law.

The effect of this ruling was to reduce sharply the F.T.C.'s powers. It now conducts investigations into fair trade practices, and issues numerous rulings on minor unfair trade practice cases. But major actions have reverted back to the courts, since everyone recognizes that an unfavorable F.T.C. decision can be appealed to the courts. The F.T.C. has, however, played an important role in policing cases of seller misrepresentation (e.g., artificial silk as silk, domestic lace as Irish lace), and in arranging voluntary agreements among business competitors on fair trade practices. For some interesting reading, go through one of the annual reports of the F.T.C. listing the many cases of misrepresentation throughout the economy that have received cease and desist orders. These actions are taken to protect competitors against the unfair competitive practice of misrepresentation, but they of course also serve to protect the consumer.

New Deal Legislation of the 1930's. The New Deal was mainly concerned with recovery, security, and help for the lower-income classes. Anomalously, the legislation aimed at these goals was by and large anti-competition rather than antimonopoly in nature. The famous NRA, the Bituminous Coal Act, the AAA legislation for farmers—all required producers to join together in cartel-like arrangements and to refrain from cutting prices below specified levels, in the hope that these measures would stimulate recovery and raise wages and farm incomes. In these government-sponsored cartels, the focus was on producer rather than consumer interests. And the measures went far to set the tone of business competition in the American economy, even though both NRA and AAA were declared unconstitutional within a few years. Substitute legislation in the agricultural field has persisted ever since; and coal and other industries still rely on cartelization.

Other New Deal legislation was also more concerned with protecting producer than consumer interests. The Robinson-Patman Act of 1938 was aimed at chain stores that might "unfairly" undersell independents in their areas. The Miller-Tydings Act of 1937 guaranteed protection from Sherman Act prosecution to manufacturers and retailers who participated in "fair-trading" arrangements, whereby the manufacturer specifies that no retailer may sell his product below a specified price (so that prices are in effect made identical for all sellers). Too much competition was feared more than too little—reflecting the widespread fear of unemployment and depression.

"Fair Trade" and the McGuire Act. The Miller-Tydings Act provided an umbrella under which retailers could avoid the trials of price competition, because minimum prices were specified by manufacturers. But Miller-Tydings specified only that such fair-trading was not to be considered a violation of federal antitrust legislation. The heart of fair-trading was the "non-signer" clause, under which all sellers of a product within a state were bound to maintain the manufacturer's prescribed minimum price as soon as any one seller within the state signed an agreement to do so.

In 1951, the non-signer clause as a basis for fair-trading was thrown out by the federal courts. This decision created a furor among sellers of fair-traded products, especially drugs and appliances. Price competition spread rapidly. Then, in 1952, the McGuire Act was passed, which specifically declared that fair-trading under the non-signer arrangement was not illegal under federal legislation if it was approved by the state legislature concerned.

But this was not the end of the controversy. Since 1952 most state legislatures have made non-signer arrangements legal. But state courts have declared such clauses unconstitutional in a number of states, and the exact status of fair-trading is still uncertain in many states. Fair-trading with the essential non-signer clause is now apparently legal in about three-fourths of the states.

The Celler Anti-Merger Act of 1950. In the boom period following World War II, many corporations found acquiring other companies outright a profitable path of expansion. Such mergers were sometimes prompted by market-expansion goals, sometimes by special tax considerations, sometimes by the desire for diversification, sometimes by other considerations. Extension of market power through direct merger was not covered by earlier antitrust legislation, and in 1950 a new act was passed forbidding the acquisition of, or merger with, other companies where the effect "may be substantially to lessen competition, or to tend to create a monopoly."

In the first postwar decade, some two thousand corporate mergers occurred in manufacturing and mining alone. The merger movement reflected again the adaptability of American businessmen in finding ways to achieve their aims. The Anti-Merger Act showed again the response of the law to hold business within the broad antitrust goals of our time. And the first major court test under the new law showed its potency. Bethlehem Steel and Youngstown Sheet and Tube, the second and sixth largest steel producers, announced plans to merge, and were brought to court in 1958 by the Justice Department under the Anti-Merger Act before the merger took place. Upholding the government's argument that the proposed merger would substantially lessen competition, the circuit court forbad the merger in a major case that appears to say that mergers are illegal whenever the companies involved are in significant competition, whether on several products or merely one major product line (such as steel plates). Moreover, the court applied the potential elimination of competition test to limited areas as small as a single state, not merely to large areas or the whole country. Under this case, any merger of competing firms above very small size appears to be of doubtful legality.

The Broad Pattern of Legislation. In perspective, over the past quarter-century a rough pattern of antitrust policy appears to have emerged. The policy seems to have two facets, though the pattern is far from sharp.

1. In general, antitrust policy is to attack oligopoly and to try to establish more competition where producers are large and few. This objective is in keeping with the traditional goals of antitrust.

2. But simultaneously, policy seems to have been to encourage quasi-cartelization where producers are many (farmers, miners, storekeepers) and where the individual is small and impotent to exercise control in the market. Security and income protection for the small producer and seller appear to have been dominant objectives here, with little recognition of the potential wastes of cartels with unlimited entry.

If this size-up of the nation's antitrust policy is correct, it suggests significant divergence from the competitive "norm" that economists have often suggested for the economic system. Quasi-cartelization with a substantial number of not-too-big firms may be the norm that implicitly underlies a significant part of our governmental policy. Is this the norm, or objective, that our federal and state legislation should be aiming at? Or is the blunt Sherman Act philosophy more appropriate?

The Law in Operation. The law is what its administrators and the courts make it. And its administrators and the courts by and large make it what the public wants, often very roughly and usually with a considerable judicial lag, but fairly effectively none the less.

Nowhere has this been truer than in antitrust legislation. The most naive observer can see that the Sherman Act states only a broad intent. What degree of monopoly and what restraint of trade does the act really forbid? No one knows, and probably most of the congressmen who voted for it had only a hazy idea themselves.

The first big enforcement campaign under the Sherman Act was President Teddy Roosevelt's, conducted with a total staff of seven lawyers and four stenographers. With this tiny staff, but with the big stick of aroused public opinion, the government tackled and broke a series of trusts. Finally, in 1911, the Supreme Court required both Standard Oil and American Tobacco, two of the biggest trusts, to divest themselves of a large share of their holdings and to desist from numerous specific unfair competitive practices. But there, too, for the first time, the Court enunciated the now-famous "rule of reason." Only trusts that "unreasonably" restrained trade were illegal. In a series of earlier cases, the Court had given a broad interpretation to the interstate commerce clause, permitting federal regulation to apply to all firms who had any direct dealing across state lines or (later) in products or materials crossing state lines; this interpretation brought most big businesses within the purview of federal antitrust legislation.

By 1920, the attitude of the times toward big business had altered, with the checking of the flagrant abuses of the late 1800's. In the U.S. Steel case of 1920, the Supreme Court refused to dissolve the company. It held specifically that neither mere bigness nor unexerted monopoly power was illegal as such; that actual unreasonable restraint of trade must be proved under the Sherman Act.

The tenor of the 1920's was one of prosperity and "leave well enough alone." Little effort was made to do more than check minor unfair competitive practices like fraudulent advertising through the F.T.C. The total budget allocated the Antitrust Division averaged only $250,000 annually for the decade. Big business was popular during the twenties.

With the strong anti-business sweep of the New Deal, the last major change in the application and interpretation of the antitrust laws began in the late 1930's. A mixture of government-sponsored cartels on the one hand and stronger enforcement of the antitrust law on the other makes generalization difficult. But under Thurman Arnold, Antitrust began an aggressive drive in the late 1930's against several of the industrial giants. Antitrust's budget was upped to $1 million (to police the entire economy). Its investigations in the construction field disclosed eye-openers that aroused the public, and actions were begun against labor, agricultural, and professional groups as well as against business. The government secured application of the Sherman Act to a labor union (under somewhat special circumstances) in the Apex Case in 1940. It dissolved a glass-container monopoly based on patents in the Hartford Empire Case in 1944 with a decision that greatly weakened the use of patents to support monopoly practices. In the Alcoa Case of 1945, it obtained a strongly worded ruling that size itself, even though not used to restrain competition, is objectionable under the act. It outlawed "basing-point pricing" (under which a few leaders set industry-wide prices f.o.b. at selected factory "basing points"), in the Cement Case of 1948. Application of federal legislation through the interstate commerce clause was steadily broadened.

Although the Eisenhower administration was generally more friendly than its predecessors toward business, it continued active prosecution of offenders under antitrust legislation. Actions were brought against both large and small firms. Appropriations to both the Federal Trade Commission and the Antitrust Division of the Department of Justice were further increased. DuPont's ownership of approximately one-fourth of General Motors' common stock was condemned. Other cases were pushed effectively in the courts, and many "consent decrees" were obtained, under which the accused company agrees to forego certain practices though it does not admit guilt. Often these decrees are worked out without formal court trial.

But the government does not win all the cases it brings. For example, in 1956 it lost a major battle against DuPont. It argued that DuPont held a monopoly in the manufacture of cellophane. But the Supreme Court held that competition should be construed to include reasonably close substitutes as well as the product itself. DuPont produced almost 75 per cent of all cellophane, but cellophane constituted less than 20 per cent of all "flexible packaging material" sales. Thus the majority declared DuPont's position legal, even though it was a monopolist in cellophane, because it held only a relatively small part of the total "flexible packaging material" market. But there was a strong minority protest that this interpretation would emasculate the entire Sherman Act prohibition against monopoly, since any product has some more-or-less close substitutes.

Why has Antitrust again become a potent force? First, the budget given it by Congress is larger than before (averaging between $3 and $4 million annually during the 1950's); even so, this is a tiny sum compared with the vast resources of the billion-dollar corporations it has to prosecute. More fundamental has been the changing temper of the times. The New Deal and public sentiment during the 1930's were frankly critical of big business. Antitrust was only one phase of a broad program of criticism, legislation, and administrative controls. Even with the weakening of this attitude in the 1940's and 1950's and the strong pro-business sentiment of the Eisenhower administration, it was clear that public wariness of bigness and of abuse of monopoly power was real and persistent. The Roper survey results cited above were mirrored in federal administrative practice on a broad antitrust front.

One last point on the law in action. The main impact of the antitrust law is preventive, not punitive. Since 1890, less than 700 suits have been brought under the Sherman Act. Of these, the government won about 475 and lost about 120, with the rest still in the courts. Total fines paid by defendants over the half-century, including fines where the defendant did not contest the case, were only a few million dollars—very little compared to the billions of dollars of assets in the companies concerned. In a number of cases, especially in recent years, the government has arranged consent decrees, which usually represent at least partial victories without the time and expense of formal court trials. The F.T.C. has brought formal charges in about 1500 cases, with something over half resulting in cease and desist orders.

But most observers are agreed that Antitrust has been a surprisingly powerful force in the American business scene since 1890. No business likes to be called criminal, or even antisocial. It does not like to have its affairs dragged into open court, even though it thinks it may win out in the end. Besides, most businessmen are law-abiding citizens, and they have no more stomach for breaking the law than anyone else. American businessmen talk the strongest case for competition you can find anywhere. The difficulty comes in defining what everyone means by competition, and what interpretation of the law is the right one. The power of the law is far-reaching, even when no one is quite sure just what the law means.

But although Antitrust has been an ever-present danger to monopolists, Congress and the state legislatures themselves have steadily eaten away at the Sherman Act's prohibition against price-fixing agreements in some areas, especially retailing. The Robinson-Patman Act of 1938 forbade sellers to discriminate in price among purchasers of like grade and quality where the effect might be to reduce competition (by driving out competitors who cannot meet the price cuts). Although this provision was consistent with the Sherman Act's objectives, it was a step toward discouraging strong price competition. The Miller-Tydings and McGuire acts went much further, specifically assuring manufacturers the power to establish retail prices below which their products could not be sold.

Legalizing resale price maintenance effectively estops antitrust prosecution of open agreements to fix prices and to eliminate retail price competition. Some observers feel that the loss to consumers through this legal type of monopolistic price-fixing may outweigh the gains provided by the Antitrust Division. But one strong ally for the consumer has stubbornly reappeared—the retailer's profit motive. Many retailers object to price-maintenance policies and cut prices surreptitiously or openly in defiance of manufacturers' rules. "Discount houses" in most major cities are a major manifestation of this revolt. The lure of potential profits from increased sales remains a potent force, whatever type of retail price maintenance the law may permit. By the late 1950's, most leading manufacturers had given up fair-trading even in states that approved the non-signer clause, because it was so hard to keep retailers from cutting prices in order to sell more goods.

THE PATENT PROBLEM

Thomas Edison invented the electric light bulb in 1879. Should he have received the rewards from selling this invention for commercial exploitation? If you say yes, how about this question: Suppose he had charged an exorbitant price for the use of his invention, so that only a few rich people could afford it. Would that still have been all right? If people objected, suppose he had said that the price wasn't exorbitant at all, that he had worked hard on his invention, and that he had a perfect right to put the price as high as he liked.

This simple example points up the patent problem. Nearly everyone agrees that an inventor should have the right to the fruits of his invention. But how much fruit? And how tightly are we willing to let the invention be withheld if it promises great benefits to mankind?

The Constitution gave the federal government power to encourage invention and to establish a patent system. Ever since, the inventor has been able to hold exclusive control over his invention for at least 17 years by patenting it. Until the Hartford-Empire Case in 1944, there was virtually no limit on the way patents could be used as the basis for monopoly. While the patent holder can still do as he likes with his own patent, under the Hartford Case patent pools or interfirm licensing agreements may not be used to develop or maintain monopolies otherwise illegal. But the exact status of the matter is not clear.

What should be done about patents? Those who advocate leaving the law as it is argue that this is an equitable arrangement, and that such protection is necessary to stimulate the hard work and large expenditures that go into inventive research in modern corporations. DuPont is said to have spent over $100 million on the development of nylon before it sold a dollar's worth.

On the other hand, there's a good chance that people would go right on researching even if they couldn't get 17-year patents. The competitive drive to get a cheaper, better product than your competitor's is the main force behind industrial research. In fact, many leading corporations (for example, Standard Oil of New Jersey) make most of their patents available to everyone. By then they're working on something newer still, and they doubt that the patent law could do much for them if they relied on it to keep out competition; other oil companies have smart scientists too. But many companies follow more restrictive policies, and it is hard to justify permitting patents to be used as a basis for maintaining "unreasonable" monopolies. The current state of the law looks more encouraging from this viewpont than it did a few years ago, even though recent rulings leave many unanswered questions on just how far the patent holder can go.

Many observers feel that a period shorter than 17 years would be just as good and would avoid the dangers of long-period restriction. Others argue that every patent-holder ought to be required to license his invention to anyone who wants to use it, at a reasonable price. (What price?) Still others favor compulsory licensing *if* the patent holder himself doesn't put the invention to active use. (Many other nations, e.g., Canada, have such compulsory use or licensing provisions.) And almost everybody agrees that higher standards of patentability would help. Now just about any minor invention or modification seems to be patentable. A firm with a basic patent must take out a bevy of surrounding ("defensive") patents on closely comparable ideas lest some competitor get a patent so close as to negate the exclusive value of the original invention. Other firms do the same thing with their inventions. The result is a mass of patent squabbles and litigation that has to be seen to be believed. Defending a patent violation, or an alleged violation, can almost bankrupt a small concern—and there have been cases where competitors have seemed to initiate lawsuits for just that purpose.

PUBLIC-UTILITY MONOPOLIES

You don't have to be much of an economist to see that most local communities can support only one efficient electric-power system, one water system, one gas system, and one telephone system. To encourage competition in these fields by insisting on three or four firms in each area would probably end up in higher prices for the consumer, certainly a big social waste of duplicated facilities. Moreover, under a competitive system maybe none of the companies would be willing to serve the isolated Jones house, way out by itself on the far side of town, except at some fantastic price.

Public opinion has generally insisted on detailed government regulation of "public utilities" where two conditions exist:

1. The industry is a "natural monopoly"—that is, the efficient scale of enterprise is very large relative to the market, so that splitting the market would involve higher-cost production.

2. The industry is vital to the public welfare—e.g., electricity, public transportation, gas, water. (How about milk delivery? Steel?) Public utilities are usually given exclusive franchises, or at least the entrance of other firms is controlled by the government to keep the number down in accordance with public interests. Then the public utility is required to provide service satisfactory to the regulating government agency, and its prices are controlled by the government.

Public utilities are usually required to serve all comers at established prices. But how to set the prices? Most people agree that the price should be as low as possible, so long as the public utility earns a "fair return" on its investment. The courts have often selected 5, 6, or 7 per cent as the fair rate. But this doesn't solve the problem. On what investment? A water works is a complex piece of apparatus, buildings, and pipes. Part of it is usually new, part old. Shall we use (1) original cost less estimated depreciation, or (2) estimated current reproduction cost? If you take the latter, the companies will be happy, because the price level has moved up a long way over the past couple of decades and they'll have a lot bigger investment base on which to calculate their 6 per cent that way. Besides, they say, that's what it will cost to replace the plant as it wears out; the customers ought to be willing to pay for today's cost, not for some unrealistic figure picked up from 1930. But the customers are more likely to plump for original cost less depreciation, for obvious reasons.

Which scheme is better? Much depends on whose interests you put first and on your ideas of equity. The courts have vacillated between the two approaches. If the price level were constant, the two would amount to pretty much the same thing. In periods of changing price levels, neither is quite satisfactory from the economist's point of view, but reproduction cost looks better since it gears public-utility costs, prices, and earnings more directly to the general level of the times. You can find lots of learned books on the subject if you'd like to investigate it further.

Where to from here? Should we be fighting back toward a highly competitive system such as the one envisaged in the economists' pure-competition model, even though we recognize we'll never get to that "ideal"? Or should we be satisfied to muddle along with the mixed economy, perhaps not getting all the theoretically possible benefits of strong price competition but getting a lot of other benefits that come with big, stable business concerns? Or should we be looking toward more government control to see that firms do operate efficiently and in the public interest? It's only a hop, skip, and an easy slide from a slightly broadened conception of public utilities into government ownership and operation of a lot of the nation's major industries—and into a full-fledged socialist economy with government ownership of most major productive resources.

Antitrust in a Mixed Economy.   Nobody thinks the modern American economy can look like the economist's perfectly competitive model. It never has, even back in the pre-Civil War days, and it certainly doesn't now. We're in for a mixed economy of some sort. Where does this leave antitrust?

Now we are back to the problems raised at the beginning of the chapter. The issues go far beyond economics in any narrow sense. But the economist might ask four questions to help in evaluating how far it may be sensible to try to push the modern economy toward more active competition through antitrust:

1. *Would stronger antitrust action really help the consumer through lower prices and higher quality?* The presumption of the past few chapters against monopoly seems clear. Simple monopoly restricts output and raises price. Monopolistic competition leads to competitive demand creation and higher prices. Oligopoly produces strong pressures toward avoidance of price competition.

Would antitrust really help by attacking big business more vigorously? Here one central question is, how big does business need to be for maximum efficiency? There's no one easy answer. It varies from case to case. Clearly, business has to be pretty big in many industries, and it is. Look back at Figure 26-1 for the dominance of leading firms in some major industries. But big business can get too big, even from the cost standpoint. Various studies have indicated that in most industries middle-sized to big companies are likely to have lower costs than gigantic ones. But not always, and not in all industries.

Table 27-1 summarizes possibly the best research study currently available on the problem of optimum (least-cost) size of plant and firm in a sample of manufacturing industries. It reflects the wide diversity just mentioned. Column 1 shows the percentage of national industry capacity contained in one plant of optimum size; the range indicates the variation in the best available estimates. Column 2 provides the same information for a firm of optimum size. Where the firm figure is larger than the plant figure, there are additional significant economies from combining a number of optimal-size plants in one firm; where the figures are the same, there is no such advantage costwise. Column 3 shows the wide variation in the amount of capital needed to set up one additional plant at about the optimum size in each industry, presumably some measure of what it would take a newcomer to enter the industry. Lastly, column 4 shows the per-

Table 27-1

ESTIMATED SIZE OF OPTIMAL PLANTS AND FIRMS IN
MANUFACTURING INDUSTRIES *

Industry	*Percentage of National Industry Capacity in One Plant of Optimal Size*	*Percentage of National Industry Capacity in One Firm of Optimal Size*	*Capital Required for One Efficient Plant (In Millions)*	*Percentage Share of National Market Held by Average of First 4 Firms*
Shoes	.14 to .5	.5 to 2.5	$.5 to 2	7
Canned fruits and vegetables	.25 to .5	.25 to .5	2.5 to 3	7
Metal containers	.5 to 3	No estimate	5 to 20	20
Cement	.8 to 1	2 to 10	20 to 25	7
Steel	1 to 2.5	2 to 5	265 to 665	11
Distilled liquor	1.25 to 1.75	No estimate	30 to 42	19
Petroleum refining	1.75	1.75	193 (without transport)	9
Gypsum products	2.5 to 3	27 to 33	5 to 6	21
Tires and tubes	3	No estimate	25 to 30	19
Cigarettes	5 to 6	15 to 20	125 to 150	23
Autos	5 to 10	5 to 10	250 to 500	23
Tractors	10 to 15	10 to 15	125	17
Typewriters	10 to 30	10 to 30	No estimate	20

* From J. S. Bain, "Economies of Scale, Concentration, and Entry," *American Economic Review*, March 1954, pp. 30, 36. Data as of late 1940's.

centage share of the national market actually held about 1950 by the average of the four largest firms in each industry. This figure is obtained by dividing the total share of the four largest firms by four. The percentage so obtained is thus smaller than the actual share of the largest firm in the industry by amounts that vary with the firm's position in the top four. For example, General Motors' share of the auto market approached 50 per cent in comparison with the 23 per cent average for the four largest firms. Similarly, U. S. Steel had around 30 per cent of the market compared to the average of only 11 per cent for the four top firms.

The estimates of Table 27-1 suggest that the actual share of market held by many of the biggest firms is far above that justified by the necessity for having firms big enough to obtain lowest-cost production. In this sample, for example, this is true for shoes, canned fruits and vegetables, petroleum refining, steel, and autos. It is probably true also for metal containers, distilled liquor, and tires and tubes, though the certainty is not great enough to justify a definite estimate. Even in such industries as typewriters and cement, the market share of the biggest firm (as distinct from the average of the four biggest) is well above the minimum optimal size. Moreover, many of these firms have regional monopoly positions that are much stronger than is suggested by the national figures; an example is cement, where transport costs are very high relative to the value of the product.

But the other side of the picture is impressive too. In several industries the cost of an efficient plant is so high there is no point pretending that competition can be readily open to new producers; note the figures for cigarettes, petroleum refining, tractors, autos, and steel. But there are a number of industries where the minimum cost of entry is so small that entry for potential competitors should be fairly easy, if enterprising firms want to try; note the cases of shoes, canned fruits and vegetables, and gypsum products.

The same author has summed up the over-all difficulty new firms might have in trying to enter a sample of the nation's major industries, taking into account size of firm needed for efficiency, capital requirements, established product names, and other relevant factors. These ratings must obviously be extremely rough, but nevertheless here they are: [3]

Very Difficult	*Moderately Difficult*	*Relatively Easy*
automobiles	petroleum refining	canned goods
cigarettes	men's shoes	cement
copper	steel	flour
farm machinery		gypsum products
liquor		meat packing
soap		metal containers
tractors		rayon
typewriters		tires and tubes

Don't forget that these are only *rough estimates,* on which many competent observers would differ. But they will help to give you some impressions on a very difficult, and important, problem.

2. *Would stronger antitrust action help prevent unfair, antisocial competitive practices?* Strong action against unfair competition designed to drive out weaker competitors and establish monopoly prices is surely desirable. But a lot of the talk about "unfair" competition boils down to talk *against* competition when you look into it carefully. Widespread antagonism to "cut-rate" drugstores in the

---

[3] From J. S. Bain, *Barriers to New Competition* (Cambridge: Harvard University Press, 1956).

1930's underlay state fair-trade legislation and the Miller-Tydings Act of 1937. The conservative, established druggists liked these actions fine. But why shouldn't a competitor be free to sell Colgate toothpaste for 59 cents instead of 69 if he thinks he can make a profit by doing so? Some manufacturers argue that people lose confidence in their products if price-cutting like this goes on. They argue that the established stores have to know where they stand if they're to stock manufacturers' items, and that the price-cutters are just scabs who fail to carry their own weight in the selling process. But from the consumers' point of view, it's not abundantly clear why price-cutting isn't just what competition is supposed to produce.

3. *Would stronger antitrust action make for a more progressive economy?* Anything that speeds us on our way toward a fuller life, new products, and less work ought to be encouraged. *Prima facie,* monopoly in all its forms tends to slow down progress. It lessens the competitive push for better products and more efficient methods. It permits companies to use up the old before introducing the new.

But even here the picture isn't as clear as you'd expect. The fact is that the big companies like Standard Oil, DuPont, G.E., and others, who are dominant figures in their industries, have been in the forefront of economic progress, new processes, and new products. They do have big potential powers of suppression, and maybe they haven't always done as well as they should. But it's clear that bigness and research are closely tied together in modern industry. How big does a firm have to be to be a leader in research, development, and introduction of modern technology? Probably pretty big, but there's no clear answer to the question, and it surely varies from industry to industry.

4. *Can antitrust do anything about the problem of the sheer power of bigness?* This may be the most basic question of all in many people's minds. Political power, social power, power over other people's lives, just the power that goes with a billion dollars—these may be the things that worry people most about big business.

The power of big business management seems especially alarming to some observers because in many firms, where the stock is widely scattered, inside management has a substantially free hand in exercising its vast power. While the stockholders theoretically direct the management and could oust it any year, as a practical matter few stockholders know much about the details of management or have any interest in interfering in it. To whom is big management really responsible in the exercise of its economic power?

A. A. Berle, a long-time observer of the business corporation, has recently pointed up this problem. Only 500 corporations control two-thirds of the entire American non-farm economy, he writes, and within each of those 500 a relatively small group holds the ultimate decision-making power. "Since the United States carries on not quite half of the manufacturing production of the entire world today, these 500 groupings—each with its own little dominating pyramid within it—represent a concentration of power over economics which makes the medieval feudal system look like a Sunday School party. In sheer economic power this has gone far beyond anything we have yet seen." [4]

Maybe the big problem is bigness and power, not monopoly as such at all. It's not clear what people really think about this. Listen to your friends and the people you hear on the bus. Read the daily papers. Think about it. Then make up your own mind.

If we want to cut down on bigness as such, Table 27-1 above gives some evidence on the economic aspects of the problem. If the sample industries in the table are indicative, many of the huge firms today (say in the billion-dollar class) could probably be a good deal smaller without serious loss of efficiency costwise. What such a reduction would do to research and progress toward greater efficiency is only a subject for speculation. But in some industries really small firms are out of the question unless we are willing to pay the price of lessened efficiency and higher costs. Approaches aimed at dispersing the power and responsibility within each corporation raise different problems, outside the area of antitrust policy *per se*.

The dilemma of antitrust policy in the mixed economy can be summarized in two brief statements. The first is that of Henry C. Simons, one of the outstanding advocates of free-enterprise economics in the United States.[5] "Reasonable" monopoly, said Simons, is a contradiction in terms. There can be no such thing. Wide dispersion of political and economic power is the only foundation on which a democratic, free-enterprise system can long exist. The role of government is clear: (1) to maintain active competition within a general framework of free-enterprise rules of the game so as to stimulate efficiency and to disperse economic power; and (2) to own and operate directly those few industries where competition cannot be made to function effectively. Specifically, said Simons, this implies:

1. Federal incorporation of all private corporations.

2. Forbidding any manufacturing or merchandising corporation to own stock in any other such corporation.

3. An upper limit on the asset size of all corporations, far below the size of the present giants. We may need big plants for productive efficiency, but we certainly don't need gigantic corporations controlling many similar plants.

4. Provision that no firm may be big enough to dominate its industry, the F.T.C. to determine this size limit in each industry. We must recognize that cartels among a few large firms, however informal and "respectable," are probably the most wasteful of all monopoly arrangements.

---

[4] *Economic Power and the Free Society* (New York: Fund for the Republic, 1958), p. 14.

[5] See especially "A Positive Program for Laissez Faire," and "A Political Credo," in his *Economic Policy for a Free Society* (Chicago: University of Chicago Press, 1948).

5. Complete prohibition of interlocking directorates, except between unrelated industries.

6. Simplification of corporate securities to two simple types, to minimize the possibility of hidden or indirect control of corporations.

This probably strikes you as a completely impractical program, which only an ivory-tower college professor could take seriously. But think about it a little. Many thoughtful observers of the American scene consider Simons the outstanding intellectual spokesman of our time for free, private enterprise.

The other statement is that of the Pittsburgh Plate Glass Company in its answer to the government lawyers in the trial brought against it and other leading glass manufacturers for alleged violations of the antitrust laws during the late 1940's.

We certainly are a big company, said the corporation's lawyer to the judge, and we can understand why the government wanted to investigate us. It's their job to see that the competitive system stays competitive, and we believe in competition just as strongly as they do. All we want to do is to tell you something about production in the flat-glass industry and how the industry works in distributing its products. Then he went on to demonstrate the similarity of modern flat-glass making to continuous-process steel making, pointing out that today six huge, efficient glass-melting tanks and rolling lines can produce all the flat glass used in the United States. Pittsburgh Plate had three of these big plants, one to serve each part of the country, since transportation is a big cost on finished glass. He didn't deny that Pittsburgh Plate Glass might be called an oligopoly by the lawyers and economists. He just pointed to modern technology in relation to the market, huge as it is in the United States today, and led the judge to wonder what was to be gained by going back to smaller-scale, less efficient productive processes.

How did the case come out? It never went to a decision. After the company's presentation, the judge instructed the lawyers for both sides to go work out a consent decree for him to sign, making it clear that he was in no mood to find for the government and order dissolution of Pittsburgh Plate.[6]

Which road is better? The one taken by Pittsburgh Plate Glass, or the one taken by Simons? Whichever road you prefer, it is important to remember that even the PPG road is far over on the competitive side compared to prevailing practice in many of the world's industrialized economies. Throughout much of Europe, cartelization of major industries is encouraged, with little or no governmental regulation of price and output policies. Government ownership and operation are widespread, not only in the communist bloc but in the democratic socialisms of western Europe and Scandinavia. At the extreme the Soviet path leads toward complete central control over most economic activity.

---

[6] This is a much oversimplified version of the controversy, but it illustrates the essential issue on this major part of the case. The company agreed to alter several of its marketing practices, which were claimed to restrain competition.

BUSINESS
AND GOVERNMENT
IN THE NEW CAPITALISM

Antitrust action is the most conspicuous government regulation of business. But government has a much wider range of impact on business in the modern American scene. The Federal Trade Commission regulates the kind of advertising business may do. The Securities and Exchange Commission regulates its practices in issuing securities. The Federal Reserve controls the terms on which it can borrow money from the banks. Federal law regulates the minimum wages it must pay its workers, and prescribes that it must deal with them in unions when they choose. It says business cannot hire child workers, and cannot work employees overtime without special pay. Through its income tax provisions it takes half of all business profits, and in effect prescribes what kinds of accounting procedures must be followed. On the vast amount of government contracts issued to business (nearly $40 billion in 1958), it sets elaborate standards of performance; specifies that business cannot discriminate amongst employees on the basis of race, creed, or color; and often reserves the right to renegotiate prices downward retroactively when business profits appear to be excessive by government standards.

When labor disputes produce long strikes that disrupt the economy, government often calls business and labor together and brings pressure for settlement on terms that businessmen consider unfair. If the business is an airline, it is regulated in detail by the Civil Aeronautics Authority and the Civil Aeronautics Board as to where it can fly and when, how much it can charge, the kinds of equipment it can use, and the safety standards it must meet. If it is a radio or TV station, the Federal Communications Commission decides when it can broadcast, on what wave lengths, and what proportion of "public service" time it must program. At the local level, government tells business what land can be used for, and how much taxes it must pay to help support the community's schools and roads. Beyond all this, government constantly hovers in the background, ready to impose new restrictions or bring new pressures to bear if a considerable portion of the public becomes seriously dissatisfied with what business is doing.

Some businessmen feel that this government interference with the freedom of managers to manage as they please has sapped the essential force of traditional private-enterprise "capitalism." But others believe that it has marked a gradual change in the role of business to a status of more clearly recognized responsibility to the general public—a change that has modified the nature of "capitalism" but has not fundamentally altered the basic forces of the profit motive, self-interest, and private ownership of property. The old automobile has had its face lifted; tail fins have been added; horsepower has been stepped up and gas consumption along with it; a governor and safety padding are compulsory; the carburetor has been adjusted; balloon tires and power steering have become standard equipment. Sometimes the machine works better as a result of this tinkering, sometimes worse. But on the whole it is now a better automobile. And above all, the motor that makes it go still relies on the same basic force—the gasoline that the profit motive still provides in the American economic system. Writers sometimes speak of "the new capitalism." Government in business is a big element in the new capitalism, but private capital and management still take the major risks, make the major economic decisions, and reap the major gains or losses those decisions produce.

There is by no means complete agreement whether this analogy is a fair one, whether the essential driving force of the traditional American private-enterprise system is as strong or stronger than before. To make an intelligent judgment you need to look at more aspects of the record, and to do some comparing with other kinds of economic systems. But it may be helpful to try a tentative summing up for yourself now.[7]

FOR ANALYSIS AND DISCUSSION

1. Do you think the problem of bigness as such is more important than the problem of monopoly?

2. How, if at all, does the problem of business monopoly affect you personally?

3. What are the main characteristics of an industry that determine whether a large or small number of firms is most beneficial to the public interest?

4. "State fair trade laws which help eliminate retail price competition on the items covered do far more harm to consumers than all the giant corporations combined." Do you agree or disagree?

5. Critics of big business corporations often argue that most huge modern corporations could be broken up into several competing units without loss of productive efficiency, because most of these corporations control many quite separate plants, each one of which could just as well operate as a separate, competitive business. Does this argument seem to you a sound one? If so, how would you suggest we ought to go about implementing the proposal?

6. What is a "reasonable" restraint of trade? Give examples of what would appear to you "reasonable" and "unreasonable" restraints of trade.

7. Trucks, buses, and airlines now are at least as important as railroads in freight and passenger transportation in many areas. Has the time come to abolish the Interstate Commerce Commission and turn the transportation field back to open competition, which is often claimed to provide the most effective prods to efficiency and progress?

8. "Any inventor ought to be able to do what he likes with his invention. If he wants to hold it off the market, or to price it sky-high, what business is it of anyone else's?" Do you agree with this philosophy? Is it inconsistent with the general philosophy of the Sherman Act?

9. Would you favor tripling the congressional appropriation to the Department of Justice for antitrust enforcement?

---

[7] Note to instructors: Chapter 34, "Wage-Price Policy and Direct Government Controls," may equally well be used here or where it is printed.

Current Research

A s with the Appendix to Part 2, the purpose here is to suggest a sample of recent research in economics that may be of interest to students who want to know more of what economists do, and especially of the excitement that goes with research—the probing for new knowledge and new understanding. Here again the items listed are merely a sample, selected to show some of the many types of research under way on the problems covered by Part 3. They are not necessarily the best, or even a careful cross section, of current research in the area. They are chosen because I hope some of them may be intriguing to you, and make you want to look further. Since they vary widely in approach, substance, and difficulty, do a sampling of your own.

The Theory of the Firm and Markets. Two major books illustrate alternative approaches to a better understanding of the firm and market behavior: *Barriers to New Competition* (Harvard University Press, 1956), by California's J. S. Bain, combines theory with intensive empirical testing and investigation. *Business Behavior, Value and Growth* (Macmillan, 1959), by Princeton's William Baumol, attempts a new theoretical approach linking business behavior to both market pricing and the theory of economic growth. For a sample of recent analysis of the role of marginalism in business decisions, add "Marginal Policies of 'Excellently Managed' Companies," by Wisconsin's James Earley in the *American Economic Review* for March 1956.

In recent years, economists have turned to new approaches to the theory of the firm. One approach, developed by a group at Carnegie Tech, has emphasized the dynamics of the firm as an organization for understanding business decisions and their relation to markets. See Herbert Simon, "Theories of Decision Making in Economics and Behavioral Science," *American Economic Review,* June 1959; and R. M. Cyert and J. G. March, "Organizational Factors in the Theory of Oligopoly," *Quarterly Journal of Economics,* February 1956. For a further challenge to the traditional theories of monopoly and the size of firms, try H. A. Simon and Charles Bonini's "The Size Distribution of Business Firms," *American Economic Review,* September 1958.

An alternative approach, using "game theory" to understand business behavior, is illustrated by Martin Shubik's *Competition, Oligopoly, and the Theory of Games* (Wiley, 1959). A related new approach to the analysis of complex market interactions—linear programming—is illustrated by *Linear Programming and Economic Analysis* (McGraw-Hill, 1958), by R. Dorfman, P. A. Samuelson, and Robert Solow of Harvard and M.I.T. These are heavy going unless you know a good deal of mathematics.

Empirical Industry and Market Studies. Many economists believe that the path to better understanding of business and market behavior lies in empirical studies of individual industries and markets, from which present theories can be validated or rejected, and new theories constructed. Bain's *Barriers to New Competition* (cited above) is partially in this tradition.

For a sample of two recent intensive industry-market studies, built largely around the traditional theoretical framework, look at Daniel Hamilton, *Competition in Oil: The Gulf Coast Refinery Market, 1925-1950* (Harvard University Press, 1958); and J. W. Markham, *The Fertilizer Industry: A Study of an Imperfect Market* (Vanderbilt University Press, 1958). A broader study of pricing practices in several large individual firms is presented by A. D. H. Kaplan, J. B. Dirlam, and R. Lanzillotti in *Pricing in Big Business: A Case Approach* (Brookings Institution, 1958). Linear programming is also increasingly used as the framework for particular industry studies. For an example, see James M. Henderson, *The Efficiency of the Oil Industry: An Application of Linear Programming* (Harvard University Press, 1958).

Two British studies aimed especially at investigating industrial organization and business policies in relation to technological change illustrate the growing modern attention to this big problem. See C. F. Carter and B. R. Williams, "The Characteristics of Technologically Progressive Firms," in the *Journal of Industrial Economics* for March 1959; and D. C. Dague, *Economics of Man-made Fibres* (Duckworth, 1957).

If you're especially interested in the role of little businesses, try J. D. Phillips' *Little Business in the American Economy* (University of Illinois Press, 1958).

Government Policy. A collection of articles by leading economists, prepared under the auspices of the American Economic Association, *Readings in Industrial Organization and Economic Policy,* R. B. Heflebower and G. W. Stocking, editors (Irwin, 1958), provides a good starting point for sampling research on industrial organization and government policy toward business. Try first the articles by M. A. Adelman and Edward Mason. Last, for an example of economic analysis applied to a very specific policy problem, see Fritz Machlup, *An Economic Review of the Patent System* (U. S. Superintendent of Documents, 1958), a study prepared for the Senate Committee on the Judiciary.

On farm policy, *Agricultural Adjustment Problems in a Growing Economy,* E. O. Heady, *et al.,* editors (Iowa State College Press, 1958), provides a similar sample of analysis and prescriptions for government policy on the farm problem. Try the papers by Earl Heady, D. G. Johnson, and R. Brandow as starters.

PART 4

The Distribution
of Income

28

How Is Income Distributed?

One of the hottest issues in economics has long been the distribution of the national income—between wages and profits, rich and poor, the farmer and the industrial worker, the "haves" and the "have-nots." Governments have risen and fallen on the struggle for income shares. The revolutionary doctrines of Karl Marx, which underlie the Soviet Russia of today, center around the "exploitation of the worker" by the "rich and greedy capitalist." In a different setting, this same struggle over income shares is the issue when the United Steelworkers fight the steel companies for wage increases. It is the issue when Congress votes government support for "parity prices" on farm products. Over the centuries, history tells a recurrent story of the "have-nots" fighting for more and the "haves" struggling to protect and increase their share.

Thoughtful observers of the private-enterprise economy point out that we're all in the same boat. If everybody pulls together—labor, capital, management, agriculture—total output will grow and all can have more. No one who understands the basic interdependence of the modern economy

525

would deny this. There is indeed an enormous community of interest in making the private-enterprise economy work effectively.

But part and parcel of that community of interest is a basic conflict, rooted deep in our social and economic structure—in our ethics and traditions of self-interest and competition. This is the struggle of each individual and group to get more for itself. It is the struggle over who gets how much of the economic pie— at the level of the individual worker, his union, and his boss, and at the level of national policy. However rich or poor the nation is, we're all interested in our own shares—relative and absolute. Nothing is gained by refusing to face this fact.

Individual self-interest is at the core of the American economic tradition. We look with favor on the man who works hard, earns a good income, and provides well for himself and his family. Self-earned wealth and security bring widespread esteem. The man who can't earn a good living is viewed with a touch of contempt, or sympathy if there is an obvious reason beyond his own control. The "Protestant ethic" of work and reward is strong.

Yet increasingly Americans have agreed on limits to the financial success that should be permitted. Federal income tax rates reach 50 per cent above the $32,000 level and 91 per cent above $400,000. Government expenditure programs are expressly aimed at reducing income inequality. We want the incentives and productivity of an individualistic, income-motivated economy. But we don't want the extremes of income and power inequality that are the consequence of all-out adherence to individual self-interest.

WHO GETS
THE NATIONAL INCOME?

The Rich and the Poor: The Income Revolution. American incomes today are higher than ever before. Our standard of living is by far the highest in the world. Some economists have dubbed modern America "The Affluent Society," an economy in which production is no longer a pressing problem.[1]

Chapter 2 presented some of the facts. (See especially Figure 2-1.) In 1958, average family income was just over $6,000. But 14 per cent of all families received less than $2,000. Even making allowances for farm families producing their own food and single, retired folks receiving help from others, these were poverty-level incomes. At the other extreme, about the same proportion of families received over $10,000. But the under-$2,000 group received in total only 3 per cent of the total national income, while the over-$10,000 group received 34 per cent. Five per cent of the families received over $15,000, with apparently about 1 per cent over $25,000. America is still a land of the rich and the poor. And the median level of $5,050 was a long way from plushy living.

---

[1] J. K. Galbraith, *The Affluent Society* (New York: Houghton Mifflin, 1958).

Figure 28-1 suggests an interesting question about this unequal distribution of incomes in America. The bell-shaped curve is what statisticians call a "normal" distribution curve. Intelligence, physical traits, and a wide variety of other phenomena seem to approximate closely this type of normal distribution, when large numbers are considered. More people are "average," at the mid-point of the curve, than at any other level, and those above and below the average shade off about equally either way.

We might assume that general ability is something like normally distributed in the total population. But incomes received, shown by the solid line, are "skewed." That is, there are many poor and relatively low-income individuals. These account for the big hump in the curve toward the lower income end of the scale. There are a few very rich, who give the curve a long "tail" out to the right. Questions: Are human abilities more normally distributed than incomes? If so, why? Do differing economic opportunities for rich and poor explain the continuing skewedness of the income curve? Is it because some people work harder than others? Because some do more useful work than others? Why?

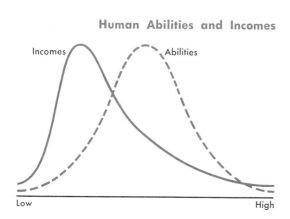

Human Abilities and Incomes

Incomes Abilities

Low High

FIG. 28-1   Ability and most other human characteristics seem to be "normally" distributed through the population, as shown by the regular bell-shaped curve. Incomes are much more unequally distributed. Why?

Looking through these inequalities, in perspective an "income revolution" has been occurring over the last two decades—a steady upward push of average incomes that has made America the land of the great middle class. From the peak of the boom in 1929 to the present, average family real income rose almost 50 per cent. In 1958, 45 per cent of all families fell in the $5,000-$15,000 range—the great American middle class that lives in modest comfort by our standards and in luxury by the standards of the world's masses. In 1958, 8 per cent of all families received less than $1,000; in 1935 half of all families, and in 1913 over 90 per cent, were in this group. At the upper end, in 1958 one family in four received over $7,500; in the middle 1930's only one family in 100. These comparisons are overdrawn because today's dollar will buy substantially less than that of earlier years, but price-adjusted data also show a comparable big upward income sweep.

One last observation. You may be struck by the fact that you have been thinking of yourself as falling in the over-$10,000 range once you get well established in a job. Maybe you'll make it, but if you do (at 1958 prices) you'll be way up toward the top of the heap.

Wages and Profits—Functional Shares. The American economy today doesn't look much like Karl Marx's picture of capitalism in its death throes, with the workers poised to seize ownership of the means of production. American labor and management exchange some violent words, and strikes are sometimes long and bitter. But the evidence is overwhelming that American workers want a basically capitalistic, free-enterprise system. In the showdown, management and labor get together; production goes on with the worker's rights pretty well looked out for and the capitalist's control over his investment substantially maintained.

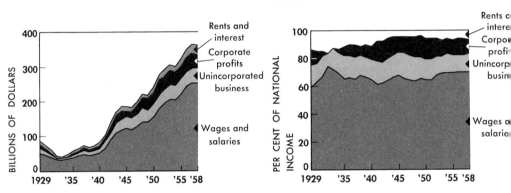

National Income Shares, 1929-1959

FIG. 28-2 Everyone's income has grown since 1929, but wage and salary earners have gradually increased their share of the total. (Source: U.S. Department of Commerce.)

When the workers go to the polls, they vote Republican or Democratic, not Socialist or Communist.

But within this framework, labor and management wrestle constantly over the division of the consumer's dollar between wages and profits. In the big-union industries, this argument comes to a boil every year or two or three, when the union's wage contract comes up for renewal. In non-unionized industries, the struggle is less sharply focused, and wages appear to follow the leaders, such as automobiles, steel, and coal.

Figure 28-2 gives an over-all picture of the outcome of this wage-profit bargaining over the last quarter-century. The left-hand part of the figure plots the actual dollar shares of national income that go to wages and salaries, corporate profits, unincorporated business incomes (a mixture of salaries and profits), rents, and interest, all before payment of income taxes. The right-hand portion shows the percentage shares that go to these various groups.

The first lesson comes from the left-hand chart. Everybody's income has grown rapidly, but in a serious depression everyone takes a beating. The second lesson, from the right-hand chart, is the general stability in the major income shares except in big business fluctuations. The wage and salary share has persistently hovered in the 60-70 per cent range. But another way of looking at the same chart is that the wage and salary share has shown a gradual long-term upward trend. In 1929 it was only about 60 per cent of the total. By the late 1950's, another prosperous period, it was about 70 per cent. Actually, the wage and salary increase came mainly in two quite different periods—during the sharp depression of the 1930's when profits vanished, and during the later 1950's when wages rose much faster than profits in spite of generally good times.

The wages and profits shares look different if we take corporate profits *after* payment of federal income taxes, as many managers during wage negotiations argue they should be taken. Using the after-tax figures drastically pulls down the share of corporate profits in recent years—for example, from 10 to 5 per cent of the total in 1958. One reason management prefers to quote the figures after taxes is obvious: Profits after taxes look like a lot smaller sum for labor to shoot at in its wage demands.

Occupational and Regional Differences.   What jobs provide the best income? In a broad way, Figure 28-3 gives an answer. The figure at the bottom shows the median income for each group; half of all incomes in the group were above and half below this figure. Managers had the highest median incomes, but the highest percentage of self-employed businessmen were in the over-$10,000 class.

Money Incomes, by Occupational Groups, 1957

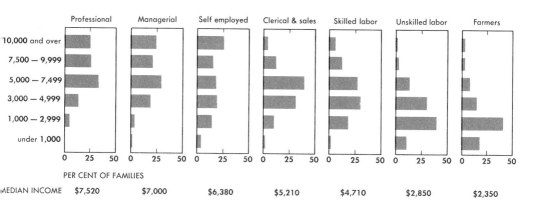

FIG. 28-3   Managers, professional men, and self-employed businessmen had the highest incomes in 1957. Farmers and unskilled labor had the biggest percentage of low incomes. (Source: Federal Reserve Board.)

Figure 28-3 suggests some other factors closely related to income level. Education is pretty clearly one. Nearly everyone now entering the three highest-paid groups has at least some college education. For business executives, doctors, and lawyers—possibly the three highest earners—advanced education is now almost a must, and has been for a good many years although there have been many notable exceptions. At the bottom, farm operators and unskilled and service workers, as groups, show the lowest levels of formal education. Education is a good investment in our society.

Regional income differences reflect these occupational and educational facts. The high incomes are concentrated in the urban areas, where high-income occupations are centered. Incomes are generally low in the South, especially in the rural areas. Per capita incomes in the deep South are still around the New York levels of a half-century ago. But the South is pulling up. New England, the traditional high-income area, is slipping relatively. And the West Coast, plus other scattered areas, is growing rapidly.

Women generally get less pay than do men for the same or similar jobs. But the much lower average income of working women reflects far more their heavy concentration in low-pay jobs—especially clerical and service work, and unskilled labor. Women are increasingly showing up in higher-paid occupations—the professions, skilled labor, and middle management. But most peak-income doors are still closed.

Older workers are another special group whose incomes are generally below average. For the highly skilled occupations—management, law, medicine—a man's earning power rises steadily until he reaches 50 or 60. But for the commonplace jobs this is not true. Workers past 40 find it hard to get new jobs, and often must move down the income ladder if they have to move. Unskilled laborers find the best-paying jobs in their 20's, or at the latest in their 30's.

Lastly, Negroes and other minority groups have a tough time raising their incomes above the poverty level. The proportion of Negro families in the below-$3,000 income range is more than twice that for whites. Less than 10 per cent of all Negro families have incomes as high as the national median. Available data for other minority groups are inadequate to justify national estimates, but evidence points clearly to the poverty of Mexican, Puerto Rican, Asiatic, and other unassimilated groups in the United States. Look at the slums of New York or Chicago. Private, state, and federal measures to decrease discrimination against these groups have made headway, especially during the labor shortages of World War II. Equal pay for equal work has become the rule in some industries. But the Negro or "foreigner" is generally the last to be taken on and the first to be laid off, regardless of his performance; and most of the best-paying jobs still are, for practical purposes, closed to these minority groups.

What accounts for these widely varying incomes? To answer this question is the main job of the rest of this Part.

Why do all these people get the incomes they
do—some large, some small; some stable,
some insecure? The answer is still the subject
of heated controversy among economists. Although we know a good deal about
the problem, there are still a lot of dark corners. But here, as in many other areas
of economics, there is substantial agreement among the experts on the fundamentals. We shall make little attempt to go beyond these simple fundamentals. They're
the important things to remember, in any case. The purpose of this section is to
provide a preliminary model, or framework, that will be filled out with more
realism and detail in the following chapters.

Incomes Are Payments for Productive Services.   Most incomes are received
as payments for productive services. Wages and salaries are payments for labor
services. Rents are payments for services of land and buildings. Interest is payment for the services of funds, but more fundamentally for the real productive
powers hirable with those funds. Profits are harder to classify simply. In a fundamental sense, they're merely the residual for businessmen and risk-takers that's
left over after all the other income payments are made out of business' gross receipts from consumers—but they're also the incentive to entrepreneurs that makes
the whole private-enterprise system go.

Thus, most incomes are the prices paid for productive services. Like any other
price, they're basically determined by supply and demand. And, as with any other
price, to understand any particular situation we need a detailed analysis of the
particular demand and supply conditions involved. The following paragraphs
map out a simple supply and demand model for analyzing productive service
markets.

The Supply Side.   First, we need a supply curve, or schedule. Look at the
supply of some given type of laborer in your community as an example (although
we could equally well take some other productive resource, like land). The supply
of such labor this month may be highly inelastic—fixed by the number of workers
there and by their strong preference to work about 40 hours a week. Or the supply
may be elastic, if comparable workers can readily be drawn in from neighboring
areas. Or overtime work may be feasible. Or maybe unskilled workers can be
easily upgraded. Another source of elasticity may be school children and retired
old people, if the job is relatively unskilled. The whole attitude of all potential
workers toward the job is important in setting the relevant supply conditions.
Over the long run, in the background are all the factors influencing the size of
the labor force as a whole, factors that were discussed back in Chapters 3 and 12.
All these things together produce a labor supply curve for the market for the time
period under study, probably an upward-sloping supply curve.

The Demand Side.[2]   Next, a demand curve. The demand for productive services is primarily a *derived demand*. The local drugstore hires clerks because customers want clerks to wait on them—not because the druggist wants clerks in the same way he wants shirts, gasoline, and the other consumer goods he buys. The demands of business for productive services thus reflect ultimate consumer demands. If consumers want lots of Coke and ice cream, the demand for drugstore clerks will be strong. But if the customers stay away, the druggist doesn't need many clerks. Begin with competitive conditions.

How many workers will a firm demand at any given wage rate? *If it is out to maximize profits, it will hire additional workers as long as each additional worker adds more to the firm's income than he adds to its total costs. If the wage the firm has to pay for another worker is more than what that worker adds to income, to hire him would lower the firm's profits. Workers' contributions to the firm's profits will be maximized, therefore, when workers are hired just up to the point where the additional income equals the additional cost for the last worker taken on—no more workers and no fewer.*

The additional income obtained by hiring one additional worker and selling the output he adds is called the "marginal revenue product" (or sometimes the "marginal value product"). Additional *physical* output ("marginal physical product") is what the worker may contribute directly. But from management's point of view it is the increase in sales income when the product is sold that matters most; hence, it is the marginal *revenue* product in which we are most interested. It is the marginal revenue product that the businessman compares with the additional cost incurred by hiring another worker in deciding how many workers to hire to maximize his profits. To summarize, the marginal revenue product of any type of productive service sets the upper limit that a business will ordinarily pay for that service; and businesses will always have an incentive to hire more productive services as long as their price is less than their marginal productivity.[3] Thus, the lower the wage, the more hours of labor will be demanded in any given labor market, other things equal.

[If you remember the process by which firms maximized profits through equating marginal cost and marginal revenue back in Chapter 21, it will be obvious that the firm's decision on how much labor to hire at any wage is precisely the same process. The only difference is that here the marginal cost–marginal revenue comparison is made in terms of additional workers, whereas in Chapter 21 it was in terms of additional units of output. The logic of increasing output (hiring more resources) as long as the additional cost involved is less than the addition to revenue, is identical in both cases; and the equilibrium level of output (of re-

---

[2] The Appendix to Chapter 20, "Physical Production Relationships Underlying Cost Curves," provides the logical foundation for this section. If you studied this Appendix it may be useful to review it before proceeding. The "marginal product" of that Appendix is identical with the "marginal *physical* product" of this chapter.

[3] The existence of monopoly raises some special problems, which will be considered in the next chapter.

sources hired) will obviously be the same either way the firm goes at it. Looking at the number of productive resources hired is looking at the volume of output from the back side, so to speak.[4]]

Moreover, our old friend from Chapter 3, the law of diminishing returns or of variable proportions, comes into play in explaining why the demand curve for labor will slope down. If more workers are hired, their marginal value product will fall as the ratio of workers to other factors of production rises. This is both because marginal physical product declines and because the price of the final output will drop as more units are put on the market with unchanged market demand. A similar analysis might be carried out for land, machinery, or any other productive service.

Generally, more workers will be demanded at lower wage rates than at higher. We can thus envisage a downward-sloping demand curve for labor, with fewer workers demanded at higher wage rates. The exact shape of different firms' demand curves for labor of different types will depend on numerous factual considerations, at which we will look in more detail in the next chapters. The purpose here is merely to map out the general nature of the firm's demand for productive resources. Remember that the use of wages of labor has been merely an example. We might equally well have been talking about the demand for farm land.

The Interaction of Supply and Demand.   The broad outlines of the market for productive services should now be apparent. We have a supply curve and a demand curve for each type of productive service in each market area, whether it be local or national. The supply curve of labor in our local area is, as we saw above, easy in principle though complex in practice. On the demand side, the marginal *physical* productivity of any type of labor in any job will be determined by its background and skills, by the equipment it has to work with, and by how many workers there are in relation to the machinery and other capital equipment available; and the marginal *revenue* productivity will be determined by adding on consumer demand for the ultimate product. Marginal revenue productivity will generally fall as more labor is hired, other things equal; the demand curve will slope downward. As long as the wage is lower than labor's marginal revenue productivity, businesses will compete for labor. *This competition will bid up wages to about the level of labor's marginal productivity, and no higher. And so the wage will be set.*

---

[4] Although the above statements indicate only how much of one single resource it will pay the business to hire, this approach can readily be generalized to cover all productive resources the firm hires. It will pay to hire more of *each* resource as long as the additional cost this involves is less than the revenue it adds (in technical terms, as long as its marginal cost is less than its marginal revenue productivity). In equilibrium, therefore, each resource will be hired up to the point where its marginal cost just equals its marginal revenue product, which is the same as saying that marginal cost equals marginal revenue for the firm as a whole, the profit-maximizing condition stated in Chapter 21. (For a more complete statement, see the Appendix to this chapter.)

Figure 28-4 pictures a simple supply and demand market equilibrium for one type of labor in a local market this week. The supply curve is inelastic; in one week not many more labor hours will be supplied at moderately higher wage rates. The demand curve slopes down for the reasons suggested above. A wage of $2 per hour just clears the market, at 400 hours of labor per week demanded and supplied. At a higher wage more would be supplied but less demanded; at a lower wage, the reverse.

All this is very fundamental on the one hand—but it may lead to a dangerous oversimplification on the other. Stop now and look at some of the assumptions we have been tacitly making: (1) Firms try to maximize their profits. (2) Businessmen know the marginal productivity of labor, which involves estimating both physical marginal productivity and consumer demand for the relevant period ahead. (3) Active competition in the market for productive services bids wages up to the marginal productivity level. (4) There is active competition among workers for jobs; they don't join together in a union to withhold labor services in order to get higher wages than they would obtain in a competitive market. (5) The government doesn't intervene to control the market price (wage).

These assumptions have a familiar look. They are pretty much the same ones involved back in Part 3 when we were looking at the behavior of business firms. If all these assumptions held in the real world, the simple competitive analytical model would give us an armchair device for predicting the level of wages and other incomes. Maybe the assumptions do hold, by and large, in a rough sort of way, for a lot of the economy. But in much of the economy this simple model provides only a beginning step and actual conditions do violence to the assumptions. Some economists think the real world is so far from these assumptions that the competitive model is of very limited use. But most economists agree that this model provides a good starting framework, and one that is a real help in explaining at least major differences in wages among different individuals, industries, areas, and classes of jobs.

Almost everyone can agree on the basic supply and demand approach to the

Supply and Demand for Labor

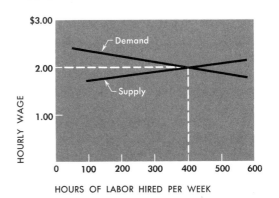

FIG. 28-4   Wages, like other prices, are determined by the interaction of supply and demand. Here the equilibrium wage is $2.00 an hour, with employers hiring 400 hours per week.

problem—if they think economic analysis has anything to say about it at all. (Some sociologists apparently believe that non-financial motives so dominate both worker and business behavior that traditional demand and supply economics is simply not the right tool to do the analytical job.) The complications come when we start looking at the demand and supply sides in detail.

The following five chapters use the basic analytical framework just suggested to look briefly at the major income shares. In a sense, the following chapter on wages and salaries is a case study, indicating the kind of analysis that is useful for understanding the broad forces at work in any given wage or salary area.

THE INTEGRATION OF PRICE AND DISTRIBUTION THEORY Under a basically competitive, private-enterprise economy, we count largely on two forces to produce an efficient allocation of resources —the profit urge of businessmen, and the income urge of workers and resource owners. Businessmen, in trying to maximize profits, hire those productive resources which contribute most to producing the goods and services consumers want, taking into account differing prices they must pay for productive resources. Individuals sell their labor and other productive services to businessmen so as to maximize their earnings, taking into account their personal preferences as to type and location of work. The incomes individuals earn provide the wherewithal to buy consumer goods in the market, providing thereby the consumer demands to which businessmen respond in hiring goods and services to produce what consumers want to buy. At each stage of this circular process, markets and prices serve to integrate the many diverse preferences of consumers and resource owners, and to equate amounts offered and demanded of productive resources and of final goods and services.

Part 3 looked in detail at how the economy responds to consumer demands, emphasizing especially the role of business firms in meeting consumer wants through striving to maximize profits. The present chapter shows that this same process determines the distribution of incomes, through setting the prices firms pay for productive services. By responding to consumer demands, businesses offer most for resources in producing what consumers want most. By trying to minimize costs, businesses hold down income payments (costs) to the minimum required to get the resources needed to meet consumer demands.

On page 480, the long-run equilibrium of a competitive economy was described. In equilibrium:

1. Competition has forced each price down to the lowest total cost of production that is consistent with the costs of the resources used in producing the good.

2. All productive resources in the economy are employed in those industries where their contribution to fulfilling consumer demands is greatest.

3. All owners of productive resources (including labor) are earning the maximum return consistent with consumer demands for final products and consistent with the owners' own preferences as to type of occupation. They will earn this maximum when productive resources are allocated as in (2). Incomes everywhere are proportional to marginal value products times the quantity of the productive service provided.

Thus, distribution theory and price theory are essentially the same thing, looked at in different ways. The costs of the business firm are the incomes of its workers and other suppliers of productive services. Both price and distribution theory center on the firm, trying to make profits. Price theory focuses on product pricing and output decisions. Distribution theory focuses on decisions as to how many and which productive services to hire. They are the same business price-output decisions in both cases, and it is the same productive resources that determine costs in both. Either way of looking at it gives the businessman the same maximum profit, hiring, output, and price position. (For a rigorous proof, see the Appendix.) Whichever way one looks at the market process, monopoly and partial monopoly disturb the smooth working of the system described under pure competition. The analytical tools useful in examining the process are the same in both cases. Only the point of view is different.

DISTRIBUTION THEORY IN MICRO- AND MACRO-ECONOMICS This chapter and those following analyze the determinants of individual incomes in particular markets. Part 4, like Part 3, is concerned primarily with micro-economics—the analysis of individual prices and incomes, rather than the aggregate national income components emphasized in Part 2. In a broad way it is easy to see how these two approaches fit together. The economy-wide forces of aggregate investment, saving, consumption, and government fiscal decisions determine the aggregate level of national product, national income, and so on. Micro-economics analyzes the allocation of resources, individual prices, and incomes within these national aggregates.

But fitting the two together rigorously is a complex job that goes beyond the goals of an elementary course. For example, the distribution of an individual firm's income between wage payments and profits seems reasonably clearcut in micro-analysis. Wages are a cost the firm must meet, largely given by the labor market. But in macro-economics, looking at the aggregate economy, we must recognize that the wages paid also constitute the incomes that largely determine final consumer demand for all firms' products. Wages are both costs and incomes. The income-expenditure model of Chapter 11 emphasizes this dual role.

Why have wages and salaries in the aggregate been a relatively stable share of total national income over many decades? Why has this share grown moderately during the past decade? Micro-analysis offers little to answer these questions, although it can throw light on what determines particular individual wages, salaries, and profits. For the aggregate shares we must turn back to our macro-analysis, but must modify it by the micro-conditions considered in this Part.

For the individual firm, an aggressive union may certainly push up wages at the expense of profits. But if all wages are pushed up, costs and incomes rise throughout the economy. In the absence of monetary-fiscal restrictions, selling prices may rise roughly in proportion as firms try and are able to protect their profit margins. Obviously, a number of factors are important here: the marginal propensities to consume of different groups in society; the pricing policies of business firms; the responsiveness of investment plans to these developments; governmental tax, expenditure, and monetary policies. Understanding the forces determining the distribution of the national income is perhaps the most difficult and complex job in economics—and in many ways the most intriguing.

It is clear that a huge mass of individual and aggregate adjustments go on simultaneously in the economy, each depending on the others. Mathematically inclined economists are fond of representing all of these by a complex set of simultaneous equations, which can be solved in principle to provide a highly abstract model of the entire integrating, adjusting process of the economy. But short of such a set of formal equations, try to envisage roughly for yourself how the macro- and micro-adjustments proceed simultaneously, with each micro-unit largely taking market supplies, demands, and prices as given, but with these millions of micro-actions combining to produce the macro-forces that in turn largely establish the framework for the micro-decisions.

REVIEW—CONCEPTS TO REMEMBER

Check your understanding of the following new concepts introduced in this chapter. You ought to be able to relate them directly back to Part 3, especially to the various cost and demand concepts there.

derived demand marginal value product
marginal physical product distribution theory
marginal revenue product

1. Would the equalization of incomes in the United States, as is proposed by some socialists, solve the problem of poverty? Use the figures on national income (in Chapter 6) and those on income distribution in this chapter, insofar as you think they are relevant, to support your answer.

2. The two biggest shares of the national income are wages and profits. Are the basic interests of wage-earners and of their employers competitive or complementary?

FOR

ANALYSIS

AND

DISCUSSION

3. In Figure 28-2, the percentage share of the national income going to wages and salaries rises sharply during the great depression of the 1930's. Yet it is commonly said that depression means mass unemployment and low wages. Can you resolve the apparent contradiction between these two observations? If so, how?

4. According to Figure 28-3, farmers and unskilled laborers have made substantially lower incomes than have the other groups shown. If this is so, why do people continue to become farmers and unskilled laborers?

5. Do you agree that a distribution of income based on marginal productivity would give everyone about what he is worth? Explain.

6. "The distribution of incomes to factors of production is no problem to one who has studied the behavior of business firms. In determining what prices to charge and what output to produce, the firm simultaneously determines how many workers to hire and what wages to pay out, what rents and interest charges to incur, and so on for the other income shares." Do you agree that your analysis of Part 3, just preceding, has in effect explained the distribution of incomes?

7. "To each according to his need, and from each according to his ability," is a slogan of diverse groups. Do you accept this slogan? Why or why not?

Appendix
Production Theory,
Price Theory, and Distribution Theory

This Appendix provides (for students who studied Chapter 21) a more rigorous statement of what economists call the theory of production and its relation to price theory and distribution theory.

The Theory of Production. The theory of production is concerned with the physical relationship between the factors of production used (input) and the product produced (output). The central principle is the law of diminishing returns, or of variable proportions. As was explained in the Appendix to Chapter 20, this law states that as the proportion of any productive resource to other productive resources is increased, the additional units of output per unit of input of that factor may rise at first, but will sooner or later begin to fall, and fall persistently thereafter (other things, such as technology, being unchanged). In its simplest form, the law concerns the effect on output of adding additional units of one variable productive factor to a fixed combination of other factors (say, hiring more units of labor in a fixed plant); but the proportional statement above is the more general one.[5]

Since the law of variable proportions applies to each productive factor as more of it is used relative to others, it constitutes a powerful analytical tool in deciding the optimal proportions among the various factors of production if we want to obtain the most efficient, or least-cost, production of any commodity. As more of each factor is added relative to the others, its marginal physical product will decline. To obtain the lowest possible cost of production for any given output, we should add more of each productive factor until the last (marginal) dollar spent on each provides the same addition to total output—that is, the same marginal physical product. This is so because under any other condition more physical product could be obtained for the same cost by switching a dollar from a lesser contributing factor of production to a higher contributing factor. Thus, in equilibrium:

$$\frac{\text{Marginal physical product of A}}{\text{Price of A}} = \frac{\text{Marginal physical product of B}}{\text{Price of B}}, \text{etc.}$$

Another (equivalent) way of saying the same thing is that in the least-cost condition, the marginal physical products of the factors of production must be proportional to their prices. That is:

$$\frac{\text{Marginal physical product of A}}{\text{Marginal physical product of B}} = \frac{\text{Price of A}}{\text{Price of B}}, \text{etc.}$$

This proposition implicitly underlies the discussion of the unit-cost curves back in Chapters 20 and 21. The U-shape of the firm's cost curve derives in part from the physical relationships described by the law of variable proportions. Most important, assuming the prices of factors of production to be given, the minimum-cost point on the firm's unit-cost curve is given by the conditions described in the preceding paragraphs—that is, by the most efficient combination of the factors of production for some given output.

This theory of production provides the answer to how much a change in the price of any factor will affect its use. If the price of one resource (say labor) falls, its use will be increased until its marginal physical product falls to the same proportion with other marginal physical products as the new proportion among the factor prices concerned. In other words, more labor will be hired until the marginal dollar spent on labor again produces the same marginal physical product as when spent on any other factor of production. Hiring more labor becomes feasible even though to do so reduces labor's marginal physical product under the law of variable proportions.

---

[5] A more complete analysis of these relationships may be found in most economic theory textbooks. See, e.g., M. J. Bowman and G. L. Bach, *Economic Analysis and Public Policy* (Englewood Cliffs, N.J.: Prentice-Hall, 1949), Chapters 18 and 19.

Maximum-Profit Positions in Price Theory and Distribution Theory. The statement of the least-cost conditions above does not necessarily specify the maximum-profit position of the firm. It only specifies the conditions for obtaining the least-cost production for any given production level. The condition for maximum-profit (or minimum-loss) production is to increase production as long as marginal cost is less than marginal revenue ($mc = mr$). This is identical with the proposition that maximum profit (or minimum loss) will be obtained by adding units of each factor of production as long as its marginal cost (price, under competitive conditions) is less than its marginal *revenue* product. Each proposition follows because as long as spending another dollar on costs adds more to total revenue than it does to total cost, total profit must be increased. The statement in terms of individual factors of production merely specifies in more detail the *mix* of productive factors that must be used in arriving at the maximum-profit position. The $mc = mr$ proposition of earlier chapters is silent on the optimal factor combination; it implicitly takes the optimal combination for granted. We can now add the equilibrium condition that for maximum profit the marginal costs of the factors used must be proportional to their marginal revenue products:

$$\frac{\text{Marginal cost of factor A}}{\text{Marginal cost of factor B}} = \frac{\text{Marginal revenue productivity of A}}{\text{Marginal revenue productivity of B}}$$

Wages and Salaries

Wages and salaries account for over two-thirds of the total national income. Most people get nearly all their income from wages and salaries, and almost everybody gets part of his income that way. By the same token, wages and salaries constitute around two-thirds of total business costs. So it is not surprising that people have been spinning out wage theories, to explain why wages are what they are, ever since they began to write about economics.

The theories of economists mirror the times in which they live, and over the last two centuries we have passed through at least three different accepted theories of wage determination. Today, most objective economists recognize that we have only the broad outlines of a satisfactory theory of wages, and that this analytical model falls far short of explaining all the cases of wages we can observe in the world around us. Yet the simple mechanics of supply and demand analysis, spelled out briefly in Chapter 28, do provide a basic framework that nearly everyone agrees is a sound and useful one.

There are nearly 75 million people in the American labor force. In some respects, every one of these is unique; no two people are exactly alike.

541

Thus it is meaningless to talk of "labor" and "wages" as if they were homogeneous. We have to look separately at many different types of labor, with different capacities, different education and training, different attitudes, living in different places, if we are to have groups homogeneous enough to be analyzed together. On the other hand, unless we lump individuals into different types of labor in different market areas, we're left with the job of looking separately at 75 million individuals. We can group workers together somewhat and talk meaningfully of different types of labor in different areas, even though no two individuals in any type are identical and even though people are continually shifting from one type and location to another.

WAGES UNDER COMPETITIVE CONDITIONS As in Part 3, it is useful to begin with a simple, purely competitive model—not because this model describes the real world closely, but because it gives a simple framework for moving on to more complex cases. This framework is the one provided in Chapter 28 for analyzing the pricing of any productive service.

To make the problem concrete, consider a hypothetical Joe Smith—a welder who works in a middle-sized eastern city for the Acme Plumbing Company, a small plumbing-fixtures manufacturer. There is no welders' union in the area. Joe's abilities are substantially undifferentiated from those of many other welders in the area. There are many businesses and construction contractors in the area who hire welders. And there are many plumbing-supplies manufacturers in the United States who compete actively with each other in the product market. So there is active competition at three levels—among welders for jobs, among businesses for the services of welders, and among businesses for the consumer's sales dollar.

What determines Joe's wage? Joe's boss sets the wage he pays, so it might be sensible to ask him. He'd probably have a simple answer. Joe gets the going hourly rate for welders—say $3 an hour. Acme Plumbing doesn't haggle over wage rates with each man it hires. It pays the going rate. The president of Acme Plumbing never heard of marginal productivity and vaguely distrusts economists and all their high-brow talk. So it's clear that that approach won't get us very far.

Something beyond Acme determines the "going rate" for welders in the area. Joe's wage is nothing but the hourly price of his type of labor service multiplied by the number of hours he works during the month, or any other time period. By now, the answer "supply and demand" ought to come easily to you as the framework for looking at this price. The next few pages outline some of the important supply and demand considerations. Then we can put them together as the determinants of the going wage.

The Supply Side.   What determines the supply of welders in the area? In any real-world case we could write a book on the subject, but the essential points would probably boil down to these:

Number of Welders in the Area. Welding is a skilled trade. There are only so many people in the area who qualify as skilled welders at any given time.

Availability of Additional Welders. The existing group of welders might be expanded either by training new welders or by bringing in men from other areas. If a small increase in the wage rate draws welders into the area and draws new recruits into the three-month training programs required to pick up the minimal skills, the supply of welders will be highly elastic. But if welders are immobile and the field doesn't look attractive, the supply will be inelastic. The elasticity of supply will thus depend on the wide range of factors that determine the desirability of the job and labor's mobility into it. It depends on information on job openings, security of positions once obtained, cost of learning the trade, costs of moving from one area to another, "non-economic" attachments to particular jobs or localities, possible restrictions on entry into the job (by unions or legal regulations), and so on. If we were looking at professional or managerial jobs, the whole educational process required for the job would be of much greater importance than in welding.

Hours of Work per Welder. For the most part, welders either put in the workweek stated by their employer or they don't get the job. But there are some ways they can control the amount of work they want to do. Pressures for overtime work can be resisted, and there's no way, short of firing him, to force a man to come to work if he decides to stay home now and then. Here again we have a problem of elasticity of supply. Will higher wage rates call forth more hours worked?

Elasticity of Supply Dependent on Time Period. On any given day, the supply of welders in our area is pretty much fixed. If there are 100 welders available, that's how many there are and no more. Firms may put on overtime schedules, but they can't get more men. But given a week's time, they may be able to lure in a few men from neighboring areas. And given six months, the possibility of training new welders opens new supply possibilities. In most cases, supply becomes increasingly elastic as a longer time period is considered. But in the professions and management, many years rather than a few months are required for big increases in supply. A doctor goes through about 10 years of college, medical school, and internship before he's ready to go out on his own.

The Demand Side.   The demand for welders' services is a *derived* demand, derived from the ultimate consumer demand for the plumbing fixtures Acme produces. Acme (and other businesses) will demand more welders whenever they have unfulfilled demand for their product at profitable prices. More precisely, Acme will demand more welders as long as the wage is below welders' marginal revenue productivity to it. Other firms will do likewise. By aggregating the demands of all firms, we could draw a demand curve for welders' services at any time. Since welders' marginal revenue productivity may be different in different firms, some firms' demand will drop off rapidly as the wage rate rises; others' will drop off only slowly.

If the marginal revenue productivity of welders is so crucial in determining employers' demand for welders, we need to look at the determinants of marginal revenue productivity—which, remember, is compounded of marginal physical productivity and a product price factor. But while you're reading these paragraphs, keep asking yourself a question: Can and do businesses really think about marginal productivity in their hiring?

Determinants of Marginal Physical Productivity. Joe Smith's marginal physical product is the additional physical product Acme Plumbing turns out by having Joe on the job, compared with the output without him, all other productive factors being identical in both cases. This marginal physical product depends on Joe's own mental and physical abilities, training, morale, and so on. It also depends on the other productive agents with which he works. With an old-style welding torch and in poor working conditions, Joe will have a low marginal physical product. Well equipped and working on a well-designed, balanced production line, his marginal physical product will be higher.

Joe's marginal physical product depends on the *proportion* of welders to other productive agents, as well as on the quality of the machinery and tools he works with. For example, if welding is one operation on a metal-sink production line, the addition of the first welder to that line means a big increase in the firm's output. Addition of a second and third welder may skyrocket output further, until the line is roughly balanced between welders and other workmen. Beyond this point, addition of more welders may increase output somewhat by speeding up the line or by having a spare welder around to spell anyone who takes a coffee break, but the additional (marginal) product is much lower than it was when the first few welders were added.

This is the law of diminishing returns. You will remember that this principle states that when additional units of one productive service are added to a fixed group of other productive services, the marginal product of the increasing service will rise at first and then diminish after some maximum marginal product combination is reached. It means that adding more welders in any plant will sooner or later mean a declining marginal physical product for welders, assuming the size of the plant and the combination of other productive agents remain unchanged. This is a fundamental physical fact, observable everywhere in the realm of productive activity.

Determinants of Marginal Revenue Productivity. The production manager is interested mainly in how many sinks get turned out in a day. But the president and the stockholders are more interested in the profit figures—in dollars and cents rather than in numbers of sinks and faucets. To be meaningful for general management purposes, physical productivity figures have to be converted into *sales-dollar terms.*

Suppose the marginal physical product of welders like Joe in Acme Plumbing is estimated at around one sink per day, and that the wholesale price of the sink is $30. Then welders' marginal revenue productivity at Acme Plumbing, with the existing number of welders, is $30; marginal revenue productivity is found by multiplying the marginal physical product by marginal revenue (price). Consumer demand for the ultimate product is just as important as the worker's physical output in determining his value to the business.

To re-emphasize: It is important to see that Joe's marginal revenue productivity depends on a lot of forces completely outside his own control. Any change in consumer demand (because a depression comes along, because competing companies turn out a better sink, or because consumers decide they want more sinks per house) will change Joe's dollar contribution to Acme's sales revenue. And any change in Acme's general production set-up may have the same result.

In summary: The marginal revenue productivity of welders will eventually decrease as more and more welders are put to work producing sinks, for two reasons. First, the law of diminishing returns will eventually bring decreasing marginal physical productivity as the ratio of welders to other factors of production increases. Second, as more sinks are produced by this and competing firms, their price will fall, consumer demand conditions remaining unchanged—although Acme alone is too small to influence market price. Acme's downward-sloping demand for welders rests on welders' diminishing marginal physical product as more are added, since each sink is sold at a constant price, so far as Acme is concerned. A larger firm whose increased output might depress the price of sinks would have a downward-sloping demand curve dependent on both diminishing marginal physical product and declining price of sinks as it hired more welders.

Thus the demand curve for welders will generally be downward-sloping, as in Figure 29-1. Starting from any equilibrium position, firms will hire more welders only as wage rates fall. In effect, the marginal revenue product curve for welders in the firm is that firm's demand curve for welders.[1]

Interdependence of Demand for Productive Services. In fact, pretty much anything that happens to any aspect of the production of sinks and substitute commodities, or to any process that uses welding, will affect Joe's marginal value productivity and the demand for his services. Suppose, for example, a new machine is invented that cuts in half the amount of welding required on a metal

---

[1] Note that if firms are prepared to increase the amount of other resources with which welders work (e.g., the scale of plant), the effect of diminishing physical productivity can be avoided. But the declining price effect may nevertheless pull down marginal value productivity in firms not perfectly competitive. We need some modifications where the market for labor is not perfectly competitive—to be noted in a later section.

sink. This will obviously mean a *substitution* of machinery for welders. But the machine will be *complementary* to other types of labor—for example, workers required to build and service the new machines. The new machinery might even lower the cost of sinks so much that total sales would boom enough to require more welders, even though each sink required less welding. Here the elasticity of ultimate consumer demand for sinks is obviously crucial.

There is an almost infinite number of possibilities in these interrelationships. Formal analysis of the interactions can become almost a game. Try thinking through, for example, the impact on the demand for welders of a new process that lowers the cost of producing bathtubs (not made by Acme Plumbing). There's no use trying to memorize all the kinds of interrelationships. The main thing is to watch out for the major interrelationships that may affect the demand for any type of labor you are considering.

Do Firms Really Use Marginal Revenue Productivity? How can businessmen ever estimate anything so complex as a worker's marginal revenue productivity? In fact, few businessmen have ever heard of marginal revenue productivity. But a lot of them are perfectly familiar with the notion. Ask them how much another welder is worth to them, and they'll have some kind of an answer, even though it may not be much more than an informed guess.

Firm's Downward-Sloping Demand Curve for Labor

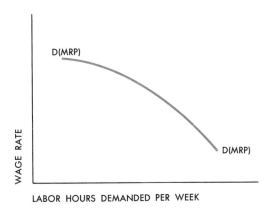

FIG. 29-1   The competitive firm's demand curve for labor is downward-sloping. The demand curve is labor's marginal revenue product curve in the firm, since it will pay to hire more workers as long as marginal revenue product is more than the wage.

In a little firm like Acme Plumbing, with only a small number of employees and simple processes, the boss may have a pretty good idea of how much his daily output will go up if he puts on an extra man. And he probably knows just about the price that extra output will bring. This was the kind of situation economists had in mind when they developed the marginal-productivity approach to explaining the demand for labor.

But what about the marginal revenue productivity of a welder like Joe in U.S. Steel? U.S. Steel has nearly 300,000 employees scattered over the United States, with hundreds of welders among them. Welders work on jobs many steps removed from the ultimate steel products sold to the company's customers. For example, one welder may do repair work on the company's railway cars that shuttle materials around the mills. What is his marginal revenue productivity?

Obviously, no one knows. It would be impossible to isolate the effect on the ultimate production of cold-rolled steel sheets of laying off that one welder, even waiving the problem of estimating the price at which that marginal output of sheets could be sold. And there are millions of workers in American industry who present similar problems in getting any useful estimate of marginal physical productivity.

Still, U.S. Steel has to decide somehow how many welders it will hire. Company officials might tell you it's simple. They hire enough welders to get the steel produced for which they have orders. But this answer, which is probably quite correct, drives us back to the question of the price at which U.S. Steel will book orders, and how many it will book for delivery this year. Clearly these decisions are dependent in large part on the costs estimated by the steel people for producing steel sheets. Somehow all these interrelated variables have to be put together, and somehow the hiring officials down at the plant level have to estimate when it will pay to hire another welder.

Where does all this leave us? First, it's clear that no very precise estimate of marginal physical productivity is possible in many cases. There are many places where a pretty good estimate is feasible, but many more where it is out of the question. Second, hard as the estimating job is, businessmen have to make some such calculation (consciously or unconsciously) in their hiring decisions if they are intelligently trying to maximize profits. Third, in many cases several types of labor must be hired as a group to operate as a production unit. You either have the people it takes to run a modern assembly line, or you just shut the line down. In this common type of situation, it is very difficult to separate out any marginal physical product of each kind of laborer.

Out of all this probably emerges some rough notion that businessmen are willing to pay workers only what they are "worth," sometimes viewing workers as individuals but often as groups required for an integrated operation. What workers are worth *logically* boils down to a notion of marginal revenue productivity. But since this figure can't be estimated with any precision in most cases, many businesses use their cost-accounting systems to get working ideas of when it pays to take new orders and hire more workers. Cost-accounting records in big concerns typically break down the cost of producing different commodities into a good deal of detail. Behind these money-cost data are time and motion studies of how much labor time should turn out how much product. Using these studies, the businessman can get a rough idea of the cost of different labor components per unit of output, and hence a rough estimate of the "productivity" of workers of different types.

Economists often shudder at the roughness of the calculations. They point out the misleading results that may arise from the use of standard-cost data rather than actual-cost figures at varying levels of output. Still, businessmen are the ones who do the hiring, and their approximations may often be closer to the marginal-productivity "ideal" than you'd guess from their methods. These problems have a familiar ring. They are the same ones we worried about back in Chapter 25. Do businessmen really try to maximize profits, and how efficient are they in carrying out their aims? The whole notion that businessmen act roughly *as if* they were comparing marginal productivity with going wage rates when they hire workers goes back to the assumption that businesses actually do act roughly to maximize their profits. Sometimes they do. Maybe sometimes they don't. Competition pushes them strongly in this direction. Remember that the model need not be an exact description of every firm's behavior. It's useful if it gives us a workable first approximation to typical behavior.

Lastly, the market has a way of smoothing out any wide deviations in the estimates of different concerns on what labor of different types is "worth." It's the summation of *all* their demands against the *total* supply in each market that sets the wage rate.

SUPPLY, DEMAND, AND PURELY COMPETITIVE WAGES In a competitive market, price (the wage rate) is determined by the interaction of supply and demand. Assume (1) that welders are all substantially identical, (2) that employment conditions are pretty much the same at different plants in the area, and (3) that information on wages offered at different plants is circulated freely. Then all plants will have to pay about the same wage to get welders, just as there tends to be a single price for any other identical commodity within any given market area.

Suppose that the going wage for welders is $24 a day, but that Acme Plumbing and some other plants figure that welders are worth more than that to them, up to around $30 per 8-hour day, on the basis of their productivity estimates. In technical language, they estimate that the marginal revenue productivity of such labor is more than $24 in their plants. What will happen? All those plants will try to hire more welders. When they do, (1) the wage rate will be bid up, and (2) the value (marginal revenue productivity) of welders in these plants will fall as more labor is added (because of the law of diminishing returns and possibly a lower price for sinks). Each firm will bid for additional welders as long as the rising wage is lower than what it can afford to pay additional men. At some rate between $24 and $30 an equilibrium wage will tend to be established, with market supply and demand in balance at that new wage. Figure 29-2 shows this equilibrium for the whole labor market; this is a summation of all the firms demanding welders, and here the supply curve is upward-sloping. Figure 29-3 shows the equilibrium for Acme Plumbing when the hourly wage is set by the market at $27; remember that Acme simply has to pay the going wage rate to get all the welders it needs.

In this equilibrium situation, we would expect to find the following:

1. Welders' wages are substantially identical at all plants in the area.
2. Each firm is hiring as many welders as it "can afford" at that wage, because each firm continues to hire welders as long as the wage is lower than what it gains by hiring additional welders. In technical language, welders' marginal revenue productivity in each plant that is hiring welders is approximately equal to the going wage.
3. All welders in the area who are seeking work at that wage are employed. If any were still looking for work at that wage or less, the market wage rate would be bid down, since employers could hire unemployed workers at less than they were paying employed welders.

**Market Equilibrium
for Welders' Wages**

**Acme Plumbing Company
Equilibrium**

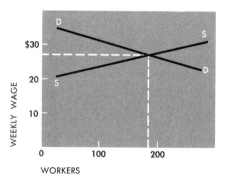
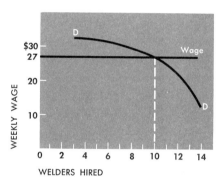

FIG. 29-2   Welders' wages are set by the interaction of supply and demand in the market, just like other prices.

FIG. 29-3   When the market wage for welders is $27, Acme maximizes profits by hiring welders until their marginal value productivity equals $27. As shown in Fig. 29-1, Acme's demand curve for welders is their marginal revenue productivity curve in the firm.

In this sense, a competitive market tends to establish a wage for any type of labor roughly equal to its marginal revenue productivity when all workers of that class are employed. But don't forget the crucial assumptions underlying this conclusion—active competition in the product and labor markets, identical welders, perfect information on job opportunities, and similar employment conditions in all plants. Moreover, don't forget that we've been talking about a small geographical area, where workers are highly mobile between jobs. If we were to try to generalize this model for application to the whole country, we would have to recognize the widespread immobilities and other barriers that divide the country into many submarkets, among which there are only partial mobility, imperfect flow of information, and widely varying employment conditions.

So what we have is a simple analytical model for a homogeneous purely competitive market, which gives us a useful starting framework for looking at wage problems. Again, the model is a big help in understanding the behavior of the labor market. Again, it provides a first approximation, not an answer.

WAGE DETERMINATION IN MONOPOLIZED INDUSTRIES What difference does it make if the plumbing-supplies industry is monopolized by one or a few major producers? This is a common, real-world situation. Continue our basic assumption that each firm does the best it can to maximize profits within the existing market arrangements, and that firms compete actively for workers.

As under competition, each firm will continue to hire more welders as long as the wage is lower than welders' estimated worth to the concern. But the total number of welders hired in the industry will be lower than under competition, given the same minimum cost level under competition and monopoly. This is because the monopolist restricts output to get higher prices and higher profits.

This means that fewer welders will have jobs in plumbing manufacture. If welders could work only there, clearly wages would be forced down by their competition for the reduced number of jobs. But welders forced out of plumbing can look for jobs elsewhere. Since we assume welders to be identical and highly mobile, those forced out of plumbing will compete for jobs elsewhere, forcing down welders' wages there. Wages will again be identical everywhere in the new equilibrium, but at a lower level than without the monopoly. By restricting output below the consumers' sovereignty "ideal," the monopolist forces an inefficient allocation of labor and produces a lower wage for welders than under competition, both in the plumbing-supplies industry and in other industries as well. Too few workers are employed in making plumbing supplies, too many in the rest of the economy.[2]

WAGE DETERMINATION UNDER EMPLOYER MONOPSONY Now assume a different situation, where there is little or no competition among employers for labor. An example might be an isolated company mining town, where there is no sig-

---

[2] The argument can be stated rigorously, as follows. Since the monopolist always faces a downward-sloping demand curve, marginal revenue is always less than price. The marginal revenue product obtained by hiring more labor is therefore always less than marginal physical product times the product price; instead, it is marginal physical product times marginal revenue. Since the marginal-revenue-product curve is in effect the firm's demand-for-labor curve, the firm's demand for labor under monopoly will thus always be less than in a comparable competitive case, where marginal revenue would be equal to price rather than below it.

nificant alternative to working in the mine. The mine operator has a substantially complete monopsony—i.e., a monopoly in hiring workers. There is no reason to suppose that he will pay a wage as high as the workers' marginal revenue productivity to him. If the workers are immobile, he may "exploit" them—that is, he may pay them a wage below their marginal revenue productivity to him. This case is similar to that of a fixed resource like a desirable land site, whose price (or rent) is largely determined by demand. Here the monopsonist may be able to hold the demand side very low and still get all the labor he needs. But even here the operator doesn't have a completely free hand. If his wages get too far below going rates elsewhere, the workers may pick up and move away to areas where they can earn more.

To hear workers tell it, monopsony is a common case; the worker needs a union to protect himself against exploitation. According to employers, this is a rare case. The evidence suggests a very mixed world, but everywhere the strength of monopsony positions tends to diminish as job-information channels improve, as workers have more time to move to new jobs, and as income levels rise high enough to permit expensive moves between jobs.

A look ahead to implications for union behavior: Where monopsony exists, the union can clearly do a job for the workers. By banding together, the employees may be able to bargain their wages up to their full marginal revenue productivity without inducing any unemployment. As long as the wage rate is less than the value of additional workers to the operator, it will pay him to keep on hiring all the workers he was previously getting at a lower rate, even at the higher union wage. The union merely recoups for the workers the "exploitation" that had previously swollen the operator's profit. An equally good way to eliminate "exploitation," less popular in union circles, may be to increase workers' mobility among jobs.

WAGE DETERMINATION UNDER BILATERAL MONOPOLY

The fourth model is one that comes close to real-world conditions in some of the big union–big business areas of today. "Bilateral monopoly" is the case where employers with monopsony power bargain with unions with monopoly power in selling labor. A very simple case would be the mining-town example above after the workers formed one single union to represent them as exclusive bargaining agent. A more realistic example, though not a "pure" case of bilateral monopoly, is wage bargaining in the steel industry, where the United Steelworkers represent the big majority of the workers and the major firms in the industry in effect act together in bargaining for new contracts. Such industry-wide bargaining is not common. But approximations are.

There are many other cases that might be called bilateral oligopoly, or bilateral oligopoly-monopoly. The auto industry, for example, has only three major firms, and they undoubtedly consider each other's positions as they bargain; but they do not bargain jointly as do the major steel firms. Heavy electrical equipment, with G.E. and Westinghouse, is a similar case. In all these cases, workers are represented by more than one union. But one union represents the great bulk of the production workers.

Under bilateral monopoly or bilateral oligopoly the wage outcome is logically uncertain. The employer will be unwilling to pay more than the labor is worth to him at the margin without cutting back the number employed. (Remember that this cutback may come as a result of higher prices resulting from higher wage costs, with a consequent drop in real sales volume; it need not come directly as a result of the higher quoted wage to make the logic sound.) Under oligopoly this uncertainty is emphasized by the kinked-demand-curve analysis illustrated on page 485. Since the firm is reluctant to disturb the existing price in such a situation, the union may push up wages without inducing a higher price or re-duced output and employment.[3] In this case, the union may have a relatively strong bargaining hand, so long as it doesn't force firms to disturb the prevailing price. But since often in such industries a similar union bargain is struck with all companies, an industry-wide price increase (with resulting lower output and employment) is likely.

Just how far an employer may be able to hold the wage below the marginal productivity level—conversely, how high the union can force the wage—is a question to which economic theory has no answer. To a considerable extent labor is immobile. Workers do not move readily from one job or location to another. Thus, in one sense, a major employer or group of employers can probably keep its labor supply at whatever wage rate is bargained, unless the wage is substan-tially below wages in alternative industries. Again, this is somewhat comparable to the case of a resource in fixed supply, where the price or rent is largely demand-determined. But here the union provides a strong force countering employer monopsony. Bargaining power—force and strategy—holds the key to the outcome, within a considerable margin.[4]

WAGE AND SALARY DIFFERENTIALS

The huge salaries of movie stars, corporation presidents, and home-run hitters are always fascinating. Why should anyone get $100,000 a year when most of us have to be content with a small fraction of that? And epecially, why should they get it when their work by and large looks so easy and

---

[3] The footnote on page 486 demonstrates rigorously why this may be optimal employer behavior. Since the marginal-revenue curve is discontinuous at the "corner" of the kinked-demand curve, marginal cost can increase up to peak of this discontinuity without calling for any change in output (employment).

[4] A new analytical approach from mathematics—"game theory"—presents some interest-ing insights into alternative outcomes under different types of bargaining strategies.

pleasant compared with ditch-digging or pounding a typewriter, which pay only a dollar or two an hour?

Even within the range of occupations which seem reasonably likely for most of us, why are differentials what they are? A recent study showed that the average pay of college presidents was $11,000, of clergymen $3,100, of lawyers $8,000, of major-league ball-players $15,000, of bricklayers $7,300, of college professors, $5,400, of labor-union presidents $18,000, of physicians $16,000, of motion-picture first cameramen $26,000. Table 29-1 shows some typical weekly earnings figures for non-supervisory workers in industry in 1959. The average annual wage was about $4,700. Within any one of these industries—for example, steel—there is again a wide spread, even for non-supervisory employees.

Table 29-1

AVERAGE WEEKLY EARNINGS, 1959 *

Industry	Earnings	Industry	Earnings
All manufacturing:	$ 87.38	Nonmanufacturing:	
Furniture	72.57	Soft coal mining	$114.71
Steel making	120.08	Metal mining	103.94
Electrical machinery	88.88	Petroleum mining	111.92
Other machinery	99.31	Construction	111.03
Automobiles	109.06	Telephone	80.81
Aircraft	105.52	Local bus lines	92.44
Meatpacking	95.65	Wholesale trade	88.44
Canning & preserving	66.85	Retail-general stores	48.23
Bakery products	80.19	Retail-food	68.43
Tobacco mfg.	63.63	Retail-automotive	87.07
Textile mfg.	60.89	Banks	66.71
Apparel	55.08	Hotels	45.66
Industrial chemicals	103.73	Laundries	45.20
Petroleum refining	117.55	Cleaning and dyeing	51.98
Shoes	60.76	Electric utilities	103.32

* Figures are average weekly earnings of non-supervisory employees before taxes or other deductions, for January 1959. Data from U.S. Department of Labor.

For instance, in early 1959, under the United Steelworkers contract with major firms, $1.96 per hour was the basic rate for completely unskilled labor. Above this, there were 32 different major classes of labor specified, each with a different base rate, up to $3.97 per hour at the top. Electricians, crane operators, machinists, lift-truck operators—all received different classifications and base rates. Beyond this, special incentives were open to many groups in different firms, which paid higher effective hourly rates if the man produced above "standard." In some cases, these incentives made possible earnings much larger than would appear feasible from the base hourly rates. From a standard bottom-rate annual-full-time income of around $4,000, actual worker incomes ranged up to above $10,000 and even toward $15,000 in exceptional cases for highly skilled workers who also produced far above standard.[5]

Supply and Demand Again.   The most fundamental things about wage and salary differentials can be said within the framework of the analytical models outlined in the preceding section. Salaries are extremely high where the supply is tiny and the demand is large. Wages are low where there are lots of workers relative to the demand. How "hard," how unpleasant, how tedious the job is—such considerations aren't likely to be very important except as they influence either the supply or the demand side of the picture.

Why did Babe Ruth in the past and Mickey Mantle now collect astronomical salaries just for playing baseball on warm summer afternoons? Mainly because they were better at hitting, catching, and throwing baseballs than almost anybody else; and we Americans lay our dollars on the line with enthusiasm to see good baseball players.[6] How can a surgeon get away with charging hundreds of dollars an hour for his time? He gets away with it because his skills are very scarce, and the demand for them is very strong. In contrast, it's easy to be a delivery boy, or a typist, or a retail clerk, and lots of people try these jobs.

The biggest factor accounting for big wage differentials thus lies in the ability of the individual to do something that few others can do—something that is highly demanded by consumers with money to pay for it. There are enormous difference in the capabilities of different people. Some of these differences we can't do much about. Joe Louis' split-second timing was largely born, not made, in spite of all the years of training that went into it. Psychologists tell us that our basic intelligence (sometimes called our I.Q.) changes relatively little over the years, no matter how hard we study. But our capabilities also depend on education, training, family background, hard work, and other things that are at least partially controllable. One reason that top-notch corporation lawyers are so scarce is that not many people have both the brains and personality *and* the drive to put in the 25 years of hard work in college, law school, and practice that it takes to make a fine corporation lawyer. The competition is tough for the top jobs, and most of them aren't won by fellows who work eight-hour days with Saturdays and Sundays off.

---

[5] Obviously, if the "standard" is set low, this makes it easy for workers to earn more than the base rate; if the standard is high, the reverse is true. It is not surprising, therefore, that the proper level of such standards for different classes of workers is a matter of persistent argument between management and union representatives in companies using this plan.

[6] Anomalously, Babe Ruth may have been more susceptible to wage exploitation than most common laborers. This is because there could be little active competition for his services to force the New York Yankees to pay him more; almost no one else had a big enough ball park in a city large enough to push Ruth's salary up to what he was probably "worth" to the Yankees in marginal revenue productivity (marginal cash drawing power). Moreover, under organized baseball's "reserve clause," other clubs couldn't hire Ruth away anyhow; they would have had to "buy" him from the Yankees. But Ruth obviously had a monopoly in selling his own services. Thus the situation was one of bilateral monopoly.

But ability and hard work aren't the whole story. Some occupations are hard to get into. You can't become a lawyer or a surgeon unless you've got the money to get into and through law or medical school, however smart and ambitious you may be. The only way to become a senior airline pilot is to move up through a long period of training and experience, where the job openings are limited. Becoming a master plumber is almost impossible unless you meet the union's requirements in many areas, and the union may not want an increase in the number of master plumbers. Many occupations are still substantially closed to Negroes, though the doors are gradually opening. Women are in effect excluded from many high-pay occupations, though here again the barriers are gradually dropping. Geographical location may play an important role. Many people can't, or won't, move far from where they are, and hence are effectively eliminated from a chance at good jobs elsewhere.

Consider another example. When a new area develops and needs new workers, we would expect wages to be unusually high for a while. People are unlikely to give up other jobs and move across the country to take a fling at a new and untried occupation unless the monetary incentive is clear. And this checks out. As the Southwest developed, wages there were generally higher than in, say, the Midwest. Any rapidly growing area tends to bid up wages, because labor is relatively scarce.[7] The same is true of new industries. Table 29-1 shows exceptionally high earnings in the aircraft industry. This high level partly reflects overtime and special work on government contracts, but it also reflects the premium that must be paid to get qualified workers into a new industry of unstable and unpredictable demand.

Increasingly, the higher-paid occupations require formal education, at least through college and many through additional graduate or professional school. This is a form of restriction on supply, as well as training for the job. Business, engineering, science, law, medicine, dentistry—all are increasingly difficult for the non-college man to enter. Salary studies consistently show the dollars-and-cents value of education. Roughly speaking, every year of additional school above eighth grade seems to be worth an extra $300 to $400 a year earning power over one's entire life span. Thus, the college graduate's average lifetime earnings will probably be some $1,500 (in 1958 prices) annually higher than the high-school graduate's, even allowing for his four years of college with no income at all. Over a working life span, this means that college may be worth some $50,000 to $75,000, a nice return on investment by any standards. (There is some trickery in these figures, of course, since we know that generally the more able people go on to college and would presumably earn above average even without the extra

---

[7] Per capita income in California in 1958 was about $2,600, in Missouri about $1,950, in Michigan about $2,150, in Vermont about $1,700, in South Carolina about $1,200, in New Jersey about $2,500, and in Mississippi about $1,000, the lowest in the nation. Can you explain these differences on the new-area hypothesis? If not, how can they be explained?

schooling. But even making a rough allowance to eliminate that factor, higher education pays handsomely on the average.)

Unions have some influence on wage differentials. Especially where the situation approximates employer monopsony, it is clear that unions may improve the position of workers compared to non-union shops. Since in fact workers are notably immobile and insensitive to even substantial wage differentials between industries and locations, unions may significantly change relative incomes by forcing wages up when workers won't eliminate "exploitation" on their own by moving to higher-paying jobs. Just how much difference unions really make is a subject of much dispute, to be postponed till the next chapter.

A supply and demand model would predict that some particularly dirty, disagreeable, dangerous jobs will command pay differentials because these factors restrict the supply of labor for the jobs—not because the dirt, danger, or unpleasantness themselves justify higher wages. Workers ordinarily get more pay for night and Sunday work; it takes that to get many people to work those shifts. Extra-hazard pay goes with dangerous jobs; "sand-hogs," for example, make good money, but not many people line up for the job of drilling tunnels underwater. Conversely, people like white-collar jobs. The low wages paid to clerks in banks and other pleasant working places attest to the appeal of such jobs in increasing the supply even though wages are lower than elsewhere for comparable workers.

But the striking fact is that the cleanest, most attractive, most pleasant jobs are generally the ones with the *highest* pay—unless you classify responsibility as a disadvantage. Just about everybody would agree that the corporation president has a nicer job than the ditch-digger, that the lawyer leads a nicer life than the coal-miner. Then why don't more people become corporation presidents, brain surgeons, and lawyers, so that the salaries there and in ditch-digging will move toward equality? You answer the question. Thinking it through should give you some insights into the complex set of factors limiting the supply of certain kinds of abilities in our society, relative to the demand for those abilities. At the end, ask yourself one more question: Do existing wage differentials reward most highly those who make the greatest contribution to human welfare (movie stars, surgeons, corporation presidents, ball-players, clergymen, schoolteachers, dope-peddlers, factory workers, farm laborers)?

ANALYTICAL MODELS AND THE REAL WORLD

The four simple analytical models above cover, as first approximations, a wide range of real-world situations. They suggest some of the useful questions to ask about almost any real-world wage problem that may arise. But the old warning is very much in point here again: These simple models, with their limiting assumptions, can seldom be fitted without change onto a real-world situation.

In the vast majority of cases, for example, businessmen have only a loose approximation of what they "can afford" to pay the various types of labor they hire. This means there is always a substantial area of uncertainty about just how high a wage it is worth while to pay for any class of labor. Thus even in substantially competitive markets, marginal-productivity analysis may be far from giving a precise guide to wage determination. In highly monopolistic and monopsonistic markets this is even more true, since the competitive pressure of the market toward profit maximization is less predictable.

Worker immobility, lack of information, "non-economic" preferences among jobs and localities, and other impediments to the operations of a perfect theoretical market are everywhere present in the real world. Studies have shown repeatedly that workers are often slow and reluctant to move to higher-paying new jobs, even in nearby areas. This means that there are many different wage rates for substantially identical labor throughout the nation, though each may be quite consistent with the marginal-productivity analysis in its own area. Widespread unionization has gone far to standardize wage rates for similar jobs and to eliminate arbitrary discrimination among slightly differing workers in the wage market. But unions also erect barriers between occupations, which further segment the labor market. The labor market is a shifting mixture of fluidity and non-competing occupational and geographical groups.

Demand and supply analysis is the best economists have to offer for understanding why wages are what they are for different jobs, and it's a powerful tool. The basic notion of marginal productivity provides a useful though rough guide to thinking about business demand for labor services. The look at labor unionism in the next chapter will give you some indication of how much these models can help you in thinking straight about some of the major public-policy issues of the day.

One last comment: Be sure you don't get your ethics mixed up with your analysis. Just because real-world labor markets diverge from perfectly competitive conditions doesn't necessarily mean they're bad or inefficient. Some people think that unions (labor monopolies) are very good—because they do raise wages above competitive levels, or because they give downtrodden workers a way of standing up to overriding employers, or because they provide good picnics and free beer, or because they've won job-security for workers and guaranteed old-age pensions. There are lots of bases for judging how well our economic institutions function. The wage and salary effects focused on by the preceding models are surely important questions to worry about. But don't let the neutral analytical models twist around your ethical judgments about what is important and good for society—unless, of course, you change your mind after thinking through the issues on their merits.

WAGES AND TECHNOLOGICAL ADVANCE

Technological change is a dominant characteristic of the modern American economy. New products, new machines, new methods—

these are the lifeblood of a dynamic, growing economy. Without the Linotype we'd still be setting print by hand, and books and newspapers would still be for the elite few. Without the electric light bulb, we'd still be lighting our homes with candles, oil, and gas. Technological advance is a boon to the national standard of living.

But not everybody is for technological advance—at least not when it puts him out of a job. The painters still hold out firmly against using spray guns and rollers, though these admittedly get more work done faster. The railway brotherhoods oppose longer freight trains, though modern locomotives can easily pull more freight than their predecessors could. The type-setters showed little enthusiasm for the introduction of the Linotype.

What does technological advance do to wages? Take a hypothetical example, going back to Joe Smith, the welder. Suppose a new machine is invented that stamps out metal sinks complete, eliminating entirely the need for welding. Trace through the results.

1. Sink producers will adopt the new method if it's cheaper per sink produced than the old one was.

2. Welders will lose their jobs in plumbing-supply companies. Joe will be out of a job.

3. Employment will increase in plants that manufacture the new machine, and in plumbing-supply companies that need men to install, service, and operate the new machines.

4. At the lower price of sinks, more sinks will be sold and consumers will be better off.

In all of this, what has happened to the wages of different labor groups and to the wage share in the national income?

First, welders' wages drop. Some welders are thrown out of work. They look for other jobs. If they stay employed total wages of welders are clearly down. Even if they get jobs elsewhere, welders' wages there will tend to be pulled down.

Second, the demand for other types of labor rises—for workers to make the new machines and to service and operate them. If the cost saving is substantial, if firms pass the saving along through lower prices, and if consumer demand for sinks is elastic, then total wage payments in the sink industry may actually rise as a result of the innovation. If consumer demand is inelastic, wage payments in the sink industry will probably drop, though profits may rise.

Third, if we assume constant total expenditures in the economy, welders thrown out of jobs can get work elsewhere or at different jobs in the sink industry, as consumers switch their expenditure patterns. This pleasant conclusion, however, skips lightly over all the problems of retraining and readjustment of individual workers. It's not hard to understand why the workers displaced by new machines and new products often fight the change. At best, the worker stands to lose prestige and salary. If he is middle-aged or older, any other job may be hard to find, and it's tough for him to have to pull up stakes and move to another city to hunt for a job. Only the young man, still without highly developed skills and established position, can move easily to other jobs, and this may not be a pleasant process even for him. Increasingly, unions, in cooperation with employers, try to arrange transfers to other jobs within the firm for workers who have been displaced by technological change. Often no one has to be laid off, because displaced workers move to vacancies created by normal labor turnover within the firm.

Fourth, the total wage share in the national income will depend largely on the elasticity of demand for the product concerned and on the ratio of labor to capital used in the innovating industry, relative to the rest of the economy. This gets pretty complicated, and we seldom know enough about the various elasticities involved to be able to predict very precisely what the over-all result will be for labor's income share in the aggregate. But since labor clearly benefits in its role as consumer, it would be the rare case in which labor's *real* income was lowered by technological advance, whatever happens to its *relative* share of the national income. The reasonably steady, and gradually rising, share of wages and salaries in the national income over many years characterized by rapid technological change suggests that labor and non-labor incomes may share about equally in the benefits of technological progress. If anything, the labor share has grown gradually.

AGGREGATE WAGES IN THE NATIONAL INCOME What determines the share of wages and salaries in the total national income? Why has it been so stable, hovering around two-thirds of the total in spite of all the changes and growth in the American economy? At this aggregate level, the answers are probably more to be found in the study of macro-economics, in Part 2, than in analysis focused primarily on micro units. Look back at Chapters 11, 12, 15, and 16, and on to Chapter 34. The analysis of individual wage bargains in the present chapter should deepen your understanding of the general propositions there concerning aggregate investment, savings, employment, wage and price levels. A look in the next chapter at union attempts to increase labor's share in the national income will provide an opportunity to weave all these considerations together.

1. Suppose you want to maximize your lifetime income. What factors should you take into account in selecting your occupation and in timing your entry into it?

2. Make an outline of the major forces that determine wages or salaries in the occupation you plan to enter after leaving college.

3. "Labor is just another commodity, and wages are its price. All we need to understand wages is a basic understanding of supply and de-

FOR ANALYSIS AND DISCUSSION

mand." Do you agree with this quotation from an economics textbook? Explain.

4. One theory of wages holds that wages are merely the result of bargaining between workers and employers, and that the only important determinant of the outcome is the relative bargaining power of the two parties. Is this theory a good one? If not, what is the matter with it?

5. Malthus, a famous economist, argued in the early 1800's that population would tend to outrun the world's food supply, and that wages would tend to be forced back down toward a bare subsistence level.

  a. Does this seem to you an acceptable theory of wages?
  b. How, if at all, would you differentiate between its usefulness in explaining wages in America and in China?

6. To what extent are the "bargaining" and "subsistence" wages theories indicated above consistent with, or in conflict with, the supply and demand approach to the problem?

7. Unions often claim that employer monopsony is widespread, and that workers have a hard time in moving from job to job to escape exploitation. How valid do you believe this union argument is? What evidence do you have to support your belief?

8. Is inequality of economic opportunity a major factor in the present unequal distribution of personal incomes in the United States? If it is an important factor, what, if anything, do you believe should be done to reduce such inequality of opportunity?

9. Suppose you are a member of the United Auto Workers union. Would you favor a union policy opposing the introduction of automatic, labor-saving machinery, or one cooperating in the inauguration of such machinery? Explain your reasoning.

30

Labor Unionism and Collective Bargaining

Labor unions loom large on the current American scene. On the economic front, they exercise vast pressures on wages, hours, and working conditions. They are behind the worker in his differences with the foreman, the day-to-day arguments that seldom reach the public's eye. Politically, their voice is increasingly heard in the selection of candidates, and their votes are increasingly felt in elections—usually on the Democratic side. Their lobbyists are among the most effective in Washington and the state capitals, and it is a secure congressman indeed who can afford to disregard what organized labor thinks. Socially, the union has become part of the lives of millions of industrial workers. Here is an organization of which the worker is really a part. He has a unity of interest and background with his fellow members that he finds in few other associations.

Pervasive as unions are, it is also easy to overrate their importance. Look at the points above. Unions do indeed influence wages and hours, but they have had many failures along with their successes. Supply and demand still set a confining framework for labor-management negotiations.

561

Although the combined A.F.L.-C.I.O. organization loosely joins many unions, they are still separate unions, often disputing among themselves. Only about one-third of all workers are unionized. Throughout agriculture, the services, and clerical and professional workers, unions have little hold. Politically, the divisions within organized labor weaken the power it can exercise, and since World War II labor has gone down to defeat on some of its most bitterly fought issues—notably the passage of the Taft-Hartley Act, which placed important restraints on union powers, and the Landrum-Griffin Act of 1959.

To understand organized labor's position, we have to look at history. The role of labor unions has been a shifting one, and though since the 1930's unions have generally ridden high, they may again come on harder days. With the present vast powers of big unions, it may be hard for you to realize that only 30 years ago unions were hanging on by the skin of their teeth, with an active membership of only 3 million workers and little or no recognition in the great mass-production industries of the country. But it's not hard for many union members to remember.

HISTORY OF AMERICAN UNIONISM Labor historians argue about the first traces of labor unionism in America. Depending on which expert you read, you'll find that unions grew out of the old guilds and "companies of mechanics," or that unions really began in America with a new type of journeymen's association among the shoemakers of Philadelphia in 1792. There is no doubt that workers have been banding together informally for hundreds of years, but it's only since the New Deal that over one-fifth of non-agricultural workers have been union members.

In the boom of the 1830's, numerous small local unions and other worker groups sprang up. Some of them banded together in the first, loose, inter-city "National Trades Union." These groups helped agitate to cut the working day from 12 to 10 hours, and had a little influence over wages and individual working conditions. But the National Trades Union vanished with most of its locals in the business crash of 1837. Legally, unions were often considered criminal conspiracies. Public antagonism to them was great. Employers fought them by every means.

Through the mid-1800's, persistent attempts at union activities are reported. These movements achieved little success beyond local areas, and only a tiny fraction of the total labor force participated. Most unions were formed by workers in the hope of bettering their working conditions, hours, and wages. But much of the union agitation during these early days was as political as it was economic—indeed, this has been called the "hot air" period of unionism. Union leaders spoke up for free public education, free credit for homesteaders, and workers' cooperatives. Marxian socialism was sponsored by some would-be labor leaders as the workers' only hope against capitalism. In those brash, flamboyant times, socialist doctrines found listeners—but not many—in America.

After each setback, local craft unions grew up again. Gradually, a few reached national proportions. The most persistent groups were skilled workers, bound together by their trades and with enough standing to risk the perils of union membership. Their goals were direct and economic—shorter hours, more tolerable working conditions, sometimes higher wages. Theirs was no spirit of militant unionism; they made no nationwide sweep. They were small, struggling groups, fighting against great odds in little islands of worker cooperation against the dominant power of employers.

In the boom of the early 1870's, the first real national association in the union field appeared. This was the Knights of Labor, founded in 1869 as a secret society (to avoid employers' reprisals against members) to unite all kinds of workers and interested liberals for better working conditions, beneficial legislation, education, and other general benefits. Its leaders were mild people with a nonbelligerent, middle-class outlook. The national organization had little power over the local assemblies, and the organization was soon split apart over objectives and methods. The assemblies composed of skilled craft workers, the only unions with reasonably established positions, were mainly interested in pragmatic economic objectives at the local level. Assemblies of rural and middle-class members were more interested in the broader legislative, national goals; introduction of cooperatives was a major objective. They talked much, and did little.

When this difference, and the ravages of depression, led to the downfall of the Knights in the 1880's, the American Federation of Labor had arisen to collect the stronger, skilled-craft locals that deserted the Knights. But the real force of the labor movement was still in the individual crafts—independent, pragmatic, concerned with their own affairs, owing only tenuous allegiance to the federation.

Some early leaders of the American Federation of Labor were Marxian socialists by background. But the tone of the organization rapidly became one of practical, economic unionism, striving for higher wages, shorter hours, and better working conditions within the American capitalist system. Samuel Gompers, a remarkable figure in American labor history, was the dominating leader of the Federation from 1886 to 1924. His outspoken philosophy of "practical" unionism reflected the spirit of the American labor movement for a half-century—"Get more, more, more—now." Gompers was a man of action. And he reflected well the spirit of the times in organized labor. Only this pragmatic, typically American attitude began to win a little grudging acceptance for unionism from employers and the public at large. But the road of the unions was a rocky one. They were still small, distrusted, ridiculed, essentially local, and fought at every turn by employers. Their struggle was for survival first.

Union membership grew mainly in prosperity, with its biggest early burst in the World War I boom that culminated in 1920. Prosperity makes a strong demand for labor. Union leaders can show wage increases to prospective members. Employers are anxious to get workers, less bitter against pressures for higher pay. Whether the union gets more than supply and demand would have given is not always clear, but the worker sees higher wages coming out of union bargaining. Even at the peak membership of 1920, however, only about 5 million workers were unionized. Steel, autos, electrical equipment, textiles—none of the big mass-production industries recognized any union as the bargaining agent for more than a few special craft groups among its employees. Only specialists like the carpenters, electrical workers, teamsters, and painters were effectively unionized. Only railway workers, coal-miners, and workers in the ladies' garment industry approached unionization on an industry-wide basis without reference to craft.

Union Membership in the United States, 1900-1958

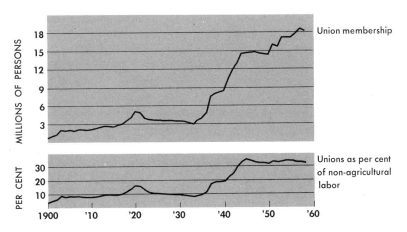

FIG. 30-1   The big growth period for unions was during the Roosevelt administrations of the 1930's and 1940's. Since then they have continued to grow, but only approximately as fast as the labor force. (Source: Florence Peterson, *American Labor Unions* [New York: Harper and Brothers, 1945], p. 56; and U.S. Department of Labor.)

The crash of 1920, together with two disastrous major strikes, swept away a quarter of the unions' members. And unions less than held their own through the prosperous decade of the 1920's. Times were good, and workers got along pretty well without help from the unions. Employers undermined unions whenever they had a chance, by open antagonism, violence, ridicule, and establishment of company unions with generous benefits to keep men out of regular unions. Labor-saving devices, which were being introduced rapidly, provided a steady pressure of temporary technological employment, weakening many of the long-established craft unions. Public opinion was in no mood for radical change, and the A.F.L. was nonaggressive, "respectable," and forced to hold on for its life, in a long period of industrial peace.

The New Deal and Modern Unionism. By 1933, the cataclysmic depression had cut union membership back to pre-World War I levels. Then came Franklin Roosevelt and the New Deal. Higher wages and higher prices were cornerstones of the New Deal's recovery policies. The National Industrial Recovery Act for the first time specifically guaranteed workers throughout the economy the right to organize and bargain collectively without interference from employers. Wage rates were raised and protected by industry "codes." Union organizers went to work, and membership picked up fast.

In 1935, there were two even bigger boosts for organized labor. First was the passage of the federal Wagner Act, which spelled out in detail workers' rights vis-à-vis employers, greatly increased labor's powers, forbade prevalent employer anti-union practices, and put teeth in the unions' powers to bargain collectively. Unions were guaranteed recognition if they won a majority vote among the workers; and elections are far easier to win than strikes, which had previously been required to gain recognition.[1] Second, 1935 was the year of the big split in the ranks of organized labor that set up the Congress of Industrial Organization (C.I.O.) and precipitated industrial unionization in the mass-production industries.

The history of the middle 1930's is stormy and violent. The newly formed C.I.O., with the fiery John L. Lewis as its first president, split off from the A.F.L., with jealousies rampant and tempers at white heat. The first big organizing drives of the C.I.O. were violent, spectacular, and successful. Open defiance of management, rather than indirection and subservience, was the tone of the drives. The famous sit-down strikes, when the unions seized possession of the major auto plants, rocked the companies and the public. But in the bloodshed and bitterness that ensued, the unions won recognition time after time—with the open support of the Roosevelt administration and local Democratic government officials. The Who's Who of American industry fell to C.I.O. organizing drives one after one during the late 1930's—U.S. Steel, Bethlehem Steel, General Motors, Chrysler, General Electric, Westinghouse, Goodrich, Goodyear, and so on down the list. By 1940, union membership had more than doubled, to about 10 million. By 1945, it was nearly 15 million, over 35 per cent of the non-agricultural labor force.

Public sympathy during the 1930's was by and large pro-labor, though many friends were lost by the violent sit-down strikes. But strong union wage demands during World War II, widespread inter-union jurisdictional quarrels and strikes, and open defiance of the federal government by a few leaders, convinced the bulk of the public that organized labor's power had gone too far. In 1947, Congress passed the Taft-Hartley Act, restricting the powers of unions and restoring some powers that employers had lost during the preceding decade. The years since World War II have seen a definite leveling off of union power. Although membership has continued to grow gradually, this growth has barely kept pace with

---

[1] For details of the Wagner Act, see Chapter 31.

the growth in the labor force. The percentage of non-agricultural labor unionized slipped after 1945, and by 1960 was still below the 36 per cent peak of 1945. About half of all union members were in manufacturing.

In 1955, the "merger" of the A.F.L. and the C.I.O. into one loose organization (the A.F.L.-C.I.O.) marked a major step toward a united labor movement. George Meany, head of the A.F.L., was chosen to lead the new organization, and an elaborate organizational structure was agreed on to provide both unity and continued independence of action for individual unions of different types. Only a few big independents, notably the United Mineworkers and the Railway Brotherhoods, remained outside the merger—though the huge International Teamsters Union was later expelled from the A.F.L.-C.I.O.

Four generalizations may point up the main lines of union development in America:

1. The trend of union membership and power has been strongly upward over the last century, reflecting a fundamental shift in the power roles of different groups in our society and a steady extension of unionism into new fields. But by mid-century, unionism had conquered most of the areas easy to organize, and there was much evidence that growth would be slower and harder in the future.

2. The growth in union membership and power has been sporadic, depending especially on prosperous business conditions and favorable political support for its spurts.

3. There has been a steady evolution of the internal structure of unionism, reflecting adaptation to industrial developments and to the temper of the times.

4. Unionism has recently moved increasingly toward active participation in political affairs, both in pushing pro-labor legislation and in supporting candidates and parties beyond issues immediately affecting organized labor.

UNION WAGE POLICY From one point of view, a union is merely a monopoly that sells the labor services of its members. Neglecting for the moment all the other things that unions do, how effective is a union monopoly in raising wages under different circumstances? And how does the public come out in the bargain?

The analytical models of the last chapter give us some simple frameworks for examining the problem. In each, let us first assume that the union is a completely effective organization in controlling its workers. It speaks for them all, and it need not worry about defections from the ranks. Assume also for the moment that total spending in the economy is constant, unaffected in the aggregate by the behavior of individual unions and employers.

Competition. First, consider the case where employers are highly competitive with each other in selling products and in hiring workers. Here, in the long run, all economic profits will tend to be eliminated. Price will be forced down to about the minimum average cost at which each product can be produced. From the labor side, wages will be roughly equal to the marginal revenue productivity of each class of labor hired.

Suppose now that a union raises wages. This raises costs, and forces up prices. At the higher prices, consumers will buy less (with total income and spending assumed constant). With less output there are fewer jobs. This is the classic case in which union wage demands lead to fewer jobs for union members. In a highly competitive industry, there isn't much unions can do to push up wages without causing unemployment in the long run, unless total spending can be increased. The workers who keep their jobs have higher incomes, but is the membership as a whole better off? (The fallacy of composition again?)

Monopoly and Quasi-Monopoly.   Second is the case where there is monopoly or monopolistic competition in selling products, but still active competition among firms for workers. Here again, if the firms are maximizing profits they will be hiring workers up to the point where the wage equals the workers' marginal revenue product. If a union raises the wage, it will, logically, pay employers to cut back on the number of workers hired and to raise price; the new maximum-profit output will be smaller than before and the price higher. Again, logically, the union can obtain higher wages only at the cost of unemployment.

But this case is different from pure competition. Under monopoly and quasi-monopoly, it is less certain that market pressures will drive firms to anything like precise profit maximization. Businessmen operate in a narrow or wide band of uncertainty about just what wages they can afford to pay and what prices they should charge. The pressures on each firm to produce at maximum efficiency are weaker. The response to union wage demands may be greater efficiency; more output rather than higher prices and unemployment may be the result of union pressures. Given this cushion of uncertainty and "play" in over-all efficiency, many other factors may influence the wage bargain—how anxious the business is to avoid a strike, how both the business and the union size up business prospects ahead, what union-management relations have been like in the past.

This range of uncertainty widens out further in oligopolistic industries where price stabilization prevails. Since price is set by the leader or the group on the basis of many tenuous variables, it is hard to tell when a wage increase will lead to a change in product price—and if it does, how much. If the business has a protected profit position, this special profit provides a melon over which the union and management can bargain. In oligopolies where firms behave as if they faced kinked demand curves, the union may have a considerable range over which it can force up the wage rate without inducing higher prices and reduced output (employment), as was indicated on page 552. But such cases may be uncommon. Wherever the union makes substantially the same bargain for all major firms in the industry, it will be obvious to all that costs have risen roughly apace and all firms are likely to expect to follow a price increase by the price leader. Where this is true, the union faces much the same likely result on employment and prices as with a single monopoly firm.

Monopsony and Bilateral Oligopoly. If union members are being "exploited" through a wage less than their marginal revenue productivity, the union can push the wage up without decreasing employment, assuming the entrepreneur is motivated solely by maximizing profits.[2] But here we get into a pure power struggle between employer and union. The employer is making a special profit by exploiting the workers, and theoretically the union can grab this sum back for the workers. But the employer isn't going to be enthusiastic about turning over the sum through higher wages. If he's been able to bargain the wage down in the past, chances are he'll fight to keep it down. Where this struggle comes out is indeterminate so far as economic theory is concerned. To guess who will win, look at the relative bargaining power of employer and union. How big is the union strike fund? How adept are both parties around the bargaining table? How badly does the employer want to get his customers' orders out on time?

Unions, the Wage Level, and Aggregate Employment. Underlying the preceding paragraphs has been an implicit assumption that we're talking about one union and one industry at a time. To the individual employer, higher wages are higher costs. The added purchasing power they give is of little significance to his sales. But when we look at the whole economy, higher wages are both higher costs and higher incomes (purchasing power), and we need to look at both sides. Suppose unions generally and persistently demand higher wages as their contracts come up for negotiation through the year. What then?

This problem was examined at length in Part 2. Some summary notes will suffice here.

1. Much depends on the size of the wage increases relative to increases in productivity. If productivity increases 3 per cent and wages by the same per cent, firms can grant the increase and also increase profits by 3 per cent without raising prices. But if the wage increase substantially exceeds the productivity gain, either prices must be raised or profits squeezed. Business pricing policies play a critical role; cost-plus, or "markup," pricing appears to be common in American industry today.[3]

---

[2] In fact, the union theoretically can *increase* employment by eliminating exploitation. Without the union, the employer bargains wages down and gets as many workers as possible at his low wage. With a union, he must pay the going wage and he can get as many workers as he wants at that wage. He thus hires workers up to the point where the wage equals their marginal revenue productivity; there is no longer any incentive to restrict output and employment to get the advantage of low wages.

[3] Remember that the wage-setting industries (steel, autos, electrical equipment) all seem to have relatively high productivity increases. Even if their wage increase only matches, say, a 5 per cent productivity increase, this sets an inflationary pattern for other industries with lower productivity gains.

2. Much depends on the state of aggregate consumer demand. If demand is strong, a substantial wage increase can be passed on through higher prices (or even used as an excuse for a still larger price boost) with little or no loss in sales. This implies a sufficient mixture of high propensity to consume, high business investment, and expansionary fiscal policy to support the higher national income necessary to maintain aggregate employment at the new higher wages and prices. In MV terms, it implies either an increase in the money supply, or elasticity in V through reduction of desired cash balances, increased extension of credit by non-bank financial intermediaries, or some other device.

3. If consumer demand is basically weak, for the converse of the reasons in 2, higher wages passed on through higher prices will reduce sales. This in turn will cut employment and profits. Business firms seldom lay off workers just because wages are increased, but reduced sales bring prompt layoffs. Here again, the propensity to consume, business investment, government fiscal policy, and the behavior of the money supply and V are of obvious importance in determining whether higher wages will mean merely inflation or unemployment.

4. How much can profits be squeezed between rising wages and stable prices without so reducing investment as to produce unemployment? Nobody knows, but the evidence suggests probably not very much. Good times have usually seen wages and profits growing at something like the same rate, once reasonably full employment has arrived. Falling profits have generally meant reduced investment spending, and full employment has seldom long survived large investment cutbacks. On the other hand, a substantial decrease in the wage and salary share under full employment is apt to slow consumer buying and bring unemployment that way. Clearly, no precise relative shares of profits and wages provide the panacea for economic instability, but wide sweeps in either direction bode serious danger.

Do Unions Really Raise Wages?   This may sound like a silly question. Everyone has read of many cases where union demands for higher wages have finally been granted by employers. But this doesn't really answer the question. Maybe supply and demand would have produced the same raises in the market without any union. Don't forget the fallacy of "post hoc, propter hoc."

Although any union man and most employers will tell you that of course unions raise wages, the dispassionate objective evidence is not clear. Careful studies have shown that wages have often risen slightly faster in strongly unionized than in non-union industries. Union wages are by and large higher than non-union. This isn't too convincing, however, because the unionized industries have been the high-wage industries anyhow, even before they were unionized— big companies with lots of skilled workmen. Over-all, labor's share in the national income since the 1920's, before the big modern union increase, hasn't changed enough to provide clear evidence that unions have raised the aggregate wage share. *Prima facie,* it seems likely that unions do raise at least *money* wages; the whole "wage-push" analysis of inflation rests on this foundation. But even here, it's clear that the demand side plays an important role too. The evidence for union wage-push is strong in some periods—for example, 1955-58; but not very convincing in many others. In particular instances, the impact of unions on wages is clear—for example, in cases of substantial employer monopsony.

Unfortunately, there is no sure way of measuring the unions' total effect on wages. But two notes of warning: (1) Don't be too impressed by the talk at the bargaining table and the wage increases that the newspapers play up afterward. A lot of these wage increases would have arrived, union or no union, especially in prosperous boom periods. (2) But don't swallow too readily the other argument either. Many businessmen will tell you that workers would really be better off without unions, that they'd be perfectly willing to pay workers every penny they're worth without unions. Maybe so—maybe not.

The Guaranteed Annual Wage.   Laborers have long wished for income security comparable to that of the salaried executive whose income goes on whether the plant is running at full capacity or not. During the 1950's widespread union pressures built up for a guaranteed annual wage (G.A.W.) as part of the regular labor-management wage bargain. In 1955, the G.A.W., in a modified form, was made part of the new auto workers' contract with Ford, then with the other major auto producers, then in steel and a few other industries. In this form, it provided that workers with a certain amount of company experience were entitled to "supplementary unemployment benefits" (S.U.B.) from the company beyond the unemployment benefits provided by the government social-security program, usually for a half-year to a year.

S.U.B. payments in the recession of 1957-58 helped substantially to ease the plight of unemployed workers, and to shorten the downswing of the recession. But the benefits were concentrated primarily on the recently hired, the young, who were laid off first. For many workers with long seniority they added little. Union contracts have long provided for discharges of recent employees first, so high-seniority workers in many firms have in effect guaranteed annual employment short of major catastrophes. Many such workers showed little enthusiasm for the G.A.W., since employer acceptance of this responsibility might well lessen the direct money wage increase the union could get in the same negotiation. The split in interest among union members along these lines should not be minimized, especially in industries with many high-seniority employees and stable employment records. Although guaranteed-annual-wage plans of some sort will undoubtedly grow, this growth may be uneven and take quite different forms in different industries.

One union argument for the G.A.W. deserves special attention. The unions generally argue that any employer operating under a guaranteed-annual-wage contract will have a major incentive to stabilize his production and employment, which, the unions argue, he ought to do anyhow but often doesn't worry about. Better planning could at least minimize the impact of seasonal and model-year fluctuations on workers' incomes. With G.A.W. it costs the employer money whenever he has to lay off workers, paying them from the fund when they don't work.

The argument sounds attractive—until you put yourself in the employer's shoes. He says that he has little control over what consumers buy and when they buy it. When demand slumps in a depression, he'd like to keep up employment, but who's going to buy the stuff? How is he to keep from partial layoffs when he must close down for model change-overs? He doesn't need G.A.W. to make him want to even out big fluctuations in his rate of operation, because he operates more efficiently at a stable rate anyhow. All G.A.W. does, in effect, is (1) raise the effective wage cost, which must ultimately mean higher prices to the consumer; and (2) make employers very reluctant to take on extra workers when they would otherwise do so, since once a worker is employed for a stated period he must be guaranteed an annual wage under many such union-proposed plans.

Which one is right? Nobody knows yet. There may be a strong element of truth on both sides, depending on the individual employer and industry.

Union and Management Motivation in Wage Bargaining.

You don't need a course in economics to tell you the main reason unions fight for higher wages. The members want more pay! But some other things aren't so easy to explain, and you hear a lot of talk about union leaders who are really out to feather their own nests rather than to help the union members.

The thing that seems to amaze people most is that unions will strike for an extra couple of cents an hour pay, when third-grade arithmetic will show that it would take months or even years at the extra rate to make up for the pay lost in a long strike. Why are the union leaders willing to keep the men out, at an apparent direct dollars-and-cents loss? The same question can be asked the other way around, too. The company's loss during the strike may cost more than years of paying the extra couple of cents to the workers. Why doesn't the company give in, and save everybody money?

Try putting yourself in the worker's shoes. What would you think? You'd think: "That so-and-so who runs the company! He gets a big salary and has everything. His plushy stockholders are getting big dividends. Yet we have to scrape along on pay that just keeps the wolf away from the door. He won't even give us a couple of cents extra when he could save himself profits by doing it instead of trying to break this strike. We'll fight it out and lick him yet!"

Now turn around and see how you'd feel as the employer. Then it all looks just the other way. You see the generous wages your company is already paying. You see the workers stubbornly holding out for unreasonable demands, even when the strike is obviously costing them more than they can hope to get out of it. You may see the union leaders as self-seeking hypocrites, out to protect their own jobs. The whole business is just one more step in the union's attempt to dictate to management and to encroach wherever possible on management prerogatives. Would you give in if you were the employer?

Now put yourself in the union president's shoes. You're probably sincerely out to do the best you can for your membership. You know that your best bet in the long run lies in getting along with management, and getting peacefully the gains you're after. But you also know that there's never enough money to go around, and that you're going to have to push hard to get the wages and other benefits the workers are (in your eyes) honestly entitled to. You know a strike is costly to everybody, but you know too that a threat often repeated but never carried out loses its force. And you don't quite trust the employer and his personnel men, even though by and large they're pretty decent people. You suspect that down underneath that surface friendliness they'd be delighted to see the unions go, and to return to the old pre-union days when the employer told the workers to do what he said—or else! All these feelings are probably shared to a considerable extent by your membership.

You know some more things too. You know that unless you produce for your members, you're likely to be just an ex-president. Especially if other unions have been getting 15 cents an hour plus fringe benefits, you've got to get at least that much from management, or you're going to have some disgruntled members. You know that your chance of rising in the union ranks, say to a position in the international, depends in part on your success in getting more than other unions do. You know that too much peace with the employer, even though it pays off handsomely in dollars and cents for the membership, is going to be interpreted by some members as "selling out." As you sit across the bargaining table with management, with tempers frayed by a long strike, would you give in on the extra two cents?

The issues at stake in a wage negotiation are seldom wages alone. Human motives are strong and complex, and many different interests usually come into play. The quarrel that the public sees in the newspapers is often only part of the real issue. Many of the fine speeches made by both sides—about the need for wage increases to prevent depression, or the impossibility of maintaining a progressive free-enterprise system without large capital expenditures out of earnings —sound good on the news broadcasts but have little to do with the settlement of the dispute on the bargaining table. To look at the issue in terms of a simple dollars-and-cents comparison is naive. There are few more complex jobs of compromise and good human relations than labor-management wage negotiations. The issues are real, and no purpose is served by pretending that nothing but common interest is involved. Unfortunately, there is seldom a simple right or wrong answer.

Union Policy on Hours and Fringe Benefits. A century ago, a 10- to 12-hour work day with a six- or seven-day work week was still common. Union men are fond of pointing to the vastly greater output per man in the present five-day, 40-hour week, both because they helped get it and because they are continually pushing for a still shorter work-week at the same pay.

If a man can turn out the same amount or more by working fewer hours, every-one is clearly better off for him to do it; and there's no reason why his weekly pay should be cut. As the unions point out, this is what happened as the work-week was cut from 84 to 72 to 60 and then to 48 hours. Every time, management protested that the result would be a big drop in output. But in fact weekly output per worker steadily rose as hours were cut, because fatigue and overwork at the longer hours had drastically reduced worker efficiency throughout the week. Hourly productivity rose with more rest and recreation, even making allowance for the increases created by technological improvements and more capital equipment. There's no doubt that the unions did a big service, both to labor and to society as a whole, by pushing hard on this front.

When the work-week dropped below about 48 hours, the gain in total productivity began to be less obvious, and there is little evidence now that weekly hours can be cut further without a loss in total weekly output per man in most industries. *If* this is so, union demands for shorter hours at the same weekly pay are in effect demands for higher pay. But many unions argue that further cuts will still increase productivity (all on the assumption of unchanged technology).

Whether union demand for shorter hours at the same pay are justifiable when hourly output is not increased thereby depends on pretty much the same considerations as apply to straight-out pay increases. Some observers believe that society should place a special premium on more leisure for the better life, rather than on more material goods. On this issue you can be your own judge. But if shorter hours mean less output, somebody is going to have to pay the cost.

Increasingly, unions have coupled their wage demands with pressures for "fringe benefits"—paid vacations, pensions and other retirement benefits, health insurance, and a dozen other such benefits. All these cost the company money. They all have to come out of somebody's pocketbook. In this sense, they all represent, in effect, wage increases, though the worker takes his pay in special forms rather than directly. Two issues are at stake here. First, should the workers get more pay, and what will be the impact of the higher wage rates in any given situation? Second, should the higher pay be tied to these special considerations? For example, should workers be allowed (or forced) to take part of their pay in health and old-age benefits? A lot of people think so, but make up your own mind. One rough estimate is that fringe benefits now account for over 15 per cent of the national wage bill; this would be around $25 to $30 billion annually. In manufacturing industries, fringe benefits in 1959 exceeded 50 cents per hour on an average hourly wage of about $2.25.

COLLECTIVE BARGAINING AND LABOR-MANAGEMENT RELATIONS

The big wage negotiations and strikes always make the headlines and news broadcasts. But the great bulk of union-management collective bargaining and negotiation goes on unheralded behind the scenes. After a union contract is signed, the day-to-day relations of the foreman and his workers take over. Wage rates have to be set for individual jobs; broad contract wage provisions must be translated into elaborate wage structures in large firms. Decisions must be made as to which jobs are on a flat hourly pay basis and which "on incentive" where the pay depends on the number of units turned out. In the latter case, standard base rates must be established for "normal" output, above which bonuses are paid. Times and rates need to be established for new work. Arrangements have to be agreed on for handling the introduction of new machinery and new methods. Wrangles between foremen and individual workers have to be adjudicated. A thousand and one problems arise in a big plant that involve disputes between labor and management.

In these disputes, the union steward is the worker's first line of protection and negotiation, just as the foreman is management's. Good feeling and cooperation between foremen and stewards can do more for effective union-management relations than almost any amount of fine top-level policy-making. Bad relations between stewards and foremen can block any good intentions at top levels. Down in the plant is where the work gets done and where most of the disputes arise, except for the major wage and hour negotiations at contract-expiration dates.

Some union-management agreements provide elaborate machinery for handling worker-management disputes that can't be settled by the foreman and the worker. These often culminate in calling on an impartial arbitrator, paid jointly by union and management, whose decision is final on disputed issues under the contract. Other contracts set up other procedures. There is no point in trying to describe the vast variety of them. The main point is that an attempt is made to set up a body of rules under which workers and management try to minimize friction and disagreement. The contract is something like the rules of law under which we operate our democratic system. This whole procedure has gone far toward creating stability and order in employee-management relations in thousands of industrial plants. But in industrial as in political democracy, the rules themselves won't make the system work. They only provide a framework within which men of reasonable goodwill, with a reasonable agreement on common objectives, can live and work peaceably together. In American labor-management relations, the uneasy jockeying for position and power goes on, on the surface and beneath.

Closed, Union, and Open Shops. If the union is to do an effective job in looking out for the interests of its members, it must be recognized and firmly established as their representative vis-à-vis management. Union security—a firmly established role for the union as such—is thus the first requirement for effective unionism. Every union leader recognizes this, and most management does too. Consequently, some of the most bitter labor-management battles are over the union-security issue.

Nowadays, recognition of the union as bargaining agent for the workers is guaranteed by federal legislation once the union wins a bona-fide election as bargaining agent. But this does not necessarily guarantee a secure status for the union and its leaders. In many cases, workers are not required to join the union and pay dues to it, and without a strong treasury the union's position is weak indeed. Union members may withdraw. And the union may or may not be able to exercise control over what workers the management hires when vacancies arise.

Management, especially when it is anxious to keep the union's position weak, tries to insist on an "open shop." An open shop is an arrangement whereby management can hire union or non-union workers alike, and where there is no obligation for workers to join the union. The union, on the other hand, often wants a "closed shop," which provides that only union members can be hired, and that every worker must belong to the union. In between are a variety of arrangements. One of the commonest is the "union shop," which permits the employer to hire non-union workers but provides that they must join the union after they are hired.

Some of the nation's bitterest struggles have been over the union or closed shop issue. Union men argue that the union or closed shop is an essential part of industrial democracy. Every man in the plant gets the benefits from union representation—higher wages, better working conditions, health and retirement benefits. He surely should belong to the union and pay dues along with the others. Freedom to stay out of the union is like giving citizens freedom to decide for themselves whether or not to pay taxes when they benefit together with everyone else from government services. A second argument for the union or closed shop may be even more fundamental. Unless the union is secure, it will always feel pressed to strengthen its position against the employer, against rival unions, and against possible deviations among the workers. Its leaders can hardly guarantee to enforce the union's side of the contract provisions. They will have to spend their time developing union morale, building up membership, and making the union secure, rather than working constructively with management on bona-fide grievances, production changes, and other matters that should be the main concern of labor-management representatives. With a union or closed shop, union leaders can concentrate on working securely with management to the common advantage of union members and the company.

But many people see the matter through different glasses. Forcing a man to join a union runs against all the principles of our free society, they argue, and they will have no part of it. Moreover, both the closed and union shops give a vast and improper power to union officials—the power to fire and (in the closed shop) to hire. Eviction of a man from the union in either case means that the company must fire him.[4] With the closed shop, he cannot even be hired without first being

---

[4] Though under Taft-Hartley expulsion from the union cannot force the employer to fire a man as long as the individual offers to pay his dues to the union.

blessed by the union leaders. Workers in union-shop or closed-shop industries have no protection against arbitrary discriminatory practices by union leaders, argue many employers. The union's power may be used by its leaders to weed out political opponents within the union, to discriminate against special groups, or for a variety of other improper purposes. In a free society no man should be forced to join an organization as a condition of getting a job, they say.

The closed shop has comparatively little support nowadays, outside some of the traditionally closed craft unions which have long followed exclusive membership policies; and it is illegal under Taft-Hartley. The union shop is a different matter. It is widely used, and it poses some tough problems of equity and operating practice, in trying to be fair to both sides.

In recent years this controversy has boiled up over state "right-to-work" laws. In many states, legislation has been proposed providing that no worker shall have to belong to a union to hold his job. Unions have fought these bills tooth and nail, but by the late 1950's over a third of the states had such laws, and bills were pending in a number of others. There is obviously a good deal to the arguments on both sides. Purely economic analysis can't help you much here. Balance the arguments out for yourself.

Seniority. Behind much of the unions' insistence on a union shop is the desire for security for their members—protection against being undermined by non-union workers. Closely related is union emphasis on seniority rights. Most union contracts now contain elaborate provisions guaranteeing preference to the workers with the longest service, especially preference on job security in the event of layoffs. Unions see seniority provisions as a major protection against employer favoritism and arbitrary discrimination. Some contracts cover the entire firm, guaranteeing that any high-seniority worker whose job vanishes can "bump" a lower-seniority worker in his general skill and aptitude group, even though the newer worker may be in a quite unrelated part of the company. Other plans limit the "bumping" area to particular divisions or departments of the company. Unions often also push for seniority preference when promotions are up. They argue that the man with the longest service generally deserves the better job. In some cases, they fear that if there is no such seniority provision employers will use promotion decisions as a club against workers who are active union men. Seniority provisions make life more secure for senior workers, but they keep the new worker on the uncertain edge, no matter how well he may do his job and how strong consumer demand may be in his particular part of the company's activities.

Most employers aren't very enthusiastic about elaborate union seniority provisions. They argue that how well a man does his job ought to be the main criterion of whether he keeps his job and when he is promoted. Moreover, they claim that seniority protection can lead to costly waste and disruption. Suppose a seniority plan calls for bumping the next-lower worker, and a steamfitter's job is eliminated because of technological advance. Joe Doaks, the displaced man, has 15 years service, so he bumps another steamfitter, no matter how much the latter's boss would like to keep him. But worse, if there isn't another steamfitter's job open, the senior man may bump a man in the next-lower job category. That man probably has seniority in his job category, so he bumps the next-lower man. If this goes through three or four men, each doing a different job that requires special training, it's easy to see why management is unhappy and tries to limit the area to which bumping extends.

How are today's elaborate seniority provisions to be evaluated? From a narrow economic viewpoint, they are probably wasteful; costs would probably be lower if employers had freedom of choice as to whether a high-seniority man is dropped or transferred when his job vanishes, and freedom of choice as to whom to promote at what pay. But seniority involves other values. Is it right that a man with 30 years' service to a company should be put out on the street, while newcomers keep jobs that he could do? And how about the tension and unhappiness generated by continual uncertainty about job security; can a company really gain from creating this atmosphere among its workers? Whatever the effect on company costs, is that the kind of industrial society we want? Some people say yes, but the steady spread of seniority preferences shows the force of the contrary view.

UNIONISM ON THE MODERN AMERICAN SCENE

Union Power and Union Politics. Unions loom large on the current American scene. Administrative decisions and settlement of differences by negotiation have taken over much of the traditional role of the market place as the governor of economic activity. The greatly increased power of organized labor means that labor-management disputes are now more a test of strength between equals—sometimes equals of prodigious strength. When Walter Reuther sits down to bargain for the United Auto Workers, he speaks for nearly a million men. Dave MacDonald across the table from the steel companies speaks for almost as many. Not millions, but billions, of dollars are at stake in these bargains; not only wages, but the pensions of tomorrow's retired families, workers' sickness insurance, their working hours, the vacations they take. In every election, the support of organized labor is eagerly sought. Labor lobbies in Washington and the state capitals are powerful and well organized.

Vast power is wielded by labor unions. And this vast power is exercised largely by a few men, as in the case of big business. Do union leaders really speak for the best interests of their members? How closely are they responsible to the workers whom they represent? Can they be trusted with the power they hold?

Now that American unionism has come of age, many careful observers believe that the issues of union power and union democracy are the biggest problems of today's unionism.[5] This concern is heightened by the shocking performances of such union leaders as Dave Beck and Jimmy Hoffa of the Teamsters, and Joe Ryan and Albert Anastasia of the Longshoremen. Shake-downs, personal theft of union funds, arson, beatings, even murder, appear to have been used in the gangster tactics of some union leaders, at national and local levels. Yet Dave Beck, now a convicted criminal for perjury and misuse of union funds, until recently could shut down a business, a major city, or even the entire economy, by calling out the 1,400,000 teamsters on strike. Jimmy Hoffa, his heir whom many consider equally unsavory, holds that power today, defying both the A.F.L.-C.I.O. which expelled the Teamsters because they would not reform, and the U.S. Congress and the federal courts. Local teamster officials have repeatedly been reported to Senate and House investigating committees to have used gangster tactics— beatings, arson, theft—to extort payoffs and protection money from businessmen for their personal gain. The record of the Longshoremen is no better. Responsible labor leaders are shocked by this behavior. Yet neither they, through the A.F.L.-C.I.O., nor law-enforcement authorities seem to be able to check such practices. Only in 1959 did Congress pass legislation (the Landrum-Griffin Bill) specifically aimed at eliminating such irresponsible, self-seeking behavior. And it remains to be seen how effective this legislation will be.

The great bulk of the labor movement is law-abiding. Yet even there, how closely checked is the power of labor leaders? In many unions (e.g., the United Auto Workers), careful constitutional safeguards protect the rights of the rank and file to choose their own leaders. Still, as in other democratic organizations, the rank and file often exercise only a very loose and indirect control over the individual actions of their leaders. Labor leaders can build up machines to maintain themselves in power, just as politicians do. In almost every union, the membership can throw out its leaders if it becomes thoroughly aroused. But this is not often or easy. In the meantime, concern over the arbitrary use of power by labor leaders has mounted in many quarters. Business power and labor power pose parallel problems.

Even though labor leaders be entirely responsible to their members, the potential recurrent struggle between labor and management giants must be a cause of concern to any thinking observer. One result is the weakened position of the consumer and the citizen who is not a member of one of these groups. Struggles between big business and big labor are likely to end in a compromise that raises both wages and prices, at the expense of the defenseless consumer. The second result, when labor and management cannot settle their differences amicably or when wage-price inflation swells, is increasing pressure for the government to step in. The halls of Congress and the hearing rooms of federal administrative agencies become the focus of major labor-management pressures and differences. In the

---

[5] See Clark Kerr, *Unions and Union Leaders of Their Own Choosing* (N.Y.: Fund for the Republic, 1958).

eyes of many observers, this is the most fundamental change of all—and in the eyes of many, potentially the most disastrous. We will return to it in the next chapter.

The Union and Its Members. But to the union man in the mill, none of these is the most important thing about unions. E. Wight Bakke, a sympathetic observer of the American labor movement, has summarized his years of experience by listing five main things that workers look for in their unions—the things that explain why they join unions, why they pay their dues, and why they go on the picket line against the corporation that employs them.[6]

1. The union gives the working man a chance to be part of the group, to gain the respect of his fellow workers, to "be somebody" in an industrial world where the boss has long been God and the worker a mere cog in an impersonal industrial plant. Everyone seeks the society and respect of his fellows, consciously or subconsciously. The union man is part of an organization that can stand up and talk back to the boss—not just to the foreman, but to the head office in New York or Pittsburgh. He may even serve as a representative of the union—within industry as member of a grievance committee or before community groups. The desire to belong to the group, to be accepted, to be important, is one of the most fundamental in most men's lives.

2. The union promises progress toward economic security—not the security of the $50,000 a year vice president, but a steady job and reasonable wages, enough to pay the bills and have a little left over for old age and a rainy day. Workers beef about the private airplanes and big incomes of their company presidents, but the evidence is strong that it's the status of the fellow just a rung or two up the ladder that matters most. Their idea of economic comforts and economic security may be based on what the foreman has, but the general manager is in another economic world.

3. The union promises the working man an increased measure of independence and control over his own affairs. As an individual the worker is powerless before the vast economic, political and social forces of modern society. The union gives him a channel to get at the employer, the huge impersonal corporation. As a union member he becomes increasingly aware that "something can be done" about depressions and inflation, about working conditions and hours, about the way congressmen vote and presidents behave. Actually, membership in a big union may leave him as an individual little more direct control over his working and non-working life than before the union. But the "feel" is often as important as the "fact," and if he has to be controlled he'd rather it would be by the union which is made up of "his people" and over which he has at least some control.

---

[6] "Why Workers Join Unions," in *Unions, Management, and the Public* (New York: Harcourt, Brace, 1948), pp. 41-49.

4. Workers want to understand the forces and factors which control their lives. Nearly everyone is uneasy when he is subject to forces he doesn't understand. The corporation, the private enterprise system, balance sheets and profit and loss statements—the working man knows that all these are somehow important, but he understands little of what they mean or how they work. The union he can trust to explain what is going on; management he doesn't quite trust. American unions have gone only a little way in developing and explaining a folklore of the economic system for workers. Unions abroad have gone further.

5. Lastly, every man looks for self-respect. He needs to be satisfied with what he is doing, to be "doing right" by his own standards. Equally, he needs to feel that other people "treat him right." Justice is hard to define, but no man who feels he is being treated unjustly is a happy, satisfied person. "They ought to treat you like a human being, you know." . . . "I'm as good as they are, any day." The worker's standards for self-respect and justice may be very different from yours, but they are important to him. For many, the union may help achieve this self-respect.

To describe unions as merely a mechanism through which workers can bargain collectively for higher wages and shorter hours is to miss much of the flavor of unionism in the American scene. Individual dignity and the feeling of belonging may be even more important to millions of workers than higher wages and better working conditions. Unionism today is a far-reaching social and psychological institution, as well as a powerful economic and political mechanism. Over the past quarter-century the rise in the status and security of the American working man has been greater than is easy to understand without having personally lived through the pre-New Deal days and the New Deal struggles of the 1930's. Much of this improvement has been due to unions. But much has also been due to the changing sympathies of the American public, and to management's own initiative in doing a better, more broadly conceived job than was true in most firms a generation ago.

Unionism versus no unions is no longer the central issue in America. Workers who want unions have them. The issue today is how well unions, as democratic organizations, can serve their members, and how the growing power of great labor organizations and their leaders can be channeled effectively toward the public welfare.

FOR ANALYSIS AND DISCUSSION

1. Some union leaders argue that the union should participate in production and price decisions of the company, since these decisions have direct consequences for the amount of work and pay received by employees. Do you agree? Defend your answer against the opposing view.

2. Most union contracts have a seniority clause, which gives preference to those with greatest seniority when layoffs occur. Do you think seniority should be the guiding rule when some employees are laid off,

even if management believes that some of the newer men are more competent and harder workers?

3. Unions have made little headway among some groups—engineers, accountants, farm workers, household servants, and college teachers. Can you suggest the reasons why? Do these help you predict union influence in other areas?

4. Should production employees have the same sort of annual wage arrangements as middle management? If not, why not?

5. "Unions are justified where employers are otherwise able to exploit their employees, but nowhere else." Do you agree or disagree? Why?

6. Suppose you are a worker in a factory. Union representatives and union members put pressure on you to join the union, though so far you have not done so.

    a. Would you, as a worker, join the union?

    b. Whatever your answer to a., do you feel that your individual freedom is being violated by the strong pressures exerted on you to join the union?

7. Would it be better to give workers the extra money involved rather than all the modern fringe benefits commonly included in union contracts, so that each member could individually decide how he prefers to spend the money?

8. If lawyers are required to take a "bar examination" before they can begin practice, is it equally reasonable for unions to set up minimum qualifications for prospective workers before they can become union members and hence eligible for jobs? If not, why not?

Government
and Labor

Economically, the continuous jockeying between labor and management centers around wages and profits—the distribution of the national income. But this is only part of what is at stake. The struggle is for power, status, and security too. Should the government encourage or discourage labor unions? Should it back up strikes, or give employers the power to obtain injunctions against strikes? How much will a minimum-wage law help the working man? How about the Taft-Hartley Act?

What does economic analysis have to contribute on questions like these? The answer is, a good deal. It can clarify the economic issues and suggest the results of alternative policies. But it can't tell you which policy you ought to like best. That's for you to decide.

THE CHANGING POSITION OF LABOR

Public and legal attitudes toward unionism through the early and middle 1800's were violently antagonistic. Until around 1850, membership in a labor union for the purpose of trying to obtain higher wages was often considered a criminal conspiracy by the courts. It was decades later before workers could be sure the law would tolerate union membership. The individualistic spirit of the times pointed to the conclusion that it was up to laborers and employers to deal with each other as individuals. The cards stacked on the employer's side were just one of the facts of economic life.

Public opinion is a tenuous, intangible thing. Over the last half of the 1800's, intolerance of the basic idea of unions gradually gave way to grudging tolerance. Certainly this was not true of most employers, who fought unionism with violence, bloodshed, economic pressure, and the law. But the criminal-conspiracy doctrine gradually crumbled, to be partially replaced by increasing employer use of court injunctions against union acts. Unions found little favor in the courts. On the contrary, most judges, conservative by training and position, disliked unions and their activities. By the late 1800's, the law tolerated unionism, but with little enthusiasm.

This slow shift from prohibition to tolerance reflected a parallel shift in the temper of the times on the role of government. During the late 1800's big business outraged millions by its blatant, monopolistic, cut-throat methods. The antitrust uprising of the 1880's and 1890's reflected a shift from the belief that uncontrolled individualism and private enterprise would unquestionably benefit all. Big business could bleed the consumer. Maybe it could also bleed the worker. On the labor front, worker susceptibility to unions grew persistently if slowly. As the economy shifted from the handicraft to the factory system, the worker lost his special skills, his biggest weapon in standing as an individual against the employer. Workers became increasingly concentrated in urban areas.

The law is a live, responsive thing, in the courts and in its administration as well as in legislative bodies. With the upsurge of labor as a major group in American society, public acceptance of labor and its objectives slowly developed. With this the law changed, too. State laws looking toward industrial safety, limitations on child labor, and minimal working conditions began to appear. Many supporters of the Clayton Act in 1914 intended that part of the act should free unions from prosecution as monopolists under the antitrust laws (though the courts soon held otherwise). Unions still seemed dangerous and radical to the staunch, solid middle class. They still represented a small minority of the labor force. But they were no longer mere isolated, struggling groups of visionaries and troublemakers. Their right to fight for members' interests gradually gained recognition.

By the 1920's, organized labor had come a long way toward winning recognition by the public and the law. But it is hard to understand today its insecure position only three decades ago, and the employer anti-union tactics that were tolerated and even encouraged under the law. A respectable, progressive businessman of the 1920's would take for granted his righteousness in using every means to break a union. He would hire private detectives as spies among his workers to ferret out union sympathizers, whom he would summarily fire. Having fired them, he would "blacklist" them with other employers in the area so they couldn't get another job. He would require every worker to sign a "yellow-dog contract" in which the employee agreed that he would not join a union. If any worker violated this contract, he would be fired. And the individual who induced him to breach the yellow-dog contract would be brought into court, where the judge would uphold the legality of the contract and probably find him guilty of conspiracy to break a legal contract.

If a union did get a foothold, the employer would not hesitate to use discriminatory pressures and threats against leaders and members. Not uncommonly, union leaders were taken to the city limits by the "cooperative" local police and advised not to return if they wanted to stay out of jail. Sometimes they went via the blackjack or tar-and-feathers route. As a counter-move to independent union activities, employers often formed captive "company unions" with special benefits for employees who joined. If an employer suspected that a strike was brewing, he would not hesitate to "lock out" the ringleaders and all other employees if necessary, and to keep them out until the economic pressure of no income made them ready to come back on non-union terms. The local magistrate could be counted on to issue an injunction prohibiting the union from striking, so that any strike would lay the workers open to legal action—and to the clubs of the local police force.

When strikes did occur, strike-breakers, private detectives, and armed guards would be called in to make things tough for the strikers. Fists and rocks would give way to blackjacks and guns if necessary to put down the radicals and ungrateful troublemakers, as the strikers were painted in the ads and editorials in the local newspapers. The police could generally be counted on to help break the "unlawful strike" against the property of the respected leading citizens.

Remember, you're reading about the 1920's—not the 1820's. Only a few decades ago. And these employer practices did not vanish with 1929. On the contrary, in some industries they became even more violent with the onslaught of depression. With no other job to go to, and with the wolf at the door, the worker had a hard time talking back.

LABOR: THE NEW DEAL AND SINCE

Even before the New Deal, the tide of public opinion had begun to swing away from such complete employer dominance. The Railway Labor Act of 1926 was a significant step toward facilitating effective union-management negotiations in the railway industry. But the Norris-LaGuardia Act of 1932, passed by a Republican Senate and a Democratic House, was the first major pro-labor legislation.

For years, the court injunction (forbidding labor to strike, picket, or engage in other activities) had been a major employer weapon. With the support of local courts, employers could get injunctions against labor groups to prohibit just about anything. Once the injunction was obtained, labor was the wrong-doer in the eyes of the law. Its only relief, in most cases, was a long and costly court proceeding to get the injunction removed.

Norris-LaGuardia outlawed the injunction in federal courts as an employer weapon against a wide variety of union activities. Courts could not issue injunctions against strikes (except possibly strikes against the government), against joining or remaining in a union, against peaceful picketing, or against giving financial aid to unions. The intent of the law was clear. It was to give unions support in achieving a more equal bargaining status with employers, and to eliminate one of the most powerful and misused employer weapons.

The New Deal, a year later, was frankly and aggressively pro-labor. Beginning with the National Industrial Recovery Act, it fathered a series of legislative acts to promote unionism and the welfare of the worker. The NRA positively guaranteed the legal right of workers "to organize and bargain collectively through representatives of their own choosing . . . free from interference, restraint, or coercion of employers." It established maximum hours of work, minimum wages, and minimal working conditions. But the NRA was short-lived. Its constitutionality was denied by the Supreme Court in 1935.

The Wagner Act. The National Labor Relations Act (the "Wagner Act") was immediately passed to take its place, and this act has since stood as the cornerstone of modern pro-labor legislation. The Wagner Act:

1. Reaffirmed the legal right of employees to organize and bargain collectively, free from employer interference or coercion.

2. Required employers to bargain with unions of the workers' own free choosing.

3. Specifically prohibited a list of "unfair" employer practices.

4. Set up the National Labor Relations Board to settle disputes over who is the legitimate bargaining agent for employees, and to act as a quasi-court to protect workers against unfair labor practices. (The NLRB does not act directly to mediate or settle labor-management disputes.)

Employer intimidation, anti-union discrimination in hiring and firing, company financing of unions, company attempts to influence union elections, and a variety of other practices were soon outlawed as unfair practices as NLRB and court decisions interpreted the law.

The robust growth of unionism under New Deal sponsorship was summarized in Chapter 30. Strikes for union recognition accounted for most of the big work stoppages and violent labor-management fights of the 1930's. Although the Wagner Act protected workers in such organizing strikes, American industry was by no means ready to give in. Blood flowed, millions of dollars were spent on anti-union activities, property destruction by striking unions was widespread, and employees actually took over huge auto and steel plants in destructive "sit-down" strikes to enforce their demands for recognition. In this struggle the Roosevelt administration used its influence wherever possible to smooth the path of labor. Employers argued with considerable evidence, moreover, that the NLRB was biased against employers. They complained they had no right even to speak up in their own defense under NLRB interpretations of the act, and that they had little protection for their property. The constitutionality of the Wagner Act was widely doubted, until it was finally upheld by the Supreme Court.

By the late 1930's, the bitterest organizing struggles were over, and industrial unionism in the mass-production industries was firmly entrenched. Employers bowed more readily to the inevitable. Emphasis began to shift to the development of more effective working relations between management and union groups.

In the courts, labor also fared better. The Supreme Court, reflecting the changing temper of the times and the presence of several Roosevelt-appointed judges, held in the Apex Case (1940) that an organizing strike was not illegal as restraint of trade under the Sherman Act, reversing a long line of judicial precedent. In the Hutcheson Case of the following year the Court went even further, virtually granting unions immunity from the Sherman Act, except (in the Allen Bradley Case of 1945) where they conspire with employers to fix prices or divide markets. The same decision extended union freedom from injunctions to cover a very wide range of union activities.

Fair Labor Standards Act of 1938.   The Wagner Act was aimed basically at strengthening organized labor's power to deal with employers. The Federal Fair Labor Standards Act of 1938 established minimum wages, maximum basic hours, and other fair labor standards for all labor in interstate commerce.

The core of the FLSA was its mandatory minimum wage and maximum basic hours provision. No covered employer could pay less than 25 cents an hour, with the minimum to rise gradually to 40 cents by 1945. A basic work-week of 40 hours was established; employees could be worked longer, but overtime work required overtime pay. A variety of other fair labor standards were spelled out in the act, notably the first federal prohibition of child labor.

The Taft-Hartley Act.   Many called the Wagner Act labor's "Magna Carta." All through the 1930's and World War II, labor rode high. It won nearly every battle with employers. Its friends in Congress, in the White House, in government administrative agencies, and in the courts stood it in good stead. But the pendulum had swung too far. More and more middle-of-the-roaders began to feel that labor had overstepped its bounds; first in the sit-down strikes of the thirties; then in the spreading jurisdictional disputes and strikes that the public and employers seemed powerless to halt; in its persistent wage demands during the World War II fight against inflation; and lastly in its outright defiance of the federal government itself in disputes of critical importance to the national economy.

The Taft-Hartley Act was passed, over President Truman's veto, in 1947, after one of the most vitriolic controversies in labor-management history. To hear Phil Murray and William Green, then heads of the C.I.O. and A.F.L., tell it, Taft-Hartley would throw labor back into the bitter defenseless days of the past. Actually, Taft-Hartley was a direct attempt to redress the balance of power between management and labor, but it retained the basic features of the Wagner Act. The free right of employees to organize and bargain collectively was re-affirmed, but stress was placed on the correlative responsibilities of unions and employers. Bitter pill though Taft-Hartley was for the unions, experience with the new act gave little evidence to support their claim that it would mean the end of labor's newly won freedoms. Nor has the public at large seemed anxious for Taft-Hartley's repeal and a return to the unamended Wagner Act, potent though labor's voice is at the polls.

What did the Taft-Hartley Act really do? First, it defined unfair labor practices of unions to parallel those of employers. Unfair labor practices by unions included failure to bargain in good faith, secondary boycotts, strikes without a 60-day notification of desire to alter a contract, jurisdictional strikes unless certified by the NLRB as representative of the workers involved, and "feather-bedding" to exact pay for no work.

Second, specific provisions to help employers were included. Nothing the employer says may now be used as evidence of an unfair labor practice, so long as it contains no threat or intimidation. And the closed shop was prohibited, against bitter union protests that this would undermine union security.

Third, there were provisions to protect the interests of the individual worker against the union. Unions may not coerce workers to join; disclosure of union financial affairs is required; and non-payment of dues was made the only ground on which the union can force discharge of a worker under a union-shop contract.

Fourth, state laws governing union security arrangements were given precedence over federal law where the state laws are more restrictive. This in effect permits states to prohibit union-shop contracts. And under this provision during the 1950's over one-third of the states enacted "right-to-work" laws that forbade union membership as a condition of continued employment.

Fifth, running through the act was a concern for the "public welfare," as distinct from either labor or management interests. This concern was foremost in the "emergency provision," which enables the president under conditions of national emergency to petition a federal court for an injunction against any strike or lockout for an 80-day period. When the 80-day clause is invoked, there must be a secret union ballot on the latest company offer before the end of the cooling-off period, a stipulation aimed at union leaders who might try to hold their members in line against a reasonable company offer.

The act also held unions more strictly accountable. They must report financial data and list their officers. All union leaders had to sign a non-communist oath if their unions were to obtain the protection of the act; this provision was as violently attacked as an infringement of labor's civil rights as the Wagner Act provisions had been attacked as an infringement of employers' freedom of speech. But in the end, most leaders signed.

This brief summary of Taft-Hartley does little to convey the deep bitterness that arose over its enactment, for the act was a symbol of strength and status, to unions and employers alike. The smashing victory of its proponents marked the end of the long dominance of labor, and both labor and management knew it— even though the act was far milder than many realize who have not studied it in detail. After 1947, repeal of Taft-Hartley became organized labor's major political goal. But Congress has failed to change Taft-Hartley substantially. This is not a sign of widespread happiness with it. But the act appears to be workable, and criticism from both extremes has generally resulted in a deadlock.

The Landrum-Griffin Act. By 1959, labor racketeering had become a national scandal. The investigations of the McClellan Committee in Congress disclosed widespread bribery, hoodlumism, blackmail, and violence in some leading unions, notably the Teamsters and the Longshoremen. High union leaders were implicated, as well as lesser officials. Scores of union officials refused to testify under the Fifth Amendment on grounds that anything they said might tend to incriminate them.

Amidst widespread public pressure for action to curb labor racketeering, Congress passed the Landrum-Griffin Act, over the violent objections of most union leaders. Nearly everyone agreed that the bill was unnecessary to regulate many American unions, which are open and law-abiding organizations. But though labor protested that the new bill made the Taft-Hartley restrictions even worse, there was no resisting the public pressure generated by the McClellan Committee disclosures. The Landrum-Griffin Act includes:

1. A new "bill of rights" for individual union members.

2. A provision tightening the restriction on secondary boycotts and organizational picketing.

3. Requirements for detailed financial reporting by unions of all payments, loans, and other transactions with all officials and members, in addition to their general financial reports.

4. A requirement for secret-ballot elections, and limitations on the term of office between elections of five years for international officials and three years for local officials.

5. A bar against any person who has been convicted of a felony or who has been a member of the Communist Party serving as a union official for at least five years after the conviction or membership.

6. A requirement that employers and middlemen must report on their spending to influence workers.

Mediation, Conciliation, and Arbitration.
Often a skillful third party can soothe hot
tempers and help get labor and management
together when they are negotiating a contract
or settling a grievance. The federal government and most state governments
provide "mediators" and "conciliators" who serve as impartial go-betweens in
trying to get disputes settled without resort to strikes. Sometimes these men enter
at the request of labor and management; sometimes they are sent by public
officials who want to be sure that work stoppages are avoided. Their work is
generally unheralded and unspectacular, but it is successful in a great number of
cases. To watch a skilled mediator at work is an intriguing experience. He has no
power to force his views on either party. He must bring them together by winning
their confidence, isolating the issues at stake, and somehow making each see the
reasonableness of the other's position—as well as reminding both frequently of
the public's interest in avoiding work stoppages.

Although the government steps in frequently as a mediator or conciliator, it
has no general power to act as arbitrator in labor disputes (except in the case of
the railways). Nevertheless, as chief executive, the president has frequently
stepped into disputes that vitally affect the national welfare, has appointed "fact-
finding boards," and in effect has brought into play the full pressure of public
opinion behind the settlement recommended. At a local level, governors and
mayors often follow similar procedures.

War Labor Board and Wage Stabilization Board.   The role of government
mediation and arbitration has varied from time to time. During World War II,
the Federal War Labor Board had extensive powers to intervene as fact-finder
and, in effect, as arbitrator. After the outbreak of the Korean War in 1950, the
Wage Stabilization Board, which succeeded the War Labor Board, temporarily
held somewhat similar powers, and President Truman made full use of this
channel in attempting to settle major industrial disputes that threatened the
national interest. The Wage Stabilization Board was abolished with the return of
peace, however. If the regular Taft-Hartley provisions fail to do the job, the president is now left with his own and the government's prestige as the only levers
for speeding settlements in disputes affecting the national welfare.

The Government as Watchdog.   Congress has long been quick to investigate
through its committees any matter that seems to congressmen to affect the
national interest. Labor-management affairs have ranked high on this list. The
wage-price spiral has been a favorite subject. Some committees have stressed
wage-push. Others have assailed business greed in its pricing policies as the
villain. Some investigations have been sober and careful. Others have focused

mainly on the headlines. But either variety exerts a strong pressure on both labor and management to be prepared to defend in public the actions they take.

The McClellan Committee of the late 1950's played a major role in exposing gangsterism, bribery, and hoodlumism in the internal affairs and operating practices of some unions, especially the Teamsters and the Longshoremen. In persistent, bipartisan hearings, labor leader after labor leader was placed on the public stand to testify about alleged conversion of union funds to personal use, blackmail, payoffs for union protection, violence, and even arson and murder. Shocking numbers of such officials retreated behind the Fifth Amendment of the Constitution, refusing to answer questions on grounds their answers might tend to incriminate them in criminal actions. Dave Beck and Jimmy Hoffa, presidents of the Teamsters, largest union in the nation, were among the most spectacular witnesses. Beck was deposed from his presidency and convicted of criminal behavior as a result of the committee's probing. Grand-jury actions for both perjury and such crimes as bribery, conversion, and blackmail were brought against numerous lesser union leaders. Some labor officials protested that the good name of all labor was being blackened improperly by such focus on the acts of a few. While most of the labor movement is undoubtedly far from the practices exposed by the McClellan Committee, such committee action points up for the public, for Congress, and for the unions themselves problems properly of national concern. And after long argument, Congress passed the Landrum-Griffin Act to correct some of the abuses disclosed.

The Government as Wage-setter.   Suppose a nation-wide steel strike is in progress. The union, pointing to rising living costs, high profits, increasing productivity, and a sweeping variety of other considerations, argues that 20 cents an hour more in pay and fringe benefits is the lowest raise it will even consider. Management in the steel industry's Big Six say they won't offer a penny more than 10 cents. They say that profits after taxes are down, that capacity is up enormously and foreign competition is rising, that steel wages have risen faster than prices, and that steel workers are already among the best-paid workers in the nation. After long months of bickering back and forth with no progress, the union calls a strike. The strike has gone on now for two long months, and the steel shortage is shutting down not only civilian production but also arms production and construction of guided-missile and other military facilities. If you were president, what would you do?

You might say, let the strike go on. It's none of the government's business. But with the economy grinding to a halt and the U.S.S.R. looming ominously on the horizon, you probably wouldn't.

You might invoke the national-emergency provision of the Taft-Hartley Act. This probably would get the union back to work and would give you 80 days to bring all the pressure you could on both sides to settle their differences. You'd get your top assistants on the job, and focus as much public pressure as you could on the negotiators. If you felt strongly that right was mainly on one side or the other, you might let your feeling be known and start building up special pressures on the other side to capitulate.

The power of the federal government is great, and chances are that this kind of pressure would bring some kind of settlement. No private business or union wants to fight the government. The odds are stacked in favor of the president. But . . . suppose this time neither the companies nor the union will give in. So the workers go out on strike again at the end of 80 days, more bitter than ever. What then?

Then is the tough time. By now tempers are really frayed. Labor and management have been over the issues *ad nauseam*. Each has been provoked into saying a lot of things better left unsaid. Everybody's dirty linen has been thoroughly aired before 175 million Americans.

You might decide to seize the steel industry and ask the workers to stay on the job. But this means seizing a vast, privately owned industry, against all the peacetime traditions of American freedom and probably against the Constitution. Or you might order the workers to stay on the job, in the interests of the public welfare. But you know perfectly well you can't make men make steel, either under the law or any other way, if they just won't go back to work and do it.

Well, what would *you* do?

SHOULD THE GOVERNMENT GET OUT? This example illustrates the problem that occurred over and over, with variations, all through World War II and the postwar period. The fact of modern economic interdependence is inescapable. Vast power over the economic life of the entire nation can be exercised by a tiny number of strategically located workers and managers. Less than 1 per cent of the nation's labor force is employed in trucking. Yet that 1 per cent, under the leadership of men widely viewed as gangsters and hoodlums, could probably bring the economy almost to a dead stop in a few weeks. An even smaller number belong to the coalminers' union, the United Mine Workers. Yet a three-month strike by the UMW through the winter months would not only shut down steel, public utilities, and other major industries, but would leave millions of homes cold and uninhabitable throughout the country. A mere handful of men can shut down the railroads and through them much of the economy, if they choose to strike. The same is true in industry after industry.

Ours is an economy of power groups. The unions and their leaders have vast power. So do employers. Wage-setting has moved from the small, competitive market place to the industry-wide bargaining table in many leading industries. The wage bargains set in steel, autos, electrical equipment, and coal go far to set the pattern for the rest of the economy. How can the government stand aside and see its arms program jeopardized, its inflation-control program split open, the operation of the whole economy periled by disputes in these industries? But if it is drawn in, what can it really do? May it be that the recent tendency of government to step in actually destroys any prospect of bona-fide collective bargaining between labor and management?

Many serious observers think there is a good chance that government intervention, when it becomes habitual, does more harm than good. They argue that when both sides know the government will eventually step in to settle the issue, there is little chance of settling the dispute beforehand. This is particularly true, they say, in inflationary periods when both labor and management know they will ultimately get much of what they want by putting on enough pressure, and the main question is how much prices will be pushed up for the consumer. Neither labor nor management expects to reach a wage agreement until government approval on the higher wages and prices is obtained.

And the government has a basically inflationary bias. In the showdown, it is likely to choose the higher wage, the higher price, to settle the dispute. Deflation and depression are greater dangers than inflation. With an open-ended fiscal and monetary policy, the danger of pricing yourself out of the market through higher wages and product prices is never too serious. When the government is intimately involved in wage negotiations, it can be counted on to see that total monetary demand doesn't fall short. The consumer pays, however brave the talk about protecting his interests. Or at least, so the argument goes. These observers generally favor putting main reliance on stabilizing monetary-fiscal policy and leaving labor and management to make their bargains freely within such an over-all stabilizing framework.

Some Final Questions. The American economy has come a long way from the highly competitive, individualistic, free-market system described by the classical economists. The leaders of big business and big labor set wages and prices by bargaining and compromise. Perhaps this concentrated power is incompatible with a smoothly functioning, free-enterprise economic system and a truly democratic political system. But concentrated economic power is here, like it or not. The problem is somehow to develop correlative economic responsibility to union members, to stockholders, and to the public as a whole; and a framework within which economic power is channeled to the public good. The hard fact is that we cannot order huge groups of workers around in a democratic society. Wage-setting must be by consensus when two powerful groups face each other across the bargaining table. And it must be by political as well as economic consensus, once the government enters the scene as a major participant in the wage-setting process.

The Swedish economy provides an interesting comparison. There, economy-wide labor-management bargaining on wages has long been accepted. Labor has a long and respected record as a powerful and responsible economic and political bargainer. The labor party often controls the Riksdag (legislature), and is always powerful in it. Organized labor's position in industry is secure, and labor participates more actively in management than it does in the United States. The result has been a stabler economy than in the U.S.—and more inflation.

Perhaps this is the alternative toward which the American economy is moving. Since labor markets cannot be highly competitive, should we frankly embrace the other extreme of economy-wide wage-making by a few representatives of labor and management, subject to the ultimate test of strength in Congress? Most Americans would be shocked at the suggestion. Or perhaps we're due to muddle through about as we have in the last two decades, with an inflationary bias. Which alternative looks best to you?

1. When the government intervenes in wage negotiations, what criteria should it use in deciding what wage settlement to support?

2. Many states have recently passed "right-to-work" laws, prescribing that no one shall be barred from any position because he refuses to join a union. Do you believe your state should have such a law if it does not now have one? Why or why not?

3. Should unions have more or less governmental support than they are now getting to assure the best public interest in bargaining negotiations between labor and management?

4. Should labor unions restrict their activities to direct economic objectives, rather than spreading out into political activities? Why or why not?

5. Would you favor or oppose legislation requiring compulsory arbitration of all labor disputes which threaten to result in strikes, with an impartial arbitrator to be chosen in each case from a panel maintained for such emergencies? What would you do about unions or employers who refused to follow the arbitrator's decision?

6. What is a "national emergency" strike which, in your judgment, would justify the government's imposition of compulsory arbitration?

7. Inflation has periodically repealed the federal minimum-wage law. Should Congress now raise the legal minimum wage to a level that will substantially raise the wages of the lowest 10 per cent or so of employed workers?

8. "As long as the government hovers in the background, ready to step into labor disputes, there is little chance that unions and management will bargain actively in good faith. One side or the other will feel that it can win a better bargain by getting the government on its side. The best thing that could happen to collective bargaining in this country is for the government to get absolutely and completely out of labor negotiations." Do you agree or disagree with this statement? List the arguments on each side of the issue.

**FOR
ANALYSIS
AND
DISCUSSION**

Appendix
The Economics of Minimum Wage Laws

What are the economic effects of a minimum-wage law covering all workers in interstate commerce? Suppose, for example, that the minimum hourly wage under the Fair Labor Standards Act were raised to $1.50. For the moment, assume a constant level of total expenditures in the economy.

1. Assuming that the legal minimum wage is higher than the going wage rate in important areas, economic theory suggests that costs will be raised, prices boosted, sales reduced, and employment cut. Workers who keep their jobs will get the new higher minimum rate. The new jobless may stay unemployed or they may go to work elsewhere in jobs not covered by the minimum-wage law. If they do the latter, the uncovered substandard wages are forced even lower as the labor supply there rises without any increase in demand.

2. However, if employers were "exploiting" labor before the law by paying wages well below labor's productivity, the minimum-wage law may simply boost wages without reducing employment. Wages get more of the consumer's dollar, profits get less. This is the situation implicitly assumed in most of the ardent arguments for minimum-wage legislation.

3. Even if there is no exploitation of labor, the law's upward pressure on wage rates may drive employers to more efficient methods, thereby absorbing the higher wages without reducing employment. This, too, is a favorite argument of minimum-wage-law advocates. How often it works this way is not clear from the evidence. A lot depends on how effective businessmen are at running their businesses without the pressures of minimum-wage laws.

4. Minimum-wage laws tend to redistribute incomes—from employers to labor and from workers who get pushed out to those who keep their jobs at higher pay. What happens to the total labor share in the national income depends basically on the elasticity of demand for labor. If employers' demand for labor is elastic, the higher wage rates required by the minimum-wage law will mean lower total wage payments. If employers' aggregate demand is inelastic, the law will mean higher total wage payments.

Which is it? Nobody knows. It's much easier to estimate what the elasticity may be in particular industries at particular times. The impact of a minimum-wage law is uneven, depending on how high wages were before the law and how strong consumer demand is in different industries.

5. Now drop the assumption of constant total spending in the economy. What does a minimum-wage law do to the total level of employment? In a boom

period, probably not a lot. Any workers thrown out of jobs in covered industries can be absorbed in uncovered fields, even though they may have to take lower-paid jobs. In depression, this re-absorption is not so easy, and persisting unemployment may result from minimum-wage legislation. These issues are essentially the same ones that arise when wages are pushed up by union action. We have already looked at some of the results in Chapters 16 and 30.

Repeal by Inflation.   As a practical matter, the minimum-wage law hasn't had much effect on the American economy. It has been repealed by inflation. By the time the act went into effect, minimum wages in almost all covered industries had already risen above the specified level. Then inflation and boom times pushed wages up faster than the gradual rise to 40 cents specified by the law. Wages in a few industries lagged behind the minimum figures, but these were mainly industries not covered by the law—agriculture, services, local shops, and so on, which are not part of interstate commerce. Then, in the 1950's, inflation and rising money wages robbed first a new 75¢ and then a $1.00 legal minimum of any widespread impact.

Today, labor is pushing for a minimum-wage revision to at least $1.25. If inflation continues, the figure may be higher. If labor's pressures succeed, we may see a more revealing test of the effects of minimum-wage legislation. Thus far, there is little evidence that the law has had a major effect on the wage structure, except in certain low-wage areas, especially in the South, and on scattered low-wage pockets throughout the economy.

Property Incomes—
Rent and Interest

About two-thirds of the national income is made up of wages and salaries. But that other third that goes to property-owners as rent, interest, and profits is a lot of money—over $100 billion in 1959. Most of these property-owners are the same people who receive part of the wages and salaries total. Only a few get their entire income from property they own—real estate, stocks, bonds, or businesses of their own. So the functional division of income between wages, rent, interest, and profits doesn't tell us directly why people receive the individual incomes they do, because so many people get income from more than one source. Still, this functional breakdown is the best approach economists have found to explaining why income gets distributed the way it does.

This chapter deals primarily with the two smaller property-income shares—rent and interest. Profits are the sole subject of Chapter 33.

RENT

"Rent" is used differently by the man in the street and by some economic theorists. In everyday usage, rent is the price paid for the use of land, buildings, machinery, or other durable goods. This is the way we shall use the term, except in one later section where a special meaning will be given to the term "economic rent."

Rent is closely analogous to wages paid for the services of workers. There are important institutional differences—we don't have a slave economy so we don't buy and sell workers the way we buy and sell land. Nevertheless, the same kind of demand and supply analysis is appropriate for explaining the rent on non-human productive resources, as for explaining the wages of human productive resources. You should be able to transfer the general analytical framework for yourself from the wages and salaries area. This section raises only a few special points about rent.

The supply of non-human productive resources, like that of labor, varies widely from case to case. At one extreme, the supply of land at the corner of Madison Avenue and 42nd Street in New York City is completely inelastic— there's just so much and no more can be manufactured. At the other extreme, garden hoes, a very simple productive resource, can be reproduced readily, and their supply may be highly elastic. Most real-world cases lie somewhere in be- tween. By and large, the supply of any productive resource is likely to be reason- ably elastic, given a long enough period for adjustment. Farm land, for example, can readily be improved through the use of fertilizer, drainage, tiling, buildings, and so forth, if it pays to do so. For practical purposes, this is the same as making more land—you still have the same number of acres, but the land has increased productivity.

The demand for non-human productive resources also varies widely from case to case, but it comes back ultimately to how much the productive service rendered is worth to the renter. Again, the problem is parallel to that of the demand for labor services. The same notion of marginal revenue productivity logically under- lies the business demand for non-human productive services. As in the case of labor services, marginal revenue productivity is often unfamiliar to the business- man, hard to estimate, and only a rough guide to our thinking about the demand side of the picture—but a useful one nevertheless.

Competitive bidding by businesses tends to draw each resource into its most productive use. Each piece of land is rented to the highest bidder, and the high bidder must use the land where its marginal productivity is greatest to permit his paying the high rent. With non-human as with human resources, monopoly or monopsony may lead to inefficient allocation of resources, to "exploitation" of resource owners, or to unemployment of some of the resources. The distribution of resources and income payments according to marginal revenue productivity is part and parcel of the process by which a competitive, private-enterprise system meets consumer demands with greatest efficiency.

An Example.   Take one simple example. What will be the rent on a half-acre site on a highway near the outskirts of a good-sized town? Look at the demand side first. One demand may be for use in truck farming. How much potential renters will pay for this use will depend on the fertility of the soil, the water supply, and other such factors. Another demand may be for use as small individual business properties, such as restaurants, garden-supply stores, and so on. Here the amount of traffic passing by, the convenience of the location for potential customers, and other such factors will be especially important. Still another demand might be for use by a single super-market, with surrounding parking area. Here again traffic flows, convenience of location for city grocery shoppers, availability of adequate space for parking and storage, and desirability of nearby neighbors might be especially important. Each potential renter would make some type of estimate as to how much he could afford to pay in rent for the site—logically, up to its estimated marginal value productivity for him.

Who will get the site, and at what rent? If there is active competition among the potential renters, the rent will be bid up until only the highest bidder is left. This will be the renter who estimates the marginal revenue productivity of the site to him as being the highest. Thus the site will be drawn into that use which promises the highest return to the renter, and through this mechanism into the use where consumers value it most highly (since the estimated high marginal revenue productivity reflects high consumer demand).

Will the rent be bid up all the way to the estimated marginal revenue productivity of the highest bidder? Not necessarily, if the value to one user is substantially higher than to others. Suppose the site is ideal for a super-market. Then the local Kroger manager needs only bid higher than the truck farmers and small shop operators, to whom the land is potentially worth far less. Kroger's may get the site at a rent substantially below its estimated marginal value productivity as a super-market site. On the other hand, Kroger's may not. Not if there's a local A&P or Safeway also in the market for sites. If there's active competition among numerous potential renters of different types, the rent is pretty sure to be bid up close to the land's highest estimated marginal revenue productivity.

This, of course, is nothing but our old problem of the degree of competition again. If we take the extreme case of lack of competition—bilateral monopoly—where there is a single landowner with this type of site and only a single potential super-market renter, the exact rent becomes indeterminant so far as economic theory is concerned. Then it boils down pretty much to bargaining strength and skill, with the limits to the bargain set by the next-best opportunity of each party. Rent is pretty much like any other price so far as the influence of the degree of competition on the ultimate price is concerned.

Rent as a Differential. The classical economists explained rent as a differential that had to be paid for the use of superior over inferior land. The reasoning went like this. If there is not enough land to go around free, rent will arise for the owners of the best land first. The rent on any given acre will be bid up to the point where it just measures how much more productive that acre is than the next-best acre. The rent on each acre, therefore, will be the differential in that acre's productivity over the productivity of no-rent land. The rent on our suburban half-acre in the preceding section, for example, would be higher than on the next-best site by the differential in the productivity between the two sites. And so on, back down to land with zero rent, where the differential between it and our site is the full amount of the rent.[1]

It should be easy to see that this reasoning gives exactly the same results as the marginal-productivity analysis. Each acre is "worth" what its use adds to the value of the total output. Since the marginal-productivity analysis is the more general approach, it is now the one commonly used. The differential reasoning makes sense, however. Some observers feel that it is a significant approach, since it emphasizes that each productive agent's relative earnings measure the amount by which it is more productive than the next-best agent.

"Economic Rent"—A Price-Determined Cost.   Economists have one special definition of "rent" that differs from ordinary lay usage. "Economic rent" is the payment for the use of a *scarce, non-reproducible resource*. For example, the rent paid for one corner of Madison Avenue and 42nd Street in New York covers a mixture of "site value" and use of the building on the space, with all the improvements available. If we could isolate the site value of a corner of Madison Avenue and 42nd Street—i.e., the land itself exclusive of any of the improvements on it —we would have a resource that is scarce and completely fixed in supply; the supply is perfectly inelastic. There are other similar cases outside the field of land values. For example, suppose a business firm develops a new process, on which it holds a patent. For the life of the patent, the process is much like the site value of our New York land; it cannot be reproduced (except by consent of the patent holder).

The rent on non-reproducible productive agents is determined exclusively by the demand for them, since the supply is completely inelastic. The supply curve is a vertical line. If there is no demand, there is no rent; the rent rises directly as demand rises, without relation to the original costs of producing the resource.[2]

Is the "economic rent" on such a resource a cost of production? It is for the individual producer, since he has to pay over the rent to the resource owner once a month. But from the viewpoint of the economy as a whole, such rents are purely price-determined (or demand-determined) costs. The economy can get

---

[1] If you fail to see why this same differential type of analysis couldn't be applied equally well to wage determination, you're right. The wage received by any type of labor could be explained as a differential measuring the extent by which such workers' productivity exceeds that of the next most productive class of labor—and so on back down to workers who aren't worth any wage at all.

[2] Economists often use the term "quasi-rent," to describe the return on *temporarily* non-reproducible resources—for example, the patented production process mentioned above. The return here is an economic rent, but one that will continue only so long as substitutes are not produced.

exactly the same productive service from the non-reproducible scarce agent for any rent. In this sense, for the whole economy economic rent is not a cost that helps to determine the price of ultimate products.

Outside the site value of land, few cases of pure economic rent exist. But there are many with some element of economic rent. Wages themselves may be an important example. Consider all labor as an aggregate for the moment. In any reasonably short period, indeed probably over long periods, the quantity of labor offered to employers is fixed (within fairly wide limits), irrespective of the wage offered. People must work to eat. They would prefer to work at high pay rather than low, but most people would work at lower pay rather than remain idle for long. At the bottom, clearly starvation sets a minimum wage below which the supply of labor would indeed vanish. But in the American economy wages are far above this. Thus, with the aggregate supply of labor somewhat fixed, most of wages might be considered a kind of demand-determined economic rent, over which employers and unions bargain. This kind of reasoning underlies what some economists call the "bargaining" theory of wages.

Were all employers to band together, this approach suggests, they might depress the wage a long way without seriously lessening the amount of labor offered. When they do not band together, of course, competition among them tends to bid up wages toward marginal value productivity. But we know that much of labor is relatively immobile, in segmented markets. In extreme cases—for example, the mining town of Chapter 29—the analogy of wages to economic rent may be a close one.

INTEREST

Real estate and some other productive resources are commonly rented. But many payments for the use of "capital" (non-human productive resources) are also made in form of interest, which is the price paid for the use of loaned funds. Which way the payment is made depends largely on custom. Rent and interest incomes can readily be converted from one form to the other.

Interest differs from rent and wages in two major respects:

1. Interest is ordinarily paid for the use of money, rather than directly for the use of productive resources. Money itself has no productivity. It doesn't build buildings or dig ditches. We can't explain interest directly as a payment for money's productivity. But money does give its owner purchasing power to obtain men and machines that will build buildings and dig ditches, and demand for loan funds traces back in considerable part to these real productive resources.

2. Interest is stated as a *rate* of return (4 per cent) rather than as an absolute sum. To say that the interest rate is 4 per cent is merely to say that the borrower pays $4 interest per year for each $100 borrowed. The statement in percentage terms as a rate is convenient because it permits ready comparison between the

payments of different amounts for widely differing resources. You can easily compare the return on money invested in an ocean liner and in a turret lathe by converting both returns into a percentage on the funds invested. For example, if the liner cost $10 million and provides an annual net return of $500,000 after depreciation and other expenses, the rate is 5 per cent. If the turret lathe cost $1,000 and provides an annual net return of $40, the rate is 4 per cent. According to these figures, funds invested in ocean liners provide a better return than funds invested in turret lathes.

The Structure of Interest Rates.   There are hundreds of different interest rates. In 1959, for example, the government paid about 3 per cent on short-term bills and about 4¼ per cent on long-term bonds. Bank loans ranged from about 4½ per cent for well-established business concerns to 5 to 7 per cent on mortgage loans to buy houses and as much as 12 per cent (1 per cent a month) on small, unsecured loans to individual borrowers. Some consumer loan agencies charged up to 40 per cent per annum. You got no interest on demand deposits, but most banks paid from 2 to 3 per cent on savings deposits. The average short-term commercial loan rate at big banks in New York was about 4½ per cent, in southern and western cities about 5 per cent. Small business borrowers typically paid 1 to 2 per cent more than large ones.

These different rates reflect differences in risk, locality, length of loan, cost of handling the loan, and a variety of other factors, as well as the "pure" interest rate that is included in each. To simplify matters, economists often talk about "the" interest rate. They mean the interest rate on a long-term, essentially riskless loan. The rate on long-term United States Government bonds is commonly considered a close approximation. At mid-1959, therefore, we might have said "the interest rate" was about 4¼ per cent. But don't make the mistake of assuming you could go out and borrow money at this rate, or even that most borrowing was done at this rate.

Interest as the Price of Loanable Funds.   Interest is the price of loanable funds. Like any other price, it is determined by supply and demand factors in the market. But the factors determining the interest rate are extremely complex on both the demand and supply sides. Interest theory is probably the most unsettled area of modern economics, and economists save some of their choicer invectives for one another on this score. The difficulties arise because of the complex interrelationships among all the motives for saving and investing, on top of all the uncertainties that surround the determination of the labor and rent shares with their uncertain dependence on marginal-productivity analysis. Add on the behavior of the monetary system, with its cyclical instability and its discretionary management by the federal government, and you begin to see why no one simple model is very satisfactory for explaining interest rates.

Understanding the interest rate is important. It not only serves as an allocator of part of the national income; it is also an important influence on the rate of capital accumulation and economic growth, and an important determinant of the rate of investment in business-cycle fluctuations. In the midst of professional controversy and uncertainty, we will make no pretense here of going beyond a very simple supply and demand analysis, plus a few insights into the impact of interest-rate changes on the behavior of the economic system.

The Demand for Loanable Funds. The biggest private demand for loanable funds comes from business firms. Businesses borrow when they think they'll make money by doing so—when they expect to make a return on the funds big enough to pay back principal and interest, and have something left over for profit. Basically, they are willing to pay interest because the borrowed funds give them control over real productive resources—machinery, buildings, labor, and so on. Their demand for funds is thus much the same, though one step removed, as for the physical productive resources themselves. It is a derived demand.

Chapter 11 looked in detail at the factors determining the "marginal efficiency of investment," analogous to the marginal revenue productivity of real productive agents. Wherever a businessman sees an investment possibility with a marginal efficiency of investment much above the interest rate he has to pay, he will want to borrow additional funds if he doesn't have them already. Since it is the *expected* return that controls business planning, anything that affects business profit expectations will affect the demand for loanable funds.

At any time there is a wide variety of possible investment opportunities. Some may *promise* a return of 10 per cent, some 5 per cent, some only 1 per cent; nobody knows for sure what they will return. The higher the interest rate required to get funds, the fewer the possibilities that will justify borrowing. The amount businesses will borrow thus depends on the interest rate relative to the marginal efficiency of investment (as in Chapter 11).[3]

The second big private demand for loanable funds comes from individual households. In 1959, total consumer credit outstanding was over $45 billion, and over half of all department-store sales were made on charge accounts or installment plans. The great bulk of house purchases involve borrowing part of the price; in 1959, total mortgage debt on houses was about $125 billion, up about $10 billion from 1958. If you have a strong positive time preference—i.e., if the present seems a lot more important to you than the future—you will be inclined to borrow to increase your consumption now, even though you know you will

---

[3] The demand for loan funds can be stated either gross or net. It is generally stated gross, to include the demand for funds to make new investments *and* to maintain existing real capital through replacement of depreciating assets. The supply side must of course be treated to match the demand side. Gross, this implies including business depreciation funds and retained earnings in the supply of loan funds, even though the business has no intention of lending the funds to anyone else. This situation is somewhat comparable to the labor market, where the demand for labor may be thought of as including the rehiring of existing workers for any time period, as well as taking on new hands.

have to cut consumption to pay off the loan later. You may borrow for other reasons—perhaps because you think prices are going up and you'll save in the end by borrowing to buy now, even though you incur some interest cost. Whatever your motives, you are likely to borrow more at a low than at a high interest rate.

The third big demand for funds is from governments—federal, state, and local. State and local governments borrow mainly to finance long-term capital improvements—highways, schools, sewer systems, water works. The federal government borrows for more purposes, partly to finance capital improvements but even more to pay for wars. Sometimes it borrows to finance deficits intentionally generated to combat depression. The motives for governmental borrowing are thus different from those for private borrowing. But here again we can safely assume that the total government demand curve for funds is downward-sloping at any time; state and local governments, in particular, will borrow less at higher rates than at lower, other things equal.

The Supply of Loanable Funds. What determines the supply of loanable funds? Your first inclination is probably to say, how much people and businesses save and how the banking system behaves. This answer would be right, but not complete. We need also to consider other financial intermediaries as crucial links between saving and the offering of savings on the loan market. In addition, people and businesses often want to change the size of their cash balances, and this swells or cuts the supply of funds.

Personal Saving. People save for all kinds of reasons—for old age, to buy insurance, to put children through college, to buy a house, for a "rainy day," just because they feel they ought to save. A lot of personal saving is more or less automatic. In 1959, the 10 per cent of families with the highest incomes apparently did around two-thirds of the total net personal saving in the country. At very high income levels, people save because they have money left over after buying all the things they want. Saving becomes much easier once a family moves into the upper-income levels. Chapter 11 looked in detail at personal consumption and saving behavior; that analysis is equally applicable here.

Business Saving. Like individuals, businesses save for a variety of reasons. Mainly, they save because it is considered sound business practice to reinvest depreciation funds and to plow back a good part of earnings each year into expansion and long-term growth, rather than paying them all out as dividends. Firms could pay out all their profits in dividends and then go into the market to borrow money for expansion purposes—but they don't. Most of their savings flow directly on into real investment; only a small part comes onto the open market for loanable funds.

Saving, Cash Balances, and the Supply of Loan Funds. Individuals and businesses may save to build up their cash balances. The motives for holding cash balances were analyzed in Chapter 10, with emphasis on transactions, precautionary and speculative motives. When savers do try to build up their cash balances, their savings may or may not become part of the supply of loanable funds. Suppose they save by building up their bank deposits. Here you need to go back to what you learned about commercial banks. In the aggregate, such saving doesn't increase the volume of bank deposits, nor does it change the volume of excess reserves in the commercial banks unless funds shift from demand to time deposits. So the net result is likely to be merely a slowing down of the velocity of bank deposits, not a stimulus to banks to lend more. If the banks do increase their loans enough to match the increased saving, it is a fortuitous circumstance.

Why should savers want to save and just build up cash balances instead of earning interest on their funds by lending them out? Beyond the general motives noted above, many business and individual savers are in no position to make loans or direct investments themselves. To them, saving means putting money in the bank.

Savings may also be put into insurance, savings and loan associations, mutual savings banks, or other non-commercial banking financial intermediaries. These generally pay interest on funds. While, unlike commercial banks, such firms can't create and destroy money directly, they can pile up or spend down their cash balances. There is no guarantee that savings flowing into these intermediaries will just match the funds being offered to borrowers by the intermediaries in any given period. As was shown in Chapter 9, shifts of funds from commercial banks to such institutions increases the supply of liquid assets and generally speeds up the velocity of circulation of money.

The Banks and the Supply of Loan Funds. You are familiar with the power of the commercial banking system to create and destroy money. Here is clearly a major force on the supply side of the loan-funds market. As long as the banks have excess reserves, they can make loans without regard to what individual and business savers do. They can contract their loans with comparable independence. If they don't have excess reserves, increased private saving won't permit them to extend more loans (unless funds are shifted from demand deposits to savings deposits with lower reserve requirements). The supply of loan funds in any time period is a complex matter. It depends on a lot of different decisions.

Determination of the Interest Rate.

Like other prices, the interest rate is determined by the interaction of supply and demand. But there are two aspects of this market that justify special mention.

The first one goes back to Part 2's analysis of the level of national income and employment. In most markets, changes in price can be expected to have significant influences upon the amount demanded and supplied. But changes in the interest rate appear to have little effect on the supply of loanable funds. A decrease in the demand for loanable funds may simply decrease the interest rate and restore a new equilibrium balance in the funds market, just as a drop in demand does in the market for wheat or steel. But often a decrease in decisions to invest and hence in the demand for funds will instead decrease the whole level of income and employment, rather than centering on the interest rate. (See Chapter 11.) A new equilibrium will indeed be achieved, but it will be through lowering national income, which in turn lowers saving to match the new lower level of investment, rather than having a lower interest rate serve as the primary equilibrating factor.

The modern theory of income and employment emphasizes that adjustments to imbalance between saving and investment decisions will come mainly through changes in the whole level of income. The traditional theory emphasized changes in the interest rate as the primary equilibrating force, with little impact on the total level of income and employment. Most economists now agree that the traditional theory placed too much weight on the interest rate as the major equilibrating factor, and glossed over the possible divergence between current saving and the supply of loanable funds. But not all truth is on the modern side. Part of the adjustment may also come through the interest rate. A more elaborate investigation of these differences is properly postponed to a more advanced course.[4]

Second, the market for loanable funds is an exceptionally complex one, in terms of the diversity of sources of funds, of financial intermediaries in the market, and of borrowers (or users) of funds. As was indicated above, there is not one interest rate, but many—a reflection of this great diversity.

Government Policy and Interest Rates.   Since the 1930's, the federal government has exerted substantial influence over the level of interest rates. Before the New Deal, interest rates were largely set in the market by the interplay of private supply and demand, though the Federal Reserve did intervene from time to time to tighten or ease the money markets. But after 1933, federal fiscal and monetary policy became more important on both the demand and supply sides of the money market. The government became a heavy borrower in the 1930's, and the dominant borrower in the 1940's. At the same time, the Federal Reserve pumped new reserves into the banking system to supply the funds needed by the government to finance the spending voted by Congress. The result was substantial government determination of the basic level of interest rates. In the 1950's, the Federal Reserve shifted to a policy of greater neutrality. But, as was emphasized in Chapters 14 and 15, government monetary and fiscal policies are powerful forces in the money market and inevitably will continue to be, even though the government does not intervene actively for extended periods.

The Interest Rate, Resource Allocation, and Capital Accumulation.   The interest rate helps potential business and individual investors allocate their funds

---

[4] Advanced texts in economic theory explain that in equilibrium the interest rate must be equal to the marginal productivity of real capital (in the aggregate), must equilibrate the loanable funds market, and must equilibrate the market for money (currency and deposits) so that everyone is just willing to continue holding the existing amount of money, rather than spending it on goods and services or securities; and that it will simultaneously do all three.

among the millions of potential investment opportunities in the economy. When funds are allocated where the expected rate of return is highest, risk and other factors taken into account, they are optimally allocated from the consumer's viewpoint as well as from the investor's. Unless an investment promises a return high enough to pay the going rate of interest under a private-enterprise economy, it does not justify exploitation, by the test of the market. Money capital is the fluid embodiment of real productive resources. Thus the money market, by channeling funds into those investments throughout the economy where the potential return exceeds the interest rate at the margin, provides a most valuable service.

The interest rate plays another, more subtle, role. The going interest rate provides a rough measure of the relative advantages of current consumption and saving. By saving, the individual or business can get a continuing return of, say, 3 per cent annually. If that return is enough to justify foregoing consumption now, it is advantageous to save. Without the interest rate to indicate the going return on saved funds in the economy, the individual saver would have no standard by which to measure the relative advantages of current consumption and saving. How important this point is hinges on how important the interest rate is in consumer and business decisions to save.

The interest rate is far from the only factor controlling saving and investment decisions. Yet it would be dangerous to write off its influence, especially on the investment side. High interest rates make money dear and discourage heavy long-term investment projects where interest is an important cost component. Low interest rates mean cheap money and encourage widespread exploitation of investment possibilities. The interest rate is a powerful influence on the rate of economic growth.

VALUATION OF INCOME-PRODUCING PROPERTY Income distribution is concerned primarily with the pricing of productive *services,* not with the prices of the productive agents themselves—land, machinery, buildings, and the stocks and bonds representing their ownership. But income-producing assets are bought and sold daily in our economy, and the interest rate plays an important part in setting the prices at which they sell.

All we need to know to estimate the price (valuation) of an income-producing asset is (1) its net annual return and (2) the going rate of interest.

Valuation of Perpetual Fixed Income. Take a very simple hypothetical case first. Suppose we have a mine that will produce *forever* ore worth $100 annually, net after all expenses are met. Suppose further that the going rate of interest on substantially riskless investments is 4 per cent. What will the mine be worth?

To get the answer, we simply "capitalize" $100 at 4 per cent. That is, we find that sum on which 4 per cent interest would amount to $100 annually. The arithmetic is simple. Four per cent of x (the unknown value) is $100. In equation form, this is: $.04 \cdot x = 100$. Dividing the .04 into 100, we get $2,500 as the value of the mine.

Can we be sure the mine will really sell for $2,500? No, but we can be pretty sure it will sell for something near that. No one will be willing to pay a much higher price, since by investing $2,500 anywhere else at equal risk he can get $100 annually. On the other hand, if the mine's price is much less than $2,500, people will find it a very attractive investment and the price will be bid up toward $2,500.

Valuation of Machinery.   The principle involved in valuing non-perpetual assets is the same. Consider a machine that will last 20 years and whose marginal revenue productivity (rent) per year is $60. The going rate of interest on comparable investments is 6 per cent. Using the same approach as before, we might capitalize $60 at 6 per cent, and find that $60 is 6 per cent on $1,000.

But there's a catch here. The annual income of $60 here only lasts for 20 years, because the machine wears out. Our problem here is: What is the present, or capitalized, value of an income stream of $60 at 6 per cent over 20 years, rather than in perpetuity as in the preceding example? The mathematicians and industrial engineers have worked out a series of tables giving the answers to the combinations of interest rates and time periods for this type of problem. The answer here is $688.

The basic reasoning runs like this: At the end of the first year, we get $60. At the end of the second year we get another $60, and so on for the 20 years. Sixty dollars today is obviously worth $60, but $60 to be received, say, five years from today is clearly worth less than $60 today, since we do not have the use of it until five years hence. How much today is equivalent to $60 a year from today; how much is equivalent to $60 two years from today; and so on? If, for example, the interest rate is 6 per cent, $56.60 invested today at 6 per cent will amount to just $60 a year from now. And we can make a similar calculation to get the amount equal to $60 two years hence, and so on up to 20 years. If now we add together all these "present values" of $60 at the end of each of the next 20 years, we will get how much we ought to be willing to pay now for the series of 20 annual $60 net returns anticipated from the machine. This calculation gives the $688 above, the "present worth" of the income stream promised if we buy the machine.

In the business world, you might find accountants dealing with the problem in a different, but equivalent, way. They might say that the machine depreciates over 20 years, so that its cost must be "charged off" over that period. Thus they might begin with the same formula as was used in the preceding section, but compute the *net* annual return on the machine *after* depreciation had been deducted each year. This approach would clearly give a much lower present value. But if we go at it this way we must remember that interest can now be earned by investing the depreciation funds we are accumulating over the 20 years.[5] Thus we could calculate the same present worth of the machine by estimating depreciation over the period and the potential earnings on the depreciation fund as it accumulated to the full cost of the machine at the end of 20 years, all at 6 per cent. But the calculations are a good deal more complicated than in the simple approach of the previous paragraph, and they offer no advantage over the simpler method.

So you'd better not pay more than about $688 for the machine if you don't want to get stung. If you stop and think, you'll see why this amount has to be a good deal less than the $1,000 the machine would be worth if it provided the $60 annually in perpetuity. If you have to pay more than about $688, you could earn more on your money by investing it elsewhere at 6 per cent for the 20 years.

One other point is significant in this example. Unless this is a patented machine, others like it can be produced. If the current cost of producing such machines, for example, is only $500, you can be pretty sure that even the $688 price is too high. As long as the price is $688, it will pay to produce more machines like this one. As more are produced, the price will gradually fall. Not until the price falls to $500 will a new equilibrium be established. With lots more machines, the marginal revenue productivity of each will be lower, both because of the law of diminishing returns and because the product of the machine will have flooded the market and will have fallen in price so that the net annual yield per machine will no longer be $60.

To summarize: (1) At any time, the capitalized value of an income-producing asset will be based on its net yield and on the going rate of interest on investments of comparable quality. (2) In the long run, the value of any asset will tend to be equal to its cost of reproduction, although it may vary widely from this figure at any given time.

Valuation of Corporate Stocks.   The same general principle holds in valuing corporate stocks and bonds, which represent claims on income earned by the issuing companies. But don't take your nest egg and rush for the stock market with this new knowledge. Corporate securities are interesting in connection with the capitalization principle especially because they point up so many of the pitfalls. So far, we've assumed that we knew the yield of each asset, its life, and the appropriate going rate of interest. But in the real world all three of these are usually uncertain, certainly on corporate stocks. The yield on most stocks fluctuates from year to year. There is no sure way of telling what it will be for any extended period ahead. Moreover, what rate of interest should we use in capi-

---

[5] Sometimes businesses set up "sinking funds" of the dollars charged as depreciation each year, and invest the sinking fund. More commonly, as was emphasized in the Appendix to Chapter 17, no separate fund is established for the depreciation on any given building or machine; the business merely considers as a current cost the estimated depreciation on its plant and machinery each year.

talizing? The appropriate one is one that prevails on other investments of comparable risk and other characteristics. But you pick it out.

Last, and most important, the market price of stocks is determined by thousands of other people who are all guessing at the same imponderables as you are. Many of them are in the market as speculators, looking for a quick dollar on the price rise rather than for a long-pull investment. There is no reproduction cost to set a fairly stable base level that anyone can count on. The actual market price will reflect what the composite of all those people thinks is going to happen. So you're betting on what other people will bet on, and they in turn are betting on what you and other people will bet on. The stock market is no place for neophytes. The capitalization principle can give you a rough steer and it can help you in comparing different securities. But the much-quoted statement of Bernard Baruch is relevant here:

> If you are ready to give up everything else—to study the whole history and background of the market and all the principal companies whose stocks are on the board as carefully as a medical student studies anatomy. If you can do all that, and, in addition, you have the cool nerves of a great gambler, the sixth sense of a kind of clairvoyant, and the courage of a lion, you have a ghost of a chance.

The point of this section is not to warn you against investing in common stocks, but rather to emphasize the wide range of special factors that may be at work in determining the actual market price of some types of income-producing assets. The analytical framework outlined in the simple cases above can help in most cases, but like all analytical models it gives only a suggestive basis for analyzing any particular situation in detail.

REVIEW—CONCEPTS TO REMEMBER

This is a difficult chapter. Recheck your understanding of the following new concepts:

functional distribution of income	"the interest rate"
rent	rate of return
economic rent	capitalization
quasi-rent	"present worth" of an income stream
interest	

1. "Rent and wages are determined by substantially the same set of supply and demand forces, even though people are human and land is not." Do you agree? If not, what are the main differences?

2. What are the major factors that determine the annual level of savings made by your family? How important is the interest rate in the list?

3. "Rent is an unearned increment for any landowner, since he does not have to do any work for the rent he receives. Therefore the govern-

FOR
ANALYSIS
AND
DISCUSSION

ment should confiscate rents through special taxes." Do you agree? Why or why not?

4. "The profits made by a company on the basis of an exclusive patent are essentially rents, not profits." Do you agree or disagree?

5. Other things equal, would you expect rapid technological advance to raise or lower the long-term rate of interest? Why?

6. Assume that you have $10,000 to invest. How would you go about deciding what is a reasonable rate of interest for you to expect to receive in investing your money?

7. Suppose the Federal Reserve tightens bank reserves and raises the interest rate. Would this increase or decrease real investment, other things equal?

8. Find out the "carrying charge" on some article you are considering buying. Then calculate the interest rate you would be paying on the funds you in effect borrow from the seller. Would you be better off to go and try to borrow the money at a bank? (See the Appendix.)

9. Suppose you inherit an 80-acre tract of farm land. You are uncertain whether to sell it, or to retain it and rent it out. How would you go about comparing the advantages of the two courses of action?

Appendix
Actual and Nominal Interest Rates

Interest rates aren't always what they seem to be. This Appendix is intended to help you protect yourself against some common mistakes through looking at two examples that arise frequently in everyday life.

1. *Installment Charges.* Most goods you buy on installment bear a "carrying charge" to pay the seller for extending credit to you. In essence, this is an interest rate, plus something extra for the nuisance of keeping the books and maybe having to dun you for the money. If you're smart, you'll compare carefully the interest rate hidden in the carrying charge with what the money would cost you if you borrowed it directly elsewhere.

Suppose you buy a $120 rug on the installment plan, with 12 months to pay and a carrying charge of $1 a month, or $12 for the year. This looks like 10 per cent, a reasonable rate for such a loan. But look again. The actual rate is far higher. You pay a dollar each month, but the total amount you have on loan from the store goes down $10 each month. The last month you owe them only $10; yet you are still paying interest at the rate of $12 per year. The actual rate on your unpaid balance during the last month is 120 per cent per annum. The average for the year is 20 per cent, just twice the apparent rate, since the average loan to you is just half the purchase price of the rug.

The actual rate each month is calculated in the following table:

	Unpaid Balance	*Interest ($1 Monthly; $12 per Year)*	*Interest Rate on Unpaid Balance*
1st month	$120	$12	10.0%
2nd month	110	12	10.9
3rd month	100	12	12.0
4th month	90	12	13.3
5th month	80	12	15.0
6th month	70	12	17.1
7th month	60	12	20.0
8th month	50	12	24.0
9th month	40	12	30.0
10th month	30	12	40.0
11th month	20	12	60.0
12th month	10	12	120.0

2. Bond Yields.   Suppose you're thinking of buying a hypothetical corporation bond that pays 4 per cent. It is a $1,000 face value bond, so the annual interest is $40. Its current market price is $1,100, and it is due in 10 years. Your alternative is putting the money into U.S. Savings Bonds, which pay about 3¾ per cent. Assume that the two investments are equally safe and attractive on all other grounds. Which one should you choose?

At first glance, the corporate bond seems to win hands down. But look again. You pay $1,100 for the bond, but you'll only get back $1,000 at the end of 10 years. To get the true net yield, you need to "write off" $10 of the value of the bond each of the 10 years, so your actual net annual yield would be only $30 rather than $40. Now you can calculate the exact yield on the corporate bond. It's $30 per year on $1,100 invested. This figures out to 2.7 per cent, appreciably under 3¾ per cent. Better buy the Savings Bond if yield over the next 10 years is your main goal.

But this example suggests still another warning. What if inflation seems likely over the years ahead? If it does, you'd better take it into account. As between the two bonds, it presumably won't make any difference, because the dollar yield of both is fixed over the period. But it may lead you to reconsider whether you want to buy a bond at all. With inflation ahead, the variable dollar yield of common stocks looks better relative to bonds than in stable-price periods. Wise investment is a complex problem.

Profits

This chapter is short, not because profits are unimportant, but because they have been discussed through all the preceding chapters. Indeed, profits are the carrot that entices the businessman to carry out his social functions of innovating and organizing productive resources in the most efficient manner to give consumers what they want, when and where they want it—just as competition is the prod that pushes him from behind. Still, since profits are the mainspring of a private-enterprise economy, it's well while to pull together what's been said about them—how they come to be and what their role is in our system.

THE ROLE OF PROFITS Profit means different things to different people. *In this book, we, as economists, have consistently used it to mean the excess of income over all "economic" costs (including in costs a "normal" return on investment). In this sense, profit (plus or minus), is a residual—what's left over for the entrepreneur after he has met all his costs.*

612

The individual businessman who predicts most successfully what the consumer will want, who meets consumer demand most effectively, who handles his production most efficiently, who buys his labor and materials most adroitly, will end up with the biggest profit. The inefficient producer who fails to respond promptly and efficiently to consumers' demands is likely to end up with red ink on his books. If a seller has a partial or complete monopoly position, he may be able to maintain positive economic profits over a substantial period without innovation, real productive efficiency, or close adaptation to consumer demands. But wherever other firms are free to enter the market, competition will tend to bid prices down and costs up, eliminating economic profits. The desire for profits plays a central organizing role for the entire economy.

Other people may have different notions about what profits are. If you ask a businessman what he means by profit, he'll probably tell you about the same thing as the economist, except that the businessman won't say excess over *economic* costs. His accounting profits will ordinarily be larger than our economic profits, because he has not charged interest on his own or the stockholders' invested funds before calculating profits. He may have handled depreciation in a way that doesn't reflect actual economic costs very accurately, and there may be other such differences.

If you ask a government statistician what profits are, he'll probably give you aggregate corporate profits (defined substantially as businessmen define them), plus possibly the incomes of unincorporated businesses (which to the economist are a mixture of profits, interest, and wages of the men who run their own businesses or professional establishments).

If you ask the man in the street, he probably won't be very sure just what profit does mean, but there's a good chance he'll have a mildly antagonistic attitude. Public-opinion polls suggest this public attitude toward profits.

But which ever definition you use, just about everyone agrees that the main function of profits in a private-enterprise system is to give businessmen and investors an incentive to produce efficiently what consumers want. This is the function we have emphasized.

Are Profits an Effective Incentive?   With professional managers (rather than owner-operators) increasingly taking over the job of running big businesses, some people question whether profit is still the most effective incentive to innovation and efficiency. The modern corporation president gets a salary plus a bonus dependent on profits, but as president he gets only a fraction of 1 per cent of the company's total profits. What motivates him? Moreover, the job big businessmen themselves do is mainly to organize and direct production. The wage-earners and salaried employees, who do the great bulk of the company's work, have to have their carrots too if the over-all job is to be done, and company profits may not rate very high on their motivation lists. So it may be easy to overrate the importance of profits as a stimulus to efficient production of the goods and services people want. But it would be easy to underrate their importance, too.

One thing is especially important to keep in mind. It's the *expectation* of profits that must be there to make the system tick, not the achievement of profits. In fact, there is some doubt whether *economic* profits over the past century have been a significant positive figure for the system as a whole, and even accounting profits over the long pull are a lot smaller than you might guess. This is a profit *and loss* system. Many a firm has gone broke. In prosperous times like the 1940's and 1950's it is easy to forget the big losses incurred across the board during past depressions.

Statistics on the rate of business failures even in prosperity are amazing. During 1958, for example, failures of incorporated businesses averaged over 1,000 per month. Total liabilities of these 1958 failures were well over a half-billion dollars. Failures among unincorporated businesses are very high. Yet each year new thousands rush in, confident that they have the knack to succeed where others have failed. Big-business failures are less common than among small firms. People who have $50 million or $100 million to venture are rare, and profitability calculations on such investments are made with a great deal more care. But even here the story is far from one of unbroken success. Think of the automobile industry, with its spectacular growth over the present century. The Oakland, Stanley Steamer, Maxwell, Hupmobile, and dozens of others were once as much household words as Ford and Pontiac are today. Yet only a quarter-century later they are as extinct as the dodo.

But hope and high expectation apparently spring eternal in the American entrepreneur's breast. Perhaps entrepreneurs are by nature overoptimistic people. Their optimism leads to a good deal of waste in resources devoted to ventures that don't succeed. But it also helps give the American economy the dynamic vigor that has pushed the American standard of living far above its nearest competitor. It is doubtful that dynamic progress in a private-enterprise system is possible without widespread losses from bad business guesses as well as widespread profits from good ones.

Management, Entrepreneurship, and Profits.   Increasingly, the job of making profits in the modern economy falls on professional managers. The return to these men is more "wages of management" than profit. Most of them work on some sort of bonus plan, however, which means that they share directly in profits and lose take-home pay when profits drop. Stockholders, who put up most of the capital and who collect most of the profits when there are any, are a very passive type of entrepreneur in most modern corporations. Thus, where to draw the line between profits, interest, and wages of management is an insoluble question, unless we arbitrarily adopt some rule of division—for example, like the one accountants use for tax purposes. The functions of management, entrepreneurship, and providing capital are thoroughly entangled in modern business firms. Just to whom and for what profits are a return is hard to separate out. It's no wonder that popular discussion about how big profits should be often generates more heat than light.

In a *static* economy, without technological advance, population change, capital accumulation, and changing consumer wants, only monopoly profits would continue. Competition would gradually eliminate all other *economic* profits as resources were shifted into high-profit industries. Capitalization would bid up the prices and rents of especially productive resources until the rate of return on them was equal to that on other resources. Throughout the entire economy, economic profits would be eliminated when equilibrium was achieved, except for those industries where new businesses were prevented from entering.[1] There, and there only, monoply profits would continue. In effect, monopoly profits would be a kind of rent on exclusive monopoly position.

But continuous, unpredictable change is the dominant characteristic of the real world. Uncertainty is everywhere. New inventions, changing demands, international repercussions, new products, political realignments, new raw materials, technological advance—all these and many more confront the entrepreneur every day. He must somehow "guesstimate" the future demand for his product, his future costs, future changes in technology, future behavior of his competitors. Then he must keep an eagle eye out for how the government is going to behave— on taxes, government spending, antitrust policy, labor relations, and international affairs. In the midst of all this, he needs to worry about keeping his costs below those of competitors, keeping the union at least tolerably happy, being sure that his sales organization is on its toes, and so on.

If he does all these things better than his competitors, he'll end up with a good profit. If he misses on many of the important decisions, the red ink will appear. The biggest job of the modern entrepreneur is to live with and make the best of uncertainty. If he doesn't thrive on this kind of life, he'd better save himself a big doctor bill for ulcers and go to work for somebody else.

Insurable Risk and Uncertainty. Many kinds of risk can be insured against. In this way, the uncertainty can be eliminated by incurring a known dollar cost. The best-known example is the risk of loss from fire or theft. Without insurance, this uncertainty would be a major problem for any business concern. But the likelihood of fire loss is reasonably predictable for a large number of buildings of any given type, even though it is highly unpredictable for any given building. By pooling together the moderate insurance premiums on a large number of

---

[1] Though accounting profits would of course continue, since they do not take into account all "economic" costs, including a normal return on stockholders' investment.

buildings, the insurance company has enough funds to pay off the fire losses on those few buildings that do burn each year. Long experience has reduced the likelihood of such occurrences to a scientific, statistical basis. Any business can now convert this type of uncertainty into a known cost through insurance.[2]

Professor Frank H. Knight has pointed out that insurable risks are really only another business cost to be included with other business costs, and that economic profits arise only from bona-fide cases of uncertainty. Economic profits beyond profits on monopoly positions, he argues, are thus analytically linked solely to a world of dynamic change and uncertainty.

Economic Profits and Dynamic Change.   Since both "economic" and "accounting" profits arise largely out of dynamic change and uncertainty, much of what happens to profits is outside the control of any individual manager or entrepreneur. The biggest profits arise in booms, the biggest losses in depressions. "Windfall profits" are widespread in the rising phase of the business cycle; in a lusty boom, it's pretty hard for any reasonably well-situated business to avoid making good profits. In a bad depression, the best management in the world has a tough time making ends meet. The business cycle—inflation and deflation—may well be the biggest single cause of profits and losses. The manager who can outguess business fluctuations and adjust successfully to them is worth his weight in gold.

Changes in consumer demand for individual products are a second big area of change largely outside the control of the individual businessman. Even General Motors is going to have a tough time making profits on automobiles if consumers decide they are going to ride in airplanes and helicopters instead. But the alert entrepreneur here is far from helpless. He can change his product to keep in step with the times, and, through his marketing methods, he can influence what consumers want to buy.

Changes in costs are a third big area of uncontrollable uncertainty. What happens to the price of steel is pretty much outside the control of Philco; yet steel represents one of the major costs in making Philco refrigerators. The same thing is true of most other materials costs, and of labor costs as well. The businessman can bargain with his local union, but he isn't going to get far with a wage rate much below the rates that prevail elsewhere for similar work.

The Profits of Innovation.   One noted economist, Joseph Schumpeter, has argued that profits boil down largely to payment for keeping a jump ahead of your competitors through innovation. The big profits come from big, successful innovations—the motor car, the radio, the diesel engine, and so on. The innova-

---

[2] Very large firms may "self-insure." If a firm has hundreds of buildings itself, it may figure that the predictable likelihood of fire loss in any given year is less than the cost of buying commercial insurance on them.

tor needs both an idea and the ability to get it into operation. An invention or an idea alone makes no profits. But the utilization of that invention, if it leads to lower costs or to a successful new product, brings dollars into the coffers.

Unfortunately, no one has yet figured out a sure way of telling in advance whether a new mousetrap or a new railway car will succeed. First, there is the technological problem of developing the idea into a usable process or product. When this is licked, there is still that capricious monarch of all he surveys—the consumer. Business history tells a fascinating story of the sure things that flopped, and the thousand-to-one shots that are the industrial giants of today.

Successful innovation in effect gives a temporary monopoly to the innovator. Like other monopoly profits, the economic profits of innovation persist only until competitors catch up and bring down profits in the industry to competitive levels. But innovations are often protected by patents that safeguard the innovator for years. And a running start on your competitor is often more important than the legal protection of patents. The firm with the know-how and experience that go with a new product or a new method is likely to have a new innovation at hand by the time competitors catch up on the last one. The continuing success of the industrial giants of today—General Motors, General Electric, Standard Oil, DuPont—rests at least as much on this kind of continuing innovation as on any other single factor.

Profits and Wages in a Dynamic Economy. Wages and profits are the two biggest shares of the national income. In every bargaining session, labor complains that wages are too low, the businessmen that profits aren't large enough to provide a reasonable return on investment and stimulate further growth. Both know that their joint welfare depends on *both* high wages and high profits; yet each would like to have more for himself.

This persistent struggle has been the recurrent theme of this section on income distribution, and indeed of much of our macro-economic analysis of problems of inflation, unemployment, and economic growth. How big must profits be to assure stable economic growth, high-level employment without inflation? This is the $64,000 question. There is no simple answer. But by now you should have the major issues well in mind. We'll take a summary look in the next chapter.

CONCLUSION Profits go largely to those who manage most efficiently to give consumers what they want in a world of continuous change. How big do profits have to be to give the incentives to management and entrepreneurs that we need for a dynamic, progressive, private-enterprise economy? Nobody knows. Profits are big enough when entrepreneurs act as if they are big enough. What matters is the desire of businessmen to innovate and to run efficient enterprises aimed at meeting consumer demands, within the economic-social-political framework established by our democratic processes.

A lot of people nowadays say that individual and corporation income tax rates are so high that there's no use working too hard, no use taking big risks when the government takes most of the profit and shoulders you with any loss. This argument may sound reasonable to you when you look at the 52 per cent tax rates applicable to corporate incomes and the peak 91 per cent marginal rates applicable to high personal incomes. Others complain that labor grabs all the gains from good management and new capital investment.

But there are many incentives to fine management and pioneering entrepreneurship. Pride in achievement, the social acclaim for success, traditions of sound management, the development of professional standards, the pure joy of risk-taking—all these and others like them may be as powerful as the purely monetary incentive of profits, especially if a substantial chunk of profit incentive remains as well. And one of the attributes of a shrewd businessman is the ability to manage affairs so as to take advantage of every possibility the law provides for minimizing taxes.

Human motivation is a very complex affair, and it varies widely from person to person. The long hours of unpaid toil that millions put in each year for causes they think are worth while are impressive evidence that money is far from everything. And the billions we spend each year on gambling devices we know are loaded against us provide impressive evidence of our love for risk-taking. The Irish Sweepstakes, slot machines, parimutuel betting on races—all are publicly announced to pay out less than the contestants put in. Yet there is always the chance that you will be a big winner. If so many of us are willing to gamble when we know that as a group we *must* lose, perhaps it is not strange that entrepreneurs continue their business risk-taking undaunted. For with business innovation there is no reason to suppose that the dice are loaded against entrepreneurs in the aggregate. Indeed, the long record of rapid growth in the economy points strongly the other way.

FOR
ANALYSIS
AND
DISCUSSION

1. "By and large, continuing profits for any firm demonstrate that it is doing a good job in satisfying consumer demand." Do you agree or disagree? Explain.

2. Higher profits generally encourage more rapid economic growth. They also tend to increase the inequality of income. Suppose you favor both more rapid growth and more equality in the distribution of income. What measures would you advocate to achieve the two goals simultaneously, or are they basically incompatible?

3. "So long as we let businessmen think they have a chance to make profits, it doesn't matter whether they actually make any profits or not." Is this a sound analysis of the incentive role of business profits?

4. "The really successful entrepreneur is the one who can guess right most of the time on the business cycle, since cyclical fluctuations are the biggest source of profits and losses." Do you agree or disagree? What is your evidence? Insofar as you agree, should you as a potential business-man concentrate on studying business cycles rather than business administration?

5. If profits would tend to be eliminated under pure competition, how could we expect a purely competitive system to get goods produced and distributed?

6. DuPont is commonly said to maintain its large profits through stay-ing ahead of its competitors on research and patents. Insofar as this is correct, are the profits shown on DuPont's income statements in fact profits or rents on their exclusive know-how?

7. "Present high corporation income taxes are killing the goose that lays the golden eggs. If we want to protect the dynamic nature of the American economy we must waste no time in reducing corporation taxes." Do you agree or disagree? What is your evidence?

8. Who actually gets the profits made by American corporations? (Refer back to Chapter 17 for some of the relevant information.)

34

Wage-Price Policy and the Role of Government

The preceding chapters have considered at length the problem of economic growth and fluctuations, and what stabilizing government monetary-fiscal policy can do. They have considered the intricate workings of the price system in allocating resources and in getting consumer wants satisfied at minimum costs. They have analyzed the ways in which these same markets distribute incomes as wages, profits, and rents.

Throughout, the persistent struggle of workers, management, and property-owners for wages and profits has played a central role. If monetary-fiscal policy cannot provide reasonably stable growth without inflation, it is probably largely because unions and businessmen press too strongly to increase their incomes. When the price system fails in allocating resources efficiently and getting goods produced at the lowest feasible costs, it is often because businessmen distort demand or seek monopolistic positions in the search for higher profits, while workers push up costs through wage demands and output-restrictive behavior. When the market place for labor exhibits smouldering resentment, or erupts into violent conflict, it is the continuing struggle over wage and profit shares that is generally near the center.

What is sound wage-price-profit policy? Does the way we handle the basic issues of wages and profits need drastic revision? Should the government take a larger hand in slicing up the national income pie between wage and profits? If it should do more, what?

WAGE-PRICE POLICY IN THE AMERICAN ECONOMY

The Traditional View: Perfect Wage-Price Flexibility. Why doesn't the private-enterprise economy maintain substantially full employment on its own? Until a quarter-century ago, most economists would have answered promptly, something like this: If all prices and wages are flexible, unemployment will automatically be eliminated. Asking prices will fall until demand absorbs all products and resources seeking markets, and full employment will be restored. Only those unwilling to work or sell at the new prices will be idle. The only real reason for unemployment is that workers ask wages higher than marginal productivity. If all prices and wages could be made completely flexible, the unemployment problem would be solved. Wage and price rigidity is the villain!

As a practical solution, this remedy to the problem of unemployment is hard to accept. Given a downward start from prosperity, a completely flexible system (without any check on monetary contraction) might well plummet downward in an all-enveloping spiral of liquidation and deflation. Most evidence, and logic, suggest that the spiral would stop short of zero prices for everything. But what happens to the money supply is a critical question here. If the money supply stays constant, its increasing purchasing power as prices fall will help check the decline. But if the banking system is engulfed in a wave of deflation and credit contraction, the downward spiral will worsen rather than halt.

In any case, such a downward spiral would be (and has been) enormously disruptive. Although a downturn *might* be checked by quick price and wage declines, this outcome is uncertain in a world of cumulative expectation changes, monetary contraction, and inventory speculation. General deflation is a dubious remedy for unemployment.

A final difficulty with the complete-flexibility remedy is this: How could we achieve it even if we wanted it? There are too many areas where competition has been dethroned, often with public approval and aid. Wage rates, utility rates, freight rates, coal prices, and agricultural prices are already supported by legislative enactment, to say nothing of unions and business groups. Perfectly flexible interest rates, rents, taxes, and salaries are equally hard to imagine.

Unions, Business Monopolies, and the Wage-Price Spiral. *Perfect* competition and *perfect* wage-price flexibility in commodity and labor markets seem out of the question. But with unions and businesses pushing up both wages and prices in the face of underemployment and unused capacity, widespread demands have developed to weaken the power of both union and business monopolies. Economists debate inconclusively how important wage-push and administered prices are in the inflationary creep. But many men in the street are convinced they are the basic cause of inflation. And government officials are painfully aware of the likely speed of wage and price increases if strong expansionary monetary-fiscal measures are used to wipe out underemployment.

Many argue that wage bargaining should be restored to a local, or at least regional, level. With unions and business as big as in the steel, auto, and coal industries, the power of each side is enormous. A strike can cripple the economy, and bring enormous pressure for inflationary wage increases. Moreover, big business can readily pass the new higher costs on to consumers through price increases. Thus, the result is gains in both wages and profits, at the expense of the consumer. In monopolistic and oligopolistic industries, the big firms all sign about the same wage agreements and all pass along the higher costs to consumers, with little likelihood that any one firm will stand out against the wage and price increases.

Breaking up unions and business monopolies might lessen inflationary pressures. But labor and price experts have doubts, short of truly drastic measures. Unless big businesses were split into many new firms, they would still have to bargain with large union groups. Unions and employers would still be likely to settle on substantial wage increases, as long as the businessman was reasonably sure his wage settlement would not be much larger than his competitor's. No employer, large or small, wants to take a strike just to hold down the national cost of living. He wants to keep production going, and will pay higher wages if he's reasonably sure the resulting higher prices won't cut his share of the market. To reduce unions in size below the level of the entire business firm with which they bargain, in order to obtain small-unit local bargaining, would drastically undermine their power vis-à-vis employers. Lastly, at least with present industrial arrangements, large-scale industry-wide bargaining (for example, in the steel industry) has been not significantly more or less inflationary than firm-level bargaining (for example, in the auto and electrical industries).

The upshot is that, at least now, no drastic action to break up either unions or management into smaller units for wage bargaining seems likely, in spite of widespread criticism of both unions and business. But weaker measures, to bring public pressure more effectively to bear against inflationary wage and price increases, may be more likely. These are considered in the later section on direct government controls.

Wage Cuts or Higher Wages to Maintain Employment?   *Wage Cuts.* Big unions and big business are probably here to stay. Extensive downward wage and price flexibility is unlikely. But modest wage cuts may not be out of the question in depressed industries, and price cuts are a possibility in weak markets. Certainly the rate of wage increases is much affected by the level of unemployment in the bargaining industries.

Suppose the economy is soft. Demand for consumer durables is weak; investment spending is slackening; unemployment is uncomfortably large. Some economists and businessmen suggest: Now's the time for a modest wage cut, to pull down costs and permit some price bargains that will lure the customers. Or at least, they say, it's the time to forego wage increases.

Is this sound advice? The basic problem is, as we have seen, to get total spending high enough to provide jobs for all at prevailing wage rates. If wages are cut, or held stable as productivity rises, will this boost the two major components of private spending—consumption and investment?

1. Consumption first. Consumption spending will rise if incomes rise, and incomes will rise if businessmen in fact spend more on wages after the wage cut than before—that is, if the demand for labor is elastic. The number of new workers employed must more than offset the lower wage per worker. This may happen if lower wages improve business profit expectations enough to justify the increased employment and output. Or even if total payrolls don't rise, if prices and total sales remain the same with lower wages increased profits may lead to increased consumption spending by dividend receivers. But only part of profits are paid out in dividends, and those mainly to the upper-income groups. So this profits channel toward more consumption spending doesn't look very promising.

Or lower wages may lead businessmen to cut prices. Will this stimulate consumer buying? The answer is probably yes—but whether total consumption spending rises depends on the elasticity of consumer demand. Thus, the elasticity of demand for final products is a major factor in determining the elasticity of demand for labor. In looking at the demand for final products, the reason for the incipient recession is important. If the cause is a saturated market in consumer durables—for example, an 8-million-car year as in 1955—moderate price cuts on cars aren't likely to draw out a new flood of consumer buying. Under other circumstances, price bargains may increase total consumer spending more.

2. How about investment? We looked in detail at the motivations underlying investment decisions back in Chapter 11. Lower costs, other things unchanged, should encourage more investment. But present wage costs are only one element in the profit picture. And remember that investment decisions hinge on expectations. Would most businessmen view a general wage cut as a major step toward renewed prosperity and economic growth, or as a probable precursor of deflation and recession? No general answer is feasible. Each case needs to be looked at individually.

3. If signs of a downturn are centered in particular areas, special wage-price reductions in these areas might help to maintain over-all employment. Wage cuts in a weak construction industry to permit lower prices might stimulate consumer

buying, provide increased employment for construction workers, and give a broad expansionary impetus to the entire economy. Cost-price reductions in a crucial out-of-line sector of the economy look a good deal more promising for encouraging renewed spending than do economy-wide cuts in wages and prices.

Wage Increases. Wage cuts to maintain employment are of doubtful value, and in any case extremely hard to get. What about the other approach—that wages should be *raised* to stimulate spending and employment?

Union leaders hammer away at one proposition: Wages are the biggest single source of buying power in our economy. The major cause of depression, therefore, is wages that are too low, not too high. If wages don't rise fast enough, profits will swell and income will be saved, not spent. Dave MacDonald of the Steelworkers in 1959 waged a major public-relations campaign that a billion-dollar wage boost would be a boon to businessmen and workers everywhere through the increased spending it would generate.

Are the unions right that higher wages are the way to fight recession? The answer hinges on much the same considerations outlined just above. Is the demand for labor elastic or inelastic? If it's inelastic, higher wage rates increase total wage payments, which may in turn increase consumption spending. But if it's elastic, higher wage rates mean less total take-home pay for workers. In the short run, higher wages probably don't change very much the number of workers hired *unless* they lead to higher prices and reduced consumer buying. But businesses do generally pass on higher wage costs in higher prices, so we're back to the question of the elasticity of *consumer* demand in predicting the elasticity of demand for labor. Over the longer pull, it's clear that higher wages steadily push the substitution of machinery for labor.

In any case, don't be trapped by the obvious fallacy that business profits represent savings withdrawn from the income stream. Many business profits flow directly into investment spending, and there is no necessary reason for classifying big profits as a deflationary force. What matters for economic health is total spending on consumption plus investment, not just consumption.

Where does this leave us on the advantages of a high-wage policy? Uncertain, as in the preceding section. Here again, the results of expansionary monetary-fiscal action are a good deal more predictable than the results of any type of wage-price policy. One thing is sure: Even if rising wages stimulate spending and employment in the short run, without an increasing money supply rapidly rising wages will sooner or later lead to unemployment and recession, as total spending falls below what is required to provide full employment at steadily rising prices.

Thus, in the short run optimal wage-price policy to stimulate employment is unclear. The best answer depends on the particular circumstances. Realistically, the issue is generally whether wage rates should go up faster or slower. Wage cuts receive little support on the modern American scene, even among employers. And with increasing productivity, workers, management, and the public all know that wages can rise steadily without necessarily eating into profits or requiring higher product prices. Thus, problems of short-run wage-price policy become inextricably intermingled with the fundamental long-run questions of who will get how much of the growing national product, and what division of the national product is most conducive to rapid economic growth without inflation.

WAGES, PROFITS, AND PRODUCTIVITY

A free price system gives people incomes roughly corresponding to the value of the contributions they make, with economic profits a residual. But everybody knows the free price system is shot through with quasi-monopolies and rigidities. And people are increasingly unwilling to let the free market determine their shares of the national income pie. Prices and wages are widely administered. They are administered to get more for the people and groups doing the administering.

Economic growth and productivity are central to the American economic process. Real output grows 3 or 4 per cent a year on the average. Of this, 2 to 3 per cent is generally increase in productivity—that is, increase in the output produced by the same number of workers. Over a decade, increasing productivity may account for a hundred billion dollars of additional income. Who should get this bonanza? How should it be divided between wages, profits, and other income shares? What is the right basis for determining wage increases at bargaining time, or when the government intervenes—productivity, ability to pay, or contribution to over-all economic stability?

Four major alternatives of wage-price policy are evident.

1. *Stable price level and rising money wages.* Perhaps the most popular notion nowadays is that wages should be based on productivity increases, and that with this wage policy the price level could be held stable. Assume for the moment three big income groups—wage-earners, profit-receivers, and fixed-income recipients. They are the worker, the capitalist, and the widow. Suppose that average productivity output per worker and total output both rise 3 per cent and money wages are increased 3 per cent. Then the workers and the capitalists divide the increased output between them, as wages and profits both rise. (Note that the wage increase buys only the wage share of the increased output.) The widows are no worse off (except relatively), but certainly no better. Their fixed incomes will buy just the same as last year, since prices are stable. But they get no share of the increase. Over-all, national income has risen 3 per cent in both money and real terms.

Many people look upon this as the ideal solution. They say that wages ought to rise just as fast as productivity, and no faster. Then we can preserve full employment without inflation, and both workers and owners get a fair share of the increase. But there are problems.

First, if you don't think the present income distribution between wages and profits is fair, preserving it won't necessarily be very attractive. Many union members believe that profits are already exorbitant, and that business has the ability to pay much more without raising prices. Businessmen are understandably reluctant to see higher wages erode profits.

Second, how about the fixed-income people—the pensioners and old folks? Should they share in the fruits of progress?

Third, as a guide to noninflationary wage policies, the rule looks deceptively simple. Productivity increases very widely from industry to industry. If individual unions push for productivity-based settlements and the pattern-setting unions are in high-productivity industries, the pattern may be set at a 6 per cent annual wage increase, though the average productivity rise for the economy is only half that. As this wage rate spreads through other bargains, it is highly inflationary indeed. Never forget that wages are set in individual firm and industry bargaining, where both sides are trying to get all they can. Fine issues of national policy and equity for wage-earners and profit-takers on the national scene get talked about in the publicity releases, but they're not what determines the settlement in the showdown.

2. *Falling prices and stable money wages.* A second alternative is product prices falling apace with improving productivity as unit costs are reduced. Under this alternative, money wages would stay constant, but workers would benefit from technological progress through falling prices for the goods they buy. Again assume a 3 per cent annual productivity increase. Prices could then fall 3 per cent each year, and both money wages, money profits, and money national income would be unchanged, while real national income rose 3 per cent. This way fixed-income receivers would share in the fruits of progress through falling prices. The increased output would be divided up among workers, capitalists, *and* widows.

Here again there are loud objections. First, why should the non-workers share in the fruits of economic progress which comes from our hard work, say many workers and owners. Second, here again productivity increases vary widely. The industries advancing fastest in productivity would cut their prices sharply for the benefit of others, but would gain little of the benefit themselves except insofar as they bought their own products. Third, and perhaps more important, wouldn't falling prices act as a drag on economic growth and efficiency? Often, falling prices have been associated with declining business activity. Rising wages and profits make people feel better, spend more, and invest more, it is argued. Lastly, even if it were desirable, realistically how could you ever enforce a national policy of falling prices and constant money wages? Businessmen would fight cutting their prices at every turn, and who can imagine unions and union leaders being content with no wage increase at all year after year?

3. *Stable prices and stable money wages.* If both product prices and money wages remain stable, all the gain from increasing productivity goes to profits. While some businessmen might like this, it doesn't get many other supporters.

Something like this occurred during the 1920's. Looking back, many economists call it "profit inflation," and argue that it overstimulated investment and stock-market speculation as profits soared, leading to the collapse of 1929.

4. *Rising price level and rising money wages: inflation.* The fourth alternative is inflation. Here the total share of wages plus profits is the highest of any alternative, since rising prices cut down the real buying power of the fixed-income group. Workers and capitalists get all the benefits of economic progress plus some of what the widows had before. What happens to the *relative* shares of wages and profits depends on how fast wages rise relative to product prices.

Chapter 7 looked at the effects of inflation in some detail. While moderate inflation is far less disruptive than is often claimed, most people consider its redistributional effects inequitable, and fear the possibility that "a little inflation" may turn into a runaway spiral. Certainly inflation based on speculation and large credit expansion threatens collapse and recession. A few economists have argued that moderate inflation, of a few per cent a year, is a beneficial social lubricant. It stimulates economic growth, they say; avoids the painful pressures of deflation and wage cuts where demand falls; and eases the transfer of resources into new industries by bidding resources away through higher wages and profits. Moreover, gently squeezing out the *rentier* class is good, this argument runs. Inflation gradually wipes out the deadening burden of debt.

Which of these alternatives is the most equitable? Make up your own mind. The issues are reasonably clear. The stakes are big.

THE PROBLEM OF MAINTAINING STABLE GROWTH WITHOUT INFLATION

Equity is only part of the problem in deciding on the best long-run wage-price policy. Which policy will do the most to promote stable economic growth without undue inflation, ruling out alternative (4) for the moment?

This is a complex problem, about which we have been talking off and on through a good share of the book. In brief summary, there are two main sets of issues here: How fast should wages grow *relative* to profits, and how fast should the *combined* total of profits and wages (i.e., roughly the national income) grow?

1. How fast should wages grow relative to profits? Here we first need to rank our main goals. Take our three old friends: (a) rapid growth; (b) avoidance of unemployment and depression; and (c) over-all price stability.

If the main goal is (a) rapid economic growth, the answer is, not too fast. For rapid growth, clearly a little profit inflation is a fine thing, to stimulate more investment. Better be sure the unions don't get too much.

But if profits and investment get *too* large relative to wages and consumption spending, the boom is likely to collapse. Then we're in trouble on objective (b)

—the avoidance of underemployment and recession. If preventing unemployment is the main problem, it's less clear that wage restraint is the best policy. Here we're back with the problems of the first section of this chapter—and no very conclusive answer. Wages are purchasing power. But so are profits.

On this point, the central problem was succinctly stated by a famous economist at the end of World War II, when the general concern was avoiding depression, rather than inflation. He wrote:

> It seems likely that the total amount of profits in an economy such as ours is subject to both maximum and minimum limits. Both are presumably rather elastic and capable of shifting with changes in business psychology and business risks, and in the spending-saving habits of the population. The minimum is the amount necessary to afford sufficient incentive to invest. The maximum is the amount beyond which people and business receiving these concentrated incomes will undertake to save more than can be invested, with resulting idle funds and shrinking total income and employment. The interesting question is what will happen if the maximum gets below the minimum, if, in order to avoid oversaving, total profits must be so low as to afford insufficient incentive to invest, by current business standards. In a very rich country, this dilemma seems entirely possible. In that case, something would have to give.[1]

What should give? It is hard to say. Perhaps it can most easily be investors' idea of the return they feel they must have to make it worth their while to continue investing. But this is more easily said than done. The main point is that it is combined consumption-investment spending that must be kept growing roughly in balance with total full-employment output, and that if either investment (profits) or consumption (wages) gets too far out of line with the other, we're in for trouble.

The third goal of sound wage-price policy was (c) to avoid inflation. Here the fight rages in today's labor-management negotiations. Management says rising wages push up costs and force price increases. Unions say that management can well afford to pay higher wages out of swollen profits without raising prices. Here we're back at the old questions of productivity and ability to pay as criteria for wage increases.

Productivity increases provide a rough measure of the wage increase any firm can afford to give without pushing up its prices, *so long as* the present level of profits is a proper one. But the present level of profits may be either unjustifiably high or low. Moreover, productivity increases vary widely from firm to firm and year to year. Wage increases which are noninflationary for General Motors in a particular year may be highly inflationary when spread to the rest of the economy, or even for General Motors another year if the productivity rate slows down. Here again, there is no simple answer to just how fast wages can rise without pushing prices up, given any rate of productivity increase. Clearly wage in-

---

[1] J. M. Clark, in *Financing American Prosperity* (New York: Twentieth Century Fund, 1945), p. 108.

creases far beyond productivity increases put strong pressures on management to raise prices; profits can be squeezed some, but no management can afford to see its profits vanish.

2. How fast should the *combined* total of wages and profits grow? Here one of our three policy goals has been increasingly questioned. Some ask, shouldn't a little inflation be *encouraged* to stimulate growth and to permit both money wages and profits to grow faster than real output?

Here merely a brief reminder, harking back to Chapter 7, is in order. Historical evidence suggests there is no clear relationship between inflation and the rate of economic growth. Moderate inflation has apparently stimulated economic growth when there has been a wage lag behind rising prices, leading to higher profits and investment. But rapid growth has also occurred in noninflationary periods—for example, the 1920's. Certainly, insofar as wages rise at least apace with prices in inflation, as they have recently done, there is little reason to expect inflation to stimulate investment and faster growth.

Neither is there clear evidence that moderate inflation either stimulates or reduces current employment and output. Again, examples on both sides of the argument abound. Clearly, speculative, credit-based, runaway inflation is a highly disruptive force, leading to widespread economic waste and collapse. But the economic effects of modern creeping inflation appear to be primarily in redistributing wealth and income, and in easing temporarily the struggle between capital and labor for ever-larger shares of the national income pie. A little inflation brings no major economic disaster. But neither does it do any significant economic good. And its distributional inequities may be highly objectionable. Last, and perhaps most important, a policy of encouraging a little inflation seems certain to increase the inflationary pressures of income-receivers throughout the economy, and to intensify the problems of holding inflation down to a creep.

DIRECT CONTROLS **Direct Action to Check the Wage-Price Spiral.** Restrictive monetary-fiscal policy to check creeping inflation won't work if unions and management keep on pushing up wages and prices in the face of growing unemployment. While wage-push and administered-price inflation can be stopped by monetary-fiscal policy, the cost may be unacceptably widespread unemployment and recession.

In this dilemma, many have suggested some type of direct government action to halt wage and price increases. In the peacetime economy, almost no one is for extensive direct government controls over wages and prices. But plans to require official notice to government agencies of coming wage and price increases, in order to expose these to advance public attention, have obtained considerable support in Congress. One bill would require most corporations to file price increases with the Federal Trade Commission a month before they go into effect. Another would require the Council of Economic Advisers to investigate all proposed wage and price increases that might controvert the purposes of the Employment Act of 1946, and to call such cases to the attention of the president so that he could bring public opinion to bear against them.

Nobody likes these measures very much, not even their sponsors. Both business and labor are generally against them, unless the government pressure is to apply only against the other. Businessmen, more than unions, have generally opposed all such steps on the grounds they are a first step toward direct government controls and away from individual freedom and the free price system. But frustration at our inability to maintain full employment without inflation through the private economy and monetary-fiscal policy alone has led more and more Americans to consider tentative steps toward more government intervention in the wage and price setting process.

Americans don't like any kind of direct control. Under the pressure of war, we tolerate individual price and wage controls, rationing, and government allocation of materials and manpower. But tolerate is the word. Even in war, these controls worked only moderately well. And once peace returns, our enthusiasm for repealing the controls has been paralleled only by our ability to pay little attention to them if they persist beyond the period of popular support.

Although the problems of peacetime and wartime direct government controls over wages and prices are different, in many fundamentals they are the same. A brief look at the World War II experience may thus be useful in thinking through the likely consequences of direct government wage-price intervention on today's scene.

Direct Controls in World War II.

1. During the armament boom of 1940-41 production and income increased rapidly. Acute shortages of materials, facilities, and manpower developed in particular industries long before full employment was reached. Some prices skyrocketed while millions were still unemployed and plants lay idle. Since a repressive fiscal policy seemed undesirable with many unemployed resources still available, individual price ceilings on individual scarce goods were authorized by Congress.

2. As the defense program grew by leaps and bounds, the government had to see that manufacturers of defense products obtained scarce vital materials. Thus "priorities" were established, to ensure that scarce materials would go to defense products ahead of nonessential civilian goods. A high government-granted priority rating gave a producer preference over other users in buying available supplies. Price competition for such scarce supplies was to be eliminated.

3. The priorities system soon proved inefficient. Evasions were commonplace. So the government began to make direct allocations of scarce materials. Producers of scarce materials were directed to supply certain amounts to users designated by the government. No one could be served except by government order. The economists and industrial experts of the government gradually took over the traditional function of the price system in allocating especially scarce resources.

4. Meanwhile, tax increases were too small to check the inflationary pressure. National income and private spending power rose rapidly, but total goods available to consumers increased only gradually as war production took more and more resources. More and more commodities were put under legal price ceilings, and in 1942 the General Maximum Price Regulation was issued, in effect putting ceilings on all prices.

5. Under these arrangements, prices could no longer allocate the available goods. This job had to be done some other way. Consumer rationing, difficult and unattractive as it was, was instituted as the best way to obtain a "fair" distribution of the limited goods available.

With critical materials and all major prices under direct controls, war production was expedited and the price rise was slowed. But difficulties soon arose. First, allocations of critical materials to war uses were very difficult to control without controlling other uses as well. Every producer of "nonessentials," from toasters to pianos, pleaded for just a little more steel, free from allocations. When the pinch became tight, black markets in allocated materials became intermittent war scandals. Second, in spite of general price controls and rationing of "essential" goods, rising incomes put almost irresistible pressure on price ceilings. Black markets and under-the-counter dealings became common. In the political arena, every seller seemed to descend sooner or later on the Office of Price Administration and on his congressman with plaintive or outraged demands for "price relief."

6. With wages, salaries, and profits spurting upward, it was apparent that the purchasing-power was too great to be restrained by price ceilings alone. Thus all wages and salaries were also put under direct control—no wage or salary increases could be granted except under specified circumstances. Price control had come around full circle—all wages and prices were now under ceilings, well supplemented by War Production Board allocations and OPA rationing.

But only wage *rates* could be administratively fixed; take-home pay swelled as a result of longer hours, overtime, and up-grading of jobs into higher pay brackets. Moreover, labor pressure for general wage adjustments to cover increased living costs forced the War Labor Board to approve higher wages to this extent, in addition to increases to correct "gross inequities" or to recognize shifts to more difficult or valuable work.

Thus wage rates crept upward. Take-home pay soared. On the price front, OPA concessions to political pressures and "legitimate" relief demands permitted prices also to creep upward. On the labor front, War Labor Board decisions gradually conceded wage increases, as union pressures grew and ways had to be found to get workers shifted into war jobs.

7. Ultimately, direct manpower controls were added. Workers were frozen in their jobs. Transfers were permitted only from less essential to more essential occupations. Selective-service deferments were granted to "war workers," refused to those in "nonessential" jobs. In default of the free price system, manpower allocation was managed by direct control and by the deferment system, though

control in this area was loose and spotty. The system of direct controls had finally reached to every major segment of the economy.

What lessons can we learn from our wartime experience with direct controls? In summary, these appear to be the most important:

1. Price-fixing can play an important role in restraining inflation, but without major assistance from fiscal-monetary policies to hold down spendable income it can succeed at best only temporarily.

2. "Just a little bit" of direct control to help check major inflationary pressure is unlikely to be practicable. To be effective, direct controls are forced by the intimate interrelationships of prices, materials, and manpower to move in all directions from the original point of impact, wherever it may be.

3. Government rationing, materials allocations, and direct manpower controls are essential if price-fixing incapacitates the price system as a resource allocator.

4. Much of wartime inflation was merely postponed to the postwar period. The war's end found an enormous pent-up demand for consumers' and producers' durables that were unavailable during the war and a huge accumulated supply of liquid assets created by wartime deficit financing. The 1946-51 period saw one of the biggest price rises in United States history, in spite of the huge increase in civilian-goods output over the same period.

These lessons in World War II are suggestive for the future. The economic system behaved very much as fundamental economic analysis suggests it would. Inflation may be suppressed but hardly avoided unless we get at the root of the unbalance between total purchasing power and goods and services available for purchase. With large excess demand, no one is satisfied with his income share, and upward wage-price pressures from all groups intensify the inflation problem. The allocation of resources, finished goods, and incomes cannot be handled by the price system unless we let the price system work, and imposition of widespread price controls merely switches the problem into the area of administrative determination.

What lessons can we draw as to the likely success of government intervention to check creeping inflation by persuasion or limited direct controls? Some economists answer that the World War II experience showed that direct controls are the right approach to restraining inflation. But most others were impressed with the difficulty of making direct controls work without widespread public support, engendered by a sense of urgency; with the political pressures for easing restraints whenever they pinch; and with the need for ever-spreading controls to keep the direct regulation of prices from collapsing. Perhaps some government restraint on creeping inflation could be exercised by requiring advance reporting of price and wage increases, so as to mobilize public opinion against inflationary moves by labor and business. But the World War II experience with direct controls gives little basis for confidence in such informal, voluntary controls without a monetary-fiscal policy that keeps aggregate demand roughly in line with aggregate supply at the desired price level.

1. During the late 1950's, President Eisenhower repeatedly called on both unions and management to exercise restraint in seeking higher wages and prices in order to avoid inflation. Is such a request consistent with the self-interest and profit incentives on which our system rests? If you were a union leader or a businessman, would you forego wage or price increases in response to such a plea?

2. Do you believe that wage increases in excess of productivity increases are inflationary? If so, what would you advocate to halt such inflation?

3. What wage-price policy do you believe is most equitable and best for the country over the long run, on the assumption that productivity increases continue at something like their past rate?

4. The United Steelworkers have repeatedly argued that higher wages are an effective measure to prevent the development of future depressions, since higher wages will provide rising purchasing power and forestall any drop in consumer buying. Do you agree with this argument? Why or why not?

5. It is more important for profits to be adequate than for wages to be increased annually, since without continued business investment there will be no jobs for anyone. Do you agree with this statement from a business magazine? Why or why not?

6. Suppose that with gross national product roughly stable at $500 billion and with full employment in the economy, the government decides to increase its arms spending from $40 billion to $60 billion. Imposition of individual price controls on selected consumer goods is suggested to restrain inflationary pressures, since an increase in taxes is not considered practicable. Would you expect this policy to be successful in restraining inflation? Why or why not?

7. If primary reliance is placed on direct price controls in a situation like that in the preceding question, would you expect that the need for maintaining the controls would become greater or less in two or three years, assuming the government deficit to continue at the same level? Explain.

FOR

ANALYSIS

AND

DISCUSSION

Current Research

Recent research on wages, unions, and the other shares of the national income has been lively, but focused more on descriptive analysis of unions, bargaining, and the behavior of wages, than on the theoretical-econometric approaches which have been prominent in other areas of modern economics. This descriptive-empirical flavor is reflected in the items below, though the sprinkling of more theoretical and statistical pieces is indicative of a gradual shift in research emphasis throughout the field. Here the warning that this is merely a sample in a widely dispersed field is even more necessary than in the research appendices to the other Parts.

Do Unions Really Raise Wages? The impact of unions on wages has long been a major research focus in the labor area and for distribution theory generally. For a recent installment in the continuing controversy, see Lloyd Ulman, "The Union and Wages in Basic Steel," *American Economic Review,* June 1958; and Albert Rees' reply. Professor Rees has summarized the state of research and knowledge on the related issues in "Do Unions Cause Inflation?" in *Labor Problems: Cases and Readings,* G. P. Shultz and J. R. Coleman, editors (McGraw-Hill, 1959).

An approach through the application of modern theory is illustrated by Frederick Meyers, "Price Theory and Union Monopoly," in the *Industrial and Labor Relations Review* for April 1959. Robert Ozanne's "Impact of Unions on Wage Levels and Income Distribution," *Quarterly Journal of Economics,* May 1959, combines theoretical and empirical approaches.

Wage and Distribution Theory. A good place to begin on the modern theory of wages is a volume reporting a conference of many of the world's top labor economists, *The Theory of Wage Determination,* John Dunlop, editor, (Macmillan, 1957). For a recent book aimed at extending the theory of wages and income distribution along relatively traditional lines, try Sidney Weintraub, *An Approach to the Theory of Income Distribution* (Chilton, 1958). A drastically new approach, leading toward simulation of major elements of the economic system on large electronic computers, is introduced by Guy Orcutt, "A New Type of Socio-economic System," *Review of Economics and Statistics,* May 1957. A leading report on wage structure is *The Evolution of Wage Structure,* by Lloyd

Reynolds and Cynthia Taft (Yale University Press, 1956). Then, on the problem of labor's share in the national income, see Robert Solow's statistical analysis, "A Skeptical Note on the Constancy of Relative Shares," *American Economic Review,* September 1958.

Last, another compendium, *New Concepts in Wage Determination,* Frank Pierson and George Taylor, editors (McGraw-Hill, 1957), provides a lively account by a group of the nation's leading labor economists on where our knowledge of this thorny problem stands.

Technological Change, Unions, and Wages.   The impact of technological change on workers and their wages, and conversely the attitudes of workers toward technological change, has long played a central role in both labor-management relations and research about them. For a sample: On the impact of technological change, try F. Pollock, *Automation: A Study of Its Economic and Social Consequences* (Oxford: B. Blackwell, 1957), and Robert L. Aaronson, "Automation—Challenge to Collective Bargaining," in *New Dimensions in Collective Bargaining,* H. W. Davey, editor (Harper, 1959). L. F. Adams and R. L. Aaronson's *Workers and Industrial Change* (Cornell University, 1957) is a detailed analysis of the experience of displaced workers. On the impact of union resistance to technological change, try William Haber and Harold Levinson, *Labor Relations and Productivity in the Building Trades* (University of Michigan Press, 1956).

Union Democracy and Internal Union Processes.   How decisions get made in unions and how much control the individual union member has over union policies have been the subjects of intensive research in recent years, especially since the widespread publicity given by congressional investigations to alleged racketeers and "bosses" in high union positions. In most big strikes, too, the claim is widely heard that the individual union members would go back to work if they really had the say on union policies.

Economists, sociologists, and social psychologists have all participated in the research aimed at answering these questions. Three recent studies give a good cross section: A. S. Tannenbaum and R. L. Kahn, *Participation in Union Locals* (Row Peterson, 1958); Joel Seidman, *et al., The Worker Views His Union* (University of Chicago Press, 1958); and Seymour Lipset, Martin Trow, and James Coleman, *Union Democracy: The Internal Politics of the International Typographical Union* (Free Press, 1956). A noted lawyer, Archibald Cox, analyzes the problem of legal intervention in "The Role of Law in Preserving Union Democracy," *Harvard Law Review,* February 1959. For a report pulling together a wide range of research, and also incidentally illustrating the kind of research study sometimes prepared for congressional committees, see *Government Regulation of Internal Affairs of Unions Affecting the Rights of Members,* a set of selected readings prepared by the Legislative Reference Service of the Library of Congress for the Senate Committee on Labor and Public Welfare (U.S. Government Printing Office, 1958).

International Comparisons.   Many labor economists believe that the changing problems of labor and labor-management relations reflect in large part the continuing industrialization that characterizes most of the modern world. For comparative international studies, try John Dunlop's *Industrial Relations Systems* (Holt, 1958), and Adolph Sturmthal's *Contemporary Collective Bargaining in Seven Countries* (Cornell University Press, 1957). If you want to try studies focused on particular countries, see Charles Myers, *Labor Problems in the Industrialization of India* (Harvard University Press, 1958); S. Levine, *Industrial Relations in Post-War Japan* (University of Illinois Press, 1958); and E. Brown, "Labor Relations in Soviet Factories," *Industrial and Labor Relations Review,* January 1958.

The Public Economy

35

The Public Economy

How far should the government intervene in economic affairs? The influential nineteenth-century English liberals argued that the primary function of the state was merely to set up and enforce certain "rules of the game" under which private enterprise could then be counted on to get goods effectively produced and distributed. At the other extreme, the communists argue that all productive resources should be owned by the state, and that production and distribution should be directed in detail by the government.

The present attitude in America is in between, but much closer to the private-enterprise position. Most Americans believe strongly in capitalism and the virtues of a free, private-enterprise economy. Yet government action has grown far beyond the regulatory duties prescribed by laissez-faire advocates. The five chapters already devoted to government economic policy (Chapters 14, 15, 16, 27 and 34) bespeak the big role of government in modern economic life. But beyond these regulatory and stabilizing activities, government participates *directly* in the stream of economic activity. More taxes have been collected and more services provided by governments at all levels—federal, state, and local. Today, taxes amount to nearly one-fourth of the gross national product.

**GOVERNMENT EXPENDITURES
AND REVENUES**

"Public finance" is thus no longer a minor part of economic life. With total tax collections in 1959 estimated at over $115 billion and government expenditures even larger, how our governments get their funds and spend them has assumed enormous importance. You may not like having government so big, but there it is.

Figure 35-1 gives an over-all picture of the expenditures made by all govern-

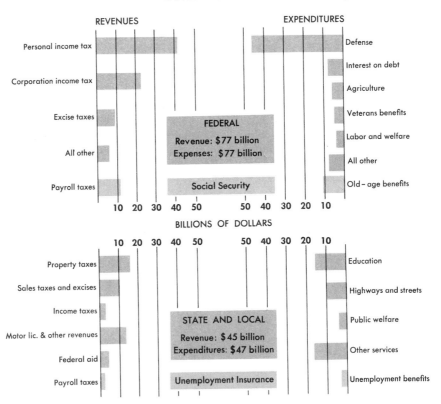

FIG. 35-1   Federal, state, and local governments collected and spent about $120 billion in 1959. Each bar shows the amount of a major tax or expenditure program. Data are preliminary estimates from the President's budget message and made by the author. Chart does not include expenses or revenues of government-operated businesses, such as public utilities or state liquor stores.

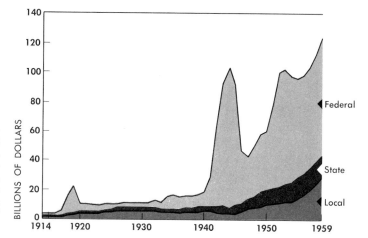

Government Expenditures, 1914-1959

BILLIONS OF DOLLARS

140

120

100

80

60

40

20

0

◀ Federal

State

◀ Local

1914   1920   1930   1940   1950   1959

FIG. 35-2   Federal spending on wars has shot up total government spending fastest. Since Korea, federal spending has not come down much, and state-local spending has risen steadily. (Source: U.S. Treasury and Department of Commerce.)

ments in the United States in 1959, and of the taxes used to finance them. The length of each bar shows the size of the tax or expenditure involved.

Clearly, federal government expenditures and taxes now dominate the picture —about 70 per cent of the total. This was not always so. Every war has brought a vast increase in federal government spending, but in the intervening peace periods state-local expenditures have usually grown again relatively as well as absolutely.

The Growing Role of Government.   Figure 35-2 provides a little historical perspective. It shows federal, state, and local expenditures for the period since 1915. If we look back further—say back to 1800—the growth is even more spectacular. In 1800, our governments spent $11 million; in 1959, the total was about $120 *billion.* In 1800, per capita federal tax collections were about $2; today they are over $450, or about $1,800 per four-person family. If we add state and local governments, the per capita figure is about $675, or about $2,700 per average four-person family. Over 8 million people now work for some governmental unit, about one of every eight jobholders. Of these, contrary to many preconceptions about the federal bureaucracy, nearly 6 million work for state or local governments.

These increases are phenomenal. Why have they come?

1. One big answer is war—past, present, and future. War is fabulously expensive, and it's getting more so every day. One modern jet bomber costs more than the total annual expenditures of the federal government a century and a half ago. Today, three-fourths of the federal budget is directly or indirectly attributable to fighting present wars, being prepared for future ones, and mopping up the obligations of past ones.

2. But civilian expenditures account for over half the combined federal-state-local total. Population has grown fast, and more people need more government

services. Even if per capita expenditures had remained constant, the increase in population from 5 million to 180 million would have meant a whopping increase in government spending.

3. We want governments to do more for us today. Big cities require more government spending on sewers, roads, police, and so on, than a rural economy would. The shift from a rural to an urban economy accounts for a big share of the state-local increase. But there's lots more than that. Now we want six-lane highways instead of dirt paths. Education is expensive. So are subsidies to farmers. Social security has been made a government responsibility, with higher minimum standards than would have been dreamed of a century ago.

Some of this suggests a bigger increase in government's role than has actually occurred, for even during the 1800's the government intervened in economic life in many ways. The Homestead Acts passed out millions of acres of free land to westward migrants. The Land Grant Acts provided large subsidies to railroads to extend their lines to the west. Already a hundred years ago we read of citizens complaining loudly about the high state and local taxes imposed to finance roads, streets, schools, sewage systems, and the like; and of others complaining just as loudly about the inadequacy of these services. Taxes and government spending have grown prodigiously, but don't get them out of perspective with the past. Government spending didn't begin with F.D.R. and the New Deal.

4. Partly, the increase simply reflects higher prices. Today's price level is the highest in our history. Go back and look at Figure 7-1 to see how important this factor is.

THE PUBLIC ECONOMY TODAY   The present federal budget is worth a more detailed look. Table 35-1 gives the picture for the fiscal year 1960.

The dominant role of national defense in federal expenditures is painfully clear. Even excluding veterans' benefits and interest on the national debt (which was accumulated largely to finance past wars), $46 billion of the $77 billion total goes for defense. Adding in interest and veterans' benefits brings the total to $59 billion, over three-fourths of all regular federal spending. (As Table 35-1 notes, the self-supporting federal social security system for old-age benefits and the like is handled separately from the regular federal budget.) If we look at total government expenditures, including state and local spending, the national defense figure of $59 billion comes to just about half the total. Actually, defense spending as a percentage of the total gradually declined during the 1950's, although its dollar size crept up, because civilian spending at federal, state, and local levels was steadily expanded. Still, with only a 25 per cent reduction on total war-related spending we could double our national standard of education, from kindergarten through college, build a whole new system of superhighways, or clear mile upon mile of city slums. Past, present, and future wars are a huge drain on the national standard of living—about 15 per cent of the total national income.

But don't forget the other big items in Figure 35-1. Total spending on education was over $15 billion, on highways and roads $10 billion. Special aid to agriculture alone was $6 billion. Even omitting the $10 billion annual federal social security system, spending on welfare benefits of all sorts was about $8 billion. General government (the courts, police, legislatures, administrative agencies—in short, the bureaucracy) cost about $2 billion at the federal level, about $5 billion more for state and local governments. We have voted ourselves wide-ranging services from our governments.

Table 35-1

FEDERAL BUDGET FOR FISCAL YEAR 1960 [a]

Receipts		*Expenditures*	
Personal income tax	$41	National defense	$46
Corporation income and		Veterans' benefits	5
profit taxes	22	Interest on public debt	8
Excise taxes	9	Agriculture	6
Other	6	Labor and welfare	4
		International aid	2
		General government	2
		All other	4
	$77		$77
Payroll taxes			
(social security)	11 [b]	Social security payments	11 [b]
Total	$88	Total	$88

[a] In billions of dollars. Data from President's budget message. Figures are his estimates for the fiscal year from July 1, 1959, to June 30, 1960. Columns may not add because of rounding.

[b] Social security is handled outside the regular budget. See Chapter 42.

The result is taxes to pay for the services. The big ones are shown by Figure 35-1. Personal income taxes took about $43 billion, all told; corporation income taxes another $23 billion. Sales and excise taxes at $20 billion and property taxes of $15 billion were the other biggest levies.

This means that we turn over a big chunk of our incomes to the government each year—some of it knowingly and a lot more through hidden taxes passed on to us in higher prices or lower incomes. The average family of four paid about $2700 in 1959. This average was pulled up by taxes on rich families. The millionaire may have had to turn over as much as 60 to 80 per cent of his income. To keep $50,000 after taxes in 1959, you had to have an income well over twice that. Even very low-income families had to contribute several hundred dollars.

Redistribution of Resources and Incomes Through the Public Economy. Nobody wants to pay taxes unless he has to. Generally, we decide first what the government is to do and then figure out how to get the money to pay for it. Congress is always happy to be able to cut taxes, always reluctant to raise them unless growing expenditures make it imperative. At the state and local levels, the pressure of making expenditures conform to tax income is a real one. These governmental units can borrow within limits, but they have to hold their spending programs fairly close to current tax receipts. The federal government, on the other hand, is a lot freer from this compulsion. In World War II, we covered only about a third of our total expenditures by taxes. Still, except during wars, the great bulk of government expenditures has been, and ought to be, covered by tax collections.

For the most part, then, the public economy produces a reallocation of resources and incomes, rather than a change in the total product to be divided up. In a full-employment economy, this is necessarily so. Since the total product cannot then be expanded appreciably, all the government can do is rechannel productive resources (e.g., into producing rockets instead of refrigerators) or redistribute money incomes directly (e.g., by taxing the rich and giving the money to the poor). In depression periods, the situation is different. As we saw in Part 2, then government spending may create jobs and increase the national output. But even with unemployment, insofar as government spending is financed by tax collections the effect is primarily a transfer of resources and purchasing power rather than an increase.

Figure 35-1 gives a broad picture of the reallocation of resources through the public economy. Instead of the many things taxpayers would have demanded privately, the government spent tens of billions on missiles, ammunition, troop maintenance, and other military items. It spent smaller sums, but still billions of dollars, on education, highways, police protection, and a multitude of other peacetime government services. Additional billions represented pure money transfers from taxpayers to recipients—interest on the public debt, old-age social security payments, unemployment benefits.

Another way of looking at this transfer effect is to ask, what does it do to the distribution of money incomes—does it level them off or make them more unequal? This is an important question, and a hard one to answer precisely. On the tax side, the man who turns the money over to the government often doesn't ultimately pay the tax; he may simply pass it on to someone else. A well-known case is the tax on movie admissions, which is noted separately in the price. In other taxes too, part or all may be passed on to consumers or back to workers or other resource owners. On the expenditure side, it is even harder to estimate what income levels get the ultimate benefits from government spending. Assistance to needy old people is relatively easy. But interest on the public debt is harder, since banks and other institutions own lots of bonds. And when you come to

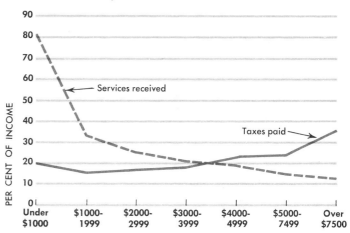

Taxes Paid and Services Received from Government, 1946-1947

FIG. 35-3 Low income groups receive much more from the government than they pay for in taxes. Upper income groups pay for more than the services they receive. (Source: J. H. Adler in *Fiscal Policies and the American Economy*, Prentice-Hall, Inc., 1951, pp. 382 and 388.)

military outlays and foreign aid, about all you can do is make an arbitrary allocation that seems not unreasonable.

A few experts have tried such over-all allocations. One set of estimates is summarized in Figure 35-3. The solid line shows the tax burden as percentage of income at different family income levels. The dashed line shows government services received as percentage of income at the same family income levels. For example, in the $1,000-$2,000 income group, taxes took about 16 per cent of the average family's income. Somewhere around the $3,000-$5,000 range, tax payments and services received from government balanced off at around 20 per cent of income. At higher income levels, families paid in a sum much larger than the value of the services received. These estimates are *very rough* and arbitrary in many respects, especially in the upper range of the income scale. Yet it is clear that at the income extremes the public economy exercises a major effect on incomes.[1]

SOCIAL POLICY AND THE PUBLIC ECONOMY

How much should our governmental units spend each year, and on what? Should they get the money through taxes or borrowing? If taxes, what taxes? These questions can be answered meaningfully only if we ask ourselves first: What are we really trying to achieve through the public economy? Without knowing where we're heading, we'll have a tough time judging what is the most effective way of getting there.

---

[1] The data in Figure 35-3 are for 1946-47. Since then, both taxes and government expenditures have increased greatly. But incomes have also risen greatly. The best evidence is that the *percentage* data in Figure 35-3, relating taxes paid and benefits received to income level, are still *roughly* applicable except that both curves should be somewhat higher at all except the very low income levels. Table 36-2 shows more recent data on tax burdens only.

Goals in the Public Economy.   Chapter 5 tentatively set up five fundamental social goals as guideposts to help in evaluating how the economic system works. If these are useful in judging the entire economic system, they should be useful in evaluating how the public economy ought to be managed. The goals were suggested because they seem to have widespread acceptance. But if you don't agree with them, substitute your own. It is essential to recognize what your own goals or standards are before you can judge intelligently how well the economic system or any part of it is performing. Here are our earlier goals:

1. A higher national standard of living.
2. Economic freedom.
3. Economic security.
4. Production in accordance with consumer demands.
5. An equitable distribution of income.

In a basically private-enterprise economy, the main job of achieving these goals has to fall on the private economy. Government steps in when it can help, in the view of the majority of voters, by regulating private behavior or by directly intervening through the public economy. Earlier chapters have looked in detail at some of the major areas where government regulation has been widespread. The present chapters are concerned with areas where the government directly uses productive resources (e.g., by providing education or ammunition) or directly redistributes money income (e.g., through assistance to the needy), leaving aside government fiscal policy to avoid depressions and inflations, which was covered in Chapter 15.

Special Characteristics of the Public Economy.   Certain special characteristics of the public economy go a long way toward determining the sphere of direct governmental action in moving toward the goals listed above.

1. The state has the power of compulsion, which no private agency has. This power is necessary for regulatory action, for effective redistribution of income (by taxing some to spend for the benefit of others), for restricting production and consumption of particular commodities such as opium, and so on.

2. The state, by virtue of being made up of all its citizens, is in a position to provide many goods and services that are generally desired but not marketable under a price system in the private economy. We all want police protection, adequate national defense, sanitation, and so on. Yet these services could not effectively be sold to individuals on a per-unit basis. The government has to take over to implement people's wants.

3. Owing to its long life and financial resources, the state is able to undertake long-run, expensive projects, which, though desirable, would not be feasible for private enterprise. Highways are an example.

4. The state, being free from the "profit motive" and having the power of compulsion, is able to make its revenues fit its expenditures (within limits) rather than the reverse. This characteristic is especially important when the government wants to unbalance its budget in order to mitigate booms and depressions.

These and other considerations indicate that the scope of the public economy must be large. A tradition of trying private enterprise first, and introducing government only where private enterprise falls short, has exerted a continuous and powerful check to the expansion of government action in this country. But wide-reaching government activities have come to be regarded as necessary, aside from such emergencies as war and depression. And some observers in recent years have argued that government spending should expand steadily in a healthy, growing economy.

Consumers' Sovereignty and Citizens' Sovereignty.   As has been stressed many times, the allocation of resources through the private economy is primarily in response to consumers' money demands for goods and services. The government may follow the same policy. If a government undertaking is run to maximize profits, for example, it may play a role much like that of private enterprise. Or a government enterprise (such as a public utility) may be operated to satisfy consumer demands at cost rather than to maximize profits.

But in the vast majority of cases, government services are not sold to consumers on a price basis. Here the allocation of resources in the public economy is ideally carried out through the process of political voting. We as citizens express our preferences for roads, rockets, zoos, and so on, through voting for representatives who subscribe to our views. They in turn should vote funds to procure resources to produce the goods and services that we have indicated we want. Thus there is, ideally, a sort of "citizens' sovereignty" analogous to the "consumers' sovereignty" in the private economy. There are, however, significant differences. Three, especially, deserve attention:

1. In the private economy, voting for resource allocation is on a *one-dollar-one-vote* basis. In the public economy, in a democratic country, it is on a *one-person-one-vote* basis. In the private economy, the rich man has many more votes than the poor man. In the public economy, a democratic system attempts, though not always with complete success, to provide each citizen with equal voting power, regardless of whether he is rich or poor.

2. In the public economy, there is little such comparative weighing of specific benefits and sacrifices by consumers as occurs in the private economy. In private life Mr. X can consider carefully whether he prefers to spend $10 on football tickets, an electric razor, a new pair of shoes, or on nothing at all. But when Mr. X votes to elect his representative, he votes on a whole group of issues. He has little opportunity to distinguish in detail between the things of which he

approves and those of which he disapproves—he votes for one complex and usually ill-defined combination against another when he chooses among candidates. Only when a specific decision is put up to the voters is there an exception —for example, when a special bond issue to finance a new school must be approved by the voters.

3. The legislative and administrative processes of government favor some groups over others. Our government is more responsive to the folks back home than many give it credit for. Yet it is particularly responsive to the organized interests, the vocal pressure groups. Unless the little man is organized to speak through such a group or through his local political organization, he may have no voice at all except on the broad sweep of issues at election time. Both markets and political systems respond imperfectly to the people's choices, but they favor different groups.

Balancing Gains and Costs in the Public Economy. *The Principle of Maximizing "Social Welfare."* In a democracy of 180 million people, there are inevitably many conflicting views on what the government should do. Even if the public were reasonably well agreed on the five social goals listed above, they would have very different meanings for different people—especially the fifth, on what is an "equitable" distribution of income. And conflicts can easily arise among the five objectives themselves.

In trying to give useful advice, economists have often suggested that the problem of reallocating resources and incomes within any total given output should be separated from that of trying to raise total output. If we concentrate on the former, where total output is what it is, all the government can do through the public economy is to redistribute resources and incomes. Government expenditures necessarily mean a transfer of resources from one group (taxpayers) to another (recipients of government services).

In this situation, some economists have suggested a rough guide to the proper level of government expenditures and tax collections. Government expenditures should be increased up to the point where the marginal loss to those who give up control over resources is just equal to the marginal gain in benefits from public expenditures. As long as the marginal gain is greater than the marginal loss, there is a net gain in over-all social welfare.

The same approach of comparing gains and losses at the margin gives guidance for determining the distribution of government expenditures. For every potential government expenditure, the same question can be asked: Will the gain from the use of resources in this manner be greater than the loss in withholding them from the use to which they would otherwise be put? This is simply one application of the general marginal principle that the total advantage to society will be maximized when resources are distributed among all uses, public and private, so that no one unit of resources could contribute more in any other use.

If society were a single unity, and *if* government were the all-comprehending brain of that unity, application of this principle would be fine. The government could then easily weigh satisfactions lost against those gained and could determine its policies accordingly. But in fact society is far from being such a unity and government is far from being an all-comprehending brain. Practical application of this principle would involve comparison of the marginal satisfactions of millions of different people who might be gaining or losing from any proposed policy. Obviously no precise interpersonal comparison of satisfactions is possible. At best, only the roughest sort of approximation is possible. Even a very wise man would quail before the task of evaluating precisely the marginal effect of taxing and spending another million dollars on military aid to Europe. Yet, over-all, we agree fairly well on the amount we are willing to spend on this purpose. However rough its application, the marginal principle of economizing the use of scarce resources suggests a rough guide to intelligent behavior.

The Problem of Government Expenditures. Perhaps the toughest problem in the public economy is how much the government should spend on what functions. National defense is the worst—here the issues are largely military and beyond the scope of economics. The economist says only, we can afford the defense we need. Not to have it because we think we cannot pay for it would be foolish. Higher taxes are unpleasant, but the American economy is so rich we could pay far larger taxes for defense and still have a national standard of living above any other nation's.

With other expenditures, the issues are more directly comprehensible to the layman. In a $500 billion economy, should we divert more of our resources to education, slum clearance, highways, parks, and other such public services? These decisions are made through the political process. Although the voter has little control over how his congressman votes on a particular public expenditure, ultimately the decisions on the scope of the public economy are made by the public.

Total government spending of about $60 billion on non-war-related services and transfer payments amounts to about 15 per cent of the national income. Is this enough, or too much? In a recent best-selling book, *The Affluent Society,* a noted economist, Harvard's J. K. Galbraith, has argued that the American economy is now so rich that we are driven to wasteful consumption just to keep the machinery going. Tailfins on automobiles are only the symbol of conspicuous consumption, meeting demands developed by high-pressure advertising. Yet our public services are barely adequate. School teachers earn less money than janitors. Half of our most able youths do not go on to college. Our cities are marred by slums. Our highways are jammed. Our police forces and local government rolls are often peopled by incompetent individuals, so poorly paid as to be constant targets for graft. Few of our symphonies and art museums receive adequate public support. The scientist who invents a new gadget is greeted with public acclaim, but the politician who suggests a new public service is deemed a wastrel. All this, Professor Galbraith argues, reflects a basic social unbalance in the affluent American economy. Somehow, we have no machinery to translate into reality the obvious need for greater public expenditures.

There is little doubt that the public would like to have more and better highways, education, symphony orchestras, and other public services. But there is little corresponding enthusiasm for raising taxes to provide them. At first glance, this appears a convincing reason for dismissing Galbraith's thesis. But is it instead, as he suggests, merely that people have become so accustomed to assuming that any government spending is prima facie bad that they do not really examine the alternatives carefully? Why, indeed, do we so generally assume that a dollar spent on taxes is wasted, while a dollar spent on ourselves produces a valuable return?

Economists recognize that economics provides no simple answer to how large government expenditures and taxes should be. Political scientists recognize equally that the democratic political process provides a very imperfect channel for the individual citizen to express his views in detail on how much the government should spend for what. Yet with over a quarter of his total income spent through the government, it is obviously to the citizen's interests to have a say on how his money is used, parallel to the say he has over his disposable income after taxes. As with an adequate national defense, America can clearly afford more public services if we want them. The test of Galbraith's position lies both in whether we really do want more public services badly enough to pay for them, and in whether we will make these wants effective if indeed they exist.

The Government as Entrepreneur. At the extreme, the government may go into business itself, instead of buying from private producers the goods it needs. For example, it may build missiles itself instead of hiring Boeing or Douglas to do the job. If efficiency is the criterion, the government should act as entrepreneur when it can do the job at a lower cost than can private enterprise. In America, however, there has been a strong presumption that private enterprise is more efficient, as well as more desirable on non-economic grounds. People believe the government should "stay out of business." Whether or not the presumption against efficiency in government enterprise is valid, these other criteria may swing the decision.

Whether the government purchases the goods and services it needs or acts as entrepreneur in producing them need make no difference in its basic policy on the distribution of real income. Thus the postal system under government entrepreneurship may be operated to make a profit, to break even, or to suffer any loss up to 100 per cent (that is, be made a free service). If the government paid private enterprises to carry on the work of the present postal system, it would still be necessary to choose among exactly the same alternatives. Whether the government acts as producer itself or buys its services is only a question of economic means to the more basic ends sought.

1. If a copy is available (e.g., in *The New York Times* of about the third week in each January), read over the President's most recent budget message to Congress. What are the major increases and decreases proposed from the preceding year? Do these changes seem to you desirable? What criteria have you used, implicitly or explicitly, in making these judgments?

2. In your judgment, does "consumers' sovereignty" or "citizens' sovereignty" provide a better basis for the allocation of society's productive resources?

3. J. K. Galbraith and many others in the "liberal" wing of the Democratic Party argue that the social priorities are higher on better public services—education, public health, cleaner cities, slum clearance, etc.—than on more consumer goods, now that America has so nearly abolished poverty. This is especially true, they argue, because more consumer goods tend to go to the already well-to-do, while public services can benefit the whole population. Analyze this argument. How do you think we should decide what our governments should do and who should pay for it?

4. Locate your family income level roughly on Figure 35-3. Assuming these data are still roughly accurate, do you feel your income level is being treated equitably in the government's over-all redistribution of income? Why or why not?

5. Recently, much concern has been expressed that our educational facilities are inadequate in many areas, especially in some rural areas in the South. Should the federal government spend more money to improve these educational facilities, say by building new schoolhouses or making grants to raise teachers' salaries? If your answer is yes, how much would you be willing to see your taxes raised to help pay for such new expenditures?

6. a. Many people believe that there is always a presumption in favor of reducing government expenditures. Do you agree? Why or why not?

b. Why, if at all, is the above presumption more defensible than a presumption that government spending should be kept up on any activity, once it has begun?

7. Government is commonly alleged to be inefficient, compared with private enterprise. Using the postal system as an example, assess this argument as scientifically as possible, considering both reasonable ways of judging comparative efficiencies and *a priori* reasons why government operation might be expected to be more or less efficient.

FOR
ANALYSIS
AND
DISCUSSION

Taxes

36

Nearly everyone beefs about high taxes. But if we're going to have our governments spend, we have to get resources transferred from private to public use. Taxes are the most straightforward way to get the funds needed. If we don't use taxes, the transfer will be accomplished through increased government spending without correspondingly reduced private spending—through inflation, with its erratic and inequitable distribution of the real burden of government spending, unless there are unemployed resources to draw on.

Government spending sets the general level of taxes we need to collect. But what taxes are the best, and who should pay them? With government spending at present levels, and with a good chance that it's headed higher, construction of a sound and equitable tax system is of foremost importance. The multi-billion-dollar federal budget may not mean much to you—the figures are too big. But the fact that you, when you leave college with an average middle-class income of perhaps $5,000, will start turning over to Uncle Sam and to local governmental units nearly $1,500 each year, puts the dollars and cents in more meaningful terms.

DISTRIBUTION
OF THE TAX BURDEN
Who pays the taxes? Table 36-1 summarizes the answer on one basis—what taxes provided the revenue in 1959.

Over one-third of all tax income in 1959 came from the personal income tax, almost exclusively a federal tax. Another 20 per cent came through corporation income and profits taxes, again predominantly a federal tax. Next came excise and sales taxes, shared about equally by federal and state-local governments. The property tax is basically a local tax, whereas payroll taxes are again primarily federal.

Table 36-1

FEDERAL, STATE, AND LOCAL TAX PAYMENTS IN 1959 *

Taxes	In Billions	Percentage of Total
Personal income and related taxes	$ 43	36
Corporation income and profits taxes	22	19
Excises and sales taxes	19	16
Property taxes	15	13
Payroll taxes	13	11
Other, excluding licenses	6	5
Total	$118	100

* Data on federal taxes are from President's budget message; state and local data are author's estimates based on latest available information. Includes social security and unemployment payroll taxes not in regular government budgets.

Income and payroll taxes are levied directly on individuals. The other half of all taxes are levied on businesses, on products, or on property. Ultimately, these taxes have to paid by people. A business is only a group of people. And products and property can't pay taxes; their owners either pay the taxes or shift them on to someone else. From a fundamental human point of view, the significant question is: Who ultimately pays all these taxes?

Table 36-2 gives a rough answer to this question. Estimating the final resting place (incidence) of taxes is a tough, uncertain job, and no one thinks it can be done very precisely. The estimates in Table 36-2 are the best now available, and they are almost certainly of the right general order of magnitude. Although the estimates are for 1954, the tax system changed little between then and 1959, so they can reasonably be compared with the 1959 data in Table 36-1, except that by 1959 the burden was somewhat higher at all levels.

All in all, the American tax system conforms moderately well to the notion of "ability to pay," *if* we take family income as the measure of ability to pay. As income rises, the percentage taken by taxes goes up. On the other hand, effective tax burden rises only slightly as a percentage of income from very poor families around the $2,000 level to families at the $5,000 level, and a sharply rising effective burden sets in only above the $10,000 level. Looking back at Figure 35-3, we see that effective burden was a *higher* percentage of income for *very* low-income families (under $1,000) than at slightly higher levels, and this situation apparently still continues.

Table 36-2

EFFECTIVE TAX BURDENS BY INCOME LEVELS *

Family Income Level	Tax Burden as Percentage of Income
Under $2,000	23
$2,000 to 2,999	26
$3,000 to 3,999	26
$4,000 to 4,999	27
$5,000 to 7,999	29
$8,000 to 9,999	31
Over $10,000	39
Average for all	30

* Estimates for 1954. Data from R. A. Musgrave, "The Incidence of the Tax Structure and Its Effects on Consumption," in *Federal Tax Policy for Economic Growth and Stability* (U.S. Government Printing Office, 1955). Income data are for "spending units," to compare with the income data used in Chapters 2 and 28. Tax data include social security taxes. These data differ slightly from those in Figure 35-3, largely because they cover different years.

Convert these estimates into dollars and you get a picture something like this for some typical families in early 1960, though remember that particular families at the same income levels may be very different from any average.

Typical family A, with a poverty-level income of around $1,000, paid about $250 in taxes, a quarter of its total income. Most of this $250 was "hidden" in the form of higher prices paid for taxed products, higher rents, and the like, or in the form of lower wages received. Over half the total went to local governments, largely through the property tax (whether paid directly or through higher rents).

Typical family B, with a $5,000 income, paid nearly $1,500 in taxes. This family, which was at a very typical income level in 1959, paid only $400 or so in federal income tax, but it was hit hard by the hidden excises and property taxes that caught family A as well. In total, family B paid a lot more taxes than A, but it is striking that in percentage of income paid the two are not very different.

Typical family C, with an income of $7,500, probably paid up toward $2,500 in taxes, or slightly less than one-third of its income. Family C had a nice income; only about 25 per cent of the total population was better off. Here the federal income tax begins to bite in, though it was still well under $1,000. Family C also bore a small chunk of the corporation income tax, plus its share of all the same excise and property taxes that hit "A" and "B."

Family D, with an income of $100,000, can't be called typical, since there are so few such families. Moreover, its tax burden depended so heavily on the way in which it received its income and how adeptly it utilized tax loopholes that no typical tax figure is possible. Probably it paid between $40,000 and $60,000 in taxes, around half its income. Its federal income tax would normally be nearly $50,000, depending on the various deductions taken, unless part of the income was received as "capital gains" (see later section) in which case the tax would be smaller. D, being a substantial corporate stockholder, also may have paid heavily through the corporation income tax. In addition, it was subject to most of the same hidden taxes as the lower-income families, and it paid them on a lot bigger volume of expenditures.

In one sense, these figures may be misleading. The wealthy family pays a big part of its income to the government in taxes. But for every rich family there are hundreds of thousands of poor and middle-income families. Thus, nearly one-third of all taxes were ultimately paid by the half of all families below the $5,000-income level in 1959, even though the tax per family wasn't large; well over another one-third by the $5,000-$10,000 group; and the last third by the 5 million families with incomes over $10,000. Put another way, about two-thirds of all taxes came from the under-$15,000 group. The reason was simple—that's where over 80 per cent of the income was.

GOOD AND BAD TAXES

Few subjects generate as much heat in popular discussion as taxes. All too often, this heat is unaccompanied by light. You can't judge intelligently what are good and what are bad taxes until you've straightened out in your mind the criteria on which you're judging. Since this effort is seldom made as a prelude to discussion, it is little wonder that people often disagree violently on what taxes should be used. Next time you hear taxes being discussed, see if you can ferret out the implicit criteria by which they are being judged. Then ask the participants and see whether they can tell you the tests they have been applying.

The same five broad social objectives we've used before can be pointed up conveniently in three questions:

1. Does the tax system encourage or hinder investment, employment, and economic growth? Will it tend to damp economic fluctuations or accentuate them?

2. Does the tax hinder or aid the allocation of resources in accordance with consumer preferences? Does it impede or encourage the free choice of occupation and investment channels? In short, how much does it interfere with the free choices of the individual in spending and earning his money?

3. How equitably is the tax burden distributed? Here again, what is an equitable distribution of income is a central issue. Government taxing and spending inevitably affect the distribution of income. Unless government tax collections

exactly equal benefits provided to each family, the issue is not *whether* the government shall redistribute income, but *how*.

Taxation for Growth and Stability.   Economic growth, as was emphasized in Chapters 3 and 12, depends on an intricate complex of considerations, but especially on research and technological advance, on saving and investment, on education, and on hard work by the labor force. If taxation is to stimulate economic growth, it probably must stimulate one of these factors. If taxes deter growth, it is probably because they deter one of these factors.

It is hard to see how taxes can stimulate economic growth, in comparison to no taxes at all (eliminating consideration of the effects of the resulting tax-financed expenditures), for taxes are a drain on someone's income. But one tax structure may be more conducive to rapid growth than another. In general, taxes that bear on savings and on returns from investment will discourage growth, compared to taxes that fall on consumption. Similarly, taxes that give special advantages to expenditures on research and development activities, or on education, are especially conducive to economic growth. In general, any taxes that stimulate longer and harder work are favorable, while those that reduce the incentive to work are disadvantageous. A tax system designed to stimulate economic growth will place these considerations uppermost. Unfortunately, as will be evident presently, some of them conflict with commonly held ideas of what is an equitable tax structure.

How about damping business fluctuations? For this purpose, the graduated personal income tax is best. To damp fluctuations, we want government tax receipts to rise more rapidly than the national income in booms, thereby withdrawing additional funds from the income stream as the boom progresses. Conversely, total government tax receipts should fall more rapidly than the national income when recession occurs, thus softening the impact of reduced incomes on private spending. The least useful tax, from this point of view, is one that remains constant with changing income, or even moves counter to incomes. For example, a fixed property tax is relatively inflexible.

Any tax tends to restrict private spending and output. But some cut private spending more directly and surely than do others. For example, an inheritance tax is unlikely to restrain current spending very much, while a general sales tax directly reduces the buying power of any given amount of income. An income tax on low incomes is sure to cut consumption, since low-income families have no savings cushion, while the impact of an income tax on rich families is less sure. Quite aside from dynamic effects on growth and fluctuations, it is desirable to minimize the restrictive effect of taxes on employment and output, except when the goal is to fight inflation.

"Equity" in Taxation.   A tax system should be equitable, as well as conducive to growth and stability. Three tests of equity are often advanced. One is to levy taxes on the people who get the benefits. Another is to levy taxes according to ability to pay. The third stresses equal treatment of taxpayers equally situated.

The "Benefit" Principle. It seems fair to a lot of people that those who benefit from government services should pay for them. No one argues that this benefit principle should be rigidly applied, but wouldn't it be a good general rule?

One obvious problem is how the principle could be applied practically. If the city is putting in a new sewer, it's easy to see who the primary beneficiaries are going to be and to assess the cost against these property-owners through a "special assessment." But how can the benefits derived from national defense, or the judicial system, be divided up among the citizens? Everywhere the principle runs into such difficulties.

An even more fundamental question: Would we really want the benefit principle applied? Look at the school system, for example. Now we have free public schools for everyone. But suppose we put all education on a benefit tax basis. Then each parent would have to pay a special school tax depending on how many children he had in school—for example, $400 per child. This might work out fine for the local banker and doctor. But how about the poor family on the other side of the tracks, with eight school-age children? Where would the $3,200 come from? The benefit principle applied to school taxation would mean the end of equal elementary and high-school education for all. The well-to-do could continue sending their youngsters to school (and at less expense than now), but millions of poor children would be priced out of the market. Government activities like poor relief would be completely ruled out by the benefit principle, since there would be little point in imposing special taxes on the poor just to return the funds to them.

Broad use of the benefit principle would thus be far more revolutionary than it sounds at first blush. It would mean in effect direct sale of government services to the consumer. It would preclude any redistribution of income through the public economy. Put otherwise, as soon as government deviates from strict benefit-principle taxation (i.e., direct sale of all government services at cost), it is in effect redistributing income, whether we like to admit it or not. This is the meaning of the statement above that, for practical purposes, the issue is not *whether* the government will redistribute incomes, but rather *how* it will redistribute them.

The "Ability To Pay" Principle. Taxation according to ability to pay is widely favored. But how shall we measure ability to pay? Net money income received in the current year is the most widely accepted criterion.

Even if we agree on net income as the best measure of ability to pay, there is still the problem of the rate at which different incomes should be taxed. Some argue that the rate should be *proportional*—that is, the same percentage of each person's income. For example, the tax rate might be 1 per cent, giving a $10 tax on $1,000; $100 on $10,000; $1,000 on $100,000. Though the rate is proportional, this procedure of course takes more dollars from high- than from low-income groups. Others argue that rates should be *progressive*—that is, a higher percentage tax on high incomes than on low (for example, $5 on $1,000; $100 on $10,000; $2,000 on $100,000). This places a still heavier burden on the well-to-do. All ability-to-pay advocates argue against *regressive* taxation, in which a larger percentage of income is taken from the lower-income groups (for example, $20 on $1,000; $100 on $10,000; $500 on $100,000).

You should be clear that ability-to-pay as a base for taxation has no exactness or "absolute" validity. There is no objective way of deciding whether rates should be proportional or progressive, and, if progressive, how steeply progressive. The "ability" phrase is, however, convenient for conversational purposes, since in America there seems to be substantial agreement that progressive taxation of income and inheritances represents the primary application of the ability-to-pay principle. When the term is used in this book, therefore, it will mean progressively higher tax rates as net income rises, without specifying any particular rate of progression. Many writers have attempted to reach some more basic justification underlying the ability-to-pay principle, but without success. In the last analysis, the issue of how much progression is "equitable" is an ethical and moral one. It boils down largely to the question of who should get how much of the limited national income pie—a fundamental and explosive question.

"Equal Treatment of Those Equally Situated." A third principle of equity states that persons equally situated should be taxed equally. This is a powerful guide to tax policy, and one that is accepted by most observers. But what is "equally situated"? Are two people with the same income always equally situated? For example, is a disabled, elderly, retired man with an income of $5,000 annually from a pension equally situated with a healthy young single man in his twenties who has the same income? Are both equally situated with the $5,000-a-year laborer who has a wife and ten children to support? Does it matter where the income comes from? For example, is a factory superintendent who gets $15,000 a year equally situated with a rich young man who gets $15,000 by clipping bond coupons on a fortune left him by his father? How about a gain of $15,000 on General Motors stock which has gone up in price between your buying and selling it?

In general, the federal income tax law takes equal income as evidence that persons are equally situated. But there are lots of exceptions. There is a special $600 income exemption for each dependent relative, other special exemptions for the elderly and the blind. The "capital gain" on the General Motors stock is taxed at only half the rate on ordinary income, and at a maximum of 25 per cent compared to 91 per cent on ordinary income. Increasingly, the federal personal income tax base has been eaten away by special exemptions of different sorts. Just what does equally situated mean when it comes to the practical problem of writing tax laws in Congress?

How Much Taxation Can We Stand?   Hardly a day goes by but someone complains that we've reached the limit of our ability to pay taxes—that for the government to raise taxes further would be the last straw. Is there some definite limit to how much taxation the country can stand? Have we reached it?

The general answer to both questions is no. But to answer more fully, we have to ask, what is the meaning of "can we stand"? The usual connotation is that with more taxes the system would grind to a halt, people would stop working, there'd be no incentive for businessmen to invest. Faced with predictions of such a debacle, the economist asks, how will it come about, and why? Let us explore these questions.

Economic analysis suggests that if more taxes are going to bring disaster, it will probably be through one or more of the following effects:

1. *Heavier taxation may remove the incentive to work.* If the government takes too big a share of the income I earn, I may say it's just not worth the candle and quit working—or at least work less. Maybe there is some level of taxation at which there'd be no more incentive at all to work, but then there's always the pressing problem of how to eat. As long as something remains after taxes and most people still have much less than they want, the incentive to earn is a powerful one, even when earnings must be shared with the government. But for well-to-do people who feel less income pressure, the amount of work *may* fall off as tax rates rise. And even for middle-income people too, when it's a question of overtime work or a second job. This is a complex problem, and the plain fact is that the evidence isn't clear enough to settle the question. Most formal studies find little evidence that higher income taxes seriously reduce the work at any income level. But somehow, this runs contrary to most people's intuitive notions. More of this later.

2. *Heavier taxes may reduce the incentive to invest,* especially if the taxes fall heavily on income from investment. Again, this may seem intuitively reasonable but there's little clear evidence to support the point. If taxes fall differentially on one type of investment, investors will flee from it in droves. But taxation on all investment income leaves no escape. And there's little evidence that corporations and wealthy individuals just eat more instead of investing. More likely, they complain bitterly about the low return on investment, and go on investing—*if* times are good (which is the more fundamental stimulus to investment). But here too there is surely some deterrent marginal tax effect, and the impact of differential taxes is strong in shifting investment behavior.

3. *Heavier taxes may lead to legal tax "avoidance."* The law provides many loopholes for people who feel taxes heavily enough to hire a good tax lawyer. Congressional tax committees have repeatedly been told that almost no one, no matter how rich, needs to pay more than half his income in taxes, although the personal income tax reaches a 91 per cent peak rate. The capital-gains provision is the big loophole, but there are many others. A large amount of energy already goes into legal tax avoidance. At last count, the Treasury listed about 100,000 tax counselors and tax lawyers whose business was to help on income tax returns.

And the effort pays off. The legal rate listed for income in excess of $200,000 is 78 per cent. Yet in a recent year Treasury statistics showed that only 37 per cent of all income above that level was collected in personal income taxes.

4. *Heavier taxes may lead to illegal tax "evasion."* The case of France is often cited, where for years the government has been able to collect only a modest fraction of the taxes due because of the expense and energy required to run down the individuals who just don't pay. By and large, we Americans report and pay our taxes without being pursued. But a recent National Bureau of Economic Research estimate suggested that 5 per cent of all wages, 30 per cent of unincorporated business income (farmers, doctors, lawyers, etc.), 13 per cent of dividends, and no less than 63 per cent of interest on bank deposits went unreported, a total of perhaps $25 billion in a then $300 billion economy. How much harder it would become to collect taxes at higher rates nobody knows. We don't spend much money on the effort now.

5. *Higher taxes might lead to inflation.* This seems a perverted argument, since counter-cyclical fiscal policy rests on the premise that higher taxes check inflation. The new argument is that if taxes get too high everyone will start raising his asking prices to offset them—unions, businessmen, lawyers, farmers, everybody. Some careful thought will show that this behavior can result in continuing inflation only if the government helpfully puts in more money to support total purchasing power at the higher prices. But don't forget the pressures on government to do just that, if the price of inaction or restraint is recession and unemployment.

What do all these points add up to? Not a conclusion that we can't stand any more taxation. Clearly we can, and a lot more if we want the government services urgently enough. Our standard of living is so high we could divert far more resources to the public economy and still have the highest living standard in the world. But they do point to some real dangers as the level of taxation climbs relative to the national income. And clearly how much taxation we can stand without getting into trouble depends partly on what the taxes are.

One last point, which creates some of the sharpest controversy among people who don't look at the facts. If we want a lot more tax revenue it has to come from the middle- and lower-income groups, because that's where the income is. Thomas Jefferson's ideal of "a country made a paradise by the contribution of the rich alone" won't work any more—the country's too big and there aren't enough rich. Complete confiscation of all personal incomes over $100,000 would add less than $5 billion to the total federal tax take. So if someone is going to "stand" more taxes, it has to be the general public, not just a rich few.

SHIFTING, INCIDENCE, AND EFFECTS OF TAXATION

Often the person who pays over the funds to the government does not actually bear the burden of the tax. The federal tax on cosmetics, for example, is paid to the government by manufacturers. But it may be ultimately "shifted" forward to consumers through higher prices, or backward to cosmetic workers through lower wages, and to owners of other resources used in the cosmetics industry through lower rents or raw materials prices. The final "incidence" (or resting place) of a tax may be far from the man who turns the money over to the government. Obviously it is this final incidence of the tax that is most important.

The difference between taxes, however, may lie even deeper than the question of who ultimately pays them. Some taxes may especially hinder investment, or reduce saving, or have other broad economic effects. It is difficult to draw any sharp line between the incidence of a tax and its broader economic effects, but it is convenient to make a rough distinction for expository purposes.

It is safe to assume that in most cases a taxpayer will shift a tax whenever he can. The question generally is, therefore, when *can* a tax be shifted? A tax can be shifted only when, as a result of the tax, the taxpayer is able to obtain a higher price for something he sells or to pay a lower price for something he buys. Hence a price transaction of some sort is essential if shifting is to occur.

Generally, taxes do nothing to increase demand for taxed commodities of business (remember that we are examining the impact of the tax alone, quite apart from what is done with the money collected). But taxes do often raise costs and thus reduce supply as resources move elsewhere to look for more profitable employment. This reduced supply pushes price up. If, as a result of a tax, the prices a taxpayer receives or pays are higher or lower than they otherwise would have been, the tax has been shifted to that extent.

Since tax-shifting depends on the prices charged and paid by taxpayers, it is in effect merely an application of the general price and output analysis of Part III. Will an excise tax be considered a part of business costs, and if so will these higher costs be passed on in higher prices? In a competitive market? In a monopolistic market? How about a tax on business net profits? This tax doesn't change business costs as usually defined; will it therefore not affect the prices charged? How about the personal income tax? What price does the individual have through which he can try to pass the tax on, and what are his chances of doing so? These questions need to be investigated tax by tax if we want to know who really pays the taxes. Here we can only look briefly at a few of the more important taxes.

One more advance warning is necessary. A rise in price following the imposition of a tax in the real world is not necessarily proof that the tax has been shifted. The price rise may have come from some other cause. Empirical verification of tax-shifting is very difficult, since it is so hard to isolate one cause and its effects in the multitude of forces simultaneously at work in most parts of economic life. Analytically, however, we can trace through the effects of any tax *assuming "other things equal"*—that is, assuming the tax to be the only new element in the situation. Such theoretical analysis is of necessity oversimplified, and the conclusions drawn are only tentative. But unless we know at least roughly where any tax ultimately falls, there is little sense in talking about its place in a good tax system.

PERSONAL INCOME TAXES

Personal income taxes account for over a third of all tax revenues. They are levied by the federal government and by about two-thirds of the states, but about 95 per cent of the revenue is accounted for by the federal tax.

Income tax rates and exemptions are changed frequently. Thus detailed discussion of the tax in any year may soon be out of date. But a brief description of the early 1960 federal tax will give a general picture of the levy, its procedures, and its impact.

The federal personal income tax applies to all money income in excess of certain deductions. (1) A personal exemption is allowed for the taxpayer and for each dependent member of his family ($600 per person in 1960); thus low-income families escape the tax altogether. (2) Additional deductions are permitted for expenses necessary to earning one's income (such as traveling expenses for traveling salesmen and operating expenses for farmers). (3) Deductions are also allowed for gifts to charitable and nonprofit institutions, for most other taxes paid, for interest paid, for exceptionally large medical expenses, and for certain other expenses. An alternative, simplifying, deduction of 10 per cent of gross income is permitted to cover all these deductions, up to a maximum of $1,000.

The tax is progressive—large incomes are subject to higher tax rates than are small ones. In 1960, an average family of four persons would have paid no income tax unless its income exceeded about $2,700—$2,400 personal exemptions for four persons plus an automatic $270 (10 per cent) expenses deduction. On the first $4,000 of income over these exemptions, the family was taxed 20 per cent; on the next $4,000, 22 per cent. Rapidly increasing marginal rates applied to each increment of income thereafter. The marginal rate was 50 per cent at $32,000, and reached a maximum of 91 per cent on all income over $400,000. This does not mean that the 91 per cent rate applied to the entire taxable income of a very wealthy family; only that portion *above* $400,000 was subject to the peak rate. The effective average rate is always less than the top applicable marginal rate paid.

But the law has several provisions that permit taxpayers to cut their actual rates well below those listed. The four most important are:

1. *Capital gains provision.* Capital gains (profits on assets bought and sold) on assets held over six months are taxed at only half the rates on other income, and at a maximum rate of 25 per cent. This provision encourages investment in growing industries, and seems to most people more equitable than taxing such special gains as regular income. But by the same token it provides a major escape from peak rates for wealthy persons who invest their funds in growing firms, the stock market, or other assets where they can obtain capital gains rather than current income. They thus cut their effective tax rates at least in half on such income, and far more if they are very wealthy. A special variant of this plan now widely

used in paying executive salaries is to pay part of the salary, in effect, in the form of a privilege for the executive to buy the company's stock at or below present market price at any later date. If the stock goes up (as it probably will for a growing company) he can buy in later, and take the gain on the stock's value as a capital gain rather than as regular income taxable at full personal income tax rates.

Wealthy investors often thus prefer companies which plow back their earnings and thereby grow faster. The growing value of the company's stock represents merely a capital gain, subject to tax at the reduced rate when sold to realize the profit. The capital gains provision is thus said to contribute to rapid growth.

2. *Postponed remuneration.* Income is generally taxable when it is received. Corporate executives, TV stars, and other high-salaried individuals increasingly work out elaborate deferred-compensation plans that provide for large post-retirement incomes. This pushes some of their peak incomes over into their retirement, when they'll be subject to lower tax rates. This provision has a certain equitable appeal, since it avoids soaking the recipient to the hilt when he's working and thereby making it harder for him to prepare adequately for retirement. The same loophole exists for low-income people, if they can find someone willing to convert their present earnings into special retirement benefits. But for them, in any case, there's no significant tax saving, because their incomes before and after retirement will probably be subject to about the same tax rates.

3. *Expense accounts.* Today's corporate executive travels in luxury, holds membership in the best clubs, and has frequent thorough health checkups, all at company expense. A TV or movie star goes to London, ostensibly to advertise a new movie. Are these really necessary business expenses of the company that employs them, or merely concealed employee income that doesn't get taxed? No one doubts the legitimacy of business expenses, and the mores of the times are that business executives entertain well and do a lot of business out of the office. But sometimes the well-to-do with access to expense accounts stretch them pretty far. Is maintaining a yacht a legitimate expense? How about a safari through Africa? Both were recently permitted as business expenses, and hence not taxable to the executives involved. What worries the Treasury as much as the income that goes tax-free through plush expense accounts is the resentful feeling of millions of other taxpayers who don't have expense accounts, but who may feel it's all right to fudge a little when they think of those big fellows who seem to get away with so much.

4. *Tax-exempt state and local bonds.* Traditionally, interest on state and local government securities has been exempt from the federal income tax. For the rich man, this makes a whopping difference. If you are in the 66 per cent tax bracket, a tax-exempt yield of 4 per cent on a local bond is equal to a taxable yield of 12 per cent on another security. This provision makes state and local bonds easier to sell, but it provides a nice loophole for the well-to-do to avoid high federal income tax rates on income from their investments.

At high income levels it pays to take advantage of these legal loopholes. A good tax lawyer may be worth his weight in gold if you're rich enough. The raw political fact that there are many more low- and middle-income families than rich makes open advocacy of increased taxes on the lower-income groups dangerous, higher taxes on the rich easy and often popular. But tax observers increasingly suggest that the important escape openings left for the wealthy reflect a basic feeling by many lawmakers that the peak rates stated in the present law are punitive and dangerously high, on grounds of both incentive and equity. Maintaining such loopholes for legally reducing the effective tax rate is politically more realistic than slashing the formal rates themselves. But it surely violates the principle of equity that people situated equally should be equally taxed.

Incidence and Effects.   The incidence of the personal income tax is relatively easy to determine. Generally, the incidence is on the taxpayer; the tax is hard to shift. Neither the demand for nor the supply of any good or service is likely to be much affected by the tax to permit shifting. If individuals are receiving the maximum income they can before the tax, no change will enable them to make more merely because of the tax.

The only important exceptions arise where the tax does lead people to work less, where the taxpayer's ability to get more income was not being fully exploited before imposition of the tax, or where for some reason employers are willing to pay higher wages after imposition of the tax. The effects of taxes in reducing incentives to work are considered below. Another example of income tax shifting might be increased union wage demands to offset increased taxes. But in such cases there is always the intriguing question—why didn't the union push up its wages before the tax instead of waiting until after? Still, with unions as potent as they are, such market "imperfections" may be common. Here, as with other taxes, final incidence of any tax in oligopolistic and monopolistic situations depends partly on bargaining power and administrative decisions.

1. *Effects of growth and stability.* The impact of the personal income tax on economic growth depends largely on the structure of rates. Heavy rates on high incomes reduce saving, and probably impair the incentive to invest. Thus they are adverse to rapid economic growth compared to rates that place the burden lower down the income scale. Conversely, a rate structure that hits lower incomes reduces current consumption and correspondingly encourages growth by permitting larger saving.[1]

---

[1] Predicting the differential effect of taxes on consumption and saving at different income levels is tricky business. If the marginal propensity to save is higher at high income levels, then any given total tax bill on the poor will reduce consumption more than will the same tax bill on the rich. Conversely, taxes on the rich will reduce saving more. But remember that Chapter 11 pointed out that the propensity to consume apparently depends on many things, of which the level of income is only one. The difference in the *marginal* propensity to consume at high and low incomes is far less than the difference in their *average* propensi-

Present high marginal income tax rates are often said to reduce the incentive to work at upper income levels. These may be crucial levels for rapid growth; they include managers, entrepreneurs, top scientists, and others of the kind. Empirical studies have failed to show this deterrent effect. But people in high tax brackets generally claim that high tax rates do affect their behavior, and the evidence is not yet sufficient to brush their arguments aside. Many economists and sociologists believe that the desire to improve one's *relative* position will keep most people working hard, even when Uncle Sam gets a big chunk of the increase. Moreover, most high-income jobs are closely associated with social prestige, power, and status. At the top of the income scale, these incentives to work and advancement may overshadow desires for more take-home pay.

At lower income levels, substantial marginal tax rates may cut down on over-time work, second jobs, and working wives. But here the pressures for more income are strong, and it is not clear that taxes are a major deterrent to work in most cases, so long as the earner keeps the bulk of the marginal income for himself.

A parallel argument is that peak marginal tax rates seriously deter risky investment. If you win, the government takes most of the killing; if you lose, you bear the loss. So why take the chance? This argument may deter investors from risky ventures—but remember that most such gains would be subject only to the maximum capital gains rate of 25 per cent, and that much of the risk investment essential to growth is done by business firms, which are permitted substantial offsets of losses against gains in computing taxable income.

Everything considered, tax experts increasingly feel that lower peak personal tax rates combined with closing some of the present loopholes would make a better system for taxing incomes in an economy that wants rapid growth. Actually, present extremely high rates have more value as symbols than as sources of revenue. Eliminating all rates above 60 per cent would cost the government less than $2 billion. Only 1,000 taxpayers are subject to the 91 per cent peak rate. There simply isn't very much aggregate income to tax away in the hands of the very rich, compared to the government's present-day tax needs.

How about damping down instability? The income tax rates high as a built-in stabilizer. When national income soars in a boom, income tax receipts rise even faster, because a bigger proportion of people's incomes falls in the higher tax brackets. This puts a damper on the boom. Conversely, when national income slides in a recession, personal income tax receipts slide even faster, thus cushioning the recession's impact on personal disposable income.

---

ties. Moreover, there is growing evidence that age, family status, asset and debt position, and other such variables significantly influence the propensity to consume out of any given level of disposable income. Over-all, the evidence still suggests that heavy taxation on the rich will bite into saving more than the same taxation on the poor, but except at the rich and poor extremes the differences may not be very great. The text generally assumes a differential effect at different income levels, but keep an open mind.

2. *Effects on income distribution and resource allocation.* From the point of view of equity, the personal income tax is widely agreed to be a good tax, though there is a disagreement on the optimum rate structure. It is a progressive tax on the basis of net income received, probably the best available indicator of ability to pay. Moreover, we can be surer than with other major taxes that the incidence will be where it is intended. A further advantage of the tax in a free society is its minimal interference with freedom of consumer, investor, and worker choices. Although the income tax takes a certain percentage of net income, this percentage is the same whatever the source of income,[2] and the taxpayer is left free to spend or invest his remaining income wherever he pleases without government interference. The personal income tax may stimulate leisure as against work, since it can be avoided by not working, but, as was indicated above, there is limited evidence to substantiate this effect.

With the present pattern of government expenditures, the progressive personal income tax results in an obviously altered pattern of resource use. When taxes bite into upper-level incomes, the demand for fur coats, Lincolns, and fine houses suffers; when lower-income families receive the funds, the increased demand for more commonplace goods and services draws resources to their production.

Death and Gift Taxes. Death and gift taxes provide an important supplement to the personal income tax. The federal government levies a progressive "estate tax" on the estate of everyone who dies with property totaling more than $60,000. Above that level, rates climb rapidly to 77 per cent on that portion of estates over $10 million, but the large exemption, plus a further special exemption of half the estate if it's given to one's husband or wife, keeps most families free from the tax. Most states have comparable taxes on the inheritances received by beneficiaries in estates, but at much lower rates, and there is a partial exemption under the federal tax for state taxes paid. The federal tax is accompanied by a gift tax to limit evasion of death taxes by giving away property before death, though there are generous exemptions for gifts spread out over several years, and maximum gift tax rates are only about two-thirds the estate tax rates.

The total yield of these taxes in 1959 was about $1 billion. Their net effect is almost purely redistributional. Together, they make it hard to pass on to heirs a huge estate, but special trust arrangements can mitigate the tax blow considerably for all, including the largest fortunes. Death and gift taxes are good taxes from the ability-to-pay standpoint, since they hit only high-income levels; and many people believe it is proper for large fortunes to be returned to the public rather than being passed on indefinitely within families. On the other hand, by making it harder for large fortunes to be perpetuated, death and gift taxes run the risk of lessening society's rate of capital accumulation. By putting most large

---

[2] Except for the qualifications noted above on tax loopholes and tax evasion.

estates into trust funds, moreover, the law pushes toward more conservative investment patterns. For their justification, these taxes rely mainly on the desire to redistribute income and wealth more equally.

CORPORATION INCOME TAXES The federal government and most states levy taxes on corporation incomes. These taxes were estimated to yield $22 billion in 1959, second only to the personal income tax. The federal tax accounted for the great bulk of this total.

The federal tax applies to all corporate net income, with a 52 per cent rate in 1959—except that the first $25,000 of income is taxed at only 30 per cent and over 80 per cent of the nation's million corporations make less than $25,000 annually. Thus most companies escaped the 52 per cent rate, but the great bulk of corporate income, earned by the big companies, paid it. Companies may offset losses in bad years against profits in good years to a considerable extent, a privilege not available to individuals.

Just what constitutes "taxable income" for any corporation is a vital issue under the corporate income tax, though it is largely hidden from the public view. We must leave this highly technical problem mainly to the lawyers and the accountants. But two questions are so important and controversial that to overlook them is to miss the essence of the corporate income tax issues that come up in session after session of Congress.

One is the issue of "depreciation allowances." How fast should companies be permitted to depreciate new plant and equipment for tax purposes? If they can "accelerate" depreciation, depreciation charges (allowable as business costs) will be larger and taxable profits correspondingly smaller during the years immediately ahead, than with slower depreciation. This permits the corporation to postpone taxes, giving it for current reinvestment funds that would otherwise have to be paid sooner as taxes. If the government wants to speed up investment in a particular area (say steel), an effective way is to offer accelerated depreciation of privileges on new plants.

Second is the issue of "depletion" allowances for companies drilling for or mining such natural resources as oil and coal. Under present law, oil companies can charge as a business cost a special depletion allowance of 27½ per cent of the gross income received from their oil wells. This special income exclusion, supported as necessary to encourage expensive exploration and drilling activities, totaled about $3 billion in 1959, and succeeded in holding the average tax rate on oil company incomes down to about 24 per cent, compared to just under 52 per cent for most major companies. Critics of the provision attack it as a blatant subsidy to the oil interests. Similar, though smaller, automatic percentage depletion allowances are provided for most other minerals.

Incidence and Effects. The incidence of the corporation income tax is uncertain. In a highly competitive economy, with firms striving to maximize profits, we could be sure the tax would fall primarily on stockholders. If a company was maximizing profits at some price-output level before the tax, this would still be the most advantageous level after the tax. The government would take some of the profits, unfortunately for the stockholders, but their profits after taxes would still be maximized at the same output and price. This situation might drive investment completely out of the corporate form into other kinds of investment opportunities. But for big business, incorporation is almost essential, and comparable investment possibilities at lower tax rates are hard to find. Or it might lead stockholders to give up investing entirely and to consume their funds. But this too seems unlikely on any large scale.

In the real world of oligopolies and partial monopolies, of imperfect information on costs and markets, of multiple motives for corporate management among which profit maximation is only one—the incidence of the corporate income tax is much less certain. Prices are set administratively, markets are shared, big buyers bargain with big sellers. If a firm does not want to disturb its position in the industry, it may be willing to absorb an increase in income taxes. Or the tax increase may prod the firm into breaking the inertia of established prices and venturing a big price increase. Although "logically" business output and price policies should be unaffected by corporate income taxes if business' main goal is to maximize profits, undoubtedly such taxes are shifted in many cases.

What has happened to post-tax corporation profits when corporation tax rates have been increased in the past? In general, profits have been squeezed, compared to lighter tax periods. This is far from convincing evidence on incidence, since many other factors influenced corporation profits in each period. But opponents of the tax point to it as evidence that taxes have eaten away at profits available for stockholders and, more important, for reinvestment.

High marginal tax rates encourage current corporation expenditures, whatever the incidence of the tax itself. With a 52 per cent marginal tax rate, each dollar spent on advertising, research, or other such business purposes costs the company only 48 cents. The government (the taxpayer) in substance pays the other 52 cents. There is no way of estimating precisely the importance of this effect, but tax experts and businessmen agree that business takes a more lenient attitude on spending when the marginal tax rate is high. This was vividly demonstrated during World War II, when peak tax rates were 82 per cent and corporations could spend "18-cent dollars." But as long as the corporation keeps part of each dollar of profits, it has an incentive to hold down costs to build up profits. Spending "cheap" dollars costs less than spending tax-free dollars, but it still costs potential profits.

All in all, economic analysis suggests that corporation income taxes are borne partly by stockholders and partly by consumers. In addition, the expenditure-inducing effects of high marginal tax rates may place the cost of some business expenditures on the taxpayer rather than on the consumer or stockholder.

1. *Effects on Growth and Output.* A tax on corporate net income imposes no direct burden on costs and hence does not have the same direct deterrent effect on output and employment as do sales, excise, and payroll taxes. On the other hand, the level of business investment depends largely on profits and the expectation of profits. A tax that draws away a large share of profits from direct reinvestment, and that sharply reduces the yield on invested capital, surely has some effect in slowing investment and growth. Just how much is not clear.

The burden of the corporation income tax is especially severe in inflation periods, when depreciation allowances set to cover the original cost of the plant or equipment fail to cover *replacement* cost. Since the tax law permits businesses to charge depreciation costs only up to the original cost of the plant or equipment depreciated, businesses in effect must pay income tax on partially "paper" profits. This special drain on profits, businessmen argue, amounts to billions of dollars a year when prices rise.

The expenditure-inducing effect of high corporate profit rates provides some offsets for some kinds of investment—those that can be charged as current costs. When the government pays 52 cents of each dollar, businesses put more into research, education, and other such activities than they otherwise would. But this is only a partial offset to the tax's deterrent effect on corporate investment.

On the score of built-in countercyclical flexibility, the tax comes off better. With good times, corporation profits rise rapidly, pushing up tax liabilities and draining off funds to the government. When business declines, corporate profits show the drop fast, and there is a correspondingly fast reduction in corporation tax liabilities. Together with the personal income tax, the corporation income tax tops the list for built-in flexibility.

2. *Effects on the distribution of income.* Taxes on corporate income conform fairly well to the criterion of ability to pay. The tax falls partly on corporate stockholders, and most such securities are held by the upper- and middle-income groups. But income from securities is often not a satisfactory measure of tax-paying ability. For example, Mr. A may have an income of $5,000 annually, and own a few shares of General Motors. He loses 52 per cent (at 1960 rates) of his potential income from dividends because of corporate income taxes. The millionaire owner of General Motors stock loses the same percentage. Clearly, high-income stockholders are taxed less progressively than if all corporate income had been paid out to them for taxation as personal income, and low-income ones more so. Over all, the corporate income tax makes the tax burden somewhat more progressive for low-income stockholders, less progressive for rich.[3]

---

[3] For estimates at different income levels, see Daniel Holland, *The Income Tax Burden on Stockholders* (Princeton Univ. Press, 1958), pp. 126 ff.

The benefit principle is also invoked in support of corporate income taxes. The benefit argument makes lots of sense at the local level, for fire protection and such services. At the federal and state levels where income taxes are used, it is far less convincing.

One of the biggest equity issues in the present corporate income tax is the "double taxation" of dividends, when they are taxed first as corporate profits and then as personal income to the stockholder. Critics argue that this arrangement is highly inequitable. No other type of income is subject to similar double taxation. This double taxation seizes a huge share of the profits away from the stockholder, and discourages precisely the type of enterprise and risk-taking that we need for economic growth and innovation. Supporters of the present arrangement retort that these are just arguments for reducing the tax burden on the rich (the stockholders), and shoving a bigger share of total taxes back onto the poor. Moreover, they argue, dividends are "unearned" income and deserve to be taxed at a higher rate than wages and salaries. In 1954, double taxation of dividends was reduced somewhat by allowing dividend receivers a partial credit against their tax liability; families can now exclude the first $100 of dividends from their taxable income and credit 4 per cent of all additional dividend income against their personal tax liability, as a partial elimination of the double-tax effect. But neither side was satisfied with this makeshift compromise.[4]

EXCISE AND SALES TAXES Excises are taxes on particular commodities, usually collected from the manufacturer or wholesaler. You probably don't realize the range of excises you pay. Many of them are hidden in the over-all price, although some are by law quoted separately from the price. The federal government lists 66 such excises—on liquor, tobacco products, sugar, automobiles, electrical energy, safe deposit box rents, and a wide variety of others. Many states and localities have comparable taxes, ranging all the way up to general sales taxes which levy a flat percentage of the sales price on all items sold at retail. All told, sales and excise taxes accounted for $19 billion in 1959.

One reason for the popularity of excises is that they are easy to hide. They mean plucking the feathers where the squawk will be least. In the political processes of tax-making, levies that are relatively invisible to the voters make a strong appeal to legislators.

Incidence and Effects. What is the incidence of a new excise tax on, say, playing cards? Most people assume it will be passed on to the consumer, and most of the time they're probably right. But not always. The answer comes

---

[4] In England, a large offset is allowed to stockholders for taxes paid by the corporation on distributed profits.

directly from an application of the supply and demand analysis of Part 3. A lot depends on how competitive the card industry is, on the demand for cards, and on the supply of labor and raw materials to the industry. Excise tax incidence is a nice exercise in the use of your price analysis from Part 3.

Competition. If competition is active in the industry so that economic profits tend to be eliminated, it is reasonably sure that the tax will be shifted. It raises costs and does nothing to increase demand, so net losses will result until the tax is shifted. Firms may put prices up by the amount of the tax, or may reduce their costs by paying less for labor and raw materials.

In the higher-price case, fewer cards will be sold at the higher price and resources will gradually be shifted out of the industry in search of better returns elsewhere; consumers pay a higher price and get fewer cards. Equilibrium will be restored when the price has risen just enough to cover total unit costs, *including the new tax,* at the lowest point on the typical firm's cost curve. Then there will be no incentive for more resources to move out of the industry. In the second case, workers and raw-materials producers bear the brunt of the tax through less pay for the same amount of work or materials. Equilibrium is re-established with the same output and price, but with costs lower by just the amount of the tax. (Look back at pages 410-417 for the complete analysis.)

Which way will the tax be shifted? Whichever way is easier. If demand is highly elastic, so that sales fall rapidly as price is put up, forward-shifting is hard. If there is a strong union in the industry, so that wages are hard to push down (i.e., so that the supply of productive resources is highly elastic), backward-shifting is difficult. How much of the tax goes each way depends on the relative elasticities of demand and supply in the two directions. The basic assumption underlying the common presumption of forward-shifting is that the elasticity of supply of productive resources is higher than consumers' elasticity of demand for the taxed product.

In industries using highly specialized resources, backward-shifting is more likely than elsewhere. To illustrate, suppose the playing-card industry takes the whole output of some grade of paper pulp that is not useful in any other industry. Then the supply of paper pulp to the card industry would be very inelastic, at least in the short run; even if the card industry offered a much lower price it could probably still get about as much pulp, since there is no place else for the pulp to be sold. The tax would be largely shifted backward in lower pulp prices. But the more unspecialized and mobile resources are, the less they are forced to take lower payments as a result of decreased demand. And in the long run, most resources are unspecialized.

Monopoly and Oligopoly. In monopolistic or oligopolistic markets where competition has not eliminated profits, the final outcome is less certain. Part of the tax may fall on profits and stay there without driving resources out of the industry. Here we are up against the whole uncertainty of price-making in imperfectly competitive areas. The partial monopolist may immediately pass on the tax through a higher price. Or he may be willing to absorb it rather than chance driving away his customers. Or he may use the tax as an excuse for an even larger price boost. Or he may follow some other course of action.

But through all this uncertainty, two fundamental facts stand: (1) A large tax cannot be absorbed by monopoly profits, and will be largely shifted, as under competition. (2) A non-shifted tax eats into profits, and few businessmen like to see profits sink, whatever their other management motives; they will shift the tax whenever they feel they reasonably can. There is little evidence, theoretical or empirical, that excises in noncompetitive industries are mainly borne by the profits in those industries.

In all cases, the process of shifting may be slow and jerky. General business conditions have a big influence on the ease and speed of shifting—taxes are easier to shift in good times than in bad. Businessmen often don't know the elasticities of demand and supply for their own firms. Often they don't set prices and output in a carefully calculated way. Here, as everywhere, economic theory provides only a framework for looking at individual problems—not ready answers to them.

General Sales Taxes. A general sales tax differs from an excise in one major respect. It hits all commodities and hence leaves fewer untaxed alternatives toward which productive resources can shift. A sales tax, like an excise, raises costs; firms will try to pass it on. If we assume a constant total money demand (as we have implicitly been doing so far), forward-shifting of a general sales tax through higher prices will mean reduced sales volume. This will reduce the demand for productive services, leading to partial backward-shifting through lower wages and materials prices, and to lower employment as output drops. This effect may, of course, be quite different from industry to industry, even though the sales tax rate is the same in all industries.

The one generalization that can be made about the over-all incidence of a general sales tax is this: It will decrease the incomes of productive agents relative to the prices of finished commodities. A general sales tax covers all commodities consumed and affects almost everybody as both consumer and seller of productive services. Therefore, in the aggregate it makes little difference whether technically the burden is passed forward through higher prices or backward through lower money incomes; the total population involved is the same either way. However, the differential effects on different individuals are likely to be great, depending on the direction of shifting.

1. *Effects on growth and employment.* The direct impact of sales and excise taxes is highly deflationary. They impose a direct burden on costs or effective purchasing power. But if we are mainly interested in rapid growth, and must obtain some given amount of tax revenue, then sales and excise taxes may be the best bet. For they bear directly on consumption, while leaving investment untaxed. Moreover, they are generally regressive, bearing relatively more heavily

on low than on high incomes. Thus they do little to impair the saving and invest-ment that come largely from the upper-income levels.

By the same token, a general sales tax is a strong anti-inflation weapon. It hits directly at the consumption expenditures of the lower- and middle-income groups. Whether this anti-inflation advantage overweighs its regressiveness is a question of judgment. Some writers feel that even inflation would be less inequitable than a heavy general sales tax. Others disagree. This leads us directly on to the question of equity.

2. *Effects on income distribution and resource allocation.* A *general sales tax* is seriously regressive. A $2,000-income family will spend almost the entire amount, except for rent payments, on taxed consumption. Assuming a forward-shifted tax of 5 per cent, it will pay a tax of $100, disregarding rent—5 per cent of total income. But a $100,000-income family will spend only part on consump-tion goods (say $40,000). The wealthy family is thus taxed 5 per cent on only $40,000, making a total sales tax burden of $2,000, or only 2 per cent of total income. Even though the wealthy family pays many more dollars, it pays a smaller percentage of its income.

But increasingly, major "necessities" like food and clothing have been ex-empted to soften his inequity. With these exemptions, plus rent, sales taxes lose most of their regression, and don't differ greatly, except at high income levels, from raising the same funds with a broad-based income tax. As a result, popular acceptance of sales taxes has risen considerably, even among "liberals" who generally favor taxes on the rich, and such sales taxes are widely supported for state and local use in view of already high federal income tax rates.

Whether an *excise* is regressive depends on the commodity taxed. Whatever its equity, an excise clearly discourages consumption of the taxed product.

Most people think we ought to avoid taxing "necessities," but that it is all right to tax "luxuries." Taxes on "necessities" are thought to be regressive; taxes on "luxuries" progressive. These loose generalizations depend, however, on how "necessities" and "luxuries" are defined. If "necessities" are goods that everyone consumes heavily (e.g., bread), taxes on necessities are clearly regressive, since a larger proportion of income will be spent on them by low- than by high-income groups. But consider taxes on two major "luxuries"—liquor and tobacco. In fact, the demand for both these products by rich and poor is relatively inelastic. The cigarette tax of about 8 cents per pack in many states often leads to lower ex-penditures on clothing and food, not to less smoking, since many people give up what are usually called "necessities" rather than cigarettes. The same is true of liquor. Thus liquor and tobacco taxes (on "luxuries") may be among the most regressive taxes.

"Necessities" can be defined in any way you like. But definitions based on moral standards should not blind you to the inelastic demand by both poor and rich for many products labeled "luxuries," nor to the real effect of taxes on these products. If excises are imposed on such goods as mink coats and caviar, grounds for criticizing them as regressive vanish; but taxes on such articles can yield little revenue, since so few of them are purchased. If excises are to yield large sums, they must fall on goods heavily consumed by the middle- and lower-income groups.

PAYROLL TAXES

Payroll taxes are used largely to finance the federal old-age insurance program and the combined federal-state unemployment insurance plans. A few cities levy additional payroll taxes.

Most payroll taxes fall in two equal parts, half levied on the employee and half on the employer. Note that payroll taxes differ significantly from personal income taxes, in that payroll taxes fall on only one type of income—wages and salaries. Dividends, rents, interest, and all other non-payroll income are exempted. This focus on payrolls is justified by the use of the funds for the special benefit of the workers. Indeed, the payroll taxes to finance the federal old-age retirement program are not officially termed taxes in the regular federal budget. Instead, Old Age and Survivors' Insurance is considered an insurance plan in which payroll taxes are compulsory premiums.[5]

Incidence. The incidence of both parts of the payroll tax (that deducted from wages and that paid by employers) is primarily on the workers covered. But the widespread imperfections in the labor market, coupled with legal and extra-legal controls over wages, make the process of shifting uncertain and jerky. Where wages are inflexible, moreover, the incidence may well take the form of unemployment for the workers involved. Look separately at the tax collected out of wages and that imposed on the employer.

1. The incidence of the tax deducted directly from the employee's wage is almost sure to be on the employee. There is no one onto whom he can shift it backward, and there is nothing in the tax to increase the demand for labor. Powerful unions may be able to use the tax as an excuse to demand wage increases—but if they can get higher wages after the tax we have to explain why they couldn't do it before. There is little likelihood that the tax will be shifted to the employer by a withdrawal of labor to "non-covered" occupations, partly because there are few such areas and partly because workers don't want to give up the benefits of the social security program.

2. The likely incidence of the tax on the employer is also on employees. The tax increases the effective wage cost. If the firm was previously in a maximum profit adjustment, after the tax it will be advantageous to raise selling prices or to curtail employment directly, both restricting output and substituting machinery

---

[5] Details on the federal social security program are given in Chapter 42.

for labor. If wages are flexible, they may move down to permit the same number of workers to be employed after the tax as before. If wage rates are inflexible, the more likely effect of the tax is unemployment. Notice that this analysis assumes either competitive conditions or monopolistic conditions where economic profits have been eliminated. When firms have a substantial protected profit position, a union may be able to bargain wages up to offset part or all of the higher payroll taxes.

If we want workers to bear the major costs of unemployment and old-age insurance, payroll taxes may be an acceptable means of financing social security. They are widely supported. But some observers object.

First, payroll taxes are regressive. They are borne mainly by the wage-worker, not by the higher-income groups. How much of the cost of social security should be borne by the workers themselves?

Second, wage rates are far from flexible downward. Imagine what the union would say if a company proposed cutting wages to pay its share of the tax. The result has to be higher prices, with decreased sales and employment, unless the employer can be forced to absorb the tax out of profits or unless total purchasing power is expanded. Payroll taxes on the employer may thus cause the very unemployment they are intended to insure against. Putting the tax on the employer in the present fashion, even though we *want* him to pay it, doesn't necessarily mean that he *will* pay it.

PROPERTY TAXES

Property taxes were, until World War II, by far the most important single tax source in the United States. They are also the oldest major source of tax revenue. The federal government levies no property taxes, and state governments now receive only a small sum annually from them. But local governmental units obtain over $15 billion annually—virtually their entire income—from property taxes.

Administration. How does the property tax actually "work" in practice? Most local units—towns, water districts, school districts, counties, road districts, and the like—annually or biennially estimate the expenditures required for the coming year or two years. Meanwhile, the property to be taxed has been assessed. Then the amount to be raised is compared with the assessed property values, and the tax rate necessary to raise the funds is determined. For example, if $1 million is to be raised and the total assessed valuation is $100 million, a tax rate of 1 per cent on assessed valuation is necessary.

The administration of this process has been very inefficient. Land and houses cannot hide. Yet in many cases efficient assessment surveys (sometimes now conducted by aerial photography) have revealed large numbers of rural and urban properties that have never even been listed for taxation. For property that is assessed, there is a wide variation in the level of assessment. Low-priced real property is widely over-assessed relative to high-priced real property (that is, assessment is "regressive")—partly because of "influence" with assessors and partly because most assessors have no idea of the value of expensive properties and hence depend on the figures suggested by the owners or simply follow past assessments.

The assessment of personal property is even worse. There have been many cases where entire counties have failed to show any bank deposits on the tax lists, in spite of the fact that banks were operating openly within the county. Most personal property taxes put a penalty on honesty, fostering a public attitude that it is quite justifiable to evade not only these taxes but others "if you can get away with it." Many local and state authorities make little pretense of enforcing them. Only the especially conscientious or conspicuously liable taxpayer pays, a highly inequitable arrangement.

Incidence and "Capitalization."   There is nothing peculiarly hard about figuring out the incidence of many property taxes. Taxes on personal property, such as household furniture, are borne by the taxpayer. There's no one he can shift them to. Taxes on buildings and other "improvements" on land may be gradually shifted if the tax drives investment out of these areas into others where taxes are lower, thereby reducing the supply and raising the price of these taxed improvements. This is the same analysis as in the case of other taxes that hit only special areas or products.

An interesting point concerns the tax on land itself, as distinct from improvements on it. The first effect of the tax on land is the same as on any other investment opportunity—the net return on the property is correspondingly reduced. Since the price that any buyer is willing to pay for a productive agent is determined largely by the capitalized value of the future net income that he expects to receive from it, buyers will be willing to pay less for the land after the tax has been levied. The capital value of the land is thus decreased by the imposition of the tax.

The tax is then said to have been "capitalized." Any future buyer of the land will not invest in the land unless the price is low enough to provide a net return *after real estate taxes* equal to that obtainable on investment elsewhere. Capitalization thus puts the burden of the capitalized tax exclusively on the owner of the land at the time the tax is levied, by forcing him to pay the unshiftable tax and by forcing down the capital value of his property. Any future buyer will not bear the burden of the tax, because he anticipates the tax in the price paid for the land. Future owners buy "tax-free."

Although capitalization does not always work out so precisely, it is an important factor in connection with the real-property tax. Consider a proposal to decrease the tax on real property. Present buyers have bought at lower figures because of the tax, capitalizing the burden on earlier owners. To lower the property tax now would be to give a subsidy to present owners through increasing the capital value of the land. The fact of capitalization is a strong argument against drastic reductions in long-established property tax rates.

Property ownership is sometimes defended as a good indication of ability to pay taxes. But even if all property were reached by the property tax, this guide to ability would be a weak one. The major portion of national income is received in wages and salaries that have no direct connection with property holdings. Moreover, in practice the property tax is largely only a real-property tax; the vast amount of wealth held in the form of tangible and intangible personalty largely escapes taxation. Lastly, on that part of the tax which is capitalized, there is no incidence in a meaningful sense on present property owners.

The real-property tax is also sometimes supported on the "benefit" principle. Owners of real property receive many important special benefits, such as police and fire protection; and the larger the property holdings, the greater are the benefits received. There is obviously merit in this view, although property taxes are used to finance many activities unconnected with the property taxes—for example, education and the courts.

One last serious defect of the property tax as the main local revenue source needs mention—its inelasticity in periods of rising income. Since increases in property assessments lag substantially behind rising values in inflation, local tax revenues tend to decrease in real purchasing power during inflation, unless tax *rates* are increased. This phenomenon has severely pinched the provision of local governmental services during the past two decades of inflation, even with large increases in local borrowing to finance improvements.

The property tax has some virtues on the benefit criterion, and a few on ability-to-pay. But the main case for it is that it's there, and everything is pretty well adjusted to it. There is no other local tax source that looks better which could realistically replace it.

"A MODEL TAX SYSTEM"

What would a model tax system look like? After this long look at the different major taxes now in use, what changes would you make in the tax system? As a citizen, this is one issue on which you will repeatedly get a chance to say your piece. At federal, state, and local levels, tax changes are continually being made.

Some economists have proposed a model tax system along the following lines. It would make some drastic changes in the present system. By now, you should be in a position to organize your own views on an ideal tax system. This unusual program should stimulate your thinking.

The model tax system would have four major taxes:

1. There would be a progressive personal income tax that would account for at least three-fourths of all tax revenue. This would mean more than doubling

present income tax revenues. Rates would reach down through the middle-income levels and into the low-income groups to produce the revenue needed. This tax places the burden directly on individuals where it ultimately must rest, and it makes clear who is paying how much. It would be supplemented by progressive death and gift taxes. All these provisions conform to commonly held criteria of ability to pay and together meet most of the tests of good taxes.

To encourage incentive and economic growth and to improve equitable treatment of similarly situated people, the present punitively high peak rates of the federal tax would be lowered to about 60 per cent, but at the same time the sieve of avoidance loopholes for high-income taxpayers would be closed. Averaging of uneven incomes over a five-year period would be permitted. State income taxes would be levied through the federal income tax system, with rebates to the states concerned, since this mass tax would be the backbone of both federal and state tax systems.

2. Both to stimulate economic growth and to improve equity by switching to the personal income tax, present corporation income tax rates would be lowered considerably. The new tax would fall on all businesses, not merely corporations. At the same time, again to encourage growth, depreciation restrictions would be eased to permit faster charge-offs. But major loopholes like the present "depletion allowance" would be closed. Undistributed profits above generous reinvestment levels would be prorated out to stockholders for taxation, to avoid use of corporations as tax-avoidance devices.

3. Taxes on real property would be continued at roughly present levels, not so much because the real-property tax is a good tax as because it is a major revenue source for local governments to which economic life has become well adjusted, and because its removal would mean a large subsidy to present real-property owners.

4. There would be special taxes that are clearly justifiable on the benefit principle. In this group would be: (a) special assessments, (b) highway taxes (on fuel and on vehicles), with the revenue to be spent on highways and streets, and (c) payroll taxes on the worker (not on the employer), with the revenue to be spent on social security. All three of these have strong claim to use as benefit levies.

This "model" tax system would differ drastically from the present one in administration as well as in make-up. Centralized collection of income taxes would be more efficient for the government, more equitable, and more convenient for the taxpayer, since he would then file only one set of returns. Therefore, there would be only one over-all income tax with a basic set of federal rates, and state rates added where desired by the states, all collected by the federal government. A similar collection and sharing system would be used for death, gift, and business taxes, for substantially the same reasons. More efficient administration of the property tax would also be attained, either through state administration of the tax or through closer state supervision to assure that local units did the job more efficiently. There is no reason why the governmental unit that spends funds should be the most efficient unit to collect them, though our fiscal system is shot through with this tacit assumption.

Taxes are going to take over a quarter of the income you earn during the rest of your life, if something like present conditions continue. Getting a good tax system is important to everybody. Stop and ask yourself, what does *your* model tax system look like? Then ask another question: In the day-to-day world of practical politics, how much support in Congress do you think could be mustered for your major reforms, and what arguments would you use to win converts?

REVIEW—CONCEPTS TO REMEMBER

Public finance involves mainly the application of analytical concepts already learned in the preceding chapters. But it has some concepts and terms of its own that you need to have firmly installed in your economic tool kit:

incidence	progressive taxation
shifting	regressive taxation
benefit principle	capital gain
ability-to-pay principle	tax capitalization

1. Some tax experts argue that taxes should be highly visible (like the personal income tax) in order to make citizens keenly aware of the taxes they are paying. Others argue that hidden taxes are better because citizens don't feel the burden so strongly and are less unhappy about the costs of government services. Analyze these arguments. What are the main issues, and where do you stand on them?

FOR ANALYSIS AND DISCUSSION

2. Suppose a substantial tax reduction becomes feasible. Which of the following would you favor, so far as the personal income tax is concerned, and why?

    a. An increase in personal exemptions from $600 to $800, thereby increasing the amount of income and the number of citizens free of tax.

    b. An across-the-board reduction of the same percentage in the personal income tax bill of all taxpayers.

3. "The government's taxing and spending policies should leave the distribution of income roughly as it would be through the private economy."

"Every child should receive a good education at least through the grade-school level."

Can you consistently accept both these propositions? Analyze carefully why or why not, examining specifically any apparent inconsistencies.

4. Suppose a new excise tax were imposed on the following products, at the producer's level:

   a. Steel (where there is considerable price leadership and some competition, plus strong labor unions).

   b. Potatoes (where the market is highly competitive and little unionized labor is involved).

   c. Ladies' garments (where the market is highly competitive and there is a strong labor union).

   d. Refined oil and gasoline (where the market is oligopolistic and little strongly unionized labor is involved).

Without making special investigations of cost and market conditions in the various industries, explain in each case whether you would expect the incidence of the tax to be on the consumer, labor in the industry, the producing firm, or some combination. Applying the analytical procedures of Chapter 36, explain in each instance why your presumption is as it is.

5. Assume a period of strong inflationary pressures as a result of government arms spending. If you were forced to vote for one of these alternatives, which would you consider the more equitable, and why?

   a. A general sales tax to balance the budget.

   b. Inflation.

6. "High income taxes on large incomes are bad policy, because they take away the incentive for top management to do a better job in getting more goods produced for consumers at the lowest cost." Do you agree? Why or why not?

7. Given a full-employment situation and the need for more taxes to finance more defense spending, what tax program would you propose to raise an additional $10 billion? Defend your program against likely criticism from those who would bear the major burden.

Current Research

$\mathbb{R}$esearch in the area of public finance has focused heavily since the decade of the 1930's on fiscal policy to avoid depression and inflation. But in recent years, research aimed at the allocative and distributional effects of government taxes and expenditures has come back into fashion, as it becomes increasingly clear that big government spending and taxes are here to stay—at federal, state, and local levels. Since the Appendix to Part 2 included research on fiscal policy, the following paragraphs are limited mainly to the areas covered by Chapters 35 and 36, arbitrary though this division may be.

Federal Tax Policy for Economic Growth and Stability, a volume of papers prepared by 75 leading tax experts for the Joint Economic Committee of Congress in 1955, provides a good introduction to recent research in the field of taxation. The volume has papers on nearly every phase of modern federal taxation. If you don't have any special interests, try R. A. Musgrave's "Incidence of the Tax Structure and Its Effects on Consumption"; Keith Butters' "Effects of Taxation on the Investment Capacities and Policies of Individuals"; or Clarence Long's "Impact of the Federal Income Tax on Labor Force Participation." The first presents one of the few available integrated estimates of the incidence of the entire tax system. The others deal with major problems in the impact of taxes on investment, growth, and output.

California's George Break looks further at the alleged deterrent effect of high personal income taxes on work, without finding much evidence of it, in "Income Taxes and Incentives to Work," *American Economic Review,* September 1957. Nicholas Kaldor, one of England's leading economists, proposes a major tax on expenditures, rather than on incomes, as a preferable device for controlling excess spending and in some ways a more equitable tax, in a lively little book, *An Expenditure Tax* (Allen and Unwin, 1957). An interesting current comparison of personal income tax burdens in the U.S.S.R. and the United States is provided in a careful study by Franklin Holzman: "Income Taxation in the Soviet Union: A Comparative Study," *National Tax Journal,* June 1958.

Turning to the corporation income tax, try M. A. Adelman's "The Corporate Income Tax in the Long Run," in the *Journal of Political Economy,* April 1957, for an installment in the continuing controversy over the incidence of the tax on corporate profits. Extensive statistical analyses of quite different sorts are presented by R. P. Collier, "Some Empirical Evidence on Tax Incidence," *National Tax Journal* for March 1958, and Daniel Holland, *The Income Tax Burden on*

Stockholders (National Bureau of Economic Research, 1958). Collier bases his analysis of business tax shifting mainly on a series of industry case studies, while Holland uses mainly aggregate data for the whole economy to investigate what taxes corporation stockholders really do end up paying. George Lent, in "The Excess Profits Tax and Business Expenditures," *National Tax Journal,* September 1958, tries to find out just how much high marginal corporation income tax rates do induce free and easy spending.

On the whole taxation picture, a final reference to *Readings in the Economics of Taxation* (R. A. Musgrave and Carl Shoup, editors; Irwin, 1959) is appropriate. Though many of the articles reprinted go back several years, they were selected by editors appointed by the American Economic Association as the leading recent studies on the problem.

Unfortunately, in spite of the enormous importance of government expenditures economists have devoted comparatively little research attention to the expenditure side of the government budget picture. *Federal Expenditure Policy for Economic Growth and Stability,* another compendium of papers prepared for the Joint Economic Committee of Congress (in 1957), provides a good survey of professional thinking on every phase of the subject—but unfortunately it is more a survey of views and attitudes than of research findings. For a careful analysis of the broad problem of determining optimal public expenditure policies, see Walter Heller's "Economics and the Applied Theory of Public Expenditures." Good historical reviews of government spending are provided by Arnold Soloway and Paul Trescott, in their opening papers. For fresh looks at major aspects of government expenditure decisions—especially on major civilian services and on defense spending—try O. H. Brownlee, "Using Market Mechanisms in Making Government Expenditure Decisions," and Fred Hoffman, "The Economic Analysis of Defense: Choice Without Markets," in the *American Economic Review* for May 1959, and the evaluative comments that follow.

Finally, have a look at J. K. Galbraith's *The Affluent Society* (Houghton Mifflin, 1958), mentioned in the closing section of Chapter 35. Though not research in any formal sense, the last quarter of Galbraith's book, beginning with "The Theory of Social Balance," argues for a major change in our approach to the problem of setting government expenditure levels, so as to redress the unbalance he sees between spending on private and on publicly furnished services.

PART 6

The International
Economy

International Trade and Lending

37

In the "one world" of today, the close interdependence among nations is painfully obvious. The dominating issues are war and peace—the international political tensions that fill the newspapers. But intimately related are the economic issues—foreign aid, higher protection for our domestic industries and workers, the "dollar shortage," trade with the Soviet bloc, the International Monetary Fund and the International Bank.

On aggregate statistical grounds, foreign trade doesn't look very important to America. We import and export only about 5 per cent of our gross national product. Yet to many industries foreign trade is the blood of life—they export a quarter to a half of their total output or else import their basic materials from abroad. More important, our foreign economic policies in a world of international tension are inseparable from our political and military policies. For to most of the world foreign trade is far more urgent than to us. England must import most of her food or starve, and she can pay for her imports only by selling her exports abroad. And so it is with most of the world's nation's. Only the United States, the U.S.S.R., and

685

possibly China are so large and so rich in resources that they need rely only a little on imports to maintain their standard of living. And even for them, foreign trade plays a major role in crucial sectors of their economies.

In spite of the pressing importance of foreign trade, governments have long followed many policies that restrict rather than encourage such trade—tariffs, quotas, exchange controls. *Prima facie,* the case for international division of labor and exchange is clear, as it is in domestic affairs. On the surface, there would appear to be no reason to suppose that human welfare would be improved by obstructing the processes of specialization and exchange. Why, then, have the layman and the lawmaker so often distrusted foreign trade and favored the tariff? Why have nations so often flown in the face of apparent economic reason? Nowhere else in economics is there a better opportunity to apply relatively simple economic analysis to popular fallacies.

THE BASIC CASE FOR INTERNATIONAL TRADE

Inter-regional and International Trade. The advantages of inter-regional specialization and division of labor within nations are everywhere recognized. Iowa produces corn and hogs, Florida specializes in citrus fruits, and Alabama raises cotton. Few would suggest that Iowa should raise her own oranges and cotton, Florida her own corn and pork. Differences in geography and climate, in the tastes and aptitudes of the people, and in the supplies of capital goods available in different localities go far to determine each area's best specialization. These productive resources and conditions are more or less fixed in the areas where they now exist. Allowing for this given geographical distribution, resources will be most efficiently utilized when each is used in that occupation where its marginal productivity is highest. In this way, the greatest quantity of wanted goods will be produced, and residents of all participating areas will gain in the resulting exchange.

In the example above, we might say that Iowa has an "absolute advantage" in producing corn, and Florida an "absolute advantage" in producing oranges That is, identical amounts of variable productive resources will clearly produce more corn in Iowa than in Florida, more oranges in Florida than in Iowa. Under these circumstances, it is obvious that both more corn and more oranges can be produced with inter-regional division of labor.

At first glance, the same advantages from specialization and exchange would seem to hold if we substituted England and Greece, or any other two countries, for Iowa and Florida. Different regions and different nations have great differences in efficiency in producing different goods, differences that persist largely because of international immobility of resources. These differences arise largely out of five considerations:

1. Over the face of the earth climatic and geographical conditions vary widely. Brazil is admirably suited for raising coffee; Newfoundland is convenient to the

fishing waters of the Grand Banks; the lower Nile Valley is ideal for cotton production. Texas and Oklahoma are great oil-producing centers; Chile has rich nitrate deposits. Such geographical and climatic differences alone would justify world-wide specialization.

2. Just as soils and climates vary over the globe, so do human capacities. Some groups are large and strong, adept at physical labor. Others excel at dexterity and manual skills. Still others stand out in enterprise and organizational ability. These differences may be due to long-standing racial characteristics, or they may be due to the political, social, and economic environment in which individuals are raised and live. Whatever the reasons, they constitute a major reason why international specialization and trade will be beneficial.

3. The accumulated supply of capital goods varies greatly from nation to nation. In some countries, centuries of accumulation have produced large supplies of fixed and mobile capital—railroads, buildings, machinery, and so forth. Examples are the U.S. and England; they specialize in industrial products. In other countries—for example, Greece and Nigeria—capital is scarce; they specialize in farming and simple production which requires little elaborate productive equipment. Moreover, vast differences exist between the kinds of capital accumulated in different nations.

4. The *proportions* between different types of resources vary widely from country to country. Australia has vast plains but relatively few people and capital goods. Therefore, she specializes in agricultural products that require a high proportion of natural resources to labor and capital goods. In England, on the other hand, land is scarce relative to human beings and capital. Therefore, she is best fitted for manufacture and industry, even though her soil may be as good as Australia's for wheat-growing.

5. In addition to these "economic" considerations, great differences exist in the political and social climate in different countries. In countries of stable government and conservative traditions, vast industrial organizations requiring large long-period capital commitments are likely to grow up. In backward, illiterate, badly governed areas, conditions may be almost prohibitory against mass-production industry. A hustling, mechanical-minded nation like the United States could hardly be expected to be satisfied again with a small-unit, predominantly rural economy, any more than the South Sea Islanders could be expected to be happy or efficient auto-makers.

The Law of Comparative Advantage.   Given these differences between nations, it is clear that international trade will be advantageous. But how far each nation should specialize and how far international trade should go are not so obvious.

If the greatest possible advantages of foreign trade are to be obtained for all, each nation must devote itself to what it can do most cheaply. In the simple case of Iowa and Florida, where the absolute advantage of each in its representative product is clear, Iowa should raise all the corn, Florida all the oranges. The greatest total of corn plus oranges will be obtained that way. But the concept of absolute advantage is a slippery one when it comes to comparing costs between different nations that have different monetary units, different proportions of factors of production, different labor standards, and different productive techniques. Most people would probably agree that as between coffee and factory machinery, Brazil has an absolute advantage in the former, the United States in the latter. Yet even in such an extreme case, it is hard to be precise on just why we are sure that these absolute advantages exist. When less-striking cases are considered, such as woolen manufacture in the United States and England, this difficulty becomes insurmountable. Monetary comparisons mean little, since different monetary units prevail in the two countries, and no one has been able to find a satisfactory measure for comparing absolute costs in different countries.

Fortunately, we don't have to say anything about the absolute advantage of different nations to determine how far specialization and trade can profitably be carried. The critical factor is the *comparative,* or *relative,* costs of producing the commodities *within* each of the two countries. To illustrate this fact and the principle underlying the advantage to be gained from international trade, consider a simple example of the United States vis-à-vis the rest of the world with respect to the production of two commodities, wheat and cloth.

Take some unit for measuring cost of production within each nation. This may be dollars or any other unit of measurement. Now let us arbitrarily define units of wheat and cloth in such a way that the cost of producing one unit of each is the same. Say that each costs x cost-units to produce, as indicated in the example below. (For this purpose, you can think of x as, say, $1, or as a group of productive services—a bundle of land, labor, and capital.) This might mean, concretely, that with $1 one bushel of wheat or one yard of cloth can be produced. Then one bushel would be one unit of wheat, and one yard would be one unit of cloth. *The important thing is that we can produce one bushel of wheat by giving up the production of one yard of cloth, and vice versa.*

	Cost of Production in the U.S.	Cost of Production Abroad
Unit of wheat (1 bushel)	x	y
Unit of cloth (1 yard)	x	$2y$

Let the cost of producing the same unit (one bushel) of wheat abroad be y. Again, costs abroad may be measured in francs or some other unit quite unrelated to dollars; we just need a basis for comparing the cost of producing wheat and cloth within the foreign country. Let us further suppose that the cost of producing one unit (one yard) of cloth abroad is $2y$, assuming thereby that abroad it costs twice as much to produce a yard of cloth as a bushel of wheat. *Abroad, production of two bushels of wheat must be given up to produce one more yard of cloth.* This situation is also shown in the above example.

Suppose there is no trade in wheat and cloth; each country produces its own supply of both. Will it pay the countries to begin specializing? The answer is yes. In the United States, we can obtain one more bushel of wheat by giving up one yard of cloth. But abroad, giving up one yard of cloth will produce two more bushels of wheat. *Therefore there will be an increase in total world output if the United States uses more of her resources to produce cloth while resources abroad are shifted to raising wheat. By transferring resources from cloth to wheat abroad, foreigners produce two additional bushels of wheat for each yard of cloth they forego; by transferring productive resources from wheat to cloth, the United States produces an extra yard of cloth for each bushel of wheat she foregoes. Obviously, we should shift more of our resources to producing cloth, while the foreign nation should shift more of hers to wheat. Then by exchanging we can both live better.*

It might appear from the table on page 688 that the United States has an *absolute* advantage in production over foreigners, since abroad it takes 2y to produce a yard of cloth while here it takes only 1x. Actually, we have not made this assumption at all. Since cost-units x (maybe dollars) and y (maybe hours of French labor) bear no necessary relation to each other, the table shows only the *comparative* costs of producing wheat and cloth in the United States and the *comparative* costs of producing the two abroad. The situation might have been equally well indicated by substituting ½y for y, and y for 2y, in the example. Both notations represent identical facts; exactly the same advantage from specialization and trade is indicated by both, as you can readily see by tracing through again the resource shift discussed in the preceding paragraph.

The principle illustrated by this simple table is that gain in total world output is possible from specialization and trade if the cost ratios of producing two commodities are different in different countries. This same principle would have applied in the above example had the cost ratios been 3:2 in the United States and 5:1 abroad, or any other set of differing ratios. Absolute costs in the two countries are not relevant. It would make no difference, for example, if one day's work in the United States would produce five times as much wheat and ten times as much cloth as abroad. Total output could be increased by specialization, because the cost ratios differ. *This principle, that total output will be maximized when each nation specializes in the lines where it has the greatest comparative advantage or the least comparative disadvantage, is called the "law of comparative advantage."*

From this principle we can easily tell in principle how far it is advantageous to carry specialization and trade. Gain from trade is possible until the cost ratios of producing the two commodities are the same in the United States and abroad. As production of cloth increases in the United States, and as production of wheat increases abroad, the cost ratios will move together. In the United States, the cost of producing cloth will ultimately rise relative to wheat as more cloth is produced. Abroad, the cost of producing wheat will rise relative to cloth.

Finally, at some levels of output the cost ratios will become identical here and abroad. Thereafter, there is no advantage in further specialization and exchange, since no further increases in total output can be obtained thereby.[1]

When the law of comparative costs is generalized to the real world with its many countries and thousands of products, no new principles are introduced, but the picture becomes immensely more complex. Gain will still be maximized if each country specializes in those goods and services in which its comparative advantage is greatest or in which its comparative disadvantage is least; and if this specialization is carried to the point where the cost ratios involved are equal to those of other countries producing the same products. In any given country, production of many products will never take place, because the country's comparative disadvantage in their production is so great. Most nations will find it advantageous to produce a variety of products. Introduction of transportation costs into the picture further strengthens the likelihood that each commodity will be produced in several countries and that each country will produce a variety of products. Trade is profitable only when the gain is sufficient to overcome transport charges. This is the abstract reasoning. Now look at its practical operation.

The Law of Comparative Advantage, Free Trade, and the Price System.   In a country like ours, the search for profits and the price system tend to bring about this optimal allocation of resources automatically. If we are relatively inefficient in producing coffee but very efficient in producing machine tools, American producers are going to have a tough time competing with Brazil in the world's coffee markets, but we'll beat out Brazilian machine tool makers in the market place. Under a free-trade system, in each country the greatest profits can be obtained by producing those commodities most desired by consumers at home and abroad. If the United States' comparative advantage is great in producing automobiles, this fact will be reflected in high returns to resources in the automobile industry. If our comparative advantage is low in producing spices, American spice producers will be unable to pay wages high enough to bid resources away from the more efficient automobile industry, since the world price for spices is set by rela-

---

[1] This principle of gain from trade can be shown in a simple diagram. Let one axis represent cloth and the other wheat. Any point on *OA* shows the relative cost of producing wheat and cloth in country A, while any point on *OB* shows the cost ratio in country B. Thus for any given output of wheat (say *OQ*) in country A an identical cost is required to produce *QM* of cloth. In B, the cost of *OQ* wheat will produce *QM′* cloth. Therefore, gain clearly will accrue if A specializes in wheat and B in cloth. As this specializaton proceeds, wheat will be subject to increasing costs in A and cloth to increasing costs in B. Thus lines *OA* and *OB* will move toward each other. When they become identical, say along the intermediate dotted line, the cost ratio will be *OQ:QN* in both countries, and further gain from trade will be impossible.

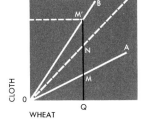

tively efficient East Indian production. Thus under a free-price system and free trade, the resources of each nation would tend to be drawn through the search for income into its most efficient industries.

Barriers to free international movement of goods impede specialization and trade, and reduce the gains from trade. The case for free trade internationally is the same as the case for free trade domestically—that in the absence of restrictions resources will be effectively allocated by the price system in accordance with consumers' demands and resource owners' preferences on jobs.

THE BASIC CASE FOR INTERNATIONAL LENDING   Society benefits when individuals and institutions save and invest, because useful capital goods and durable consumer goods are thereby accumulated. The saver gains individually from the return on his investment, and society gains from the increased efficiency of roundabout mechanized production. Both the saver and society gain most when savings are invested where their productivity is highest.

In the domestic economy, we mainly trust the price system to allocate savings to the most desirable investments. Savers (directly or through such institutions as banks and insurance companies) invest their funds where the combination of safety, liquidity, and rate of return seems most attractive. Since the rate of return tends to be highest where investments fulfill the strongest consumer demands, savings are drawn into those industries where consumers most want output increased. Consumer choices direct the allocation of savings among investments.

Internationally, as domestically, society is generally best off if savings are allocated where their marginal productivity is greatest. International loans are "better" than domestic loans when the anticipated rate of return on them (including liquidity and risk allowance) is greater. For decades, both England and the New World gained from heavy loans by Britishers to individuals and businesses in the rapidly developing Western Hemisphere. British lenders gained by receiving good returns on their investments; borrowers gained by getting additional capital to combine with the plentiful natural resources of the New World. Today the United States is the main international lender. Internationally, as domestically, lending may be unwise if the loan is unsafe, or undesirably illiquid. But here again national political boundaries do not invalidate the basic economic principles of gain from exchange and lending.

INTERNATIONAL TRADE AND DOMESTIC EMPLOYMENT   Do international trade and investment increase or decrease domestic employment? The answer is not easy. Over the long pull, probably their impact on the level of domestic employment is neutral—their effect is rather on the allocation of workers and non-human resources among jobs. But in the short run, one nation may temporarily increase its own employment by increasing its net exports. Production for export provides domestic jobs; imports cut into the market for domestic production. The net export balance is one form of investment. Like other investment, it may exercise a multiplier effect on domestic income and employment—usually called the "foreign trade multiplier."

But this short-run reasoning leads to obviously wrong results. It would lead every nation to want to export, none to want to import. This situation clearly can't be. Moreover, as soon as one country adopts such a policy, others are quick to retaliate. The result is thus an over-all shrinkage of the volume of international trade without gain to any nation.

In a world preoccupied with the problem of avoiding depression, concern over the impact of international trade on domestic employment may overshadow the more traditional interest in an optimal allocation of resources. Harmonizing these two goals is not always easy, though in the long run they are clearly complementary. We will look at the problem in more detail in Chapter 39.

INTERNATIONAL COMMUNITY AND CONFLICT OF INTERESTS Free international trade and lending are in the interest of the world as a whole. Removal of restrictions on international exchange permits more wanted goods and services to be produced in the world. For the most part, but not always, such free trade and lending also benefit each of the individual countries concerned. One of the major exceptions often mentioned is the possibility that an individual nation can increase its domestic employment in depression by shutting out competing foreign goods; this type of anti-unemployment argument is considered in the following chapters. But several other possible conflicts of interest merit attention here, assuming that relatively full employment exists:

1. *Personal Migration.* If the "economic welfare" of the world as a whole is the aim, then international migration probably should occur whenever the real wages obtainable in one country are higher than in another. But for the workers in high-wage countries, immigration of workers from low-wage countries might prove a major financial blow. Consider such an influx into the United States, assuming that the immigrants are substitutable for American workers. Average real wages for workers throughout the world would rise, but the shift in the labor supply would surely lower the wages and incomes of present American workers. U.S. wages might not go as low as present levels in other countries, because of the superior complementary American resources and better training of American workers; foreign labor might be a far from perfect substitute. But this conflict of national and international interest should not be glossed over by loose application of the law of comparative advantage. Given the international distribution of resources, the law of comparative advantage applies. But the law does not say that

each nation will gain from an international shift of resources, even when the shift raises the world's average standard of living.

2. *Monopoly-type Action by One Country.* Just as a domestic monopolist can benefit himself by restricting output, so a country may sometimes be able to benefit itself by restricting trade. But this effort is by no means sure to be successful. For one thing, the international monopolist must always face the potential competition of other countries. More important, any one country's restrictions on imports are likely to provoke retaliatory restrictions by other countries, and then there is no doubt that both are worse off from the reduced exchange of goods and services. Thus, it may be that a country can gain temporarily from restricting trade at the cost of the rest of the world, but the more likely result is a loss to all countries involved.

The extreme cases of nations endeavoring to act as monopolists are those where foreign trade is centralized under government control—Soviet Russia, for example. But to a smaller extent, other countries have also centralized their foreign-trade activities. Brazilian coffee is an example.

3. *Growth of Underdeveloped Areas.* When a rich country lends to underdeveloped areas, the lender may eventually find itself worse off because of the loans. This result occurs if the new areas develop industries to compete with the lender's. More often, however, the new industries are not directly competitive. In any case, as the new country sells abroad it can begin to buy abroad. A major portion of United States international trade is and has been with other highly industrialized nations. The problem of the "underdeveloped" countries vis-à-vis the industrialized nations is a major one for the decades ahead, and is the subject of Chapter 43.

4. *War.* The most important potential conflict goes beyond economics. It centers around war and preparation for war. No nation wants to be dependent on its potential enemies for vital raw materials and finished goods. We may not want to help build up the strength of potential enemies. With this major exception, however, economic and political considerations point in the same direction. Wide-ranging international trade and finance are probably the soundest bases for lasting peace.

THE BALANCE OF PAYMENTS

The United States exports and imports commodities and services. It also exports and imports capital and gold. Table 37-1 summarizes the complete United States "balance of payments" in 1958.

Basically, the table shows what we paid to foreigners and what they paid to us. The dark blue (I) shows what they paid us, for goods, services, and interest on our investments abroad. The light blue (II, IV, and V) shows what we paid them—for goods and services, in government and private aid, and in net new U.S. investments abroad. (III is merely a memorandum item included to show where we stood on exports vs. imports of goods and services alone.) The bottom section (VI, VII, and VIII) shows the "balancing" items; since we, on balance, owed them more than they owed us, they took the difference partly in gold ($2.3 billion) and partly by building up their bank deposits and short-term investments in the United States ($1.2 billion).

Table 37-1

U.S. BALANCE OF INTERNATIONAL PAYMENTS, 1958 [a]

(*In Billions*)

I. U.S. Exports:		
Merchandise	$16.2	
Services	4.1	
Income from investments abroad	2.9	
Total		$23.2 [b]
II. U.S. Imports:		
Merchandise	12.9	
Services	3.1	
Military purchases abroad	3.4	
Income on foreign investments here	.7	
Total		21.0
III. Net balance due U.S. on goods and services		2.2
IV. Net unilateral transfers: public and private U.S. aid		2.3 [b]
V. U.S. capital exports		3.8
VI. Accumulation of foreign capital in U.S.		1.2
VII. Net gold flow from U.S.		2.3
VIII. Errors and omissions		.4

a Data from U.S. Department of Commerce.
b Excludes $2.5 billion of military aid not considered part of the balance of payments.

This same balance-of-payments picture can be shown in T-account form. The left-hand side shows transactions involving payments *to* the United States (dark blue). The right-hand side shows transactions involving payments *from* the United States (light blue). The uncolored items—accumulation of foreign capital in the United States and gold flows—are the "balancing" or adjusting items, just as in Table 37-1. They arose from the fact that on other transactions we made more payments to foreigners than foreigners made to us—we had a "payments deficit."

Look at some of the particular items. We exported $2.3 billion more goods and services than we imported. But we gave foreigners $2.2 billion of unilateral aid, mainly through the government's foreign-aid program but partly through private gifts; and we made $3.8 billion (net) of new investments abroad. These big capital transfers meant that we ended up owing foreigners $3.9 billion more in payments than they owed us. They might have taken all this difference in gold, and they did take $2.3 billion. But they also chose to take $1.2 billion in bank accounts and short-term investments in the United States. U.S. *military* aid of $2.5 billion is excluded completely from the table. Such exports of military equipment (planes, missiles, etc.) might have been included in the exports figure (I)

Table 37-2

U.S. BALANCE OF PAYMENTS—T-ACCOUNT FORM

Payments to U.S.		*Payments from U.S.*	
	(In Billions)		*(In Billions)*
U.S. exports:		U.S. imports:	
Merchandise	$16.2	Merchandise	$12.9
Services	4.1	Services	3.1
Income on investments		Military purchases	
abroad	2.9	abroad	3.4
	$23.2	Income on foreign	
Accumulation of foreign		investments here	.7
capital in U.S.	1.2		$21.0
Net gold flow from U.S.	2.3	Net U.S. unilateral aid	2.3
	$26.7	U.S. capital exports	3.8
Errors and omissions	.4		$27.1
	$27.1		

and in the balancing net unilateral transfers figure (IV). But such goods are not considered regular exports, and if they're not included in exports they can't be included either under unilateral grants, since to do so would throw the balance-of-payments figures out of balance.

THE "BALANCE OF PAYMENTS" AND THE "BALANCE OF TRADE" This table points up the importance of being clear about the difference between the "balance of payments" and the "balance of trade." The balance of payments includes all payments between the countries concerned (all of Table 37-1). The balance of trade includes only trade in goods and services (items I and II of the table).[2] Popular discussion, which generally runs in terms of the balance of trade, is often confused because of failure to consider the entire balance of payments. For example, the massive $15 billion gold inflow into this country during the 1930's, which accounts for much of our current gold stock,

---

[2] It is the difference between these two (i.e., III in the table) which is the "net exports," or "net foreign investment," figure sometimes shown separately in the g.n.p. accounts. When not shown separately, it is usually included as part of gross private investment.

was due primarily to a huge flow of funds to this country for long- and short-term investment and simply for safekeeping—not to a "favorable balance of trade," as a surplus of exports over imports is sometimes popularly called. Similarly, the outflow of gold shown for 1958 clearly can't be on account of the balance of trade, since we exported $2.2 billion more than we imported. You have to keep clear the distinction between the balance of payments and the balance of trade if you want to think straight about international economic problems.

Since World War I, the United States has consistently had a net export surplus —that is, exports of goods and services have consistently exceeded imports. But the total balance-of-payments picture has varied widely. During the 1920's and 1930's, we generally accumulated gold and short-term balances abroad, because payments were due us on balance. During the 1950's, by contrast, we have run a consistent balance-of-payments deficit. That is, foreigners have steadily accumulated gold and dollar balances, as our imports have risen faster than our exports, our investments abroad have grown rapidly, and we have annually provided a substantial amount of government and private foreign unilateral aid. The large gold drain shown for 1958 was exceptional, however. Foreigners have generally preferred to build up their deposits and investments in this country, and our gold stock declined only from about $24 billion to $20 billion over the decade. We still have over half the world's known monetary gold stock.

You have probably heard that gold is shipped back and forth to settle differences between exports and imports in international trade. Some gold does move this way. But international unbalance in the trade accounts may equally well be settled by capital transfers. If we export more than we import, we may simply build up our bank balances or short-term investments abroad, rather than requiring payment in gold. Conversely, foreigners may simply accumulate dollar balances or short-term investments here when their sales to the United States exceed purchases here. Like a business balance sheet, the international balance-of-payments statement pictures an interrelated set of transactions, no one of which can properly be considered a direct offset against any other. Each item represents largely independent transactions, with gold and short-term capital accumulations by and large the "balancing" items.

Composition of the Trade Balance.   Exports and imports of goods and services are the biggest part of the balance of payments. While services (foreign travel, shipping, etc.) and interest on investments abroad amount to billions annually, trade in commodities is by far the biggest single item. Commodity exports and imports between the United States and the principal countries with which we traded in 1958 are shown in Figure 37-1.

Figures 37-2 and 37-3 fill out the picture, showing the actual commodities that were our most important exports and imports in 1958. Note that how the commodities are grouped makes some difference in their rank. For example, if all machinery were not grouped under one head, machinery would not stand first on

United States International Trade, 1958

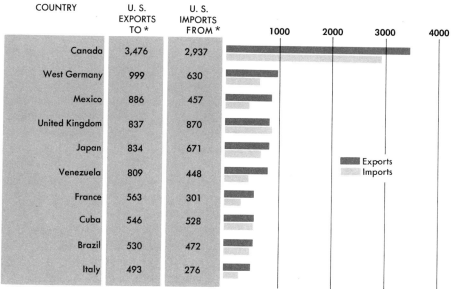

COUNTRY	U.S. EXPORTS TO *	U.S. IMPORTS FROM *
Canada	3,476	2,937
West Germany	999	630
Mexico	886	457
United Kingdom	837	870
Japan	834	671
Venezuela	809	448
France	563	301
Cuba	546	528
Brazil	530	472
Italy	493	276

*All figures in millions of dollars

FIG. 37-1   Canada is the United States' best customer, and four other western hemisphere nations are in the top ten. (Source: U.S. Department of Commerce. Military exports excluded.)

Chief Exports of the United States in 1958

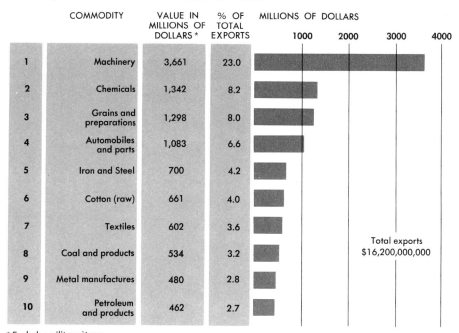

	COMMODITY	VALUE IN MILLIONS OF DOLLARS *	% OF TOTAL EXPORTS
1	Machinery	3,661	23.0
2	Chemicals	1,342	8.2
3	Grains and preparations	1,298	8.0
4	Automobiles and parts	1,083	6.6
5	Iron and Steel	700	4.2
6	Cotton (raw)	661	4.0
7	Textiles	602	3.6
8	Coal and products	534	3.2
9	Metal manufactures	480	2.8
10	Petroleum and products	462	2.7

Total exports $16,200,000,000

* Excludes military items

FIG. 37-2   Machinery, chemicals, and other manufactured products dominate United States exports, a big change from the dominance of farm products a century ago. (Source: U.S. Department of Commerce. Excludes military products.)

the export list. Raw materials are predominant among the imports, whereas finished and semi-finished products bulk large among the exports. Our comparative advantage has shifted away from farm products (where it was through the early history of the United States) toward manufactured products. Although some raw materials (especially grains and cotton) remain important exports, a substantial part of the totals shown for them are government sales of surpluses accumulated under the farm-aid program.

International Trade and the Gross National Product.   How important is international trade to the United States? During the prosperous 1920's, about 7 per cent of all goods and services produced in the United States were exported. During the depression, this figure fell off to around 4 per cent, partly because of bad business conditions and partly because of growing trade barriers here and in other countries. After World War II, the ratio rose sharply, then fell back to around 5-6 per cent, where it has hovered since. United States exports and imports as percentages of gross national product since 1919 are shown in Figure 37-4.

The percentages above may seem to indicate that international trade isn't very

Chief Imports of the United States in 1958

	COMMODITY	VALUE IN MILLIONS OF DOLLARS *	% OF TOTAL IMPORTS	MILLIONS OF DOLLARS
1	Petroleum and products	1,637	12.6	
2	Coffee	1,172	9.1	
3	Non-ferrous metals	1,023	7.9	
4	Paper	986	7.6	
5	Textiles	637	4.9	
6	Machinery	598	4.4	
7	Automobiles and parts	554	4.2	Total imports $12,900,000,000
8	Sugar	523	4.0	
9	Meat products	337	2.5	
10	Iron and Steel products	330	2.5	

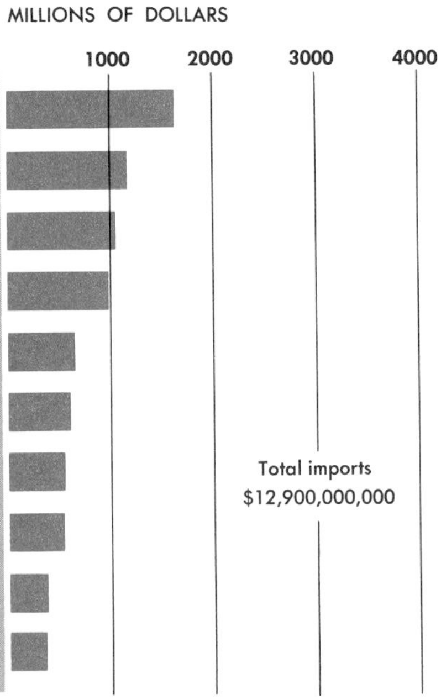

* Excludes military items

FIG. 37-3   Raw materials and foodstuffs are our biggest imports, but some manufactured products are included in the top ten. (Source: U.S. Department of Commerce.)

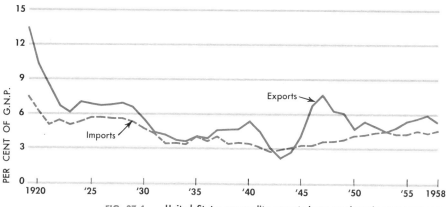

United States Exports and Imports as Percentage of Gross National Product

FIG. 37-4   United States commodity exports have consistently exceeded commodity imports. During the 1950's both have generally stayed in the range of 4 to 6 per cent of g.n.p. (Source: U.S. Department of Commerce. Military exports and World War II lend-lease excluded.)

important. But don't jump to conclusions. Even 5 per cent was over $20 billion in 1958, a recession year. As high as 70 per cent of the total cotton crop has been exported in certain years, with the annual average around 50 per cent. Foreign markets largely determine the welfare of a big part of U.S. agriculture, except as Uncle Sam steps in to hold up American prices. Look at Figure 37-2 to see how heavily other industries depend on export markets. Similarly, as was demonstrated dramatically by war shortages, many domestic industries depend heavily on foreign-produced raw materials (for example, rubber and chrome); and it is virtually impossible to get some consumption goods except from abroad (for example, coffee). For the industries shown in Figures 37-2 and 37-3, foreign trade looks very important indeed. And to most nations abroad in a tense, uncertain world, United States demand in world markets and United States policies on foreign aid and investment are matters of vital concern.

The United States—World Creditor.   Every growing country tends to pass through four stages in its economic development, with corresponding stages in its international balance-of-payments position.

1. *Net Borrower.* A new, undeveloped country often borrows heavily abroad to obtain the working and fixed capital it needs to develop natural resources. This was the position of the United States until about 1873. Capital came largely from Europe. Commodity imports (supplies, machinery, consumption goods) consistently exceeded exports. In this stage, the trade balance must be "unfavorable" (imports must exceed exports) if the goods and supplies needed are to be obtained, and this "unfavorable" balance is covered by borrowing.

2. *Debt Repayment.* After 1873, debt repayment by the United States began to exceed new borrowing, though we were still a heavy debtor. In this stage, exports tend to exceed imports—the trade balance is "favorable." Our net export balance transferred the real goods to other nations as we paid off our debts. As

in stage (1), money transfers are only the first step. It is the real transfer of goods and services that counts.

3. *Net Creditor.* Stage 3 is entered when the nation shifts over to a net creditor basis—when loans outstanding abroad exceed debts to foreigners. World War I and the 1920's thrust the United States abruptly into this stage, as we made heavy loans to our European allies. Government and private lending following World War II repeated the World War I experience with even greater intensity. Today, the United States is the one great creditor nation of the world. In this stage, a continued export surplus is to be expected. This surplus transfers abroad in real form the loans we make as we increase our creditor position.

4. *Mature Creditor.* The shift to stage 4 comes when the creditor nation finds its outstanding loans so great that current income on foreign investments more than offsets the net new loans being made abroad. In this stage, the trade balance must shift to an import surplus in order to transfer to the "mature creditor" nation the excess of its current return on investment over new loans being made abroad. England was a mature creditor early in this century.

As a nation passes through these four stages, slowly or rapidly, a changing trade balance is normal and essential. Whether a "favorable" balance of trade is in fact favorable depends basically on how well it fits in with the country's over-all balance of payments position. Severe disequilibrium will result if the trade balance is maintained (by tariffs or other controls) in a position unsympathetic to general balance-of-payments requirements.

Whether the United States is yet a mature creditor nation remains to be seen. But whether we are in stage 4 or only stage 3, one fact remains: Unless we are willing to continue heavy net lending abroad, we cannot hope to maintain our traditionally large surplus of exports over imports. As the one major world creditor, it is clear that we can sell abroad only by buying abroad or by lending or giving others the funds to purchase our goods and services.

**THE GREAT
AMERICAN RESPONSIBILITY**

In the century before World War I, England was the world's great creditor nation and the financial center of the world economy. This was a century of expanding production. It was an era of free international trade in which a high degree of specialization was developed among the world's nations. Trade was multilateral—based on an intricate web of exchanges in which no two countries balanced out directly with each other. There was no need for France to find another country that wanted what France had to sell and simultaneously could provide what France wanted to buy. The gold standard assured stable exchange rates among the world's currencies, to facilitate foreign trade. The British pound provided a standard currency and London was the financial center of world trade and lending. The system was complex, but it operated, like the free-price system, in an essentially automatic fashion—through the multitude of buying and selling activities of individuals in the many countries of the world.

The day of British leadership has passed. On America falls the enormous responsibility of providing leadership in the twentieth-century world economy. That task is incomparably more difficult than was Britain's in the nineteenth and early twentieth centuries. The world has gone through a period of elaborate schemes to restrict international trade. The old gold standard with its automatic regulation of exchange ratios among the various national currencies has broken down. "Planned" domestic economies have replaced free private enterprise in many countries. Maintenance of domestic full employment has become the first objective of most nations' economic policies. Many nations have come to look upon the United States as a continuing source of military and economic aid.

In the face of these conditions, it has been widely suggested that the United States must do three things:

1. Find a way to maintain a stable, prosperous United States economy as a crucial step toward international economic prosperity.

2. Lead the way toward reducing trade barriers and restoring multilateral trading. This means not only preaching "good" policies, but living up to them ourselves. The rest of the world is more sensitive to what we do than to what we say.

3. Give strong financial and moral backing to international institutions for providing international monetary stability and for facilitating investment programs for underdeveloped countries.

What is America's responsibility in these matters? What steps shall we take? In the one world of today, few questions are more important to the American citizen.

REVIEW—CONCEPTS TO REMEMBER

International economics is essentially fundamental economics applied to the field of international economic activity. But it has a number of new terms and concepts that you must have in your tool kit if you want to be able to operate effectively on international problems:

law of comparative advantage	capital movements
comparative costs	export surplus or deficit
balance of payments	balance of payments
balance of trade	surplus or deficit
commodity exports and imports	net creditor or debtor position

1. State the basic case for specialization, division of labor, and free exchange. In your judgment, are there reasons why this case applies in different degree within a nation and across national boundaries? If so, what are they?

2. Explain how imbalance in the international accounts between two nations can be settled through short-term capital movements as well as through gold movements.

3. Explain the difference between the balance of payments and the balance of trade. On which do the data in Figures 37-1, 37-2, and 37-3 throw the most direct light?

4. "Anyone who believes in free trade ought equally to believe in free international migration of labor, unrestricted by immigration barriers." Do you agree? Why or why not?

5. "Because of its wide diversity of natural resources, high development of technical skills, and great accumulation of capital, the United States can produce almost every major commodity more cheaply in terms of real effort than other countries. Obviously, therefore, we must lose rather than gain from most foreign trade." Do you agree? Explain carefully why or why not.

6. "In the absence of restrictions on international trade, the total real income of the world as a whole would be maximized, just as within any given country real income is maximized when resources move freely into those industries where consumers bid for them most strongly." True or false? Why? If you think the issue is not clean-cut, in what sense is the statement true or false?

7. If you were wealthy, would you invest any of your money abroad? Why or why not? What would be the crucial considerations in your mind?

8. Does the United States, by virtue of its large creditor position and dominant size in the world economy, have a responsibility to help stabilize other nations' economies? Think through carefully why you would answer this question yes or no. Make a list of the major reasons pro and con, weighting them if you have implicitly done so in reaching your own decision.

Financing International Transactions

Domestic trade and international trade are essentially similar, but there is one crucial difference between them: In domestic trade one common currency is used, but in international trade the parties to any transaction are likely to use different currencies. There must be a conversion of currencies. How is this managed?

The purpose of this chapter is to explain very briefly how international transactions are financed under different international monetary arrangements, as a basis for understanding the policy issues considered in Chapter 40.

FOREIGN EXCHANGE

If you're an importer buying woolens from England, the English woolen manufacturer wants English pounds, not American dollars. You need to convert your dollars into pounds if you're going to buy his cloth.

There is a continuous demand for this sort of conversion, and certain institutions have made it their business. In the United States, these institutions are primarily big New York banks; in other countries, large firms have grown up with this exclusive function. Other banks or financial institutions receive demands from customers for foreign currencies and simply pass on the transaction to one of these regular dealers.

Let us trace through a very simple transaction of this sort.[1] Suppose that you, an American importer, have agreed to pay a Britisher £1,000 in British money for some woolen goods. What do you do? You go to a bank, say the Chase Manhattan in New York, to buy 1,000 British pounds. The Chase Manhattan, a regular dealer in foreign currencies, sells you the pounds at the going rate—say $3 for £1. You pay the Chase Manhattan $3,000 and get a special check, made out to the bearer, for £1,000 This special type of check is called "foreign exchange."

Then all you have to do is send the check over to the British manufacturer. He can take it to his bank in London and get his £1,000. His bank presents the check to the Chase Manhattan's London Branch for payment, and the transaction is completed (except that we have omitted the small commission made by the Chase Manhattan on the deal).

The rate at which British pounds can be bought with American dollars is called the "exchange rate." When you buy pounds with dollars, you are purchasing foreign exchange. Foreign exchange is merely a claim on some foreign currency, and the rate of exchange is the number of units of one currency it takes to purchase one unit of another currency. If the dollar-franc exchange rate is 1 to 333, for example, then the price of one franc is about one-third of a cent.

The Foreign Exchange Market

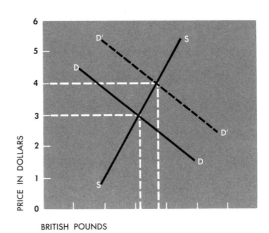

FIG. 38-1   The supply and demand for British pounds in terms of dollars looks just like the supply and demand for a commodity.

Like other prices, the exchange rate is determined by supply and demand. Suppose American importers need large numbers of pounds to pay British manufacturers. When they try to buy these pounds with dollars, the increased demand will force up the price of pounds—the dollar-pound exchange rate will move in

---

[1] This example is not an exactly accurate statement of how such a transaction would probably be executed. However, the actual procedure, though sometimes more complicated, follows the same general principle.

favor of the pound, say to 4 to 1. In other words, the price of a pound will become $4. Conversely, when Britishers want to make payment here, they buy dollars, bidding up the price of dollars, and the exchange rate goes down toward 2 to 1.

This situation can readily be represented by a simple supply and demand diagram, as in Figure 38-1. With the solid supply and demand curves, the price of pounds is $3. If demand increases to $D'D'$ (when American importers need pounds to pay for their British woolens), the price of pounds goes up to $4, given the supply of pounds shown. Try for yourself showing the effect of an increased British demand for dollars to pay for automobiles bought in America.

There are always Americans buying British pounds with dollars, and Britishers buying dollars with pounds. This is what keeps things reasonably well in balance on both sides of the Atlantic. The demand for pounds in America comes from American importers, people planning to travel or invest in Great Britain, and people owing other debts in Great Britain. The British demand for dollars comes from comparable British sources. Thus, there might well be an exact offset to your payment of £1,000 to the British manufacturer—say by a $3,000 payment to General Motors in Detroit by a British motor-parts dealer, who bought the dollars at the Chase Manhattan's London Branch. In effect, the two payments would be canceled off against each other. Fundamentally, goods would be exchanged for goods (woolens for motor parts), with the help of the foreign-exchange markets.

Of course, the British parts dealer might not have gone to the Chase Manhattan Branch of London, but instead to some other foreign-exchange dealer. This would have caused no difficulty. In both London and New York there are regular foreign-exchange markets. If the Chase Manhattan in New York has large demands for pounds, but a small supply of pounds in England, it can readily go into the New York exchange market and buy pounds from other dealers who happen to have larger supplies on hand in London. As long as the total demand for pounds in New York equals the total demand for dollars in London, all transaction can be settled without any change in the exchange rate or any international shipment of gold. Here again the market place does the complex job more or less automatically.

EXCHANGE RATES

Exchange Rates with "Free" Currencies.
Exchange rates depend on the demand for, and supply of, the currencies in question, except where rates are somehow fixed by government decree. In a completely "free" exchange market, exchange rates would fluctuate freely in response to varying demands for the different currencies. With fluctuating demands for currencies, large swings in foreign exchange rates could be expected, especially since capital movements (e.g., shifts of funds for investment abroad) affect exchange rates as directly as do merchandise exports

and imports. On the other hand, as long as supply and demand for the various currencies remain reasonably in balance, stable exchange rates would prevail under free-exchange markets.

Exchange Rates under the Gold Standard. For many years before World War I and again during the 1920's, most important countries were on the gold standard. During these periods, no direct control was exercised over exchange rates by governments, but, through the gold standard, exchange fluctuations were held within narrow bounds.

Under the gold standard, the monetary unit "contained" (was convertible into) a fixed number of grains of gold. For example, the prewar dollar was 23.22 grains and the prewar British pound 113 grains of fine gold. Thus the pound had 4.86 times as much gold as the dollar, a relationship that established a par of exchange between the currencies.

Under these circumstances, suppose there was an increased demand for dollars which sent the price of dollars up so that one pound would buy less than $4.86 (say the exchange rate moved up to 1 to 4.80). Then, instead of buying dollars and getting only $4.80 for £1, Britishers could simply convert their pounds into gold, send the gold to America, and there get $4.86 for the 113 grains of fine gold in each pound. Obviously therefore, the exchange rate could not vary far from 4.86 to 1 or gold would be shipped instead of foreign exchange being used at all. Actually, shipping costs and interest losses in transit made it unprofitable to ship gold unless the exchange rate varied more than 3 cents either way from the 4.86 to 1 ratio. Hence exchange rates could fluctuate within these "gold points" of 4.89 and 4.83, but no farther.

This stability of exchange rates was a great boon to international traders. They always knew just what foreign currencies would cost to make payments abroad and just what price they could get for foreign currencies received. Such stable exchanges may prevail without the gold standard, but as soon as one country is off the gold standard the *guarantee* of stable rates vanishes.

"Controlled" Exchange Rates. Today, the traditional international gold standard has been discarded, and there are no gold points to set limits on exchange-rate fluctuations. On the other hand, there are virtually no cases where exchange rates are left free to move up and down purely in response to private demands for, and supplies of, exchange. All over the world, foreign-exchange markets fall into an intermediate classification—unfixed by gold points but controlled to some extent by government action.

Government intervention in foreign-exchange markets has varied all the way from intermittent purchases and sales of currency to mitigate short-run exchange fluctuations, to complete fixation of rates with government rationing of all foreign exchange. The simplest approach is for the government to enter the foreign-exchange market as a temporary buyer or seller when it wants to influence rates; several governments have set up "exchange stabilization funds" for this purpose. A more drastic step is direct government control over the ways in which foreign exchange may be used. For example, a government may tell its nationals that they can spend foreign exchange only an approved imports; this is a kind of rationing procedure for the use of foreign exchange. Going a step further, the government may seize all foreign exchange received by its nationals and parcel it out only for approved purposes. At the extreme, the government may simply take over all foreign-exchange transactions itself, eliminating anything approaching a free foreign-exchange market.

A wave of controls over foreign-exchange transactions swept the international economy during the world-wide depression of the 1930's. Since World War II, there have been repeated efforts, with considerable success, to re-establish freer international trading and foreign-exchange markets. The whole problem is considered in more detail in Chapters 39 and 40.

INTERNATIONAL ADJUSTMENTS

International Adjustments under the Gold Standard. The international gold standard provided a more or less automatic procedure for keeping different countries "in balance" with one another. Most people thought this was a big advantage. If we eliminate capital movements for simplicity, a simple example will show how the gold standard was supposed to do this equilibrating job.

Suppose the United States begins to sell more goods and services to France without a corresponding increase in imports from France, both countries being on the gold standard. The French will need an increasing number of dollars to pay for their imports, and dollars will become increasingly expensive in terms of francs. But as soon as the dollar-franc rate moves to the gold point, the French will begin to ship gold rather than dollars to pay for their additional imports from America.

What happens when gold moves from France to America? In France, there is less gold backing for the money supply; currency and credit are contracted. Other things equal, this movement will mean depressed prices, costs, and incomes in France. In the United States, the reverse effect occurs. The new gold provides more bank deposits and more excess reserves. Currency and credit expand, with rising prices, costs, and incomes.

As these effects proceed, it will become harder for the French to buy in the United States, and easier for Americans to buy in France. Americans have larger incomes to spend on French goods and prices of French goods are falling. On the other hand, the French have lower incomes to spend on American goods and American prices are rising. This combination gradually shuts off the excess of U.S. exports to France, pulling the exports and imports of the two countries back into balance. When exports and imports are restored to balance, the gold flow ceases and international equilibrium has been restored.

With a larger number of countries, gold flows lead to equilibrium in international trade in essentially the same way. They will not long continue in the same direction without automatically bringing about a check to themselves by raising prices, costs, and incomes in the gold-receiving nation, and the reverse in the nations losing gold. But remember that gold flows tend to bring equilibrium *only* if they are permitted to affect prices, costs, and incomes in the countries involved. It was when countries became increasingly unwilling to have domestic monetary and fiscal policies controlled by gold flows that the international gold standard broke down and gave way to other arrangements.

International Adjustments under Fluctuating Exchanges.   How do international adjustments take place when the international gold standard is absent?

Assume the same United States-France situation as before, with American exports overbalancing imports from France. As before, the French will buy dollars to pay for their imports, and will thereby drive up the exchange rate—i.e., the cost of dollars in terms of francs. American goods will become more expensive to the French, and French goods will become cheaper to Americans. American incomes will rise because of our increased exports, without any such corresponding increase in France. These circumstances will gradually cut down on French purchases from the United States and will increase American purchases from France, until finally exports and imports between the two countries are restored to balance. As under the gold standard, there is an automatic tendency for the payments between the two countries to be brought back into equilibrium.

But the adjustment process is restricted to a smaller segment of each economy in the flexible exchange case. The rising dollar exchange rate effectively raises the price of American exports to the French, but it does so without raising American domestic prices generally in terms of dollars, as a gold inflow would have done. Similarly, the falling franc exchange rate effectively lowers the price of French exports to Americans, but it does so without imposing deflationary pressure on the whole French economy, as a gold outflow would have done.

This advantage of the flexible exchange method is especially important when large short-term capital "flights" are likely to occur as a result of unsettled world political and economic conditions. Under the gold standard, such drastic and unpredictable gold flows would lead to tremendous expansionary and deflationary pressures in the countries concerned. No economy could stand the shock of such expansions and contractions without suffering severe booms and depressions. On the other hand, the importance of stable exchange rates to international trade and finance is not to be underemphasized. Here is a real dilemma. Some of the ways countries have tried to solve it are considered in Chapter 40, which looks in more detail at alternative international monetary policies.

This chapter adds a few more concepts worth adding to the list at the end of Chapter 37:

foreign exchange
exchange rate
"free" exchange rates

flexible exchange rates
gold points
controlled exchange rates

1. Using Figure 38-1 on page 704, trace through the effects of the following, beginning from the equilibrium shown by *DD* and *SS:*

   a. General Motors decides to buy a British automobile plant to get production facilities there.

   b. British students come to study in America.

   c. British citizens decide to buy General Electric stock in America at the same time as American imports from England decline.

FOR

ANALYSIS

AND

DISCUSSION

2. Most European countries have advertised extensively in the United States in recent years to persuade Americans to travel in Europe. Why?

3. Suppose that you and many others decide to travel to France next summer. Trace through carefully the effect your trip might have on dollar-franc exchange rates, gold flows, and prices in each country under:

   a. An international gold standard.

   b. A flexible exchange rate system.

4. Domestically, free-price movements serve to equilibrate supply and demand in the markets concerned. Since foreign exchange rates are substantially frozen under the gold standard, how can the gold standard be said to be an international equilibrating system?

5. Under "exchange rationing" the government, through its allocation of exchange to importers, in effect decides what a country's imports shall be.

   a. Under uncontrolled conditions (i.e., without exchange rationing), who decides what a country shall import?

   b. Which system would seem to you to give the best determination of the goods to be imported? Explain carefully why you answer as you do.

6. "Short-term capital movements (hot money) seeking protection from monetary and political uncertainty first in one country and then in another were the real cause of the downfall of the gold standard. No country could afford to let its monetary system be subjected to such random violent shocks." Evaluate this argument in the light of the 1930's; of the future.

Commercial Policy

During the 1600's, "mercantilism" was the prevalent economic doctrine. Mercantilism held that a primary aim of government policy should be to get more gold and silver, especially from abroad. Treasure could be obtained simply by seizing it in the New World, but a "favorable balance of trade" was required to get it from other established countries. By exporting more than it imported, a nation could receive gold for the balance.

This preoccupation with gold and silver as the major ends of international trade has continued to the present in the minds of many people. Added to this venerable argument have been others: that a "favorable balance of trade" increases domestic employment, that it increases domestic wages and raises the nation's standard of living, and so on. All these arguments claim that there are advantages in exporting more than we import—all spring fundamentally from the old favorable-balance-of-trade position.

The publication of Adam Smith's *Wealth of Nations* in 1776 signaled a major attack on protectionism and the beginning of a strong swing

710

toward free trade, internationally as well as domestically. Under the leadership of England, which clearly stood to gain from extensive international trade, trade restrictions were whittled away. But popular acceptance of the free-trade position was never complete; gold loomed large in the layman's mind, and foreign imports seemed an obvious threat to the jobs of domestic workers. Thus, with the uneasy nationalism of the twentieth century, tariffs were steadily boosted. And the massive depression of the 1930's brought a wave of foreign trade restrictions, designed to stimulate employment and recovery at home, whether or not at the expense of other nations.

In retrospect, the restrictionism of the 1930's stifled international trade and helped no one very much. Thus, following World War II most nations began an earnest search for ways to increase the volume of international trade without threatening their domestic economies. From this search, new approaches are emerging, as well as concerted efforts to move back toward the older patterns of free, multilateral international exchange.

The first section of this chapter looks thoroughly at the tariff, the main device for restricting imports and producing a "favorable balance of trade." The latter portion, and the following chapter, examine some of the more recent intergovernmental efforts to combine freer international trade with protection to national economic sovereignty and domestic full employment policies.

THE TARIFF   A tariff is a tax on imports, sometimes at so much per "specific" article imported and sometimes at a certain percentage of the value of entering products ("ad valorem"). Either way, the main objective of modern tariffs has been to restrict the volume of imports—to protect American industry and workers. A secondary effect is to produce revenue. But the two effects are in conflict—the more the tariff keeps out imports, the less revenue it raises; the more revenue it raises, the less it shuts out imports. If the tariff is mainly for protection, it won't be much of a revenue-producer.

Tariff regulations are complex. Under the Smoot-Hawley Tariff of 1930, which imposed the highest barriers in American history, merely listing the commodities covered, with rates of duty, took 212 pages of fine type on 8½ by 11 inch paper.[1] Almost half of the commodities listed had effective duties exceeding 100 per cent of their value before payment of the duty. And of all the commodities listed, less than one out of ten was admitted free of duty.

Precise measurement of the effects of the U.S. tariff is difficult, especially because it shuts out many commodities completely. Tariff duties collected as a percentage of the value of all imports reached a peak figure of about 33 per cent

---

[1] In the *Statistical Classification of Imports into the United States,* Bureau of Foreign and Domestic Commerce (Washington, D.C.: 1937).

in 1933. But this figure is far too low to describe the real force of the tariff, both because it gives no effect to the many commodities shut out completely by prohibitively high rates and because well over half the commodities that do come in do so completely duty-free. We have no tariff at all on some products which do not compete at all with domestic production, and this group pulls down the average tariff rate on all imports to perhaps half what it would otherwise be. Since 1933, the average tariff burden on imports received has been cut by more than 50 per cent, and reductions have been made on almost 90 per cent of all items subject to tariff. Thus, the effective tariff wall has been reduced substantially since the peak of the 1930's, but it remains a major barrier to the import of foreign products.

Consider now the major arguments for a protective tariff. All we need to analyze them are a few simple economic principles. The central principles are those of specialization and division of labor, and of comparative advantage. The problem is to keep the emotional, nationalistic words from making you forget the principles.[2]

Partially Valid Arguments. *The "Infant Industry" Argument.* A protective tariff may help "infant industries" until they are firmly established and able to stand on their own feet. For example, in 1816 the newly founded iron industry found it difficult to get established in the face of strong competition from British iron-makers. If foreign competition were shut out for a few years, it was argued, the American iron industry could soon not only meet, but outstrip, foreign competitors.

There is some validity to the "infant industry" argument. It is hard for a new industry to establish itself in the face of vigorous competition from older competitors, even though the new industry once established will be more efficient than the old. The protective tariff on iron and steel probably speeded the growth of an industry that would in any case have prospered. Perhaps the most significant fact is, however, that the tariff still stands to protect the steel industry—indeed a lusty "infant" by now. By the time the infant industry has grown up, other arguments are found for continued protection.

Because of the nature of tariff-making in the United States, protection, once achieved, can usually be retained. Congress passes tariff acts covering thousands of products, and most of the actual decisions are made by small subcommittees in the House and Senate. No congressman can know about more than a comparatively small number of these thousands. But each congressman is pressed by his constituents to vote for protection for the goods that they produce. Each congressman, in attempting to get votes for his particular duties, has to agree to vote for his fellows' duties in exchange. Thus, the congressman from one state

---

[2] This section is purposely written in more "one-sided" language than is the rest of the book. In reading it, test yourself to see whether you can see significant counterarguments that seem to you to be glossed over.

will agree to vote for a tariff on shoes if the congressman from another state will vote for one on sugar. The tariff is the classic example of congressional log-rolling.

The "National Self-sufficiency" Argument. In a world of international tension, every nation wants to be as nearly self-sufficient as possible. United States dependence on the Far East for tin and rubber at the beginning of World War II, for example, left us painfully exposed. In such a situation, the desire for economic self-sufficiency may overbalance all other considerations, regardless of what the costs of such economic self-sufficiency may be.

The economist cannot say whether a nation should try to become partially or wholly self-sufficient in the face of such considerations. But he can point out what self-sufficiency costs in terms of poor allocation of resources and a lowered standard of living, so that this factor will be weighed with others in deciding whether or not we will seek more self-sufficiency. And the cost for most nations would be great.

The "Diversified Economy" Argument. When a nation is highly specialized in producing one or a few major products, its economy is highly vulnerable to variations in foreign demand. Cuba's sugar economy and Brazil's coffee economy are examples; usually such one-product nations export a foodstuff or raw material. If foreign markets weaken, the result is domestic disaster. For such nations, greater economic diversification may be desirable, even though the new industries be comparatively inefficient. Tariffs may be used to shelter them in a diversification program. But for widely diversified countries like the United States, this argument has little relevance.

Largely Fallacious Arguments.   *The "Favorable Balance of Trade" Argument.* Most naive of all arguments advanced in support of the tariff is the desire for a "favorable balance of trade" for its own sake. Two major fallacies are involved. First, there is nothing generally favorable about a "favorable" balance of trade. A continued "favorable" balance means that a nation continually gives foreigners more goods and services than they give it; the nation receives in exchange gold (often to be held idle at considerable storage expense) or investments abroad. Thus it means a *reduced* standard of living for the country sending away goods and services, certainly in the short run and indefinitely if the "favorable" balance of trade continues without willingness to accept goods from abroad in payment of foreign indebtedness. We don't eat gold. Our standard of living is made up of the goods and services we have.

Second, a favorable balance of trade is substantially impossible as a continuing policy.[3] Foreigners can't buy from us unless they get dollars to pay for our products. The way they get dollars is by selling us their goods and services. For a while, they can continue to buy more from us than they sell us, by paying the

---

[3] Considering only the trade components of the balance of payments.

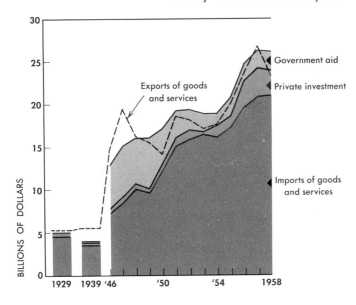

FIG. 39-1   Other countries get dollars to buy United States exports mainly through our payments for imports. But U. S. private investment abroad and government aid help a good deal. (Source: U.S. Department of Commerce. Military aid and exports excluded.)

balance in gold or by giving us investments in their industries. But fundamentally it is only by buying from foreigners that we can expect to sell to them, unless they mine the required gold or we continually lend or give them the money to buy from us.

There is no point more fundamental than this—that we will sell abroad only if we buy abroad. It is fundamental to understanding the fallacy in nearly every argument for protective tariffs and other trade-restriction policies. Figure 39-1 shows where other countries obtained the dollars to buy our exports from 1929 to 1959. In many years we lent them large sums and gave them large grants under our foreign-aid programs. But throughout, our purchases of goods and services abroad were the dominant source of dollars with which foreigners bought our exports.

The "Protect Home Industry" Argument. Probably the most popular basis for advocating tariff duties is that we ought to protect home industry against low-cost foreign competition.

A domestic industry asking for tariff protection argues that without protection its market will be lost to foreign competitors, thus forcing the domestic industry out of business, throwing workers out of jobs, and generally decreasing national welfare. Actually, industries seeking protective tariffs would often be able to retain their markets without tariffs; tariffs enable them to raise domestic prices with lessened fear of foreign competition. Indeed, the tariff has been called "the mother of monopolies," since it may permit domestic monopolies to exist without fear of foreign competition. But suppose that if the industry does not receive protection it *will* lose its market to foreign competitors. What will be the effects of giving the protection the industry wants?

The first and most obvious effect is that domestic consumers must pay more for the protected product than if it had come in free. If sugar comes in over the tariff, consumers must pay the regular price of the foreign sugar plus the tariff duty. If the tariff succeeds in shutting out the product, domestic consumers must pay a higher price for domestic sugar, since domestic producers cannot, without a tariff, produce and sell at a price low enough to meet foreign competition.

The second effect is that domestic sugar producers are subsidized by the tariff; they are permitted to charge higher prices than would have been possible had not foreign competition been shut out. It's clear that domestic producers are the great gainers from a tariff on their product.

In effect, therefore, a tariff is a subsidy to domestic producers, financed by consumers through higher prices for the protected product. Moreover, the more inefficient domestic producers are, the higher tariff they need to protect them against foreign competition and the larger subsidy they receive from such protection.

Indeed, industry's argument for a tariff is often that the tariff should be high enough to "equalize domestic and foreign costs of production." A suggestion in Congress that special taxes be levied on consumers to finance subsidies to producers, each subsidy to be based on producers' inefficiency, would horrify everyone. Yet this is substantially the result of a protective tariff so designed to protect home industry.

A noted economist, Bastiat, put the free-trade case against "protection" tellingly over a century ago in his satirical "Petition of the Candle-Makers." We need protection, said the candle-makers of Paris in their petition. Foreign competitors are bad enough, and we cannot give work to the workers of France and good candles to the people unless their inferior products are shut out. But, they pleaded, it is the sun who is our most unfair competitor. Each day he shines and throws light over all, at no cost at all. If you will only shut out the sun, pleaded the candle-makers, we can have a magnificent candle industry, giving employment to untold numbers of workers.

Should we protect American domestic industry against cheap foreign competition today using the same arguments as Bastiat's candle-makers pleaded a century ago?

The "Protect Our High Wages and High Standard of Living" Argument. In the United States, a major argument for the tariff is that it protects high domestic wages and the high American standard of living. In other countries, wages and living standards are much lower than here. Therefore, it is argued, unless we have a protective tariff international competition will push down high American wages to the level of foreign wages.

The "Petition of the Candle-Makers" should suggest a fallacy here; how high could the wages of French workers have been raised by shutting out the sun? But consider the argument in more detail.

First, why are wages now higher in the United States than in other countries? Fundamentally, because of the high productivity of American workers. Anything that raises their productivity makes it possible for them to receive higher wages.

And each worker can receive his highest possible wage when he is working in that industry where his marginal productivity is highest.

What happens when a tariff is passed to "protect" high American wages? The tariff will mean that relatively inefficient American industries will grow up where otherwise they could not have existed, giving jobs to American workers. But, at the same time, American exports will fall off, because foreign countries cannot buy from us for very long unless we buy from them. (Remember Figure 39-1.) Therefore fewer workers and other resources can be employed in the export industries. The net result will be a shift of workers from relatively efficient export industries (where they would be situated under free trade) into less efficient protected industries. As workers move to lower marginal productivity positions in protected industries, the wages they can receive in the new jobs are necessarily lower than they could have been before the shift. *The long-run result of a protective tariff is to lower real wages, not to raise them.*[4]

To illustrate this point, consider an extreme example cited by proponents of a tariff to protect American wages. Suppose that Japanese labor is paid only a dollar per day. It is argued, then, that if we permit the free import of Japanese goods American workers will be forced to take much lower wages to compete.

In considering this argument, first we need to recognize that even though Japanese daily wages are much lower, it is not necessarily true that the labor costs of Japanese producers (say of china plates) are correspondingly lower. The Japanese worker gets lower wages, but he also produces less in one day. Therefore the labor cost per plate may be as much for the Japanese producer as for the American. If, for example, the daily output per worker in Japan is 40 plates, the labor cost per plate is 2.5 cents. If the daily output per American worker is 500 plates and the daily wage $10, the labor cost per plate would be only 2 cents. The wage cost per plate is the wage cost that counts.

But this by no means answers the tariff argument, for probably labor costs on many articles are lower in Japan in spite of the higher output per worker here. Suppose, to continue the hypothetical example, that Japan can far undersell us on china plates, and that we remove the tariff on such plates. This move, of course, would mean that workers in the American chinaware industry will be thrown out of jobs. But since Japan would then be selling more to us, she would have the power to buy more from us. She would buy from us those goods that we were able to produce more efficiently and cheaply (say, machine tools). Workers thrown out of jobs in making china would gradually be drawn into the machine-tool industry. But since the United States is, by assumption, comparatively more efficient in producing machine tools than china, workers can receive higher wages making tools. Workers in the china industry would surely be temporarily unemployed and, if personally unadaptable, might never be re-employed. But the

---

[4] This is not to deny that a protective tariff on a particular product may raise the real wages of workers *in that industry* by increasing the demand for labor there, so long as there are immobilities in the domestic labor market that keep other workers from moving in to take advantage of the higher labor demand provided by protection.

general public would clearly gain by obtaining cheaper china plates, and more workers would be drawn into the high-productivity industries where wages are highest. Removal of an existing tariff may ruin protected producer groups; yet a net gain in standard of living accrues to the whole economy.[5]

The "Increased Employment" Argument. In the long run, it should by now be clear, a protective tariff neither increases nor decreases employment, but merely shifts resources from "more efficient" to "less efficient" industries. However, the *short-run* adjustments in moving toward the new long-run equilibrium may be slow and painful (as with any shift in demand). It is small consolation to the china-maker to know that eventually his wage *may* be higher if in the meantime he is unemployed, his children are underfed and ill-clothed, and his home and insurance policy are forfeited. His producer interest is dominant, and he *as an individual* may never be able to shift to the machine-tool industry. Removing an existing tariff may result in temporary unemployment, unemployment that may persist stubbornly if total demand is weak.

But the protectionist argument is that, at least *in the short run,* raising tariffs will generate new jobs as domestic firms begin selling to the customers who previously bought imported goods. With the development of multiplier analysis, this argument was cloaked in more elegant analytical terms. Creation of an export surplus through tariff increases *is* increased investment, in the national income accounts. This investment rise would yield a "foreign trade multiplier" effect, and a substantial rise in income and employment might be induced.

But this is a short-sighted argument. Suppose America puts on a tariff to shut out foreign goods and to export our unemployment. What would you do if you were Belgium or England or France? You'd come right back with restrictions against American exports. And that's just what they did. During the 1930's, each country sought to gain a temporary advantage by raising tariffs, and the net result was much higher tariff walls all around without any country getting much short-run advantage. For illusory short-run employment gains, nations imposed long-run burdens on themselves and on each other. And once a tariff is imposed, the process of removing it is slow and doubtful.

Conclusion. From this analysis, we can draw a broad summary of the major economic effects of protective tariffs. *In the long run,* a protective tariff lowers real wages and the standard of living; it diverts resources from self-sustaining export industries to protected domestic-consumption industries; and it forces consumers to pay higher prices. *In the short run,* advantages *may* be gained from imposing new tariffs to aid infant industries or to stimulate employment during depression periods. However, infant-industry tariffs are seldom removed later on, and new tariffs can increase employment only if almost inevitable retaliatory steps are not taken by other nations. Lastly, history demonstrates dramatically that the tariff works strongly toward long-run restriction of trade and toward cumu-

---

[5] This argument applies strictly only if labor costs are the same proportion of total costs in the two industries concerned. In most real-world cases in the United States, this approximation is close enough to permit the above example to apply in substance.

lative international friction. A variety of special cases can be postulated where particular circumstances would make it possible to obtain beneficial national results through imposition of tariff restrictions. But, for the most part, these are artificial, academic examples, and the basic economic case for free trade, specialization, and division of labor remains fundamentally unimpaired.

Tariff-making in the United States. If the protective tariff is open to such serious criticism, and if it benefits only particular groups at the cost of the rest of society, why have we had high protective tariffs so long? There are two big answers.

First, public opinion on the tariff has been greatly influenced by self-seeking propaganda, and many citizens are uninformed on the nature of international trade. Groups seeking protection have presented their propaganda effectively in Congress and to the general public, and the appeal to nationalism against the interests of foreigners is a potent rallying cry.

Second, in the log-rolling processes of tariff legislation, small groups seeking protection can trade votes; as a result, each group can win much higher duties than it could have on its own. With the tariff as with much other economic legislation, consumers are unrepresented and often forgotten; they are the great unorganized mass. But the groups seeking protection have strong, effective lobbies. The result is legislation that favors the groups who bring the most pressure to bear.

Experience suggests that the most hopeful channel for scaling down the tariff is to take the job of rate-setting as far as possible out of congressional politics and to put it into more insulated administrative hands. Under the Trade Agreements Act of 1934 (still in force), the president was given wide tariff-making powers, including the power to lower United States tariffs on specific commodities as much as 50 per cent if the other country most vitally interested in the product would make reciprocal concessions. Succeeding congressional renewals have permitted even further cuts. Under this arrangement, over 30 reciprocal trade agreements have been entered into, a large portion of them with other American countries. Over 1,600 individual rates had been reduced by 1958, and many reductions were big ones. Moreover, since the "most-favored-nation clause" was made a part of the agreements, concessions made in the reciprocal agreements were generalized to other countries (except those specifically excluded because of discriminatory action against United States exports). If, for example, we lowered our tariff on lumber in an agreement with Canada, this concession would also apply to lumber imports from other countries. Any concession made to the most-favored nation is generalized to other nations.

The Reciprocal Trade Agreements Program reversed the long trend toward protectionism. Every president since Franklin Roosevelt has shared his enthusiastic support for the program. Yet it comes under violent attack each time it requires congressional renewal, especially in recession periods. Then the argument for action to create new American jobs is strongest. Because the average level of American tariffs has been cut by more than 50 per cent under the Reciprocal Trade Agreements Program, it has become the focal point for attacks by widespread and powerful protectionist groups. And in recent renewals Congress has inserted growing safeguards to be sure that domestic producers are not hurt by negotiated tariff reductions. A "peril point" provision assures that no cut will be approved if it involves "peril" to a domestic producer. These special safeguards have substantially halted presidential negotiation of further large reductions.

QUOTAS, SUBSIDIES, AND ALLIED DEVICES The theories and proposals of economists and politicians mirror the times in which they live. Tariffs were the simplest type of interference with international trade when private-enterprise economies with a minimum of government participation in economic life were the rule. The long depression of the 1930's raised the specter of mass unemployment throughout the western world. In this atmosphere, tariffs became a technique for increasing domestic employment at the expense of workers abroad. But the difficulty of escaping retaliation soon became obvious. Thus both economists and practical politicians turned to devising other, less familiar techniques to achieve the same end without facing certain retribution. Moreover, many of the domestic "planned" economy programs would work only if they were supplemented by special controls over international trade. Import quotas supplemented tariffs; subsidies were given to encourage exports; exchange controls were introduced and elaborated.

Import quotas prescribe the amount of any foreign-produced commodity that may enter per year. The import quota is like the tariff in shutting out foreign commodities and permitting domestic producers to charge higher prices because foreign competition is eliminated. Like the tariff, the import quota is a direct consumer-financed subsidy to domestic producers. The quota is more drastic than the tariff, since it sets an absolute maximum of imports that cannot be exceeded.

Quotas have long been used, but until recent years they were commonly limited to special cases, such as the importation of narcotics. During the 1930's, however, quotas rose to major importance as a means of attaining the traditional tariff goals. Although the United States has not imposed quotas so widely as many other countries, cattle, milk and cream, fish, potatoes, fox furs, certain types of lumber, molasses and other sugar syrups, crude petroleum products, and miscellaneous other products were still subject to quota in 1958. Some countries have had virtually their entire list of imports under such restrictions. All the analysis of tariff restrictions above is substantially applicable here, with one exception.

When a country must rely heavily on imports and finds itself short of foreign exchange (for example, short of dollars), it feels that it must husband its scarce exchange carefully. Import quotas and exchange controls have been widely imposed in such cases. Through these devices, the government hopes to allocate its scarce dollars to the most vital imports and to purchase other less essential goods elsewhere with more plentiful non-dollar exchange. Basically, this balance-of-payments deficit argument for controlling imports is restrictionist only in the sense that is restricts some imports in order to obtain others. It is quite a different matter from the more common arguments to "protect home industry," which try to reduce aggregate imports.

Export subsidies are government grants to producers of exportable goods to enable them to employ more workers by making it possible for them to sell abroad at prices lower than costs. The theory is that this arrangement will increase markets for domestic producers by stealing foreign markets from foreign producers. The domestic taxpayer finances the subsidy.

Recently the government has been financing a kind of export subsidy through the farm-aid program. It buys up farm surpluses to support domestic prices and then tries to sell the surpluses abroad—the only market where it will not undercut its supported domestic prices. Large gifts of wheat have been made to India and other crop-disaster areas. But for the most part the government tries to sell the surpluses abroad at world prices, below what it paid to buy up the crops here. This gets back at least some of the money invested in surpluses, cuts down on storage costs, and avoids sheer waste through spoilage. But it doesn't make our friends in Canada, Australia, and other big wheat-exporting nations very happy. To them it looks like "dumping" American wheat to get the world market away from them, just as if direct export subsidies had been given to American farmers.

Export subsidies, like tariffs and quotas, may temporarily increase domestic employment and help keep domestic prices high. But other nations are almost sure to retaliate. When they do, the export subsidies on both sides are nullified, though their costs remain in both countries as burdens on domestic taxpayers. And it doesn't promote international friendship on either side.[6]

INTERGOVERNMENTAL
AGREEMENTS
TO EXPAND TRADE

The International Trade Organization and GATT.   After World War II the spirit of internationalism was strong. All the victorious nations except the U.S.S.R. moved to extend their wartime collaboration into economic cooperation that would reverse the restrictionist wave of the 1930's. Within the framework of the United Nations,

---

[6] Perhaps the most controversial American protectionist device is the "Buy American" provision, under which Congress directs the president to give preference to American bidders on government contracts even when foreign bids are up to 25 per cent lower, when to do so appears to be in the national interest. Under this provision, numerous contracts for heavy electrical equipment (e.g., large turbines and generators) have been given to G.E., Westinghouse, and other American companies even when foreign bids were far lower, largely on national defense grounds. The rejected British, German, and Italian companies and their governments have protested bitterly. But other times, low foreign bids have been accepted, often amid floods of protest from American producers.

several member nations pushed for an International Trade Organization, which would attempt to expand and stabilize the volume of world trade. Negotiations on the founding of this new organization were long and involved. From the outset, the United States representatives urged a strong charter that would emphasize the restoration of free multilateral trade, vigorous attacks on such restrictive devices as import quotas, close trade cooperation through the ITO, and ITO supervision of international commodity agreements to assure emphasis on trade expansion and consumer interests. Other nations, facing dollar shortages and uncertain of the future, were less ready to bargain away their rights to use restrictive commercial policies. Many were frankly worried about the possibility of another major depression in the United States. They feared that such a depression would spread abroad rapidly, in view of the United States' dominant position in world trade; and direct trade controls were one weapon still held by the smaller nations to help insulate their economies.

Prolonged debate failed to bring agreement on a charter for ITO that could command support of most of the nations concerned. Out of these discussions, however, came the General Agreement on Tariffs and Trade (GATT), now with 37 signatory countries. GATT provides for regular discussion of means to reduce international trade restrictions among the members, and each member nation agrees to work toward approved trade practices, insofar as these practices are not in conflict with the country's national legislation.

The success of GATT has been modest. No spectacular results have been achieved. But GATT has provided a steady pressure in the direction of freer, multilateral trade. Most nations are anxious to encourage freer trade, yet wary of giving up national powers that might protect their national interests. The limited progress made in both ITO and GATT reflects the uneasy times in which we live, and the inevitable difficulty in persuading sovereign nations to give up restrictive weapons that may some day be useful to them.

The European "Common Market."   The major postwar move toward international economic cooperation has come in Europe, and a major move it is. In 1951, six European nations—Belgium, France, Italy, Luxembourg, the Netherlands, and West Germany—broke long precedents of political and economic rivalry and formed the European Coal and Steel Community. This was an agreement to cooperate in rationalizing and improving the efficiency of coal and steel production in the entire six-country economy. In 1957, after success with ECSC, the same countries joined in creating a European Atomic Energy Community (Euratom). And in 1958 they banded together in the European Economic Community, generally called the "Common Market"—a precedent-shattering agreement to eliminate all tariff and similar trade barriers against each other over a period of 12 to 15 years. Moreover, they will gradually equalize all their restrictions on trade with nations outside the six.

Together, "the six" have a total population of over 170 million, just short of the United States and only about 20 per cent below the U.S.S.R. In 1958, they accounted for nearly one-fourth of the world's exports, and some $2 billion more than the United States' $20 billion. Their steel production was 66 million tons, compared to 86 million for the U.S. and 60 million for Russia. Their electricity generation was only one-third the U.S.'s, but greater than Russia's. The Common Market, once integrated, will be a trade area to rival the United States, and probably the second-largest free-trade sector in the world economy.

Establishment of EEC is not proceeding without strain. But proceeding it is, on the foundation of the highly successful Coal and Steel Community. Small reductions in internal tariff and quota restrictions have already been made, and private international agreements within the six countries are growing rapidly.

Establishment of the Common Market poses major problems for other nations. Will this huge common market shut out outside products and leave old suppliers high and dry? England and the Scandinavian countries have stayed out of the Common Market because they are unwilling to give up special preferential trading arrangements with other countries—especially with other nations in the British Commonwealth, which has a wide-ranging system of preferential trading agreements. Britain has, therefore, suggested that the Common Market be gradually expanded into a larger European free-trade area, encompassing all the western bloc allied nations but not requiring complete equalization of treatment of outside exporters and importers. The extension of the Common Market to this wider area now seems problematical. But if the Common Market is successful, the pressure for other nations to join in freer trade arrangements will be enormous. And a true economic United States of Western Europe would mean a huge free-trade area surpassing both the United States and the U.S.S.R. in population. Thus far there is little evidence that the Common Market will be used as a device to eliminate outsiders. Rather, it appears a powerful force toward freer international trade on a broad front.

The Soviet Bloc and Foreign Trade. The Soviet bloc has stayed outside these major postwar moves toward international trade. But the U.S.S.R. has increasingly stepped into foreign markets with its exports, which amounted to some $4 billion in 1958. Soviet policy in foreign trade is mixed. Partly, the U.S.S.R. wants imports, and trades to get them in the same way as western nations do. Partly, she uses foreign trade and economic aid as a political and economic device to draw the uncommitted nations into the Soviet bloc and away from the West. Special bargains and concessions in South America and Asia have clearly been designed as part of an "economic warfare" program, according to western observers. Russia is building steel mills for India, a huge dam for Egypt. In such cases, she sends in Soviet technicians and creates strong ties for maintenance and replacement activities in the future.

Vis-à-vis the major western powers, the Russian strategy appears to be mixed. In 1958 Russian aluminum was offered in world markets at prices well below prevailing levels, and below what western observers thought Russian costs must be. American and other western producers feared this might be the opening gun of a price war for foreign markets by the Soviet state monopoly which would seek political and military gain without having to worry about covering costs. Similar moves have been made in other markets. But over-all, this may be more a move to gain purchasing power to buy what the Russians need from abroad than a politico-economic offensive to ruin western producers. Russia needs supplies from abroad and must have foreign currencies to pay for them outside the Soviet bloc, just as other countries must. In general, she has been more cooperative on matters of international trade than on political and military issues. Only time will tell what her role will be in the world economy of the future.

FOR

ANALYSIS

AND

DISCUSSION

1. What is the fallacy in the "Petition of the Candle-Makers" for protection against the sun? If there is a fallacy, is the same fallacy present in other arguments for protective tariffs?

2. List the factors that explain the high wages received by American workers in the steel and chemical industries. Which, if any, would be affected, and in which direction, if American tariffs were raised on steel and chemicals?

3. Should the U.S. government always accept foreign bids on its projects when the foreign bids are lower than those from American companies, assuming that the bids meet the specifications established? If your answer is no, how would you answer a taxpayer who says he wants to get the most for his tax dollar? In general, does the "Buy American" provision seem to you sound economic policy today?

4. Are there any industries in the United States today that seem to you clearly to deserve tariff protection as "infant industries"? Explain your answer carefully, considering what factors may put an "infant industry" at a disadvantage, and ways in which these disadvantages might be overcome.

5. One leading economist has argued: "Removal of tariffs is clearly desirable, but the associated transition effects would be tolerable only in times of prosperity and in the absence of monopolistic restrictions in the more efficient American industries." Can you explain this apparently paradoxical statement?

6. Can you suggest any ways whereby, in a period of depression, the United States could raise its tariffs against foreign goods so as to avoid probable retaliation?

7. What do you think America's attitude toward the European "Common Market" should be? In what respects will this new, large, internal free-trade area help or hurt us?

8. "The United States should agree to put the level of her tariff rates, import quotas, and export subsidies under control of the United Nations if at least 20 other major nations agree to do likewise." Do you agree? Why or why not?

International Monetary and Fiscal Policy

40

The pre-1914 gold standard was, in theory and to a substantial degree in practice, an "automatic" system (see pages 707-708). Its essence was the correspondence of domestic money supply changes to international gold flows. "Management" of the money supply by central banks played a minor role in modifying the impact of gold acquisitions and drains. Gold was, in a very real sense, the center of a "religion" of money. It was accepted by most economists and the public alike without real questioning as an ultimate repository of value. In the rapidly expanding, reasonably flexible pre-1914 world, this gold standard supplied an important element of international exchange stability, and the requisite domestic price-income adjustments were generally accomplished without excessively painful consequences.

THE DOWNFALL OF THE GOLD STANDARD

The monetary disruptions of World War I were extreme. Wild inflations occurred in several European nations; serious inflation in every one.

Re-establishment of the international gold standard in the 1920's was thus fraught with difficulties. What should the re-established gold values, or "contents," of the various national currencies be in light of the preceding inflations? In other words, what should exchange rates be? In Britain, the financial center of the prewar world, the pound was finally put back "on gold" in 1925 at the prewar gold content, and the prewar dollar-pound exchange rate of $4.86 = £1 was restored. In other countries, new gold contents were prescribed for currencies in an endeavor to place them in "equilibrium" balance-of-payments positions vis-à-vis the rest of the world.

The new currency relationships were only moderately satisfactory. In retrospect the British pound was "overvalued." That is, at the new exchange rates it was hard for foreigners to buy in Britain, and the British economy was under steady deflationary pressure. Some currencies were undervalued, with resulting inflationary pressures.

The depression of the 1930's dealt the death blow to the gold standard. Losing gold in a period of growing unemployment meant even further deflationary contraction of national money supplies. First England in 1931, then most other major nations, decided this price was too high to pay. They "went off gold," devaluing their currencies to avoid the domestic deflation implicit in adherence to the gold standard and to encourage foreign purchases of their domestically-produced products. Thus, the American dollar was devalued in 1934 to 59 per cent of its earlier gold content. Eventually every major currency was devalued.

In retrospect, the major factors that led to the downfall of the gold standard were three:

(1) Increasing severity of business cycles and increasing public pressure to lessen unemployment made adherence to financial orthodoxy increasingly difficult. (2) Greater rigidity in the cost-price structure aggravated the impact of price and income deflation, and thwarted the equilibrating forces previously at work under the gold-standard system. Labor unions, industrial monopolies, agricultural groups—all contributed to holding up prices as incomes declined. (3) With waning faith in the gold-standard religion, and with growing political instability, capital flights to "safer" countries became common. Cumulative mass-capital withdrawals—"hot money" drains—were more than any nation could stand. The religion of gold worked admirably so long as no infidels entered the temple to whisper misgivings and suspicion. Once doubt spread, however, capital flights never envisaged in a stable, well-behaved international system spelled doom to the gold-standard structure in a rigid, depression-conscious world.

EXCHANGE DEPRECIATION AND EXCHANGE CONTROLS Widespread desertion of the gold standard and currency devaluations failed to bring the results expected. One country acting alone could clearly expand its exports by exchange depreciation (currency devaluation). But when everyone's currency was depreciated, the actions offset each other and no one ended up with much of a gain in exports.

In retrospect, thus, the main result of the competitive depreciation race of the 1930's was disruption of international trade and investment, widespread friction, and ill will, with no very important continuing gains to any of the competitors. As with tariff increases, exchange depreciation was a "beggar-my-neighbor" attempt to shift the onus of unemployment to other nations. Like tariff increases designed to improve domestic employment, it was doomed to defeat and mutual loss by the virtual certainty of retaliation.

As exchange depreciation failed to eliminate the unemployment that plagued the western world, cross currents of conflict and cooperation were everywhere apparent in international economic relations. New types of exchange controls proliferated. Nations fixed their exchange rates at varying levels, searching for the one to maximize their gain from foreign trade. Many countries, especially Nazi Germany, "blocked" the use of foreign exchange from their foreign sales, and rationed the foreign exchange received to prohibit its expenditure on unwanted imports.

At the same time, the disruption caused by uncertain, fluctuating exchange rates was so great that some nations tried to introduce area-stabilization arrangements. The broadest area of cooperation began with the British Commonwealth nations—the "sterling bloc." These nations agreed, at least temporarily, to keep their currencies in a stable relationship to the British pound sterling, although the pound might still fluctuate vis-à-vis other major currencies. The strong trade relationships of the sterling bloc countries made this modified exchange-stabilization plan eminently sensible in bread-and-butter terms. A weaker "Tripartite Agreement" among England, France, and the United States made some progress in avoiding sharp fluctuations in pound-franc-dollar relationships, as each government bought or sold its own foreign exchange to maintain reasonably stable rates.[1] But on the whole, the 1930's were a decade of restrictionism and attempted beggar-my-neighbor policies, on the foreign exchange front as well as in the commercial policy area.

THE INTERNATIONAL MONETARY FUND	To the nations mapping peacetime reconstruction at the end of World War II, the international monetary disruption and conflict

---

[1] The United States "Exchange Stabilization Fund" was set up in 1934 with $2 billion of the "profits" that arose from the reduction of the gold content of the dollar. The power of such stabilization funds to change rates, or to hold them stable, is set by their monetary resources, which may be quickly exhausted if balance-of-payments pressures are severe. At best, such funds are only able to eliminate moderate short-term fluctuations in exchange rates. They cannot hope to hold existing rates against continuing balance-of-payments pressures.

of the 1930's were bitter memories. There was little sentiment for restoring the old gold standard. But there was widespread agreement on the need for reasonable exchange stability and for lessening the restrictive, discriminatory exchange controls prevalent before and during the war.

In 1946, some 40 nations established the International Monetary Fund to help attain these goals.[2] The Fund consists of about $8 billion of gold and member-country currencies made available for stabilizing activities in accordance with the Fund's charter. Each country's contribution was based on its national income; the United States put up about one-third of the total. Voting control over the Fund is roughly in proportion to contributions to its capital.

The officially stated purposes of the Fund are:

1. To promote international monetary cooperation through a permanent institution that provides the machinery for consultation and collaboration on international monetary problems.

2. To facilitate the expansion of international trade and thereby to promote and maintain high levels of employment and real income.

3. To promote exchange stability, to maintain orderly exchange arrangements among members, and to avoid competitive exchange depreciation.

4. To assist in the establishment of a multilateral system of payments on current transactions and in the elimination of exchange restrictions.

5. To give confidence to members by making the Fund's resources available to them under adequate safeguards, thus providing them with an opportunity to correct maladjustments in their balances of payments without resorting to measures destructive of national and international prosperity.

6. In accordance with the above, to shorten the duration and lessen the degree of disequilibrium in the international balances of payments of members.

Organization and Operations.   The primary operating purpose of the Fund is to help member nations provide exchange-rate stability, coupled with reasonable flexibility to make any long-run adjustments required in case of fundamental disequilibria in individual balances of payments. In this respect, the philosophy of the Fund differs substantially from that of the old gold standard, whose keynote was exchange stability at all costs.

The Fund is intended to help member countries meet temporary exchange deficits only—to give them time to correct balance-of-payments maladjustments without being forced to adopt harmful and disruptive measures under exceptional strains. The Fund can thus relieve the position of any country that might otherwise be caught temporarily short of exchange. Whereas previously the only likely alternative would have been imposition of exchange controls, with the Fund's assistance imposition of such controls may be avoided. The Fund stands

---

[2] After participating in the planning, the Soviet bloc countries did not join.

ready to "lend" to any member country up to one-fourth of its quota in any year, if the proposed use of the exchange is in keeping with the Fund's stated objectives.

If any country faces a fundamental, lasting disequilibrium in its balance of payments, more fundamental steps are called for. Here the Fund tries to play a useful but different role. First, member countries agree that they will consult through the Fund on all major international monetary problems, and that each will continuously submit to the Fund's expert staff full information on its own international monetary position. Facilities for continuous consultation are the Fund's first contribution. Second, any country may, if it finds its balance of payments in fundamental disequilibrium, devalue its currency by as much as 10 per cent on notification, but without official permission, of the Fund. But any greater devaluation must be approved by the Fund, which will judge on the basis of the need for such a step to restore equilibrium. This is the second aspect of the basic philosophy underlying the Fund—exchange stability, but with flexibility where required to correct fundamental disequilibria.

Two last important observations should be made. First, the Fund specifically avoids prohibiting member-country exchange controls over *capital* movements. Over the past two decades, thinking has shifted strongly in the direction of prohibiting "hot money" movements, even though exchange controls are required for this purpose.

Second, the Fund's charter contains a special "scarce-currency" provision, aimed mainly at the United States. If any one currency becomes generally and continuously scarce, so that a substantial share of the rest of the world is out of balance vis-à-vis that currency, the Fund may declare the currency "scarce." Then all other member nations have the right to impose exchange controls on current as well as capital transactions with the offending country, in order to check the continuous drain on their own reserves. This scarce-currency provision reflected widespread fear that the United States would not always abide by the spirit of the Fund sufficiently to avoid running large balance-of-payments surpluses, or that we would not be able to escape another disastrous depression like that of the 1930's.

The Fund in the Postwar World. When it was first established, the Fund's potentialities were widely overrated, especially by the press and the lay public. On the short experience thus far, the Fund appears to be a significant step toward international monetary collaboration and stabilization after the disastrous decade of the 1930's. But it can work satisfactorily only in a relatively stable world, where cases of "fundamental disequilibrium" are rare. Indeed, member countries have already defied the Fund's regulations, devaluing their own currencies when they thought it essential, without the Fund's approval.

The fundamental question is thus whether world economic affairs can be held in a general state of trust and reasonable order. In such a world, the Fund can play a useful role in preventing the temporary stringencies that have often snowballed into major international monetary crises. But in a world characterized by general instability, distrust, and discriminatory commercial policies, it would be folly to expect more than minor results from the Fund.

POSTWAR
BALANCE-OF-PAYMENTS
PROBLEMS

What has the international economy of the postwar world been like? On the whole, developments have been encouraging. The period falls roughly into two contrasting parts, which illustrate the importance of considering the total balance of payments.

"The Dollar Shortage." After World War II, Europe's rehabilitation and reconstruction needs were enormous. Only the American economy had escaped the war unscathed. Europe's demand for American goods of every kind was almost inexhaustible. To this, the rest of the world's demand was added. But foreign nations, intent on rebuilding their war-torn factories and feeding their people, had little to offer in exchange, and their gold and dollar reserves had been exhausted early in the war.

Thus everywhere, but especially in Europe, "the dollar shortage" dominated the international economic situation. No one seemed to have enough dollars to pay for the goods and services he needed. Understandably, the American balance of trade showed a large surplus, which was covered only by large U.S. government loans and gifts abroad. On the financial side, the "Marshall Plan," under which we extended billions of reconstruction aid to allied nations, was a major attempt to alleviate this dollar shortage, paralleling the political and military objectives of strengthening our friends in the deepening East-West struggle for world domination.

What is a dollar shortage? In one hardboiled view, it is merely a situation in which the rest of the world wants to buy more from the United States than it can pay for—and hopes to get financed by American grants or other government aids. In a more sympathetic view, it was a special postwar situation in which many foreign nations found themselves strapped for gold and dollar reserves by the long expensive war, just when they most needed imports from America. The latter view was strengthened by the fact that during the war our vast productive machine, unharmed by hostilities, had continued to turn out war and civilian products, many of which had been sold abroad until our allies' monetary reserves were virtually exhausted. At the war's end, we held over 75 per cent of the world's known monetary gold stock. The entire gold and dollar holdings of the rest of the world were less than $15 billion, a perilously small cushion to finance a rapidly growing volume of world trade and capital movements.

This crisis was heightened by two further developments. One was the burgeoning cost of military preparedness and the cold war against Russia. The other was the awakening of the underdeveloped countries of the world, most of which looked to the United States for economic or military aid. The result was enormous pressure on this country to finance both military and civilian exports to our friends, and to many of the neutrals as well, through foreign aid that would supplement their scarce gold and dollar purchasing power.

The U.S. Payments Deficit of the 1950's.   By the late 1950's, international balance-of-payments statistics began to mirror a dramatic change. The United States was running a substantial balance-of-payments deficit. In 1958 alone we lost $2.3 billion of gold, and in addition foreigners built up their dollar holdings by another $1 billion. Over the decade, foreign gold and dollar holdings more than doubled, to over $30 billion in 1959.[3] In nearly every year, the United States had a payments deficit, some large, some small.

By the end of the decade, many voices were raised in alarm. Were we in danger of losing our gold stock? Was there a run on the dollar? Had the world lost faith in the stability of America's currency? Should we impose restrictions on gold withdrawals and on foreign-exchange uses? In short, wasn't this the sign of a major international crisis for America?

Most economists were agreed that the answer to the last question was an emphatic no. But no nation can indefinitely run a payments deficit without trouble. What was behind this one? Three big factors furnish most of the answer:

1.   The cold war called forth a huge, continuing American foreign-aid program for our allies and for many neutrals too. During the decade, U.S. government military and economic aid to foreign nations totaled nearly $50 billion. Well over half was military assistance, but nearly $20 billion was in direct grants and loans.

2.   American private investment abroad has risen steadily, averaging over $3 billion a year and amounting in total to nearly $40 billion by 1960, double 1950 American foreign investment.

3.   American imports have risen rapidly, and more than in proportion to our exports, as prosperity has increased American purchasing power and as foreign products have become more attractive. Thus our traditional large export surplus has lessened in the total balance of payments. Inflation in America has raised American costs and prices, making it harder for other countries to buy here and easier for us to buy there (although this applies only in those countries whose inflation has been less than ours).

Some economists see no harm in letting the situation continue. They argue that still wider distribution of the world's monetary reserves would provide a stronger base for continuing world trade and prosperity. Others, agreeing with many businessmen, emphasize that we must check inflation if we don't want to

---

[3] Reflecting this change, Britain (with the sterling bloc) and 9 other major European nations in 1959 substantially removed foreign-exchange restrictions on all their currencies.

make it still harder for foreigners to buy here and for American producers to compete abroad. Still others argue that our basic foreign-aid programs need thorough reconsideration. Perhaps we can no longer afford the large foreign assistance we provide; more important, it is no longer so clear that many of our allies any longer need it, as healthy prosperity has replaced postwar poverty in Europe especially. Very few economists see a crisis in our international monetary position or favor measures to restrict imports. Economists, often alleged to disagree on everything, are almost unanimous on the case for freer and expanding world trade.

INTERNATIONAL LENDING The basic case for foreign lending is simple and clear-cut. Both lender and borrower gain when funds are made available across national borders to those areas where the net return on investment is greatest, if due regard of risks is taken. From the viewpoint of the world economy, resources are properly allocated when such lending occurs; the world's real income is increased through commercialization and industrialization of relatively backward areas. Ordinarily, both lending and borrowing nations share this gain. This is the basic argument for the optimum allocation of resources.

U.S. Investment Abroad. U.S. private investment abroad has burgeoned since World War II. Fig. 40-1 shows total U.S. private investment abroad in selected years since 1929. The three lower areas in each bar are direct American investments. The light blue area at the top is investment in securities, including short-term investments. Even allowing for inflation, the rise since 1939 has been phenomenal.

Figure 40-2 shows the picture in terms of annual new investment abroad and annual earnings on total American foreign investment. Here again, the picture of steadily growing American investment abroad is clear. More surprising may be the earnings bars, which show that we now earn about as much each year on our investments abroad as the entire new investments we make. And, as with domestic firms, a big part of new U.S. investment abroad each year consists of plowing back earnings on the investments already there. In recent years, this reinvestment has totaled about three-fourths of total new investment, and new funds from the United States only about one-fourth.

Figure 40-2 suggests a central fact about foreign lending, government or private. To collect earnings and amortization on loans and investments abroad, either we must accept payment basically in the form of goods and services (imports) or we must be prepared continually to reinvest the principal and earnings abroad. (Remember the net creditor and mature creditor positions from Chapter 37.) Government and private lending abroad has been a major factor in permitting us to continue our traditional export surplus of goods and services. If we ever stop our annual net lending abroad, we will be able to collect our earnings and any repayments due us on loan principal only by running a net import surplus of goods and services.

American foreign aid has combined loans and direct grants. U.S. government gifts are gone forever, whatever the gain they buy. Loans appear to have the great virtue of promising a return of the funds invested. But remember Figure 40-2. Are we going to be prepared to take the import surpluses implied in collecting the large loans made to other nations since World War II? Perhaps even more fundamental, will the borrowing nations—especially the poor ones—be prepared to suffer the heavy balance-of-payments pressures implied in eventually paying off the loans without offsetting replacements from the United States or some other outside source?

To make loans abroad to stimulate American trade, especially in Latin America, Congress established the Export-Import Bank back in 1934. This bank finances mainly private exports, and imports between the United States and other nations which could not be financed through regular

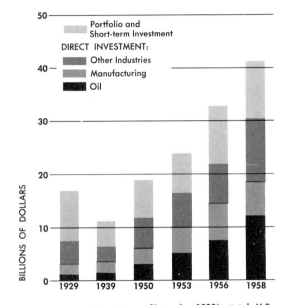

Total U.S. Private Investment Abroad

FIG. 40-1   Since the 1930's, total U.S. private investment abroad has soared. Oil investments have grown most, but American funds are widely diversified. (Source: **U.S. Department of Commerce.**)

channels at reasonable cost. It uses funds borrowed from the federal Treasury for its loans; often it guarantees private loans rather than advancing funds itself. Within its sphere the "Ex-Im Bank" has been a great success. But it has stuck largely to businesslike loans.

More recently, the Development Loan Fund was established by Congress to supplement direct government grants to other countries. This agency also uses U.S. government funds, and is designed especially to help finance the development of underdeveloped countries. But it is unclear whether we should realistically expect net repayment of such loans. And with growing European prosperity and the continuing American payments deficit, our government has increasingly moved toward plans to provide such foreign loan funds through international

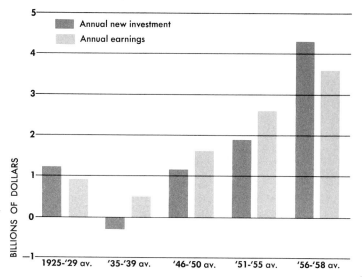

New Investment and Earnings of U.S. Private Capital Abroad

■ Annual new investment

☐ Annual earnings

BILLIONS OF DOLLARS

1925-'29 av.   '35-'39 av.   '46-'50 av.   '51-'55 av.   '56-'58 av.

FIG. 40-2   Annual new U.S. private investment abroad has grown steadily. Annual earnings on investments abroad have grown almost as fast. (Source: U.S. Department of Commerce.)

organizations whose resources are jointly provided and administered by several nations.

International Bank for Reconstruction and Development.   Parallel to the International Monetary Fund, the same countries established, in 1946, the $8-billion International Bank for Reconstruction and Development. The Bank was set up to facilitate the flow of sound long-term foreign lending for postwar reconstruction and for development of "backward" areas. Additional objectives are "to help develop the balanced growth of world trade," and "to help develop the multilateral character of international investment." The organization and management of the Bank closely parallel those of the Fund. The Bank's main offices are in the United States and its operating head is from this country, in recognition of the dominant size of the United States contribution to the Bank's capital and the dominant demand for dollar loans.

Although the Bank may lend out its own capital, it operates primarily through two other channels—attaching its guarantee to private loans, and borrowing funds in the various member countries to finance its loans. For example, if Peru wants a loan to develop its industries and plans to spend most of the loan in the United States, the Bank will either try to arrange a direct loan for Peru from American lenders, attaching its own guarantee to the loan; or it will float a bond issue in the American market to obtain funds for the Peruvian loan. In either case, the United States representative on the Bank's board would have to approve, since every loan must be approved by the major country or countries in which the loan is to be raised and spent, as well as by the Bank's officers.

The Bank is the success story of the postwar international economy. By 1958, it had lent over $3.5 billion to 53 different nations. Railways, highways, agriculture, industry, and electric power development have been the main classes of loans. Careful checking before loans are made has kept policies near to private banking standards, and the Bank has returned a profit on its activities. Yet the international nature of the Bank has given it power and resources in areas where private capital alone would fear to tread. Sixty-eight nations are now members.

The Bank operates as an international institution; risk and responsibility are shared by the member nations. All nations thus have a stake in a good repayment record. Supervision of loans is by an international agency, not by a single, "imperialistic" lender. This wide distribution of risks and responsibilities seems preferable to most observers to direct foreign loans by the American government.

Some people say the Bank has been too careful, too much like a private institution. World Bank funds are seldom available to the underdeveloped nations except for projects that clearly promise repayment in the lending country's currency —often dollars or one of the other "hard" currencies. But many such nations look to the United States for general help on economic development. To replace such direct American government loans and grants, America and others in the United Nations have been pushing for the establishment of a new affiliate of the Bank, an International Development Association. IDA would pool the resources of many nations, much as the World Bank has done. But it would finance less "bankable" projects and, most important, would be prepared to accept repayment in local currencies, thus avoiding the painful pressure faced by borrowing countries in getting dollars or other "hard currencies" to repay World Bank loans in the same currencies in which they were received.

CONCLUSION From the wave of growing controls over international economic relations between World Wars I and II—tariffs, quotas, export subsidies, exchange controls, and others— three conclusions stand out: (1) Such controls contributed to the stifling of international trade without gaining much advantage for any country. (2) Retaliatory measures increased international political friction and helped precipitate World War II. (3) Increasing government control over international trade was closely associated with increasing government control over domestic economic activity.

The period since World War II has seen a major swing back toward freer trade and more international cooperation. How can this trend be continued and strengthened? In broad perspective, perhaps four foundation stones are essential:

1. There must be a continuing downward revision of tariffs and other barriers to free international trade and lending. Any given level of tariffs and other barriers is costly to all nations because of the inefficient allocation of resources it causes. But the greatest costs come in the kind of competitive restrictive struggles between nations that characterized the decade of the 1930's.

2. There must be a reasonable degree of exchange stability; competitive exchange depreciation must be eliminated.

3. Reasonably free access must be provided for all nations to the raw materials they need. This is the logical counterpart of the general free-trade argument; not only should nations be free to sell where they will, but they should also be able to buy where they will.

4. Stable domestic economies (especially in the United States) and rising standards of living are perhaps the greatest safeguards against international economic confusion and conflict. With prosperity, nations feel little pressure toward cutthroat international economic practices. Depression, unemployment, and poverty are the most basic threats to a stable world economy.

1. The traditional gold standard has been abandoned by all major nations and few economists favor its restoration. Yet a number of leading bankers and businessmen advocate re-establishment of the gold standard, with the United States taking the lead even if other countries don't go along at the outset.

List all the reasons you can why these men might take this position. Do you find the list convincing?

2. Should the United States be concerned about its continuing balance-of-payments deficit through the 1950's? If so, what should we do about it?

3. If you were president of an American company considering the establishment of a branch abroad in a blocked-currency area, would the necessity of spending your local profits in that area rule out the project for you? Why or why not? If your answer is yes, how do you explain the fact that American companies do invest in such areas?

4. "If any major country depreciates its currency against the dollar to sell more here, the United States should retaliate by import restrictions or other comparable measures." Do you agree? Think through carefully why or why not.

5. "It is unrealistic for a mature creditor nation like the United States to expect to collect the principal and interest on its foreign loans in the aggregate. Instead, it must continue increasingly to export capital if it expects to be paid principal and interest on outstanding loans. Thus, if the U.S. government wants to help foreign nations, it is better to make outright gifts than to pile up future problems by expanding foreign loans." Do you agree or disagree? Why?

6. "If private American investors are unwilling to invest their capital abroad, this is evidence that the risks are not good ones under prevailing conditions. Then why should this government make investments abroad and use the taxpayers' money in ways they would not use it themselves?" How would you answer this question? Why?

7. "United States government development loans to foreign countries are an effective way of buying the economic and political friendship of those countries." Do you agree? (Assess carefully the evidence and reasoning you use in arriving at your position.)

FOR ANALYSIS AND DISCUSSION

Current Research

With the upsurge of interest in international affairs since World War II, economic research in the area has grown apace. Immediately after the war, the big emphasis was on investigations related to the establishment of the International Monetary Fund and Bank, and associated problems of re-establishing international trade on a freer, multilateral basis. Then the "dollar shortage" monopolized research attention. More recently, economic development of the underdeveloped countries has drawn the most attention. Leaving aside the underdeveloped countries for Chapter 43, a look at the following will provide some impression of the lively probing that has characterized this area in recent years. With the vast mass of recent research, it is especially important to remember that these suggestions represent only one economist's notion of what may prove interesting to you. The items vary widely. Skip to another if the first ones don't hit the spot.

The General Analysis of International Trade and Finance.   A good place to start is with Herbert Woolley's paper, "Transactions Between World Areas in 1951," on the intricate mesh of international trade relationships, which opens a special supplement to the *Review of Economics and Statistics* for February 1959, devoted to problems in international economics. Glance at the other papers in this issue too. Two major books, which represent combined theoretical and empirical approaches to the area, are Oskar Morgenstern's *International Financial Transactions and Business Cycles* (National Bureau of Economic Research, 1959), and John Letiche's *Balance of Payments and Economic Growth* (Harper, 1959); neither is easy going, but both are worth a look. Briefer articles which represent comparable research are Gerald Meier's "International Trade and International Inequality," *Oxford Economic Papers,* October 1958; and Arnold Harberger's "Some Evidence on the International Price Mechanism," *Journal of Political Economy,* December 1957. Easier going and perhaps more fascinating is Henry G. Aubrey's *United States Imports and World Trade* (Oxford Univ. Press, 1957), which attempts to forecast roughly the level and structure of America's imports in the rapidly changing world of the 1970's.

Commercial Policy.   An encyclopedic introduction to research across the whole field of commercial policy is another volume of special papers, *Foreign Trade Policy*—this one prepared for the Foreign Trade Policy Subcommittee of the House Committee on Ways and Means (Government Printing Office, 1958). Many of the papers are partisan pleas by industry representatives, but try Howard Piquet's thorough analysis of the effects of tariff reductions on the volume and structure of U.S. imports; Walter Salant's analysis of the broader effects on the American economy of tariff reductions; and Irving Kravis' special study of the claim that protective tariffs are needed to protect American wages against undercutting by low-paid foreign labor. Then, if you're intrigued by the Piquet analysis, look at Lawrence Krause's related argument, "United States Imports and the Tariff," *American Economic Review,* May 1959, that recent tariff reductions have had less real impact in stimulating imports than appears at first glance.

Two recent books by Dr. Percy Bidwell make concrete, easy reading on the effect of the tariff on specific American industries (*What the Tariff Means to American Industries,* Council on Foreign Relations, 1956), and on the importance of foreign-produced raw materials to the American economy (*Raw Materials: A Study of American Policy,* Harper, 1958). Pick out an industry that interests you and sample it. These are strong anti-tariff arguments. E. E. Hagen's "An Economic Justification of Protectionism," in the *Quarterly Journal of Economics* for November 1958, illustrates how tariff protection *may* in special cases lead to positive benefits—in this case in helping along industrialization in underdeveloped countries.

For a look at the European Common Market and something of what it may mean to the United States, try the brief, readable study prepared by the Committee on Economic Development, *The European Common Market and Its Meaning to the United States* (1959). And for an introductory look at Soviet Russia's use of foreign trade and economic aid to extend and tighten her sphere of international influence, see Joseph Berliner, *Soviet Economic Aid* (Council on Foreign Relations, 1959).

International Monetary and Financial Policy. The balance-of-payments problem has precipitated the greatest research flood of all. A careful overview and analysis of the postwar period is provided by Fred Klopstock and Paul Meek's "Structural Shifts and Recent Trends in United States Trade and Payments," in the *Foreign Trade Policy* volume cited above. Herbert Furth's "U.S. Balance of Payments in the Recession," *Quarterly Journal of Economics,* May 1959, re-examines some of the standard propositions about the impact of domestic recession on our balance of payments. And Randall Hinshaw's "Implications of the Shift in the U.S. Balance of Payments," *American Economic Review,* May 1959, is a stimulating argument that our recent payments deficit mainly results from so much prosperity in the United States that we want to buy much more abroad, so that our imports have risen faster than our exports. If you're interested in gold, try M. A. Kriz' *Gold in World Monetary Affairs Today* (Princeton Univ. Press, 1959).

For a good introduction to work on international lending, sample Raymond

Mikesell's *Promoting United States Private Investment Abroad* (National Planning Association, 1957). A comparable work on the International Bank and its achievements is Alex Cairncross' little book, *The International Bank for Reconstruction and Development* (Princeton Univ. Press, 1959). Neither is technical or difficult, but each is by a recognized authority, and will lead on to other work.

Much of the research in this area is being done at the new international agencies themselves, as well as in the American government. See, for example, J. M. Fleming, "Exchange Depreciation, Financial Policy, and the Domestic Price Level," in the *International Monetary Fund Staff Papers* for April 1958; and, for a sample of the statistical work under way, *International Reserves and Liquidity* (1958), by the staff of the Fund. A good sample of the currently available research by our own Department of Commerce staff is S. Pizer and F. Cutler's "Private Foreign Investments Near $37 Billion," *Survey of Current Business,* September 1958.

PART 7

Some Current Economic Problems

Managerial Economics

This is a chapter on managerial economics. Its purpose is to suggest some ways in which economic concepts and economic analysis can be used in making managerial decisions, just as they can be used in making decisions on public policy issues. In other words, this is a chapter from the businessman's point of view—a chapter on how to make more profits. As such, it will be of greatest interest to students headed toward careers in business.

Making good managerial decisions is a complex and difficult job. Usually the problems are partly economic, partly noneconomic. A decision on where to locate a new factory will hinge largely on economic considerations, such as nearness to raw materials and to markets, availability of skilled labor, and so on. But it may also depend on the pleasantness of the community for living, on local attitudes on race and religion, on likelihood of bomb damage in any future war, and so on. A decision on introducing a new automatic machine will hinge largely on its economic benefits relative to its cost—but the decision may also rest on human-relations problems in the plant. How will foremen and workers react to the new machine?

Are you prepared to see employees with long seniority laid off? In the end, many economists are fond of saying, it's the dollars-and-cents answer that counts. But managers spend a lot of time worrying about other factors too. This is no different from public policy problems, where economic and noneconomic considerations must be combined too.

This chapter presents a sample of relatively simple managerial problems, chosen mainly to illustrate how even the elementary economic concepts of a first course can serve as useful, and often powerful, tools for the manager—in pointing up fundamental ways of looking at problems and in helping to reach well-reasoned conclusions. Many managerial problems are more complex, but a surprising number hinge on the fundamental issues raised here.

THE FIRM AND ITS ENVIRONMENT

Economics' greatest contribution to the manager is the light it throws on the environment in which he operates. Only a small portion of managerial decisions can be made entirely within the factory walls. The level of consumer demand the company faces; the prices it must pay for raw materials and for labor; the supply of money and credit available to it and other firms; the tax and spending policies of the government; booms and depressions; growth in aggregate demand—all these are largely determined outside the individual firm. To make wise decisions for the firm, the manager must understand the forces that shape these external conditions. For they are as important influences on his firm's profits as are any purely internal policies he may follow. This will be obvious in most of the examples that follow.

But to understand what has gone in all the preceding chapters is not enough. There is the further problem of adapting this understanding and the use of these analytical tools to the specific decision problems faced by the manager. In most of the following examples, adjustment to the external environment plays an important role. But, properly used, the concepts of economics can be of powerful use to the manager in his internal decision-making too—especially in the analysis of demand and of costs.

ELASTICITY OF DEMAND AND PRODUCT PRICING

Demand is often elastic. And when demand is elastic, a price policy that doesn't recognize this fact can mean disaster. A price policy founded on full knowledge of demand elasticity can make life pleasant for the stockholders, and unpleasant for competitors.

The phonograph record industry is a classic case. For decades classical records were high-priced luxury items, aimed at a small market. In 1938, Columbia reduced the price per record (on the old shellac 78-rpm records) from $2 to $1.

The response was overwhelming. Total expenditure on classical records, to the amazement of almost everybody else, rose drastically. Demand turned out to be highly elastic.

About the same time, the railroads, desperate for revenue, *raised* their fares. The result was equally impressive. The customers switched to cars and buses, or just stayed home in droves; total revenue dropped as the railroads learned about elastic demand the hard way.

Of course individual product demand is sometimes inelastic. But over and over again, businessmen have underestimated the gain to be had from reducing prices and expanding markets where elastic demand prevails. Economists sometimes describe this as "elasticity pessimism." Mass markets based on low costs and low prices have been the foundation of the growing American economy.

Now try a simple problem. Suppose you are sales manager for a small company that has just developed and patented a revolutionary new type of lawn sprinkler. You are confident, from your tests, that this sprinkler will outperform and outlast the makes on the market. The company's engineers and manufacturing people tell you that with a monthly sales volume of less than 1,000, costs would be prohibitively high. From roughly 1,000 to 2,000, unit cost will be in the range of $5 to $6. Above 2,000 units up to capacity of about 4,000 units weekly, cost should run about $4.50 per sprinkler. All costs include the normal company allowance for overhead and selling costs.

You have tried the market by putting a few dozen trial-run sprinklers in some local hardware stores, pricing them to sell at retail for $7.95, $8.95, and $9.95 in different stores (with recognition that this sales price must include a markup of about 60 per cent over wholesale to provide reasonable expenses and profit for retailers). In a few days, each store has sold its dozen sprinklers. They went fastest at $7.95, next fastest at $8.95, but not strikingly faster than at $9.95. Unfortunately, you have no good way of telling whether store salesmen were more effective one place than another.

Problem: What price should you set on the sprinkler? You are convinced you can sell, with your present distribution channels, at least 2,000 sprinklers weekly through the summer season even at the $9.95 price. But will you sell many more, with higher total profits, at $8.95 or $7.95? The answer, it is easy to see from Chapter 18, depends largely on the elasticity of demand for the sprinklers. This fundamental concept focuses the problem for you, and gives you a framework for some further investigation of your demand's elasticity, possibly doing a more thorough market study. Modern statistical methods can give you a big helping hand.[1]

---

[1] For further descriptions of the use of economic concepts in the analysis of demand, readily comprehensible with the background you now have, see M. H. Spencer and L. Siegelman, *Managerial Economics* (Homewood, Ill.: Richard D. Irwin, 1959), Chapter 5; and Joel Dean, *Managerial Economics* (New York: Prentice-Hall, Inc., 1951), Chapter 4.

CASH VS.
ECONOMIC PROFITS

You're in business for yourself, doing miscellaneous repairs on plumbing, electrical wiring, carpentering, and so on, at a minimum charge of $5 per call and $2 per hour additional after the first hour. Your only equipment is your family station wagon, the back end of which you have converted to carry your working tools. You are prepared to answer calls anywhere in your general area. You've spent $20 for an ad in the local paper and for a supply of mimeographed postcards mailed at random to names from the phone book.

After a month, you've collected a large amount of experience, considerable boredom waiting for the phone to ring, and $310. Have you made a profit? Should you stay in business?

The answer to the profit question hinges on what your costs have been. If you deduct the original $20 outlay, you have $290 left. Not bad for a summer month. But look again. There is clearly gas and oil for the station wagon. And wear and tear on the same, which may be appreciable from this use. Then, aside from any materials (for which you may have charged extra), there's the question of your own time.

Suppose gas and oil allocable to this work have cost $40. And you make a rough estimate of $25 a month extra depreciation on the car. That still leaves you $225. Is that more or less than a reasonable wage for your own full time and energy for the month? Here the concept of opportunity cost provides a guide to the answer. What could you hope to make elsewhere, doing work you consider about equally interesting, difficult, and convenient? If the answer is above $225, you've made a loss, even with $250 in the bank. If it's less than $225 you've made a profit, though maybe a very small one. Central concepts from economic analysis: the distinction between cash and income, and opportunity cost. Without them you're apt to pull a real business boner.[2]

NEW-PRODUCT DECISIONS—
MARGINAL COST
VS. AVERAGE COST

Suppose you manage a filling station. Thus far, you have handled only gasoline, oil, and a few miscellaneous supplies like auto polish, windshield wiper blades, and so on. The local wholesaler approaches you to put in a small line of a good brand of batteries and tires. He argues there will be very little extra expense, since you're not pressed for space, and that you have a small but ready-made market in your regular customers who don't want to go to the inconvenience of shopping around for these items.

---

[2] This and the following five cases all hinge on the proper analysis of costs. The central concepts are drawn from Chapters 20, 21, and 22. For more detailed analyses of their use in managerial decision making, see Spencer and Siegelman, *op. cit.,* Chapter 7; Dean, *op. cit.,* Chapters 3 and 5; and M. Colberg, W. Bradford and R. Alt, *Business Economics* (Homewood, Ill.: Irwin, 1957), Chapters 4 and 5.

You've had a course in economics and you know about costs. So you calculate carefully what the marginal (extra) cost of putting in these lines would be relative to the likely increase in revenue. The answer looks good. The only marginal cost you can see is the money tied up in keeping an inventory on hand, and it looks as if you might sell $200 to $300 a month worth of tires and batteries. At a markup over wholesale that will keep the final price roughly competitive with other retailers, this should yield an extra $50 to $75 a month even after allowing for interest cost on the money tied up in inventory. On the other hand, if you allocate against the tires and batteries their approximate share of other costs (space, your time and that of the help, taxes, electricity, and so on), the line would probably show a small loss. Should you put in the tires and batteries?

The answer clearly hinges on whether you use marginal or average costs, assuming your sales estimates are reasonable. Adding the line will pretty clearly increase revenue more than cost for the enterprise as a whole, unless you've overlooked some new costs associated with the tires and batteries. Following the principles of Chapter 21, you'll increase your total profit by expanding, even though comparing the "total" cost of the batteries and tires against their selling prices they wouldn't appear to provide a profit. If it's total profit that matters to you, the comparison based on marginal cost will point the best answer.

But this is a rule to be used with care. It depends on careful analysis of costs, to be sure what is truly marginal and what is not. Suppose you add the tires and they seem a great success, selling more than you'd expected and taking up more and more space and time. You have to add a new man and expand your building. Where do you allocate the cost—to the gasoline, the tires, where? You can look at any one part of your output first, and then the other looks marginal.

Many businessmen use the above kind of marginal (or incremental) analysis in adding products, but only when the addition is small relative to their total activity, and understandably so. Adding some expense to develop "by-products" (e.g., getting glue from animals' hooves in a meat-packing firm) will clearly pay if it doesn't increase other costs and if the revenue from glue exceeds the added expense, even though the glue wouldn't pay if it carried its full share of all costs. But when any product line becomes relatively large, they expect it over the long pull to carry its regular share of the "overhead," or the "burden," as indirect costs of running the business are sometimes called. In principle, comparing marginal cost with marginal revenue always gives the right answer in deciding whether or not to take on a new product or to expand output. The trick lies in applying the principle carefully.

SUNK COSTS AND OPERATING DECISIONS Try another case—similar but somewhat different. You are a manufacturer of men's suits. Your costs fall roughly into two groups—those variable with the level of output (mainly labor and materials), and those fixed for a considerable period without reference to the level of output (rent, management salaries, and so on). You know that for the range of output in which you usually operate, you must add about 30 per cent to your variable costs to get a price that permits you to break even; you normally price by adding 40 per cent to variable costs, with the prices of individual suits varying largely with differences in cloth and the amount of hand labor.

This season, demand has been slow and you are operating well under your normal rate. It has been a bad year, and you probably will not even break even. You have a chance to make a thousand suits on a special order from a wholesaler who is not a regular customer. However, he will only pay a price that would cover variable costs plus 20 per cent. Should you take the order?

Your fixed costs are "sunk." That is, they go on and must be paid, at least for the short run, whether you operate at capacity or with large excess capacity. Since they are sunk, economic analysis says they should have no effect on your decision to accept or reject the order, if your goal is to maximize profits or minimize loss in the short run. By taking the order you will cover all your variable costs and will have the 20 per cent additional to apply on your fixed costs. You may not make a profit on your total operations, but your loss will be smaller than without the order.

But many businessmen would think a long time before taking the order. They might agree with your analysis above, that sunk costs are sunk and only marginal costs should be considered to maximize short-run profits. But they worry about the long run, and properly so. Suppose you cut the price on this order and your regular customers hear about it. Might this break your whole price line, with dire results for profits over the longer run? If the answer is yes, looking only at the particular gain from taking this order would be wearing blinders to the long-run result. In the short run you may minimize losses by taking orders at less than total cost, but both economic analysis and managerial common sense say that in the long run your price has to cover all costs or you'll end up in bankruptcy.[3]

DEPRECIATION AND **EQUIPMENT REPLACEMENT**	You operate a fleet of taxicabs. With the hard use the cabs receive you estimate that after three years they will have depreciated to the

point it is no longer economical to operate them. At that time you anticipate you will be able to sell or trade them for about 10 per cent of the original cost of $2,000 each. Thus, you account as a cost an annual depreciation charge of 30 per cent ($600) per cab, in addition to regular operating and maintenance costs.

At the end of three years you have fully depreciated the cabs, except for the small turn-in value. Yet they seem to be still in reasonably good condition. Should

---

[3] A somewhat similar problem arises when a firm using break-even charts (see pp. 466-467) receives an order for goods that will more than pay their marginal cost but will leave the firm below its break-even point. Should the manager accept the order? What are the critical considerations?

you turn them in on new cabs, using the accumulated depreciation reserve to finance the new cabs, or continue to use the old ones?

The forward-looking nature of economics, and the "sunk costs are sunk" point above, suggest the answer. The fact that you estimated a three-year life and have now accumulated a 90 per cent depreciation reserve does not give you an answer to when you should replace these particular cabs. Don't be over-impressed by the bookkeeping. The optimal choice depends on analyzing the cost and performance of new cabs against the cost and performance of continued use of the old cabs. If the total profit by continuing to use the old cabs exceeds the profit with new cabs,[4] then keep the old ones. If not, buy new ones. The crucial point is the importance of the forward-looking decision, not the fact that three years is the end of your estimated depreciation period. If you made a mistake in estimating the cabs' useful life, it may pay you to replace long before the cabs are fully depreciated, or to wait until long after. Depreciation charges represent only an estimate of the proper cost to be currently charged for the use of durable assets, not a determinant of when assets should be replaced.

DETERMINING OPTIMUM LEVELS OF PRODUCTION AND INVENTORIES Consider now a different kind of problem. Given the amount of a commodity to be produced over a year, what is the optimal (cheapest feasible) pattern in which to produce it? Suppose you are a factory manager. Your factory produces various products, and some machines are used for several products. To shift a machine to a new product involves substantial "set-up" costs, so it is cheaper to plan a long "run" on a machine than to be continually shifting from one product to another. But if you program a machine for a long run, this means you will pile up inventory of the finished product before it is needed, which will involve tying up funds and storage space to carry the inventory. How should you decide the optimal pattern for production, and, by the same token, the optimal level of finished-goods inventory to hold?

Economic theory says that it is the variable costs that matter. Leave out all the costs and benefits that are not affected by this decision. Then the relevant costs are the carrying costs for inventory (roughly, storage and interest on the funds tied up), and the manufacturing costs involved in using the machines in question. Your goal is to minimize the total cost of producing the quantity needed for the year, including the inventory holding as part of the cost. For large "lot

---

[4] Remembering possible consumer preferences for new models and all such relevant considerations, and recognizing that the assets of the business can be used another way if they are not used to buy new cabs.

[5] For a detailed analysis of just how to go about making this judgment on the best time to replace durable plant and equipment, a more advanced text is needed. See, for example, E. L. Grant, *Principles of Engineering Economy* (New York: Ronald Press, 1950), Parts II and III.

sizes" the manufacturing cost will be low, but inventory cost will be high, and conversely for small ones.

If the total cost of carrying inventory is proportional to the amount of inventory held, this cost will rise linearly (in a straight line) as the average inventory for the year rises. But the total manufacturing cost will fall steadily as the average lot size increases; this is comparable to the spreading-the-fixed-cost (or "spreading-the-overhead") phenomenon back in Chapter 20. If we graph these two curves and add them vertically to get the total cost for different lot sizes, we can readily see what production plan will provide the lowest total cost in this simple case.

Suppose we want to manufacture 10,000 units this year. In Figure 41-1, *SC* (for set-up costs) shows the decreasing total set-up cost for the year's output as the average "lot size" increases—that is, as the number of set-ups during the year is reduced. *IC* (for inventory cost) shows the steadily rising annual cost of holding inventory as the average lot size increases; it is a straight line because we have assumed that inventory carrying cost is proportional to the average amount of inventory held. If we simply add these two curves vertically to get total cost (*TC*), we find that we get the lowest total machine plus inventory cost of producing 10,000 units (about $200) if we manufacture in lot sizes of about 2,000 units, with about 5 separate "runs" of the product during the year. To produce in smaller lots would involve too much set-up cost; to produce in larger lots would involve too large inventory costs.[6]

A combination of economic theory and modern mathematics has produced comparable decision rules for optimal behavior in more complex production-

---

[6] For students mathematically inclined, the derivation of lot-size formulae, or models, which give optimal production and inventory levels for specified cost conditions, is explained simply in E. H. Bowman and R. B. Fetter, *Analysis for Production Management* (Homewood, Ill.: Richard Irwin, 1957), Chapter 9; and Grant, *op. cit.*, Chapter 18.

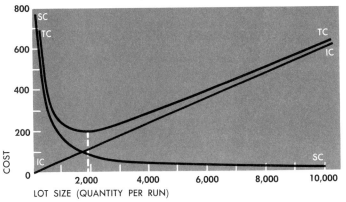

Calculation of Optimum Lot Size in Manufacturing

FIG. 41-1   The lowest total set-up plus inventory cost for 10,000 units during the year is provided by manufacturing in lot sizes of about 2,000 units.

planning situations. The best known of these approaches is "linear programming," a mathematical technique for considering simultaneously a large number of interdependent variables. Suppose, for example, we have various grades of crude oil coming to a refinery; that we want varying mixes of final product as among high-octane gasoline, motor fuels, heating oil, and residual tars; and that refinery costs vary depending on the input and output mixes and on the frequency with which the mixes are changed. This is obviously an enormously complex problem, but a very real, even typical, one in modern industry. Linear programming provides a mathematical model for combining all the costs (recognizing the technological production "constraints" that only certain inputs will produce certain outputs through the refinery in question) and for comparing alternative patterns to obtain the optimum (cheapest feasible) program to achieve the desired results.[7]

Modern managerial economics is developing rapidly in its ability to handle such complex industrial problems, aided by modern statistics, digital computers, and the rapidly developing tools of "operations research." These techniques may well be the wave of the future in managerial economics, and their use is spreading rapidly. But their description still belongs in more advanced texts.

STANDARD COSTS, ECONOMIC COSTS, AND PRODUCT PRICING

Turn back now to the problem of costs in relation to product pricing. The basic steel industry produces thousands of products—from pig iron to highly finished steels; from basic steel to intricate alloys; from cast-iron pigs (blocks) and steel ingots, through semi-finished shapes, to finished steel sheets, plates, wire, tubes, girders, and highly specialized forms and shapes. Some of these, such as cold-rolled sheets, are relatively standard products, though they vary as to exact type of steel, width, and thickness. On these, the mills have a large amount of experience on which to base cost estimates. Some highly specialized products, such as elaborate steel shapes for construction purposes, represent essentially a new job when each one comes along, on which cost estimates are inevitably rougher. In all cases, costs per ton drop rapidly as volume rises. Steel is a heavy-fixed-cost industry. In many parts, it is a continuous, day-and-night operation with high costs of shutting down and starting up. It is a mass-production industry par excellence.

As was suggested in Chapter 25, most steel companies operate on "standard costs" as a basis for their pricing. That is, their accountants and engineers determine as accurately as possible the cost per ton (or other unit of output) for a standard run of each regular product when the mill is operating at some satisfactory level of output, say 80 per cent of capacity. This is the "standard cost" of

---

[7] Bowman and Fetter, *op. cit.,* Chapter 4, present a relatively simply statement of linear programming, but you're not likely to get far without some grasp of college-level mathematics.

manufacturing that product. To this is added a relatively standard mark-up (which may vary somewhat from one product line to another) to cover selling, administrative, and all other non-manufacturing costs, plus a reasonable profit. This gives the list price. The company typically issues a "price list" or "price book" giving prices for its major products. To these list prices, "extras" may be added for additional specifications prescribed by buyers, such as quick delivery or special fabricating costs. From them may be deducted discounts, when the salesmen find it necessary to shade prices to get orders in periods when demand falls short of a satisfactory sales volume.

Are standard costing and cost-plus pricing consistent with the incremental economic concepts and analysis of Part 3 above? At first blush, the answer appears to be no. The economic models there suggested that costs per unit *vary* with changes in the level of output. If costs vary substantially depending on the level of output, is it reasonable to base prices on a standard cost figure, which often will not be the actual cost of the tonnage being sold? Similarly, is it reasonable to use a standard mark-up or cost to set prices, rather than recognizing the continually varying nature of selling costs and the continually shifting nature of market demand? May the steel industry executives need a lesson in elementary economics?

Maybe, but don't jump to the conclusion. For one thing, in a firm selling a billion dollars' worth of steel per year there are enormous advantages in having standardized policies and practices. If each order was priced on an individual salesman basis, trying to take into account *de novo* all the cost and demand considerations involved, chaos would be the likely result. Heaven knows what cost and demand estimates he might come up with. Worse, what would other customers do if they found they had just been charged 20 per cent more for a similar product by another salesman of the same company? In large transactions involving long-continued supplier-customer relationships, reasonably consistent, understood pricing practices contribute to stability and goodwill. And goodwill is extremely important in business relationships, as elsewhere.

Second, however, even with the standard cost and pricing practices commonly followed by the leading firms, list prices often become merely a starting point for bargaining on large orders. This is not to belittle the importance of list prices, for actual prices seldom vary far from them. But steel producers and customers both know that on major orders the company may be prepared to concede a little on price in slack markets, perhaps by reducing the extras charged in tighter times. Both know that the buyer can shop around—steel according to specifications is a precisely defined product where prices can be compared closely. Steel prices may even sag below the profit line for particular types when excess capacity is large, if this is what it takes to get orders. But like the suit manufacturer above, the steelmaker worries about "spoiling" his entire market with price cuts, and he suspects strongly that his price cuts will be met promptly by major competitors, thus neutralizing his advantage in drawing away their customers. Steel prices are oligopoly prices. Would you set them differently if you were president of a major steel company? [8]

BUSINESS FORECASTING   Turn now to a quite different problem of managerial economics—business forecasting. This takes us back to macro-economics.

Forecasting for What?   Businessmen must make economic forecasts all the time. Many of these forecasts are related closely to the general level of economic activity and prices; almost all are related at least indirectly. The manager must forecast the level of his own sales for weeks or months ahead to plan purchases of raw materials, to schedule production, to determine the size of inventories he needs, to set sales goals for his marketing department, to establish management bonus goals, and so on. These are short-run action decisions. He must forecast years ahead if he is to do long-range planning for the company—facilities planning (when to build new plant and equipment), personnel planning (when he will need how many of what classes of skilled workers and managers), financial planning (when the firm may need to go into the market for external funds), and so on. And in most cases his company's outlook is closely or indirectly related to the general level of business activity, its growth and fluctuations. The businessman has to make economic forecasts, explicitly or implicitly, whether he likes it or not. Sometimes he forecasts without recognizing what he's doing.

Economics has two important guidelines on forecasting at the outset. The first is: No one can forecast reliably and precisely very far into the future, no matter how glibly he talks or how much he charges for his services. The best economists can improve appreciably on just assuming the future will be like the present, but don't expect too much. And the further out the forecast goes, the more sensible it is to take a range of likely outcomes rather than trying to get one precise, most likely figure.

The second guide-line is: Don't pay more attention to uncertain forecasts than you need to. For a decision today on whether to buy ten tons of steel sheets for next quarter's refrigerator output, the manager needs to have a clear sales forecast in mind. He may be able to maintain some flexibility, but not much. He has to have steel on order if he's going to get it only a few weeks away. But if the issue is long-range facilities planning, only part of the decision needs to be made now. A forecast that says his sales for 1965 will probably be not more than 100,000 and not less than 75,000 units can serve adequately to indicate he won't need a new plant in operation before about 1962 at the earliest if his present annual capacity is, say, 65,000. At the same time, the range suggests he'll almost cer-

---

[8] The basic economic analysis involved was presented in Chapters 20-26. For more detailed managerial analyses, see Dean, *op. cit.,* Chapters 7-9; and Spencer and Siegelman, *op. cit.,* Chapters 1-3.

tainly need more capacity by 1963 or 1964. This kind of range forecast, which often can be made quite reliably, can serve his current purpose adequately; and it avoids the danger of taking some one relatively unreliable figure (say 85,000 units) for 1965 and resting present action decisions on it when it may turn out to be significantly wrong. By 1961, his forecasters will be able to make a lot better estimate for 1962-1965. Until economists and statisticians get to be better forecasters, intelligent use of uncertain forecasts is one of the greatest skills for the manager to have.

Short-range Forecasting.   Suppose you manufacture home sewing machines. It is spring, and you must make the production decisions for machines to be ready for the market in the autumn, which has traditionally been the big sales season for you, culminating in the Christmas rush. You have found in the past a quite stable relationship between consumer purchases of sewing machines and the level of disposable personal income. While this relationship has been by no means perfect and while your share of the market varies depending on advertising expenditure, model changes, and so on, forecasting disposable personal income for the whole economy is one important step in your production-planning procedures. How would you go about it?

Maybe you'll want to spend your time reading and thinking about the predictions of others—professional forecasting services, business magazines, government economists, academicians. But even if you rely on these, you need to have some criteria for judging among the almost certainly conflicting predictions you will find.

First, your economics should tell you that business fluctuations are complex, ever-changing phenomena, and that there is no sure-fire way of predicting aggregate business activity, even six months ahead. Beware of the man who has the sure-fire answer.

Second, economics suggests that there is a large amount of inertia in such a huge, diverse economy as ours. Disposable personal income next autumn is very unlikely to be enormously different from this spring. Partly this is for some very definite reasons associated with "built-in countercyclical flexibility" in government taxes and expenditures, noted below. But partly it is just because the economy is so big, with so many different factors influencing disposable personal income, that only in major expansions or contractions will most of them be moving strongly in the same direction over a short period. Employment in autos may be rising, but construction is easing off and the stock market is soft. Government spending moves up, but international developments have oils and chemicals in the doldrums. And so it goes.

So one simple type of short-run forecast, which has a higher batting average than most, is just to assume the next half-year will be about like the present one, unless there is a *strong* reason to modify this prediction. A slightly more sophisticated "inertia" approach is just to extend the rate of change of the present six months out a half year—this assumes that the present direction will continue at about the same rate. This one will do better in strong expansion or contraction periods, but it will miss more widely around the turning points. Still another inertia approach, preferred by many economists, is merely to extrapolate, say, a 3 per cent per annum growth for the next half-year, since disposable personal income has shown a long, persistent growth at about that rate over the past two decades. None of these is very elegant, but each recognizes the very basic fact of inertia for short-run forecasting.

Third, if you want a more elaborate forecast, most leading economists (in industry, government, and the universities) now use the gross national product accounts as a framework, and try to estimate each major component separately. Then they fit the parts together to see whether they are consistent, and check for likely interactions that may have been missed in studying the individual parts. Chapter 6 provides the breakdown commonly used, though many forecasters look in considerably more detail.

For example, we may want to forecast private investment, consumer expenditures, and government expenditures to get gross national product. Then we need separate estimates on government taxes and depreciation accounts to get to national income, and then estimates of transfer payments and personal income taxes to get to disposable personal income. How, for example, shall we estimate that most volatile item, business investment?

For plant and equipment spending, we now have businessmen's own forecasts of their investment spending a year ahead, collected and published regularly by the U.S. Department of Commerce and the Securities and Exchange Commission. Businessmen don't always do what they say, but these figures give a pretty good short-run benchmark. We can check them to see whether projected spending is way out of line with historical relationships to, say, consumer buying of final goods. The more extreme the estimates look, the more we may want to modify them.

For investment in inventories, we again have the published plans of businessmen from time to time. But these forecasts have proved less reliable. We need to look at the ratio of inventories to sales (probably separately in manufacturing, wholesaling, and retailing) in relation to historical standards. More important, we need to look at how fast businesses have been accumulating or using up inventories over the past year or two. The "inventory cycle" (from Chapter 13; see especially Figure 13-5) is one of the somewhat regular phenomena of business fluctuations; businesses seldom accumulate or reduce inventories on a large scale for more than a year or two at a stretch except during really major booms or depressions. If inventories have been accumulating at, say, an $8 billion annual rate for the past couple of years, you can be pretty sure a drop-off in this rate isn't far away in anything except a big, inflationary boom. Over the long pull, businesses won't continue to produce large inventories they can't sell. Nor will they be willing to deplete their inventories below what they consider sound business levels. And so it would go. We'd need a separate analysis of home construction, of foreign investment, and so on through the investment categories.

Similarly, the study of consumer spending might take several tacks. The Federal Reserve has financed and published a major study of consumer buying intentions at least once a year, and the University of Michigan's Survey Research Center, which does the work, often releases supplementary interim survey results. These will give some clues. But consumer spending depends mainly on consumer disposable income received, so we need to rely heavily here on the forecasts of private and business investment plus transfer payments, adjusted by all the special factors that may affect the propensity to consume in the short run (consumer credit, the current stock of consumer durables, the rate of family formation, and so on—see Chapter 11).

Then you would want to look at the government—at tax and expenditure rates, at monetary policy expectations, at special government activities in any field that might affect economic activity. In particular, you should recognize that with government tax revenues so heavily dependent on personal and business income taxes, government receipts will drop rapidly as national income falls and will rise rapidly as national income rises. That is, taxes will absorb a substantial part of income increases from the businesses and individuals, and will substantially lessen the impact of income declines. At the same time, unemployment insurance will produce government transfer payments to supplement private incomes if unemployment develops, and private unemployment insurance plans have the same effect. Thus, disposable personal income will be considerably more stable than gross national product, national income, or industrial production.

Put all this analysis of the individual categories in the national income accounts together, verify to see whether the individual estimates appear consistent with one another, and you will have a major check on the simpler inertia type of forecast you may have begun with.

A fourth approach, often called "econometrics," uses the same variables but combines them more formally in a mathematical model. The model, stated in a series of interrelated equations, is based on the relationships among such major variables as investment, profits, income, consumption, and so on. For example, if past experience shows that consumption in any period is 80 per cent of income in the same period, the equation would be: $C = .8Y$.

Business Week, while poking a little fun at econometricians, has summed up the method of econometric model building in the accompanying sketch. You can readily see that, in effect, this approach is much like the former one, except that it states precisely the interrelationships that were floating somewhat fuzzily before. Not everyone agrees it's good to try to be so explicit and precise, but the econometricians have scorn for people who don't face up to the job of knowing just what they are saying and what their hidden assumptions are. In any case, take a special look at steps 1 and 4; they're the crucial ones. Making up the formal mathematical model from the theory (at least in simple cases like this one)

The Junior Econometrician's Work Kit.

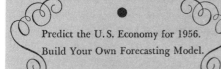

Predict the U.S. Economy for 1956.
Build Your Own Forecasting Model.

DIRECTIONS:

1. Make up a theory. You might theorize, for instance, that (1) next year's consumption will depend on next year's national income; (2) next year's investment will depend on this year's profits; (3) tax receipts will depend on future Gross National Product. (4) GNP is the sum of consumption, investment, and government expenditures. (5) National income equals GNP minus taxes.

2. Use symbols for words. Call consumption, C; national income, Y; investment, I; preceding year's profits, P_{-1}; tax receipts, T; Gross National Product, G; government expenditures, E.

3. Translate your theories into mathematical equations:

(1) $C = aY + b$ (4) $G = C + I + E$

(2) $I = cP_{-1} + d$ (5) $Y = G - T$

(3) $T = eG$

This is your forecasting model. The small letters, a, b, c, d, e, are the constants that make things come out even. For instance, if horses (H) have four legs (L), then $L = aH$; or $L = 4H$. This can be important in the blacksmith business.

4. Calculate the constants. Look up past years' statistics on consumption, income, and so on. From these find values for a, b, c, d, and e that make your equation come out fairly correct.

5. Now you're ready to forecast. Start by forecasting investment from this year's profits. Look up the current rate of corporate profits — it's around $42-billion. The model won't tell what federal, state, and local governments will spend next year — that's politics. But we can estimate it from present budget information — it looks like around $75-billion.

6. Put all available figures into your model. (We've put in the constants for you.)

(1) $C = .7Y + 40$ (4) $G = C + I + 75$

(2) $I = .9 \times 42 + 20$ (5) $Y = G - T$

(3) $T = .2G$

7. Solve the equations. You want values of C, I, T, G, Y. Hints: Do them in this order — (2), (1), (4), (3), (5). In solving (1), remember that I and E are both part of G, $Y = G - T$, and $T = .2G$.

8. Results. (See if yours are the same.) For 1956, consumption will be $260.0-billion; investment, $57.8-billion; GNP, $392.8-billion; tax receipts, $78.6-billion; national income, $314.2-billion. These results are guaranteed — provided that the theories on which they're based are valid.

Reprinted with permission from *Business Week*, September 24, 1955

is relatively easy, and solving the equations once the figures are filled in isn't hard if you know a little mathematics or have access to a computer. But finally, read the last clause of the last sentence with great concentration. No econometric model is better than the theory on which it is based and than the empirical relationships used in its constants. It's all too easy to believe that the answer ground out of an elaborate mathematical model must be good. Some modern econometric models are very elaborate and sophisticated indeed. Most economists think they're making real headway. But never forget that the answers are no better than the foundation theories and empirical constants on which they rest.

A fifth approach emphasizes leads and lags. Some economists, especially in the National Bureau of Economic Research, have studied past fluctuations in detail and have found that some economic series generally tend to lead others. Typically leading series include construction contracts, new orders for durable goods, common-stock prices, business failures (inverted), length of the manufacturing work-week, and new business incorporations. If most of these series are moving up, this suggests that other parts of the economy may follow. Figure 13-3 presented some of the data. But none of the leaders has proved to be infallible, alas, nor has even the entire group together. Study of leading indicators can supplement other approaches, but most economists (including the National Bureau) are wary of using them as a predictor all by themselves.

It should be clear by now that short-run business forecasting is a tough and complex problem indeed. And the preceding paragraphs only begin to suggest the avenues that need investigation and the ways of analyzing the problem. Yet you need to decide how many sewing machines to schedule into production next month. Most businessmen use a mixture of personal feel for the market, reading of business publications, hearsay, and heavy reliance on their own salesmen's forecasts. This practice reflects the fact that most businesses depend heavily on the special circumstances visible in their own product markets, not on the behavior of the whole economy. But increasingly the larger firms do a sophisticated job of general economic forecasting, either with a staff of their own or by buying professional services from outside. Nobody has a clear crystal ball. But forecasters who understand and use the tools of modern economic analysis can generally improve on hearsay, casual reading, and business talk, and even on inertia forecasts. A decade hence their abilities should be still better, as our understanding of the economic system steadily grows.[9]

Long-range Forecasting.   Long-range economic forecasts are needed for different purposes. Generally, a reasonably wide range of likely figures for five years ahead will serve the company's planning purposes just about as well as a specific figure, since what is usually needed is an order-of-magnitude picture of the firm's total market several years ahead. Many businessmen insist on having a specific figure for such long-range estimates, but this is pure wishful thinking. No economist, statistician, businessman, government official, or anyone else can forecast an exact figure for the gross national product or any other major eco-

---

[9] The bookstores are full of books on business forecasting, especially on forecasting the stock market. Measured scientifically by tests of what their success would have been had they been used in the past, many of them, alas, aren't much good. A recent careful, standard text that spells out alternative approaches without claiming too much is Sherman Maisel, *Fluctuations, Growth, and Forecasting* (New York: Wiley, 1957). See also Chapters 1, 2, 3, and 5 of Spencer and Siegelman, *op. cit.*

nomic series three or five years ahead with firm expectation of 1 or even 5 per cent accuracy (which would allow an error margin of some $5 to $25 billion on g.n.p.).

A good economist can lay out the major factors determining the economy's long-term growth rate. He can point out the importance and likely effects of alternative government policies aimed at providing purchasing power sufficient to assure full employment. He can provide careful forecasts of the major variables involved, and of their interaction. Some suggestions on this procedure were outlined in Chapter 12.

But he cannot forecast any of these factors with accuracy for a given future year—for example, the growth in productivity per man-hour, the size of the labor force, private investment spending, consumer spending on durables, and so on. Most important, three or five years ahead he has no reliable way of predicting the stage of the business cycle, even if he can forecast roughly the full-employment level of gross national product for the economy in the year concerned. His only real answer-giving recourse that far ahead is to assume that government policy will assure reasonably full employment. But few economists today would accept this assumption as more than a rough approximation. Many believe that government monetary and fiscal policy can and will avoid massive depressions and inflations, but there is little evidence that government policy can hold the level of unemployment continuously below, say, 4 or 5 per cent while keeping the price level stable—or even either one alone.

But these warnings need not be discouraging to the thoughtful manager. For long-range forecasts *can* be made that will provide reasonably reliable order-of-magnitude estimates for the total economy, estimates that are close enough to provide a rough basis for individual-firm long-range planning. In any case, individual industry and product forecasts are the critical requirement for the business firm. What the total-economy forecasts can do is only provide the general setting for the individual market studies required. The bare statement that g.n.p. in 1965 will probably be *at least* $600 billion in 1960 prices, and may be higher, is enough alone to pose the growth problem squarely to any firm that expects to hold or increase its share of the market.

THE IMPACT
OF INFLATION

This has been called "the age of inflation." As a businessman, you feel it is prudent to analyze just what the effect of continuing inflation is likely to be on your business. You need this information to decide how, if at all, you should change your operating policies in light of the widely voiced prediction of persistently rising prices. How can economics help you?

Economics can tell you some of the important questions to ask. It can give you a framework for studying the problem. And it can warn you against some of the common fallacies.

First, the fallacies. The closing section of Chapter 7 had something to say on these, especially the ones that arise from failing to look through the veil of money to the real goods and services underneath. There is little reason analytically or historically to suppose that moderate, "creeping" inflation will bankrupt the economy, impoverish everybody, or bring about an economic debacle. In real terms, what matters is the output of real goods and services, the distribution of that output, and the ownership of society's stock of durable goods. The main impact of creeping inflation will probably be in what it does to those real factors. If it stimulates or deters real production, if it shifts the shares of the national income, if it stimulates or deters saving and investment, if it transfers ownership of wealth —then we can assess these effects and evaluate them. The consequences of inflation may be unhappy ones, but it is not rational to begin with sweeping clichés.

Economic analysis suggests a framework for looking at the effects of inflation on your firm. (1) If inflation raises the prices you pay faster than the prices you charge, it will lower your real profits (even though your money profits may be higher), assuming it does not change the real output and sales of your firm. (2) If inflation increases your sales volume in real terms, to this extent it will help your profits, other things equal. (3) If your firm is on balance a debtor, inflation will improve your position relative to creditors; conversely, it will worsen your relative position if you are on balance a creditor.

Try thinking through for yourself the likely impact of inflation on some typical firm, say a shoe manufacturer. On (1), what are the main prices you pay? For leather, machinery, rent, insurance, interest, and, probably most important, wages for your workers. What are the main prices you charge? Which are likely to rise fastest in a period of creeping inflation over the next year? Which if the inflation continues year after year? The traditional rule of thumb was that profits would rise fast in inflation, because selling prices would go up faster than other costs, especially wages, salaries, interest, and rents. But during the long inflation of the 1940's and 1950's, money wage rates outdistanced rising prices, and the wage-salary percentage share of the national income rose substantially. What about the prospects for the future, for the economy and for your particular firm?

Consider two particular elements of your costs—depreciation charges and the prices you pay for raw materials. In inflation it is clear that depreciation charges will not be sufficient to replace the machine depreciated, since depreciation covers only the original cost of the machine while the replacement cost will be higher. How important will this be for you? Should you raise your depreciation charges to a replacement-cost basis? Remember that you pay corporation income taxes with depreciation charged on only an original-cost basis.

Now consider the related problem of raw materials and inventories. If you charge for your shoes on the basis of actual costs for the leather used, your price will not be high enough to replace the leather for the next round of production. Your present leather inventory cost, say, $2 per pair of shoes; but to replace it will cost $2.50. Do you include $2 or $2.50 in the cost of shoes currently produced in setting your prices? The accountants look at it this way: Should you charge for your leather inventory used up on a FIFO basis (first in, first out), a LIFO basis (last in, first out), or a replacement cost basis? FIFO was the traditional way, which assumes you use up the first-bought leather first, and hence charge the first-paid lower cost for it. With persistent inflation, many firms have switched to LIFO, which charges the cost of the leather bought most recently. Accounting practice does not smile on the use of replacement price costing, which would give a still higher cost for the leather in inflation. Would your economics confirm or contradict this accounting position?

(2) Will inflation raise or lower your real volume of business? This is a complicated problem on which there is no clear general answer. The best judgment, based on a combination of economic theory and examination of historical experience, seems to be that creeping inflation probably won't make much difference one way or the other for the economy as a whole. Take a look back at Chapters 7 and 12 for some of the considerations, and try applying them to your shoe business.

(3) Are you a net debtor or a net creditor, and how much difference will this make? Compute from your balance sheet all the debts you owe in fixed dollar terms (bank loans, accounts payable, bonds, taxes due, etc.) and compare them with all the assets you have in fixed dollar terms (accounts and notes receivable, bonds you own, bank deposits, currency, etc.). If your debts are bigger, you're a net debtor; you're a net creditor if your debts are smaller. As prices rise, the value of each dollar you owe, or have due you, drops correspondingly. You can compute roughly what the effect is likely to be on your balance sheet. In the aggregate, business firms are net debtors to a substantial extent, but this varies widely from firm to firm. At different recent times studies have shown about one-third of all nonfinancial corporations to be net creditors, and that many firms shift back and forth from one category to the other. How about your company?

If you sum up these effects, you can get some idea of the likely effect of any assumed amount of inflation on your firm. It may not be easy, but it may be very much worth while if it suggests changes in your policies to take advantage of the inflation where possible and to avoid its bad effects on the other side. What does it suggest about desirable policies at wage-bargaining time; about financing patterns; about the timing of investment and inventory purchases; about depreciation practices? Try listing the main changes you would make for an age of creeping inflation. The main purpose of this section has been to provide guidance in suggesting some of the important questions to ask.

CONCLUSION Managerial economics is merely economic analysis applied to the problems of managers. As such, it offers no more ready-made answers than it does on public policy problems. This is because economic analysis is only a guide to thinking about and investigating problems as they arise; and because managerial, like public policy, problems often involve noneconomic considerations that need to be weighed carefully along with the economic. But managerial economics has grown rapidly over the last decade, both among academic economists and within business firms. Economics today offers useful tools for both public and managerial policy-making.

FOR
ANALYSIS
AND
DISCUSSION

1. Suppose you are president of a small sporting goods manufacturing establishment. Make a list of the main ways in which the external economic environment is likely to influence the operating problems with which you have to deal.

2. Officials of major steel firms consistently argue that the demand for steel is inelastic—that by cutting prices they would sell very little more steel. Yet in both the cases cited in the text (phonograph records and rail travel) demand proved to be highly elastic. What reasons can you see to explain the apparent differences among the industries involved?

3. Economic theory points out that "sunk costs are sunk," and should have no influence on future operating decisions. Can you think of any exceptions to this rule?

4. Look back at the gasoline-station problem in the chapter, where the owner must decide whether or not to add the new line of batteries and tires. What would you decide? If you don't think there's enough information, make a list of the extra things you would need to know in order to make a wise decision, and indicate how you might go about getting that information.

5. Suppose you are president of the Acme Paint Company, back in the Appendix to Chapter 17. Would you use standard costs to set your paint prices, and stick to the prices set in that way? Now suppose you were in charge of pricing electric fans for Westinghouse. What would be your answer to the same question? If your answers are different, explain why.

6. Explain how you can use the analytical framework developed in Chapter 12 to gather information and make a long-range forecast of the gross national product in 1970.

7. If you were president of a major steel firm, would you favor or oppose creeping inflation in terms of its likely effect on your profits? What would your answer be if you were president of the United Steelworkers? Explain fully in both cases.

Social Security—
A Case Study

Modern industrialization over the past century brought all groups face to face with the problem of economic insecurity. The family farm, reasonably secure against hunger and physical privation, became less and less important. With increased mobility, the tradition of family care for aged parents and relatives was drastically weakened. Concurrently, depressions became more severe and far-reaching.

During the long depression of the 1930's, two groups—wage-earners and farmers—bore the special brunt of this hazard, which some social scientists have called the greatest bane of modern civilization. The outcome was the New Deal unemployment programs and wide-ranging aid for farmers. But with two decades of prosperity, the center of the problem of economic insecurity has shifted to another group—the aged. In 1900, there were only 3 million people over 65, about one out of 25 in the population. Today there are over 15 million, nearly one of every 10; and only a small fraction of the 15 million are gainfully employed. By 1975 this total will be over 20 million and growing steadily, while the labor force as a percentage of the population will surely contract over the next decade as both the very young and the very old grow more rapidly than the 14-65 group. In 1958, the personal income of three-fifths of all persons over 65 was less than $1,000.

Is our present unemployment insurance plan adequate to protect workers against depressions and loss of livelihood through shifting demand and technological advance? Perhaps more pressing, how are the growing millions of older people to be supported after they retire? Should we leave it up to each individual to look out for himself, either to save for old age or face poverty? Should federal compulsory old-age insurance be expanded to cover everyone at a rate sufficient to guarantee freedom from want? Should private pension plans in industry be expected to absorb the bulk of the burden?

The purpose of this chapter is not to give a summary of the state of public and private measures to provide social security. Rather, it is to use the problem of social security as a brief case study in the application of a few fundamentals of economic analysis to a major social-economic problem of the day. The following pages therefore make no pretext of being comprehensive. Instead, they ask: What are the major economic problems involved in providing reasonable social security, and what does economic analysis suggest about the likely consequences of alternative courses of action? Here again, you should find that your elementary economic concepts and principles are adequate to help you think through for yourself the fundamental aspects of the problem.

SOCIAL SECURITY IN THE MODERN ECONOMY [1]

Until only a quarter-century ago, private charity, plus some state-local government help, was depended on to shoulder the major burden of caring for persons unable to support themselves. Inability to provide for self-support was considered a social stigma, and the outspoken general attitude was, "If he can't make his own way, why should we carry him on our shoulders?" Workers were expected to take jobs at their own risk; special compensation for industrial injuries was almost impossible to collect. The specter of poverty in old age was one of those uncomfortable subjects to be avoided in polite conversation. Although local "poor laws" existed in most communities from early times, they were in most cases so ineffectual as to be only a sop to the consciences of the more fortunate.

With the continued spread of industrialization, urban concentration, factory production, and recurrent business depressions, the problem of economic insecurity became more widespread, more insistent. Some remedial steps were

---

[1] A comprehensive survey of social-security systems throughout the world has been prepared by the Federal Security Agency, *Social Security Legislation throughout the World* (1949). J. G. Turnbull, C. A. Williams, and E. F. Cheit, *Economic and Social Security* (New York, Ronald Press, 1957), provides a summary of the American system.

taken, but it was the nationwide economic debacle of the 1930's that brought the problem inescapably to public and governmental attention. Under widespread pressure for action, the federal government took over the job of caring for the unemployed and needy. Part of the program was "work relief" aimed at mitigating unemployment caused by depression. The other part, reflecting the Roosevelt Administration's desire to help the "underfed and underprivileged third," culminated in the Social Security Act of 1935, which provided a long-run program of aid for the aged and other needy groups.

The federal Social Security Act of 1935 is still the cornerstone of the nation's governmental social-security program. Its two main facets are a nationwide program of unemployment insurance and compulsory old-age insurance for workers and self-employed throughout the economy. In 1958, total federal and state funds paid to beneficiaries under the act were about $15 billion. This included about $3.4 billion to nearly 7 million individual recipients of direct aid, such as assistance to the needy aged, mothers, children, and the blind; $3.6 billion in unemployment compensation under cooperating state programs; and $8.4 billion to over 12 million beneficiaries under the old-age insurance system, the latter a figure that will grow rapidly.

Today there are nearly 47 million workers in occupations covered by unemployment compensation and over 75 million covered under Old Age, Survivors', and Disability Insurance (O.A.S.I.). Another 20 million have accumulated some claim under old-age insurance. Thus, social security blankets most of the population, although only a small fraction of the total have received actual cash benefits thus far. Nine out of 10 workers are covered, and 9 out of 10 of the nation's mothers and children are eligible for benefits should the family breadwinner die. Figure 42-1 on page 764 summarizes the operations of combined federal, state, and local governmental social-welfare programs in 1958.

Governmental social security provides a minimum protection against unemployment, poverty in old age, and destitution from lack of support for most of the nation's population. But benefits under all these programs are small, rising to a maximum of only $174 a month for a retired couple and $232 a month for a widow with three or more children. Thus, unions and other workers have increasingly pressed for supplementary private retirement plans. In 1929, employer contributions to employee security programs totaled less than 1 per cent of the total wage bill, almost entirely for executive pensions and workmen's compensation for injuries. Figure 42-2 shows what has happened to these private contributions since. In 1958, they totaled nearly $14 billion, nearly 7 per cent of the entire wage bill. Of this, only about one-third went into the governmental unemployment, disability, and old-age insurance plans. Over $7 billion represented employer contributions to private employee pension and welfare funds, and this total is growing faster each year.

Social security has become big business. It accounts for a sizable chunk of total personal income now, and that chunk will grow rapidly over the years ahead, as more people begin to collect benefits under the federal and private old-age insurance and pension plans. Another depression would send the number of recipients of unemployment compensation soaring.

The problem of unemployment is far from solved. Yet the most striking aspect of the social-security problem over the years ahead lies in the old-age problem. Figure 42-3 points this up. Today there are only about 15 million people over the age of 65, often considered retirement age. This is only about 8 per cent of the total population. But over the next 15 years, this over-65 group will

Governmental Social-Security Programs, 1958

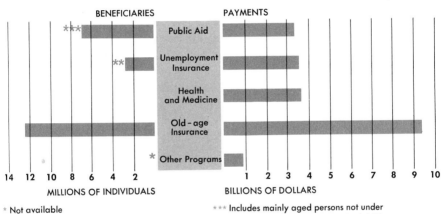

FIG. 42-1   Old-age insurance dominates the governmental social-security picture, but unemployment insurance, health, and other aids run into the billions. (Source: Social Security Administration.)

probably increase by about 50 per cent, to at least 22 million—while the working-age group between 20 and 65 will rise by less than 20 per cent. Add on the phenomenal increase in the under-20 group, if anything like the recent baby boom continues, and the problem becomes obvious. The non-working section of the population will increase by some 50 per cent (37 million people) over the next 15 years, while the working section, even when all women in that age group are included, will increase by only about 18 million people. Even if we assume that two-thirds of the 20-65 group enter the labor force, this will be an increase of only about 12 million workers to support over 35 million more non-workers.

How shall we assess this development? How much social security can we afford under these circumstances? Who should pay for it, and how?

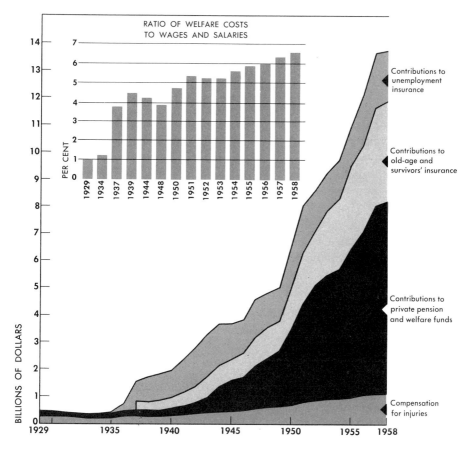

FIG. 42-2   Employer payments for employee pension and benefit funds have soared. Private pension and welfare funds are now the biggest category. (Source: National Industrial Conference Board.)

Age Distribution of U.S. Population

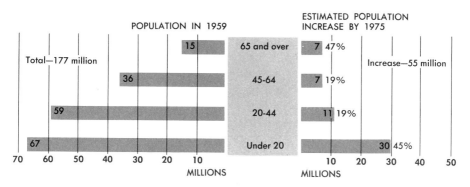

FIG. 42-3   Those of working age in the population will increase only about 18 million by 1975, while non-workers will increase by nearly 40 million. (Estimates of U.S. Census Bureau.)

Consider unemployment insurance first. The federal Social Security Act does not establish a federal unemployment-insurance system. Instead, it provides for special aid to those states that establish acceptable systems, and penalizes those that do not. The law imposes on employers a federal tax equal to 3 per cent of wages and salaries paid up to $4,200 per annum to each employee. However, in states having unemployment-insurance plans approved by the Federal Social Security Administration, employers are granted exemption from the federal tax to the full amount of the state tax paid for unemployment insurance up to nine-tenths of the federal tax.[2] The obvious intention of the law was to induce all states to adopt acceptable insurance plans, and they did. Except for a few basic federal requirements to assure fiscal solvency, to protect workers' union rights, and to set certain administrative requirements, states can set up the type of unemployment insurance they like. Regulations on benefits, eligibility, period of unemployment covered, and other such matters therefore vary considerably.

When unemployment insurance was established in the 1930's, the problem of depression unemployment held the center of attention. Today, after two decades of prosperity, attention is focused also on the problem of temporary unemployment—between jobs, in seasonal industries, and such cases. Let us first consider depression unemployment, and then look at the smaller-scale unemployment associated with individual job losses because of shifts in consumer demands, technological change, personal difficulties, and so on.

Is "Unemployment Insurance" Really Insurance?

Unemployment insurance as a protection against depression unemployment is fundamentally different from life, fire, theft, and other regular types of insurance. Ordinary insurance rests on two assumptions: (1) the predictability of the risk involved when a large number of cases are considered, and (2) the strong improbability of a mass occurrence of the insured event. Neither of these conditions, necessary for ordinary insurance, exists in depression unemployment protection.

1. Although a private insurance company cannot tell whether any given building will burn down in any year, it can estimate closely from experience how many of a very large group of buildings of a particular sort will burn per year. On the basis of this estimate, the company can tell about how much in benefits it will have to pay out per year on a large number of buildings. It can then set a premium rate sufficient to cover the probable payments to be made, plus expenses of operation. Because of the actuarial basis of likely fire losses for the large groups of insured buildings, any individual owner can convert the danger of an unpredictable large loss into a relatively small annual insurance cost. The same

---

[2] The 10 per cent allocated by the federal government goes for administrative expenses and for varied-purpose grants to the state insurance programs.

sort of actuarial calculation underlies life, accident, theft, and other such sorts of insurance. By contrast, the total amount of unemployment in any given year, or over any group of years, is highly unpredictable. There is no actuarial basis for predicting the number of workers who will be unemployed in any given period.

2. Mass unemployment comes in depression periods. Unemployment of one worker is likely to be associated with, and partially the cause of, unemployment of other workers. It is as if all the buildings insured by a fire insurance company were attached, so that if one burned all the rest would be endangered. In fire insurance this is termed the "conflagration risk," and no company would think of assuming such a risk on a large scale. To afford to do so, it would have to charge extremely high premiums, and it still might be wiped out financially by a single fire. Instead, by insuring individual buildings in scattered localities or by reinsuring with other companies in case of risk concentration, most insurance companies hold their payments to actuarial expectations and operate on roughly a current basis; their current income is sufficient to cover current claims payments, and they keep their reserve funds in investment.

These considerations indicate the special problems of unemployment "insurance." Depression unemployment cannot be predicted with any real accuracy, and it is a mass risk not susceptible to the "spreading" that is the essence of regular insurance. Moreover, in the case of ordinary insurance, the insured person can often contribute to a lower premium rate by reducing the likelihood of fire, accident, or theft in his own case. But the mass-unemployment problem centers largely in economy-wide depressions. There is relatively little the individual employer can do to lessen the likelihood of unemployment for his workers in such periods.[3]

Economic Aspects of Unemployment Insurance.   If insurance against depression unemployment is not insurance in the strict sense of the word, what is it? Fundamentally, it is a special, systematic program of unemployment relief, financed by payroll taxes on employers. The present plan aims to collect large premiums during prosperous periods, and to disburse them when unemployment arrives. The plan might simply provide for "relief" to the unemployed equal to present insurance benefits and might finance these relief payments out of special employer taxes without changing much except the name. Yet there is a good case for retaining the name of insurance, on the psychological grounds of removing the stigma of charity from payments made. And the "insurance" flavor undoubtedly helps to keep the plan from becoming a highly controversial political issue.

---

[3] Many states have "experience rating" plans that give lower employment-insurance premiums to firms that show low lay-off records. These provisions have economic justification largely in the pressure they exert on employers to reduce the "individual" type of unemployment considered later.

Looked at economically, the basic problems are: when unemployment payments should be made, how large benefits should be, how the funds should be raised, and how the payments should be distributed. These are the same questions we examined at length when we analyzed alternative fiscal and monetary policies to check depressions. What was said there applies here. How much should be spent to stimulate re-employment? Should the funds flow through public works, subsidies, or direct unemployment benefits? To be most effective, should anti-depression spending be financed by borrowing or taxation? If by taxes, by what taxes? The answers to these questions provide, as far as economic considerations go, the basic answers to the problems faced in planning for unemployment insurance.

Unemployment insurance has performed well since World War II. Each time recession struck—in 1948, 1954, and 1958—transfer payments under unemployment compensation rose rapidly to offset falling incomes under unemployment. There was no need for wise economic forecasters, prescient congressmen, or foresighted administrators. Under unemployment insurance, payments begin automatically when unemployment strikes. This plan clearly deserves significant credit for keeping postwar recessions from snowballing into depression.

But experience has also pointed to weaknesses, especially in the recession of 1958 when unemployment approaching 6 million put severe strains on the resources of state unemployment compensation funds.

1. *Coverage.* Limitation of coverage to employees and self-employed who fit readily under the present financing arrangement makes sense for an insurance plan. An insurance plan is solvent only if it collects the premiums to meet its obligations. But if the main rationale of unemployment insurance is really counter-recession transfer payments plus aid to the unemployed, then widespread coverage of almost everyone in the working population would be advantageous. Moreover, benefit payments should be extended beyond the 16 to 30 week limits now imposed by most states. The need to fight recession does not end when labor has been unemployed 16 weeks, nor does the unemployed family's need for assistance vanish.

2. *Financing.* These same considerations raise serious questions about present financing arrangements. The present tax on employers builds up compensation funds sufficient to meet recession demands *if* prosperity periods in between are substantial. But even in the mild recession of 1958, numerous state funds reached near or complete exhaustion. Special federal financial aid was needed to keep payments going to workers entitled to them under the plan, and to extend payments beyond state time limits. Perhaps reliance on separate state funds and on the employer payroll tax is justified by the desire for state autonomy and by the "non-depression" unemployment insurance goals of the plan, considered later. But for counter-recession effectiveness, the broader resources of the federal Treasury would be a more secure source of the needed transfer payments.

This re-emphasizes the questions raised since the plan's establishment about the wisdom of relying solely on a payroll tax on employers for funds. During depression periods, payroll taxes to finance any expansionary purpose tend to be self-defeating, since they raise employers' costs without increasing the demand for output. They tend to cause the very unemployment they are supposed to protect against. In boom times, payroll taxes are also deflationary, which may then be desirable. Since they are probably largely shifted to the covered employees and consumers, payroll taxes are regressive, placing much of the burden of financing relief directly upon the working class and consumers. The entire strong emphasis on a self-financing "insurance" plan leads to difficulties insofar as the goal is economic stabilization. The general case for countercyclical fiscal policy points to budget surpluses in booms, to deficits in depression. New-money borrowing in depression, on those grounds, would be the most advantageous basis for financing unemployment compensation. But to give up the present insurance connotation, which is strong in the public's mind, would involve a real political and sociological loss.

Insurance Against "Non-Depression" Unemployment.   How does the unemployment-insurance plan look as applied to non-depression types of unemployment? Smaller-scale ("individual") unemployment arises constantly through shifts in consumer demand, technological change, personal failures of workers, frictions between employer and employee, seasonal fluctuations, and other such causes. Even in "full employment" periods, holding unemployment to two million or so workers appears to be very difficult in the United States free-enterprise system; and in only moderately prosperous years the figure creeps up. In booming 1959, for example, unemployment in the Detroit area remained a serious problem, as auto output stayed around 6 million cars compared to nearly 8 million in 1955.

Much of this "individual" unemployment is temporary and frictional in a reasonably prosperous economy. The temporarily unemployed worker may take a day, a month, or even a year to get a new job, depending on his skills, his mobility between types of work and parts of the country, his personal qualities, and so on. But clearly the problem is quite different from that of depression mass unemployment.

With "individual" unemployment, the social problem is to help tide the worker and his family over their temporary lack of income and to increase his job mobility. Unemployment benefits give the worker a chance to look around for another job he will like and some possibility of moving to a new location if necessary. Without any income, the typical low-income worker is in desperate straits. His savings, if he has any, are quickly exhausted. He must usually take the first job he can find in his own vicinity, whether it is a good job for him or not; and sometimes finding another job is tough even in good times, especially for older and handicapped workers and for members of minority groups. Unemployment insurance can be a big help to the worker, and to the economy as a whole, too, since it facilitates adjustment to the inevitable shifts in demand and productive methods of our free and dynamic economy.

Shorter-term, small-scale unemployment of this sort is much more amenable to unemployment *insurance* than is the depression type. Although the predictability of the risk probably falls short of usual insurance standards, at least the conflagration risk is absent. Here, too, the need for long-continued unemployment benefits is much smaller than in the depression case, since with reasonable help and good fortune most of the "individually" unemployed workers can hope to get re-employment within the four-to-six month limit placed on unemployment benefits under most state laws. Viewed in this light, the present system of unemployment insurance stands up well under economic analysis.

OLD-AGE PENSIONS AND AID TO NEEDY GROUPS   Beyond the unemployed, social-security programs have focused on two broad groups—the aged, and special groups unable to provide for themselves, such as the blind, widows, and orphans. The social-security legislation of 1935 provided minimal federal aid to these groups. Increasingly, private pension plans have supplemented federal old-age insurance benefits.

The Federal Old-Age Insurance Program.   The federal old-age, survivors', and disability program now covers some 75 million people, plus about 20 million others who have built up some claim under the program. By 1975, it is estimated, 20 million people will be collecting benefits. The insurance plan is supplemented by joint federal-state old-age assistance to the needy aged who are not adequately cared for by private sources and who have no substantial benefits built up under the old-age insurance program. This assistance is simple direct relief; it will presumably decline in importance as O.A.S.I. takes over, but about 2½ million people received such aid in 1958.

The old-age insurance plan is set up to resemble an ordinary insurance company. Compulsory premiums (taxes) are to be calculated on roughly an actuarial basis, and reserves are accumulated to strengthen the fund and to assure payments when policyholders' claims come due. A payroll tax on the employer, matched by an equal tax on the worker (2½ per cent each in 1959 on the first $4800 of income, and scheduled to rise gradually to 4½ per cent each by 1969), provides the funds. The taxes collected must be invested in special United States government securities. Payments to most policyholders begin at age 65. The annuity received depends roughly on contributions made. If the insured dies before 65, his widow, children, or other beneficiaries receive the payments, beginning at age 62 for the widow. Women may also draw benefits beginning at 62 on a reduced basis from their own accumulations if they so choose. Payments begin at age 50 if a worker is totally disabled.

Benefits, as of 1959, rose to a maximum of $116 monthly for a single retired worker, and $174 monthly for a worker and his wife. Widows with children draw the largest benefits—up to $254 for a widow with three or more dependent children. All these figures apply only where the covered worker has participated in the program over a long period. Many participants are still eligible only for smaller benefits.

Inflation and steadily rising income levels have repeatedly led Congress to raise benefits under the program, and usually to raise tax rates to provide the needed revenue. The benefits and tax rates now planned for after 1969 are nearly twice the levels in the original act. Even so, tax premiums are now considerably short of the levels needed to keep the plan on an actuarially sound basis. Increasingly, it appears that Congress will be content to raise taxes only fast enough to match current benefit payments, rather than accumulating the reserves required under a regular insurance program. This means, actuarially, that present generations when they retire will need to be subsidized by the workers at that time. Even so, with the combined employer-employee wage tax now scheduled to reach 9 per cent, further increases in benefits will require substantial burdens indeed on productive workers. Yet with each burst of inflation and each annual rise in average family income, present pension and aid levels seem less and less adequate. Social security for a major fraction of the population cannot be provided in any year without a major drain on the productive workers in the economy, who must provide the goods and services transferred to beneficiaries under the program.

From the viewpoint of the worker, O.A.S.I. is much like a private annuity plan. But on four points, it is significantly different.

First, participation in the old-age program is compulsory. The worker has no voice in how he allocates his earnings between insurance and other uses. Make up your own mind on whether this compulsion is desirable; most people think it is.

Second, half the cost is financed by a payroll tax on employers. This would appear to represent a redistribution of income from businesses to workers. Maybe so, but more likely the tax is shifted onto the workers involved or onto consumers. (See Chapter 36.) Merely putting the tax on employers does not guarantee that they will ultimately pay it.

Third, individual benefits under O.A.S.I. are not solely determined by that individual's contributions, as they would be under a private old-age retirement annuity. Once a person has made contributions for a certain number of years, he is entitled to the same full benefits, whether he contributes all his life or only the required minimum period. Benefits are also more generous in relation to contributions for low-income than for high-income earners. Most important, tax rates are currently set too low to cover the benefits planned, so in a real sense present workers will be subsidized by future workers.

Fourth, when the system becomes as large as O.A.S.I., it is important to look at its economy-wide implications. On a going basis, O.A.S.I. amounts to an annual transfer of money income from the working portion of the population to non-workers amounting by 1960 to over $10 billion. This money transfer is soon reflected in real goods and services shifted to O.A.S.I. beneficiaries. Ten billion dollars is only 3 per cent of the current national income, but that's a lot of money, and both the absolute amount and the percentage are scheduled to grow rapidly.

Private Pension and Welfare Plans.   In 1935, private pension and welfare plans, whereby businesses systematically provided for pensions and related welfare benefits for employees, were almost nonexistent. Today, as Figure 42-2 shows, they have substantially outdistanced even the burgeoning O.A.S.I., and their lead is growing. Since World War II, unions have stressed pension plans as part of the "package" to be bargained for at each contract negotiation. Most of these plans are fully financed by company contributions, unlike O.A.S.I. By 1958, private employer contributions to employee pension and welfare funds exceeded $7 billion, and were growing at a rate of over $1 billion per year. The plans covered retirement pensions, death benefits, and accident, hospital, and health insurance. These, plus required contributions under O.A.S.I., totaled nearly 7 per cent of the total wage bill.

Almost all these welfare plans are new. They are currently piling up potential employee benefits at an enormous rate, but few of the benefits have yet been collected. Private firms are faced with a monumental financial problem in planning for such future benefits. Most plans require the firms to set aside in some form annual funds roughly equal to the current cost of the promised pensions, calculated on an insurance basis. But practices vary widely. Sometimes the corporations manage their own pension funds (e.g., U.S. Steel and General Electric), but increasingly corporations have turned the job over to banks, or to insurance companies by buying special insurance policies to provide the benefits agreed on.

Figure 42-4 shows what has happened to the assets of public and private pension funds since 1950. In only eight years, they rose from $37 billion to $89 billion. In 1950, government programs accounted for 70 per cent of the total; by 1958, the government share had fallen to about half, and was declining steadily. Put another way, private corporate pension funds held assets of over $40 billion, and were adding to them over $6 billion each year. By 1965, the private pension funds alone may well pass the $100 billion mark. This is in addition to over $50 billion of private individual and family trust funds, often administered by the same banks, set up against old age and for the later benefit of widows, children, and grandchildren.

Control and investment of such huge funds pose new problems. Where should they be invested? In stocks, to protect pensions against erosion from possible inflation? If so, what if the stock market goes down? In bonds, to give security of dollar income? If so, will the unions be content to live with the pensions bargained now if inflation comes and the income level rises substantially?

More broadly, what about the impact of such funds on the financial markets? Already, many observers believe they are the biggest single factor driving up the prices of "blue-chip" common stocks during the bull market of the 1950's. What of the implications for control of companies as more and more billions are poured into comomn stocks? Will the managers of pension funds come to wield vast power over the management of American business? [4]

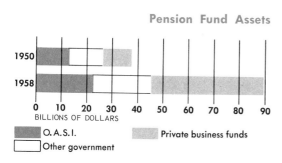

Pension Fund Assets

0 10 20 30 40 50 60 70 80 90
BILLIONS OF DOLLARS

O.A.S.I.   Private business funds
Other government

FIG. 42-4   Total assets of public and private pension funds have reached astronomical figures already, and are growing faster every year. (Source: Securities and Exchange Commission.)

Still another question arises on the impact of such plans on the mobility of labor. Few of the programs "vest" the pension benefits in the individual workers as the funds are set aside to provide future benefits. Thus, if the worker leaves the company he cannot take his pension benefits with him; he loses his accumulated pension rights. As potential pension benefits mount over the years, what will this do to the mobility of workers which has played a major role in the flexible, growing American econ-

omy? At the executive level, where pension plans are oldest, pension losses are clearly a major barrier to job changes, as many companies intend them to be. So far, the effect is not clear for the mass of workers. Vesting benefits in individual workers would eliminate the immobility problem, but companies understandably fight this more expensive provision. Under present plans, it is estimated that not more than half the workers currently covered by private corporate pension plans will actually draw benefits from the plan they are now under, because they will change jobs.

WORKMEN'S COMPENSATION   Workmen's compensation—insurance against industrial accidents—is unlike unemployment and old-age insurance in several respects. But as a major element in the over-all social-security program, it is worth a brief look. In 1958, workmen's compensation payments totaled about $1 billion.

The risk of industrial accident, with its attendant loss of working time, medical

---

[4] For a careful survey of the whole pension problem, see Robert Tilove's *Pension Funds and Economic Freedom* (Fund for the Republic, 1959), which sees no crisis ahead. However, A. A. Berle, in *Economic Power and the Free Society,* cited in Chapter 17, finds cause for alarm.

expenses, and often permanently impaired earning capacity, has long constituted a major insecurity for wage-earners. Industrial accidents have taken a devastating toll of workers.

There is no comprehensive federal law that requires employers to protect employees against this insecurity, but most states now have workmen's compensation legislation of some sort. About 43 million workers are covered—over three-fourths of all non-agricultural employees. The core of most of these acts is the provision that the employer is responsible for injuries resulting from any accident "arising out of or in the course of employment," or for insuring workers against such injuries. The worker need not prove employer negligence to collect for accidents occurring on the job. Under most state laws, employers are required to take out accident insurance with approved companies. Some states have set up their own insurance funds, to which employers must contribute premiums on a regular insurance basis.

The social-security argument for workmen's compensation is simple: the working man needs protection against personal disaster. Loss of working time through accident may not worry the $20,000-a-year man, but it is a constant specter for one earning $4,000. The high-income employee is usually hired on an annual basis, with adequate allowance for sick leave with pay. Furthermore, the risks of industrial accidents are low for most upper-income jobs. Were their incomes higher, wage-earners might be expected to save enough to protect themselves against the "rainy day" when they are laid up by an accident; but many workers are unable to make such provision, or even to purchase individual accident-insurance policies.

In addition, compensation acts have helped to reduce the number of accidents. When employers become liable for damages arising out of industrial accidents, they have a stronger incentive to install safety devices and to take all possible precautions to prevent the occurrence of accidents.

Third, many people argue that injuries to workmen are as much a cost to be assumed by the employer (through insurance or payments to injured workers) as is wear and tear on buildings and on machinery.

Nearly everyone now agrees that compulsory workmen's compensation is a good thing. But who really pays for the benefits? Probably a mixture of the employer and the employee himself, with part of the cost passed on to the public through higher prices. If the cost is borne by producers and consumers of products that involve high accident losses, real social costs are being allocated to the industries incurring them. If the cost is shifted back to the worker, workmen's compensation amounts to compulsory accident insurance paid for by the worker. Even then, workers may be better protected at less cost to themselves in this way than through any available form of personal insurance. Either way, there is reasonable assurance that the rights of injured workers will be protected and that unforeseen accidents will not constitute complete disaster for low-income wage-earners. And pressure toward adoption of safer production methods probably increases the national output over the long run, even though its main immediate effect may appear to be higher costs.

CONCLUSION   The main economic effect of our widespread social-security program is to provide incomes for persons unable for some reason to earn for themselves. Unless social security increases the total product, it means a transfer of purchasing power from those who work to those who don't.

Some social-security expenditures may increase the current national product. Unemployment insurance, which helps temporarily unemployed workers to find new jobs, and helps to reverse recessions, clearly falls in this category. Other such expenditures decrease total output through facilitation of no-work. Others contribute directly to increased *future* productive power—this is notably true of public health, child-care, and rehabilitation expenditures. But, by and large, social security means that the current "workers" who produce the national product help support the currently "idle" who are eligible for benefits.

This is not necessarily an argument against social security. The whole social-security program rests largely upon ethical and moral foundations. The major premise is that it is the responsibility of society to care for those who for some reason are temporarily or permanently unable to care for themselves, or at least to force the improvident to save for themselves. Some also argue that income is too unequally distributed and that social security helps a little to give more to the poor. Make up your own mind what you think about these ethical "redistribution" questions; economics can't answer them for you.

You can be sure that the social security issue is going to produce some strains in the American society over the years ahead. With over $18 billion already being set aside annually by the working portion of the population (employers and employees) to take care of the voluntarily or involuntarily "idle," and with this figure scheduled to grow rapidly, social security for those not working is going to put an increasing strain on the current standard of living of the workers. For with full employment, goods and services provided in any year for the aged, the disabled, and others not working, can come from only one place—the current production of the "workers." And, as Figure 42-3 shows vividly, for the next two decades at least, the "idle" are scheduled to grow much faster than the "workers." But don't forget that the worker of today is the pensioner of tomorrow. Over the long pull, the cost-benefit balance looks different than it does in any given year.

A few years ago, the American public joshed about the British "cradle to the grave," or "womb to tomb," system of social security introduced by the newly elected Labor Government. But steady expansion has been the rule in American social security too. With company-financed pensions firmly established and the federal social-security system extended to almost the entire population, many observers think the next big push will come on health and medical services. Already many firms provide minimal health services on the job. Many pay part of the cost of "Blue Cross" or other hospitalization insurance. Some unions (e.g., the United Mineworkers) already maintain elaborate health and hospitalization plans for members, all financed by employer "welfare" contributions—and probably ultimately by consumers and workers. When will "Health for the Worker and his Family" turn up as the next big fringe benefit on union negotiating lists? Or will some other area see the next big demand for government or private action to broaden social-security benefits?

FOR
ANALYSIS
AND
DISCUSSION

1. Until only a quarter-century ago, people were largely expected to look out for their own economic security. Do you think the sweeping moves toward guaranteed governmental and private social security have been, on the whole, good or bad? In answering, consider the costs of the programs, their possible effects on incentives, and any other factors that seem to you important.

2. Do you agree with the Social Security Act that you ought to be forced to save $120 out of your income each year (at 1959 rates) under the Old Age and Survivors' Insurance program toward an old-age pension, once you start working? What would you say to someone who argued that the program ought to be voluntary, covering only people who choose to be insured?

3. Is it the responsibility of society (in effect, of employed workers) to care for those who for some reason are temporarily or permanently unable to care for themselves? Examine your own thinking to try to discover why you believe what you do on this point. In doing so, is it useful to discriminate among the following different groups claiming social-security benefits?

    a. Unemployed because of depression.
    b. Unemployed because of technological change.
    c. Unemployed because of accidents (such as industrial, auto).
    d. Orphaned children.
    e. Aged who haven't saved enough to support themselves.
    f. "Ne'er-do-wells" and people who "just can't hold jobs."

4. "Unemployment insurance, federal old-age insurance, aid to needy children, and other such programs should be financed out of general tax revenues, with the cost distributed on the same 'equity' basis as the costs of other general government services." Do you agree or not? Explain carefully why or why not.

5. "The only defensible basis for financing old-age insurance is an actuarial plan, with current premium (tax) collections set aside by the Treasury until they are needed to meet old age payments." Do you agree or not? If not, defend your answer against a private insurance man who argues that this is the way private companies operate.

6. "The responsibility for all old-age pensions and unemployment insurance should be placed squarely on private industry, as it is for workmen's compensation insurance, as a regular cost of running a business." Do you agree or not? Analyze the consequences of such a plan.

43

Economic Development: The Underdeveloped Countries

The Anatomy of Economic "Backwardness."

Strategic Factors in Economic Development.

The Underdeveloped Areas: Present and Prospect.

The United States and the Underdeveloped Areas.

Two-thirds of the world's population—over 1,800,000,000 people—live in economically "underdeveloped" or "backward" countries,[1] where the great mass of people live in abject poverty, where starvation is an ever-present danger, and where disease and malnutrition hold the average lifespan down to around 40 years, compared with 70 in the United States. In 1959, per capita income in the United States was about $2,300; in the underdeveloped countries it averaged less than $100—less than one-twentieth of what we enjoy. Even if a major allowance is made for the fact that incomes in underdeveloped countries may be underestimated because so much home-produced food and clothing does not go through the market, still the over-all picture is not significantly altered.

---

[1] There are many good references now available on the underdeveloped areas and their problems. Two excellent, readable ones are Charles Kindleberger, *Economic Development* (New York: McGraw-Hill, 1958), and Eugene Staley, *The Future of Underdeveloped Countries* (New York: Harper and Bros., 1954). Kindleberger provides more detailed material on most of the points covered in this chapter, and some of the charts here are patterned closely after his.

For most of the world, poverty is still far and away the number one economic problem.[2]

Which are the underdeveloped countries? What do we mean when we say "underdeveloped" or "backward"? In the last analysis, income per capita is probably the best measure we have, imperfect as it is, for judging how well off economically the people of a country are. Using this measure, most writers have classified economies as "underdeveloped" or "highly developed" according to the income per capita they provide for their people. Just where we draw the line on what we call economically "underdeveloped" or "backward" is obviously an arbitrary decision. The preceding paragraph adopts one widely used classification, which gives the results shown in Table 43-1.

Here countries are called "highly developed" if their per capita income around the mid-1950's was above about $600. They are in the "intermediate" group if their per capita income was between about $200 and $600. They are in the "underdeveloped" group if their per capita income was less than about $200.

What has led the few countries in the top group of Table 43-1 to develop economically to their present high-income levels, while the rest of the world has lagged far behind—and indeed in many cases has not grown at all over the past century by our test of real income per capita? Besides poverty, what are the characteristics that differentiate the underdeveloped from the more highly developed economies? Perhaps most important, how, if at all, can the undeveloped countries raise their standards of living above their present poverty levels? Will two-thirds of the world's population be content to stay poverty-stricken and economically "underdeveloped"?

Economic development of these economically "backward" countries has become perhaps the most explosive socio-economic problem of our times. Poverty has become a source of acute discontent for hundreds of millions of people aroused by their nationalistic leaders. In China and India alone there are over a billion people—two huge nations gradually or violently awakening to their potential power and to the fact that poverty and misery may not be the inescapable lot of the masses in the Orient. A great change is moving eastern society to its depths, compounded of growing nationalism and the desire for economic progress and power. Justice William O. Douglas reported after his long tour of the East and Middle East in the early 1950's that he had not seen a village between the Mediterranean and the Pacific that was not stirring uneasily.

Today, India and China, Egypt and Burma, nearly all the underdeveloped countries, share a fierce determination to raise their living standards. We neglect their drive for economic development at our peril, even if we have no humani-

---

[2] Some experts believe that the very low per capita incomes of Asia and Africa are underestimated substantially. But views differ, and the much longer average working hours in the underdeveloped rural economies provide an offset to this possible income understatement. If we place any value on leisure, incomes in highly developed countries are relatively understated on this score. See Kindleberger, *op. cit.,* Chapter 1, for some estimates.

tarian interest in their plight. A revolution of rising expectations—of economic progress, individual status, and national prestige and power—is sweeping the underdeveloped nations. And national leaders are well aware that national power is inevitably tied to economic strength. Whether China and India become world powers comparable to the United States and the U.S.S.R. will depend on how successful they are in building powerful economies. The decline of England and

Table 43-1

COUNTRIES GROUPED BY LEVEL OF ECONOMIC DEVELOPMENT [a]
(Figures Show Per Capita Annual Income in Dollars)

Highly Developed Countries (about 400 million people)			
In the Americas:		*In Europe:*	
United States	$1900	Switzerland	$1000
Canada	1300	United Kingdom	930
		Sweden	910
In Oceania:		Denmark	740
New Zealand	970	Norway	720
Australia	920	Belgium	720
		Luxembourg	710
		France	600
		Netherlands	600

Intermediate Countries (about 500 million people)			
In Africa:		*In Asia:*	
Union		Israel	450
of South Africa	280	Japan	200 [b]
		Turkey	200
In the Americas:			
Venezuela	530	*In Europe:*	
Puerto Rico	430	W. Germany	480 [b]
Uruguay	420	U.S.S.R.	440 [b]
Argentina	370	Ireland	420
Cuba	330	Hungary	370
Panama	300	Poland	370
Chile	250	Austria	290 [b]
Columbia	250	Spain	240
Brazil	220	Yugoslavia	200
Mexico	200		

Underdeveloped Countries (about 1.7 billion people)			
All of Africa except		All of Asia except Israel,	
Union of South Africa	about 50-75	Japan and Turkey	about 60
All of the Americas except		India	60
countries listed above	about 125-150	China	50
		Southeast Europe	about 150-175

[a] Data for 1953 in most cases. Estimates of M. H. Watkins, Center for International Studies, Massachusetts Institute of Technology. Estimates are very rough in many cases, especially for the less-developed countries.

[b] These countries grew especially fast during the 1950's, and would rank considerably higher in a list for only a few years later.

France as world powers is an eloquent lesson on the parallel between deteriorating economic and political power.

Are the Underdeveloped Countries Really "Backward"?   Although many economists refer to regions with low output per capita as "backward," sociologists and anthropologists often protest against the imposition of our standards of economic well-being on other societies. The warning is well-taken. It may be that some societies prefer to devote themselves to aesthetic values and leisurely living rather than to accumulating material possessions. Perhaps they are happier and in that fundamental sense more "advanced" than the western industrialized states. Moreover, much of our material wealth may be pointless in the eyes of other nations. Cars so long they crowd the highways and can't be parked; elaborate subways to get us around the teeming cities we have created; work-filled days and activity-filled nights. All these raise the national income, but do they really raise our happiness?

There are no easy answers to these questions. It is important to remember that we *are* looking at only one part of human life when we focus on economic well-being, and that there is no objective way to say that our western standards of well-being and happiness are better than those of the Hindu or the South Sea islander, who have very different standards from ours. When we speak of "backward" or "underdeveloped" here, we are speaking only economically.

But having taken this warning to heart, remember that poverty and hunger are very real and unpleasant facts for hundreds of millions of people in other lands. The idyllic picture of the Indonesian who basks in the sun on the beach all day, spearing a fish for dinner and drinking coconut milk provided by nature, appears more often in romantic novels than in the reports of careful observers of life in the Far East. The number of economies that have rejected additional material goods when given a practical choice is small indeed. It is precisely the leaders of the newly awakening "underdeveloped" countries who have protested most violently against the poverty, disease, and misery that envelop the masses in their countries. We must remember the dangers in imposing our values on other societies, but in the world of today the drive for increased material well-being dominates economic thinking around the world.

THE ANATOMY OF ECONOMIC BACKWARDNESS   Poverty is the central economic fact of the underdeveloped areas. To understand what this poverty means and what the problem of the underdeveloped areas is in trying to raise their living standards, we need to look in more detail at the anatomy of the economic situation that prevails in most of them. Actually, there are wide differences among the far-flung parts of the world classified as underdeveloped, but they do have important similarities, and in a short chapter like this we will emphasize the similarities. What is the problem they face?

The Pattern of Consumption and Production. In the underdeveloped countries, with total income averaging under $100 per capita, food is the main category of consumption. It has to be, with starvation hovering uncomfortably near. For the entire group of underdeveloped countries, about 70 per cent of all income goes for food, according to the best (but very rough) estimates available. In the United States, the comparable figure is only a little over 20 per cent. Total calories per day in such major underdeveloped areas as China and India apparently average between 1,500 and 2,000, with the diet composed almost entirely of rice, other cereals, and potatoes. Although this is enough to preserve life, it is probably inadequate to fend off many diseases or, even allowing for the small bodily stature of most Asians, to provide enough energy for continued hard work for many of the population. The comparable calorie figure for the United States is above 3,000 per day, and our diet is rich in milk, vegetables, and other health-building foods. Calorie intake per day rises directly with the level of per capita income, if we compare poor and rich nations.

A mud or thatched hut and a little simple clothing make up most of the rest of the consumption pattern of the most underdeveloped economies. If you remember that something less than $30 per year is left to cover everything except food, you will have some notion of the prevailing level. Formal education, medical care, plumbing, highways, and other such services that we take for granted have little place in such standards of living. The masses in these nations save little or nothing at all, either in money assets or in the consumers' durables and housing that comprise a major type of asset accumulation in the western economies.

In nearly all the underdeveloped economies, income is very unequally distributed. There are a few very rich landowners, often with vast holdings. Sometimes the rich live abroad, spending prodigiously in Paris, New York, or Monte Carlo. The great masses are abysmally poor. In some countries, recently, the huge estates have been seized by the government and the land divided up among the people in small lots, sometimes in plots too small for any except the crudest hand-farming methods. Strikingly, there is generally no "middle class" of shopkeepers, professional men, and skilled workers, such as makes up a major portion of western populations.

The pattern of productive activity parallels these consumption patterns. Agriculture accounts for from 70 to 80 per cent of total population in most of the underdeveloped countries. Production is mainly at the handicraft stage. Since human labor is almost costless, even the most laborious and minute details are done by hand. Workers, ranging from young children to aged men and women, often walk miles to spend the day at menial tasks. Human and animal power are used almost exclusively; mechanical power per capita is infinitesimal in comparison with the highly industrialized economies. Tractors and other mechanized farming equipment are substantially unknown, and would be unusable in many areas, even if available, because of lack of fuel, maintenance facilities, and know-how, absence of sufficient education to use them properly, and, sometimes, cultural barriers against the adoption of drastically new methods.

Figure 43-1 points up the close correlation between energy use per capita and the stage of economic development. The highly developed countries use large amounts of electrical, water, and mineral energy per capita. The poor nations must rely mainly on human and animal energy. (In this and the following figures, income per capita, from Table 43-1, is always shown on the vertical axis. Here both income and energy use are plotted on ratio [logarithmic] scales to make relative [percentage] comparisons easy.)

The non-agricultural population is often clustered in a few cities, where small-scale industry, services for the wealthy, and government employment account for much of the remaining employment and output. Simple textiles, sometimes not much beyond the handicraft stage, are important in many underdeveloped economies; the cloth is used for clothing and home furnishings. In a few cases, one major basic industry dominates the non-agricultural picture—oil in the Middle East, rubber in Malaya.

A large part of production is consumed directly on the farm or bartered for other goods and services. Only a small part of total output is exchanged through the market. The elaborate systems of commodity distribution we take for granted are unknown. There is no large commercial class of individual enterprisers. Transportation facilities are crude, restricting movement of both commodities and people and drastically limiting the size of the market. There is commonly little production for export except for the one-product economies centered around such basic products as oil, rubber, and coffee, where natural resources and climatic conditions provide major comparative advantages. Where major capital investment is required—e.g., in oil refining—it has typically been provided from abroad. Except for countries with special export industries of this sort, foreign exchange to procure needed industrial equipment, foodstuffs, or other supplies from abroad is invariably scarce. And with the exception of such major export industries, as we shall see, foreign capital has not found the underdeveloped countries highly attractive for investment.

Population. *In one fundamental sense, overpopulation is the crux of the underdeveloped economies' problem. In most underdeveloped economies, the population is so large that, given the natural resources and capital available, there is barely enough output per person to maintain life. And when output increases because of improved technology or capital accumulation, population seems to increase just as fast, so there is no improvement in the average standard of living.* This is not the picture in all the underdeveloped economies, but it is in most.

Yet don't be too quick to jump to the conclusion that overpopulation is the

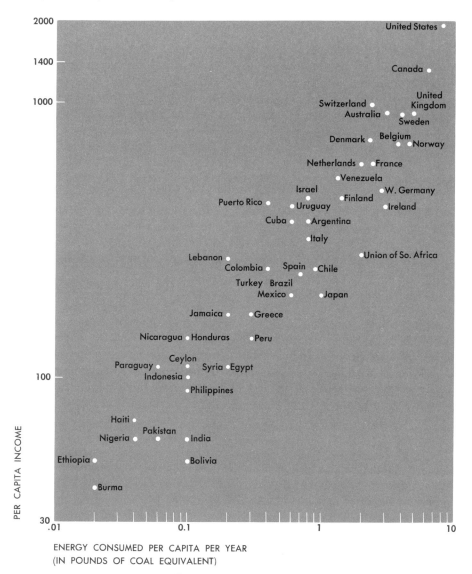

FIG. 43-1   Energy consumption per capita is closely correlated with the degree of economic development. (Figures are for the early 1950's; see Table 43-1. Source of energy data: United Nations.)

whole problem. Indeed, if more capital equipment per capita could somehow be obtained and if modern methods of production could be introduced, many of the underdeveloped economies could support much larger populations at much higher levels of living. Natural resources vary widely, but in most nations they could, if effectively used, support many more people at higher per capita incomes than now prevail. Populations are "too large"—but we must ask, too large given what supplies of capital, technology, and other resources, and given what form of economic organization?

What are the facts about population? In most underdeveloped economies, the annual birth rate is between 30 and 45 per thousand people; in the United States and western Europe, the comparable rate has generally declined to around 20 per thousand. But in the underdeveloped economies death rates until recently typically ran from 25 to 35 per thousand, compared with 10 or below in the western world. Malthus' specter of famine has always been near, aided by inadequate diet and low resistance to disease. Since it is the difference between birth and death rates that determines the rate of population growth, population growth rates in the two types of economies have until recently not been grossly different, running around 10-15 per thousand (1-1½ per cent per year). But population has steadily pushed on the food supply in the underdeveloped countries, while it has been limited by other means in more developed nations.

Recently, this picture has changed dramatically. Introduction of western methods of disease prevention has drastically reduced the death rate in many underdeveloped countries, especially the rate of infant mortality. DDT alone has saved millions of lives through checking the spread of infectious disease. Other simple modern sanitary practices, public health measures, and medicines have had similar results, even without the use of many trained doctors. In Ceylon, for example, the death rate was cut almost in half in three years by the virtual elimination of malaria. During the 1940-1950 decade, the death rate declined by 46 per cent in Puerto Rico, 43 per cent in Formosa, 23 per cent in Jamaica. But birth rates have dropped slowly if at all in most cases. The result is a population explosion in some of the underdeveloped nations. In Mexico, Ceylon, Venezuela, and El Salvador, population has been growing at 3 per cent per annum recently, a rate that means a doubling every 25 years. China's growth rate is nearly 2.5 per cent. Her 640 million population is growing by 15 million per year, and at the present rate will reach 1 billion before 1980. By contrast, both birth and death rates have been relatively stable in most highly developed countries.

Figure 43-2 shows this contrast dramatically. Note the high birth rates in most underdeveloped countries, and the rapid rates of population growth there implied by the big spread between birth and death rates, compared to the stable, highly developed European nations.

Labor and Natural Resources. The Malthusian hypothesis suggests that per capita incomes will be lowest where the ratio of population to natural resources is highest—where people outrun the ability of the land to feed them. But this hypothesis, at least in this simple form, is not supported by the facts. While the richest nations (the U.S., Canada, Australia) have low ratios of population to arable land, most of the highly developed countries of western Europe are among the world's most densely populated. The ratios for Switzerland, Belgium, and the

Netherlands are virtually identical with those for Bolivia, Peru, and Egypt. Plentiful rich land helps, but it doesn't explain much by itself.

Nor do other natural resources, except possibly in the extreme cases of the U.S., Canada, and the few other big unoccupied nations. Switzerland has one of the world's highest per capita incomes on virtually no natural resources; China one of the lowest on vast natural resources. There is no adequate way of con-

Birth and Death Rates in Different Countries

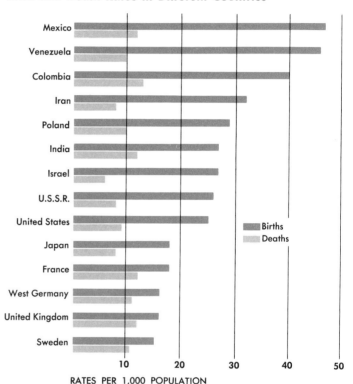

FIG. 43-2   The underdeveloped countries have the fastest growing populations. For the whole world, the birth rate is about 34 per thousand and the death rate about 12 per thousand. (Figures are mainly for 1956. Source: United Nations.)

RATES PER 1,000 POPULATION

verting natural resources other than land to a per capita basis, but rough calculations don't suggest that much weight can be put on the natural resources variable alone in explaining the stage of economic development.

But variations in the quality of the labor force do look important. People who cannot read or write are seldom highly productive workers. Surely they are unfitted for work in the occupations that mark the highly developed nations—science, engineering, business, the professions, even work in modern factories or use of modern farming methods. Yet in most underdeveloped nations over half the population is illiterate. New methods which involve even the simplest changes often meet barriers of superstition and inadequate understanding—for example, use of chemical fertilizers and crop rotation. The first problem in such nations is providing hoes and simple education in how to use them, not tractors and mechanical cultivators for the illiterate natives. Figure 43-3 shows the strong

Literacy and Per Capita Incomes

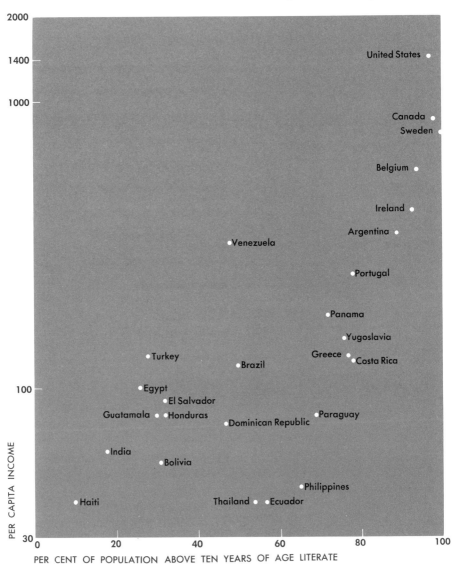

FIG. 43-3   Degree of literacy is highly correlated with the extent of economic development, probably both as cause and as effect. (Figures for about 1949. Source: United Nations.)

correlation between literacy and living standards. Plotting daily newspaper circulation per 1,000 inhabitants against per capita income gives an even more striking correlation (though here the causal chain may run strongly from income level to newspapers as well as the other way).

The absence of a middle class is striking in the underdeveloped countries—businessmen, doctors, lawyers, clerks, white-collar workers. This is largely a reflection of underdevelopment itself, but it also reflects the absence of a qualified labor force. The absence of even qualified clerks and minor administrators poses a major problem for any commercial or business activity. Basic education and the mores of reasonable honesty and efficiency in work which we take for granted are the foundation for most economic activity as we know it in the western world. Without them, economic development faces major barriers.

The Shortage of Capital and Lagging Technology.   Natural resources don't explain much about how economically developed countries are. The stock of capital explains more. No underdeveloped country has a large stock of capital goods per capita; every rich nation has a large stock. Modern factories, highways, machinery and equipment, hospitals—all are scarce in the backward nations. Without them, high output per capita is very difficult.

The reason is easy to find. When nations are poor, they find it hard to save. Saving in India means cutting back an already pitifully low standard of living. Saving in America is easy. The underdeveloped country can divert resources from producing consumption goods to investment only at the risk of further want and privation. Yet without capital goods it can never hope to raise the standard of living of the masses.

In many of the underdeveloped nations, net capital formation runs around 5 per cent of net national product, scarcely enough to keep up with growing populations. By contrast, in America recent rates have been around 10 per cent; in West Germany over 30 per cent; in Australia 25 per cent; in much of western Europe around 15 per cent. It is easy for the rich to become richer. The poor, like the Queen in *Through the Looking Glass,* must run as fast as they can merely to stay in the same place, as population grows constantly.

Most underdeveloped countries use little modern technology. To the illiterate native of Peru or Nigeria, Detroit's mass-production methods and Pittsburgh's steel mills have little relevance. For him the problem is to learn to use a hoe and to rotate crops. Moreover, much of modern technology is enormously expensive; without heavy capital investment it is out of the question. Modern technology can be imported from the advanced countries, but it requires an educated work force to use and maintain it. Much of modern technology is related to mass markets and large-scale production. It might seem easy for the backward nations to leap ahead by importing the readily available know-how of advanced nations. But in fact crude and lagging technology is everywhere prevalent in the low-income countries.

Environment and Initiative.   Rapid growth in output per capita has come mainly in countries that emphasize individual initiative and that provide social and political institutions conducive to individual work and advancement. Every country in the "highly developed" group of Table 43-1 falls in this category (although some others showing rapid growth in recent years—e.g., the U.S.S.R. —have used western-style individual initiative to a lesser extent).

By and large, these conditions are lacking in the underdeveloped economies. Apathy and ignorance characterize the great mass of their populations. Except for government leaders and small educated groups, there is generally little individual initiative or effective impetus toward economic development. The peasant who owns no land of his own and who must give up much of what he produces to an absentee landlord sees little gain in working harder to increase output. If he gets enough to eat and has a place to live, he feels little need to work harder to try to get ahead economically. If his lot has been one of poverty and misery for untold generations, and he has not been educated to enjoy better things, there is little to give him hope of a better lot through his own efforts.

Nor in most cases does the general environment encourage him to activities calculated to produce national growth. Entrepreneurship in establishing small shops and factories is rare. Mores often do not favor such activities, nor can the necessary capital be borrowed or saved. Savings by the rich often fail to produce socially desirable investment, since there is no effective market to channel funds along these lines. Financial institutions that encourage saving and channel savings to business borrowers are lacking. Governments are typically weak and unstable, lax in enforcing the rules which underlie business behavior as we know it in the western world—or ruthlessly dictatorial.

The Vicious Circle of Poverty.   The economically underdeveloped countries vary widely. But in many the problem seems to be a vicious circle of poverty, something like this: Incomes and living standards are so low that productivity is low and saving is impossible for the mass of the population. Without more saving to accumulate more capital goods, build highways, and provide education, total output per capita cannot be increased. Total output does increase as population produces more workers, and some saving provides some additional capital goods and public services. But the birth rate is high, and population grows about as fast as does total output, thus holding down living standards to present poverty levels and preventing the saving that might permit faster capital accumulation and a break-through to higher real incomes per capita.

A special aspect of the vicious circle of poverty in many nations is the surplus farm population. It has been estimated that throughout the underdeveloped economies as much as from 20 to 40 per cent of all farm population is "surplus," in the sense that its marginal product is substantially zero. It could be removed from the farms of the countries concerned without any reduction in total farm output. Such conclusions have been reached within the last decade for southeastern Europe, Egypt, India, and parts of Indonesia. For widespread other areas, the situation may not be much different.

But to move this surplus population to productive employment seems impossible. How shall millions of people be uprooted from their farms and villages? What will keep them from starving until they become established in industrial jobs? How can uneducated people be made into effective industrial workers? Where will the industrial jobs come from—who will provide the tools for new factory workers, capital for factory equipment, and the enterprise to establish new concerns? How could the newly made industrial goods be sold, either domestically with the absence of adequate transportation and commercial facilities, or abroad? Could such a wholesale shift be made without destroying the non-economic values of peoples whose traditions and whole lives have for centuries moved in different channels?

There are other aspects of the vicious circle of poverty. Government assumption of the investment function is required to channel investment into socially desirable channels; yet government taxation of high incomes stifles the private investment desired in the private sector. Poor countries, which need strong governments to provide the environment for economic growth, seldom have them because of the unrest generated by poverty in an unsettled world. It seems that everywhere they turn, the underdeveloped nations face insoluble dilemmas.

STRATEGIC FACTORS IN ECONOMIC DEVELOPMENT

What are the strategic factors in economic development? Why have some nations grown fast, others not at all? How can the underdeveloped countries break out of the vicious circle of poverty?

There is no single answer. Some of the factors that are probably important are considered below. But for the time being at least, how to rise from poverty to sustained economic growth remains a controversial and unsettled issue.

Environment and Institutions for Economic Development. It is striking that every country in the "highly developed" group of Table 43-1 is either in western Europe or has inherited much of western European culture and traditions. Max Weber, a famous sociologist, in his *The Protestant Ethic and the Spirit of Capitalism,* argued that the rapid economic development of western Europe was linked intimately with what he called the "protestant ethic"—the belief that work is good for its own sake and that the individual should be free to seek after his own welfare through work.

Parallel with the impetus of the protestant ethic, Weber emphasized the institutions of capitalistic society that have accompanied rapid economic development in the West: (1) private ownership and control of the means of production; (2) freedom of the market from such irrational restrictions as guild monopolies, social class barriers, and government price-fixing; (3) the reign of calculable law, enabling people to know in advance what rules they operate under in economic life; (4) freedom of individuals to work for wages; (5) "commercialism" of economic life through a market system of wages and prices to mobilize and allocate productive resources; and (6) speculation and risk-taking (which had been largely prevented in the preceding feudal and guild societies).

Were the protestant ethic and the institutions of capitalism essential to the rapid economic growth of today's richest countries? The facts fit Weber's description reasonably well. But these are not the only countries that have had rapid economic growth, and other kinds of impetus and institutions seem to have been effective elsewhere.

The rise of industrial Germany during the last half of the nineteenth century, for example, showed strong government encouragement of economic development within an essentially private-enterprise economy. The spectacular industrialization and economic development of Japan during the half-century preceding World War I was a clear case of deliberate and positive government leadership on at least a quasi-authoritarian basis. A small group of national leaders within the governing group were determined to modernize Japan, and to do so they deliberately altered the entire Japanese economic and social system. An authority on Japan writes:

> Japan skipped from feudalism into capitalism omitting the laissez-faire stage and its political counterpart, Victorian liberalism.... [Her leaders] were so far in advance of the rest of their countrymen that they had to drag a complaining, half-awakened nation of merchants and peasants after them.[2]

Perhaps the most striking case of all those outside the Weber pattern is modern Russia, whose rapid economic development has been accomplished through a drastically centralized economic control, with results examined in detail in the next chapter. Communist China is the great experiment of the present generation.

Nevertheless, the predominance of western private-enterprise nations in the highly developed group suggests the importance of the profit motive and the free-price, market-type economies they represent. The absence of a commercial, business-oriented middle class is striking in the backward nations. So is the absence of financial institutions to encourage private saving, and mores that support private initiative and risk-taking. Do the underdeveloped countries need something like the protestant ethic and the institutions of modern capitalism to facilitate economic growth? Or do the patterns of Japan or the U.S.S.R. offer greater promise? Or can the underdeveloped nations grow best with quite different institutional frameworks of their own?

In the underdeveloped nations, recognition of the importance of appropriate environment has been growing. National leaders, many of whom are educated abroad, have seen that a better life may be feasible. They are trying to stir their

---

[2] E. H. Norman, *Japan's Emergence as a Modern State* (New York: Institute of Pacific Relations, 1946), p. 47.

populations, to give leadership to development programs, and to revise local institutions (like land-ownership) that stand in the way of popular initiative and development. The United Nations, in its *World Economic Survey for 1955,* reported optimistically (p. 3):

> Perhaps the most significant advance in the underdeveloped countries to date, however, lies . . . in the evolution of a social climate favorable to economic development. The change in social philosophy, especially in countries which have only recently acquired national independence, is of revolutionary proportions; the vision of social and economic progress is taking its place alongside religion and language as a basis for social integration. . . . Perhaps the outstanding change is . . . that governments are increasingly coming to view themselves as engines for the promotion of economic and social welfare; this has already had far-reaching implications in converting the government budget into an instrument for the development of both natural and human resources . . . and also for widespread reforms of private institutions—most notably in connection with land ownership—which have in the past stifled economic development.

Most observers today think this report was too optimistic. Local governments have had far less success than at first seemed possible. Democratic approaches have faced serious problems in areas unprepared for popular assumption of such responsibilities. But change is the order of the day.

Innovation and Technological Advance.   Development of the western economies has been marked by widespread innovation and technological advance. The industrial revolution rested in considerable part upon a remarkable series of inventions and their steady introduction into practical use. At least in the United States, as we saw in Chapter 12, there is evidence that this rate of technological advance has increased in recent years, and has played a major role in raising output per capita. In recent years, large research expenditures have stimulated invention and provided widening opportunities for profitable innovation.

How can the underdeveloped countries obtain such technological stimulation? In one sense their problem is easier than for the western economies. They can adopt present techniques outright from the older economies which have developed them by slow experimentation and innovation. Thus, Germany, as it developed industrially in the nineteenth century, was able to borrow productive processes developed in England, which had pioneered in industrial development. More recently, the spectacular industrial growth of the U.S.S.R. represents a similar mass adaptation of industrial methods and techniques from the West—in many cases whole factories were reproduced.

Today India and China are both importing technology heavily from the developed countries, China mainly from the U.S.S.R. and India from both East and West. But the problems of such importation were outlined above—the necessity for heavy capital investment; the need for skilled laborers, technicians, and managers; the need for mass markets to justify many modern methods. In most nations (Japan is an exception), experience suggests the need for a modest approach first, to introduce simpler methods which can be used effectively by backward populations. Simple technical assistance to farmers, provision of fertilizers, improved farming methods, above all education—at least in the smaller countries, these steps seem to pay off with more certainty than do attempts to import complex modern technology. Centuries-old habits, superstition, mistrust, above all lack of education, have made introduction of even simple reforms slow and uncertain. Similar problems have been met in introducing new industrial technology, and commercial and managerial innovations from the developed nations.

Education and Creation of an Industrial Labor Force. Economic development in western Europe may not have required the improvement in mass-education levels that accompanied it, but there is little doubt that this improvement in basic education and technical skills helped greatly. The even greater success in America, Australia, and New Zealand is, perhaps significantly, associated with even broader standards of mass education. Look back at Figure 43-3; it speaks for itself. Investment in education does not pay fast returns. But it is probably necessary for substantial economic development, and the long-run payoff is big.

Industrialization requires the transfer of workers from agriculture to industry and the cities. Occupational mobility is necessary. Here again, the "open economies" of western Europe and her colonies, with their freedom of movement and opportunity, have encouraged the development of industrial labor forces anxious to raise their living standards. Even the centrally directed economies, such as the U.S.S.R., have found this development essential to industrialization and economic growth; they have used both forced movement of labor and the incentives of monetary rewards. Education and training increase the productivity of workers leaving the overcrowded land for industrial jobs. At a more advanced level, the training of scientists and engineers on a large scale has marked the recent advances of the most rapidly growing nations, in both the free economies and the centrally directed states. No less important—possibly most important of all—is creation of a merchant, business-oriented, educated class for private activity and government service.

Capital Accumulation and Industrialization. *Substantial capital accumulation has marked every major case of rapid economic development.* In the western economies, net capital formation has averaged well over 10 per cent of net national product during periods of rapid growth—for example, in the United States, Russia, England, and Germany. Peak rates of 20-30 per cent have been not uncommon in the post-World War II period, in West Germany, Russia, Japan, and (apparently) Communist China. Economies with low ratios have almost invariably had low per capita growth rates.

Saving and capital accumulation are essential for industrialization, for more transport facilities, for better education, for more fertilizer, for better public health measures—in fact, for just about every important step that can be taken to raise output per capita. There is rough evidence that it takes about $3 to $4 of new capital goods to increase current income by about $1 annually in these countries (a "capital-output ratio" of say 4 to 1). In this case, an economy that saves 4 per cent of its income will, other things equal, increase its national income by about 1 per cent annually. Then, if population grows at about 1 per cent annually, per capita income is just held constant. Thus improved living standards require either higher saving or lower population growth rates. Any saving rate below 4 per cent will mean *decreasing* per capita incomes.

This relationship between the capital-output ratio and the rate of saving is pointed up by Table 43-2. The left-hand side of the table shows a capital-output ratio of 4, and what happens to the annual increase in total output with increasing ratios of saving to income. Thus, if 4 per cent of total income is saved, as above, there will be a 1 per cent increase in total annual output. If 5 per cent is saved, this goes up to 1.25 per cent. But if saving can be raised to 10 per cent of income, the annual growth in output jumps to 2.5 per cent. You can readily calculate the output growth rate implied by any savings ratio, given the capital-output ratio of 4.

Table 43-2

CAPITAL-OUTPUT AND SAVINGS RATIOS

Capital-Output Ratio	Savings-Income Ratio	Annual Increase in Output (Percentage)	Capital-Output Ratio	Savings-Income Ratio	Annual Increase in Output (Percentage)
4	.04	1.0	3	.04	1.33
4	.05	1.25	3	.05	1.67
4	.10	2.5	3	.10	3.33
4	.15	3.75	3	.15	5.0

The right-hand part of the table shows comparable data for a capital-output ratio of 3. Since less new capital is required to produce an additional unit of output, the annual increase in output is larger for each savings ratio. For example, a 4 per cent saving rate produces a 1.33 per cent annual increase in output. This side of the table, compared to the other, illustrates how important the capital-output ratio is in governing how fast output will grow as the result of any given savings ratio.

In fact, saving in the underdeveloped economies seldom exceeds 5 per cent of national income; and even this is often accomplished only through government collection of taxes to finance capital improvements, or through inflationary government spending to bid resources away from consumption. If the capital-output ratio is high (say 4 or above), the problem of breaking out of the vicious circle of poverty is difficult indeed, since correspondingly more saving and capital is required to produce 1 unit of additional output. If the ratio is lower, the saving problem is correspondingly easier.

Although industrialization may not be essential to sustained economic growth, it has played a central role in the capital formation of every economy that has

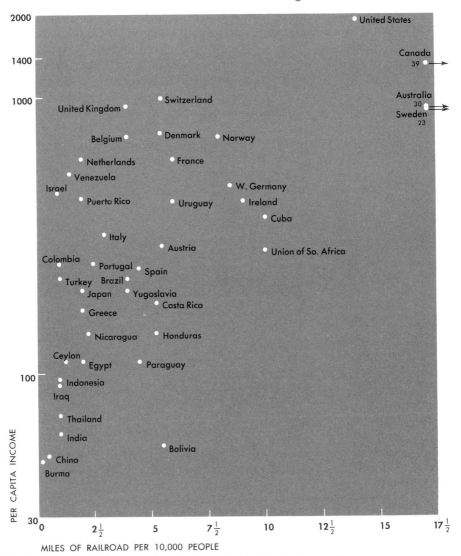

Railroad Mileage in Different Countries

FIG. 43-4   Railroad density is also closely correlated with the degree of economic development, again probably both as cause and as effect. (Figures are for early 1950's; see Table 43-1. Railroad data from United Nations and *Statesmen's Yearbook*.)

grown rapidly over the past century. In most countries industrialization has come gradually, spreading through the economy first through fabrication of locally available raw materials and then growing into full-fledged industrial activity. The much-discussed "industrial revolution" in England is probably more accurately,

Annual Steel Consumption in Different Countries

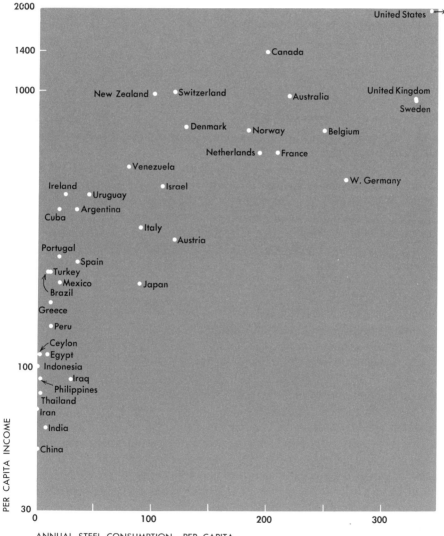

FIG. 43-5   The highly developed nations use vastly more steel per capita than do the underdeveloped ones. (Figures are for early 1950's; see Table 43-1. Steel data from United Nations.)

if less spectacularly, termed industrial evolution. But there are exceptions. Japan's forced-draft industrialization and modernization of a century ago and the modern Russian economy, for example, are both cases of spectacularly rapid industrialization, both under strong government direction and control. Today's Communist China may be the beginning of another spectacular case.

Transport and steel appear to have played prominent roles in most instances of rapid industrial development. Adequate transport facilitates communication, permits specialization and division of labor, and underlies mass production and mass markets. Steel is used in nearly every facet of modern industrial activity. Without steel, development to intermediate or high living standards is virtually impossible. Figure 43-4 shows the close correlation between miles of railroad per 10,000 people and per capita income levels. Figure 43-5 shows a similar correlation between per capita steel consumption and per capita incomes. It is not surprising, therefore, that most underdeveloped countries and their advisers stress the importance of investment in adequate transportation facilities first of all; and the necessity to import or produce steel domestically once substantial industrialization begins.

Some industrialization is necessary for rapid economic growth; a purely agricultural economy could never hope to achieve modern American living standards. But history is far less clear on how fast an economy must industrialize for an optimal rate of economic development, as it breaks out of the trap of poverty. Many responsible economists urge that concentration on improving agricultural productivity and food production is the first need if the underdeveloped nations are to break out of their vicious circle. To try to leap to modern industrialization is too costly and too difficult. Evolution rather than revolution, they say, is the realistic path to progress.

Population Growth in Relation to Capital Formation. *Living standards have risen most rapidly in countries having high rates of capital formation and low rates of population growth.* Strikingly, birth rates have generally declined in nations whose living standards have risen; rates of only 15 to 20 per thousand are common in highly developed countries, compared to 40 or more in underdeveloped areas. Net annual population increases of around 1 to 1½ per cent are common in the highly developed nations. In combination with rapid rates of capital formation, these low population growth rates permit substantial annual increases in per capita incomes, ranging as high as 2 to 3 per cent over long periods in countries like the United States. For example, using the capital-output ratio of 4 in Table 43-2, a saving ratio of .15 would give a 3.75 per cent annual increase in total output, which would imply about 2 per cent per capita even with a high 1.75 annual population growth.

This pattern contrasts sharply with that of the underdeveloped economies, with rapid population growth and little or no increase in per capita incomes. Unless output increases can be speeded greatly through higher saving rates or lower capital-output ratios, per capita incomes in most underdeveloped nations can be increased substantially only if ways can be found to slow the explosive population growth that has followed rapid reduction in death rates. One way to hold down population growth would be to let people die younger, as they have for centuries past. But few would advocate this step backward. The other way is to reduce the birth rate. But this is difficult, partly because of religious objections, but especially because of the absence of cheap, readily available means of birth control for use by the uneducated millions of the underdeveloped countries. Governments concerned with forcing economic development have become increasingly concerned with this problem. In many of the underdeveloped nations, Malthus' gloomy predictions still look more right than wrong.

The Take-Off into Economic Growth.   Economists are fond of talking about the take-off into economic growth. What is the magic factor that will permit an underdeveloped nation to break out of the vicious circle of poverty into self-reinforcing growth? Alas, we don't know. Probably there is no simple answer, certainly not the same answer for all cases.

Some economists stress the need for a big original burst of capital investment in one or two lines, especially transport and electric power, with the funds perhaps provided from outside economy—say a large loan from the United States. Others stress the need to improve agricultural productivity and food supplies, so human energy levels can be raised and manpower can be freed for other tasks. Still others stress "balanced growth," with parallel action on farm and industrial fronts. Still others say that education is the only answer, to improve worker productivity and the whole climate for expanding economic activity. As disillusion has descended after the first burst of enthusiasm for various of these approaches, some observers have turned to a very prosaic answer indeed—people in the backward countries need, above all, just to work harder. The experience of Communist China is cited by some as a successful case in point.

But the fact is that no one knows for sure which is the best path to take.

THE UNDERDEVELOPED AREAS: PRESENT AND PROSPECT   Where do the underdeveloped areas stand today, and what are their prospects for the future? These are not easy questions to answer, and perhaps the best we can do is to point up some of the questions that will determine their future paths. What's been said above can be given focus in the following big questions.

1. Do the underdeveloped countries have the impetus required for breaking out of their poverty levels into sustained economic growth? And what kind of impetus is required? Are individual enterprise and desire for self-advancement the answer, or must the initiative come from a powerful government?

2. Can the underdeveloped economies develop the institutions and customs needed for economic development? Indeed, what are these institutions? Should the underdeveloped economies try to develop free markets of the private-enterprise type? What kinds of monetary and credit institutions can do most to encourage capital accumulation and investment?

3. What is the optimal pattern of economic development? Should they seek rapid industrialization, involving mass shifts of population from agriculture to industry? Or is a slower path that attempts to raise productivity in agriculture along with gradual industrialization sounder in the long run? How much stress should be placed on development of the intermediary kinds of investment—highways and transport, education, commercial establishments? If population must be moved from agriculture to industry sooner or later, how can this shift be achieved without running the risk that the families moved to the cities will starve to death?

4. How can the accumulation of savings and capital, so vital to economic development, be increased? Table 43-2 showed the major impact of higher saving rates. Can populations at poverty level be forced to save more, or must the saving come entirely from the rich few? Should saving be forced through government taxes, with the proceeds used for desirable investment projects? Is the government issue of money to finance investment projects a desirable way of forcing saving, as resources are bid away from the masses in the resulting inflation? If population is moved from farming to industry, how can consumption of the remaining farmers be held down to shift food to the new industrial population (i.e., how can the remaining farmers be forced to save more)?

5. How can the rate of population growth be reduced? Continuing reduction of the death rate is surely desirable on moral grounds, but unless this reduction is accompanied by lower birth rates it deals rapid economic growth a heavy blow. Are local religious and cultural beliefs a serious barrier to birth control, and if so should they be respected? Can and should cheap, effective means of birth control be disseminated?

6. Can help be obtained from abroad? Are foreign gifts or loans the answer to the great lump of investment that seems to be required in some countries to break out of the vicious circle of poverty? How can investment be made more attractive to investors from the highly developed areas with excess savings? Is it the moral or economic responsibility of the wealthy nations, or of international organizations, to help raise the living standards of underdeveloped areas, even if such investments look relatively unpromising on a dollars-and-cents basis?

Economic Planning or the Price System. The problems faced by the underdeveloped areas must often seem insuperable. If only they could get the millions of surplus population off the farms into some newly established industry where their marginal product would be positive, food output would be undiminished and industrial output would rise. Total output per capita would be increased.

Saving could then be increased more easily to provide further capital equipment, education, and public services. And continuing, self-perpetuating growth might be established.

Some American economists have argued that the price system is the best guide to what should be done, and the marketplace the best channel for getting it done. But this view has found little sympathy in the underdeveloped countries. There is too much to be done, and little evidence that sitting back to rely on individual initiative and the marketplace will bring the desired changes fast enough—if at all. There is no simple profit-maximation rule to guide the complex process, to assess the long-range importance of alternative uses of resources in building roads, developing better schools, distributing fertilizer to farmers, building irrigation ditches, establishing better commercial and marketing channels, improving banking facilities, and building industrial plants. And even in the successful developed countries, the growth process took generations under private enterprise —too slow in the eyes of many nationalist leaders. Thus, government intervention on a wide scale is the active agent in underdeveloped nations. The main issue is whether it shall involve substantially complete government control over economic life (as in Communist China) or merely government direction of broad lines of activity with considerable scope left to private initiative (as in India).

In nearly all nations, it is agreed that the government must take steps to increase saving and investment; the most obvious way is through heavy taxation with the proceeds used to finance desired investment. Nearly everywhere, the government decides on the main lines of investment—highways, fertilizer plants, electric power facilities, and so on. Even where most of the economy stays private, these investment priorities have become the province of the government. Nearly everywhere, foreign exchange is under government control, so that scarce foreign currencies are used for high-priority imports rather than for private luxuries.

Whether we like it or not, the American private-enterprise economy is not generally viewed as a very useful model for solving the problems of the underdeveloped countries. To them, the choice lies between communism and complete government control of economic life on the one hand, and a kind of partial socialism with considerable private initiative under broad government planning on the other. China and India typify these two approaches, and the eyes of the underdeveloped world are upon them.

Monetary-Fiscal Policy and Economic Growth. If you remember Part 2, expansionary monetary-fiscal policy to eliminate underemployment and stimulate investment may seem an obvious answer to the underdeveloped countries' problems. Why can't the government create some money, set up factories, and through deficit-financed spending lure the surplus farm population away from disguised unemployment into useful work in the newly created industry, thereby increasing output and improving everybody's welfare?

The answer is that the main result would probably be inflation rather than increased output. The differences between such a plan in underdeveloped economies and the use of deficit financing to cure unemployment in the United States are great. Analyze the problem.

Suppose the government of an underdeveloped country prints money to lure workers into industry. There are no idle factories where output can be increased by calling the unemployed back to work. First the government must build the factories and provide the tools for the new workers. Where will it get the steel, machinery, skilled labor, and management to accomplish this? There is no mass of trained unemployed workers, ready to troop through the factory doors. Who will train the workers and managers? How will the government provide new living quarters for the families drawn into industrial life, even if the reluctance of such families to give up their traditional ties and way of life can be overcome? Suppose the people are somehow drawn to the city and housed. How will the government get food to the cities to feed them in an essentially non-market economy, with no regular distribution channels? Suppose all these obstacles are overcome. How long will it take before salable output begins to come out of factories manned by untrained workers, and where will the goods be sold when they are produced? Suppose the product is cloth; will there be a domestic market and distribution channels to tap the market, or will the government have to try to find markets abroad in the hectic international competition of the textile trade?

With all these obstacles to the increase of real output, government spending without corresponding tax collections is likely to lead mainly to higher prices as the new money bids for an unchanged quantity of goods. The inflation might help stimulate investment through forcing the economy to save more, as government spending bids resources away from consumers. Inflation has been consciously used in this way. But there are limits to how much can be accomplished. Too rapid inflation may endanger not only economic activity but the stability of the government as well. And inflation makes it harder to sell domestic production in world markets, a telling blow when foreign exchange is badly needed to finance imports. The problems of the underdeveloped economies are basically "real" problems. There is little basis for supposing they can be solved by using the modern monetary and fiscal policies that seem so promising against unemployment in the western economies.

Two Important Cases: India and China.   With over a billion people, India and China together include nearly two-thirds of the population of the underdeveloped areas and over a third of the world's total population. They are, potentially, two of the most powerful nations on the face of the globe. The undeveloped areas are not just lazy South Sea islands or hard-to-remember small nations of Indonesia or Africa. And India and China exemplify two drastically different approaches to the problem of economic development.

In many respects, India and China face similar problems. They are both vast land masses, heavily populated in many areas but with great reaches of mountains and wasteland. Both, at about 1950, had per capita incomes around $50; China's was somewhat the lower of the two. In both, around 80 per cent of the total population is engaged in agriculture. And both, since World War II, have undertaken vigorous planned programs of economic development.

But their programs differ drastically. In her first "five-year plan," covering 1951 to 1956, India chose an essentially democratic approach, leaving freedom to private enterprise under broad government planning and alongside government projects in such major areas as irrigation, transportation, education, and improved technology for farmers. Over half of total investment comes from private saving. Taxes were raised only a little. Although the plan pushed industrialization, it put primary emphasis on increasing agricultural productivity. Total investment under the plan was allocated more heavily to agriculture and irrigation than to industry. Industrial investment concentrated on both small-scale industry such as textiles, and on larger projects such as power development, fertilizers, coal, and heavy manufacturing. After agriculture, transport facilities received the greatest emphasis. The plan called for a small increase in per capita consumption, with most of the planned increase in output devoted to capital accumulation in agriculture and industry, plus added government services. Foreign capital did not provide more than 5 per cent of total capital formation.

Results were encouraging, but far from spectacular. Output of food was increased somewhat, that of major industrial items appreciably. Investment rose 2 or 3 per cent in relation to gross national product. Per capita income rose a little, but only a little. Achievements generally fell short of goals. Resources, only loosely controlled by government plan, were siphoned off from planned investment into consumption throughout the period.

The second five-year plan (for 1956-61) is more ambitious. It sets higher goals for both agriculture and industrial expansion. Recognizing the continuing scarcity of capital and of foreign exchange, the new plan concentrates heavy, modern capital-equipment investment in such basic industries as steel, where it is essential for efficient production, and in the export industries, where Indian costs must be as low as possible to compete effectively. Weaving of cloth for local consumption and other such local production is left largely in the handicraft stage, to take advantage of cheap labor and to economize scarce capital. Increased imports from abroad play a central role in expansion plans.

As during the first plan, India is making progress. But early in the period it became clear that the plan was overambitious. India faced a major foreign-exchange crisis, as her exports failed to pay for badly needed imports for the industrialization program; and major industrial goals had to be scaled back. Continued loose government controls have proved insufficient to channel current output as heavily into investment as the plan calls for. Private saving has risen less than was hoped, and the government has been reluctant to press down living standards with new heavy tax burdens.

China's first five-year plan, covering 1952-57, called for drastic increases in industrialization, collectivization of agriculture, and ruthless suppression of consumption to obtain the resources required for capital accumulation. The plan centralized all control in the communist government. It called for mass transfer of agricultural population into industry, where the bulk of the capital formation was centered. Voluntary private saving played only a small part; high government taxes on the masses were used to seize a far larger portion of total income for government investment than in India, and government-monopolized necessities were sold at high prices yielding large government profits. The government channeled these funds largely into heavy investment. Hard work and long hours were forced on the Chinese population.

Under the plan, steel production was the largest class of investment, with machine tools and other heavy equipment also programmed for large increases. In sharp contrast to the Indian plan, comparatively little capital was channeled into agriculture, fertilizers, and transportation. Strikingly, China has only 15,000 miles of railroads over an area more than twice that of India, which already has over 34,000 miles of railways. No reliable information is available on the amount of outside capital and technical aid provided to China by the U.S.S.R. Clearly it was large, and there is some evidence of wholesale transfer of Russian technology into China in the construction of new plants of all types.

China's second five-year plan continues these same policies, and calls for an even larger (50 per cent) increase in total output by 1962, an increase of about 10 per cent a year. Again, the primary focus is on heavy industry, although food targets are also up substantially this time. Government seizure of great land masses and forced concentration of millions of agricultural families in huge "communes," virtually abolishing individual family units and treating the peasants as hardly more than draft animals, was introduced in 1958. Women were pressed into all areas of work on substantially the same basis as men, with children raised under state auspices. Communist dictation of even thought patterns makes George Orwell's *1984* seem very real indeed.

Communist leaders claim spectacular advances since 1950. Real gross national product almost doubled in less than 10 years. Investment as a percentage of gross national product rose from 9 to 22 per cent. Industrial output increased by 10-12 per cent per annum. Food output doubled. Qualified western observers discount many of the more extreme communist claims, and in 1959 Chinese leaders were forced to lower both their claims and goals for the second five-year plan. But nevertheless nearly everyone agrees that growth on both industrial and agricultural fronts has been rapid indeed.

The Chinese have had problems. Reports of serious resistance to the commune movement of the late 1950's have continued to trickle out, and there are signs of a major communist retreat from the commune program. Massive floods drasti-

Economic Growth in India and China, 1950-1958

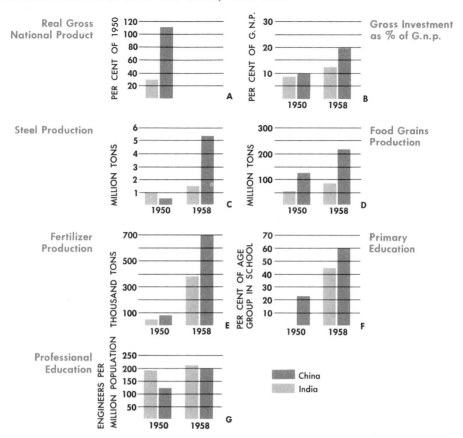

Real Gross National Product — PER CENT OF 1950: 120, 100, 80, 60, 40, 20 — A

Gross Investment as % of G.n.p. — PER CENT OF G.N.P.: 30, 20, 10 — 1950 1958 — B

Steel Production — MILLION TONS: 6, 5, 4, 3, 2, 1 — 1950 1958 — C

Food Grains Production — MILLION TONS: 300, 200, 100 — 1950 1958 — D

Fertilizer Production — THOUSAND TONS: 700, 500, 300, 100 — 1950 1958 — E

Primary Education — PER CENT OF AGE GROUP IN SCHOOL: 70, 60, 50, 40, 30, 20, 10 — 1950 1958 — F

Professional Education — ENGINEERS PER MILLION POPULATION: 250, 200, 150, 100, 50 — 1950 1958 — G

China
India

FIG. 43-6   During the 1950's, China outdistanced India by most economic measures. By 1958 her per capita real income had probably about caught up to India's. (Source: W. Malenbaum, "India and China: Contrasts in Development," *American Economic Review*, June 1959.)

cally reduced food production in 1959. Uneven industrial expansion has led to serious unbalance and bottlenecks in major areas. Chinese exports have not competed effectively in outside markets, because of low quality and unsatisfactory trading techniques, and China has faced a major foreign-exchange shortage in recent years to pay for heavy imports from Russia and other areas. Low quality generally may be a serious problem that hasn't shown up yet in the aggregate output statistics. Nonetheless, on grounds of output expansion alone results have been spectacular—unless later data disclose wholesale misrepresentation and overestimation of results.

There is little doubt that economic growth in China under rigid regimentation outdistanced growth in India under democratic planning during the decade of

803

the 1950's. Figure 43-6 summarizes the comparison, using estimates by an unbiased western observer. The results don't make pleasant reading for us.

But on human values, communist results have been achieved at incredible costs, utterly unacceptable to westerners, and to most Indians as well. And the race is not over. Can the Chinese communists maintain a loyal, or even an acquiescent, population in the face of their ruthless abolition of traditional Chinese family values, their relentless pressure for more and harder work, their repression of consumption, their grim redirection of all economic activity? How much are they dependent on help and technological know-how from Russia, and how lastings is this bond which so far has involved mainly exports from Russia with little return? Is the quality of Chinese industrial output adequate to support further industrialization and growth? How far can industrialization go on the basis of sheer mass of manpower, which has accounted for much of the progress to date?

On the other hand, India faces a basic problem of human incentives too. Can the Indian government implement its program of low consumption and capital accumulation among the people on a voluntary basis, and can it count on individual management to do a good job in the major areas of business and industry left in private hands? Persuading a poverty-stricken population to hold down consumption and to save more is hard—perhaps impossible—in a democratic society. Many western economists believe there has been too much hope and too little realism in the Indian five-year plans to date. India must succeed faster if the democratic, non-communist way is to win the race in the eyes of the watching underdeveloped nations.

The Future of the Underdeveloped Areas.   What is the future of the underdeveloped areas? Can they hope to "catch up" with the more developed nations?

Clearly many of the underdeveloped nations are economies in motion. India and China are major examples, but their focus on economic development is mirrored in nearly every other underdeveloped country. It will be surprising if some improvement in output per capita does not come out of all these activities. But for such nations to catch up with U.S. per capita income is an almost insuperable task. Even on the most optimistic assumptions of rising annual growth rates in the underdeveloped countries, the *absolute* spread in per capita income levels seems certain to widen. A 2 per cent *annual increase* on $2,300 (the present U.S. per capita figure) is $46, almost the *total* present annual per capita income in India and China.

Look at the comparison between the United States and Latin America. In the late 1950's, per capita income in Latin America stood at around $250, perhaps one-eighth of the United States figure. If we make the highly optimistic assumption that total Latin-American output will rise faster and population growth will slow down enough to provide a 2.5 per cent annual growth in output per capita, it would still be some 40 years before Latin-American per capita income reached one-third the *present* U.S. per capita income. But if U.S. income continues to grow at around 2 per cent per year, it would be over 250 years before Latin-American per capita income would reach one-third of then-current United States income levels. Even if Latin-American per capita income rose at 4 per cent per year, more than 50 years would be required to reach one-third of then-prevailing U.S. levels, assuming only a 2 per cent U.S. growth rate. The underdeveloped countries face an enormously difficult job to keep the gap between their living standards and those in developed nations from rapidly widening further. The international world of the "haves" and the "have nots" seems likely to grow more disparate, not less.

THE UNITED STATES AND THE UNDERDEVELOPED AREAS What interests does the United States have in the underdeveloped areas? First of all, there are political and military interests. In a world of continuing East-West tension, it is critical for us to keep the underdeveloped areas out of the communist orbit. Although many of these nations are small and unimportant in a direct military sense, others are vitally situated—India, the Middle East with its oil, Africa, the masses of Indonesia. If we want to maintain the prestige and attractiveness of the western way, it is important that economic development in India and the free societies not lag far behind that in China and the communist satellites. Perhaps we will need to be concerned one day even about communist infiltration into Latin America. Whether we can buy political friendship and allegiance through help in economic development remains to be seen. That this is a precarious and uncertain business is clear. The countries that take our aid one day sometimes seem to turn on us almost before the money is spent; Egypt's startling seizure of the Suez Canal in 1956 following substantial western aid and presumed firm friendship is a striking case. But clearly we must try.

Second, our interests are economic. It would be foolish to overstress this element. Trade with the underdeveloped areas does not bulk large in the American economy. But it does include vital raw-material imports (nonferrous metals, oil, and rubber) and significant markets for both machinery and foodstuffs; remember that much of Latin America, one of our best customers, falls in the under-developed category. Moreover, developing economies abroad may provide markets where our comparative advantage will be highest—in machinery, highly fabricated metals and equipment, and so on. Except for foodstuffs and raw materials, there is relatively little direct competition in world markets between the developing economies and American exports. The advantages of international exchange with such areas look especially favorable for us.

Lastly, we have a humanitarian interest in the relief of starvation, the lessening of disease and misery, and the improvement of education and living standards generally in the underdeveloped areas. American public opinion appears to be strongly in favor of activities devoted to these humanitarian goals—at least so long as they do not cost too much.

Guidelines to United States Aid. If we want to help many of the underdeveloped nations along the path to economic growth, for political, economic, or humanitarian reasons, we need first to ask the question: Can we really make any difference? The task of helping a billion people to higher standards of living, even if we neglect the large communist bloc, may seem a hopeless one. And it is clear that American aid alone, however well-intended, can do only a small part of the job of getting any underdeveloped area out of the vicious circle of poverty. But we should remember one fact: The *total* annual income of *all* the billion inhabitants of those underdeveloped areas is not more than about $125 billion. United States national income *alone* in 1959 was about $400 billion, at least three times that of the *entire* friendly and neutral bloc of underdeveloped nations.

What can the United States do to be of help? What should it do? Five types of aid have received wide attention.

1. *Government loans and gifts.* The most direct path is United States government loans or gifts. Over the past decade, such government aid to underdeveloped areas has averaged between $500 million and $1 billion annually; the total was about $9 billion for the ten years following World War II. Additional loans of a similar amount have been provided by the Export-Import Bank and the International Bank for Reconstruction and Development, both with capital obtained largely in the United States. Some government aid has been in the form of direct gifts of foodstuffs and needed materials to disaster areas. Most has been in the form of monetary loans or grants that the underdeveloped nation can spend on imports of both consumption and capital goods.

These are large dollar figures. But they are not large in relation to the total capital needs of the underdeveloped economies, and they are less than one-half of 1 per cent of American national income. They have financed mainly foodstuffs, public improvements such as highways and sanitation, and capital imports for industrialization.

2. *Private United States capital investment.* The large growth potentials of the underdeveloped economies might seem attractive to American capital seeking investment at good rates of return. But they have not proved so on any large scale. The problems of breaking the vicious circle of poverty are apparent to any private investor who seriously investigates an underdeveloped economy. Moreover, many of the underdeveloped economies have not made private foreign investment attractive or easy. Foreign control of business is distrusted and resented in many areas, especially where developing nationalism is strong. Far-reaching government regulations, special taxes, and restrictions on withdrawal of profits are commonplace; and there is great uncertainty over whether today's rules will be changed tomorrow. Many of the governments are unstable, and the next government to take over may decide to seize foreign property. Returns are often high, but risks of all sorts are great.

These barriers have not completely discouraged private American investors.

Over the past decade, private United States investments in the underdeveloped areas.have averaged somewhat over $500 million annually, with around two-thirds of this total going into Latin America. Such investments are fairly well distributed among oil, manufacturing, and mining activities, with smaller amounts going into trade and public utility projects. Total accumulated United States private investments in the underdeveloped nations in 1959 were around $8 billion, most of them made during the postwar period.

3. *Technical assistance.* After the postwar burst of enthusiasm for aid to the underdeveloped economies came the sobering recognition that many of the crucial problems were internal ones—ignorance and apathy among native populations, lack of real impetus for development, unstable governments and legal institutions. Even billions of American dollars might have little effect unless such factors were attacked vigorously and effectively by the underdeveloped countries themselves.

Emphasis on "technical assistance" programs to help local governments and local peoples to help themselves has grown steadily during recent years, partly because it seems a crucial step to effective aid, partly because it is far cheaper than mass capital investment grants. Technical assistance now reaches into many phases of local life. Better farming techniques, use of fertilizers and simple tools, training of workers for simple industrial jobs, and other direct help in increasing output have played a central role. Assistance in establishing better schools, efficient local government administration, sanitation and public health projects, low-cost highways, and other such programs have apparently proved equally useful.

Throughout the technical assistance program, stress has been placed on training natives to teach other natives, and to take over essential jobs themselves at the earliest possible moment. Direct contact on day-to-day problems of native existence, though less spectacular than huge government grants, has sometimes seemed to provide better results—and very often more friendly, responsive attitudes on the part of native populations. In most cases, United States technical assistance has been provided on a matching basis, with half the cost of the joint programs being borne by local governments. The stated purpose of the program is the complete transfer of all activities to local governments as rapidly as is feasible. Comparable technical assistance programs are provided by the United Nations.

4. *Lowering of international trade barriers and purchase of local products.* In order to grow, the underdeveloped countries often must sell basic products abroad if they are to secure foreign exchange with which to finance needed imports. Many of the economies are centered around one or two basic products—oil, rubber, nitrates, coffee, tin. One-product economies are highly susceptible to fluctuations in foreign demand, and the United States is a huge buyer of their basic products in the world market. Trade barriers that shut these products out of American markets strike a serious blow at the economies concerned, and raise understandable resentment among natives who hear American propaganda that

we are anxious to help the underdeveloped countries. Although reduction of trade barriers hinges on many issues in the United States, there can be little doubt that freer trade would be a direct help to many of the underdeveloped economies. Anomalously, these countries themselves are among the leaders in imposing exchange restrictions and special barriers on withdrawal of foreign profits— perhaps understandably so, in view of their need to hoard their scarce foreign exchange for the most essential imports.

5. *Military aid.* Military aid to underdeveloped countries is presumably given mainly for direct military purposes. But it has an important economic effect as well. In a country that would otherwise spend part of its national product on military activities, U.S. military aid provides direct relief to the local government budget and permits local government spending to be focused on nonmilitary projects that are more conducive to economic development. United States military grants to the underdeveloped areas have been relatively small—about $5 billion since World War II—but they have supplemented direct economic aid.

Perspective on United States Policy.   How successful has American aid to underdeveloped countries been thus far? To answer, we must have criteria for judging. If the test is maintenance of military alliances with America or neutrality vis-à-vis the communist bloc, the verdict seems to be generally favorable but still uncertain. If the test is friendliness and "thankfulness" in response to American generosity, the verdict is at best mixed. Few people like to consider themselves objects of charity, and we probably make a great mistake to expect thankfulness and specific reciprocity in return. If the test is improvement of living standards and lessening of human misery abroad, the verdict is—a little progress, but not much headway yet on a huge problem that will inevitably take many decades to solve, if it can be solved at all. American aid has helped, but the major solution for the underdeveloped areas must probably be worked out at home.

Recognition of the powerful force of growing nationalism and the desire for status and respect in nearly every underdeveloped country must be the corner-stone of successful aid, whatever our basic motives are. The battle for the friend-ship, or at least the neutrality, of the underdeveloped areas is real and earnest; the communist bloc has proved itself highly effective in many of our propaganda and technical-aid skirmishes. As J. J. Singh, President of the India League of America, reported following a visit to Asia: ". . . One of the main causes of re-sentment against the western powers is their arrogant assumption that the 'white fathers' know what is good for the backward Asian peoples. . . . A little friendly gesture, a little consideration, a little less of 'see what I am doing for your country,' a little respect for the aspirations and hopes of the Asian peoples will go a long way." [3]

If this analysis is correct, it suggests that we minimize our interference in the

---

[3] *The New York Times Magazine*, Sept. 28, 1952.

domestic affairs of underdeveloped countries, even on how they spend the aid we provide and on what reciprocal trade advantages they provide to Americans. Insistence on active support of United States policies and on active opposition to those of the U.S.S.R. may be an erroneous condition to tie to American aid, much as we desire such behavior. Our long-run objectives require tolerance and understanding, slowness to interfere or criticize. To insist on imposing American economic patterns on the underdeveloped economies is short-sighted indeed. To win the intense competition for their friendship and cooperation will take more than blunt force and dollars alone.

1. Why is it so hard for people in many of the underdeveloped countries to accept what seems to most Americans the obvious superiority of the American way of life?

2. A rapid increase in population is generally regarded as a major cause of poverty in underdeveloped countries like India, but is often thought to be an important cause of prosperity in the United States. Is this distinction a valid one? Explain your answer.

3. "Modern economics tells us to pump in purchasing power in order to eliminate unemployment and raise living standards when depression occurs in the western world; but this approach simply has no relevance for the underdeveloped nations, where a shortage of real capital is the basic problem." Is this statement correct? Explain your answer.

4. The United States has spent over $40 billion annually for defense expenditures in recent years. Yet it has spent less than $1 billion annually on direct aid to the underdeveloped economies. Would it be sound policy to divert $10 billion annually from the military budget to an all-out effort to speed economic development and to win friends and allies among the underdeveloped nations of the world?

5. If you were economic adviser to the government of an underdeveloped economy, what measures would you advise to improve the environment for development and to increase the economic initiative of the native population? Why?

6. Is the private-enterprise approach really superior to the communist, government-dominated approach to economic development? If your answer is yes, how would you go about justifying it to a fellow student from an underdeveloped area who is convinced that central government direction and control are needed to break the apathy and vicious circle of poverty in his country?

7. Some writers have referred to the South as the United States' underdeveloped economy. Per capita incomes have been below those in the rest of the country; the economy has been largely rural; "disguised unemployment" has been common in many rural areas.

   a. Does this seem to you a proper description of the American South?

   b. Whatever your answer, how do you explain the rapid increase in industrial development and per capita real income in the American South over the past quarter-century, while there has been little increase in many of the world's underdeveloped nations?

FOR ANALYSIS AND DISCUSSION

Comparative Economic Systems: U.S.S.R. and U.S.A.

44

The Comparison
of Economic Systems.

How Does
the Soviet Economy Work?

Comparative Economic Systems
in Perspective.

Conclusion.

The dominant problem of the modern world is war and peace—the relentless struggle between East and West for power and position, for men's minds, even for survival. In three short decades Soviet Russia has become indubitably the world's second great industrial and military power. Perhaps militarily today she is the most powerful. We in the United States no longer stand as the unchallenged leaders.

How has Russia achieved this great advance? What is the Russian communist system, and how does it work? How different is it in actual operation from the private capitalist system that has produced such spectacular results in the United States over the past two centuries? Are we in danger of being overtaken by the U.S.S.R., and of losing the battle for world supremacy on the economic front without a shot having been fired? Who will win the respect and emulation of the world's uncommitted billion in the underdeveloped nations?

At the end of a long look devoted largely to the American private-enterprise system, it is well to look in detail at the great economic challenge to that system, and to think through how the two systems get their jobs done. For many years, capitalist observers sagely observed that national economic planning couldn't work and confidently predicted the collapse of the Soviet economy. But after some 40 years of experience, it is clear that planning *does* work in Russia, and at least in some respects seems to work well. And few competent observers are any longer predicting the imminent collapse of the Russian economy.

THE COMPARISON OF ECONOMIC SYSTEMS   To us, ours is the normal way of life; private enterprise is the usual type of economic system. Only 35 years ago this feeling would have been substantially justified for the whole western, industrialized world. World War I was over. The postwar revolutions were done. Capitalism seemed securely re-established everywhere except in Russia, and the new communist regime there tottered precariously. Millions of Russians died of starvation; total Russian production appeared scarcely higher than it had been far back in the 1800's under the czars; internal strife split the communist nation.

Today, only three decades later, the United States stands as one of a small minority of the world's nations with a thoroughly private-enterprise, capitalist economy. Communism is the economic system of far more of the world's population than is the private-enterprise system we know. The U.S.S.R. and China alone account for 850 million people, almost a third of the world's total. The democratic socialism of Sweden, Britain, and India, too, typifies more of the world than our system does, hard as this may be for us to realize. In all of Europe, only Switzerland and the new West Germany enthusiastically embrace the private-enterprise philosophy that we take for granted in analyzing our economy. And there is little reason to expect that in the "backward" countries of Asia and Africa private-enterprise economics will win out over at least substantial central control and collectivism. It is hard indeed to see other systems as the people who live in them see them—to recognize that many other people do not share the ideals and values we Americans hold so dear. But this recognition is a first step toward understanding how other economic systems work.

Capitalism and Communism.[1]   When someone says "communism," what comes to your mind? Dictatorship? International aggression? Slave labor? Ruthless oppression of political opponents? Poverty and starvation? The secret police and torture?

---

[1] There are many volumes on comparative economic systems and on the "isms." Two easily readable summaries are A. R. Oxenfeldt, *Economic Systems in Action* (New York: Rinehart, 1957), and George P. Adams, *Competitive Economic Systems* (New York: Crowell, 1955). References to more specialized works can be found in these two books. For comparative looks focused primarily on the American economy, try Calvin B. Hoover, *The Economy, Liberty, and the State* (New York: Twentieth Century Fund, 1959); F. A. Hayek, *The Road to Serfdom* (Chicago: University of Chicago Press, 1944); and J. A. Schumpeter, *Capitalism, Socialism and Democracy* (New York: Harper, 1942).

All of these apparently exist to at least some extent in communist Russia as we know it today. But you may be amazed to learn that you would find none of them in Karl Marx's famous *Das Kapital,* the foundation of modern communism. Marx wrote a detailed critique of capitalism, but he was conveniently vague when it came to blueprinting the communist economy to be. Still, one thing is sure. He wasn't looking for any political and economic dictatorship, except the dictatorship of the proletariat—of the whole working class.

Communism today has heavy overtones of politics as well as economics. To look at the economic side of any "ism" alone is to miss its essence. Communism has become inseparably associated with political and economic dictatorship because we see these together in Soviet Russia, the country that dominates our thinking about communism today. Yet in its original form, Marxian communism or socialism was highly democratic in spirit. Evolutionary socialism has much the same roots, but it is today found in varying degrees in England, Sweden, Australia, New Zealand—all countries with the highest traditions of political democracy and protection for individual rights.

From an *economic* viewpoint, there are two big differences between capitalism and communism. *Under private-enterprise capitalism as we know it, most productive resources are privately owned, and economic activity is largely directed by prices established through the interaction of supply and demand in the market. Under communism, conversely, most productive resources are publicly owned, and economic activity is directed largely by central physical planning, not through a price system.* The two critical questions are: (1) are productive resources privately or publicly owned, and (2) is economic activity directed by the price system or by governmental planning?

Obviously, both are matters of degree. Not all productive resources are privately owned under American capitalism—governments own land, highways, dams, buildings, and so on. Nor are all resources publicly owned in Russia. Similarly, not all economic activity is price-system-directed in the United States, nor is all economic activity centrally planned in Russia. Too, an economy can have private ownership of resources and nevertheless be centrally planned. The American economy during World War II was a partial example. Hitler's fascism in Germany was a more complete example.

Thus economic systems fall along a spectrum on both these conditions, something like the following:

Private ownership	U.S. ———— U.K. — India ———————— China — U.S.S.R.	*Public* ownership

Price- directed	U.S. — U.K. ——————— India ——————— China U.S.S.R.	*Centrally* planned

The location of the countries is only approximate, but it is intended to suggest the variation on the two scores.

The American and Russian systems differ widely on both scores. They are thus especially worth a careful comparison. But don't forget that most of the world's economies lie in between, on one or both of the spectrums shown.

Through Whose Eyes?   Through whose eyes shall we judge these widely differing systems? If the answer is, through ours, then remember that things may look very different to the Russian, the Spaniard, and the Frenchman. Every nation has its own ideals, its own mores, its own history. Maybe the Russian and Egyptian economic systems look terrible to us; but if they're doing all right in the eyes of the Russians and the Egyptians, who's to say they're worse than ours? We know that our system doesn't look so good to many foreigners.

How, then, can we intelligently compare economic systems? The answer is: (1) Get clearly in mind the main functions we expect each system to perform; (2) recognize the main standards we use to evaluate the performance of each; (3) apply these standards systematically to each system's performance; and (4) then never forget that what looks rose-colored to us may be a dismal gray through someone else's glasses. In the one world of today, understanding how things look to other peoples is a first step toward getting along with them. Your views may look just as queer to the Russian as his look to you.

The Functions of Every Economic System.   We have the basis for this sort of comparison—from back in Chapters 4 and 5. As we saw there and again in Chapter 43, every economic system, no matter what it's called or what political arrangements go with it, has to do four main jobs:

1. It must decide what is to be produced.
2. It must decide how it is to be produced.
3. It must decide how the products are to be distributed among the people.
4. It must decide between the present and the future—how many of society's resources should be devoted to growth and how many to current consumption.

The Tests of a Good Economic System.   Every economic system gets the jobs done somehow, whether it's the U.S., the U.S.S.R., or a primitive South Sea island economy. So by answering these four questions we get only a comparative description. If we want to *evaluate* the different systems, we need to set up criteria for judging each. This, too, we did long ago—but remember, we did it through *our* eyes. The five criteria tentatively outlined back in Chapter 5 were:

1. Does the system provide a progressively higher standard of living for all—economic growth with stability?
2. Does it provide economic freedom for the individual?
3. Does it provide reasonable economic security for all?
4. Does it produce the goods and services consumers want?
5. Does it provide an equitable distribution of income?

Substitute your own criteria if you don't like the five listed. But keep some set in mind as you read the following pages.

This chapter is mainly an analysis of how the Soviet economy operates, and an evaluation of how well it does its job. But all the way through, there's a running comparison with the way the American economy accomplishes the same tasks, and how well it does. One of the most valuable results of this chapter should be to force you to pull together your own understanding and evaluation of the American economy which you've been studying all year, by checking at each point to see how it stacks up against the Soviet system. Such a comparison, often charged with emotion, is an easy place to go wrong. Watch out for the fallacies back in Chapter 5—colored words, facts that aren't facts, wishing it were so.

HOW DOES THE SOVIET ECONOMY WORK?

Objectives. The modern Soviet economy rests on the doctrines of Karl Marx. "From each according to his abilities, to each according to his needs," was Marx' foundation for the communist society. The rule of the masses, with productive resources used for the common benefit of all, remains, on paper, the foundation of the modern communist economies—China as well as the U.S.S.R.

The goals stressed by modern communist leaders look very much like the five listed above for the American economy. While there is no one set of official goals for modern Russia, the following have been repeated over and over by Soviet leaders:

1. Expansion of the productive capacity of the nation, both to raise the Russian standard of living and to permit an adequate national defense against aggression.
2. Improvement in literacy and higher cultural levels.
3. Improvement in national health standards.
4. Reduction in hours and unpleasantness of work.
5. Elimination of insecurity.

Soviet leaders eulogize the virtues of democracy and personal participation in achieving the goals of the factory, the community, and the state. Freedom of speech and assembly, and all the other basic freedoms of the American Constitution are guaranteed in the Soviet Constitution—plus some others we don't include, such as freedom from "racial or national exclusiveness or hatred and contempt." From the words, it would be hard to distinguish Soviet Russia from the western democratic societies.

What actually goes on is often very different. Although everyone can vote in Russia, effective political and economic power is highly concentrated in the Praesidium, composed of a handful of communist leaders. Only a small percentage of the population are actually members of the Communist Party, and it is they who apparently exercise most of the political control, insofar as any real power exists beyond Nikita Khrushchev and the small central group around him. From the evidence we can get, the freedoms guaranteed in the constitution seem to be honored mainly when to do so seems to the leaders to further the welfare of the state.

Certainly it would be foolish to accept at face value everything the Soviet leaders say about their motives. Yet it would be equally foolish to disregard their statements completely. The Soviet rulers have often been cruel, tyrannical, power-hungry men. But there is much evidence that many of the Russian leaders and the Russian people actually believe that they are truly democratic, and that we are so only in form. And it seems clear that personal freedom has been considerably expanded in Russia since the Stalin regime. The most favorable description of modern Russian "democracy" might be that it provides widespread participation in the discussion stage but acceptance of the decision once it has been made by the communist officials at the top.

The centralization of political power in Russia is especially significant for our economic survey, because all basic economic plans and policies are made by the controlling political group. The Soviet economy is the most highly planned and controlled in the world, save possibly Communist China. In America, we leave everyone pretty much free to use his private property and his income as he wishes within the law, and accept the outcome as by and large the best one for the public welfare. The Russian leaders decide specifically what they want to happen economically, and use a comprehensive system of plans and controls to see that it happens.

So much for Russia's stated objectives and basic approach. How do the Soviets go about solving the four big economic problems faced by every system?

(1) Deciding What to Produce and (2) Getting It Produced.[2]   In Russia, the central planners decide in complete detail what is to be produced. They do this through an enormously elaborate system of planning. After the Russian revolution of 1917-18, the communists made an almost fatal mistake. They assumed that central economic control was easy—all you had to do was confiscate private productive resources, use a little common sense in shifting over to a communist system, tell people in general what to produce, and everything would go along nicely. It didn't! Russian total output in 1919-20 dropped back to nearly the 1890 level. The Russian peasants didn't see why they should produce just to have their crops taken away and given to someone else. There was virtually no modern industrial capacity in Russia. The economy was thrown into chaos by war and revolution.

Drastic steps were called for. Lenin and his followers took them. They com-

---

[2] A good recent study of the Russian economy is Harry P. Schwartz, *Russia's Soviet Economy,* 2nd ed. (Englewood Cliffs, N.J.: Prentice Hall, 1954).

promised on the collectivization of farms, permitting many farmers to retain part of their land, though they nationalized vast acreages and apparently "liquidated" literally millions of protesting peasants through starvation and oppression. The rest of the economy they put under complete central control, setting up a broad plan of industrialization. Industrial machinery, dams, electrification—these came first. A bare minimum for subsistence was allocated to consumers.

The central planners made many mistakes, and those who made the mistakes seldom stayed around to make them again. The vast complexities of a completely planned economy were gradually realized. After years of experimentation and a series of "five-year plans" for economic development since 1928, the general pattern of Soviet economic control is this:

First, the basic decisions are made by the central communist authorities—what industries to develop, which to let lag, how much for consumption, how much for industrial expansion, how much for the military. Then the planners map out detailed directions for all units of the economy to follow in implementing these decisions. Lastly, these plans have to be carried out by millions of Soviet officials, managers, and workers throughout Russia. Consider the process in more detail.

Making the Plan.   The broad goals for the economy are set by the Praesidium and the Central Committee of the Communist Party. Since 1928, these have focused around a series of comprehensive five-year plans, each concentrated on a few special objectives (mainly industrialization) by mapping out major product goals for the entire economy. In 1958, Premier Khrushchev announced two new seven-year plans, which would lead, he said, to Russia's overtaking the United States economically by 1970. The current plan covers the period 1959 through 1965. Table 44-1 gives a preliminary impression of the plan for a few important products. We'll look at it in more detail presently.

Table 44-1

SOVIET SEVEN-YEAR PLAN GOALS

	1958	1965 Goal	Percentage Increase
Steel (million tons)	54	91	68
Iron ore (million tons)	81	247	179
Cement (million tons)	32	82	152
Natural gas (billion cubic meters)	30	150	400
Wool fabrics (million meters)	300	500	66
Silk-type fabrics (million meters)	843	1458	73
Leather shoes (million pairs)	352	515	46

Given these broad objectives, the detailed annual plan for each year is worked out by the "Gosplan" (State Planning Commission), working with a huge Central Statistical Administration which provides data on available resources and technological capacities. Imagine their job. Suppose you had to schedule production of only aircraft. How would you plan production of all the thousands of components that go into a single modern airplane, scheduling each to be on hand just when it was needed? Now back up and decide how you would plan the production of all the sub-components to produce the parts you need for the airplanes. By now you'll be up in the hundreds of thousands of individual decisions, just for one industry. And the complexities multiply geometrically when you add other products because of all the linkages between materials, labor, and manufacturing facilities needed.

This is the complexity that leads private-enterprise economists to favor the impersonal price system, leaving the interaction of supply and demand to work out all these interacting decisions through the price system. But the Gosplan does it another way.

First, the Soviets don't start from scratch each year. They use last year as a benchmark, which enormously simplifies the task. Second, they apparently concentrate largely on some 1,500 major commodities (industries). For each of these, they construct a "materials balance," a "labor balance," and a "geographical balance." These show the materials, labor, and other resources needed to produce the desired output throughout the economy, and the new output required to add to present inventories in order to meet the plan goals. By combining these balances for all major products, they have a reasonably complete picture of the over-all materials, labor facilities, and regional balances for the entire economy. From this "input-output" model, they can see roughly where there are likely to be materials shortages, where labor surpluses, and so on, and can adjust the plans accordingly.

But planning can be simplified further. The Gosplan apparently focuses each year primarily on some 50 basic products and industries that are of critical importance in attaining the prime goals of the over-all plan.[3] We can safely assume, for example, that the military missile program is currently on that list. With central planning, the Russians can, and do, put first things first. We, or even the Russian people, may not agree that they're the right first things, and that consumers' goods, for example, ought to go well down the list—but it's clear that planning does get resources devoted effectively to the prime planned objectives.

Even with this focus on prime industries, the Gosplan must then still carry out the enormously complex job of planning in detail each individual product and its production. They do the best they can, making adjustments in minor industries to accommodate the major goals. But it is important to recognize that such detailed planning doesn't have to be precisely accurate. Plans are continuously

---

[3] During World War II, when the U.S. industrial economy was extensively but by no means completely planned, the whole planning process hinged largely on allocation of three major materials—steel, copper, and aluminum. A crucial difference, aside from the more complete Russian planning, may be the scarcity of numerous types of skilled labor which the Gosplan now faces.

adjusted. If the electric light bulb plan runs into labor shortages while that for razor blades turns up a labor surplus, the planners don't have to wait until next year to make an adjustment. This probably doesn't make for a quiet life among Gosplan employees, but it is a practical way of getting the job done.

Moreover, once an annual plan is completed in draft form, it is cleared in advance with the various economic ministries concerned—for the coal industry, the steel industry, and so on. Each ministry checks the goals down through its industry. For example, the Ministry of Food Products checks to see whether the goals look workable for each sub-product, such as bread. If the Ministry finds from its regional or local managers or from the trade union leaders in the plants that the goals are not feasible, it can protest back to the Gosplan. Local plant managers might protest that their machinery is out of repair, or workers that they are already too speeded up to maintain efficiency. Then it's a subject for negotiation with the planners. We know that the Soviet planning process involves lots of talk. After the complete annual plan is settled by the Gosplan, it is approved by the Central Committee of the Communist Party and becomes the law of the land.

This may seem to you very different from the way things get produced in the United States—largely in response to consumer demands. And it is. The consumer sovereignty that dominates goal-setting in the American market is notably lacking in Russia. But it should be clear that in principle the Soviets, should they want to do so, could plan production to meet consumer demands, just as would occur in a purely competitive market economy. In principle, the only serious complication would arise from communist doctrine on the interest rate (see p. 826). But as a practical matter, the Soviets have quite different goals and hence produce quite different plans.

Carrying Out the Plan.   The annual plan is a *physical* blueprint for the use of productive resources and production of intermediate and final products for the year. (Note that nothing whatsoever has been said about money, prices, or profits.) How do the Soviets get their plans carried out?

In essence, by telling people what to do and by paying them for doing it. This is an oversimple answer, and one that perhaps puts too much emphasis on the impetus of direct personal reward. But it seems to be substantially accurate.

Managerial Incentives. The plant manager gets a quota, together with detailed information on the supply of materials he will receive, the equipment he will be allocated, the labor he is to use, and so on. But it's still up to him to get the final product out with the minimum use of resources. If he exceeds his quota, he is praised by the party and gets substantial economic rewards. These are money, and special rewards such as better housing, a car, paid vacations, and other such benefits not available except through the official reward system. These are powerful incentives in a low-consumption society. On the other hand, if his plant ends the year below quota, or if he requires more labor and materials than he's been allocated, he's done a bad job. His income may be scaled down next year, his special perquisites taken away; in extreme cases he may be demoted or even expelled from the party, of which he is probably a member if it's an important plant.

The Soviets are thoroughly aware of the importance of good managers to the success of their plans. Managers get among the largest incomes in the economy. They are subject only to a 13 per cent income tax, the same low rate as for factory workers. They receive medals and public commendation for exceeding quotas. But the communists are also harsh critics when managerial performance falls short.

How is this different from the American scene? In many respects, not at all. It's still up to the manager to run the plant effectively in the last analysis, though the Soviet test is real output in relation to resources allocated while the American test is low costs and high profits. The Soviet manager can't accumulate property and live well off interest and dividends to supplement his salary and bonus. His absolute standard of living, and certainly his ability to save for his children and his future, are much lower. But *relatively* speaking, he apparently can do about as well as his American counterpart.

The Soviets have some serious problems on managerial incentives. If the manager can somehow convince the planners that his quota should be lower, he can easily make a good showing and collect handsomely. Moreover, Russian managers have learned to make their own performances look good by hoarding labor and materials, bootlegging scarce materials outside the plan, and even fudging the basic performance reports on which they are judged. This is not utterly different from the American case, where local managers often try to make their own units look good by devices that deter rather than advance the total corporate profit. But in America the dollars and cents on the income statement at year-end, the per cent return on investment, and the per share earnings for the stockholders provide widely visible, objective measures that probably permit more objective evaluation of management performance. Still, effective goal-setting and control over local and district sub-managers is one of the major unsolved problems facing many big American corporations, somewhat as it is in Russia.

Innovation is apparently another special managerial problem. New ideas involve risks and the Soviet system lacks effective rewards for risk-taking. In the Soviet climate, doing reasonably well is more conducive to the manager's peace of mind and health than is taking a chance on a new idea that may flop. The top planners complain about lack of managerial initiative, but haven't figured out what to do about it. There's nothing like the American private-enterprise entrepreneur out to make a million (or go broke) in a gamble on a new product or new method. Maybe this means less waste under Soviet planning; it probably means less imaginative innovation except on the big problems that get the central attention of the planners.

Lastly, there is the problem of how much decentralization of decision-making and operating authority is optimal to make the plan work most efficiently. The parallel to the problem faced by a large American corporation, like General Motors, is striking. In America, decentralized decision-making and authority, under only broad rules from headquarters, has been widely accepted as the best way of maintaining local managerial initiative and coupling the advantages of central planning with local, first-hand management. Strikingly, the communists seem to be moving in the same direction. Khrushchev has repeatedly complained that the Moscow central ministries were out of touch with real operating problems in industry and agriculture. And in 1958 he announced sweeping steps to decentralize many central ministry planning and control functions to new widespread regional offices. But Gosplan continues to make the basic plans and the blueprints for carrying them out.

Labor Incentives and Labor Unions. In carrying out their plans, do the Soviets use slave labor and just tell the workers what to do? The answer is no. There are apparently still some forced labor camps, mainly for political prisoners; nobody outside knows just how many. But they are no longer an important source of labor, if they ever were. The great bulk of the work is done by ordinary Soviet citizens. And money is the big incentive used, supplemented by continuous emphasis on national pride and party loyalty for members.

The planners decide how much is to be paid for each type of work, and they do it mainly so as to get the plan carried out most effectively. The biggest pay goes to scientists, artists, inventors, and managers who overproduce their quotas. About 75 per cent of all industrial workers are on "piece rates," whereby each worker gets paid according to how much he turns out. This is a much higher percentage than in the United States. Money wages thus play much the same role in pulling labor into jobs and stimulating good performance as they do in America, *except* that in Russia they are set by the planners to channel workers into occupations and industries where the planners want them, rather than freely by market supply and demand. It is striking that money incentives—differential pay for workers and managers turning out more output with higher skills—are used more strongly than in such "capitalist" countries as the United States. And resulting *worker* pay differentials are considerably *wider* in the U.S.S.R. than here, where union pressures have tended to lessen wage differentials.

How free are Soviet workers to work where they wish? Apparently substantially free, given the immobility inevitably associated with low incomes and limited geographical fluidity—except where workers have been "recruited" for special projects or where they have received special training or education at state expense. Workers may be transferred against their wishes, but the complaints of managers about labor turnover suggest that labor moves from job to job with considerable freedom.

Most Soviet workers belong to unions. But they are quite different from unions in America. Soviet unions have nothing to do with setting wages; wages are established by the central planners. The unions are worker organizations which are expected to help in implementing plans. As such they apparently have a substantial role in channeling labor from surplus to shortage occupations. They administer most worker benefits. They handle worker grievances. But they are more like workmen's clubs than like unions as we know them; and their main role seems to be in helping to get workers to work hard on the jobs where they are needed most. Make your own comparison with the role of unions in America, where there is far more union power, and far more conflict. Which plan seems better to you?

Checking on Performance: The Gosbank. All basic planning is done in physical terms. But the Gosplan also makes up a complete set of "value" (or financial) plans to parallel the basic physical plans. Using these financial plans, the Gosbank (state banking system) provides the money to managers needed to pay for labor and materials to carry out the production plans. For example, if the annual plan calls for 10 million pairs of shoes, the Gosbank provides shoe plant managers just enough rubles to pay for the labor, leather, and so on, allocated to the production of those shoes. It does the same for all other products. And managers must deposit their receipts in the Gosbank, except for cash payments made to workers. Except for wages and citizens' purchases of consumer goods, all transactions in Russia are made by check through the Gosbank.

The Gosbank plays two significant roles. First, it provides a financial control over all managers. If they run out of money, this is a sign they are buying more than the inputs allocated to them under the physical plan. And since they can get materials and labor only by paying for them, the control is close and effective. When the manager reports his income to the Gosbank, this provides an automatic check on whether he has produced the amount specified in the plan. Field representatives of the Gosplan continuously check on how well different parts of the over-all plan are being carried out, and the Gosbank checking accounts provide the major source of information. Second, the Gosbank provides a regular banking function, transferring funds, advancing working capital, and creating a money supply for the economy.

In some respects, the Gosbank is thus like banks in the United States. It advances working capital to carry out productive processes, transfers funds, and creates money for the economy. But in other respects it is very different. It is strictly government-operated, and its main goal is to help police and implement the physical plan. It will advance new checking accounts (create credit) when this seems desirable to stimulate desired production. It reduces funds available to industries that have been absorbing too much labor or material. (Its policies are also designed to help insure that total purchasing power is about equal to goods and services available at the desired state prices, as we shall see presently. Thus, it is a little like our Federal Reserve, but with far more direct control over the supply of money.)

How does this checking on performance compare with the private-enterprise process? In America, too, the availability of funds to carry out any economic service exercises a basic control over what is done and who does it. In America, the firm gets funds continuously from selling its products; thus consumers exercise a continuous check on whether any firm is doing its job effectively. If a firm wants to expand, it must either have stored up its own profits to risk or it must go to the competitive capital markets for funds. There its project is evaluated by bankers, private investors, and other lenders against other alternative demanders of funds. If the firm's prospects look good, it will be able to borrow; if they look bad, it will have trouble raising funds.

Which checking process is more effective? It obviously depends on your point of view. The Soviet procedure gives a direct control to the planners through the Gosbank. In America, again, we place most of our faith in the impersonal market, where lenders and business firms themselves are counted on to look out for their own incomes and thereby to get our resources allocated most effectively. Here is one place the socialists criticize the American economy vigorously. They say that capital markets are not really competitive—that capital is rationed out by monopolistic lenders to big, favored borrowers in a way that makes it hard for new, smaller firms to compete effectively with the established giants. Think back to the chapters before on monopoly and competition and on the American banking and credit system to decide how much weight to give this criticism.

The Recalcitrant Problem of Agriculture. Since the communists took over after World War I, agriculture has been their knottiest problem. Their early attempts to collectivize Russian agriculture, carried through by bloody force during the 1920's and 1930's, met bitter and sullen resistance. Forced to work on collective farms, farmers produced less than before, and kept crops and animals for themselves rather than turning them over to Soviet authorities for export to the cities. Frustrated communist planners tried one tack, then another—but with little success in meeting expanded food goals for the rapidly growing industrial population, or in freeing farm labor for industrial jobs.

In theory, a collective farm is a cooperative, democratic association of farmers who have pooled their land, tools, and labor to make a large farm, which they operate in common. Proceeds are shared in proportion to the quantity and quality of work they do. Large-scale operation produces the economics of large-scale, mechanized farming, eliminating the waste and inefficiency which for centuries have characterized Russian agriculture.

It sounds fine, but not to the Russian peasants. Soviet planners found crops vanishing into farm consumption, and total production declining. Bloody reprisals brought only temporary compliance and smoldering resentment. Over millions of acres, effective control was impossible.

The present pattern of planning and production for Soviet agriculture is something like this. There are now some 100,000 collective and state farms, compared to perhaps 25 million small peasant farms four decades ago. About 5,000 of these are huge state farms of many thousand acres, operated outright as "business" firms by the Ministry of Agriculture in much the same pattern as prevails for industrial production. Some 95,000 are collective farms, ranging from a few "communes" (which involve complete sharing of property, labor, and results) to many cases where the collective farm is scarcely more than a sharing of major machinery and some exchange of labor. In most cases, part of the land is farmed collectively but each family retains a small plot for its own individual operation. A significant part of total Soviet farm output still comes from these private family holdings.

Nominally, all Russian farms are under the Ministry of Agriculture. A plan is made for them, much like the plan for industrial products. But getting the plan carried out is another story. In addition to the farmers themselves, there are apparently some 500,000 supervisors of collective farms whose job is to get the farm goals carried out. This cumbersome bureaucracy has come in for scathing top-level communist criticism, but neither it, nor other variants that have been tried, have succeeded in bringing agricultural output up to plan.

Payments to farmers are calculated on a complicated basis. For work on collective farms they receive largely payment in kind, but they also receive some money income. Apparently about a third of total output is delivered directly to the state, about a third is used on the farms for further output (seed, feed for animals, and so on), and about a third is given to the farmers themselves. A substantial portion of the latter finds its way onto the free market for food consumption in the cities. This is augmented by products from the millions of small family holdings. No one knows just how much escapes outside the formal procedures of the plan.

It appears that the Soviets have recently been moving in the direction of more and larger "state" farms, which are directly operated by the state and on which farmers are employed directly as workers and paid largely on a direct salary basis, in money or in kind. Mechanization and modern farming methods play a major role, especially in the huge "virgin lands" areas beyond the Ural Mountains. Direct money incentives for farm workers are simultaneously being expanded, paralleling the incentive plans used in industry.

Up to the mid-1950's it was not clear that total farm output was much greater than it had been during the 1920's. Recently, substantial increases have been reported, though they still leave Soviet agriculture far behind the rapid per capita advances reported for farm workers in many other nations. By the late 1950's grain output appeared to be at least 20 per cent higher than a decade before, while cotton, meat animals, milk, and other products showed smaller gains. The new seven-year plan calls for a 70 per cent increase in farm output by 1965. Few outside observers believe this is a realistic goal. But expansion of farm output per capita with fewer farmers will have to be a major objective for the Soviet planners if they are to succeed in raising Russian food consumption at the same time as they obtain more badly needed industrial workers from the present farm population.

(3) Deciding How Income Is to Be Distributed. Marxist doctrine says, to each according to his need. The Soviet economy today seasons this liberally with, to each according to how hard he works and how much he contributes. Incomes are much more equally distributed than in the United States, because in Russia no income from property is permitted and many of the highest American incomes are from dividends, interest, and capital gains on private property. There are no millionaires in modern Russia. But money incomes derived *from work* are probably more unequally distributed in Russia than in America. This inequality reflects the strong use made of incentive payments to achieve the goals established by the central planners.

Artists, scientists, professors, managers, and government officials apparently receive the highest incomes, including special supplements in premium housing, use of government automobiles, paid vacations, and so on. Common labor is at the bottom of the totem pole, as in America, except for farmers, many of whom take much of their income in kind from their farms. It is reported that the average salary of scientists, professors, and managers in Russia is about eight times that of typical factory workers. For managers, this relationship seems not unlike that in America, but for scientists, artists, and professors the Russian pay is *relatively* much higher than for their American counterparts. Within the ranks of factory workers and comparable laborers, apparently the spread between lowest and highest monthly incomes is nearly 1 to 8, far wider than in America.

Wage rates are adjusted up and down frequently for different occupations and industries, to help implement the over-all plan. The Soviets may be good Marxists, but their behavior on wages suggests they have learned a good deal too about monetary incentives.

Government Services and Income Redistribution. Although it uses money incentives freely to stimulate production and allocate resources, the Soviet state provides widespread social services to help the masses. Soviet authorities claim (without outside verification) that one-third of the income of low-income groups is provided by free government services, beyond individual money earnings. Virtually all housing is government-owned, and rents are extremely low; on the average, Soviet citizens apparently pay only 2 to 3 per cent of their income for housing, far under the 15 to 25 per cent common in America. Russian housing is bad, but it's cheap. Paid vacations, government nurseries, special grants to large families, completely subsidized education, and extensive health services all supplement money incomes.

What taxes are used to finance these services and other government expenditures? A general sales ("turnover") tax accounts for about half of all government receipts. Profits on state enterprises provide another third, and the income tax, plus some forced sale of government bonds, the remainder. All told, government collections and expenditures somewhat comparable to our combined federal-state-local governmental taxes and expenditures apparently amount to about 35 per cent of the gross national product, though estimates vary substantially.

Since the turnover tax varies widely from product to product and from year to year, estimation of its incidence by income levels is extremely difficult. Increases and decreases in the tax are used in adjusting the prices of individual products up and down to discourage or stimulate consumption in order to make consumer demand match the goods produced under the plan, somewhat as free market prices provide this adjustment in the United States. Tax rates vary from only a few per cent to over 1,000 per cent. Since the government depends on this tax for the bulk of its revenue and since few products are completely exempted, the tax may be more or less proportional to income in its impact; there is comparatively little personal saving like that in America to make the tax regressive. This tax, therefore, is a substantial offset to the apparent big government supplement to low incomes.

On the other hand, apparently the Soviets use especially low prices on some major commodities besides housing to subsidize low-income consumers. This means that such goods are sold below "cost." Prices are set very high on such luxuries as automobiles. Just how important such differential pricing is in equalizing incomes is impossible to estimate from present information. Here again, pricing is used by Soviet planners to promote all the goals they consider important —stimulation or restriction of consumption, redistribution of income, equating aggregate spendable income to aggregate supply available.

The relatively unimportant personal income tax is progressive in rate structure (from 13 to 48 per cent in 1958). But the rates vary widely for different occupational groups; equal treatment of those equally situated (by income) has no place in the Soviet tax system. Workers, managers, and most government employees pay only 13 per cent on their entire income. Farmers are taxed under a special arrangement (permitting partial payment in kind) that provides roughly equivalent rates. But professional people (doctors, for example) engaged in private practice and others engaged in occupations not considered to contribute directly to planned social goals face rates that rise rapidly to the 48 per cent peak. There are no low-income exemptions comparable to those in the United States, so the apparent progression applies to only a small portion of the population.

Thus, government services to the general public are financed by widespread taxes that apparently provide little transfer of income from the rich to the poor, except for the substantial portion financed by profits from state-owned industry. The extensive government social services help to equalize the distribution of income, but the actual equalizing impact may be less than in the United States, where, at least at the extremes, federal income taxes shift income strongly from the rich to the poor. Nevertheless, since incomes are far more unequally distributed before taxes in the United States, reflecting especially large property incomes, even after taxes and government services this greater inequality clearly remains.

(4) *Deciding Between Economic Growth and Current Consumption.* In America the choice between economic growth and current consumption depends on a complex set of factors, including consumer saving behavior, business investment decisions, private educational and research decisions, and government tax and investment behavior. In Russia, the choice is simple. It is made and implemented by the central planners. And their choice has been in favor of rapid growth at the expense of current consumption.

The basic data have been cited before. The Russian economy over-all has grown at perhaps 7-10 per cent per annum over the past decade, and at perhaps 10-12 per cent in industrial output. This is something like double the American rate in the aggregate, more than double in industrial output. In recent years, about 57 per cent of the Soviet gross national product appears to have been allocated to consumption goods and services (including those provided by the government); about 28 per cent to what would correspond to our gross private investment plus government non-defense investment; and, according to Soviet figures, about 15 per cent to direct defense. Comparable figures for the United States have run around 70 per cent for total consumption, 18 per cent for investment, and 10 per cent for defense. (It is clear that the Soviet "defense" category is narrower than that used in the American budget, and that some upward adjustment should be made in the 18 per cent to make the figures comparable.)

Soviet emphasis on growth is implemented through the planning process. Priority is given to expansion of industrial capacity, even though this permits per capita consumption to rise very little with the rapid expansion in total output. The Gosplan and Gosbank give growth their first emphasis. Even with this control, there is evidence that the path of Soviet industrial expansion has not been smooth. During the late 1950's, Russia faced a serious shortage of real capital goods, in spite of restricted consumption, and a new five-year plan announced in 1956 had to be scrapped a year later as, in effect, unrealistically ambitious for capital goods. It was replaced with the new seven-year plan of 1958, with industrial goals spaced out over a longer period. Even with central planning and control rather than individual choice and the price system, Russia faces the same fundamental problem in growth as does any other economy—she must divert scarce resources from consumption to investment, improve her technology, and step up the ability and performance of her labor force. There is no other way, for either communism or capitalism. And the Soviet growth rate since World War II has severely strained her ability to maintain the growth in both capital goods and military spending in an economy where living standards are still low.[4]

---

[4] Under Marxist doctrine, only labor is truely productive. Thus interest on money or real capital plays no role in communist planning doctrine. Western economists properly point out that this position, if followed, will lead Soviet planners to improper decisions in allocating resources among capital goods. Some producers' goods involve a heavy use of productive resources per unit of output, others a low investment. Some render productive services over a long period, others over a short one. Only by taking into account these differences can optimal decisions be made as to what capital goods should be produced. And the interest rate, as was pointed out in Chapter 32, is the price system's tool in making such comparisons

It should be clear that how fast the Russian economy grows depends on the decisions of the central planners. But it depends also on fundamental political forces—on how long the population will be content to see most of the increased output go into capital expansion and military products. In the American economy, the public speaks on this division continuously, through its own saving-spending behavior and through its directions to congressmen on government spending and taxes. Under the Soviet system there is little evidence that the man-in-the-street has any voice in the decisions. Yet the Soviet leaders constantly face the need to keep the masses reasonably content if they are to stay in power. Persistent, though small, increases in consumption goods output per capita attest to this concern, much as the communist leaders would like to see total productive capacity rise faster. Although the standard of living is far higher in Russia, the problem of the Soviet planners is the same as that of the planners in the underdeveloped nations like India and China—the choice between present and future, complicated by the heavy drain of military spending.

Soviet planning for growth extends to every phase of economic life. Soviet education, in the European pattern, is deadly serious from kindergarten on. While all youths go through elementary and high-school level education, only those with special capacities are sent on to what corresponds to our college-level training. For these, education is more specialized and more sharply focused on specific job training than is ours, but it is intense and thorough in those specialties, especially science, engineering, medicine, and the like. The National Science Foundation reports that Russia is currently training twice as many scientists and engineers as we are (about 125,000 a year as against our 60,000), and that her lead will apparently grow. Again, the contrast with the privately determined, free-choice advanced education system of the United States is striking.

No reliable estimates on the total Soviet expenditure on research are available, but apparently, with a national income only 40 per cent of ours, Russia spends at least as much as we do on basic research.

Government Monetary-Fiscal Policy and Economic Stabilization.

The Soviet central planners do not program men or machines into unemployment. If there is unemployment, it is because planning has gone awry or because someone is not behaving according to plan. But there is still the problem of keeping total spending power roughly equal to goods to be bought. If buying power gets too

---

among such alternatives. Interestingly, there is recent evidence that Soviet planners (who are smart fellows too) are beginning to slip the interest rate into their calculations through the back door.

From a *managerial control* point of view, the Soviet position on interest costs turns out to be correct. Since managers are properly held responsible only for resources over which they exercise control and since all allocations of machinery (fixed capital) are made by the planners alone, to charge the manager interest on real capital allocated him would be improper inasmuch as this is a cost over which he has no control. This fact may help explain the planners' slowness to see the essential role of the interest rate in allocation decisions.

large, inflationary pressures will mount. If buying power is too low, either prices must be cut or unsold goods will pile up.

The Soviets manage this balance largely through the turnover tax (fiscal policy) and the Gosbank (monetary policy), the same two tools now most widely accepted in America. In Russia, most of the burden falls on the turnover tax. The Gosplan sets wages and prices in the over-all financial balance approximately to match the physical goods available for consumer and intermediate purchase. The Gosbank provides about the appropriate amount of checking balances for managers throughout the economy. Nevertheless, physical and financial plans frequently do get out of balance. People decide to buy more shoes than was planned, or men's suits pile up in the stores. More fundamentally, Russia is persistently subject to inflationary pressure, since per capita incomes are low and resources must continually be wrenched away from consumption for investment and defense spending. Voluntary saving is low, and the planners seldom need worry about the public's generating over-all unemployment by piling up idle savings.

Whether an individual product or total demand gets out of balance, the answer is much the same. Raise or lower the turnover tax to bring things back into balance. If too many shoes are being demanded, the turnover tax on shoes is increased (raising the price) until demand is cut back to fit the production programmed. If men's suits are piling up, the turnover tax is cut to make the price more attractive. If total demand is excessive and inflationary pressure exists, the turnover tax is raised all along the line, or on those products where demand seems most excessive, raising prices and siphoning off income to the government. If total demand should be inadequate, turnover taxes would be lowered. In a real sense, the Russians have adopted "functional finance" as the core of their stabilization and allocation mechanism.

In spite of this plan, inflation has been a persistent problem for Soviet Russia. The Russians are human beings too, and when there isn't enough to go around they apparently tend to plan a little more resources for all the demanders than there are to parcel out. The result is a demand pressure that tends to bid up prices all along the line as shortages occur. In 1947 a drastic monetary reform confiscating most private monetary balances and government bond holdings was proclaimed to reduce excess buying power. For a while, the Russians used compulsory purchase of government bonds as an important device for soaking up excess consumer purchasing power. But as large amounts of these bonds began to come due just when inflationary pressure was mounting again in 1957, the Russians virtually repudiated the entire national debt of 260 billion rubles.

The basic pressures that make for inflation—shortage of goods relative to the purchasing power provided by incomes paid out—are the same in communist and capitalist societies. But monetary and fiscal controls are managed differently in the two economies. And the difficulties faced by the capitalist stabilizers are far greater. They must work almost entirely through trying to match total demand to total supply, while the Soviets can rely on the closely controlled physical plan, supplemented by the turnover tax, to absorb most of the responsibility for programming resources into useful employment. Russia faces no serious danger of a cumulative income contraction leading to collapse of private investment and consumption spending; there isn't any private investment to fluctuate. Russian workers thrown out of jobs by technological change are quickly programmed into other work. There is little doubt that the American private-enterprise market economy is more vulnerable to economic instability and the waste of recession unemployment. The basic fact that America is rich means that excess saving may present an unemployment problem substantially unknown to the Russian planners, who face a constant shortage of both capital and consumption goods.

COMPARATIVE ECONOMIC SYSTEMS IN PERSPECTIVE At the end of a long book, it may be useful one last time to recall your criteria for evaluating the performance of any economic system, and to apply them briefly in comparing the performance of our American system with that of Soviet Russia—not because Russia is the best standard against which to measure our performance, but because this is the comparison we have just been making and because it is the comparison being made by much of the world. Most important, it should provide a last chance for you to organize your own ideas on the performance of the American system and what, if anything, you think needs to be done to improve it.

Raising the National Standard of Living—Growth with Stability. Some of the communist achievements have been spectacular. No other nation in history has industrialized as fast as the Soviet economy since the 1920's. From a backward, rural economy, in three decades Russia has become the world's second-greatest industrial power. Since World War II, there is no doubt that Russia's annual growth rate in total output has far exceeded that of the United States, and probably that of every other major nation.

If Russia achieves the continued growth in industrial capacity that is budgeted in her current seven-year plan, by 1965 the Russian economy will be far ahead of any other in the world except that of the United States. The *increase* in Russian steel-making capacity over the seven years will substantially exceed the *total* capacity of England. Total growth is planned for nearly 9 per cent a year, well over 9 per cent for industrial goods and about 7.3 per cent for consumers' goods. This compares with a probable 3 to 5 per cent for the United States.

But as time goes on, Russia may find it increasingly hard to close this gap with America. A big part of her spectacular growth since 1946 represents rebuilding from war devastation—merely a catching up to previous growth trends. Thus far, she has depended on taking over technology and plans for industrial plants from the western world, for she was far behind when she began; now this will be harder, since she has pretty well caught up on many types of facilities. Thus far, she has had plentiful labor. Since most of the workers were drawn from the farms, and had no industrial skill, their performance improved rapidly. This source is no longer so plentiful. Moreover, Russian manpower losses in World War II were enormous, and as a result there will be a drop in the number of workers entering the labor force over the next decade. Thus Russia now faces a critical shortage of skilled labor. Thus far, the communist leaders have been able to hold consumption at low levels while concentrating on industrial growth; there is some evidence that they will have to pay more attention to raising current consumption if the people are to be kept content with the ruling regime. But, with all these reservations, Russia has become the industrial giant of Eurasia, surpassed only by the United States.

But in this spectacular expansion of output, consumption has been ruthlessly suppressed to permit rapid industrial growth. Russian per capita income of around $500 in 1959 U.S. dollars puts her well above the poverty class, but still far short of such highly developed western nations as the U.S. and Canada. Still, the communist leaders in the U.S.S.R. as in China have made a clear choice, and have stuck to it with few deviations—industrial growth and military strength ahead of more consumption goods. Housing, especially outside the major cities, is appallingly crowded and poor. Food for the masses is no more than adequate, with little variety. Consumer "hard goods" are scarce. Only the very powerful have private automobiles. In 1959, there were only 6 million radio sets in the entire U.S.S.R., compared to over 100 million in the United States. Still, most Americans who visit Russia are surprised to find living standards as high as they are. In part, the national income statistics contribute to this underestimate, because in the communist system of accounting many personal services (which make up a big part of our consumption total) are not considered "productive" and hence are not included in the national income data.

Agriculture has been a nagging problem to the planners. It is not clear that total agricultural output today is greatly above the levels of the 1920's. Clearly, Russian farm output per capita has fallen far behind the growth pattern of the western economies. Collectivization of the farms never worked well; the peasants refused to cooperate, stealing crops for themselves and sometimes destroying crops and animals outright in protest against communist seizure of their lands. World War II took a terrible toll of Russian farmers, livestock, and farm buildings. Although Russian agriculture has managed to feed the Russian economy at a tolerable level, in this area communist central planning can hardly be rated much above a failure.

Viewed in perspective, how efficient is the Russian economy? Most responsible opinion holds that in industry Russian technology and productive efficiency at their best match any to be found in the world. But this best is concentrated in the vital capital-goods industries, and in military production. In consumer-goods industries, shoddy, expensive products seem to be more common. And the Russian press carries persistent complaints of worker and managerial deficiencies—defective products, missing replacement parts, excess labor turnover, idle manpower and machines caused by poor scheduling, "hoarding" of labor and materials—difficulties not unreminiscent of the American wartime scene. Over-all, output per industrial worker in Russia appears to be about half what it is in the United States, roughly comparable with that in England and above that of most of the rest of Europe. But the figures for agriculture, as indicated above, show the Russian economy in a far worse comparative position.

How efficient is the over-all planning process? It works far better than most economists here guessed it could, given the immensity of the problem. Still, it appears to be rough, and the Russians periodically face major balance and capital-shortage problems.

How about the American economy on the same scores? Viewed in perspective, the record is one of solid achievement. There is no gainsaying the per capita American income of some $2300, far above the rest of the world. True, the American economy has only grown at about 4 per cent during the postwar period, compared to much higher rates for other countries. But many rapid growth rates have occurred in countries rebuilding from World War II devastation, and most have benefited greatly by importing technology and know-how from the United States. It is unlikely that Russia or others of the recent rapidly growing nations will be able to continue their postwar rates indefinitely.

Premier Khrushchev boasts that Russia will overtake the United States by 1970, but this is clearly just propaganda. Even if Russia achieves the goals set by the new seven-year plans, her real gross national product in 1970 will be only moderately over $400 billion in 1959 U.S. dollars—still well below even the 1959 American level. By 1970 the American g.n.p. will surely be at least $650 billion in present dollars, which means that Russian g.n.p. is unlikely to be more than 60 per cent of ours at the most, compared to about 40 per cent now. On a per capita basis, the present spread may narrow somewhat, but hardly enough to change the general picture of a Soviet per capita income well under half of ours.

On the score of stability and avoidance of waste through unemployment, the American system doesn't come off so well. The great depression of the 1930's and even the smaller recessions of 1948, 1954, and 1958 have no parallels in the Soviet system. Although Russian production was set far back by the original communist revolution and again by World War II, communism has avoided the scourge of modern capitalism—depression and mass unemployment. Although Soviet steel capacity is less than half ours, in the recession year 1958 Soviet *production* of steel was 60 million tons compared to only 80 million tons in the United States, where our mills were running at only 60 per cent of capacity. Perhaps modern reforms plus effective monetary-fiscal policy have eliminated the worst of cyclical instability from the western economies; the past decade provides some basis for this hope. But this failure in the past presents a weakness the communists are fond of emphasizing.

On the inflation side, neither communism nor capitalism can point to a clean slate. Inflation has plagued both systems through the postwar period. There is no evidence that either has the problem effectively in hand. The tools in the hands of the Soviet planners should make it possible for them to assure reasonably stable prices through their elaborate system of physical and monetary-fiscal controls. A nagging question: Does capitalism have an adequate answer to the inflation problem?

Economic Freedom for the Individual. How much "economic freedom" the Soviet economy provides for the individual depends on what you mean by the phrase. Today, the Soviet citizen has considerable freedom to move to another job, and apparently complete freedom to spend his income on whatever he can find to buy. But the meaning of this freedom is subject to dispute, since the government determines completely what goods will be available for purchase, and the government not infrequently tells him where he must work. And the government further restricts this freedom of choice through the large part of production it siphons off through heavy turnover taxes and provides "free" to all citizens. Russian unions have little voice in determining the wages at which the citizens will work.

By contrast, the American private-enterprise system provides almost complete freedom on where to work, where to live, how to spend our money, and other such economic choices. The freedom to go into business for yourself is completely unmatched in the Soviet system. American unions are a powerful device for equalizing the economic power of employers and employees. Government taxes are heavy and to this extent economic freedom may be said to be curtailed— though less so than in Russia and in many other major economies.

It seems obvious to us that our individual economic freedom far surpasses that available in Russia. But the question "Through whose eyes?" is relevant again. The following quotation from a recent speech by Khrushchev illustrates how different things can look to someone else. He said: [5]

> Indeed, there is freedom in the capitalist countries, but for whom? Of course, not for the working people, who are forced to hire themselves out to capitalists on any conditions to avoid finding themselves in the huge army of people who are unemployed. Neither is there freedom for the peasants, who are constantly threatened by "liberation" from their holdings as a result of bankruptcy. Nor is there freedom for the intelligentsia, whose creative activity is in the grip of material dependence on the moneybag. . . . Freedom in the capitalist countries exists only for those who possess money and who consequently hold power.

---

[5] Speech before 21st Party Congress in Moscow, Jan. 31, 1959.

Clearly, political and economic freedom are intimately intertwined. If in fact the Russian people completely controlled the Soviet officials who make the nation's economic plans, the communists could reasonably claim a high degree of individual economic freedom, exercised through voting for central economic planning rather than through the marketplace. In America we freely choose to have our governments take part of our income from us and provide certain goods and services through non-market channels, and there is no reason why for others to do likewise would imply lack of economic freedom. But without effective democratic control over the central planners, the Soviet system, even with its greatly increased sphere of individual economic and personal freedom under Khrushchev, can hardly escape the designation of economic as well as political dictatorship. Inability to speak out against the government and to elect new representatives characterizes for us a system of dictatorship and oppression.

Economic Security.   What is economic security? Is it freedom from the fear of unemployment? Freedom from the fear of arbitrary discharge? Freedom from the fear of poverty and disaster in old age or ill health? Is economic security separable from political security—security against government dictation of where we work, and against retribution if we speak out or act contrary to the wishes of those in power?

How economic security is defined will partly determine the rating of the American and Soviet systems on this score. By one test, the Soviet citizen is secure economically. The state will not let him and his family starve. He is assured of a minimum of public services and of a job if he works reasonably hard and conforms to the rules of the leaders in power. In a planned economy, workers aren't planned into unemployment. Probably the Soviet leaders believe their system provides more economic security than does capitalism, where (to them) the worker lives in constant fear of discharge by the all-powerful capitalist and of unemployment in the periodic "crises" that communist doctrine says must ultimately destroy capitalism.

Fundamentally, the greatest protection to economic security under the American system is the vast productive power it provides—the high per capita incomes that make it possible for workers to look out for themselves and for them to be supported reasonably by others if for some reason they are unable to support themselves. Although our governmental social-security system is less elaborate and far-reaching than that of many other countries, it now offers protection against most of the types of insecurity likely to strike the average individual. Private welfare and pension funds have developed rapidly in recent years. Still, the capitalist system has some serious weaknesses here—weaknesses that will persist until we learn to substitute stable economic growth for intermittent depressions and inflations. Depression unemployment, even with unemployment insurance, represents a major form of economic insecurity, largely centered in the industrialized capitalist countries.

Just how much security should an economic system provide? Many Americans believe the system ought to deal out big rewards to those who work hard and "produce," and that those who don't produce have no right to economic security. This is the incentive that has made the American economic system such a spectacular success so far, they argue, and to substitute guaranteed economic security would be to undermine the very foundation of the system. Others disagree. It is clear where the American system stands on this type of incentive compared to most other economies. Whether it ought to provide more security, and if so how, is for you to decide.

Production in Response to Consumer Demands.   Here the Soviet system rates low according to our criteria. The communist planners, not the consumers, decide what is to be produced. The "free choice" of consumers in spending their money is strictly limited—they can spend it only on goods available. In Moscow in 1958, 10 minutes of work was required to earn enough to buy a loaf of bread; in New York 5 minutes was enough. For potatoes (per pound) the times were 6 minutes and 2 minutes. But the ratios changed drastically for other products—33 minutes against 7 minutes for a quart of milk, 33 days against 4 days for an overcoat, 25 days against 1 day for a table radio. The central planners dictate how hard it is to get different products. And consumers have almost nothing to say about the division of resources between present and future.

Don't forget, though, that in the Russian's eyes maybe a centrally planned allocation of resources makes more sense than the kind of unplanned allocation that we get through the free-price system. Maybe the political process reflects the people's needs better than the marketplace would. The communists say it does— but from here it looks as if the voter doesn't have very much to say about it in practice.

Does the American system produce the goods and services consumers want? By and large yes, *if* we take one-dollar one-vote as our criterion. Over three-fourths of the gross national product is allocated through the private economy, pretty much in response to consumers' dollar demands. In 1958, the American system produced fewer bicycles per capita than did the Russian, twice as much sugar and cotton cloth, three times as much meat, ten times as many TV sets, washing machines, and refrigerators, fifty times as many autos.

The way the private-enterprise system responds to consumer demands is not perfect. Varying degrees of monopoly and monopsony throughout the economy impede allocations of resources exactly in accord with the purely competitive "ideal" of consumers' sovereignty. Development and introduction of new products depend on private profit incentives, with widespread failure and waste along with the successful ventures. Consumers seem to have little control over the allocation of resources to advertising and other selling costs. Social costs and social benefits not mirrored in prices and costs permit poor resource allocations by the pure-competition criterion. And other "imperfections" are not hard to find.

But is consumers' sovereignty as specified in the model of "pure competition" necessary to give consumers what they want? Maybe they like the quality competition and demand creation that have become prevalent. Maybe some oligopoly price stability is by-and-large better for consumers than continuous sharp price competition. And the "waste" of market failures and bankruptcies may be a fair price to pay for the freedom it mirrors and the progress the system has brought. These are issues on which you can make your own judgment by now. However they look to you, surely, over-all, consumer choice is *the* powerful director of economic production in our basically price-directed, unplanned economy.

Lastly, there is the 20-odd per cent of the gross national product produced through the public economy—presumably on a one-person one-vote criterion rather than one-dollar one-vote. Is this one-fifth a truer reflection of what consumers really want than goods and services produced in response to market demand? Is individual choice on economic matters effectively reflected through our present political processes? There are obvious problems, in addition to the fundamental choice between one-person one-vote and one-dollar one-vote. Here the economist cannot answer. Your own answer will go far to determine how highly you rate the system on this criterion of consumer choice, compared with systems that put much more stress on government direction of economic activity.

Equitable Distribution of Income.   Does the Russian system provide an equitable distribution of income? By substantially eliminating incomes from property, the communists have eliminated the very high incomes of capitalist systems. Do you think this is good or bad? Worker money incomes, on the other hand, are probably more unequally distributed than in the United States, but then somewhat equalized by government services and pricing policies. This condition reflects the heavy emphasis placed on monetary work incentives by the communists. The over-all result is a much more equal distribution of incomes than in the United States, both before and after taxes.

How about American capitalism? Our incomes are unequally distributed, before and after taxes. But over the past quarter-century there has been a strong tendency toward greater equality, perhaps arising from the growth of trade unions, perhaps from government tax and expenditure policies, perhaps from other causes. The emergence of a huge, reasonably well-to-do middle class is one of the striking developments of recent American history. But how equal should incomes be? And if we want greater equality, can it be obtained without incurring prohibitive costs through destroying incentives to work and invest which underlie our high standard of living? The question of how equally distributed incomes should be is, in the last analysis, one of how the basic income pie should be sliced up. On this ethical question, again make your own judgment. But remember the problems we will face if the wage and profit shares get badly out of line with the requirements for a continued productive, growing economy. Any income redistribution that reduces total output is hard to defend.

CONCLUSION Since the beginning of recorded history, men have sought the perfect society. In the books that fill the libraries, many of these utopias promise peace and plenty for all. But it is a long step from dream to reality. In the real world, the utopias that look best in the writing sometimes turn sour for quite unforeseen reasons.

Over the years, some economists have worked out the details of an "ideal" democratic society. In it, resources would be allocated in accordance with consumer demands, individuals would be free to work and spend as they wish, state-owned capital resources would be devoted to producing what consumers want, and the proceeds from state enterprises would be distributed among the people to provide as much income equality as the public desired. This is much like the utopia of the early socialists, with state ownership of resources and operation of enterprise, with political democracy, and with economic implementation spelled out through the price system. Its advocates claim it combines the best features of private enterprise and of socialism.

But in the real world, are centralized economic control and democratic freedom in fact compatible? The Russian blueprint looks surprisingly like this model, but in operation it looks very different indeed. Wise observers have often noted that dispersion of economic power and dispersion of political power are usually handmaidens—that centralized economic power and political democracy seldom live long together. If this is true, the attempt to "plan" and centrally control economic activity toward the goals we want may be a false dream, likely to lead to political and economic slavery rather than to organized plenty.

The economic system must be our servant, not our master, in an effective society. If the society has fundamentally democratic, individualistic ideals, most people must be at heart satisfied with the way the system works—not in detail and all the time, but by and large. Lewis Carroll, in *Alice in Wonderland,* put his finger tellingly on the basic problem:

> The Dodo suddenly called out, "The race is over!" and they all crowded round, panting, and asking, "But who has won?"
> This question the Dodo could not answer without a great deal of thought, and it sat for a long time with one finger pressed upon its forehead, while the rest waited in silence. At last the Dodo said, *"Everybody* has won, and all must have prizes."

In a working, democratic society all must win and all must have prizes. What shall the prizes be, and how can the economic system keep everyone satisfied with his reward? The American economy provides prizes in abundance, compared with all the other nations of the world. Any reasonable evaluation must count it highly successful. But to be pleased should not make us smug. The American economic system is not perfect. And it will change in many respects over the years ahead, as it adapts to changing needs and changing objectives.

You should now be able to do a good share of your own thinking on how the

American economy should steer over the years ahead. Economic analysis can help greatly in pointing the way in a changing world. Not to use this powerful tool is to waste a valuable resource. But never forget, too, that the problems of modern economic life here and in the tense world around us reach far into the ethical, political, and social realms—they often cannot be solved by economic analysis alone. It would be a simpler world if they could.

FOR ANALYSIS AND DISCUSSION

1. In the light of your study of the American economic system and alternative systems, make a careful list of the major defects, if any, you see in the American system. What, if any, reforms do you think are needed, and how feasible do you think each of your reforms is?

2. During the past quarter-century, the economic climate of the world has shifted markedly in the direction of central economic planning and collectivism, away from major reliance on private-enterprise capitalism. Make a list of the factors that you think have been most important in bringing about this change.

3. Since World War II, the two major nations showing the highest growth rates are Russia (a communist state) and West Germany (a basically private-enterprise economy). How do you account for this fact? Does it indicate that the two types of economic organization are equally fitted for producing continued, rapid growth?

4. The United States' standard of living is undeniably the highest in the world. Yet many other countries seem relatively uninterested in adopting an economic system like ours. How do you explain this fact?

5. In Russia, wages are set by the central planners to keep total purchasing power about in line with the supply of goods to be bought. Would some variant of this plan be a good approach to our problem of avoiding creeping, wage-push inflation? If you think so, defend your answer against the likely attack of a union member.

6. Make a list of those attributes of present-day communist Russia that seem to you most objectionable. How many of these attributes are economic, how many social, how many political?

7. What does your own utopia look like? How do its economic and political characteristics compare with the best to be found anywhere in the world today?

Current Research

With four broad areas covered briefly in Part 7, the selection of suggestive samples of current research is especially difficult. Each area is so big that research varies widely in both method and subject matter. The previous warning that these are merely samples which one economist thinks may be interesting to you is therefore doubly appropriate here. There is no pretense that the items cited are necessarily either the best or the most significant research in recent years. Especially in managerial economics, advanced mathematical analysis is being used more and more, so that much of the pioneering research is out of reach unless you have a good mathematical background.

Managerial Economics.   To some, managerial economics includes analysis of the total economic environment in which business operates. But since other Appendices have focused on this part of the managerial problem, the examples here deal mainly with managerial decision-making in the narrower sense.

First, consumer behavior. How can the manager understand and predict what consumers will buy? Probably the toughest problems lie in the area of consumers' durables. For a start, look at L. R. Klein and J. B. Lansing, "Decisions to Purchase Durable Goods," *Journal of Marketing,* October 1955, which summarizes the findings from a decade of intensive consumer surveys by the Survey Research Center at the University of Michigan. Daniel Suits focuses on the demand for perhaps the most important single product—automobiles—in his "The Demand for New Automobiles in the United States, 1929-56," *Review of Economics and Statistics,* August 1958. A broader look at the whole problem of consumer buying attitudes and behavior is provided by *Consumer Behavior* (Lincoln Clark, ed.; Harper, 1958), which includes studies by psychologists, sociologists, and market-research experts as well as economists. The articles by Mueller, Neilson, and Reisman may be of special interest.

If predicting consumer spending on durables is difficult, predicting business investment spending is even more so. One of the major aids is a quarterly series of reports collected by the Department of Commerce and the Securities and Exchange Commission from businessmen on their investment plans. For a sober analysis of the results, see M. F. Foss and V. Natrella, "Ten Years Experience with Business Investment Anticipations," *Survey of Current Business,* January 1957. A more sophisticated, and difficult, analysis of the problem is Franco Modigliani and M. Weingartner's "Forecasting Use of Anticipatory Data on Investment and Sales," *Quarterly Journal of Economics,* February 1958.

Beyond these studies of particular sectors of the g.n.p., many economists are at work on the general problem of forecasting. Geoffry Moore, reflecting the approach of the National Bureau of Economic Research, has summarized his analysis in *Measuring Depressions* and *Business Cycle Indicators* (National Bureau of Economic Research, 1959 and 1960). A related but significantly different analytical approach is suggested by Sidney Alexander in "Rate of Change Approaches to Forecasting," *Economic Journal,* June 1958.

Managerial decision-making on production planning and intra-firm problems generally has moved rapidly along lines involving considerable mathematics, under the titles of "management science" and "operations research." An excellent introduction for the non-mathematical layman is provided by Carnegie Tech's M. L. Anshen, C. Holt, F. Modigliani, J. Muth, and H. Simon in "Mathematics for Production Scheduling," *Harvard Business Review,* March 1958—a report on one of the first actual attempts in industry to schedule production using these new techniques. A complete account of the underlying analysis is provided by the same authors in "A Linear Decision Rule for Production and Employment Scheduling," in *Management Science,* October 1955.

If you find the introductory analyses in this area offered in Bowman and Fetter's *Analysis for Production Management,* cited in Chapter 41, accessible, try the collection of current research reports collected by the same authors in *Analyses of Industrial Operations* (Irwin, 1959). The selections by W. W. Cooper and A. Charnes and by G. Dantzig will provide an insight into the work of the real pioneers in the development and application of linear programming to industrial operations.

Social Security.   Though the problem is surely no less pressing, recent research in the area of social security has been more traditional and, at least to many economists, less exciting. But Peter Steiner and R. Dorfman show how careful statistical and analytical work can be applied to one major sub-area in *The Economic Status of the Aged* (Univ. of California Press, 1957). A comparable study, emphasizing careful factual presentation, is H. Sheldon's *The Older Population of the United States* (Wiley, 1958).

Some of the liveliest recent controversy in the social-security field has been over the financial implications of the huge sums being accumulated in private pension funds. Daniel Holland provides a thorough analysis of the facts and issues in "What Can We Expect from Pensions," *Harvard Business Review,* July 1959. Robert Tilove's *Pension Funds and Economic Freedom* (Fund for the Republic, 1959) takes a broader look at the social, political, and economic implications of the pension funds.

For a sample of research on the unemployment-insurance problem, try C. Spivey's *Experience Rating in Unemployment Insurance* (Univ. of Illinois Press, 1958), a study of the costs of unemployment insurance allocable to individual employers and the effects of varying these costs with individual company employment records.

The Underdeveloped Economies.   Over the past decade there has been a flood of research on economic development and the underdeveloped economies. After World War II the debate centered around broad issues of policy. More recently research has turned toward studies of individual countries, to provide the facts to help resolve these unsettled issues. But the controversy over the big issues continues.

W. Malenbaum's "India and China: Contrasts in Development," *American Economic Review,* June 1959, is a good introduction to research in the area. A more detailed study on China is Choh-Ming Li's *Economic Development of Communist China* (Univ. of California Press, 1959). A. Coale and E. M. Hoover focus mainly on India and Mexico in their *Population Growth and Economic Development in Low Income Countries* (Princeton Univ. Press, 1958). W. S. Woytinsky's *India: The Awakening Giant* (Harper, 1957) is somewhat more impressionistic, but illustrates a broad historical and cultural approach combined with economic analysis in highly readable form. For good case studies of smaller countries, see Henry Oliver, *Economic Opinion and Policy in Ceylon* (Duke Univ. Press, 1957), and D. Warriner, *Land Reform and Development in the Middle East* (Oxford Univ. Press, 1957)—both fascinating accounts of the intricate interactions which seem to produce economic growth or to bar it in specific settings.

Meanwhile, the search for general principles to explain economic development continues. A good introduction is W. W. Rostow's "The Take-Off into Economic Growth," *Economic Journal,* March 1956. At book length, different approaches are exemplified by Gunnar Myrdal's *Rich Lands and Poor* (Harper, 1957); H. Leibenstein's *Economic Backwardness and Economic Growth* (Wiley, 1957); and A. J. Youngson's *Possibilities of Economic Progress* (Cambridge Univ. Press, 1959). The work of Myrdal is of special interest; he is one of the world's leading social scientists, with extensive experience in the United Nations as well as in academic channels. Youngson's study differs from the others in focusing mainly on the development of Britain, Sweden, Denmark, and the southern United States during their periods of early growth, in the search for controlling factors.

Two quite different individual studies may help suggest further the widely diverse lines along which research is moving. E. E. Hagen's "Population and Economic Growth," *American Economic Review,* June 1959, takes a new look at the population problem in undeveloped countries. Richard Meier's *Modern Science and the Human Fertility Problem* (Wiley, 1959) goes far beyond the problem of the underdeveloped countries *per se* to examine the factors controlling the shifting balance between population growth, science, and technological change now and over the decades to come.

Comparative Economic Systems: The U.S.S.R.   While our factual knowledge about the Russian economy has increased enormously in recent years, there is still a lively dispute over just how Russian output compares with that of America and other nations. *Soviet Economic Growth: A Comparison with the U.S.,* a special study prepared for the Joint Economic Committee of Congress (Government Printing Office, 1957), provides a good summary. Two new National Bureau of Economic Research studies by Warren Nutter, *Industrial Production in the Soviet Union,* and Gregory Grossman, *Soviet Statistics of Physical Output of Industrial Commodities,* suggest that the spread between Soviet and American growth rates may not be as wide as has been commonly supposed. But the problem of comparisons is a complex one, and more work is in progress.

The Soviets are concerned about the performance of managers, a crucial link in the communist system. A new volume by David Granick, *The Red Executive* (Doubleday, 1959), draws an intriguing parallel between managerial problems and behavior in Russia and the United States. Another good study of the same problem is Joseph Berliner's *Factory and Manager in the U.S.S.R.* (Harvard Univ. Press, 1957). A. Nove takes a look at a specific Soviet approach in "The Problem of 'Success Indicators' in Soviet Industry," in *Economica* for February 1958.

With the increased information flowing out of Russia, American researchers are beginning to dig into every facet of Russian economic performance. Useful samples are provided by papers given at two recent major sessions of the American Economic Association, on Soviet planning and economic prospects (*American Economic Review,* May 1959). See especially the reports on Soviet agriculture under Khrushchev by L. Volin and on the current role of the price system in Russia by Grossman. Intriguing studies of the income tax in Russia and the comparative performance of the Russian transport system are offered by F. Holzman, "Income Taxation in the Soviet Union," *National Tax Journal,* June 1958; and Ernest Williams, *Freight Transportation in the Soviet Union: A Comparison with the United States* (National Bureau of Economic Research, 1959).

For a look at the role of Russia outside the U.S.S.R., try N. Spulber, *The Economies of Communist Eastern Europe* (Wiley, 1957), which pieces together the scattered information available on economic performance in the "satellite nations" of eastern Europe; and J. Berliner, *Soviet Economic Aid* (Council on Foreign Relations, 1958), an account of Russia's use of foreign economic aid to extend her sphere of international influence.

Lastly, though to us many of its articles smack more of propaganda than of research, sample the publication, *Problems of Economics,* if your library has it. This is a monthly translation into English of current papers by leading Soviet economists on all phases of Russian economics and the performance of the Soviet system.

Index

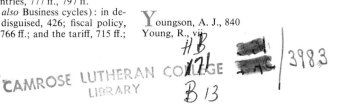